Travel Discount Coupon

This coupon entitles you to special discounts
when you book your trip through the

🌊 *TRAVEL NETWORK* ®
RESERVATION SERVICE

Hotels ♦ Airlines ♦ Car Rentals ♦ Cruises
All Your Travel Needs

Here's what you get: *

♦ A discount of $50 USD on a booking of $1,000** or
more for two or more people!

♦ A discount of $25 USD on a booking of $500** or more
for one person!

♦ Free membership for three years, and 1,000 free miles
on enrollment in the unique Miles-to-Go™ frequent-
traveler program. Earn one mile for every dollar spent
through the program. Earn free hotel stays starting at
5,000 miles. Earn free roundtrip airline tickets starting
at 25,000 miles.

♦ Personal help in planning your own, customized trip.

♦ Fast, confirmed reservations at any property
recommended in this guide, subject to availability.***

♦ Special discounts on bookings in the U.S. and around
the world.

♦ Low-cost visa and passport service.

♦ Reduced-rate cruise packages.

Visit our website at http://www.travnet.com/Frommer or
call us globally at 201-567-8500, ext. 55. In the U.S., call
toll-free at 1-888-940-5000, or fax 201-567-1838. In
Canada, call toll-free at 1-800-883-9959, or fax 416-922-
6053. In Asia, call 60-3-7191044, or fax 60-3-7185415.

---

* To qualify for these travel discounts, at least a portion of your trip must
  include destinations covered in this guide. No more than one coupon discount
  may be used in any 12-month period, for destinations covered in this guide.
  Cannot be combined with any other discount or program.
**These are U.S. dollars spent on commissionable bookings.
***A $10 USD fee, plus fax and/or phone charges, will be added to the cost of
  bookings at each hotel not linked to the reservation service. Customers
  must approve these fees in advance.

Valid until December 31, 1997. Terms and conditions of the Miles-to-
Go™ program are available on request by calling 201-567-8500, ext 55.

GRE123

Frommer's®

1st
Edition

Greece

by John S. Bowman, John Bozman,
Michael C. Goldstein, Sherry Marker,
and Tom Stone

Macmillan • USA

MACMILLAN TRAVEL

A Simon & Schuster Macmillan Company
1633 Broadway
New York, NY 10019

Find us online at **http://www.mgr.com/travel** or
on America Online at Keyword: **Frommer's.**

Copyright © 1997 by Simon & Schuster, Inc.
Maps copyright © 1997 by Simon & Schuster, Inc.

ISBN 0-02-860902-6
ISSN 1089-6007

Editor: Peter Katucki
Production Editor: Michael Thomas
Design by Michele Laseau
Digital Cartography by Ortelius Design and Roberta Stockwell

SPECIAL SALES

Contents

ABOUT THE AUTHORS

John S. Bowman has been a freelance writer and editor for more than 30 years. He specializes in nonfiction work ranging from archeology to zoology to baseball. He first visited Greece in 1956, and has traveled and lived there over the years. He is the author of numerous guides to regions of Greece and is best known for his *Traveller's Guide to Crete*. He currently resides and works in Northampton, Massachusetts.

John Bozman has degrees in sociology-psychology, English, and creative writing, and he has studied Spanish, French, Thai, German, Italian, and Greek. He served four years as an intelligence officer in the U.S. Air Force, including a year in Southeast Asia, and taught survival, escape, resistance, and evasion. He writes novels, plays, and screenplays; his most recent effort is *Maria & Ari,* a drama about Maria Callas and Aristotle Onassis. He has traveled extensively in Europe, Latin America, and Southeast Asia, and is the author of *Frommer's Comprehensive Travel Guide to Thailand,* and a co-author of *Frommer's Greece from $45 a Day,* and a contributor to *Frommer's Europe from $50 a Day* and *Frommer's Complete Guide to Europe.*

Michael C. Goldstein has worked and played in Asia, Africa, South America, and Europe, and presently resides in Jerusalem, where he organizes cultural events.

Sherry Marker's love of Greece began when she majored in Classical Greek at Harvard, studied archeology at the American School of Classical Studies in Athens, and did graduate work in Ancient History at the University of California at Berkeley. In 1975, she bought a two-room house in the Peloponnese, where she spends every summer with her family and laptop computer. The author of a number of guides to Greece, she has also had articles published on Greece, Puerto Rico, England, and New England in the *New York Times, Travel & Leisure,* and *Hampshire Life.* In addition, she has written books on a variety of subjects including a history of London for young adults, an account of the Plains Indians Wars, and biographies of Norman Rockwell and Edward Hopper. When not in Greece she lives in Massachusetts, where she teaches a writing seminar at Smith College.

Tom Stone graduated from Yale in 1958 and made his first trip to Greece the following spring as an assistant stage manager for Jerome Robbins' Ballets: USA. Since then, alternating a career in the theater with that of writing, he has worked as a stage manager on the original productions of such notable Broadway hits as *Funny Girl, Fiddler on the Roof,* and *Cabaret,* while publishing several short stories, a novel, and numerous writings about Greece. In 1970, he settled on the Greek island of Patmos, where he met and married the French painter Florence Messager, now highly regarded in the Greek art world. They have two children: Samantha, recently graduated from Princeton with high honors, and Oliver, presently a student at Wesleyan. After 22 years of living almost exclusively in Greece, mostly in Thessaloníki, Mr. Stone returned to the professional American Theater in 1992 when he directed the London and Vienna companies of the musical *Kiss of the Spider Woman* for Harold Prince. Currently he is back in his hometown of Baltimore, where he is hard at work on a number of writing projects, including a novel set in classical Athens.

List of Maps

INVITATION TO THE READER

In researching this book, we discovered many wonderful places—hotels, restaurants, shops, and more. We're sure you'll find others. Please tell us about them, so we can share the information with your fellow travelers in upcoming editions. If you were disappointed with a recommendation, we'd love to know that, too. Please write to:

Frommer's Greece, 1st Edition
Macmillan Travel
1633 Broadway
New York, NY 10019

AN ADDITIONAL NOTE

Please be advised that travel information is subject to change at any time—and this is especially true of prices. We therefore suggest that you write or call ahead for confirmation when making your travel plans. The authors, editors, and publisher cannot be held responsible for the experiences of readers while traveling. Your safety is important to us, however, so we encourage you to stay alert and be aware of your surroundings. Keep a close eye on cameras, purses, and wallets, all favorite targets of thieves and pickpockets.

WHAT THE SYMBOLS MEAN

✪ Frommer's Favorites

Hotels, restaurants, attractions, and entertainment you should not miss.

⑤ Super-Special Values

Hotels and restaurants that offer great value for your money.

The following abbreviations are used for credit cards:

AE	American Express	EU	Eurocard
CB	Carte Blanche	JCB	Japan Credit Bank
DC	Diners Club	MC	MasterCard
DISC	Discover	V	Visa
ER	enRoute		

ACCENT MARKS

To aid the reader in the pronunciation of Greek words, we have added an accent mark to indicate where you should put the stress. Getting the right pronunciation *can* be important, especially if you are asking for directions or are buying, say, a train or bus ticket. Thus, for example, in Leofóros Vassiléos Konstantínou (King Constantine Avenue, in Athens), the accents tell you that the words should be pronounced Leh-oh-*FOH*-rohs Vahssee-*LEH*-ohs Kohn-stahn-*TEE*-noo.

The Best of Greece **1**

by John Bozman

From Santoríni's Caldera to the gray pinnacles of rock of the Metéora, Greece is spectacular. There aren't many places in the world where the forces of nature have come together with such dramatic results. Greece is, of course, the land of ancient sites and architectural treasures, the Acropolis in Athens, the Amphitheater of Epidaurus, the excellent museum at Delphi, and the reconstructed palace at Knossos.

It can be bewildering to plan your trip with so many options vying for your attention. Take us along and we'll do the work for you. We've traveled the country extensively, and chosen the very best that Greece has to offer. We've explored the archaeological sites, visited the museums, inspected the hotels, reviewed the tavernas and ouzeríes, and scoped out the beaches. Here's what we consider to be the best Greece has to offer.

1 The Best Ancient Sites

- **The Acropolis** (Athens): One of the world's greatest architectural treasures. Built to last, it's an enduring testimony to an illustrious people. See Chapter 4.
- **Akrotíri** (Santoríni): The best preserved of all Minoan cities, a mine of knowledge and beauty, and believed by many to be the legendary lost Atlantis. Try to find time for its murals in the National Archaeological Museum in Athens. See Chapter 8.
- **The Amphitheater of Epidaurus** (Palaiá Epídavros, Argolídi, eastern Peloponnese): The world's most magnificent amphitheater, with incredible acoustics, hosts world-class performances of the immortal tragedies of Aeschylus, Sophocles, and Euripides and the comedies of Aristophanes. Nearby are the remains of the most renowned Asclepion (center of healing arts) in the Hellenic world and a fine museum. See Chapter 6.
- **Delphi** (Delphí, Stereá Elládos): The center of the earth to the ancients, Delphi was home of the greatest of ancient oracles, sacred to Apollo (god of light, learning, and music), and the site of the Pythian Games. It's one of the richest repositories of ancient treasures. Word reached this mountain retreat at the foot of sacred Parnassus, home of the Muses, that Christians were coming to destroy it; a few incredible treasures were quickly buried and saved, and they're now exhibited in its excellent museum. See Chapter 10.

- **Knossos** (Iráklion, Crete): Don't let anyone persuade you reconstruction has ruined this marvel, where King Minos ruled over the richest and most powerful of Minoan cities and, according to legend, his daughter Ariadne helped Theseus kill the Minotaur and escape the Labyrinth. See Chapter 7.
- **Mycenae** (Mikínes, Argolídi, eastern Peloponnese): The ruins of the greatest of all Mycenaean fortress palaces, where the vault was perfected in beehive burial chambers. From Mycenae, Agamemnon led the Greeks to conquer Troy. You can walk through its famous Lions Gate and around the palace; look out over the kingdom it commanded. See Chapter 6.
- **Olympia** (Olympía, Elía, western Peloponnese): The Olympics, the greatest of all games, were begun here in 776 B.C. You can still run in the original Stadium, wander among the impressive ruins of the Sacred Precinct, and enjoy the treasures of its fine museum, including the Hermes of Praxiteles. See Chapter 6.

2 The Best Beaches

- **Elía Beach** (Mýkonos): The longest beach on one of the world's premier fun-in-the-sun islands, Elía is sheltered, broad, and sandy. There's some green protection from the golden rays and a good restaurant. It's the last stop on the south coast caïque (skiff) run—the last time we were there, anyway. Occasionally you can even find peace and privacy here. See Chapter 8.
- **Kolymbíthres Beach** (Páros): Sheltered in Náoussa Bay, Kolymbíthres has sparkling clear water and small golden sand coves separated by giant smooth rock formations that have been sculpted by the elements. Several good hotels and tavernas are nearby. It's within walking distance of pleasant and picturesque Náoussa, so it's far from secluded. See Chapter 8.
- **Lalária Beach** (Skiáthos): Lalária is not nearly as popular nor accessible as famous Koukounariés, which is one of the reasons why it's still gorgeous and pristine. This gleaming white pebble beach has white limestone cliffs, with natural arches cut into them by the elements, and vivid aquamarine water. See Chapter 11.
- **Psilí Ámmos Beach** (Pátmos): A kilometer stretch of fine sand (from which it takes its name), Psilí Ámmos lies on secluded and sheltered Stávrou Bay. Shaded by pretty tamarisk trees, it's accessible only by caïque from Skála or reached by a two-hour hike. The water is shallow and calm in the morning, but afternoon breezes bring waves. There's a good taverna, too. See Chapter 9.
- **Platís Yialós Beach** (Sífnos): Not so very large or beautiful but gently sloping and well protected, this beach is perfect for children. Not yet overdeveloped, Platís Yialós has several good hotels and a few decent places to eat; on a charming, hospitable island famous for good cooks. See Chapter 8.

3 The Best Museums

- **National Archaeological Museum** (Athens): Simply the best in the world. It contains the golden "Treasure of Agamemnon," discovered by Schliemann; an unsurpassed collection of ceramic vessels; an incomparable bronze Poseidon preserved 2,000 years by the sea; and two incredibly beautiful Aphrodites, one smacking Pan with her sandal for daring to get randy with her. See Chapter 4.
- **Archaeological Museum** (Iráklion, Crete): This fine museum contains Neolithic, Archaic Greek, and Roman finds from throughout Crete. Its Minoan collection is especially important and includes superb frescos from Knossós, elegant bronze and stone figurines, and exquisite gold jewelry. See Chapter 7.

- **Archaeological Museum** (Olympia): Besides the much-celebrated Hermes of Praxiteles, there are the magnificent pediments and metopes of the Temple of Zeus, remarkable for their preservation and attention to anatomical detail and expression, as well as a number of objects related to the Olympic Games. See Chapter 6.
- **Archaeological Museum** (Thessaloníki): Some may think that seeing the skeleton of Alexander the Great's father and his funerary treasures spread out for your viewing pleasure is a bit macabre. See it before you make up your own mind, but we think Philip II would approve. See Chapter 14.
- **Delphi Museum** (Delphi): This museum alone would be worth the three-hour trip from Athens. Besides its famous life-size bronze charioteer with his sparkling eyes, there are two magnificent Archaic koúri; a room of silver and gold treasures; the celebrated Naxian Sphinx; the graceful and powerful Acanthus Column of the Dancing Girls; and an excellent statue of Antinoös, which is an eloquent recapitulation of classical sculpture. See Chapter 10.
- **Goulandris Museum of Cycladic and Ancient Greek Art** (Athens): An impeccable display of astonishing Cycladic and ancient Greek treasures, well labeled and beautifully displayed, in the handsomest small museum in Greece. It's only half a dozen blocks from the center of Athens. See Chapter 4.

4 The Most Spectacular Natural Wonders

- **The Caldera of Thíra** (Santoríni): One of the world's most dramatic geological sights, this crater averages 5 miles in diameter. It was left by the explosion of a colossal volcano between 1647 and 1628 B.C. See Chapter 8.
- **Metéora** (Kalambáka, Thessalía): These awesome gray pinnacles of rock were left when the sea retreated from the plain of Thessaly 30 million years ago. They look like some strange and beautiful set from a sci-fi movie. See Chapter 10.
- **Samaria Gorge** (Crete): The "Grand Canyon of Greece" is 18 kilometers long (the longest gorge in Europe). Its vertical walls reach up to 500 meters, and in the spring it's liberally sprinkled with an incredible array of wildflowers. See Chapter 7.

5 The Most Picturesque Ports

- **Chaniá** (Crete): Handsome Venetian remains line Crete's most beautiful and impressive harbor. You can wander its narrow lanes, filled with a heady mix of colorful local culture, charming hotels, excellent restaurants, swinging nightspots, and interesting shops. See Chapter 7.
- **Hóra** (Mýkonos): Overexposed on a million postcards, overpriced, overrun by tourists in the summer—it somehow manages to hold on to its rugged good looks, ample charm, and more than a vestige of self-respect. Hóra is still a thrill. See Chapter 8.
- **Hýdra** (Ýdra): A national monument and treasure, Hydra has a perfect horseshoe-shaped harbor surrounded by grand slate-gray Italianate architecture. Motorized vehicles are banned from the entire island, and strolling the meandering cobblestone lanes is a very special pleasure. The town offers some very good restaurants, interesting shopping, and excellent accommodations. See Chapter 5.

- **Náfplion** (Argolída, Peloponnese): A city of Venetian fortresses, Náfplion was the first capital of modern Greece, with much of its glory still evident. From its *paralía* (waterfront), across from its picturesque little harbor island Boúrtzi, there is very little but serene beauty in any direction. See Chapter 6.
- **Rhodes:** Imagine its Collosus, one of the Seven Great Wonders of the ancient world, as the famous hind and stag welcome you to one of the world's most cosmopolitan resorts. It has the best-preserved medieval town in Greece, if not all Europe. Too popular, too expensive, too much—but still a must-see on every dedicated traveler's list. See Chapter 9.
- **Sými:** This picture-perfect little harbor is surrounded by pastel-yellow neoclassical homes that are being preserved by archaeological decree. See Chapter 9.
- **Skópelos** (Skópelos): An amazingly well-preserved whitewashed traditional town, Skópelos is adorned everywhere with pots of flowering plants. It has a rather sophisticated local life, several excellent restaurants, some very good hotels, and plenty of interesting shopping. See Chapter 11.

6 The Most Intriguing Religious Treasures

- **Dafní Monastery:** The biggest and best preserved of Greece's many Byzantine monasteries, Dafní has handsome architecture and impressive mosaics. It's very accessible from Athens/Corinth Highway. See Chapter 4.
- **Eleusis:** The site of the most sacred of ancient Mysteries, Eleusis was destroyed by Alaric the Goth in A.D. 396. But you can still see the Ploutarion Cave into which Hades abducted Persephone and the well where her mother, Demeter, wept for her and, in her grief, neglected the earth and caused the seasons. See Chapter 4.
- **Church of Panayía Evangelístria** (Tínos): The most revered Eastern Orthodox shrine in Greece, Evangelístria is a neoclassical gem, filled to the gills with treasures. It's above the pleasant port of Tínos town, on one of the friendliest, most hospitable islands in Greece. See Chapter 8.
- **Monasteries of Metéora** (Kalambáka, Thessalía): The Byzantine monasteries atop the awesome pinnacles of rock are serene, mysterious, and truly otherworldly. See Chapter 10.
- **Mount Athos** (Macedonia): The impressive "Holy Mount," on the easternmost of Halkidíki's fingerlike peninsulas, is an independent religious state composed of 20 monasteries. It can be entered only with special permission; women have been excluded since 1060. Cruise excursions around Mount Athos are offered from Thessaloníki. See Chapter 14.
- **Néa Moní** (Híos): One of the most beautiful and important religious sites in Greece, Néa Moní is among the country's oldest monasteries, despite its name, which means "New Monastery." Barely functioning, it dominates the center of the craggy island and has a grand view. The skulls of those slaughtered in a Turkish massacre are matter-of-factly displayed. There may be better preserved Byzantine mosaics than those of its ruined chapel, but none are more mysterious and moving. See Chapter 16.
- **Pátmos:** The entire island of Pátmos has a rare spiritual quality; you will seldom find people who love, respect, and revere their home more. Pátmos is dominated by a fortress monastery above the cave where the exiled disciple John the Younger (The Theologos) Theologian had his vision of Apocalypse and wrote his Revelations. See Chapter 9.

7 The Most Beautiful Villages & Towns

- **Hóra** (Folégandros): The most beautiful and least spoiled capital in the Cyclades, Hóra sits high atop a spectacular cliff. Mercifully free of vehicular traffic, it boasts a picture-perfect old *kástro* (castle), the handsome all-white Panayía Church on the hillside above it, and surprisingly good accommodations. See Chapter 8.
- **Ía** (Santoríni): The most beautiful and pleasantly unconventional village on spectacular Santoríni, Ía is at the north end of the Caldéra. It survived a devastating 1956 earthquake better than any place on the island and profits from some tasteful reconstruction. Ía is world famous for its sensational sunsets, when it can be quite crowded. It gets quieter and more sophisticated after dark, with some very good restaurants, interesting shops, and excellent accommodations. See Chapter 8.
- **Métsovo** (Epirus): Superbly situated in the mountains east of Ioánnina, Métsovo is serene and chock-full of rustic charm. It's refreshing in the summer and invigorating in the winter ski season. Métsovo has a number of excellent small hotels and an interesting local cuisine. See Chapter 12.
- **Mistra** (near Sparta, Lakonía, southern Peloponnese): A long-abandoned Byzantine city gracefully fading away, Mistra is the most haunting ghost town in Greece. It's a delight to explore—especially in the spring when it's still cool and decked out in wildflowers. See Chapter 6.
- **Piryí and Mestá** (Híos): These are the two most interesting and attractive of the villages of southern Híos, where mastic (the chief ingredient of chewing gum) is grown. Piryí is the only village in Greece decorated predominantly with white-and-gray graffiti in geometric patterns that give it a surreal op art quality. Nearby Mestá is a 14th-century medieval fortress village with meter-thick walls and a labyrinth of interconnected streets. See Chapter 16.

8 The Best Luxury Hotels

- **Hotel Belvedere** (Rohári, Mýkonos; ☎ 0289/25-122): The newest and finest hotel in Mýkonos town, the Belvedere was built and furnished in traditional island style, with specially designed double doors and windows for extra quiet. It has a handsome pool and a faithfully restored 1850 mansion, where a full American breakfast is served. See Chapter 8.
- **Hotel Bratsera** (Hýdra; ☎ 0289/53-971): The best hotel on lovely, serene Hydra, the Bratsera was an old sponge factory. Recently lovingly restored, it has a handsome spacious lobby, a nice pool surrounded by a colonnade and trellis covered with wisteria, and an excellent restaurant. Decorated in typical Hydriot style, each room is different. See Chapter 5.
- **Chateau Zevgoli** (Hóra, Náxos; ☎ 0285/22-993): A recently restored Venetian mansion, the Chateau Zevgoli is in the charming labyrinthine old quarter. Its lobby/dining area has been decorated with antiques and family heirlooms by the gracious and discerning owner. Cozy rooms are distinctively furnished in traditional style with modern bathrooms and central heat. See Chapter 8.
- **Doma** (Chaniá, Crete; ☎ 0821/51-772): A former neoclassical mansion east of downtown, the Doma has been converted into a comfortable and charming hotel by its gracious owner; she has furnished it with her family heirlooms. Its top-floor dining room offers a unique Cretan dining experience. See Chapter 7.

- **Hotel Kyma** (Híos; ☎ 0271/44-500): Built as a private villa in 1917, the Kyma was later converted into a very special hotel with a friendly, capable, and hospitable staff. The original architectural details have been preserved in the dining room, where an especially good breakfast is served. The older front rooms have big whirlpool baths; the newer wing is plain, modern, quiet, and comfortable. See Chapter 16.
- **Skála Hotel** (Skála, Patmos; ☎ 0247/31-343): The Skala is a very attractive and comfortable hotel, with an excellent and hospitable staff. It's just far enough from the harbor and behind its own charming garden and cascading bougainvillea to escape the noise and hustle. See Chapter 9.

9 The Best Hotel Bargains

- **Attalos Hotel** (Monasteráki, Athens; ☎ 01/321-2801): An excellent location near the major sights and the Monasteráki metro station is the chief asset of this comfortable, clean hotel, which is skillfully managed and staffed. From the rooftop bar, there's a good view of the Acropolis. The Attalos is quiet enough for a good night's rest, especially if you take advantage of the air-conditioning, and there's an ample breakfast. See Chapter 4.
- **Loucas Hotel** (Firá, Santoríni; ☎ 0286/22-480): These cool, white rooms, with vaulted ceilings, are attractively and comfortably furnished. Ably managed, the Loucas is an especially good value, considering the priceless Caldera view and all the exciting sightseeing, dining, and shopping possibilities nearby. See Chapter 8.
- **Marble House Pension** (Koukáki, Athens; ☎ 01/923-4058): On a quiet cul-de-sac in a nontouristic neighborhood south of the Acropolis, the Marble House has clean, comfortable rooms with ceiling fans and an exceptionally friendly, helpful, and caring staff. See Chapter 4.
- **Hotel Pelops** (Ancient Olympia, Elía; ☎ 0624/22-213): An attractive, excellent-value hotel, the Pelops has clean, comfortable rooms and a charming Australian owner/manager. See Chapter 6.

10 The Best First-Class Restaurants

- **Chez Cat'rine** (Hóra, Mýkonos; ☎ 0289/22-169): Justifiably the most famous restaurant in the Cyclades, Chez Cat'rine is small and intimate. It has a limited menu of seafood, grilled meats, and a few French dishes, all meticulously prepared and professionally served. Very expensive, but a very special dining experience; reserve as far ahead of time as possible. See Chapter 8.
- **Lalula** (Náoussa, Páros; ☎ 0284/51-547): The menu is imaginative and eclectic—sweet-and-sour chicken with rice and ginger chutney, vegetable quiche, fish steamed in herbs—depending on what's fresh at the market. The cooking is lighter and more refined than usually found in Greece, the decor is chic but subdued, and the music is interesting but unobtrusive. See Chapter 8.
- **To Liotrivi** (Artemóma, Sífnos; ☎ 0284/32-051): The favorite taverna on an island famous for its excellent cooks serves delectable local specialties such as *povithokeftédes* (croquettes of ground chick peas). More international dishes are available, too, such as beef fillet with potatoes in wine sauce baked in an envelope of foil. See Chapter 8.

11 The Best Inexpensive Restaurants

- **Naoussa Restaurant** (Firá, Santoríni; ☎ 0286/24-869): This friendly family-run place serves ample portions of a large variety of dishes—Mexican salad, souvlaki oriental, chicken Americaine—at surprisingly reasonable prices. See Chapter 8.
- **Panathinea Pizzeria/Cafeteria** (Makriyánni, Athens; ☎ 01/923-3721): An unpretentious place across from the Center for Acropolis Studies (Melina Mercouri's office) that serves good pizza, country salads, moussaka, and chicken souvlaki in generous portions at fair prices. See Chapter 4.
- **Thanasis** (Monasteráki, Athens; ☎ 01/324-6229): This ever-busy souvlaki stand, just off Monasteráki Square, has the best french fries in town as well as tasty souvlaki, brusque service, and no-nonsense prices. See Chapter 4.
- **Yiannis Taverna** (Old Town, Rhodes; ☎ 0241/36-535): Generous portions of hearty moussaka, stuffed vegetables, and meat dishes, friendly service, and exceptionally good prices for the pricey Old Town. See Chapter 9.

12 A Few Other Bests

THE BEST CRUISE

- **The Seven-Day Cruise of the Cyclades Aboard the *Viking Star*** (☎ 01/898-0729, fax 01/898-0729; U.S. 800/341-3030; E-mail: vikings@ars.forthnet.gre): You'll see the highlights of Greece's best and most varied island group on this cruise, aboard a vessel small enough to feel like a well-kept older yacht. You can actually feel the Aegean Sea. Not luxurious, but comfortable, with a good friendly crew and plenty of excellent food.

THE BEST DRIVE

- **The coastal highway between Arepolis and Kalamáta** (the southern Peloponnese): Unspoiled, varied, and spectacular scenery, with lush and lovely vegetation. See Chapter 6.

THE BEST PLACE TO GET MARRIED

- **Ía, Santoríni:** Musicians lead the lucky couple along the marble pedestrian street through this charming village to their ceremony, which can be either civil or religious. Afterwards, the bride and groom and their guests can enjoy a special feast in a local restaurant. One of the excellent nearby Caldera-view villas can provide the honeymoon accommodations. A wedding in Ía can be half the cost and hassle of one at home. See Chapter 8.

2 Getting to Know Greece

by John Bozman

Greece is both a respite and a feast for the senses: the smell of baking bread; a widow in dull black patiently sweeping the street in the morning; a weathered fisherman offering fish fresh from his yellow net; an ancient ruin glowing in the incandescent moonlight; endless olive trees silvering in the warm breeze; deep blue water and distant islands; women sitting on their doorsteps talking and knitting a mile a minute but pausing to smile and wish you health; empty streets as shopkeepers settle in for siesta.

Exotic and yet familiar, dreamlike but immediate, Greece is full of strange subtleties and stark contrasts. It's a nation struggling to be contemporary but haunted and elevated by its heritage. Greece is sometimes dazzlingly modern, and yet there is always something to remind you of the past: Alexander the Great and Homer on Greek coins; an ancient Mycenaean fortress; a classical temple you know already; a Byzantine church; a Venetian or Frankish castle; the remains of a mosque; a neoclassical building from only a century ago.

1 The Regions in Brief

Geographically, Greece is at the southern part of the Balkan peninsula in the northeastern Mediterranean Sea. It has nearly 6,000 islands—fewer than 200 of them inhabited—strewn around and far to the south. As we sometimes forget, the Balkans have been perennially troubled, caught in the crucible of several thousand years of turbulent history, but Greece itself remains somehow relatively constant.

The mainland is bordered on the north by Albania, the former Yugoslavia, Bulgaria, and Turkey, its former overlord and archenemy. For mostly historic reasons, Greece is divided into various areas, many of them much like their ancient counterparts, others truncated by history. Such is the unhappy and much contested case with the northern region we call **Macedonia** (Makedonía), most of which is part of Greece, but part of which was a republic in the former nation of Yugoslavia.

The name Thessaloníki celebrates the Macedonian victory over the Greeks at the battle of Chaeronea in Thessaly in 338 B.C. by Philip II, Alexander's dad. It's a thriving cosmopolitan capital, the second largest city and port in Greece, with Roman ruins, marvelous Byzantine churches, a superb archaeological museum, an important yearly international trade fair, and a busy but pleasant atmosphere.

Alexander the Great country itself is mostly to the west and south at Pélla, Vérgina, and Dión. To the south stretches the three-fingered peninsula of Halkidíki and holy Mt. Athos, which can be visited by men, only with permission. Kavála, the pretty port where the Apostle Paul first stepped ashore in Europe, and nearby Phillipi, where he also preached and where the armies of Anthony and Octavian (later Emperor Augustus) defeated those of Brutus and Cassius, are east.

East of Macedonia is the region that was in ancient times known for its wild red-haired people, **Thrace** (Thráki), which now has a large Muslim population. From its capital, Alexandroúpoli (city of Alexander), you can catch a ferry to Samothráki or continue on by bus or train to Istanbul (Konstantinópoli) or Bulgaria.

South of Macedonia and mighty Mt. Olympus lies **Thessaly** (Thessalía), famous since antiquity for pastoral life, which continues there today along with agriculture on the central plains around the big easygoing capital of Lárissa. Volos, from where Jason and the Argonauts set sail, is today a major seaport, where the ferries to the Sporades can be caught. The wild slopes of Mt. Pelion (Pílio) are now covered with orchards, and centaurs are no longer seen, but there are a number of very charming traditional villages, beautiful beaches, and gracious people. In western Thessaly the monasteries of Metéora perch atop their towering rocks, spectacular and serene.

West of Thessaly is the mountainous region of **Epirus** (Ípiros), with its lovely mountain villages like Métsovo and the wild and nearly deserted Zagóri, now being avidly discovered by trekkers. South of the busy capital, Ióannina, and its tranquil lake, are the remains of the famous Oracle of Zeus at Dodona (Dodóni). Unlike most of Greece, Epirus is densely forested in the north and rather overlooked by tourists, possibly partly because its people are not especially outgoing, but nature lovers, trekkers, and hikers will love it.

Then there is what we conveniently call **Central Greece** (Stereá Elládos). This includes Attica (Athens County, you might say) and sometimes the big island of Évvia. The high point is the stellar Mt. Parnassus (Parnassós), often covered with snow and shrouded with clouds—the Muses may still linger here. Delphi, in the shadow of Mt. Parnassus, is one of the most beautiful and deeply impressive places in Greece. The town itself is very pleasant, the remains of the Oracle of Apollo and the surrounding Sanctuary are endlessly fascinating, and the museum alone would be worth the trip. In the vicinity are the handsome Byzantine monastery of *Óssios Loukás,* several lovely mountain villages, including Aráchova—a ski resort in the winter—as well as Itéa on the Gulf of Corinth for those who require a dip in the sea, lovely Galaxidi, historic Dióstomo, or Lefpákto (Lepanto), where the European fleets defeated the Turkish.

In Athens, you'll find the Acropolis, the Ancient Agorá, the National Gardens, the Temple of Olympian Zeus, the Stadium (built on the site of the ancient one for the first modern Olympic games in 1896), scenic Mt. Hymettus (Imittós), and the refreshing Monastery of Kaisarianí. Piraeus, its port since ancient times, is one of the busiest in the Mediterranean and famous for its vibrant nightlife, especially its rebétika clubs.

South of Athiná you'll find wealthy and stylish Glyfáda, the Apollo Coast, and the austere Temple of Poseidon, which commands the impressive hilltop overlooking Cape Soúnio. Devotees of the goddess Artemis may want to visit her temple at Brauron (Vravróna). Marathon is to the northeast of Athens, where the Athenians defeated the Persians in 490 B.C. and from which Pheidippides ran the 26 miles to

Greece

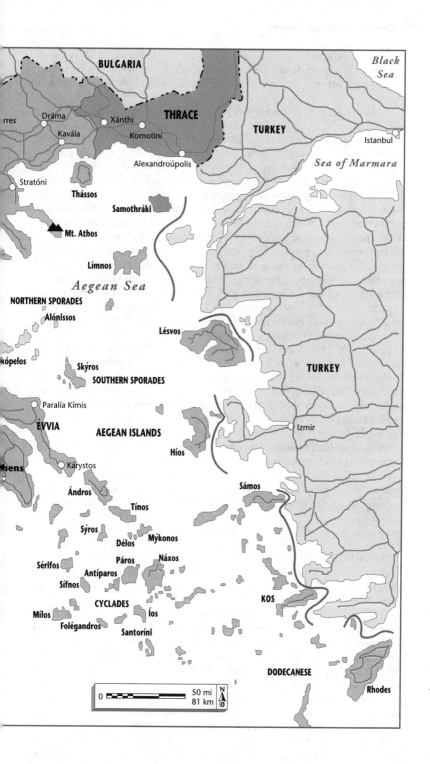

BULGARIA

Black Sea

THRACE

rres Dráma Xánthi

Kavála Komotiní

TURKEY

Istanbul

Alexandroúpolis

Sea of Marmara

Stratóni

Thássos

Samothráki

▲ Mt. Athos

Límnos

Aegean Sea

NORTHERN SPORADES

Alónissos

kópelos

Skýros

SOUTHERN SPORADES

Lésvos

TURKEY

Paralía Kímis

ÉVVIA

AEGEAN ISLANDS

Híos

Izmir

hens Kárystos

Ándros

Sámos

Tínos

Sýros

Délos Mýkonos

Páros Náxos

Sérifos

Antíparos

Sífnos

CYCLADES

KOS

Mílos Íos

Folégandros Santoríni

DODECANESE

Rhodes

0 50 mi
81 km

N

11

Athens with the news of victory. The superb Byzantine Monastery of Dafní is only 10 kilometers west of Athens on the way to Corinth, and it's only a bit further to Eleusis (Elefsís) and the remains of the most famous and revered of all ancient Mysteries.

Last comes that most distinctive peninsula, the **Peloponnese** (Pelopónnisos)—now separated from the mainland by the Corinth Canal, begun by Nero in A.D. 67 and finished just over a century ago by a French construction company. The Peloponnese is sometimes referred to as the Morea (in Italian) and fairly defies quick description. A glance at a map will find you at least a dozen places of major interest: the important seaport of Pátra; Olympia, famous for its games; Mycenae, from which Agamemnon led the Greeks against Troy; Argos, home of Jason and most of the Argonauts; Epidaurus, with its perfect amphitheater and Asclepion; the beautiful port of Náfplion; Sparta, which won the Peloponnesian War with its famous discipline, and the nearby Byzantine ghost city of Mistrá; Kalamáta; and "sandy" Pylos.

The three remote southern fingers of the Peloponnese are largely unspoiled by tourism. The Venetian fortress at Monemvassiá, the "Gibraltar of Greece," is peaceful and otherworldly except in the summer and on holidays when Greeks reclaim and overrun it. The Máni is remote and wild, its people known for their independent spirit, with the cool underworld of the caves of Pírgou. The highway along the coast from Areópoli to Kalamáta is especially varied and spectacular. Below Pýlos and past Navaríno (Navarone in Italian), where the Great Powers of Britain, France, and Russia accidentally defeated the Turkish fleet and ended the War of Independence, are "the Eyes of Venice," the lovely castles at Methóni and Koróni and good beaches.

The islands are divided mostly along geographical lines into seven major groups: the Saronic Gulf islands near Athens and east of the Peloponnese peninsula; the south-central Cyclades; the Ionian islands west of the mainland; the Sporades (sometimes including Évvia) on the east; the northeastern Aegean islands further north and east; the Dodecanese east near Turkey; and the most southerly, Crete.

The **Saronic Gulf islands** are the closest to Athens and the most easily accessible, but they are often crowded on the weekends and in the summer. Aegina is worth at least a day trip to its handsome and pleasant port, Eyina, and the lovely Temple of Aphaia (*Aphéa)*, one of the best preserved and most beautifully situated of all Archaic buildings. In another hour you can reach touristy Póros, which is pleasant and relatively inexpensive, with several good beaches. The whole island of Hydra is a national preserve on which vehicles are not allowed, a real gift, if a tad expensive. Spétses is the most distant, a pretty and sophisticated island, on which traffic is allowed.

The **Cyclades** probably need little introduction, as they are among the most popular and accessible of the islands. Spectacular **Santoríni** and swinging **Mýkonos** are world famous, sophisticated, and expensive, especially if you opt for luxury in the high season. **Páros** is the transportation hub of the Cyclades. Away from its port of Parikía, Páros is not as expensive or as crowded as Santoríni or Mýkonos, and it's an excellent place for water sports, especially windsurfing. Sýros is the capital, largest city, and administrative center of the Cyclades; it's not much acquainted with tourists, and therefore a good place to find authentic Greece without sacrificing the amenities. **Náxos** is large, mountainous, and largely self-sufficient because of its agriculture, and a pleasant place to stay, shop, and escape the hordes. Or you can join them for a beer bust on **Íos**. Tínos is a religious retreat, where little English is spoken and foreign tourists are noticed only if they seem lost, then given genuine attention. Shy Síphnos offers more enjoyable escape, and Folégandros is even more remote.

The **Ionian islands** are among the greenest and most beautiful, but they sometimes seem more Italian than Greek and their inhabitants are not known for friendliness and hospitality. These islands are quite distant from Athens, though fairly convenient for those coming from Italy. Corfu is the best known, remarkably beautiful, sophisticated, and expensive. Lefkáda is accessible by car, without having to resort to a ferry, and not especially attractive at first sight, but the interior is very pleasant and the south coast has some lovely beaches. Ithaca is more famous as the home of wily Odysseus than as a tourist destination, but it has a beautiful interior with rugged hills and evergreen valleys, plus a few pretty if rocky beaches. Unspoiled Kefaloniá is a large island with sensational scenery and several excellent beaches. Zákynthos is the most southern and convenient to the Peloponnese, with much to offer in the spring and fall, though its handsome Venetian architecture was mostly ruined by an earthquake in 1953.

The **Sporádes** are off the east coast of the mainland of Greece. Verdant and boasting particularly clear water, they are not quite as picturesque as the Ionians. They are accessible from Athens, via bus to Aýios Konstandínos then by hydrofoil or ferry, or from the port of Vólos. Skiáthos, which can also be reached by air, is the most sophisticated, most expensive, and best developed—perhaps too developed—because of its many beautiful fine-sand beaches. Skópelos is more rugged with fewer good beaches, but it is being developed more slowly and thoughtfully, and Skópelos town is one of the most beautiful ports in Greece. Alónissos is more remote and less touristy, but it has its share of attractions, and its people are friendlier. Skýros is also quite isolated, with its own ferry from Kými on Évvia, as well as its own character, traditions, and wild ponies.

The **Northeastern Aegean Islands,** to the north and east, are the most remote and least visited of the major islands—which in itself should pique some interest. Sámos is only a few kilometers from Turkey, with regular ferry service to Kuçadasi and Ephesus, plenty of good tourist facilities, good beaches, and several interesting sights. Híos is known for its wealthy ship owners, mastic (chewing gum), its handsome medieval villages, and the warm hospitality of its people. Lésvos is probably known best as the birthplace of Sappho, the greatest of all lyric poets. It is a prosperous island not dependent on tourism, though it has important resort havens in the north at beautiful Mólivos and south at Plomári. Límnos is a fertile volcanic island, strategically located at the mouth of the Black Sea, and perhaps best known today for its luxurious Akti Minini resort complex. Lonely Samothráki has its Sanctuary of the Great Gods, where important fertility Mysteries were celebrated in ancient times, but few tourist facilities. Far northern Thássos has plenty of facilities because it's very close to the mainland, maybe a little too close.

The **Dodecanese** ("Twelve Islands" in Greek) are further south and generally better connected and developed, again perhaps too well. Famous Rhodes is the best known of the Dozen; decades of unflagging popularity with foreign visitors have not ruined the island, but it is not an easy visit, certainly expensive, and unless you're careful not a good value. Little **Sými** owes its popularity to overflowing Rhodes, from which it is easily visited, its relative serenity, and its pretty yellow neoclassical architecture. Lovely **Kos** was in ancient times famous for its cure resort; now it's better known for its tour resorts, and much too popular with budget groups, though with a little effort you can still find it well worth visiting. Sponges gave **Kálymnos** it's livelihood until recently, but it's now soaking up the overflow of tourists from adjacent islands, especially along its attractive west coast. Holy **Pátmos** is a very special island, which probably needs little introduction if you know your New Testament history, a refuge for the spirit and a joy to the senses.

Crete is the largest and most southerly of the islands, something of a land unto itself, with great diversity and its own special character. It has spectacular scenery;

impressive Minoan ruins and beautiful Venetian remains; the bustling capital of Iráklion with its excellent Archeological Museum and nearby Knossós; handsome and pleasant Réthymno; lovely Chaniá with its Venetian fortifications and excursions to Samariá gorge; and excellent beaches.

2 A Look at the Past

Dateline

- **6,000 B.C.** Earliest known human inhabitants, Neolithic culture with rudimentary agriculture.
- **3,000 B.C.** Bronze Age begins; Minoan culture on Crete; Helladic (Mycenaean) on mainland.
- **2,000 B.C.** Knossós and Mycenae are being built.
- **1900 B.C.** Minoan culture is ascendant, the Palace of Knossós so large and maze-like that the myth of the Labyrinth takes shape.
- **1640 B.C.** Volcano of Santorini erupts, burying Akrotíri in ash and inundating Crete with tidal wave.
- **1400–1200 B.C.** Mycenae conquers Crete, leads Greek forces against Troy in Asia Minor (Hissarlik, Turkey).
- **1100–1200 B.C.** Mycenaean culture collapses under Dorian invasion; the "Dark Ages" ensue and writing disappears.
- **900 B.C.** Lykúrgus demands obedience in Sparta.
- **800–600 B.C.** The Aristocratic Age: Homer composes the *Iliad* and *Odyssey*; city-state (pólis) becomes most important political entity; colonization throughout Mediterranean; Athens consolidates power.
- **776 B.C.** Panhellenic Games established, help ensure peace among Greek city-states.
- **621 B.C.** Dráko proclaims notoriously severe laws in Athens.
- **600–500 B.C.** Sparta rises to prominence through

continues

The Minoan civilization (named after the mythical King Minos) arose around 3000 B.C. on Crete. The Minoans were seafarers, more interested in trade than agriculture, who had contact with Egypt and established outposts on the Peloponnese, and had a proto-Greek written language, called Linear A, which has not yet been satisfactorily translated. The unwalled capital of Knossós grew into a major city with impressive architecture, marvelous art, even plumbing, and a palace so large and elaborate that it gave rise to the myth of the Labyrinth.

Several abandoned sites on the mainland suggest that it was invaded from the north by another more warlike people in about 2,000 B.C., giving rise to the Mycenaean (or Helladic) culture, which was distinguished by a citadel; a walled palace with a warrior king; a strong central authority that levied taxes and demanded tribute by armed force; the worship of male as well as female deities; and a written language, Linear B, probably adapted from Minoan, which has been more successfully deciphered. Judging by Homer's account, warfare was waged primarily by royal kings and princes in chariots. By about 1400 B.C., Mycenae (Mikínes) had attained supremacy on the mainland, and there were Mycenaean strongholds at Tíryns, with its Cyclopean walls of huge boulders (which the ancients believed could only have been built by the giant Cyclops) and Pýlos, home of the Iliad's venerable King Nestor, with its mégaron (great room with central hearth), which would develop into the classical temple.

The eruption of Santorini, sometime between 1647 and 1628 B.C., buried Akrotíri and produced a tidal wave that inundated the Minoan cities of Crete. Knossós was able to recover, but Minoan dominance came to an end about a century later, subdued by Mycenean warriors.

About 1200 B.C. nomadic Dorians invaded from the north and destroyed the Mycenaean culture. They brought with them the worship of male deities and their own alphabet, recognizably Greek, though writing all but disappeared and Greece fell into its "Dark Ages." Where these Dorians settled, as in

Sparta in the Peloponnese, the language was a distinct dialect called West Greek, and part of the later conflict with Athens, which spoke Ionian or East Greek, was based on linguistic differences.

Sometime about 900 B.C. the legendary tyrant Lykúrgus established a totalitarian society in the landlocked settlements of Sparta that came to make its name synonymous with rigid control, compulsory military training for all males, and the suppression of liberty, luxury, and individualism.

THE AGE OF ARISTOCRACY   Elsewhere in Greece most cities grew up around an acropolis, a defensible high ground, usually near a natural harbor, to which the population could flee for protection when threatened by hostile forces. By about A.D. 800, the city-state (polis, from which we get politics) had taken shape, and Greece entered the Age of Aristocracy, rule of the elite, with power being shared among powerful families rather than given to a warrior king. From about this time we have the epic poetry of Homer (sometimes considered a composition singer or more than one person), the *Iliad* and *Odyssey,* only later written down, which tell of the lost days of glory in a more heroic time, often called the Heroic Age.

Greek civilization was by no means homogeneous, but certain aspects became more prevalent. The larger and more prosperous city-states raised armies, built navies, and began to establish colonies on the coast of Asia Minor and in southern Italy, particularly those places that supplied them with food or other valuable materials such as metal. Conflict was inevitable, and the Panhellenic Games established at Olympia in 776 B.C. were probably meant to defuse tension by channeling energy into athletic competition rather than the more destructive impulse to war. The Oracles at Delphi and Dodona were instrumental in defusing jealousies, soothing resentments, and preserving peace—if only by imposing the time to be consulted.

About 725 B.C., the poet Hesiod catalogued the pantheon of Olympian gods in his *Theogony* and described daily rural life in *Works and Days.* From sculpture and depictions on pottery we begin to get a much clearer picture of life in archaic Greece. Farmers turned from growing grain to raising livestock, not an efficient use of land, and along with deforestation to build ships denuded much of southern Greece. In Thessaly, where there was plenty of arable land, this change was hardly noticed.

totalitarian society, forms Peloponnesian League, and consolidates military power.

- 594 B.C. Sólon reforms Athenian constitution.
- 505 B.C. Cleísthenes strengthens Athenian democracy.
- 490–479 B.C. Persian Wars.
- 490 B.C. King Darius invades Greece with mightiest force yet recorded, defeated by Athenians at Marathon; Pheidíppedes runs 26 miles with news of victory.
- 480 B.C. Xérxes, son of Darius, brings even bigger force, and 300 Spartans and their allies are betrayed and annihilated at Thermópylae; Athens is captured and destroyed but manages to set fire to Persian fleet and snatches victory from jaws of defeat.
- 479 B.C. Persians decimate Thessaly but are defeated at Platéa and Mykále; Athens declares itself winner.
- 478 B.C. Athens forms Delian league, purifies Délos.
- 475–400 B.C. Classical Age, golden for Athens forever.
- 462 B.C. Pericles elected, leads Athens to its pinnacle.
- 460–445 B.C. First Peloponnesian War.
- 445 B.C. Peace breaks out.
- 432 B.C. Sparta declares war on Athens, Second Peloponnesian War.
- 429 B.C. Athens is besieged and starving, plague kills third of population, including Pericles.
- 421 B.C. Peace of Níkia (Nicaea).
- 415 B.C. Athens invades Sicily.
- 413 B.C. Athenian fleet destroyed in Syracuse Bay.
- 404 B.C. Sparta captures Athens, tears down walls.

continues

- **398 B.C.** Agesilaus seizes power in Sparta, begins aggressive foreign policy.
- **394 B.C.** Persians destroy Sparta's fleet.
- **386 B.C.** Plato opens Academy.
- **384 B.C.** Aristotle born.
- **378 B.C.** Second Athenian Confederation.
- **371 B.C.** Thebes defeats Sparta at Léfktra (Leuctra).
- **362 B.C.** Epaminóndas dies in battle of Mantínea and Thebes loses power.
- **355 B.C.** Athenian Confederacy collapses, Greece with it.
- **351 B.C.** Demósthenes warns of Macedonian threat in First Phillipic.
- **342 B.C.** Aristotle becomes tutor of Alexander.
- **338 B.C.** Philip II of Macedon defeats Greeks at Héronia (Chaeronia).
- **336 B.C.** Philip is assassinated; Alexander, 18, succeeds him and Hellenism is born; Aristotle opens Lyceum in Athens.
- **336–323 B.C.** Alexander carries Greek culture to known world.
- **323 B.C.** Alexander dies with fever in Babylon.
- **336–215 B.C.** Hellenism flourishes under Macedonian power.
- **215 B.C.** Rome attacks Macedonia.
- **146 B.C.** Rome defeats Macedonia, begins to lose culture to Greece.
- **48 B.C.** Julius Caesar defeats Pompey at Phársalus.
- **42 B.C.** Octavian Caesar and Marc Anthony defeat Brutus and Cassius at Philippi.
- **31 B.C.** Octavian defeats Anthony and Cleopatra at Actium, becomes Emperor Augustus, dooming Roman Republic.

continues

Autocratic Sparta, with its large *hélot* (serf) population, also had little difficulty coping with change.

But cities like Athens, with growing populations of free citizens and diminishing resources, were faced with the problems of internal conflict that required political innovation. Initially the emergence of tyrants—such as Dráko, with his extraordinarily stringent laws—from among the aristocracy dealt effectively with social instability, but as common people amassed land and wealth they became increasingly dissatisfied with aristocratic intransigence. Changes in warfare, which was being increasingly waged by infantry made up of common men rather than the cavalry of the aristocracy, which had itself replaced the chariots of the Heroic Age, also brought pressure for political rights and shared power.

THE RISE OF DEMOCRACY & THE CLASSICAL ERA   Eventually Solon, an aristocrat with enlightened self-interest, recognized Athens's dependence on the contributions of its common citizens and in 594 B.C. introduced the constitutional changes that allowed them to share power with the upper classes, most importantly by opening the assembly to common citizens. Aristocrats complained that they were being robbed and the hoi polloi felt they were still being cheated, but the wheel of democracy was in motion.

Athens was becoming the greatest political entity yet known, with unparalleled accomplishments in government, philosophy, art, architecture, drama, history, and it was little more than a century later that it had to meet the first major test of its mettle. Between 508 and 501, under the leadership of Cleisthenes (Kleisthenes), democratic institutions were improved and strengthened.

Sparta meanwhile had continued to perfect its absolutist society, build its army and develop new tactics, increase its state-owned slave force, and consolidate its military dominance by establishing the Peloponnesian League in 550 B.C.

THE PERSIAN WAR   In 499 B.C. the Greek colonies in Asia Minor revolted against their Persian masters, and Athens sent 20 ships to the aid of its fellow Ionians. The mighty Persians finally prevailed after four years of fighting, but their new king, Darius, was determined to punish the upstart Athenians for daring to challenge his power. He launched his first naval force in 492, but it was wrecked off Mt. Athos.

In 490, Darius launched a second force that reached the Bay of Marathon. The Athenian general Miltíades sent the messenger Pheidíppides off to Sparta to ask for reinforcement, then together with his Platáean allies prepared for battle. Pheidíppides ran 150 miles to Sparta in two days, but the Spartans were unwilling to march because of a lunar holiday. The tireless messenger ran back with the bad news, and in desperation the Athenians attacked, concentrating on the vulnerable wings of the Persian army, which gave way. Darius withdrew his troops to his ship and sailed immediately for Athens, hoping to catch it undefended. Pheidíppides ran the 26 miles back to Athens with the news of victory, giving us the name of our less urgent race (marathon), and Miltíades hurried his army back to defend but lose the city.

The Persians did not take the humiliation well, and in the spring of 480 Darius's son Xérxes, after having built a pontoon bridge across the Hellespont (Dardenelles) and dug a canal through the peninsula of Halkidíki to prevent losing his ships to another storm, set sail with a force of 180,000 men. The Greek fleet, under the command of Athens, met the Persian fleet off Cape Artemísion, north of Évvia, engaged it as best it could, then fled south to shelter at Salamís.

The Greek land defenses, 7,000 men under the command of the Spartan general Leonidas, valiantly held the pass at Thermopylae for three days, until the traitor Ephialtes led the Persians over another nearby pass. The Greeks were surrounded and badly outnumbered, so Leonidas ordered the bulk of his army south and together with 300 Spartan and Boeotian soldiers stayed behind to guard their retreat. They fought bravely to the last man, and their immortal epitaph can still be seen there: "Stranger, tell the Spartans that here we lie obedient to their word."

At Salamís the Athenian leader Themístocles, cleverly interpreting the Delphic oracle's cryptic message that Athens could be "saved only by wooden walls," mobilized its entire fleet and sent a slave to act as a traitor and urge Xerxes to attack immediately. The Persian fleet sailed boldly into the narrow Bay of Eleúsis, where the smaller and more maneuverable Athenian triremes dispersed and destroyed most of it, while Xerxes watched in dismay from a cliff above.

Xerxes withdrew to the Hellespont, but the following spring Persian forces again attacked Attica,

- A.D.125 Pausánius writes first guide to Greece.
- 260 Goths begin raiding Greece.
- 324 Emperor Constantine moves capital from Rome to Byzantium, which becomes known as Constantinople.
- 394 Emperor Theodósius declares Christianity state religion of Rome, bans pagan cults, closes Oracle of Delphi, Mysteries, and Olympic Games.
- 476 Rome falls, and Greece gets little protection from weakened Byzantine empire.
- 529 Byzantine Emperor Justinian closes schools of Athens, including Plato's Academy.
- 1054 The Big Schism: Byzantine Patriarch and Catholic Pope excommunicate each other.
- 1204 Catholic Franks and Venetians capture and sack Constantinople during Fourth Crusade and divide Greece between themselves.
- 1261–62 Byzantine Empire recovers Constantinople and most of mainland Greece.
- 1354 Ottoman Turks capture Gallípoli.
- 1429 Turks capture Thessaloníki.
- 1453 Turks capture Constantinople.
- 1460 Turks capture Mistrá.
- 1499 Turks take Náfpaktos, Methóni, and Koróni from Venice.
- 1537 Turks take Monemvassiá from Venice.
- 1540 Turks take Náfplion.
- 1571 Fleet of Holy League under Don John of Austria defeats Turkish fleet at Náfpaktos (Lepanto).
- 1685–99 Venice recovers Peloponnese (Morea).
- 1770 Catherine the Great of Russia encourages but does

continues

not support unsuccessful revolt.

- 1814 Greek merchants in Odessa, Ukraine, found Philikí Etaireía (Friendly Society) to work for Greek independence.
- 1821–29 Greek War of Independence.
- 1821 Orthodox Patriarch Gyrmanos declares independence.
- 1826 Byron dies at Messolónghi.
- 1827 Triple Alliance (Great Britain, France, Russia) intervene against Turkey and Egypt.
- 1829 Fleet of Triple Alliance is accidentally brought into fight with Turkish fleet in Navaríno Bay, defeats it and ends war.
- 1830 Attica, the Peloponnese, Central Greece, the Cyclades, and the Saronic Gulf Islands form Republic of Greece.
- 1831 President Kapodístrias assassinated.
- 1833 Prince Otto of Bavaria is imposed as King Otto I of Greece.
- 1881 Turkey relinquishes Thessaly to Greece.
- 1912 First Balkan War; Greece takes Thessaloníki, Ioánnina, Epirus, and Crete from Turkey.
- 1913 Second Balkan War; Greece takes Serbia's side against Bulgaria, wins.
- 1917 Greece joins Britain and France in World War I.
- 1919 Greece attempts to seize Smyrna (Izmir), Turkey, but without support of Allies, suffers.
- 1920–23 War between Greece and Turkey ends in catastrophe: More than 1,300,000 Christians expelled from Turkey; 400,000

and seized and destroyed Athens. As soon as they withdrew, the Athenians set about rebuilding their walls, leaving the defense of the rest of Greece to the Spartans, who met the enemy at Plataéa, near Thebes, and defeated them. The remnant of the Persian fleet was intercepted off Cape Mykále, in Asia Minor, and burned.

The Persian War should have made it clear to the Greeks that a united defense was necessary for survival, but as Thucydides tells us, the Athenians were hurrying to rebuild their walls out of fear of the Spartans, and the Spartans, forgetting their no-show at Marathon, felt they were being insufficiently rewarded for their recent victories. Distrust and enmity set in, and the first important cold war in history was soon on.

Athens took the first real action, forming the Delian League (Confederation of Delos) in 478, thinking it was necessary to counterbalance the Peloponnesian League and claiming that it meant to continue the struggle to liberate the Ionian colonies from the Persians. The island of Delos was "purified"—its dead reburied on nearby Rhenía—and a naval alliance was formed, an expensive undertaking that strengthened Athens but impoverished and alienated its allies.

ATHENS UNDER PERICLES In 462 B.C. Pericles (*Perikléos*) rose to power and Athens was on its way to the pinnacle of power and prestige. Democracy was strengthened, government was centralized, office holders were paid, and more people became involved in government. In 447 construction of the Parthenon was begun under the direction of Pericle's friend, Phidias, one of the greatest of all sculptors, with the architects ("leading workers") Iktínus and Kallikrátes in charge of building, and Phidias and his students sculpting the ornamentation. It was to become the greatest monument to civic pride ever built, as well as eloquent testimony to the clarity, harmony, and precision of the Classical mind.

Shortly thereafter, under Kallikrátes, construction was begun on the perfect little Ionian Temple of Athena Nike ("Wingless Victory") on the spot where legend has King Aegeus leaping to his death in despair at the sight of his son Theseus's ship returning with black sails, giving his name to the Aegean Sea. In 437 the construction of the Propylaia, the monumental entrance to Acropolis, was begun under the architect Mnésikles.

continues

Thinking was a national passion with the ancient Greeks, and the Athenians had a particular love of argument. Thales of Miletus had started wondering about the world. Heraclitus had some very advanced ideas about the nature of matter. Pythagoras of Samos had observed the relationship between numbers and harmony in music, formulated the theorem that bears his name, and founded a colony in southern Italy devoted to restraint and thought. Diogenes, the Cynic, who owned as little as possible, lived in a barrel, and went around with a lighted lamp in daylight looking for an honest man, taught that a simple life without obligations was best. Zeno's followers, called the Stoics because they studied under a stoa (porch), believed in universal love and divine order, that here and now are more important than ultimate questions, and that men should live free of passion, unmoved by joy or grief, submissive to natural law. Epicurus and his group argued there was no life after death and therefore happiness in this life is the highest good and only reasonable aim.

Down-to-earth Socrates brought Athens into the golden age of philosophy and the world into the investigation of knowledge and meaning. Apparently he did little but talk and question, and we would probably not know much about him if not for his star pupil Plato, who put him at the center of most of his dialogues, and the historian/general Xénophon. Through Socrates, Plato taught us to question the very nature of reality itself and to think rigorously about politics and government. Plato's "best pupil," Aristotle brought us logic and gave the European world a body of knowledge that was to go virtually unchallenged for over a thousand years, as well as passing the passions of the mind on to his pupil Alexander.

Theater also found its golden age. It had already moved beyond ritual toward drama when Thespis had introduced the hypokrites (actor) and narrative. In 477 Aeschylus, first of the great tragic poets, had added a second actor and dialogue in his *The Persians;* his *Oresteia* is a cornerstone of dramatic literature. Sophocles, who won his first prize in the dramatic competition of 468, added a third actor and painted scenery; he wrote more than 100 plays, including the masterpieces *Antigone* and *Oedipus Rex,* in which he perfected the form of tragedy. Euripides (born in 480 during the battle of Salamís) was very much a product of the Periclean age; his plays are the most modern, realistic, psychologically penetrating, and politically charged, and

Muslims expelled from Greece.

- 1924 Greece declares itself republic.
- 1924–36 Political disorder.
- 1935 Monarchy of King George II restored.
- 1936 General Metaxás suspends constitution, assumes dictatorship.
- 1939 Fascist Italy invades Albania.
- 1940 Mussolini demands access to Greek ports, and Metaxás says "Ochi!" (No!).
- 1941 Germany invades Greece.
- 1941–44 Under brutal German occupation, resistance, especially by communists, grows.
- 1946 Greece joins United Nations; plebiscite returns George II to throne.
- 1946–49 Civil war; U.S. and Britain support right-wing royalist government against communists.
- 1949 U.S. helps defeat communists.
- 1951 Greece joins North Atlantic Treaty Organization.
- 1952 Women given right to vote.
- 1967 Military coup, led by Colonel Papadópoulos, ousts King Constantine II.
- 1973 "Referendum" abolishes monarchy.
- 1974 Turkey invades Cyprus and junta collapses. Elections held, Constantine Caramanlís becomes prime minister; popular vote confirms republic.
- 1981 Greece joins European Economic Community. Liberal PASOK (Panhellinic Socialist Movement) party, under Andréas Papandréou, wins election.
- 1984 PASOK re-elected.
- 1989 Charges of corruption bring down Papandréou government.

continues

include such masterpieces as *The Bacchae, Hippolytus, Medea,* and *The Trojan Women.* He didn't shy away from technical innovation either, inventing the *deus ex machina* device to lower a god onto the stage to save a hopeless situation.

Dramas were presented every fall during the festival of Dionysus, in what must have been a very full day, in sets of three tragedies followed by a satyr-play (farce) to dispel the dark mood. Aristophanes excelled at these comedies, burlesques with lyrical passages, that lampooned social pretension and political folly—nothing was sacred. In *The Birds, The Frogs, The Wasps* and others he satirizes fashion, modern music, politicians, courts, and even state policy. In *Lysistrata,* he takes on the battle between the sexes. In *The Clouds* he makes fun of Socrates, and there are historians who claim that this play led the Athenians to condemn the venerable old philosopher to death in 399 B.C.

History itself wasn't shirked. Herodotus fathered it with his thrilling account of *The Persian Wars,* and Thucydides perfected it in his chilling no-punches-pulled account of *The Peloponnesian Wars.* Xenophon's essays enlighten us about his time and mind.

THE PELOPONNESIAN WARS   Athens, having adopted an aggressive foreign policy intended to assert its supremacy and enlarge its empire, fought a series of small wars with its neighbors, particularly commercial and naval rivals such as nearby Aegina, which it subjected and reduced. Sparta looked on with growing envy and distrust, intervening when it could, but its navy was no match for its rival's. In 445 B.C. peace was declared. Athens consolidated its gains into an empire and continued its remarkable growth under the direction of Pericles.

In 430 B.C. Athenian vessels attacked those of Corinth in the Ionian Sea. Corinth appealed to the Peloponnesian League for help, and Sparta was only too glad to jump to its defense and march on Athens. The Second Peloponnesian War was basically a series of ineffective yearly campaigns in which Sparta seized the plains of Attica and besieged Athens. Its hoplite infantry forces were masters of battle in the open field but were not prepared for siege warfare and couldn't stop the flow of supplies in by sea.

Athens was well prepared for a siege, but it couldn't field a force sufficient to mount an attack on vulnerable Sparta. Most of the devastation was wreaked on their respective allies, both sides capturing each other's colonies, killing the men and enslaving the women and children. Athens's Delian League allies were particularly resentful about the lack of protection after their many contributions and sacrifices. In 429 a plague broke out in besieged Athens, and a third of the population died, including Pericles. Without his able leadership, the city lost unity and direction. (Read Thucydides's account for the full details of the arrogance, folly, and suffering.) The Truce of Nicaea (Nikías) was declared in 421, and both sides took a breather.

Athens once again set its sights on foreign expansion and in 415 sent a large fleet to capture the prosperous colony of Sicily. Alcibiades, nephew of Pericles and a favorite of Socrates, betrayed his own forces to the Spartans, and in 413 Athens suffered a humiliating defeat in Syracuse harbor, from which only a few sailors escaped.

Sparta meanwhile had traded off its colonies in Asia Minor to the Persians for naval assistance and gradually asserted its dominance over the sea. Alcibiades betrayed the Spartans and he joined the Athenians, but it was only a matter of time until the

Athenian fleet went down in defeat. In 404 Athens surrendered and its walls were torn down, never to rise again, and the possibility of a united Greece was lost.

DECLINE   Nearly all of Greece had been devastated and most of the major city-states were all but ruined financially. Widespread unemployment, food shortages, and rampant inflation followed, as is so often the case, and the once prospering economy faltered. Farmers struggled on with meager subsidies from the wealthy, who released their slaves into poverty, and the poor hired themselves out as mercenary soldiers—for peace was not to last.

Sparta, not satisfied with victory alone, sought to build its own empire and joined Persia in attempting to subdue the Greek colonies of Asia Minor. By 398 the tyrant Agesilaus had seized control of Sparta and set it on a course of reckless expansion that eventually brought it into conflict with Persia again, and in 394 the Persians destroyed the Spartan fleet.

Sparta was not deterred in its aggression, however, but merely deflected back to its former land game, and an alliance against it was formed, the Boeotian League, composed of Thebes, Athens, and several former members of the Peloponnesian League that had been betrayed by Sparta. Persian king Artaxerxes, facing rebellions in Egypt and Cyprus and fearful of another protracted war in mainland Greece, ordered Sparta to make peace with its neighbors.

Though Athens had managed to form a second Athenian Confederation, it was now Thebes, under the capable leadership of Epaminondas, that asserted itself as the major power. Sparta meanwhile was experiencing discontent at home, as its Helots, long chafing under the yoke of oppression, began to rebel. Still, the whole Greek world was stunned when in 371 the Thebans defeated the Spartans at Léftra.

Epaminondas then set about the conquest of the Peloponnese, seizing Messenía and founding the model city of Megalópolis. Athens was so alarmed that it sided with Sparta. The final showdown came at Mantínea in 362, where Epaminondas fell in battle and the Boeotians, who were winning, lost heart and retreated. In 355 the Second Athenian Confederation collapsed and Greece was in complete disorder.

THE RISE OF MACEDONIA   Meanwhile power had been shifting away from the south, with its city-states and citizen armies, to the more rural northern states like Thessaly and Macedonia, where autocratic authority was untroubled by democratic unrest and could afford to hire mercenary soldiers. Thessaly, under Jason of Pherae, was the first to show its muscle.

Athens had regained some political stability under its greatest orator, Demosthenes, and it joined Thebes in several preemptive incursions into Thessaly and Macedonia. During one of these raids the heir to the Macedonian throne, Philip, was taken hostage, but he was soon released.

In 359 Philip became king of Macedonia and soon set out to realize his dream of conquering and uniting all Greece. He drove south and seized the vital pass at Thermópylae, then quickly took Halkidíki and Thessaly.

Demosthenes had been warning the Athenians in his Philipics that Philip was ambitious and meant to attack Athens. He convinced them to strengthen their fleet and led them into an alliance with Thebes. The combined Greek forces were defeated by the Macedonians in battle at Heronia (Chaeronea) in 338, and Philip razed Thebes for its resistance. He was less harsh with Athens, though he forced Demosthenes into exile.

The Greek city-states, joined together in the League of Corinth, had little choice but to recognize Philip as their sovereign and Macedonia as the new center of power.

ALEXANDER THE GREAT   Phillip was assassinated in 336 B.C. and was succeeded by his son Alexander, whose ambitions were even greater. Alexander had the
good fortune of having as his tutor one of the greatest of Greek philosophers,
Aristotle, who was born in Halkidíki, not far from Macedonia. Aristotle had of course
studied in Athens with Plato and picked up a number of his ideas, particularly those
of *The Republic,* which is profoundly antidemocratic and favors enlightened despo-
tism. Alexander must have already had a keen mind and a driven personality when
he met Aristotle, but under the philosopher's influence the young soldier's knowledge grew, his interests broadened, and his appreciation of Greek culture surely
increased.

Though he was only 18 at the time of his father's death, Alexander had served as
a general in the battle of Heronia and had otherwise already proven his leadership
abilities. Plutarch, who cared more for the memorable than the factual, furnished us
with a number of anecdotes to attest to this, as though any were needed; the proof
is there in the young man's accomplishments.

The king of Macedonia, Alexander was therefore the general of the League of
Corinth. He had Demosthenes arrested for continuing his anti-Macedonian propa-
ganda, but otherwise Alexander had little need to prove his lordship over Greece. In
334 Alexander set out to conquer Persia, to avenge its invasions of Greece and help
pay for his future expeditions. Among his many gifts was a remarkable sense of pub-
licity; he took along a copy of the *Iliad* and stopped at Troy to sacrifice to Athena
in imitation of Achilles, his and every young Greek man's hero.

At the cost of much hardship, death, and injury among his troops, which he wisely
did not place himself above, he took Miletus, Tyre, Phoenicia, Palestine, and Egypt,
where he spent the winter of 332–31 and founded the city of Alexandria, that great
city that still bears his name, though he was to bestow it on another 15 along his
route.

The Persian king, Darius, had fled him earlier, leaving behind his family, which
Alexander took hostage, but he now stood ground at Gaugemela, where his troops
were routed. Alexander refused to accept his offer of peace and pushed east to
Babylon, Sousa, and Persepolis, where he burned the palace of Xerxes in revenge for
Thermopylae. Bessos, the ruler of Bactria, captured and killed Darius, hoping to
impress Alexander, but Alexander gave Darius a lavish funeral and had Bessos ex-
ecuted. Then he continued his march east into the rugged mountains of what is now
Afghanistan, and in 327 he decided to invade India.

His troops were tired and homesick, as well as offended by some of the manners
he was picking up from his Persian aides, who prostrated themselves before him as
though he were a god. He began to punish any sign of insubordination and pushed
on, the loyalty of his soldiers holding. But by the time the troops reached the Indus
River, in what is now Pakistan, the monsoon rains had come in force and were spoiling their remaining morale, and the soldiers refused to cross the Hyphasis River, and
after much pleading Alexander finally agreed to turn back.

The return trip was extremely difficult, marked by several natural disasters and
chronic shortages of food and water, but after nearly a year they reached Sousa again.
There he seems to have lost his drive and even good sense. He married a Bactrian
princess and presided over the marriage of 10,000 of his men to Asian women. He
forced thousands of his loyal Macedonian soldiers into retirement, proposed replac-
ing them with Persian troops, and was amazed to find them angry and resentful.

He announced that his next objective was Arabia, but in June of 323 B.C. he fell
ill with a fever in Babylon and died. He had in fact conquered most of the known
world and introduced Greek culture there, but it was too much of an empire for one

man, and it was soon divided. Greek culture, however, continued to exert an extraordinary influence throughout the ancient world.

HELLENISM The empire was soon at war, but Macedonia remained under the control of Alexander's general Antipater, who was tolerant of the Greeks. The Olympian pantheon had replaced the original Macedonian deities, and Macedonia probably seemed more like a colony of Athens than its master. Aristotle had returned to Athens to open the Lyceum and was widely respected for his fair-mindedness and encyclopedic knowledge, but after the death of Alexander anti-Macedonian feeling ran so high that he was forced to flee Athens.

Demosthenes, whom Alexander had ordered arrested but later released, now used his oratorical power to whip up patriotic fervor and resentment of Macedonia to reunite much of Greece as the Hellenic League in an attempt to regain independence. The Greeks were easily defeated at Lamía, the Athenian navy was trounced at the Hellespont, and Athens surrendered once again. Soldiers pursued Demosthenes to Póros where his last act was to once again prove the power of his pen, committing suicide with the poison it contained. Antipater abolished democracy, disenfranchised all citizens without substantial property, and offered free land in Thrace to those who wanted to resettle there; Athens never recovered.

Antipater's son Cassander remained in control in Macedonia and placed Demetrius over Athens. Seleucus, the leader of Alexander's foot guards, held onto the Asian part of the empire and administered it from Antioch, Syria. It slowly dwindled away, as there was nothing except the memory of a dead hero to hold it together.

Ptolemy, Alexander's bodyguard, took control of the southern part of the empire and ruled it from Alexandria, Egypt. He revered Alexander, brought his body to Alexandria, and sought to sustain his ideals. The Ptolemaic Empire survived until its last heir, Cleopatra, committed suicide in 31 B.C. after the defeat of her lover Mark Anthony. Alexandria took Athens's place as the center of learning, particularly important in science and mathematics, producing the geometer Euclid, the physicist and inventor Archimedes, and the astronomer Aristarchus of Samos, who asserted that the earth revolves around the sun.

Greece itself became something of a crossroads or way station, as the mainland was drained of its more capable citizens, who moved east as sailors, soldiers, craftsmen, and officials in the growing Greek colonies of Asia Minor. But though the Greeks themselves retained little political or economic influence, their culture remained dominant. The Attic drachma became acceptable coinage throughout the eastern Mediterranean. Greek philosophy also held sway; Stoicism, with its concept of universal brotherhood and a world state ruled by a supreme power, was especially influential. Koine, a common form of Greek, became the universal language throughout the Mediterranean, and was the language of the New Testament.

THE ROMAN EMPIRE Greece sided with Carthage and Macedonia in the first Macedonian War in 215 B.C. and continued in its resistance until 205. In 146 B.C., Greek forces combined in the Achaean League were again defeated, and the Roman consul Memmius leveled Corinth, killed its male population, and sold its women and children into slavery. In 86 B.C., Sulla massacred a mob of rebellious Athenians. Wherever they resisted, the poorer classes were ruthlessly slaughtered, and property owners were rewarded with positions of power. It proved a brutal but effective means of deterring further resistance. When Greece became a Roman protectorate, conservative factions were given control of the cities.

Greece was often the battleground for control of the Roman empire. In 48 B.C., Julius Caesar defeated Pompey at Pharsalus (Phársala) in Thessally. In 42 B.C., Caesar's grandnephew and heir, Octavian, and Mark Anthony defeated Caesar's assassins, Brutus and Cassius, at Phillipi in Thrace. In 31, Octavian routed the fleet of Mark Anthony and his lover Cleopatra, ruler of the Ptolemaic Empire, in the decisive naval engagement of Actium, off Cape Áktio, near Préveza, on the Ionian coast. This internecine struggle was conducted without the slightest regard for Greek property and at some cost to its economy.

When Octavian assumed the title of Emperor Augustus and the Roman Empire was imposed in 27 B.C., Greece was made the province of Achaea. Augustus was a great admirer of Greek culture, as can easily be seen in the literature and artifacts of Augustan Rome, but he had little concern for Greece itself. Educated Romans were familiar with Greek literature and conversant in Greek, but they knew little about the actual land. In the first century A.D. Seneca wrote, "Do you not see how in Greece the foundations of the most famous cities have already crumbled to nothing?"

Gradually a sort of romanticization—for lack of a better word—set in, and there was increasing interest in Greek art: Classical sculpture was reproduced, the great tragedies were revived and copied, and old philosophies were much discussed among the well educated. Plutarch in his *Lives* praised Greek heroes, ethics, and philosophy in the early 2nd century, and helped fuel popular interest. In about A.D. 125 Pausanias wrote a detailed account of Greek archaeology that helped shore up interest, as well as contributing much to our current knowledge.

The Emperor Hadrian, who ruled from A.D. 117 to 138, was probably the biggest single contributor to Athens, possibly because he fell in love with a handsome Greek youth named Antinoös. He lavished great attention on Athens, completed the construction of the Temple of Olympian Zeus, restored other temples, built his library, constructed streets, and funded a number of public works. He also restored a number of temples elsewhere in Greece, revived religious festivals, and founded a new Panhellenic League. After the mysterious death of Antinoös on the Nile, which was linked to the prophecy of an oracle, Hadrian deified him and built a number of shrines in Greece, and there are still classical-style statues of the young man at Delphi and Eleusis.

Another important Roman contributor to Athens was Herodes Atticus, whose father is said to have found an enormous treasure in an old house with which he gave his son a classical education. Herodes greatly admired Athens and spent much of his fortune on the city, most importantly the odeum (ódeion, covered theater) that bears his name, completed in A.D. 161 and still used for performances, though it was burned in 268.

In A.D. 242, the Goths made their first ominous appearance on the frontiers of Greece. In 260, their raids began and for the next eight years they continued to wreak destruction. It was a sign of the declining strength of Rome, that it could offer little but promises of protection. Christianity had grown into a powerful force within the empire, and possibly its otherworldly focus, its resigned response to the tribulations of the present one, were partly responsible; perhaps it did not mind seeing pagan culture destroyed. The invasion was finally repulsed, but the population suffered both economic deterioration and a loss of confidence. The wealthy were reluctant to invest in public buildings, and, as two centuries passed before there was any demand for architectural skills, they were lost.

THE BYZANTINE ERA   At the end of the 3rd century A.D. Diocletian divided Greece into several dioceses and made Byzantium its capital, and for a while Greece experienced something of an economic recovery as Greek art and goods flowed into the new capital. Because of its location on the Via Egnatia, Thessaloníki became more important. In 324 the Emperor Constantine moved his capital from Rome to Byzantium, and its name was changed to Constantinople; Rome, with so significant a loss in prestige, edged closer to its eventual fall.

In 394 the Emperor Theodosius declared Christianity the state religion of Rome, banned all "pagan" rituals, and ordered the closing of the Olympic Games, the Oracles, and the Mysteries. The following year a systematic destruction of the classical sites was begun. The Virgin Mary could easily be substituted for the virgin Athena, so the Parthenon was spared. The Mysteries of Eleusis were too close for comfort to the Christian mystery, so Eleusis was leveled, its sacred statues hacked to pieces. Olympia fared a little better. We now surmise that the priests at Delphi had some warning and more time because of the remote location, and we can thank this bit of good fortune for many of the beautiful objects that can be seen there today.

In 476, Rome fell to the Goths, and Greece was left unprotected, especially in the west, where Byzantine power failed to reach. The east was considerably more fortunate. In 529 the Byzantine Emperor Justinian closed the schools of Athens, including Plato's Academy, dealing another blow to the unfortunate city's prestige and economy.

During the 7th century Goths and Slavs continued to invade western Greece as far south as the Peloponnese, destroying what was left of urban civilization and with it the Roman and Christian culture as well. The Byzantines fought back, sending missionaries to convert the Slavs to Christianity and teach them Greek, but an indication of how effectively they had destroyed the old culture is that the word *polis* came to mean Constantinople only, all other cities having been destroyed.

Much of Greece, however, prospered as the Byzantine empire grew wealthier and more powerful. During the 8th century, under the Isaurian dynasty, most of it was divided into administrative units called themes.

Dissension between the eastern and western branches of Christianity was apparent as early as 800, when the Pope usurped the power of the Patriarch by crowning Charlemagne emperor of the Holy Roman Empire. The Byzantine (or Eastern Orthodox) branch felt that it had legitimate claim to primacy from the time the capital of the empire was moved there; besides, the New Testament was written in Greek. The Roman Catholic branch based its claim on other factors. There were various offenses taken on both sides until the Great Schism finally occurred in 1054, and the Patriarch and the Pope excommunicated each other.

The peace and prosperity the Byzantines experienced under a succession of Macedonian emperors ended in 1071 when Turkoman tribes from central Asia slashed into the Byzantine army at Manzikert in Anatolia. In the next century, the Normans under Roger of Sicily invaded Greece and sacked Thebes and Corinth. The worst misfortune came in 1204 when Roman Catholic Crusaders on their way to the Holy Land seized and sacked Constantinople, shattering the empire. The former themes became feudal principalities, fought over and traded among the conquerors, Venetians, French, Sicilians, Aragonese, and Catalans. Geoffroy de Villehardouin, a Frank, was lord of the prosperous principality of *Morea* (the Peloponnese).

For the next 50 years the Paleológi dynasty fought back through mainland Greece and recovered Constantinople. In 1262, they recovered Morea, renamed it the Peloponnese, and made Mistrá the new capital. Western Greece was briefly held by the Serbs, and the Vlachs established a principality in Thessaly. Venice held on to Crete, the Ionian islands, Évvia, Náxos, and Monemvassiá, Náfplio, Argos, Methóni, and Koróni on the Peloponnese until as late as 1797, leaving the impressive architecture admired so much today.

Gallipoli fell to the Ottoman Turks in 1354, and their threat could no longer be ignored. Maybe the Byzantines actually thought they could neutralize it by arranging a few marriages between Greek princes and Turkish princesses. Like the Romans, the Byzantines lacked sufficient men to fight their wars, so maybe it even seemed politic to hire Turkish mercenaries, who more than proved their ferocity against the Bulgars on the Maritsa River in 1371 and the Serbs at Kóssovo in 1389.

Mongol attacks on Ottoman territory in the east gave the Byzantines a brief respite, but the writing was on the wall. In 1429 the Turks overran Thessaloníki. In April 1453, Sultan Mohammad II laid siege to Constantinople, and it fell in less than two months. It took the Turks another eight years to complete their conquest of the mainland. The Aegean islands held out longer; Tínos didn't fall until 1715.

OTTOMAN GREECE   The Greeks call the nearly 400 years they endured under Turkish domination the Tourkokratía, and you may still detect a note of rue and even anger when they speak of the period. The Greeks were permitted to practice their Orthodox religion, as long as they remained loyal to the Ottoman state. In fact, the Turks put an end to the raids of European neighbors, and Suleiman the Magnificent allowed considerable freedom of trade and even open instruction of the Greek language.

Freedom is an important idea to the Greeks, however, and they may be allowed to claim that they developed the very idea of political liberty, so it should be easy to understand how they chafed under Turkish rule, no matter how mild and tolerant. And they were taxed rather heavily: a per capita tax for the "privilege" of being a resident, as well as real estate and sales taxes. For nearly two centuries, a fifth of their male children were taken away to Istanbul, the strongest to be trained as Janissaries, the sultan's personal guards, and the brightest to be trained in the harem as civil servants. This was surely sorrow for some and honor for others, as many took advantage of the opportunity to improve their lot in life. Some Christians converted to Islam, others preferred to flee to the mountains.

The Greek Orthodox Church was allowed to keep its seat of power in Istanbul, which it never ceased to call *Constantinopli*, was actually granted special privileges, and in time acquired some power and prestige and even a certain amount of local autonomy. This did not, however, rule out oppression, as local tyrants were often capricious and abusive.

In 1571 the fleet of the Holy League (the Papal States, Spain, Genoa, Naples, Malta, and Venice) under the command of Don John of Austria defeated and destroyed most of the Turkish fleet at the Battle of Lepanto (*Náfpaktos*), in the Bay of Pátra, the last and greatest in which oar-powered vessels were used. The majority of sailors and galley slaves in both fleets, by the way, were Greek. Turkish power was effectively checked and soon began to wane.

In the 17th century the central authority of the Ottoman state began to weaken, and local tyrants were free to impose their will. Fighting between the Turks and Venetians also took its toll, especially in the Peloponnese, which Albanians fighting for the Turks ravaged in 1715 and again in 1770 during a local uprising ostensibly led by Russian prince Orloff and encouraged by Catherine the Great, which she failed to support. In 1786 when she again tried to stir up trouble in Greece, the people of the Peloponnese ignored her, though there was an unsuccessful revolt in Epirus.

Pirates and brigands had also become an increasing problem with the neglect and sometimes the compliance of Turkish authority. The location and plan of many island communities was dictated by the fear of piracy, as is still evident today. In the mountainous interior or in remote areas like the Máni roving bandits were a similar concern. In peasant lore, these Klephts (think of kleptomania) have often been romanticized as heroic resistance to Turkish occupation, but they often found it easier to plunder a Greek peasant village than a better-protected Muslim estate.

THE WAR FOR INDEPENDENCE The 18th century was a time of enormous change in Europe, which experienced the rise of nationalism, the American Revolution against their English colonial masters, and the French Revolution against its monarchy. Greeks were not so isolated that they could miss these events and their consequences.

The most important element for the development of Greek nationalism was probably the growth of the Greek merchant community, both in Greece and abroad. Commercial links with Europe allowed wealthier and better educated Greeks to travel there and become acquainted with European culture and ideas, most importantly nationalism and Philhellenism. The love of Greek culture was more than simply fashionable—it had wide appeal, to Romantics, Neoclassicists, and even to the growing middle class that knew or cared little about either—and it became particularly appealing to educated young Greeks who probably as yet had much less exposure to the subject.

In 1814 three Greek merchants in Odessa, Ukraine, formed a secret organization called *Filikí Etaireía* (Friendly Society), which proposed the betterment of the Greek nation and quickly found members in Greece itself. A number of unsuccessful attempts to spark an uprising were made. In 1820 Ali Pasha, Sultan of Epirus, broke away from the Ottoman Empire, and the revolutionaries saw their chance. On March 25, 1821, Bishop Yérmanos raised the Greek flag at the monastery of Ayía Lávra, near Kalávrita, in the Peloponnese, and the war was on, though it was by no means an immediate success.

Though the movement had the support of wealthy Greek merchants and landowners, the Orthodox Church, the Phanáriots (prominent aristocratic families in Constantinople), many common people, and a number of bandits and pirates, they rarely had each others' support. The peasants were fighting for land reform, while the landowners were fighting to keep their land. Each group fought the Turks looking over their shoulders to be sure no one got the better of them, and they occasionally fought each other. There were of course able fighters like the guerrilla leader Theodóros Kolokotrónis (that's him on the Dr 5,000 bill), who won a number of important battles, and the naval hero Andréas Miaoúlis, a man of great courage and integrity. The idea of a noble national struggle, however, was firmer in the minds of foreigners like Lord Byron than it was among the natives, and it was men such as the activist English poet who brought the idea forcefully to the minds that shaped European opinion.

The major European powers, except for Russia, which had territorial gains against Turkey in mind, were initially not much interested in Greek independence. Great Britain and France were both exhausted from the Napoleonic Wars. Most of the thousand or so Philhellenes who came to fight with the Greeks were German, but the most important one was Byron. He probably wasn't much of a soldier, but his death from a fever, probably malaria or common and unromantic dysentery, in April 1824 caused a minor sensation and put the unknown outpost of Messolónghi on the map.

Awareness of the Greek struggle had grown in western Europe, especially in England, and word of the Sultan's Egyptian army ravaging the Peloponnese caused some concern. In 1826 the news that Messolónghi had fallen to the Turks, its defenders slaughtered and the town destroyed by fire, at last sparked some action from the Triple Alliance: Britain, France, and Russia finally agreed to send a combined fleet to try to stop the massacre of innocent civilians on the Peloponnese.

The fleet of 26 ships sailed south to the island of Navaríno (Navarone), off the southwest coast of the peninsula, where the Turkish commander, Ibrahim Pashsa, was based with a fleet of 82 ships. The intention was merely to make the Turks and Egyptians aware of their presence, but as the smaller fleet entered the mouth of the bay, what the Duke of Wellington called "an untoward event" occurred: A nervous Turk must have started firing, and the fight was on. The Turkish fleet was caught without room to maneuver and was quickly destroyed. The sultan was suddenly interested in negotiation. The following spring when Russia declared war on Turkey, the Sultan was forced to recognize the existence of an independent Greece.

MODERN GREECE   Ioánnis Kapodístrias, an aristocratic diplomat with close ties to the Russians, was elected president of the new nation by a National Assembly in 1827. He urged Greek forces to push north, and in 1829 the Conference of London fixed the northern boundary along a line from Árta on the Ionian coast to Vólos on the east coast, in addition to Attica, the Peloponnese, the Saronic Gulf Islands, and the Cyclades, territory that contained less than one-third of the population that was ethnically Greek. The European powers soon began discussing the imposition of a king and were looking for a good candidate. Liberal theorists thought the new president was too likely to accept a monarch, the common people found him too high-handed, and the wealthy found him too democratic; in 1831 two aristocratic dissidents shot him as he was entering a church in Náfplion.

Political chaos reigned. Otto, son of Ludwig I of Bavaria, arrived at Náfplion on a British warship in 1833 to be crowned King Othon of the Greeks, but as he was not yet of age a series of regents ruled for him, and they ignored demands for a constitution. In 1834 there was a rebellion in the Máni, and the government troops sent to quell it were easily defeated and sent back without their equipment. In 1843 an uprising in Athens forced Otto to dismiss his Bavarian advisers and accept a constitution and parliamentary government.

The constitution of 1844 gave the country the institutions of a modern democracy and a parliament composed of a lower house, called the Voulí, and a senate, called the Yerousía. Political parties, however, didn't grow from political ideals or social classes, but rather around men valued for their charisma or patronage. Factions separated mainly out of differences on foreign policy issues, and the three major political parties might as well have been called Britain, France, and Russia.

Otto proved a clumsy and autocratic ruler, his support of Russia during the Crimean War proved too much, and he was finally driven out by a popular revolt in 1862. The Europeans quickly found a replacement in young Prince William of Denmark, and the British ceded the Ionian islands to Greece to make the deal a little more palatable. William ascended to the throne in 1863 as George I, king of the Hellenes, this change of title signifying a veiled intention of further expansion.

King George I ruled until 1913; his reign was a time of relative stability and respectable if unspectacular economic growth. He improved the roads, built the first railroad, instituted some limited land reform, and helped expand the nation's borders. In 1878 Turkey peacefully ceded Thessaly and southern Epirus to Greece, which only helped to fuel the *Megáli Idéa* (Great Idea) of expanding the borders to include all Greek people. A worldwide economic slump in 1893 hit the Greek economy especially hard and drove a large number of peasants to emigrate, especially to the United States, setting a pattern of young exiles supporting their families from abroad.

In 1896 the Greek population of Crete rose in arms against their Turkish overlords, and the following year the Greeks attacked Turkey on its mainland border in an attempt to force reunification. This proved a humiliating failure that almost bankrupted the nation. The European powers stepped in again and arranged a peace treaty making Prince George of England high commissioner of Crete under Turkish control.

This compromise was actively opposed by Elefthérios Venizélos, a prominent Cretan politician who led the continuing struggle for reunification and went on to become one of Greece's most illustrious leaders. In 1908 European troops were withdrawn from Crete. In 1909 military leaders desirous of political reform summoned Venizélos to Athens and made him prime minister. He revised the constitution, instituted economic and social reforms, and continued to work for the reunification of additional Greek territory.

THE BALKAN WARS   In 1912 Venizélos organized the Balkan League and with Serbian assistance was able to fight a successful land war against Turkey, forcing it almost completely off European soil, and winning back Macedonia, northern Epirus, Crete, and the northeast Aegean islands. King George was assassinated and succeeded by his son Constantine, who had been a hero in the war.

The Treaty of London abolished the Turkish Empire and returned occupied territory in Europe to the Balkan League, which immediately began to squabble over the disposition of this territory, leading directly to the Second Balkan War in which Greece and Serbia (also an Orthodox nation) defeated Muslim Bulgaria. In 1913 the Treaty of Bucharest left Bulgaria a small part of Macedonia and access to the Aegean and created Albania from a part of Epirus. The Turks and Italians, however, refused to relinquish their holdings in the Aegean and Dodecanese islands.

WORLD WAR I & THE CATASTROPHE   World War I soon demanded attention to more immediate concerns. King Constantine was married to the sister of the Kaiser and was probably sympathetic to the Germans, though he insisted on neutrality. Prime Minister Venizélos sided with France and Britain, which offered Smyrna as an enticement, and was dismissed. Constantine was able to maintain neutrality until June 1917, when the Allies demanded that Greece enter the war, and he left the country in protest. Venizélos returned and military successes in Macedonia resuscitated the Big Idea, and Thrace was seized when Turkey and Bulgaria surrendered at the end of the war. At the Conference of Versailles, Venizélos demanded Smyrna (now Izmir), a prosperous former Greek colony with a large Greek population, and adjacent land on the coast of Turkey.

In 1919, with the encouragement of the Allies, Greece attempted to seize Smyrna, but the Allies balked, and the Greco-Turkish War soon proved one of the most disastrous episodes in modern Greek history. Turkey, too, had an extraordinary leader, Mustafa Kemal, later called simply Atatürk ("Father of the Turks"), who was able to rally his people and army to resist the Greek invasion.

Venizélos lost the election of 1920, and right-wing royalists took power and ordered the Greek army to advance on Ankara. This Anatolian campaign stalled in 1922, and Turkish troops forced the Greeks back to the sea, where they were hurriedly evacuated. The Turks then seized Smyrna, massacred most of its Greek and Armenian population, and burned the city to the ground.

In 1923, under the Treaty of Lausanne, the League of Nations supervised a forced exchange of populations: nearly 400,000 Muslims were expelled from Greece and more than 1,300,000 Christians were expelled from Turkey. The refugee problem was so enormous that it was entirely beyond the means and control of the government. A group of army officers forced Constantine to abdicate, executed five of his ministers, and proclaimed a republic.

The refugees found themselves crowded into shantytowns around Athens, Piraeus, Thessaloníki, and other cities. A fortunate few, Aristotle Onassis and Stavros Niarchos among them, were able to escape to new lives. The large agricultural estates of Thessaly were redistributed, and some found homes there. The majority, however, remained where they were, and Athens was transformed into the megalopolis it is today. About the only winner in the political turmoil that followed the Catastrophe was the Greek Communist Party (KKE), which was established and found plenty of new members among the masses of poverty-stricken urban refugees.

In 1924 Admiral Pávlos Koundouriótis was declared president. Though Greece was nominally a democracy, the military maintained what very little control there was. Venizélos, who remained the leader of the Liberal Party, made several attempts to return to power. After one of his failed coups in 1935 the royalist Popular Party rigged a plebiscite that restored the monarchy and King George II.

The bitterness against the right-wing monarchists and the leftist Venizelists, both blamed for the Catastrophe and the misfortunes that followed, was such that the Communists won enough votes in the parliamentary elections of 1936 to form a governing coalition. Fearful of them, King George allowed a military takeover by General Ioánnis Metaxás, who imposed a fascist dictatorship that used military force to end a general strike, imprisoned and exiled political opposition, formed a secret police, and imposed censorship.

WORLD WAR II & THE CIVIL WAR   Greece again tried to remain neutral at the beginning of the Second World War, even after Fascist Italy invaded neighboring Albania in 1939 and an Italian submarine entered Tínos harbor and torpedoed the Greek cruiser *Élli* in August 1940. When Mussolini demanded passage through Greece and access to its ports in October 1940, Metaxás is said to have given an adamant negative, "Ochi!" (October 28 is now a national holiday, Ochi Day, though his actual response was probably, "*C'est la guerre.*") Greek forces drove the Italians back into Albania and occupied northern Epirus, which had long been a goal. They failed to consolidate their gains, however, or prepare a proper defense of the Macedonian border.

In April 1941, Nazi forces invaded through the Balkans, the expected British support once again failed to materialize because of poor coordination, and they swept quickly through Greece. Metaxás had conveniently died just before their arrival, and King George and his government fled to Cairo to spend the war under British protection. By the end of May, German air and naval power had completed the conquest, and Greece was occupied until late 1944.

German and Italian forces soon had firm control of the urban areas, and it proved to be an especially deadly grip. Already scarce food was requisitioned to feed the occupying troops, and nearly half a million Greeks starved to death. Throughout the mainland and on Crete, which was particularly hard hit, entire villages were slaughtered and homes destroyed at the least sign of resistance. Nearly 90% of Greece's important and diverse Jewish population was rounded up and deported to Nazi concentration camps for eventual extermination.

Axis control of the countryside was less effective, and resistance soon grew and coalesced into the National Liberation Front (EAM), which was largely communist. By 1943 EAM had control of most of the country, with its own army (ELAS), navy, and police, both civil and secret. It was quite successful, especially when working with British tactical forces, enjoyed widespread popularity, and fully expected to assume control of the government when the occupying forces were expelled.

British Prime Minister Churchill, however, was staunchly anti-Communist and determined to reimpose the monarchy. In August 1943, representatives of the resistance, including two noncommunist groups, flew to Cairo to ask the king to promise not to return unless a plebiscite proved popular support. The British refused to even consider the matter. The resistance was soon divided, as the British probably intended, into those who favored peaceful means of attaining control and hard-liners who refused to compromise and were quickly accused of being Stalinists.

By October 1943, lines had been drawn and ELAS, fearing a British takeover, launched an attack on its rivals, and by the time a cease-fire was imposed the follow-ing February it had effectively eliminated all except the EDES, a right-wing group suspected of collaborating with and receiving help from the Nazis. Britain and the United States had both infiltrated agents into the country to prevent a communist takeover even before the Germans withdrew.

In October 1944 as the Germans were pulling out, the EAM leadership agreed to participate in an interim government sponsored by the British. They were dismayed to learn that they were to receive only one-third representation and that the king was refusing to renounce his claim to the throne. In November, Allied forces demanded that ELAS disarm, and tensions were running high when on December 3 police fired on communist demonstrators in Athens and fighting broke out between ELAS and British troops.

The army and militia were already firmly in the hands of right-wing royalists, and soon the police and most of the civil service were in tow, with those suspected of left-wing sympathies being quickly excluded. Right-wing parties won the elections of 1946 and a plebiscite approved the return of the monarchy. Leftists weren't buy-ing it, inflation was soaring, the black market was thriving, random violence spread as reprisals for collaboration and other old scores were settled, and by 1947 a civil war was fully astir.

Meanwhile King George died and was succeeded by his brother Paul, whose con-sort, Frederika, was outspokenly intolerant and unconciliatory. British meddling gave way to American manhandling of what it perceived as a Cold War threat and under the Truman doctrine and the overzealous John Foster Dulles was trying to quash as quickly as possible by providing extensive military and economic aid to the Greek government, no matter how tentative its claim to legitimacy or the merits of its opponents. The Greek government detained tens of thousands of suspected leftist sympathizers and forced the evacuation of entire villages, and the rebel forces were also guilty of a number of atrocities.

Greek government forces, with American arms and advice, defeated the rebels in the mountains of northwest Greece in October 1949, but not before Greece had suffered enormous psychological damage, the worst since the Peloponnesian Wars. Democracy barely survived the conflict; the powerful right-wing security service was not dismantled, and the violation of civil rights did not end.

THE POSTWAR ERA   Greece became a charter member of the United Nations in 1946, regained the Dodecanese islands in 1948, and joined the North Atlantic Treaty Organization (NATO) in 1951. In 1952 after a series of unstable govern-ments, Field Marshall Alexander Papágos formed a new government under his Greek Rally party. A new constitution was adopted, which gave Greek women the right to vote. A program of national reconstruction was begun and continued by his succes-sor Constantine Caramanlís, who came to office in 1955, and presided over a period of relative stability, peace, and economic growth, as Greece reestablished its traditional markets in Germany. The country also unfortunately saw widespread depopulation of its rural areas as people moved to the cities, sought work in northern Europe, or emigrated to America and Australia. Greece allied itself firmly with the West and tried to settle some of its differences with its neighbor and NATO ally, Turkey. In 1959 the Zurich Accord between Greece, Turkey, and Britain granted independence to Cyprus and provided for the sharing of power between the island's Greek and Turkish communities.

In 1961 Caramanlís was reelected, and there was strong public suspicion that the army, and its commander-in-chief, the king, had arranged it. Unemployment was high, strikes were increasingly common, King Paul and especially the outspoken Queen Frederika were openly criticized, even in Parliament. In May 1963 right-wing forces arranged the assassination of the left-wing minister Grigóris Lambrákis in Thessaloníki—later made better known outside Greece by the Costa-Gavras film *Z*. Caramanlís resigned, lost the subsequent elections, and left for exile in Paris.

George Papandréou and his Center Union Party (a left-of-center coalition) won the election by a decisive majority of nearly 50 seats. King Paul died and was succeeded by his son, Constantine II. The elections of 1964 weakened the liberal majority, and a battle of wills between the elderly Papandréou, a veteran Venizelist, and the young monarch over the army's role in the elections of 1961, led to Papandréou's resignation in an attempt to force new elections. The king refused to hold new elections and persuaded Constantine Mitsotákis, a member of the Center Union, to defect and organize a new coalition government, which was met by resignations, strikes, and demonstrations. New elections were set for May 1967, which Papandréou was expected to win handily.

In April 1967, a group of colonels, headed by George Papadópoulos, staged a coup—apparently only a few weeks before one planned by the king himself—which Andréas Papandréou, the Harvard-educated son of George, termed, "the first successful CIA military putsch on the European continent." The colonels were sworn in by the king, survived his clumsy attempt at a counter-coup, then consolidated power, dissolved Parliament and banned political activity, claiming it meant to purify Greek society, rid the country of corrupting western influences, and revive Orthodoxy.

King Constantine soon found himself asked to leave the country, and a referendum was arranged to abolish the monarchy. The press was heavily censored, classics disappeared from library and bookstore shelves, production of the ancient tragedies was forbidden, even *rebétika* and other forms of popular music were banned. Thousands of liberals were arrested as communists, imprisoned, and often tortured. George and Andréas Papandréou, other prominent leftist politicians, even prominent intellectuals and artists such as Míkis Theodorákis, composer of the music for *Zorba*, were imprisoned. Melina Mercouri, Greece's most famous actress, and thousands of other prominent Greeks were deprived of their citizenship.

U.S. presidents Johnson and Nixon continued to support the colonels with substantial economic and military aid, no matter how detestable their behavior, because they were anti-Communist, and as the Junta became ever more unpopular with the Greek people so did the American government. In 1973 demonstrations broke out, often ostensibly directed against the presence of American nuclear weapons in Greece. In November students at the Athens Polytechnic occupied campus buildings, and armored vehicles were sent in, killing a still undetermined number of students. Colonel Papadópoulos, who had only recently proclaimed himself president of the new republic, was ousted and replaced by General Ioannídes, head of the secret police, who clamped martial law even tighter.

The Junta met its comeuppance within the year, however, when it attempted to topple the government of Archbishop Makários on Cyprus and annex the island, provoking a Turkish invasion that quickly occupied nearly half the island. The army mutinied and asked Constantine Caramanlís to return from exile to his former office.

Caramanlís accepted, quickly negotiated a cease-fire on Cyprus, withdrew temporarily from NATO, and informed the United States that it must remove all bases except those that served Greek interests. In the elections of November 1974, he and his New Democracy party easily defeated the newly formed Panhellenic Socialist Movement (PASOK) led by Andréas Papandréou. A plebiscite rejected the return of the monarchy, and the following year Parliament ratified a new constitution that provided for a republican form of government.

Though a conservative with a mandate, Caramanlís fostered an effective return to democratic stability that including legitimizing the Communist Party (KKE), and he was rewarded by being returned to office in 1977. In 1980 he assumed the presidency of the republic, and he presided over Greece's entry into the European Community (now European Union) in 1981. The most egregious offenders of the old military regime were brought to trial, and Greece saw renewed economic growth, though it was outstripped by inflation caused by military spending due to the continuing tension with Turkey. Greece had reentered NATO, not an especially popular move, the conservatives failed to deliver promised reforms of the bureaucracy, social services, and the notoriously backward educational system, and tax evasion had become the national sport.

Andréas Papandréou and PASOK—promising an end to corruption, bribery, and bureaucratic inefficiency, improvement of social services, socialization of industry, the expulsion of the U.S. military, and withdrawal from NATO and the European Community—took 174 of 300 parliamentary seats in the elections of 1980, the KKE took 13, and Greece had its first socialist prime minister. Laws were passed providing for civil marriage, the priority of women in the family, equal rights elsewhere, and pensions to peasant women—the later provoking much resentment among many men. Reaction from the military was feared, especially when Papandréou himself assumed the office of defense secretary, but he was careful not to offend, the promised withdrawal never materialized, and salaries and defense spending were increased.

For all his training in economics at Harvard, Papandréou could do little with the economy. A world-wide recession hit Greek shipping, the most important source of national income, particularly hard. Tourism fell off with terrorist actions getting prominent television coverage and making headlines in the West, and even remittances from Greeks working abroad slumped. The foreign debt swelled, inflation was soaring above 25%, and unemployment grew increasingly problematic.

Nevertheless, PASOK managed another victory in 1985, though it wasn't nearly so impressive, and Chrístos Sartzetákis unseated Caramanlís as president. In the fall a two-year wage freeze was imposed, the currency devalued, and the offer of a huge loan from the EC with the condition of an austerity program was accepted. The Communists deserted the government and many members of PASOK threatened to bolt; Papandréou responded by firing labor leaders and dismissing members of his own party.

New Democracy won the mayoral elections of 1986 in Athens, Thessaloníki, and Pátra, and Papandréou admitted some failures and replaced a few members of his government. In early 1987, probably in an attempt to placate voters, he fired the remaining members of his cabinet, including his son. In February a million striking workers demonstrated in Athens. Still, New Democracy was unable to field an acceptable alternative, and PASOK might well have won a third term, if Papandréou himself hadn't made a fool of himself in the minds of most Greeks.

In 1988, while in London for heart surgery, the 70-year-old prime minister made public his current affair with a 34-year-old Olympic Airways flight attendant, Dímitra Liáni, whose nickname "Mimi" was immediately a household word, and not generally one of affection, in tradition-minded Greece. Economic scandals soon added injury to insult, the most serious being the flight of the director of the Bank of Crete to the United States with nearly $2 million, in which Papandréou and several other ministers were implicated. Allegations of illegal arms deals by other ministers further tainted the government.

The June 1989 election was inconclusive, but an unlikely coalition of conservatives and communists emerged to dominate the scene for the next three months. Papandréou and three other ministers were formally charged with complicity in the Bank of Crete scandal. Surprisingly, PASOK actually made a minor recovery in the inconclusive November elections but it refused to compromise, and a caretaker government was set up while preparations were made for yet another election.

The election of April 1990 proved even more of a mixed bag, but New Democracy managed to put together a government under Constantine Mitsotákis. The new conservative government quickly set about trying to reverse liberal economic policy. Austerity measures were, however, largely a failure due to a major world recession (aka Reaganomics); inflation remained near 20% and unemployment worsened. The arrival of thousands of impoverished and uneducated Albanian refugees brought increasing social problems, especially in Athens, as well as the passage of stricter immigration laws, which have proven ineffective. Efforts to combat terrorism have proven more successful, though anti-strike laws have been largely ignored.

The Bank of Crete fiasco was turned into an extremely popular television court drama when the culprit was returned to give evidence against Papandréou and several of his ministers, one of whom obligingly died of a heart attack on camera. Two ministers drew short prison sentences, but the case against Papandréou proved unconvincing, as such politically motivated charges often do, and he was acquitted in 1992. The embezzler himself was finally convicted and is still in prison.

The disintegration of Yugoslavia in 1991 presented Mitsotákis with a major challenge when the Former Yugoslav Republic of Macedonia (still referred to in Greece by the acronym FYROM or as Skópia, after its capital, Skopje) declared itself the nation of Macedonia, injuring Greek national pride and stirring up storms of protest. (You will still see many signs reminding you that "Macedonia has always been Greek" or, nearer the facts, "Macedonia has been Greek for 3,000 years." Technically, Greece was first part of Macedonia 2,334 years ago.) New Democracy, of course, actively joined in the objections.

By 1993, the new nation had gained recognition from both the European Union and the United Nations as the Former Yugoslav Republic of Macedonia, for the time being, and thumbed its nose at Greece by placing the Star of Véryina, symbol of the family of Alexander the Great and often referred to as "the Greek sun," on its new flag, as well as the White Tower of Thessaloníki on its currency. Mitsotákis meanwhile was being accused of having the phones of rivals tapped and participating in a major contract-fixing scheme. In the summer of 1993 the foreign minister, Adónis Samarás, seized the opportunity to accuse Mitsotákis of being too eager to settle the issue and bolted from New Democracy to form his own rightist party, Political Spring. Other defections soon led to a call for new elections.

Papandréou and PASOK, needing little else to ensure reelection, fanned Greek nationalism and resentment of 150 years of foreign domination and promised to get tough with FYROM, and returned triumphantly to power. The new government immediately set about reversing conservative privatization by renationalizing the Athens bus system. A trade embargo against FYROM proved unpopular with several of Greece's allies and economic partners, though it has managed to win some concessions, such as FYROM's recent renunciation of the Star of Véryina as a national symbol.

Mimi (the flight attendant) became Mrs. Papandréou and, to many people's embarrassment, her husband's chief of staff. Papandréou himself, now in his eighties, was plagued by failing health as well as the disarray of his party, and in early February 1996 was forced to name a successor, Costas Simítis.

The 59-year-old Simítis is a staunchly pro-European technocrat known for his academic bent, mild manners, and methodical approach to problems, and he is expected to move Greece closer to EU economic and political standards. His new cabinet is a skillful blend of old Papandréou loyalists and younger socialist party reformers.

The economy remains the big issue, and PASOK can claim no successes there. Attempts to deal with the Albanian refugee problem have amounted to little but rounding up some of the more conspicuous Albanians and busing them back across the border, from where they soon return. (Does this sound familiar?)

Greeks continue to remain remarkably resilient, interested and engaged in politics, and even in general good-humored about it. Unlike in most English-speaking countries, religion and politics are not inappropriate subjects for polite conversation. Most Greeks are religious without much question, at least at Easter, and the Orthodox church emphasizes ceremony and doesn't address touchy social issues like birth control, abortion, and homosexuality. Opinions about political matters can be openly expressed—one important improvement over most of the century—and they can be dismissed with a shrug, politely deflected, or hotly denounced and debated, but finally a tolerance born of long and difficult experience usually prevails.

3 A Legacy of Art & Architecture

Greek culture is best known through and most visible in its architecture, the foundations of which were laid nearly 6,000 years ago, and the art that is integral to it, particularly its sculpture. Little is left of ancient painting except the pigment that remains on the sculpture and buildings, a few recently restored Minoan frescoes, and drawings on ceramics that are design, cartoons, pictures, stories, clues to life, and lore.

The Minoan civilization that arose on Crete in about 3,000 B.C. and built its labyrinthine palace at Knossos also produced polychrome pottery, stone vases and figurines, fine gold jewelry, and especially the impressive frescoes that can be seen in the archaeology museums of Athens and Iráklion. Though there is an undeniable stylistic influence from the Egyptians and other Near East cultures, these elegant depictions of humans, animals and plants have a vivacity, grace, and joy not seen before.

A little later on the nearby Cycladic islands, another much simpler civilization was producing smooth white marble figurines, rubbed into shape with emery stone rather than carved, that are so abstract and modern in their design and sensibility that we hardly valued them at all until modernism itself reconnected us to their eloquent simplicity earlier in this century.

The warrior Myceneans built fortresses so massive that we call their walls Cyclopean, but they also made architectural innovations, such as their beehivelike *thólos* tombs that are precursors of the vault and dome, and produced elegant weapons and objects in gold that are both primitive and powerful.

The Dorian invasion that destroyed the Mycenean culture left a "Dark Age" cultural void out of which eventually grew a more basic period we call Geometric because of the simple abstract decoration of its pottery. From this grew black-figure pottery with elemental scenes and the style of the Archaic Period, simple massive structures in limestone and figure sculpture, characterized by formal rigid poses that at first barely separate themselves from stone, which must also have had much Egyptian influence. The characteristic nude *koúros* (young man), with one foot forward and arms stiffly against his side, might be taken for an Egyptian except for his confident Archaic smile.

The *kóre* (young woman) could show more individuation in an object she held (often a dove in devotion to Artemis), her hair, her dress, the flow of its drapery rendered more realistically, until the Classical style itself began to evolve, and a goddess, Artemis or Athena usually, still demure and virginal, but ever more lifelike, began to emerge. The decoration of pottery also became more naturalistic with red figures on painted black backgrounds, superior artistry, and careful attention to line, detail, and subtlety of expression. The essence of classicism is simplicity, harmony, and poise; the pose of a statue might actually be difficult if not impossible to achieve, but it looks natural and effortless. Doric architecture gives much the same impression; though the Parthenon is massive, most of the lines aren't actually straight, and it was a major technical accomplishment, the effect one of simple symmetry, balance, lightness, and repose.

Ever more complicated ornamentation was imposed, until the baroque Corinthian capital topped the column, and statuary moved from cool repose toward more emotion and movement during the Hellenistic period. The *Venus de Milo,* turning temptingly, and the *Winged Victory of Samothrace,* with her violent movement and windblown drapery, are particularly powerful examples.

Having reached this height of passionate intensity, under the Romans, Greek art was essentially reduced to making copies of older works or new works in the old style, then it simply faded away in neglect or was destroyed by barbarian invasions.

What emerged under Byzantine influence was not measured by its likeness to the human and the real world but how well it spoke of a spiritual dimension. At its worst, it is little more than big staring eyes, flat perspective, and stiff poses, but at its best it has undeniable power, appealing not to the emotions, as Hellenistic and Western art under Catholicism does, but to the mind. It doesn't stir up passions by appealing to the senses as Renaissance art does; it calms those receptive to it, leads toward another less immediate, other world.

Art is still very much alive in Greece. In contemporary Greek art we find all these earlier qualities variously melded with borrowings from other cultures through new techniques or even the old ones faithfully reproduced. Probably the most important artist of the century is Hatzmihális Theóphilos, whose naive folk art owes much to Byzantine influences and yet expresses the human qualities so important to the Classical, some hint of Hellenistic passion, something of the Archaic in his smiles, and an echo of Minoan innocence and joy.

Greek architecture is still true to its roots, after a foolish flirtation with the modern international style that is responsible for much of the boring homeliness of Athens and many of the resorts built in the 1960s. The graceful Neoclassical architecture of the more genteel 19th century is finally valued and is being preserved and restored in Athens, especially in the Plaka and Kolonaki, and on several islands, notably Syros, Hydra, and Symi. Art deco, which is the Classical stripped to its essentials, is being restored and even revived. Traditional architecture is everywhere being valued, preserved, and continued, often under mandate, but also because people realize its distinctiveness and appeal.

Reproductions of icons are often inferior copies, but sometimes they have much of the technique and some of the power of the originals. Reproductions of Classical

The Classics Come to Life: Summer Theater Festivals

Theater is also still very much alive in the land of its birth. Athens has nearly 50 permanent theaters where drama of every conceivable variety is presented, almost always in Greek, but not usually in the summer. There are, however, various summer festivals where the classics of Aeschylus, Sophocles, Euripides, and Aristophanes are staged. The best known of these is the Epidaurus Festival, where the idyllic setting, superb performances, and perfect acoustics of the ancient amphitheater can be thrilling. There are also performances in ancient theaters of Dodona, Thassos, and Phillipi, as well as the archaeological site at Eleusis, which has an annual Aeschylia in honor of the founder of Greek tragedy.

Other summer festivals also include theater performances, notably the Athens Festival held annually in the beautiful Odeum of Heródes Atticus on the southwest slope of the Acropolis, which also includes world-class orchestral performances, opera, ballet, popular singers, and even experimental works. The Lycabettus Theater also stages a variety of performances.

The Epirotika Festival in Ioánnina, the Hippokrateia Festival on Kos, the Demetria Festival in Thessaloníki, the Aegean Festival on Skiáthos, the Mólyvos Festival on Lésvos, and the Lefkáda Festival include theatrical performances. In September the Itháki Theater Festival recognizes the work of the new generation of playwrights.

works are usually kitsch, often awful and sometimes even offensive, but occasionally there is something that truly connects with a glorious past. Ceramics are actually having a revival, and you can find excellent new work done faithfully by old techniques, touched by other old and foreign influences such as Japanese *rakú,* and of course the very latest innovations that are fanciful, stylish and contemporary indeed. Greeks also excel in jewelry design, incorporating and updating ancient motifs, reproducing and adapting more recent "antiques," finding inspiration in the art of nature, innovating new sleek and sophisticated work, all with considerable appeal.

The once famous Greek handicrafts, however, are in general unfortunately slowly disappearing despite some notable efforts at conservation and revival. There is still much needlework done, and some of it is offered for sale at fair prices, but synthetics and imports from the East are too often sold. Most of the hand-loomed carpets now offered for sale are not made in Greece, though there are still a few made in isolated areas in the north, but if you care about such things don't hesitate in hopes of finding something authentic at a better price somewhere else in the future. The woven bags so popular with young tourists are still made by hand, though they're now meant more to appeal to their potential purchasers than to preserve traditional motifs. Wood-carving is all but lost, and the shadow puppets you see were made for sale to tourists, not performance.

The quality of leather goods has improved somewhat in recent years, though much of it is produced in Turkey, and the prices are still relatively good, but you must pay attention to details and tanning technique—which is, by the way, not regulated and often does environmental damage. The quality of souvenir articles has improved in recent years too, though you will still see lots of hurriedly manufactured junk that looks as though it should have "Made in Taiwan" on the bottom, and even fine Parian marble wasted by clumsy, uncaring hands. With even a little time and effort, however, you should be able to find much that is still appealing.

4 The Cradle of Western Literature

Greek literature is part of the bedrock of our own, and few of you reading this will need to be reminded that its own foundations were laid by Homer in his immortal *Iliad* and *Odyssey*. He was a singer of heroic poetry, possibly not so much a composer as a compiler of traditional lore—once thought to be myth, but now believed to reflect actual events in the Greek conquest of Troy in Asia Minor, now Turkey. Some consider him probably more than one person, and his epics were not actually written down until long after his death. By the Classical era they were a major part of education, routinely memorized and recited, and they continued to be a cornerstone of culture through Roman times. (Virgil's epic *Aeneid* is a continuation of the Trojan saga. Chaucer, Shakespeare, Dryden, Tennyson, O'Neill—the list continues to grow of those who have recycled Homer's material.)

Hésiod wrote his more everyday poetry sometime about 700 B.C. and, though it's not much read today, his *Theogony* was very important in formalizing the various myths into a more cogent Olympian panoply, for us as well as the ancients. His *Works and Days* is the earliest and still one of the best descriptions of the daily activity of common people.

About the same time Greeks began to compose lyric poetry. Archilóchus of Páros in his few extant verses contributed our first glimpse of the spurned lover. Tyrtaéus of Sparta sang the virtues of the martial life, leaving us a good account of the military ethic, and a little later his countryman, Alcman sang loving praise of women. Early in the 6th Century the fertile island of Lésvos produced its first crop of illustrious poets in Alcáeus, who sang of the hardships of sea travel, war, and exile, and Sappho, whose subject matter is famous, so highly regarded by the ancients that Plato called her "the tenth Muse" and the precious little of her poetry that survives confirms her as one of the greatest of all lyric poets. Thebes contributed Pindar, who left us aristocratic odes celebrating the winners of the Olympic and Pythian Games.

In the 5th century Aeschylus (525–456 B.C.) began composing the Greek tragedies that are among our very greatest literary legacies. He fought at the battle of Marathon before he won his first victory in the dramatic competition at the festival of Dionysus in 484 B.C., and he later again fought at Salamís. In 467 he composed the first important trilogy about Oedipus, though all that remains of it for us is the final *Seven Against Thebes*. His most famous work is *The Oresteía,* his only surviving trilogy, which dramatizes the fall of the house of Atreus: Agamemnon, leader of the Greek expedition against Troy, sacrifices his daughter Iphigenia to placate Artemis and secure favorable winds for the voyage, gaining the hatred of his wife, Clytemnestra, who marries her other daughter Electra off to a swineherd, and with her lover Aegistheus murders Agamemnon in his bath when he returns from the long war. Their son Orestes returns and, goaded by his spiteful sister Electra, murders his mother in return. He is pursued by the vengeful Furies (euphemistically called the *Euminides)* to Athens, where the cycle of vengeance is finally broken by a court of law.

His successor Sophocles (496–406 B.C.) was the most admired of the ancient tragic poets. Only seven of his plays survive. The earliest, *Ajax,* is about the Greek hero who goes mad in his fury at being denied the armor of Achilles and is driven to suicide. In *Antigone,* a favorite of modern audiences, the heroine chooses to obey divine law and give her brother funeral rites knowing that she must forfeit her life to secular law. In his most famous play, *Oedipus Tyrannus,* which Aristotle cited as the best example of perfect form, the hero unknowingly kills his father and marries his mother, bringing a plague on Thebes, and when he learns the truth and realizes his guilt he blinds himself in horror.

Euripides (485–406 B.C.) was not so highly regarded by his contemporaries, probably because he criticized them so relentlessly and powerfully in his dramas, but he is the most accessible and appealing to modern audiences, and several of his plays continue to be produced or adapted. His most famous is probably *Medea,* who spurned by her lover Jason, for whom she has sacrificed greatly, revenges herself by murdering their two sons. His *Hippolytus* (which Racine later adapted in his famous *Phaedra* and on which O'Neill based *Desire Under the Elms),* dramatizes the destructive power of love in the tragedy of Phaedra, the young wife of Theseus, king of Athens, who falls in love with her stepson Hippolytus, who spurns her; in revenge she causes his destruction then commits suicide in despair. His powerful *The Bacchae* dramatizes the power of the irrational: Pentheus, king of Thebes, resists the mysterious god Dionysus and imprisons him; an earthquake releases the god, and he drives the women of Thebes, including Pentheus's mother Agave, into a wild frenzy, then devilishly tempts Pentheus into spying on their orgies, where he is unrecognized even by his own mother and torn apart. *The Trojan Women* depicts the suffering of the survivors of the Greek victory over Troy and was meant to remind the Athenians of their recent heartless massacre of the men of the island of Mílos.

Aristophanes (448–380 B.C.) was able to get away with criticizing his contemporaries because he did so through comedy, proving, as Shaw later claimed, that you can say anything as long as you make people laugh. His farces contain almost all the elements of modern comedy: grotesque exaggeration, ridicule of excess, reason reduced to absurdity, comic reversal of plot, bawdy jokes, puns, witty one-liners—you name it. He had such a powerful effect on his audiences that he may even have actually effected some change. (As noted earlier, *The Clouds* may have contributed to the condemnation of Socrates for impiety and the corruption of Athenian youth.)

Modern Greek literature would have a hard time matching so glorious a legacy, but it has not proven altogether a failure. The best known literary figure is surely the Cretan poet and novelist Níkos Kazantzákis (1895–1957), who created the best-known modern Greek work, *Zorba the Greek,* as well as *The Last Temptation of Christ, Report to Greco, Freedom or Death* (sometimes titled *Captain Mihalis* in the U.S.), *The Fratricides,* and many others. Alexándros Papadiamántis (1815–1911) is better known in Greece than elsewhere because his highly idiosyncratic language doesn't translate well; his collection of short stories, *Tales from a Greek Island* (his native Skiathos), is often recommended, along with the novel *The Murderess.* Strátis Myrivílis, from Lésvos, is another novelist, best known in English for *Life in a Tomb,* though his *The Mermaid Madonna* and *The Schoolmistress with the Golden Eyes* are better known in Greece.

The 20th century has produced its share of illustrious poets as well, and probably the best known and most accessible is Constantine Cavafy (Kaváphis, in Greek, 1868–1933), who lived most of his life in Alexandria, Egypt. In 1963 George Seferis (Seferiádes, 1900–71) became the first Greek to win the Nobel Prize for Literature. Odysseus Elýtis (born 1911), from Lésvos, won a second in 1980.

Greece also enjoys some attention in the English language, and its ancient legacy is probably best known through the novels of Mary Renault, notably *The King Must Die, The Mask of Apollo, Fire from Heaven,* and *The Persian Boy* (which offers a full account of Alexander the Great's exploits). Lawrence Durrell, whose family lived for many years on Corfu, writes about Greece in *Prospero's Cell* and it is the setting for *Tunc;* his excellent *Alexandria Quartet* has a number of Greek characters. John

Fowles's much-admired *The Magus* is set on the island of Spétses, where he taught English. Other often-suggested books include Henry Miller's *The Colossus of Maroussi,* Irving Stone's *The Gold Treasures of Iris Leaman,* Gore Vidal's *Creation,* Evelyn Waugh's *Officers and Gentlemen,* and Thornton Wilder's *The Woman of Andros.*

5 The ABCs of Greek Cuisine

You probably already know about the common taverna, where you can usually find a number of grilled meats, including *souvláki* (shish kebab to the Turks), commonly available in lamb, pork, and chicken, and *keftédes* (meatballs), usually fried, but on Híos they may turn out to be made of ground chickpeas and equally delicious. You may also be familiar with many of the other dishes, like the dependable Greek salad with *féta* cheese, the usually reliable *moussaká* (eggplant casserole, with lots of regional variation, often with minced meat) and *yemistá* (tomatoes or green peppers filled with rice and sometimes minced meat), and the often bland but filling *pastítsio* (baked pasta).

And to wash it down? You can play it safe and stick with bottled water, beer, or soft drinks, but you really should try one of the many excellent Greek wines— *krasí* rather than *retsína,* to begin with, in the usual red (*kókkino*), white (*áspro*), and rosé (*rosé*). *Retsína* is a pine resin–flavored wine that may taste like turpentine the first time you try it, and may grow on you only slowly, though it's surely more immediately likeable than scotch. The flavor comes from being stored in untreated pine barrels. Greeks are very proud of their wine—they often claim to have invented it, like much else. They may tell you the resin was put in retsína to keep the Italians from taking it all away, and they got to liking the flavor. Many tavernas and restaurants have their own house wines, usually in barrels. The bottled wines by Achaia-Clauss, Boutari, Carras, Kourtaki, and Tsantali are reliably good. Ask for advice, and you're likely to get a lot more information than we have space to give you here—though you can be fairly sure the opinions expressed will be colored by where the speaker is from.

In some places you'll find that the tavernas don't open for lunch and you may have to settle for a simpler *estiatório,* which sounds like a restaurant but usually isn't, and the menu may be not only limited, but nonexistent. Your few choices may all be on display in the kitchen or under steamed-over glass. Yes, it was made earlier and it's probably tepid—hot food is thought to be bad for the stomach—but it's likely to be tasty and even healthful. The oil it's "swimming" in is olive oil—no cholesterol.

Many tavernas still don't serve desserts, which are often very sweet, though there are those who like *baklavá,* (filo soaked in honey, which some Greeks insist is actually Turkish) or *halvá* (a sort of nougat, sweeter yet and undeniably Turkish). Those with a serious sweet tooth may want to stop at a *zaharoplastíon* (confectioner) or patisserie, as French bakeries are fairly common.

Another kind of eating establishment is the *oúzerie*—usually informal though not necessarily inexpensive—which serves ouzo, the clear anise-flavored national aperitif that turns milky when mixed with water. Ouzo is especially intoxicating on an empty stomach—which is why ouzeries serve food, usually an assortment of *mezédes,* hearty appetizers eaten à la grecque with bread: the common *tzatzíki* (yogurt with cucumber and garlic), *taramosaláta* (fish roe dip), *skordaliá* (hot garlic and beet dip), *melitzanosaláta* (eggplant salad), *yigántes* (giant beans in tomato sauce), *dolmádes* (stuffed grape leaves), grilled *kalamarákia* (squid), *oktapódi* (octopus), and *loukánika* (sausage).

There is also the *psarotavérna,* which specializes in fish and seafood. Fish is no longer abundant in Greek waters and trawling with nets is prohibited from mid-May through mid-October, so prices can sometimes be exorbitant. Often you'll have to settle for the smaller fish, such as *barboúnia,* which are delicious if not overcooked. Ask locals to recommend a place for a fish dinner, always choose your own fish—in reputable places you shouldn't have to insist—and try to make sure it isn't switched on you.

Fast food is fast becoming common, especially pizza, which can be okay but rarely good. Many young people seem to subsist on *gýros* (thin slices of meat slowly roasted on a vertical spit, sliced off and served in pita bread), so we want to pass along a tip from our friend Markos: If the spindle of meat is "skinny" in the morning, you should guess it isn't fresh and pass it by.

One of the most reliable of snacks is the ubiquitous *tirópita* (cheese pie), usually made with feta, though there are endless variations. On Náxos, the *tirópita* may look like the usual flaky round pastry but contain the excellent local *graviéra.* In Métsovo it may resemble cornbread and contain leeks and *metsovélla,* a mild local cheese made from sheep milk. On Alónissos, the tirópita may contain the usual feta but be rolled in a big spiral and deep fried. A close relative to the tirópita is *spanokópita* (spinach pie), which is also prepared in a variety of ways.

Breakfast is not an important meal to the Greeks. In the cities you'll see them grabbing a *koulóuri* (pretzel-like roll) as they hurry to work. Most hotels will serve a continental breakfast of bread or rolls with butter and jam, coffee and usually juice (often fresh), occasionally yogurt. Sometimes an "English breakfast" will be offered at extra cost. Better hotels will usually serve an "American" buffet with eggs, bacon, cheese, yogurt, and fresh fruit.

Lunch is typically a heavier meal in Greece than it is in most English-speaking countries, and most Greeks still take a siesta afterwards. Keep siesta hours, about 2 to 5pm, in mind when planning your own day, especially in more provincial destinations. (Even in Athens you should be considerate about contacting friends or acquaintances at home during these hours.)

Dinner is often an all-evening affair for Greeks, starting with mezédes at 7 or 8pm, with the main meal itself as late as 11pm. (You might consider a snack before joining Greek friends in their long evening meal.)

3 Planning a Trip to Greece

by John Bozman

Before any trip, you need to do a bit of advance planning. When should I go? What is this trip going to cost me? Can I catch a festival during my visit? We'll answer these and other questions for you in this chapter.

1 Visitor Information & Entry Requirements

VISITOR INFORMATION

The **Greek National Tourist Organization** (GNTO or EOT inside Greece itself) has helpful offices throughout the world that can provide you with information concerning all aspects of travel to and in Greece. Contact one of the following **GNTO** offices:

UNITED STATES **New York:** Olympic Tower, 645 Fifth Ave., 5th Floor, New York NY 10022 (☎ 212/421-5777; fax 212/826-6940). **Chicago:** 168 North Michigan Ave., 4th Floor, Chicago, IL 60601 (☎ 312/782-1084; fax 312/782-1091). **Los Angeles:** 611 West 6th St., Suite 2198, Los Angeles, CA 90017 (☎ 213/626-6696; fax 213/489-9744).

In the **United States,** the **Overseas Citizens Emergency Center,** Department of State, Room 4811, Washington, DC 20520 (☎ 202/647-5225; fax 202/647-3000, or send self-addressed stamped envelope) issues Consular Information Sheets, travel advisories that include security problems and health risks. You can also get the latest information by contacting any U.S. embassy, consulate, or passport office. Readers with computer modems can reach the bulletin board of the Bureau of Consular Affairs at 202/647-9225.

AUSTRALIA & NEW ZEALAND 51 Pitt St., Sydney, NSW 2000 (☎ 2/241-1663; fax 2/235-2174).

CANADA **Toronto:** 1300 Bay St., Toronto, ON MSR 348 (☎ 416/968-2220; fax 416/968-6533). **Montreal:** 1233 Rue de la Montaigne, Suite 101, Montreal, QC H3G 1Z2 (☎ 514/871-1535; fax 514/871-1498).

UNITED KINGDOM & IRELAND **London:** 4 Conduit St., London W1R ODJ (☎ 0171/734-5997; fax 0171/287-1369).

ENTRY REQUIREMENTS

Citizens of **Australia, Canada, New Zealand,** and the **United States** and most other countries, except members of the **European Union,** are required to have a valid passport, which is stamped upon entry and exit, for stays up to 90 days. All U.S. citizens, even infants, must have a valid passport, but Canadian children under 16 may travel without a passport if accompanied by either parent. Longer stays must be arranged with the Bureau of Aliens, Leofóros Alexándras 173, Athens (☎ 770-5711).

Citizens of the **United Kingdom** and other members of the **European Union** are required to have only a valid passport for entry into Greece, and it is no longer stamped upon entry. Children under 16 may travel without a passport if accompanied by either parent.

2   Money

The unit of currency in Greece is the **drachma** (*drachmí,* in Greek), abbreviated **Dr,** and the current exchange rate is about Dr 235 (drachmas, *drachmaí* or *drachmés*) per U.S. dollar or Dr 360 per British pound. Coins come in denominations of Dr 5, Dr 10, Dr 20, Dr 50, and Dr 100, with old Dr 1 and Dr 2 coins still occasionally seen. Bills come in denominations of Dr 50 (blue), Dr 100 (red) (both being taken out of circulation), Dr 1,000 (brown), and Dr 5,000 (mostly gray), with a Dr 10,000 bill expected soon.

ATM NETWORKS   Automated-Teller Machines are not as abundant in Greece as they are in most English-speaking countries, but they are increasingly common. Ask your bank or credit-card company if your card will be acceptable in Greece.

In commercial centers, airports, and larger towns you will find a number of machines accepting a wide range of cards. The Commercial Bank (*Emborikí Trápeza*) services Plus and Visa; Credit Bank (*Trápeza Písteos*) accepts Visa and American Express; National Bank (*Ethnikí Trápeza*) takes Cirrus and MasterCard/Access. Though transaction fees are generally larger than they are at home, Cirrus and Plus exchange rates are based on the

---

The Greek Drachma

At this writing, $1 = Dr 240 (or 1 Dr = $0.004). This was the rate of exchange used to calculate the dollar values given in the table below and throughout this edition.

Note: International exchange rates fluctuate from time to time and may not be the same when you travel to Greece. Therefore, this table should be used as a guide for approximate values only.

Drs	U.S.$	U.K.£	Drs	U.S.$	U.K.£
5	0.02	0.01	5,000	20.83	13.51
10	0.04	0.03	7,500	31.25	20.28
25	0.10	0.07	10,000	41.67	27.02
50	0.21	0.14	12,500	52.10	33.78
75	0.31	0.20	15,000	62.50	40.54
100	0.42	0.27	17,500	72.92	47.30
125	0.53	0.34	20,000	83.33	54.05
250	1.04	0.68	22,500	93.75	60.80
1,250	5.21	3.38	25,000	104.17	67.57
2,500	10.42	6.76			

What Things Cost in Athens	U.S. $
Taxi from airport to the city's center	10.00
Local telephone call	.02
Double room at a B-class hotel	96.05
Bathless double in a pension	26.80
Lunch for one at a taverna	8.75
Dinner for one, with wine, at a restaurant	32.50
Bottle of beer	1.25
Soda	1.00
Cup of Greek coffee	.83
Roll of ASA 100 Kodacolor film, 36 exp.	8.40
Admission to National Archeological Museum	6.25

What Things Cost in Corfu	U.S. $
Taxi from airport to the city's center	4.60
Local telephone call	.02
Double room at a B-class hotel	90.30
Bathless double in a pension	34.40
Lunch for one at a taverna	8.80
Dinner for one, with wine, at a restaurant	35.85
Bottle of beer	1.66
Soda	1.25
Cup of Greek coffee	1.05
Roll of ASA 100 Kodacolor film, 36 exp.	9.75
Admission to National Archeological Museum	2.10

wholesale rates of the major banks, so you may actually save money by withdrawing larger sums and paying in cash.

TRAVELER'S CHECKS   Traveler's checks are the safest means of carrying money while traveling, and they are accepted by most hotels and some restaurants, usually with a small commission charged. Most banks sell them with a charge of 1% to 3%. If your bank charges more, you can call the travel check issuers about more competitive rates. Some organizations sell traveler's checks at reduced rates. (The Automobile Association of America sells American Express checks in several currencies without commission.)

American Express (☎ 800/221-7282 in the U.S. and Canada) is one of the largest and best known issuers of traveler's checks. American Express charge card holders and members of **AAA**, as we mentioned above, can obtain checks without having to pay a commission.

Citicorp (☎ 800/645-6556 in the U.S. and Canada or **813/623-1709** collect elsewhere).

Interpayment Services (☎ 800/221-2426 in the U.S. or Canada or **800/453-4284** from most places elsewhere) sells Visa checks issued by Barclays Bank and Bank of America.

What Things Cost in Póros	U.S. $
Local telephone call	.02
Double room at a B-class hotel	56.85
Bathless double in a pension	24.45
Lunch for one at a taverna	6.30
Dinner for one, with wine, at a restaurant	22.25
Bottle of beer	1.25
Soda	1.05
Cup of Greek coffee	.95
Roll of ASA 100 Kodacolor film, 36 exp.	9.20

Thomas Cook (☎ **800/223-9920** in the U.S. or **609/987-7300** collect, elsewhere) issues MasterCard traveler's checks.

Most British banks can issue their account holders a **Eurocheque** card and checkbook, which can be used at most cash machines and at Greek banks for an annual fee and a 2% charge.

CREDIT & CHARGE CARDS Credit cards are increasingly accepted in Greece, especially at larger hotels, better restaurants, and in many shops, and they are all but required for renting a car, but many taverns and small hotels still do not accept them. **Visa** is the most widely accepted, and **MasterCard** is usually accepted where you see signs for **Access** or **Eurocard. American Express** is less frequently accepted because it charges a higher commission and is more protective of the cardholder in disagreements. **Diner's Club** is also increasingly recognized.

Many restaurants are, however, reluctant to accept payment in plastic unless the bill is above a certain amount. Many small hotels will accept them only if you agree to pay their commission (usually about 6%), and we consider this fair enough, especially in some of the more out-of-the-way destinations where negotiating and receiving payment remains difficult and time-consuming.

EMERGENCY CASH In an emergency you can arrange to have money sent from home to a Greek bank. Telex transfers from the United Kingdom usually take at least three days and sometimes up to a week, with a charge of about 3%. Bank drafts are more expensive but potentially faster if you are in Athens. From Canada and the United States money can be wired by **Western Union** (☎ **800/325-6000**) or **American Express** (☎ **800/543-4080**), and at a cost of 4% to 10%, depending on the amount, money can be available in minutes at a local Western Union or American Express office.

3 When to Go

THE CLIMATE

Greece has a generally mild climate, though in the mountainous northern interior the winters are rather harsh and summers are brief. Southern Greece enjoys a relatively mild winter, with temperatures averaging around 12° to 15°C (55° to 60°F) in Athens. Summers are generally hot and dry, with daytime temperatures rising to 30° to 35°C (85° to 95°F), usually cooled by prevailing north winds (the *meltémi*), especially on the islands, which usually cool appreciably in the evenings.

The best time to visit is late April through June, when the wildflowers are blooming and before summer arrives in force with hordes of tourists, higher prices, overbooked facilities, and strained services. Orthodox Easter—not concurrent with our western Easter because it's still determined by the Julian calendar—is a particularly delightful time to visit, though reservations are necessary and service is not the best as so many Greeks living abroad return for the holiday. After Easter most of the island resorts will be cranking up for the season. You might plan to visit the mainland attractions first, then see the islands.

In July and August the temperatures are too high for much but beach and water activities in the overcrowded south, and we strongly recommend you not go unless you have firm reservations and enjoy close encounters with overbaking northern Europeans, loud Italians, and footloose students. The higher elevations remain cooler and less crowded, very nice for hikers, bikers, and those who don't demand sophisticated pleasures.

In September the temperatures start to fall and the crowds thin, and the weather remains generally calm and balmy well into October. This is usually the best time of year for a cruise. In mid-October ferry service is reduced and facilities on the islands begin to close for the winter, but the cooler fall weather makes Athens and the mainland all the more pleasant. If you have the time, visit the islands first then return for a tour of the archaeological sites.

Winter is no time for fun in the sun, unless you want to join the Greeks for skiing and winter sports in the mountains, but some hotels and many good tavernas are open in the winter, prices are at their lowest, and the southern mainland is still inviting, especially for those interested in archaeology and authentic local culture.

HOLIDAYS

The legal national holidays of Greece are: New Year's Day, January 1; Epiphany (Baptism of Christ), January 6; Clean Monday (*Katharí Deftéra*), day before Shrove Tuesday, 41 days before Easter; Independence Day, March 25; Good Friday through Easter, including Monday; May Day (Labor Day), May 1; Whitmonday, day after Whitsunday (Pentecost), the seventh Sunday after Easter; Assumption of the Virgin, August 15; *Ochi Day*, October 28; Christmas, December 25–26.

On these holidays government offices, banks, post offices, most stores, and many restaurants are closed. Some museum and attractions remain open, however, and visitors are often included in the celebration. For more information ask at your hotel or find one of the current English-language publications, such as the *Athens News*, *Athenscope*, or *Athens Today*.

CALENDAR OF EVENTS

January
- **Feast of St. Basil** (*Áyios Vassílios*). St. Basil is the Greek equivalent of Santa Claus. Gifts are exchanged, and a special cake, *vassilópita*, is made with a coin in it; the person who gets the piece with the coin will have good luck. January 1.
- **Epiphany** (Baptism of Christ) is celebrated with the blessing of baptismal fonts and water. A priest may throw a cross into the harbor and young men will try to recover it; the finder wins a special blessing. Children, who have been kept good during Christmas with threats of the *kalikántzari* (goblins), are allowed on the 12th day to help chase them away. January 6.
- **Gynecocracy** (*Gynaikokrátia*, Rule of Women) is celebrated in Thrace, when women take over the cafes and the men stay home and do the housework. January 8.

February
- **Carnival** (*Karnaváli*) is celebrated the three weeks before the beginning of Lent with parades, marching bands, costumes, drinking, dancing, and general lack of inhibition.

Some scholars say the name comes from the Latin for "farewell meat," while others hold that it comes from "car naval," the chariots celebrating the ancient sea god Poseidon (Saturn, to the Romans). The city of Pátras shows its support of the later theory with its famous chariot parade and wild Saturnalia, private parties and public celebrations. Masked revels are also widely held in Macedonia. On the island of Skýros, the pagan "Goat Dance" is performed, again reminding us of the primitive Diónysiac nature of the festivities. Crete has its own colorful versions, while in the Ionian islands festivities are more Italian. In Athens people bop each other on the head with plastic hammers.

March

- **Independence Day** and the **Feast of the Annunciation** (the Announcement by the Angel Gabriel to the Virgin Mary that Christ is Incarnate) are celebrated simultaneously with military parades, especially in Athens. The religious celebration is particularly important on the islands of Tínos and Hýdra and in churches or monasteries named *Evanyelismós* ("Bringer of Good News") or *Evanyelístria* (the feminine form of the name). March 25.

April

- **Sound-and-light performances** begin on the Acropolis in Athens and the Old Town on Rhodes. Nightly through October.
- **Procession of St. Spyrídon** (*Áyios Spyrídon*) is held in Corfu town. Palm Sunday.
- **Feast of St. George** (*Áyios Yóryios*), the patron saint of shepherds, is an important rural celebration with dancing and feasting. Aráchova, near Delphi, is famous for its festivities. The island of Skýros also gives its patron saint a big party. April 23. (If the 23rd comes before Easter the celebration is postponed until the Monday after Easter.)

May

- **May Day** is an important urban holiday when families have picnics in the country and pick wildflowers that are woven into wreaths and hung from balconies and over doorways. **Labor Day** is still celebrated by Greek communists and socialists as a working-class holiday. May 1.
- **Folk dance** performances begin in the amphitheater on Philopáppou Hill in Athens and continue through September.
- **Sound-and-light** shows begin in Corfu and continue through mid-September.
- **Feast of St. Constantine** (*Áyios Konstandínos*), the first Orthodox emperor, and his mother St. Helen (*Ayía Eléni*), is celebrated, most interestingly, by fire-walking rituals (*anastenariá*) in Ayía Eléni and Langáda, in Macedonia. It's a big party night for everyone named Costa and Eleni. (Name-days, rather than birthdays, are celebrated in Greece.) The **anniversary of Ionian reunion with Greece** is also celebrated, mainly in Corfu. May 21.

June

- **Athens Festival.** Features superb productions of ancient drama, opera, orchestra performances, ballet, modern dance, and popular entertainers in the handsome Odeum of Heródes Átticus, on the southwest side of the Acropolis. Through September.
- **Folk-dance** performances are given in the theater in the Old Town of Rhodes.
- **Wine Festival** is held annually at Dafní, 10 kilometers west of Athens; others are held on Rhodes and elsewhere.
- **Lycabettus Theater** presents a variety of performances at the amphitheater on Lycabettus (*Likavitós*) Hill overlooking Athens from mid-June until late August.
- **Aegean Festival** on Skiáthos presents ancient drama, modern dance, folk music and dance, concerts, and art exhibits in the Boúrtzi Cultural Center in the harbor of Skiáthos town through September.

Holy Week Celebrations

Easter is the most important festival of the year, much more important than Christmas, and it is observed far more seriously than Easter is in the West and celebrated every bit as heartily as a western Christmas. Holy Week is well under way by Ash Wednesday; services are broadcast on radio and television, which seem almost worthy of the altar status so often given them. On Thursday offices are getting by with a skeleton crew as everyone heads home, where eggs are being dyed red and baked into braided bread. People greet each other with *"Kaló Páska"* (Good Easter).

The Good Friday exodus from Athens is truly amazing, and you can remain and enjoy the deserted city or, if you're fortunate—and have wisely made reservations and preceded the evacuation—you can be among the celebrants in any town or village. The evening service is the first of the important public ceremonies. The well-dressed celebrants, most of the population, gather in the church around the *Epitaphiós*, Christ's funeral bier, which is lying in state, having been decorated earlier by the local women with flowers, greenery, and ribbons. After a brief service, the bier is carried solemnly through the streets. In some places effigies of Judas are burned.

Late Saturday night the people crowd into the church again for the most impressive solemn service; at midnight all lights and candles are extinguished, the darkness signifying Christ's journey through the underworld. Then a candlelight emerges from behind the altar, and the priest, chanting "This is the light of the world," lights the nearest candle, and candlelight is spread until the church is again alight, bells ring, and fireworks are set off outside. *"Christós anésti!"* (Christ is risen!), people greet each other joyfully and the response is an even more joyful, *"Alithós Anésti!"* (Truly He is risen!) as they make their way home with lighted candles for a big meal that includes the traditional *margarítsa* soup.

Sunday morning everyone greets you with *"Chrónia polá!"* (Many years!) and you should answer with the same wish. You'll probably be given a red egg for breakfast; you should knock it against someone else's, and the one that doesn't crack brings good luck. The serious feasting has begun. The older men have already built fires in pits and are supervising the turning of the big paschal lambs slowly roasting on their spits. Nearly every woman you meet will offer you some treat she has obviously spent some time preparing. Don't insult her by refusing. A man will offer you some of his home-made wine, maybe in a plastic pop bottle, and again you shouldn't say no. Later there will be dancing, often in traditional costumes.

- **International Classical Musical Festival** is held annually for one week in June at Náfplion, in the southern Peloponnese.
- **Midsummer Eve** is celebrated by burning the dry wreaths picked on May Day to drive away witches, a remnant of pagan ceremonies now associated with the birth of John the Baptist on Midsummer Day, June 24. June 23.
- The **Feast of the Holy Apostles** (*Ayíi Apostolí*, *Pétros*, and *Pávlos*) is another important name-day. June 29.
- **Navy Week** is celebrated throughout Greece. In Vólos the voyage of the Argonauts is reenacted. On Hýdra the exploits of Adm. Andréas Miaoúlis, naval hero of the War of Independence, are celebrated. Fishermen at Plomári on Lésvos stage a festival. End of June and beginning of July.

July

- **Dodóni Festival** presents classical dramas at the ancient theater of Dodóni, south of Ioánnina. Through September.

- **Epidaurus Festival** of classical Greek drama begins in the famous amphitheater and continues through early September.
- The Northern Greece National Theater performs classical dramas in the amphitheaters in **Phillipi** and on the island of **Thássos.**
- **Diónysia Wine Festival** is held on the island of Náxos. Mid-July.
- **Wine Festival** at Réthymno, Crete, continues throughout the month.
- **Feast of Ayía Marína,** protector of crops, is widely celebrated in rural areas. July 17.
- **Feast of the Prophet Elijah** (*Profítis Ilías*) is celebrated in the hilltop shrines formerly sacred to the sun god Helios, the most famous of which is on Mt. Taíyettos, near Sparta. July 18–20.
- **Feast of Ayía Paraskeví,** continues the succession of Saint Days celebrated at the height of summer when agricultural work is put on hold. July 26.

August

- **Feast of the Tranfiguration** (*Metamórphosi*) is celebrated in the numerous churches and monasteries of that name, though it isn't much for name-day parties. August 6.
- **Aeschylia** festival of ancient drama stages classical dramas at the archaeological site of Eleusis, home of the ancient Mysteries and birthplace of Aeschylus, west of Athens. Through mid-September.
- **Feast of the Assumption of the Virgin** (*Apokímisis tis Panayías*) is an important day of religious pilgrimage. Thousands of people flock to the most important shrine on Tínos, and others take the opportunity to go home for a visit, so rooms are particularly hard to find. August 15.
- **Epirotika Festival** in Ioánnina presents theatrical performances, concerts, and exhibitions.
- **Hippocratia Festival** on Kos presents ancient drama, musical performances, a flower show, and a re-enactment of the Hippocratic Oath. Mid-August.
- **Olympus Festival** presents cultural events in the Frankish Castle of Platamónas, near Mt. Olympus.
- **Santorínii Festival** of classical music features international musicians and singers in outdoor performances for two weeks beginning at the end of the month.

September

- **Feast of the Birth of the Virgin** (*Yénisis tís Panayías*) is another major festival, especially on Spétses, where the anniversary of the Battle of the Straits of Spétses is celebrated with a re-enactment in the harbor, fireworks, and an all-night bash. September 8.
- **Feast of the Exaltation of the Cross** (*Ipsosi to Stavroú*) marks the end of the summer stretch of feasts, and even Stavros has had enough for a while. September 14.
- **Thessaloníki International Trade Fair.** Rooms are scarce in Salonica. Mid-September.
- **Thessaloníki Film Festival** and **Festival of Popular Song**. That lively and sophisticated city continues to live it up. End of the month.

October

- **Feast of St. Demetrius** (*Áyios Dimítrios*) is particularly important in Thessaloníki, where he is the patron saint, and the **Demetrius Festival** features music, opera, and ballet. New wine is traditionally untapped. October 26.
- *Ochi* **Day,** when General Metaxá's supposed negative reply to Mussolini gives a convenient excuse for continuing the party with patriotic outpourings, including parades, folk-music and dancing, and general festivity. October 28.

November

- **Feast of the Archangels Gabriel and Michael** (*Gavriél* and *Miháíl*), with ceremonies in the many churches named for them. November 8.

• **Feast of St. Andrew** (Áyios Andréas), patron saint of Pátra, is another excuse for a party in that swinging city. November 30.

December

• **Feast of St. Nikolas** (*Áyios Nikólaos*). This St. Nick is the patron saint of sailors. Numerous processions head down to the sea and the many chapels dedicated to him. December 6.

• **Christmas.** The second day honors the **Gathering Around the Holy Family** (*Synaksis tís Panayías*). December 25–26.

• **New Year's Eve,** when children go out singing Christmas carols (*kálanda*) while their elders play cards, talk, smoke, eat, and imbibe. December 31.

4 The Active Vacation Planner

BIKING   Traveling by bicycle is becoming more common in Greece, though you won't see bicyclists in crowded downtown areas. There are more foreign travelers seeing Greece on bikes every year, and those interested in the possibility can get more information from the **Greek Cycling Federation,** Odós Bouboulínas 28, Athens (☎ 01/88-31-414). **Trekking Hellas** (Odós Fillelínon 7, 10 557 Athens (☎ 01/32-34-548; fax 01/32-51-474) can also assist you in arranging mountain bike trips.

In the United States **Classic Adventures,** Box 153, Hamlin, NY 14464 (☎ 716/964-8488 or 800/777-8090) offers a 14-day cycle tour that follows the coast and includes Corinth, Epidaurus, Mycenae, Náfpaktos, Olympia, the island of Zákynthos, and a 12-day tour of Crete.

Mountain bikes are better suited for Greek terrain, and you can even bring your own along by train (for a small fee) or plane (free, though not easy), and you can take them along on ferries, usually at no extra cost. You should also bring along spare parts, as they are rarely available outside the major cities. Keep in mind also that road shoulders in Greece are not among the most generous and well maintained.

You can rent an old bike for very little in most major resorts, and good mountain bikes are increasingly available. **Crete** is an especially good place for biking, and mountain bikes are available for rent in Iráklion at **Creta Travel,** Odós Epiméndou 20-22 (☎ 081/22-70-02), which also has offices in Réthymno and Ayios Nikólaos. In Haniá, try **G&A Travel,** Odós Hálidon 25 (☎ 0821/28-817). On **Páros** the **Mountain Bike Club,** near the post office in Parikía (☎/fax 0284/23-778) rents good mountain bikes. On **Rhodes** they are available at **Mike's Motor Club,** Odós Kazoúli 23 (☎ 0241/37-420). **Kos** is also well suited to cycling, and they are widely available for rent.

CAMPING   Greece offers a wide variety of camping facilities throughout the country. Rough or free-lance, camping is no longer acceptable in most places. The Greek National Tourist Organization can give you further information on its many licensed facilities, as well as a guide, Camping in Greece, published by the **Greek Camping Association,** Odós Sólonos 76, 106 80 Athens (☎ 01/36-21-560; fax 01/34-65-262).

DIVING   Scuba diving is currently restricted throughout most of Greece because of potential harm to sunken antiquities and the environment. There is some legal diving off the coast of Attica, off the Peloponnese peninsula, and off Halkidíki and a few other places in the north. There is also limited diving off the islands of Corfu, Crete, Kálymnos, Kefaloniá, Mýkonos, Rhodes, and Zákynthos. For more information contact the **Organization of Underwater Activities** (☎ 01/98-23-840) or the **Union of Greek Diving Centers** (☎ 02/92-29-532).

There are **diving schools** on both Corfu, **Calypso Scuba Divers,** Áyios Górdis (☎ 0661/53-101, fax 0661/34-319), and Rhodes, the **Dive Med Center,** Odós Dragoúmi

5 Rhodes Town (☎ **0241/33-654**). There are **diving and underwater activity centers** on Crete, **Paradise Dive Center,** Odós Giamboudáki 51, 741 00 Réthymno (☎/fax **0831/ 53-258**), and Mýkonos, **Lucky Scuba Divers,** Órnos Beach (☎ **0289/22-813;** fax 0289/ 23-764). Even if you are qualified you must dive under supervision.

Snorkeling, however, is permitted, and the unusually clear water makes it a special pleasure. Simple equipment is widely available for rent.

FISHING Opportunities for fishing abound. Contact the **Amateur Anglers and Maritime Sports Club,** Aktí Moutsopoúlou, 185 37 Piraeus (☎ **01/45-15-731**).

HIKING Greece offers endless opportunities for hiking, trekking, and walking. Greeks themselves are only just beginning to show some interest in walking for pleasure, but there are a number of well-mapped and even signed routes.

In Greece itself we recommend **Trekking Hellas,** Odós Fillelínon 7, 10 557 Athens (☎ **01/32-34-548;** telex 226040 HIM; fax 01/32-51-474) and in Thessaloníki at Odós Aristotélous 11 (☎ **031/242-190**) for both guided tours and help in planning your own private trek.

In the **United States,** the **Appalachian Mountain Club,** 5 Joy St., Boston MA 02108 (☎ **617/523-0636**) often organizes hiking tours in Greece. **Classic Adventures,** Box 253, Hamplin, NY 14464 (☎ **716/964-8488** or **800/777-8090**) offers hiking tours of Crete and the Zagóri region of Epirus. **Mountain Travel-Sobek,** 6420 Fairmount Ave., El Cerrito, CA 94530 (☎ **510/527-8100** or **800/227-2384**) sometimes offers summer treks in the Píndos Mountains and the Zagóri. Birders and nature lovers should contact **World Nature Tours,** P.O. Box 693, Silver Spring, MD 20918 (☎ **301/593-2522**), which offers annual trips to northern and northeastern Greece, in conjunction with the University of Thessaloníki. **Questers Worldwide Nature Tours,** 381 Park Ave. South, Suite 1201, New York, NY 10016 (☎ **212/251-0444** or **800/468-8668**) also sometimes offers nature tours in Greece.

HORSEBACK RIDING There is some opportunity for horseback riding in Greece. Near Athens you'll find the **Athletic Riding Club of Ekali** (☎ **01/81-35-576**), the **Helenic Riding Club,** Maroussi (☎ **01/68-26-128**), and the **Riding Club of Parnitha** (☎ **01/24-02-413**); call for directions and reservations. Good facilities are also found near Thessaloníki, and on Corfu, Crete, Rhodes, Skiáthos, with many smaller stables elsewhere.

In the United States, **Equitour,** Box 807, Dubois, WY 82513 (☎ **307/455-3363** or **800/545-0019**), offers a six-day riding tour of the beautiful Mt. Pelion area. **FITS Equestrian,** 685 Lateen Rd., Solvang, CA 93463 (☎ **805/688-9494** or **800/666-3487**) offers riding tours of remote villages and countryside in Crete, as well as Mt. Pelion.

MOUNTAINEERING Those interested in more strenuous trekking and mountain climbing should contact the **Hellenic Federation of Mountaineering Clubs,** Odós Milióni 5, 106 73 Athens (☎ **01/36-45-904** or 36-44-687).

SKIING There are a number of attractive skiing centers in Greece. They can't compare to those further north in deep snow and posh facilities, but they don't approach them in steep prices either, and there is much charm in their little hotels and lively après-ski life. The season generally begins after Christmas and continues until the end of April, depending on the weather.

The best developed is the **Parnassós Ski Center,** near Aráchova, on Mt. Parnassus, which has 20 ski slopes, chair lifts, tow bars, classes, equipment rental, snack bars and restaurants, and even child care. For more information contact the Greek Tourist Organization (EOT) or the center itself: 320 04 Aráchova, Viotias (☎ **0234/22-689** or **0234/22-493;** fax 0234/22-695).

There is also skiing on the gentler slopes of **Mt. Pelion** and at charming **Métsovo,** in Epirus northeast of Ioánnina, where the season is somewhat shorter. Other centers are found on the Peloponnese peninsula at **Helmós,** near Kalávrita, in central Greece at **Veloúhi,** near Karpeníssi, and in Macedonia, at **Pisodéri,** near Flórina, and **Vérmion,** near Náoussa. For more information contact the **Hellenic Federation of Skiing Clubs,** Odós Karayóryi tís Servías 7, 105 63 Athens (☎ **01/32-30-182**; fax 01/32-30-142).

WATER SPORTS   Water sports of various kinds are available at most major resort areas, and we will mention the more important facilities in our individual reviews. **Parasailing** is possible at the larger resorts in the summer.

River rafting and **kayaking** are definite possibilities, especially in Epirus, with more limited opportunities on the Peloponnese peninsula. Contact the **Alpine Club,** Leofóros Syngroú 28, 117 43 Athens (☎ **01/92-45-218**).

Waterskiing facilities are widely available; there are several schools at Vouliagméni, south of Athens, and usually at least one on each of the major islands. Contact the **Water Skiing Federation,** Odós Stournari 32, 106 83 Athens (☎ **01/52-31-875**) for more information.

Windsurfing has become increasingly popular in Greece, and boards are widely available. The many coves and small bays along Greece's convoluted coastline are ideal for beginners, and instruction is usually available at reasonable prices. The best conditions and facilities are found on the islands of Corfu, Crete, Lefkáda, Lésvos, Náxos, Páros, Sámos, and Zákynthos. There are a number of excellent schools. Contact the **Hellenic Wind-Surfing Association,** Odós Filellínon 7, 105 57 Athens (☎ **01/32-30-068** or 01/32-30-330).

5 Learning Vacations

ARCHAEOLOGICAL DIGS   The **American School of Classical Studies at Athens,** 993 Lenox Dr., Suite 101, Lawrenceville, NJ 08648 (☎ **609/844-7577**), offers an early summer tour of one of their excavation sites guided by archaeologists and historians. **Archaeological Tours,** 30 East 42nd St., Suite 1202, New York, NY 10017 (☎ **212/986-3054**) offers tours led by expert guides. **Educational Tours and Cruises,** 14(R) Wyman St., Medford, MA 02155 (☎ **617/396-3188** or **800/275-4109**; fax 617/396-3096) can assist you in arranging a wide variety of cultural excursions, including tailor-made arrangements. In Greece, **Educational Tours and Cruises** can be reached at Odós Artemídos 1, Glyfáda, 166 74 Athens (☎ **01/89-81-741**; fax 01/89-55-419). **FreeGate Tourism,** 1156 Avenue of the Americas, No. 720, New York, NY 10036 (☎ **212/764-1818** or **800/223-0304**), and **Hellastours,** 1100 Glendon Ave., Suite 1700, Los Angeles, CA 90024 (☎ **310/208-8700** or **800/824-8535**), can also provide expert guides.

ART   **International Study Tours,** 225 West 34th St. No. 913, New York, NY 10122 (☎ **212/563-1202** or **800/833-2111**; fax 212/594-6953), offers studies in architecture, art, and culture. The **Athens Center for the Creative Arts,** Odós Archimídou 48, Pangráti, 116 36 Athens (☎ **01/70-12-268**), offers summer programs. The **Hellas Art Club** on the island of Hýdra, at the Leto Hotel, 180 40 Hýdra (☎ **0298/53-385**; fax 01/36-12-223 in Athens), offers classes in painting, ceramics, music, theater, photography, Greek dancing, and cooking.

CRAFTS   The **Texas Connection,** 217 Arden Grove, San Antonio, TX 78215 (☎ **210/225-6294**) offers tours focusing on the handicrafts of mainland Greece and Crete, including visits to the workshops of craftsmen and weavers.

MODERN GREEK   For the study of modern Greek, the **Athens Center** (see above) is highly recommended. The **School of Modern Greek Language** of Aristotle University in Thessaloníki also offers summer courses.

PERSONAL GROWTH   The **Skýros Center,** which can be contacted in the U.K. at 92 Prince of Wales Rd., London NW5 3NE (☎ **0171/267-4424**), offers "personal growth" vacations on the island of Skyros, with courses in fitness, holistic health, and creative writing.

6 Health & Insurance

STAYING HEALTHY   Milk is pasteurized, though refrigeration is sometimes not the best, especially in out-of-the-way places, where you might also want to take some care with meat. Diarrhea is often a minor problem with all travelers everywhere, so it's wise to take along some of your favorite remedy. Allergy sufferers should carry along some antihistamines, especially in the spring. Cola soft drinks are said to be helpful for those having digestive difficulties with too much olive oil in their food.

There are no immunization requirements for getting into the country, though it's always a good idea to have polio, tetanus, and typhoid covered when traveling anywhere.

Health services are good, if not as noticeable as they are in most English-speaking countries. For minor health problems go first to the nearest pharmacy (*pharmakío*), which will be marked with a green cross. (In the larger cities, if it is closed, there should be a sign in the window directing you to the nearest open one. Newspapers also list the pharmacies that are open late or all night.) Pharmacists are well trained and usually speak English quite well, and many medications are available without prescription. You should bring along a sufficient quantity of any prescription medication you are taking, in your carry-on luggage. Just in case, ask your doctor to write you new prescriptions, in the generic—not the brand—name.

For more serious medical problems, ask your hotel to recommend an English-speaking doctor or call a **first aid center** (☎ **166**), **hospital** (☎ **106**), or the **tourist police** (☎ **171**, in Athens, or **92-27-777**). You can obtain a list of English-speaking doctors before you leave from the **International Association for Medical Assistance for Travelers (IAMAT)** in Canada at 40 Regal Road, Guelph, ON N1K 1B5 (☎ **519/836-1002**), in the United States at 417 Center St., Lewiston, NY 14092 (☎ **716/754-4883**), or in Switzerland at 57 Voirets, 1212 Grand-Lancy, Geneva. Your embassy or consulate can also help you find a doctor.

Those with chronic illnesses should discuss their travel plans with their physician. Those with epilepsy, diabetes, or significant cardiovascular disease should wear a Medic Alert identification tag or bracelet, which will alert a health care provider to the condition and provide the telephone number of the 24-hour hotline from which your medical record can be obtained. Contact the **Medic Alert Foundation,** P.O. Box 1009, Turlock, CA 95381-1009 (☎ **800/344-3226**).

Emergency treatment is usually given free of charge in **state hospitals,** but be warned that only basic needs are met. The care in **outpatient clinics,** which are usually open in the mornings (8am to noon), is usually somewhat better; you can find them next to most major hospitals, on some islands, and occasionally in rural areas, usually indicated by good signs.

INSURANCE   Before you purchase any additional insurance, check your current medical, automobile, and home-owner's policies as well as any insurance provided by credit-card companies and auto and travel clubs. You may already have adequate off-premises theft coverage, and your credit-card company may provide cancellation coverage on tickets paid for with their card. If you are prepaying for your trip or taking a flight that has cancellation penalties, consider cancellation insurance.

The following companies can provide you with insurance and further information:

Mutual of Omaha (**Tele-Trip**), 3201 Farnam St., Omaha, NE 68131 (☎ **402/ 342-7600** or **800/228-9792**).

Travel Guard International, 1145 Clark St., Stevens Point, WI 54481 (☎ **800/ 782-5151**).

Travel Insurance Pak, Travel Insured International, P.O. Box 285568, East Hartford, CT 06128 (☎ **860/528-7663** or **800/243-3174**).

Wallach and Co., HealthCare Abroad, 107 W. Federal St., P.O. Box 480, Middleburg, VA 22117 (☎ **540/687-3166** or **800/237-6615;** fax 540/687-3172).

7 Tips for Travelers with Special Needs

FOR TRAVELERS WITH DISABILITIES   Few concessions are made for the disabled in Greece, and steep steps, uneven pavement, narrow walks, slick stone, and traffic congestion can cause problems; the archaeological sites often prove difficult; and crowded public transportation can be all but impossible. The **Greek National Tourist Organization** can provide you with a short list of hotels that may be suitable, and we will mention the special facilities in those few hotels that have them. In Greece the **Hermes Association,** Odós Patriárchou 13, Argiroúpoli, 165 42 Athens (☎ **01/99-61-887**) also offers advice.

In the **United States** a free booklet, *Air Transportation of Handicapped Persons,* can be obtained by writing to Free Advisory Circular No. AC12032, Distribution Unit, U.S. Department of Transportation, Publications Division, M-4332, Washington, DC 20590. The **American Foundation for the Blind,** 15 West 15th St., New York, NY 10011 (☎ **800/232-5463**) is the best source of information for those with visual impairment. The **Federation of the Handicapped,** 211 West 14th St., New York, NY 10011 (☎ **212/ 206-4200**), operates summer tours for members, who must pay a small annual fee. The *Itinerary,* a travel magazine published every other month, is filled with news about travel aids, special tours, information on accessibility, and much else; you can subscribe for $12 a year at P.O. Box 2912, Bayonne, NJ 07002-2012 (☎ **201/858-3400**).

The **Catholic Travel Office,** 4701 Willard Ave., Suite 226, Chevy Chase, MD 20815 (☎ **301/564-1904**), and **New Directions,** 5276 Hollister Ave. No. 207, Santa Barbara, CA 93111 (☎ **805/967-2841;** fax 805/964-7344) offer tours for the handicapped. You can obtain the names and addresses of other tour operators that offer services to the disabled by sending a self-addressed stamped envelope to the **Society for the Advancement of Travel for the Handicapped,** 347 Fifth Ave., Suite 619, New York, NY 10016 (☎ **212/447-7284**, fax 212/725-8253). The **Travel Information Service,** Moss Rehabilitation Hospital, 1200 W. Tabor Rd., Philadelphia, PA 19141-3099 (☎ **215/456-3099**), offers a $5 package that contains the names and addresses of accessible hotels, restaurants, and attractions, often based on firsthand reports of travelers who have been there.

FOR GAY & LESBIAN TRAVELERS   The **International Gay Travel Association,** P.O. Box 4974, Key West, FL 33041 (☎ **800/448-8550**) can advise you about travel opportunities, agents, and tour operators. You can subscribe to *Our World,* a gay and lesbian travel magazine, at 1104 N. Nova Rd., Suite 251, Daytona Beach, FL 32117 (☎ **904/ 441-5367**). A monthly newsletter, *Out and About,* also has information about gay travel, and can be ordered by phone (☎ **800/929-2268**).

In Athens the gay organization *Akoe Amphi* can be found at Odós Zalóngou 6 (☎ **01/ 77-19-221**), P.O. Box 26022, 100 22 Athens. The **Autonomous Group of Gay Women** can be contacted through The Women's House, Odós Románou Melódou 4, Likavitós (☎ **01/28-14-823**). The *Greek Gay Guide,* published by Kraximo Press, P.O. Box 4228, 102 10 Athens (☎ **01/36-25-249**), can be purchased at some kiosks.

FOR SENIORS   For information before you go, write for *Travel Tips for Senior Citizens* (publication no. 8970), distributed for $1 by the Superintendent of Documents, U.S. Government Printing Office, Washington, DC 20402 (☎ **202/783-5238**). Another booklet, ***101 Tips for Mature Travelers,*** is available free from **Grand Circle Travel,** which specializes in service to senior citizens, 347 Congress St., Boston, MA 02210 (☎ **617/350-7500** or **800/248-3737**). A monthly newsletter, *The Mature Traveler,* is available for $29.95 a year at P.O. Box 50820, Reno, NV 89513 (☎ **702/786-7419**).

The **American Association of Retired Persons** (**AARP**), 1909 K St. NW, Washington, DC 20049 (☎ **202/872-4700** or **800/424-3410**) offers members information on discounts on airfares, car rentals, and hotels.

The **National Council of Senior Citizens,** 1331 F St. NW, Washington, DC 20004 (☎ **202/347-8800**), publishes a monthly newsletter that includes travel tips. Membership is $12 ($16 per couple) annually, and discounts on lodging and car rental are made available.

Elderhostel, 75 Federal St., Boston, MA 02110 (☎ **617/426-7788**), offers study programs for people over 60.

Interhostel, University of New Hampshire, 6 Garrison Ave., Durham, NH 03824 (☎ **603/862-1147** or **800/733-9753**), offers two-week programs in more than two dozen countries for people over 50.

Saga International Holidays, 222 Berkeley St., Boston, MA 02116 (☎ **800/343-0273**), offers all-inclusive tours for seniors 50 and older.

FOR STUDENTS   In the **United States** the largest travel service for students is the **Council on International Education Exchange,** 205 E. 42nd St, New York, NY 10017, by mail or in person at 356 West 34th St. (☎ **212/661-1414**), with branches in Boston (☎ **617/266-1926**), Los Angeles (☎ **310/208-3551**), Miami (☎ **305/670-9261**), and many other college towns. **CIEE** provides details about budget travel, study abroad, work permits, and insurance, and it sells **ISIC** and **IYC** cards ($15) and a number of helpful publications, such as *Student Travels* magazine ($1, free in person). **Campus Connections,** 325 Chestnut St., Suite 1101, Philadelphia, PA 19106 (☎ **215/625-8585** or **800/428-3235**), specializes in student fares. **Travel Management International,** 3617 Dupont Ave. South, Minneapolis, MN 55409 (☎ **612/823-3001** or **800/245-3672**), offers student discounts, as well as other travel arrangements.

In Greece, students with proper identification (ISIC and IYC cards) are given reduced entrance fees to archaeological sites and museums, as well as discounts on admission to most artistic events, theatrical performances, and festivals.

A **Hostelling International** membership can save students money in over 5,000 hostels in 70 countries, where sex-segregated dormitory-style sleeping quarters cost about $8 to $20 a night. In the **United States** membership is available through the **American Youth Hostels,** 75 Spring St., New York, NY 10012 (☎ **212/431-7100**) or P.O. Box 37613, Washington, DC 20013-7613 (☎ **202/783-6161**).

In **Greece** an International Guest Card can be obtained at the Greek Association of Youth Hostels in Athens at Odós Dragatsaníou (☎ **01/32-34-107**).

8 Getting There

The vast majority of travelers reach Greece by plane. Many also come by ferry from Italy. There is still bus service from Europe, but few people are interested in the arduous journey. Train service from Europe has been disrupted by the trouble in the Balkans, and even when running, it's slow and uncomfortable in the summer—and a EurailPass is valid only for ferry service from Italy.

BY PLANE   The United States   British Air (☎ 800/247-9297) has service to Athens from a number of major cities, all stopping in London, most at Heathrow, but some at Gatwick. **Delta** (☎ 800/241-4141) has satisfactory service from throughout the United States, most flights stopping in Frankfurt. **KLM** (☎ 800/374-7747) has superior service from 10 major cities in the United States to Athens, all flights stopping in Amsterdam. **Lufthansa** (☎ 800/645-3880) has superior service to Athens, Thessaloníki, and Crete from 10 U.S. cities, via Frankfurt. **Olympic** (☎ 800/223-1226) has satisfactory, sometimes rude service nonstop daily from New York, twice weekly from Boston, and twice weekly from Chicago via New York. **Sabena** (☎ 800/955-2000) has good service to Athens from Atlanta, Boston, Chicago, and New York, all flights stopping in Brussels. **TWA** (☎ 800/892-4141) has satisfactory service to Athens, with a bit more leg room, from all over the United States, most flights nonstop from New York. **Virgin Atlantic** (☎ 212/242-1330 or 800/862-8621) offers fair service at fair prices, especially its low-cost promotional fares, with daily service from Los Angeles and from New York or Newark, several times weekly from several other cities, to London.

Australia   Service to Athens is offered daily from Perth and Sydney and several times weekly from Brisbane and Melbourne by **Alitalia** (☎ 02/247-1308 in Sydney), via Bangkok and Rome; **KLM** (☎ 800/505-747), via Singapore and Amsterdam; **Lufthansa** (☎ 02/367-3800 in Sydney), via Frankfurt; and **Olympic** (☎ 02/251-2204 in Sydney), via Bangkok. The lowest fares generally offered are on weekly service from Sydney on **Aeroflot** (☎ 02/233-7148 in Sydney), via Moscow, and on **Thai Airways** (☎ 02/844-0900 in Sydney) flights from Brisbane, Melbourne, Perth, and Sydney via Bangkok. **British Airways** (☎ 02/258-3000 in Sydney) and **Qantas** (☎ 02/957-0111 and 236-3636 in Sydney) have regular service to London, and a "Global Explorer Pass" that allows you to make up to six stopovers wherever the two airlines fly, except to South America.

Canada   Air Canada (☎ 800/776-3000) flies to Vienna, with connections on Olympic to Athens. **KLM** (☎ 800/361-5073) has several flights a week to Athens (via Amsterdam) from Calgary, Halifax, Montreal, Toronto, and Vancouver. **Olympic** (☎ 800/223-1226) has two flights a week to Athens from Montreal and Toronto. **Air France** (☎ 800/667-2747), **Alitalia** (☎ 800/223-5730), **British Airways** (☎ 800/668-1059), **Czechoslovak Airline** (☎ 800/223-2365), **Iberia** (☎ 800/423-7421), **Lufthansa** (☎ 800/645-3880), **Sabena** (☎ 800/955-2000), and **TAP Air Portugal** (☎ 800/221-7370) all have several flights a week from Montreal via other European cities to Athens.

Ireland   Aer Lingus (☎ 01/844-4777 in Dublin) and **British Air** (☎ 0345/222111 in Belfast) both fly to Athens via London's Heathrow. Less-expensive charters operate in the summer from Belfast and Dublin to Athens, less frequently to Corfu, Crete, Myknonos, and Rhodes. Contact **Balkan Tours,** 37 Ann St. Belfast BT1 4EB (☎ 01232/236795) or **Joe Walsh Tours,** 8 Baggot St., Dublin (☎ 01/676-0991). Students should contact **USIT,** Aston Quay, O'Connell Bridge, Dublin 2 (☎ 01/679-8833) or at Fountain Centre, College St., Belfast (☎ 01232/324073).

New Zealand   Singapore (☎ 09/303-2506 in Aukland), via Singapore, and **Thai** (☎ 09/377-3886 in Aukland), via Bangkok, presently offer the least expensive fares to Athens. **Air New Zealand** (☎ 09/309-6171 in Auckland) and **Qantas** (☎ 09/303-3209 in Auckland) offer connections through **Lufthansa** (☎ 09/303-1529 in Auckland) to Athens. **British Air** (☎ 09/367-7500 in Auckland) and **Qantas** (☎ 09/303-2506 in Auckland) can get you to Europe and offer a "Global Explorer Pass," with up to six stopovers, for very little more. **Alitalia** also flies to Athens (via Rome).

The United Kingdom   British Air (☎ 0181/897-4000), **Olympic** (☎ 0181/846-9080), and **Virgin Atlantic** (☎ 01293/747747) have several flights daily from

London's Heathrow Airport. Newer companies such as **Air UK** and **Britannia** also have regular flights. Eastern European airlines, such as the Czech **CSA** (☎ **0171/255-1898**), Bulgarian **Balkan** (☎ **0171/637-7637**), and Hungarian **Malev** (☎ **0171/439-0577**), offer service to Athens via their capitals at good prices, but with frequent delays. There are also connecting flights to Athens and some to Thessaloníki from Aberdeen, Belfast, Birmingham, Bristol, Edinburgh, Glasgow, Leeds, Liverpool, Newcastle, and Southampton, as well as flights to Athens and the major islands from Birmingham, Cardiff, Gatwick, Glasgow, Luton, and Manchester.

Charters   There are a number of companies that charter less-expensive flights to Athens from the United States; generally you must book through a travel agent and at least a month in advance to get on a flight in the summer. Flights are less expensive in the spring and fall, least expensive in the winter, and slightly less expensive during the week. One company we continue to recommend is **Homeric Tours** (☎ **212/753-1100** or **800/223-5570**), which in 1995 charged $589 for a round trip from New York in the winter and from $785 to $950 during the spring and summer. They have several flights a week between June and September, only one flight a week during the rest of the year. **Tourlite International** (☎ **212/599-3355** or **800/272-7600**) charges similar fares for its flights between New York and Athens. Both companies offer low-cost tours, car rental, cruises, and hotel accommodations at considerable savings.

Note: Greece prohibits visitors on charter flights from leaving and reentering the country—to prevent visitors from taking advantage of subsidized landing fees only to spend their time and money in Turkey—and you should determine if this rule is being observed before you break it.

Bucket Shops (Consolidators)   Bucket shops—those companies you see advertising the very low prices—buy unused seats in bulk from the various airlines at even lower prices and sell them at a profit. You must usually be prepared to leave on short notice. Not all of them are entirely trustworthy, and some will not make refunds, so take some precautions: Pay for tickets with a credit card, consider taking out cancellation insurance, and always confirm the reservation with the airline itself. Some frequently recommended consolidators are **Council Charter** (☎ **800/233-7402**), **Travac** (☎ **800/872-8800**), and **Unitravel** (☎ **800/325-2222**).

By Boat   Most people who come to Greece by boat come from Italy, though there is service from Cyprus, Egypt, Israel, and Turkey. Brindisi to Pátra is the most common ferry crossing, an 18-hour voyage, with as many as seven departures a day in summer. **Ilio Lines** now offers four-hour hydrofoil service between Brindisi and Corfu. There is also regular service, twice a day in summer, from Ancona and Bari, once daily from Otranto, and two or three times a week from Trieste. Most ferries stop at Corfu or Igoumenítsa, often at both, and occasionally at Kephaloniá.

One-way fares from Brindisi to Pátra cost about £40 or $60 for a tourist-class deck chair to about £140 to $225 for a cabin with a view. Fares to Igoumenítsa are considerably cheaper but by no means a better value unless your destination is nearby.

The number of shipping lines involved and variations in schedules doesn't permit us to give you more concrete details. Consult a travel agent about the possibilities, book well ahead of time in the summer, and reconfirm with the shipping line on the day of departure.

9   Getting Around

BY CAR   Driving in Greece is a bit of an adventure, but it's the best way to see the country at your own pace. Greece has the highest accident rate in Europe, due more to treacherous roads, mountain terrain, and poor maintenance of older cars, than to reckless driving—though Greeks are certainly aggressive drivers. Athens is a particularly intimidating place to drive in at first, and parking spaces are practically nonexistent in the center of town. Accidents must be reported to the police for insurance claims.

The **Greek Automobile Touring Club** (**ELPA**) Odós Mesoyíon 2, Athens (☎ **01/ 77-91-615**), with offices in most cities, can help you with all matters relating to your car, issue an international driver's license, and provide you with maps and information (☎ **174** 24 hours daily). The **emergency road service** number is **104,** and the service provided by the able ELPA mechanics is free, but you should definitely give a generous tip.

Driving Rules   You drive on the right in Greece, pass on the left, and yield right-of-way to vehicles approaching from the right except where otherwise posted. Greece has adopted international road signs, though many Greeks apparently haven't learned what they mean yet. The maximum speed limit is 100 kph (65 mph) on open roads, and 50 kph (30 mph) in town, unless otherwise posted. Seat belts are required. The police have become increasingly strict in recent years, especially with foreigners in rental cars; alcohol tests can be given and fines imposed on the spot. (Worse things have been known to happen to foreign tourists in rental cars, but if you feel you have been treated unfairly get the officer's name and report him at the nearest tourist police station.) Honking is illegal in Athens, but you can hear that law broken by tarrying at a traffic signal.

Driving Your Own Vehicle   To drive your own vehicle, valid registration papers, an international third-party insurance certificate, and a driver's license are required. A free entry card allows you to keep your car in the country up to four months, after which another eight months can be arranged without having to pay import duty.

Car Rentals   There is an abundance of rental cars, with considerable variation in prices. Always ask if the quoted price includes insurance. You can usually save by booking at home before you leave, and this is especially advisable during the summer. When shopping around for a bargain, be sure to carry along and display a number of brochures from competitors.

Most companies require that the renter be at least 21 years old (24 for some models), have a valid Australian, Canadian, EU-nation, U.S., or international driver's license, and have a major credit card or leave a large cash deposit.

The major rental companies in Athens, most with branches at the airport, are **Avis** (☎ **01/32-24-951**); **Budget** (☎ **01/92-14-771** or 01/06-13-634 at the airport); **HellasCars** (☎ **01/92-35-353;** fax 01/92-35-397); **Hertz** (☎ **01/92-20-102**); and **InterRent/EuropeCar** (☎ **01/92-33-452;** fax 01/92-21-440), all with offices in major cities and on most islands. The smaller local companies usually have lower rates, though their vehicles are often older and not as well maintained. **Viking Tours** (☎ **01/89-80-729;** fax 01/89-40-952) and many hotels can arrange rentals at discount rates. Daily rates start at about $60 per day, plus 40¢ per kilometer, or $600 a week with unlimited mileage for the smallest Fiat or Suziki in the high season, but at other times rates are negotiable.

Car Ferries   Car ferry service is available on most larger ferries, and there's regular service from Piraeus to Aegina and Póros in the Saronic Gulf, most of the Cyclades, Haniá and Iráklio on Crete, Híos, Kos, Lésvos, Rhodes, and Sámos. For the Cyclades crossing is shorter and less expensive from Rafína, an hour east of Athens. From Pátra there's daily service to Corfu, Itháki, and Kephaloniá. In the summer there are four car ferries daily from Kilíni to Zákynthos. The Sporádes have service from Áyios Konstandínos, Kými, and Vólos. The short car ferry across the Gulf of Corinth from Río to Antírio can save a lot of driving for those traveling between the northwest and the Peloponnese or Athens. There's also service between many of the islands, even between Crete and Rhodes, as well as car crossing to and from Turkey between Híos and Çesme, Lésvos and Dikeli, and Sámos and Kuçadasi.

BY PLANE   Air travel is one the most expensive and occasionally one of the most frustrating means of travel in Greece, and we recommend it only for those pressed for time and for the more distant destinations. **Olympic Airways** maintains a virtual monopoly on domestic air travel and thus has little incentive to improve service. Better computerized booking has reduced the possibility of finding out at the last minute that you don't actually have a seat, but delayed flights are still common, and the airline is not famous for quality maintenance. (Their domestic flight attendants tend to be more pleasant than their international counterparts.) Book as far ahead of time as possible, especially in the summer, reconfirm your booking before leaving for the airport, and try to arrive at the airport at least an hour before departure. (*Note:* Tickets are nonrefundable; changing your flight can cost you up to 30% within 24 hours of departure and 50% within 12 hours.)

Olympic Airways (☎ 01/92-69-111; fax 01/92-19-933) has a number of offices in Athens, though most travel agents also sell tickets, and offers service on the mainland to Alexandroúpoli, Ioánnina, Kalamáta, Kavála, Kozaní, Kastoriá, and Thessaloníki, and the islands of Astipálea, Corfu, Crete (Iráklio, Haniá, Sitía), Híos, Kárpathos, Kásos, Kastellórizo, Kephaloniá, Kos, Kýthira, Léros, Lésvos, Límnos, Mílos, Mýkonos, Náxos, Páros, Rhodes, Sámos, Skiáthos, Skýros, Sýros, and Zákynthos. All domestic flights leave from Athens's West Terminal, often called *Olympikí*. Most flights are to or from Athens, though there is some interisland service. The baggage allowance is 15 kilos (33 pounds) per passenger, except with a connecting international flight. All domestic flights are nonsmoking.

Round-trip tickets are sold as two one-way fares. Some sample 1995 one-way fares are: Athens-Corfu Dr 19,300 ($82); Athens-Crete (Iráklio) Dr 20,700 ($88); Athens-Mýkonos Dr 16,700 ($71); Athens-Páros Dr 16,500 ($70); Athens-Rhodes Dr 23,300 ($99); Athens-Santorínii Dr 18,700 ($80); Iráklio-Rhodes Dr 20,500 ($87). As you see, the shorter trips, such as to Mýkonos and Páros, are not good values, and though you'll probably save a little time, you'll miss all the scenery.

BY TRAIN   Greek trains are generally slow but inexpensive, efficient, and pleasant. The Railway Organization of Greece (**OSE**) also operates some bus service from stations adjacent to major terminals. (Bus service is faster, but second-class train fare is nearly 50% cheaper, and trains are more comfortable and scenic.)

For information and tickets in Athens visit the OSE office at Odós Karolou 1-3 (☎ 52-40-601), or Odós Sína 6 (☎ 36-24-402), both near Omónia Square; information is available at Odós Filellínon 17 (☎ 32-36-747), near Sýntagma Square.

Purchase your ticket and reserve a seat ahead of time, as a 50% surcharge is added to tickets purchased on the train and some lines are packed, especially during the summer. A first-class ticket may be worth the extra costs, as seats are more comfortable and less crowded. There is sleep service (costly, but a good value if you can sleep on a train) on the Athens-Thessaloníki run, and express service (six hours) twice a day, 7am and 1pm.

Trains to northern Greece (Alexandroúpoli, Flórina, Kalambáka, Lamía, Lárissa, Thessaloníki, Vólos, etc.) leave from the Lárissa Station (*Stathmós Laríssis*). Trains to the Peloponnese (Árgos, Corinth, Pátra) leave from the nearby Peloponnese Station (*Stathmós Peloponnísou*). Take trolley 1 or 5 from Sýntagma Square to both stations.

The relaxed Peloponnese circuit from Corinth, to Pátra, Pírgos (near Olympia), Trípolis, and Árgos is a good way to experience this scenic region, though the Athens-Pátra stretch is often crowded. The spectacular spur between Diakoftó and Kalávrita is particularly recommended for train enthusiasts.

BY BUS   Public buses are convenient, inexpensive, and easy to use. Local buses vary from place to place, but on most islands the bus stop is usually fairly central with a posted schedule, destinations displayed on the front of the bus, and fare collected after departure by a conductor. In Athens and other large cities, a ticket must be purchased before boarding—kiosks usually have them, as well as information—and validated after boarding.

Greece has an extensive **long-distance bus** service (**KTEL**), an association of regional operators with green and yellow buses that usually leave from convenient central stations. Current information can usually be found at a Greek Tourist Organization (EOT) or municipal tourist office.

In Athens most destinations within Attica leave from the Mavromaté on terminal, north of the National Archaeological Museum; most buses to central Greece leave from Odós Lissíon 60, 5 kilometers north of Omónia Square (take local bus no. 024 from Leofóros Amalías in front of the entrance to the National Garden and tell the driver your destination); most buses to the Peloponnese, western and northern Greece leave from the terminal at Odós Kifissoú 100, 4 kilometers northeast of Omónia Square (take local bus no. 051 from two blocks west of Omónia, near the big church of Ayios Konstandínos, at Zinonos and Menándrou).

Various express buses between major cities, usually air-conditioned, can be booked through travel agencies. Make sure you're pronouncing your destination properly, or at least are being understood—you wouldn't be the first to see a bit more of Greece than bargained for—and determine the bus's schedule and comforts before purchasing your ticket. Many buses are not air-conditioned, take torturous routes, and make frequent stops. (No-smoking signs are generally disregarded by drivers and conductors, as well as by many older male passengers.)

Organized bus tours are widely available, many of them departing from near Syntagma Square. Ask at your hotel or call **Educational Tours** in Athens (☎ **01/89-81-741**).

BY CRUISE SHIP   Travelers short on time and previous experience will want to consider a cruise, which can save a lot of time and hassle in making travel and accommodations arrangements. There are, of course, any number of day cruises from most of the major destinations, there are three- and four-day cruises that can be combined with mainland travel, and longer cruises with a range of stops, prices, and amenities. Ask your travel agent for details. In the United States we recommend the **Greek Island Cruise Center,** 4321 Lakemoor Dr., Wilmington, NC 28405 (☎ **800/342-3030**; fax 910/791-9400).

BY FERRY   Ferries are the most common, cheapest, and generally the most pleasant way to visit the islands, though the slow roll of a ferry is conducive to seasickness. There's a wide variety in the vessels sailing Greek waters—some huge, sleek and new, with comfortable TV lounges, discos, and good restaurants, some old and ill-kept, but pleasant enough if you stay outside. None of the ferries are entirely reliable, but they're usually fun and relaxing, and even the worst of them offers plenty of opportunity to meet people. Drinks and snacks are almost always sold, but the prices and selection are never good, so you may want to bring along your own.

The map of Greece offered by the Greek Tourist Organization (EOT) is very useful in planning your sea travels because the various routes are indicated. Once you've learned what is possible, you can turn your attention to what is available. There are dozens of shipping companies, each with its own schedule, which by the way are regulated by the government. Your travel agent might have a copy of *Helenic Travelling*, a monthly travel guide published by GNTO, or another similar summary of schedules. Remember that the summer schedule is the fullest, spring and fall have reduced service, and winter schedules are skeletal, and that different travel agencies sell tickets to different lines. (This is usually the policy of the line itself, and one agent might not know or bother to find out what else is being offered.) The port authority is the most reliable source of information, and the shipping company itself or its agents usually offer better prices and may have tickets when other agents have exhausted their allotment. It often pays to shop around a little to compare vessels and prices.

Photos can give you some idea, but remember any photo displayed was probably taken when the ship was new, no matter when it was reproduced, and there are few clues to actual age. It never hurts to ask. The bigger ferries offer greater stability during rough weather. Except in the summer, you can usually depend on getting aboard a ferry by showing up about an hour before scheduled departure—interisland boats sometimes depart before their scheduled time—and purchasing a ticket from a dockside agent or aboard the ship itself, though this is often more expensive.

Tourist-class fare entitles you to a seat on the deck or in a lounge. (Tourists usually head for the deck, while the Greeks stay inside, watch TV, and smoke copiously.) First class usually has roomy air-conditioned cabins and its own lounge and costs as much as flying, which is a good value however, especially on longer overnight hauls, when you're on a comfortable floating hotel. Second class has smaller cabins and its own lounge. Hold on to your ticket; crews usually conduct ticket control sweeps.

Your best bet is to buy a ticket from an agent ahead of time. In Athens we recommend **Galaxy Travel,** Odós Voulís 35, at Apóllonos, near Sýntagma Square (☎ 01/32-29-761; fax 32-29-538), open daily except Sunday. Also on the square are **HellasTours,** the Thomas Cook representative, at Odós Karayóryi tís Servías 4 (☎ 32-20-005; fax 32-33-487), a full-service agency that changes money without commission for its clients, and just up the street, in the arcade at no. 10, **Summertime Tours** (☎ 32-34-176), which offers discounts on its services.

We include more details on service and schedules with the fuller discussion of each island, as well as suggested travel agencies and sources of local information.

Those taking a ferry to Turkey from one of the Dodecanese islands must submit their passport and payment to an agent the day before departure.

Some estimated sample tourist-class fares from Piraeus are: Crete (Iráklio) Dr 6,350 ($27); Kos Dr 7,600 ($32); Lésvos Dr 5,800 ($25); Mýkonos Dr 3,900 ($17); Náxos Dr 4,100 ($18); Rhodes Dr 8,400 ($36); Sámos Dr 6,100 ($26); Santoríni Dr 4,950 ($21). A small embarkation tax and value-added tax (VAT) of 8% will be added.

BY HYDROFOIL Hydrofoils are nearly twice as fast as ferries, have comfortable airline-style seats, their stops are much shorter, and they are less likely to cause seasickness. They cost nearly twice as much as ferries, are frequently fully booked in the summer, can be quite bumpy during rough weather, and give little or no view of the passing scenery, but they're the best choice for those with limited time, and everyone should try one of the sleek little craft at least once. There is presently regular hydrofoil service to nearly all the major islands, with new service appearing every year. Longer trips over open sea, such as between Santorínii and Iráklio, Crete, may make them well worth the extra expense. (Smoking is prohibited, and actually less likely to be indulged in, possibly because the cabins seem so much like those of an aircraft.) The foreword compartment offers somewhat better views, but it's also bumpier.

The Flying Dolphin service from Zéa Marina in Piraeus to the Saronic Gulf islands is especially good, and the new Super Cats are truly super. (The fare to Spétses is about Dr 5,700 ($24) as compared about Dr 3,000 ($13) for tourist-class ferry service, but because of the number of stops in between it's better than twice as fast.) Flying Dolphin service in the Sporades is also recommended for its speed and regularity.

BY MOPED, MOTORBIKE & MOTORCYCLE There seems to be no end to the number of mopeds available for rent in Greece. They're a good, practical, inexpensive way to sightsee, especially in the islands. Roads are often poorly paved and shoulderless. Greek hospitals admit scores of tourists injured on motorbikes every summer, and there are a number of fatalities. Loose gravel is another common problem, and abrasions on knees and elbows are frequently seen. Make sure you have insurance and that the machine is in good working condition before you take it. Helmets are recommended and required by law, but you will rarely see anyone wearing one.

Frankly, we wish the larger motorbikes and motorcycles were forbidden on all the islands, as Greek punks seem to delight in punching holes in the muffler and tearing around all hours of the day and night. (Some islands are wisely banning them from certain areas and restricting the hours of use, as they are the single most important cause of complaint from tourists and residents alike.) Those motorcycles rented to tourists are usually a bit quieter, but they are more expensive and obviously more dangerous; a driver's license is usually required to rent one.

BY TAXI Taxis are the most expensive and often the most exasperating means of travel in Greece, though there have been improvements in recent years. (*Táxi*, by the way, is a Greek word, and you can easily make the word out even in Greek letters; *kaló taxídi* means "bon voyage.") You no longer have to negotiate for a cab at the airport; just find the line. Cabs are considerably less expensive in Athens than they are in London, New York, or Toronto, and not all drivers are crooks—many are good-natured, helpful, and informative. Language and cultural difficulties can make it easier for them to gouge you, and many drivers seem to relish the opportunity.

Get your hotel desk to help you in hailing or booking a taxi. Radio cabs cost Dr 500 extra, but you'll have some leverage. Restaurants and other businesses can also help you in calling or hailing a cab, negotiating a fare, and making sure your destination is understood. Take a card from your hotel, have your destination written down, or learn to pronounce it at least semicorrectly. Be willing to share a cab with other passengers picked up on the way, especially during rush hour; think of it as your contribution to better efficiency and less pollution. Always have some vague idea of where you're going on the map, so you don't end up going to Pláka from Sýntagma by way of Piraeus. Don't be bothered by bullying or bluster; try to find it amusing and counter with your own bluff, showing your superiority by keeping your cool.

Some typical taxi tricks include: The meter is left off, and the driver hopes you won't notice and will try to extort a much larger fare. Check the meter, and even if you don't speak a word of Greek besides *táxi*, point at the meter and say "meter."

The meter will be on, but the little window next to the drachma display will be on "2"—which indicates an early morning or outside-the-city-limits rate. If that's not the case with your current trip, reach over and indicate that you notice.

With a group of tourists, a driver may insist that each person pay the full metered fare. Pay one fare only. (In pairs or groups, have a designated arguer; the others can write down names and numbers, stick with the luggage, or look for help—from a policeman, maitre d', or desk clerk.)

Late at night, especially at airports, ferry stops, and bus and railroad stations, a driver will refuse to use his meter and demand an exorbitant fare. Smile, shake your head, and look for another cab; there will be one.

A driver will want more than the legal surcharge for a service such as pickup from an airport (no more than Dr 500), bus or rail station (Dr 250), or luggage (Dr 100 per piece). Ask to see the official rate sheet that he is required to carry.

A driver will say that your hotel is full, but he knows a better and cheaper one. Laugh, and insist you'll take your chances at your hotel.

A driver may want to let you off where it's most convenient for him. Be cooperative if it's easier and quicker for you to cross a busy avenue than for him to get you to the other side, but you don't have to get out of the cab until you're ready.

If things are obviously not going well for you, conspicuously write down the driver's name and number and by all means report him to the tourist police if he has the nerve to call your bluff. One of the best countertactics is to simply reach for the door latch and open the door slightly; he won't want to risk damaging it. (Two of you can each open a door.)

Again, most cabbies are honest, and we don't want to make you paranoid, just aware of the possibilities. And please be sure to reward good service with a tip, at least 10%.

BY BICYCLE   Bicycles are not nearly as common in Greece as they are throughout most of Europe, as they are not well suited to the terrain and temperament and would be downright dangerous in traffic. Older bikes are usually available for rent at very modest prices in most resort areas, and good mountain bikes are increasingly available. (See the previous section on active vacations for more information.)

FAST FACTS: Greece

Area Code   The international telephone country code for Greece is **30.** To call a number in Greece from abroad, dial the international access code plus 30 plus the area code minus the first zero, then the number. The international access code from Australia is 0011, from Canada 011, from Ireland 00, from New Zealand 00, from the United Kingdom 00, from the United States 011.

Banks   Banks are open to the public from 8am to 2pm Monday through Thursday; 8am to 1:30pm on Fridays. Some banks have additional hours for foreign currency exchange. Contact the Greek Tourist Organization (EOT) for more information.

Business Hours   Greek business hours take some getting used to, especially in the afternoon, when most English-speaking people are accustomed to getting things done in high gear. Most stores and services are still closed on Sunday. Monday and Wednesday hours are usually 8:30am to 3pm; Tuesday, Thursday, and Friday, 8:30am to 2:30pm, then again 5 to 8:30pm; Saturday, 8:30am to 3:30pm. The afternoon siesta is still generally observed from 3 to 5pm, though many tourist-oriented businesses have a minimal crew during nap time and may keep extended hours, often 8am to 10pm. Most government offices are open Monday through Friday only, 8am to 3pm. We suggest you call ahead to check the hours of businesses you plan to deal with and that you not disturb Greek friends during siesta hours.

Car Rentals   See "Getting Around" earlier in this chapter.

Climate   See "When to Go" earlier in this chapter.

Crime   Crime is not a significant concern in Greece. Athens is the safest capital in Europe. Pocket picking and purse snatching have been on the rise, especially in heavily touristed areas. (Tourists are conspicuous and much more likely to have and be carrying valuables.)

Currency   See "Money" earlier in this chapter.

Customs   You are allowed to bring into Greece duty-free personal belongings including clothes, camping gear, and most sports equipment. (Certain water sports equipment, such as Windsurfers, can be brought in only if a Greek citizen residing in Greece guarantees they will be re-exported. Scuba diving is presently restricted to a very few areas, and divers will have difficulty bringing in equipment.) You may bring two cameras with 10 rolls of film each, a movie or video camera, a portable radio, a phonograph or tape recorder, a typewriter, a lap-top computer, and new articles (including electronic equipment) worth up to Dr 10,000 ($43) or Dr 40,000 ($175) for EU members, provided they are not for resale.

Visitors from outside the European Union are allowed up to 10 kilos of food and beverage, 200 cigarettes (300 for EU members), 50 cigars (75, EU), 250 grams of tobacco (400, EU), 1 liter of distilled alcohol or 2 liters of wine (1.5 liters of alcohol or 5 liters of wine, EU), 50 grams of perfume (75 grams, EU), 500 grams of coffee (1 kilo, EU), and 100 grams of tea (400 grams, EU).

There are presently no restrictions on the amount of traveler's checks either arriving or departing, though amounts over $1,000 must be declared, and if you plan to leave the country with more than $500 in bank notes (or its equivalent in other currency) you must declare at least that sum on entry. No more than Dr 10,000 per traveler may be imported or exported.

Explosives, weapons, and narcotics are prohibited and violations are subject to severe punishment. Medication, except for limited amounts properly prescribed for your own use, and plants with soil are prohibited. Passengers from the United States and the United Kingdom arriving in Athens aboard international flights are generally not searched, and if you have nothing to declare continue through a green lane. (Because of the continuing threat of terrorism, baggage is frequently searched before boarding domestic flights.)

Dogs and cats may be brought in with proper health documentation, including rabies inoculation, not newer than six days before arrival nor older than 12 months for dogs and 6 months for cats.

Greek antiquities are strictly protected by law, and no genuine antiquities may be taken out of Greece without prior special permission from the Archaeological Service, Odós Polygnótou 3, Athens.

Remember to keep receipts for all merchandise purchased in Greece for clearing customs on your return home.

Documents   See "Visitor Information and Entry Requirements" earlier in this chapter.

Driving Rules   See "Getting Around" earlier in this chapter.

Drugstores   Drugstores (*pharmakía,* singular *pharmakío*), identified by a green cross, are the first place to go with minor medical problems, as pharmacists usually speak English well and many medications can be dispensed without prescription. Ask for directions at your hotel. In larger cities, if the one you find is closed, look in the window for a sign giving the address of one that might be open.

Electricity   Electric current in Greece is 220 volts AC, alternating at 50 cycles. (Some larger hotels have 110-volt low-wattage outlets for electric shavers, but they aren't good for hair dryers and most other appliances.) Electrical outlets require Continental-type plugs with two round prongs. U.S. travelers will need an adapter plug and a converter, unless their appliances are dual-voltage. Laptop computer users will want to check their specs; a converter may be necessary, and surge protectors are recommended.

Embassies and Consulates   See "Fast Facts: Athens."

Emergencies   For automobile emergencies, put out a triangular danger sign and telephone **104** or **174.** For fire call **199.** For medical emergencies, telephone **166,** the tourist police or police (see below). For police emergencies, dial **100.**

Holidays   See "When to Go" earlier in this chapter.

Information   See "Visitor Information" earlier in this chapter.

Language   Language is not a problem for English speakers in Greece, as so much of the population has lived abroad where English is the primary language and young people learn it in school, from English-dominated pop culture, and in special classes meant to prepare them for the contemporary world of business. Television programs are also broadcast in their original language, and American prime-time soaps are very popular, nearly inescapable. Even advertisements have an increasingly high English content.

Greek itself is usually "Greek" to most foreigners because it is not immediately identifiable with other Indo-European languages. At first glance, it looks quite unfamiliar, but most of its characters have an identifiable "Roman" counterpart, especially in printed capitals, and it is regular, each letter or group of letters almost always having the same sound. Greeks tend to speak rapidly and thus it's difficult for most foreigners to hear when one word ends and another begins. Stressed syllables are particularly important—which is why we've included accents in our rendering of Greek words—and they are marked, except over capital letters. The grammar is more complicated than German, with masculine, feminine, and neuter nouns requiring agreement in the various cases—a real chore for us who have fortunately had ours simplified through the ages—though foreigners are not expected to master it.

To complicate matters, modern Greek is quite different from ancient Greek; most Greeks don't understand the Orthodox liturgy. To further confuse matters there was an attempt to "purify" the language, called *katharévousa,* which was adopted by the founding fathers as the official language. Despite subsequent attempts by several conservative or reactionary governments to impose this artificially "improved" language, the majority of Greeks have stuck to *dimotikí,* demotic Greek, which has also been used by almost all important modern Greek writers.

Don't let all this keep you from trying to pick up at least a few words of Greek; your effort will be rewarded by your hosts, who realize how difficult their language is for foreigners and will politely and patiently help you improve your pronunciation and usage. There are various taped programs, including *Berlitz's Greek for Travelers* and *Passport's Conversational Greek in 7 Days,* which can be very helpful.

Try a little. *Káli méra* means good day. *Efharistó* means thanks; *efharistó polí* means thanks a lot. That last word isn't really difficult; it's the same one we use in "polyphonic" to mean several sounds. There are a surprising number of Greek words you will recognize from our technical language.

Mail   You can receive mail addressed to you c/o Poste Restante, General Post Office, City (or Town), Island (or Province), Greece. You will need your passport to collect your mail. Many hotels will accept, hold, and even forward mail for you also; ask first. American Express clients can receive mail at any Amex offices in Athens, Corfu, Iráklio, Mýkonos, Pátra, Rhodes, Santorínii, Skiáthos, and Thessaloníki, for a nominal fee, with proper identification.

Newspapers/Magazines   There are several English-language newspapers, including the *International Herald Tribune* and *Athens Today,* widely available at news kiosks. (We will mention important sources of English-language periodicals under separate destinations.)

Passports   See "Entry Requirements" earlier in this chapter.

Pets   See "Customs," above, in Fast Facts.

Photographic Needs   Cameras, film, accessories, and photo developing are widely available, though more expensive, in Greece.

Police   To report a crime, for help with a medical emergency, or for information or other assistance, first contact the local tourist police (telephone numbers will be found under "Essentials" in the particular destinations), where an English-speaking officer is more likely to be found. If there is no tourist police officer available, contact the local police.

Radio and Television News   The Greek ERT 1 radio and television network has weather and news in English at 7:40am. CNN, Eurochannel, and other cable networks are widely available. Many better hotels have cable television. The BBC World Service can be picked up on short-wave frequencies, often frequencies 15.07 and 12.09 Mhz.

Restrooms   Public restrooms are not common in Greece, and they are sometimes rudimentary, but they usually do work. Old-fashioned squat facilities are still found. Carry some toilet tissue with you at all times, and do not flush it down the toilet; use the receptacles provided. You can often use the facilities of a restaurant or shop, though near major attractions they are sometimes denied to all but customers because the generosity is abused. If you are permitted the use of such facilities, keep in mind the needs of future travelers, respect your benefactor, and leave a small tip.

Street Names   The Greek word for Street is *Odós*—think of our word odometer—and the word for Avenue is *Leofóros*, often abbreviated *Leof.*, usually applied to major thoroughfares, and numbers are written after rather than before as they are in English. Street names are given in the genitive (possessive) case; *Leofóros Vassilíssis Sofías* means "Avenue of Queen Sofia." *Vassilíssis* is the genitive form of *Vassilíssa*, Queen, and *Vassiléfs* is the genitive of *Vassiléos*, King; both are generally abbreviated *Vass.* (You will not be tested on grammar.)

Platía—think place or plaza—is Greek for Square, and usually means a large public square, such as Syntagma (Constitution) Square in Athens, though sometimes a *platía* may be little more than a wide area where important streets meet.

Taxes and Service Charges   Unless otherwise noted, all hotel prices include a service charge, usually 12%, a 6% value-added tax (VAT), and a 4.5% community tax. In most restaurants, a 13% service charge and an 8% VAT are added. (In Athens there's also a 5% city food tax.) A VAT of 18% is added to rental-car rates.

Telephone and Fax   The Telecommunications Organization of Greece (Organismós Tilepikinonión tís Elládos), OTE—pronounced *OH-tay*—has some pay phones on the streets and in public buildings in the larger towns and cities, but to make a long-distance call you'll usually need to go to the local OTE office, which is usually centrally and conveniently located. (Local offices are given under "Essentials" for the destination.)

Older public telephones require a Dr 10 coin—which are in short supply, so hold on to several if they come your way. Deposit the coin and listen for a dial tone, an irregular beep. A regular beep indicates the line is busy. Blue and silver telephone booths are for local calls; orange and silver booths are for long-distance (outside Athens and international) calls. Telephones using the new card-phone are increasingly common. You can buy cards at OTE or at most kiosks; Dr 1,000 will cover 100 local calls, but a card can also be used for long-distance and international calls. (Kiosks usually still let you use their phone for Dr 20 and in remote areas may even let you make a long-distance call.)

Note: Long-distance calls can be quite expensive in Greece, especially at hotels, which may add a surcharge up to 100%, unless you have a telephone credit card, which can reduce your expense considerably by avoiding hotel surcharges. Most companies also offer recorded-message service in case the number you're calling at home is busy or doesn't answer. Call your company before leaving home to determine the access number in Greece. For AT&T service dial 00800-1311; for MCI service dial 00800-1211; for Sprint service dial 00800-1411.

At OTE offices you usually have to negotiate your call at the desk and are assigned a booth with a metered phone. You can make collect calls, but this can take much longer, so it's easier to pay cash, unless you have a phone credit card. To phone abroad from Greece dial the country code plus the area code minus the initial zero (if any), then the number. Some country codes are: Australia 0061, Canada 001, Ireland 00353, New Zealand 0064, United Kingdom 0044, United States 001. (To call the United States, dial 001 plus the area code plus the number.)

You can send and receive faxes at most OTE offices. Fax machines are increasingly common in Greece, and many hotels and some travel agencies will send and receive a fax for you. Some post offices have good, inexpensive fax service.

Time Zone Greece is two hours ahead of Greenwich mean time. With reference to North American time zones, it's seven hours ahead of eastern standard time, eight hours ahead of central standard time, nine hours ahead of mountain standard time, and 10 hours ahead of Pacific standard time.

The European system of a 24-hour clock is used officially, and on schedules you'll usually see noon written as 1200, 3:30pm as 1530, and 11pm as 2300. In informal conversation, however, Greeks express time much as we do, though noon may mean 12 noon to 3pm, afternoon is 3pm to 7pm, and evening is 7pm to midnight.

Tipping A 10% to 15% service charge is included in most restaurant bills and is reflected in the two columns of prices next to the menu item. (Prices are, by the way, controlled by the government.) Nevertheless, it's customary to leave an additional 5% to 10% for the waiter, more if the service merits it. Usually, on small bills, change up to the nearest Dr 100 is left. Good taxi service merits a 5% to 10% tip. (Greeks rarely tip taxi drivers, but tourists are expected to.) Chambermaids and porters should be tipped Dr 200 to Dr 500.

Water Municipal drinking water in Greece is safe to drink, though it is often salty. You will probably prefer the bottled water commonly available at kiosks, hotels, and restaurants.

4 Athens

by John Bozman

Travelers flock to Athens from all over the world just to see the Acropolis. Side by side with the remnants of the great Classical Age, today's visitors find intriguing evidence of Athens's Byzantine heritage in its tiny, old churches and in its bustling Eastern-style markets. And a reminder of the centuries of Turkish rule are the city's many coffeehouses, exuding the pungent aroma of what we know as Turkish coffee, but what the Greeks call Greek coffee. Put all this in the midst of a sprawling, fast-growing city of four million people and you'll have some idea of the vibrancy and excitement that infuse contemporary Athens.

Some big-city problems have come to Athens in recent years. Congestion is one, aggravated by a recent influx of Eastern European refugees, many of them in search of work. Traffic and noise are another—the city has more than a million automobiles. A third problem, which stubbornly persists despite efforts by one government after another to solve it, is pollution. The city's noxious smog, called *néfos* by the Athenians, clouds the air on many days, especially during the summer.

Yet, serious as these problems are, they have not dampened the energy and vibrancy of Athens, which is at its liveliest when other cities are fast asleep: early in the morning and late at night. The shops and markets and vegetable stalls, particularly those in Monastiráki and around Omónia Square, open almost at the crack of dawn. By 8am traffic is already heavy, with taxis weaving in and out of the paths of tethered trolley buses, which are filled with Athenians on their way to work, as the sound of car horns blaring impatiently signals the start of another day. The cafes downtown are abuzz with activity as bleary-eyed office workers jostle each other for a quick cup of coffee while scanning their favorite newspaper for the latest political gossip.

At 2 or 3pm most businesses shut their doors for the officially sanctioned siesta, a period of rest and refortification, especially during the summer, at the height of the midday heat. The whole city, it seems, heads home for lunch (the biggest meal of the day) and an hour or two of an afternoon rest or nap.

Beginning around 9 or 10pm, the city gets its second wind. Crowds pour into the tavernas, restaurants, and bars, filling them until well past midnight. Sometime around 2am, Athenians wander home for a few hours of shut-eye before they begin anew.

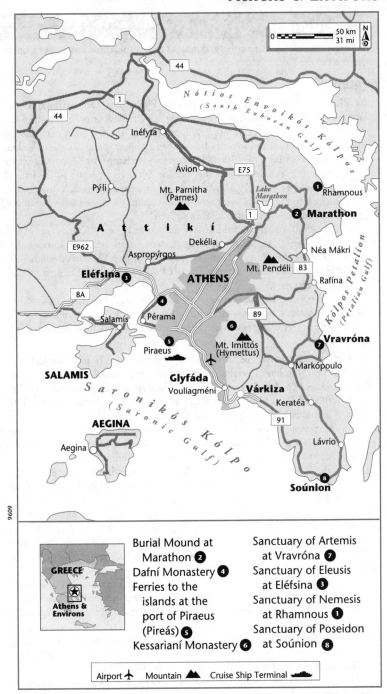

Burial Mound at
Marathon ❷
Dafní Monastery ❹
Ferries to the
islands at the
port of Piraeus
(Pireás) ❺
Kessarianí Monastery ❻

Sanctuary of Artemis
at Vravróna ❼
Sanctuary of Eleusis
at Eléfsina ❸
Sanctuary of Nemesis
at Rhamnous ❶
Sanctuary of Poseidon
at Soúnion ❽

Airport ✈ Mountain ▲▲ Cruise Ship Terminal ⛴

1 Orientation

Athens is a sprawling metropolis, and most of its transportation terminals lie outside the heart of the city.

ARRIVING

BY PLANE   Most visitors arrive by plane at **Hellenikon International Airport, East** (*Anatolikó*) **Terminal.** A plain old facility, it's 7 miles south of Sýntagma ("Constitution") Square (and sometimes heavily congested). It offers a few convenient facilities: branches of the major Greek **banks** open 24 hours giving you the official rate; **luggage carts** available for Dr 200 (85¢); **currency exchange,** while you wait for your luggage to arrive; a managed **taxi line** outside to the right; **buses** to the left. The **Greek National Tourist Organization (EOT) information desk** is inside the terminal slightly to the left as you come out of customs; it's open Monday through Friday from 9am to 7pm, Saturday 9am to 2pm.

All domestic and international flights of the national airline, Olympic, arrive at the newer **West** (*Dytikó*) **Air Terminal;** it's on the west side of the airport runways. **Bank offices** are in the arrivals area, open 7am to 11pm, with **ATMs** for after hours. The **tourist information center** and the **Tourist Police** are in the building across from the terminal entrance.

The airport's only **luggage storage,** unofficial and rather expensive (Dr 700/$3 for 24 hours) is across the parking lot from the entrance of the East Terminal.

A **shuttle** service operates between the two terminals every hour between 8:30am and 8:30pm.

Transportation into Athens   To reach downtown Athens from Ellinikón International Airport, you have several alternatives that vary in cost and speed, in the usual inverse relationship. A **taxi** from the airport to Sýntagma Square should cost Dr 2,000 to Dr 2,500 ($8.30 to $10.40). Without traffic the trip from the airport should take 20 to 30 minutes, but during rush hour it could take 1 to 1 1/2 hours.

It is, of course, far less expensive to take **bus no. 090** to Omónia and Sýntagma squares. The bus stop is outside the building, a few feet to the left. Once you are in Athens you can either walk to your hotel or take a far shorter cab ride.

From the West Terminal only, the **Olympic Airways bus** leaves every half hour from outside Olympic's international terminal (adjacent to the domestic terminal) and takes Olympic passengers to the airlines' office at Leofóros Syngroú 96 (in Koukáki) or to Sýntagma Square (where there are buses to many other parts of the city). The Olympic buses run regularly between 6:30am and 10:30pm; the fare is Dr 190 ($1.06), and you must have exact change. You can catch the Olympic airport-bound bus at Amalías Avenue on the northeast corner of Sýntagma Square or at the Syngroú Avenue Olympic office.

A second choice for Olympic passengers at the West Terminal—and the only express choice for anyone (passengers at the East Terminal included)—is the blue-and-yellow, double-decker **express bus** that runs every 20 minutes from 6am to 11pm, every 30 minutes from 11pm to 2am, and hourly from 2am to 6am, taking passengers to Sýntagma Square or Omónia Square, also for Dr 200 (80¢) with a 25% night premium from midnight to 6am. This bus leaves Amalías Avenue at Sýntagma Square or Stadíou Street at Omónia Square for the return trip to the airport.

If you're really on a budget and have the time, you can take public **bus no. 133,** which plies the coastal route and stops at Posidónos Street outside the airport grounds. For Dr 75 (33¢) it, too, will take you to Sýntagma Square. However, you must buy a ticket from the bus kiosk or a newsstand before boarding and then have the ticket stamped after boarding.

Transportation to Piraeus (Pireás) If you're skipping Athens and heading straight for the island boats, you should probably take a taxi to Piraeus; the fare for the half-hour trip is Dr 1,500 to Dr 1,800 ($6.25 to $7.50). If you're traveling on by hydrofoil, known as the Flying Dolphins, it's best to take a cab. The hydrofoils for the nearby island of Aegina leave from the western edge of the main harbor. The hydrofoils for the other Saronic Gulf islands leave from Zéa Harbor on the south side of the Piraeus peninsula from the main harbor. Be sure to tell the cab driver to what island you are heading so he will take you to the correct harbor.

Travelers at either terminal can also take public **bus no. 19** to Karaïskáki Square in Piraeus for Dr 300 ($1.25).

To those travelers who imagine returning to Athens from the islands on an overnight boat with a neat connection to an early morning homeward flight, we can only say *Good luck!* Some may succeed, but many have been foiled by delayed boat arrivals and Athens's early morning gridlock. You're better advised to allow a buffer day. You'll also face a conspiracy of taxi drivers, who meet the boats and have one fare—Dr 4,000 ($16.66)—to go anywhere. Pass them by and walk to the nearest major street, where you'll probably find an honest taxi driver. Or catch the same bus no. 19 at Karaïskáki Square.

Airline Offices Most international carriers have ticket offices in or near Sýntagma Square. The **Delta Airlines** office is at Odós 4 Óthonos (☎ 01/323-5242). The **Lufthansa Airlines** office is at Leofóros Vassilíssis Sofías 11 (☎ 01/771-6002). The **TWA** office is at Odós Xenofóndos 8 (☎ 01/322-6451).

Olympic, the national carrier, offers both international and domestic service. For information on schedules and fares, visit either Olympic's Sýntagma Square office, at Odós Óthonos 6 (☎ 01/929-2555), or its main office, at Leofóros Syngroú 96 (☎ 01/929-2251). The main reservations number is 01/961-6161.

For general and flight information at the East (International) Terminal, call 01/969-9466. For Olympic flights at the West Terminal, call 01/989-2111.

BY CAR If you arrive by car from either Corinth or Thessaloníki the signs to Athens will direct you fairly clearly to the center of town, Omónia Square, which you will enter from the west along Ayíou Konstandínou Street.

BY BUS There are two principal stations for the national bus company, **KTEL.** Some distance northwest of Omónia Square, **Terminal A** (☎ 01/512-9233), at 100 Kifíssiou St., handles buses to and from northern Greece and the Peloponnese (including Pátra, the Ionian islands, and all points south and west). If you want to take a cab out of this maelstrom, you'll have to wait your turn at the taxi rank. Public **bus no. 51** will take you from this terminal to the corner of Zínonos and Menándrou streets, near Omónia Square; from there you can catch a bus or trolley to Sýntagma. (Board at Sýntagma for the return trip.)

Terminal B (☎ 01/831-7096), at 260 Liossíon St., handles buses to and from central Greece (including Delphi, Thebes, Évvia, Metéora and other points north and east). **Bus no. 24** will take you to and from Amalías Avenue, in front of the entrance to the National Garden, just a block south from Sýntagma Square. (When taking bus no. 24 to Terminal B, from the stop you must turn right on Gousíou to see the terminal.)

Many people who travel by bus between Thessaloníki and Athens prefer to take the **OSE** bus run by the railroad company, which operates from the Peloponnese Train Station.

Buses for most destinations in Attica leave from the Mavromatéon terminal at Patissíon and Alexándras, a few hundred meters north of the Archeology Museum.

Check with the **Tourist Police** (☎ 01/171) or the **Greek Tourist Organization (EOT) office** (☎ 01/32-34-130) for current schedules and fares.

BY TRAIN   There are two train stations, close together about a mile northeast of Omónia Square. Trains from the north arrive at the main **Larissa Station** (**Stathmós Laríssis**). Trains from the west, including Eurail connections via Patrá, arrive at the older beaux-art **Peloponnese Station** (**Stathmós Peloponníssou**) across the tracks to the southwest.

Taxis are available at all hours from the parking area outside the train stations and should cost less than Dr 900 ($3.75) to Sýntagma Square. **Trolley no. 1** (in front of Laríssis) goes to Sýntagma Square and Koukáki, passing through Omónia Square. (Catch it on Amalías Avenue in front of the Parliament building at Sýntagma.) **Trolley no. 405** is an alternative route to Sýntagma Square. The fare is Dr 75 (33¢). You must purchase a ticket before boarding the trolley, either from a transit kiosk near the bus stop or from a newsstand.

You can purchase train tickets through a travel agent or at the Omónia Square ticket office, at Odós Károlou 1 (☎ 01/524-0647). The office at Odós Filellínon 17 (☎ 01/323-6747) is more convenient to Sýntagma.

BY BOAT   Athens's main seaport, **Piraeus** (Pireás), is about 7 miles southwest of its center. The fastest and most enjoyable way to reach downtown Athens is to ride the **metro** (subway). (If you're coming from abroad, however, you may find your dock far from the station; also, if you have heavy bags, you may be advised to take a bus or cab instead.) This old-fashioned subway, the fastest way to cut through Athens's traffic congestion, takes you only to certain stops within the city. The two closest stops to Sýntagma Square, the heart of Athens, are Monastiráki (about a 10-minute walk west of Sýntagma, noted for its flea markets) and Omónia Square (a major business and transportation hub). Tickets cost Dr 75 (33¢), with a Dr 75 surcharge after Omónia; they can be purchased either at the ticket machines or at the manned booths. The metro runs every 10 minutes between 5am and 12:10am.

There's also **bus service** to and from Piraeus from the green bus depot at Filellínon Street, just off Sýntagma Square. **Bus no. 40** leaves every 15 minutes between 5am and 1am and hourly between 1 and 5am. The bus stop, however, is several long blocks from the boat docks, and the metro is more conveniently located.

If you must take a **taxi**, be prepared for banditry from the taxi drivers meeting the boats. The normal fare on the meter from Piraeus to Sýntagma should be Dr 1,800 to Dr 2,000 ($7.50 to $8.30), but many of these drivers try to charge as much as Dr 4,000 ($16.70). Pay it if you're desperate, but better yet, walk to a nearby street, hail another taxi, and insist on the meter.

If you've landed by hydrofoil at **Zéa Marina** (about a dozen blocks south across the peninsula from the main harbor), you'll find the taxi choices slim and the rates exorbitant. To avoid the big fare, walk up to the main street and take **bus no. 905,** which goes between Zéa and the Piraeus subway station. Catch it up the hill from the hydrofoil marina and on the side street next to the subway station. You must buy a ticket at the small ticket stand near the bus stop or at a newsstand before boarding the bus.

If you've landed at the port of Rafína (about an hour bus ride east of Athens), you'll see a sloping bus stop with several buses in line up the hill from the ferryboat pier. Inquire about the bus to Athens; it runs often and will return you within the hour to the Áreos Park Terminal, at Odós Mavrommatéon 29, near the junction of Alexándras Avenue and Patissíon Street (about 25 minutes by trolley from Sýntagma Square or one block from the Victoria Square metro stop). From the terminal, there are buses to Rafína every half hour.

VISITOR INFORMATION

The **Greek National Tourist Organization (EOT)** has a walkup window outside the National Bank of Greece at the northwest corner of Sýntagma Square, 2 Karayióryi Servías St. (☎ **01/322-3111**). It's open Monday to Friday from 8am to 6pm, Saturday 9am to 2pm, closed Sunday and holidays. Information about Athens, free city maps, hotel lists, and other general booklets are available in English, though the line can get rather long. There's also an EOT office at Zéa Marina; ask at the hydrofoil office for directions.

The **Tourist Police** (☎ **01/171**), available 24 hours a day, are an invaluable source of information. They offer service in English, as well as other languages, and they also are the ones to call with problems or emergencies.

The **Hellenic Chamber of Hotels** (☎ **01/323-7193**) operates a desk nearby inside the National Bank of Greece on Sýtagma Square where you can book your hotel for anywhere in Greece and pick up brochures and a free map of central Athens. It's open Monday to Thursday from 8:30am to 2pm, Friday 8:30am to 1:30pm, Saturday 9am to 12:30pm, closed Sunday and holidays.

The **Quality of Life Consumer Association** (☎ **01/330-4444**) maintains an office at 43-45 Valtetsíou and is open to help tourists with problems Monday to Friday from 10am to 2pm.

The **Citizen Union's Tourist Protection Service Network** offers information, will help if you have a complaint, and provides legal advice. There's an office in the Athens suburb of Paleó Fáliro (☎ **01/982-9152**; fax 01/982-5096), open Monday to Friday from 8am to 4pm.

CITY LAYOUT

In general, finding your way around Athens is relatively easy. An exception is Pláka, with its small winding streets at the foot of the Acropolis, a labyrinth that'll challenge even the best navigators, but the neighborhood is small enough that you can't go far astray and so charming that you won't mind being lost. One excellent map, the *Historical Map of Athens*, has the sites of Athens clearly identified and an enlarged map of Plaka as well. This is produced by the Greek Archeological Service and sold for about Dr 500 ($2).

Two helpful landmarks for orientation are the **Acropolis** and to its northeast **Lykavitós (Lycabettus) Hill,** higher, with a small white church on top—both visible from most parts of the city.

Central Athens is based on an almost equilateral triangle, its points at **Sýntagma** (Constitution) **Square, Omónia** (Harmony) **Square,** and **Monasteráki** (Little Monastery) **Square,** near the Acropolis, all now construction sites for a future Athens subway. Omónia and Sýntagma squares are connected by two parallel roads, **Stadíou Street** and **Panepistimíou Street,** which is also called **Elefthériou Venizélou.** West from Sýntagma Square ancient **Ermoú Street** and broader **Mitropóleos Street** lead slightly downhill to Monasteráki Square. Here you'll find the flea market, the Ancient Agora (Market) below the Acropolis, and the **Pláka,** the oldest neighborhood, with names and monuments from ancient times. From Monasteráki Square, **Athinás Street** leads north to Omónia Square.

Most of the area within this central triangle has been sanctioned as the **Commercial Center** where, but for three cross streets (Sophokléous, Evripídou, Kolokotróni), no cars are permitted.

MAIN ARTERIES & STREETS   Five main streets radiate from the hub of Omónia Square. **Ayíou Konstandínou** leads directly west. **Pireós,** the main avenue down to Piraeus, leads southwest. The next street, **Athinás,** runs south through the city's modern **Central Market** to the flea market, Pláka, and the Acropolis. **Stadíou,** a one-way street, heads one-way southeast to Sýntagma Square. The next street above and parallel, **Panepistimíou,** is a one-way in the opposite direction. **Third of September Street** (*Trítis Septémvriou*) leads one-way north.

Third of September Street is the continuation of Athinás Street north of Omónia Square. One block to the east and parallel to this street runs another main avenue, called **Eólou** (sometimes spelled Aiolou).

Above Omónia Square, which it passes one block to the east, this street is officially referred to as **28th of October Street,** as its signs declare, but it's always spoken of as **Patissíon,** and seven blocks north of Omónia along it you'll find the **National Archaeological Museum.**

The streets northeast of and parallel to Stadíou (Stadium), **Panepistimíou** (University) and **Akademías** (Academy), bracket the 19th-century university, library, and academy buildings (from south to north). The parallel streets farther toward **Lycabettus Hill** run between the university area of **Exárchia Square** to the northwest above the Polytechnic and the fashionable **Kolonáki** area to the southeast.

Beyond this central area, Third of September Street and Patissíon mark the western border of areas you will probably want to explore. Broad **Vassilíssis Sofías** (Queen Sophia) **Avenue** runs east from Sýntagma Square and is met by **Vassiléos Konstandínou** (King Constantine) **Avenue** near the Hilton Hotel and continues north as **Kifissías Avenue,** the main road to the northern suburb of Kifissiá. **Alexándras Avenue** runs between Patissíon and Kifissías north of Lycabettus. The **Pedíon tou Áreos** (Field of Ares) **Park** is at the western end of Alexándras Avenue. The western edge of the Pedíon tou Áreos park is **Mavromatéon Street,** the point of departure for many of the buses for the more remote sites in Attica.

The **Záppion,** a large exhibition and sometime conference hall, is east and slightly north of the Acropolis. The **National Garden** is adjacent to the Záppion to the north, with the **Voulí** (Parliament Building) in its northwest corner at the intersection of **Amalías** and **Vassilíssis Sofías** Avenues. The **Temple of Olympian Zeus** is directly south of the Záppion, just across the short but wide **Vassilíssis Ólgas Avenue.** The other main road down to the sea, **Syngroú Avenue,** leaves from the southwestern edge of this large archaeological area for the sea at Fáliron. **Vouliagménis Avenue** leaves from the southeastern edge of the archaeological area for the seaside area of Vouliagméni, passing the airport on the way.

If you arrive from the airport, it is most likely that your first sight of the Acropolis will be from Vouliagménis Avenue.

FINDING AN ADDRESS   Many Greeks have some command of English and your first understanding of Greek hospitality may come in seeing how willingly strangers on the street offer assistance when asked for help in finding an address. Most cabs operate with an Athens street guide in their glove compartment, so you may simply let a cab driver find your destination. If you're going to be looking for a number of addresses outside the main tourist areas and want to be entirely independent, however, you'll need to know or learn the Greek alphabet, nearly half the capital letters of which are like our Roman version. The only complete **street guide** is in Greek.

The *Athína-Pireás Proástia A- Atlas* (available in most book shops for about $13) includes Athens, Piraeus, and the suburbs, and therefore is fairly large—250 pages of listings and 210 pages of maps. The plus side of this is that it lists all the street names in capital letters, both in its alphabetical listing and in the accompanying maps. With this book, a little practice, and some assistance you will be able to locate whatever address you might like to find relatively easily.

STREET MAPS   As already mentioned, you can get a free map of central Athens from the tourist information desk inside the National Bank of Greece office on Sýntagma Square. Larger maps of Greece can be found in the English-language book shops; the *Falk-Plan* is a good one, if you can find it. (See "Books" under "Shopping," below.)

NEIGHBORHOODS IN BRIEF

The Commercial Center   Omónia, Sýntagma, and **Monasteráki,** the three squares at the apexes of the central city triangle are standard points of reference in Athens. All three of them now are dominated by construction work on the Athens metro, which won't be open for several more years.

Omónia Square was for many years the commercial and tourist center of Athens, and it's still the city's transportation center, with a major metro (subway) stop. Many businesses have moved out of the area and the hotels have gone downhill, and it strongly resembles New York's Times Square, complete with homeless refugees from Eastern Europe's recent turmoils. Late at night some of the less respectable night-spot streets below it, to the west, can be raucous. Yet, while not the safest or most attractive part of town, it certainly remains one of the most interesting.

During the day the area is fully active, with some of the 19th century still evident in the architecture and the old stores, particularly along Athinás Street. The **Town Hall** is two blocks south along Athinás Street, on the west side of the street, and few blocks further south is the **Central Market,** selling fresh vegetables and fruit on the west side of the street, while on the east side is the marvelous covered market, selling mostly meat and fish.

Monasteráki Square and the **Pláka** area farther south are wonderful areas, full of historical interest and contemporary diversions, well worth getting to know. **Monastiráki** is a small neighborhood on the north side of the Acropolis, next to the Agora. Its name, "Little Monastery," derives from a monks' abode that was once there. There is a very convenient metro stop and an extensive labyrinth of shops, as well as the world-famous flea market, which is at its best on Sunday.

Pláka, which extends east around the base of the Acropolis is a tourist favorite. It was inhabited in ancient times and resettled in the 19th and early 20th centuries by wealthy merchants, who built luxurious multistory wood-and-marble mansions with finely crafted interiors. Today, a few of those mansions remain homes, but most have been transformed into bars, bouzouki clubs, restaurants, and shops. Yet, despite the rows of T-shirt and souvenir shops, the back lanes of this old neighborhood retain a charm that leads us to recommend a number of hotels and restaurants in the area.

Sýntagma Square is solidly in the 20th century, with several major banks, airline and other major business offices, travel agencies—including American Express and Thomas Cook—and luxury hotels—including the Grande Bretagne Hotel, the grand old lady of Greek hotels. The sidewalk cafes here are traditional points of call, and there is a large **Post Office** at the corner of Mitropóleos Street. The old royal palace stands guard over the landscaped square on the east side, and is now home to the Greek Parliament and the Tomb of the Unknown Soldier. A fun event is the delightfully theatrical changing of the guard by white-skirted, pompom-shoed *évzones*.

Athens at a Glance

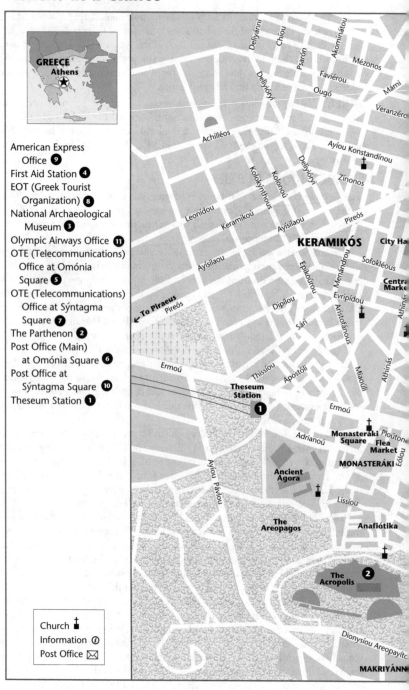

American Express
  Office **9**
First Aid Station **4**
EOT (Greek Tourist
  Organization) **8**
National Archaeological
  Museum **3**
Olympic Airways Office **11**
OTE (Telecommunications)
  Office at Omónia
  Square **5**
OTE (Telecommunications)
  Office at Sýntagma
  Square **7**
The Parthenon **2**
Post Office (Main)
  at Omónia Square **6**
Post Office at
  Sýntagma Square **10**
Theseum Station **1**

Church ✝
Information ⓘ
Post Office ✉

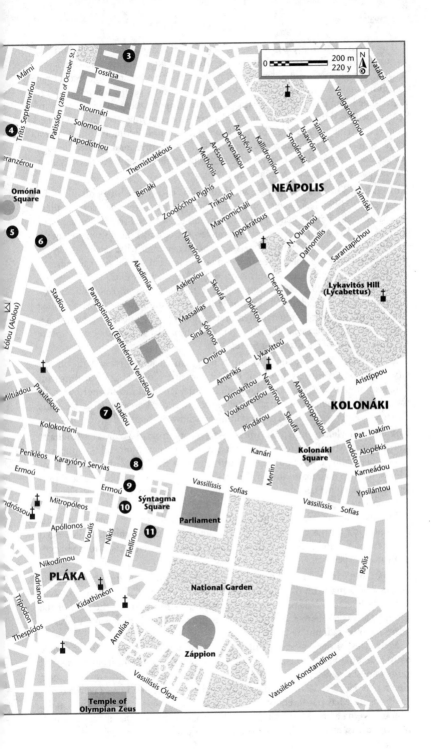

3

Márni

Tríits Septemvríou

4

Patissíon (28th of October St.)

Tossítsa

Stournári

Solomoú

Kapodístriou

eranzérou

Themistokléous

Arachóvis

Dervenakíou

Aréssou

Methónis

Kallidromíou

NEÁPOLIS

Benáki

Zoodóchou Pighís

Trikoúpi

Mavromicháli

Ippokrátous

Voulgarokónou

Tsimiskí

Issavrón

Smolénski

Tsimiskí

Omónia Square

5

6

Navarínou

Akadimías

Asklipíou

Skoufá

Didótou

Chersónos

N. Ouranoú

Dafnomílis

Sarantapíchou

Tsimiskí

Lykavitós Hill (Lycabettus)

Stadíou

Panepistimíou (Elefthéríou Venizélou)

Massalías

Síná

Sólonos

Omírou

Amerikís

Dimokrítou

Voukourestíou

Pindárou

Lykavittoú

Navarínou

Skoufá

Anagnostopoúlou

Aristíppou

KOLONÁKI

Eólou (Aiólou)

Miltiádou

Praxitélous

7

Kolokotróni

Stadíou

Perikléous

Karayióryi Servías

8

Ermoú

Kanári

Merlin

Kolonáki Square

Pat. Ioakím

Irodótou

Alopékis

Karneádou

Ypsilántou

Ermoú

9

ndróssou

Mitropóleos

10

Sýntagma Square

Vassilíssis Sofías

Vassilíssis Sofías

Apóllonos

Voulís

Níkis

Filellínon

11

Parliament

Nikodímou

PLÁKA

Adrianoú

Trípodon

Kidathinéon

Thespídos

Amalías

Vassilíssis Ólgas

National Garden

Záppion

Rhyfís

Vassiléos Konstandínou

Temple of Olympian Zeus

0   200 m   N
     220 y

77

The **downtown shopping area** is the commercial triangle enclosed by **Athinás, Ermoú,** and **Stadíou streets** connecting Monasteraki, Omonia, and Sýntagma squares. As vehicles are forbidden in most of this area, it has become, in effect, a large shopping mall, with trees and benches. Street vendors selling *kouloúria*, large pretzel-like bread rings sprinkled with sesame seeds, are frequent, as are many more vendors selling shirts, socks, kitchen appliances, and a varying assortment of other wonders, usually around the Church of Ayíi Théodori on Evripídou Street, just a couple of blocks up from the central food market. The **central food market,** through the narrow entryway at Eólou 81, is a marvelous place, full of stands selling fresh meat and fish, an eastern bazaar you shouldn't miss.

Kolonáki   The posh area in town, Kolonáki, is on the slopes of Likavitós (Lycabettus) Hill, a few blocks northwest of Sýntagma Square. The **central square** here is officially named Platía Filikís Eterías (Square of the Friendly Society) but always called Kolonáki, after the little column few notice under the trees on the south-west side of the square. Many businesses are based here, but what catches the eye is the predominance of fashionable stores and boutiques. The several sidewalk cafes on two sides of the square are favorite haunts of the Athenian idle elite.

   Although it has lost some of its glamour to the new suburbs, Kolonáki remains Athens's best in-town address. **Lykavitós Hill** offers a stunning view (when the smog clears) of the entire metropolitan area, and a contemporary outdoor theater with a diverse program of music and theater. There's a funicular railway that runs up the hill from the top of **Ploutárchou Street.**

The University Area   Kolonáki gradually merges to the northwest with the university area, spread loosely between the 19th century university buildings on Panepistimíou all the way to the Polytechnic some ten blocks to the northwest. In the northern section of this area, a few blocks from the Polytechnic, is **Exárchia Square,** a center of student activity with many sandwich shops, cafes, and bars.

Koukáki and **Makriyánni**   The working-class counterpart to Kolonáki is **Koukáki,** southwest of the Temple of Olympian Zeus between Syngroú Avenue and Philopáppos Hill (Lófos Filopáppou), also known as the Hill of the Muses (Lófos Moussón). The main road through Koukáki is Véïkou, along which buses and trolleys run, making the neighborhood a convenient place for budget travelers. There are some unpretentious cafes and restaurants here, as well as reasonably priced hotels.

   Makriyánni, the neighborhood just north of Koukáki, at the southern base of the Acropolis, is a bit more upscale. It's a very convenient location for those interested in the Acropolis and Pláka, with a few good hotels and restaurants, which are generally more expensive.

Pangráti and Mets   Surrounding the reconstructed Athens Stadium known to the Greeks as Kallimármaro (Beautiful Marble), **Pangráti** is a bit higher on the socioeconomic scale, about halfway between Kolonáki and Koukáki. At the turn of the century, it was a separate village. Now it is primarily residential, with a pleasant scattering of restaurants and tavernas.

   Mets is just to the southeast on the other side of the Stadium, between the temple of Zeus and the First Cemetery, next to Arditós Hill. It's noted for its many fine old garden houses, which give it a villagelike aspect reminiscent of Old Athens. Named after a popular cafe, Metz, that once flourished here, it has become a favorite of the city's literati. Mets has several stylish boutiques and art stores as well as bars and a famous taverna along Moussoúri Street. The nightlife reflects the understated tone of its residents, many of whom are young professionals.

The Northeast Suburbs The main thrust of the city's growth is to the northeast, between the mountains of **Pentéli** to the east and **Párnitha** to the west. Up this valley the **National Road** runs along the western side of the city and **Kifissías Avenue** runs along the eastern side of the city. Kifissias runs through many bedroom suburbs before reaching its namesake, the suburb of **Kifissiá** some 8 miles (12km) to the northeast. Higher than Athens and blessed with a good water supply, Kifissiá used to be where wealthy Athenians retreated to escape the summer heat. In recent years more and more Athenians have been coming here to live, and the area is now an active commercial hub with expensive stores and restaurants near impressive 19th-century mansions, many well shaded under large plane trees.

Piraeus and the southern suburbs Along the coast, of course, is **Piraeus** (Pireás), a city very much in its own right although you won't be able to tell precisely where Athens ends and Piraeus begins. If you're going on to one of the Aegean islands it's likely that your ship will leave from **Main Harbor,** or Mégas Limín (Great Harbor), or **Zéa Marina** (also called Pasalímani) in Piraeus. You might well come down here for any one of the many fish tavernas in the little harbor of **Mikrolímano** (Little Harbor), also called Turkolímano (Turkish Harbor)—if so, be warned that seafood prices are exorbitant anywhere in Athens and occasionally extortionate here.

Paleó **Fáliro,** a suburb of Athens down the coast to the southeast, is a city by the sea, full of apartment buildings in the occasionally deafening flight path to the airport.

South of the large yacht harbor of **Kalamáki** along **Possidónos Avenue,** the coast road, there's a big and busy public beach at **Áyios Kósmas.** Farther south, **Glyfáda,** Attica's largest resort, is busy, stylish, and pleasant enough. It's just as much in the flight path as Paleó Fáliro, but no one seems to notice. Glyfáda also has a yacht harbor, a good public beach, many good restaurants, lots of bars and discos, and upscale shopping, for its wealthy expatriate residents and Athenian visitors.

Voúla, farther southeast, has another good public beach. The major resort area of **Vouliagméni,** 14 miles (23km) south of Athens, has two good public beaches and several hotels, notably the luxury Astir Palace.

2 Getting Around

BY PUBLIC TRANSPORTATION

BY METRO (SUBWAY) The new metro is very much under construction but several years from use. The existing tram line runs between Piraeus and Kiffisiá, covering only the western part of the city. For tourists, it's most useful for the trip from Omónia or Monasteráki down to Piraeus to catch a boat to the islands. Buy your tickets at the station, validate them in the machines as you enter, and hang on to the ticket. The fare in 1996 was Dr 75 (33¢), the same as for buses, but the tickets are not interchangeable. The harbor in Piraeus is about a five-minute walk left from the end of the line.

BY BUS & TROLLEY BUS The public transportation system is inexpensive but rather difficult to understand. Buses and trolley buses run from central Athens to various suburbs but the only map of the full system is decidedly unclear. Some of the stops have schematic drawings of the route so you can learn where you might be going, but most of the buses and trolley buses are marked only by the last stop on their route. As with many things in Greece, ask. Someone will be found who regularly rides the bus to where you want to go and will tell you the steps involved. The bus service has a telephone number for information (☎ **01/185**), but because the bus system is new and many people haven't yet come to terms with it, the number is often busy. If you're stuck, call the Tourist Police (☎ **01/171**); they speak English, try very hard to be helpful, and have rich sources of information.

Tickets cost Dr 75 (33¢) each and can be bought from the kiosks (*períptera*) scattered throughout the city, one of which almost certainly is near your bus stop. The tickets are sold in packets of 10, though sometimes you can buy them one at a time. They are good for a ride anywhere on the system. Be certain to validate yours when you get on, and keep it until you get off. Occasionally, inspectors board the bus and check if everybody has paid the fare, and tourists are not spared a stiff fine.

If you're heading out of town and take a blue A line bus for transferring to another blue A line bus, your ticket will still be valid on the transfer bus. In central Athens, the minibuses numbered 60 and 150 serve the commercial area free of charge.

Buses heading out to farther points of Attica leave from Mavromatéon Street on the western edge of the Pedión tou Áreos park at the western end of Alexándras Avenue.

BY TAXI

Cabs are relatively inexpensive in Athens, costing about Dr 200 (85¢) for the meter to start running and Dr 55 (23¢) for each additional kilometer in town. There is a Dr 300 ($1.25) surcharge for fares from the airport, ports, railways, and bus terminals. An additional Dr 55 (23¢) is charged for each bag over 10 kilos.

Between midnight and 5am and outside the city the rate is double and the meter will be set on "2". Otherwise, makes sure it's on "1" and running.

In the morning and early afternoon when people are going to and returning from work, it's difficult to find an empty cab. People will stand in the street and call out their destinations to passing cabs, which will fill up with customers going in the same direction. The fare will be what the driver tells you, not necessarily what is on the meter, which may have begun long before you get in.

BY CAR

In Athens a car is more trouble than convenience. The traffic is heavy and finding a parking place can be extremely difficult. If you want to drive outside the city, there are plenty of rental agencies south of Sýntagma Square. **Avis,** 48 Amalías St., charges about Dr 15,000 ($65) per day with unlimited mileage, including insurance and tax. A little further south, **Budget,** 8 Syngroú, charges Dr 13,000 ($55), and **Eurodollar Rent a Car,** 29 Syngroú, charges about Dr 11,500 ($49).

Here's a list of some of the better agencies: **Athens Cars,** 10 Filellínon St. ☎ 01/323-3783 or 01/324-8870. **Autorent,** 94 Syngroú Ave. ☎ 01/924-0107 or 01/923-8532. **Avis,** 46-48 Amalías Ave. ☎ 01/322-4951 through 7. **Budget Rent a Car,** 8 Syngroú Ave. ☎ 01/921-4771 through 3. **Eurodollar Rent a Car,** 29 Syngroú Ave. ☎ 01/922-9672 or 01/923-0548. **Hellascars,** 148 Syngroú Ave. ☎ 01/923-5353 through 9. **Hertz,** 12 Syngroú Ave. ☎ 01/922-0102 through 4; 71 Vas. Sofías Ave. ☎ 01/724-7071 or 01/722-7391; East Air Terminal ☎ 01/961-3625 or 01/961-3530; West Air Terminal ☎ 01/981-3701. **Interrent-Europcar/Batek SA**, 4 Syngroú Ave. ☎ 01/921-5788 or 01/921-5789; East Air Terminal ☎ 01/961-3424; West Air Terminal ☎ 01/982-9565. **Rent a Reliable Car,** 29 Hatzichristou St. ☎ 01/924-2206 or 01/924-2207. **Thrifty Rent a Car,** 24 Syngroú Ave. ☎ 01/922-1211 through 3.

ON FOOT

Many of the areas you will want to visit are best reached, and enjoyed, on foot. The central commercial area, Pláka, and Monasteráki are largely pedestrian-only anyway, so there is little choice. A bus or a cab can take you to the edge of the area you wish to visit and from then on the distances are not great.

FAST FACTS: Athens

American Express   The main office (☎ 01/324-4975; fax 322-7893) is on Sýntagma Square, at the corner of Ermoú Street behind McDonalds, one flight up. It's open Monday through Friday from 8:30am to 4pm, Saturday 8:30am to 1:30pm. If you're going to be receiving mail there, the mailing address is Odós Ermoú 2, Sýntagma Square, 102 25 Athens, Greece. American Express will cash and sell traveler's checks, accept claims for lost and stolen credit cards and traveler's checks, store luggage for Dr 300 ($1.25) per day, make travel arrangements or book tours, accept mail for card members (others pay Dr 500/$2.10 per collection), and package and send parcels. The office closes one hour earlier in winter, and mail service ends at 4:30pm weekdays. Don't forget your passport. During off-hours, for lost or stolen credit cards and checks, call collect to the American Express office in London (☎ 0044/273/675-975).

Area Code   The country code for Greece is **30.** The telephone area code for Athens is **01.**

Banks   The **National Bank of Greece** on Sýntagma Square (☎ 01/322-2255) is open Monday to Thursday from 8am to 2pm and 3:30 to 6:30pm, Friday 8am to 1:30pm, and 3 to 8:30pm, Saturday 9am to 3pm, Sunday and holidays 9am to 1pm. The extended evening and weekend hours are for foreign exchange only and are shorter October to April. There's also a machine teller that will exchange foreign bank notes into drachmas 24 hours a day.

Official banking hours throughout Greece are Monday to Thursday from 8am to 2pm, Friday 8am to 1:30pm. The General Bank across the street has similar hours. International banks with local offices include **Citibank,** Odós Óthonos 8 (☎ 01/322-7471); **Bank of America,** Odós Panepistimíou 39 (☎ 01/324-4975); and **Barclays Bank,** Odós Voukourestíou 15 (☎ 01/364-4311). Americans with Cirrus cards may be able to access automatic cash machines, if they have their four-digit PIN code. (Check with your local bank or credit card company.)

Currency Exchange   Banks give the best exchange rates for converting foreign currency into drachmas; exchange bureaus add a surcharge. Remember that the exchange is one way, into drachmas. You will not be able to convert any surplus drachmas you may have back into dollars before leaving.

Beside the **National Bank of Greece** (see above) the **Post Office** on Sýntagma Square, at the corner of Mitropóleos Street, has an exchange office, open Monday to Friday from 7:30am to 7:30pm.

Dentists and Doctors   Embassies (see below) usually keep a list of dentists and physicians prepared by the embassy's medical officer. You can also call **01/105.**

Drugstores   See "Pharmacies," below.

Embassies/Consulates   Australia, Dimitríou Soútsou 37 (☎ 01/644-7303); **Canada,** Ioánnou Yenadíou 4 (☎ 01/725-4011); **Ireland,** Vassiléos Konstandínou 7 (☎ 01/723-2771); **New Zealand,** Semitelou 9 (☎ 01/771-0112); **United Kingdom,** Ploutárchou 1, Kolonáki (☎ 01/723-6211); **United States,** Vassilíssis Sofías 91 (☎ 01/721-2951). U.S. citizens in need of emergency assistance when embassy is closed, call the **embassy receptionist** at **01/722-3652** or the **duty officer** at **01/729-4301.**

Emergencies For police emergencies, call **01/100.** For a doctor between 2pm and 7am, call **01/105.** The first aid emergency number is **01/166.** For ambulances, call **01/178.** See also "Embassies/Consulates," above.

KAT, the emergency hospital in Kifissiá (☎ 01/801-4411 through 9) and **Asklépion Voúlas,** the emergency hospital in Voúla (☎ 01/895-3416 through 8), both have emergency rooms open 24 hours a day. They have vast experience and they are good. If you need medical attention fast, don't waste time trying to telephone these hospitals. Just go. Their doors are open and they will see to you as soon as you enter.

In addition, one of the major hospitals takes turns each day being on emergency duty. A recorded message in Greek at ☎ **01/106** tells which hospital is open for emergency services and gives the telephone number.

The **SOS Doctor** in Athens can be reached at ☎ 01/331-0310 or 01/331-0311; this is a 24-hour service that can send you a physician promptly for a fee of approximately Dr 15,000 ($65).

Hospitals Except for emergencies as described above in "Emergencies," hospital admittance is gained through a physician.

Information See "Visitor Information" earlier in this chapter.

Lost Property The **lost property office** is at Alexándras 173 (☎ 01/642-1616).

Luggage Storage/Lockers Many hotels and hostels will store your excess luggage for you while you gallivant around the country, often for free. You can store luggage at **Pacific Ltd.** (☎ 01/322-3213), 24 Níkis St., just southwest of Sýntagma Square, open Monday to Saturday from 7am to 8pm, Sunday and holidays 7am to 2pm; each piece costs Dr 500 ($2.10) per day, Dr 1,000 ($4.15) per week, Dr 2,500 ($10.40) per month. There are storage facilities at the metro station in Piraeus, at both train stations, and across from the entrance at the East Air Terminal.

Maps See "City Layout" earlier in this chapter.

Newspapers/Magazines The major English newspapers and the *International Herald Tribune* are readily available at kiosks. *Time, Newsweek,* the major English weekly magazines, and the major U.S. and English monthly magazines are well distributed. The local daily English language newspaper is *The Athens News.* Greece's *Weekly* newspaper comes out, as its title proclaims, every week. *Athenscope,* a weekly guide to what's on in Athens, lists current movies, restaurants, and bars. The monthly magazine, *The Athenian,* has interesting articles on Athenian life, as does the bimonthly *Odyssey.*

Pharmacies *Pharmakía,* identified by a green Greek cross, are scattered all over the city. The usual hours are Monday through Friday from 8am to 2pm. One drugstore in each area, however, is open all the time, and each drugstore prominently displays in its window a list with the names and addresses of the drugstores open when it's not. Newspapers also list the drugstores open outside regular hours. Call **01/107** to hear recorded announcements in Greek of open drugstores in Athens; in the suburbs, call ☎ **01/102.**

Police The central office for the traffic police is at 5 Aghiou Konstantinou St., five blocks west of Omonia Square (☎ 01/523-0111 through 5). If there is an emergency, call ☎ **01/100.**

Post Office The main post offices in central Athens are at 100 Eólou St., just off Omónia Square, and on Sýntagma Square at corner of Mitropóleos Street. Both are open Monday through Friday from 7:30am to 8pm, Saturday 7:30am to 2pm,

Sunday 9am to 1pm. The post offices at both air terminals also keep these extensive hours. The office at 29 Koumoundoúrou St., just north of Ayíou Konstandínou Street west of Omonia Square, primarily for packages, is open Monday through Friday from 7:30am to 8pm, as is the office at 60 Mitropóleos St., just past the Athens Cathedral toward Monasteráki. Most neighborhoods also have post offices, open Monday to Friday from 8am to 2pm.

Restrooms   There are public restrooms in the underground station beneath Omónia Square and beneath Kolonáki Square. Otherwise your best bet is the restroom of a hotel or restaurant. (Toilet paper is often not available; carry some tissue with you. Do not flush paper down the commode; use the receptacle provided.)

Safety   Athens rates among the safest capitals in Europe, and there are few reports of violent crimes. Pickpocketing, however, is not uncommon, especially in Pláka and the Omónia Square area, on the metro and buses, and in Piraeus. We advise travelers to avoid the back streets of Piraeus at night. As always, leave your passport and valuables in a security box at the hotel. Carry a photocopy of your passport, not the original.

Taxes   Unless you are working in Greece, your only brush with taxes probably will be the value-added tax (VAT), which in Greek abbreviates to FPA. It is the same for all customers, Greek or foreign, and varies between 4% on books to 36% on electronic goods.

Telephones/Telefaxes/Telegrams   The main office of the **Telecommunications Organization of Greece** (**OTE**) is 15 Stadíou St., two blocks from Sýntagma Square. This and the Omónia Square branch are open daily from 8am to 10pm. The OTE office at 85 Patissíon St., near Victoria Square, is open 24 hours. There are other, smaller OTE exchanges in Athens; they generally have more limited hours of operation.

Telegrams, telexes, and telefaxes can also be sent through the OTE offices. Some post offices also have fax service.

Most kiosks (*períptera*) have phones with meters that the public can use. There are increasing numbers of telephone stands, some with plastic hoods for shelter and acoustic protection. The telephones in these stands operate with a telephone card that can be bought for about Dr 1,300 ($5.50) from OTE offices and most kiosks; the card is good for 100 local calls.

Transit Info   For bus routes, ferry schedules, and other transit information, call the Tourist Police at **01/171.**

3 Accommodations

Don't expect high style and ornamentation in most Greek hotels. They're usually plain and unadorned but should be clean and comfortable. The area south and west of Sýntagma Square, and the neighborhoods of Pláka, Koukáki, Makriyánni, and Monastiráki offer the most convenient and comfortable choices. We especially recommend Koukáki for its quiet residential back streets and the feeling it offers of a real Greek neighborhood; although it's not as conveniently situated as Pláka or Sýntagma Square, it's only a short walk or bus ride from those areas. For pure convenience, the Sýntagma hotels, as well as those in the lively Pláka area, can't be beaten.

Note: We strongly advise that you reserve well in advance if you're coming in the summer.

Athens Accommodations

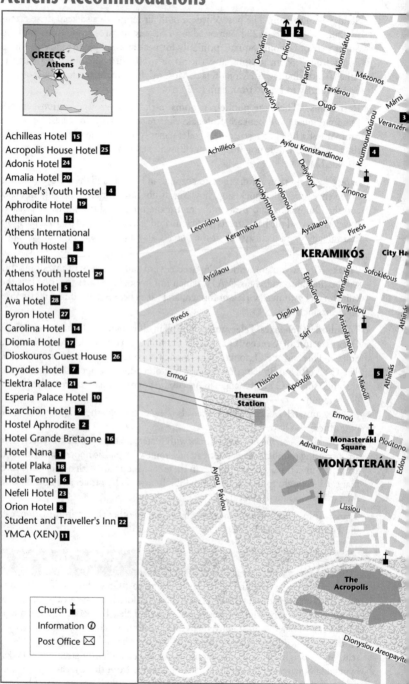

Achilleas Hotel **15**
Acropolis House Hotel **25**
Adonis Hotel **24**
Amalia Hotel **20**
Annabel's Youth Hostel **4**
Aphrodite Hotel **19**
Athenian Inn **12**
Athens International
  Youth Hostel **3**
Athens Hilton **13**
Athens Youth Hostel **29**
Attalos Hotel **5**
Ava Hotel **28**
Byron Hotel **27**
Carolina Hotel **14**
Diomia Hotel **17**
Dioskouros Guest House **26**
Dryades Hotel **7**
Elektra Palace **21**
Esperia Palace Hotel **10**
Exarchion Hotel **9**
Hostel Aphrodite **2**
Hotel Grande Bretagne **16**
Hotel Nana **1**
Hotel Plaka **18**
Hotel Tempi **6**
Nefeli Hotel **23**
Orion Hotel **8**
Student and Traveller's Inn **22**
YMCA (XEN) **11**

Church ✝
Information ⓘ
Post Office ✉

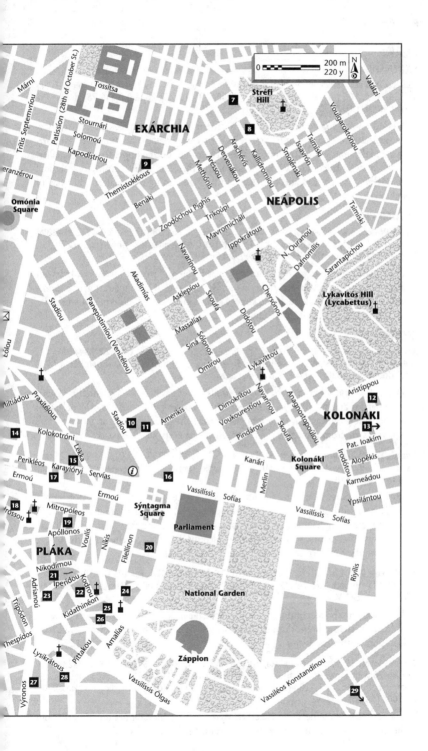

PLÁKA
EXPENSIVE

Elektra Palace. 18 Nikodímou St., Pláka, 105 57 Athens. ☎ **01/324-1401** through 7. Fax 01/324-1875. 106 rms, all with bath. A/C MINIBAR TV TEL. Dr 26,500 ($112.75) double (including breakfast). AE, DC, MC, V.

A good choice for comfort and a convenient location, the Elektra is just a few blocks southwest of Sýntagma Square at the edge of Pláka. The rooms are comfortable and decorated in warm muted tones. The rooms on the upper levels are smaller, but their larger balconies have a view that merits their use. There's a nice rooftop pool for soaking up the rays and the view and for a refreshing splash after a hot day of sightseeing.

MODERATE

Hotel Pláka. 7 Kapnikeréas St. at Mitropóleos, Pláka, 105 56 Athens. ☎ **01/322-2096** through 8. Fax 01/322-2414. 67 rms, 15 with bath, remainder with showers. A/C TV TEL. Dr 21,000 ($89) double. Dr 2,000 ($8.50) extra for A/C. AE, MC, V.

The bright new white lobby is impressive, as is the roof garden's wonderful view of the Acropolis, particularly in the evening. Request one of the more attractive rooms facing the Acropolis, though the street-facing rooms have double-paned windows. Mini fridges are available by request.

INEXPENSIVE

Acropolis House Hotel. 6-8 Kodroú St., Pláka, 105 58 Athens. ☎ **01/322-2344.** Fax 01/324-4143. 25 rms, 4 suites, 15 with bath. Dr 11,500 ($49) double without bath; Dr 17,000 ($73) double with bath and A/C. No credit cards.

This 150-year-old house at the end of Voulís Street has been well restored by Panos Choudalakis and his family. The "new" wing, 60 years old, has less of neoclassical Athens, but its toilets (one per room, across the hall) are fully tiled and modern. The best views are from rooms 401 and 402. Breakfast costs $6.50 extra.

Adonis Hotel. 3 Kodroú, Pláka, 105 58 Athens. ☎ **01/324-9737.** Fax 01/324-9737. 25 rms, 1 suite, all with shower. TEL. Dr 12,600 ($54) double; Dr 16,000 ($70) suite (including breakfast). No credit cards.

This clean, quiet hotel, near Voulís Street, has central heat, an elevator, and a pleasant rooftop garden with a great Acropolis view. The rooms are quite plain but comfortable enough, some with balconies large enough for sunbathing. If you stay more than two nights, request the 20% discount. Breakfast, included in the bill, is served on the roof terrace, which doubles as a cafe in the evening.

Ava Hotel. 9-11 Lysikrátous, 105 58 Athens. ☎ **01/323-6618.** Fax 01/323-1061. 11 rms, 7 suites, all with bath. A/C TEL. Dr 10,100 ($43) double; Dr 17,000 ($72) suite. A/C Dr 2,000 ($8.50) extra. DC, V.

These well-equipped, comfortable utility apartments are for those who would like to make themselves at home during a lengthier visit. They're a half block from Hadrian's Gate across Amalías Avenue.

Byron Hotel. 19 Výronos St., Pláka, 105 58 Athens. ☎ **01/325-3554.** Fax 01/323-0327. 22 rms, 20 with showers, 2 with separate bathrooms. A/C TEL. Dr 10,000 ($43) double with separate bathroom; Dr 17,200 ($73) double; Dr 20,800 ($89) triple (including breakfast). A/C Dr 2,000 ($8.50) extra. V.

The rooms here are neat and cheerful. Výronos Street doesn't get much traffic, but the front rooms are a bit noisier than the rooms in back.

Dioskouros Guest House. 6 Pittakoú St., Pláka, 105 58 Athens. ☎ **01/324-8165.** 12 rooms (none with bath) Dr 6,000 ($26) single; Dr 8,000 ($34) double. No credit cards.

This small guest house occupies an old home that has seen better days. The staff, however, keeps the place clean, and it's fairly quiet, as it's shielded from busy Amalías by a much larger building. Breakfast is Dr 700 ($3) extra.

Nefeli Hotel. 16 Iperídou St., Pláka, 105 58 Athens. ☎ **01/322-8044.** Fax 01/323-1114. 18 rooms, all with bath, 6 with A/C. TEL. Dr 13,800 ($59) double (including breakfast). No credit cards.

This charming, well-run little hotel is at the end of Voulís Street, in a quiet corner in the heart of Pláka. The rooms are small but spotless, some with old-fashioned ceiling fans.

MONASTERÁKI
INEXPENSIVE

✪ **Attalos Hotel.** 29 Athinás St., 105 54 Athens. ☎ **01/321-2801.** Fax 01/324-3124. 80 rms, all with bath. A/C TEL. Dr 9,500 ($40) double. A/C Dr 1,500 ($6) extra. V.

The Attalos has a good location: two blocks north of Monasteráki metro station, a short walk to the Acropolis, Pláka, and Sýntagma Square. Excellent management, a friendly and attentive staff, and comfortable lodgings make this an exceptional value. Bustling Athinás Street is nearly deserted and quiet at night, and there's a handsome roof garden with fine views of the city and the Acropolis. Rooms are plain, but very well maintained and especially clean. A good buffet breakfast costs Dr 1,100 ($4.50) a person. The Attalos provides free luggage storage.

✪ **Hotel Tempi.** 29 Eólou, 105 51 Athens. ☎ **01/321-3175.** Fax 01/325-4179. 24 rms, 10 with showers. Dr 7,000 ($30) double, separate bathroom; Dr 8,000 ($34) double with bathroom; Dr 9,000 ($38) triple, separate bathroom. AE, MC, V.

This clean, low-budget alternative for the student crowd is three blocks north of Monasteráki Square. No cars are allowed on Eólou, so it's quiet. The staff is friendly, and there's a laundry room with ironing facilities, free luggage storage, and a small paperback library.

AROUND EXÁRCHIA SQUARE
INEXPENSIVE

Exarchion Hotel. 55 Themistokléous, 106 83 Athens. ☎ **01/380-1256.** Fax 01/380-3296. 49 rms, all with bath. TEL. Dr 8,000 ($34) double. No credit cards.

The Exarchion is right on Exárchia Square, the heart of the university district. The lobby is decorated with large photos of archaeological sites, and there's a rooftop, where you can relax and watch students debate in the square below. The rooms are comfortable, have ceiling fans, and most have a balcony.

Dryades Hotel. 4 Dryadón at Anexartisías Sts., 114 73 Athens. ☎ **01/362-0191** or 01/362-7116. 19 rms, 10 with shower. Dr 9,500 ($40) double. No credit cards.

This is the slightly better of the two hotels run by the same management in a pleasant nontourist area on the slopes of Stréfi Hill. Both hotels are used by students and seasoned visitors. Each floor has a common kitchen and living room.

Orion Hotel. 105 Emmanouíl Benáki at Anexartisías. 114 73 Athens. ☎ **01/382-7362.** Fax 01/380-5193. 23 rms, 10 with bath. Dr 7,500 ($32) double. No credit cards.

This hotel is less expensive than its sister hotel, the Dryades, and it's just down the street, also on Stréfi Hill. The terrace is available for guests, as are kitchen facilities.

SÝNTAGMA SQUARE
VERY EXPENSIVE
Hotel Grande Bretagne. Sýntagma Square, 105 63 Athens. ☎ **01/323-0251.** Fax 01/ 322-8034. 365 rms, 33 suites (all with bath). A/C MINIBAR TV TEL. Dr 63,000–Dr 125,650 ($268–$535) double; suites from Dr 86,000 ($366). AE, CB, DC, MC, V.

This grande dame is still a favorite for old-world elegance. Built in 1864, it remains a venerable institution; its beaux-arts design is without equal in all of Greece. The polished marble floors and classical pillars of the lobby, with its ornately carved wood paneling and soaring ceilings, lend a true continental air, a feeling that the clientele only enhances. Yet, the Greek flavor prevails, as the movers and shakers of Greek society pass through for power lunches at the popular GB Corner.

Softly lit hallways with marble wainscoting lead to old-fashioned rooms with 12-foot ceilings and wall-to-wall coziness. The hotel was renovated in 1992, but we occasionally hear of a room that was apparently overlooked. The front rooms, with views of Sýntagma Square and the Acropolis are usually preferred, but inner court-yard rooms are quieter.

EXPENSIVE
Amalia Hotel. 10 Amalías Ave., 105 57 Athens. ☎ **01/323-7301** through 9. Fax 01/ 323-8792. 98 rms, all with bath. A/C MINIBAR TV TEL. Dr 25,800 ($110) double (including breakfast). AE, DC, MC, V.

This is one of the best values in Athens, especially considering its convenient Sýntagma Square location. Rooms are large, comfortable, and quiet, and the busy staff is helpful, if sometimes a bit curt.

Esperia Palace Hotel. 22 Stadíou St., 105 61 Athens. ☎ **01/323-8001.** 185 rms (all with bath). A/C MINIBAR TV TEL. Dr 30,000 ($127) double (including breakfast). AE, DC, MC, V.

Another good value hotel with a convenient location. The rooms are rather plain but large and comfortable, with direct dial telephones. The buffet breakfast is especially good. Many tour groups stay here and the staff is used to handling a high turnover well. (You can make reservations through Best Western.)

INEXPENSIVE
🟢 **Achilleas Hotel.** 21 Lékka St., 105 62 Athens. ☎ **01/323-3197.** Fax 01/324-1092. 34 rms, 7 with bath, 27 with shower. A/C TEL. Dr 15,700 ($67) double (including continental buffet breakfast). AE, V.

On a quiet street just off Sýntagma Square. Don't be put off by the entrance off the street; this hotel was completely renovated in 1995, and all the rooms are spacious and bright. It's a very good value, especially for families, who will enjoy the twin bed-rooms that share a sitting room and bath.

Aphrodite Hotel. 21 Apóllonos St., 105 57 Athens. ☎ **01/323-4357** through 9. Fax 01/ 322-5244. 84 rms A/C TEL. Dr 14,300 ($61) double (including breakfast). AE, DC, MC, V.

The entrance looks rather bleak, but the staff is friendly and helpful. The rooms are plain but comfortable, and those at the back overlook an abandoned church surrounded by a school with the Acropolis above. The buffet breakfast is also quite good.

Carolina Hotel. 55 Kolokotróni St., 105 60 Athens. ☎ **01/331-1784** and 01/331-1785. Fax 01/324-0944. 31 rooms, 16 with separate bathroom. Dr 8,000 ($34) double with separate bath-room; Dr 9,000 ($39) double with bathroom. AE, EURO, MC, V.

This old budget favorite is still holding up. The rooms are small and worn, but com-fortable and clean, with ceiling fans. Solar heating units were installed in 1996 for a regular supply of hot water. Rates are cheaper before August 1 and after October 31. Breakfast is another Dr 1,000 per person extra.

Diomia Hotel. 5 Diomías St., 105 63 Athens. ☎ **01/323-8034.** Fax 01/324-8792. 71 rms, 6 with bath, 65 with shower. A/C TEL TV. Dr 19,200 ($82) double. AE, EU, DC, MC, V.

The Diomia has been through some ups and downs, but it was renovated in early 1996. Choose your room carefully, as the upper ones are brighter and more spacious, some with good balcony views.

KOLONÁKI
MODERATE

Athenian Inn. 22 Háritos St., Kolonáki, 106 75 Athens. ☎ **01/723-8097.** Fax 01/724-2268. 28 rms, all with bath. A/C TV TEL. Dr 23,500 ($100) double; Dr 29, 500 ($125) triple. AE, DC, V.

This is a favorite hotel for many return visitors. The quiet location three blocks east from Kolonáki Square is a blessing, as are the clean accommodations and friendly staff. (A quote from the guest book: "At last the ideal Athens hotel, good and modest in scale but perfect in service and goodwill. Hurrah. Lawrence Durrell.") Many of the balconies look out upon Lykavitós Hill. You can have breakfast in the cozy lounge with a fireplace and piano.

THE EMBASSY DISTRICT
VERY EXPENSIVE

Athens Hilton. 46 Vassilíssis Sofías Ave., 115 28 Athens. ☎ **01/722-0301.** Fax 01/721-3110. 427 rms, 19 suites (all with bath). A/C MINIBAR TV TEL. Dr 66,000–Dr 140,000 ($280–$595) double; suites from Dr 155,000 ($660). Plaza Executive Dr 117,000 ($498) double. AE, DC, EC, MC, V.

The Athens Hilton, near the U.S. Embassy, is something of an institution in the capital. Not only is it home to many international businesspeople and diplomats, but for years it has been a place to meet for a swim or a drink or to dine in one of its many restaurants. Of polished marble and quietly elegant, the lobby and other public spaces are a bit too cool and impersonal for some. Guest rooms are comfortable, with marble bathrooms and a pleasantly neutral style.

The Hilton often runs promotional sales, so check with your travel agent about special weekend rates before booking. For those on business, there's the Plaza Executive floor of executive rooms and suites, a separate business center, and a higher level of service.

Sports options include a great pool and a health club. The lobby Polo Club and top-floor Galaxy Roof Terrace, with superb city views, are fine venues for a drink.

MAKRIYÁNNI
VERY EXPENSIVE

✪ **Divani-Palace Acropolis.** 19-25 Parthenónos St., Makriyánni, 117 42 Athens. ☎ **01/92-22-2945.** Fax 01/92-14-993. 242 rms, 11 suites (all with bath). A/C MINIBAR TV TEL. Dr 52,000–Dr 72,000 ($221–$306) double; suites from Dr 72,500 ($308). AE, DC, MC, V.

For luxury, comfort, and location, you'd have a hard time beating this recently renovated beauty, just three blocks south of the Acropolis. The rooms are quietly elegant; service is friendly but professional; the spacious modern lobby is appointed with copies of classical sculpture; and sections of the actual walls built by Themistocles during the Persian Wars are exhibited in the basement. The hotel has a small, handsome pool and a bar, a good restaurant, and a lovely roof garden with the view you expect.

EXPENSIVE

Herodion Hotel. 4 Rovértou Gáli St., Makriyánni, 117 42 Athens. ☎ **01/923 6832** through 6. Fax 01/923-5851. 90 rms, 78 with bath, 12 with shower. A/C TV TEL. Dr 32,000 ($135) double (including breakfast). AE, DC, MC, V.

This attractive hotel is just a block south of the Acropolis, near the Herodes Atticus theater. The lobby leads to a lounge and patio garden where you can have drinks and snacks under the trees. The dining room has a set three-course menu for about Dr 4,500 ($20). The large rooms are tastefully decorated, many with a balcony, some with good views. The roof terrace has a fine view of the Acropolis, and you can have room service bring up snacks and meals.

MODERATE

Acropolis View Hotel. 10 Webster St., Acrópolis, 117 42 Athens. ☎ **01/921-7303** through 5. Fax 01/923-0705. 32 rms, 20 with bath, 12 with shower. A/C TEL. Dr 20,000 ($85) double. AE, MC, V.

This is a fine little hotel on a small winding side street with no traffic near the Herodes Atticus theater, between Rovérto Gálli and Propiléon. The rooms are small but have most modern amenities; some have the view from which it takes its name. The view from the rooftop bar is sensational, especially at sunset and at night.

Hera Hotel. 9 Falírou St., Makriyáni, 117 42 Athens. ☎ **01/923-6682.** Fax 01/924-7334. 45 rms, 4 with bath, 35 with showers. A/C TEL. Dr 19,500 ($83) double. No credit cards.

This is an attractive, modern hotel with a rooftop bar looking out on the Acropolis. The spacious lobby includes a coffee shop and breakfast lounge and bar with a view of the back garden. The compact rooms are simply furnished and carpeted. Some rooms have TVs. Garage parking is provided at no extra cost.

Hotel Philippos. 3 Mitséon, Makriyáni, 117 42 Athens. ☎ **01/922-3611.** Fax 01/922-3615. 50 rms, all with shower. A/C TV TEL. Dr 16,500 ($70) single; Dr 22,500 ($96) double. AE, DC, MC, V.

Completely renovated in 1993 in keeping with its sleek art deco design, this hotel is amazingly quiet for its busy location three blocks south of the Acropolis. The rooms are small but pretty and quite comfortable, and there's a laundry service.

KOUKÁKI
MODERATE

Austria Hotel. 7 Moussón St., Filopáppou, 117 42 Athens. ☎ **01/923-5151.** Fax 01/902-5800. 37 rms, all with bath. A/C TEL. Dr 22,000 ($94) (including breakfast). AE, DC, EU, MC, V.

This quiet, well-maintained little hotel at the base of Philopáppou Hill is operated by a nice Greek-Austrian family. The rooms are rather spartan but especially neat and clean. The view from the rooftop is especially fine, and it's a good base for taking in the sights.

INEXPENSIVE

Art Gallery Pension. 5 Erechthíou St., Koukáki, 117 42 Athens. ☎ **01/923-8376.** Fax 01/923-3025. 22 rms, all with bath. TEL. Dr 12,000 ($51) double; Dr 13,900 ($59) triple; Dr 15,700 ($67) for four people. V.

The Art Gallery Pension takes its name from the many paintings displayed here by artists who have lived in this 40-year-old family house. Polished hardwood floors, ceiling fans, and a tiny cage elevator provide a warm, homey atmosphere.

⑤ Marble House Pension. 35A Zinní St., Koukáki, Athens 11741. ☎ **01/923-4058** or 01/922-6461. 17 rms, 9 with bath. Dr 8,900 ($38) double without bath; Dr 9,990 ($43) double with bath. From October to May, rooms can be rented by the month for $277. No credit cards.

Accommodations & Dining
South of the Acropolis

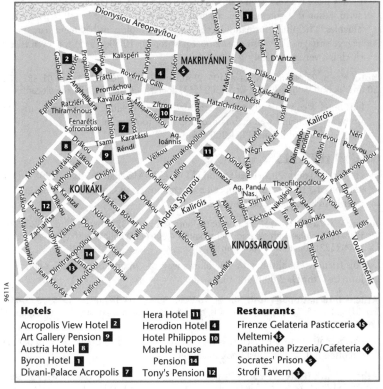

Hotels

Acropolis View Hotel **2**
Art Gallery Pension **9**
Austria Hotel **8**
Byron Hotel **1**
Divani-Palace Acropolis **7**

Hera Hotel **11**
Herodion Hotel **4**
Hotel Philippos **10**
Marble House
  Pension **14**
Tony's Pension **12**

Restaurants

Firenze Gelateria Pasticceria **15**
Meltemi **13**
Panathinea Pizzeria/Cafeteria **6**
Socrates' Prison **5**
Strofi Tavern **3**

This place is a favorite of repeat visitors for its good value and friendly atmosphere. It's two blocks from Syngroú Avenue and the Olympic Airlines Office, on a cul-de-sac just after the church on Zinní Street, and decked in fuchsia-colored bougainvillea. The rooms facing the cul-de-sac have balconies; all are small, simple, functional, clean, with solid ceiling fans. The affable Thanos and his staff are informative, caring, and helpful.

Tony's Pension. 26 Zacharítsa, Koukáki, 117 41 Athens. ☎ **01/923-6370** or 01/923-5761. 15 rooms, 11 studio apartments, all with shower. TEL. Dr 9,000 ($38.50) double. Dr 9,000–Dr 12,000 ($38–$51) studio apartments. EU, MC.

Tony's is about halfway between Philopáppou Hill and Sýngrou Avenue. Each floor has a common kitchen and TV lounge. Students, models, and singles stay here in this congenial atmosphere. The roof is comfortably arranged with chairs for the fine view, and there's a barbecue for guest use. Monthly rentals in the winter are 20% less than the day rate.

NEAR THE RAILROAD STATION

The only reason to stay near the railroad station is to make a convenient overnight connection between trains, saving time and taxi fare.

INEXPENSIVE

Hostel Aphrodite. 12 Einárdou St. and Michaíl Vodá 65, 104 40 Athens. ☎ **01/881-0589** or 01/883-9249. 28 rms, 12 with shower. Dr 1,800 ($8) for single bed; Dr 4,500 ($19) single without bathroom to Dr 10,000 ($43) for quad with bathroom. No credit cards.

Hostel here means "small hotel," not "youth hostel," and this clean, unpretentious, friendly place is a very good deal. It's a few blocks northwest from the Victoria Square metro station in a quiet residential/small shop area. They have hot showers, a safe for valuables, a helpful information desk, a sun roof, a pleasant basement bar, and free luggage storage. They also offer a boat pass for Dr 10,500 ($45) for seven islands, which is a very good deal.

Hotel Nana. 27 Neófitou Metaxá, 104 39 Athens. ☎ **01/884 2211.** Fax 01/882 3220. 50 rms (all with bath). A/C TEL. Dr 12,500 ($53) double (A/C included). No credit cards.

This hotel is conveniently near the railroad station if you're heading out early. The rooms are clean and well maintained. Ask for a room at the back, which is quieter. Breakfast is an additional Dr 1,200 ($5).

YOUTH HOSTELS

The Greek Youth Hostel Federation (☎ 01/323-4107; fax 01/323-7590), 4 Dragatsaníou St., 105 59 Athens, operates several hostels in Greece. Call to learn if any other hostels not listed here are operating.

Annabel's Youth Hostel. 28 Koumoundoúrou St., 104 37 Athens. ☎ **01/524-5834.** Dr 3,000 ($13) single with separate bathroom; Dr 4,000 ($17) double with separate bathroom; Dr 5,000 ($22) double with bathroom.

This friendly establishment a few blocks west of Omónia Square also offers single dorm beds for Dr 2,000 ($8.50).

Athens International Youth Hostel. 16 Victor Hugo, 104 38 Athens. ☎ **01/523-4170.** Fax 01/523 4115. Only beds, not rooms, are available here for Dr 1,500 ($6.50) a night. No credit cards.

This recently renovated facility is the best youth hostel in Athens. It's very popular, and often full, so you must book in advance.

Athens Youth Hostel. No. 5, 75 Damaréos St., Pangráti, 116 33 Athens. ☎ **01/751-9530.** Fax 01/751-0616. Beds Dr 1,500 ($6.50); single rooms Dr 3,500 ($15); double rooms Dr 5,000 ($22). No private bathrooms. No credit cards.

This facility is acceptable, if not especially clean, but it's in a nice quiet neighborhood east of Athens Stadium.

Student and Travellers' Inn. 16 Kidathenéon St., Pláka, 105 58 Athens. ☎ **01/324-4808** or 01/324-8802. 45 rms, none with bath. Dr 2,800 ($12) single bed in room with four beds; Dr 5,500 ($24) single; Dr 7,000 ($30) double. No credit cards.

This hostel/hotel, which is being refurbished, is a good deal for inexpensive accommodation in the heart of Athens.

YWCA (XEN). 11 Amerikís St., 106 72 Athens. ☎ **01/362-4291.** Dr 4,200 ($18) single without bathroom; Dr 5,500 ($24) single with bathroom; Dr 3,500 ($15) per person double or triple room with bathroom.

Women will find spotless lodging at bargain prices at the YWCA (XEN in Greek) on Amerikís Street between Panepistimíou and Akadamías streets. There's a Dr 600 ($2.50) membership fee, and breakfast costs an additional Dr 800 ($3.40).

4 Dining

You'll find every sort of ethnic food in the capital, but Greek cooking is still the best and least expensive. Seafood is almost always very expensive, and we often have doubts about its freshness. There are plenty of places for a quick snack, such as a gyro (yíro or souvlaki me píta), which you are probably already familiar with, a tirópita (cheese pie), spanakópita (spinach and cheese pie), or any number of pastries and sweets. For dining choices in nearby Piraeus, see "Side Trips from Athens: Attica," below in this chapter; some of the restaurants we have listed there are where Athenians go when they want to splurge on a good fish dinner.

PLÁKA
MODERATE
Eden Vegetarian Restaurant. 12 Lissíou St. ☎ **01/324-8858.** Main courses Dr 1,200–Dr 2,100 ($5.10–$8.95). No credit cards. Daily noon–midnight. From Adrianoú take Mnissikléos up two blocks toward Acropolis. VEGETARIAN.

One of the few vegetarian restaurants in Greece, this place serves up good low-cost food in an attractive contemporary setting. The decor includes 1920s-style prints, mirrors, and wrought-iron lamps, and there are views of a pretty Pláka street. They have a good mushroom, wheat germ, and onion pie; wonderful soya moussaká; and several other inventive dishes. The brown bread is delicious. They also have separate sections for smokers and nonsmokers, a blessing in this country.

Piccolino Restaurant. 26 Sotíros St. ☎ **01/324-6692.** Main courses Dr 1,500–Dr 2,800 ($6.40–$11.90). No credit cards. Daily 6pm–3am. At corner of Kidathenéon, near the Metamórfossi Church. GREEK/ITALIAN.

Piccolino is popular with both Greeks and tourists. Dishes include generous portions of spaghetti carbonara, macaroni and cheese, pastítsio, octopus with french fries, mussels stewed in white wine, fish and chips, and 10 varieties of pizza baked in a traditional wood-fired oven.

Platanos Taverna. 4 Dioyénous St. ☎ **01/322-0666.** Main courses Dr 1,500–Dr 2,500 ($6.40–$10.65). No credit cards. Mon–Sat noon–4:30pm and 8pm–midnight. From Adrianoú take Mnissikléos up one block toward Acropolis. GREEK.

This traditional taverna is on a quiet pedestrian square near the Tower of the Winds. Inside is a pleasant ambience of paintings, photos, and certificates on the walls beneath the modern wooden ceiling. If it's warm, sit at a table beneath the eponymous plane (sycamore) tree in front. Platanos is famous for its Greek specialties and large list of white, red, and rosé wines.

Ta Bakaliarakia Taverna (Damigos). 41 Kidathenéon St. ☎ **01/322-5084.** Main courses Dr 1,500–Dr 2,600 ($6.40–$11.05). No credit cards. Daily 7pm–12am; closed July–Sept. On Kidathenéon just before Adrianoú. GREEK.

Down a short flight of steps, this long-time budget favorite is where you'll find solid Greek food at low prices. Bakaliarákia are deep-fried patties made from salted cod, soaked for hours to reduce the salt, and served with garlic sauce. There are many other dishes as well.

Taverna Poulakis. 6 Pános St. ☎ **01/321-3222.** Meals Dr 1,400–Dr 2,500 ($5.95–$10.65). No credit cards. Daily noon–midnight. Just west of the Tower of the Winds. GREEK.

You'll be served good home-style Greek food you can select at the counter. The menu includes dolmádes (grape leaves stuffed with ground meat), pastítsio (baked pasta with meat), and country salad with feta cheese. This typical taverna has seating for 20 inside and 100 outside.

✪ **Taverna Xinos.** Angélou Yéronda 4. ☎ **01/322-1065.** Reservations recommended. Main courses Dr 2,000–Dr 2,800 ($8.50–$12). No credit cards. Mon–Fri 8pm–12:30am. Closed Sat–Sun and all July. On a narrow lane near Iperídou Street. GREEK.

This classic taverna with live music as well as superb food is worth making reservations for, but make them for after 9pm. Its informal atmosphere draws guests in aloha

Athens Dining

L'Abreuvoir **15**
Apollonian Bakery **18**
Apotsos **13**
Bajazzo **28**
Café Neon (Omónia) **8**
Dimokritos **14**
Diros Restaurant **21**
Eden Vegetarian
    Restaurant **6**
Epirus **2**
Far East **11**
GB Corner **12**
Grill House Plaka **25**
Kioupi **16**
Kouklis Ouzeri
    (To Yeráni) **23**
Mrs. Rose **19**
Myrtia **29**
Neon (Sýntagma) **20**
Piccolino Restaurant **24**
Platanos Taverna **5**
Restaurant Costoyanis **7**
Restaurant Kentrikon **10**
Restaurant Nea-Olympia **9**
Rodia Taverna **17**
Ta Bakaliarakia Taverna **26**
Taverna Poulakis **4**
Taverna Sigalas **1**
Taverna Xinos **22**
Thanasis **3**
To Tristato **27**

Church ✝
Information ⓘ
Post Office ✉

9612

94

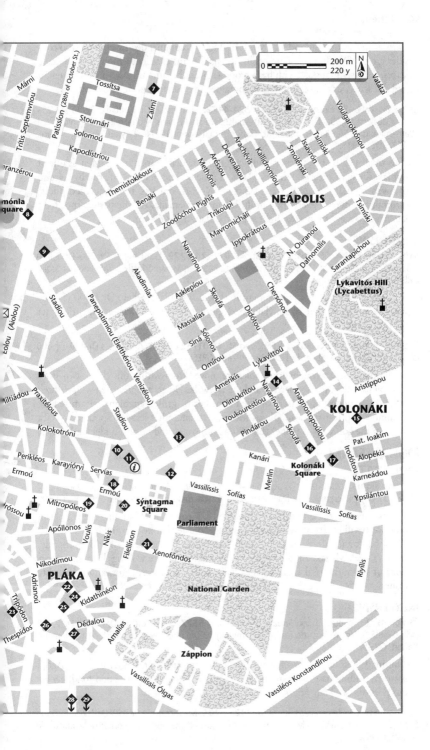

shirts as well as the suit-and-tie crowd. It's highly recommended by Greeks, who consider it one of the finest restaurants in Athens. Try the excellent lemony stuffed grape leaves, the tasty moussaká with fresh ground spices, the lamb fricassee in an egg-lemon and dill sauce, or the veal stew with tomatoes and potatoes in rich olive oil.

✪ **To Tristato.** 34 Dédalou St. ☎ **01/324-4472.** Light meals Dr 1,000–Dr 2,000 ($4.25–$8.50); desserts Dr 800–Dr 1,500 ($3.40–$6.40). No credit cards. Mon–Fri 2pm–midnight; Sat 10am–midnight, Sun 11am–midnight. Closed Aug 10–Sept 10. Near Ayíou Yéronda Square. SNACKS/DESSERTS.

This small 1920s-style tearoom, adjoining a triangular-shaped rose garden, is one of our favorite light-meal and dessert places in Athens. This new age cafe run by a group of lovely women has it all: fresh fruits and yogurt, omelets, fresh-squeezed juices, scrumptious cakes—everything healthful and homemade. It's the perfect spot for a late breakfast, afternoon tea, light supper, or late-night dessert.

INEXPENSIVE

Grill House Plaka. 28 Kidathinéon St. ☎ **01/324-6229.** Light meals Dr 900–Dr 1,800 ($3.85–$7.65). No credit cards. Daily 11am–1am. Between Metamórfossi Church and Acropolis. GREEK.

A simple, clean, family run gyro joint in the heart of Pláka, where Dr 1,800 ($7.65) will get you a full plate of souvlaki (beef, pork, or chicken), fresh greens, fries, pita bread and tzatzíki.

Kouklis Ouzeri (To Yeráni). 14 Tripódon St. ☎ **01/324-7605.** Appetizers Dr 400–Dr 800 ($1.70–$3.40). No credit cards. Daily 11am–2am. GREEK.

In summer, small wrought-iron tables are moved from within this classic two-story town house to the rooftop terrace and the sidewalk. Diners are presented with a dozen plates of mezédes: appetizers of fried fish, beans, grilled eggplant, taramosaláta, cucumber-and-tomato salad, olives, fried cheese, and other seasonal specialties. With a liter of the house krassí (wine) (Dr 800/$3.40), you can dine on a budget at Kouklis.

MONASTERÁKI
MODERATE

Taverna Sigalas. 2 Monasteráki Square. ☎ **01/321-3036.** Main courses Dr 1,000–Dr 1,800 ($4.25–$7.65). No credit cards. Daily 7am–2am. East across square from metro station. GREEK.

This worthy taverna is housed in a vintage 1879 commercial building, with a newer outdoor pavilion. Its lively interior has huge, old retsina kegs in the back and dozens of black-and-white photos of Greek movie stars on the walls. After 8pm nightly, there's Greek Muzak. At all hours, Greeks and tourists are wolfing down large portions of stews, moussaká, grilled meatballs, baked tomatoes, gyros, and other tasty dishes.

INEXPENSIVE

Ⓢ **Epirus.** 15 Ayíou Filíppou Square. ☎ **01/324-5572.** Main courses Dr 1,200–Dr 2,000 ($5.10–$8.50). No credit cards. Daily noon–midnight. Two blocks west of the Monasteráki metro station. GREEK.

This marvelous restaurant a few yards from the entrance to the Ancient Greek Agora is worth finding past the awnings in the square. No pretensions, good food, generous portions, and fair prices.

Ⓢ **Thanasis.** 69 Metropóleos St. ☎ **01/324-4705.** Main courses Dr 350–Dr 1,700 ($1.50–$7.25). No credit cards. Daily 8:30am–1 or 2am. Just off the northeast corner of Monasteráki Square. GREEK.

This specialized souvlakatzídiko ("souvlaki stand") is truly an institution. It serves souvlaki wrapped "to go" or on a plate with pita bread at one of two dozen wooden tables. The french fries are superb and cooked in olive oil—no cholesterol. It's almost always packed with locals who don't seem to notice the brusque service or blaring TVs.

SYNTAGMA

EXPENSIVE

Far East. 7 Stadíou St. ☎ **01/323-4996.** Reservations recommended. Main courses Dr 1,400–Dr 7,000 ($6–$30). AE, EU, DC, MC, V. Daily 11:30am–2am. CHINESE/JAPANESE/KOREAN.

Several Oriental restaurants have opened in central Athens in recent years, but this is the only one we can fully recommend. Though expensive, it turns out the town's best chicken and beef dishes, some tofu and mixed-vegetable dishes, and light, steamed dumplings. The decor is 1960s Chinatown, with teak paneling and floral patterns and with waitresses (some even Chinese) in classic cheongsam.

GB Corner. In the Grande Bretagne Hotel, Sýntagma Square. ☎ **01/323-0251.** Reservations required for lunch. Main courses Dr 4,000–Dr 9,500 ($17–$40). AE, DC, EU, MC, V. INTERNATIONAL.

The atmosphere is British men's club, with dark leather booths and hunting pictures on the walls. The menu has a full international/continental range, as well as breakfast and late night offerings.

MODERATE

Apotsos. 10 Panepistimíou St. ☎ **01/363-7046.** Appetizers Dr 400–Dr 2,000 ($1.70–$8.50) AE, DC, MC, V. Mon–Sat 11am–5pm. At end of arcade by the Zalotas jewelry store, two blocks from Sýntagma Square. GREEK.

This quintessentially Greek establishment specializes in mezédes, small plates of delicacies that fill your table. Regional cheeses and various salads are also served. It has been an Athenian haven for decades and maintains a 1920s atmosphere.

Diros Restaurant. 10 Xenofóndos St. ☎ **01/323-2392.** Main courses Dr 1,400–Dr 2,500 ($5.95–$10.65). AE, DC, V. Daily noon–midnight. One block south from Sýntagma Square. GREEK.

Many demanding Greek regulars frequent this air-conditioned restaurant, so you can count on getting good home-cooked food. Menu items include avgolémono (rice, egg, and lemon soup), bean soup, a large selection of spaghetti dishes, and roast chicken with french fries. There's seating for 50 both inside and out, and the waiter and manager speak some English.

Neon. 3 Mitropóleos St. ☎ **01/322-8155.** Sandwiches Dr 500–Dr 900 ($2.10–$3.85); main courses Dr 1,000–Dr 2,500 ($4.25–$10.65). No credit cards. Southwest corner of Sýtagma Square. INTERNATIONAL.

This new addition to the Neon chain offers yet another choice for this busy area. The sleek art deco style is perfect for the no-nonsense food and cafeteria service. You're sure to find something to your taste—maybe a Mexican omelet, a Green Forest salad, spaghetti Bolognese, or sweets ranging from Black Forest cake to tiramisú.

Restaurant Kentrikon. 3 Kolokotróni St. ☎ **01/323-2482.** Main courses Dr 1,600–Dr 4,000 ($6.80–$17). No credit cards. Sun–Fri noon–6pm. One block up Stadíou, on left. GREEK/INTERNATIONAL.

This spacious air-conditioned restaurant caters mostly to local workers and businesspeople. The decor will march you back to the early 1960s, with its large open dining room with wood panels covered by prints of ancient Athens and glass-ball chandeliers. We suggest the delectable lamb ragout with spinach or chicken with okra.

INEXPENSIVE

Apollonion Bakery. 10 Níkis St. ☎ **01/331-2590.** Snacks Dr 300–Dr 1,000 ($1.25–$4.25). No credit cards. SANDWICHES/PASTRIES.

This new arrival, off the southwest corner of Sýntagma Square, is a branch of a well-known chain. Their sandwiches and croissants are good and fresh.

Mrs. Rose. 18 Voulís St. ☎ **01/322 3158.** Snacks Dr 250–Dr 800 ($1–$3.40). No credit cards.

This new stand-up shop specializes in delicious cookies as well as good sandwiches.

KOLONÁKI

EXPENSIVE

L'Abreuvoir. 51 Xenokrátous. ☎ **01/722-9106.** Reservations recommended. Main courses Dr 4,600–Dr 8,700 ($19.60–$37). AE, DC, MC, V. Daily 12:30–4:30pm, 8:30pm–midnight. FRENCH.

This fine French restaurant has tables set under mulberry trees, a wonderful place to have lunch or dinner. From the fluffy spinach tart or smoked trout to the steak au poivre, *entrecôtes Provenççale* (a filet cooked in marvelous garlic, mushroom, and parsley sauce) to the soufflé au Grand Marnier or chocolate mousse, it's all a delight. L'Abreuvoir has all the attributes of a perfect splurge evening: a quiet, elegant setting, wonderful food, and good service. For what you get, the prices are reasonable.

MODERATE

Dimokritos. 23 Dimókritou St. ☎ **01/361-3588.** Meals Dr 2,500–Dr 4,000 ($10.65–$17). No credit cards. Mon–Sat 1–5pm and 8pm–1am. Four blocks northwest of Kolonáki Square on Skoufa Street, turn right on Dimokritou off Skoufa; one block up, up one floor, marked only by the word *taverna* on doors. GREEK.

Overlooking the Church of Áyios Diónysíos, this two-room taverna serves good food to a dedicated clientele. The large menu, in both Greek and English, features grilled veal, rabbit, fish, and lamb, though many knowledgeable locals swear by the swordfish souvlaki. A variety of Greek salads are displayed in a case by the entrance. It's a spotless, pretty interior.

Rodiá Taverna. 44 Arístípou St. ☎ **01/722-9883.** Main courses Dr 600–Dr 2,500 ($2.55–$10.65). No credit cards. Mon–Sat 8pm–2am. GREEK.

This is a romantic, old-fashioned taverna below street level in one of Kolonáki's oldest homes, at the foot of Lykavitós Hill. In the winter, dining is in Rodiá's dark interior, with its patterned tiled floors and lace curtains; kegs of the house krassí (wine) are on display. During the other seasons, the small tables are put in the vine-shaded back garden. Specials include octopus in mustard sauce; oregano or lemon beef; fluffy bourékis (vegetable pastries); and, for dessert, fresh halvá.

INEXPENSIVE

Kioupi. 4 Kolonáki Square. ☎ **01/361-4033.** Meals Dr 1,200–Dr 2,100 ($5.10–$8.95). No credit cards. Daily 11am–11pm (closed evenings in summer). GREEK.

This friendly basement restaurant is a favorite with people who want good food without frills, and it's an especially good value for this expensive neighborhood. Once you've gone down the steps, turn left toward the kitchen and point out what you want.

OMÓNIA SQUARE
EXPENSIVE

Restaurant Costoyanis. 37 Zaími St. ☎ **01/822-0624.** Meals Dr 2,400–Dr 6,000 ($10.20–$25.55). No credit cards. Mon–Sat 8am–2am. Two blocks behind the Archeological Museum. GREEK/SEAFOOD.

As you enter the Costoyanis, you'll see an impressive display of fish and other foods, and you can choose the items you'd like to sample. You can also order from the menu. The attractive dining room has wooden ceiling beams and a long array of windows covered by curtains.

MODERATE

Café Neon. 1 Dórou St. ☎ **01/523-6409.** Main courses Dr 1,000–Dr 2,600 ($4.25–$11). No credit cards. Daily 8am–2am. Northeast side of square. INTERNATIONAL.

The Kafeníon was built in 1924 and was one of Omónia Square's grandest old edifices; it was recently completely restored as an air-conditioned "free-flow" restaurant. The staff, clad in sailor suits, assist customers at several self-service stations. You can choose from the salad bar (Dr 1,000/$4.25 for a bowlful), the omelet kitchen, the hot-entrée counter, or the pastry counter. Everything is freshly made, tasty, and a good value. Vegetarians will appreciate the cold and hot vegetable dishes, and all will enjoy the breakfast choices.

Restaurant Nea-Olympia. 3 Emanuíl Benáki St. ☎ **01/321-7972.** Meals Dr 1,300–Dr 3,200 ($5.75–$14.25). No credit cards. Mon–Fri 11am–midnight, Sat 11am–4pm. Two blocks southeast of Omónia Square, left (north) off Stadíou Street. GREEK/INTERNATIONAL.

This is one of the largest restaurants in town, with a slightly more attractive decor than some of the area's other budget picks. Windows overlook the street and Greek prints adorn the blond-wood walls. Daily specials are posted at each table in Greek, so make sure to ask the waiter for a translation; the regular menu is in English.

METS
VERY EXPENSIVE

Bajazzo. 14 Anapafseos & Tiriteou sts., Mets. ☎ **01/921 3013.** Reservations required Fri–Sat. Dinner for two Dr 35,000 ($150). AE, DC, MC, V. Mon–Sat 8pm–1am. HAUTE CUISINE.

This is the most expensive restaurant we've been to or know of in Athens. There's no menu; the many possibilities are brought to you uncooked by the waiters for your selection. The owner and chef, Klaus Feuerbach, cooks your choice to perfection. The service and the surroundings are excellent. If you want to let out all the stops, this is the place to go. It's located on Anapafseos, the street running up to the First Cemetery in Athens, southeast of Athens Stadium.

Myrtia. 32-34 Trivonianoú St. ☎ **01/924-7175.** Reservations recommended. Fixed price menus Dr 10,000–Dr 17,000 ($42.55–$72.35). AE, DC, EU, MC, V. Mon–Sat 8:30pm–2am. Closed August. GREEK.

You'll want to dress your best and take a cab up to the serious feast at this most famous of the fixed-menu tavernas in Athens, up the hill behind the Olympic Stadium in Mets. The atmosphere is charmingly bucolic, like a Greek village, with strolling musicians, outdoors in the summer. You'll be served a full array of mezédes, tender roast chicken, delicious lamb, fruit, sweets, various wines, and much more—all you can eat, prepared to perfection.

MAKRIYÁNNI
MODERATE

Socrates' Prison. 20 Mitséon St. ☎ **01/922-3434.** Reservations recommended. Main courses Dr 1,400–Dr 2,700 ($6–$11.50). Mon–Sat 7pm–1am. Closed Aug. Half block down from southeast corner of Acropolis. GREEK/CONTINENTAL.

This is a local favorite for travelers and hip young locals, situated near the Acropolis. You dine at long, family style tables or outdoors in summer. The meat dishes are well prepared and come in large portions; the salads are fresh; and the retsina is flavorful. New additions on the menu include continental dishes such as pork roll stuffed with vegetables and salad niçoise.

✪ **Strofi Tavern.** 25 Rovértou Gálli St. ☎ **01/921-4130.** Reservations recommended. Main courses Dr 2,400–Dr 3,500 ($10–$15). Mon–Sat 7pm–2am. Two blocks south of Acropolis. GREEK.

The view of the Acropolis from the rooftop garden of this long-time favorite restaurant is wonderful. The Strofi Tavern offers a varied cuisine marked by interesting cheeses, fine olive oil, and fresh ingredients. Every dish is well presented and served. We especially like the fine mezedes (appetizers) and the excellent lamb and veal courses. In the winter, there's a Saturday brunch with 20 mezedes and ouzo.

INEXPENSIVE

Panathinea Pizzeria/Cafeteria. 27/29 Makriyánni St. ☎ **01/923-2721.** Main courses Dr 900–Dr 2,600 ($3.85–$11.05). V. Daily 8:30am–1am. Across from the Center for Acropolis Studies. GREEK/ITALIAN.

An unpretentious place that serves really good food at very reasonable prices. If the street side is too noisy for you, go inside for air-conditioned comfort. The pizza is especially good, the country salad is fresh and ample, the chicken souvlaki is tender and juicy, and the moussaká is delicious.

KOUKÁKI
MODERATE

Firenze Gelateria Pasticceria. 42 Dimitrakopoúlou St. ☎ **01/922-7156.** Pastries, ice cream: Dr 600–Dr 2,000 ($2.55–$8.50). No credit cards. 9am–2am. At corner of Drákou St. DESSERTS.

This comfortable and hip spot serves superb gelati and graniti (sorbets)—strawberry, melon, banana, kiwi, and more, all pure and fresh—outdoors under the trees or in the marbled modern indoor space. The pastries—tarts, cheesecakes, rich cream cakes—are superior, with cappuccino and espresso that are the best in town. You'll find it well worth the walk. Across the plaza is Gargareta Pizza, which serves reasonably decent pizza.

INEXPENSIVE

Meltemi. 26 Zinní St. ☎ **01/902-8230.** Main courses Dr 750–Dr 2,000 ($3.20–$8.50). No credit cards. Mon–Sat noon–1:30am. GREEK.

If you are arriving at or leaving from the Olympic Airways office on Syngroú Avenue, the Meltemi is a nearby ouzerí that's a good stopover for a light meal or drink. Trees and shrubs shade the distinctive blue chairs and tables. Go inside and choose from the fresh shrimp or stuffed green peppers. A bottle of ouzo costs Dr 600 ($2.50).

5   Exploring the Acropolis

The Acropolis is open in summer, Monday through Friday 8am to 7pm; Saturday, Sunday, and holidays hours are 8:30am to 7pm. Admission is Dr 2,000 ($8.50), half price for students. (Check with the Greek Tourist Office (☎ 01/323-4130) for reduced spring, fall, and winter hours.) Photographing with a camera without flash and amateur videotaping is allowed free of charge. The main approach to the Acropolis is the path from near the intersection of Dioskoúron and Theorías streets in the southwest corner of Pláka. You can also approach it through the Ancient Agora from Adrianoú St. or from the south side to the left of the Odeum of Heródes Átticus.

The Acropolis is the most famous site in Greece; for more than 3,000 years, it has been the center of life in Athens. Once the center of religious cults, it draws us today as the most impressive site in Greece from the Classical period, when Athens was at the peak of its artistic and intellectual strength.

THE BEULÉ GATE

The only entrance to the Acropolis is from the west, where the ascent is less precipitous, through the Beulé Gate, named after the French archaeologist who discovered it in 1853. This gate was probably built, using parts from older monuments, by the Roman emperor Valerian in A.D. 267.

The wide steps and angled stone path lead up what was in antiquity the steep, wide ramp to the Propylaia, the commanding entrance to the Acropolis. The bastion to the right holds the Temple of Athena Nike and the towering pedestal on the left is the Monument of Agrippa. The pedestal was built in 178 B.C. by King Eumenes of Pergamum to celebrate his victory in a chariot race. Statues of Antony and Cleopatra replaced King Eumenes's chariot when the lovers stayed in Athens, before their defeat by Octavian at the battle of Actium in 31 B.C. Agrippa, a close friend of Octavian's who commanded Octavian's forces at Actium, became first minister when Octavian was made Augustus. Agrippa treated Athens generously, and the Athenians erected a four-horse chariot on the pedestal in his honor.

THE TEMPLE OF ATHENA NIKE

The Temple of Athena Nike high up on the right is the first reminder of the primarily religious function of the Acropolis. The temple is positioned to overlook the right side of anyone ascending; the right side was the vulnerable side, for soldiers carried their shields on their left arm. It was fitting that city's protector should be in this crucial defensive position. This site had probably been associated with Athena since archaic times. The beautiful little Ionic temple was completed in approximately 424 B.C., about eight years after the sculptural decoration on the Parthenon was finished. What you see today is the second reconstruction, completed in 1940.

The larger structure on the right is the **Pinakotheke** (picture gallery), which contained couches upon which visitors to the sanctuary could rest. No trace of the paintings have survived, but Pausanias describes some of them.

THE PROPYLAIA

The Propylaia was built immediately after the Parthenon (437–432 B.C.) to provide a commanding entrance, which it still does. Six large Doric columns provide five doorways to the deep outer porch, which is supported by six somewhat more delicate Ionic columns.

The view of the sanctuary from the Propylaia, looking ahead and slightly to the left to the Erechtheum and, higher and to the right to the Parthenon, is still impressive more than 2,400 years later. In front of the Propylaia, the 5th-century B.C. visitor would have seen the colossal **statue of Athena Promachos,** a bronze statue so tall that the reflection of Athena's helmet and spear could be seen by ships at sea. The only indications today of where the statue stood are cuttings in the rock and a block

Athens Attractions

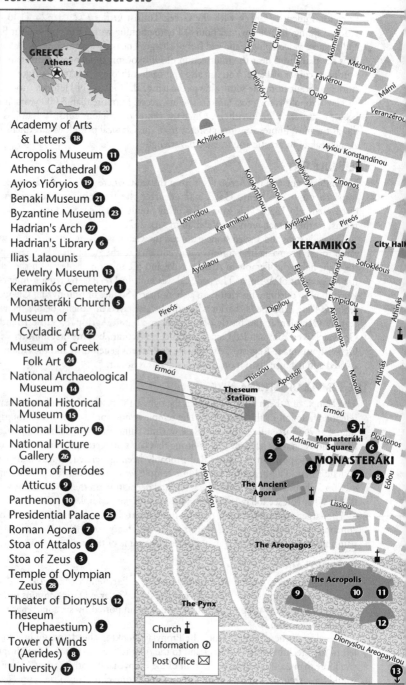

Academy of Arts
 & Letters 18
Acropolis Museum 11
Athens Cathedral 20
Ayios Yióryios 19
Benaki Museum 21
Byzantine Museum 23
Hadrian's Arch 27
Hadrian's Library 6
Ilias Lalaounis
 Jewelry Museum 13
Keramikós Cemetery 1
Monasteráki Church 5
Museum of
 Cycladic Art 22
Museum of Greek
 Folk Art 24
National Archaeological
 Museum 14
National Historical
 Museum 15
National Library 16
National Picture
 Gallery 26
Odeum of Heródes
 Atticus 9
Parthenon 10
Presidential Palace 25
Roman Agora 7
Stoa of Attalos 4
Stoa of Zeus 3
Temple of Olympian
 Zeus 28
Theater of Dionysus 12
Theseum
 (Hephaestium) 2
Tower of Winds
 (Aerides) 8
University 17

GREECE
Athens

KERAMIKÓS   City Hall

Church
Information
Post Office

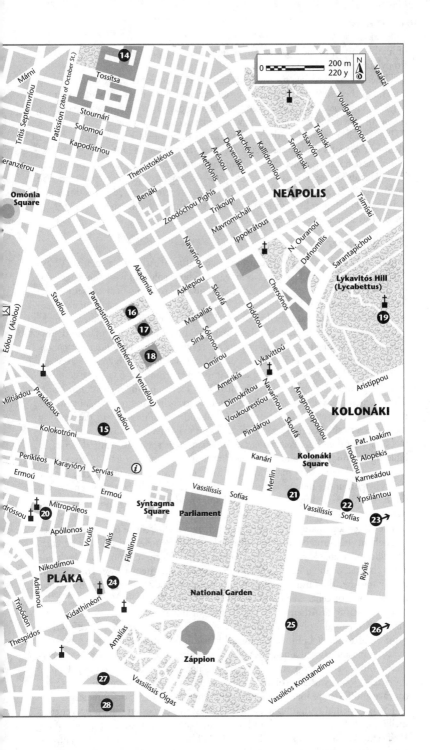

of marble carved in the egg-and-dart design, about 35 yards directly in front of the Propylaia.

The entire way between the Propylaia and the Parthenon's entrance at the far, eastern end of the temple was lined with innumerable shrines, most of them sculptures, of gods and heroes. The ancient visitor would have passed through these shrines along the north side of the Parthenon over what today seems empty rock.

The area immediately to the right, south, of the Propylaia was occupied by the **Shrine of Artemis Brauronia,** a cult imported from Brauron in Attica.

The next building along the southern ramparts was used for storing bronze objects—shields, armor, vessels, votive offerings—belonging to the many sanctuaries on the Acropolis. The only traces of it evident today are a few squared poros stones and a shallow foundation line cut into the stone that interrupts the steps leading up to the southwest corner of the Parthenon.

THE PARTHENON

The name *Parthenon* comes from the huge statue of Athena Parthénos (Virgin Athena), once inside the temple. Nothing of this huge gold and ivory statue remains, but a small Roman copy of it is in the National Archaeological Museum. The Parthenon was erected between 447 and 438 B.C., although the sculptural decorations were not completed until 432 B.C. Archaeologists are uncertain about how many temples have been built here, but there may have been an archaic temple on the site that was pulled down to accommodate what is referred to as the Older Parthenon, on which work began a few years after the Athenian defeat of the Persians at Marathon. When the Persians occupied and burned Athens in 480 B.C., they destroyed everything on the Acropolis, including this Older Parthenon still under construction. The Athenians vowed not to rebuild the desecrated shrines and temples, but after 33 years Athens had reached a point of political and economic strength that enabled them to adopt the plan proposed by Perikles for major temple construction.

To support the Older Parthenon the Athenians had created an artificial terrace by building retaining walls south of the building and laying many courses of poros stone foundation. There are as many as 22 of these courses, approximately five times a man's height, under the southeast corner where the Acropolis falls off steeply to the south. Perikles added to the rampart wall and raised the terrace to the present level just before work began on the new Parthenon.

The Athenians spared no expense on their new temple. The only material used throughout the entire building was marble from Mt. Penteli, and sculptural decoration filled all available space. The Parthenon had 17 Doric columns along each side and 8, instead of the usual 6, at each end. The columns are narrower and set more closely together than usual, giving an impression of solidity in contrast to the large central room, or cella. The cella was large to accommodate the 36-foot-high gold-and-ivory statue of Athena. The visual effect of the architecture is extraordinarily subtle, unsurpassed for balance and harmony. The architect ("master builder") Iktinus maintained a strict 9:4 ratio in length/width, width/height, and the distance between the columns and their diameter. Any possible appearance of disproportion was corrected: Lines were slightly curved to appear straight, an optical illusion called *éntasis* (intensifications), with the columns bowed slightly inward (6cm) to avoid appearing concave and the steps inclined 12 centimeters over their length of 70 meters.

The pedimental sculptures left after the disastrous explosion caused by Venetian shelling in 1687 were carted off to London by Lord Elgin in the first decade of the 19th century. Those that survived the process of being taken down, and the journey, are still on display in the British Museum, although the Greek government has repeatedly requested their return. On the west pediment, the only remnants still in their original position are the badly damaged remains of statues of Kekrops and his daughter and, in the southern corner, of a nymph. On the east pediment, the only original sculptures are the heads of two horses from the sun god's chariot in the southern corner and the head of one horse from the moon goddess's chariot in the northern corner. (The reclining figure on the east pediment, probably Diónysos, is a modern copy.) The western pediment once showed the contest between Athena and Poseidon for the city, and the eastern pediment, over the entrance to the temple, showed the birth of Athena.

Beneath the pediments a frieze consisting of triglyphs and metopes, continued around all four sides of the temple (*triglyphs* are three vertical bands separated by grooves, and *metopes* are the panels between them). All 92 of these metopes—the first Greek temple to have this number, for they were very expensive—had sculptural decoration. The triglyphs and traces of the badly damaged metopes can be seen easily. The west side showed the battle between King Theseus and the Athenians against the Amazons, the east side the battle between the gods and the giants, the south side the battle with the centaurs, and on the north side were scenes from the Trojan War. Most of the surviving metopes are from the southern side and are now in the British Museum.

The sculptural decoration took on a new dimension for a Doric temple—the frieze was decorated all the way around the temple building itself, inside the columns of the peristyle. The last remaining section still in its original position was recently taken down by Greek archaeologists for repair, and will be replaced by a cast. This frieze, just over a meter high and 160 meters long, shows the Panathenaic procession, the most important religious festival Athenians held to honor their goddess.

If you want a better idea of what the Parthenon and its decoration look like, visit the **Center for Acropolis Studies** (see "The Museums of Athens," below), southwest of the Acropolis, where admission is free.

The Parthenon continued in use as a religious building after Christianity replaced the pagan cults. Late in the 6th century, the temple was converted into an Orthodox church, and when the Crusaders occupied Athens, they made this church Catholic. The Turks, in turn, converted the church into a mosque. During these changes, the building was altered only slightly. The ancient structure remained in good condition until September 26, 1687, when Venetian cannon fire ignited the munitions the Turks had stored in the Parthenon, blowing off the roof and doing major damage to the building. When the Turks returned shortly thereafter, they built a small mosque in the ruins, dismantled by archaeologists in 1844. The next major blow to the building was the removal, between 1801 and 1811, of much of the greatest sculpture on the Acropolis, in particular the Parthenon pediment sculptures, by Lord Elgin. Many pieces were destroyed in this process. Fighting between Greeks and Turks for the Acropolis in 1821–22 and 1826–27 contributed further damage. Archaeological research and restoration began in 1834. The most recent danger is from air pollution and tourism. To protect the site, buses no longer drive up toward the entrance nor may visitors walk into the Parthenon.

The first temple on the Acropolis is thought to have been built in the 8th century B.C. in what is now the wide area between the Parthenon and the Erechtheum. No traces of such a temple exist, but Homer mentions it in both the *Iliad* and the *Odyssey*. Prevailing archaeological opinion holds that this early temple was replaced by another temple around the end of the 7th century B.C., of which the only remains are the two column bases covered by iron grillwork in the eastern end of the Old Temple of Athena near the southeastern corner of the Caryatid Porch. This temple, in turn was replaced in the 6th century B.C. by the Peisistratid tyrants. It is the foundations of this 6th century temple, known as the Old Temple of Athena, which you can see today.

Until it was destroyed in 480 B.C., the Old Temple of Athena housed the ancient wooden statue of Athena Pólias, the goddess as protector of the city, which was the focus of the Panathenaic Festival. This festival seems to date from Mycenaean times. In 566 B.C., it was reorganized to include the Greater Panathenaic Festival, perhaps the most important religious festival held in ancient Athens. The central act in this festival was the bringing of a newly woven cloth gown in which to dress the sacred statue. Every four years, the new gown was placed on the mast of a wooden ship on wheels which was pulled along the Panathenaic Way through what we call the ancient Greek Agora until the ascent became too steep. The gown was then carried on foot up to the Acropolis and placed on the statue. Many other activities, such as plays and athletic contests, were associated with the festival.

The ancient wooden statue of Athena Pólias must have been saved from the Persian destruction, for when the Athenians rebuilt their shrines and temples on the Acropolis, they placed the statue in the Erechtheum. For the intervening 74 years between the Persian destruction and the building of the new temple, the statue of Athena Polias may have been placed in the surviving western end of the Old Temple of Athena. Athenian resources had been reduced during the long years of the Peloponnesian Wars, and the death of Perikles in 329 B.C. removed the strongest advocate of the plan to glorify the Acropolis, but nonetheless, the Athenians could not leave their most revered statue in a temporary accommodation.

THE ERECHTHEUM

The Erechtheum, the most complex of all the temples on the Acropolis, was constructed between 421 and 406 B.C. It was the tomb of Erecteus and housed the most ancient Athenian cults. Erechtheus was the mythical king of Athens, the son of the god Hephaistos and Earth, who was raised by Athena. Because of his close association with the earth he is often represented as half man, half snake or simply by a snake, and Athena, because of her association with him, is often represented with a snake or snakes.

The Erechtheumn consists of the main temple (divided into two sections) and two porches at its western end, all built in the Ionian order on four different levels. Archaeologists differ over whether the statue of Athena Polias was in the eastern or the western section of the main temple, but they agree that the Erechtheum was built on the site Athenians associate with the contest between Poseidon and Athena for the city. The ancient builders left a hole in the ceiling of the northern porch to show where Poseidon's trident was thrust to make the salt spring gush forth. They also left a hole in the floor so visitors could look down and see the marks the trident had made in the rock. Today the site is roped off, but the holes in the roof and the floor can easily be seen.

Altars to several other gods were in or near the Erechtheum. An altar to Zeus Hypatos (Supreme) was just outside the entrance. Inside the building were three altars: one on which sacrifices were offered to both Poseidon and Erechtheus, one to Boutos (Erechtheus's brother), and one to Hephaistos. The building also contained an ancient wooden statue of Hermes, the tomb of Erechtheus and the sacred snake, a chair made by Daidalos, spoils taken from the Persians, and an "eternally burning" golden lamp made by Kallimachos, the man who invented the Corinthian capital. A cistern holding the saltwater from Poseidon's salt spring was said to have been beneath the building. The tomb of Kekrops was beneath the southwestern corner of the main temple and the northwestern corner of the southern porch, the famous Caryatid Porch. (Kekrops was the mythical first king of Athens sometimes, as was Erechtheus, said to be the son of Hephaistos and Earth and often represented as half man, half snake.)

The **Caryatid Porch** is named after the six draped maidens, 1 1/2 times life size, supporting the porch roof. The name may have come originally from *kórai*, the Greek word for "maidens." All of the Caryatids now supporting the roof are modern copies. One Caryatid was removed during the Ottoman occupation and has since disappeared and one, now in the British Museum, was taken by Lord Elgin. The four remaining Caryatids are in the Acropolis Museum, where they are kept in a controlled environment behind glass, safe from the ravages of atmospheric pollution.

The area immediately west of the Erechtheion was also sacred ground, containing a **sanctuary to Pandrosos,** Kekrops's daughter and the first priestess of Athena, and an **altar to Zeus Herkaios,** Zeus as god of the household. The altar to Zeus Herkaios was said to have been beneath the Athena's olive tree, which won her the city in the contest with Poseidon. According to Herodotus, the 5th-century B.C. "father of history," Athena's olive tree was burned during the Persian sack of the Acropolis, but fresh shoots grew from the old trunk. The tree was still standing in the 1st century A.D. An olive tree, albeit a modern one, grows on the same spot today.

THE ACROPOLIS MUSEUM

The Acropolis Museum is in the southeastern corner of the acropolis, set low in the ground to be as inconspicuous as possible. (Entrance is included with that to the site.)

Room 1 contains remains of pedimental sculpture from archaic temples on the Acropolis, possibly from the archaic temple built on the site of the Parthenon. The most impressive piece is a lioness killing a calf.

Room 2 also has archaic remains, notably two large pedimental sculptures. The pedimental sculpture on the left has two large serpents facing each other. The center is missing from the pedimental sculpture on the right, but you can see the headless torso of Hercules fighting with Triton, a pre-Greek mythological figure with a serpent's tail, while on the right waits Nereus, "the old man of the sea" with three serpentlike bodies and three human heads. The most famous sculpture in this room is the *Calf-Bearer, Moschophoros,* a koúros (archaic statue of a young man) carrying a calf across his shoulders, dating from 570 B.C.

Room 3 is dominated by the pedimental sculpture of two lions tearing at a bull. Only part of the bull's trunk and the hind legs of the lions remain. The other statues in this room all date between 540 and 520 B.C.

Room 4 has some of the most beautiful archaic korai (statues of young women). The Peplos Kore, the smaller Maiden of Chios, the Kore with the Almond Eyes, all with gentle archaic smiles. The so-called Rampin Rider, also in this room, is the oldest statue of a mounted rider in Greek art, dating to the mid-6th century B.C.

Room 5 contains the pedimental sculpture of the battle between the gods and the giants, representing the triumph of Greek civilization over barbarism, from the Old Temple of Athena. The restored figure of the goddess leans dramatically forward and to the left, wearing a cloak edged with snakes.

Room 6 has slightly later work, dating from the first half of the 5th century B.C. Both the head known as the Blond Youth (because, when found, the yellow color of his hair still could be seen) and the Kritios Boy date from 480 B.C. They are much more lifelike than the stiffer, archaic koúroi, and the magnificent forepart of a horse is also fully alert. The famous Mourning Athena relief, showing Athena leaning on her spear before a stele, is on the wall by the door between rooms 5 and 6.

Rooms 7 and **8** contain the reliefs remaining in Athens from the Parthenon frieze, the Erechtheum frieze, and the temple of Athena Nike.

Room 9 has the four remaining Caryatids from the Erechtheion, safe behind glass.

Before leaving the Acropolis, you may wish to go the raised rampart with the flagpole on the northeast wall known as the **Belvedere,** which offers a wonderful view over the city immediately below and much of the Attic Plain.

6 Sites North of the Acropolis

THE AREOPAGOS

The rocky hill below the Acropolis to the northwest—to the right and down the slope as you leave the Acropolis entrance—is the **Areopagos (Hill of Ares),** which gave its name to the Council of the Areopagos. At first a body of advisors to the king, the council became a court of law and its decisions were final. In the 4th century B.C. the council met in the Royal Stoa in the Agora, but for murder cases it always convened on the Areopagos.

The name comes from the myth about Ares, the god of war, who was tried here and acquitted for killing Halirrhothios, Poseidon's son, who had raped Ares's daughter. In the last act of the tragedy of the house of Atreus, Orestes was acquitted by the Council of the Areopagos for killing his mother, Clytemnestra. Athena cast the deciding vote for acquittal, after which, according to Aeschylus, the Furies fled underground down a cleft in the Areopagos.

The Council of the Areopagos had jurisdiction over constitutional and religious matters, so when the Apostle Paul visited Athens in A.D. 49 with "new teaching," he was summoned to appear before it. The Greek text of St. Paul's speech before the Areopagos (Acts 17:22–31) is inscribed in a large plaque on the east side of the stairs climbing the Areopagos. Dionysios the Areopagite became St. Paul's first Athenian convert; he was later canonized as St. Dionysios, the patron saint of Athens.

If you are going to visit the Ancient Greek Agora after the Acropolis, take the pleasant downhill walk through the trees to get there. An opening in the fence to the east (right as you face the Areopagos) leads to a path bending down to the right that joins the ancient **Panathenaic Way,** clearly evident by large cobblestones, alongside which cement has been laid. The descent will take you about five minutes.

THE ANCIENT GREEK AGORA

The Ancient Greek Agora, Below the Acropolis, just North of Monastterák Square. ☎ **01/ 321-0185.** Admission Dr 1,200 ($5) half price for students. Daily 8:30am–3:45pm.

We don't have the space to describe all the myriad remains in the Agora. What follows is a selection of the most prominent, in terms of their historical importance.

The Ancient Greek Agora was used for virtually all public pursuits—religious, commercial, political, civic, educational, philosophical, theatrical, and athletic. In ancient Greek the word *agorá* meant "gathering place," but today it means "market." It was the center of Athenian life.

Throughout late antiquity, the Byzantine period, and the Latin and Ottoman occupations, the area was residential, but the fighting during the War of Independence destroyed most of the houses. After the war was over, the area became densely populated. The first archaeological dig was made in 1859, and in 1890–91 the construction of the railway uncovered ancient remains. The American School of Classical Studies, backed by funding from John D. Rockefeller Jr., proposed to compensate the people living in the area and undertake archaeological excavations. The Greek government agreed, and most of the Agora was made an archaeological site. Excavations began in 1931 and, except for the period of World War II, have continued ever since.

Today what you see are the remains of many different periods of life in the Agora. The buildings of the archaic Agora were located on the west, before the hill of Kolonos Agoraios (Market Hill). If you have entered the Agora from the main gate on Adrianou Street, ignore the urge to continue on the wide path up to the reconstructed Stoa of Attalos, and turn right after coming down the entrance ramp, and head in the direction of the hill and the Hephaisteion. The development of the area below the hill as a civic center of ancient Athens came at the same time as the laws defining civil life. In the western part of the Agora were the many stoa (porticos) where civic functions took place. The **Panathenaic Way,** the road cutting diagonally through the Agora from the **Dipylon Gate** (in the Keramikós cemetery, about 500 yards west on Ermoú Street) to the Acropolis, was used for theatrical performances and various athletic events, which were viewed by spectators from temporary wooden stands. The Peisistratid tyrants probably were responsible for constructions in the southeast and southwest parts of the Agora.

After the Peisistratid tyrants were removed from power, Kleisthenes instituted reforms in 508–07 B.C., which broke the power of the aristocracy and laid the foundations of Athenian democracy. All Athenian citizens were assigned to 10 tribes, each of which provided 50 men to serve in the senate for a year. The senate met every day except during festivals. (The assembly of all citizens met about every ten days on the Pnyx.) The **Old Bouleuterion (senate house)** was built on the west side of the Agora to accommodate these 500 newly created senators. The **Royal Stoa,** the first Athenian stoa, was constructed at about the same time.

When the Persians occupied Athens in 480 B.C. they destroyed all they could in the Agora as well as on the Acropolis. The Athenians responded with a flurry of building activity, no doubt encouraged by their vow not to rebuild the desecrated shrines and temples on the Acropolis.

Right after the final defeat of the Persians at Plataia in 479 B.C, the Athenians built the Painted Stoa and the Tholos, and rebuilt the Royal Stoa and the Old Bouleuterion, all on the west side of the Agora.

The three most important administrators of Athens were the military commander; the archon, responsible for civil administration; and the so-called "king archon," responsible for religion and certain legal aspects associated with religion. The king archon had the title "king" but not kingly power, for the archons (including six judicial archons, making a total of nine) were elected to office by the popular assembly and served for one year, after which they all became members for life of the Council of the Areopagos. The king archon worked in the Royal Stoa. By about 400 B.C., the city's laws were inscribed on stone and set up in the stoa so any citizen could refer to them. The Royal Stoa is in the northwestern area of the archaeological site, between the railway line and Adrianou Street.

Outside the archaeological site across Adrianou Street you can see the remains of part of the **Painted (Poikile) Stoa,** which was just across the Panathenaic Way from the Royal Stoa. Souvenirs of Athenian military victories were kept here—the name comes from the many paintings of Athenian military exploits displayed on wooden panels—but the building's fame comes from its popular use. Sword swallowers, jugglers, and hawkers attracted crowds here, and so did philosophers. The Stoic school of philosophers derives its name from this stoa, because Zeno, founder of the school, taught his followers here regularly.

Inside the archaeological site running up to the railway line are the remains of the **Stoa of Zeus Elefthérios** (Freedom), which was immediately south of the Royal Stoa. It was built in 430–420 B.C. in honor of Zeus, who had helped keep the Athenians free from the Persians. This stoa seemed, unusually, to have functioned both as a temple and as a civic building. Socrates met his followers here.

Behind the Stoa of Zeus on the low hill is the **Hephaístion** (often called the **Theseum** [*Thissío*]), built between 460 and 420 B.C. This Doric temple was dedicated to Hephaistos and Athena and is the best preserved ancient Greek temple in the world. Since part of the frieze depicts the exploits of Theseus, the temple was originally thought to have been dedicated to Theseus; the nearby rail station is still called Theseum (*Thissío*). In the 7th century, the temple was converted into the Church of St. George.

Leaving the Hephaístion, walk to your right, south, along the paved path until you come to an open area with a large reconstructed site plan displayed in a case. This gives a clear view of the Agora together with an impression of what it looked like in A.D. 150.

If you continue on the path down to the Agora you will pass the round **Thólos,** built in 465 B.C. basically as a dining hall for the senate's executive committee. The 50 members of each tribal contingent took turns serving for approximately one month on this executive committee, responsible for the city's daily business. During this month they were fed at public expense in the Tholos. At night at least 17 senators slept in the Tholos so decisions could be made quickly in case of emergency. Immediately north of the Tholos is the **Old Bouleuterion,** built after the reforms of Kleisthenes in 508 B.C. Adjacent to it on the west is the **New Bouleuterion,** built in 415–06 B.C. The Old Bouleuterion (under the name Metroon) continued in use as the storage place for official archives.

East of the Old Bouleuterion and across the **Great Drain,** which cleared the Agora from rain water flowing from the surrounding hillsides, are the long, narrow foundations of the **monument of the Eponymous Heroes.** When the ten tribes were created, the oracle at Delphi helped select 10 early Athenian heroes to give their names to the tribes, from which the word *eponymous* ("giving name") derives. Statues of these heroes were erected late in the 5th century, although it is not known exactly where; the foundations you now can see date from approximately 330 B.C. Notices for members of the tribes were posted beneath the statue of each tribe's hero. Pending legislation and other matters of public concern were also posted here so, in effect, this was the city's bulletin board, a fundamental democratic tool.

South of the Tholos slightly to the west is the **Strategion,** the office of the military commander and the ten generals.

The ancient Athenians had an extremely active legal system, with juries ranging in size from 201 to over 2,500. A **large law court** was built in the northeast section of the Agora to supplement the smaller 6th-century B.C. law court (Heliaia). Stoas that could accommodate large juries were used as law courts, and cases were held in the open as well. Crimes were usually paid for with fines or exile, but some people were detained and certainly the death penalty was imposed upon Socrates in 399 B.C. It has been argued that the prison where this took place may have been approximately 100 meters to the southwest of the Strategeion, outside the boundaries of the Agora.

The southern area of the Agora has the remains of a **Classical stoa,** known as **South Stoa I** to distinguish it from the **Hellenistic stoa** later built on the same site. This may have been used by the city officials in charge of weights and measures and coinage, for the **city mint** was at the eastern end of the building behind the **Southeast Fountainhouse** near the restored 11th-century **Church of the Holy Apostles.**

The Peisistratid tyrants probably were responsible for the Southeast Fountainhouse as well as the large almost square law court (Heliaia) in the southwest.

There was no major construction under Macedonian rule, although the **Southwest Fountainhouse** and a **water clock** were built in the southwest corner of the Agora and the small **Temple of Apollo Patroös** was built immediately south of the Stoa of Zeus.

The big change in the Agora took place with the construction in the 2nd century B.C. of the **Stoa of Attalos.** King Attalos II of Pergamum (159–38 B.C.) in Asia Minor had, apparently, enjoyed his time studying in Athens in his youth, and built the huge stoa on the east side of the Agora. In the 1950s the stoa was reconstructed by the American School of Classical Studies to provide museum and office space. You should not miss the **small museum** it contains (see the Agora Museum, below).

Another large stoa, the **Middle Stoa,** was built towards the south of the Agora, and, parallel to it to the south, **South Stoa II.**

During Roman rule the structure of the Agora was fundamentally altered when the large open central space was filled with the **Temple of Ares** and the much larger **Odeum** (*Odíon*, covered concert hall) **of Agrippa.** The Temple of Ares was, in fact, a 5th-century B.C. temple dismantled and moved from its original, unknown site and re-erected here in the Agora during the reign of Augustus. The huge Odeum of Agrippa, probably completed by 12 B.C., was at least three stories high and could seat 1,000 people. After 150 years, the 25-meter unsupported span of the Odeum roof collapsed. It was reconstructed with an interior supporting wall for the roof, which cut the size of the auditorium in half, to seat only 500. The remodeling included the huge Giants (half man, half snake) and Tritons (half man, half fish) which so command attention when you enter the Agora from Adrianoú Street.

The Agora Museum. ☎ 01/32-10-185. Admission fee included with that to site. Tues–Sun 8:30am–2:45pm.

The museum, on the ground floor of the Stoa of Attalos, is one long room, taking up what would have been space for ten ancient shops. It displays representative finds from 5,000 years of Athenian history, all clearly marked. To me, the most interesting displays in the museum are the bronze ballots, the allotment machine, and the ostraka.

Displayed along the left wall in a case just before the allotment machine are the **bronze ballots,** used in determining votes by juries. They have the form of small wheels with axles: Those with solid axles indicate a vote for acquittal, the ones with hollow axles meant a vote for conviction. ("There's a hole in his story," says one archaeologist.) Each juror was given a ballot with a hollow and a solid axle, which he held between thumb and forefinger so his vote would be secret.

On the left wall a little past the center of the room from the entrance, the **marble allotment machine** shows how far the Athenians went to make sure that courts were fair. Each tribe had to have a minimum of 20 men available for jury duty, who served for a year. Each juror was issued a bronze identification ticket that fit into the slots in the allotment machine. On the day of a trial the men appointed jurors would appear before the magistrate, who would collect all the identification tickets in baskets by tribes. The magistrate would then insert the tickets from each tribe in vertical rows of slots, one vertical row for each tribe. Into a hollow tube at the top of the machine he would then insert a mixture of black and white balls that would line up in the tube in random order. A crank at the bottom of the machine released a single ball. If the first ball was white, then all the jurors from the first horizontal row of identification tickets were on jury duty. If the second ball was black, then the jurors on the second horizontal row were free for the day, and so forth, until a full complement of jurors was selected. This procedure guaranteed that all tribes participated in the court decision and, as well, jurors for a particular case could not be bribed because they were selected just before the trial began.

Óstraka, the origin of our word *ostracism,* are potsherds, small pieces of pottery. These are in a case by the right wall just past the allotment machine. Every year, the ancient Athenians voted by scratching on ostraka the name of any individual they thought was becoming too powerful and might become a tyrant. If a majority of the required 6,000 votes cast had one name, the individual named would be exiled from Athens for ten years. The practice proved not to be the safeguard it was intended. In 443 B.C., Pericles arranged to have his chief rival ostracized. In 417 B.C., Alcibiades and Nikias, the two main rivals for power, had their followers vote against a third man so neither of them would be ostracized. The practice was abandoned after this fiasco.

THE ROMAN AGORA

The **Roman agora** is just south of Hadrian's Library, up Areos past the sidewalk hawkers, left on Dexipou past the wicker shops and then right past the **Church of Ayíi Taxiárchi** (**the Archangels**). The area is known as the Roman agora because most of the remains excavated date from the Roman period, but this entire area had been used as the commercial center for Athens since earliest times. What is referred to today as the ancient Greek agora was the civic center for administration offices, law courts, and temples.

The monumental **Gate of Athena Archéyetis** (Athena the Leader) consists of four Doric columns supporting an architrave and pediment. Paid for by Julius Caesar and Augustus, this was the entrance to the Roman agora, a huge (111 by 98 meters) rectangular court surrounded by columns, behind which were shops. Parts of many of the columns have be re-erected, particularly in the southeast corner of the colonnade, so you can easily see the extent of the building.

Just inside the archaeological site at the corner of Pános and Pelopída streets is the **Fethiye Mosque** (**Mosque of the Conquest**), built shortly after the Ottomans occupied Athens in 1456. It's named after Sultan Mehmet II, the Conqueror, who captured Constantinople in 1453. The mosque, which has been restored by the Greek Archaeological Service, is used as a storeroom and is not open to the public.

Pelopída continues across Aiolou as a wide walkway just outside the **Tower of the Wind,** *Aérides* to the Greeks, but known to archaeologists as the Clock of Andronikos Kyrrestos (*Kyrrestos* means "of Kyrros," a town in Syria). This octagonal building, built in the middle of the 1st century B.C., is famous for the relief carvings still clearly visible of the winged personifications of the winds. A weathervane on top of the building pointed to the appropriate relief as the wind blew. There were sundials on each of the eight sides, and inside was an intricate water-driven 24-hour clock.

In the 18th century, the Tower of the Winds was used as a religious lodge (*tekke*) by a community of Mevlevi dervishes, the famous whirling dervishes, who based their order on the teachings of the 13th-century Sufi mystic Jalal al-Din Rumi. In their dance, the dervishes sought to unite good and evil into the reality underlying both; that is, God. They danced every Friday after midday prayers.

The remains of a rectangular building in front of the Tower of the Winds adjacent to Pelopida are the **public latrines** built by the Roman emperor Vespasian (A.D. 70–77). The stone slab toilet seats can easily be seen. They must have been cold. Continuously running water flushed the waste down to the city's main sewer.

Facing the Tower of the Winds to the north is the ornate entrance gate of an **Islamic school** founded in 1721. Toward the end of the Ottoman period the buildings were used as a **prison** and the Turks hung condemned prisoners from a large plane tree in the courtyard. When the new Greek government arrived, it carried on the same practice, confirming the school's blackened reputation. The prison was closed in 1911.

Next to the Islamic school on the left as you walk up the slight incline is the **Museum of Greek Popular Musical Instruments,** a fine exhibition of musical instruments from all over the country, with clear English texts and earphones by every display so you can hear what you are seeing. If this is the way modern Greek museums are going, it's an excellent precedent. Open Tuesday through Sunday from 10am to 2pm, Wednesday to 7pm. Entrance is free.

7 Sites South of the Acropolis

The Odeum (Odíon) of Heródes Átticus. Dionyssíou Areopayítou Street, on the south slope of the Acropolis.

In a beautiful setting, this odeum was built by Herodes Atticus in A.D. 174 and originally had a cedar roof. Reconstructed in 1858 by the Greek Archeological Society, it's now used for concerts and plays in association with the Festival of Athens.

The long stoa to the right (east) of the odeum is 535 feet (163 meters) long and was built by Eumenes II of Pergamum (197–58 B.C.). His younger brother, Attalos II (159–38 B.C.), built the Stoa of Attalos, reconstructed in the Ancient Greek Agora.

Theater of Dionysos. Entrance on Dionyssíou Areopayítou on the south slope of the Acropolis. ☎ **01/322-4625.** Admission Dr 500 ($2). Daily 8:30am–2:30pm.

Scattered remains of a sanctuary to Dionysos are just inside the entrance to the archaeological site, but you will be drawn to the theater, built in approximately 330 B.C. to seat 15,000 people. The front row had 67 thrones; the central one was for the high priest of Dionysos.

Hadrian's Arch. Outside the archaeological site on Amalías Avenue, between the Temple of Olympian Zeus and Pláka.

This large arch, through which Hadrian probably marched in triumph to dedicate the Temple of Olympian Zeus in A.D. 132, separated the Greek and Roman cities. Each side of the architrave bears an inscription. On the west of the gate, the side of the old city, the inscription reads "This is Athens, the ancient city of Theseus." Another on the east side says "This is the city of Hadrian, not of Theseus." This would not be very apparent to the modern visitor, for few Roman remains are obvious other than the Temple of Olympian Zeus east of Hadrian's Arch. There are, however, extensive remains south of the Temple of Olympian Zeus, including a 2nd-century A.D. temple (probably dedicated to Kronos and Rhea) and a 3rd-century A.D. cemetery. Recent excavations on the east side of Vassilíssis Ólgas Avenue have revealed extensive Roman construction. These excavations are hard to see, but you can get a glimpse of them from the third-floor windows of the Jewish Museum of Greece at 36 Amalías (see Museums below).

The Temple of Olympian Zeus. Vassilíssis Ólgas and Amalías aves. (entrance on Vassilíssis Ólgas). ☎ **01/922-6330.** Admission Dr 500 ($2). Open Tues–Sun 8:30am–3pm.

The huge Temple of Olympian Zeus was first planned in 515 B.C. when Athens was ruled by the Peisistratids. Construction on the temple stopped when these tyrants were overthrown and was resumed only three centuries later under Antioches Epiphanes in 174 B.C. When Antioches Epiphanes died in 164 B.C., work stopped again, this time for slightly less than three centuries. The Roman emperor Hadrian decreed that work on the temple would resume, and finally in A.D. 132 he dedicated the largest temple to Zeus ever built. The temple is 360 by 143 feet (110 by 44 meters). The temple enclosure is 674 by 423 feet (206 by 129 meters).

North of the temple are the remains of a three-aisled early Christian basilica built late in the 5th century mostly of material taken from the temple. The church, probably dedicated to St. Nicholas, was in use until the 14th century. Northwest of the church are the remains of one of the many baths built by the Romans in Athens.

The Stadium. Vassiléos Konstandínou Avenue.

The modern stadium across from the Záppion park is a reconstruction of the ancient stadium first built in 330 B.C. for the athletic events held every four years as part of the Greater Panathenaia. The stadium was completely remodeled by Herodes Atticus for the Panathenaic Festival of A.D. 143–44, making it able to seat 50,000 people. Very little of this stadium remained in the 19th century when it was rebuilt again at the expense of a private Athenian citizen, Georgios Averoff, in time to be used for the first modern Olympic Games in 1896. The Greeks call it *Kallimármaro,* meaning Beautiful Marble.

The Vassiléos Konstandíou entrance is often closed. The small park on both sides of and behind the stadium is known by few visitors. It's a wonderful oasis of green from the summer heat, perfect for a picnic lunch. Enter from Archimídous Street in Pangráti behind the stadium through the gates to the sporting club. Pass the club building on the right and climb up to the running track behind the stadium. Down to the right you have a fine view over the Temple of Olympian Zeus and the Acropolis. The large Roman sarcophagus now next to the running track may have been used for Herodes Atticus.

8 The Museums of Athens

The National Archaeological Museum. 44 Patissíon (October 28 Avenue). (About ¹/₃ mile north of Omónia Square.) ☎ **01/821-7717.** Admission Dr 2,000 ($8.50), half price for students. Mon 11am–5pm, Tues–Fri 8am–5pm, Sat–Sun and holidays 8:30am–3pm. Take trolley no. 2, 4, 5, 9, 11, 12, 15, or 18 from Amalís St. south of Syntagma Square.

The large 19th-century building looks imposing, and its contents can appear daunting, but if you are selective you can see some beautiful museum pieces and learn something without undue strain. Below is a selection.

Room 4, directly in front of the main museum entrance, contains finds from the Mycenaean period (1600–1100 B.C.). The most famous of these are the gold objects excavated by Heinrich Schliemann in Mycenae in 1876, in particular the gold funerary mask Schliemann enthusiastically but erroneously identified as that of Agamemnon. The detail work on some of the gold cups, on the gold decorations on knives, and especially on signet rings is extraordinary. The rock crystal vase made in the shape of a duck is particularly graceful. Linear B, the script understood only after World War II to be an early form of Greek, is written on clay tablets that were found at Pýlos.

Room 5, to the left as you enter the Mycenaean room, contains prehistoric finds.

Room 6, to the right, is the Cycladic room, named after the circular island group in the central Aegean. Most of the distinctive Cycladic figurines in this room date from 3000 to 2000 B.C. The most famous is the small marble harp player gazing skyward as he plays, in the end of the room near the entrance.

The main sculptural collection begins with **Room 7,** the room to the left of the entrance lobby as you enter the museum. Most of the works in this and the following rooms on this side of the museum are from the Archaic period, but the central display in Room 7 is a huge clay funerary amphora from the Kerameikos cemetery dating from the middle of the 8th century B.C. The geometric decoration on the amphora illustrates why this period in Greek art is referred to as the Geometric period.

Room 8 has the Sounion Kouros, dating from the late 7th century B.C. These idealized statues of youths, standing solidly with their left feet forward, are a basic element in ancient Greek art. This particular kouros stood in the Temple of Poseidon at Cape Sounion until it was damaged by the Persians in 480 b.c. It was found in 1906.

Room 9 has a kouros, on the right as you enter, dating from the mid-6th century B.C. from the Cycladic island of Mílos. In the far left of the room is a kore, a female counterpart to a kouros, dating from the end of the 6th century B.C. The kore was found in Merenda (near Markópoulo) in Attica in 1972.

Room 10, through the door at the far left of Room 9 (as you enter) has the kouros that was found together with the kore in Room 9, perhaps brother and sister. Room 10A beyond has the Volomandra Kouros, also dating from the mid-6th century B.C.

Room 11, next to Room 8 away from the courtyard, has the Kéa Kouros, found on the Cycladic island of Kéa and dating from approximately 530 B.C., and the tall, delicately carved funerary stele of a bearded warrior made approximately 20 years later.

Room 12, in the far northwestern corner of the museum, has the funerary relief of a naked running soldier, also dating from approximately 510 B.C.

The outstanding exhibit in **Room 13** is the Anavyssos Kouros, dating from approximately 520 B.C. The inscription on the base says, "Stop and lament over the grave of dead Kroiros, whom furious Ares destroyed one day as he fought in the front rank."

Room 14 has funerary sculpture from the 5th century B.C., notably the relief of the so-called Self-Crowned Athlete from the Temple of Athena at Sounion.

Room 15 is dominated by the large bronze statue of Poseidon, known as the Poseidon of Artemision because it was found off Cape Artemision in Évvia. Few such large bronze statues survive from antiquity; this one dates from approximately 460 B.C.

Room 16 has a large white funerary vase of a young woman named Myrrine with a relief showing her being led to the underworld by Hermes while her relatives look on.

Room 17 has votive sculpture from Rhamnous in northern Attica, Fáliro, and Piraeus, all from the late 5th century B.C.

A door in the right (as you enter) of Room 17 leads to **Rooms 19** and **20** which have Classical sculpture and Roman copies of Classical sculpture. At the end of Room 20 is the very interesting, small, poor quality Roman copy in marble of the huge gold and ivory statue made by Phidias for the Parthenon.

Room 18 has more 5th-century B.C. funerary sculpture, notably that of a woman named Hegeso, shown seated on a chair and looking at something in her right hand while a young slave girl stands before her. This graceful relief, dating from approximately 410 B.C., is framed as though it were in a temple.

Room 21, outside Room 4 with the Mycenaean finds, has the wonderful bronze galloping horse and rider found together with the Poseidon of Artemision in Room 15. The horse and rider are much later than the Poseidon, dating from the 2nd century B.C. This room also has a fine marble Roman copy (1st century B.C.) of the 5th-century B.C. original of Apollo as a young man.

The primary exhibit in the long **Room 34** is the altar dedicated by the Athenian parliament early in the 2nd century B.C. to Aphrodite Hegemone and the Graces.

Room 36, to the left of Room 35 (with the stairs), has finds discovered by the archaeologist Konstantinos Karapanos.

Room 37 has small bronze finds from the Geometric, Archaic, and Classical periods.

Rooms 40 and 41 contain a new exhibit of Egyptian material. In the context of Greek art, it is interesting to see how the ancient Egyptian statues resemble Archaic Greek kouri.

The **upper floor** of the museum, reached by taking the stairs in Room 35, has seven rooms with the museum's extensive collection of ancient Greek pottery, from the Geometric period through the 4th century B.C. The real attraction of the upper floor, however, is the museum's extraordinary display of Minoan frescoes from Akrotíri, on Santoríni.

Return to **Room 21** with the Hellenistic bronze horse and rider and turn left into **Room 22,** which has 4th-century B.C. finds from Epidaurus in the Peloponnese.

Rooms 23 to **28** have 4th-century B.C. funerary and votive reliefs, of which the most outstanding is the monument in Room 28 of a man named Aristonautes, shown as a soldier in fighting posture, almost in the round, dating from the late 4th century B.C. Room 28 also has the famous bronze statue of a young man with his right arm raised dating from approximately 340 B.C. The statue was found with an ancient shipwreck off the coast of the southern island of Andíkythera in 1900.

Rooms 29 and **30** contain Hellenistic sculpture, including several fine bronze works. Toward the right wall at the far end of the room is the famous marble statue of Aphrodite threatening to hit Pan with her sandal while Eros hovers. This statue, dating from approximately 100 B.C., was found on the Cycladic island of Délos.

Rooms 31 through **33** contain Roman sculpture. By far the most interesting is the bronze equestrian statue of Augustus, the first Roman emperor, in Room 31. It dates from the last decade of the 1st century B.C. and was found in the sea off the coast of Évvia in 1979.

Stairs in the entrance lobby lead down a flight to a **cafeteria** and the **museum shop.**

The large building immediately south of the archaeological museum, toward the Acropolis, is the **Athens Polytechnic,** the place where a spontaneous student revolt against the junta in 1973 first revealed the extent of popular distaste for the dictatorship. The army drove a tank through the front gate and crushed the demonstration, killing many students. Flowers and wreaths are placed on the gate in commemoration each November 17 and a large, usually unruly, demonstration is held at night.

The Goulandris Museum of Cycladic and Ancient Art. 4 Neoph´ytou Douká, Kolonáki. ☎ **01/722-8321.** Admission Dr 400 ($1.70). Mon, Wed, Fri 10am–4pm, Sat 10am–3pm.

The Nicholas Goulandris Foundation opened this superb private museum in 1986. It contains masterpieces of Cycladic art from prehistoric times to the 4th century B.C. These wonderful, almost modern looking figures are exceptionally well displayed and labeled on three floors of a handsome marble facility.

The Byzantine Museum. 22 Vassilíssis Sofías Ave. at Vassiléos Konstandínou Ave. ☎ **01/723-1570.** Admission Dr 500 ($2), Dr 250 ($1) for students. Tues–Sun 8:30am–3pm. Twelve blocks west of Syntagma Square.

This museum is devoted to the art and history of the Byzantine era. Greece's most important collection of icons and religious art, along with sculptures, altars, mosaics, bishops' garments, bibles, and a small-scale reconstruction of an early Christian basilica, are exhibited on three floors around a courtyard.

The Museum of Greek Folk Art. 17 Kydathenéon St., Pláka. ☎ **01/322-9031.** Admission Dr 500 ($2), Dr 250 ($1) for students. Tues–Sun 10am–4pm. Across from the Metamórfossi Church.

Embroideries and costumes from all over the country are displayed here, but the most interesting collection is the series of folk paintings from the eccentric artist Theofilos Hadjimichael in the early years of this century.

The National Historical Museum. 13 Stadíou St. ☎ **01/323-7617.** Admission Dr 500 ($2), Dr 250 ($1) for students. Tues–Sun 9am–1:30pm. Two blocks northeast of S´yntagma Square, on left.

The country's primary ethnological museum contains traditional costumes and the personal effects of famous Greeks. There are objects relating to local life from the Byzantine period, the Turkish occupation, the Balkan Wars, and the War of Independence.

Benáki Museum. Vassilíssis Sofías Ave. at Koumbári. ☎ **01/361-1617.**

The private collection of the late Anthony Benáki, a wealthy Greek from Alexandria, Egypt, should reopen soon after a lengthy restoration. It's a rich collection of Hellenic, Byzantine, and post-Byzantine objects, including some fine icons, several rare manuscripts, and an extensive collection of Greek folk art, which should appeal to those interested in traditional handicrafts.

The Center for Acropolis Studies. 2-4 Makriyánni St. ☎ **01-923-9186.** Free admission. Open daily 9am–2:30pm and Mon, Wed, Fri 6–10pm. Southeast of the Acropolis.

This former military barracks was transformed under the direction of Melina Mercouri, as minister of culture, into a fine museum that offers significant insights into the former splendor of the Acropolis, as well as a welcome respite from the sun and traffic. It contains plaster casts of the most significant sculpture from the Parthenon, artifacts, reconstructions, photographs, drawings, and other exhibits.

The Ilias Lalaounis Jewelry Museum. 12 Kallispéri (corner with Karyátidon, below the Herodes Atticus theater). ☎ **01/922-1044.** Admission Dr 800 ($3.40). Mon & Wed 9am–9pm; Thurs, Fri, Sat 9am–3pm; Sun 10am–3pm.

The highly successful jewelry designer Ilias Lalaounis, in a burst of humility, established this museum to display his creations. The ground floor has a small workshop and a store. The first and second floors house the displays, and explanations tell where the artist got his inspiration. Some of the work is, indeed, impressive.

The Jewish Museum. 36 Queen Amalías Avenue, 3rd floor (not far from Hadrian's Gate). Free admission Sun–Fri 9am–1pm. (The museum is expected to move to new premises a few blocks away at 39 Níkis St.)

This museum traces the more than 2,000-year history of the Jewish community in Greece. Maps and illustrations showing the origins of this community are in the first room. Objects used in religious festivals and services, costumes, and photographs are displayed in the following four rooms. Maps and artifacts from the holocaust, which was catastrophic for Greek Jewry, are in room 6. Artifacts from the Zionist movement in Greece are displayed in room 7. Room 8 is a reconstruction of the Alkabetz Synagogue in Pátras, a traditional Romaniote synagogue.

9 Exploring Elsewhere in Athens

THE PNYX & THE PHILOPAPPOS MONUMENT—SOUTHWEST OF THE ACROPOLIS

The law courts and the representative assembly met in the Agora, but the full assembly of all citizens met every 10 days on the Pnyx, the central one of three heights west of the Acropolis and Agora, to vote on laws proposed by the senate. For votes to be valid, a minimum of 6,000 citizens—men, of course; women, children, and slaves did not vote—met in the curved slope of the hill overlooking the Agora and the Acropolis. Today the Pnyx is fenced off, formally accessible only when the **Sound and Light show** is being performed. The rock cuttings and large retaining wall of the assembly area are immediately southwest of the area where the chairs are placed for the Sound and Light show, that is, behind, higher, and to the right from the seating area as you face the Acropolis.

Southwest of the Acropolis and almost on a level with it on Philopáppos Hill, also called the Hill of the Muses, is the Philopáppos Monument. It's not within any archaeological site and can be reached at any time. It commands a wonderful view of the Acropolis.

This monument was built as a tomb for Philopappos, the last pretender to the throne of Commagene, a small kingdom in Asia Minor that existed from 80 B.C. until A.D. 72 when it was incorporated into the Roman empire. Philopappos settled in Athens and became a benefactor of the city, for which the citizens awarded him with this tomb dating from between A.D. 114 and 116. The tomb stands 43 feet (13 meters) high and is almost square. The rich architectural facade included statues of Philopappos; Antiochus IV, the last king to rule Commagene; and Seleucus I, the son of Antiochus IV and the founder of the Seleucid empire.

LYKAVITÓS (LYCABETTUS) HILL—NORTHEAST OF THE ACROPOLIS

This hill is 278 meters above sea level, higher than the Acropolis. The road up enters from Sarandapichou Street on the northwest side of the hill. A path begins just across the street from the St. George Lycabet Athenstus Hotel, on Kleomenous Street. A funicular lift operates from the corner of Doras D'Istria and Ploutárchou streets.

If you are blessed with a clear day, the view from the top of Lykavitós is incomparable, including much of Athens, Piraeus, and extending past Aegina down to Hýdra in the Saronic Gulf. On the summit, the small church dedicated to St. George may have been built on the site of a Byzantine church dedicated to Profítis Elías (the Prophet Elijah), which was probably built on a site sacred to the sun god Helios in ancient time. The restaurant here offers little more than a view.

STROLLING AROUND PLÁKA

Easily accessible by foot, Pláka extends from the curving northern walls of the Acropolis east to Amalías Avenue, west to the ancient Greek Agora, and north to Mitropóleos Street. In it you will find classical, Roman, Byzantine, and Ottoman antiquities; restaurants, tavernas, and small sandwich shops; modern boutiques offering fine jewelry, clothes, antiquities, and tourist glitz; and wonderful views.

Pláka is for casual walking and discovery. Cars are banned from much of Pláka so the area is an oasis from the automobile that Athenians, like the rest of us, are just

Sýntagma Square & Pláka

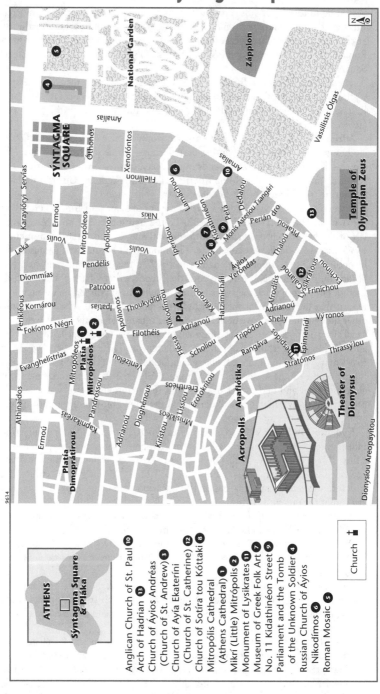

ATHENS

Sýntagma Square & Pláka

Anglican Church of St. Paul ⑩
Arch of Hadrian ⑬
Church of Áyios Andréas
(Church of St. Andrew) ③
Church of Ayía Ekateríni
(Church of St. Catherine) ⑫
Church of Sotíra tou Kóttaki ⑧
Mitropólis Cathedral
(Athens Cathedral) ①
Mikrí (Little) Mitrópolis ②
Monument of Lysikrates ⑪
Museum of Greek Folk Art ⑦
No. 11 Kidathinéon Street ⑨
Parliament and the Tomb
of the Unknown Soldier ④
Russian Church of Áyios
Nikodimos ⑥
Roman Mosaic ⑤

✝ ■ Church

119

beginning to learn need not completely dominate our lives. The main commercial street is Adrianoú, running from the Library of Hadrian all the way to Kydathinéon Street. The major archaeological excavations are directly north of the Acropolis in the Roman agora by the Tower of the Winds and the Library of Hadrian by Monasteráki Square.

The area known as **Anafiótika**—because its first residents came from the small Cycladic island of Anáfi in the 19th century—is higher up the slopes of the Acropolis. Restaurants and tavernas are scattered throughout this quarter, but the better ones are near the periphery.

Adrianoú Street offers a pleasant walk past stores of every description selling bags, clothes, jewelry, pottery, glow-in-the-dark T-shirts, all the necessities of life. After crossing Kydathinéon, Adrianoú ends by a sunken courtyard containing two Ionic columns built during the Roman period. The 12th-century **Church of Saint Catherine (Ayía Ekateríni)** is to the left in the courtyard.

If you look down Lyssikrátous Street to the left of Saint Catherine's, you will see the **Arch of Hadrian,** built in A.D. 132. To the right on Lyssikrátous Street is the last of the major archaeological monuments standing in Pláka, the **Monument of Lysikrates,** in a small, pleasant square. The monument has survived because it was incorporated into a Capuchin monastery in 1669. In the 19th century, it was a small library and reading room, used by both the French writer Chateaubriand and the English poet Byron when they were visiting Athens. An inscription on the architrave reports that the monument was built by Lyssikrátes in 335 B.C. The bases for nine other such monuments have been found in the square and another eight were excavated along Tripódon Street, the continuation of what the Greeks spell Séllei (Shelley, after the English poet) to the north, past Kydathinéon. These monuments were built to celebrate victory in the annual drama contests in honor of the god Dionysos at his theater on the southeast slope of the Acropolis. All of the 10 Attic tribes entered one chorus of men and one chorus of boys, and the victorious chorus was awarded a bronze tripod. Lyssikrátes proudly displayed the tripod on top of the carved floral arrangement on the conical roof.

Kydathinéon Street is the second main commercial street in Pláka, running from Fillelínon toward the southern slopes of the Acropolis. Number 11 Kydathinéon is a fine 19th-century house. Across the street is the **Church of the Sotíra tou Kóttaki,** dedicated to the Virgin Mary and built in the late 11th or early 12th century. The structure was rebuilt and enlarged in 1908, leaving the original church at the eastern end of the present structure.

Across the street, at 17 Kydathinéon, what looks like a modern office building is the **Museum of Greek Folk Art** (see Museums below).

Philómousou Eterías Square, the focal point for many visitors to Pláka, is past the next intersection. Several restaurants and cafes and ice cream stores are along here, good for a break.

For a taste of how wealthy Athenians used to live, visit the **Folk Art Center,** at the corner of Angélou Yerónda and Angeliki Hatzimichali streets. Open Tuesday through Friday from 9am to 1pm and 5 to 9pm, Saturday and Sunday 9am to 1pm. Admission is free.

Toward the west end of Adrianoú, a few blocks from the ancient Greek agora the street is interrupted by the still impressive remains of the **Library of Hadrian,** built late in the reign of the Roman emperor Hadrian (A.D. 117–138). Much of this large rectangular building was destroyed probably in the 3rd century by the Herulian raid. Late in the 19th century, a market occupying the site was burned down, clearing the area for the excavations that have been going on and off ever since.

STROLLING AROUND MONASTERÁKI & THE FLEA MARKET

Monasteráki Square is now cramped by ongoing construction of the new subway line, which we all hope will put some convenience into getting around Athens, preferably before the end of the century. Cars are no longer allowed here at all, and pedestrians have to squeeze along the sidewalk by the construction fence.

The square is named after the monastery founded here in the 17th century, of which there remains only the heavily reconstructed main **Church of the Panayía Pándanassa** (Church of the Virgin Mary, Queen of All Things). However unattractive the early 20th-century reconstruction, including the present bell tower, this is the "little monastery" that gives its name to what most visitors to Athens know as the flea market.

The center of the **flea market** proper is in **Abyssinia Square,** down Iféstou from Monasteráki Square, but the market extends into shops along Iféstou and the nearby streets, even east of Monasteráki Square up Pandróssou to **Mitropóleos Square.** You find everything ranging from good taste to kitsch here, with better quality merchandise up Pandróssou. The focus near Abyssinia Square is on music tapes, tools, shoes, and what appears to be army surplus clothes and jackets. In the square itself the emphasis is on secondhand furniture, with temporary stands offering coins, glass, old lamps, aged radios, and everything else gleaned from some communal grandfather's attic.

This is fun, a thoroughly vibrant area. On Sundays when the flea market is in full swing, Iféstou is so packed you can move only at a snail's pace with the human current.

OFF THE BEATEN TRACK—THE KERAMIKÓS CEMETERY

The main cemetery of ancient Athens is in the area known as the **Keramikós,** about 500 yards from the ancient Greek Agora. The entrance to the archaeological site is on Ermoú Street to the west about 200 yards from Assómaton Square. (The 12th century Church of Ayíi Assómati, crowded by construction for the new Athens metro, is across from the Theseum metro station somewhat below the modern street level.) The site and small museum are open Tuesday through Sunday (including holidays) from 8:30am to 3pm. Entrance is Dr 500 ($2).

The protected space within city walls was too valuable to be used as a cemetery, so the ancient Greeks buried their dead outside the walls. The Keramikós area had been used for burials since the end of the 3rd millennium B.C. A small river, the Eridanos, used to run along the north side of the ancient Greek Agora down through the Keramikós. The Eridanos today is evident only as a small channel of water through the Keramikós archaeological site, but along its banks the ancient Greeks found substantial clay deposits. Clay and skill made Athens preeminent in the production of pottery, which was exported throughout the ancient Greek world. The name Keramikós means "Potters' Quarter" (our word *ceramics* comes from the Greek word), and potters worked here both because the clay deposits were at hand and because burial urns and funerary pottery were an important market.

The Keramikós area was cut in half when the Themistoclean Walls were built in 479 B.C. In the **archaeological site** today we can see substantial remains of the city walls and two gates, the Sacred Gate and the Dipylon Gate, the latter of which was the main gate into the ancient city.

After entering the site, take the small footpath down to the right, where you will soon cross the still water of the Eridanos. The remains of the **Sacred Gate** are on both sides of the water, for the Sacred Way between Eleusis and Athens ran next to the Eridanos through the Sacred Gate. The Sacred Way and Sacred Gate were so named

The Acropolis & Monasteráki Square

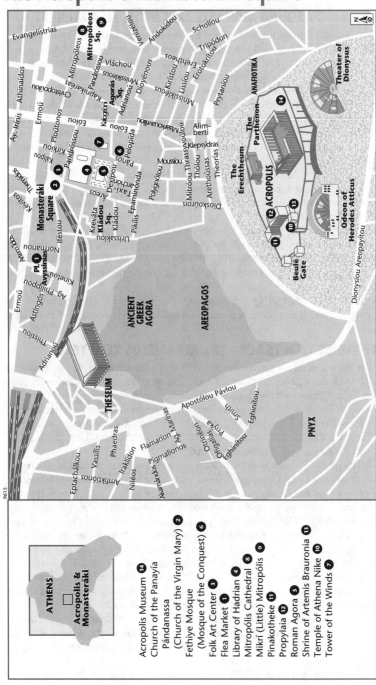

ATHENS

Acropolis & Monasteráki

Acropolis Museum **14**
Church of the Panayía Pándanassa
(Church of the Virgin Mary) **2**
Fethiye Mosque
(Mosque of the Conquest) **6**
Folk Art Center **3**
Flea Market **1**
Library of Hadrian **4**
Mitropólis Cathedral **8**
Mikrí (Little) Mitropólis **9**
Pinakotheke **11**
Propylaia **12**
Roman Agora **5**
Shrine of Artemis Brauronia **13**
Temple of Athena Nike **10**
Tower of the Winds **7**

because the annual procession from Eleusis, celebrating Demeter's descent into the Underworld in search of her daughter Persephone, came along this road and through this gate.

The remains of the **Dipylon Gate,** the main gate into the ancient city along a road that was known as the Dromos ("road") outside the walls and as the Panathenaic Way inside the walls, are 50 yards farther on. A modern cement path runs between the remains of the two massive square outer towers of the Dipylon Gate. The gate, the largest gate in ancient Greece, was 22 yards across and 41 yards deep, creating a large courtyard in which attackers were subjected to fire from high walls on three sides. Built in 479 B.C. and rebuilt at the end of the 4th century, the Dipylon Gate stood until the Herulian sack of Athens in A.D. 267, after which it was abandoned.

Between the Dipylon and Sacred gates was the **Pompeion,** the large peristyle court where people assembled for processions, notably the Panathenaic Procession. The Pompeion stood from approximately 400 B.C. until the Roman general Sulla sacked Athens in 86 B.C.

The city's honored dead were buried at public expense along the **Drómos,** the road to the Academy from the Dipylon Gate, but there is little to be seen of these graves today. More graves, many of them impressive, are along the **Sacred Way,** which parallels the Eridanos until forking to the right of the hill while the Street of the Tombs forks to the left.

10   Organized Tours

Three large companies run regular Athens sightseeing tours through Athens, tours of Athens by night, and a visit to Soúnion. They also offer tours beyond Attica, such as to Delphi, Mycenae, Epidauros, and Metéora. These make good sense if your schedule is tight.

GO Tours (Greek Organized Tours). 31-33 Voulís St., 5th floor. ☎ **01/322-5951** through 4.

The GO Tours buses leave from the corner of Amalías Avenue and Souri (one block south of the Amalias Hotel). The Athens sightseeing bus leaves at 9am and returns at 12:30pm. Its stops include the Athens cathedral and the Acropolis. The cost is Dr 8,400 ($36).

GO Tours operates three evening tours. One, for Dr 8,200 ($35), includes the Sound and Light show and a presentation of Greek dances at the Dora Stratou. A second, for Dr 11,300 ($48) takes you to the Sound and Light show and dinner at a taverna. The third, only offered on Tuesdays, Thursdays, and Fridays, offers dinner at the Old Stables restaurant in an area called Karella near Markopoulos (about a 30-minute drive) for Dr 14,000 ($60). All these trips leave at 8:15pm and return shortly after midnight.

The GO Tours Soúnion bus leaves at 3:30pm and returns at 7pm; the cost is Dr 6,400 ($27).

C.H.A.T. (Hermes en Grece) Tours. 4 Stadíou (just off S´yntagma Square). ☎ **01/ 322-3137.**

The C.H.A.T. Tours Athens sightseeing bus leaves at 9:15am from in front of the Amalia Hotel (10 Amalías Ave., just off Sýntagma Square) and returns at about 1pm. The cost of this city tour is Dr 8,400 ($36). The Athens by night trip leaves from the same place at 8:30pm, and the trip to Soúnion leaves at 3pm (returning at about 6pm) for about Dr 6,400 ($27).

Key Tours. 4 Kallirois St. Athens 117 43. ☎ **01/923-3166.** Fax 01/923-2008.

The Key Tours sightseeing bus leaves from 4 Kallirois at 9:15am, tours Athens, and returns at 1pm. The cost is Dr 8,400 ($36). Their Athens by night tour, from 8:30pm until about midnight, also leaves from here; it includes the Sound and Light show and dinner at a taverna for Dr 11,300 ($48). The excursion bus to Soúnion leaves at 3pm and returns at about 7pm; the cost is Dr 6,500 ($27).

11 Shopping

THE SHOPPING SCENE

In recent years individual neighborhoods have been developing their own shopping areas. Some of these neighborhoods include **Kallithéa,** down Syngroú toward the sea; **Glyfáda,** on the sea after the airport; **Halándri,** to the east, right, off Kiffissias Avenue after Filothei when heading toward Kiffissiá; **Kifissiá;** and **Néa Ionía,** due north of central Athens and most easily reached by taking the Kifissiá-Piraeus train. If you want to see what Athens is like outside the center head to one of these areas. Probably the most interesting is Néa (New) Ionía, settled by Greek refugees from Asia Minor after 1922 and now a thriving urban center, but it still has some old shops established 70 years ago.

The main shopping areas, however, are in central Athens, notably the so-called **commercial triangle** formed by **Athinás, Ermoú,** and **Stadíou streets,** where cars are banned except for a few cross streets. Much of Ermoú Street has upscale shops such as Sinanis and Tsandilis for women's clothes, but there is a Marks and Spencer's farther down toward Monasteráki.

Nearby **Pláka** focuses on the tourist trade, but there are some fine antique and jewelry stores here, and a particularly good sweater store on Pandróssou. **Monasteráki** has good jewelry and antique shops as well as souvenirs, and here you can also find inexpensive clothes and travel gear. **Kolonáki** has a full complement of expensive designer clothing boutiques, with a selection no better and prices probably higher than you'd find at home.

SHOPPING A TO Z
ANTIQUES

Pandróssou Street in Monasteráki has several antique shops, particularly in the last block before Monasteráki Square. The eponymous proprietor of Argyriadis, 42 Patriárchou Ioakím (Kolonáki), ☎ 01/725-1727, specializes in 18th-century furniture, but he has many smaller items, and an even larger collection in his nearby storeroom. **Giannoukos** is at 4 Amalías (near Syntagma Square), ☎ 01/324-1700. **Orpheus,** 28B Pandróssou St., Monasteráki, ☎ 01/324-5034, has accurate museum copies, including classical and Byzantine material.

BOOKS

Although many bookstores in Athens carry English books in addition to their Greek titles, the following stores have mainly, or only, English books. The range of the English titles they have available is impressive. **Compendium,** Nikis 28 (near Pláka), ☎ 01/322 1248. **Eleftheroudákis** (☎ 01/331-4180) has recently moved to new and larger quarters at 17 Panepistimíou Ave.,near Syntagma Square; they now have eight stories with a full range of subjects including travel, language, art, architecture, and literature, as well as children's books, CD-ROM and multimedia. There's also a cafe and music shop on the 6th floor. **Kakoulides** (The Book Nest), 25-29 Panepistimíou, ☎ 01/323 1703, has the greatest selection of books about Greece;

it's across from the university in the stoa, one flight up. **Pantelides,** 11 Amerikís (up from Panepistimíou), ☎ 01/362-3673. **Reymondos,** 18 Voukourestíou (up from Panepistimíou), ☎ 01/364-8189. **Romvos,** 6 Kapsali (Kolonaki), ☎ 01/724-2082.

For **religious books** and articles, go to either of these two bookstores: **Grafeion Kalou Typou,** 2 Sina (up from Panepistimíou), ☎ 01/362-6091; or **Filokalia,** 38 Voulís (near Pláka), ☎ 01/323-4411.

CLOTHES

In general, except for work clothes available in Monasteráki, clothes imported into Greece are expensive. The poshest stores are in the Kolonáki area. **Artisti Italiani,** 5 Kanári (Kolonáki) ☎ 01/363-9085, has Italian-designed clothes for men and women. **Giannetos,** 18 Panepistimíou, ☎ 01/361-6793, has men's clothes. **Jade,** 3 Anagnostopoúlou (Kolonáki), ☎ 01/364-5922, sells women's clothes. **Lacoste,** 5 Sólonos, ☎ 01/361-8030, offers men's and women's clothes. **Laura Ashley** is at 28 Heródotou (Kolonáki), ☎ 01/724-6869. **New Man,** 25 Sólonos (corner of Voukourestíou), ☎ 01/360-8876, has men's clothes. **Ritsi,** 13 Tsakalof (Kolonáki) ☎ 01/363-8677, sells women's clothes. **Sinanis,** 9 Ermoú ☎ 01/324-5316, has women's clothes. **Sofos,** 5 Anagnostopoúlou (Kolonáki), ☎ 01/361-8713, has women's clothes. **Tsandilis,** 4 Stadíou, ☎ 01/323-0026, sells women's clothes; there's another branch at 23 Ermoú, ☎ 01/323-9401.

CRAFTS

The **Center of Hellenic Tradition,** 3 Mitropóleos and 36 Pandróssou (arcade, Pláka), ☎ 01/321-3023, has quality traditional Greek art, antiques, icons, pottery, embroideries, and much more. The **Greek Women's Institution,** 3 Kolokotróni, ☎ 01/325-0524, specializes in embroidery from the islands and copies of embroideries from the Benáki Museum. The **National Welfare Organization** (Ethnikós Organismós Prónias), 6 Ypátias (and Apóllonos, just east of the Cathedral), ☎ 01/325-0524, offers embroideries, tapestries, rugs, pottery, copperware, and icons. At **To Anoyi,** 1 Sotíros (Pláka, across from the Nefeli Hotel), ☎ 01/322-6487, Kati Epostolou paints the luminous icons she sells in her shop. She also has hand-painted eggs, traditional pottery, weaving, and ceramics from other artists.

DEPARTMENT STORES

All the following are located near Omonia Square. **Lambropoulos,** 99 Eólou (and Lykoúrgos), ☎ 01/324-5811. **Minion,** 17 Veranzerou at Patissíon, ☎ 01/523-8901. **British Home Stores (BHS)/Klaudatos,** 3-5 Kratínou at Athinás, ☎ 01/324-1915. BHS occupies the first two floors including mezzanine, Klaudatos all the upper floors. (The building faces north on Kótzia Square three blocks south of Omónia on Athinás and isn't easy to see until you're right at one of the two entrances.) The self-service restaurant on the 8th floor is just a bit lower than the Acropolis and treats the startling view casually.

JEWELRY

High-quality jewelry is produced in Greece. If you take the time, you will find some excellent buys. The two long established gold jewelry stores of high quality and high prices are **Lalaounis** and **Zolotas,** both near Syntagma Square. Many stores sell silver jewelry and other silver objects worth investigating.

Kaisaris, 18 Ermoú, ☎ 01/321-4606, sells gold jewelry. **Lalaounis,** 6 Panepistimíou, ☎ 01/361-1371, also carries gold jewelry. **Nisiotis,** 23 Lékka, ☎ 01/324-4183, is one of the best silver shops in Athens. **Stathis,** 2 Pal. Venizélou, Mitropóleos Square, ☎ 01/322 4691, has offered us fair prices and courteous service over several years. **To Mati,** 20 Voukourestíou, ☎ 01/362-6238, has gold, silver, and glass articles of high quality at reasonable prices; it's one of the most interesting little jewelry stores in Athens. **Zolotas,** 10 Panepistimíou, ☎ 01/361-3782, sells gold jewelry.

MUSEUM SHOPS

Several museums operate small shops offering reproductions of some of the articles in their collection. In particular, at the **Goulandris Museum of Cycladic Art,** 4 Neoph´ytou Douká (Kolonáki), ☎ 01/722-8321, you will find some wonderful items. The **Benáki Museum,** at 1 Koumbári (Kolonáki), ☎ 01/361-1617, should reopen soon, and its museum shop will be worth a visit. Also check out the shop at the **National Archaeological Museum,** 44 Patissíon, ☎ 01/822-1764.

SHOES

Good shoes are available in Greece at reasonable prices. **Kaloyirou** has two locations: one at 12 Pandróssou (Pláka), ☎ 01/331-0727, and 4 Patriárchou Ioakím (Kolonáki), ☎ 01/722-8804. **Mouriadis,** 4 Stadíou, ☎ 01/322-1229, sells men's and women's shoes. **Moschoutis,** 12 Voulís (and Ermoú), ☎ 01/324-6504, specializes in women's shoes.

SWEATERS

Nick's Corner, 48 Pandróssou (Monasteráki), ☎ 01/321-2990, has a good supply of heavy-knit sweaters, which are bargains in Greece. Look downstairs.

SWEETS

The traditional Greek sweet shop **Aristokratikon,** 9 Karayórgis Servías (near Sýntagma Square), ☎ 01/322-0546, has excellent chocolates, glazed pistachio nuts, and loukoúmia (nougats).

12 Athens After Dark

Check the daily *Athens News,* sold at most major newsstands, for current cultural and entertainment events, including films, lectures, theater, music, and dance. The weekly *Athenscope* is even better, filled with a good list of nightspots, restaurants, movies, theater, and much else.

THE PERFORMING ARTS

The **Greek National Opera** (☎ 01/361-2461) performs at the **Olmypia Theater** (☎ 01/361-2461), 59 Akadimías St., at Mavromiháli.

The **Mégaron Mousikís Concert Hall** (☎ 01/729-0391), 89 Vasilíssis Sofías Ave., is a new, acoustically marvelous music hall that hosts a wide range of classical music programs, which includes quartets, operas in concert, symphonies, and recitals. The box office is open Monday through Friday from 10am to 6pm and Saturday 10am to 2pm. Tickets run from Dr 5,000 to Dr 20,000 ($21.30 to $85.10) depending on the performance.

The **Pallas Theater** (☎ 01/322-8275), 1 Voukourestíou St., hosts most major jazz and rock concerts, as well as some classical performances. It's an older, acoustically imperfect hall.

The **Hellenic American Union Auditorium** (☎ 01/362-9886), 22 Massalías St. (between Kolonáki and Omónia), hosts English-language theater and American-oriented music. Ticket costs vary with each performance but are usually around

Dr 3,000 ($12.77) or lower. Arrive early and check out the art show or photo exhibition at the adjacent art gallery.

THE ATHENS FESTIVAL

The **Athens Festival** at the **Odeum of Herodes Atticus** has famous Greek and foreign artists performing music, plays, opera, and ballet from the beginning of June through the beginning of October. The open-air setting at this ancient odeion beneath the Acropolis is beautiful. The only drawbacks are that the stone seats are hard and there are no backrests. Find out what's being presented through the English-language press or at the **Athens Festival office,** at 4 Stadíou, ☎ 01/322-1459 or 01/322-3111 through 9, ext. 137. The office is open Monday through Saturday from 8:30am to 2pm and 5 to 7pm, Sunday 10am to 1pm. If they are available, tickets can also be purchased at the Odeum of Herodes Atticus, ☎ 01/323-2771, on the day of performance. The better-known performances are fully attended by Athenians, so get tickets in advance if there is something you particularly want to attend. Performances begin at 9pm.

THE LYCABETTUS FESTIVAL

This outdoor amphitheater near the top of Lykavitós is sometimes used for modern music and theater in association with the Athens Festival. Consult the **Athens Festival office** at 4 Stadíou, ☎ 01/322-1459 or 01/322-3111 through 9, ext. 137).

THE EPIDAURUS FESTIVAL

If you want to really make a long evening of it, arrange to attend a performance of an ancient Greek tragedy (in modern Greek) in this famous ancient **amphitheater of Epidaurus.** The festival runs from the end of June through the end of August. The drive takes well over an hour, but buses convey the devoted down to the theater and back to Athens after the show. Request information at the Athens Festival office (above).

SOUND & LIGHT SHOWS

History is glorified by lights on the Acropolis, on the Pnyx. The shows are held from April 1 to October 31. English performances begin at 9pm and last for 45 minutes. Get tickets from the **Athens Festival office** (☎ 01/322-7944), at 4 Stadíou St., or at the entrance to the **Sound and Light** (☎ 01/922-6210). Tickets are Dr 1,200 ($5) adults, students Dr 600 ($2.50). Grab seats farthest away from the public address system.

TRADITIONAL FOLK DANCING

The Dora Stratou Folk Dance Theater. Philopáppou Hill, ☎ 01/924-4395 8am to 2pm, 01/921-4650 after 5:30pm. Performances nightly at 10:15, with additional matinees Sunday and Wednesday at 8:15pm. Tickets can be purchased at the theater's office, 8 Scholío St., Pláka; prices range from Dr 1,800 to Dr 2,500 ($7.65 to $10.65).

As opposed to the contrived boúzouki dances in the ultratouristy tavernas, here is a theater that provides one of the few opportunities to see genuine Greek folk dances. Since her company's first performance in 1953, Dora Stratou has achieved the status of grande dame of all Greek traditional dances; a night's concert will feature up to seven different styles. Typically, a program will include dances from Macedonia, the Peloponnese, and several island groups. The choreography is accompanied either by a *zyghiá,* an instrumental group of two or three musicians, or by a *companía,* an orchestra of five musicians (clarinet, drums, violin, *sandoúri,* and lute). Each dance is performed in costumes from the appropriate region; in between dances, while the dancers change outfits, the musicians play folk music.

BOUZOÚKI

Bouzoúki clubs—with abundant but expensive wine, amplified bands, and guests dancing up a storm—are enjoyed by many in spite of the loud music, high prices, and late hours. Plate-smashing, the accepted method of showing appreciation, has been outlawed, but the tradition persists in some clubs; check with the management before you join in, because you'll be charged by the plate. (If you really get into it, they're sold before the show begins, by the dozen.)

The boundaries between *dimotiká* (country folk music) and *rebétika* (music of the urban poor), which is what many people consider bouzoúki (after the most important instrument used to play it), have blurred, and purists seeking authentic rebétika will have to look harder and pay a lot more.

Pláka has always been the center of the tourist-oriented bouzoúki clubs. It's an area where a few key streets are just wall-to-wall sound, and the clubs have only pink or blue neon signs to differentiate them. Many of the tavernas with musicians or elaborate floor shows serve a high-priced meal beforehand to get you in the mood; count on spending at least Dr 6,000 ($25) a head.

Those who are serious about bouzoúkiing should consult their hotel receptionist or the current issue of *Athenscope* magazine (in English and available at newsstands) to find out which clubs are featuring the best performers. The really Greek clubs are a distance from the Sýntagma/Pláka area, so budget another Dr 2,500 to Dr 4,000 ($10 to $17) for round-trip taxi fare. Two of the better known nightspots are **Dias,** 25 Ionías and Ayíou Melétiou (Patíssia), ☎ 01/832-6888; and **Fantastiko,** 140 Syngroú Ave. (Kallithéa), ☎ 01/922-8902. The downscale smoke-filled **Rebétiki Istoría,** ☎ 01/642-4937, housed in a neoclassical building at 181 Ippókratous St., near the University, features old-style rebétika music, played to a mixed crowd of older regulars and younger students and intellectuals. The music usually starts at 11pm, but arrive earlier to get a seat.

TRADITIONAL MUSIC CLUBS

Pláka also has a good number of venues where dimotiká is played. **Taverna Mostroú,** ☎ 01/324-2441, 22 Mnissikléos St., Pláka, is one of the largest, oldest, and best-known clubs for traditional Greek music and dancing. Shows here begin about 11pm and usually last until 2am. The entrance cost of Dr 3,500 ($14.89) includes a fixed-menu supper. An à la carte menu is available but expensive. Of the many other tavernas offering traditional live music, **Neféli** (☎ 01/321-2475), 24 Pános St.; **Dioyenís** (☎ 324-7933), 3 Séllei (Shelley) St.; and **Stamatopoúlou** (☎ 01/322-8722), 26 Lissíou St., are the most reliable.

If you want some background, buy a copy of *Greek Dances* (Lycabettus Press), by Ted Petrides, available at many bookstores for Dr 1,000 ($4.25); it has a lively, informative introduction to the country's various dances, accompanied by explicit foot diagrams, so that even a klutz can learn the *syrtáki,* one of the easiest dances.

POPULAR MUSIC CLUBS

If you want to check out the local rock and blues scene along with small doses of metal, go to where Athenian popsters play—**Memphis,** ☎ 01/722-4104, 5 Ventíri St. (near the Hilton Hotel); it's open Tuesday through Friday from 10:30pm to 2:30am.

In the heart of Pláka, **Zoom,** ☎ 01/322-5920, 37 Kydathinéon St., is the place to go to hear the best of Greek pop music. Performers, who are likely to have current hit albums, are showered with carnations by adoring audience members. The minimum order is Dr 4,500 ($19.15).

Other clubs in which modern Greek popular music is served up at high decibels include: **Gazi** (☎ 01/345-0038), 9 Ierofánton and 96 Piréos; **Diogenes Palace** (☎ 01/942-5755), 259 Syngroú (Néa Smʹyrni); **Neráïda** (☎ 01/981-2004), 2 Vassiléos Yióryiou (Kalamáki); and **Rex** (☎ 01/381-4591), 48 Panepistimíou St.

DANCE CLUBS

Hidden on the outskirts of Pláka, the second-floor **Booze** (☎ 01/324-0944), 57 Kolokotróni St., blasts danceable rock music to a hip student crowd. There's art on every wall, jelled stage lights, and two bars. Admission is Dr 1,500 ($6.38), plus Dr 700 ($2.98) per drink. If it's disco you're craving, head east to **Absolut,** 23 Fillelínon St. If you feel a bit too old there, head north to **The Wild Rose,** in the arcade at 10 Panepistimíou St. Up the street, **Mercedes Rex** (☎ 361-4591), 48 Panepistimíou St., has an even more diverse crowd.

GAY CLUBS

The current gay scene in Athens is still fairly discrete; it's mostly centered along Syngroú Ave. in Makriyáni, where there's a transvestite cruising area. **Granazi** (☎ 01/325-3979), 20 Lebési St., is popular, and the best known alternative is **E . . . Kai?** ("So What?") (☎ 01/922-1742), across Syngroú at 12 Iossíf ton Rogón. In more upscale Kolonáki, **Alexander's,** 44 Anagnostopoúlou, is more sedate.

JAZZ CLUBS

The fine **Half-Note Jazz Club** (☎ 01/921-3310), 17 Trivonianoú (Mets, near the Athens First Cemetery), brings in good artists from Europe and the United States. **Jazz Bar** (☎ 01/360-5889) serves up music at 10 Tsakálof (Kolonáki). **Rock and Roll** (☎ 01/721-7127), is at 6 Loukianoú (Kolonáki).

13 Side Trips from Athens

PIRAEUS

Although many of its citizens are chauvinistic, Piraeus, the port of Athens since antiquity, is essentially an extension of Athens and of interest mostly because it's where you catch boats to the islands. It's one of the most seen, least appealing places on the Greek itinerary. It has the seamier side of a sailors' port of call, yet the color and bustle of an active harbor. The restaurants in or near Mikrolímano (Tourkolímano) are the other main reason people go down to Piraeus, though we no longer recommend them.

ESSENTIALS

GETTING THERE   By Metro   The fastest and easiest way to Piraeus is to take the metro from Omónia Square or Monastiráki to the last stop (Dr 75/33¢), which will leave you one block from the domestic port.

By Bus   From Sýntagma Square take the Green Depot bus no. 40 from the corner of F**i**llelínon Street; it will leave you one block from the international port, about a 10-minute walk along the water from the domestic port. From the airport, bus no. 19 goes to Piraeus; the fare is Dr 300 ($1.25).

By Taxi   A taxi from Sýntagma Square will cost up to Dr 1,800 ($7.50). A taxi from the airport to the port costs about Dr 1,500 ($6.25).

GETTING BACK TO ATHENS   The easiest way is to take the metro to central Athens, to either Monastiráki or Omónia Square. Taxi drivers have a conspiracy to overcharge tourists disembarking from the boats. They often charge Dr 4,000 ($16.70), two or three times the legal fare. If you stand on the dock, you'll get no mercy. The only option is to walk to a nearby street and hail a cab.

VISITOR INFORMATION   For boat schedules, transit information, and other tourist information 24 hours a day, dial ☎ **01/171.** The closest **Greek National Tourist Organization (EOT) office** (☎ **01/453-7107**) is inconveniently located on the street above Zéa Marina (the hydrofoil port) on the second floor of a shopping arcade stocked with yacht supplies. It's open Monday through Friday from 9am to 2:30pm, but its limited resources probably won't warrant the 20-minute walk from the ferry piers.

If you need a travel agency to make reservations or to recommend a particular service, try **Explorations Unlimited** (☎ **01/411-6395** or 01/411-1243), at 2 Kapodistríou St., just off Aktí Posidónos near the metro station, open Monday through Friday from 8am to 7pm, Saturday 9am to 2pm.

FAST FACTS   There are several banks in Piraeus along the waterfront. The **National Bank,** on Ethnikí Antistáseos Street, has extended hours in summer. A portable post office branch opposite the Aégina ferry pier also offers currency exchange; it's open Monday through Saturday from 8am to 8pm, Sunday 8am to 6pm. The **main post office** is at Ethnikí Antistáseos and Dimitríou streets. The **EOT** (phone center) is a block away from the post office. There is another branch by the water, on Aktí Miaoúli at Merarchías Street, open daily from 7am to 9:30pm. You'll find secure but expensive **luggage storage** in the metro station, at the **Central Travel Agency** (☎ 01/411-5611); the cost is Dr 1,000 ($4.10) per piece per day.

FERRIES TO THE ISLANDS   Ferry tickets can be purchased at a ticket office up to one hour before departure; after that they can be purchased on the boat. For booking first-class cabins or for advance-sale tickets, see one of the harborside travel agents (around Karaïskáki Square by the domestic ferries and along Aktí Miaoúli, opposite the Crete ferries). Most open at 6am and will hold your baggage for the day (but there is no security). The EOT publishes a list of weekly sailings, and the **tourist police** (☎ 01/171) or the **Port Authority** (☎ 01/451-1311) can provide you with schedule information.

The boats to the islands are opposite the metro station. Both normal boats to the Saronic Gulf and hydrofoils (Flying Dolphins) to Aegina are found opposite and to the left of the metro station; the hydrofoils leave from the foot of Goúnari Street. Boats to the other islands are around to the right and away from the station. Boats to Italy and Turkey are found a mile or so to the left. Hydrofoils to other destinations leave from Zéa Marina, a separate harbor some distance from the metro station.

WHAT TO SEE & DO

On midsummer evenings, open-air theatrical performances are given at the **Kastélla Theater,** a few blocks inland from Mikrolímano. In the wintertime performances are staged indoors, at the **Public Theater,** on the green at King Constantine Avenue. The Piraeus **Sunday flea market** on and around Alipedou and Skylitsi streets is an equally crowded variation on the Monasteráki flea market with, generally, lower quality goods. In addition, there are two museums you might consider visiting.

The Piraeus Archaeological Museum. 31 Hariláou Trikoúpi St., Piraeus. ☎ **01/452-1598.** Admission Dr 500 ($2). Tues–Sun 8:30am–3pm.

On the second floor this small museum has three unusual large cast bronze statues, two of Artemis from the 4th century B.C. and one of the young Apollo from 530 to 520 B.C. The statue of the young Apollo is the only kouros with the right foot instead of the left foot forward.

Maritime Museum. Aktí Themistokléous, Piraeus. ☎ **01/451-6264.** Admission Dr 400 ($1.70). Tues–Fri 9am–2pm, Sat–Sun 9am–1pm.

This small museum to the left of the curving ramp running down from Akti Themistokleous to the Flying Dolphin departure dock by Zéa Marina is worth coming down to the harbor a little early. The museum has models and explanations of and artifacts from some of Greece's major sea battles from antiquity down to the Second World War.

WHERE TO STAY

We don't recommend an overnight stay in Piraeus, but if it makes sense in your travel plans, here are some decent choices.

Lilia Hotel. 131 Zéas St., Passalimáni, 185 34 Piraeus. ☎ **01/417-9108.** Fax 01/411-4311. 20 rms, all with bath. TEL. Dr 16,500 ($70) double (including breakfast). AE, V.

The Lilia has clean, bright, and comfortable rooms, with ceiling fans; it's a 20-minute walk from Passalimáni, the small boat harbor by Zéa Marina (a taxi ride costs Dr 600/ $2.50). The neighborhood is good for strolling, and there are some authentic ouzerís that are great for a sunset drink and contemplation of the pleasure boats.

Ideal Hotel. 142 Notará St., 185 31 Piraeus. ☎ **01/451-1727.** 29 rms, all with bath. A/C TEL. Dr 12,000 ($51) double. AE.

The Ideal is just two blocks inland from the waterfront, opposite the international ferries. It's clean, pleasant, air-conditioned, and well maintained.

Hotel Mistral. 105 Vassiléos Pávlou St., Kastélla, 185 33 Piraeus. ☎ **01/412-1425.** Fax 01/ 412-2096. 100 rms, 3 suites, all with bath. A/C TEL. Dr 26,000 ($110) double (including breakfast). AE, EU, MC, V.

The modern Hotel Mistral is only two blocks inland from the lively seafood dining capital of Mikrolímano. Spacious rooms have views of the Aegean from sunny balconies. There's a nice roof garden, with a swimming pool, that may be open.

WHERE TO DINE

While there are undoubtedly some good restaurants in Piraeus, the places to eat along the harbor are generally mediocre and sometimes awful. Island-bound travelers may want to get to Piraeus early enough to buy their tickets, find their ferry, and have time to walk into the market area behind Aktí Posidónos and the Aégina hydrofoils. There are a lot of outdoor fruit vendors, shops selling dried fruit-and-nuts, bakeries, and knickknack traders.

We've received a number of letters complaining of rip-offs, especially in seafood restaurants in Mikrolímani and Piraeus. Before ordering, make sure you know the price. Insist on a receipt, and take any complaints immediately to the tourist police.

Expensive

Dourambeis. 29A Dilavéri St., Piraeus. ☎ **01/412-2092.** Reservations suggested. Fish Dr 9,000–Dr 14,000 ($38–$60) per kilo. No credit cards. Mon–Sat 8:30pm–1am. SEAFOOD.

If you must have seafood we suggest this fish taverna near the Delphinario theater in Piraeus. It's where Greeks go when they want to splurge on a good fish dinner.

The decor is simple, the food excellent. The crayfish soup alone is worth the trip and their lettuce salad still remains in our memory, but the whole point of going here is for their excellent grilled fish.

Moderate

Aschimopapo (The Ugly Duckling). 61 Ionón St., Áno Petrálona. ☎ **01/346-3282.** Reservations suggested. Meals Dr 2,500–Dr 4,000 ($10.65–$17). No credit cards. Mon–Sat 8:30pm–1am. GREEK.

Áno Petrálona is the neighborhood between the western edge of the Philopáppos Hill and the Athens-Piraeus train line. It's not far from the center of town, but you'll need a cab driver who either knows this taverna or has the Athens street guide to get here. The Aschimopapo is on the last stretch of Ionón before the ring road around the Philopáppos Hill, and the entrance is marked only by a light. This place offers much more than the regular taverna fare, and you can eat well for Dr 3,000 ($13) a person, so it's worth the trouble. Their specialties are lamb cooked in a clay pot, snails, and exóchiko (pork baked in aluminum foil in individual servings), and they have many other good dishes, good mezédes, and wine from the barrel.

Stou Delivoria. 8 Milónos St. Paleó Fáliro. ☎ **01/985-0257.** Meals Dr 2,000–Dr 3,500 ($8.50–$14.90). No credit cards. Mon–Sat 8:30pm–midnight. GREEK.

If you want very good, very unusual Greek food, take a cab to this restaurant run by Nikolaos Delivorias just off Filikí Etairías Square in Paleó Fáliro, south of town. The decor is reconstructed Byzantine and the food is prepared from very old Greek recipes: lamb with plums and almonds, chicken with almonds, stuffed peppers with cheese, eggplant salad with walnuts, and Greek broad beans with spinach—all are dishes we'd never heard of and found surprisingly good.

☺ **Vasilainas.** 72 Etolikoú, Ayía Sofía. ☎ **01/461-2457.** Reservations recommended Fri–Sat. Meals Dr 4,000 ($17). Mon–Sat 8pm–midnight. No credit cards. SEAFOOD/GREEK.

There's no menu at this interesting restaurant in a suburb just north of Piraeus; for a flat fee of Dr 4,000 ($17) per person you're presented with a steady flow of more than 15 dishes. Come here hungry, and even then you probably won't be able to eat everything set before you. There's plenty of seafood, plus good Greek dishes. In the winter you eat downstairs in what used to be a grocery store; in the summer tables are set on the roof. This is a deservedly popular spot, well worth the trip.

Inexpensive

Ariston. 415 Bouboulínas St. Pastries Dr 140–Dr 1,100 (60¢–$4.70). Off Aktí Miaoúli (south side of the harbor) one block before Olympic Airways office.) PASTRIES/DESSERTS.

This excellent zacharoplastío (confectioners), which lives up to its name (*áriston* means "excellent"), sells delicious pastries, sweets, miniature tirópitas, and rich spanokópitas, which are cheaper and considerably better than the snacks you'll find on a ferry.

Da Nicola Pizzeria. 8 Merarchías St. ☎ **01/451-9623.** Main courses Dr 1,400–Dr 2,800 ($6–$12). V. Mon–Sat 11:30am–11pm. From the Olympic Airways office on Aktí Miaoúli (south side of the harbor) follow Merarchías southeast. ITALIAN.

This inexpensive restaurant and snack cafe is one of the better dining choices in the area. It's quite large, air-conditioned, and comfortable, with a pizza oven in the front window. There are tables indoors or outside on the bustling street.

Rio-Antirion. 14 Merarchías St. ☎ **01/451-4583.** Main courses Dr 800–Dr 1,800 ($3.40–$7.65). No credit cards. Open daily 8am–1am. Near Da Nicola Pizzeria. GREEK.

A very clean, modern taverna with good salads, souvlaki, pasta, and chicken. You can make your choice from the display case. Everything is tasty, freshly prepared, and inexpensive.

Tzaki Grill. 7 Goúnari St. ☎ **01/417-8932.** Main courses Dr 800–Dr 2,500 ($3.40–$10.65). Open daily 8am–2am. Off Aktí Possidónos east of Karaïskáki Square. GREEK.

You'll find this unpretentious but clean little grill, with octopus hanging out to dry, near the Aégina hydrofoil pier and the ticket agents' offices. It's a good place for inexpensive and delicious charcoal-grilled fresh fish, octopus, or chicken specialties.

SOÚNION

43 miles (69km) from Athens

Cape Soúnion is the southernmost point of Attica, where the 5th-century B.C. marble **Temple of Poseidon** stands majestically on the promontory. The history of the Temple of Poseidon at Soúnion parallels that of the Parthenon in Athens in that work on a temple began here after the defeat of the Persians at Marathon in 490 B.C., and the Persians destroyed this temple in 480 B.C. before it was completed. The Greek vow not to rebuild the temples and shrines destroyed by the Persians lasted here for 36 years; the Classical temple we see today was built from 444 to 440 B.C.

ESSENTIALS

The Temple of Poseidon is open daily from 10am until sunset. Admission is Dr 1,000 ($4).

The easiest way for you to visit the site is on an organized tour run by Chat, Key, or GO tours. (See "Organized Tours," above.) If you want to go on your own for far less money, take the Soúnion bus leaving from Mavromatéon St. along the west side of the Pedíon tou Áreos park (off the eastern end of Alexándras Avenue). Buses leave about every half hour, take two hours to reach Soúnion, and cost under Dr 1,200 ($5). To verify times, ask a Greek speaker to telephone the local **ticket office** (☎ **01/823 0179**). Once you're in Soúnion, you'll have to walk from the main road up to the temple, about 1 kilometer.

THE SANCTUARY OF POSEIDON

The Classical temple was built right on top of the foundations of the earlier temple, raising the floor level by one step to just over 240 feet (73 meters) above sea level. The temple is approximately 44 by 102 feet (13.5 by 31 meters) and had six columns on the eastern and western ends and 13 columns on the northern and southern sides. The columns are just over three feet (one meter) in diameter and just over 20 feet (6 meters) high. The nine columns on the southern side, the one eastern porch column, and the third and fourth columns from the eastern corner on the northern side are in their original positions. The other columns were reset in 1908. The frieze apparently dealt with the battle between the Lapiths and centaurs, the battle between gods and giants, and the feats of Theseus. Some of the blocks of this frieze are in the National Archaeological Museum in Athens. None of the pedimental sculpture remains on the site, although the figure of a seated woman now in the National Archaeological Museum is probably from here. The other figures probably were removed in antiquity.

The modern stone path from the ticket booth leads through the sanctuary walls and turns left toward the temple, passing the ancient propylaia on the right. The propylaia was built of porous limestone and marble soon after the Classical temple.

Immediately west of the propylaia was a small square room, followed by a stoa almost 125 feet (38 meters) long and 33 feet (10 meters) deep. Another stoa, in far more ruinous condition, ran from its western end south.

Work on the sanctuary's defensive walls began in 412 B.C. so Soúnion could function, as did Rhamnous, to defend grain ships coming from Évvia to Athens.

Beneath the western end of the wall is a cutting in the rock for a ship shed, at the end of which the floor slopes upward steeply. Two cuttings in this slope made it possible to draw two boats up out of the water. The remains of stairs can be seen on the north.

If you have your own transportation and want to have a pleasant dinner, go to the fish taverna known as **Theodoros and Eleni's** in Legréna. The clean, unpretentious surroundings are in the finest tradition of what a country Greek taverna should be. The road directly from the sea at Legréna goes 500 meters to a small square, then angles slightly to the left. The taverna is another 100 meters down the road on the left. It's open every evening in the summer after 6pm and for lunch on weekends. Eleni is English, and her three children help as waiters. They use light, high quality oil and the cooking is delicious. The bill will also be to your liking.

THE MONASTERY OF KESSARIANÍ, MT. IMITTÓS (HYMETTUS)

10 miles (16km) east of central Athens

A refreshing half-day trip for tourists weary of the Big City is to the beautiful **Kessarianí Monastery,** in a cool, bird-inhabited forest at the foot of Mt. Imittós. The spring waters pouring forth from the marble goat's head at the monastery's entrance have distinguished this as a holy site for centuries.

The Kessarianí Monastery (☎ 01/723-6619) is open Tuesday through Sunday, and admission is Dr 800 ($3.40).

Bus no. 224 leaves from Panepistimíou and Vassilíssi Sofías, northeast of S´yntagma Square, every 20 minutes to the suburb of Kessarianí. It's a pleasant 2-kilometer walk up the road to the wooded site.

Kessarianí, dedicated to the Presentation of the Virgin, was founded in the 11th century and prospered in the 12th and 13th centuries. It was built over the ruins of a 5th-century Christian church, which in turn probably covered an ancient Greek temple. The small church is constructed in the form of a Greek cross, with four marble columns supporting the dome. The lovely frescoes date from the 16th century, with the exception of those in the narthex, signed "Ioánnis Hýpatos, 1689." On the west side of the paved, flower-filled courtyard are the old kitchen and the refectory, which now houses some sculptural fragments. To the south, the old monks' cells and a bathhouse are being restored (exploration at your own risk is permitted).

On a clear day, Mt. Imittós offers prospects over Athens, Attica, and the Saronic Gulf. At every scenic parking spot, you'll find men playing backgammon, couples holding hands, and old people strolling. After sunset, Imittós becomes Athens's favorite lovers' lane. The road winds around these forested slopes for nearly 11 miles (18km), and the choice of sun, shade, cool breezes, and picnic spots is unlimited.

In antiquity, Mt. Imittós is believed to have been crowned with a statue of Zeus Hymettios, and ancient caves (including a 6th-century B.C. altar) have been found near the summit. More recently the mountain was cherished by Athenians for the honey produced by bees that fed off the mountain's fragrant flowers and herbs. Most of the bees have migrated now, although a few apiaries still exist for heather-fed bees.

THE SANCTUARY OF ARTEMIS AT VRAVRÓNA

22 miles (38km) east of central Athens

Vravróna (or Vraóna), ancient Brauron, is between Pórto Ráfti and Loútsa on the east coast of Attica. The site is small and easy to reach only by car; but since it's in a farming area with no buildings nearby, it's the most pleasant ancient site in Attica near Athens.

ESSENTIALS

The site of the **Sanctuary of Artemis at Vravróna** (☎ **0294/71-020**) is open Tuesday, Wednesday, Saturday, Sunday and holidays 8:30am to 3pm. Admission to the site is Dr 500 ($2). The museum is open Tuesday to Sunday from 8:30am to 3pm; its separate admission is Dr 500 ($2).

Take the bus for Ayía Paraskeví from Akadamías Street and get off at the end of the line in front of the Greek national television station. From there, take bus 305 to Loútsa, asking the driver to let you off at the Vravróna intersection about 300 yards from the site.

Take the road through Peanía and Markópoulo towards Pórto Ráfti, which the road signs also call Port of Mesóyia (the Midland plateau). Turn left at the first turn after Markópoulo. The sign indicates Mesogea's Port (Pórto Ráfti) straight ahead 6 kilometers and has an arrow to the left toward Vravróna and Artemída, written only in Greek. The ancient sanctuary is just over 4 kilometers from this turn. About 600 yards before the site, on the left, are the remains of a 6th-century church. Traffic often backs up on the road between Stávrou and Markópoulo, particularly in Peanía, so the trip probably will take the better part of an hour.

THE SANCTUARY

The small hill above the chapel on the site was inhabited since Neolithic times, but the cult of Artemis seems to have begun here in the Geometric period. The **sanctuary** was founded in the 6th century B.C. by Peisistratos, the tyrant of Athens, who was born here and wanted to strengthen the base of his support. Peisistratos also built the shrine of Artemis Brauronia on the Acropolis between the Propylaia and the Parthenon. The sanctuary became prosperous in the late 6th and early 5th century B.C. because several Athenian leaders were born in Brauron, including Miltiades, the general who commanded the Greeks at their victory over the Persians at Marathon in 490 B.C.

The legend about the founding of the sanctuary was that an epidemic appeared in Athens immediately after a boy had killed a bear that had attacked his sister near the sanctuary. The oracle consulted replied that to keep themselves free of disease, the Athenians should institute a ceremony in which young girls would act like bears. The Athenians were to "not allow any virgin to live in the same house as a man before she had acted like a bear in honor of the goddess."

Every year a procession of girls went to the sanctuary wearing yellow robes. While the priestess sacrificed an animal the girls imitated bears in a ceremony that was at least in part mystical. The girls stayed in the sanctuary only for the ceremony, but orphan girls who had been dedicated to Iphigenia lived here permanently. Some girls danced wearing clothes that had been dedicated to Artemis by women who had given birth easily, apparently in the belief that wearing the goddess's clothes would ensure that they, in turn, would bear children easily.

The most striking structure at Brauron is the **stoa,** restored in 1961. The stoa was built in the shape of an incomplete Greek letter *pi* (π) facing south toward the hill. Six rooms on the north of the stoa contained 11 small beds for the children, with stone tables by the beds. Four rooms on the west of the stoa may also have been used as bedrooms for the children.

The **ancient stone bridge** west of the stoa is the only remaining example of a horizontal bridge built in the middle of the 5th century B.C. Ruts worn by ancient wheels are clearly evident.

To the south, on a small plateau on the lower level of the hill, are the foundations of the **Classical Temple of Artemis.** It was built in the early 5th century B.C. on the site of an earlier temple destroyed by the Persians in 480 B.C.

Southeast of the temple, to the left of the 16th-century **Chapel of St. George,** is an area which used to be a cave. The roof has long since fallen in, but the rising rock walls are obvious, as are the four small rooms. This is the **tomb of Iphigeneia.**

The **sacred spring** still forms a small pond of clear water west of the temple and north of the retaining wall below the Chapel of St. George.

The small (five rooms) **museum** is one of the better local museums, with some superb Geometric vessels, worth the visit although you do have to pay another entrance fee. The museum is an easy three-minute walk from the sanctuary if the back gate in the southeast corner of the sanctuary is open; otherwise it's just under 1 kilometer by road, to the left around the hill behind the chapel.

There are two pleasant fish tavernas in the area, one north and one south of the site. The more sophisticated is **Alexander's Taverna,** with good food, below the large white hotel complex toward Loútsa. Head back toward Markópoulo and turn right at the first intersection, some 300 yards from the site. One kilometer farther on there is a dirt road to the right, toward the sea, as the paved road turns left to go up the hill. The taverna is 500 yards down this dirt road on the left.

To reach the other taverna, turn left from the museum and follow the road over the hill and down to the left to the sea. Turn right with the road along the shore to find the taverna a bit more than a kilometer on the left.

THE MONASTERY OF DAFNÍ

5¹/₂ miles (9km) West of Athens on highway to Corinth

The mosaics in the Monastery of Dafní are masterpieces of Byzantine art, dating from approximately 1100. The other two roughly contemporary survivors of this quality of mosaics are in the Monastery of Óssios Loukás (near Delphi) and the Monastery of Néa Moní on the island of Híos.

ESSENTIALS

The Monastery of Dafní (☎ **01/581-1558**) is open daily except major holidays from 8:30am to 3pm. Admission is Dr 800 ($3.40).

Take bus no. 860 from Panepistimíou St. north of Siná (behind the University), bus no. 853, 862, 873, or 880 from Elefthería Square off Piréos Ave. (northwest of Monasteráki), or bus no. A 15, marked Eléfsina, from Sachtoúri Street, southeast of Elefthería Square. The trip should take about half an hour, and the bus stop at Dafní is about 150 yards from the monastery.

If you are driving, head for Corinth on Athínon Avenue. After the National Road overpass the road rises steadily for 5 kilometers to the gentle crest of the hill. There is a traffic light just over the crest and another traffic light approximately 500 yards further on. Turn left at the second traffic light and then right along the parallel road some 300 yards to the monastery.

THE MONASTERY

Dafní means laurel, and in ancient times the laurel was associated with the god Apollo. A temple dedicated to Apollo was on the site, although all that remains of it today is a column near the southern entrance to the compound. The other columns, now in the British Museum in London, were carted off by Lord Elgin in the early 19th century.

The first monastery on the site was built in the 6th century. Square walls approximately 100 yards on a side were built around the monastery to seclude it from the then and now well-traveled road to Athens. Two Corinthian capitals from this period are to the right and left of the church entrance.

The present monastery was built in the late 11th century, possibly by one of the Comneni (1081–1185) Byzantine emperors. After the Crusaders captured Constantinople in 1204, Daphní was used as a Catholic monastery by the Cistercian monks who installed the twin Gothic arches in front of the west entrance to the church. After the Ottomans captured Athens, the monastery was returned to the Greek Orthodox Church.

Excellent restoration work has been going on in the monastery for the last several years, and most of the mosaics are brilliantly clear. The central dome has the commanding **mosaic of Christ Pantocrator** (the Almighty), whose powerful gaze looks left. The image is of an awesome judge rather than the Western conception of a suffering mortal. Sixteen prophets are displayed between the windows of the dome. The Annunciation, Nativity, Baptism, and Transfiguration are in the squinches supporting the dome. The Adoration of the Magi and the Resurrection are in the barrel vault inside the main (southern) entrance of the church; the Entry into Jerusalem and the Crucifixion are in the northern barrel vault.

Mosaics showing scenes from the life of the Virgin are in the south bay of the narthex (passage between the entrance and nave). In the north bay are the Washing of the Disciples Feet, the Betrayal, and the Last Supper.

A **Wine Festival** is usually held on the grounds every year from mid-August to mid-September. It goes from 8pm to midnight, and admission is Dr 600 ($2.50); for Dr 1,800 ($7.65) you get to sample many different kinds of wine. Check with the **Athens Festival box office (☎ 01/322-7944),** 4 Stadíou St., near Syntagma Square, for more information.

ANCIENT ELEUSIS

14 miles (22.5km) west from central Athens on the highway to Corinth

Eleusis was the site of the most famous and revered of all the ancient Mysteries. The names of the illustrious people initiated into the sacred rites here would fill pages, yet we know almost nothing for certain about those ceremonies. We can only guess at what the initiates into their cult were taught during the rites, held in two degrees, in March and September. All but those rituals performed in public were kept secret from the uninitiated, including us, and remain truly a mystery, the very source of that word.

We do know that in March those who wanted to be initiated into the Mystery gathered in the Ancient Greek Agora in Athens and solemnly prepared themselves before joining a procession along the Sacred Way to Eleusis. (The Sacred Way began by the present entrance to the archaeological site.) We know also that during the autumn ritual, initiates who had undergone the spring ritual performed sacrifices in the precinct on the first day and then marched in procession with the priestess of Demeter along the Sacred Way into the Agora in Athens. A festival was held in Athens for the following four days, from which those not speaking Greek or guilty of murder, sacrilege, or other serious crime were excluded. On the fifth day, the initiates returned to Eleusis and became full members of the cult during the following two days. A reenactment of the story of Persephone's kidnapping may have been part of this last stage.

ESSENTIALS

The site of Eleusis (☎ 01/554-6019) is in the modern industrial city of Eléfsina. It's open Tuesday to Sunday and holidays 8:30am to 3pm; admission is Dr 500 ($2), free Sunday.

Take bus no. 853 or no. 862 from Elefthería Square off Piréos Avenue (northwest of Monasteráki), or bus no. A 15, marked Eléfsina, from Sachtoúri Street, southeast of Elefthería Square. (This trip can be combined with a visit to Daphní Monastery.) Ask the driver to let you off at the Sanctuary (herón), which is off to the left of the main road, before the center of town.)

If you're driving, take the national road and exit at Eléfsina, follow the signs, and then turn left at the third traffic light.

THE SANCTUARY OF ELEUSIS

The **Sanctuary of Eleusis** was used from Mycenaean times through the Roman period and was famous throughout the Greek and Roman worlds. It was destroyed by barbarians and Christians in the 4th century A.D.

The site and its history are complex. The path from the entrance leads south past a **Temple of Artemis,** on the right. To the left of the huge sculpted marble medallion of Antonius Pius, its builder, is the **Greater Propylaea,** which was built in the second century A.D. and modeled after the Propylaea in Athens. To the left of the Greater Propylaea, you can see one of two triumphal arches dedicated to the Great Goddesses and to the Emperor Hadrian. (This arch inspired the Arc de Triomphe, on the Champs-Elysées in Paris.) Nearby is the **Kallichoron Well,** where Demeter wept, and where women later danced and chanted in her honor.

A little further south the **Lesser Propylaia,** the entrance into the main part of the sanctuary, is distinguished by two curved grooves for the doors. (You can see one of the two colossal caryatids that supported the Lesser Propylaia in the museum; the other was carted off to Cambridge, England, in 1801.)

Beyond the Lesser Propylaia on the right is the **Ploutonion,** a cave said to be sacred to Pluto and that, according to the Hymn to Demeter, was an entrance to Hades.

The path continues to the **Telesterion,** the temple of Demeter, where initiates were presented with the cult's mysteries. Tradition holds that the first temple to Demeter built by King Keleos was here. It was built in four distinct phases, and the last phase can be seen clearly in the lines of seats cut into the acropolis rock.

The **museum** is above the Telesterion to the south. The collection isn't large or well labeled, but it does contain the greater part of a famous Demeter by Agoracritis, a caryatid from the Lesser Propylaia, a cast of Demeter and Persephone sending Triptolemos off to teach mankind agriculture, and several Roman statues, including one of the Emperor Hadrian's beloved Antinoös in the cloak of an initiate into the Mystery.

MARATHON

26 miles (42km) northeast of Athens

The battle of Marathon in 490 B.C. was fought on a plain by the sea 26 miles (42km) northeast of Athens between the villages of Néa Mákri and Marathóna. You can visit the burial mound of the Athenians, the burial mound identified by the excavator as that of their Plataian allies, and the archaeological museum.

ESSENTIALS

The museum (☎ 0294/55155) is open Tuesday to Sunday from 8:30am to 3pm. Admission is 500 ($2); it includes both the mound and the museum.

Buses leave for Marathon from Mavromaté Street along the east side of the Pedión tou Áreos Park approximately every half hour in the morning and every hour in the afternoon. The trip costs about Dr 700 ($3) and takes two hours and 20 minutes. For departure times, call the tourist police at ☎ 01/171, or ask a Greek speaker to call the local ticket office (☎ 01/821-0872).

If you have your own transportation you can reach Marathon by driving north from Athens on along Kiffisías Avenue, the more scenic route that rounds Mt. Pendéli through Dionissós to the sea at Néa Mákri, or along the National Highway toward Thessaloníki, from which signs will direct you to Marathon. The burial mound of the Athenians is between Marathóna and Néa Mákri; there are good road signs to mark the site.

THE BURIAL MOUND

A memorial to a magnificent Athenian military victory, the burial mound is simply a circular mound of earth 9 meters high, 50 meters in diameter, and 185 meters in circumference; it's about 700 meters from the highway. The stele on the mound is a modern copy; the original is in the National Archaeological Museum in Athens.

Persia, the largest empire in the world, sent an army of a least 20,000 to Marathon; they were supported by a huge fleet. Approximately 9,000 Athenian soldiers marched alone to meet this threat, and they were joined by 1,000 soldiers from Plataia, a town in Boeotia. According to Herodotus, who was alive in 490 B.C. and later collected reports from men who fought in the battle, the runner Pheidippides was sent to ask the Spartans for help. Pheidippides is said to have run the 150 miles to Sparta in two days, but the Spartans were holding ceremonies in honor of the moon and refused to march to Marathon at once.

The Athenians were camped in the foothills northeast of the plain of Marathon, near the present site of the archaeological museum. The Persians were camped near the shore. Pheidippides returned to Marathon with the bad news, and the dismayed Athenian commanding general Kallimachos accepted the tactical advice of Miltiades, another leader. Kallimachos reduced the number of men at the center of their line and strengthened their flanks. The uneasy confrontation had held for eight days, when apparently some of the Persian forces began withdrawing toward their ships, probably to sail for undefended Athens. Miltiades seized the opportunity and attacked at once. When the two armies met, the Athenian center fell back before the Persians, while its wings drove hard with the determination of free men protecting their homeland and overcame their opposition, then turned inward to trap the center of the Persian line, routing the invaders. According to tradition, the Persians lost 6,400 men, and the Athenians 192.

Miltiades dispatched a runner—Plutarch named the swift and tireless Pheidippides—back to Athens with the news of victory. Legend says the runner covered the 26 miles without pausing for breath, gasped out his glad news, then died of exhaustion.

The 192 Athenian dead from this astonishing victory were cremated and buried together in this mound, which was excavated in the late 19th century. The mound identified as being that of the Plataian warriors is near the archaeological museum about 3 kilometers to the west. There is nothing to mark where the Persians were buried, but most authorities place their mass grave to the northeast, in the area around the small Church of the Panayía Mesosporitíssa.

To visit the **archaeological museum** and the **mound of the Plataians,** return to the Néa Mákri-Marathóna road and turn to the right, toward the modern village of Marathóna. The sharp turn to the left for the archaeological museum is 1.7 kilometers from the intersection. Follow the small yellow signs to the museum $2^1/_2$ kilometers after this left turn.

The five rooms of the archaeological museum contain finds from several ancient sites in the area, including the capital from the column of victory which stood on the mound of the Athenians. The one find, however, which brings the battle near is the Persian helmet in the entrance hall, to the right before you enter the first room.

Outside the museum to the right as you face the museum entrance is a large protective structure over two Middle Helladic grave mounds dating from approximately 1600 B.C. The first tomb was found to be empty, but the second contains the remains of five people and one horse.

Approximately 100 yards in front of the museum is the mound identified by the excavator as being the burial mound for the Plataians. The entire mound was not excavated, but 11 graves, nine of young men approximately 20 years old, one of a 10-year-old boy, and one of a 35-year-old man, were found. There is no doubt about the date of these graves, but there is some disagreement about the identification.

Plutarch's accounts of the battle of Marathon may be doubted; the biographer wasn't born until about A.D. 46 and he often embroidered an account for effect or a moral point. Herodotus, the Father of History, was a more scrupulous historian, and in the early 1970s his account of Pheidippides's feat was tested by five English Royal Air Force men running from Athens to Sparta. The first man to reach Sparta covered the distance in $34^1/_2$ hours. The event is now repeated every four years.

Herodotus also reported that, while he was running, Pheidippides was visited by the god Pan, and the god complained that the Athenians did not give him honor. During the battle itself, Pan is supposed to have struck terror into the hearts of the attacking Persians, the origin of our word *panic.* The appearance of Pan to Pheidippides is explained by the fact that long distance runners often suffer hallucinations under extreme exhaustion. It's a fact that after the battle, shrines were dedicated to Pan all over Attica where there had been none before.

THE TEMPLE OF NEMESIS AT RHAMNOUS
33 miles (53km) northeast from Athens

Rhamnous was a fortress town on the northern borders of Attica. For the last several years, the Greek Archaeological Society has been carrying out extensive excavations in the area. The ancient entrance road to the site has now been cleared, and several tombs at the beginning of this road have been reconstructed.

ESSENTIALS

The temple (☎ **0294/69477**) is open daily from 8:30am to 3pm. Admission is Dr 500 ($2).

Rhamnous can be visited easily only by car, and it can be handily combined with a trip to Marathon, as it is only a dozen or so kilometers beyond the site of the famous battle. From Athens, take the Néo Mákri-Marathóna road, turn right toward Káto Soúli. The unmarked road to Rhamnous branches left 3 kilometers from Káto Soúli and continues another 2 $^1/_2$ kilometers beside vineyards to the site. There's only the fence and the small ticket stand to tell you that you have reached the archaeological site.

The Sanctuary

The **Sanctuary of Nemesis** is just over the crest of the hill from the entrance of the archaeological site. Nemesis was the goddess of righteous vengeance. She changed into many forms to flee Zeus but finally was caught by him when she was in the form of a goose. The result of their union was an egg from which Helen, the wife of Menelaos and the cause of the Trojan War, eventually was born. Nemesis gave the egg to Leda, who raised Helen and often is considered Helen's mother.

The sanctuary of Nemesis is approximately 100 meters above sea level on a natural terrace, which is extended to the north by a retaining wall almost 125 feet (38 meters) long. The remains of two temples of Nemesis are in the sanctuary. The smaller temple, the first as you enter, is sometimes called the Temple of Themis because a statue of Themis was found here. It is in fact the older Temple of Nemesis, built just after the battle of Marathon in 490 B.C. The statue of Themis found here is now in Athens's National Archaeological Museum (Room 28). Themis, the personification of justice, shared the temple with Nemesis.

The larger Temple of Nemesis is immediately north, almost touching the older Temple of Nemesis. It was built of locally quarried white marble in 436–32 B.C. A darker marble, also quarried locally, was used for the foundations and the bottom step of the three-step platform. The order is Doric, with an outer colonnade of six columns at the east and west and 12 columns on the north and south. Both the east and west porch have two columns in antis (between the projecting pilasters of a cella wall, known as antae). The name of the architect is not known, but he also designed the Temple of Hephaistos in the Agora in Athens, the Temple of Ares moved by the Romans to the Agora in Athens, and the Temple of Poseidon at Soúnion.

The town of ancient Rhamnous flourished in the 5th and 4th centuries B.C., primarily as a garrison town protecting grain ships from Évvia. The walled town is approximately 830 meters from the sanctuary of Nemesis on a low hill at the bottom of the valley by the water. The fortifications probably were begun late in the 5th century B.C. and completed toward the end of the 3rd century B.C. The hill was surrounded by defensive walls and a smaller area at the hill's summit had defensive walls as well.

Because excavations are going on, the fortress cannot be visited without special permission from the archaeological service in Athens. The area below the Sanctuary of Nemesis has been fenced off.

5 The Saronic Gulf Islands

by John Bozman

The calm Saronic Gulf, sheltered between Attica and the Peloponnese peninsula, has a number of attractive islands, each with a unique identity, but all so convenient to the mainland that their easy accessibility and popularity have paradoxically been their main drawbacks, especially during the summer and on weekends. Our advice about visiting in the off season is especially important here. Besides, these islands are at their most beautiful in the spring before the hordes have trampled the wildflowers and in the fall when they seem to take a long luxurious sigh of relief. Unless you have reservations, go only for day-trips during the summer, and then only during the week.

Aegina (Éyina) is the closest to Athens and was an important commercial center in ancient times—an important rival of Athens then and something of a suburb of today. Well developed, its hills are covered with pines and its fertile valleys are extensively cultivated, especially with numerous pistachio orchards. Its graceful Doric temple of Aphaia is one of the best preserved of all Archaic buildings and is especially appealing because of its situation atop a pine-covered hill.

We're sorry to have to skip over **Salamís,** famous for the Athenian victory over the Persian fleet and as the birthplace of Euripides, but today it's a suburb of Piraeus and blighted by industrial development.

Póros is an attractive if less cultivated island, very popular with the younger budget crowd and increasingly with tour groups, but it manages to keep its head above water and can be a pleasant place to enjoy good beaches, sightseeing on the Peloponnese, and inexpensive nightlife.

Hýdra (Ýdra), with its superb natural harbor, elegant stone mansions, and monasteries, is the most strikingly beautiful of all the Saronic Gulf Islands. The whole island has been declared a national monument and vehicles have been banished, so it is a particular delight, fashionable and rather expensive.

Spétses offers much better beaches than Hýdra, some architectural distinction, more sophisticated nightlife, and traffic, which you can escape with a little effort.

The Saronic Gulf islands are all inundated with visitors on summer weekends, though by midweek some semblance of calm has been restored and sand can be seen on the beaches, tables are

The Saronic Gulf Islands

0   50 km
    31 mi

N

Salamís
Pérama
Ambelákia
Piraeus
ATHENS

SALAMÍS
Peristeriá   Peráni
Glyfáda

Saronikós Kólpos
(Saronic Gulf)

DIAPÓRIA

LÁOUSSES
Souvála   Váia
IPSILÍ
Kórfos
❶
Messágros ❷
Aegina
Ayia Marína
Paleohóra
KIRÁ Anghístri
Marathónas
Pórtes
ANGHÍSTRI
MONÍ   Pérdika
AEGINA
Néa Epídavros

Kounoupítsa

Epidavrikós
Kólpos
(Gulf of
Epídavros)
Vathý
Méthana
Ag. Eléni
Kaloní
PÓROS
Trizína
Póros ❸
Galatás ❹
Dídima
Loukaíti
Piepi   Metochi
TSELEVINIÁ
Kraníd   Ermióni
Zoúrvas
Dokós
Hydra
Episkopí
❺
DOKÓS
HYDRA
Spétses
SPÉTSES
SPETSOPOÚLA

Monastery of Áyios Nektários ❶
Monastery of the Prophet Elijah
   (Profítis Ilías) ❺
Monastery of Zoödóches ❹
Temple of Aphaia ❷
Temple of Poseidon ❸

GREECE
Athens
The
Saronic
Gulf

Airport ✈
Ferry Service
Prehistoric Site
Archeological Site

143

available at restaurants, and rooms can be found at hotels. You could scout all these islands during a single day, or rely on our advice for a brief respite from Athens.

1 Aegina

Triangular Aegina (Éyina), the largest of the Saronic Gulf islands, continues to be the most visited island of Greece, due to its proximity to Athens, just 17 nautical miles (30 kilometers) southwest of Piraeus. If you have only one day for one island, it's a good choice, especially during the week or off-season, because of its famous Doric temple of Aphaia. The island has a permanent population just over 10,000, with many people commuting to Athens to work. Most ships arrive and depart from the main port and capital of Aegina town on the west coast, though there are a few that stop at the group-tour town of Ayía Marína on the east coast—not recommended.

Despite massive tourism and rapid development, the fertile soil of Aegina is still cultivated, and along the roads you see many gardens and olive, almond, and pistachio orchards. The gnarled pistachio trees are especially distinctive—and thirsty, contributing to the island's chronic water shortage—and the nuts are sold everywhere, not inexpensively, as the island's specialty.

ESSENTIALS

GETTING THERE   One of the main advantages of touring the Saronic Gulf is the convenience of transportation: You can go from one island to another almost any time of day. Car ferries, excursion boats, and hydrofoils run almost constantly during the summer, and you will rarely have to wait long for a boat.

Car ferries, excursion boats, and hydrofoils to Aegina leave from the main harbor of Piraeus; the Ceres terminal is on the north side. Hydrofoils to Póros, Hýdra, and Spétses leave from the far southwest corner of Zéa Marina in Piraeus.

By Hydrofoil   Hydrofoil service is particularly efficient; the Ceres **Flying Dolphins** are twice as fast as ferries and only about 35% more expensive. The sleek little yellow-and-blue hydrofoils are outfitted like broad aircraft with airline seats, toilets, and a minimum of luggage facilities. (The fore sections offer better views, but they are also bumpier.) The newer **Super Cats** are bigger, faster, and more comfortable, with food and beverage service.

By Organized Tour   A good way to see the Saronic Gulf is via a three-island day cruise, which can be booked through a travel agent, such as **Viking Star Cruises** (☎ **01/89-80-729** or 01/89-80-829) or at your hotel desk. **Epirotiki Lines** (☎ **01/42-91-000**) provides transportation to and from your hotel in Athens to Flísvos Marina, where their *Hermés* departs daily about 8:30am for Hýdra (swimming and shopping), Póros (lunch and sightseeing), and Aegina (to visit the Temple of Aphaia or swimming), returning to Athens about 7:30pm. Lunch is served on board, and there's a small pool. For about Dr 16,500 ($70) you get a good tour and an introduction to travel aboard a luxury cruise ship.

Ferry and excursion boat tickets can be purchased at the pier. Call the **Piraeus Port Authority** (☎ **01/45-11-456**) for schedule and departure pier information. Hydrofoil tickets can be purchased in advance from **Ceres Hydrofoils** (☎ **01/42-80-001**), Aktí Themistokléous 8, midway on the waterfront in Piraeus, or at the nearby departure pier.

VISITOR INFORMATION   There are several travel agents on the island. **Pipins Tours** (☎ **0297-24-456;** fax 26-656), one block inland from the hydrofoil pier, is very helpful and serves as the Ceres Hydrofoil agent. **Aegina Island Holidays**

(☎ **0297/25-860;** fax 25-860), just off Odós Dimokratís, the waterfront street, near the church, is also helpful. Currency **exchange** can be made at the National Bank of Greece, on the *paralía* (waterfront); some travel agents also exchange money at later hours.

For **medical emergencies**, the island hospital (☎ **0297/22-251**) is on the northeast edge of town. The **telephone center** (**OTE**) is five blocks inland from the port, on Odós Aiákou. The **police** (☎ **0297/22-391**) are on Odós Leonárdou Ladá, about 200 meters from the port. The **post office** is to the left and around the corner from the hydrofoil pier.

GETTING AROUND   The **bus station** is on Platía Ethneyersías, to the left from the ferry pier, and there is good service to most of the island, every hour during the summer to the Temple of Aphaia and Ayía Marína, Dr 350 ($1.50); tickets must be purchased at the small temporary office before boarding. **Taxis** are available nearby; fare to the temple should cost about Dr 2,400 ($10). **Bikes, mountain bikes,** and **mopeds** can be rented at the opposite (south) end of the paralía, near the beach. Careful, prices can be exorbitant. An ordinary bike should cost no more than Dr 1,000 ($4) a day, and mopeds should cost about Dr 3,500 to Dr 6,000 ($15 to $26) a day.

EXPLORING THE ISLAND

Aegina town itself is a pleasant sight, its large crescent-shaped harbor almost picturesque with its busy scene of caïques (skiffs) selling fresh fruit and vegetables brought over from the mainland and fishermen mending their nets and offering the local day's catch. Handsome neoclassical architecture, dating from the time the town was briefly the capital of Greece, is visible behind the tourist facilities that crowd the waterfront. If you take a horse-drawn carriage (about Dr 4,000/$17) or wander the streets back from the port, you can find much that will take you back to Aegina's charming past.

In the middle of town you'll find the restored **Markélos Tower,** the seat of the first Greek government, near the large church of Áyios Nikólaos. North of the harbor, behind the town beach, you'll find the lone worn Doric column that marks the site of the **Temple of Apollo,** open Tuesday through Sunday, 8:30am to 3pm, but hardly worth the Dr 500 ($2) admission, unless you're interested in the view. Nearby the new **Archaeology Museum,** Odós Mitrópoleos 10, open Tuesday through Sunday, 8:30am to 3pm, Dr 500 ($2), contains ceramics from the Neolithic through the Classical era; some good sculpture from the 5th century B.C., including decorations from the temple of Aphaia; and even mosaics from an ancient synagogue.

Those interested in shopping should visit **Eleftéris Diakoyiánnis** on the waterfront, Odós Demokratías 39 (☎ **0297/24-593**), open daily 9am to noon and 4 to 7pm, who has excellent ceramics from all over Greece, jewelry, and superb reproductions of ancient and classical works of art; he accepts credit cards.

The **Temple of Aphaia** is on the east side of the island, near the resort town of Ayía Marína, which is popular with tour groups and which we recommend only to those interested in our idea of tacky overdevelopment. The temple itself is one of Greece's foremost archaeological treasures, the best preserved Archaic temple on any island, set appealingly on a lovely pine-wooded hill. (Take your binoculars and you can see the Parthenon and the Temple of Poseidon at Soúnio, with which it forms the points of a triangle, important for ancient telecommunication.)

The sanctuary was constructed of local limestone in the late 6th or early 5th century B.C.—earlier than the Parthenon—over older temples, and 25 of the original 32 Doric columns are now standing, due partly to reconstruction. Originally it was covered by a coat of stucco and painted with bright colors. The original pediments of Parian marble depicting scenes from the Trojan war are among the greatest works of Archaic art. In 1812 King Ludwig of Bavaria bought them from the Turks—probably saving them from destruction by peasants who may have used them in their lime kilns—and they are now at the Glyptothek in Munich.

Aphaia was a prehistoric goddess, often identified as the Great Goddess in her virginal aspect, a protector of wild animals, and thus associated with Artemis. Later myths made her a child of Zeus and Leto, sister of Artemis, and recount her flight from Crete pursued by King Minos, who had fallen madly in love with her. He pursued her for nine months until they reached Aegina, where in despair she threw herself into the sea. Later she became identified with another important virgin, Athena.

On the way to the temple from Aegina town you'll pass the huge new **Monastery of Áyios Nektários.** (Nektários was a bishop of Libya, who retired to Aegina and died in 1920; he was canonized in 1961, and the 9th of November, the anniversary of his death, is celebrated by a pilgrimage and festival honoring his crowned skull.) About a kilometer east on the hill behind the monastery, a steep drive or a hike requiring good shoes, is the ghost village of **Paleohóra,** built in the 9th century as a refuge from the Saracens and reputed to have had 365 churches. The pirate Barbarossa slaughtered its men and enslaved the women and children in 1538. In 1654 Morosini overthrew it again and built the Venetian castle, which shows its age as well. In 1826 the population deserted their town to move to Aegina, and only about 15 of the churches remain recognizable. Anne Yannoulis's *Aegina* (Lycabettus Press) is recommended reading for those with a deeper interest in the island.

You can cycle down the west coast to find less crowded beaches or take the bus to the pretty fishing village of **Pérdika,** near the southwest corner of the triangle, 9 kilometers south of Aegina town, which has a small beach, a wildlife sanctuary, and some of the best accommodations on the island. From Pérdika you can catch a caïque (Dr 300/$1.25, one way) to the nearby little island of **Moní** for better and more secluded swimming, and possibly see a *kri kri* (a rare ibex from Crete) being rehabilitated by the wildlife sanctuary. (The Greek National Tourist Organization (EOT)-sponsored campground in Moní has apparently been abandoned, and though there is a taverna in the summer, you should take a picnic lunch.)

Those interested in relative isolation, during the week or off-season, might try the island of **Angístri** ("Hook"), which is a half-hour caïque ride from Aegina town; boats cost about Dr 400 ($1.75) one way and leave every couple of hours, or whenever the boat is full. There are plenty of inexpensive basic accommodations, a few taverns, and a few nudist beaches.

WHERE TO STAY

Pipins Tours (☎ 0297-24-456), one block inland from the hydrofoil pier, and **Aegina Island Holidays** (☎ 0297-25-860), just off port-side Odós Dimokratías near the church, are both good sources for rooms to let around the island. Doubles with private bath start at about Dr 8,000 ($34).

Eginitiko Archontiko (Traditional Hotel). Odós Eakoú 1 and Ayíou Nikoláou, 180 10 Aegina. ☎ **0297-24-968.** 12 rms (all with bath). Dr 8,000 ($35) single; Dr 11,500 ($49) double; Dr 23,000 ($98) suite. Rates include breakfast. No credit cards.

This mansion, near the Markélos Tower, was built in 1820 and renovated in 1988 with some loss of original detail. The rooms are rather small and modern but traditionally furnished, comfortable, and quiet, and the pleasant downstairs lobby retains much 19th-century charm.

⑤ Eleni Rooms to Let. Odós Káppou, 180 10 Aegina. ☎ **0297/26-450.** 7 rms (4 with bath). Dr 7,000 ($29.80) single/double without bath; Dr 8,800 ($37.40) single/double with bath. No credit cards.

This top budget choice is in part of a house built in 1888. Rooms are cool, quiet, and exceptionally clean, with refinished pine floors and whitewashed walls. Each room is different, and the second-floor rooms with baths are the best.

Moondy Bay Bungalows. Profítis Elías, Pérdika, 180 10 Aegina. ☎ **0297/25-147** or 01/ 36-03-745 in Athens. Fax 0297/61-147. 80 rms (all with bath). A/C TEL. Dr 16,300 ($69.40) double. Rates include breakfast. No credit cards.

This bungalow complex, 7 kilometers south of Aegina town in well-kept grounds overlooking the sea, is generally considered to have the best accommodations on the island, though it could be improved by better maintenance. There's a good seawater pool, tennis court, minigolf, and children's playground.

WHERE TO DINE

Most visitors will probably not venture past the paralía, where the food is typically overpriced but rather good, considering how bad it might be with a captive clientele. Not surprisingly, seafood is expensive. The local pistachios are a delicious snack, worth the price.

Estiatórion Económou. Odós Dimokratías. ☎ **0297/25-113.** Reservations not required. Appetizers Dr 400–Dr 2,500 ($1.70–$10.65); main courses Dr 900–Dr 2,800 ($3.85–$11.90). AE, EURO, MC, V. Daily 9am–1am. GREEK/INTERNATIONAL.

A reader suggested this excellent port-side taverna with a dark blue canopy about midway along the paralía, and several visits have confirmed its high quality. We recommend the lemony fish soup, grilled sfirída (a local fish), and tender lamb souvláki with chips. Grilled local lobster is sometimes available for about Dr 12,000 ($51) a kilo.

Maridáki Cafe. Odós Dimokratías. ☎ **0297/24-014.** Reservations not required. Appetizers Dr 450–Dr 1,500 ($1.90–$6.40); main courses Dr 1,000–Dr 1,250 ($4.25–$5.30). No credit cards. Daily 8am–midnight. INTERNATIONAL.

This lively newer port-side cafe, near the port police station, serves a little of everything, including good omelets, fresh mezédes, grilled octopus, and savory stewed okra and tomatoes.

Taverna Vatsoúlia. Odós Ayii Assómati. ☎ **0297/22-711.** Reservations not required. Dr 600– Dr 1,000 ($2.55–$4.25). No credit cards. Wed, Sat, Sun 6pm–1am. GREEK.

The local favorite, said to be the best and least expensive on the island, is about a 10-minute walk out of town on the road to the Temple of Aphaia, but call ahead before you go to make sure it's open. The menu is limited, rabbit a specialty, and live music is sometimes provided.

AEGINA AFTER DARK

At sunset the harbor scene gets livelier as everyone comes out for an evening *vólta* (stroll). **Kanella's Piano Restaurant** usually has live pop music, and **N.O.A.,** a portside ouzerí, offers a more traditional scene. Dancers will want to find **Disco Elpianna** or the **Inoi Club** in Fáros for Greek music, and the scene in Ayía Marína is sure to be lively, if a bit sordid. For more sedentary entertainment, there are two outdoor cinemas, the **Anesis** and **Olympia,** and several bars, including the **Bel Epoque,** at the corner of Aiándos and Piléos, and the **Rainbow** on Mitrópolis.

2 Póros

Lively Póros ("ford") is 31 nautical miles (55 kilometers) southwest of Piraeus and only 370 meters from the Peloponnesian Peninsula, which explains its popularity with both weekending Athenians and package tourists. It's an attractive island, with some good beaches, fair tavernas, and considerable nightlife. More importantly, it allows easy access to the many attractions on the mainland, especially Epidaurus, Náfplio, Mycenae, and Trizína (ancient Troezen). It says much that there is a car ferry across the narrow strait every 20 minutes in the summer.

Even if you're just passing through be sure to take a gander as you pass down the busy "grand canal." You're sure to find it interesting if not quite as exciting as it was to Henry Miller, who wrote, "To sail through the straits of Póros is to recapture the joy of passing through the neck of the womb. It is a joy too deep almost to be remembered."

The island is irregularly shaped, with a convoluted coastline with many coves and beaches, and nearly divided into two islands joined by a narrow isthmus. The smaller part, Sfería, contains the port and major city of Póros and the biggest concentration of the tourist facilities. Kalávria, the much larger half, is densely wooded with many natural harbors and beaches, where wealthy Athenians have built secluded villas.

ESSENTIALS

GETTING THERE   Most people come and leave on ferries or hydrofoils from Piraeus or the other Saronic islands, but others cross the narrow strait to and from Galatás by ferry, which costs Dr 60 (25¢) and takes only a few minutes. For information call the **Piraeus Port Authority** (☎ 01/45-11-311) or **Ceres Hydrofoils** (☎ 01/42-80-001) in Piraeus or **Marinos Tours** (☎ 0298/23-423) in Póros.

The other Saronic islands are all easy to reach, and Marinos Tours also runs a weekly round-trip hydrofoil excursion to Tínos (3½ hours each way) for Dr 15,000 ($63.80), and to Mýkonos via Hýdra (four hours each way) for Dr 17,500 ($74.50). (The one-way fare to Mýkonos is Dr 12,500/$53.20)

VISITOR INFORMATION   The **tourist police** (☎ 0298/22-462), **post office,** and **telephone center** (OTE) are on the paralía (waterfront); the OTE is open Monday through Friday from 8am to 11pm and on weekends 8am to 1pm and 5 to 10pm. Currency **exchange** can be made at the National Bank of Greece, on the far right of the port, or at several travel agencies, which keep extended hours.

GETTING AROUND   You can walk anywhere in Póros town. The island's bus can take you to the beaches; the conductor will charge you according to your destination. The taxi station is near the hydrofoil dock or you can call for one at 23-003; the fare to or from the beach at Askéli should costs about Dr 700 ($3). **Kóstas Bikes** (☎ 0298/23-565), opposite the Galatás ferry pier, rents bicycles for about Dr 700 ($3) a day and mopeds from about Dr 1,700 ($7.25) a day; the use of helmets is offered free.

WHAT TO SEE & DO

The waterfront of Póros town itself is quite a sight, with its constant boat traffic and tourists parading up and down the paralía, and at night you're sure to find people dancing to Greek music, notably the quick, energetic *hasápiko*, which will give you some idea how many Greeks stay fit. Póros town has a **Naval Training School,** a private school that might be of interest to some, and a small **Archaeology Museum,** with finds from ancient Troezen; call **0298/23-276** for an appointment to visit it.

The island's most famous sight is the **Temple of Poseidon,** now little more than a few broken columns and some rubble on a hill near the center of Kalávria. Most of the marble was hauled away to build a monastery on Hýdra. Póros was in ancient times an important refuge for political exiles, especially those ostracized from Athens. (Our word *ostracize* comes from the Greek *óstrakon*, "potsherd," from the Athenian custom of voting to exile offending politicians by writing their name on a piece of broken pottery. Don't you sometimes wish it were still so easy?) In 322 B.C., after the defeat of the Greek forces by the Macedonians at Lamía, Demósthenes, one of the greatest of Athenian orators and statesmen, fled to the Temple of Poseidon for refuge, but Antípater's forces pursued him, and he committed suicide by swallowing poison hidden in the nib of his pen, proving, as some wags observe, that the pen is sometimes quicker than the sword.

Those with a special interest in monasteries might want to visit the 18th-century **Monastery of Zoödóches Piyí** ("Life-giving Spring"), about 4 kilometers southeast of Askéli, though there are no longer any monks there—only a caretaker and a couple of tavernas nearby.

There is a beach northwest of town at **Neório,** though it is not always very clean. Better beaches are found southeast of town at **Askéli** and **Kanáli.** Those with the time or keener interest in the island should read Níki Stavrolákes's *Póros* (Lycabettus Press).

Instead of touring Póros, you might want to catch the ferry across to **Galatás,** especially in the middle of June during the **annual Flower Festival,** when there are parades with floats and marching bands and floral displays. (Greece exports flowers, even to Holland.) From Galatás you can catch a bus the 8 kilometers west to **Trizína** (ancient Troezen), birthplace of Theseus and the scene of the tragedy of his wife Phaedra and son Hippólytus, and site of an **ancient temple of Asclepius.** There's not a lot to see at the site, but the walk through fields of carnations and along the **Devil's Causeway,** which is supposed to have the old fellow's face on one of its walls, is very pleasant and may be of even greater interest to those who have read Mary Renault's *The King Must Die.*

About 4 kilometers south of Galatás near the beach of **Alíki,** you'll find the olfactory wonder of **Limonodássos** (Lemon Grove), where more than 25,000 lemon trees fill the air with their fragrance. Follow the signs to **Taverna Kardássi,** where you can have freshly squeezed lemonade for about Dr 550 ($2.10) or the potent local retsina.

WHERE TO STAY

The waterfront hotels are generally too noisy for all except heavy sleepers, so if you want to stay in town we suggest you check with **Marinos Tours** (☎ **0298/23-423**), which books several hundred rooms and apartments, as well as the hotels on the island. Expect to pay about Dr 7,000 to Dr 15,000 ($29.80 to $63.80) for a double, depending on the season, location, and facilities.

Hotel Latsi. Odós Papadopoúlou 74, 180 20 Póros, Trizinías. ☎ **0298/22-392.** 39 rms (most with bath). Dr 5,000 ($21.30) without bath; Dr 8,800 ($37.45) with bath. No credit cards.

This older hotel is on the quieter north end of the port, near the Naval School, opposite the Galatás ferry, with balconies overlooking the port and the Peloponnese. Rooms are worn but clean and comfortable.

Hotel Sirena. Monastíri, Askéli, 180 20 Póros, Trizinías. ☎ **0298/22-741.** Fax 0298/22-744. 120 rms (all with bath). A/C TEL. Dr 12,250 ($52.10) single; Dr 19,200 ($81.75) double. Half-board optional. MC.

The best hotel on the island is east of town beyond Askéli, on the road to the monastery, but as it's popular with tour groups, it must be booked early. The rooms, all spacious, in the six-story building have excellent views, and there's a nice saltwater pool near the lovely private beach.

⑤ Maria Christofa Rooms to Let. 180 20 Póros, Trizinías. ☎ **0298/22-392.** 6 rms (none with bath). Dr 5,500 ($23.40) single/double. No credit cards.

Our favorite budget choice is the home of Maria Christofa, in a narrow lane high above the town. The high-ceilinged rooms are simple but clean and comfortable, and some have great views of the town and harbor.

WHERE TO DINE

There's plenty of fast food and some good Greek cooking all along the paralía, but our particular recommendations are the following.

Caravella Restaurant. Paralía, Póros town. ☎ **0298/23-666.** Reservations not required. Appetizers Dr 600–Dr 1,500 ($2.55–$6.40); main courses Dr 1,250–Dr 3,800 ($5.30–$16.15). No credit cards. Daily 10am–1am. GREEK.

This port-side taverna specializes in seafood and traditional dishes such as veal stifádo, moussaká, souvláki, and stuffed eggplant.

Lucas Restaurant. Paralía, Póros town. ☎ **0298/22-145.** Reservations not required. Appetizers Dr 400–Dr 750 ($1.70–$3,20); main courses Dr 1,000–Dr 3,600 ($4.25–$15.30). No credit cards. GREEK

You'll find this pleasant outdoor place across from the private yacht marina. Fresh seafood and traditional dishes are well prepared and reasonably priced, especially for the upscale area.

PÓROS AFTER DARK

There's plenty of evening entertainment in Póros town, especially if you're in the mood to dance. The best disco is probably still **Scirocco,** about a kilometer south of town. The elegant music bar **Artemis,** in Askéli, draws a more sophisticated crowd, including the yachting set.

3 Hýdra

35 nautical miles (65km) S of Pireaus

Hýdra (Ýdra) has both natural physical beauty and superlative architectural distinction, plus the blessing of no traffic. Pedestrians are free to wander the port and the peaceful back lanes with only an occasional donkey, mule, or horse, and a rare appearance of a motorized garbage truck—there's one or two. The whole island has been declared a monument by both the Greek government and the Council of Europe.

The barren rocky island is at first sight almost forbidding until your ship enters the perfect horseshoe harbor surrounded by gray and white mansions, topped with red-tiled roofs, and churches, and suddenly you see cause for all the excitement. The island was briefly an artist colony in the 1960s; the artists have since fled because of rising real estate prices, leaving behind an artistic flavor. If you avoid the midday crush of cruise-ship visitors and the weekend inundation of Athenians, you will find Hýdra delightful and refreshing, if rather expensive. The island's one major drawback for some tourists is lack of good beaches, though there are a few places for swimming.

ESSENTIALS

GETTING THERE   Several ferries and excursion boats make the four-hour voyage between Piraeus and Hýdra daily, and there is connecting service to several ports on the Peloponnese peninsula, as well as with the other Saronic islands. Contact the

Piraeus Port Authority (☎ 01/45-11-311) or the **Hýdra Port Authority** (☎ 0298/52-279) for schedules. **Ceres Hydrofoils** (☎ 01/42-80-001) has several daily Flying Dolphins, some of them direct (a 1¼-hour trip), as well as Super Cat service between Piraeus's Zéa Marina (the southwest corner) and Hýdra. Reservations are recommended during the summer and on weekends.

VISITOR INFORMATION   The free publication *This Summer in Hýdra* is widely available and contains much useful information. **Saitis Tours** (☎ 0298/52-184), in the middle of the harbor front, can exchange money, give you information on rooms and villas, book excursions, and help you make long-distance calls or faxes.

GETTING AROUND   Walking is the only means of getting around on the island itself, unless you come upon available four-legged transport. Caïques provide water-taxi service to the island's beaches and the nearby island of Dokós, as well as to secluded restaurants in the evening; rates run from about Dr 200 to Dr 2,000 (85¢ to $8.50) depending on destination, with an extra Dr 600 ($2.55) charge if booked by phone.

FAST FACTS: HÝDRA

Area Code   The telephone area code for Hýdra is **0298.**

Banks   The National Bank of Greece and the Commercial Bank both have offices on the harbor; they're open Monday through Thursday 8am to 2pm, Friday 8am to 1:30pm, and on Saturday during the high season from 11am to 2pm.

Currency Exchange   The post office offers the best rates, but several travel agents, including Saitis Tours on the harbor, will exchange money from about 9am to 8pm.

Doctors and Pharmacies   There's a pharmacy and doctor's office on Odós Rafaélia, right off Odós Miaoúli, above the small square a couple of blocks inland from the port. There are other doctor's offices nearby and another pharmacy off the left of the harbor. Call the police for medical emergencies.

Hydrofoil Office   The Ceres Flying Dolphin office is on a back street, up the first street on the left from the ferry pier and to the right. (Look for the small signs.)

Police   The tourist police (☎ 0298/52-205) are on the second floor at Odós Votsí 9, two lanes up from near the right-hand side of the harbor front. They can usually provide the free publication *This Summer in Hýdra*, which has a map, a list of rooms to rent, and other useful information.

Post Office   The post office is just off the harbor front on Odós Ikonómou, the street between the two banks, open Monday through Friday from 7:30am to 2:15pm, and exchanges money at the best rates.

Telephones   The telephone center (OTE) is across from the police station on Odós Votsí, open Monday through Saturday from 7:30am to 10pm, Sunday from 8am to 1pm and 5 to 10pm.

WHAT TO SEE & DO

Hýdra town is the port, capital, and only town on the island, but it's chock-full of enough charm and history to keep you interested for several days. Some streets have names, but signs are scarce, and getting lost is part of the fun. The **mansions** that give the steep-sided port its special character were built in the late 18th century by Italian architects with the fortunes made by audacious Hýdriot captains, who had the skill and the courage to transport cargo wherever it was in demand regardless of embargoes and blockades, which was especially lucrative during the Napoleonic Wars. Find a copy of *This Summer in Hýdra* for a map to help you find the places we mention. *Hýdra*, by Catherine Vanderpool (Lycabettus Press), is a good companion guide.

On the right (west) side from the ferry pier you'll find the **Tombázi mansion,** now a branch of the **School of Fine Arts,** with a hostel for students. Call the mansion (☎ **0298/52-291**) or the Athens Polytechnie (☎ **01/61-92-119**) for information about the program or exhibits). The nearby **Ikonómou-Mириklís** (sometimes called the **Voulgaris**) **mansion** has an interesting interior. Higher up the hill is the largest and handsomest, the **Koundouriótis mansion,** built by an Albanian family that contributed generously to the cause of independence and still contributes to the confusion of tourists in those places where streets are named after both of the two most prominent members, Lázaros and Pávlos. There's plenty of interesting shopping on this side of the harbor, particularly at the **Hermes Art Shop** (☎ **0298/52-689**), which has an amazing array of jewelry, some good antique reproductions, and a few textiles—not local, but interesting.

On the left (east) side of the waterfront you'll find the **Spilopoúlou mansion** and the **Tsamados mansion,** now the **Merchant Marine School,** Greece's oldest college for sea captains. (You can visit if classes are not in progress.) A small **archaeology museum** can be found next door, though it wasn't open during out last visit. By making your way carefully up the worn stairs, you can visit the fortress that once protected the harbor. Further on, behind the **port police,** you'll find the **Kriezis mansion.**

Hýdra is famous for the number of its churches, said to be one for every day of the year, and several of them are well worth a visit. (Greek Easter is a great time to visit the island, provided you've booked a room ahead of time.) The most beautiful, the **Monastery of the Assumption of the Virgin Mary,** is found conveniently on the central waterfront at the **Clock Tower.** The former cells are now municipal offices, but the marble courtyard offers a serene retreat. (Most of the marble came from Póros's Temple of Poseidon.) There's a small chapel with precious Byzantine art, including an exquisite marble iconostasis, well worth the donation requested, Dr 150 (65¢), for which you also get a postcard. The statues are of Lázaros Koundouriótis and Andréas Miaoúlis.

If you're interested in more religious sites, feel like stretching your legs, and you're wearing sturdy shoes, continue on up Odós Miaoúli past **Kalá Pigádia** (Good Wells),

Miaoúlis and the War of Independence

Andréas Miaoúlis was the commander-in-chief of the Greek Navy during the War of Independence, and you will find many a waterfront named Aktí Miaoúli. He achieved his position through his skill, daring, and ability to persuade his men to follow him into battle. (At that time Greek ship crews had more automony, and crews often voted not to fight, gaining the Greek naval forces little respect from their more autocratic European neighbors.) One very effective Greek tactic was to take an old vessel, fill it with explosives, have a small crew ease up on a Turkish vessel at night, light the fuse, and swim for their lives. Admiral Miaoúlis's flagship, the *Hellas*, was his pride and joy, made in America with the very latest technology at enormous expense. But after independence was achieved when he was ordered by the Great Powers to surrender it to Russian control, he chose to blow it up and avoid a civil war. Every June 20, Hýdra honors him with its festive *Miaoúlia*, often celebrating his exploits with reenactments of battles and setting fire to old boats.

where the town still gets much of its water, about an hour to the **Convent of Ayía Efpraxía** and the **Monastery of the Prophet Elijah** (*Profítis Ilías*). Offering superb views of the town and beyond, both are still active, and the nuns sell their hand-woven fabrics. (*Note:* Men and women in shorts and tank tops will not be allowed inside.) By continuing further northeast you can reach the **Monastery of Ayía Triáda** (Holy Trinity), which also still has a few monks and excludes women. Two hours further east will bring you to the **Cloister of Zourvás** and the east end of the island.

The only real beach on the island is at **Mandráki,** a 20-minute walk east of town. West of town you can swim off the rocks at **Kamíni,** and further west along a don-key trail you'll find **Kastéllo,** with the small fort that gives it its name, and another rocky beach with less crowded swimming. Further west is the pretty pine-lined cove of **Mólos,** favored by jet-setters. The donkey path continues west to the cultivated plateau at **Episkopí,** from which a faint trail leads on west to **Bísti** and **Àyios Nikólaos** for more secluded swimming.

One fairly good beach on the south coast, **Limióniza,** can be reached with strong legs, sturdy shoes, and a good map from Ayía Triáda, though it's much easier to take a water taxi. The island of **Dokós,** northwest off the tip of Hýdra, an hour boat ride from town, has a good beach and excellent diving conditions—it was here that Jacques Cousteau found a sunken ship with cargo still aboard believed to be 3,000 years old—but few facilities, so you should take a picnic lunch.

WHERE TO STAY

As all the hotels are rather small, you would be wise to book well ahead of time, pref-erably for the middle of the week. In the summer reservations are a must. All hotels are open from early April until late October unless otherwise noted. Low season prices should be 20% to 30% less, often including breakfast.

🟢 **Hotel Angelika.** Odós Miaoúli 42, 180 40 Hýdra. ☎ **0298/53-202.** 22 rms (all with bath). Rates include breakfast. Dr 9,500 ($40.45) single; Dr 15,200 ($64.70) double. No credit cards.

This friendly pension, a 10-minute walk up from the port, is open most of the year. The rooms are simple, clean, and a good value, all overlooking a quiet arbor court-yard, where breakfast is served. Rooms 6, 8, 9, and 10 have large rooftop terraces with panoramic views.

🔵 **Hotel Bratsera.** Odós Tombázi, 180 40 Hýdra. ☎ **0298/53-971.** Fax 0298/53-626. 23 rms (all with bath). A/C TEL. Dr 29,500–Dr 35,500 ($125.50–$151) double, Dr 46,000–Dr 48,000 ($195.75–$204.25) suites. Rates include breakfast. AE, DC, EURO, MC, V.

The newest and best hotel on the island is in a lovingly restored 1860 sponge factory, a couple of minutes from the port. The lobby is spacious and charmingly fur-nished, with a fireplace for winter, as the hotel is open 11 months of the year, and there are good conference facilities. Rooms are all unique, distinctively decorated in typical Hýdriot style, quiet, with ample light and very comfortable. The swimming pool is especially nice, if not large, surrounded by a colonnade and trellises covered with wisteria, under which meals are served in fair weather.

Hotel Greco. Odós Kouloúra, 180 40 Hýdra. ☎ **0298/53-200.** Fax 0298/53-511. 19 rms (all with bath). A/C TEL. Dr 12,800 ($54.50) single; Dr 17,000 ($72.35) double. Rates include breakfast. AE.

In a quiet neighborhood, this stone factory, in which fishing nets were once made, has been converted into modern hotel. All rooms are spotless, with blue tiled floors and designer-print fabrics. The taverna on the large enclosed stone patio is a pleas-ant place for fresh grilled meats and Greek fare in the evenings.

🟢 **Hotel Hýdra.** Odós Voulgari 8, 180 40 Hýdra. ☎ **0298/52-102.** 13 rms (8 with bath). TEL. Dr 7,500 ($31.90) single; Dr 10,250 ($43.60) single with bath; Dr 13,500 ($57.45)double without bath; Dr 16,000 ($68.10) double with bath. Rates include breakfast. MC, V.

One of the best bargains in town if you don't mind a hike up to this beautifully restored two-story, gray-stone mansion on the western cliff, to the right as you get off the ferry. The rooms are carpeted, high ceilinged, and simply furnished, many with balconies overlooking the town and harbor. Open all year.

Hotel Leto. 180 40 Hýdra. ☎ **0298/53-385.** Fax 01/36-12-223 in Athens. 24 rms, 6 suites (all with bath). TEL. Dr 12,500 ($53.20) single; Dr 17,250 ($73.40) double; Dr 20,000 ($85.10) double with A/C; Dr 25,500 ($108.50) suites for 3 to 4 persons. Rates include breakfast. No credit cards.

The recently renovated Leto has new hardwood floors, contemporary furnishings, modern-art posters, and big bathrooms. The staff is young and eager to please. The garden is particularly delightful. An American-style buffet breakfast is served in the smoke-free basement.

You may want to ask about enrollment in the **Hellas Art Club**, which offers classes in painting, ceramics, music, theater, photography, Greek dancing, and cooking.

Hotel Miranda. 180 40 Hýdra. ☎ **0298/52-230.** Fax 0298/53-510. 16 rms (all with bath). Dr 19,200–Dr 24,800 ($81.70–$105.55) single/double; Dr 30,250 ($128.70) suite. Rates include breakfast. AE, V.

This homey 1820 sea captain's mansion is eclectically decorated with oriental rugs, antique cabinets, worn wooden chests, marble tables, contemporary paintings, and period naval engravings. The warm hospitality of Miranda and Yannis makes it especially pleasant. We particularly recommend that families stay in the suites, which have three comfortable beds, Greek country antiques, and large balconies with harbor views.

Hotel Mistral. 180 40 Hýdra. ☎ **0298/52-509.** Fax 0298/53-411. 20 rms (all with bath). TEL. Dr 14,400 ($61.30) single; Dr 19,200 ($81.70) double; Dr 19,800 ($84.25) double with A/C. Rates include breakfast.

The three-story Mistral (named for the strong northerly winds that cool the late summer) is fairly new and has a spacious stone courtyard with flowers. Sofia, the friendly proprietor, keeps her large, comfortable rooms spotless. Only guests can take advantage of dinner in the courtyard—a chance to sample the freshest seafood at bargain prices. Open February to November.

Hotel Orloff. Odós Rafalia, 180 40 Hýdra. ☎ **0298/52-564.** Fax 0298/53-532. 10 rms (all with bath). A/C TEL. Dr 27,600–Dr 34,000 ($117.45–$144.70). Rates include breakfast. AE, DC, EURO, MC, V.

This recently restored 200-year-old mansion is distinctively decorated with antique furnishings, professionally and graciously managed, and just a short walk from the port. Each room is unique, quiet, and comfortable, and there's a very nice basement lounge with a bar. Breakfast is superb.

Pension Efi. Odós Sachíni, 180 40 Hýdra. ☎ **0298/52-371.** 15 rms (all with bath). Dr 8,850 ($37.70) single/double. No credit cards.

This newer pension offers good views of the harbor and the town's rooftops from its simple modern rooms. You'll find the affable proprietor at a tourist shop opposite the Clock Tower. His English is limited, but his hospitality makes up for it.

WHERE TO DINE

The harborside eateries are predictably expensive and not generally suggested for anything but coffee or a snack. **To Roloi** (The Clock) has especially friendly and attentive service, and nearby **The Three Brothers** has a good reputation for the quality of its food. The **Ambrosia Cafe,** back from the port, serves vegetarian fare and good breakfasts. There are some good places west of town at Kamíni, notably **Christina's,** which serves seafood and excellent simple Greek fare.

Bratsera. Odós Tombázi, Hýdra. ☎ **0298/52-794.** Reservations recommended in summer and on weekends. Appetizers Dr 600–Dr 1,400 ($2.55–$5.95); main courses Dr 1,400–Dr 3,500 ($5.95–$14.90). AE, DC, EURO, MC, V. Daily 8am–11pm. INTERNATIONAL.

This new restaurant—up the first street left from the ferry pier, left from near the Flying Dolphin office—may prove itself the best on the island. The indoor dining area is charmingly rustic, decorated with antique maps, but outdoors under the wisteria-covered trellis beside the pool may be more enjoyable. The menu is small but varied, with pastas, fresh seafood, grilled meats, and even a few Chinese specialties.

Marina's Taverna. Vlihós. ☎ **0298/52-496.** Reservations not required. Appetizers Dr 400–Dr 1,200 ($1.70–$5.10); main courses Dr 1,000–Dr 3,200 ($4.25–$13.60). No credit cards. Daily noon–11pm. GREEK.

One of the island's most special dining experiences can be had at this seaside taverna, also appropriately called the **Iliovasílema** ("Sunset") because of its spectacular sunsets. Perched on the rocks west beyond Kamíni, it's a 45-minute walk or Dr 2,000 ($8.50) water taxi ride from town. The menu is basic, but the food is fresh and carefully prepared by the lovely Marina; her *kléftiko* (pork pie, an island specialty) is superb.

O Kípos (The Garden). Hýdra. ☎ **0298/52-329.** Reservations recommended in the summer. Appetizers Dr 500–Dr 900 ($2.10–$3.85); main courses Dr 1,600–Dr 2,600 ($6.80–$11). No credit cards. Daily 7pm–midnight. GREEK.

This very popular *psisteriá* (grill) is in a tree-filled garden behind whitewashed walls, several blocks up from the left side of the harbor near the stadium. Grilled meat is, of course, the specialty, but there is also excellent swordfish souvláki. The *mezédes* alone will be enough for some. The specialty is *exochikó*—lamb wrapped in *phýllo* (thin leaves of pastry).

☉ To Steki. Odós Miaoúli. ☎ **0298/53-517.** Reservations not required. Appetizers Dr 125–Dr 1,250 (55¢–$5.30); main courses Dr 1,200–Dr 2,400 ($5.10–$10.20); daily specials Dr 2,200–Dr 3,500 ($9.35–$14.85). No credit cards. GREEK.

This local favorite—on the left a couple of blocks up the main street from the port—has simple food at reasonable prices. Inside the walls have framed folk murals of typical island life. The daily specials, basic meals that sometimes include locally caught seafood, come with salad, vegetables, and a desert.

HÝDRA AFTER DARK

The **Veranda** is up from the right (west) end of the harbor, near the Hotel Hýdra; look for the sign Savvas Rooms to Let. It's an excellent place to sip a glass of retsína or café frappé and watch the sunset. There are several discos, most of them fairly low key, usually open June through September. **Heaven** (☎ 0298/52-716), which has grand views, is up the hill on the west side of town, and **Kavos** (☎ 0298/52-716), west above the harbor, has a pleasant garden for a rest from the dancing. The louder **Scirocco,** is fortunately well outside of town, on the way to Kamíni.

Port side, there are plenty of bars. The **Pirate** (☎ 0298-52-711), near the Clock Tower, is the best known, though nearby **To Roloi** is probably a more pleasant place for a nightcap.

4 Spétses

53 nautical miles (98km) SW of Piraeus
2 nautical miles (3km) from Ermióni

Spétses (sometimes Spétsai) is the farthest of the Saronic islands from Athens, though it's less than 2 miles from Ermióni, on the Peloponnese. It's greener, better watered, more relaxed, and less expensive than Hýdra, and though its architecture is less impressive it's nevertheless distinctive. In recent years it has become increasingly popular with both Athenians and foreign tourists, especially the British, partly in response to descriptions of the island in John Fowles's masterful *The Magus*, so there are a few too many signs advertising English Breakfast and far too many mopeds.

The oval island has the best beaches in the Saronic Gulf, and it's not difficult to escape the crowds and noise into the back streets or the pine forests of the interior. There's a wide variety of accommodations, and nightlife is especially lively and sophisticated.

ESSENTIALS

GETTING THERE   Several ferries and excursion boats make the five-hour voyage from Piraeus daily, connecting with the other Saronic islands; contact the **Piraeus Port Authority** (☎ 01/45-11-311) for schedules. (*Note:* Cars are not allowed on the island without express permission.) Several hydrofoils (Flying Dolphins and Supercats) leave Piraeus's Zéa Marina daily, most connecting with the other Saronic islands; express service takes 90 minutes. Contact **Ceres Hydrofoils** (☎ 01/42-80-001) in Piraeus or **Bardákos Tours** (☎ 0298/73-141) in Spétses for schedules. (Reservations are recommended for weekends.)

There is less frequent service to the island of Kýthira and various ports on the Peloponnese.

VISITOR INFORMATION   Currency **exchange** can be made at the port-side banks or at nearby travel agencies, which are open daily from 9am to 8pm in the summer. There's a **medical clinic** (☎ 0298/72-201) inland from the east (left) side of the port. The local **police** and the **tourist police** (☎ 0298/73-100) are to the left off the Dápia, where the hydrofoils dock, on Odós Botássi. The **post office** is up the street from the police station. The **telephone center** (**OTE**), open daily from 7:30am to 3pm, is to the right off the Dápia, behind the Hotel Soleil. **Pine Island Tours** (☎ 0298/72-464; fax 0298/73-255), across from the water taxi stop, can help you with day tours, ferry tickets, travel plans, and yacht charters; the manager, Kostas, is exceptionally well-informed about the island.

GETTING AROUND   The island's limited public transportation consists of two municipal buses and three or four taxis. Mopeds can be rented everywhere, beginning at about Dr 2,800 ($11.90) per day. Bikes are also widely available, and the terrain along the road around the island makes them sufficient means of transportation; three-speed bikes should cost about Dr 1,000 ($4.25) a day, while newer 21-speed models will go for about Dr 2,000 ($8.50).

Horse-drawn carriages can take you away from the busy port into the quieter back streets where most of the island's handsome old mansions are to be found. (Take your time choosing a driver; some are friendly and informative, others are surly and bent on getting the trip over with.) Inquire at the art shop near the post office about the possibility of private horseback riding.

The best way to get to the various beaches around the island, as well as to the beach at Kósta, on the Peloponnese, is by water taxi (locally called a *venzína,* "gasoline"); these little powered boats can hold about eight to 10 people. A tour around the island should cost about Dr 4,500 ($19.50), and shorter trips, such as from Dápia to the Old Harbor should cost about Dr 2,250 ($9.60). Save money by joining a group; schedules are posted on the pier.

WHAT TO SEE & DO

Unlike most island capitals, Spétses (also called Kastélli) is quite spread out. Many of the island's neoclassical mansions are inland, screened from the busy port by all the greenery.

The square where the ferries and hydrofoils arrive, the **Dápia,** is more or less the heart of the town. It once was the center of the island's defenses, but now it's the center of its society. The black-and-white pebble mosaic, called *votsalotá*—distinctive of the island and similar to those found on Rhodes—commemorates the beginning of the Revolution on Spétses, when the first flag with the motto "Freedom or Death" was raised. (You will see other such mosaics throughout the town.)

The biggest and most colorful celebration of the year falls on the weekend closest to the 8th of September, the anniversary of the island's victory over the Turks in the Straits of Spétses in 1822.

Around the esplanade to the right (west) you'll find one of the island's most important landmarks, the grand old **Hotel Possidónion,** one of the first major tourist hotels in Greece, built in 1911 by the island's greatest benefactor, Sotíris Anáryiro. In front of it the **statue of Bouboulína,** the island's heroine.

Laskarína Bouboulína was the daughter of a naval captain from Hýdra. One of the many stories about her is that she was born in prison, which helps explain her rather piratical nature. She was already twice a widow, with six grown children when the war began, and she spent her fortune building her *Agamemnon,* a superb vessel on which she sailed to Náfplio and successfully blockaded the port. Both brave and shrewd, she was responsible for several naval victories, gaining the love and admiration of her countrymen, even those who said she could drink any man under the table and that she was so ugly the only way she could keep a lover was with a gun.

The **Laskarína Bouboulína House** (☎ 0298/72-077) in Pefkákia, just off the port, has been restored and is now open to the public from 10am to 5:30pm Monday through Saturday, with an English-speaking guide giving a half-hour tour. Admission is Dr 800 ($3.40) for adults, Dr 400 ($1.70) for children. You can see her bones, along with other artifacts, archaeological relics, and more recent folk objects, at the **Mexís Museum,** beyond the post office, behind the clinic, open daily from 9:30am to 2:30pm, free admission.

Near the OTE, behind the Hotel Soleil, you'll find a very good craft shop, **Pityoússa** (no phone), which has a collection of decorative folk paintings, ceramics, and interesting gift items. Across the street, **Gorgóna** has a similar collection and some antiques.

A little west of town, you'll find **Anáryiros College,** another gift from the great benefactor, who modeled it after an English public school. It's now most famous for having had John Fowles as one of its teachers, and is closed most of the year except during August when it hosts the *Anaryíria* **festival** of art exhibits, lectures, and theatrical performances.

East of the Dápia along the cannon-studded port you'll find the picturesque **Old Harbor** (*Paleó Limáni*), where the wealthy moor their yachts. The **Cathedral of Àyios Nikólaos** (St. Nicholas) is the oldest church in town; it has a lovely bell tower on which the Greek flag was first raised on the island. Nearby is a pebble mosaic picturing the event. (There are nearly a dozen similar mosaics in the vicinity.)

Continue east to **Baltíza,** where boatyards continue to make caïques (*kaíkia*) the traditional way. Beyond it at the tip of the peninsula is the **Fáros** (Lighthouse.)

South along the road takes you to **Ayía Marína,** the town's closest beach and most important nightlife suburb.

You can continue south and clockwise around the island to search for various isolated beaches. The enticing little island off the eastern shore is **Spetsopoúla,** once the private domain of that modern-day pirate extraordinaire, Stavros Niarchos, who was upstaged only by Aristotle Onassis. Though he died in early 1996, his black yacht, the largest in Greece, is sometimes seen moored offshore.

Àyii Anáryiri, on the south side of the island opposite Spétses town, has the best sandy beach anywhere in the Saronic Gulf, a perfect C-shaped cove lined with trees, bars, and two tavernas (the **Taverna Tássos** is considered one of the best on the island), so naturally it's very popular. You can reach it by bike, though in either direction it's a hilly trip, or by hike via Vígla, though this isn't as pleasant as it once was, due to several forest fires, the most recent in 1990. The best way is by water taxi.

Continuing clockwise, by caïque or foot, you'll reach **Ayía Paraskeví,** which is smaller and more private because it's more closely bordered by pine trees. There's a cantina and the **Villa Yasemía,** residence of the Magus himself, which can now be rented, for a price (see "Where to Stay," below). West over some rocks is the island's official nudist beach.

Picturesque **Zogeriá,** a difficult hike by foot, northwest back over to the north side of the island—or west from Dápia—has a few places to eat and some pretty rocky coves for swimming. Back to the east—the best place west of Spétses town—is pleasant **Vrelloú,** in a wooded valley that is locally known as "Paradise," which you may think of as Paradise Littered because of all the plastic bottles and aluminum cans. (When is someone going to figure out that the stuff is actually worth a little something—or at least that clean beaches are more economically productive—and start collecting and recycling?) Closer to Dápia there's **Lambroú beach** near **Ligonéri,** and closer still to town is **Blueberry Hill,** which if not exactly a thrill is usually somewhat cleaner, though threatened by development.

Andrew Thomas's *Spétses* (Lycabettus Press) has more details on the island.

WHERE TO STAY

Finding a good, quiet, inexpensive room in spread-out Spétses can be a bit of a hunt, so try our suggestions or inquire at **Pine Island Tours** (☎ 0298/72-464), across from the water taxi stop, which can even rent you the Magus's old digs at Villa Yasemía. Avoid the main street hotels and the group "villas," which can be noisy. Expect to pay about Dr 7,000 to Dr 9,000 ($29.80 to $38.30) for a plain double with bath. The hotels we recommend below are a little removed from the main streets and open from late April to mid-October, unless otherwise noted.

Anna-Maria Hotel. Dápia, 180 50 Spétses. ☎ **0298/73-035.** 20 rms (all with bath). TEL. Dr 8,300 ($35.30) single; Dr 13,000 ($55.30) double. Rates include breakfast. No credit cards.

This bright new lodging with a second-floor reception and breakfast lounge, above the post office, has clean simple rooms. Unfortunately, like much of the town, it's often monopolized by British tour groups, but check it out.

Hotel Fáros. Platía Kentrikí (Central Square), 180 50 Spétses. ☎ **0298/72-613.** 40 rms (all with bath). TEL. Dr 8,850 ($37.70) single; Dr 11,400 ($48.45) double. No credit cards.

Though there's no *fáros* (lighthouse) nearby, this older hotel shares the busy central square with a Taverna Fáros, a Fáros Pizzeria, and other establishments whose tables and chairs curb the flow of vehicular traffic. Try for the top floor, where simple, comfortable, twin-bedded rooms are quietest, with balcony views of the island.

Hotel Possidónion. Dápia, 180 50 Spétses. ☎ **0298/72-006** or 0298/72-308. Fax 0298/72-208. 55 rms (all with bath). TEL. Dr 15,400 ($65.55) single; Dr 17,700 ($75.30) single with garden or sea view; Dr 20,200 ($85.95) double; Dr 22,850 ($97.25) double with sea view. Rates include breakfast. AE, DC, MC, V.

The landmark Poseidon (as we would call it) is a grand and gracious hotel that was built in 1911 and, under new management, was recently completely renovated. This belle epoque classic boasts two grand pianos in its lobby and the statue of Bouboulína guarding the plaza in front. The high-ceilinged rooms are spacious and sparsely but elegantly furnished. The old-fashioned bathrooms have large tubs. The view from the tall front windows is superb.

🟆 **Star Hotel.** Dápia, 180 50 Spétses. ☎ **0298/72-214** or 0298/72-728. Fax 0298/72-872. 50 rms (all with bath). TEL. Dr 8,625 ($36.70) single; Dr 11,500 ($48.95) double. No credit cards.

This blue-shuttered five-story hotel is fortuitously situated on a pebbled mosaic, making it off-limits to vehicles. It's the best of the older budget establishments. All rooms have balconies, the front ones with views of the harbor. The large bathrooms have a bathtub, Danish shower, and bidet. Breakfast is available à la carte in the large lobby.

WHERE TO DINE

Spétses's reputation for good living comes partly from its number of fine restaurants, which can get really packed on weekend evenings. To avoid the Greek crush, try to be seated before 9pm. The island also has some of the best bakeries in the Saronic Gulf, and all serve an island specialty called *amygdalóta*, small cone-shaped almond cakes flavored with rosewater and covered with powdered sugar.

Vegetarians should try **Lirákis,** above the supermarket of the same name on the harbor, which also serves some unusual Greek specialties. The **Red Dragon Chinese Restaurant,** above the Yacht Club, serves the expected cuisine.

The Bakery Restaurant. Dápia. No phone. Reservations not required. Appetizers Dr 600–Dr 1,500 ($2.55–$6.40); main courses Dr 1,200–Dr 3,000 ($5.10–$12.75). EURO, MC, V. Daily 6:30pm–midnight. CONTINENTAL.

This contemporary restaurant is on the deck above one of the island's more popular patisseries. The food is prepared fresh, with little oil, and served hot. The chef obviously understands foreign palates and offers smoked trout salad, grilled steak, roasted lamb with peas, as well as the usual Greek dishes.

Exedra Taverna. Paleó Limáni. ☎ **0298/73-497.** Reservations not required. Appetizers Dr 400–Dr 750 ($1.70–$3.20); main courses Dr 1,000–Dr 3,000 ($4.25–$12.75). No credit cards. Daily noon–3pm and 7pm–midnight. GREEK/SEAFOOD.

This traditional taverna on the Old Harbor, where yachts from all over Europe moor, is also known by locals as **Siora's,** after the proprietor. The specialties are fish *Spetsiotá* (a broiled fish and tomato casserole) and *Argó* (shrimp and lobster baked with sharp feta cheese). The freshly cooked zucchini, eggplant, and other seasonal vegetables are also excellent. If you can't find a table for supper, try the nearby Taverna Liyerí, also known for good seafood.

Lázaros Taverna. Dápia. No phone. Reservations not required. Appetizers Dr 600–Dr 1,000 ($2.55–$4.25); main courses Dr 1,000–Dr 2,500 ($4.25–$10.65) Daily 6:30pm–midnight. GREEK.

This traditional place is decorated with potted ivy, family photos, and big kegs of homemade retsina lining the walls. It's popular with a lively local crowd that comes here for the good, fresh, reasonably priced food. The menu is small and features grilled meats and daily specials, such as goat in lemon sauce. The Lázaros is inland and uphill about 400 meters from the water.

SPÉTSES AFTER DARK

There's plenty of nightlife on Spétses, with bars, discos, and bouzouki clubs from the Dápia to the Old Harbor to Ayía Marína, and even the more remote beaches.

For bars, try **Socrates** in the heart of Dápia. The **Anchor** is more upscale, and there's the **Bracera Music Bar** on the yachting marina. For something a little more sedate try the **Halcyon** or the **Veranda,** for softer Greek music. To the west of town, in Kounoupítsa, near the popular Patralis Fish Taverna, are the nicer upmarket bars, **Zorba's** and **Kalia.**

As for discos, there's the trendy and hot **Figaro,** with a seaside patio and international funk until midnight, when the music switches to Greek and the dancing follows step. The **Delfina Disco,** opposite the Dápia town beach on the road to the Old Harbor, has become increasingly popular. **Disco Fever,** with its flashing lights, draws the British crowd, and **Naos,** which looks more like a castle than a temple, features techno pop. The **Fox** is expensive but offers live Greek music and dancing—any tourists present are urged to join in the fun, which gets livelier after everyone has had a few drinks.

The Peloponnese   6

by Sherry Marker

What's special about the Peloponnese? It's tempting to answer, "Everything." With the exception of Athens and Delphi, just across the Gulf of Corinth, virtually every famous ancient site in Greece is in the Peloponnese—the awesome Mycenaean palaces of Kings Agamemnon and Nestor at Mycenae and Pýlos; the mysterious thick-walled Mycenaean fortress at Tiryns; the magnificent classical temples at Corinth, Neméa, Vassae, and Olympia; and the monumental theaters at Árgos and Epidaurus, still used for performances today.

But the Peloponnese isn't just a grab bag of famous ancient sites: This peninsula, divided from the mainland by the Corinth Canal, is studded with medieval castles and monasteries, bounded by sand beaches, and dominated by two of Greece's most impressive mountain ranges: Taygetos and Parnon. Tucked away in the valleys and hanging precipitously from the mountainsides are hundreds of the villages that are among the Peloponnese's greatest treasures. An evening under the plane trees in tiny Andrítsena, where the sheep bells are the loudest sound at night and oregano and flowering broom scent the hills, is every bit as memorable as a visit to one of the famous ancient sites. This is perhaps especially true in the mountains of Arcadia and deep in the Máni peninsula, where traditional Greek hospitality hasn't been eroded by one too many busloads of camera-snapping visitors.

While many of the Aegean islands sag under the weight of tourists from May until September, the Peloponnese is still relatively uncrowded even in midsummer. That doesn't mean that you're going to have Olympia to yourself if you arrive at high noon in August, but it does mean that if you get to Olympia early in the morning, you may have an hour under the pine trees all to yourself. If you're traveling with a car and can set your own pace, you can visit even the most popular tourist destinations of Corinth, Mycenae, Epidaurus, and Olympia early in the morning or late in the afternoon—and have them virtually to yourself.

Still, even the most avid tourists do not live by culture alone, and one of the great delights of spending time in the Peloponnese comes from the quiet hours spent in seaside cafes, watching fishermen mend their nets while Greek families settle down for a leisurely meal. *Leisurely* is the word to remember in the Peloponnese, an ideal place

The Peloponnese

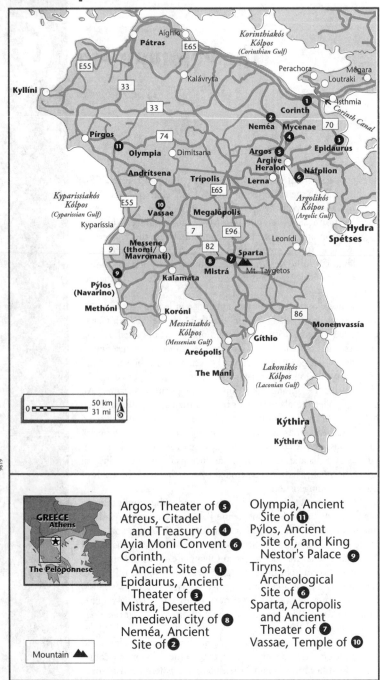

Argos, Theater of ⑤
Atreus, Citadel
    and Treasury of ④
Ayia Moni Convent ⑥
Corinth,
    Ancient Site of ①
Epidaurus, Ancient
    Theater of ③
Mistrá, Deserted
    medieval city of ⑧
Neméa, Ancient
    Site of ②

Olympia, Ancient
    Site of ⑪
Pýlos, Ancient
    Site of, and King
    Nestor's Palace ⑨
Tiryns,
    Archeological
    Site of ⑥
Sparta, Acropolis
    and Ancient
    Theater of ⑦
Vassae, Temple of ⑩

Mountain ▲▲

to make haste slowly. And what better place to watch shepherds on the hills or fishing boats on the horizon as you wait for dinner?

Although Greek food doesn't have the strong regional contrasts of French or Italian cuisine, there are some Peloponnesian favorites, such as rabbit stew (*kouneli stifado*) with a surprising hint of cinnamon, or *fish à la Spetsai* (fish baked with tomato sauce). In summer—when it seems that every tree on the plain of Árgos hangs with apricots and every vine is heavy with tomatoes—Peloponnesian food is at its freshest and best. If you're here in the spring, keep an eye out for the delicious fresh artichokes and delicate little strawberries. Even in winter, the fresh lettuce grown here is superb, citrus fruits are at their peak, and there's less competition in restaurants to get the best and freshest fish.

A few suggestions for your trip to the Peloponnese. Don't forget sunscreen, a broad-brimmed hat, good walking shoes, and some books to read while you're sitting in that cafe. Bookstores with a good selection of English titles are few and far between here, although you'll find excellent bookstores in Náfplion and Olympia. At the time of my most recent visit, cash machines were not available in the Peloponnese, but all banks, most hotels, and many post offices change money at competitive rates. Speaking of competitive rates, don't hesitate to ask if there's a cheaper rate for a room than the one first quoted at hotels. This is especially true off-season, when many hotels are willing to be quite flexible in their prices.

You'll probably be pleasantly surprised at how very impressed locals are if you master the linguistic basics of hello (*yia sas*) and thank you (*eucharisto*). And if you have trouble pronouncing *eucharisto,* here's a suggestion: It sounds a lot like the name *F. Harry Stowe.* If you're still having trouble, try *merci* (French for *thank you*), which most Greeks use interchangeably with eucharisto.

And however relaxed you get on your Peloponnesian holiday, it's a good idea to remember that this is still one of the more conservative areas of Greece, and virtually the only area where there's strong sentiment to restore the monarchy and bring back the good old days. Most Peloponnesians are at best amused and at worst deeply offended by public drunkenness, elaborate displays of affection, and swim suits or shorts and halters worn anywhere but on the beach. That said, *kalo taxidi* (bon voyage) on your trip to the Peloponnese, the most beautiful and historic part of Greece.

1 Corinth

55 miles (89km) W of Athens

Today, as in antiquity, Corinth, along with Pátras, is one of the two major gateways to the Peloponnese. Still, gates are there to pass through, not to linger in. There's no reason not to stop to see the ships slipping through the impressive Corinth canal that cuts across the isthmus and then head straight for Ancient Corinth, bypassing the modern city altogether. The contemporary English classicist and philhellene Peter Levi wasn't exaggerating when he wrote that "A night in a hotel in Corinth is not to be recommended to anyone." Mycenae and Náfplion both have excellent hotels and restaurants—and are only about an hour's drive from Corinth.

In fact, the entire modern town of Corinth (pop. 24,000) has remarkably little to recommend it. The town was moved here in 1834, after an earthquake devastated the settlement at Ancient Corinth; successive earthquakes in 1858, 1928, and 1981 destroyed virtually every interesting building in the new town. As a result, Corinth is now a thicket of undistinguished, flat-roofed buildings, supposedly built to withstand future quakes.

All this makes modern Corinth a far cry from Ancient Corinth, which was famously splendid and lively. As one Greek proverb had it, "See Corinth and Die," suggesting that there was nothing to look forward to after visiting the splendid monuments (and fleshpots) of the city that dominated trade in Greece for much of the 7th and 8th centuries B.C. and had a second golden age under the Romans in the 2nd century A.D.

ESSENTIALS

GETTING THERE   By Train   There are several trains a day from Athens's Stathmos Peloponnisou (Train Station for the Peloponnese) to the Corinth station off Odos Demokratias (☎ 0741/225-22). These trains are almost invariably late, often taking three hours or more. Refreshments sometimes are and sometimes are not available on board. For information on schedules and fares call **01/51-24-913.**

By Bus   There are at least 15 buses a day, taking two to 2 ¹/₂ hours from the Stathmos Leoforia Peloponnisou (Bus Station for the Peloponnese) at Odos Kifissou 100 in Athens to the Corinth station at Ermou and Koliatsou Streets (☎ **0741/ 256-45**), where you can catch a bus (15 to 20 minutes) to Archaia Korinthos. For information on Athens-Corinth-Athens schedules and fares call **01/51-28-233.**

Buses for the Peloponnese leave Corinth from the station at the corner of Konstantinou and Aratou streets (☎ 0741/244-03). For most destinations beyond Tripolis, you'll find yourself changing buses at Tripolis.

By Car   The National Highway runs from Athens to Corinth. The toll is Dr 400 ($1.70). The highway is in the process of being widened to seven lanes, but still contains some three-lane stretches that are particularly dangerous. The highway ends just before the Corinth canal; just after the canal, you'll see signs for Corinth (the modern town), Ancient Corinth (the archaeological site), and Isthmia (site of the Isthmian games). Allow at least 1 ¹/₂ hours for the journey from Athens.

FAST FACTS   The area code for Corinth is **0741.** There are several banks on Leof. V. Konstantinos and elsewhere in the town. The **OTE** at 33 Odos Kolokotronis (open 6am to midnight) and the **post office** by the park on Adimantou Street (open 7:30am to 2pm weekdays) are both signposted. The **police station** is at 51 Ermou (☎ **0741/221-43**), near the bus station for Athens.

A LOOK AT THE PAST

Historians are fond of saying that "Geography is destiny," and much of Corinth's power and prosperity came from its strategic location overlooking the sea and land routes into the Peloponnese. No enemy could sneak across the isthmus without being spotted by the soldiers stationed on Corinth's towering acropolis, Acrocorinth (1,863 feet).

During the 8th and 7th centuries B.C., Corinth controlled much of the trade in the Mediterranean and founded colonies as far away as Syracuse in Sicily. This was when Corinth made and exported the distinctive red-and-black figured pottery decorated with lively animal motifs, examples of which are on display in the excavation museum. Great sailors, the Corinthians were credited with refining the design of the trireme, the standard warship in Greek antiquity. The only obstacle Corinth couldn't overcome was the isthmus itself: Ships had to be dragged from the port of Kenchreai on the east to the port of Lechaion on the west.

Although Corinth's greatest period of prosperity was between the 8th and 5th centuries B.C., most of the ancient remains here are from the Roman period. Razed and destroyed when the Romans conquered Greece in 146 B.C., Corinth was refounded by Julius Caesar in 44 B.C. and began a second period of wealth and prosperity. When Saint Paul visited here in A.D. 52, he found Corinth all too sophisticated and chastised the Corinthians for their wanton ways.

By the 2nd century A.D., with some 300,000 citizens and 500,000 slaves, Corinth was much larger and more powerful than Athens. During the next hundred years, a series of barbarian invasions and attacks undermined Corinth's prosperity. Thereafter, although the long series of invaders—Normans, Franks, Venetians, and Turks—fought for control of the strategic citadel of Acrocorinth, Corinth itself was a provincial backwater with a glorious past.

WHAT TO SEE & DO
THE CORINTH CANAL

Almost everyone stops here for a coffee, a souvlaki, and a look at the Corinth canal that separates the Peloponnese from the mainland. There's a small post office at the canal, a kiosk with postcards and English language newspapers, and most of the large souvlaki places have surprisingly clean toilet facilities (and very tough souvlaki). One word of warning that is necessary here and almost nowhere else in Greece: Be sure to lock your car door. This is a popular spot for thieves to prey on unwary tourists.

The French engineers who built the Corinth canal between 1881 and 1893 used lots of dynamite, blasting through 285 feet of sheer rock to make this 4-mile-long, 30-yard-wide passageway. The Corinth canal utterly revolutionized shipping in the Mediterranean: Ships that previously had made their way laboriously around Cape Matapan at the southern tip of the Peloponnese could dart through the canal. The journey from Brindisi, Italy, to Athens was immediately shortened by more than 200 miles.

Although it took modern technology to build the canal, the Roman emperors Caligula and Nero had tried, and failed, to dig a canal with slave labor. Nero was obsessed with the project, going so far as to lift the first shovelful of earth with a dainty golden trowel. That done, he headed back to Rome and left the real work to the 6,000 Jewish slaves he'd had brought here from Judea.

The Archaeological Museum. Old Corinth, on the site of Ancient Corinth. ☎ **0741/31-207.** Admission Dr 1,000 ($4.26) includes admission to the site. Summer Mon–Fri 8am–7pm, Sat–Sun 8am–3pm; Winter Mon–Fri 8:45am–3pm, Sat–Sun 8:30am–3pm.

As you'd expect, the museum has a particularly fine collection of the famous Corinthian pottery that is often decorated with charming red-and-black figures of birds and animals. There are also a number of statues of Roman worthies and several mosaics, including one in which Pan is shown piping away to a clutch of cows. The museum also has an extensive collection of finds from the shrine of Asclepeios; as many of these are graphic representations of intimate body parts, they are kept in a room that is usually locked. If you express a scholarly interest, a guard may unlock the room. The museum courtyard is a shady spot to sit and read up on the ancient site.

Ancient Corinth. Old Corinth. ☎ **0741/31-207.** Admission Dr 1,000 ($4.25) includes admission to the museum, see above. Summer Mon–Fri 8am–7pm, Sat–Sun 8am–3pm; winter Mon–Fri 8:45am–3pm, Sat–Sun 8:30am–3pm.

If at all possible, visit here first thing in the morning or late in the afternoon: There'll be fewer tourists and the sun on this virtually shadeless site will be less fierce.

The most conspicuous—and the most handsome—surviving building at Ancient Corinth is clearly the 6th-century B.C. **Temple of Apollo,** which stands on a low hill overlooking the extensive remains of the **Roman Agora** (marketplace). Only seven of the temple's 38 monolithic Doric columns are standing, the others having long since been toppled by earthquakes.

From the temple, ancient Corinth's main drag, a 40-foot-wide marble-paved road that ran from the port of Lechaion into the heart of the marketplace, is clearly visible. Pottery from Corinth was carried down this road to the ships that took it around the world; back along the same road came the goods Corinthian merchants bought in every corner of the Mediterranean. Everything made here and brought here was for sale in countless shops, many of whose foundations are still clearly visible in the agora.

Two spots in the agora are especially famous: the **Bema** and the **fountain of Peirene.** In the 2nd century A.D., the famous Roman traveler, philhellene, and benefactor Herodes Atticus rebuilt the original modest fountain house. Like most Romans, Herodes seemed to think that bigger was better: When he was done, the spring was encased in an elaborate two-storied building with arches and arcades and a 50-square-foot courtyard. Peirene, by the way, was a woman who wept so hard when she lost her son that she finally dissolved into the spring that still flows here. As to the Bema, this was the public platform where Saint Paul had to plead his case when the Corinthians, irritated by his constant criticisms, hauled him up in front of the Roman governor Gallo in A.D. 52.

Acrocorinth. Old Corinth. Summer daily 8am–7pm, winter daily 8am–5pm. During the current restoration project, there is no admission fee.

A road twists from the ancient site to the summit of Acrocorinth, the rugged limestone sugarloaf mountain that looms 1,885 feet above the plain. On a clear day, the views from the summit are superb, although it's been a long time since the atmosphere was clear enough to spot the glistening columns of the Parthenon on the Athenian acropolis.

A superb natural acropolis, Acrocorinth was fortified first in antiquity. Everyone who came later—the Byzantines, Franks, Venetians, and Turks—simply added to the original walls. Today, there are three courses of outer walls, massive gates with towers, and a jumble of ruined houses, churches, and barracks. Before you head down, you might like to have a cold drink at the small cafe here and reflect on the fact that there was a Temple of Aphrodite on this summit in antiquity, staffed by an estimated 1,000 temple prostitutes, whose prospective customers walked here from Corinth.

WHERE TO STAY

As noted, if at all possible, do not stay in Corinth, a noisy and unappealing town.

Hotel Bellevue. Odos Damaskinou 41, Corinth, 20007. ☎ **0741/22-587.** 22 rms. TEL. Doubles Dr 9,000 ($36). AE, MC, V.

This hotel overlooking the harbor has as much of a *belle* view as you'll have in Corinth. The rooms in the front with balconies have the best views (and also the most street noise). The staff here has been praised as being helpful.

WHERE TO DINE

None of the cafes or restaurants along the Corinth canal out of town or the waterfront in town deserves to be singled out; most deserve to be avoided. Similarly, the restaurants near the ancient site tend to have high prices and mediocre food. That said, here are two suggestions, if you find yourself hungry in Corinth.

Archaeologists of the American School of Classical Studies who excavate here give the nod to the grandly named **Splendid** restaurant across from the site; lunch or dinner of simple stews, chops, and salads starts at Dr 1,725 ($7.34).

In the modern town, locals speak well of the **Pantheon Restaurant,** Odos Ethnikis Antistasis, Corinth (☎ 0741/25-780), which serves standard Greek fare such as chops, salads, and a hot dish or two such as moussaka or pastitsio (macaroni with cream sauce). Lunch or dinner from Dr 1,725 ($7.34).

SIDE TRIPS FROM CORINTH: ISTHMIA, LOUTRAKI & PERACHORA

ISTHMIA

Isthmia was one of the four places in Greece where Panhellenic games were held (the others being Delphi, Olympia, and Neméa). According to legend, the games here were founded in 582 B.C. in honor of a certain Meliertes, whose body was carried ashore by a dolphin at the very moment that the Delphic Oracle had revealed that a harsh famine would end only when the Corinthians honored someone who had died at sea. The Isthmiam games took place every two years at the **Sanctuary of Poseidon,** of which regrettably little remains.

From Ancient Corinth, drive back toward the Canal. Isthmia is signposted on your right just before you reach the canal.

What to See & Do

The **Site and Museum of Isthmia** are officially open summer Tuesday through Saturday 8:45am to 7pm, Sunday 9:30am to 2pm; winter 8:45am to 3pm; Sunday 9:30am to 2:30pm. Admission is Dr 500($2.15) for each.

The **principal temple** in Isthmia was dedicated to Poseidon and foundations remain of the structure built in the 7th century B.C., first rebuilt after a fire in the 5th century B.C., and then rebuilt once again when the Romans refounded Corinth in 44 B.C. Even the excavator here, Oscar Broneer, admitted of the temple that, "The casual visitor will marvel chiefly, perhaps, at the thoroughness of its destruction." The **ancient stadium,** with its elaborate starting gate, which Broneer lovingly reconstructed and equally lovingly demonstrated until his recent death, is better preserved.

Isthmia's interesting **small museum** seems to be closed as often as it is open. If you get in, you'll see exhibits on the Isthmian games and some handsome **glass-mosaic panels** showing land- and townscapes and the figure of a philosopher, sometimes identified as Plato. These panels were found, carefully packed in the wooden crates that preserved them for posterity after the ship they were on sank in the harbor of Kenchreai. Archaeologists speculate that the panels may have been intended to decorate the elegant home of one of the Roman officials who lived at Corinth.

LOUTRAKI

To get to Loutraki from Corinth, cross the Corinth Canal. Once you are on the mainland, you'll see that Loutraki is signposted on your left.

Loutraki is the famous Greek spa whose springs churn out a good deal of the bottled water you'll see in restaurants. If possible, don't visit Loutraki or Perachora (see below) on summer weekends when it's slow going to get through Loutraki, which bursts at the seams with the Athenians who stream here each weekend to enjoy the beaches and "take the waters" at the **Hydrotherapy Thermal Spa** at 26 G. Lekka St. (☎ 222-15). The spa is open Monday through Saturday 8am to 1pm.

En route to Perachora from Loutraki, you'll pass **Lake Vouliagmeni,** a saltwater inlet from the Gulf of Corinth. There are a number of equally good fish restaurants along the lake; make your choice depending on what's on the menu and whether you do, or do not, want to listen to Muzak.

PERACHORA

Perachora, especially after sprawling Corinth, seems like a miniature model of an ancient site. The site was founded in the 8th century B.C. and had several temples to Zeus's wife Hera, several stoas, and a number of useful water cisterns. Perched at the end of the peninsula, around a tiny cove, this is an idyllic spot, with just enough to see, as well as a picturesque lighthouse chapel. There would be more antiquities to see here if the Romans hadn't dismantled the temples and stoas and ferried the stones across the gulf to rebuild Corinth.

To get to Perachora, from Corinth, head back across the Corinth Canal and take the left turn signposted Loutraki; continue through Loutraki to Perachora, 20 miles (32km) or 30 minutes away by car.

The **Site of Perachora** is open daily in summer 8am to 7pm; winter 8am to 5pm. Admission is Dr 500 ($2.15). The ancient Corinthians called this spot Perachora, which means "the land beyond," meaning the land beyond the gulf. From here on a clear day, you can see the land beyond just about everything: There are superb views south across the Gulf to Acrocorinth and the mountains of the Peloponnese and along the north coast to the mountains of Central Greece.

This is an ideal spot for to spend a few lazy hours swimming and picnicking (but not on weekends, when too many other people have the same idea). You may prefer simply to dangle your toes in the water and not swim in the cove: Sharks are not unknown just outside the harbor in the Gulf.

2 Náfplion

90 miles (145km) SW of Athens

It's easy to overlook contemporary Greece as you travel from one ancient site to another in the Peloponnese. Náfplion (population 10,000) brings you face to face with the beginnings of modern Greece. For several years after the Greek War of Independence (1821–28), this was Greece's first capital. Although the palace of Greece's young King Otto—a mail-order monarch from Bavaria—burned down in the 19th century, you can still see the **former mosque** off Synta-gma (Constitution) Square where Greece's first parliament met. Another legacy of those years is the impressive number of handsome **neoclassical civic buildings and private houses,** as well as the generous number of **commemorative statues of revolutionary heroes** in Náfplion's squares and parks.

All this would be reason enough to visit this port on the east coast of the Gulf of Árgos, but Náfplion also has **two hilltop Venetian fortresses,** a **miniature castle** on an island in the harbor, shady parks, an interesting assortment of small museums, and better than average hotels, restaurants, and shops.

In short, Náfplion is far and away the most charming town in the Peloponnese. You could spend several pleasant days here simply enjoying the port town itself, but you'll probably want to use Náfplion as your home base for day trips to the ancient sites at Árgos, Neméa, Mycenae, Tiryns, Epidaurus, and—if you didn't see it on the way to Náfplion—Corinth.

ESSENTIALS

GETTING THERE   By Train   Unless you are a totally dedicated train buff, it makes no sense to come here by train. That said, there are several trains a day from Athens to Corinth and Árgos, where you can catch a bus on to Náfplion.

Information on schedules and fares is available from the **Stathmos Peloponnisou** (railroad station for the Peloponnese) in Athens (☎ **01/51-31-601**).

By Bus   There are at least a dozen buses a day to Náfplion from the **Stathmos Leoforia Peloponnisou** (bus station for the Peloponnese) in Athens at 100 Odos Kifissou (☎ **01/51-34-110** and 51-34-588). The trip is a slow one (about four hours) because the bus goes into both Corinth and Árgos before reaching Náfplion.

By Boat   There is **Flying Dolphin hydrofoil service** from Marina Zea, Piraeus to Náfplion Monday through Saturdays, weather permitting. The hydrofoil makes a number of stops and takes almost as long as the bus to reach Náfplion. The hydrofoil usually leaves Athens for Náfplion in the late afternoon and leaves Náfplion for Athens in the early morning. For information on fares and schedules, call ☎ **01/ 32-42-281** or 01/45-36-107.

By Car   From Athens, head south to the Corinth canal. If you want to stop at Mycenae and/or Neméa en route, take the winding old road to Náfplion. If you want to stop at Epidaurus en route, turn left just after the canal at the sign for Epidaurus. If you want to get to Náfplion as quickly as possible, take the new Corinth-Tripolis road as far as the Árgos exit (exit 2). Follow the signs first into Árgos itself, about 6 miles (10km) from the exit) and thence on to Náfplion. You will almost certainly get lost at least once in Árgos, which has an abysmal system of directional signs. Allow at least three hours for the drive from Athens to Náfplion, including a brief stop at the Corinth canal and some time thrashing around in Árgos.

Parking   When you reach Náfplion, park in the large municipal lot (no charge) by the harbor.

VISITOR INFORMATION   The **Greek National Tourist Organization Office (EOT)** is at 16 Photomara Street, catercorner from the bus station in Plateia Nikitara. The tourist office is usually open 9am to 2pm weekdays (☎ **0752/28-131**). Information and tickets for special events, such as the concerts in the **Náfplion Music Festival,** usually held during the first half of June, are often available from the Town Hall (Demarkeion) in the old high school building on Iatrou Square.

FAST FACTS   The telephone area code for Náfplion is **0752.** The **post office** (open Monday through Friday from 8am to 2pm) and the **OTE telephone and telegraph offices** (open 8am to 2pm, Monday through Friday) are signposted from the bus station. There is a branch of the **National Bank of Greece** on the main square, Plateia Syntagma (Constitution Square). There are a number of travel agencies in Náfplion, such as **Staikos Travel** by the harbor (☎ 0757/27-950), where you can get information on car rental and day trips from Náfplion. The **best place to swim** is at the beach beneath the Palamidi. With the Bourtzi on your right, walk as far as you can along the quay until you come to the beach. The **weekly market** on Saturday from around 7am to 1pm occupies most of the road alongside Kolokotronis Park. You can buy everything from handsaws to garlic here.

WHAT TO SEE & DO

Náfplion is a stroller's delight and one of the great pleasures here is simply wandering along the harbor, through the parks, and up and down the stepped side streets, discovering unexpected Turkish fountains and small churches. Don't make the mistake of stopping your harborside stroll when you come to the last of the large seaside cafes by the Hotel Agamemnon: If you continue on, you can watch fishing boats putting in at the pier, explore several cliff-side chapels, and wind your way past the small beach on a cliff-side path under the Acronafplia. And don't ignore Náfplion's lush green parks at the foot of the Palamidi: You can usually find a cool spot to sit here even at midday. Náfplion is so small that you can't get seriously lost, so have fun exploring. Here are some suggestions on how to take in the official sights after you've had your initial stroll.

ACRONAFPLIA & PALAMIDI

Náfplion's two massive fortifications, the **Acronafplia** and the **Palamidi,** dominate the skyline. As you'll realize when you visit these fortresses, whoever held the heights here could keep a close watch on both the gulf and the plain of Árgos. The Greeks began to fortify Acronafplia and Palamidi, and the Romans, Byzantines, Venetians, Franks, and Turks added a wall here and a turret there, with the results you see today. If you're here in the summer, try to visit the fortresses in the relative cool of either the morning or the evening; there's no admission to visit Acronafplia. If you're in Náfplion in June during the **Music Festival,** check to see if any evening concerts are being held at the Palamidi, which is open summer weekdays from 8am to 7pm; winter from 8:30am to 5pm, with an admission of Dr 500 ($2.15).

The easiest way to get up to the cliffs above Náfplion, known as the Acronafplia, is to drive or hitch a ride on the elevator that conveys guests from the lower town to the Xenia Palace Hotel. If you want to walk up, follow signs in the lower town to the **church of St. Spyridon;** one of its walls has the mark left by one of the bullets that killed Ianni Kapodistria, the first governor of modern Greece. From Saint Spyridon, follow signs further uphill to the Catholic **church of the Metamorphosis.**

This church is as good a symbol as any for Náfplion's vexed history: Built by the Venetians, it was converted into a mosque by the Turks, and then reconsecrated as a church after the War of Independence. Inside, an ornamental doorway has an inscription listing philhellenes who died for Greece, including the nephews of both Lord Byron and George Washington. Greece's first King, young Otto of Bavaria, worshiped here, wearing the Greek national costume, the short pleated skirt known as the foustanella, which he adopted to show solidarity with his new subjects. Ironically, while Otto wore his foustanella, the more fashion-conscious of his subjects here abandoned their Greek costumes and copied the western clothes worn by the members of Otto's court.

As you continue to climb toward Acronafplia, you may see several **carvings of the winged lion** that was the symbol of Saint Mark, the protector of Venice. The most important fortifications on Acronafplia were built during the first (1388–1540) and second (1686–1715) Venetian occupations. In the days before the Greek historical preservation movement dug in its tentacles, both the Xenia and the Xenia Palace Hotels were built over the fortifications, one reason that the original structures have been obscured. Unless you are a military historian, you may have to take it on faith that what you're looking at here is a Frankish castle and Venetian defense tower to the east and a Byzantine castle to the west. Náfplion retained its strategic importance well into this century: During World War II, the German occupying forces had gun emplacements here.

If you're not staying in the **Xenia Palace Hotel,** where bedrooms overlook the harbor, be sure to enjoy the view from Acronafplia of the **Bourtzi fortress** in the harbor. The Venetians built the Bourtzi to guard the entrance to the harbor in the 15th century. Since then, it's had a checkered career, serving as a home for retired executioners in the 19th century and briefly as a small hotel in this century.

From Acronafplia, you can look down at the Bourtzi and up at the Palamidi. If you are not in the mood to climb the 800-plus steps to the **summit of Palamidi,** you can take a taxi up and then walk down. The Venetians spent three years building the Palamídi, only to be conquered the next year by the Turks in 1715. You'll enter the fortress the way the Turkish attackers did, through the main gate to the east. Once inside, you can trace the course of the massive wall that encircled the entire summit and wander through the considerable remains of the five defense fortresses that failed to stop the Turkish attack. Kolokotrónis, the hero of the Greek war of Independence who later tried to subvert the new nation and seize power for himself, was held prisoner for 20 months in **Fort Miltiades,** the structure to your right as you enter the Palamídi.

NÁFPLION'S MUSEUMS

If your heart sinks at the thought of four museums to do in a town as small as Náfplion, it shouldn't: All four are within easy walking distance of each other, and one, the Folk Art Museum, is one of the most delightful museums in Greece.

The Folk Art Museum. Odos V. Alexandros 1. ☎ **0752/28-379.** Admission Dr 400 ($1.70). May–September Wed–Mon 9am–2pm and 5–7pm; October–April Wed–Mon 9am–2pm. Closed February.

Everything about this museum is charming: It's housed in an elegant 18th-century house with a shady courtyard and welcome snack bar, has a superb shop, and one of the finest collections of costumes in Greece. Throughout, labels are in English as well as Greek, which means that you can learn just how cotton was harvested and silk was spun and what kind of loom was used to make what kind of costume. Life-sized photos of women spinning, men shearing sheep, and a wide-eyed bridal couple posing in front of their wedding bed make the exhibits here come alive. The excellent museum shop has interesting books, records, old embroidery, and rugs, as well as inexpensive but stylish small purses made from old fabrics at Dr 1,150 ($4.90).

The Archaeological Museum. Syntagma Square. ☎ **0752/27-502.** Admission Dr 500 ($2.15). Year-round Tuesday–Sunday 8:30am–1pm.

The Archaeological Museum is housed in the handsome 18th-century Venetian arsenal that dominates Syntagma Square. The thick walls make this a deliciously cool place to visit on even the hottest day. Displays are from sites in the area and include pottery, jewelry, and some quite horrific Mycenaean terra-cotta idols as well as a handsome bronze Mycenaean suit of armor.

The Military Museum. Leoforos Amalias. ☎ **0752/25-591.** Free admission. Year-round Tuesday–Sunday 9am–2pm.

If you like old prints and old photographs, not to mention muskets, you'll enjoy strolling through the exhibits here, which cover Greek wars from the War of Independence to World War II.

The Museum of Childhood. Stathmos, Kolokotronis Park. Admission Dr 400 ($1.70). Year-round Mon–Fri 4–8pm; Sat 9am–1pm; frequent unscheduled closings.

An offshoot of the Folk Art Museum, this museum has an eclectic collection of dolls, baby clothes, and toys. It seems to keep especially fluid hours; if you arrive and the door is locked, you can see a fair amount by peering through the windows.

WHERE TO STAY

Náfplion has enough hotels that you can usually find a room here, although you may end up on the outskirts of town in high season. Be sure to make a reservation if you want a view of the harbor or if you are going to be here when there is a performance at Epidaurus, when tour groups reserve entire hotels.

Hotel Agamemnon. Akti Miaouli 3, Náfplion 21100. ☎ **0752/28-021.** 40 rooms (all with bath). TEL TV. Dr 23,000 ($97.90) double. Rates include breakfast and lunch or dinner. AE, EU, MC, V.

The Agamemnon is on the harbor just past the string of cafes, which means that you're bound to hear voices if you have a front room with a balcony. Still, friends who have stayed here claim that they were not bothered by noise and loved the view. The rooms are of the generic variety found in hotels throughout Greece. They're furnished with two single beds with pine bed frames and bedside tables.

Hotel Amphitriton. Plateia Speliadon, Náfplion 21100. ☎ **0752/27-366.** 42 rooms (all with bath). TEL. Dr 20,000 ($85.10) double. Rates include breakfast. AE, MC, V.

Many of the rooms in this pleasant, usually quiet, in-town hotel have views of the harbor and Bourtzi castle. Like many Náfplion hotels, the Amphitriton does a brisk tour business and you can feel a bit odd-man-out here if everyone else is with "the group." Still, the rooms are large, clean, and comfortable, and the hotel itself is just steps from the shops that line Spiliadou Street.

✪ **Byron Hotel.** Plateia Agiou Spiridona, Náfplion 21100. ☎ **0752/22-351.** Fax 0752-26338. 13 rooms (all with bath). TEL. Dr 12,118 ($51.60) double. AE, EU, MC, V.

This very pleasant small hotel, painted a distinctive pink with blue shutters, is in a quiet, breezy location overlooking the Church of Agiou Spiridona. There are a number of nice bits of Victoriana in the bedrooms and sitting rooms. Word has gotten out about the Byron's charm, and it's almost impossible to stay here in July or August without a reservation.

✪ **King Otto.** Farmakopoulou 4, Náfplion 21100. ☎ **0752/27-585.** 12 rooms (4 with showers). Dr 9,200 ($39.15) double. AE, MC, V.

The small, venerable, King Otto Hotel, in a pleasant neoclassical building with a handsome suspension staircase, is the best bargain in town. Don't expect frills here, but the rooms have high ceilings and some overlook a pleasant small garden.

Xenia Palace Hotel. Acronaufplia, Náfplion 21000. ☎ **0752/28-981.** Fax 0752/28-987. 48 rooms, 50 bungalows, 3 suites, all with bath. A/C MINIBAR TEL TV. Dr 46,000–Dr 60,000 ($195.75–$253.55) double. Rates include breakfast and either lunch or dinner. AE, DC, EU, MC, V. Off-season reductions possible.

The Xenia Palace has the best view in town; whether you think it has the best location depends on whether you want to be in town or up here on the slopes of Acronafplia looking across the harbor to the Bourtzi and the mountains of the Peloponnese. This may be the only hotel in the Peloponnese where you'll find such luxurious touches as a telephone in your bathroom; that said, the rugs and chairs in many of the bedrooms are showing signs of wear. The dining room has indifferent "international" and Greek cuisine, but people-watching can be fun here when elegant Athenian families appear on weekends. One big plus: a swimming pool, which is the perfect place to cool off after a day sightseeing. You can sometimes make arrangements to use the pool here if you're staying at the nearby Xenia Hotel, the Xenia Palace's less-expensive sister hotel, where rooms are usually at least $20 cheaper (same phone number and fax).

WHERE TO DINE

Oddly enough, the restaurants in and just off Syntagma Square are not the tourist traps you'd expect. Furthermore, you'll see a good number of Greeks at the big harborside cafes on Akti Miaoulis. In short, Náfplion has lots of good restaurants—as well as one superb pastry shop and any number of ice cream parlors selling elaborate gooey confections.

Hellas Restaurant. Syntagma Square, Náfplion. ☎ **0752/27-278.** Appetizers Dr 345–Dr 900 ($1.50–$3.85); main courses Dr 1,035–Dr 1,725 ($4.40–$7.35). AE, MC, V. Daily 9am to midnight. GREEK.

Kostas, the patron of the Hellas, says that there's been a restaurant here for more than 100 years. Shady trees and awnings make this a cool spot to eat outdoors; there's also an inside dining room, where locals tend to congregate year-round. Excellent dolmades with egg lemon sauce are usually on the menu, as well as stuffed tomatoes and peppers in season. Just about everyone in town passes through Syntagma Square, so this is a great spot to watch the world go by.

Karamanlis. Bouboulinas 1, Náfplion. ☎ **0752/27-668.** Appetizers from Dr 345 ($1.50); main courses Dr 1,035–Dr 1,725 ($4.40–$7.35). Fresh fish priced by the kilo. AE, EU, MC, V. 11am to about midnight.

This simple harbor-front taverna several blocks east of the cluster of harbor-front cafes tends to get fewer tourists than most of the places in town and serves up good grills and several kinds of meatballs (*keftedes, sousoutakia,* and *yiouvarlakia).* If you like the food here, you'll probably also enjoy the Kanares Taverna and the Hundalos Taverna, both also on Bouboulinas.

Ta Phanaria. Staikopoulos 13, Náfplion. ☎ **0752/27-141.** Appetizers from Dr 334 ($1.50); main courses Dr 1,150–Dr 2,300 ($4.90–$9.80). AE, EU, MC, V. Daily from about 11am to midnight. GREEK.

The shaded tables under Ta Phanaria's enormous scarlet bougainvillea are one of the prettiest places in town for lunch or dinner. Ta Phanaria usually has several inventive vegetable dishes on the menu in addition to such standbys as moussaka. The stews and chops here are also good, and in winter there are usually hearty bean dishes on the menu. Like the Hellas, Ta Phanaria continues to attract steady customers, despite doing much of its business with tourists.

⑤ The Pharos. Akti Miaoulis by the children's playground, Náfplion. ☎ **0752/26-043.** Ouzo and standard mezedes plate from Dr 575 ($2.45). Ouzo and a meal of mezedes from Dr 1,725 ($7.35). Daily from around 10am until midnight. OUZO BAR.

It's easy to stop at the Pharos for a drink and a snack and end up eating enough octopus, keftedes (meatballs), and *saganaki* (fried cheese) to make a meal. This is a great spot for enjoying the waterfront away from the main tourist bustle.

The Pink Panther. Odos Staikopoulou, Náfplion. No telephone. Ice cream sundaes from Dr 1,035 ($4.40). Daily from about 10am until around midnight. SWEETS/ICE CREAM.

There are those who swear that this place has the best ice cream in town. Anyone wanting to test the assertion might do a comparison taste test at the Fantasia, also on Odos Staikopoulou, and then try the mango sherbet at the Napoli di Romania cafe on Akti Miaoulis. Perhaps not all in one day.

✪ Savouras Psarotaverna. Leoforos Bouboulinas 79, Náfplion. ☎ **0752/27-704.** Fish priced by the kilo according to availability. AE, EU, MC, V. Daily from about noon until 11pm. FISH.

This restaurant has been here more than 20 years and its fresh fish attracts Greek day-trippers from Tripolis and even Athens. What you eat depends on what was caught that day. Expect to pay at least $30 for two fish dinners, a salad, and some house wine. On summer weekends, this restaurant can be terribly crowded.

Stathmos Cafe. Náfplion (the old railroad station). No telephone. Coca-Cola Dr 345 ($1.50); bag of potato chips Dr 300 ($1.30); mezedes from Dr 575 ($2.45). Daily from about 9am until midnight. DRINKS/SNACKS.

This is a nice shady spot to sit and take a break from tourist Náfplion, perhaps after visiting the Museum of Childhood next door. The old train station is decorated with a splendid painting of an old steam engine, has elaborate wooden gingerbread trim, comfortable chairs under shady trees, and a cozy inside room for cold weather.

⊙ **The Yatagan.** Plateia Saint George, Náfplion. ☎ **0752/21-221.** Pastries from Dr 3,000 ($12.75) a kilo. Usually 10am–10pm. ANATOLIAN SWEETS/ICE CREAM/COFFEE.

If you arrive in Náfplion by bus, you could do worse than to take the first turn on your left as you face the bus station and head straight to the Yatagan. The different varieties of honey-drenched Anatolian pastries here are the next best thing to the pastries sold at the superb Karavan pastry shops in Athens. You can eat your pastries at the shop or get them to go—or both.

SHOPPING

Náfplion has not escaped the invasion of T-shirt and mass-produced souvenir shops that threatens to overwhelm Greece, but there are also some genuinely fine shops here, many on or just off Odos Spiliadou, the street immediately above Plateia Syntagma. As in most Greek towns heavily dependent on tourism, many of these shops are closed in winter.

Aelios. 4 V. Konstantinou, Náfplion 21100. ☎ **0752/28-149.**

This jewelry store sometimes has unusually distinctive rings and bracelets for both men and women from around Dr 23,000 ($97.90). The shop's owner speaks excellent English and can show you pieces done by a number of fine Greek jewelers. Virtually everything on sale here is a pleasant departure from the more customary mass-produced gold jewelry on sale elsewhere in Náfplion.

To Enotion. Odos Staikopoulou. No telephone and no visible street number.

You'll know you've found To Enotion when you see a window full of handsome museum-quality leather and wood reproductions of characters from the Greek shadow theater, including Turkish pashas, country bumpkins, military heroes, and damsels in distress. The smallest of the colorful marionettes begin at about Dr 10,000 ($42.55), but it's easy to spend much more here.

Helene Papadopoulou. 5 Spiliadou, Náfplion. ☎ **0752/25-842.**

Helene Papadopoulou sells dolls made of brightly painted gourds, priced from Dr 10,000 ($42.55), and traditional weavings, from Dr 10,000 ($42.55), in her shop near the waterfront end of Odos Spiliadou. Next door, her husband has a wide collection of excellent quality Greek costume dolls from Dr 10,000 ($42.55), as well as some nice ceramic jewelry of Greek ships and flowers from Dr 1,500 ($6.38).

Konstantine Beselmes. 6 Athan. Siokou Street, Náfplion. ☎ **0752/27-274.**

Konstantine Beselmes sells his own quite magical paintings of village scenes, sailing ships, idyllic landscapes, and family groups. Although new, the paintings are done on weathered boards, which gives them a pleasantly aged look. Priced from Dr 15,000 ($63.85).

Odyssey bookshop. Syntagma Square, Náfplion.

The Odyssey has a wide selection of newspapers, magazines, and books in English, as well as a startling collection of pornographic drink coasters. This is also a good place to pick up a copy of Timothy Gregory's *Náfplion* (Lycabettus Press), the best guide to the city.

SIDE TRIPS FROM NÁFPLION: AYIA MONI CONVENT & TIRYNS
AYIA MONI CONVENT
1¹/₂ miles (3km) outside Náfplion

Although this peaceful hillside convent is just minutes outside Náfplion, it seems a world away. To get there by car, head out of Náfplion on the Epidauros road. Turn right at the sign for Agia Moni and continue on a partly bumpy road to the convent. Don't go during the afternoon siesta time when the convent is usually closed. The convent was founded in the 12th century, and the church is a fine example of Byzantine church architecture. Many of the other buildings here are modern and were built after a series of fires destroyed much of the original convent. The nuns sometimes have embroidery to sell and are usually more than willing to show you the church and garden.

The spring that feeds a small pond just outside the convent walls is one of a number of springs in Greece identified as the one in which Zeus's wife Hera took an annual bath to restore her virginity and renew Zeus's ardor. Today, the spring water is considered both holy and delicious and pilgrims here often fill bottles here to take home.

TIRYNS
3 miles (5km) outside Náfplion on the Árgos road

From the moment that you see Tiryns, you'll understand why Homer called this Mycenaean citadel "well-walled." The **Archaeological Site of Tiryns** is open in summer from 8am to 7pm and in winter from 8am to 5pm. Admission is Dr 500 ($2.15). If you have a car, this is an easy drive; if you don't, take one of the Árgos-Náfplion-Árgos buses and ask to be let off at Tiryns. Taxi drivers in both Árgos and Náfplion will take you to Tiryns and wait while you visit; expect to pay at least Dr 5,750 ($24.50).

Tiryns stands on a rocky outcropping 87 feet high and about 330 yards long, and the entire citadel is girdled by the massive walls that so impressed Homer. Later Greeks thought that only the giants known as Cyclopes could have positioned the wall's 14-ton red limestone blocks, and archaeologists still call these walls "cyclopean." Even today, Tiryns's walls stand more than 30 feet high; originally, they were twice as tall—and as much as 57 feet thick.

According to Greek legend, the great hero Heracles (Hercules) was born at Tiryns after Zeus deceived and impregnated Alkmene, one of many maidens to catch his fancy. Zeus's wife Hera, infuriated that her attempts to win back her husband's love had failed yet again, sent serpents to strangle the infant Hercules in his cradle. Instead, Hercules strangled the serpents. Hera, however, was nothing if not determined; years later she made Hercules kill his wife and children in a fit of temporary insanity.

As at Mycenae, people seem to have lived at Tiryns virtually forever. And, as at Mycenae, Tiryns seems to have increased its fortifications around 1,400 B.C. and been destroyed around 1,200 B.C. Most scholars assume that Tiryns was a friendly neighbor to the more powerful Mycenae, and some have suggested that Tiryns was Mycenae's port. Even today, Tiryns is only a mile from the sea; and in antiquity, before the plain silted up, it would have been virtually on the seashore.

Tiryns is a good deal better preserved than Mycenae and once you climb the ramp and pass through the two gates, you'll find yourself in an impressive **series of**

storage galleries and chambers on the east side of the citadel. Ahead, there are more galleries and chambers, including one long passageway with a corbelled arch whose walls have been rubbed smooth, probably by the generations of sheep that took shelter here after Tiryns fell.

The citadel is crowned by **the palace,** whose **megaron (great hall)** has a well-preserved circular hearth and the base of a putative throne. This room would have been gaily decorated with frescoed walls; you can see the surviving frescoes, some with scenes of elegant women riding in a chariot, in the National Archaeological Museum in Athens. These women, who would have lived in the royal apartments west of the megaron, probably freshened up in the bathroom, whose floor is a massive 20-ton limestone slab. Lesser folk would have lived below the citadel on the plain. Two tunnels led from the lower slopes of Tiryns out into the plain to the **large subterranean cisterns** that held the secret water supply that allowed Tiryns to withstand even a lengthy siege.

As at Mycenae, there's no knowing why Tiryns finally fell into decline, with some scholars suggesting civil wars, others natural disasters, still others invasions by the mysterious "People of the Sea," sometimes credited with invading Greece about this time.

3   Mycenae

71 miles (115km) SW of Athens; 31 miles (50km) S of Corinth

According to Greek legend and the poet Homer, King Agamemnon of Mycenae was the most powerful leader in Greece at the time of the Trojan War. It was Agamemnon, Homer says, who led the Greeks from Mycenae, which he called "rich in gold," to Troy (ca. 1250 B.C.). There, the Greeks fought for 10 years to reclaim fair Helen, the wife of Agamemnon's brother Menelaus, from her seducer, the Trojan prince Paris.

The German archaeologist Heinrich Schliemann, who found and excavated Troy, began to excavate at Mycenae in 1874. Did Schliemann's excavations here prove that what Homer wrote was based on an actual event—not myth and legend? Scholars are suspicious, although most admit that Mycenae could have been built to order from Homer's descriptions of Mycenaean palaces.

After you visit here, see if you agree with something that the English philhellene Robert Liddell once wrote: "Mycenae is one of the most ancient and fabulous places in Europe. I think it should be visited first for the fable, next for the lovely landscape, and thirdly for the excavations."

ESSENTIALS

GETTING THERE   By Bus   There is frequent bus service from the Peloponnesian bus station (☎ 01/51-34-100) in Athens at 100 Kifissou to Corinth, Árgos, and Náfplion (allow three to four hours). From any of these places you can travel on by bus to Mycenae (allow an hour).

By Car   From Corinth: Take the old Corinth-Árgos highway south from Corinth for about 30 miles, and then take the left turn to Mycenae, which is about 5 miles down the road. **From Náfplion:** Take the road out of town toward Árgos. When you reach the Corinth-Árgos highway, turn right and then, after about 10 miles, right again at the sign for Mycenae. (If you are going to Náfplion when you leave Mycenae, try the very pleasant back road that runs through villages and rich farmland. You'll see the sign for Náfplion on your left shortly after you leave Mycenae.)

FAST FACTS   The area code for the modern village of Mycenae is **0751.** You can buy stamps and change money at the **mobile post office** at the ancient site, weekdays from 8am to 2pm. This office is sometimes open on weekends and after 2pm, but don't count on it.

INSIDER TIP   If at all possible, visit here early in the morning and wear a hat and sturdy shoes: There's no shade at the site (except in the cistern and the beehive tombs) and the rocks are very slippery.

WHAT TO SEE & DO
The Citadel and the Treasury of Atreus. Admission Dr 1,000 ($4.25). Summer Mon–Fri 8am–7:30pm, Sat–Sun 8am–3pm; winter 8am–5pm, Sat–Sun 8am–3pm.

As you walk uphill to Mycenae, you begin to get an idea of why people settled here as long ago as 3,000 B.C.: Mycenae straddles a low bluff between two protecting mountains and is a superb natural citadel. The site overlooks one of the richest plains in Greece and whoever held Mycenae could control all the land between the narrow Dervenakia Pass to the north and the Gulf of Árgos, some 10 miles to the south.

By about 1,400 B.C., Mycenae controlled not just the Plain of Árgos, but much of mainland Greece, as well as Crete, many of the Aegean islands, and outposts in distant Italy and Asia Minor. Then, some unknown disaster struck Mycenaean Greece; by about 1,100 B.C., the Mycenaeans were on the decline. By the time of the classical era, almost all memory of the Mycenaeans had been lost, and Greeks speculated that places like Mycenae and Tiryns had been built by the Cyclopes. Only those enormous giants, people reasoned, could have moved the enormous rocks used to build the ancient citadels' defense walls.

You'll enter Mycenae through just such a wall, passing under the massive **Lion Gate,** whose two lions probably symbolized Mycenae's strength. The door itself (missing, like the lions' heads) would have been of wood, probably covered with bronze for additional protection; cuttings for the door jambs and pivots are clearly visible in the lintel. Soldiers stationed in the **round tower** on your right would have shot arrows down at any attackers who tried to storm the citadel. Since soldiers carried their shields on their left arms, the tower's position made the attackers vulnerable to attack on their unprotected right side.

One of the most famous spots at Mycenae is immediately ahead of the Lion Gate: the so-called **Grave Circle A,** where Schliemann found the gold jewelry now on display at the National Museum in Athens. When Schliemann opened the tombs and found some 14 kilos of gold here, including several solid gold face masks, he concluded that he had found the grave of Agamemnon himself. At once, Schliemann fired off a telegram to the king of Greece saying, "I have looked upon the face of Agamemnon bare." More sober scholars have concluded that Schliemann was wrong, and that the kings buried here died long before Agamemnon was born.

From the grave circle, head uphill past the low remains of a number of **houses.** Mycenae was not merely a palace, but a small village, with the palace at the crest of the hill and administrative buildings and homes on the slopes. The **palace** was considerably grander than these small houses and had a several court rooms, bedrooms, a throne room, and a large megaron (ceremonial hall). You can see the imprint of the **four columns** that held up the roof in the megaron, as well as the outline of a **circular altar** on the floor.

If you're not claustrophobic, head to the northeast corner of the citadel and climb down the flight of stairs to have a look at Mycenae's enormous **cistern.** You may find someone here selling candles, but it's a good idea to bring your own flashlight. Along with Mycenae's great walls, this cistern, which held water channeled here from a spring 500 meters away, helped to make Mycenae impregnable for several centuries.

If it's not too hot when you visit, try to give yourself some time to sit on the citadel and contemplate the sad history of the House of Atreus and enjoy the view of the farm fields below. On your way back down, take a look at the **little bathtub** in the palace, which Schliemann thought was the very bathtub where Agamemnon was stabbed to death by his wife Clytemnestra.

There's one more thing to see before you leave Mycenae: the massive tomb known as the **Treasury of Atreus,** the largest of the tholos tombs found here. You'll see signs for it on your right as you head down the modern road away from Mycenae. This treasury may have been built around 1300 B.C., at about the same time as the Lion Gate, in the last century of Mycenae's real greatness.

This enormous tomb, with its 118-ton lintel, is 43 feet high and 47 feet wide. To build it, workers first cut the 115-foot-long passageway into the hill and faced it with stone blocks. Then, the **tholos chamber** itself was built, by placing slightly overlapping courses of stone one on top of the other until a **capstone** could close the final course. As you look up toward the ceiling of the tomb, you'll see why these are called **"beehive tombs."** Once your eyes get accustomed to the poor light in the tomb, you can make out the **bronze nails** that once held hundreds of bronze rosettes in place in the ceiling. This tomb was robbed even in antiquity, so we'll never know what it contained, although the contents of Grave Circle A give an idea of what riches must have been here. If this was the family vault of Atreus, it's entirely possible that Agamemnon himself was buried here.

WHERE TO STAY

La Belle Helene. Mycenae, Argolis, 21200. ☎ **0751/76-225.** 8 rooms (none with bath). Dr 11,500–Dr 15,000 ($48.95–$63.80) double, sometimes less in the off-season. Rates include breakfast. DC, V.

The real reason to stay here is to add your name to that of Schliemann and other luminaries in the guest book. Sentiment aside, this small hotel, one of the most famous in Greece, is usually very quiet and the simple rooms are clean and comfortable. If you stay here, be sure to drive or walk up to the ancient site at night, especially if it's a full moon.

✪ **La Petite Planete.** Mycenae, Argolis, 21200. ☎ **0751/76-240.** 30 rooms (all with bath). TEL. Dr 17,250 ($73.40) double, sometimes less off-season. Rates include breakfast. AE, V.

This would be a nice place to stay even without its swimming pool, which is irresistible after a hot day's trek around Mycenae. I've usually found it quieter here than at La Belle Helene, and friends who stayed here recently praised the restaurant and enjoyed the view over the hills from their window.

WHERE TO DINE

Most of the restaurants in Mycenae specialize in serving up fixed-price set-meals to groups. You won't starve if you eat at one of these big, impersonal roadside restaurants, but you're likely to be served a bland, lukewarm "European-style" meal of overcooked roast veal, underripe tomatoes, and—not out of the realm of possibilities—canned vegetables. You'll have better luck trying the smaller restaurants at **La Petite Planete** or **La Belle Helene hotels** (see above). It's also sometimes possible to avoid tour groups at the **Achilleus,** on Main Street, Mycenae (☎ 0751/76-027), where you can eat lunch or dinner, priced from Dr 2,000 ($8.50).

4 Epidaurus

39 miles (63km) S of Corinth; 20 miles (32km) E of Náfplion

The **Theater of Epidaurus** is one of the most impressive sights in Greece. Probably built in the 4th century, possibly by Polykleitos, the architect of the Tholos, this theater seated—and still seats—some 14,000 spectators. Unlike so many ancient buildings, including almost everything at the Sanctuary of Asclepios, the theater was not pillaged for building blocks in antiquity. As a result, it is astonishingly well preserved; restorations have been minimal and tactful.

ESSENTIALS

GETTING THERE   By Bus   Two buses a day run from the Peloponnesian bus station (☎ 01/51-34-100) in Athens at 100 Kifissou to Epidaurus. Buses take about three hours. There are three buses a day from the Náfplion bus station off Plateia Kapodistrias (☎ 0752/273-23) to Epidaurus, as well as extra buses when there are performances at the Theater of Epidaurus. The bus takes about an hour.

By Car   If you're coming from Athens or Corinth, turn left for Epidaurus immediately after the Corinth canal and take the coast road to the Theatro (ancient theater), not to Nea Epidavros or Palaia Epidavros. From Náfplion, follow the signs for Epidaurus. If you drive to Epidaurus from Náfplion for a performance, be alert: The road will be clogged with tour buses and other tourists who are driving the road for the first time.

WHAT TO SEE & DO

The Sanctuary, Museum, and Theater at Epidaurus. Combined admission Dr 1,500 ($6.40). Open hours to all three are summer Mon–Fri 8am–7pm, Sun–Sat 8:30am–3:15pm; winter Mon–Fri 8am–5pm, Sat–Sun 8:30am–3:15pm.

Although it's pleasant to wander through the shady **Sanctuary of Asclepios,** it's not at all easy to decipher the scant remains here—visit the excavation museum first (see below). As at Olympia, the Asklepion had accommodations for visitors, several large bath houses, civic buildings, a stadium, gymnasium, and several temples and shrines. The remains here are so meager that you may have to take this on faith, but try to find the round **tholos** that you'll pass about halfway into the sanctuary. The famous 4th-century B.C. architect Polykleitos, who built similar round buildings at Olympia and Delphi, was the architect here. If you wonder why the inner foundations of the tholos are so convoluted and labyrinthine, you're in good company: Scholars still aren't sure what went on here, although some suspect that Asclepios's healing serpents lived in the labyrinth.

Next to the tholos are the remains of **two long stoas,** where patients slept in the hopes that Asklepios would reveal himself to them in a dream. Those who had dreams and cures dedicated the votive offerings and inscriptions now in the museum.

At the entrance to the site, the **excavation museum** helps to put some flesh on the bones of the confusing remains of the sanctuary. It has an extensive collection of architectural fragments from the sanctuary, including lovely **acanthus flowers** from the mysterious tholos. The **terra-cotta body parts** are votive offerings that show precisely what part of the anatomy was cured. The display of **surgical implements** will send you away grateful that you didn't have to go under the knife here, although hundreds of inscriptions record the gratitude of satisfied patients.

If you climb to the top of the **ancient theater,** you can look down over the 55 rows of seats, divided into a lower section of 34 rows and an upper section with 21 rows. The upper seats were added when the original theater was enlarged in the 2nd century B.C. The theater's acoustics are famous and you'll almost certainly see someone demonstrating that a whisper can be heard all the way from the round orchestra to the topmost row of seats. Just as the stadium at Olympia brings out the sprinter in many visitors, the theater at Epidaurus tempts many to step stage center and recite poetry, declaim the opening of the Gettysburg Address, or burst into song. Still, there's almost always a respectful silence here when a performance of a classical Greek play begins as the sun sinks behind the orchestra and the first actor steps onto the stage (see "Epidaurus After Dark," below).

WHERE TO STAY

Epidaurus Xenia Hotel. Ligourio, Nafplias, Peloponnese. ☎ **0753/22-005.** 26 rooms (12 with bath). TEL. Dr 17,250 ($73.40) double, sometimes less off-season. Rates include breakfast.

The best place to stay overnight at Epidaurus is this hotel at the site itself. Once everyone leaves, this is a lovely, quiet spot, in a pine grove. The 26 bungalow-like units go quickly on the night of a performance, so book well in advance. The restaurant serves bland but acceptable food.

WHERE TO DINE

There are several kiosks selling snacks and cold drinks near the ticket booth at Epidaurus. There are a number of boring restaurants in Nea and Palaia Epidaurus, most of which cater to large groups.

EPIDAURUS AFTER DARK
CLASSICAL PRODUCTIONS AT THE ANCIENT THEATER

Performances at the ancient theater are usually given Saturdays and Sundays from June through September. Many productions are staged by the **National Theater of Greece,** some by foreign companies. For information and ticket prices, contact the **Athens Festival Box Office,** Odos Stadiou 4 (☎ 01/32-21-459). It's also possible to buy tickets at most of the travel agencies in Náfplion and at the theater itself, from 5pm on the day of a performance. The performance starts around 9pm. The ancient tragedies are usually performed either in classical or modern Greek; programs (Dr 1,000; $4.26) usually have either a full translation or a full synopsis of the play. The excellent Odyssey bookstore in Náfplion (see "Náfplion: Shopping," above) usually has English translations of the plays being performed at Epidaurus.

A MUSIC FESTIVAL

In 1995, the Society of the Friends of Music sponsored a festival during the last two weekends of July at the recently restored 4th-century theater at Palea Epidaurus, 7 kilometers from Epidaurus. The Society hopes to hold a music festival every year at the small theater, which seats 4,000; check with the Greek National Tourist Office to see if the festival is taking place the year of your visit.

5   Neméa

15 miles (25km) SE of Corinth; 21 miles (35km) north of Árgos

Panhellenic games were held every four years at Olympia and Delphi and every two years at Isthmia, near Corinth, and at Neméa, in a gentle valley in the eastern foothills of the Arcadian mountains. The first Olympic games were held in 776 B.C. and didn't begin at Neméa until 573 B.C. By about 100 B.C., Neméa's powerful neighbor Árgos moved the festival from Neméa to Árgos itself, putting an end to the games here. But, thanks to the Society for the Revival of the Neméan Games, games will be held again at Neméa on June 1, 1996—and, it is hoped, every two years thereafter. So when you visit Neméa, you won't just see the stadium where athletes once contended, but the site of the new Neméan games.

Two excellent site guides are on sale at the Museum (*Neméa* at Dr 3,500 ($14.90) and *The Ancient Stadium of Neméa* at Dr 500 ($2.15), and you'll find shady spots to read them in both at the site and at the stadium.

ESSENTIALS

GETTING THERE   By Car   From Athens, take the National Road to Corinth and then follow signs for Árgos and Tripolis. The road divides just after the sign for Ancient Corinth. The speedy new Corinth-Tripolis toll road has green signposts with a drawing of a highway. The toll is Dr 700 ($2.97). Take the Neméa turnoff and then follow signs to the site. If you take the old road, you'll see signs for Neméa just after the Neméa train station, where the main road bends sharply left, and you continue straight toward Neméa. Allow 30 minutes from Corinth to Neméa on the new road and an hour on the old road.

By Bus   There are about five buses a day from the Peloponnesian Bus Station in Athens at 100 Kifissou St. (☎ **01/51-34-110**) to Neméa. Allow about two hours for the trip and ask to be let off at the ancient site of Neméa (Ta Archaia) on the outskirts of the hamlet of Archaia Neméa, not in the village of Nea Neméa.

By Train   It's possible to take the train from Athens to the station several kilometers from the ancient site. The train, however, is very slow and it makes better sense to take the bus.

FAST FACTS   The area code for Neméa is **0726.** If you want to swim, check to see if the **municipal pool,** or *piscina,* about 1 mile from the stadium, is open (☎ 0726/22-168); an entrance fee of Dr 400 ($1.70) is charged.

WHAT TO SEE & DO

The Museum and Ancient Site. Admission Dr 500 ($2.15). Open year-round daily 8:30am–3pm (closed Mondays).

The Neméa Museum, set on an uncharacteristically Greek green lawn, is one of the most charming small museums in Greece. You'll get an excellent picture here of the history of the excavation of Neméa and the Neméan games, as well as the early Christian village here, much of which was built from material pillaged from ancient Neméa.

A display map just inside the museum's main gallery shows all the cities in the Greek world whose coins were found at Neméa and illustrates just how far people came to see these games. There are a number of excellent photographs of the excavations and enlarged photos of important finds, such as the small bronze figure of the infant Opheltes, in whose honor the Neméan games may have been founded.

According to legend, the Seven Theban Champions founded the games in memory of the infant, who—not as agile as Heracles (Hercules)—was killed by a serpent. Because the games were perceived as funeral games, the judges wore black mourning robes, just as they will in June 1996 at the revived Neméan Games. Another legend says that the games were established not to honor Opheltes but to honor Heracles, who killed a fierce lion that had his lair in one of the caves in Evangelistria hill, just behind the stadium. Fortunately, lions are unknown in today's Greece.

When you're in the museum, be sure to take a look out of one of the large picture windows that overlook the ancient site where the coins, vases, athletic gear, and architectural fragments on display were found. A raised stone path tactfully suggests the route from the museum to the site, passing a carefully preserved early Christian burial tomb and skirting a large Christian basilica and Roman bath before arriving at the Temple of Zeus.

This temple was built of local limestone around 330 B.C. on the site of an earlier temple, which may have burned down. Today, only three of the original 32 exterior Doric columns are still standing: The drums of the others are scattered on the ground. When Pausanias came by here in the 2nd century A.D.., he felt that the temple was worth seeing but complained, "that the roof has collapsed." Sometime later, the columns followed suit, perhaps when early Christian squatters pillaged the temple for building blocks, or after one of the many earthquakes that rocked the Peloponnese.

The Stadium. Admission Dr 500 ($2.15). Year-round daily 8:30am–3pm (closed Mondays).

To reach the stadium, leave the site and head several hundred yards back along the road that brought you into Neméa.

The Ancient Stadium of Neméa on sale at the ticket booth contains a self-guided tour of the stadium. The locker room just outside the stadium caused quite a stir when it was discovered in 1991, with few journalists able to resist cracks about what a locker room must smell like after 2,500 years.

Athletes would have stripped down in the locker room, oiled their bodies with olive oil, and then entered the stadium through the vaulted tunnel, just as football players today rush onto the playing field. Once you pass through the tunnel, you'll see where the judges sat while spectators sprawled on earthen benches carved out of the hillside itself. When they got thirsty, they could have a drink from the water carried around the race track in a stone channel. If you want, walk down onto the 178-meter race course and stand at the stone starting line where the athletes took their places for the footraces. Running barefoot, the athletes kept their balance at the starting line by gripping the indentations in the stone with their toes.

If you'd like to take your place at the starting line and run at the New Neméan Games on June 1, 1996, register by sending your name, address, date of birth, and gender to Mr. Konstantinos Demetriou, Secretary, Society for the Revival of the Neméan Games, Neméa GR-20500, Greece. Then all you have to do is show up at the stadium by 8am on June 1, 1996.

In a compromise between historical accuracy and contemporary sensibilities, athletes will run barefoot, but not naked, wearing short tunics. The less athletic can write the above address for information on the games and on how to join the Society for the Revival of the Neméan Games (membership $10).

WHERE TO STAY & DINE

There's no hotel here as yet. The **Pisina Restaurant** in New Neméa next to the swimming pool keeps irregular hours.

6 Árgos

30 miles (48km) from Corinth

Árgos was the most powerful city in the Peloponnese in the 7th century B.C. when it was ruled by its skillful tyrant, Pheidon, often credited with inventing coinage in Greece. There should be lots of impressive remains to visit here, but since modern Árgos (population 20,000) is built precisely on top of the ancient city, there's little to see in town except the 4th-century theater and the excellent museum. Out of town is a different story: The fortifications on Árgos's twin citadels, the Aspis and the Larissa, are very impressive.

As for the modern town itself, repeated earthquakes have left Árgos with an undistinguished agglomeration of flat-roofed buildings, with only the occasional neo-classical house as a reminder of how nice this town once was. That said, the central plateia is very lively and the street market on Wednesday and Saturday mornings is one of the largest in the Peloponnese.

If your time in the Peloponnese is limited, you might consider saving Árgos for a return trip. If you can spend a few hours here, give the theater a passing glance, concentrate on the museum, and try to drive up to Larissa and Aspis citadels to take in the Venetian fortifications and the view over the plain.

ESSENTIALS

GETTING THERE   By Train   There are about five trains a day from Athens to Árgos. Information on schedules and fares is available from the Stathmos Peloponnisou (railroad station for the Peloponnese) in Athens (☎ **01/51-31-601**) or at the Corinth train station (☎ **0751/272-12**). Trains take at least three hours.

By Bus   There are five buses a day to Árgos from the Peloponnesian Bus Station at 100 Odos Kifissou (☎ **01/51-34-588**). Buses usually take just under three hours. Árgos is also served by frequent buses from Náfplion (buses take about 30 minutes).

By Car   From Athens, take the National Road to Corinth, and then follow signs for Árgos and Tripolis. The road divides just after the sign for Ancient Corinth. The speedy new Corinth-Tripolis toll road has green signposts with a drawing of a highway. The toll is Dr 700 ($3). Take the Árgos exit (the second exit) and follow the exit road until it reaches an obvious main road (the old Corinth-Árgos road). Turn right, cross the bridge, and you'll soon enter Árgos. If you take the old road to Árgos, it runs straight into the town.

It's never easy to park in Árgos, but you'll probably find a place on one of the side streets off the central square or by the ancient theater.

FAST FACTS   The **area code** for Árgos is **0751.** There are several **banks** on the central square, Plateia Agios Petros. The **OTE** at 8 Nikitara St. is usually open weekdays from 7am to midnight. The **Post Office,** 16 Odos Danaou, off the central square, is open from 7am to 2pm, Monday through Friday. The **train station** on Leoforos Vas. Sophias is about a kilometer from the central square. Árgos's has **two bus stations:** The Athinon Station (buses to and from Athens) is on Leoforos Vas. Georgiou B. (☎ 0751/673-24); the Arcadia-Laconia Station (buses for Tripolis) is at 24 Odos Peithonos (☎ 0751/673-24). The **police** at 10 Odos Agelou Bobou (☎ 0751/672-22) sometimes speak English.

CITY LAYOUT   Árgos's confusing system of one-way streets and potentially lethal three-way intersections makes driving here almost as chaotic as the night in 272 B.C. when Pyrrus of Epirus stormed the city with a large force including two war elephants, one of which overturned, blocking the main gate into the city.

WHAT TO SEE & DO

The Theater at Árgos. Admission Dr 500 ($2.15). Year-round Mon–Sat 9am–6pm; Sun 10am–3pm. Sometimes closed unexpectedly.

If you've already seen the theater at Epidaurus, you'll find it hard to believe that Árgos's 4th-century theater was not just larger, but probably the largest in classical Greece. Twenty thousand spectators could sit here, in 89 tiers of seats, many of which were carved from the hillside itself.

The thronelike seats in the front rows were added by the Romans and reserved for visiting big wigs, including the Roman emperor himself. The Romans remodeled the theater, so that the orchestra (stage) could be flooded and mock naval battles staged here. Fortunately, the Romans had a genius for building the aqueducts needed to channel enough water here to create a temporary inland sea. There was enough water left over to service the baths, whose remains are next to the theater.

The Museum at Árgos. Admission Dr 500 ($2.13). Open Tues–Sun 8:30am–3pm.

This small museum has a handful of superlative pieces that you'll want to take in, including the fragment of a 7th-century B.C. clay krater showing a determined Ulysses blinding the one-eyed Cyclops Polyphemus, from whose blood already drips. Nearby are a handsome lyre made from a tortoise shell and a stunning late geometric bronze helmet and suit of body armor. Downstairs, in the Lerna room, the tiny, stout Neolithic clay figure of a woman or goddess found at Lerna is one of the oldest known sculptural representations of the human body yet found in Europe. Nearby, is a handsome pitcher in the shape of a bird with its head thrown back in song—and ornamental breasts on its chest.

Outside, in the museum's shady courtyard with its rose bushes, there are some terrific Roman mosaics showing the god Dionysios and the seasons. The figures in the seasons mosaics are bundled up in cloaks and heavy leggings in the cold months and casually dressed in light tunics and filmy cloaks in the summer months.

If you visit the museum (which has a welcome icy cold water fountain and very clean toilets) on Wednesday or Saturday morning, don't miss the street market that runs for several blocks to your left as you leave. This is the place to get anything from water glasses, baseball caps, and farm implements, to live chickens and every possible seasonal fruit and flower.

If you're here on a nonmarket day and need supplies, there's a large supermarket (Pharmatetras) just off the main square. To reach the supermarket, turn right as you leave the museum and then right again in the Plateia.

The Larissa and the Aspis. Usually open sunrise to sunset. Free admission.

You can climb up to the Larissa from the theater (allow at least an hour), and then hike across the ridge called the Deiras to the Aspis. If you drive, ask for directions to the Kastro, or castle, as the Larissa is called, at the museum or the police station, as roads in Árgos are in a seemingly constant state of flux.

Árgos was famous in antiquity for its two citadels and the 905-foot-high Larissa was well fortified by the 6th century B.C. When you reach the Larissa summit, you'll be able to spot the more elegant ancient blocks that were reused in the medieval battlements. There's an inner and outer system of walls here, with several towers and the ruins of a church. The view's the thing here, and you get a bird's-eye view of the plain, Árgos, the Gulf of Náfplion, and the lower citadel, the Aspis (328 feet high).

The Greek word *Aspis* means "shield," which is what the Argives thought this hill looked like. This was the city's first acropolis, abandoned when the higher Larissa was fortified. With the exception of one tower, the summit here really is a confusing jumble of low walls and the indeterminate depressions in the earth that mark building foundations. Still, the views are tremendous. If you're properly dressed and not here at siesta time, you may want to stop at the convent of the Panagia tou Brakou, although the building is not of enormous architectural interest.

You can wander around the Larissa or Aspis as you wish. Not many visitors come here, so be especially cautious about doing any dangerous climbing on the walls if you're here alone.

WHERE TO STAY & DINE

With Náfplion just down the road, there's really no reason to stay overnight in Árgos unless you prefer the bustle of this crowded Greek market town to Náfplion's more sybaritic pleasures. If you do stay here, the **Hotel Mycenae,** Plateia Aghio Petrou (Saint Peter's Square) 10, Árgos 21200 (☎ 0751/28-569) is probably your best bet. Doubles with breakfast from Dr 16,100 ($68.15). Although the Hotel Mycenae is on Árgos's energetic main square, the rooms are relatively quiet and you're certainly where the action is in Árgos.

None of the small **cafes** and **restaurants** in Árgos are worth seeking out, but the conveniently located **Aigle,** on the main square between the General Bank and the Ionian Bank, has the usual chops, salads, and souvlaki. Lunch or dinner from $8.

SIDE TRIPS FROM ÁRGOS: THE ARGIVE HERAION & LERNA

The two sites of Argive Heraion and Lerna are easy to reach from Árgos, and although neither has spectacular remains, each is worth visiting for its lovely locale, stirring legends, and great antiquity.

THE ARGIVE HERAION

The Argive Heraion is a lovely spot to come in the early evening, when the heat haze has diminished, and the views over the plain are particularly fine. The earliest settlement here probably dates from the Neolithic era, but the remains you see are from an important sanctuary to Zeus's long-suffering wife Hera; it was built between the 7th and 4th centuries B.C., although the Romans constructed the inevitable bath here in later years.

The Argive Heraion is about 8 miles (13km) outside Árgos. To get there, head out of Árgos on the inland road to Náfplion and take the left-hand turning toward Prosimna. At Nea Irea, the road divides; turn left for the Heraion.

As is often the case at the smaller ancient sites in the Peloponnese, you'll probably enjoy the setting here more than the actual remains, which include several stoas, two temples, an altar, and the Roman baths. Admission is Dr 500 ($2.13), and the site is open Tuesday through Sunday from 8am to 5pm. The sanctuary occupied three terraces, and the 7th-century B.C. temple on the highest terrace may have been the first building in the Peloponnese to be built with columns on all sides, rather than just in front. The 5th-century temple on the middle terrace contained a massive chryselephantine statue of Hera made by the sculptor Polykleitos that rivaled Pheidias's similar statue of Zeus at Olympia. Nothing of these temples remains but low foundations, and you'll probably have more fun finding the nicely carved doves that ornament some building blocks than trying to decipher the ruins.

According to legend, Agamemnon was officially named leader of the Greek expedition against Troy at the Argive Heraion. And, according to the historian Herodotus, two of the happiest mortals ever to have lived died here: Cleobis and Biton. Herodotus tells us that when King Croesus of Lydia asked the Athenian statesman and sage Solon who was the happiest mortal in the world, Solon named Cleobis and Biton, whose mother was a priestess at the Argive Heraion. One day, when the oxen customarily yoked to the family chariot failed to turn up, the devoted Argive youths pulled their mother's chariot here from Árgos so that she would arrive in time for a festival of Hera. Moments after they arrived, Herodotus says, "The two boys fell asleep in the temple and never awoke." As Solon pointed out to King Croesus, "Call no man happy until his death"—words Croesus would remember years later when he lost his great empire.

If you think this is only a pretty story, and that there never was a Cleobis or a Biton, consider this: Herodotus says that the Argives dedicated statues of the two boys at Delphi; the statues are lost, but their bases, inscribed in honor of Cleobis and Biton were found in the excavations at Delphi and are now on display in the museum there.

LERNA

As you travel around the Peloponnese, you're often told that the sites you are visiting were occupied as long ago as the Neolithic era, but you very seldom see any actual building remains from that period. That's what makes Lerna's 4th-millenium B.C. palace known as the House of the Tiles so special. People lived at Lerna from the Neolithic period through the Mycenaean era, and pottery from as far away as Troy has been found here.

From Árgos, take the old road to Tripolis to Myloi. Lerna is just outside Myloi on the left hand side of the road. The sign is very modest. Look for a straight path running through citrus groves to the site, which is protected by a metal roof.

The **Archaelogical Site at Lerna** is open Tuesday to Sunday from 8am to 3pm. Admission is Dr 500 ($2.15). Although Lerna's remains are scant, the final fire that destroyed the House of the Tiles calcified its mud brick walls, leaving the remains you see today, including several enormous pottery storage vessels. According to legend, Heracles killed the nine-headed Lernan Hýdra in a nearby swamp. The swamp, long since drained, is now a fertile plain with citrus and fruit trees.

Where to Dine

If you're hungry when you visit Lerna, head back into Myloi. Just as you enter the hamlet, drive steeply downhill to the **nameless souvlaki place** on the right hand side of the road across from the blue and white house that serves as the Nea Demokratia headquarters. The souvlaki is delicious and, at the time of my visit, the french fries were still homemade, not the increasingly ubiquitous flabby prepackaged frozen fries. A stick of souvlaki is Dr 150 (65¢); $6 will get you four souvlaki, salad, fries, and an ice-cold beer. Accept no substitutes: The souvlaki here is much better than that peddled at the other souvlaki stands in Myloi.

7 Sparta

153 miles (248km) SW of Athens; 36 miles (58km) S of Tripolis

Few sights in the Peloponnese are more imposing than the immense bulk of Mount Taygetos towering above Sparta. There's often snow on Taygetos until well into the summer, and when the sun sinks behind the mountain, the temperature seems to plummet instantly. The rich plain watered by the bottle-green Eurotas River that has made Sparta prosperous since antiquity stretches between the Taygetos and Parnon mountain ranges. Lush olive and citrus groves run for miles between the ranges, and there are even ornamental orange trees planted along Sparta's main avenues.

In a famously accurate prediction, the 5th-century B.C. Athenian historian Thucydides wrote that if Sparta were ever "to become desolate, and the temples and the foundations of the public buildings were left, no one in future times would believe that this had been one of the preeminent cities of Greece." The ancient remains here are so meager that only the truly dedicated will seek them out. Others will prefer to take in the small archaeological museum, enjoy the bustling town of Sparta itself, and head 8 kilometers down the road to the very impressive remains of the Byzantine city of Mistra (see "A Side Trip from Sparta: Mistra," below).

ESSENTIALS

GETTING THERE   By Bus   From Athens, seven buses a day depart from the Peloponnesian Bus Station (for information call **01/51-24-913**) at 100 Kifissou for the Sparta bus station at Odos Vrasidou (☎ **0731/264-41**). There are frequent buses from Sparta to Mistra.

By Car   From Athens, allow five hours; from Corinth, three hours; from Pátras, three hours; from Tripolis, two hours. From Athens or Corinth, the new Corinth-Tripolis road is well worth taking.

VISITOR INFORMATION   It is usually possible to get **visitor information** in the Town Hall on the Main Square (open weekdays, 8am to 3pm). In recent years, there has been a **summer music and drama festival** in Sparta; information is available at the Town Hall.

FAST FACTS   The area code is **0731.** Both the **Post Office,** on Kleombrotou Street, and the **OTE,** at 11 Kleombrotou, are signposted. The police and tourist police are at 8 Odos Hilonos (☎ 0731/262-29). The weekly market is on Saturdays. Lampropoulou, the **bookseller** on Odos Paleologou, sells English-language guides, newspapers, magazines, and books.

A LOOK AT THE PAST

The Spartans earned their reputation for courage and military heroism in 580 B.C. when the Spartan general Leonidas and a band of only 300 soldiers faced down the invading Persian army at Thermopylae. From 431 to 404 B.C. Sparta and Athens fought the Peloponnesian War; Sparta finally won, but was exhausted by the effort. From then on, Sparta was a sleepy provincial town with a great future behind it. Greece's first king, young Otto of Bavaria, paid tribute to Sparta's past by redesigning the city with the wide boulevards and large central square that make it still charming today.

WHAT TO SEE & DO

Sit in the square almost any evening and around 9pm you'll see the famous Spartan Volta, or promenade. For years, this was a highly stylized affair, with men and women walking on separate sides of the square. This was where much courting went on under the watchful eye of parents; today, most young men and women stroll in couples with no attending chaperones. Especially on weekends, this is a lively scene, as entire families stroll up and down and up and down again, sometimes taking a break to sit at one of the cafes for an ice cream.

The Acropolis and Ancient Theater. Free admission. Usually open sunrise to sunset.

The ancient Spartans boasted that they didn't need fortifications because the Taygetos and Parnon mountains were their defense walls. Consequently, there's very little to see on the Spartan acropolis. The acropolis is at the north end of town, just beyond the monumental statue of Leonidas near the supposed site of his tomb. The grove of trees here makes this a pleasant place to sit and read at sunset, but you'll enjoy the view of Taygetos more than the scattered remains of the 2nd-century B.C. theater. Originally, this was one of the largest theaters in Greece; it was dismantled and the blocks were carted off for reuse when the Franks built Mistra in the 13th century.

The Temple of Artemis Orthia. Free admission. Usually open sunrise to sunset.

If you continue out of town on the Tripolis road, you'll see a small yellow sign for the Temple of Artemis Orthia, where little Spartan boys were whipped to learn courage and endurance. Today the site, which dates from the 10th century B.C, but was extensively remodeled by the Romans, is often crowded with gypsy children, begging for money.

The Menelaion. No admission. Usually open sunrise to sunset.

To visit the Menelaion, take the Tripolis road north out of town and turn right immediately after the bridge; the Menelaion is signposted about 3 miles (5km) down the road. The shrine in honor of Helen's long-suffering husband Menelaus, has three terraces of gray limestone blocks and is about a 10-minute walk uphill from the chapel, where you'll park your car.

Beside the shrine are the low remains of several Mycenaean houses, none of which seems remotely grand enough to have belonged to Menelaus. Again, as with the acropolis of ancient Sparta, the real reason to come here is for the view of the plain and Taygetos.

The Archaeological Museum. Admission Dr 500 ($2.15). Tues–Sat 8:30am–3pm; Sun 8:30am–12:30pm.

The prize of this museum is a handsome 5th-century marble bust, believed to show Leonidas and to have stood on his tomb. The Spartans, however, were famous as soldiers, not as artists, and the museum's collection reflects Sparta's lack of a lively artistic tradition. Still, it's worth stopping here to see the statue of Leonidas, several fine Roman mosaics, and a small collection of objects found at Mycenaean sites in the countryside near Sparta. The museum's rose garden, peopled with decapitated Roman statues, is a nice spot to sit and read. Be warned: This museum has no toilet facilities.

WHERE TO STAY

☉ Hotel Byzantion. Mistra 23100, Laconia. ☎ **0731/93-309.** Fax 0731/20-010. 22 rooms (all with bath). TEL. Dr 9,200 ($39.15) double; less off-season. AE, EU, MC, V. Seasonal closings: Usually closed Nov 1–May 1.

This is the place to stay if you want to be poised to visit Mistra first thing in the morning. There's very little traffic on the road through Mistra at night, but whatever there is passes the Hotel Byzantion, which may make you decide to opt for a back room. Bedrooms and bathrooms are on the small side, but very clean, and the staff is helpful. There are several small tavernas in Mistra if you don't want to go to Sparta for dinner.

Hotel Maniatis. Odos Paleologou 72, Sparta, 23100 Laconia. ☎ **0731/22-665.** 80 rooms (all with bath). A/C, TV, TEL. Dr 11,500 ($48.95) double. MC, V.

Despite its location at the corner of Paleologou and Lycourgou, Sparta's two main streets, the Maniatis is reasonably quiet (the rooms in back are by far the best). The marble and glass lobby is considerably grander than the bedrooms that, if not Spartan, are simple, with functional bedside tables, a straight chair, and a small bathroom. The hotel restaurant, the Dias, is decorated in pastels that should be soothing but somehow aren't. The food here is okay, but the restaurant is often filled with noisy tour groups and it's worth walking a block or two to the excellent Diethnes restaurant.

Hotel Sparta Inn. Thermopilion and Acropoleos, Sparta 23100, Laconia. ☎ **0731/25-021.** Fax 0731/24-855. 160 rooms. A/C TV TEL. Dr 13,800 ($58.70) double.

This large hotel has a quiet location on a side street, but is often taken over by not-so-quiet tour groups. Still, the hotel does have two (small) pools, a real plus in Sparta. Bedrooms are air-conditioned, with firm beds, decent reading lights, and good-sized bathrooms. There's nothing charming about this hotel, but its quiet location and pools are real pluses in Sparta, which tends to be noisy and hot in the summer.

WHERE TO DINE

✪ **Diethnes.** Paleologou 105, Sparta. ☎ **0731/28-636.** Appetizers from Dr 460 ($1.95); main courses from Dr 1,150 ($4.90). No credit cards. Daily from about 8 am–midnight. GREEK.

On summer Saturdays, all of Sparta seems to eat lunch in the Diethnes's shady garden after shopping at the street market around the corner. If you're only going to eat one meal in Sparta, it should be here; in fact, unless you really don't like eating in the same place more than once, why go anywhere else? The grills (including local lukanika sausages) are excellent, the vegetables are drizzled, not drenched, in oil, and the waiters move with the speed of light through the crowds.

Elysse Restaurant. Odos Paleologou 113. ☎ **0731/29-896.** Appetizers from Dr 575 ($2.45); main courses from Dr 1,150 ($4.90). No credit cards. Daily from about 11am–11pm. GREEK.

If the Diethnes Restaurant weren't just a few doors away, this would be a very tempting place to eat. The food is good, the staff is efficient, but in the summer it's much more pleasant to sit in the garden at the Diethnes than in the Elysse's indoor dining room. If you are tired of Greek food by the time you reach Sparta, check to see whether any of the Continental dishes listed on the Elysse's menu are actually being served: Chicken Madeira has been known to appear here.

The Stoa Cafeteria. 140 Lykourgou. No telephone. Coffee and an order of loukoumades for Dr 700 ($3). Daily from 8am–late evening. LOUKOUMADES/SNACKS.

This little hole in the wall next to a florist is the place to go for a Spartan favorite: loukoumades, airy deep-fried puffs of pastry drenched in honey syrup.

A SIDE TRIP FROM SPARTA: MISTRA

The deserted medieval city of Mistra, now Greece's most picturesque ghost town, sprawls down a distinctive conical hill on Taygetos's lower slopes. So much remains of Mistra and so little of ancient Sparta that it's not surprising that the early travelers here identified Mistras as ancient Sparta, lovingly describing the 13th-century A.D. Palace of the Despots, now undergoing restoration, as Menelaus's Mycenaean palace—a cautionary tale for all travelers trying to make sense of Greek ruins.

Sir Stephen Runciman, a British scholar who spent a lifetime studying Mistra, has admitted that the site has a certain "picturesque incoherence"—not surprising, when you consider that there are the remains of at least 75 churches and more than 2,000 houses on the slopes.

To reach Mistra, leave Sparta on Odos Lykourgou and follow the signs for Mistra 5 miles (8km). If you arrive here alone by car, you'll have to decide whether to park at the main gate and climb up to the castle (Kastro) or park at the castle entrance, work your way downhill to the main gate, and then climb back up to your car. If you are not traveling alone, try to persuade your companion to let you out at the castle entrance and meet you at the main gate. There are frequent buses from the main square in Sparta to Mistra.

If you visit Mistra in the summer, try to visit in the relative cool of the morning. There's very little shade, and you'll find yourself climbing up and down a very steep hill for several hours. Be warned: There are no toilet facilities at Mistra. Vendors sometimes sell water and soft drinks outside the Kastro and main entrances to Mistra.

A LOOK AT THE PAST

In 1204, the Frankish leader William de Villehardouin chose this site as the headquarters for his Greek empire. De Villehardouin crowned Mistra with a fortress and defense walls, built himself a palace on the slopes below, and had 10 good years here, until the Byzantine Greeks defeated him at the Battle of Pelagonia in 1259. According to legend, de Villehardouin would have escaped capture if a Greek soldier had not identified him by his famously protruding buck teeth.

Mistra's real heyday came under the Byzantine Greeks, when most of its churches and more than 2,000 houses, as well as the enormous Palace of the Despots, were built. Some 25,000 people lived in Mistra—twice the population of Sparta today. Among them were the philosophers and writers, architects, and artists who made Mistra something of an international center of culture.

Mistra was such an important city that many Byzantine emperors sent their heirs here for some on-the-job training. After Constantinople and the Byzantine empire fell to the Turks in 1453, Mistra held out; the last emperor of Byzantium was crowned in the Cathedral at Mistra, which finally fell to the Turks in 1460.

The Venetians captured Mistra from the Turks in 1687 and ruled here for a half century, during which time Mistra swelled to an enormous city of more than 40,000, largely supported by a flourishing silk industry. When the Turks regained power, Mistra began its long decline into what it is today: Greece's most picturesque ghost town.

THE ARCHAEOLOGICAL SITE OF MISTRA

The site is open from 8am to 3pm and sometimes later in summer. Admission is Dr 1,500 ($6.40). If you start your tour of Mistra at the top, you can orient yourself by taking in the fine view over the entire site from de Villehardouin's Castle (the Kastro). As you head down, you'll begin to pass Mistra's churches, most of which have elaborate brickwork decoration, a multiplicity of domes, and superb frescoes. Despite Mistra's "picturesque incoherence," the churches are signposted, and you should be able to find the most beautiful ones—the **Saint Sophia,** the **Pantannasa,** the **Panagia Hodegetria,** the **Peribleptos,** and the **Cathedral.**

Give your eyes time to adjust to the poor light inside the churches; once they do, you'll be able to pick out vivid scenes, such as the Raising of Lazarus and the Ascension in the 15th-century frescoes in the Pantannasa Monastery, the Marriage of Cana in the 14th-century Panagia Hodegetria, and the stunning Birth of Christ in the 14th-century Peribleptos Monastery. The frescoes that decorated Greek churches have been described as the "Books of the Illiterate"; any devout Byzantine Greek could have "read" these frescoes and identified every New and Old Testament scene, just as their descendants can today.

8 Vassaé & Andrítsena

27 miles (45km) from Megalopolis to Andrítsena; 15 miles (24km) from Andrítsena to Vassaé

Vassaé is one of the most impressive 5th-century Greek temples, its gray granite columns the perfect complement to its remote mountain setting. Unfortunately, the temple, badly damaged by time and earthquakes, is now hidden under a bizarre protective tent that looks rather like the Sydney opera house. If you want to see what the artist Christo might do to Vassaé, this is your chance, and probably will be for some time. Every year the guard here says that he hopes that Vassaé will be mended and the tent removed "next year," a phrase that in Greek does not carry the specificity that its English translation suggests.

Although it's perfectly possible to visit Vassaé on a day trip from Olympia, Andrítsena, with the scent of oregano and the sound of sheep bells everywhere, is one of the most charming of the Peloponnesian mountain villages. There's one decent hotel here and a number of small restaurants. The main street is punctuated by enormous plane trees, several of which have been fitted with pipes gushing forth the delicious local spring water. In the evening, villagers stroll the main street while sheep bells echo in the hills. In short, if you want to "get away from it all" and spend the night in a Greek mountain village, try to make it Andrítsena.

ESSENTIALS

GETTING THERE   By Bus   There are several buses a day to Andrítsena from Athens and from Árgos, Tripolis, Olympia, and Megalopolis. The Greek National Tourist Office in Athens should have information on these services.

By Car   All the routes to Andrítsena go through spectacular mountain countryside. The roads are excellent, but each winding mile takes about twice as long to drive as you might have anticipated.

FAST FACTS   The telephone code for Andrítsena is **0626.** Everything you might need—the bus station, the OTE, the post office, the bank, the police—is clearly signposted on or just off Andrítsena's main street.

WHAT TO SEE & DO

The Temple of Vassaé. Admission Dr 500 ($2.15). Usually open daily 8am–7pm.

Coming around the last turn in the road and suddenly seeing the severe gray limestone columns of this 5th-century Doric temple to Apollo used to be one of the great sights in the Peloponnese. It seemed almost impossible that such a staggeringly impressive building should have been built in such a remote location—and designed by none other than Ictinus, the architect of the Parthenon. Evidently, the temple was built by the inhabitants of the tiny hamlet of Phigaleia, to thank Apollo for saving them from a severe plague.

If you saw the temple before it disappeared under its tent, cherish your memories and don't bother to visit there now. The tent fits so snugly that the only way to get a sense of what the temple actually looks like is to buy a postcard.

If you haven't seen Vassaé, you'll have to decide whether you want to see it this way, or hope that the guard will be right and that "next year" the tent will be gone.

THE VILLAGE OF ANDRÍTSENA

Tiny Andrítsena has one of the finest libraries in Greece, the legacy of a 19th-century philhellene. If you like old books, check to see if the **library,** recently moved into a grand new building just off the main street, has opened.

The small **folk museum** on the plateia below the main street, is usually locked, despite its posted hours. Admission is Dr 200 (85¢); contributions welcomed. To see the endearing collection of local wedding costumes, rugs, farm tools, and family photographs, ask to be let in at the house nearest to the museum.

If you can, plan to be in Andrítsena on Saturday, when the main street is taken over by the **weekly market,** an excellent place to buy every manner of sheep, goat, and cow bells, mountain tea, and herbs.

WHERE TO STAY

Theonexia Hotel. Andrítsena 27061, Eleia. ☎ **0626/22-219.** 45 rooms. TEL. Double Dr 11,500 ($48.95). MC, V.

This 1950s hotel has clearly seen better days, and it was heartening to see that some public rooms and bedrooms were being freshly painted during my visit to research this guide—less heartening to see that the painting hadn't been completed a month later. Still, the views from the front rooms overlooking the valley below Andrítsena more than compensate for the basically shabby decor, although students of kitsch will appreciate the needlework pictures. The sometimes less-expensive rooms in back have almost as good a view and are much quieter; trucks and buses tend to turn around in front of the hotel. The room rates here are somewhat flexible and you might bargain if you are quoted a high rate. Avoid the restaurant, and hold onto your room key, as there's often no one at the front desk.

WHERE TO DINE

The Andrítsena Kafezakeroplasteion (Coffee-Sweetshop). Main Street. No telephone. Full breakfast Dr 1,150 ($4.90). No credit cards. Daily from about 8am–11pm. COFFEE/SWEETS.

You can avoid the desultory breakfast at the Philoxenia Hotel by coming here for bread and honey, yogurt, or an omelet. In nice weather, you can sit outside under the red and white striped umbrellas, looking at the elegant lace curtains in the cafe's six decorative fan windows.

Sigouri. Odos Sophokleos, Andrítsena. No telephone. No credit cards. Open most days for lunch and dinner, usually closing by 10pm. GREEK HOME COOKING.

Kyria Vasso is usually to be found cooking lunch and dinner at this small restaurant across from the metalworker's shop above the main Plateia. Her *briam* (vegetable stew) is excellent, as are her stuffed tomatoes, and barrel wine. Expect to pay about Dr 1,880 ($8) for a salad, main course, and the local wine. If you like *kourouloudes* (rag rugs), ask to see the ones she makes and sells by the meter; for about Dr 5,750 ($24.50), you can take home a colorful hand-loomed bedside rug.

The Trani Brisi. Main Street. No telephone. No credit cards. Open most days for lunch and dinner, usually closing by 10pm. GREEK.

This small restaurant has tables outside under extralarge beach umbrellas in a widening of the road between the two upper plateias (squares). The menu varies from day to day, but often features some kind of lamb stew, fresh vegetables, and the local wine. As at Kyria Vasso's, expect to pay about Dr 2,000 ($8.50) if you have a meat dish. If you like the wine here, you can usually buy some to take away with you.

9 Monemvassía

210 miles (340km) S of Athens; 60 miles (97km) S of Sparta

Nicknamed "the Gibraltar of Greece" because of its strategic importance during the Middle Ages, Monemvassía was a virtual ghost town by the 20th century. Today, this rocky island just off the easternmost tip of the Peloponnese has a new lease on life: Wealthy foreigners and Greeks are buying and restoring old houses here. Furthermore, word is getting out that in addition to its medieval fortress, handsome churches, and drop-dead sunsets, Monemvassía has several of the most stylish small hotels in the Peloponnese.

Although Monemvassía is an island, it's connected to the mainland by a causeway that you can drive or stroll across. Once you step through the massive Venetian Gate that is Monemvassía's only entrance (*mone emvasis* means "one entrance" in Greek), you're in a separate world. Cars are banned here—a wise decision, since the only approximation of a street on "the rock" is barely wide enough for two of the donkeys that bring in supplies to squeeze past each other.

ESSENTIALS

GETTING THERE **By Bus** There is one direct bus a day from the Peloponnesian Bus Terminal at 100 Kifissiou in Athens to Monemvassía and six daily buses via Sparta. Call ☎ **01/24-913** for schedule information.

By Car Take the National Road from Athens-Corinth-Tripolis. Then head south to Monemvassía via Sparta. Allow at least six hours for the trip.

By Boat The Flying Dolphin Hydrofoil leaving from Marina Zea in Piraeus links Athens and Monemvassía for most of the year and is the fastest way to reach Monemvassía from Athens. For information, call ☎ **01/61-219.**

FAST FACTS You'll find the post office, a bank, and several grocery stores in the town of new Monemvassía on the shore across the causeway from the old town. The **Malvasia Travel Agency** (☎ **0732/61-432**) has several helpful English-speaking staff members.

WHAT TO SEE & DO
A STROLL

Monemvassía is a great place to wander: Sure, you'll get lost in the winding cobbled lanes, but how lost can you get on an island 1,600 feet long and half again as wide? The answer (at least at night) is pretty lost: It's a good idea to wear decent walking shoes, bring along a flashlight, and save the 880-foot ascent of the citadel for daytime.

From the **citadel,** there are truly spectacular views down to the red-tile roofs of Monemvassía, out across the sea and deep into the mountains of the Máni peninsula. While you're on the citadel, try to figure out just how the 13th-century **Church of Agia Sophia** (Holy Wisdom), was built not just on, but virtually over, the edge of the cliffs.

After taking on the climb to the citadel, you'll probably want a swim, so head down to the **bathing jetty.** En route, you'll pass the **Church of Christos Elkomenos** (Christ in Chains), across from a Venetian canon, as well as a tumble-down **mosque** and the **Venetian chapel of Panagia Chrissafitissa.** The churches sometimes are and sometimes are not locked; if they're locked, content yourself with the thought that the handsome stone houses lining Monemvassía's winding lanes are the real treat to see here.

On the subject of treats, Monemvassía is one place in the Peloponnese where you don't have to contemplate yet another moussaka. Strung out along Monemvassía's main street are a number of restaurants: **Martina's** has a varied Greek menu and **To Canoni** has pasta, including spaghetti Carbonara. No wonder knowledgeable travelers come back to Monemvassía every year: excellent food, marvelous sunsets, medieval ruins—and, as yet, few tourists.

WHERE TO STAY

There are so few rooms on "the rock" that this is one place where it's a good idea to try to make a reservation. I say "try" because records of reservations sometimes disappear mysteriously, even after several phone calls.

Byzantion. Ritsos Street, Monemvassía. ☎ **0732/61-351.** Fax 0732-61-352. 17 rooms, 1 suite. Doubles Dr 10,000–Dr 12,650 ($42.55–$53.85); suites for four Dr 11,500–Dr 17,250 ($48.95–$72.40). AE, DC, EU, MC, V.

There's only one problem with staying in this small hotel in a beautifully restored and furnished house: A number of the rooms are built flush against a hillside, do not get cross-ventilation and can be stuffy, with a strong odor of mildew. Ask for a room with a balcony and cross-ventilation. Some rooms have air-conditioning, televisions, and refrigerators.

Kellia. By the Panagia Chrysafiotissa church, Monemvassía. ☎ **0732/61-520.** 12 rooms. TEL. Sea-view doubles Dr 17,250–Dr 20,000 ($73.40–$85.11). Ground-floor doubles Dr 11,500 ($48.94). Rates include continental breakfast. AE, EU, MC, V.

This former convent is run as a hotel by the Greek National Tourist Organization, which, alas, does not seem to be keeping an eye on the place. Service is slow to slack, and although the rooms are nicely furnished with hand-loomed rugs and many have lovely sea views, the haphazard service means that you shouldn't stay here unless the Byzantion and the Malvasia are full. The ground-floor rooms lack the sea view but are usually as quiet as the higher rooms.

Malvasia. Headquarters on Ritsos Street, Monemvassía. ☎ **0732/62-223.** Fax 0732/61-722. 20 rooms and 15 suites. Doubles from Dr 17,250 ($73.40); suites from Dr 57,500 ($244.70); substantial reductions possible off-season. AE, EU, MC, V.

This is far and away the finest hotel in Monemvassía and one of the most charming in Greece. Over a number of years, the owners have bought up a number of old houses, restored them, and furnished the rooms with old copper, hand-loomed rugs and bedspreads, and handsome wooden furniture. This would be a wonderful place to stay a week, or a month (long-term reduced rates available). If you can't do that, at least to stay for one night and hope for a sea-view room in the Stellaki Mansion on the ramparts or in the hotel's original building on Ritsos Street. If you're here in the winter, ask for a room with a fireplace. Some rooms have telephones and refrigerators; some suites have full kitchens.

SHOPPING

There's no shop on the Rock that's truly outstanding, but the shops strung out along **Ritsos Street** have thus far avoided the infestation of T-shirts and cheap museum reproductions so common elsewhere. Just inside Monemvassía's gate, **Costas Lekakis** has a good selection of books in English, including R. Klaus and U. Steinmuller's excellent guide *Monemvassía* ($6). **Bentouraki** has nice linen caps and straw boaters from around $40—expensive, but a hat is a necessity to ward off the harsh sun here. **Ioanna Angelatou's shop** next to the Byzantion Hotel often has a good selection of the deep blue glassware made in Greece and well-done reproductions of antique wood carvings and copper.

10 The Máni

Githion is 186 miles (301km) S of Athens; 27 miles (45km) S of SpartaAreopolis is 20 miles (32km) W of Githion

The innermost of the Peloponnese's three tridentlike prongs, the Máni is still one of the least-visited areas in Greece. That's changing fast, as word gets out about the good beaches near Githion and Kardamili and the haunting landscape of the Inner Máni (the southernmost Máni). Good roads mean that you can now drive the circuit of the entire Máni in one day, but it's more fun to spend at least one night here in one of the restored tower house hotels.

ESSENTIALS

GETTING THERE   By Bus   It's possible to get a bus from Athens to Sparta and from Sparta to Githio or Areopolis, but this is a trip that takes a full day. For schedule information, call **01/24-913.**

By Car   Again, a long trip, but not as tedious as the bus, which makes many stops. Take the National Road Athens-Corinth-Tripolis, and then head south to Githio and Areopolis via Sparta.

FAST FACTS   The **GNTO Máni office,** along with the **post office,** a **bank,** the **bus station,** and several **restaurants,** is on the main square in the capital of Areopolis. There are also banks and a post office in Githion, but do not count on finding banks, post offices, or much in the way of restaurants elsewhere in the Máni.

GETTING AROUND   Long-time visitors to Greece wax nostalgic about the days when they had to hoof it around the Máni. You can get around today by local bus, but by far the most efficient method is by car.

A LOOK AT THE PAST

The Inner Máni's barren mountains are dotted with tiny olive trees and enormous prickly pear cactuses. It's hard to believe that 100 years ago, this was a densely populated area, with almost every hillside cultivated. If you squint, you can still make out the stone walls and terraces that farmers built on the deserted hillsides.

Now that most Mániotes have moved away, to Athens or abroad, many of the handsome gray stone tower houses are deserted. Originally, the Mániotes chose to live in tower houses because they were easy to defend, an important consideration for these constantly feuding Peloponnesians, who spent much of their time until the 20th century lobbing cannon balls at their neighbors. Fortunately, many tower houses survived, and the towers of the virtually deserted villages of Koita and Nomia look like miniskyscrapers from a distance.

When the Mániotes weren't trying to destroy their neighbors' homes, they seem to have atoned by building churches: The area is dotted with tiny medieval chapels tucked in the folds of the hills. Keep an eye out for the stands of cypress trees that often mark the chapels, many of which have decorative brick work and ornately carved marble doors. If you don't want to tramp around the countryside in search of chapels, at least take a look at the **Church of the Taxiarchoi** (Archangels) in Areopolis. Don't miss the droll figures of the saints and signs of the zodiac carved on the church's facade.

WHAT TO SEE & DO

The Caves of Dirou. Pirgos Dirou, The Máni. Admission Dr 2,500 ($10.64). The visiting hours for the caves vary unpredictably; in general, the caves are open 9am–5pm in summer and shorter hours off-season.

These caves, a very popular holiday destination for Greeks, are mobbed in summer, so try to arrive as soon as they open. Guided tours through the Glyfada cave take about 30 minutes and are not recommended for the claustrophobic: You take your place in a small boat that your guide poles through the clammy caverns. The crystal-studded stalactites (the ones hanging from the ceilings like icicles) and stalagmites (the ones rising up from the cave's floor) are spectacular, in shades of rose, green, amber, black, blood red, and purple. It may be best not to trail your fingers in the cool water: Giant eels live just beneath the surface.

The Pirgos Dirou Caves were discovered in 1955 by a dog that crawled through a hole into the caves and returned several days later coated in red clay. Fortunately, his owner, spelunker Anna Petroclides, was curious about the red clay and followed her dog when he next set off on explorations. What she found was a vast network of caves, of which some 5,000 meters have now been explored. The caves themselves are impressive, but what has made them famous is the Paleolithic and Neolithic remains found here. In short, the Pirgos Dirou caves are one of the oldest inhabited spots in Greece and the pottery, bone tools, and even garbage found here has shed light on Greece's earliest history.

Before you leave Pirgos Dirou, check to see if the small museum, with displays of artifacts found in the caves, is open. Admission is Dr 500 ($2.15).

The Demaglion Folklore Museum. Thalames, The Máni. Admission Dr 700 ($3). Usually open daily from 9:30am–5pm, May 1–September 30.

This small private collection in the village of Thalames, some 12 miles (20km) north of Areopolis, has old prints, costumes, olive presses, farm tools, ceramic plates commemorating various Greek monarchs—and just about anything else you'd expect to find if you cleaned out a number of Mániote attics. The owner, Mr. Demaglion, is a local schoolteacher who speaks a little English and a lot of German and enjoys lecturing visitors. From time to time, Mr. Demaglion sells duplicate items from his collection and you may be able to buy an inexpensive antique wood carving or piece of embroidery here. Items for sale are usually on display in front of the museum.

WHERE TO STAY

Hotel Itilo. Neo Itilo, Lakonia 23062, Máni. ☎ **0733/59-222.** Fax 0733/29-234. 26 rooms. TEL. Dr 17,250 ($73.40) double (with breakfast). AE, MC, V.

This beachfront family run hotel on the Gulf of Itilo just north of Areopolis attracts lots of French, German, and Greek families whose usually well-behaved children enjoy the little beachside playground. Many of the large bedrooms, furnished with the ubiquitous simple pine furniture found in most newer Greek hotels, overlook the sea. If you show up here for just a night or two in high season, you may be relegated to the annex, just across the road from the beach. The hotel food, with lots of fresh fish, is excellent, but, as always with fish, expensive.

Limeni Village Hotel. Areopolis, Limeni, Laconia 23062, Máni. ☎ **0733/51-111.** Fax 0733/ 51-182. 85 beds in main hotel and 18 tower units. TV TEL. Dr 14,950 ($63.60) double. AE, EU, MC, V.

With the Máni filled with deserted tower house villages, it's hard not to wonder whether this new hotel north of Areopolis built as a Mániote tower village isn't a glaring example of bringing coals to Newcastle. Some of the bedrooms here are quite charming, with nice rag rugs, stone floors, and balconies overlooking the Bay of Itilo. Like so many wannabe luxury hotels in Greece, the main lobby, unfortunately, has all the cozy ambience of an airport waiting room. For several years, we've been told that the swimming pool will be open "next year." It remains to be seen if 1996 will be the year. At the time of my visit, this hotel was marvelously quiet with only a handful of European guests, but be warned: The management is trying to attract groups.

Tsitsiris Castle. Stavri, Laconia 23071, Máni. ☎ **0733/56-297.** 20 rooms. TEL. Dr 11,500– Dr 15,000 ($48.95–$63.85) double (with breakfast). MC, V. Usually closed Nov 1–Apr 15.

This tower house hotel—10 kilometers south of Areopolis, in the virtually deserted hamlet of Stavri—has its lobby and dining room in a 200-year-old restored tower, with most of the bedrooms in two new wings flanking a lush rose garden. The lobby and dining room are handsome, with lots of exposed stone walls and floors and interesting woven rugs and chair covers. The bedrooms are more mundane, although when we stayed here, we had our own icon shrine and wonderful views across the hills. Not many independent travelers make their way here, and you may have the place all to yourself. The restaurant is excellent when there are a good number of guests; otherwise, choice is limited and the cooking is desultory.

Kapetanakou Tower Hotel. Areopolis 26062, Laconia, Máni. ☎ **0733/51-233.** 8 rooms (two baths on each floor). Dr 8,000 ($34) double. AE, EU, MC, V.

One of the first of the traditional settlement hotels managed by the Greek National Tourist Organization, the 180-year-old Kapetanakou Tower stands in a walled garden just off the main street in Areopolis. Some of the rooms have sleeping lofts, and most have colorful rag rugs and locally handmade weavings. This is a wonderful place to stay to get an idea of what it was like to live in a Mániote tower—despite the intrusive TV in the breakfast room. There's no restaurant here, but it's only a five-minute stroll to Areopolis's restaurants. The hotel attracts independent travelers, including Greek families of Mániote origins who come here to explore the region and their roots.

Tsimoba Guesthouse. Areopolis 26062 Laconia, Máni. ☎ **0733/51301.** 10 rooms (8 with bath). Two rooms with TV. Dr 5,750 ($24.50) double. No credit cards. Reductions possible off-season.

If you speak some Greek and want to find out about the Máni, this private home in a 300-year-old tower with gun slits is the place to stay. Owner George Bersakos has lived all his life in the Máni and turned much of his house into a small museum, stuffed with Mániote memorabilia, including marvelous photographs and an impressive range of pistols. If you don't speak Greek, Mr. Bersakos will entertain you in his distinctive English, French, or German. You'll be beautifully taken care of here, but you'll inevitably have less privacy than you would in a hotel.

Vathia Tower Hotel. Vathia 23071, Laconia, Máni. ☎ **0733/55-244.** 32 beds in 6 tower houses. TEL. Dr 10,350 ($44) double. AE, EU, MC, V.

This hotel should be nicer than it is. Vathia is one of the most handsome tower villages, and a cluster of six tower houses has been restored as a small hotel by the Greek National Tourist Organization. Unfortunately, no one has bothered to clean up the building debris around the towers, the staff is bored witless by the slow pace, and the restaurant serves appallingly bad food—and there's no other restaurant for miles. We'll keep checking on this hotel and hope that it eventually lives up to its potential.

WHERE TO DINE
GITHIO

I've eaten at most of the seaside seafood restaurants on the harbor in Githio and still haven't found one that's good enough to make me come back over and over. You should get good, fresh fish at any one of these restaurants, so you may want to make your choice on factors such as how best to avoid the loud Greek pseudo-folk music at some restaurants.

AREPOLIS

The three basically interchangeable restaurants, on Areopolis's main square serve equally good—or bad, depending on your point of view—food, featuring grilled meats and salads. Lunch or dinner at any one of these costs from about Dr 2,000 ($8.50).

Fish Taverna To Limeni. Limeni, Areopolis. ☎ **0733/51-327.** Starters from Dr 460 ($1.96); fish priced by the kilo. No credit cards. Usually open for lunch and dinner; sometimes closed in the winter.

The superb fresh fish in this small restaurant in Limeni, the harbor of Areopolis, draws customers from as far away as Kalamata. If you can, chose your fish from the live tanks floating just offshore rather than from the refrigerated display case inside.

This is not the place to eat if you are squeamish about seeing fish cleaned a few feet away from where you are eating. We paid Dr 3,500 ($14.90) for 600 grams of delicious fresh barbouni.

11   Pýlos (Navarino)

196 miles (317km) SW of Athens; 67 miles (108km) W of Sparta; 31 miles (50km) west of Kalamata

I must admit that all too often in the Peloponnese the modern village with a famous ancient name—Olympia or Corinth, for example—is a disappointment. That's not the case at Pýlos (also known as Navarino), where the modern harbor town has considerable charm. Pýlos is developing some sprawling suburbs and some of the nearby beaches are being developed with a vengeance, but the harbor and leafy main square are still very pleasant—so pleasant that it's hard to realize that Pýlos's harbor has seen some very bloody battles. The Athenians trapped a Spartan force on the offshore island of Sphakteria in 424 B.C., and in 1827, a combined French, Russian, and British armada defeated the massed Ottoman fleet here. More than 6,000 Ottoman sailors were butchered in what proved to be one of the critical battles of the Greek War of Independence. There's a monument to the three victorious admirals in Pýlos's main square, which is understandably called the Square of the Three Admirals. Ancient Pýlos, site of the Mycenaean palace of King Nestor, is located about 10 miles (17km) north of the town. Homer described Pýlos as "sandy Pýlos, rich in cattle," and the hilltop palace still overlooks sandy beaches flanked by rich farmland. Ancient Pýlos seems to be a site that people take to—or don't. For every visitor who complains about the protective plastic roof over the site, another raves about the palace's idyllic setting. Some call the remains here "scanty," while others find the low walls remarkably "evocative." You decide.

ESSENTIALS

GETTING THERE   By Bus   There are several buses a day to Pýlos from the Peloponnesian Bus Station at 100 Odos Kifissiou in Athens (☎ 01/51-34-293). There is also bus service to Pýlos from Kalamata (☎ 0721/285-81).

By Car   Pýlos is a full day's drive from Athens and three to four hours from either Pátras or Sparta. The drive from Sparta to Pýlos is via the Langada pass to Kalamata, one of the most beautiful mountain roads in the Peloponnese.

FAST FACTS   The telephone area code for Pýlos is **0723.** The **post office** and **OTE** are signposted in the main plateia, where the **police** and several **banks** are located.

WHAT TO SEE & DO

Neokastro. Pýlos. Admission Dr 800 ($3.40). Daily 8am–7pm.

The Turkish fortress known as NeoKastro, to distinguish it from an earlier fortress, now contains a splendid small museum in a restored 19th-century barracks. The museum features the extensive collection of maps, prints, and watercolors of the French philhellene Rene Puaux, as well as a number of marvelously kitsch porcelain figurines of the English philhellene Lord Byron. Neokastro also contains a small church, clearly a former mosque, and some impressive fortification walls.

Ancient Pýlos (Nestor's Palace) and Museum. Admission to each Dr 500 ($2.15). Tues–Sat 8:30am–3pm; Sunday 9:30am–2:30pm (closed Mondays). Directions: To visit the Palace of Nestor and its Museum at Chora, head north out of Pýlos on the main road and follow the signs for Chora.

The palace at Pýlos belonged to Nestor, the garrulous old king who told stories and gave unsolicited advice while the younger warriors fought at Troy. The palace was rediscovered in 1939 by the American archaeologist Carl Blegen, who had the un- believable good fortune to discover the palace archives on his first day working here. Blegen uncovered some 600 clay tablets written in a mysterious language ini- tially called Linear B, and later shown to be an early form of Greek.

Unlike Mycenae and Tiryns, Pýlos was not heavily fortified: You'll see a sentry box, but no massive walls here. The royal apartments are well preserved, and include a more-than-adequate bathroom with the tub still in place. The palace, with its cen- tral courtyard, was originally two stories high and richly decorated with frescoes, some of which are on display at the small archaeological museum a mile away in the vil- lage of Chora.

WHERE TO STAY

Karalis Hotel. 26 Kalamateas St., Pýlos 24001, Messenia. ☎ **0723/22960.** 21 rooms (all with bath). TEL. Dr 11,500 ($48.95) double. AE, DC, EU, MC, V. Usually closed Nov 1–May 1.

This hotel is owned and managed by the Karalis Beach Hotel, which often sends its overflow here. Rooms here are perfectly pleasant, and those in front overlook the harbor. Unfortunately, they also overlook the main road into town, and a certain amount of traffic noise is unavoidable.

Karalis Beach Hotel. Paralia Street, Pýlos 24001, Messenia. ☎ **0723/23021.** Fax 0723/ 22970. 14 rooms (all with bath). TEL. Dr 11,500 ($48.95) double. Rates include breakfast. AE, DC, EU, MC, V. Usually closed Nov 1–May 1.

This hotel clearly has the best location in town, at the end of the harbor, below the Turkish kastro, far from any traffic. Perhaps someone could tell the very pleasant management that placing an enormous television in front of the lobby picture win- dow so that it blocks a good deal of the sea view is not the way to please guests. Rooms here are not enormous, but nicely furnished; some have balconies and all have decent-sized bathrooms.

Hotel Miramare. Paralia Street, Pýlos 24001, Messenia. ☎ **0723/22751.** Fax 0723/22226. 20 rooms (all with bath). TEL. Dr 12,650 ($53.85) double. AE, EU, MC, V.

The Miramare is just above Pýlos's public bathing beach and has its own small res- taurant. The rooms are simply furnished, but most have balconies overlooking the harbor. This hotel is usually considerably quieter than the Karalis Hotel, but not as quiet as the Karalis Beach Hotel.

WHERE TO DINE

Diethnes Taverna. Paralia Street. No telephone. Appetizers from Dr 500 ($2.10). Fish priced by the kilo. Noon to at least 11pm. GREEK/SEAFOOD.

In bad weather, you can eat indoors, but in good weather tables are set up on the quay overlooking the harbor. As you'd expect from a restaurant on the sea and next to the government fish inspection station, the seafood here is very fresh. Fish in Greece is never cheap, so be sure to ask how much your fish will cost before ordering. There are also usually a number of chicken and meat dishes on the menu.

Philip Restaurant. On Pýlos-Kalamata Road. ☎ **0723/22-741.** Appetizers from Dr 460 ($2); main courses from Dr 1,150 ($4.90). Daily for lunch and dinner. GREEK.

This good restaurant has an unfortunate location on the main road into town. It's not easy to park here; if you walk uphill from town, you're all too aware of trucks thundering past you downhill. That said, the food is a bit more imaginative here than at many restaurants, with swordfish shish kebab, inventive vegetable dishes, and the occasional European entree on the menu.

SIDE TRIPS FROM PYLOS: METHONI & KORONI

Methoni is 8 miles (13km) from Pýlos
Koroni is 18 miles (30 km) from Pýlos

Methoni and Koroni are two of the most impressive medieval fortresses in Greece and would be worth seeing for that reason alone. But that's not the only reason to go here: Methoni has one of the best restaurants in Greece, and the drive through the lush Messenian countryside between Methoni and Koroni is ravishing. The route from Pýlos to Koroni via Longa is especially blissful; by contrast, the southerly seaside route, takes in the village of Finikoundas, which is in the throes of overdevelopment.

The long, sandy Methoni beach has won several awards for its ecosensitivity, including Greece's Golden Starfish and the Common Market's Blue Flag. Happily, ecosensitivity seems to include not just a clean beach, but an absence of loud music at the children's playground and beach side cafes. In short, although it's perfectly possible to visit both Methoni and Korone on a day trip from Pýlos, the superb Klimataria Restaurant and pleasant Methoni Beach Hotel make it tempting to spend the night here. Not many Americans get to this part of the Peloponnese, but Methoni and Koroni are popular with both Greeks and Germans.

The Venetians built Methoni on the Ionian Sea and Koroni on the Gulf of Messenia in the 13th century to safeguard their newly acquired Greek empire. In some of the bloodiest fighting on record, the fortresses, almost immediately nicknamed "the twin eyes of empire," passed back and forth between various powers for the next several centuries. In 1500, the Turks slaughtered all 5,000 Venetian defendants at Methoni and in 1685, the Venetians wiped out the 1,500-man garrison at Koroni.

Methoni stands at the end of a spit of land and covers enough ground to have contained a city of several thousand inhabitants during the Middle Ages. Ships filled with pilgrims bound for the Holy Land put in here for supplies; in 1571, Miguel de Cervantes was an unwilling visitor here, one of many Spanish seamen captured and forced to work as galley slaves by the Turks after the Battle of Lepanto. Methoni's exterior walls are stupendous, although little remains inside the fortress itself. Don't worry about being locked in here when the gates close at 7pm: a very officious guard on a motorcycle rounds up any stragglers. The fortress is usually open from 8am to 7pm. No admission.

Whereas Methoni's fortress is deserted except for visitors, the fortress at Koroni encloses a number of village houses, a flourishing convent, and several small cemeteries. Although the main road in town leads directly to the fortress gate, park before the road heads steeply uphill to the gate, unless you would enjoy backing up over a sheer drop to the sea. The grounds inside the fortress walls are lovingly planted with roses and very welcome shade trees, with piles of canon balls and the occasional cannon to remind visitors of Koroni's bloody past. There's a string of seafood restaurants at the harbor below, but nothing here to compare with Methoni's Klimataria Restaurant. This is a good place not to come on summer weekends, when there's an influx of day-trippers from Kalamata.

WHERE TO STAY

Hotel Amalia. Methoni, Messenia 24006. ☎ **0723/129-31.** Fax 0723/31-195. 36 rooms (all with bath). TEL TV. Dr 13,800 ($58.70) double. AE, DC, EU, MC, V.

This new hotel, with its large lobby and dining room, straddles a low hill outside Methoni, with fine views of the sea and fortress. The bedrooms here are larger than usual, as are the bathrooms. Each room faces the sea and is entered through a freshly planted rose garden that will be quite lovely in a year or two. The only drawback here is that although you can see the sea, you aren't on the sea.

⑤ Hotel Methoni Beach. Methoni, Messenia 24006. ☎ **0723/31-455.** 15 rooms (all with bath). TEL. Dr 9,200 ($39.15) double. AE, MC, V.

This hotel on a long sand beach has drawn many Greek families back year after year, which gives it a comfy feeling. The bedroom furnishings have been here a while, but being just steps from the beach and fortress makes that easy to forgive. The wretched reading lights are less easy to forgive. Rooms 208, 209, and 210 have especially fine views of both the fortress and the sea, and most rooms have balconies. The very engaging Manoleas Brothers own both this hotel and the Klimateria Restaurant; hotel guests get a 10% deduction at the restaurant.

WHERE TO DINE

The Akroyiali. Waterfront, Methoni. No phone. Snacks from Dr 575 ($2.45); fish priced by the kilo. Open all day. FISH/SNACKS.

This is a pleasant spot for a snack by the sea. Even though this place has good fresh fish, it's hard to resist the Klimateria (see above) at mealtime.

The Kaggelarios. Waterfront, Korone. No phone. Snacks from Dr 575 ($2.45); Ouzo and octopus Dr 1,150 ($4.90). OUZO/SNACKS/LIGHT MEALS.

This cafe seems to attract more locals than the other waterfront fish tavernas in Korone. The octopus is certainly fresh—the day's catch can be seen hanging on a line at the restaurant.

Taverna Klimateria. Methoni. ☎ **0723/31544.** Appetizers from Dr 700 ($3). Main courses from Dr 1,150 ($4.90). Lunch (served at the Hotel Methoni Beach) and dinner. Open May–about November 1. SOPHISTICATED GREEK/ANATOLIAN CUISINE.

This restaurant, serving the best food we've eaten in the Peloponnese, is reason enough to visit Methoni. The chef somehow manages to take standard dishes familiar from any Greek menu (fried zucchini, eggplant salad, briam) and turn them into elegant delights. Then there are the delicately seasoned stews, the chicken breasts in puff pastry, and the fresh fish and lobster. The restaurant is in a pleasant garden, and the service is fast and attentive. It's easy to be seduced by the wide variety of food here, and this is one of the few restaurants in the Peloponnese where it's not difficult for a couple to spend $50 for dinner.

12 Messene (Ithómi/Mavromáti)

16 miles (25km) from Kalamata; 39 miles (60km) from Pýlos

Between 370 and 369 B.C., the great Theban general and statesman Epaminondas built the sprawling city of Messene and its almost 6 miles of walls below Mount Ithómi in the hopes of checking the power of Sparta. Today, the defense wall, with its two-story towers and turreted gates, is the best preserved classical fortification in the Peloponnese.

ESSENTIALS

GETTING THERE   By Car   From Pýlos, Kalamata, or Tripolis, take the main Kalamata-Pýlos road to the modern town of Messini, where the road to ancient Messene is signposted. The site of ancient Messene (also called Ithómi) is in the village of Mavromáti, aproximately 13 miles (20km) N of Messini.

WHAT TO SEE & DO

Ancient Messene. Admission Dr 500 ($2.15). Tues–Sun 8am–3pm.

The most impressive stretches of the ancient wall are outside the site, north of the village of Mavromáti. As you drive there through Mavromáti, you can pick up a copy of the excellent site guide at the postcard shop next to the village spring for Dr 1,000 ($4.25). Even at a distance, the sheer size of the wall, with its towers and gates, makes most visitors gasp. The **Arcadian Gate** is especially well preserved, with the grooves cut in the marble pavement by ancient chariot wheels still clearly visible.

As you drive back toward Mavromáti, you'll pass more of the defense wall and the site museum, which has been closed for some time and shows no signs of reopening.

The excavated ruins of Messene are clearly signposted past the museum. This is a vast, sprawling site, with a **Sanctuary of Asclepios** so large that it was originally thought to be the agora (marketplace). The partially excavated **Stadium,** with many of its marble benches well preserved, lies along the dirt road beyond the Asclepeion. To walk the entire site takes a minimum of several hours, but it's possible to see the Asclepeion alone in an hour.

WHERE TO STAY & DINE

At present, there is no hotel here, although signs indicate that there are rooms to rent in homes. The **Ithome Restaurant** (☎ 0724/51-298), across from the Spring of Gramatikon, serves souvlaki and chops and has a nice view over the ancient site. Lunch or dinner from Dr 1,725 ($7.35).

13 Olympia

199 miles (311km) W of Athens; 55 miles (90km) S of Pátras; 13 miles (921km) E of Pirgos

With its shady groves of pine, olive, and oak trees, the considerable remains of two temples, and the stadium where the first Olympic races were run in 776 B.C., Olympia is the most beautiful major site in the Peloponnese. When you realize that the archaeological museum is one of the finest in Greece, you'll see why you can easily spend a full day here.

ESSENTIALS

GETTING THERE   By Train   There are several trains a day from Athens to Pirgos, where you change to the train for Olympia. Information on schedules and fares is available from the Stathmos Peloponnisou (railroad station for the Peloponnese) in Athens (☎ 01/51-31-601).

By Bus   There are three buses a day to Olympia from the Peloponnesian Bus Station in Athens at 100 Odos Kifissou (☎ 01/51-34-110). There are also frequent buses from Pátras to Pirgos, with a connecting service to Olympia. In Pátras, KTEL buses leave from the intersection of Zaimi and Othonos streets (☎ 061/273-694).

By Car   Olympia is at least a six-hour drive from Athens, whether you take the coast road that links Athens-Corinth-Pátras and Olympia or head inland to Tripolis and Olympia on the new Corinth-Tripolis road. Heavy traffic in Pátras means that the drive from Pátras to Olympia can easily take two hours.

VISITOR INFORMATION   The **tourist office (EOT),** on the way to the ancient site near the south end of the main street (Leoforos Kondili), is usually open 9am to 10pm in summer and 11am to 6pm in winter. This is the place to ask for a map to ancient and modern Olympia and accommodations and transportation information (☎ 0624/23-100 or 0624/23-125). The **tourist police** (☎ 0624/22-100) are at

Odos Ethnossinelefseos 6. The **OTE** (telephone and telegraph office) on Odos Praxitelous is open Monday through Friday only, 7:30am to 10pm.

FAST FACTS   The telephone area code for Olympia is **0624**. The **train station** is at the north end of town, one street off Leoforos Kondili. You can call for a **taxi** at 0624/22-580. Everything is well signposted in Olympia, and there are a number of banks and groceries, as well as lots of souvenir shops, on the main street.

A LOOK AT THE PAST

There's really no modern equivalent for ancient Olympia, which was both a religious sanctuary and an athletic complex, where the games took place every four years from 776 B.C. to A.D. 395. Thereafter, the sanctuary slipped into oblivion, and buildings were toppled by repeated earthquakes and covered by the flooding of the Alpheios and Kladeos rivers. When the English antiquarian Richard Chandler rediscovered the site in 1766, most of Olympia lay under ten feet of mud and silt. The Germans began to excavate here in 1852 and are still at it today.

Reports of the rediscovery of Olympia prompted the French Baron de Coubertin to work for the re-establishment of the Olympic game in 1896. The first modern games were held in Athens in 1896, and Greece was very sorry to lose the 1996 hundredth anniversary games to Atlanta.

OLYMPIA TODAY

The straggling modern village of Olympia (confusingly known as Ancient Olympia) is bisected by its one main street, Leoforos Kondili. The town has the usual assortment of tourist shops selling jewelry, T-shirts, and reproductions of ancient pottery and statues, as well as more than a dozen hotels and restaurants. Two things worth visiting in town: the Museum of the Olympic Games and the excellent Galerie Orphee bookstore.

The ancient site of Olympia lies an easily walkable 15 minutes south of the modern village, but if you have a car, you might as well drive: The road teems with tour buses and the walk is less than relaxing.

WHAT TO SEE & DO

The Archaeological Museum. Admission Dr 1,200 ($5.10). Open summer Mon noon–6pm, Tues–Sat 8am–5pm; winter Mon noon–6pm, Tues–Sat 11am–5pm.

If ever a building shouldn't be judged by its facade, this is it: From outside, the museum has all the charm of a small factory. Inside, one of the finest collections in Greece is beautifully displayed in well-lit rooms, some of which look onto an interior courtyard.

Even though you'll be eager to see the ancient site, it's a good idea to begin your visit to Olympia with the museum whose collection makes clear Olympia's astonishing wealth and importance in antiquity: Every victorious city and almost every victorious athlete dedicated a bronze or marble statue here. Nothing but the best was good enough for Olympia, and many of these superb works of art are on view here. Most of the exhibits are displayed in rooms to the right and left of the main entrance and follow a chronological sequence from severe Neolithic vases to baroque Roman imperial statues, neither of which will probably tempt you from heading straight ahead to see the museum's superstars.

The monumental sculpture from the Temple of Zeus is probably the finest surviving example of archaic Greek sculpture. The sculpture from the west pediment shows the battle of the Lapiths and Centaurs raging around the magisterial figure of Apollo, the god of reason. On the east pediment, Zeus oversees the chariot race between Oinomaos, the king of Pisa, and Pelops, the legendary figure who wooed and won Oinomaos's daughter by the unsporting expedient of loosening his opponent's chariot pins. On either end of the room, sculptured metopes show scenes from the Labors of Hercules, including the one he performed at Olympia: cleansing the foul stables of King Augeus by diverting the Alphios River.

Just beyond the sculpture from the Temple of Zeus are the 5th-century B.C. winged victory done by the artist Paionios and the 4th-century B.C. figure of Hermes and the infant Dionysios known as the Hermes of Praxiteles. The Hermes has a room to itself—or would, if tourists didn't make a bee-line to admire Hermes smiling with amused tolerance at his chubby half-brother Dionysios. If you want to impress your companions, mention casually that many scholars think that this is not an original work by Praxiteles, but a Roman copy.

In addition to several cases of glorious bronze heads of snarling griffins and the lovely terra-cotta of a resolute Zeus carrying off the youthful Ganymede, the museum has a good deal of athletic paraphernalia from the ancient games: stone and bronze weights that jumpers used, bronze and stone discuses, and even an enormous stone with a boastful inscription that a weight lifter had raised it over his head with only one hand.

Before you leave the museum, have a look at the two excellent site models just inside the main entrance. As the models make clear, ancient Olympia was quite literally divided by a low wall into two distinct parts: the Altis or religious sanctuary, containing temples and shrines, and the civic area, with athletic and municipal buildings.

The Ancient Site. Admission Dr 1,200 ($5.10). Usually open summer Mon–Fri 7:30am–7pm, Sat–Sun 8:30am–3pm; winter Mon–Fri 8am–5pm, Sat–Sun 8:30am–3pm.

In antiquity between festivals, Olympia was crowded with thousands of statues, but every four years during the games, so many people thronged here, that it was said by the time the games began, not even one more spectator could have wedged himself into the stadium. So, if the site is very crowded when you visit, just remember that it would have been much worse in antiquity.

Olympia's setting is magical: Pine trees shade the little valley, dominated by the conical Hill of Kronos, that lies between the Alphios and Kladeos Rivers. The handsome temples and the famous stadium that you've come here to see, however, are not immediately apparent as you enter the site. Immediately to the left are the unimpressive low walls that are all that remain of the Roman baths where athletes and spectators could enjoy hot and cold plunge baths. The considerably more impressive remains with the slender columns on your right mark the gymnasium and palestra, where athletes practiced their foot racing and boxing skills. The enormous gymnasium had a roofed track, precisely twice the length of the stadium, where athletes could practice in bad weather. Still ahead on the right are the fairly meager remains of a number of structures including a swimming pool and the large square Leonidaion, which served as a hotel for visiting dignitaries until a Roman governor decided it would do nicely as his villa. If you want, you can continue around the outskirts of the site, identifying other civic buildings, but you'll probably want to enter the sanctuary itself.

The religious sanctuary was, and is, dominated by two temples: the good-sized temple of Hera and the massive temple of Zeus. The temple of Hera with its three standing columns is the older of the two, built around 600 B.C. If you look closely, you'll see that the temple's column capitals and drums are not uniform. That's because this temple was originally built with wooden columns and as each column decayed, it was replaced; inevitably, the new columns had variations. The Hermes of Praxiteles was found here, buried under the mud that covered Olympia for so long due to the repeated flooding of the Alphios and Kladeos Rivers.

The Temple of Zeus, which once had a veritable thicket of 34 stocky Doric columns, was built around 456 B.C. The entire temple—so austere and gray today—was anything but austere in antiquity: Gold, red, and blue paint decorated it everywhere, and inside the temple stood the enormous gold and ivory statue of Zeus seated on an ivory and ebony throne. The statue was so ornate that it was considered one of the Seven Wonders of the Ancient World—and so large that people joked that if Zeus stood up, his head would go through the temple's roof. In fact, the antiquarian Philo of Byzantium suggested that Zeus had created elephants simply so that the sculptor Pheidias would have the ivory to make the statue of Zeus.

Not only do we know that Pheidias made the 13-meter-tall statue, we know where he made it: the Workshop of Phedias was on the site of the well-preserved brick building clearly visible west of the temple, just outside the sanctuary. How do we know that this was Pheidias's workshop? Because a cup with "I belong to Phedias" and artists' tools were found here.

Between the temples of Zeus and Hera you can make out the low foundations of a round building. This is all that remains of the shrine that Philip of Macedon, never modest, built here to pat himself on the back after conquering Greece in 338 B.C.

Beyond the two temples, built up against the Hill of Kronos itself, are the curved remains of a once-elegant Roman fountain and the foundations of 11 treasuries where Greek cities stored votive offerings and money. In front of the treasuries are the low bases of a series of bronze statues of Zeus dedicated not by victorious athletes but by those caught cheating in the stadium. These statues would have been the last thing that competitors saw before they ran through the vaulted tunnel into the stadium.

Ancient tradition is clear that the Olympic games began here in 776 B.C. and ended in A.D. 395, but is less clear on just why they were held every four years. According to one legend, Heracles initiated the games to celebrate completing his 12 labors, one of which took place nearby when the hero diverted the Alphios River to wash out the fetid Augean stables that King Augeas had neglected for more than a decade. With the stables clean, Heracles paced off the stadium and then he ran its entire length of 600 Olympic feet (192.27 meters) without having to take a single breath.

The Museum of the Olympic Games. Admission Dr 500 ($2.15). Open Mon–Sat 8am–3:30pm; Sun and holidays 9am–2:30pm.

When you head back to town, try to set aside half an hour to visit the Museum of the Olympic Games. Not many tourists come here and the guards are often glad to show visitors around. Displays include victors' medals, commemorative stamps, and photos of winning athletes, such as former King Constantine of Greece and the great African-American athlete Jesse Owens. There's also a photo of the bust of the founder of the modern Olympics, Baron de Coubertin. (The bust itself stands just off the main road east of the ancient site and marks the spot where de Coubertin's heart is buried.)

WHERE TO STAY

Olympia has more than 20 hotels, which means that you can almost always find a room, although if you arrive without a reservation in July or August, you may not get your first choice. In the winter, many hotels are closed.

The Ancient Olympic Games

The five-day Olympic festival was held every four years between 776 B.C. and A.D. 395 at full moon in mid-August or September, after the summer harvest. Participants came from as far away as Asia Minor and Italy and the entire Greek world observed a truce to allow athletes and spectators to make their way to Olympia safely. During all the years that the games took place, the truce was broken only a handful of times.

By the time that the games opened, literally thousands of people had poured into Olympia and much of the surrounding countryside was a tent city. Women were bared from watching or participating in the games, although women had their own Games in honor of Hera, Zeus's long-suffering wife, in non-Olympic years. Any woman caught sneaking into the Olympic games was summarily thrown to her death from a nearby mountain.

No one knows precisely what the order of events was at the games, but the five days included foot races, short and long jumps, wrestling and boxing contests, chariot races, the arduous pentathlon (discus, javelin, jumping, running, and wrestling), and the vicious pankration, which combined wrestling and boxing techniques.

The 3rd-century A.D. writer Philostratos recorded that participants in the pentathlon "must have skill in various methods of strangling." The most prestigous event was the stade, or short foot race, which gave its name to the stadium. Each Olympiad was named after the winner of the stade, and athletes like the 2nd-century B.C. Leonidas of Rhodes, who won at four successive Olympics, became international heroes. In addition to the glory, each victor won a crown made of olive branches and free meals for life in his home town.

Hotel Europa. Ancient Olympia 27065, Peloponnese. ☎ **0624/22-650** or 0624/22-700. Fax 0624/23-166. 42 rooms, all with bath. A/C TV TEL. Dr 28,750 ($122.35) double. Rates include breakfast. AE, DC, MC, V.

This member of the Best Western Hotel chain, a few minutes' drive out of town on a hill overlooking both the modern village and the ancient site, is clearly the best hotel in town—and one of the best in the entire Peloponnese. The only reason not to stay here is if you want to be able to walk out the door and be in the village of Ancient Olympia. The lobby and large restaurant gleam with marble, have unusually comfortable chairs, and great views out the picture windows. Most of the bedrooms overlook the large pool and garden, and several overlook the ancient site itself. The bedrooms are large, with colorful rugs, extrafirm mattresses, and sliding glass doors opening onto generous balconies. Friends who travel through the Peloponnese every summer rave about the Hotel Europa's unusual tranquility. The Europa plans to be open year-round.

Hotel Neda. Odos Praxiteles, Ancient Olympia 27065, Peloponnese. ☎ **0624/22-563.** Fax 0624/22-206. 43 rooms (all with bath). TEL. Dr 17,500 ($74.50) double. AE, V.

With a pleasant rooftop cafe, comfortable lobby, serviceable restaurant, and a distinctive red and white facade, the Neda offers good value. The double rooms, many decorated in shades of pink and rose, are large, with colorful shaggy flokaki rugs on the floor and good bedside reading lamps. Some of the double rooms have double beds, but most have twin beds, so specify what you want. Each room has a good-sized balcony, and the bathrooms are better than those usually found in hotels in this price category thanks to the presence of shower curtains, which help you to avoid spraying the entire room. Bedrooms here are usually quieter than at hotels on the main street.

⑤ Hotel Pelops. Odos Varela 2, Ancient Olympia 27065, Peloponnese. ☎ **0624/22-213.** 25 rooms (all with bath). TEL. Dr 11,500 ($48.95) double. Closed Nov–Feb. EU, MC, V.

The English-speaking owner, Susanna Spiliopoulou, described by many visitors here as especially helpful, makes this one of the most welcoming hotels in Olympia. There are flokaki rugs on the floors, good mattresses on the beds, and plants and vines shading the terrace.

Hotel Praxiteles. 7 Spiliopoulou, Ancient Olympia 27065, Peloponnese. ☎ **0624/225-92.** 10 rooms, all with bath. Dr 5,750 ($24.50) double. AE, EU, V.

The small, inexpensive family run Hotel Praxiteles is the best bargain in town. It's just one street back from Olympia's main street, Odos Spiliopoulou, and the neighborhood has a nice feel, with children often playing ball in the street in front of the police station. Although bedrooms are small and very spare, the beds are decent, and the front rooms have balconies. If you want to avoid the murmurs of conversation from the Praxiteles's excellent restaurant on the sidewalk below the balconies, ask for a room at the back (and hope that the neighborhood dogs don't bark too much).

WHERE TO DINE

There are almost as many restaurants as hotels in Olympia. The ones on and just off the main street with large signs in English and German tend to have indifferent food and service, although it's possible to get good snacks of yogurt or tiropites (cheese pies) in most of the cafes.

Taverna Ambrosia. Behind the train station in Ancient Olympia. ☎ **0624/23-414.** Appetizers Dr 460–Dr 1,000 ($2–$4.25); main courses Dr 1,150–Dr 2,875 ($4.90–$12.25). AE, V, MC. Daily 7pm–11pm. Serving lunch some weekends. GREEK.

This large restaurant with a pleasant outside veranda continues to attract locals although it does a brisk business with tour groups. You'll find the usual grilled chops and souvlaki here, but the vegetable dishes are unusually good, as is the lamb stew with lots of garlic and oregano.

Taverna Kladeos. Behind the train station in Ancient Olympia. ☎ **0624/23-322.** Appetizers Dr 345–Dr 690 ($1.50–$2.95); main courses Dr 1,000–Dr 1,725 ($4.25–$7.35). EU, MC, V. Daily 7pm–11pm. GREEK.

The charming Kladeos, with the best food in town, is at the end of the little paved road that runs steeply downhill past the Ambrosia restaurant. You may not be the only foreigner, but you probably will find lots of locals here. In good weather, tables are set up under canvas awnings and roofs made of rushes. If you sit in the hillside, you'll be serenaded by the frogs that live beside the river. Rather than offering an inflexible menu, the Kladeos varies its menu according to what's in season. In summer, the lightly grilled green peppers, zucchini, and eggplant are especially delicious. The house wine, a light rose, is heavenly. If you want to buy a bottle to take with you, give your empty water bottle to your waiter and ask him to fill it with krasi (wine).

Taverna Praxiteles. 7 Odos Spiliopoulou, Ancient Olympia. ☎ **0624/23-570** and 0624/ 22-592. AE, EU, V. Appetizers Dr 460–Dr 1,035 ($1.95–$4.40); main courses Dr 700–Dr 2,300 ($3–$9.80). Daily lunch and dinner. GREEK.

The reputation of the Hotel Praxiteles's excellent and reasonably priced restaurant has spread rapidly—and it's packed almost every evening, first with foreigners, eating unfashionably early for Greece, and then with locals, who start showing up around 10pm. Although the main courses are very good, especially the rabbit stew with onions (stifado), it's easy to make an entire meal out of the delicious and varied appetizers. A large plate of mezes (appetizers) is only Dr 1,500 ($6.40) and may include octopus, eggplant salad, taramasalada and Russian salad, meatballs stuffed with zucchini, fried cheese, and a handful of olives. In good weather, tables are outside on the sidewalk; for the rest of the years, meals are in the pine-paneled dining room.

SHOPPING

Galerie Orphee. Ancient Olympia. ☎ **0624/23-555.**

Antonios Kosmopoulos's main street bookstore, with its extensive range of cassettes and CDs of Greek music, and frequent displays of contemporary art, is a pleasant contrast to Olympia's other shops, which have all too many T-shirts, museum reproductions, and machine-made rugs and embroideries sold as genuine handmade crafts.

14   Pátras

128 miles (207km) SW of Athens.

The third-largest city in Greece and far and away the largest in the Peloponnese, Pátras's unappealing urban sprawl now extends for miles north and south of the city center. Although Pátras does have sights worth seeing—the Cathedral of Saint Andrew, the Archaeological Museum, a Roman Odeon (music hall) on the slopes of the ancient Acropolis, and a Medieval Castle on the summit—there's nothing here sufficiently worth seeing to linger unless you have to mark time until catching the ferry to Italy.

ESSENTIALS

GETTING THERE   By Train   There are frequent trains from Athens's Peloponnesian Train Station (☎ 01/51-31-601 for schedule information). If you are catching a ferry boat, keep in mind that Greek trains usually run late.

By Bus   There are some 15 buses to Pátras daily from Athens's Peloponnesian Bus Terminal at 100 Odos Kiffisiou (☎ 01/52-24-914 for schedule information). The Pátras train station, at Odos-Othonos Amalias 14, is on the waterfront near the boat departure piers.

By Car   The drive on the National Highway from Athens to Pátras takes about six hours. *Note:* In the city center, the system of not always obviously marked one-way streets means that you should drive with particular care.

VISITOR INFORMATION   The **Greek National Tourist Office (EOT)** is at Odos Iroon Polytechniou 1, on the harbor near ferry boat gate 6. The office is usually open Monday through Friday from 7am to 9pm weekdays and Saturday and Sunday from 2 to 9pm weekends (☎ 061/420-305).

FAST FACTS   The area code is **061.** The **Tourist Police** office is at Odos Patreos 53, off Plateia Georgiou (☎ 061/220-902). There are a number of **banks** on the waterfront and on Plateia Georgiou. Most of the **car-rental agencies** (Avis, Hertz, Kemwell) have clearly marked offices on the waterfront, as do the ferry boat companies.

WHAT TO SEE & DO

If you do find yourself with a few hours in Pátras, here are some suggestions: First, head for **Plateia Georgiou** (George Square). Sit at one of the cafes and take in the facades of the handsome neoclassical theater and banks on the square. Pátras has been hit repeatedly by earthquakes, and these buildings are among the few that remain from the 19th century, when the city was famous for its arcaded streets and neoclassical architecture.

Then, head down to the waterfront to the **Cathedral of Saint Andrew.** Although the present rather hideous church was only built after World War II, the mosaics give a vivid picture of old Pátras. Be sure to dress appropriately to visit the cathedral, a major pilgrimage shrine, thanks to the presence of Saint Andrew's skull in an ornate gold reliquary to the right of the altar. There are several pleasant cafes in the shaded park across from the cathedral.

If you're in Pátras in July or August, you may be able to take in one of the concerts or plays given during the **International Festival.** Or, you may prefer to concentrate on the **Wine Festival,** featuring wine tastings at the Achaia Clauss winery. (Schedule information available from the EOT.) Pátras also has a vigorous **carnival,** with parades, costumes, and floats, to mark the beginning of Lent.

WHERE TO STAY

Astir Hotel. Agiou Andreas 16, Pátras 26223. ☎ **061/277-502.** 120 rooms (all with bath). TEL TV. Dr 25,000 ($106.40) double.

If you arrive too late to continue your journey or have an early morning boat to catch, this is a convenient, if overpriced, hotel. The rates here are higher than they should be since the bedrooms are nothing special, and many seem to have been decorated by someone who couldn't decide on just which color to go with. Some rooms have harbor views, as does the rooftop terrace. For Pátras, this is a quiet place to spend the night—which is to say that the street noise here is usually endurable.

Porto Rio Hotel. Rion 26500. ☎ **061/992212.** Fax 061/992115. 267 rooms and bungalows (all with bath). A/C TV TEL. Dr 28,500–Dr 37,200 ($121.30–$158.30) double in the high season (Jun 16–Sept 15); Dr 20,200–Dr 28,750 ($85.95–$122.35) double in the low season. Service and government taxes included. Full board supplement Dr 5,000 ($21.30) per person.

This sprawling hotel complex on the beach, a 20-minute drive north of Pátras, does a brisk business with business conventions and European families on holiday. The Rio has a several swimming pools, a health club (with saunas and Jacuzzi), and two tennis courts. The bedrooms are large, and most have either a terrace or a balcony overlooking the extensive gardens. This is a good place to stay if you have a day to kill before catching a ferry in Pátras. The only drawback is the unimaginative food.

WHERE TO DINE

The restaurants along the harbor near the train station serve consistently mediocre food to the hordes of tourists arriving from and departing for Italy. You won't starve at any one of these places, but you can do better. If you want an ouzo before dinner or a sweet after, head for any of the cafes in the main square, Plateia Georgiou.

Trikoyia. Amalias 46. No telephone. AE, DC, V. Appetizers from Dr 1,000 ($3); fresh fish priced daily by the kilo. SEAFOOD.

This hole-in-the-wall taverna serves up excellent fresh fish and octopus. Chops are usually available and you can often get one or two more ambitious meat dishes, such as stifado (beef or rabbit stew with onions). It's a 15-minute walk along the harbor from the main port.

☉ Pharos Fish Taverna. Amalias 48 (number not on building). ☎ **061/336-500.** No credit cards. Appetizers from Dr 920 ($2.80); fresh fish priced daily by the kilo. SEAFOOD.

Next door to Trikoyia, the Lighthouse Fish Taverna has equally fresh fish and outdoor dining in an alleyway. There are usually lots of locals eating here, always a good sign. Head inside first and chose your fish; if you arrive and sit at a table, the waiter will probably ignore you thinking that you haven't made up your mind yet.

SIDE TRIPS FROM PATRAS: ARCHAIA CLAUSS WINERY, CHLEMOUTSI & RIO

ARCHAIA CLAUSS WINERY

This winery is located above Pátras in the hills, which are usually noticeably cooler than Pátras itself. Tours of the winery, with its old barrels and grape presses, are given most weekdays (☎ 061/325-051 for information). The German vintner Clauss named his sweet dessert wine "Mavrodaphne" in memory of his beloved Greek wife, who died young. You may be offered a free sample of Mavrodaphne at the end of your tour. Be warned: The wine is as sweet as molasses.

THE CASTLE AT CHLEMOUTSI

This astonishingly well-preserved 13th-century Frankish castle with crenelated walls, cavernous galleries, and an immense hexagonal keep, is a relic of the days when Geoffrey de Villehardouin dominated the Peloponnese. Like most castles in the Peloponnese, it passed back and forth between the Franks, Venetians, Turks, and Greeks. The gaps in the outer wall were caused by Ibrahim Pasha's cannon during the Greek War of Independence. The castle is open sunrise to sunset most days. Admission is free. The turn-off to the castle is signposted some 34 miles (55 km) out of Pátras on the main Pátras-Olympia road.

THE BEACH AT RIO

If you are really desperate for a swim, head 3 miles (5km) out of town on the National Road and take the turn off to Rio. The coast road runs along the narrow pebble beach for about 6 miles (10km). This excursion is recommended only for the diehard sunbather or swimmer: Traffic is heavy, the beach is crowded, and the sea is not the cleanest. There are a number of perfectly okay restaurants along the coast road, but if there's one that's really special, I haven't found it yet, despite many attempts.

Crete 7

by John S. Bowman

In a world where increasing numbers of travelers have "been there, done that," Crete remains a still endlessly fascinating and satisfying destination. Per square mile, it must be one of the most loaded places in the world—loaded, that is, in the diversity of history, archaeological sites, natural attractions, touristic amenities, and more. Crete happens to be almost the exact size of Puerto Rico, yet it has only about one-seventh of the permanent population—some 500,000 people. That leaves a lot more space for visitors, whether they are seeking to relax on a beach or pursue exotic encounters.

Every year, many hundreds of thousands of foreigners spend time on Crete, and an elaborate service industry has grown up to please them. There are facilities now for everyone's taste—ranging from luxury resort complexes, which can hold their own with the finest in the world, all the way to cafes and guest rooms in villages that have hardly changed over several centuries. You can spend a delightful day in a remote mountain environment where you're treated to some fresh goat cheese and olives; then within an hour, you can be back at your hotel on a beach and enjoying a cool drink.

Yet Crete isn't always and everywhere a gentle Mediterranean idyll—its terrain can be raw, its sites austere, its tone brusque. But for those looking for a distinctly defined place, Crete will be rewarding.

One more word: Crete has become an island on overload during July and August, so if you possibly can arrange it, go in June or September, even late May or early October—unless you seek only a sun-drenched beach.

A LOOK AT CRETE'S PAST

Crete's diversity and distinction begins with its history, a past that has left far more remains than the Minoan sites many people first associate with Crete. You cannot take 10 steps without tripping over Crete's past. Its full history, of course, began with its emergence from the primeval Mediterranean sea over millions of years as a massive ridge of mainly limestone. After being settled by humans about 6500 B.C. Crete passed through the late Neolithic and Early Bronze ages, sharing the broader eastern Mediterranean culture.

Sometime after 3000 B.C., new immigrants came over; by about 2500 B.C., there began to emerge a fairly distinctive culture that's been dubbed Early Minoan. By about 2000 B.C., the Minoans were

Crete

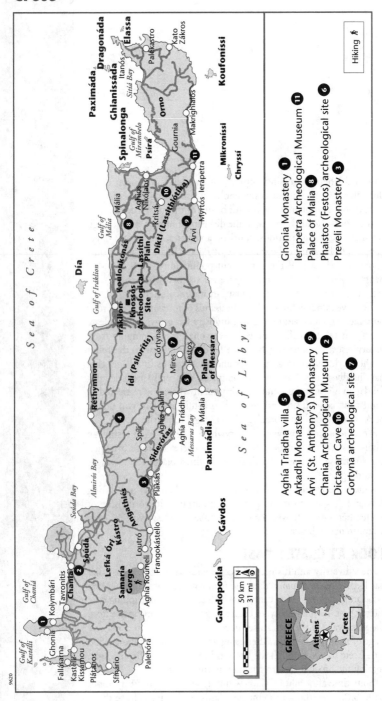

Ghonia Monastery **1**
Ierapetra Arkeological Museum **11**
Palace of Malia **8**
Phaistos (Festos) archeological site **6**
Preveli Monastery **3**

Aghía Triádha villa **5**
Arkadhi Monastery **4**
Arvi (St. Anthony's) Monastery **9**
Chania Archeological Museum **2**
Dictaean Cave **10**
Gortyna archeological site **7**

Hiking ⚐

moving into a far more ambitious phase, the Middle Minoan—the civilization that gave rise to the palaces and other structures and the superb works of art and artifacts that now attract hundreds of thousands of visitors to Crete every year.

Mycenaean Greeks appear to have taken over the palaces by 1500 B.C., and by about 1200 B.C., this Minoan-Mycenaean civilization had pretty much gone under. For several centuries, Crete was a relatively marginal player in the great era of Greek classical civilization.

When the Romans conquered the island in 67 B.C., they revived certain centers (including Knossos) as imperial colonies. Early converts to Christianity, the Cretans slipped into the shadows of the Byzantine world, but the island was pulled back into the light when Venetians in 1204 broke up the Byzantine Empire and took over Crete. The Venetians made Crete a major colonial outpost, revived trade and agriculture, and eventually built quite elaborate structures.

By the late 1500s, however, the Turks were conquering the Venetians' eastern Mediterranean possessions, and in 1669 they captured the last major holdout on Crete, the city of Candia—today's Iráklion. Cretans suffered considerably under the Turks, and although some of Greece finally threw off the Turkish yoke in the late 1820s, Crete was left behind. A series of rebellions marked the rest of the 19th century, resulting in the Great Powers' sponsoring a sort of independent Crete in 1898.

Finally in 1913, Crete was for the first time formally joined to Greece. Crete had yet another cameo role in history when the Germans invaded it in 1941 with gliders and parachute troops; the ensuing occupation was another low point for the people of Crete.

Since 1945, Crete has advanced amazingly in the economic sphere, powered by its agricultural products as well as by its tourist industry. Not all Cretans are pleased by the development, but all would agree that, for better or worse, Crete owes much to its history.

1 Iráklion

Iráklion is one Greek city you have to visit, not because it's the capital and transportation/commercial center of Crete, but because it's home to the world's only comprehensive collection of Minoan artifacts and because it's the gateway to Knossos, the major Minoan palace site (see the listings for the Archaeological Museum and the Site of Knossos, in "What to See and Do," below). Beyond that, it does have several attractions of its own—at the very least, its magnificent fortified walls and several other memorials to the Venetians' time of power. Although Minoan remains have been found on its outskirts and a few Roman, Byzantine, and Arab remains within, it's the Venetian and Turkish survivals that give Iráklion whatever picturesqueness it has.

Iráklion is also big enough (Greece's fifth-largest city) and confident enough to have its own identity as a busy modern city. Tourism may be a big business here but it hasn't totally monopolized the character of the city. Why then does Iráklion often get such bad press? Precisely because it's a big modern city, bustling with traffic and commerce and construction—the very things most travelers are trying to escape. Iráklion can also be noisy at night, what with airplanes from the nearby airport flying over your hotel and motorcycles and scooters buzzing around the surrounding streets. (We've worked to find some quieter alternatives.) Anyway, give Iráklion a chance. If you follow some of the advice we proffer, you may come to like it.

ESSENTIALS

GETTING THERE   By Plane   Most people fly from the **Athens Airport** to Iráklion on an **Olympic Airlines** flight at a cost of some Dr 21,150 ($90) one way. Reservations are a necessity during the high season. During the summer, Olympic also offers service between Iráklion and Santoríni, Iráklion and Rhodes, Iráklion and Corfu, and Iráklion and Mýkonos—again, these are heavily booked in high season so you would have to commit yourself well in advance.

There is now another alternative to Olympic—**Air Greece,** a new (1995) privately owned airline that offers cheaper (by about 15%) flights (albeit in smaller planes) between Iráklion and Athens, Thessaloniki, and Rhodes. It may not yet be on the international booking computers, but you can ask your travel agent to look into these flights, or you can contact Air Greece's general agent in Iráklion (☎ 081/330729); fax 081/241377.

Iráklion's airport is about 3 miles (5km) east of the city, along the coast. Major car-rental companies have desks at the airport. A taxi to Iráklion costs about Dr 1,500 ($6.40), and the public bus is Dr 200 (85¢).

To get back to the airport, you have the same two choices—taxi or public bus (no. 1). You can take both from Platia Eleftheria (Liberty Square) or at other points along the way. Inquire in advance at your hotel about the closest possibility.

By Ferry   If you have come over from the mainland by one of the overnight ferries (or from Santoríni or any other port), you'll probably want to take a taxi up into the town. Depending on where you want to go, the fare may be Dr 500 to Dr 1,000 ($2.15 to $4.25). It's quite a steep climb (a solid 15 minutes) from the port to the city, but certainly many do choose to do so. A compromise is the public bus described below.

By Bus   The third common mode of arrival is by bus from elsewhere on the island, and where you end up depends on where you've come from. Those arriving from points to the west or east or southeast—Chaniá or Réthymnon, for instance, or Ághios Nikólaos or Ierapetra to the east—will end up down along the harbor and will have a choice of three approaches to the center of town: walking (you're only a few hundred yards closer to the town than if you got off a ship), taxi, or the public bus. The bus starts its route at the bus terminal where vehicles from the east and southeast stop (directly across the boulevard from the station for the Réthymnon-Chaniá buses). Those arriving from the south—Phaestos, Matala, and such—will end up at the Chaniá Gate on the southwest edge of town; walking will not appeal to most, but you have the choice of a public bus or a taxi.

VISITOR INFORMATION   The **National Tourist Office Information Desk** is at Odos Xanthoudidou 1 (opposite the entrance to the Archaeological Museum), Iráklion 71202 (☎ **081/244462,** 244633, 228203, or 228225). It's open Monday through Friday from 8am to 3pm.

GETTING AROUND   Most people will find it easiest to walk around Iráklion—the points of interest are never that far apart. A car is really no asset in Iráklion, what with so many one-way streets and so much traffic—it's best is to park it somewhere safe. There is frequent public bus service to all points and there are taxis. The main taxi stand is on Liberty Square, across from the Archaeological Museum.

FAST FACTS: Iráklion

American Express   The official agency for American Express is **Cretan Travel Bureau** 20-22, Iráklion 71202 (☎ 081/227002).

Area Code   The area code for Iráklion is **081.**

Car/Moped Rentals   Every second doorway in Iráklion seems prepared to rent a car or motorbike. We have found one of the most helpful agencies to be the **Motor Club,** at Platia Agglon 18 (at the foot of Odos 25th Avgusto, overlooking the traffic circle and the old harbor) Iráklion 71202 (☎ 081/222408; fax 081/222862). They also have offices at the Iráklion Airport, Malia, and Réthymnon. See also "Getting Around," above.

Embassies/Consulates   The British Consul is at Odos Papa Alexandrou 16 (opposite the Archaeological Museum). There is no American consul in Iráklion.

Hospitals   The main hospital of Iráklion is the **Venizelou Hospital** (☎ 081/ 237502) on Knossos Road. For general **first-aid information,** call 081/222222.

Luggage Storage   There are several places along Odos 25th Avgusto that will keep your luggage for a fee, the most established one being at no. 48 (☎ 081/281750). It's open only April through October. The fee here has been Dr 400 ($1.70) per piece per day. Most hotels will hold luggage for brief periods. You can leave luggage at the airport, too, but it costs Dr 800 ($3.40) per piece per day.

Mail and Post Office   The main post office (☎ 081/289995) is on Platia Daskaloyiannis; it's open daily from 7:30am to 8pm. There's a branch post office (☎ 081/212963) down at the harbor, open Monday through Friday from 7:30am to 8pm; closed Saturday and Sunday.

Police   The **Tourist Police** (☎ 081/283190 or 081/289614) are at Odos Dikiosenis 10 (linking top of Odos 25th Avgusto to Platia Eleftheria). It' open daily from 7am to 11pm.

Restrooms   There are public toilets in El Greco Park, at the far end of the Archaeological Museum's garden-cafe area, and in the city's public gardens at the far edge of Liberty Square.

Taxis   For a radio-directed taxi from anywhere in or around Iráklion, call 081/ 210102 or 081/210168.

Telephone, Telex, and Fax   The **OTE,** or national telecommunications office, is at Odos Minotaurou 10 (the far side of El Greco Park), Iráklion 71202. Open daily from 6am to 11pm.

Transit Info   For KTEL buses to Réthymnon-Chaniá and points west, call 081/ 221765. For buses to Mallia, Ághios Nikólaos, Sitia, Ierapetra and points east, call 081/245019. For buses to Phaestos and other points to south, call 081/255965. For information about all ships, call the Port Authority at 081/244956.

Travel Agencies   There seems to be no end to the city's travel agencies. Among the oldest and most reliable are **Adamis Tours** (see American Express, above); **Creta Travel Bureau,** Odos Epimenidou 20-22, Iráklion 71202 (☎ 081/227002); and **Arabadzoglou Travel,** Odos 25th Avgusto 54, Iráklion 71202 (☎ 081/226697).

Useful Telephone Numbers   For car accident assistance, call 081/193.

WHAT TO SEE & DO

✪ The Archaeological Museum. Odos Xanthoudidou (far corner of Platia Eleftheria), Iráklion 71202. ☎ **081/226092.** Admission Dr 1,500 ($6.40); free on Sunday; students with official ID half price. Apr to mid-Oct, Tues–Sun 8am–7pm, Mon 12:30–7pm; mid-Oct to Mar, closed every day at 5pm.

This is the world's premier collection of art and artifacts from the Minoan civilization. Although many of its most spectacular objects are from Knossos, it does have finds from other sites. It also includes some finds from the pre-Minoan and post-Minoan cultures, but most visitors will have enough to do to take in the Minoan remains. The museum is well laid out (and now air-conditioned) and on a chronological plan, with finds from specific sites then grouped within periods.

The variety of objects, styles, techniques, and materials will amaze all who have not previously focused on the Minoans—ceramics of every kind, stone vases, ivory figurines, and metal work from large bronze axes to delicate gold jewelry.

Among the most prized objects are the **snake goddesses** from Knossos, the **Phaestos Disc** (with its still undeciphered inscription), the **bee pendant** from Mallia, the **carved vases** from Aghia Triadha and Kato Zakros, and various objects testifying to the famous bull-leaping.

Upstairs are the **original frescoes from Knossos** and other sites, their restored sections clearly visible (the frescoes now at Knossos are copies of these). Even those meeting the Minoans for the first time will end up with a good sense of their distinctive spirit—a sense of aesthetics, a love of nature, an enjoyment of life.

A hint about visiting this museum: During the high season, it can be overwhelmed by large tour groups, and the noise level (in various languages) and visibility problem can detract from your enjoyment. So plan to get there either very early or late in the day (allowing one to two hours for your visit)—and visit Knossos in the other time frame, if you are limited to one day. Most displays have decent labels in English, but you might prefer to invest in one of the guidebooks on sale in the lobby. And if you're really serious, ask at a travel agency about a guided tour.

✪ **The Knossos Site.** Knossos Road (5 kilometers south of Iráklion). ☎ **081/231940.** Admission Dr 1,500 ($6.40), free on Sunday. April to mid-Oct, Mon–Fri 8am–7pm, Sat–Sun, 8:30am–3pm; mid-Oct to Mar, Mon–Fri 8am–5pm, Sat–Sun 8:30am–3pm.

We include this as an attraction under Iráklion because it is for most people just that—indeed, it's the main show, perhaps for some people preferable even to the museum if it comes down to one place to meet the Minoans.

Until Arthur Evans began excavating here in 1900, little was known about this ancient people—although others had begun to dig a bit on the site and the great Schliemann, of Troy and Mycenae fame, almost bought the site. Evans turned up most of the more spectacular parts of the palace and its contents in the first few years, but he continued to oversee the excavations—and pay for much of the work from his personal fortune—almost till his death in 1939. Excavations continue to this day.

Evans also did something else quite controversial then and even now: Using every possible clue and remnant, he rebuilt large parts of the palace—walls, floors, stairs, windows, and columns. He insisted that he had solid evidence for all his restorations (color-coded to indicate the original materials) and they certainly help the average visitor appreciate the palace. Realize that you are seeing the remains of two major palaces plus several restorations that were made from about 2000 B.C. to 1250 B.C. Realize, too, that this was not a palace in the modern sense of a royal residence but a combination of that and the Minoans' chief religious-ceremonial center as well as their administrative headquarters and royal workshops.

You can now wander through its rooms and up and down the stairs and gain a true sense of why this "house of the double-ax" (or *labrys*) inspired the myth of Daedalus's constructing a labyrinth to contain the Minotaur, half man, half bull, and then of Theseus, after making his way in to kill the Minotaur, getting out thanks to a ball of thread given him by Ariadne, daughter of the tyrannical King Minos.

Thoroughly exploring the place and its adjacent buildings can take a solid three to four hours, but you can get a good sense of it in a one- to two-hour walk-through.

Here is one place that a guided tour might be worth the expense; your hotel or a travel agency can arrange for this. Alternatively, buy one of the guidebooks that give a detailed account.

Historical Museum of Crete. Odos Kalokorinou 7 (street behind Xenia Hotel on coast road), Iráklion 71202. ☎ **081/283219.** Admission Dr 500 ($2.15); students with official ID, half price. Mon–Fri 9am–2pm, closed Sun and holidays.

This museum picks up where the Archaeological Museum leaves off, displaying artifacts and traditional popular art from the early Christian era up to the present. Coming into focus here are the Byzantine-medieval realm, the Venetians' long occupation (1210–1669), and the Turkish occupation (1669–1898). You also get some sense of the role the Cretans' long struggle for independence still plays in their identity. You see a choice collection of **traditional Cretan folk arts;** the **recreated study of Nikos Kazantzakis,** Crete's great modern writer; and finally the fairly recently acquired **works attributed to the painter El Greco,** another of Crete's admired sons. Even if you take only an hour for this museum, it will reward you with some surprising aspects to round out your image of Crete.

Venetian Walls. The Harbor Fort, and Kazantzakis' Tomb, Harbor Fort. Daily 9am–1pm, 4–7pm. Dr 500 ($2.15).

You need not be a student of Renaissance military engineering to appreciate the **great walls** and **bastions** of the once proud fortress-city the Venetians called Candia. There had been crude walls and a basic fort at the harbor from the time of the Arab occupation (A.D. 824–961) and the Byzantine period (A.D. 961–1204). The Venetians began to enlarge and improve these from fairly early on, but it was not until the 16th and 17th centuries that the truly magnificent wall was erected—in part under the supervision of the great Italian engineer **Michele Sammicheli.**

The **harbor fort,** also built on earlier forts on this site, went up between 1523 and 1540, and although greatly restored, is essentially the grand Venetian original. Two of the great city gates have survived fairly well: the Pantocrator or Panigra Gate— better known now as the **Chaniá Gate** (dating from about 1570) at the western edge; and the **Gate of Gesu,** or Kainouryia Gate (dated to about 1587) at the southern edge. You can walk around the outer perimeter of almost the entire walls and get an impression of their sheer massiveness. They were built, of course, by the forced labor of Cretans. Numerous carvings and lions attest to the Venetians' role in all this.

But one non-Venetian presence has now come to rest on one of the bastions, the Martinengo Bastion at the southern corner. Here is the **grave of Nikos Kazantzakis** (1883–1947), a native of Iráklion who went forth to travel much of the world and appropriate many of its ideas and convert these into several modern classics, including *Zorba the Greek* and *The Last Temptation of Christ.* His self-chosen epitaph ("I hope for nothing, I fear nothing, I am free") expresses the defiant individualism that gained him the enmity of the Orthodox Church in his lifetime. Now many people pay pilgrimage to his grave, and he seems more like some spiritual master.

It's standing here at Kazantzakis's tomb, by the way, that you get one of the best views to the south of Mt. Iouktas, which appears in profile to be the head of a man. According to one ancient myth, this is the head of the buried god Zeus. Kazantzakis would have appreciated your making the connection.

A Stroll Around Iráklion

You will bump into a lot of Iráklion's past just making your way at random around the city—old Italian or Arabic inscriptions, archways and other architectural elements—but a neat two- to three-hour walking tour can include the major points of interest.

Start off at **Fountain Square** (a.k.a. Lions Square, officially Venizelou Square), perhaps fortified with a plate of *bougatsa* at one of the two small cafes serving this distinctive filled pastry—it's not Cretan but was introduced by Greeks from Armenia, which is why you won't find it in many other places. The fountain was installed here in 1628 by the Venetian governor of Crete, Francesco Morosini. The lions were brought from some 14th-century structure. Note the now fading but still elegant relief carvings around the basin.

Across from the fountain is the **Basilica of St. Mark,** restored to its original 14th-century Italian style and used for exhibitions and concerts.

Proceeding south 50 yards to the crossroads, you see before you the **Market Street** (officially 1866 Street), now, alas, increasingly taken over by tourist shops but still harboring some purveyors of fresh fruits and vegetables, meat, wine, and other products of the Cretan countryside. As you stroll up it, note on the left the legendary **Dirty Alley,** lined with tiny tavernas that sell basic meals.

At the far end of Market Street, you come out onto **Kornarou Square,** with its lovely Turkish fountain (now housing a snack bar/cafe); beside it is the **Venetian Bembo Fountain** (1588), with a Roman statue incorporated into it. The modern statue in the center of the square commemorates the hero and heroine of Vincenzo Kornarou's Renaissance epic poem *Erotokritos*, a Cretan-Greek classic.

Turning right onto **Vikela Street,** you proceed (always bearing right) until you come out at the **Cathedral of Aghios Menas,** dedicated to the patron saint of Iráklion; an imposing if not artistically notable structure, it was built between 1862 and 1895. Below and to the left is the medieval **Church of Aghios Menas,** which boasts some old wood carvings and icons.

At the far corner of the cathedral (thus to northwest) is the 15th-century **Church of St. Katherine.** During the 16th and 17th centuries, this hosted the Mt. Sinai Monastery School, where **Domenico Theotocopoulou** is alleged to have studied before moving on to Venice, Spain, and fame as **El Greco;** it now houses a small museum of icons, frescos, and wood carvings, the most valuable being six late 16th-century paintings by **Michael Damaskinos,** a contemporary of El Greco's. (Hours Monday through Saturday from 10am to 1pm; Tuesday, Thursday, and Friday also from 4 to 6pm. Admission Dr 400; $1.70.)

Taking the narrow street that's directly perpendicular to the facade of St. Katherine's—Odos Aghii Dheka—you come out onto Leoforos Kalokerinou, the **main shopping street** for ordinary Iraklians. Turn right onto it and proceed on up to the crossroads of the Market and 25th Avgusto. Turn left and proceed back down past Fountain Square and, on the right, the (totally reconstructed) **Venetian Loggia,** originally dating from the early 1600s. Here the leading Venetians met to conduct affairs; now its upper floor houses offices of the city government, with others in the connecting building to the rear, the original Venetian armory.

A little farther down 25th Avgusto, also on the right, is the **Church of Aghios Titos;** dedicated to the patron saint of all Crete (the Titus of the Bible, who introduced Christianity to Crete). The church has gone through several restorations under the Venetians and then the Turks. You proceed down to the **harbor** (with a side visit to the **Venetian fort,** or *Koules,* if you have the energy at this time), then pass, along the right, the two sets of great **Venetian *arsenali***—where ships were built and repaired (the sea then came in this far). Climbing the stairs just past the arsenali, you turn left onto Odos Bofort and curve up under the **Archaeological Museum** to **Liberty Square** (Platia Eleftheria)—where you can take a much deserved refreshing drink at any one of the numerous cafes.

WHERE TO STAY

Iráklion has actually been losing hotel rooms and overnight visitors in recent years as the trend is to beach hotels, but there is still a big choice and there can still be a need for reservations in the high season. Single rates are always available, as are special arrangements for families. At the more expensive hotels, by the way, you are expected to dress up a bit for dinner.

And let's be frank about the noise factor. At the moment, Iráklion lies annoyingly close to the flight patterns of both commercial airliners and occasional jet fighters of the Greek Air Force. Not to deny the nuisance element, but the total time of the overhead airplane noise adds up probably to less than a half hour every 24 hours—and many would agree that the sound of scooters and motorcycles outside your hotel at night is more annoying. For that matter, we've stayed in a luxury hotel and had our sleep ruined by a barking dog. In any case, there's now a plan to add a runway out into the sea to eliminate the flights over Iráklion. It will take some years for this to happen. All we can say is that we have made the search for some quiet a major criterion in our selection of hotels.

INSIDE THE CITY
Expensive

Atlantis Hotel. Odos Igias 2 (behind the Archaeological Museum), Iráklion 71202. ☎ **081/229103.** Fax 081/226265. 130 doubles, 30 singles, 4 suites. A/C MINIBAR TV TEL. High season, Dr 32,000 ($135) double; low season, Dr 25,000 ($106) double. Rates include buffet breakfast. Surcharge (Dr 1,000; $4.25) for one night's stay, but reduction possible for longer stays; special rates for business travelers; half-board rates (which include breakfast and dinner) available. AE, DC, EU, MC, V.

This is a superior Class A hotel in the heart of Iráklion, yet just enough removed that it can offer some isolation from the noise of the city (especially if you use the air conditioning). They have made major renovations in 1994 and 1995 and by the time of your visit hope to have added still other features such as a taverna, health club, and swimming pool. Even without these facilities, it's a fine hotel. The staff is friendly and helpful—it's run by the sons of the founder so still has a family feel. It has been especially popular with conference groups but individuals get individual attention. Rooms are not plush but they are certainly comfortable. The Atlantis is probably your best bet if you can afford it and want to be in the center of things.

Dining/Entertainment: A ground-floor restaurant offers a Greek and international menu. Two bars and a rooftop garden offer refreshments.

Services: Concierge, room service, dry cleaning and laundry, massage, baby-sitting, pickup at airport arranged.

Facilities: Video rentals, Jacuzzi, sundeck, outdoor tennis court (across the street), bicycle rental, children's playground across the street, conference rooms (up to 650), car rental arranged, tours arranged, hairdresser, boutiques, parking around the hotel (with special arrangements for conference groups).

Galaxy Hotel. Avenue Dimokratias 67 (about ¹/₂ mile out main road to Knossos), Iráklion 71306. ☎ **081/238812.** Fax 081/211211. 144 rms (some with shower only, some with tub only). A/C MINIBAR TV TEL. High season, Dr 36,800 ($157) double; low season, Dr 28,750 ($122) double. Rates include buffet breakfast. AE, DC, EU, MC, V. Parking on street. Frequent bus to center within yards of entrance.

In recent years, this has gained the reputation as one of the finer hotels in Iráklion, and it's classy—once you get by its rather forbidding exterior. The main level public areas are striking, and there is (for now at least) the largest swimming pool in Iráklion (also a sauna). Ask for an interior room since you lose nothing in a view and gain in quietness. The rooms are stylish in a masculine rather than feminine fashion. The restaurant offers the standard Greek and international menu. The pastry shop and ice cream parlor attract outsiders, their fare is so delicious. There's a Presidential Suite with several rooms and extra amenities. The desk, of course, will handle all the usual requests for special services. And the hotel is fully equipped to handle conferences of up to 80. If its attractions described above appeal to you, then give this a try.

Moderate

Atrion Hotel. Odos Paleologou 9 (behind Historical Museum), Iráklion 71202. ☎ **081/229225.** Fax 081/223292. 65 doubles (33 with tub, 32 with shower); 4 suites, all with bath. A/C TEL. High season, Dr 19,500 ($83) double; low season, Dr 18,000 ($76) double. Rates include buffet breakfast. Reductions for children. AE, EU, JCB, MC, V. Parking on street. Public bus within 200 yards.

This relatively new hotel has well-appointed public areas—the lounge area, a restaurant, cafeteria, bar, and a refreshing patio-garden. Its rooms are good sized and pleasant while its suites offer color TV and a minibar. The front desk can arrange for such services as laundry, baby-sitting, and rentals. All this is to be expected in a Class B hotel. What's not is that its location gains it more quiet, both day and night, while still leaving you within a 10-minute walk to the center of town. The adjacent streets are not that attractive but they're perfectly safe, and once inside you can enjoy your oasis of comfort and peace.

Lato Hotel. Odos Epimenidou 15, Iráklion 71202. ☎ **081/228103.** Fax 081/240350. 50 doubles (some with shower only, some with tub only). A/C TV TEL. High season, Dr 18,375 ($79) double; low season, Dr 12,650 ($54) double. Rates include continental breakfast. AE, DC, EU, MC, V. Parking in street.

One of several hotels on this street (east off the bottom of Odos 25th Avgusto), this one offers many rooms with an especially fine view of the harbor. It provides meals only for groups, but you're so close to the center that you'll never lack for restaurants. It has offered room service for breakfast and snacks (but this can change depending on the availability of staff). It can host meetings of up to 50 (and will arrange to feed them). Once again, what earns this otherwise standard hotel its inclusion here are its harborside rooms offering relatively more quiet at night.

Inexpensive

Marin Hotel. Avenue Bofort 12 (the street winding down below Archaeological Museum), Iráklion 71202. ☎ **081/224736** or 081/224737. Fax 081/224730. 48 doubles/triples, some with showers, some with tubs. High season, Dr 13,800 ($59) double; low season, Dr 11,500 ($49) double. Rates include continental breakfast. AE, EU, MC, V. Closed Nov–Mar. Parking on streets.

This is a Class C hotel that has the advantage of offering good views over the sea, easy walking from the harbor as well as to the center of town, and some isolation from the worst of the street noise. The rooms are decorated with a nod to the traditional Cretan style—nothing fancy but adequate. The front desk will help arrange for all the basic services, from laundry to car rentals. The restaurant is used only for breakfast, but there's a bar. (The rooftop garden is temporarily out of service.) Definitely for people on a budget who use a hotel mainly for nights, not for days.

Poseidon. Odos Poseidonos 46, Póros (above New Harbor), Iráklion 71202. ☎ **081/222545** or 081/245360. Fax 081/245405. 26 doubles, all with shower. High season, Dr 16,100 ($69) double; low season, Dr 10,350 ($44) double. All rates include continental breakfast. *Note:* Ask about a 10% reduction for Frommer's users making reservations. Frequent public buses 200 yards at top of street; about 1 mile from Liberty Square off main road east out of Iráklion.

We include the Poseidon because it's a favorite of Frommer's loyalists, and for a reason. Its owner-host John Polychronides and the desk staff (fluent in English) personify all that is best about old-fashioned Cretan hospitality. They provide useful support (making calls, directing you to services, etc.) and more important, they show genuine concern for your stay on Crete. Yes, it's on a not especially elegant street—but that's true of the city hotels, and few can match the fresh breezes and its view over the port of Iráklion. Yes, it gets the airplane noise—but so do virtually all the other hotels in and around Iráklion. And it is a budget hotel—no elevator, a basic shower, but everything is clean and functional. Frequent buses and cheap taxi fares let you come and go into Iráklion center (a 20-minute walk). This remains a choice for those who travel to experience the true Crete but have limited funds.

OUTSIDE THE CITY

One solution to avoiding the city noise is to stay in one of the hotels on the coast to either side—although those immediately to the west also get the occasional over-flight, the hotels to the east we single out are far enough away so as not to be under the usual flight patterns. We're assuming here that you want to be fairly close to Iráklion—if you just want a remote beach anywhere on Crete, such accommodations are described elsewhere. A couple of the hotels described are truly luxury class. Although all can be reached by public buses, a car or taxi would certainly save you some valuable time.

Expensive

Candia Maris. Amoudara, Gazi (on beach about 2 miles west of Iráklion center) Iráklion 71303. ☎ **081/314632 to 9.** Fax 081/250669. 261 rms, including 28 seafront bungalows. A/C TV TEL. High season, Dr 19,350–Dr 20,450 ($82–$87) double, Dr 25,350–Dr 30,600 ($108–$130) bungalow; low season, Dr 9,600–Dr 10,250 ($41–$44) double, Dr 11,800–Dr 14,600 ($50–$62) bungalow. All rates are per person per day, buffet breakfast included. Reductions for extra person in room and for children; half-board (including breakfast and dinner) plan available for additional Dr 5,500 ($23). AE, DC, EU, JCB, MC, V. Public bus every half hour to Iráklion.

In recent years, the coast west of Iráklion has begun to emulate the coast to the east by building more and more hotels. Although the beach itself is not always as pleasant and you have to pass through a rather dreary edge of Iráklion to get there—this west coast has the advantage of being really close to town (yet farther from that airport). The grandest and newest of these west coast hotels is the luxury Candia Maris, and as the description above indicates, it offers just about everything. It's also one of the first hotels in Greece to be handicapped accessible. It's too bad that the exterior and layout is rather severe, because the rooms are especially cheerful. (If it looks like a brick factory owner's idea of a hotel, it's because the owner is just that.) Considering that you don't spend much time looking at the construction but are either inside it or on the beach or on the road, this shouldn't deter you from trying this first-class resort hotel.

Dining/Entertainment: Three restaurants and four bars cater to every type of appetite at any time of day. Light music is provided in the evening and special Cretan nights feature traditional music and dancing.

Services: Concierge, room service, dry cleaning and laundry, baby-sitting, airport transport arranged.

Facilities: 2 outdoor swimming pools, 1 indoor pool, children's pool, health club/gymnasium, sundeck, tennis, squash court, volleyball, bowling, full water sports center, bicycle rental, game room, children's program, full conference facilities (up to 700), car rental and tours arranged, hairdresser, boutiques.

Minoa Palace. Amnisos Beach (about 9 miles east of Iráklion), Iráklion 71110. ☎ **081/ 380404 to 6.** Fax 081/380422. 127 rms. A/C TV TEL. High season, Dr 33,000 ($140) double; low season, Dr 19,000 ($81) double. Rates include buffet breakfast. Half board (including breakfast and dinner) may be arranged for Dr 3,500 ($15) extra. AE, DC, EU, MC, V. Closed Nov–Apr. Public bus every half hour to Iráklion or points east.

This is Iráklion's answer to the grand resort hotels that first appeared close to Ághios Nikólaos and Réthymnon. On the one hand, the facilities, services, meals, and accommodations are what have come to be standard at these places—namely, deluxe. What makes the Minoa Palace special is its location: east of that airport yet only 9 miles from the center of Iráklion. The rooms are comfortable and with views of the sea, the beach is beautifully maintained, and there are as many activities (volleyball, water polo) as you care to engage in. With your own vehicle, you are only a couple of hours from any point of interest on the whole island. This is your chance to visit the Minoans while living in a palace with greater comfort than anything they knew.

Dining/Entertainment: The main restaurant offers a view of the sea to complement its reliance on seasonal and local foods. The taverna is down between the pool and the beach with more informal fare. Weekly "Cretan Night" with traditional music and dancing.

Services: Concierge, room service, dry cleaning and laundry, newspapers available, baby-sitting, airport transport arranged, children's activities.

Facilities: Large swimming pool and one for children, aerobics, sundeck, tennis court (lit at night), water sports equipment, bicycle rental, table tennis, billiards, video games, children's playground, conference rooms hosting 60, car rental and tours arranged, hairdresser, gift shop, minimart.

Xenia-Helios. Kokkini Hani (about 8 miles east of Iráklion), Iráklion 71500. ☎ **081/761502.** Fax 081/418363. 108 rms. A/C TEL. High season, Dr 23,000 ($98) double; low season, Dr 17,250 ($74). Rates include half-board. EU. Closed Oct–Mar. Buses every half hour to Iráklion or points east.

We single this out from the many fine beach hotels both east and west of Iráklion because it's one of three such hotels run by the Greek Ministry of Tourism to train young people for careers in the hotel world. (One is outside Athens, the other outside Thessaloniki.) It offers many of the services and facilities of the luxury resorts—the front desk will arrange for everything from laundry to tours. There's a swimming pool as well as a beautiful beach, two tennis courts, a hairdresser, water sports equipment, a fine restaurant, and a conference room for up to 200. The physical accommodations may not be quite as glitzy as some of the other beach resorts, but they're certainly first class and the service is especially friendly. You can pamper yourself, be convenient to anyplace on the island, and help support the young Greeks in training for the future.

WHERE TO DINE

There is a school that holds that the best Cretan meals are to be had in bare rooms with unshaded lightbulbs and a chef who looks more like a butcher. The corollary to this: Avoid all Greek restaurants that have plastic-sealed pictures of their food on display. We can't pretend to have held strictly to these rules in the literal sense, but what we have done is try to identify restaurants that have something special about their menu, location, and atmosphere. One thing, though: Don't plan on eating a meal on either Fountain Square or Liberty Square unless you simply want to have the experience, because the food at the establishments operating there now is, to put it mildly, nothing special. Save these squares for a coffee or beer break.

A word on prices: In Iráklion (as indeed throughout much of Greece), the prices per item do not vary greatly from the cheapest to the most expensive. Virtually every restaurant has a cheap omelet or stuffed tomatoes or moussaka at the low end. What becomes expensive are a few special items—the finer steak cuts, lobster, and certain fishes. The cover charge, pricey appetizers, wine—these also make a restaurant more expensive.

EXPENSIVE

Kyriakos. Leoforos Dimokratias 45 (about ¹/₂ mile from center on road to Knossos), Iráklion 71202. ☎ **081/224649.** Reservations recommended for evening in high season. Main courses Dr 1,200–Dr 3,800 ($5.10–$16.20). AE, DC, EU, MC, V. Daily except Wed noon–4pm, 7pm–2am; has been known to close in mid-June to mid-July. GREEK.

In recent years, this restaurant has gained the reputation of offering the most style as well some of the finest cooking in Iráklion (although this may be in part due to its location close to the equally posh Galaxy Hotel). Certainly its dining area is more formal (although it must be pointed out that you are actually dining alongside one of the major thoroughfares of Iráklion) and the service more continental. In fact, the menu is essentially traditional Greek—from the *taramasalata* to the *stifado* (rabbit with onions), pork with celery or octopus with onions—but everything's done with special care and brio. Snails are a specialty, and if that doesn't tempt you, come back at Christmas for their turkey. The wine choices are appropriately fine (and expensive). A couple should expect to drop Dr 15,000 to Dr 20,000 ($64 to $85) for the full works here, but think what you'd pay at home for such a fine meal. Dress well. Frequent public bus service to the restaurant.

Louloukos. Odos Korai 5 (one street behind Daedalou), Iráklion 71202. ☎ **081/224435.** Reservations recommended for evenings in high season. Main courses Dr 1,500–Dr 3,500 ($6.40–$15); fixed-price lunch about Dr 2,400 ($10). AE, DC, V. Mon–Sat noon–1am, Sun 6:30pm–midnight. ITALIAN/GREEK.

Another restaurant that has gained a reputation, this is almost the opposite of the Kyriakos in that it's cramped into a tiny patio on a back street and features fanciful umbrellas over the tables. (In winter you dine indoors.) But the chairs are comfortable, the table settings lovely—at night you get cloth napkins. Their selection of *mezes* is varied (and expensive), their basic Greek salad is truly crisp. Meanwhile, the menu is creative Italian—lots of pasta dishes, such as a rigatoni with a broccoli and Roquefort-cream sauce that was delicious (if seldom tasted in Italy). Treat yourself to Iráklion's "in" place (and save by settling for the house wine). Dress up a bit for evening.

MODERATE

Giovanni. Odos Korai 12 (on street behind Daedalou), Iráklion 71202. ☎ **081/246338.** Main courses Dr 1,000–Dr 2,800 ($4.25–$12); fixed-price meals, Dr 2,100–Dr 3,150 ($9–$13.40). AE, EU, MC, V. Mon–Sat 12:30pm–2am, Sun 5pm–1:30am. GREEK.

A taverna with some pretensions to chic, it appeals to a slightly younger and more informal set than its neighbor, Louloukos (described above). It has only a few tables on the narrow street—others must sit inside. Service is casual. For some reason it, instead of Louloukos, has the Italian name while its fare is traditional Greek. House specialties include shrimp in tomato sauce with cheese, baked eggplant with tomato sauce, baked lamb, and *kokhoretsi* (a sort of oversize sausage made from the innards of lamb; much better than it may sound). It's all tasty and with the house wine you actually come out with a modest tab.

I Vardia. Old Harbor (on jetty that forms the right arm of harbor, opposite the Venetian arsenali) Iráklion 71202. ☎ **081/223731.** Main courses Dr 1,100–Dr 2,500 ($4.70–$10.65). No credit cards accepted. Mon–Sun 10am–2am. Closed Nov–Apr.

Here's a restaurant with no pretensions, but what it does offer is solid Cretan fare, especially fresh seafood, and a prime location down on the harbor and away from the tourist hustle. It is, in fact, a favorite with Iráklion's citizens, who come to sample its squid or octopus and the catch of the day, or meat dishes such as pork with wine sauce. One of its old Cretan specialties is *kritharokouloura*—a sort of Cretan toast (*paximadhia*) covered with oil and tomatoes and a touch of oregano. As so often, the house wine goes just fine with the meals. You won't score points with French gourmets but you'll have an enjoyable meal.

Pantheon. Odos Theodosaki 2 ("Dirty Alley," connecting Market Street and Evans Street). ☎ **081/241652.** Main courses Dr 1,200–Dr 3,000 ($5.10–$12.75). No credit cards. Daily 11am–11pm, closed Sunday.

Anyone who spends more than a few days in Iráklion should take at least one meal in "Dirty Alley." (Stories vary as to the origin of this name, but you need not fear that it refers to the food or dishware.) The menus (all much the same at the half-dozen little "Dirty Alley" locales) offer the relatively few taverna standards—stews of various meats, chunks of meat or chicken or fish in tasty sauces, vegetables such as okra or zucchini or stuffed tomatoes—and for that reason there's not much on the cheap end (the omelets and spaghetti that other restaurants offer). These places are not especially cheap—you pay for atmosphere—but it's all tasty and if you sit in the Pantheon, on the corner of Market Street, you get a choice view of the passing scene.

INEXPENSIVE

Ionia. Odos Evans 3 (just to the left of the market street), Iráklion 71202. ☎ **081/283213.** Main courses Dr 800–Dr 2,200 ($3.40–$9.35). EU, JCB, MC, V. Mon–Fri 8am–10:30pm, Sat 8am–4pm, closed Sunday.

This is the Nestor of Iráklion's restaurants. Founded in 1923, it has served generations of Cretans as well as all the early archaeologists and visitors. In the late 1980s, it had to cut back on its once generous space and it now occupies only a triangle, but the food is as good as ever—lots of tasty stews and gravy dishes. It's one of the traditional places that encourages foreigners to step into the kitchen area and select from the warming pans. (It's also one of the last restaurants where the waiters must pass every bit of food by the manager-cashier, who checks the portions and adds up what the waiter owes the house.) You may get more refined food and fancy service elsewhere on Crete—the waiters seem to have trained in the New York delicatessen school—but you won't get heartier dishes than the Ionia's green beans or lamb joints in sauce. We recommend a visit to what is clearly a fading tradition.

Ippocampus. Odos Mitsotaki 3 (off to left of traffic circle as you come down 25th Avgusto), Iráklion 71202. ☎ **081/282081.** Main courses Dr 800–2,000 ($3.40–$8.50). No credit cards. Mon–Fri 1–3:30pm, 7pm–midnight, closed Sat–Sun.

This is something of an institution among native Iraklians—they line up on hot summer evenings for the privilege of sitting at one of the small tables on a sidewalk that doesn't even command the best view of the harbor. What they come for is a typical Cretan village meal, the kind made up of a lot of little dishes—essentially a meal of appetizers. The zucchini slices, dipped in batter and deep-fried, are fabulous. A plate of tomatoes and cukes, another of sliced fried potatoes, some small fish, perhaps the fried squid—that's enough. The main course prices are deceptive—most people get out of the whole meal, house wine, and all, for about $10—because they assemble a meal from a variety of cheap plates. But go early.

SHOPPING

Barko (The Barque). Odos Korai 7, Iráklion 71202. ☎ **081/246335.**

This curious little shop has something you won't see elsewhere: original paintings of traditional Greek/Mediterranean ships and models of the same—the former by the wife, Mali Xaniotaki, the latter by the husband, Socrates. The shop also has a small selection of equally original ceramics, jewelry, and small prints and paintings. Mali herself is usually on hand to explain each work in what is obviously a personal collection of talented artists and crafts workers. It's located on the street behind Daedalou, where we also recommend a couple of restaurants. Open Monday to Sunday from 9:30am to 2pm, 6 to 9pm.

Dedalou Galerie. Odos Daedalou 11 (between Fountain Square and Platia Eleftheria), Iráklion 71202. ☎ **081/246353.**

Costas Papadopoulos, the proprietor, has been offering his tasteful selection of traditional Cretan-Greek arts and crafts for several decades now—icons, coins, jewelry, porcelain, silverware, pistols, and more. Some of it is truly old, and he'll tell you when it isn't. It's not cheap, but this is a shop that might hold its own in a large cosmopolitan city. Open Monday to Sunday from 9am to 2pm, 6 to 8pm (with some irregularities in winter).

Eva and Helmut Grimm Handicrafts of Crete. Odos 25th Avgusto 96 (opposite the Venetian Loggia), Iráklion 71202. ☎ **081/282547.**

Founded by a Cretan-German couple—and now maintained by their son, Heinrich—this store boasts one of the finest selections of antique and old Cretan textiles (rugs, spreads, coverlets, etc.) along with some unusual pieces of jewelry and other objects, most made from silver and gold. And when the items are not old, you'll be so informed. The finest objects are not cheap, but you get what you pay for here, and the textiles are stunning. Open Monday to Sunday from 9am to 3pm, 5 to 9pm, but closed Sundays in winter.

Eleni Kastrinoyanni-Cretan Folk Art. Odos Ikarou 3 (opposite the Archaeological Museum), Iráklion 71202. ☎ **081/226186.**

Long the premier store in Iráklion for the some of the finest in embroidery, weavings, ceramics, and jewelry that reflect traditional Cretan folk methods and motifs. We put it that way to make it clear that these are not old pieces—indeed, the embroidery and weavings are done expressly for this store by workers under contract to the proprietor. The point is that these are fine pieces made by skilled craftspeople—the store almost feels like a museum. Get out your credit card and go for something you'll enjoy for years to come. Open Monday to Saturday from 8:30am to 8:30pm, and on Sunday from 10am to 6pm; closed October through February.

Voltone. Odos Idomeneou 25 (street off Liberty Square by Astoria Hotel), Iráklion 71202. ☎ **081/226443.**

In a city flooded with imitation old ceramics and, frankly, a lot of tasteless original work, here's a little shop that sells some handsome ceramics in the modern vein. Most are by Cretan potters, some are from the mainland. What makes them distinctively Cretan are their earthy colors and archaic shapes. There's also a selection of original jewelry, but what also distinguishes this shop is its collection of gemstones and fossils. The unifying sensibility behind all these works is that of the proprietor, a geologist by training. Open Monday to Sunday from 9am to 9pm.

IRÁKLION AFTER DARK
THE *VOLTA* & CAFES

One way to spend the evening is to do what most Iraklians themselves do: strolling about (the famous Mediterranean *volta*), then sitting in a cafe and watching others stroll by. The prime locations for the latter have been Platia Eleftheria (Liberty Square) or Fountain Square, but it must be said that the packed-in atmosphere of these places—and the overly aggressive solicitation of your presence by some waiters—has considerably reduced their charm.

On the square beside Aghios Titos, the church midway up 25th Avgusto, is **O Yero Platanos,** a cafe-restaurant (taking its name from the 300-year-old plane tree that shelters it). This is the perfect place to enjoy a coffee or ice cream while watching the local kids play as their elders come and go in the church.

Or perhaps even more entrancing, go down to the old harbor and the **Marina Cafe** (directly across from the restored Venetian arsenals). With as little as Dr 350 ($1.50) for a coffee or as much as Dr 1,200 ($5.10) for an alcoholic drink, you can enjoy the breeze as you contemplate the illuminated Venetian fort looking much like a stage set.

There are quiet cafes in virtually every little square or clearing. Here's another alternative: the **Four Lions Roof-Garden Cafe** (☎ 081/222333), entered by an interior staircase in the shopping arcade on Fountain Square. It tends to be frequented by a younger set of Iraklians, but it's not a rowdy or noisy place and foreigners are made to feel welcome. The background music is usually Greek. You get to sit above the crowded crossroads, and with no cover or minimum, enjoy anything from a coffee (Dr 300; $1.30) or fresh juice (Dr 600 to Dr 800; $2.60 to $3.40) or ice cream (Dr 900 to Dr 1,100; $3.85 to $4.70) or an alcoholic drink (Dr 600 to Dr 1,200; $2.60 to $5.20).

DISCOS

There are no end of bars and discos featuring Greek popular music and/or international rock 'n' roll—their names, at least, change from year to year to reflect the latest fads in music and slang. **Disco Athina** (Odos Ikarou 9, just outside the wall on the way to the airport; ☎ 081/245035) is an old favorite; the **Cotton Club,** just down the same road, is another one. For just plain modern Greek popular music, the **Doré Club** (☎ 081/229970) on Liberty Square is a popular music-bar/restaurant.

TRADITIONAL CRETAN MUSIC & DANCING

For those seeking traditional Cretan music and dancing—and by the way, almost every Class A hotel now has a **Cretan night,** when performers come to the hotel—there are a couple of clubs where you can hear the traditional music: the **Aposperides** (out on the road toward Knossos) and **Sordina** (about 5 kilometers to the southwest of town) are well regarded; you'd take a taxi to either.

OUTDOOR FILMS

Another delight during the long summers is to attend an outdoor movie. There are now three such theaters in Iráklion—the **Romantika,** the **Pallas,** the **Galaxy**—and a fourth in nearby Halikarnassos, the **Studio.** The current films are posted at several bulletin boards around the center of town. The movies start only as darkness settles. (And as throughout Greece, most foreign films are shown in their original language, with Greek subtitles.)

The Iráklion Arts Festival

For many years now, Iráklion has hosted an **arts festival** that, although hardly competitive with the major arts festivals of Europe, certainly provides some interesting possibilities for those spending even a few nights in town. The schedule usually begins in late June and ends up about mid-September. Some of the groups and individuals have world-class reputations—ballet troupes, pianists, and such. Mostly, though, the performers come from the Greek realm and do ancient and medieval-renaissance dramas, dances based on Greek themes, and Greek music both traditional and modern. Most performances take place outdoors in one of three venues: on the roof of the *Koules* (the Venetian fort in the harbor), the **Kazantzakis Garden Theater**, or the **Hadzidaksis Theater**. Ticket prices vary so from year to year and for individual events that it's meaningless to list them here, but they are well below what you'd pay at such cultural events elsewhere. Maybe you didn't come to Crete expecting to hear Vivaldi, but why not enjoy it while here.

SIDE TRIPS FROM IRÁKLION

Travel agencies have excursions setting out from Iráklion practically every day during the high season to virtually every point of interest on Crete—from the **Samaria Gorge** in the far southwest to the Minoan palace at **Kato Zakros** in the far southeast. In that sense, Iráklion can be used as the home base for all your touring on Crete. One destination or excursion above all should be made from Iráklion if you have only one extra day on Crete, and that's to **Gortyna** (see below).

Day Trips by Ship to the "Lost Atlantis" Island

Those seeking some changes from the usual sightseeing are now offered a variety of activities. For one, there are now as many as three different ships (during the tourist season only) offering day-long excursions to **Santoríni**, the "Lost Atlantis" island about 65 miles due north of Crete. You board early in the morning (about 7am), spend the hours between about 11:30am and 5pm taking in what you want on Santoríni, and then are served dinner on board ship so as to arrive in Iráklion between 9 and 10pm. (These same ships offer the same excursion from Ághios Nikólaos or Réthymnon on various days.) The cost has been about Dr 16,000 ($68), evening meal included. Any number of travel agents in Iráklion (or the other cities) can sell you a ticket.

The Islet of Dia

For those not up to quite such an ambitious voyage, there is the shorter day excursion to **Dia,** the islet visible just 7 miles off the shore east of Iráklion. Since the 1950s this has been used as a preserve for the wild goats of Crete that seemed threatened with extinction. Now that the goats are well established, the authorities have allowed some touristic development there, and boats take people over for a day of swimming, hiking, and observing the once elusive wild goats, and eating at one of the tavernas. The cost (only for boat fare) has been Dr 3,000 ($13) for a trip lasting from about 9:30am to 5:30pm. Tickets are sold by most travel agents.

Gortyna, Phaestos, Aghia Triadha, Kommos & Matala

If you have an interest in history and archaeology, this is probably the trip to make if you have only one other day after visiting Knossos and Iráklion's museum. The distance isn't that great (a round trip of some 100 miles/165km) but it would be a full day to take it all in: If you don't have your own car, a taxi or guided tour is advisable because bus schedules won't allow you to fit in all the stops. (You can, of course, stay at one of the hotels down at the south coast, but they're largely booked up in high season.)

The road south takes you right up and across the **mountainous spine** of central Crete, and at about the 25th mile you get the experience of leaving the **Sea of Crete** (to the north) behind and seeing the **Libyan Sea** to the south. You then descend onto the **Messara,** the largest plain on Crete (some 20 miles by 3 miles), long a major agricultural center. At about 28 miles (45km) you see on your right the **remains of Gortyna;** many more lie scattered in the fields off to the left. Gortyna (or Gortyn or Gortys) first emerged as a center of the Dorian Greeks who moved onto Crete after the end of the Minoan civilization. By 500 B.C., it was advanced enough to have a law code that they inscribed in stone (some 17,000 letters, in the ox-plow manner—that is, you read a line from left to right, then the next right to left, and so on). The inscribed stones were found in the late 19th century and reassembled here, where you can see this unique—and to scholars, invaluable—document testifying to the legal and social arrangements of this society.

Then, after the Romans took over Crete (after 67 B.C), Gortyna enjoyed yet another period of glory: It was the capital of Roman Crete and Cyrenaica (Libya) and as such was endowed with the full selection of Roman structures—temples, a stadium, and all. They are the ones to be seen in the fields to the left. On the right, along with the **Code of Gortyna,** you will see a small **Hellenistic odeon,** or theater, as well as the remains of the **Basilica of Aghios Titos**—dedicated to the Titus commissioned by Paul to head the first Christians on Crete; the church was begun in the 6th century but was later greatly enlarged.

Proceeding down the road another 10 miles (15km), you turn left at the sign and ascend to the ridge where the **palace of Phaestos** sits in all its splendor. Regarded by scholars as the second most powerful Minoan center, it is also regarded by many visitors as the most attractive because of its setting—on a prow of land that seems to float between the plain and the sky. Italians began to excavate Phaestos soon after Evans began at Knossos, but they made the decision to leave the remains pretty much as they found them. As at Knossos, you see the remains from several palace phases; and as at Knossos, excavations continue to this day. The **ceremonial staircase** is as awesome as it must have been to the ancients, the **great court** remains one of the most resonant public spaces anywhere. Again, to truly understand all the elements you should take a guided tour or at least have a fairly detailed guidebook, but anyone should be able to appreciate that the people who built this must have had a real sense of their place in nature.

Leaving Phaestos, you continue down the main road 2^1/$_2$ miles (4km) and turn left onto a side road where you park and make you way to at least pay your respects to another Minoan site, a minipalace complex known as **Aghia Triadha.** To this day, scholars cannot be certain exactly what it was—something between a satellite of Phaestos or a semi-independent palace. Several of the most impressive artifacts now in the Iráklion Museum were found here, including the painted sarcophagus (on the second floor). Aghia Triadha as a site may not grab the casual visitor, but it's worth a brief diversion.

Back on the road, follow the signs to **Kamilari** and then **Pitsidia.** In this village lies another brief diversion for archaeological buffs: the Minoan harbor town of **Kommos,** which Joseph Shaw and his wife Maria, from the University of Toronto, have been excavating since 1976. We recommend this side trip not only because of the increasingly more ambitious set of remains, from the Minoan through the Hellenistic periods, but because it reveals how almost a century after Evans's first dig, it's still possible to be discovering more from these remarkable people.

And now you have earned your **rest** and **swim,** and at no ordinary place: the nearby **beach at Matala.** It's a small cove enclosed by bluffs of age-old packed earth in which humans—possibly beginning under the Romans but most likely no earlier than A.D. 500—have dug **chambers,** some complete with bunk beds. Cretans long used them as summer homes, the German soldiers used them as storerooms during World War II, and hippies took them over in the late 1960s. Now they are off limits except for looking at during the day. Matala has become one more overcrowded beach during the peak season, so after a dip and a bit of refreshment, you'll be glad to depart and make your way back to Iráklion (going up via **Mires** and so bypassing the Phaestos-Kommos stretch).

2 Chaniá

Until the 1980s, Chaniá was one of the best-kept secrets of the Mediterranean: a delightful seaside town, nestling between mountains and sea, a labyrinth of atmospheric streets and structures from its Venetian-Turkish era, with just enough restaurants and diversions to make life interesting. Since then, tourists have flocked there to enjoy Chaniá's charms—and the locals have rushed to satisfy them. There's hardly a square inch of the Old Town, which fans back from the harbor, that's not dedicated to satisfying visitors—restaurants and cafes, pensions and hotels, gift shops of every variety. Chaniá was heavily bombed during World War II, and some its atmosphere is due to still unreconstructed buildings that are now used as shops and restaurants.

What's amazing, then, is how much of Chaniá's charm has persisted. The Venetians and Turks effectively stamped the old town in their own image between 1210 and 1898, and they were pushed out early in the 20th century. Then, as the western end of Crete did not produce the fabulous Minoan remains of central and eastern Crete, Chaniá was bypassed by the first great waves of tourism as a provincial town. (Yet, the last 20 years have seen the excavation of quite ambitious Minoan remains right at the apex of the old town.) Now the town has caught up with a vengeance. All we can say is try to visit it any time except July and August, but whenever you come, dare to strike out on your own and see the old Chaniá.

ESSENTIALS

GETTING THERE   By Plane   Olympic Airways offers at least three flights daily to Chaniá in high season. There's also one flight weekly to and from Thessaloniki. Occasional charter flights connect to European cities. The airport is located 10 miles (15km) out of town on the Akrotiri. Public buses meet all flights except for the last one at night, for which a taxi is required. Olympic Airways (Odos Tzanakaki 88, ☎ 0821/57701) provides bus service to the airport, departing 90 minutes before flights, to its clients; fee Dr 500 ($2.15).

By Ship   There is one ship sailing daily between Chaniá and Piraeus, usually leaving early in the evening. This ship departs from Souda, a 15-minute bus ride from the stop outside the Public Market. Many travel agents around town sell tickets. In high season, those with vehicles should make reservations well in advance.

By Bus   There are frequent buses from early in the morning until about 9 or 10pm (depending on the season) connecting Chaniá to Réthymnon and Iráklion. There are less frequent (and often inconvenient) buses between destinations in western Crete.

VISITOR INFORMATION   The **National Tourist Office (EOT)** is, at least temporarily, located in the new town (off 1866 Square) at Odos Kriari 40, on the ground floor. ☎ 0821/92624 or 0821/92943. Open Monday through Friday from 8am to

3pm. On the harbor, in the mosque, is the local merchants' own tourist information office, open April through October only, Monday through Saturday from 10am to 5pm.

A useful source of insider's information is **The Bazaar,** a shop that sells used foreign-language books, some household objects, and used clothing; owned and staffed by non-Greeks, it maintains a listing of all kinds of helpful services. It's somewhat hard to find, but is best approached from Odos Hadzimichali Daliani, off Odos Daskaloyiannis, where it is a right turn.

GETTING AROUND   Almost anyplace you will want to visit in Chaniá is best reached by foot. There are public buses to nearby points, but a taxi is probably your best buy. If you intend to go off into the countryside or more distant points in western Crete, a rented car is advisable to make the best use of your time.

FAST FACTS: Chaniá

Area Code   The area code for Chaniá is **0821.**

Banks/ATMS   Several of these are located just where the old town adjoins the new town.

Consulates   There's neither a U.S. or a British consul in Chaniá.

Etiquette   The harbor area and touristic enterprises everywhere tolerate beachwear, but it's frowned upon elsewhere in town.

Hospital   The city's hospital (☎ **0821/27231**) is on Odos Venizelou in the Halepa Quarter.

Luggage Storage/Lockers   The only organized place to store luggage is at the **KTEL Bus Station** on Odos Kidonias.

Newspapers and Magazines   A good selection of foreign periodicals can be found at the newsstand on the corner at the top of Odos Halidon.

Police   Call **0821/73333.**

Post Office   The main **post office** is on Tzanakaki Street (leading away from the Market). Open Monday through Friday from 8am to 8pm, Saturday 8am to noon. The yellow "branch office" in front of Cathedral on Odos Halidon deals only in stamps (and foreign exchange); it's open April through October, Monday through Saturday from 8am to 8pm; November through March, Monday through Saturday 8am to 2pm.

Restrooms   There are public toilets outside the Market and in 1866 Square.

Taxis   There are plenty around town but to get one accustomed to dealing with English speakers, call **Mikhali** (☎ **0821/46855**).

Telephone, Telex, and Fax   The national telephone office (OTE) is at **Odos Tzanakaki** (beside the post office). Open daily from 7:30am to 11:30pm.

Travel Agencies   There are many travel agencies around town. Two that we have found helpful are **Spa Tours** (☎ **0821/57444;** fax 0821/55283), Odos Mihelidaki 10 (side street off Dimokratias, the main street opposite Public Market leading to stadium); and **InterKreta,** Odos Kanevaro 9 (just off Santrivani Square at the harbor), ☎ **0821/52552.**

Transit Info   The main bus station (to points all over Crete) can be reached by calling **0821/93306** or 0821/93052.

WHAT TO SEE & DO

Archaeological Museum. Odos Halidon 20. ☎ **0821/90334.** Admission Dr 500 ($2.15). Mon 12:30–7pm, Tues–Fri 8am–7pm, Sat–Sun 8:30am–3pm.

This is perhaps the one cultural institution in Chaniá that even short-term visitors should exert themselves to see, if only for a brief walkthrough. For one thing, it's housed in the 16th-century Venetian Catholic Church of St. Francis (carefully restored in the early 1980s). For another, it gives a fascinating glimpse of the different cultures that have played out on Crete, from the Neolithic through the Minoan and on to the various periods of Greek civilization and then to the Romans and early Christians. You'll come away with a sense of how typical people of the time lived, as opposed to the palace elite.

A Walk Around Old Chaniá

As good a place as any to start is **Santrivani Square,** the large clearing at the far curve of the old harbor. (Its name is from the Turkish for "fountain," which once stood here.)

Before setting off around the harbor, you could make a brief side trip up Odos Kanevarou, to the right, to see the **ongoing excavations** of the Minoan city of Kydonia—nothing exciting, except the fact that on this site there's been continuous habitation for at least 4,000 years.

Back at Santrivani Square, you head along the east side for the prominent **Mosque of Djamissis** (or of Hassan Pasha), erected soon after the Turks conquered Chaniá in 1645. It's currently being restored but for exactly what function is not clear. (The **merchants' tourist information office** uses one side room.)

Proceeding around the **waterfront** toward the **new harbor,** you come to what remains of the great *arsenali,* where the Venetians made and repaired ships; exhibits are sometimes held inside. (If you have the time, go to the far end of this inner harbor and walk out along the breakwater to the lighthouse, which is from the 19th century.)

Turning inland at the near end of the arsenali onto Odos Daskaloyianni Arnoleon and proceeding up, you'll come, on the left, to the **1812 Square,** and the present **Orthodox Church of St. Nicholas.** Begun as a Venetian Catholic monastery, it was converted by the Turks into a mosque—thus its campanile and minaret! The square is a pleasant place to sit and have a cool drink. Proceeding along, you come to Odos Trouderon, where you turn right and (passing another minaret) come to the back steps of the great **Municipal Market** (1911)—definitely worth a walkthrough. If you will exit at the opposite end of where you entered, you come out on the edge of the **new town.** You proceed right along Hadzimichali Giannari till you come to the top of Odos Halidon, the **main tourist shopping street.** As you make your way down, you pass on the right the now famous **Odos Skridlof,** with its leather workers; then the **Orthodox Cathedral,** the Church of the Three Martyrs (from the 1860s); and then on the left the **Archaeological Museum** (described above).

As you come back to the edge of Santrivani Square, you turn left one street before the harbor onto **Zambeliou.** You hardly need a guidebook to point out the sights along this narrow old street, but when it comes to Odos Moskhou (opposite the Casa Delfino), you turn right onto it and pass through the **Renieri Gate** (1608). Continuing on you come out onto **Odos Theophanos,** where you take a right turn and, again taking in the sights of this Venetian-style street, you come out to the sea. You are now just outside the harbor, and you turn right and pass below the walls of the **Firkas;** this is the name given to the fort here, a focal point in Crete's struggle for independence at the turn of the century. Now it houses the **Naval Museum,** with exhibits on Crete's naval history. (☎ 0821/91875 or 0821/74484. Open daily from 10am to 4pm. Closed public holidays. Admission is Dr 400 [$1.70].) Whether or not you visit the museum, you can now sit at the **Cafe Meltemi,** on the slope just before the entrance to the museum, and join Chaniá's smart set in a much-deserved refreshment.

We have said nothing about the remains of the **Venetian walls** of Chaniá, because they really don't stack up to those of Iráklion, but there are fragments here and there. And for true history buffs, you could get a bus (or even walk) to the **Halepa Quarter** at the far east of town; there you will see some fabulous turn-of-the-century houses, as well as the home of the Cretan-Greek statesman, Eleftherios Venizelos (1864–1936). Some would claim Venizelos was the only truly world-class statesman of modern Greece, but in any case he led Crete into union with Greece and then led Greece through several tumultuous episodes. (If you are really interested in pursuing this man, his tomb and that of his sons are on the Akrotiri, a 4-mile (6km) drive from the center of town. It's most impressive in its setting and view.) Also in Halepa is the **Historical Museum,** with important displays of the Venetian and Turkish eras and Crete's struggle for independence and union (☎ 0821/92606; open Monday through Friday, 9am to 1pm; admission free).

WHERE TO STAY
EXPENSIVE

Hotel Creta. Paradise P.O. Box 89, Gerani, Crete (12 miles west of Chaniá on coast road). ☎ **0821/61315.** Fax 0821/61134. 148 doubles and triples, 38 bungalows, 4 suites, all with bath. A/C TEL. High season Dr 36,000–Dr 42,000 ($153–$179) double, Dr 42,000–Dr 47,000 ($179–$200) bungalow; low season Dr 23,000–Dr 35,000 ($98–$149) double, Dr 33,000–Dr 39,000 ($140–$166) bungalow. Rates include continental breakfast. Considerably lower rates for tour groups include half board (breakfast and dinner). AE, DC, EU, MC, V. Closed Oct–Mar. Ample parking. Taxi or bus to Chaniá.

This is the most luxurious and ambitious hotel-resort in the western half of the island and might prove an attractive alternative to staying in Chaniá for those expecting to spend most of their time either sunning on a beach or touring western Crete. Among its more unusual charms is a small petting zoo—in general, kids would have a fine time here. A unique delight are the turtles that come onto the hotel's beach to lay their eggs from May to June; these hatch in late August. The hotel boasts the largest and most technically advanced conference facilities in western Crete (for up to 550 delegates). Rooms are a bit severe for Americans accustomed to upholstered luxury (don't expect plush beds), but everything is tasteful, modern, and appropriate to the setting—lots of Grecian marble! Beautifully landscaped in the style of a Mediterranean villa, the resort lives up to its image. The clientele has been mostly European but the manager is American-trained and Americans will also be made to feel most welcome.

Dining/Entertainment: International cuisine (a bit bland but with some Greek touches) is served in the main dining room, but other meals can be taken at the poolside restaurant or the lobby cafeteria, with a children's menu. There is an in-house orchestra and weekly "theme nights" offer Greek music and dance troupe.

Services: Virtually anything can be provided on request, from TV or a minibar in your room to baby-sitting or a massage, from scuba diving lessons to the use of a computer. Secretarial and other business services can be provided. Vehicle rentals and tours can be arranged. Laundry and dry cleaning can be done. A doctor and a dentist are on call. There is an "animation team" that leads everything from aerobics to "theme" parties.

Facilities: A large swimming pool plus a children's pool; small health club gym and sauna; tennis and volleyball courts; water sports (with professional tuition available); children's video games and TV; hairdressing salon and boutiques.

Casa Delfino. Odos Theofanous 8, Chaniá, Crete. ☎ **0821/93098** or 0821/87400. Fax 0821/ 96500. 7 studios, 4 suites, 1 VIP suite, all with shower. A/C TV TEL. Dr 32,000–Dr 40,000 ($136–$170) double. Breakfast extra. AE, EU, MC, V. Open all year (with central heating). Free parking in nearby area.

A late 17th-century mansion (but named after a 19th-century Italian owner) was converted in the late 20th century into stylish independent suites. Each has a refrigerator and stove so that whatever you pay for the room could be saved on certain meals. Tastefully decorated rooms—most with bed on an upper level—are combined with the latest in bathrooms. Services of all kinds are provided, from meeting you at the airport to arranging for tours. Refreshments and drinks can be enjoyed in the courtyard. You're only a block or so behind the harbor but you are far removed from the harbor's bustle and noise. This is an ideal way to combine a convenient location and comfortable amenities with old-world charm in a 17th-century neighborhood. Incidentally, the adjacent Hotel Contessa or Hotel Porto del Colombo can provide much the same facilities should you arrive without reservations to find the Casa Delfino booked up.

Doma. Odos Venizelou 124, Chaniá, Crete. ☎ **0821/51-772** or 0821/51-773. Fax 0821/ 41-578. 22 rms. (shower only), 3 suites, all with bath. TEL. Dr 18,400–Dr 25,300 ($78–$108) double; Dr 34,500–Dr 51,750 ($147–$220) suite (with A/C and TV). Rates include continental breakfast. Reduced rates for longer stays and/or more than two in suite. EU, MC, V. Closed Nov– Mar. Free parking on nearby streets. Bus to Halepa or Chaniá center; can be reached by taxi, car, or foot; 2 miles from town center along coastal road to airport.

There are some hotels that are singled out in every guide and for a reason: They're truly wonderful. The Doma is one such hotel. It was among the first in Greece, if not the first, converted from a fine old building into a fine hotel—in this case, a neoclassical mansion from the turn-of-the-century that was once, among other things, the British consulate. The owner-manager, Mrs. Irene ("Rena") Valyraki, sees to every detail—from the authentic Cretan heirlooms that decorate the public spaces to the freshly squeezed orange juice served at breakfast. The atmosphere is quietly elegant, the amenities are there for the asking (including laundry on the premises, an elevator for those who can't take stairs). The new ground-floor bar offers a civilized ambience. Among the Doma's many pleasures is the third-story dining room, with fresh breezes and a superb view of old Chaniá; breakfast here includes several homemade delights, while evening dinner includes Cretan specialties. Front rooms have the great view of the sea and some sound of passing traffic, but the hotel is far from the noise of the center of town. The Doma proves that the provincial can be world class.

MODERATE

Hotel Porto Veneziano. Enetikos Limin, Chaniá 73122. ☎ **0821/5931,** 0821/5932, or 0821/5933. Fax 0821/44503. 57 rms with showers, 6 suites with baths. A/C TEL. High season Dr 24,200 ($103) double, Dr 39,000 ($166) suite; low season Dr 21,300 ($91) double, Dr 34,000 ($145) suite. Rates include buffet breakfast. AE, DC, EU, MC, V. Free parking nearby. Walking distance to everything.

This solid hotel is located at the far end of the so-called Old Harbor (follow the walkway from the main harbor all the way around to the east, or right) and gives the maximum of closeness (to the center of activities) with the minimum of noise (from the activities of the center). It has been thoroughly renovated in the early 1990s, and its rooms and public areas are tastefully done. (The suites have TVs.) Meals are served only to organized groups, but refreshments from the hotel's own Cafe Veneto may be enjoyed in the garden. The desk personnel are genuinely helpful and will make any arrangements from car rentals to laundry. All in all, an excellent choice for those who would appreciate being down on an old harbor.

Louis Maleme Beach Hotel. P.O. Box 9, Chaniá (14 miles west of Chaniá on coast road). ☎ **0821/62221** or 0821/62226. Fax 0821/62406. 96 doubles, 114 bungalows, all with bath. A/C TEL. High season Dr 40,250 ($171) double, Dr 29,900 ($127) bungalow; low season Dr 31,050 ($132) double, Dr 21,850 ($93) bungalow. Rates include breakfast and dinner. Children under 2 free, aged 2–12 half price. AE, DC, EU, JCB, MC, V. Closed Oct–Mar. Ample parking. Taxis and frequent buses to Chaniá.

The closest to the Creta Paradise—in both the facilities and distance, as it happens—is the Louis Maleme (and now under the same management). Practically the same as the Creta Paradise in terms of the physical environment and services, the Louis Maleme tends to be more family oriented and even a bit like a Club Mediterrané. That means it has an "animation team" of young people who lead an endless round of activities and diversions from water polo to instantaneous games (all voluntary, of course). There are lots of activities for children, from video games to organized water sports. The turtles (described under Creta Paradise, above) also come to this beach, which has been awarded a Blue Flag of the European Community for its fine condition. As at Creta Paradise, its rooms are not plush but are comfortable and modern—a stripped-down holiday mode. Likewise, its main clientele has so far been European, but it would welcome Americans who appreciate its lovely landscaping and lively activities.

Dining/Entertainment: Its main restaurant serves buffet breakfast and dinner; the dinner menu is the now standard International with some Greek specialties. Beach taverna. Bars in the lounge and at the pool. Disco club. Weekly "Greek night" with music and dancing, and other special entertainments.

Services: The desk clerks can arrange for services from laundry and dry cleaning to baby-sitting and secretarial assistance. Car rentals and tours can be arranged.

Facilities: Large pool and a small children's pool; tennis, basketball, and volleyball courts; a minigolf course; table tennis; water sports include waterskiing, windsurfing, water-parachuting, canoeing; 400-person conference room.

Halepa Hotel. 164 Eleftherios Venizelou St. (on the street in Halepa just past the right turn to the airport) Chaniá. ☎ **0821/53544** or 0821/53546. Fax 0821/43335. 46 singles, doubles, triples, all with bath (some with tub only, some with shower only) 3 suites with bath. A/C TEL. High season Dr 15,900 ($68) double; Dr 20,800–Dr 28,800 ($89–$123) suite; low season Dr 13,400 ($58) double; Dr 17,300–Dr 28,800 ($73–$123) suite. Breakfast Dr 1,500 ($6.40). Open year-round with central heating. MC, V. Parking nearby. Frequent public buses to Chaniá or 15-minute walk along coast.

Like the better-known Doma, this is in a converted 19th-century neoclassical mansion—in this case, one with a dramatically curved exterior staircase. Some of its neighboring buildings are famous in Cretan history. The quiet of the neighborhood is further enhanced by the hotel's being set well back and buffered by its front garden—with its distinctive palm trees—where drinks and light refreshments can be enjoyed. (Meals are available only for groups.) There is a full bar; a sunroof offers a spectacular view of Chaniá and the bay; and there is a room set up to host small (12 to 20) conferences. Mary and Anthony Spanoudakis, the proprietors (she grew up in America), have created a restful oasis, with classical music often wafting through the air (each room also has a radio and most rooms have TV). They can take care of your every need, from laundry to car rentals. We would place one condition on staying here: Demand a room in the main, or traditional, mansion; otherwise you must settle for a room (albeit quiet and comfortable) in the rather nondescript new wing.

Hotel Pallazo. 54 Theotokopoulou St. (around the corner of far left/west arm of harbor), Chaniá, Crete. ☎ **0821/93227.** Fax 0821/93229. 8 doubles, 3 triples, all with only shower. A/C TEL. High season Dr 13,800 ($59) double; low season Dr 11,500 ($49) double. Rates include breakfast. EU, MC, V. Closed Nov–Mar but would open for special groups. Ample parking 100 yards away. Within easy walking distance to all of Chaniá.

This is a Venetian town house that once knew grander days, fell into disrepair, and has now been converted into a handsome little hotel. The use of wood, from the staircase to the furniture, and other decorative details give the feel of Old Crete, but certain amenities make it a first-class hotel—a small refrigerator in every room, TV in the bar, a roof garden with a spectacular view of the mountains and sea. Rooms are good sized; those on the front have balconies. It's generally quiet, and if occasionally the night air is broken by rowdy youths (true of all Greek cities), that seems a small price to pay for staying on Theotocopoulou Street—the closest some will come to living on a Venetian canal. The manager, Yiannis Papadakis, can provide laundry services, car rentals, and tours.

WHERE TO DINE

Chaniá has quite an amazing selection of restaurants and eateries of all kinds. Although most are around the harbor, you can find tasty meals in various locales.

EXPENSIVE

O Anem. Akti Tombazi, Chaniá. ☎ and fax **0821/58330.** Reservations for large parties. Main courses Dr 1,300–Dr 3,900 ($5.54–$16.60). Seafood platters for two, Dr 6,800 ($29). MC, V. Daily 10am–12pm. Closed Dec–Jan. At the corner where the new and old harbors meet. GREEK.

Competing with the Nykterida for title of the finest restaurant in Chaniá, this is in fact owned and run by the same couple, Babis and Mette Mastoridis, who opened it in 1994. Cloth napkins, a pitcher of ice water, quality table settings, more attentive service than at your typical Greek restaurant—these are the things that signal its intentions. The food lives up to this (and emerges from an amazingly small but state-of-the-art kitchen). Try one of its specialties—chicken santos (boned breast of chicken stuffed with spinach, cheese, and bacon); or if you're adventurous, stuffed goat. Its special seafood platter (lobster, shrimp, squid, a fillet of whatever's in season) plus various side dishes including taramasalata) at Dr 3,400 ($14.50) is a bargain anyplace else in the world. (Purists might ask them to "hold" the sauces.) Having a meal here— the epitome of Mediterranean dining—is a treat, especially as you sit overlooking the harbor yet removed from its hustle and bustle.

Nykterida. Korakies, Crete (right turn off road to airport directly opposite NAMFI Officers Club, on road signed "Korakies"). ☎ **0821/64215.** Reservations recommended for parties over 6. Main courses Dr 1,200–Dr 2,480 ($5.10–$10.55). MC, V. Mon–Fri 8pm–midnight. Open all year. Parking on site. Taxi required if you don't have a car. GREEK.

Many would nominate this as the finest restaurant in all Crete. Certainly none can beat its setting, high on a point providing nighttime views of Chaniá or Soudha Bay that must rank with the most spectacular in the world. Established in 1938, it's now run by the founder's son, Babis Mastoridis, and his Danish wife, Mette, and there is a low-keyed elegance that makes you feel you are in a world-class restaurant. Diners are expected to dress up a bit. The cuisine is traditional Cretan-Greek, but many of the dishes have an extra something. For an appetizer, try the *kalazounia* (cheese pies with specks of spinach) or the dolmades made with squash blossoms stuffed with a spiced rice (served with a dollop of yogurt) or the crepes stuffed with chicken and mushrooms, almost a meal in itself. Anything from the main course is going to be well done, from the basic steak fillet or generous portion of lamb chops to the chicken with okra (but you have to like okra). Service is a bit casual, but it's hospitable. Complimentary *tsoukoudia* (a very strong traditional Cretan liqueur) is served at the end of the meal. On Monday, Thursday, and Friday evenings through the high season (to end of October), traditional Cretan music is performed. Surprisingly, the tab for an unforgettable dining experience at "The Bat" (its name in Greek) is only a few dollars above that at more pedestrian locales (perhaps because they use the same silly paper napkins).

MODERATE

Alana. 19 Zambeliou St. (one street back from harbor, between Halidon and Kondilaki) Chaniá. ☎ **0821/95774** or 0821/56176. Main courses Dr 1,200–Dr 2,800 ($5.10–$11.90); combination plates Dr 3,000–Dr 3,500 ($12.80–$14.90). AE, MC, V. Daily high season 6pm–1am; off season daily noon–4pm, 6pm–1am. Closed early Nov to late Mar. GREEK.

Yet another conversion of an old structure for modern usage, but this one can claim priority, in both its age and its inspiration. The building was erected about 1290 by Venetians; originally a soap factory and oil warehouse as well as the residence of the owner, it served many functions over the years, then fell into disrepair until the present proprietor, Yiannis Nannadakis, restored it. He was the first on Crete to convert such an old structure into a restaurant when he opened his first nearby in 1976. The menu is the traditional one and almost anything will be tasty: as an appetizer, try *kalokithikephthedes* (zucchini meatballs); their onion soup is a meal in itself. The moussaka is just fine. Heartier specialties include the *stifado* (beef with onion) or pork in wine sauce. But there's no denying that the interior space contributes to your dining experience, while live music adds to it every evening except Sunday.

Amphora Restaurant. 49 Akti Koundouriotou, Chaniá, Crete. ☎ **0821/73131.** Fax 0821/93224. Reservations accepted. Main courses Dr 1,150–Dr 3,500 ($4.90–$14.90). Fixed-price meals Dr 2,200–Dr 6,500 ($9.40–$28). Combination plates Dr 1,800–Dr 5,000 ($7.70–$21.30). EU, MC, V. Daily 11:30am–midnight. Closed Oct–Apr. GREEK.

Of the seemingly endless circle of restaurants on the harbor, this emerges as a favorite when it comes to balancing price with quality, choice with taste. As with any Greek restaurant, if you order the lobster or chateaubriand, you'll pay a hefty price. But if you're looking for a bargain menu, you can assemble a delicious meal here at modest prices. For an appetizer, try the aubergine croquettes, or the *spetsofai* (little sausages with a tomato sauce and peppers). The speciality of the house is also a best buy—a fish soup, a chunk of fresh fish in a lemony liquid, with potatoes and onions filling it out. Sometimes they offer rabbit, sometimes chicken with rice; always they have a lamb in wine sauce. This restaurant belongs to the Amphora Hotel, a Category A, and although its tables and location suggest a basic harbor taverna, its food and friendly service make it first class. Near the far right western curve of the harbor.

Kavouria. 4 Akti Tobazi, Chaniá, Crete. ☎ **0821/23558.** Fax 0821/71675. Reservations recommended for parties over 6. Main courses Dr 1,100–Dr 4,000 ($4.70–$17). AE, DC, EU, MC, V. Daily 11am–midnight. Closed some days off-season. On harbor, so park elsewhere and walk. GREEK.

This is one of the oldest, now more traditional restaurants on the harbor. It's an unpretentious place where stiff wooden chairs and no-nonsense waiters (and alas, tiny paper napkins) let you know you're actually on Crete and not in some International-Restaurant Land. Service is prompt and courteous, and the waiters will be as chummy as you invite them to be. Best of all, it's located at the far edge of the now-claustrophobic wall-to-wall carpet of restaurants, so you can have some sense of space while enjoying a view of the entire harbor. The menu includes all the standard Greek items; seafood and steak fillets are its specialties. The tzatziki is pungent, the Greek salad hearty. (Assemble your own meal, avoiding, if possible, combinations that include veggies and potatoes.) Wines are also standards—try the Peza Minoa Palace (red) or Boutari (white). Its main concession to the new wave of tourism is that it now serves coffee, desserts, and ice cream. Far right corner of the new harbor.

The Well of the Turk. 1-3 Kalinikou Sarpaki, Chaniá, Crete. ☎ **0821/54547.** Reservations recommended for parties over 6. Main courses Dr 1,100–Dr 1,800 ($4.70–$7.65). No credit cards. Daily 6pm–midnight. MIDDLE EASTERN.

If it seems strange to be eating Middle Eastern food on Crete, remember that the Turks possessed Chaniá for some 250 years. This restaurant is located in the heart of the old Turkish quarter, known as Splanzia. Tucked into maze of back streets, it's best reached from Daskaloyianni Street, which in turn is reached from the harbor by turning up alongside the old Venetian shipbays onto Archoleon Street. The establishment is in a historic old building with an interior well; its marble fountain depicts scenes from Istanbul. Diners usually sit outside in a quiet street-court. It's entirely the creation of Jenny Perschke Payalas, who brings to the cuisine an imagination that makes it more than standard Middle Eastern. From several interesting appetizers you might try the plate with a mixture of delicious salads. In addition to tasty kebabs, there are such specialties as meatballs with eggplant mixed in, and the *laxma bi azeen,* a pita-style bread with a spicy topping. Middle Eastern musicians sometimes play here, and you can settle for a quiet drink at the bar.

Elisabeth Restaurant. Akti Eneseos (at farthest corner of Old Harbor), Chaniá. ☎ **0821/ 45236.** Main courses Dr 800–Dr 1,800 ($3.40–$7.70) (much depends on cost and size of seafood order). Daily 11am–midnight. Closed late Nov to Mar. GREEK TAVERNA.

This would be an even cheaper restaurant if it weren't for the seafood, which is what draws most people. Starting with an unusual appetizer such as sea urchins roe in oil through a fish soup to whatever is in season, you'll be eating fresh produce of the sea. (Warning about the famous fish soup, which is really a Cretan version of the more famous French bouillabaisse: It can be very boney, because all kinds of fish go into the pot along with potatoes.) Trust the owner-cook Elisabeth to direct you to whatever is best that day.

INEXPENSIVE

Apostolis II. Akti Enosis 6, Chaniá, Crete. ☎ **0821/41767.** Reservations recommended for large parties. Main courses Dr 700–Dr 3,000 ($3–$12.80) AE, EU, MC, V. Daily 10am–midnight. Open all year. Parking a block behind harbor if you approach from behind; otherwise walk from harbor. GREEK.

If you're looking for a typical harbor taverna with decent traditional food, you might want to try Apostolis II, located at the far end of the old harbor. (For that matter, his Apostolis I, a little closer to the new harbor, is not that much different in its menu or prices—perhaps just a tad fancier.) Like most such Greek locales, Apostolis a family run place, and despite the hordes of foreign tourists, it still has the spontaneous feel of a waterfront taverna—the type of place where the villager selling mountain herbs for tea is invited to sit down and take a meal with strangers. All the standards are tasty; try their stiffado (lamb and onions in a rich sauce). Accompany the appetizers or dessert with the house wine—it's almost like a Madeira or a port.

O Mathios. 3 Akti Enoseos, Chaniá. ☎ **0821/54291.** Main courses Dr 800–Dr 2,500 ($3.40–$10.65). No credit cards. Daily 11am–2:30am. About midway around the old harbor. GREEK.

This is a traditional harborside taverna, a place where you enjoy a decent meal watching the boats bobbing at the quay and the cats stalking beneath the tables. In general, it has not been patronized by that many foreigners, but this is no reflection on its table settings (colorful red tablecloths), service (prompt no-nonsense), or food (as good as any in its class). Try the basic tzatziki and Greek salad, moussaka, or stuffed tomatoes—you can't go wrong. Fish dishes are their specialty (and as elsewhere can cost considerably more). It's worth a try if you want to have a quiet night in Old Chaniá.

SHOPPING

You hardly need a guidebook to locate the jewelers and leather goods shops and tourist souvenir stores of Chaniá—they're everywhere. But truth to tell, it's hard to find that very special item that's both tasteful and distinctively Cretan. Go ahead and buy your souvenirs as you enjoy them, but be wary of overpriced jewelry that is in fact no different from what can be found in cities throughout the world. Also be circumspect of all claims made for the age of objects. There's something for all tastes in Chaniá, but we try to confine our recommendations to some shops that sell authentic Cretan objects—or at least items you will not find anyplace else.

Anatolia. 5 Odos Halidon. ☎ **0821/41-218.** AE, EU, JCB, MC, V. Open Mon–Sat 10am–9pm.

This gets a listing as an exception to the rule of recommending distinctively Cretan things, because it's a collection of jewelry that the proprietors, Juliette and Patrick Fabre, have assembled from around the world—principally from the Middle East, Asia, and Africa. Why then list it? Because it's such a fabulous selection. Some of it is of museum quality and all of it is displayed in museum fashion. It's not cheap, but it might be the cheapest way for most of us to acquire such exotic objects. At least give a look—and then indulge yourself just once. Years later you will probably be glad you did. Located at the bottom of Halidon Street, just above Santrivani Square on the harbor.

Carmela. 7 Odos Anghelou, Chaniá. ☎ **0821/90-487.** AE, EU, MC, V. Open daily 11am–3pm, 6–11pm.

In this rather small shop you will find some of the finest ceramics, jewelry, and original art works in all of Crete. The proprietors, ceramist Carmela Iatropoulou and her husband, the painter Dimitris Katziyiannis, display and sell their own works along with those of some 30 other Greek artists and craftspeople. What unites them beneath their diversity is a mastery of the various techniques combined with a modernist aesthetic. Many of the items of ceramics and jewelry have been inspired by ancient works of art—Minoan, classical Greek, Byzantine, even Asian—but while employing some of the old techniques these creators have produced original works. There is a range of prices from simple but elegant earrings to museum-quality ceramics. On narrow street above entrance to Naval Museum, just up from the rug store.

Cretan Rugs and Blankets. 5 Odos Anghelou, Chaniá. ☎ **0821/98-571.** AE, EU, MC, V. Daily 9am–2pm, 5–9pm. On the narrow street across from the entrance of the Naval Museum at the far left, west arm of the harbor.

To step into this shop is to enter a realm probably not to be experienced anywhere else on Crete—an old Venetian structure filled with gorgeously colored rugs and blankets and kilims (these latter referring to a special weave that makes for what most of us regard as a light rug or wall hanging). The owner, Kostas Liapakis, says that much of his stock is at least several decades old—that their bright, unused appearance is due to their having been saved by families as dowry gifts. All we can say is buy what you like and can afford. And there is so much to like! Prices range from Dr 30,000 to Dr 400,000 ($128 to $1,700), with his prize piece at Dr 650,000 ($2,766)—actually not that much if you know prices of old weavings elsewhere. On the narrow street across from the entrance of the Naval Museum, at the far left, west arm of the harbor.

Khalki. 75 Zambeliou St., Chaniá. ☎ **0821/75379.** EU, MC, V. Open daily 10am–10:30pm.

Being one of so many little shops that sell ceramics along with other trinkets and souvenirs, this one could easily be overlooked, but seek it out. It carries the work of several local and Greek ceramists who produce some distinctive work—not in the modern vein but traditional Greek motifs and colors that both dazzle and refresh. Some platters are stunning. Past Roka Carpets (below) on well-traveled Zambeliou.

Roka Carpets. 61 Zambeliou St., Chaniá. ☎ **0821/74736.** AE, EU, MC, V. Daily 10am–10:30pm.

This establishment, about midway on this shopping street, should be visited if only to see a traditional weaver at his trade. Mikhali Manousakis works away here (while his mother, the shop's founder, works in her home) to produce an endless succession of varied rugs, blankets, coverlets, and wall hangings. There are patterns and colors and sizes for every taste, with prices from Dr 4,000 ($17) and up. These are not artsy textiles but traditional Cretan weaving.

CHANIÁ AFTER DARK

Chaniá's nightlife mostly comes down to two possibilities: Either you go into some ear-shattering club/bar/disco packed with young people, or you walk around the harbor and Old Town and enjoy the passing scene (a ritual known in Greece as the *volta*). As you stroll, wander into the back alleys and be amazed at the extent of both the old Venetian and Turkish remains and the modern touristic enterprises—it's perfectly safe, by the way. Sit in a quayside cafe and enjoy a coffee or drink. Perhaps this is the time to treat yourself to a ride in one of those horse-drawn carriages found down at the harbor. Or at the other extreme, stroll through the new town and be surprised at the modernity and diversity (and prices) of the stores patronized by typical Chaniots.

There are several **movie houses** around town, too—three outdoor in the summer months, three indoor. They usually show foreign movies in the original language. (The one in the Public Gardens is especially enjoyable.) Viewing a movie on a warm summer night in an outdoor cinema in Greece is one of life's simpler pleasures.

There's not much regular or residential cultural activity in Chaniá that would be of interest to foreigners on holiday, yet in recent years, there's been an effort to provide a **summer cultural festival** of sorts—occasional performances from July into September of **dramas, symphonic music, jazz, dances,** and **traditional music.** These performances take place at several venues: the **Firka** fortress at the far left of the harbor; the Venetian arsenals along the old harbor; the **East Moat Theatre** along Nikiforou Phokas Street; or in the **Peace and Friendship Park Theatre** on Dimokratias Street, just beyond the Public Gardens. Admissions, times, schedules, and such are too unpredictable to list, but if this kind of thing appeals to you—and these can be both professional and entertaining evenings—inquire at one of the tourist information offices as soon as you arrive in town.

In addition, there are frequent **performances of traditional Crete** and **Greek music** and **dances** in many restaurants. One locale that attracts some authentic Cretan musicians, singers, and dancers is **Lyrakia,** at 22 Kallergon St., one block behind Akti

Enoseos, the quay of the Old Harbor (☎ 0821/58661). There's no cover or minimum. This is for true aficionados—it's not primarily a tourist production. In recent years, there have been fairly regular performances through the summer of **Greek folk dances** by a fully costumed troupe at the **Firka's outdoor theater;** again, inquire when you come into town.

That then leaves the young set seeking their type of culture. Clubs come and go, from year to year, of course, so there is no use getting excited over last year's in-place. One is tempted to say that you need only follow the noise, but in fact several of the more popular locales have been forced to barricade themselves behind several doors and entryways precisely to keep the noise from disturbing the neighbors. There are many such—**El Mondo** on Kondilaki (the street leading away from the center of old harbor); **Pyli** on the ramparts (the outermost wall at the northeast corner of the harbor); **Idaeon Andron** on Odos Halidon 26; **Ariadne** on Akti Enoseos (just around to the right of the old harbor). On Odos Anghelou (up from the Naval Museum) is **Fagotta,** a bar that sometimes offers jazz music. **Meltemi** (at far left/west corner of new harbor) is one of the more cosmopolitan cafes, attracting both locals and foreigners, some young, some old.

For those whose idea of a night out is to be drinking a cold beer, there are several such **pubs** or **stubes**—one of the favorites being **Rudi's Beer House** at Odos Sifika 24 (a street to the east of Santrivani Square/Odos Halidon).

Let it be also said that Chaniá has for decades had something of an international reputation as a **popular hangout for gay males,** and it remains something of a favorite way station, for both transient travelers and a more permanent expatriate community. At this writing, however, there seems to be no single bar or nightclub where the gay community gathers unless it's the **Triiris Club,** on Odos Mousourou (along the west side of the Public Market).

A SPECIAL CAFE RESTAURANT

After saying all the above, rather than just cop out on Chaniá's nightlife, we can recommend a find we feel should appeal to many—from young lovers to old marrieds. It's a place for anyone seeking to get away from the crowds, celebrate a special occasion, or just enjoy a lovely vista and a refreshing drink.

Pallas Roof Garden Cafe-Bar. Akti Tobazi (right at the corner where the New Harbor meets the Old Harbor), Chaniá. ☎ 0821/45688. Drinks Dr 800–Dr 1,500 ($3.40–$6.40). No cover or minimum. No credit cards. Daily 6pm–1am. Closed mid-Oct to Apr. Walk from any point around the harbor.

In some ways, the Pallas Roof Garden is the best-situated locale on the harbor. This cafe-bar—the only solid food is a deliciously fresh fruit salad (Dr 1,200 /$5.10)—offers everything from coffees and chocolate to milk shakes and ice-cream sundaes (Dr 1,000–Dr 1,200/$4.25–$5.10). Its good selection of alcoholic beverages includes champagne. Mellow and discreet background music plays constantly—mostly old soft-rock and pop favorites, occasionally some jazz; just make a request and see what they can dig up. With little lanterns at each table, you sit high above the harbor and listen to the murmur of the crowds and watch the blinking lighthouse. There has to be some drawback and there is—you must climb 44 stairs to get there. But as the sign says, it's worth it.

SPORTS & OUTDOOR ACTIVITIES

Tourists may not likely be seeking athletic activities in Chaniá, but there are some possibilities. **Joggers,** of course, will always find their own routes: Try going along the **waterfront road** from the east edge of town and over into the Halepa Quarter.

Chaniá has a most impressive stadium (over by the Public Gardens) with night lights big enough for world cup competition. It also supports a semiprofessional **soccer team** (football) and a professional **water polo team;** ask at the information center if you are interested in seeing a match.

SIDE TRIPS FROM CHANIÁ

Chaniá can serve as a home base for a number of interesting day trips. If your interests lie in the historical/cultural vein, there are countless **medieval Byzantine chapels** throughout the villages and hills of western Crete, but it would take a specialized guide—both a book and individual—to get you to most of them. But just as an example, if you were to take the main road west out of Chaniá to Tavronitis (some 12 miles/20km) and turn south at that point, you would come to a whole string of villages—Voukolies, Floria, Kandanos, Kadodiki, and Kadhros—all of which have interesting frescoed medieval churches. Or if you continue on that coast road west, you come (at about 15 miles/23km) to a turnoff to the right to the village of Kolymvarion and just outside it, the **Monastery of Ghonia**—noted not for frescoes but for icons. Back on the road west, another 2 miles (4km) brings you to a right turn that leads (in 3 miles/5km) to the village of Rodhopou: Here you could get a guide to take you on an arduous walk of several hours to either the pilgrimage **Church of St. John Giona** or the remains of the **Hellenistic-Roman temple of Dictyna.**

Again back on the main road west, you would come in another 10 miles (16km) to the little port town of **Kastelli-Kissamou.** A post-Minoan and then Roman settlement, its most important remains unfortunately have been "re-buried"—mosaic floors that are being protected until the experts can decide what to do with them. (Kastelli, by the way, is the port for a little-used boat service that links Crete to the Peloponnese and Piraeus. It does have a modest hotel or two so it can become an overnighter.)

More people are more likely to be interested in two other destinations once they have come this far: the beaches of **Phalasarna** and **Elefonissi**—each quite different from the other but both prized for their natural settings and (relatively) undeveloped locales. Phalasarna is some 10 miles (16km) from Kastelli, all the way to the northwestern coast. It's backed by dramatic slopes and a rocky shore and provides a sense of being at the end of the earth. Elefonissi (some 30 miles/48km from Kastelli) is the opposite—it's on the southwest corner and evokes a more tropical feeling. Both have been "discovered" in recent years, but they still reward those who have gone this far.

THE SAMARIA GORGE

There remains the one excursion that everyone with an extra day on Crete—and steady legs and solid shoes—should consider: the descent through the Gorge of Samaria. First, this involves getting to the top of the gorge (a trip of some 26 miles/42km from Chaniá). Second comes the descent by foot and passage through the gorge itself (some 11 miles/18km). Third, a boat takes you from the village of Aghia Roumeli, at the end of the gorge, to Khora Sfakion; from there, it's a bus ride of some 46 miles (75km) back to Chaniá. (Some boats go westward to Paleochora, about the same distance by road from Chaniá.)

Most people do it all in a long day, but there are modest hotels and rooms at Aghia Roumeli, Khora Sfakion, Paleochora, and elsewhere along the south coast where you can put up for the night. In any case, it's advisable for most people to sign up with one of the many **travel agencies** in Chaniá that get people to and from the gorge. Unless you are really unaccustomed to this sort of excursion, there is no need to sign up for a guided trip; one of many little books available will tell you what you'll need to know. The point of signing up with an agency is that you get a comfortable bus ride to the top of the gorge, a guaranteed boat trip from Aghia Roumeli to Khora Sfakion, and, most important, a guaranteed (and now even more welcome) seat on that comfortable bus back to Chaniá.

In recent years, the Gorge of Samaria has been so successfully promoted as one of the great natural splendors of Europe that on certain days it seems that half of Europe is trekking through. It's only open from about April to October (depending on weather conditions), so your best chance for a bit of solitude is clearly near those two extremes. On the most crowded days, you can find yourself walking single file with several thousand other people many of those 11 miles. As a hike or trek, it rates as relatively easy, but here and there you scramble over some boulders, and if you haven't done any such exercise for a long while, your legs will let you know this the next day. But we've seen elderly people go through in street shoes and kids in sandals—even young girls in heels. (Germans will insist on wearing solid boots.) So don't imagine that it's a killer. But yes, bring your own water and snacks and just make sure that your feet are going to be comfortable with whatever you have on them.

After all this, is it worth it? Some of us still think so. The gorge has enough "breathing space" that you can still break away from the crowds in places. There are wildflowers to be seen, dramatic geological formations, the fun of crisscrossing the water, the sheer height of the gorge's sides, and several chapels that you come across. It's one of these, about midway through the gorge, dedicated to a Mary in Egypt who converted when an icon of the Virgin Mother appeared before her, that has given it the name Sa(int)maria.

The descent, the crossings of the stream, the passage through the rocky narrows, the emergence onto the south coast—all seem to add up to a worthwhile experience, if not a metaphor of your visit to Crete.

3 Réthymnon

Whether visited on a day trip from Chaniá or Iráklion or used as a base for a more extended stay in western Crete, Réthymnon can be a delightful town—*if* you pick the right Réthymnon.

Its history is much closer to Chaniá's than Iráklion's—that is, its defining centuries came under the Venetians in the late Middle Ages and the Renaissance, then under the Turks from the late 17th century to the late 19th century. Like Chaniá, too, neither it nor its immediate environs has produced major Minoan sites, so that the first wave of post–World War II tourism did not affect it. But finally—also, alas, like Chaniá—it has so welcomed the latest wave that at times this once-quaint provincial town seems almost to have been swept away by the tourist locales and services.

Its maze of streets and alleys are now lined with shops and signs offering every possible service, its old beachfront is lined with restaurants and bars, and its new beach-resort development (to the east of the old town) is an incredible example of how a small town can exploit its seacoast. This stretch of resorts may not be the Réthymnon you've come to see, however, and you can focus your time and interests in the old town. This is the place that inspired a minor classic of modern Greek literature, *The Tale of a Town*, by Pandelis Prevelakis. One of the more admired writers of 20th-century Greece, Prevelakis was a native of Réthymnon.

ESSENTIALS

GETTING THERE   By Ship   Réthymnon lacks an airport but now has its own ship line, offering daily trips direct to (about 7:30pm) and from Piraeus (also about 7pm).

By Car   Traditionally, most people arrive by car, taking the highway from either Iráklion (some 49 miles/79km) or Chaniá (45 miles/72km).

By Bus   If you don't have your own vehicle, the bus service is frequent to and from Iráklion and Chaniá—virtually every half hour from early in the morning until midevening (in high season, buses have departed Réthymnon as late as 10pm). The fare has been about Dr 1,300 ($5.55) one way. The **KTEL** bus line (☎ **0831/ 22212**) that provides service to and from Chaniá and Iráklion is located at Akti Kefaloyianithon at the western entrance to the city (so allow extra 10 minutes to get there).

By Taxi   A taxi might be an alternative for a small group (two to four persons), with one-way fares some Dr 15,000 ($64) from Iráklion and Dr 9,600 ($41) from Chaniá.

VISITOR INFORMATION   The **National Tourist Information office** (☎ **0831/29148**) is on Odos Venizelou, near the center of the town beach. Open weekdays from 8:30am to 2:30pm.

GETTING AROUND   Réthymnon is a walker's town—bringing a car into the maze of streets and alleys is more trouble than it's worth. The sites you'll want to see are never more than a 20-minute walk from wherever you are. Taxis, meanwhile, are there for anyone who can't endure a short walk—especially in the heat of the day. The younger set might consider renting a motorbike or scooter but even this is not that much of an asset if all you intend is a day in the old town.

FAST FACTS: Réthymnon

Area Code   The area code for Réthymnon is **0831**.

Hospital   The state hospital (☎ 0831/27491) is on Odos Trantallidou Street 7-9.

Police   The **Tourist Police** (☎ 0831/28156) share the same building with the Tourist Information Office.

Post Office   The post office (☎ 0831/22571) is located on Leoforio Kountounati 100. It's open Monday through Friday from 8am to 8pm, Sat 8am to noon.

Telephone, Telex, and Fax   The main **OTE** or national telecommunications of-fice (☎ 0831/131) is on Leoforio Kountounoti 40; it's open daily from 7:30am to midnight. There is a kiosk station on Odos Venizelou; it's open Monday through Saturday from 8am to 11:30pm, Sunday 9am to 2pm and 5 to 10pm.

Travel Agencies   One of the oldest on Crete, **Creta Travel Bureau** has an office at Odos Venizelou 3, ☎ 0831/22915; it can arrange trips to virtually anyplace on the island.

WHAT TO SEE & DO
A STROLL THROUGH THE OLD TOWN

Réthymnon's attractions are best appreciated by a stroll through the old town that allows visitors to pick out what appeals to them. Get a good map, free from the Greek National Tourist Organization office.

If you have only limited time, the one place you should visit is the **Fortezza,** the Venetian fortress that dominates the headland of the town (☎ **0831/28101**). It's open from 8:30am to 7pm, and admission is Dr 300 ($1.30). You'll approach it by a fairly rugged and steep pedestrian road off Odos Melissinou; vehicles have another route, up the adjacent Odos Kheimara, that brings you close to the entrance.

Built under the Venetians but by Cretans from about 1573 to 1580, it remains an imposing work of Renaissance military engineering. Its massive walls (some 1,130 yards in perimeter) were designed to deflect the worst cannon fire of the day. In the end, of course, the Turks simply went around it and took the town in 1646 by avoiding the fort. There's a partially restored mosque inside as well as a Greek Orthodox chapel. Around the interior are remains of a prison, wells, and other structures. It's in this vast area, by the way, that most of the performances of the annual **Réthymnon Festival** take place (see below).

Before you enter the Fortezza, on the right is a former Turkish prison that since the early 1990s has been converted into an **Archaeological Museum** (☎ 0831/ 54668), displaying the ancient artifacts found in Réthymnon Nome—from the Minoan through Roman periods. It's open Tuesday through Sunday from 8:30am to 3pm, closed Monday. Admission is Dr 500 ($2.15), and it's free on Sunday. To be frank, despite the fine museum space, most people will find the objects unexciting, especially in comparison with the splendors of Iráklion's Museum. Unless you're serious about these ancient cultures—and there are some fine Neolithic tools that were found in the nearby Yerani Cave in recent years—here's one museum you're allowed to skip.

Rather, save your energy for some of the more unexpected sights in the old town. Leaving the Fortezza, you make your way to the corner of Odos Mesologiou, with the Catholic church at the corner. If you have the time and inclination turn into Odos Mesologiou and visit the **Historical and Folk Art Museum,** with its collection of artifacts, implements, clothing, and other vivid testaments to the traditional way of life of most Cretans across the centuries. It's open Monday to Saturday from 9am to 1pm and 6 to 8pm. Admission is Dr 400 ($1.70).

Proceeding down Odos Salaminos to the **old harbor,** you come to an unexpected sight in the bad sense—the wall of restaurants and bars that effectively obliterate the quaint harbor that drew them there in the first place. Emerging at the southeast corner of this curved harbor, you come to a square that faces the town's long beach, its broad boulevard lined with even more restaurants and cafes. You turn right up Odos Petikhaki and at the first crossroads will see the **Venetian Loggia** (ca. 1600)—for many years the town's museum but now vacant and awaiting restoration. Continue up past it on Odos Paleologou to the next crossroads where you come, on the left, to the **Arimondi Fountain** (1623), built by a prominent Venetian of that time.

Leaving the fountain at your back, proceed onto Odos Antistaseos and come to the **Mosque of Nerantzes** with its minaret (open for climbing Monday through Friday, 11am to 7:30pm; Saturday 11am to 3pm. Closed during August). Beyond it is the Venetian Catholic **Church of San Francesco** (now used for civic meetings and exhibitions). If you follow Odos Antistatheos to its top, you come to the **Porta Guora,** the only remnant of the Venetian city walls.

Across the main east-west road and to the right are the Town's **Public Gardens.** On your left is the Orthodox **Church of the Four Martyrs,** worth a peek in as you walk east along Odos Gerakari until you come to the **Heroes Square** (Platia Iroon)— the border of the old town and the new beachfront development.

Turning back into the old town on Odos Arkadhio, you will see on your left the **Mosque of Kara Pasha,** now restored and used as a botanical museum (daily 9am to 6pm). As you continue along Arkhadiou, in addition to the modern shops and their offerings, note the several remains of the Venetian era that survive—as, for instance, the **facade of no. 154.** From this point on, you're on your own to explore the various narrow streets, to shop, or just to head for the waterfront and enjoy some refreshment.

WHERE TO STAY

There is no shortage of places to stay in and around Réthymnon—but it has become increasingly harder to find a place that offers a convenient location, some authentic atmosphere, and a good night's sleep. Our choices try to satisfy the last-mentioned criterion first. We also feel that you do not travel all the way to this town to be crammed into a honky-tonk beachfront. Note that many places in Réthymnon shut down over the winter—at which time, of course, the noise dims considerably and many of the more central places are quite acceptable.

VERY EXPENSIVE

Rithymna Beach Grecotel. P.O. Box 23, Réthymnon 74100, Crete. (7 kilometers east of Réthymnon on the old road to Iráklion). ☎ **0831/29491** or 0831/71002. Fax 0831/71668. 463 rooms including 120 bungalows, 11 villas with 2 bedrooms (7 of which have private pools). All with bath. A/C TV TEL. High season Dr 30,000–Dr 32,200 ($127–$137) double; Dr 34,500–Dr 37,000 ($147–$158) bungalow; Dr 86,250 ($367) villa or suite. Low season Dr 15,000 ($64) double, Dr 15,000 ($64) bungalow, Dr 43,125 ($184) villa or suite. All rates are per person, daily, including breakfast and one other meal. Reduction for third person sharing room of two fully paid persons; baby free. AE, DC, EU, MC, V. Parking on premises. Buses to and from Réthymnon (and Chaniá) or Iráklion every half hour.

This is an alternative that few Americans have taken advantage of—one of the luxury beach hotels now found outside all of Crete's major cities. The Rithymna Beach is one of five such in the Grecotel chain on Crete and one of the finest of any facilities on the island. The advantages are obvious: You escape the noise and bustle of the city, and especially with a rented car you can get to see as much of the island as you like, always returning to your more than comfortable hotel (which is not much more than two hours from most sites of interest anywhere on Crete).

Definitely pricey—although well within international rates at similar hotel resorts—but you get a lot of first-class facilities and services. A bit glitzy and probably not for those intending to be on the go most of their time on Crete, but something to consider if you like to mix occasional sightseeing with luxurious facilities, pampered relaxation, and water-based activities.

Dining/Entertainment: There is a bottomless cornucopia of fine food and drink to be enjoyed from the main restaurant (more French than anything), a cafeteria, a taverna (Cretan dishes), a cafe, the main bar, a beach bar, and a pool bar.

Services: Concierge, room service, dry cleaning and laundry, newspaper delivery, massage, baby-sitting, secretarial services, courtesy car, children's activities.

Facilities: Four pools (outdoor seawater, outdoor freshwater, outdoor children's, indoor heated from October to April), health club, aerobics, Jacuzzi, sauna, sun areas (deck chairs and umbrellas free), bridge room, video room, 5 outdoor tennis courts (2 with lights), squash court at nearby Creta Palace, water sports equipment (windsurfing and scuba diving instructions), bicycle rental, nature trails, children's programs, conference rooms (up to 600), car rental desk, tour desk, beauty salon, and boutiques.

EXPENSIVE

Hotel Fortezza. Odos Melissinou 16 (at eastern edge of town, just below the Venetian Fortezza, which is approached by this road) Réthymnon. ☎ **0831/23828.** Fax 0831/54073. 51 doubles, 3 suites, all with bath. Rates high season Dr 24,150 ($103) double, Dr 29,900 ($123) suite. Low season Dr 18,400 ($78) double, Dr 22,080 ($94) suite. All rates are per room, with continental breakfast. Surcharges for third person sharing room with two fully paid persons, baby free. AE, DC, EU, MC, V. Parking nearby. Public bus service 100 yards.

This has emerged as one of the more appealing of the better hotels in Réthymnon, for its location isolates it from the noise of the inner town. This is especially true of its inside rooms, which overlook the modest but welcomed swimming pool. There's a pleasant restaurant, although most people will prefer to frequent the restaurants of the town. You're only a few blocks from the inner old town and then another couple of blocks to the town beach or the Venetian harbor.

The common areas aren't especially spacious but there's a fancy bar, a TV room, and a working fireplace (and central heating when necessary). All rooms are good-sized, modern, comfortable and most have balconies. Half of the rooms have air-conditioning and telephones. This relatively new hotel has become so popular that you are advised to make reservations for the high season.

Kyma Beach Hotel. Platia Iroon (at the eastern edge of the old town and its beach) Réthymnon. ☎ 0831/55503. Fax 0831/27746. 35 doubles, all with bath. A/C TEL. Rates high season Dr 22,130 ($94) double; low season negotiable. Rates include continental breakfast. AE, EU, MC, V. Parking nearby. Public buses nearby.

This is one of the newer hotels yet close to the major attractions of the old town. It's a hotel with an exterior of some style as opposed to the rather stodgy construction of most Greek hotels, which often are designed and built by engineer/owners. Although its rooms are hardly spacious, they too are well furnished. Some, however, have loft beds and if this doesn't appeal, speak up beforehand. All rooms have balconies, but ask for a higher floor to escape street noise. The outdoor cafe is a popular watering hole for Rethymnians, so you feel you're part of the town and not in a foreigners' compound. Perhaps a bit overpriced given its location, but a first-rate modern establishment.

Kournas Village Hotel Bungalows. Kavros (¹/₂ hour west of Réthymnon, on the main road to Chaniá). ☎ and fax **0831/61416/8.** 141 rooms (singles, doubles, triples) all with bath. A/C TEL. High season Dr 27,140 ($115); low season Dr 13,420 ($58) double. Rates include breakfast and dinner. Closed Nov–Mar. Parking on site.

Here's an alternative for those who may want to focus their Cretan stay on Réthymnon and Chaniá and western Crete, yet who prefer to be based on a beach that's not an annex to a noisy town. Everything about this place—and by the way, its jointly owned twin, Mare Monte, is just down the road—is first class, yet you feel you're living on a remote Cretan beach with the sea before you and the mountains behind. The village of Georgioupolis is close enough for an evening stroll, and various restaurants and shops have sprouted along the road to handle the guests from several similar beach resorts along this stretch. It lacks the luxury of the grand resorts to the east of Réthymnon, but it's more than adequate.

Dining/Entertainment: The main restaurant, cafeteria, bar, and lounge provide some variety in the choice of foods and drink, but you should go to outside restaurants for more indigenous Greek food.

Services: Concierge, dry cleaning/laundry arranged, rentals and tours arranged.

Facilities: Two pools plus a children's pool, health club (aerobics, bodybuilding), sauna, massage, sundeck, tennis court (with flood lights), table tennis, water-sports equipment, bicycle rental, playground nursery, conference room (150 persons), video games, car rental arranged, safety deposit boxes, boutiques.

Hotel Ideon. 10 Plastira Square (on coast road just outside the Venetian harbor) Réthymnon. ☎ **0831/26667** to **9.** Fax 0831/28670. 89 doubles, some with shower only. A/C TEL. Rates high season Dr 19,600 ($83) double; low season Dr 11,900 ($51) double. Rates include buffet breakfast. Half-board plan (including breakfast and dinner) available, reduced rate for third person in room and children 2–12 years. AE, DC, EU, MC, V. Closed Nov to mid-March. Parking in adjacent street.

This old favorite has totally renovated itself so that it now has both the appearance and facilities of a better hotel. Its friendly desk staff can arrange for everything from laundry to car rental. It now boasts a swimming pool and a sunning area as well as a conference room that can handle up to 80 persons. Rooms are the standard modern of Greek hotels. We like it most of all because it offers an increasingly rare combination in a Cretan hotel: that of being near the active part of the town, near the water (although it doesn't have a beach, and relatively isolated from night noises. A solid choice for sheer convenience.

MODERATE

Hotel Olympic. Corner Moutsou and Demokratias (one block up from main street), Rehymnon. ☎ **0831/24761 to 4.** 65 rooms (singles, doubles, triples) all with bath. A/C TEL. Dr 16,100 ($69) double. Breakfast Dr 1,000 ($4.25). Open all year. Parking in front. Public local buses and buses to Iráklion within few hundred yards.

This is your standard Class C hotel, but it offers a few advantages that would make it a possible choice for budget travelers. It's only about 225 yards (200 meters) up from the midsection of the town beach, yet it's somewhat removed from the main traffic of the city. The desk staff will help with every need. Rooms all have balconies, most have no special views, and the interior ones are the quietest. There is a breakfast room, a lounge bar, and a roof garden. The decor throughout is modified Cretan village. Again, it's nothing grand, but it does offer an alternative to those who find the old town a bit claustrophobic and noisy.

WHERE TO DINE
EXPENSIVE

Cava d'Oro. 42 Nearchou St. (Venetian Harbor). ☎ **0831/24446.** Main courses Dr 1,100– Dr 3,200 ($4.70–$14). AE, DC, EU, MC, V. Daily 11am–midnight. Closed Nov–Mar. GREEK.

In recent years, this has emerged as the Venetian harbor restaurant with the reputation for the most pleasant ambience and with food at least as good as any other's. But part of its appeal is based on its air-conditioned dining room—not everyone's idea of being on a Cretan harbor—and its very reputation has made it crowded, especially when tour groups move in. Seafood is its specialty, naturally, and this means the high end of the menu prevails. You'd hardly go here for the cheaper dishes. Save this for a special occasion, and go off hours or off peak season.

MODERATE

Taverna Mourayiou Maria. 45 Nearchou St. (Venetian harbor) ☎ **0831/26475.** Main courses Dr 900–Dr 2,500 ($3.85–$10.65). AE, EU, MC, V. Daily 9am–midnight. Closed Nov–Mar. GREEK.

Another of the necklace of restaurants on the Venetian harbor, this is a more modestly priced alternative to the Cava d'Oro. Like all of them, it specializes in lobster and fish in season, but it also offers a choice of traditional Greek dishes at the lower end of the price scale. The popularity of the Venetian harbor has somewhat overwhelmed the picturesque charm that originally led to its attracting restaurants such as this, but everyone will want to try at least one meal on the harbor and this is as good a choice as any.

Famagusta. 6 Plastira Square (near Ideon Hotel, on coast road just to west of Venetian Harbor), Réthymnon. ☎ **0831/23881.** Main courses Dr 1,100–Dr 3,200 ($4.70–$14). Daily combination plates Dr 1,500–Dr 2,000 ($6.40–$8.50). AE, DC, EU, MC, V. Daily 10am–midnight. Closed during Christmas–New Year holidays. Parking nearby. GREEK/INTERNATIONAL.

A well-tested restaurant in a location that's removed from the hustle of the harbor yet convenient to the center's attractions and enjoying a view of the sea. The menu offers several Cretan specialties such as breaded zucchini deep fried with yogurt lightly flavored with garlic, or *halumi* (a grilled cheese). Grilled fish and steak fillets are the core of the main courses, but the adventurous chef also includes such dishes as Chinese-style mandarin beef and that old basic chili con carne. Eating here makes you feel like you're at an old-fashioned seaside restaurant, not some touristic confection.

INEXPENSIVE

Fanari ("The Lantern"). 16 Kefalogianithon St. (on coast road just west of Venetian harbor—past Ideon Hotel and Famagusta Restaurant), Réthymnon. ☎ **0831/54849.** Main courses Dr 900–Dr 2,500 ($3.85–$10.65). Daily special combination plates about Dr 1,500 ($6.40). Cash only. Daily 11am–1:30am. Closed late Nov to early Jan. Parking nearby. GREEK TAVERNA.

We list this place not because its menu or cooking is so exceptional, but because of its pleasant location, overlooking the sea and well removed from the bustle of the center of Réthymnon, and its prompt and pleasant service. The proprietor is a repatriated Canadian-Greek and will welcome all English speakers. The old harbor and the old beach strip have now become so geared to tourism—with those tacky plastic photos of meals that are somehow supposed to lure us in—that an unpretentious taverna like this should come as a relief and retreat. Take a table at the railing, order a cool drink, and enjoy your meal: You can't go wrong with the standard fare, and fish here can be as tasty as at most of the more expensive locales.

SHOPPING

Here, as in Chaniá and Iráklion and so many Cretan cities, the visitor will be overwhelmed by the sheer numbers of gift shops offering much the same objects—most not much more than souvenirs. All you need, though, is to see one object that appeals. Those looking for something a bit different might try one of the two shops named **Nymphe** that sell traditional Greek icons (painted by contemporary artists) and other forms of traditional Greek art: One shop is at 63 Eleftherios Venizelou St., the other at 233 Arkadiou St. Another shop with something special is called **Olive Tree Wood,** at 51 Arabatzoglou St.; its name clearly announces its products—various bowls, containers, and implements carved from olive wood. A nice selection of Cretan embroidery and various other popular craft work is to be found in either of the two shops of **Evangelia Manolaki-Paximada**—one at Adelianos Campos (next to the Hotel Paladium) and the other at 4 Titou Petichaki St. The shop **Hobby** at 143 Arkadiou St. also has a fine selection of traditional handmade Cretan embroidery.

SPECIAL EVENTS

THE RÉTHYMNON WINE FESTIVAL

Réthymnon has been holdings its annual "wine festival" a lot longer than many other Greek communities that now make much of such occasions. Réthymnon's is held in the last 10 or so days of July, centered in the Public Gardens, with music and dancing to accompany the samplings of local wines. It's a modest affair, but a welcome change from some of the more staged festivals.

THE RÉTHYMNON CULTURAL FESTIVAL

For some years now Réthymnon has hosted a cultural festival that concentrates its events—mostly musical and theatrical—in August and early September. The stated theme has been "The Renaissance in Réthymnon," but this has been interpreted loosely to include anything from productions of ancient Greek dramas to more contemporary artistic endeavors. Most performers are Greek but some are foreigners. Most performances are in the Fortezza itself; there's nothing quite like listening to some 17th-century music or seeing the performance of a Renaissance drama in this setting. If this appeals to you, inquire at the NTO office or the International Press Store on first arriving.

OUTDOOR ACTIVITIES

Among the newer diversions offered in Réthymnon are the daily **excursion boats** that take people on **a day trip for swimming** on the beach either at **Bali** (to the east) or to **Marathi** (on the Akrotiri to the west). The price (which has been about Dr 8,000/$34 for adults) includes a midday meal at a local taverna as well as all the wine you care to drink. The **Nias Tours** (Odos Arkadhiou 4, ☎ 0831/23840) also offers an **evening cruise** with refreshments that provides a view of Réthymnon glittering in the night. There's the **Riding Center** for horseback riding, located southeast of town at Platanias, 39 N. Fokas St. (☎ **0831/28907**). **Guided "nature hikes"** through local areas are conducted daily by the **Happy Walker,** Tombazi Street (☎ 0831/52920).

SIDE TRIPS FROM RÉTHYMNON

For the younger backpack set and various European charter groups, Réthymnon has become known as the turnoff to the south coast and **Plakias,** a beach that has been developing in recent years—upgraded or downgraded, depending on your taste in these matters—into a resort. Its appeal is that its sea water seems to remain warmer longer than at other points; its beach is certainly not that great. In any case, Plakias does not seem to warrant a detailed description: Its pensions—sometimes completely booked in the high season—are all standard as are the many eating places.

A much more meaningful excursion—one that should be made by anyone who wants to say they have some sense of modern Cretans—is to the **Monastery of Arkadhi.** It sits some 15 miles (23km) southeast of Réthymnon and can be reached by public bus. A taxi might be in order if you don't have a car, and you'll only need it to wait about an hour—it should cost about Dr 5,000 ($21). What you see when you arrive is a surprisingly Italianate-looking church facade, for although it belongs to the Orthodox priesthood it was built under Venetian influence in 1587.

Like many monasteries on Crete, Arkadhi provided support for the rebels against Turkish rule. During a major uprising in 1866, many Cretan insurgents, along with their women and children, had taken refuge there. Realizing they were doomed to fall to the far larger besieging Turkish force, the abbot, it is claimed, gave the command to blow up the powder storeroom. Whether an accident or not, hundreds of Cretans and Turks died in the explosion. This occurred on November 9, 1866, and the event became known throughout the Western world, inspiring writers and revolutionaries and statesmen of several nations to protest at least with words. To Cretans it became and remains the archetypal incident of their long struggle for "freedom or death." (An ossuary outside the monastery contains the skulls of many who died in the explosion.) Even if you have never had occasion to think about Cretan history, a brief visit to Arkadhi should go a long way to explaining the Cretans you deal with.

4 Ághios Nikólaos

Until the 1970s Ághios Nikólaos, now a major resort center, was a lazy little coastal settlement. Having no archaeological or historical structures of any interest, it had little to attract tourists—it's really a town built up only since the late 19th century. So the few foreigners who did drop by usually did little more than take a drink on the harbor, take in its indigenous character, and then take to the road. Then the village got discovered, and the rest is the history of organized tourism in our time.

For about five months of the year, Ághios Nikólaos becomes one gigantic resort town—literally every square inch taken over by the package-tours industry and their clients—most from Northern Europe (although it's popular with the Italians and Spanish, too). Most of these people stay in beach hotels along the adjacent coast, but they come into Ághios Nikólaos and concentrate around the little harbor and what's still a surprisingly pleasant lake, to snack, to eat, to shop, to stroll. During the day, Ághios Nikólaos vibrates with people. During the night, it vibrates with music—the center down by the water becomes like one communal nightclub.

Part of the appeal of Ághios Nikólaos to so many tourists is that there's so little that they have to feel guilty about not visiting. The one point of interest is right there for everyone to sit on the edge of while enjoying a meal or drink. This is the little pool, formally called **Lake Voulismeni,** just inside the harbor. Inevitably, it has given rise to all sorts of tales—that it's bottomless (it's known to be about 215 feet/ 65 meters deep); that it's connected to Santoríni, the island some 65 miles to the north; that it was the "bath of Athena." Originally it was a freshwater pool, probably fed by some subterranean river draining water from the mountains inland; the channel was dug sometime early in the 20th century and so now the water mixes with sea water.

Ághios Nikólaos remains a pleasant place to spend a little time in and is a fine base for excursions to the east of Crete. And if you're willing to stay outside the very center of town, in one or another of the places we've selected, you can take only as much of Ághios Nikólaos as you enjoy and then retreat to your beach or explore the east end of the island.

ESSENTIALS

GETTING THERE   By Plane   Ághios Nikólaos does not have its own airport but can be reached in 1¹/₂ hours by taxi or bus from the Iráklion airport. Olympia also offers some flights to Sitia, but the drive from there to Ághios Nikólaos is a solid two hours.

By Ship   There are several ships a week each way (at least during tourist season) that link Ághios Nikólaos to Sitia (just east along the coast) and on, via the islands of Kassos, Karpathos, and Khalki, to Rhodes. There are also several ships that link Ághios Nikólaos to the island of Santoríni and then via several other Cycladic islands to Piraeus. Schedules and even ship lines vary so from year to year that you should wait until you get to Greece to make specific plans.

By Bus   There is service almost every half-hour of the day each way (during the tourist season) linking Ághios Nikólaos to Iráklion and almost as many buses to and from Sitia. This is provided by the **KTEL bus line** (☎ 0841/22234 or 0841/28284), with its terminal at Akti Atlantidos (by the town marina, around the headland).

VISITOR INFORMATION   The **Municipal Information Office** (☎ 0841/ 22357) is one of the most helpful in all of Greece, perhaps because it's staffed by eager young employees instead of jaded veterans. It is open daily 8:30am to 10pm, from April 1 to the end of October. In addition to providing maps and other ready services, it issues a **Visitor's Card,** which entitles you to certain free items and discounts when presented at the Municipal Beach.

GETTING AROUND   The town is so small that you can and should walk to all points, although there are taxicabs to take you any place—say, with your luggage to or from the dock or bus terminal and your hotel. The **KTEL buses** (referred to above) service towns, hotels, and other points along the coast highway.

FAST FACTS: Ághios Nikólaos

Area Code   The area code for Ághios Nikólaos is **0841**.

Car/Moped Rentals   It seems like there are car and moped/motorcycle rentals at every other doorway. We found some of the best car rates at **Alfa Rent a Car** (☎ 0841/24312; fax 0841/25639) Odos Kap. Nik. Fafouti 3 (small street between the lake and harbor road), Aghios Nikoloas 72100. Fotis Retakis is the man to deal with.

Emergencies   Dial **0841/100** for all emergencies.

Holidays   Ághios Nikólaos adds a special touch to the Orthodox Easter by having its celebrants make a candlelit procession around the inner lake after the midnight service.

Hospitals   The town's new **general hospital** (☎ 0841/25221) is on west edge of town at junction of Odos Lasithiou Street and Odos Paleologos.

Luggage Storage/Lockers   Luggage may be stored at the main bus station, **Akti Atlantidos** (around headland and down by Town Marina). The charge is Dr 300 ($1.30) per piece per 24 hours.

Mail and Post Office   The **post office** (☎ 0841/22062) is at Odos 28th Octobrio 9. In summer, it's open Monday through Saturday from 7:30am to 8pm; hours in winter are Monday through Saturday 7:30am to 2pm.

Newspapers and Magazines   The best selection of foreign-language newspapers and magazines is at the **4 Epoxes** (4 Seasons) at Odos Koundounarou 27 (also distinguished by the young clerk's fondness for European classical music).

Police   The **Tourist Police** (☎ 0841/26900) are at Odos Koundoyianni 34.

Telephone, Telex, and Fax   The **OTE,** or national telecommunications office (☎ 0841/131), is on Odos Sfakinaki 10 (at the corner of March 25th Street). It's open Monday through Saturday from 7am to midnight; Sundays and holidays, 7am to 10pm.

Toilets   Public toilets are located at the Marina, the ferry boat dock, and on Odos Filellinon Street (a small street off Odos N. Plastiras, which runs high above the back of the lake).

Transit Info   The main **bus station** (☎ 0841/22234 or 0841/28284) is at Akti Atlantidos (by town marina, around the headland).

Travel Agenices   Among the scores of travel agencies, ticket offices, and such, we have always found one of the old establishments to be among the best: **Creta Travel Bureau** (☎ 0841/28496), at Akti Koundourou (just out of the harbor on the coast road to Elounda).

WHAT TO SEE & DO

Archaeological Museum. Odos Paleologou 120, Ághios Nikólaos. ☎ **0841/24943.** Admission Dr 400 ($1.70), free on Sunday. Tues–Sun 8:30am–3pm. Closed Mondays.

This is a fine example of one of the relatively new provincial museums that are appearing all over Greece in an effort to decentralize the country's rich holdings and also allow the local communities to profit from the finds from their region. This museum has a growing collection of Minoan artifacts and art that is being excavated in eastern Crete. Its prize piece is the eerily modern ceramic *Goddess of Myrtos,* a woman clutching a jug, found at a Minoan site of this name, down on the southeastern coast. There are also objects from post-Minoan to medieval times. It's worth at least a brief visit.

LATO CULTURAL FESTIVAL

For some years now Ághios Nikólaos has sponsored a modest arts festival. Usually beginning in late July and continuing into early September, these events include Cretan choral groups, Cretan traditional dance troupes, both classic and modern plays (usually in Greek), and concerts by Greek instrumentalists and vocalists. Admission runs from Dr 1,000 to Dr 3,000 ($4.25 to $12.75), usually less for children. To show their appreciation for the foreigners who come to their town and support these and other events, the sponsors have also given parties about midway through the season and then at the end of September—a nice touch, suggesting that perhaps mass tourism need not totally wipe out local customs.

WHERE TO STAY
INSIDE TOWN
Very Expensive

Minos Beach. Elounda Road (a 10-minute walk from center), Ághios Nikólaos 72100. ☎ **0841/22345.** Fax 0841/22548. 12 rms in main building, 118 bungalows. A/C MINIBAR TEL. High season, Dr 29,670–Dr 31,550 ($129–$176) double; low season, Dr 14,030–Dr 26,000 ($60–$110) double. All rates include buffet breakfast. Special rates for children; one meal a day for Dr 6,000 ($26). AE, DC, EU, MC, V. Closed end of Oct to early April. Frequent public buses to Ághios Nikólaos center or Elounda.

This was the first of the luxury beach-bungalow resorts on Crete and remains a favorite of many loyal returnees. Its grounds now look a bit cramped (the greenery seems out of control), and its common areas are not as glitzy as newer resorts. As with almost all Greek deluxe hotels, the mattresses seem a bit thin (to Americans, at least). The hotel has a civilized air, enhanced by the original works by world-famous modern sculptors, which are located around the grounds. It's a great place to enjoy complete peace and quiet and yet not be that far from Ághios Nikólaos.

Dining/Entertainment: The main restaurant offers a Greek/International menu; Terpsis Taverna serves a Greek menu and hosts a weekly Cretan Evening, with barbecue and traditional Cretan music and dances; three bars; and their greatest boast, *La Bouillabaisse*, member of the exclusive *Chaine des Rotisseurs*) is located at the water's edge and serves (very expensive) French-style food.

Services: Concierge, room service, dry cleaning, laundry, newspaper delivery, massage available, baby-sitting, secretarial services, valet parking, airport transportation arranged.

Facilities: TV in VIP Bungalows and large TV room, saltwater pool, "beauty farm" sauna, sundecks, 1 outdoor tennis court lit at night, water sports equipment, bicycle rental, table tennis, snooker table, video games, conference center hosts up to 60, car-rental desk, tours arranged, hairdresser, boutiques.

Expensive

Hotel Hermes. Akti Kondourou (on the shore road around from the inner harbor), Ághios Nikólaos 72100. ☎ **0841/28253.** Fax 0841/28754. 207 rms. A/C TEL. High season, Dr 36,800 ($157) double; low season, Dr 26,450 ($113) double. Rates include half board (breakfast and dinner). Cheaper rate for breakfast only; special rate for longer stays. AE, DC, EU, MC, V. Closed Nov–Mar. Parking in adjacent street.

This is perhaps the best you can do if you want to stay as close to the center of town as possible, yet be free from as much of the noise as possible. It's just far enough and around the corner from the inner harbor to escape the nightly din. This won't be attractive to everyone, but it's a compromise between the deluxe beach resorts and the cheaper in-town hotels. Rooms are done in the standard style, and most enjoy a view over the sea. There's a private terrace (not a beach) on the shore, just across the boulevard. On the roof is a swimming pool, with plenty of space to sunbathe. There's also a sauna and exercise room. All rooms have fridges, and suites have TVs. Other diversions include video games and billiards. The main restaurant is on the fifth floor. A conference room can accommodate up to 250.

Moderate

Hotel Coral. Akti Koundourou (on the shore road, next to Hermes Hotel), Ághios Nikólaos 72100. ☎ **0841/28253.** Fax 0841/28754. 170 rms, some with shower, some with tub. A/C TEL. High season, Dr 30,475 ($130) double; low season, Dr 22,425 ($95) double. Rates include half board (breakfast and dinner). AE, EU, MC, V. Closed end of Oct to Mar. Parking on street.

This is directly next door to the Hotel Hermes and under the same management. It's a Class B (rather than a Class A) establishment with a few less facilities, and perhaps its physical appearance is a bit less classy. But in fact it's hard to see many differences between the Hermes and Coral. It has a restaurant and bar, a rooftop pool, and a gift shop. We can recommend it as a perfectly decent alternative to the Hermes if your budget is a bit strained.

OUTSIDE TOWN

Very Expensive

Elounda Beach. Elounda (about 4 miles from center of Ághios Nikólaos), Ághios Nikólaos 72100. ☎ **0841/61303** or 0841/61325. Fax 0841/61383. 275 rooms and bungalows, 5 VIP bungalow suites with private swimming pools. A/C MINIBAR TV TEL. High season, Dr 54,510–Dr 184,000 ($232–$783) double, Dr 220,000–Dr 255,000 ($936–$1,085) VIP bungalow suites; low season, Dr 22,000–Dr 92,000 ($94–$390) double, Dr 120,000–Dr 140,000 ($510–$596) VIP bungalow suite. Rates are per person per day and include half board (breakfast and dinner). AE, DC, EU, MC, V. Closed early Nov to Mar. Public buses to Ághios Nikólaos or Elounda every hour; Elounda is a 15-minute walk.

Just in case you think Crete has some fine facilities but nothing to really compete with the true world-class resorts, we've included the Elounda Beach. Staying here is like buying a yacht: If you have to ask the price, you can't afford it. (Note that its rates are per person.) There are even more extras than we can list, including the gala dinner every Sunday might and open-air movies each Monday night. There's not much more to say about such a place except that it's truly grand. From the prunes at the breakfast buffet to the mini-TV at your bathroom mirror, they've thought of everything. Yes, we stayed there and the meals are fabulous. And oh, in case you're concerned, they do have their own heliport, so you can come in that way.

Dining/Entertainment: The Artemis Restaurant, serving Greek and international cuisine, overlooks the swimming pool. Other restaurants are located throughout the vast property and include the beachfront Agonaut. There are several locales that offer discreet background music, and a disco for night owls.

Services: Concierge, room service, dry cleaning, laundry, newspaper delivery, nightly turndown, baby-sitting, secretarial services, valet parking, airport transport arranged.

Facilities: VCRs and videos available from desk, main pool, health and fitness center, Jacuzzi, sauna, sundecks, 2 floodlit tennis courts, water sports equipment, bicycle rental, table tennis, billiards, basketball, volleyball, minigolf, supervised children's activities during day, business support can be arranged, conference center for up to 450 (at adjacent sister hotel, Elounda Bay), car rentals and tours arranged, hairdresser, boutiques.

Istron Bay. Istron (8 miles east of Ághios Nikólaos), P.O. Box 68, Ághios Nikólaos 72100. ☎ **0841/61303.** Fax 0841/61383. 112 rms, 6 suites, 27 bungalows. A/C MINIBAR TV TEL. High season, Dr 52,900 ($225) double, Dr 71,300 ($303) suite; low season, 28,175 ($120) double, Dr 40,250 ($170) suite. Rates include buffet breakfast. Special rates for extra beds in room, for children, and for half board (breakfast and dinner). AE, DC, EU, JCB, MC, V. Closed Nov–Mar. Public buses every hour to Ághios Nikólaos or Sitia.

Still another new and beautiful beach resort, this one is a few miles to the east of Ághios Nikólaos and is nestled against the slope on its own bay. It is this location, plus its own beach and the sense of being in some tropical paradise, that makes this such a special place. Plus, it's family owned and thus maintains a touch of the traditional Cretan hospitality—inviting newcomers to a cocktail party to meet others, for instance. The rooms have spectacular views. If you can tear yourself away from here, you're well situated to take in all the sights of eastern Crete.

Dining/Entertainment: The main dining room, high up the "sloped" hotel, has a fabulous view to go with its award-winning cuisine; it takes special pride in its selection of Greek wines. A Greek taverna, an à la carte restaurant down on the beach, a poolside cafe, two bars, and a disco provide further diversion.

Services: Concierge, room service, dry cleaning, laundry, newspapers available, baby-sitting, children's activities.

Facilities: A swimming pool and a children's pool, aerobics, sundeck, one outdoor tennis court (lit at night), water sports equipment, table tennis, volleyball, video games, bicycle rental, conference rooms for 30, car rental and tours arranged, hairdresser, boutique.

WHERE TO DINE

Ághios Nikólaos and nearby Elounda have so many restaurants that it's hard to know where to start or stop. The thing is, too, that almost any place you'd select is going to be in the same price range. Most every locale offers the cheaper omelets and stuffed tomatoes or moussaka, and most every place offers the expensive steaks, fish, and lobster. So what you want to consider are the location and atmosphere, and to that end we're pointing you to a variety of places.

MODERATE TO EXPENSIVE

Cretan Restaurant. Akti Koundourou 10 (on right arm of the harbor). ☎ **0841/28773.** Reservations accepted. Main courses Dr 990–Dr 3,400 ($4.20–$14.50). AE, DC, EU, JCB, MC, V. Mon–Sun 11am–midnight. Closed mid-Nov to mid-Mar. GREEK.

This was one of the first of the fancy restaurants to spring up on the harbor, and it remains a perennial favorite. Beachwear is not accepted. It tends to draw a more conservative, not to say older, set. Inside you can enjoy the cool and shade and a slightly overwrought decor, or you can sit outside at the seven or so tables. (In either case, you're a bit removed from the noise, and fumes, of the locales right on the curve of the harbor.) The menu is traditional but done well—the *stiffado* is made with rabbit, as it should be. For something different, try the perch à la Spetsiota (in a tomato sauce); for an appetizer, sample the mussels braised in wine. One final bit of trivia that you can interpret as you please: The owner hires only women, as cooks and waitresses.

Zefiros. Akti Koundourou 1 (just around the left arm of the harbor). ☎ **0841/28868.** Main courses Dr 900–Dr 3,750 ($3.85–$16). AE, EU, MC, V. Daily 11am–midnight. Closed Nov–Mar. GREEK/INTERNATIONAL.

This is typical of the many restaurants that have grown up in recent years to cater to largely a Northern European crowd. So the menu ranges widely, from cheap omelets and spaghetti to very expensive sole. Just off the harbor, it enjoys a view of the sea. It's usually well patronized but still maintains an intimate atmosphere, with its lamp-lit tables. We would say that this is a place to go to when you are looking for a night off from standard Greek taverna food—and want to treat yourself to something like melon with prosciutto (at Dr 1,200/$5.10).

Hollands Restaurant—De Molen (The Mill). Odos Dionysos Solomos 8 (the road at the highest point above the lake). ☎ **0841/25582.** Reservations accepted. Main courses Dr 1,100–Dr 2,600 ($4.70–$11). Combination plates offered. EU, V. Daily 10am–11:30pm. Closed Nov–Mar. A taxi is your only choice if you can't make it up the hill. DUTCH/INDONESIAN.

Yes, we know: Who would go to Crete to eat Dutch cuisine? But aside from offering a new experience for your palate, this place happens to command just about the most dramatic view of Ághios Nikólaos at night. The proprietors, Petra and Rolf Demmenie, are longtime residents and play host to a lot of their fellow Dutch compatriots. But they'll make you feel equally welcome as they explain some of their specialties such as the pork filet in a cream sauce or pepper sauce or mushroom sauce. Vegetarian? Try their crepe with eggplant, mushrooms, carrots, and cabbage, tied up with leeks. We tried something even more exotic, one of their Indonesian dishes, *Nasi Goreng*—a heaping plate of rice with vegetables and pork, with a sate (peanut) sauce. Somehow it seemed to go with sitting overlooking exotic Ághios Nikólaos.

Blue Lagoon. Omirou 8 (on the lake). ☎ **0841/25706.** Main courses Dr 950–Dr 2,950 ($4–$12.50). Fixed-price meal at about Dr 2,700 ($13.40). AE, EU, MC, V. Daily 8:30am–midnight. Closed Nov–Mar. GREEK/INTERNATIONAL.

Everybody who comes to Ághios Nikólaos for one or more days should eat at least one meal overlooking the inner lake. And there are plenty of restaurants waiting to satisfy that goal—some a bit too ready, as the waiters try to steer you into their locale. The Blue Lagoon is no worse or better on this score, but it does offer pleasant tables, a nice location, and at least well-presented and tasty food. Their Greek salad seemed a cut above in its crispiness; the moussaka uses fresh ground meat; the boned chicken with mushroom sauce was just fine. So you overlook the pushy "barker" and concentrate on the ducks in the lake and the bobbing boats and the passing scene as you sip your Cretan white. Isn't this what traveling is all about?

Vritomartes. Elounda (on the breakwater). ☎ **0841/41325.** Reservations recommended for evenings in high season. Main courses Dr 900–Dr 3,500 ($3.85–$14.90). Offers a fish platter special for Dr 3,000 ($12.75). EU, MC, V. Daily 10am–11pm. Closed Nov–Mar.

This taverna involves a slight exertion—you have to get out to Elounda—but there are buses every hour and always taxis for the 8-mile (12km) trip, and everyone who's come as far as Ághios Nikólaos should get out to Elounda. Once there, you can't beat dining at this old favorite—there's been at least a lowly taverna here long before the beautiful people discovered Elounda. (They're the reason you should either come early or make a reservation.) The specialties, no surprise, are the seafood. The proprietor literally was "out at sea" the last time we stopped by, catching that night's fish dinners. If you settle for the red mullet and a bottle of Cretan white Xerolithia, you can't go wrong. The dining area itself is rather plain, but this is one kind of a dining experience you won't forget.

INEXPENSIVE

Itanos. Odos Kyprou 1 (just off Platia Iroon, at top of Koundourou). ☎ **0841/25340.** Reservations not accepted, so come early in high season. Main courses Dr 900–Dr 2,100 ($3.85–$8.95). No credit cards. 11am–midnight. GREEK.

A now familiar story on Crete: A simple local taverna where you go to get authenticity gets taken up by the tourists and the scene changes somewhat. But the fact is that the food and prices haven't changed that much. It's still standard taverna oven dishes—no-nonsense chicken and lamb and beef in tasty sauces and hearty vegetables—and grilled meats. The house wine comes out of barrels. During the day, you sit indoors, also with no-nonsense decor and service. But at night during the hot months, tables appear on the sidewalk, a roof garden is opened up on the building across the narrow street, and your fellow tourists take over. Come here, though, if you need a break from the harbor scene and want to feel you're in a place that exists when all the tourists go home.

SHOPPING

Maria Patsaki. Odos Sfakianakis 2 (next door to Pegasus, just off Koundounari), Ághios Nikólaos 72100. ☎ **0841/22001** or 0841/24619.

Here on this little side street in Ághios Nikólaos is a shop chock-full of handsome and obviously well-made items that might well be found in many a more cosmopolitan city. Its forte are handwoven textiles of all kinds: rugs (some old), tablecloths, lace, even some women's clothing. It also carries some blown glass, ceramics, brass work, lampshades, small paintings, and trinkets of various sorts. None of it is cheap, all of it is tasteful. The store is open all year from 10am to 2pm, then from 5 to 10:30pm.

Marieli. Odos 28th October 33, Ághios Nikólaos 72100. ☎ **0841/28813** or 0841/28247.

Sofia Kana, the shop's proprietor and weaver of the wonderfully imaginative rugs and other works, studied law and then worked as a journalist until 1972, when she decided her true vocation was to weave. But not just any old yarn: She uses only natural plants for her dyes and produces her distinctively colored yarns, which she weaves into patterns that evoke the Greek realm, without reproducing either stale traditional forms or obvious modern clichés. You can often find her weaving away and ready to show her wares. She also carries some interesting jewelry. Her store is open from 11am to 1:30pm and from 6:30 to 11pm most of the year.

Petrakis Workshop for Icons. Elounda 72053 (on left, coming down incline from Ághios Nikólaos, just before town square). ☎ **0841/41669** or 0841/41461.

What is more Greek than an icon, a religious painting on a wooden plaque? The tradition is kept alive by generation after generation of young painters who master the old materials (such as egg tempera) and techniques. Here in their studio-store, a young couple, Georgia and Ioannis Petrakis, work seriously at maintaining this art. Their icons are in demand from Orthodox churches in North America as well as in Greece. Stop by and watch them at painstaking work—some of which are copies, but often with their original touches. You don't have to be Orthodox to admire or own one. They also have a selection of original jewelry, blown glass, and some paintings in a more popular tradition. They're open from 10am to 2pm and 5 to 11pm.

Talos. Akti Koundari 2 (on shore road around the corner from harbor), Ághios Nikólaos 72100. ☎ **0841/23178.**

This goes against our rule of selecting only shops with Cretan wares, but it satisfies another with its unusually attractive selection of ceramics. These are from the Greek mainland (most from Pátras), and they so stand out from the ware in most tourist shops that we couldn't resist. Serving platters, vases, bowls of all sizes, lampshades—they all have a light, summery feel. There's also a selection of jewelry and minerals, but if you're really into the latter, go to the owner's other shop, also called Talos at no. 2 Akti Koundari (around the corner on the harbor), which offers a large collection of minerals (mostly from Brazil). Both Talos shops are open every day from 10am to 10pm, both close mid-November till mid-March.

Pegasus. Odos Sfakianakis 5, (on corner of main street, R. Koundourou), Ághios Nikólaos 72100. ☎ **0841/24347.**

Here's one of the more interesting selections of small objects we've seen on Crete: jewelry, knives, icons, and trinkets. Some of these are old, some not, and you have to trust the owner, Kostas Kounalakis, to tell you which is which. Likewise, he has a few genuine antiquities, on which you have to take his word. (Get the proper export documents if you purchase a genuine antiquity.) Meanwhile, his wife runs a somewhat similar shop, Syllogi, right on the harbor (Akti Skordidou 5, ☎ 0841/22929); it, too, features interesting jewelry, old silver, and some antique trinkets, but it also has such items as maps, prints, and marionettes. Pegasus and Syllogi are open all year from 10am to 3pm, then from 6 to 10pm.

SIDE TRIPS FROM ÁGHIOS NIKÓLAOS

Almost everyone who comes to Ághios Nikólaos makes the two short excursions to Spinalonga and Kritsa. Each can easily be visited in a half day.

SPINALONGA

Spinalonga is the **fortified islet** in the bay off Elounda. The Venetians built another of their fortresses there in 1579, and it enjoyed the distinction of being their final outpost on Crete, not taken over by the Turks until 1715. When the Cretans took possession in 1903, it was turned into a leper colony, but this ended after World War II, and now Spinalonga has become a major tourist attraction. Boats depart regularly from both Ághios Nikólaos harbor and Elounda as well as from certain hotels.

KRITSA

Although a walk through Spinalonga can resonate as a byway of history, if you had time to make only one of these short trips, we advise making the short (8 miles/12km) trip up into the hills behind Ághios Nikólaos to the village of Kritsa and its 14th-century **Church of Panaghia Kera.** Not only is the church of some interest architecturally but its **frescoes,** dating from the 14th and 15th centuries, are regarded as among the jewels of Cretan-Byzantine art. They have been restored, but the power emanates from the original work. Scenes depict the life of Jesus, the life of his mother, Mary, and the Second Coming. Guides can be arranged for in Ághios Nikólaos at any travel agency or the Town Information Office. After seeing the church, go into the village of Kritsa itself and enjoy the view and the handicrafts for sale.

KATO ZAKROS & GOURNIA

This is a full day's excursion of interest primarily to archaeology buffs. The distance to Kato Zakros from Ághios Nikólaos is some 74 miles (118km), which means traveling 150 miles in one day if you want to be back in Ághios Nikólaos the same night. In terms of mileage, that isn't so much, but it represents about five hours total driving time. Many do it—a reasonably early start gets you there late morning; you do the site, then a leisurely lunch; a stop at Gournia on the way back; and you're in Aghios Nikalaos by early evening.

Why exert yourself? Well, Kato Zakros is the fourth of the **major Minoan palace sites,** with a number of interesting elements, including the cistern and fountain, well within the palace proper and a paved road leading to the port. It's also the site where several stunning works in the Iráklion Museum were found.

But above all, it's the story of the site itself that may inspire you: A few Minoan remains had been found here in 1901, but it was dismissed as a minor site. Then in 1961, an American couple, Mr. and Mrs. Leon Pomerance, read in the guide to the Iráklion Museum a statement by the then curator, Nicholaos Platon, that there were still major Minoan remains to be dug on Crete. The Pomerances guaranteed Platon financial support to prove this, and he began digging at Kato Zakros in 1962. The digging, and discoveries, have never ceased (although all three principals are now dead). So a visit to Kato Zakros pays tribute to both an ancient people and a modern fairy tale.

As for Gournia, this, too, has an American connection. It lies on a hill some 13 miles (20km) from Ághios Nikólaos. You get your best view of it as you drive beyond it on the road to Kato Zakros. It's another **Minoan site,** but unlike the other famous ones, it was not a palace but an apparently ordinary small town. It has a so-called "palace" at the pinnacle, but this is really more like a governor's mansion. You wander up and down the narrow streets, marveling at the cramped quarters, realizing that the Minoans must have been rather small people. Gournia is an antidote to the image of all Minoans living in the palatial splendor of Knossos or Phaestos. The original excavation (1901–04) was directed by a young American woman, Edith Boyd (later Hawes), the first woman to head a major archaeological dig.

The Cyclades 8

by John Bozman

Still spiraling around Délos, the spiritual, cultural, and commercial center of the eastern Mediterranean in ancient times, the Cyclades (*Kykládes*, meaning "Circling Islands") are the best known and most popular of the Aegean islands. Most look like rather barren piles of rocks jutting out of the clear blue sea, with small harbors and hills topped with little villages of asymmetrical white sugar-cube houses, labyrinthine lanes, and handsome churches. As a whole, they are the single most enjoyable group of islands to visit, particularly by ferry, cruise ship, or yacht.

Those islands nearest Athens are more visited by weekending and vacationing Greeks than by foreign tourists, though Ándros is starting to see more international visitors. **Tínos,** often referred to as the "Lourdes of Greece," is the most important destination for religious pilgrimage for Greeks, but it also has much to offer foreign visitors. **Mýkonos** is so famous for its excellent beaches, sophisticated amenities, and swinging social life that it needs no introduction, but be warned that it's expensive and reservations are necessary in the summer. **Páros** has similar attractions, including nightlife and excellent windsurfing, and it's nearly as overrun in the summer, though it remains both less intense and less expensive. **Náxos** is the largest and most fertile of the Cyclades, largely self-sufficient and not so dependent on tourism, which is therefore less prominent.

Íos is the get-drunk capital of the Aegean, if not the entire Mediterranean, and strictly for the young in summer. Rugged Amorgós, the easternmost of the Cyclades, was off the beaten path until it recently became popular with backpackers, who overwhelm its meager resources. Anáfi, the most southerly, just isn't ready for tourists (for some idea of its architecture and people, visit Anafiótika on the southern slope of the Acropolis in Athens). **Santoríni** is the spectacular remains of an ancient volcanic eruption, one of the most recognized and admired islands in the world, and still a thrill to visit. There's simply too little to see and do on Síkinos. **Folégandros** is also quite spectacular, rather remote, and not yet on the map in most tourists' minds. **Mílos** is large and self-sufficient because of its mining industry, which also mars its interesting landscape; it's getting ready for big-time tourism, but doesn't yet have a lot to offer independent travelers. Sérifos has a fairly attractive port and a pretty hilltop Hóra, but it doesn't quite make our cut because of a significant mosquito problem and a lack of hospitality. **Sífnos** is close

The Cyclades

0   50km
30mi

N

ATTICA

A e g e a n

ÁNDROS
Gávrio
Bássi

S e a

KÉA
Kéa

Gyáros

TÍNOS
Koúmaros
Falatados ➊
Tínos

MÝKONOS
Áyios
Stéphanos ➋
Platís Yialós

SÝROS Áno Sýros
Ermoúpolis
Possidón
DÉLOS

Kýthnos
KYTHNOS

Serfopoúla

SÉRIFOS
Sérifos
Livadi

Náxos
(Hóra) ➌ ➎
Náoussa

Apóllonas
Kóronos

Donoússa
Donoússa

Parikía ➍ Aliki
Artemóna
SÍFNOS Kástro
Kamáres Apollonía
Platis Yialós

PÁROS
Antíparos

Ay. Anna
Ay. Prokópios

NÁXOS

Koufoníssi
Káros

AMORGÓS
Lefkés

Iráklia

Mílos
Adámas

MÍLOS

Yialós

Hóra
ÍOS

Folégandros

SANTORÍNI (THÍRA)

Ia
Fira ➏
Kamári
➐
Embório Périssa

Anáfi

GREECE
Athens ★
The
Cyclades

Akrotíri ➐	Panayía
Kamári Beach ➏	Evanyelístria ➊
Kolymbíthres Beach ➌	Panayía Paraportianí
Panayía	Church ➋
Ekatontapylianí ➍	Temple of Apollo ➎

Ferry Route
〰️ - - - - -

enough to Pireaus to be popular with Athenians, and foreign tourists are discovering it, but it still retains its quiet charm and remains both relaxed and relaxing. Kýthnos and Kéa have no archaeological sites or museums, no good restaurants and hotels, and they're not especially attractive. **Sýros** is the most populous of the Cyclades, and handsome old Ermoúpolis is the administrative capital of the Cyclades; thus the island is not exactly a backwater, but not many foreign tourists visit yet, making it a refreshing contrast to its neighbors.

More than any other island group, the Cyclades are affected by the winds, and you'll want to keep this in mind while planning your trip. In the spring the sirocco brings warm, dry air off the Sahara desert and warms the islands, which are green from the winter rains, and dries them to their usual summer sere. In July the *meltémi*, cool winds off the Russian steppes, arrive, sometimes playing havoc with excursion and hydrofoil schedules. The larger ferries can stand up to the winds and still usually run; though precautions against seasickness must be taken by those susceptible to the malady. In the winter the strong north *voriás* make sea travel impossible much of the time, and many of the islands are nearly deserted for more comfortable accommodations and company in Athens.

Water continues to be a problem on several of the islands, particularly Santoríni. Even on the greener and better-watered islands, such as Náxos, you should conserve water and be prepared for shortages. Local tap water is almost always potable, though you may prefer the better-tasting bottled variety.

1 Tínos

87 nautical miles (161km) SE of Piraeus and 66 nautical miles (122km) SE of Rafína

Tínos is the most important place of religious pilgrimage in Greece, and yet it remains one of the least commercial of the Cyclades and a joy to visit for that very reason. Besides the famous church of Panayía Evangelístria, where the miraculous icon that excites so much religious interest is enshrined, Tínos has an attractive port town, a lovely green landscape with hundreds of white Venetian dovecotes for which the island is also famous, some beautiful beaches, charming traditional villages, and friendly people who don't speak much English but make up for it with warm hospitality.

ESSENTIALS

GETTING THERE   There are several ferries to Tínos daily from Piraeus and three daily from Rafína; schedules should be confirmed with **Tourist Information** in Athens (☎ 01/143), the **Piraeus Port Authority** (☎ 01/45-11-311), or the **Rafína Port Authority** (☎ 0294/25-200). **Ilio Lines** (☎ 01/42-24-772 in Athens or 0294/22-888 in Rafína) has hydrofoil service from Rafína. Several times a day, ferries connect Tínos with nearby Ándros, Mýkonos, and Sýros. There are several daily excursions from Tínos to Mýkonos and Délos, costing about Dr 10,000 ($42.55).

There are two piers in Tínos harbor, the newer one 600 meters north of the main one; be sure to find out from which your ship will depart. The **Tínos Port Authority** can be reached at **0283/22-348.**

VISITOR INFORMATION   **Tínos Mariner** (☎ 0283/23-193) provides information and has a good map of the island. The **Nicholas Information Center** (☎ **0283/24-142;** fax 0283/24-049) is at Odós Evangelístria 24, the main market street to the left and perpendicular to the port. It's open 6:30am to midnight and provides information, sells ferry tickets, and has rooms for rent. The **tourist police** have an office opposite the bus station (☎ **0283/22-255**).

GETTING AROUND   The taxi stand and bus station are on the harbor. KTEL has an office there; bus schedules are erratic. On the harbor are several shops renting mopeds (from about Dr 4,000 or $17 a day); **Nicholas** (☎ **0283/24-142**) and **Moto Mike** (☎ **0283/23-304**) are reliable. Cars can be rented from about Dr 15,500 ($66) a day with insurance.

FAST FACTS   There are several banks and travel agents along the waterfront. The **telephone office** (**OTE**), open 8am to midnight, is on the main street leading up to the church of Panayía Evangelístria at Odós Lazárou Dóchou. The **first-aid center** can be reached at **0283/22-210**.

WHAT TO SEE & DO

The **church of Panayía Evangelístria** ("Our Lady of Good Tidings"), the "Lourdes of Greece" draws thousands of pilgrims every year from all over Greece seeking the aid of a miraculous icon enshrined there. In 1822, during the War of Independence, Pelayía, a nun at the Kehrovouníou Convent, had a dream that an icon was buried on a nearby farm. She summoned her neighbors to help excavate, and they soon discovered the foundation of a Byzantine church, where a workman found a gold icon, said to be the work of St. Luke, depicting the Annunciation of the Virgin Mary, which is believed to have been sent by her to cure the faithful. Work was begun immediately on the elegant neoclassical church that can be seen today.

Almost any day of the year you can see people, particularly elderly women, with padded arms and knees, crawling from the port up the street to church in supplication, usually, it's said, to ask for intercession for a loved one. Some will find this a disturbing sight, and they should concentrate on the colorful stalls that line Leofóros Megaloháris ("Avenue of Great Grace"), the street leading up from the left of the port, which sell icons, incense, candles (up to six feet tall), gold and silver medallions, and *támata* (tin, silver, and gold votives), or hurry on up to the church, which is a spectacle well worth the short climb. (The church and its galleries are open from noon to 6pm year-round, and from 8am to 8pm in the summer. Men must wear long pants and shirts with sleeves, women must wear skirts and sleeves to enter.)

Grand marble stairs lead up into the church itself, which is filled with the offerings of those who have received the miracle or blessing they sought. Hundreds of lamps overhead light a truly fantastic array of gold, silver, precious jewels, and thousands of flickering candles. The object of adoration is to the left of the central aisle, but even if you manage to make your way through all the faithful you won't be able to see the icon itself, because it's encased in gold, diamonds, and pearls. (Reproductions, however, can be seen in various shops.) Services are held regularly throughout the day, and if you haven't yet attended an orthodox service and experienced its resonance and mystery, you might wait for one. Notice the marble; the white is Parian, of course, and the green-veined is from Tínos itself and justifiably prized.

Below the church is the crypt where the icon was found, surrounded by smaller chapels; the spot in the rocks where the icon lay is now lined with silver. The crypt is always crowded, but especially so in August, with Greek parents and children in white waiting to be baptized with water from the font, which is filled with gold and silver offerings. The water from the spring here is believed to be both curative and beneficent. The church is surrounded by various museums, galleries, and hostels for the pilgrims. One of the galleries contains 19th-century works of religious art, including many from the Ionian school, as well as paintings said to be by Rembrandt and Rubens.

Another houses Byzantine icons. One museum contains sculpture by a famous local artist, Lázarou Sóchou, and above it another contains works by other Greek sculptors, such as Vitális and Ioánnis Voúlgaros. You could spend half a day and not take in half the sights.

The **Archaeological Museum,** open Tuesday through Sunday 8am to 3pm, admission Dr 500 ($2.10), is about half a block below the church. The small collection includes finds from the ancient sanctuary of Thesmophoríon, near Exóbourgo. Some red clay vases from the 8th century B.C. are particularly prized. In the museum's courtyard are marble sculptures, including a sundial, from the 2nd century A.D. found at the Sanctuary of Poseidon and Amphitrite (his wife) at Kiónia.

The town is a pleasant place for a ramble, with a **flea market** area behind the port, up the street from Ferry Boat Naias office. Besides a huge variety of candles and religious paraphernalia, you'll find local embroidery, weavings, and the delicious local nougat, as well as *loukoúmia* (Turkish delight) from Sýros. Several ceramic shops on the waterfront, **Margarita, Bernardo,** and **Manina,** have interesting pottery, jewelry, and copper ware at moderate prices.

Harris Prassas Ostria-Tínos, Odós Evangelístrias 20 (☎ **0283/23-893;** fax 0283/ 24-568), is particularly recommended for his fine collection of gold and silver jewelry in contemporary, Byzantine, and classical styles, silver work, and beautiful religious objects, including reproductions of the miraculous icon. Harris is friendly, informative, famous for the quality of his work, and he accepts credit cards.

Those interested in authentic hand-painted icons should find the small shop of **Maria Vryoni,** the first left from the port off the street up to the church, the second shop on the left. Maria spends at least a week on each of her works of art, so they aren't cheap, costing up to Dr 50,000 ($212) for a large one, but they are superb, and she accepts credit cards.

The famous **Venetian dovecotes,** many dating from the 17th century, are scattered throughout the island. You can see several, as well as the **Temple of Poseidon and Amphitrite,** by taking the coastal road 2 kilometers west of town to **Kiónia** ("Columns"), a pleasant 30-minute hike past the Hotel Aigli. There are two dovecotes behind the tennis courts of the large luxury resort complex, the Tínos Beach Hotel, and past the hotel on the beach road you'll find the scant remains of the excavated temple.

A pleasant day trip from Tínos to **Pírgos** will take you through many island villages to the region where the green marble is quarried and local sculptors work. Buses leave the port five times a day for the one-hour trip beginning at 6:30am; check the schedule at the stop in Pírgos for the return time. From Pírgos you can go to **Pánormos,** from where the marble was once exported, where there is a nice beach and rooms to let. Dovecote devotees may want to include a detour along the way, to **Tarambádos** and **Smardákito,** which has some of the most elaborate ones.

The scenery above Tínos town in the vicinity of the Venetian fortress of **Exóbourgo** is particularly appealing. The fortress itself was ruined by the Turks, but it still contains the remains of some houses, three churches, and a fountain, as well as a superb view. **Tripótamos** is known for its lovely architecture. **Xinára** is a Catholic village, seat of the island's bishop. **Loutró** is an especially attractive village with a 17th-century Jesuit monastery that is now an Ursuline convent and carpet-making school.

You can continue on to **Krókos,** which has a couple of nice restaurants, and from where it's an hour hike to one of the highest and most remote villages on the island, **Vólakas,** known for its excellent baskets. You can also continue on another 5 kilometers to **Kómi,** where an unimproved road leads down to the island's best beaches at **Kolimbíthres,** where there's a taverna and some rooms to let.

There's a bus to the **Convent of Kehrovouníou,** one of the largest in Greece and still active, where Pelayía dreamed of the icon. You can visit her former cell and see her mummified head. Nearby **Dío Horiá** and **Arnádos** are both well worth a visit.

BEACHES

Beach enthusiasts may want to head east of town. The first beach, about 2 kilometers out, is busy **Áyios Fokás,** which has the very nice little **Golden Beach Hotel** (☎ **0283/22-579**), with a lovely garden and clean comfortable doubles from about Dr 10,500 ($44.70). A little further east is the place called **Vyrócastro,** which has the walls of an ancient town and a ruined Hellenistic tower. The nearby beach of **Livádi** is rather exposed to the wind and waves. From Tínos, there is bus service on the south beach road (usually four times a day) to the resort of **Pórto,** 8 kilometers to the east. Porto has two beaches and several hotel complexes but little in the way of eateries, so you may want to bring a picnic. If the beaches at Pórto are crowded, walk back southwest to the beach at **Xerés,** which is less developed.

WHERE TO STAY

Unless you have hotel reservations, you shouldn't plan an overnight visit to Tínos during important religious holidays, especially March 25 (Feast of the Annunciation) and August 15 (Feast of the Assumption)—though a summer night under the stars wouldn't be too high a price to pay for such an experience—and on summer weekends.

If you avoid the religious holidays and summer weekends, you'll have no trouble finding a room. Because it has been a popular destination for travelers of modest means for more than a century, the town has plenty of economical accommodations. People will offer you their rooms, more politely than on some of the other Cyclades, at the landing. **O Yánnis** (☎ **0283/22-515**), next to the Hotel Oceanis on Odós Gízi, has large, homey, high-ceilinged rooms with clean shared facilities for about Dr 5,000 ($21.25) for a double. Strátis Keladítis, at the **Nicholas Information Center** (☎ **0283/24-142**), Odós Evangelístrias 24, has plain rooms upstairs for about Dr 4,800 ($20.40) for a double with shared facilities.

Avra Hotel. Tínos town, 842 00 Tínos. ☎ **0283/22-242.** 14 rms (all with bath). Dr 8,200 ($34.90) single, Dr 12,300 ($52.35) double. No credit cards.

This century-old hotel, east (right) on the waterfront, has simple, spacious, high-ceilinged rooms off a tiled plant-filled courtyard.

Ⓢ **Hotel Eleana.** Platía Ierarchón, Tínos town, 842 00 Tínos. ☎ **0283/22-561.** 17 rms (all with bath). Dr 6,600 ($28.10) single, Dr 8,600 ($36.60) double. V.

Tínos's best value hotel is about 400 meters from the port, up the street from the right of the Hotel Posidónios. It doesn't have harbor views, but the rooms are large, comfortable, clean, and quiet. The management makes up for a lack of proficiency in English with friendly hospitality.

Porto Tango Hotel. Áyios Ioánnis, Pórto, 842 00 Tínos. ☎ **0283/24-441.** Fax 0283/24-416. 57 rms, 7 suites (all with bath). A/C, MINIBAR, TV, TEL. Dr 13,250–Dr 22,500 ($57.45–$95.75) single, Dr 23,800–Dr 30,500 ($101.30–$129.80). AE, EU, MC, V.

The island's most luxurious resort has all the amenities of a major resort complex, including a large swimming pool, tennis court, gym, sauna, and water sports on the nearby beach.

Tinion Hotel. Odós Alaváno 1, Tínos town, 842 00 Tínos. ☎ **0283/22-261.** 20 rms (all with bath). Dr 10,500 ($44.70) single; Dr 13,250 ($56.30). EU, MC.

This venerable old hotel to the right from the harbor retains its old-world charm with marble floors, dark polished wood, and lace curtains. The rooms have high ceilings, old tile work floors, and large terraces.

WHERE TO DINE

Tínos has a number of very good restaurants, probably because most of their customers are other Greeks, who won't settle for second-rate food. As usual, you should avoid harbor-front joints, where food is generally inferior and service can be rushed.

Leftéris. Harborfront, Tínos town. ☎ **0283/23-013.** Appetizers Dr 170–Dr 900 (70¢–$3.85), main courses 800-2,600 ($3.40–$11.05). No credit cards. Daily 11am–midnight. GREEK.

On the harbor front, look for a blue sign over an arched entrance that leads to a large courtyard decorated with fish plaques. The menu is large and varied; it offers grilled sea bass, veal stifádo, and dolmádes (stuffed grape leaves in lemon sauce). There's plenty of room for dancing, and the waiters often demonstrate and urge diners to join them.

Ⓢ O Kipós (The Garden). Tínos town. ☎ **0283/22-838.** Appetizers Dr 160–Dr 800 (69¢–$3.40), Dr 900–Dr 2,400 ($3.85–$10.20). No credit cards. Daily noon–midnight. GREEK.

Take the first street to the right of the Posidónion Hotel and wander inland through the quiet residential area, about four lanes, until you see the bright lights of this small, friendly taverna.

Peristeriónas (Dovecote). Odós Paksimádi Fraiskóu 12, Tínos town. ☎ **0283/23-425.** Appetizers Dr 500–Dr 1,200 ($2.15–$5.10), main courses Dr 1,600–Dr 2,400 ($6.80–$10.20). No credit cards. Daily noon–3pm and 7–11:30pm. GREEK.

This restaurant, decorated like one on the island's famous dovecotes, is found on a small lane uphill behind the Lido Hotel; its outdoor tables fill the walkway. It serves excellent grilled meats and fish, and delicious marathotiganítes (vegetable fritters with onions and dill).

TÍNOS TOWN AFTER DARK

As you surely already suspect, wild nightlife is not found on the island, but there's a small enclave of music bars off the left of the port, including **Argonautis,** the **Sibylla Bar,** and **George's Place,** which features Greek dancing.

2 Mýkonos

96 nautical miles (177km) SE of Pireaus, 81 nautical miles (150km) SE of Rafína

Jet-setty Mýkonos is one of the smaller of the Cyclades (only 29 square miles or 75 square kilometers) and yet the busiest. A permanent population of 15,000 hosts an average of 800,000 visitors annually. It's an arid rocky island, with excellent beaches, attractive architecture, numerous and often expensive accommodations, good restaurants, chic shopping, and wild nightlife. Yet it somehow manages to hold on to much of its charm and self-respect as well as the continuing interest of international visitors of every kind. Millionaires have little choice but close contact with bottom-budget backpackers in the narrow lanes of Hóra. (*Hóra* means "chief town," and many island capitals are called by this name, the name of the island, and sometimes even by another, usually from the time when the Venetians had control of many of the islands.)

Note: We strongly recommend that you not plan a stay on Mýkonos without reservations in the high season, unless you enjoy sleeping out of doors.

ESSENTIALS

GETTING THERE   By Plane   Olympic Airways has seven flights daily (10 in the high season) between Mýkonos and Athens. Olympic has one flight daily between Mýkonos and Iráklio, Crete; Rhodes; and Santoríni. Olympic flies three times a week between Mýkonos and Híos, Lésvos, and Sámos. It's difficult to get a seat on any of these flights, so make reservations early and reconfirm them at the Olympic office in Athens (☎ **01/96-16-161**) or Mýkonos (☎ **0289/22-490**).

By Ferry   From Piraeus, the **Ventouris Lines** (☎ 01/42-82-900 in Piraeus) has departures for Mýkonos at least once daily, usually at 8am, with a second in the afternoon in the summer. (Check schedules in Athens with the Tourist Police at ☎ **01/171** or the Port Authority at ☎ **01/45-11-311.**) From Rafína, **Strintzis Lines** has daily ferry service to Mýkonos; schedules can be checked at **0294/25-200.** There is daily ferry connection between Mýkonos and Ándros, Páros, Sýros, and Tínos. Five to seven times a week, ferries connect Mýkonos with Náxos and Íos. Ferries sail four times a week between Mýkonos and Iráklio, Crete. Several times a week there's ferry service from Mýkonos to Kos and Rhodes. Twice weekly, there are sailings to Ikaría, Sámos, Skiáthos, Skýros, and Thessaloníki.

   Sea and Sky Travel (☎ **0289/22-853;** fax 0289/24-753) on Taxi Square represents the Strintzis, Ilio, and Agapitos ferry lines; this travel agency also offers excursions to Délos. The **Veronis Agency** (☎ **0289/22-687;** fax 0289/23-763), also on Taxi Square, offers ferry information.

By Hydrofoil   Ilio Lines (☎ **01/42-24-772** in Athens or 0294/22-888 in Rafína) has daily hydrofoil service to Mýkonos from Rafína. Hydrofoil (catamaran) service from Mýkonos to Crete, Íos, Náxos, Páros, and Santoríni is often irregular. For information call the **Piraeus Port Authority** (☎ **01/45-11-311**), **Rafína Port Authority** (☎ **0294/23-300**), or the **Mýkonos Port Authority** (☎ **0289/22-218**).

VISITOR INFORMATION   The **Mýkonos Tourist Office** (☎ **0289/23-990**) is on the west side of the port near the excursion boats to Délos. Look for a copy of the free *Mýkonos Summertime* magazine. **Sea and Sky Travel** (☎ **0289/22-853;** fax 0289/24-753) on Taxi Square represents the Strintzis, Ilio, and Agapitos ferry lines; the agency changes money and offers excursions to Délos. The **Veronis Agency** (☎ **0289/22-687;** fax 0289/23-763), also on Taxi Square, offers information, safekeeping of baggage, and other services.

GETTING AROUND   One of the best things to happen to Mýkonos was the government decree that made Hóra an architectural landmark and prohibited motorized traffic from its streets. You will see a few small delivery vehicles, but the only way to get around town is to walk. Much of the rest of the island is served by a good transportation system.

By Bus   Mýkonos has one of the best organized bus systems in the Greek islands. Buses run frequently, on schedule, and cost Dr 200 (85¢) to Dr 800 ($3.40) one way. There are two bus stations in Hóra. The **north station** is near the middle of the harbor below the Leto Hotel. From there, buses leave for Toúrlos, Áyios Stéfanos, the northwest coast hotels, the inland village of Áno Méra, and the far east coast beaches of Elía, Kaló Livádi, and Kalafátis. Schedules are posted, though subject to change, and buses usually leave when they're full. Ask the driver when there will be bus service back to Hóra from your destination.

   The **south station** is about a 10-minute walk from the harbor, near the Olympic Airways office; follow the helpful blue signs. From this stop, buses leave for the airport, Áyios Ioánnis, Órnos, Psárou, and Platís Yalós. There are posted schedules, though buses often leave as soon as they're full.

By Boat   Caïques (skiffs) to Super Paradise, Agrári, and Elía depart from the town harbor every morning, weather permitting. Caïques to Paradise, Super Paradise, Agrári, and Elía leave from Platís Yalós every morning, weather permitting. (Caïque service is almost continuous during the high season, and they also depart from Órnos Bay.)

Excursion boats to Délos depart every day from the west side of the harbor near the tourist office at 9am. (For more information see a travel agent; guided tours are available.)

By Car and Moped   Rental cars and Jeeps are available from travel agents for about Dr 22,500 ($95.75) per day, including full insurance, during the high season, and substantially less at other times if you bargain. Mopeds are available from shops near both bus stations, with a better selection beyond the south bus station. Expect to pay about Dr 3,500 to Dr 11,000 ($14.90 to $46.80) a day, depending on engine size, during the high season. The roads on the island can sometimes be treacherous.

Parking   If you park in town or in a no-parking area, the police will remove your license plates, and you, not the rental office, will have to find the police station and pay a steep fine to get them back.

By Taxi   Getting a taxi in Hóra is easy; walk to Taxi (Mavro) Square, near the statue, and join the line. There's a notice board that gives rates for each destination for both high and low seasons. You can also call **0289/22-400.** For late hours and out-of-town service, call **0289/23-700.**

FAST FACTS: MÝKONOS

Area Code   The telephone area code for Mýkonos is **0289.**

Currency Exchange   The **Commercial Bank** and the **National Bank** of Greece are conveniently located on the harbor a couple of blocks west of Taxi Square, both open from 8am to 2pm and 6 to 8:30pm Monday through Friday. The National Bank is open for exchange only on Saturday from 9am to 12:30pm and 5:30 to 8:30pm, and on Sunday from 5:30 to 8:30pm. Traveler's checks can also be cashed at the post office, as well as at many travel agents and hotels, at less-than-bank rates.

Hospitals   The **Mýkonos Health Center** (☎ **0289/23-944**) handles minor medical complaints. The **Mýkonos Hospital** (☎ **0289/23-994**) offers 24-hour emergency service and is open for general visits from 9am to 1pm and 5 to 10pm.

Police   The **tourist police** (☎ **0289/22-482**) are on the west side of the port near the ferries to Délos. The local police (☎ **0289/22-235**) are behind the grammar school.

Post Office   The post office is on the east side of the harbor near the Port Police; it's open 7:30am to 2pm Monday through Friday.

Telephones   The **OTE** office (☎ **0289/22-499**) is on the east side of the harbor beyond the Hotel Leto; it's open daily from 7:30am to 10pm.

WHAT TO SEE & DO

You'll be relieved to learn that the streets of **Hóra,** or Mýkonos town, were designed purposely to confuse pirates, so your own confusion will be completely understandable. As you get off the ferry you can see the main square across the harbor beyond the small town beach and a cluster of buildings; we refer to it as **Taxi Square,** though it's officially called **Platía Mandó Mavroyénous,** after the island's heroine, who lead a local resistance to successfully repulse an invading Turkish force during the War for Independence, then took her forces on the offensive in Évvia, Thessaly, and Turkey itself. Here you'll find several travel agents, kiosks, snack bars, and of course the town's taxi stand. You might want to buy a map from one of the kiosks; the one published by Stamatis Bozinakis (Dr 400/$1.70) is particularly good.

The "main" street, **Matoyánni** leads south off Taxi Square behind the church; it's narrow, but you can hardly miss it for the bars, boutiques, and restaurants. Several "blocks" along it you'll find a "major" crossroad, **Kaloyéra,** and by turning right you'll find several of the hotels and restaurants we recommend.

By continuing along Kaloyéra on into the maze you're sure to get pleasantly lost, and by bearing generally to the right you'll come out on the harbor again.

You can stroll along the waterfront beyond the excursion boats to Délos and the tourist office, and near the northwest corner you'll find the **Folk Art Museum.** It contains old artifacts and a re-created kitchen and bedroom with a big four-poster bed; it's open daily from 4 to 8pm, Sundays 5 to 8pm. Beyond the museum is the old Venetian **Kastro** and the most famous little church on the island, **Panayía Paraportianí** ("Our Lady of the Port"). This is a whitewashed asymmetrical joining of four smaller chapels in a style variously called vernacular, folk, or Cycladic, because it defies categorization. The church is a favorite subject of photographers and artists because of the endless variations of light and shadow that play upon it. (The island claims to have nearly 400 churches, and some people say it needs more.)

Beyond this charming little church is the quarter known as **Little Venice,** officially called **Alefkánda,** a neighborhood of mansions built right on the water, many of them now converted into fashionable bars prized for their sunset views. Along **Ayíon Anaryíron** you'll find some of the island's best shopping for art and crafts; and after several blocks, you'll reach the **Greek Orthodox Cathedral** and, to its right, the smaller **Roman Catholic Cathedral.** The famous windmills of **Káto Mýli** crown the hill above and can be easily reached.

By continuing on up the main street, Matoyánni, past Kaloyéra, you'll soon come to another major street leading off to the right, **Énoplon Dinaméon,** and the neighborhood called **Tría Pigádia** ("Three Wells"). Local legend says that if a virgin drinks from all three of the wells she is sure to find a husband, but today she is more likely to contract a disease. On the left is the grammar school, and on the right the **Nautical Museum,** which contains models of ancient ships, nautical paintings and prints, and old coins. It's open daily in the summer 10:30am to 1pm; admission is Dr 400 ($1.70). Next door is **Lena's House,** a 19th-century mansion in which the furnishings, housewares, utensils, and needlework of Léna Scrivanoú are displayed; it's open from 7 to 9pm. The next major street is **Mitropóleos;** a right will take you back to the harbor and a left will take you into the neighborhood called **Laka,** toward the south side of town.

The **Archaeology Museum** (☎ 0289/22-325) is on the north side of town beyond the OTE, across from the bus stop. It contains a display of ceramic vases dating from 2,500 B.C.; gravestones and funerary jewelry recovered from the nearby island of Rhénia, which served as the cemetery of Délos; a large 7th-century B.C. storage jar with Trojan war reliefs; and a Parian marble statue of Hercules. It's open daily except Tuesday from 9am to 3:30pm, Sunday and holidays 10am to 3pm; admission is Dr 600 ($2.55).

We don't want to be unduly negative about **shopping** in Hóra, especially as it's such a prominent possibility and the prices are sometimes lower than they are in similar boutiques in Athens. (Greece is really not the place to buy designer clothing, if you care about selection and value.) Our chief complaint is that local sales techniques are state-of-the-art sharp, and people are often pressured or charmed into making purchases they later regret. If you will be visiting less-expensive islands, such as Náxos, you should postpone purchasing leather goods, ceramics, and textiles, little of which is manufactured locally.

The one thing Mýkonos does have in spades is fine jewelry, not at bargain prices of course, but skillfully handcrafted in a variety of designs, some of them unique. The best-known jeweler is **Ilias Lalaounis,** Odós Polykandrióti 14 (☎ **0289/22-444**), near the taxi station, which has an international reputation for superb craftsmanship and design, especially in classical, Byzantine, and natural motifs. **Délos Dolphins,** Matoyánni at Énoplon Dimaméon (☎ **0289/22-765**), specializes in copies of museum pieces. **Mýkonos Gold,** on Áyios Efthímios (☎ **0289/22-649**), in Little Venice, specializes in traditional Mykonian designs. **Vildiridis,** Matoyánni 12 (☎ **0289/ 23-245**), has designs based on ancient jewelry as well as the very latest styles.

Mono Ena ("Only One") **Center for Contemporary Art,** Odós Koúzi Yorgoúli 43 (☎ **0289/26-868**), behind the Orthodox Cathedral, has works of art by well-known and newer Greek artists, including paintings, sculptures, engravings, and ceramics. **The Studio** (no phone), left off Matoyánni at the Vengera Bar and a couple of blocks up, features neo-Byzantine mosaics, fantastic painted-wood objects, and washable T-shirt art. Works of culinary art can be found at **Skaropoulos,** on Matoyánni (☎ **0289/24-983**), including almond sweets such as *amygdalotá* and almond biscuits, claimed to be a favorite of Winston Churchill.

To work off the extra calories and get your body ready for the beach, visit the **Bodywork Gym** (no phone), near Alexis Snack Bar off Taxi Square.

The famous pelicans can usually be found along the port, and there is an article on them in *Summertime Mýkonos* for those who want to know more.

The only other town on Mýkonos is **Áno Méra,** 4 miles (7km) east of Hóra near the center of the island, a fairly easy walk or a quick bus ride from the north station. A trip to Áno Méra is especially recommended to those who are interested in religious sites. The **Monastery of Panayía Tourlianí** is southeast of town; it was begun in 1580 and has a handsome carved steeple. Inside the church are a huge Italian baroque iconostatis (altar screen) with icons of the Cretan school, an 18th-century marble baptismal font, and a small museum containing liturgical vestments, needle-work, and wood carvings. Another kilometer southeast is the 12th-century **Monastery of Paleokástro** in one of the greenest spots on the island.

Áno Méra has the most traditional atmosphere on the island, with a fresh produce market on the main square selling excellent local cheeses, and it's the island's place of choice for Sunday brunch. It also has one of the best hotels on the island, the **Ano Mera Hotel** (☎ **0289/22-404;** fax 0289/24-814), with a pool, restaurant, and disco; doubles begin at about Dr 15,000 ($63.85).

BEACHES

For those who can't wait to hit the beach, the closest is **Megáli Ámmos** ("Big Sand"), about a 10-minute walk south of town, but don't be surprised if it's crowded and don't expect to see topless bathing here. The nearest to the north is 2 kilometers away at **Toúrlos,** though it's barely acceptable; another better but crowded one is 2 kilometers further north at **Áyios Stéphanos,** a major resort center with water sports.

We suggest you take a little time to research the subject, ask around as conditions change quickly on Mýkonos, and then catch the bus or a caïque to the beach of your choice. With close to a million visitors a year, the island doesn't have pristine or secluded beaches (except some not worth visiting), but there are those less crowded than others, as well as those suited to particular interests. We'll adopt a counterclock-wise order south from Hóra in discussing the island's beaches.

As you will notice in passing, Kórfos Bay is not especially pleasant, so the nearest possibility is **Áyios Ioánnis,** about a half-hour hike south of town—not recommended during the hotter months. It can be reached five or six times a day by bus from the south station. The village has a chapel and a lovely view of its bay, but its beach is too small and rocky to be recommended. **Órnos** is the first real possibility, and buses run hourly from the south station from 8am to 11pm. The town has a fair beach, a few acceptable tavernas, a number of overpriced rooms, and the **Lucky Divers Scuba Club** (☎ **0289/23-579**), which offers lessons as well as daily dive excursions. (Mýkonos offers unusual opportunities for scuba diving, possibly because its regulating agencies are lax, figuring damage has already been done.)

Platís Yialós is your best bet because, though the beach is likely to be crowded, the bus runs every 15 minutes from 8am to 8pm, then every 30 minutes until midnight during the summer. From here, you can catch a caïque to the more distant beaches of Paradise, Super Paradise, Agrári, and Elía. Nearby **Psaroú** is less overwhelmed by resort hotels and has a lovely pale-sand beach that you can actually see except in the high season. Its water sports facilities include the **Diving Center Psarou** (☎ **0289/23-579**), waterskiing, and windsurfing.

Paránga, further east, which can be reached easily by foot on an inland path from Platís Yialós, is a small cove popular with nudists and usually not too crowded.

It's only a few little semiprivate beaches further to **Paradise,** the island's most famous beach, which has regular bus as well as caïque service. This was the original nude beach of the island, which does not officially sanction nudism, though you wouldn't know that from all the flesh exposed on the crescent of fine pale gold sand. It remains a remarkably beautiful beach, despite the crowds and activity, with especially clear water, and it's still where the beautiful people look for each other.

Super Paradise (Plindri) is accessible only by a very poor road, footpath, or caïque, so it's less crowded. It's still predominantly gay and bare, but clothed sunbathing by heterosexuals is tolerated, and there's a cafeteria-style taverna with nonstop pop music and even some water sports facilities.

Further east across the little peninsula is **Agrári,** a lovely cove sheltered by lush foliage, with all states of dress common and a good little taverna.

Elía, a 45-minute caïque ride from Platís Yialós and the last regular stop, is one of the island's best and largest beaches with clean pale sand. It's usually one of the least crowded, though bus service from the north station via Áno Méra and accounts like this will probably soon put an end to that. If it gets too crowded, head back west to Agrári.

The next major beach is **Kaló Livádi,** which means "Good Pasture." In a farming valley, this beautiful beach is accessible by a scramble over the peninsula east from Elía and by bus from the north station in the summer. It even has a good restaurant. Further east, accessible by a very poor unpaved road, is the lesser known **Ayía Ánna,** which has a good sand beach.

The last resort area on the southern coast accessible by bus from the north station is at **Kalafáti.** This fishing village was once the port of the ancient citadel of Mýkonos, which dominated the little peninsula to the west. Today, Kalafáti is dominated by the large Aphrodite Beach Hotel complex. Several kilometers further east, accessible by a fairly good road from Kalafáti, is **Lía.** This beach has fine sand, clear water, bamboo wind breaks, and a small taverna.

The north coast beaches, except for sheltered **Pánormos Bay,** are too exposed to the meltémi winds and troubled by tar and litter to be considered among the choices for beach recreation. **Ftelía**—about 4 kilometers northwest of Áno Méra and only a 15-minute walk down from the road—is the only accessible choice. It's a good place for windsurfing because of its sandy bottom and the strong cross currents in its recessed cove. Further north, **Pánormos** has a very nice fine-sand beach that is one of the least crowded on the island, probably because it's still difficult to reach.

WHERE TO STAY

Greece's most popular resort destination seems to have developed every possible spot on the coast and on the roads from town, and yet there's still a shortage of desirable and affordable accommodations during the high season. If you arrive by ferry, you will be met by a throng of people hawking rooms, most of which are up the hill from Hóra and not especially pleasant. Accept one of these for one night only if you don't have a reservation and you're too exhausted for a lengthy search.

Many hotels are fully booked in advance by tour groups, others by their regular clientele, so we urge you to start making arrangements well in advance. Mýkonos is a much easier and more pleasant place to visit in the spring or fall. Hotel rates in April, May, and October are sometimes nearly half the quoted high-season rate. Those determined to visit the hottest spot during the hottest season should make reservations at least a month and if possible three months in advance. Most of the hotels we list below will accept reservations only if accompanied with a deposit equal to at least a third of the cost of your total stay, subject to penalty for cancellation, and even they will reserve their better rooms for past customers.

If a hotel doesn't respond to your query, you don't have any particular preferences for accommodations, or you just want to save the time and effort of making a booking yourself, contact the **Mýkonos Accommodations Center** (**MAC**), at Odós Énoplon Dinaméon at Malamatenias (in Tría Pigádia), 84600 Mýkonos (☎ **0289/ 23-160** or 0289/23-408; fax 0289/24-137). Its helpful multilingual staff will correspond, talk by phone, or meet with you to determine the best accommodation for your budget. They charge 15% of the rental or a Dr 5,000 ($21.30) minimum, a reasonable price for avoiding disappointment and frustration, especially in the high season. You can also contact the parent company, **Accommodation Centers of Greece,** Odós Voúlis 7, 10562 Athens (☎ **01/322-0000** or 01/322-3400; fax 01/ 24-137).

IN HÓRA

Expensive
Hotel Maria. Odós Kaloyéra 18, Hóra, 846 00 Mýkonos. ☎ **0289/24-212.** Fax 0289/ 24-213. 10 rms (all with bath). TEL. Including breakfast: Dr 26,000 ($110.65) double. V.

Kaloyéra is a busy pedestrian street, but this area remains fairly quiet because there are no bars or discos nearby. The rooms here are clean, modern, and comfortable, some with plenty of sunlight.

Hotel Matina. Odós Fournakíon 3, Hóra, 846 00 Mýkonos. ☎ **0289/22-387** or 0289/ 24-501. 14 rms (all with bath). Including breakfast: Dr 22,900 ($97.45) single, Dr 30,750 ($130.90) double. No credit cards.

Rooms are small but clean, modern, and inside a large garden that makes them especially quiet for their central location.

Moderate
Hotel Apollo. Paralía, Hóra, 846 00 Mýkonos. ☎ **0289/22-223.** 20 rms (8 with bath). Including breakfast: Dr 20,500 ($87.25) double with bath. No credit cards.

This harborside hotel, one of the island's oldest and best values, is a little worse for wear, but the management is friendly and the rooms are clean and comfortable.

Hotel Marios. Odós Kaloyéra 24, Hóra, 846 00 Mýkonos. ☎ **0289/22-704.** 12 rms (all with bath). A/C TEL TV. Including breakfast: Dr 22,100 ($94.05) single or double. No credit cards.

This quaint hotel has spotless doubles with dark wood-beamed ceilings and modern facilities, some with balconies overlooking a garden.

Hotel Phílippi. Odós Kaloyéra 32, Hóra, 846 00 Mýkonos. ☎ **0289/22-294** or 0289/
22-295. 12 rms (all with bath). Dr 19,900 ($84.70) double. No credit cards.

Each room in this homey little hotel is unique, so you may want to check yours out
before accepting it. The owner tends a lush garden that often provides flowers for her
son's restaurant, the elegant Phílippi's, which can be reached through the garden

PENSIONS & ROOMS TO LET IN & AROUND TOWN

There are a number of **pensions** and **rooms to let** in and around town. Many of
these are larger, more comfortable, and have better views than the older hotels. Most
of them don't serve breakfast, and some of them are quite a hike up the hill and not
in the most fashionable neighborhoods. Try the two we list below first. If the **Tourist
Office** (☎ 0289/23-900) is open, check with them to see what's available. If you
arrive without a reservation and a lot of luggage, you may want to stop at **Meridian**
(☎ **0289/24-702**), Platía Ayía Ánna (two blocks behind the post office, left before
you reach Taxi Square) to inquire about rooms. (You can leave your luggage in the
office and check the room out before you accept it.) If you aren't carrying much luggage, continue on through town following the blue arrows that direct you to Platís
Yialós to the south bus station, where there are several tour operators who usually have
an odd room or two that they're anxious to fill.

Maria and Mike Mitropia. Platía Laka, Hóra, 846 00 Mýkonos. ☎ **0289/23-528.** 20 rms
(13 with bath). Including breakfast: Dr 15,000 ($63.85) double without bath, Dr 17,200
($73.20) double with shower. V.

Tidy, comfortable rooms above Mike's locksmith shop on central Laka Square opposite the Mýkonos Market. Write or call to reserve one of their quiet, good-value
rooms.

⑤ Pension Stelios. Odós Apóllonos 9, Hóra, 846 00 Mýkonos. ☎ **0289/24-641.** 12 rms
(all with shower). Including breakfast: Dr 21,500 ($91.50) double. No credit cards.

Conveniently located near the ferry pier on the northeast end of the harbor, on the
hill above the OTE office. It's easily reached by broad stone steps above the road.
Rooms are clean, modern, with twin beds and balconies with good views.

ON THE EDGE OF TOWN

Most of the new hotel construction in town in recent years has been along the District Road (Odós Ayíou Ioánnou), which is the road that circles the older Hóra. There
also are new hotels along two other roads: the one that leads south to Platís Yialós
and that leading north to Áyios Stéphanos. All three areas have good views of Hóra
and the sea; they're easily accessible by car, and it's an easy 10-minute walk down to
the nightlife spots. Many of the newer places have a swimming pool, larger rooms,
private telephones, and balconies or patios.

Very Expensive

✪ Hotel Belvedere. Rohári, 846 00 Mýkonos. ☎ **0289/25-122** or 0289/25-125. Fax 0289/
25-126. 19 rms, 6 suites (all with bath). A/C MINIBAR TEL TV. Including American breakfast:
Dr 43,000 ($183) double, Dr 72,000 ($306.40) suite. AE, EU, DC, MC, V.

This brand-new hotel, just below the District Road and across from the School of
Fine Arts, is easily the finest anywhere near Hóra. It has large bathrooms with full
tubs, balconies overlooking the town and sea, and even fireplaces. Rooms are tastefully decorated in traditional island style and all have specially designed double doors
and windows for extra quiet. The courtyard contains a handsome pool, bar, and a
faithfully restored 1850 mansion, where a full American breakfast is served.

Expensive

Hotel Aegean. Tagoú, 846 00 Mýkonos. ☎ **0289/23-544** or 0289/22-869. Fax 0289/24-927. 28 rms (all with bath). TEL TV. Including breakfast: Dr 33,000 ($140.40) double, Dr 55,000 ($234) family room. AE, EU, MC, V.

This pleasant bungalow hotel is beyond the north bus stop above the road to Áyios Stéphanos. Rooms are large and comfortable. Some have sea views, others have views of the hills. The hotel has a good pool, transportation to and from the airport, and an attentive staff.

Hotel Edem. Áyios Loúkas, 846 00 Mýkonos. ☎ **0289/25-620** or 0289/22-774. Fax 0289/25-619. 24 rms (all with bath). TEL Including breakfast: Dr 23,400 ($99.60) single, Dr 30,000 ($127.65) double. AE, EU, DC, MC, V.

This new hotel is just above the District Road around the town, near the south bus station, and far enough away from town for quiet but close enough for convenience. The rooms are spacious, well furnished, and comfortable. All have balconies with views over the town and the sea. Some rooms have half bathtubs with shower curtains. A new pool should be ready soon.

Hotel Ilio Maris. Despotiká, 846 00 Mýkonos. ☎ **0289/23-755.** Fax 0289/24-309. 26 rms (all with bath). TEL TV. Including American breakfast: Dr 32,500 ($138.30) single, Dr 40,650 ($172.85) double. AE, V.

This attractive hotel, on a slope down from the south beach road, has balconied rooms with views of the pool and the sea beyond. The comfortable bar, lounge, and rooms are decorated with traditional Greek art—a stylish touch. Some rooms are air-conditioned.

Hotel Poseidon. Hóra, 846 00 Mýkonos. ☎ **0289/24-441.** Fax 0289/23-812. 41 rms (all with bath). Including breakfast: Dr 32,000 ($136.15) double. AE, EU, MC, V.

The Hotel Poseidon is located near the sea on the road to Órnos and has attractive surroundings, a pool, and particularly attentive service. The newer wing, Poseidon B, has air-conditioning.

K Hotels. P.O. Box 64, 846 00 Mýkonos. ☎ **0289/23-435** or 0289/23-431. Fax 0289/23-455. 135 rms (all with bath). A/C. Including breakfast: Dr 37,000 ($157.45) single, Dr 38,500 ($163.95) double. AE, EU, MC, V.

The four K Hotels (Kalypso, Kohili, Korali, and Kyma) form a complex just off the south beach road. Clean, modern, air-conditioned rooms are stacked on two levels to give views of the sea, hills, pool, or tennis courts. Each building has a small bar and breakfast lounge, and there's a common restaurant.

Kouros Apartment Hotel. Tagoú, 846 00 Mýkonos. ☎ **0289/25-381** or 0289/25-383. Fax 0289/25-379. 20 apts, 5 suites. TEL, TV. Including full American breakfast: Dr 34,000 ($144.70) double, Dr 54,500 ($231.80) suite. AE, DC, EU, MC, V.

This new apartment hotel just outside of town above the road to Áyios Stéphanos isn't as well known as the nearby Cavo Tagoo, but its rooms are much more spacious. All have kitchenettes, large modern bathrooms, and large balconies with sea views. Its pool has fresh water, and the staff is friendly. Infants younger than two stay free and children younger than 12 stay half price, so it's a good place for families.

AROUND THE ISLAND

There are hotels clustered around many of the more popular beaches on the island, but most people prefer to stay in town and commute to the beaches. Those who prefer the more serene beach scene can consider these suggestions:

There are private studios and simple pensions at both **Paradise** and **Super Paradise** beaches, but rooms are almost impossible to get, and prices more than double in July and August. Contact **MAC** (☎ **0289/23-160**), or for Super Paradise, **GATS Travel** (☎ **0289/22-404**) for information on the rooms they represent. The tavernas at each beach may also have suggestions.

At **Kalafáti,** the **Paradise Aphrodite Hotel** (☎ **0289/71-367**), has a large pool, two restaurants, and 150 rooms, which are a good value in May, June, and October, when a double costs about Dr 25,000 ($106.40).

Costa Ílios

This village over a small cove on Órnos Bay is one of the most beautiful spots on the island, with its own beach, swimming pool, children's pool, and tennis court. Private homes, in the traditional style, offer accommodations for two to six people, with twice-weekly maid service; these can be rented by the week for Dr 248,000 to Dr 375,000 ($1,055 to $1,595; DC, MC). Contact **LEMA,** Odós Makrás Stoás 1, 185 31 Piraeus (☎ **01/41-75-988** or 01/41-76-741; fax 01/41-79-310); or write Maria Koulalia, Cósta Ílios, 846 00 Mýkonos (☎ **0289/24-522**).

Órnos Beach

This beach on calm Órnos Bay is especially recommended for families because of its shallow water, water sports facilities, and good tavernas. The comfortable, family owned **Hotel Asteri** (☎ **0289/22-715**), near the beach, has doubles for Dr 26,000 ($110.65), breakfast included, no credit cards. The handsome new **Hotel Yiannaki** (☎ **0289/23-393;** fax 0289/24-628), 200 meters from the beach, has a large pool and doubles for Dr 26,900 ($114.45). **Club Mýkonos Hotel** (☎ **0289/22-600;** fax 0289/24-560) has doubles overlooking the water for Dr 38,000 ($161.70) and studios for Dr 41,700 ($177.45). Bungalow-style rooms are also offered. Breakfast and transportation to and from the airport is included; AE, EU, MC, and V accepted.

Platís Yialós

This sandy, crescent-shaped beach is just a 15-minute bus or a half-hour walk from Hóra. Its the caïque stop for shuttles to Paradise, Super Paradise, Agrári, and Elía beaches. There are several excellent hotels, some very similarly named.

✪ **Hotel Petassos Bay.** Platís Yialós, 846 00 Mýkonos. ☎ **0289/23-737.** Fax 0289/24-101. 21 rms (all with bath) A/C MINIBAR TEL. Dr 32,500 ($138.30) single, Dr 34,400 ($146.40) double. AE, MC, V.

Rooms here are large and comfortable with balconies overlooking the beach, which is less than 40 yards away. The hotel has a good-sized pool and sundeck, a Jacuzzi, gym, and sauna. It offers free round-trip transportation from the harbor or airport, safe deposit boxes, and laundry service. The new seaside restaurant has the best view in town and a large wine list, and it serves a big buffet breakfast. The gracious family that owns and operates this hotel—as well as the larger **Hotel Petassos Beach** next door and the **Petassos Town Hotel** in Hóra—and their well-trained and friendly multilingual staff win a star.

Hotel Petinos. Platís Yialós, 846 00 Mýkonos. ☎ **0289/22-127.** Fax 0289/23-680. 66 rms (all with bath). A/C TEL TV. Including breakfast: Dr 30,500 ($129.80). AE, EU, MC, V.

This hotel has good, clean, attractive rooms with large balconies. The owners also have the smaller, slightly more expensive **Nissaki Hotel** up the hill, as well as the more luxurious **Petinos Beach Hotel,** which has a pool and doubles for Dr 54,500 ($231.90).

Myconian Ambassador Hotel. P.O. Box 64, Platís Yialós, 846 00 Mýkonos. ☎ **0289/ 24-233** or **0289/24-166.** Fax 0289/24-233. 66 rms, 2 suites (all with bath). A/C MINIBAR TV TEL. Dr 57,200 ($243.50) double, Dr 88,900 ($378.30) suite. AE, EU, DC, MC, V.

The island's most luxurious hotel and biggest pool is on the hill above the beach. Rooms are large, tastefully furnished, and comfortable, all with sea views. Guests are offered a tennis court, sauna, Jacuzzi, gym, minigolf, squash court, and both room and laundry service. The hotel has a lobby bar, pool bar, snack bar, restaurant, TV room, and a large meeting hall.

Áyios Stéphanos

The popular resort of Áyios Stéphanos, about 2¹/₂ miles (4km) north of Hóra has a number of hotels, including the luxurious **Princess of Mýkonos** (☎ 0289/23-806; fax 0289/23-301), with 26 rooms, a pool, sauna, and Jacuzzi; doubles go for Dr 50,000 ($212.75). The **Hotel Artemis** (☎ 0289/22-345), near the beach and bus stop, has 23 rooms (all with bath); doubles cost Dr 21,000 ($89.35), breakfast included. The small **Hotel Mina** (☎ 0289/23-024), uphill behind the Artemis, has 15 doubles with bath for Dr 13,500 ($57.50). The **Hotel Panorama** (☎ 0289/ 22-337), about 80 meters from the beach, has 27 rooms (all with bath) doubles for Dr 19,400 ($82.40).

CAMPING

Paradise Camping. Paradise Beach, 846 00 Mýkonos. **0289/22-852.** Fax 0289/24-350. Dr 2,400 ($10.20) per person, Dr 1,500 ($6.40) for tent. MC, V.

Showers and transportation to and from the port and town are provided. There's a bar, restaurant, and minimarket. Rooms and bungalows are also available.

Paranga Beach Camping. Paranga Beach, 845 00 Mýkonos. ☎ **0289/24-578.** Dr 2,400 ($10.20) per person, Dr 1,500 ($6.40) for tent.

Newer than Paradise Camping, this nice facility provides cooking and laundry facilities, as well as showers and transportation.

WHERE TO DINE

Mýkonos has a number of excellent restaurants and plenty of fast food, most of it edible. As usual, the harborside joints are mostly expensive and mediocre. One of the best places for a snack is **Alexis Snack Bar** on Taxi Square; practically a landmark, it's open all hours and features a salad bar, as well as good inexpensive gyros and burgers. The **Andreas Pouloudis Bakery,** Odós Flórou Zuganéli 3 (☎ 0289/ 22-304), off Taxi Square in the little lane behind the gold store, has good cheese, spinach, and zucchini pies, as well as other baked treats. The more refined **Hibiscus Croissanterie** (☎ 0289/24-899), Odós Kaloyéra 38, near the Hotel Phílippi, is a good place for a light breakfast; it offers a large variety of croissants, good quiche lorraine, and other authentic delights.

VERY EXPENSIVE

✪ **Chez Cat'rine.** Odós Áyios Yerásimos, Hóra. ☎ **0289/22-169.** Reservations recommended. Appetizers Dr 2,000–Dr 6,000 ($8.50–$25.55); main courses Dr 4,000–Dr 6,500 ($17–$27.65); fish Dr 17,000–Dr 24,000 ($59.55–$102.10) per kilo. AE, EU, DC, MC, V. Daily 6:30pm–midnight. FRENCH/INTERNATIONAL.

This elegant, intimate little place is only a couple of blocks off the harbor behind the Hotel Apollo, and it might be difficult to find if it weren't the most famous restaurant in the Cyclades. The menu is small and includes seafood and grilled meats in addition to a few French entrees. All is meticulously prepared and professionally served.

EXPENSIVE

Edem Restaurant. Above Panahrándou church, Hóra. (Walk up Matoyánni, turn left on Kaloyéra, and follow the signs up and to the left.) ☎ **0289/22-855.** Reservations recommended Jul–Aug. Appetizers Dr 1,200–Dr 4,200 ($5.10–$17.85); main courses Dr 3,200–Dr 6,500 ($13.60–$27.65). AE, DC, EU, MC, V. Daily noon–1am. GREEK/CONTINENTAL.

This excellent restaurant recently moved to larger quarters, where you can swim and have a drink, lunch, or dinner around the very nice pool. Edem is famous for its meat dishes, but its large menu also includes traditional Greek and continental dishes. The service is still excellent.

El Greco/Yorgos. Platía Tría Pigádia, Hóra. ☎ **0289/22-074.** Appetizers Dr 750–Dr 4,000 ($3.20–$17); main courses Dr 1,800–Dr 5,000 ($7.65–$21.30). AE, DC, EU, MC, V. Daily 1pm–1am. GREEK/CONTINENTAL.

This sophisticated traditional taverna, with a large patio on central "Three Wells" Square, has a large menu that includes pastas, grilled meats, and traditional Greek specialties, including delicious eggplant bouréki.

Phílippi. Off Matoyánni, Hóra. ☎ **0289/22-294.** Reservations recommended Jul–Aug. Appetizers Dr 2,000–Dr 4,200 ($8.50–$17.85), main courses Dr 2,200–Dr 5,000 ($9.35–$21.25). AE, MC, V. Daily 7pm–1am. GREEK/CONTINENTAL.

You'll find this excellent restaurant in a quiet garden just off the main street and Kaloyéra, or you can come in the back way through the garden of the Hotel Phillipi. It's one of the island's most special dining experiences, and it certainly has the most romantic atmosphere. The menu includes French classics, curry, and superbly prepared traditional Greek dishes. The wine list is also impressive.

To Steki Manthos. Toúrlos Beach. ☎ **0289/23-435.** Dr 700–Dr 2,800 ($2.90–$11.90); main courses Dr 1,400–Dr 3,600 ($5.95–$15.30). No credit cards. Daily 9:30am–3pm, 7pm–1am. INTERNATIONAL.

Drive, take the bus to the Yephiráki stop, or walk (it's well worth the 15-minute hike) north toward Áyios Stéphanos to find this excellent place with a large and varied menu, a gifted chef, and a fine view of the sea and the nearby cruise-ship pier.

MODERATE

Sesame Kitchen. Platía Tría Pigádia, Hóra. ☎ **0289/24-710.** Appetizers Dr 750–Dr 2,600 ($3.20–$11.05); main courses Dr 1,500–Dr 3,200 ($6.40–$13.60). V. Daily 7pm–12:30am. GREEK/CONTINENTAL.

This small health-conscious taverna, which serves some vegetarian specialties, is next to the Naval Museum. Fresh spinach, vegetable, cheese, and chicken pies are baked daily. There's a large variety of salads, brown rice, and soya dishes, including a vegetable moussaka, and lightly grilled and seasoned meat dishes.

INEXPENSIVE

Antonini's. Taxi Square, Hóra. No telephone. Appetizers Dr 725–Dr 1,500 ($3.10–$6.40); main courses Dr 1,500–Dr 2,400 ($6.40–$10.20). No credit cards. Daily 11am–3pm, 7pm–1am. GREEK.

This busy taverna on the east side of the main square serves good typical Greek fare at reasonable prices.

Delphines. Odós Matoyánni, Hóra. ☎ **0289/24-269.** Appetizers Dr 600–Dr 1,250 ($2.55–$5.30); main courses Dr 1,500–Dr 3,600 ($6.40–$15.30). No credit cards. GREEK.

This busy little family owned spot on the main street serves generous portions of good traditional taverna fare.

⑤ **Niko's Taverna.** Near Paraportianí church, Hóra. No phone. Appetizers Dr 650–Dr 1,500 ($2.75–$6.40); main courses Dr 1,000–Dr 3,200 ($4.25–$9.85); fresh fish Dr 3,000 ($12.75) for 300 grams. Daily noon–11pm. GREEK/CONTINENTAL.

A good budget choice, this bustling little taverna is off the southwest corner of the harbor, and it's a favorite with locals and tourists. The menu is standard taverna fare, with a little variety. It's inexpensive for Mýkonos, and the staff is friendly and energetic.

MÝKONOS AFTER DARK

Mýkonos has the liveliest, most abundant, and most varied nightlife in the Aegean. Hóra is one place where you can get gussied up to your heart's content and not feel the least bit conspicuous. It's a bar-hopper's paradise, and you will actually enjoy wandering through the maze of streets looking for the right bar and looking at everyone else looking. Don't be too disappointed if some of the places we suggest are closed, have moved, changed their name or image; such is the nature of nightlife on an island where everything is seasonal. And be warned, drinks cost more here than they do in London or New York.

If you're visiting during July through September, you may want to find out what's happening at the **Anemo Theatre** (☎ 0289/23-944), an outdoor venue for the performing arts in a garden in Rohári, just above town, which presents a variety of concerts and performances.

Catch the sunset in one of the sophisticated bars in **Little Venice.** The **Kastro** (☎ 0289/23-070), near the Paraportianí church, is famous for classical music and frozen daiquiris. If you find it too crowded or tame, sashay on along to the **Caprice** up the block on Scarpa, which also has a seaside perch and rocks a little harder, or across the street to **Diva.** The **Montparnasse** (☎ 0289/23-719), on the same lane, is cozier, with classical music and Toulouse-Lautrec posters. The **Veranda** (☎ 0289/23-290), in an old mansion overlooking the water with a good view of the windmills, is as relaxing as its name implies. **Galleraki** (☎ 0289/27-188), a little further along, also has tables near the water, to drink in the sunset with a fancy cocktail. The similarly named **Gallery** (☎ 0289/22-526) is more discoish, as is **La Mer** (☎ 0289/23-124).

If all this just isn't quite up to your speed, you should probably hit "Main Street," starting near the harbor with the "king of the scene," **Pierro's,** which rocks all night long to American and European music and draws a range of people in sufficient quantity to impede your progress up the narrow street. If you'd like something a little more laid-back, back up and check out the **Nine Muses,** on Taxi Square, or the **Piano Bar,** which has live music. Or squeeze past the throng to the **Lotus** (☎ 0289/22-181), for good music, good food, and an interesting scene, or the **Anchor,** which plays blues, jazz, and classic rock for its 30-something clients. Or mosey on up Matoyánni to No. 42 to check out **Bar Uno** (☎ 0289/26-144); its slogan promises "a night to remember." From **Véngera** (☎ 0289/22-800), which remains a favorite of the more mature and discerning, hook a right to find **Bolero,** which has live music, and **1900** (☎ 0289/23-290) another block along on the right, or a little further along, **Argo** (☎ 0289/24-674), which is considered especially hip.

Head right back toward the harbor for some wilder action. **Stavros Irish Bar** (☎ 0289/23-867), behind the Town Hall, is still among the most unrestrained places—sometimes it's almost like an orgy—on the island with girls dancing on the table. Nearby the **Scandinavian Bar** rivals it in the anything-goes competition. The music is quieter at the **Windmill Disco,** which draws a younger crowd who seem to be more interested in actually getting to know each other. And if you'd like to sample some Greek music and dancing, you're in the right neighborhood. **Thalami** (☎ 0289/23-291), a small club underneath Town Hall, may have room for you to experience something very nearly authentic. Nearby **Four Roses** (☎ 0289/23-350) offers lively Greek music and dancing.

The other end of the harbor also has some nightlife, especially at **Remezzo Disco,** near the OTE, where you can boogie into the morning under the stars. If you'd like to visit an actual **Hard Rock Cafe** (☎ 0289/24-913) look for the pink bus that makes the trip from the port a couple of kilometers east of town to the "Acropolis of Rock" and back every 30 minutes from noon to 5am.

We read in another guide that the **City Club** has a nightly transvestite show, and maybe we saw part of it. Who can be sure on Mýkonos? Another source names the **Factory,** near the windmills, as a place for gay striptease. **Manto, Icaros,** and **Nefeli** are said to be popular gay and lesbian bars; we didn't find them, but that doesn't mean they're hidden. If you're interested, ask; on Mýkonos no one will bat an eyelash—or maybe they will, and that might be even more interesting.

So, now it's well after midnight and you're still up for more. You haven't exhausted the possibilities. **MADD,** on Taxi Square is only just coming alive at 1am, and the view of the port is sensational. The **Anchor Club**—remember it?—on Main Street is now a disco, and not far away at Three Wells (Tría Pigádia), the **Astra** is playing some even harder stuff.

3 Délos

The small island of Délos, where according to myth Leto gave birth to Artemis and Apollo, was considered by the ancient Greeks to be the holiest of sanctuaries, the sacred center around which the other Cyclades circled. Though it has suffered much theft, pillaging, and wanton destruction during the two millennia since it was the most important commercial center in the eastern Mediterranean, it's still one of the most remarkable archaeological preserves in the world with ample evidence of its former wealth and sophistication.

Just as in ancient times when people were not allowed to die or be born on the sacred island, today they are not allowed to spend the night, and the site can be visited only between the hours of 8:30am and 3pm.

THE MYTH OF DÉLOS

The myth, which perhaps reflects a rapprochement between the northern male deities and the Minoan Great Goddess, tells us that great Zeus was smitten with the Titan Asteria and pursued her. Trying to escape his amorous advances she changed into a quail, but he became an eagle and continued in hot pursuit until she turned into a rock that plummeted into the Aegean. Asteria floated around beneath the surface, becoming an unseen island called Adélos ("Invisible"). The ever-ready Zeus then fell in love with her sister Leto and came to her more successfully in the form of a swan. His jealous wife, Hera, as usual gave her rival no rest and persuaded Gaea, Mother Earth, to forbid the earth to give Leto shelter. The unfortunate woman was pregnant with twins and searched in vain for a place of refuge to deliver them. Zeus's brother Poseidon took pity on her and raised Adélos from the sea, making it Délos ("Visible"), and Poseidon anchored the island to the ocean floor with four diamond pillars.

While Zeus watched from Mt. Kýnthos, Leto clung to a palm tree near the Sacred Lake and gave birth first to Artemis, the virgin goddess of the hunt and patron of childbirth. Nine days later Apollo was born; he is the god of light, truth, learning, music, and prophecy.

ESSENTIALS

GETTING THERE   Délos can be reached by sea only. Most people visit on excursion boats from nearby Mýkonos and other neighboring islands. The island is a prominent stop for cruise ships and yachts. From Mýkonos organized guided and unguided excursions leave Tuesday through Sunday from the west end of the harbor; the trip takes about 40 minutes and costs about Dr 2,750 ($11.70) round-trip for transportation alone. **Yiannakis Tours** (☎ **0289/22-089**) offers guided tours for Dr 8,500 ($36.15) that depart at 9 or 10am and return at 12:30 or 2pm.

Note: We recommend visiting Délos early as possible in the day, especially in the summer, when the afternoon heat gets intense and the crowds get worse. Sturdy shoes and water are necessary; a hat or cap and food are advised. (There is a cafe near the museum, but the prices are high, the quality is poor, and the service is even worse.)

WHAT TO SEE & DO

The three hours allotted by most excursion boats should be enough for all except the most avid archaeological enthusiasts to explore the site. To the left (north) of the new jetty where your boat will dock is the **Sacred Harbor,** now too silted in for use, where pilgrims, merchants, and sailors from throughout the Mediterranean used to land. The commercial importance of the island in ancient times was due to the protection its harbor offered in the shelter of surrounding islands, the best anywhere between mainland Greece and its colonies and trading partners in Asia Minor.

Entrance to the site costs Dr 1,500. At the ticket kiosk you'll see a number of site plans and picture guides for sale. One of the better ones is *Délos: Monuments and Museum,* by P. Zaphiropoúlou (Kreve Edition), which has a well-translated text, good pictures, and a foldout map.

If you're not on a tour and have the energy, you may want to head up to **Mount Kýthos,** the highest point on the island. It offers an overview of the site and a fine view of most of the Cyclades: the neighboring island of Rhénia with Sýros beyond it to the west, Tínos to the north, Mýkonos to the northeast, Náxos and Páros to the south.

Nearest the jetty is the **Agora of the Competialists,** built in the 2nd century B.C. when the island was a bustling free port under Rome. Roman citizens, mostly former slaves, worshipped the *lares competales,* who were minor "crossroad" deities associated with the Greek god Hermes, patron of travelers and commerce. From the far left corner of the Agora of the Competialists, the **Sacred Way**—once lined with statues and votive monuments—leads north toward the **Sanctuary of Apollo.** By retracing the steps of ancient pilgrims along it, you will first pass on your right the remains of the **South Stoa** (a *stóa* is a roof supported by columns, though the columns here are long gone). It was built in the 3rd century B.C. by Pergamon, a wealthy Greek colony in Asia Minor. Just beyond the stoa is the **Agora of the Delians.** On the left of the agora is the remains of the **Stoa of Philip,** built by Philip V of Macedonia in 210 B.C. (Most of the stone from the site was taken away for buildings on neighboring islands, especially Mýkonos and Tínos.)

At the far end of the walkway was the **Propylaea,** a monumental marble gateway that led into the Sanctuary. In ancient times, the sanctuary was crowded with temples, altars, statues, and votive offerings. Just inside the sanctuary and to the right is the **House of the Naxians,** built in the 6th century B.C. to store offerings to Apollo. Next to it stood a monumental statue of the god, which Plutarch tells us was toppled in a storm by an even larger bronze palm tree erected by the Athenians in 417 B.C. Next come the three **Temples of Apollo,** the first and largest built by the Delians in the early 5th century B.C., the second built by the Athenians about a half century later, and the third an even earlier one built by the Athenian tyrant Pisístratos in the 6th century B.C.

The long narrow foundation to the right (east) of the temples is called the **Shrine of the Bulls,** named after a pair of bulls found at the entranceway. It is thought to have contained a trireme (a war galley with three banks of oars), dedicated to Apollo in thanks for a naval victory. (Another theory holds that it honored Theseus's successful trip to Crete where he slew the minotaur, which signifies the end of Minoan dominance.) Toward the Museum on the left is the **Sanctuary of Dionysus,** built in the late 4th century B.C. It's flanked by marble phalluses on pillars erected by winners of the choral competitions held during the Delian Games, similar to the Olympic games. The presence of this sanctuary to the god of revelry on the island where the god of reason was born is an early indication of the religious tolerance that would prevail here.

The **Museum** itself, open the same hours as the site, contains finds from the various excavations on the island. It displays some fine statuary, reliefs, masks, and jewelry, and is well worth a visit. Admission to the museum is included in the entrance fee to the site.

North of the **Tourist Pavilion** on the left is the **Sacred Lake,** where the oracular swans once swam. The lake is now little more than a dusty indentation most of the year surrounded by a low wall. Beyond it is the famous guardian **Lions,** made of Naxian marble and erected in the 7th century B.C. (There were originally at least nine. One was taken away to Venice in the 17th century and now stands before the Arsenal there. The whereabouts of the others remain a mystery.) Just south of the dry lake is the **Agora of the Italians.** South and parallel to the agora are the remains of the **Stoa of Antigonos**, and through the stoa is the **Temple of Leto,** which was built in the 6th century B.C.

North of the lake are the remains of two **Palaestras** ("wrestling schools"); to their east the foundation of the **Archiyession,** where the ancient ancestors of the Delians were worshipped. Beyond it to the northeast is the large square courtyard of the **Gymnasium** and the long narrow **Stadium,** where the athletic competitions of the Delian Games were held. East of them are the remains of a **synagogue** built by Phoenician Jews in the 2nd century B.C.

Follow the path from the Tourist Pavilion south toward Mt. Kýnthos, and you'll find the **Sanctuary of the Syrian Gods,** dating from about 100 B.C. Beyond it are the **Temples of Serapis,** about a century older. (This deity combined the attributes of the Egyptian gods Osiris and Apis; he was introduced by Ptolemy I, Alexander's bodyguard.) On the west of this complex of temples is the **Shrine of the Great Gods** (dedicated to the Cavíri, underworld fertility deities worshipped on Samothráki) and to the south, the **Temple of Isis,** with the remains of a statue, and the **Temple of Hera**, from the late 6th century B.C. Next up the hill is the **Shrine of Good Luck,** and near the top is the **Sacred Cave,** where an oracle of Apollo gave prophecy and later Hercules was worshipped.

West of the temple complex is the **Theater Quarter,** a residential area with the remains of houses from the Hellenistic and Roman era, when the island reached its peak in wealth and prestige. About 10,000 humans were sold daily in its slave market, and cosmopolitan merchants and bankers built their luxurious villas around central courtyards. There is still some evidence of the cisterns under their houses and a sewer system.

Mithridates of Pontus sacked Délos in 88 B.C., killed 20,000 people, enslaved the women and children, and carried them off with much of the island's treasure. Sulla retook the island, but two decades later pirates again sacked the island and carried the population off into slavery. Triarius retook the island and fortified it, too late. Hadrian tried to revive the cult of Apollo, with a glimmer of success, and in 363 A.D. Julian the Apostate tried again. After Theodosius declared Christianity the state religion and banned pagan activity, a small Christian population tried to take hold of the island. But the island was increasingly at the mercy of pirates, and little more than a century later, it was finally abandoned to them. In time, without water, even the pirates found Mýkonos more attractive.

All that remains in vivid testimony of the island's glory are the exquisite mosaics, the work of Syrian artists. South of the **Theater,** which seated 5,500 people and was the site of the choral competitions during the Delian Games, you'll find the **House of the Dolphins,** with the mosaic from which it takes its name, and the larger **House of the Masks,** with the island's most famous image, the astonishingly vibrant mosaic of Dionysus riding a leopard.

Behind the theater is a handsome arched **reservoir,** and below it the **House of the Trident** and the **House of Dionysus** also contain excellent mosaics. Near the new harbor in the **House of Cleopatra,** headless statues eloquently express the sad centuries of abuse and neglect since the island fell from grace and became the domain of archeologists, tourists, guides, and lizards.

4 Páros

91 nautical miles (168km) southeast of Piraeus

Geographically near the center of the archipelago, Páros has become its transportation hub. It's one of the largest and most fertile of the Cyclades. Thousands of visitors, including many tour groups, have only slightly diminished the island's considerable charm. It remains remarkably attractive, rivaling even Mýkonos for good beaches and surpassing it for windsurfing conditions, and its inhabitants are friendlier and more hospitable. Parikía, its lively capital with an enticing *agorá,* has the remains of a Venetian castle, a good archaeology museum, and the finest Byzantine cathedral in Greece. The island also has the pretty fishing village of Náoussa, which has grown into a major resort center, as well as a number of other resort areas.

ESSENTIALS

GETTING THERE   By Plane   Olympic Airlines has five flights daily (ten in the summer) between Páros and Athens. For schedule information and reservations call Olympic Airlines at **01/96-16-161** in Athens or 0284/21-900 in Parikía.

By Ferry   The main port, **Parikía,** has ferry service at least once daily (six hours), four times daily in the summer, from Piraeus. Confirm schedules with tourist information in Athens (☎ **01/171** or 01/45-11-311). **Strintzi Lines** (☎ **01/42-25-000** in Athens) and **Ventouris Ferries** (☎ **01/48-28-901** in Athens) have service three or four times a week from Piraeus via Sýros. **Ilio Lines** (☎ **01/42-24-772** in Athens) has hydrofoil service almost daily from Rafína.

Daily ferry service from Parikía links Páros with Íos, Mýkonos, Náxos, Santoríni (Thíra), and Tínos. Daily excursion tours link Parikía and Náoussa (the north coast port) with Mýkonos. The F/B *Golden Véryina* has overnight service to Ikaría and Sámos four times a week. (From Sámos you can arrange a next-day excursion to Ephesus, Turkey.)

For ferry information, call the **port authority** in Parikía (☎ **0284/21-240**). Ferry tickets are sold by several agents around Mavroyénous Square and along the port.

Vintsi Travel (☎ **0284/21-830;** fax 0284/23-666), toward the north end of the port, has the best service. Schedules are posted along the sidewalk.

VISITOR INFORMATION The **Páros Information Bureau** (☎ **0284/22-079**) is inside the windmill on the harbor. It's open from 9am to 11pm daily, June through September. The staff speaks English and French, provides local schedules, and changes traveler's checks.

GETTING AROUND **By Bicycle** Páros's rolling fertile hills make it especially well suited to exploration by bike; the pebble-and-dirt roads require tires with good air pressure. A good regular bike should cost about Dr 2,000 ($8.50) per day. Mountain bikes are about twice as expensive but better suited to the terrain. **Mountain Bike Club Páros** (☎ **0284/23-778**), left from the bus station, just off the water-front, offers organized tours, as well as such essentials as a helmet, insurance, repair kits, and water bottles.

By Bus The **bus station** (☎ **0284/21-233**) in Parikía is on the waterfront left from the windmill. There is hourly **public bus** service between Parikía (leaving on the hour from 8am to 8pm) and Náoussa (leaving on the half hour from 8:30am to 8:30pm). The other public buses from Parikía run hourly from 8am to 9pm in two general directions: south to Alíki or Poúnda (for boats to Antíparos) and southeast to the beaches at Píso Livádi, Chrissí Aktí, and Dríos. Schedules are posted at the stations, or you can call for information (see the number above).

By Car A Jeep or dune buggy are good ways to see the island, and there are several rental agencies along the waterfront. (Except in July and August you should be able to bargain some.) We recommend **Rent-A-Car Acropolis** (☎ **0284/21-830**), left from the windmill on the waterfront, which has wildly painted dune buggies for about Dr 16,000 ($68.10) per day, or Suzuki Jeeps for about Dr 25,000 ($106.40) per day. Full insurance, which is recommended, costs an additional Dr 3,000 ($12,75). **Budget Rent-a-Car** (☎ **0284/22-320**), also on the waterfront, is another good choice.

By Moped There are several moped dealers along the waterfront, left from the windmill. Depending on size, mopeds should cost about Dr 4,000 to Dr 6,000 ($17–$25.50) per day.

By Taxi Taxis can be booked (☎ **0284/21-500**) or hailed at the windmill taxi stand. If you're coming off the ferry with lots of luggage and are headed for a hotel in Náoussa, it's worth the Dr 2,000 ($8.50) to take a taxi directly there.

FAST FACTS: PÁROS

Area Code The telephone area code for Páros is **0284.**

Banks There are three banks in Parikía on Mavroyénous Square (to the right behind the windmill); they're open weekdays 8am to 2pm, and evenings and Saturdays during the high season.

Medical Clinic In Parikía the new private **Medical Center of Páros** (☎ **0284/ 24-410**) is left (west) of the Central Square, across from the Post Office, a block off the port. The public **Parikía Health Clinic** (☎ **0284/22-500**) is down the road from the Ekantopylianí church. There are **medical stations** in Anyeria (☎ **0284/ 91-277**), in Antíparos (☎ **0284/61-219**), in Léfkes (☎ **0284/41-728**), in Márpissa (☎ **0284/41-205**), and in Náoussa (☎ **0284/51-216**).

Police Call **0284/100** or 0284/23-333. The **Tourist Police** (☎ **0284/21-673**) are in Parikía behind the windmill on the port. In Márpissa, call **0284/41-202.** In Náoussa, call **0284/51-202.**

Post Office   The post office in Parikía (☎ **0284/21-236**) is left from the windmill on the waterfront road, open Monday through Friday 7:30am to 2pm, with extended hours in July and August. They offer fax service (☎ **0284/22-449**). There's a branch on the main street in Náoussa.

Telephones   The telephone center (OTE) in Parikía is to the right from the windmill; it's open 7:30am to midnight. (If the front door is closed, go around to the back, as wind direction determines which door is open.) There's a branch in Náoussa with similar hours.

WHAT TO SEE & DO
IN PARIKÍA

Parikía, site of the ancient capital, is the main port and largest town on the island. Its best-known and most important landmark is the squat, whitewashed **windmill** just off the main pier. To the windmill's left is the open triangular **Central Square.** Behind the windmill to the right is the long, irregular **Mavroyénous Square,** which contains the town's banks, several hotels, restaurants, and various stores. There's a scowling bust of Mandó Mavroyénous in the garden. (After her exploits in the War for Independence, Mavroyénous returned to Páros, where she died in poverty and all but forgotten in 1848.)

On the left side of Mavroyénous Square near the port are travel agents, ferry-ticket vendors, excursion operators, and offices that can help you find accommodations. By following the main street through the square, between the banks, you'll reach the town's picturesque **agorá** (market) section, where you'll find some interesting shopping in a wide range of galleries, clothing boutiques, handicraft shops, and food markets. Near the end of Market Street you'll find the **Aegean Center for the Fine Arts,** where artists, photographers, and writers study year-round. If you're interested in studying at the center, you can write them at Parikía, 84400 Páros, Cyclades, or fax them at 0284/23-287.

By bearing to the right back toward the sea, you'll find yourself near or in the maze of the heart of the old town, the **Kástro** (Venetian castle) neighborhood. The 13th-century fortress was built from marble taken from the ancient temples of Apollo and Demeter. Local housing is now incorporated into the fortress. You'll see ancient blocks and columns, recognizably part of the Venetian fortifications, forming the walls of neighborhood homes built in the traditional Cycladic style.

The town's most famous sight, the beautiful cathedral of **Panayía Ekaton-dapyliání** (Our Lady of a Hundred Doors), can be found by turning left from the windmill and taking the street up off the Central Square. You'll pass a park with pine trees all blown aslant by the island's strong winds, and up ahead you'll see the white gate of the high wall built to protect the church from pirates. According to local tradition, the church was founded by St. Helen, mother of the first Byzantine Emperor Constantine, in gratitude for the shelter the port had given during a storm. The massive yet graceful sanctuary you see today wasn't constructed until 200 years later, in the 6th century A.D., by Justinian. Though it actually incorporates three churches, the older chapel from the early 4th century (on the left) is thought to have originally been a pagan temple. It was badly damaged by an earthquake in the 8th century and rebuilt in the 10th century.

Legend says that the emperor hired the master architect Isodorus of Miletus, one of the builders of the famous Ayía Sophía in Constantinople, to design Panayía Ekatondapyliání, but that the architect sent an apprentice, Ignatius, in his place. When the old architect came to Páros to inspect the work he was so impressed by beauty and majesty of the church that he was consumed with jealousy and tried to push his apprentice off the dome, but the younger man caught the elder's foot in falling and both were killed. Legend also says that if you count there are only 99 doors, and when the 100th is found, Constantinople, the holiest of Eastern Orthodox cities, will be returned to the Greeks.

You can visit the church daily from 8am to 1pm and 5 to 8pm; admission is free. The ceiling and walls were once covered with frescos, and you can still make out some remnants. Of particular interest is the iconostasis of the luminous local marble. The doors to the altar are painted to look like marble, but the floors and columns are the real thing. Take the time to visit the baptistery, to the left of the church, where you may have the good fortune to witness a baptism, and the various chapels and galleries.

The island's **Archaeology Museum** (☎ 0284/21-231), behind the baptistery of Ekatondapylianí, is open Tuesday through Sunday from 8:30am to 2:30pm. Admission is Dr 600 ($2.55). The museum's most valued holding is a fragment of the famous Parian Chronicle (no. 26); the Ashmolean Museum at Oxford University has a larger portion. The chronicle, carved on marble tablets, was found in the 17th century and contains valuable information from which many of the events of Greek history are dated. (Interestingly, it gives us information about artists, poets, and playwrights, but doesn't bother to mention political leaders or battles.) The museum also contains a Winged Victory from the 5th century B.C.; some objects found at the local temple of Apollo; and part of a marble monument with a frieze of and information about the poet Archilochus, the important 7th-century B.C. lyric poet who first used iambic meter and ironic detachment—one of Páros's most famous sons. ("What breaks me, young friend, is tasteless desire, lifeless verse, boring dinners.")

AROUND THE ISLAND

The free booklet *Páros Windsurfing Guide* has a good small map of the island, maps of several beaches, and useful information; it's especially recommended to those interested in water sports. The free *Summer Páros/Antíparos* also has a map of the island, a fairly good map of Parikía, and information.

There are beaches north along Parikía Bay, but beach seekers will probably want to head east to Náoussa Bay. On the road you'll pass **Tris Ekklisíes** ("Three Churches"), a 7th-century basilica built over the tomb of the poet Archilochus. The **Monastery of Logovárdas,** on the mountainside to the east, which has an icon-painting school, can also be visited by a side road, though only properly dressed men are allowed inside.

Until recently **Náoussa** was a fishing village with simple white houses in a labyrinth of narrow streets, but it's now a growing resort center with good restaurants, trendy bars, and sophisticated boutiques. Most of the new building has been concentrated along the nearby beaches, and the town itself still retains much charm, with colorful caïques in its harbor, the nearby half-submerged ruins of a Venetian fortress, and fishermen still calmly going about their work. There are a number of good beaches within walking distance of town, or you can catch a caïque to the more distant ones.

Coming from Parikía you'll pass a number of new hotels and restaurants along the paved road. After crossing a street-level bridge, Archilochus Street and Náoussa's main square are on the right. The long irregular square, shaded by tall eucalyptus trees, has a bus stop, a taxi stand, cafes, and stores. If you cross the square to an arched entryway, you'll be at the gates of the old city. Within are the charming cobblestoned back lanes of the town, best explored in the midafternoon when the inhabitants are taking siesta.

Beyond the National Bank is the busy harbor of **Áyios Dimítrios Bay.** It's most active at sunrise and in the late afternoon when the fishermen are setting out or returning with the day's catch, spreading out and folding their nets, mooring and cleaning their blue, green, yellow, and orange caïques. You can relax at one of the port-side cafes or ouzeries to watch. The small whitewashed **church of Áyios Nikólaos,** patron saint of sailors, stands out among all the bright primary colors.

The half-submerged ruins of the **Venetian fortress** are on the east end and are most impressive when lighted at night. The most colorful local festival is held on August 23, when the battle against the pirate Barbarossa is reenacted by torch-lit boats converging on the harbor; this is followed by feasting, dancing, and general merriment.

The ever helpful **Nissiótissa Tours** (☎ **0284/51-480** or 0284/52-094; fax 0284/ 51-189) can be found off the left side of the main square near the bus station, across the lane from the Náoussa Sweet Shop. Cathy and Kostas Gavalas, Greek Americans who are experts on this area of the island, can help you find accommodations (hotels, rooms to let, apartments, or villa), book Olympic flights, and arrange other plane, ferry, and excursion tickets, island tours, and rental cars (EURO, MC, V accepted). They also have a book exchange, as well as used books for sale, and they can even arrange horseback riding tours with experienced guides.

The town **police** (☎ **0284/51-202**) are on the road to Parikía, across from the **OTE.** (You can also use metered phones at travel agencies.) The **post office** is 600 meters out on the road to Ambelás. The town medical **doctor** is on the main square, on the right before the church. There's a shop that sells **foreign periodicals** on the square.

Náoussa offers transportation to other destinations on the island, as well excursion boats to other islands. **Buses** to Parikía leave the main square on the half hour from 8:30am to 8:30pm, more frequently in July and August, and there's service to Santa Maria beach twice a day. The service to other villages on narrow dirt roads is infrequent. (Check the schedule at the station.)

Daily **excursion boats** leave Náoussa harbor for Mýkonos and Délos; the two-hour trip costs Dr 5,300 ($22.50) one way, and the full-day excursion costs Dr 10,500 ($44.70) round trip. In the summer there are excursions to Náxos for Dr 4,800 ($20.45) and Santoríni for Dr 11,900 ($50.65); one-way tickets are half price. Lo-cal caïques provide service to Kolymbíthres, Monastery, and Langéri beaches, west of town, for about Dr 700 ($2.95) round trip. There's caïque day trips to the beach at Santa Maria, about 4 miles around the eastern peninsula, for about Dr 1,700 ($7.25) round trip.

There are several **moped** dealers on the main square; prices are comparable to those in Parikía, and bargaining may be successful except in the high season. **Nissiótissa Tours** rents Suzuki Swifts for about Dr 16,000 ($68.10) plus 18% tax, including third-party insurance and free mileage; expect to pay about half this in the low season.

One of the island's best and most famous beaches, picturesque **Kolymbíthres** ("Fonts"), is an hour's walk or a 10-minute moped ride west from Náoussa. It has smooth giant rocks, some reminiscent of baptismal fonts, that divide the smooth golden sand beach into little coves. There are several tavernas nearby; we recommend the **Dolphin Taverna,** to the south, open 7am to 2am, for traditional Greek food. Nearby, to the north is the sprawling **Porto Páros** (☎ **0284/52-010;** fax 0284/ 51-720), the largest resort complex in the Cyclades. It has a huge pool, tennis courts, and a video game arcade, 145 rooms and 45 villas; it will soon be under new management and wouldn't give its rates. To the south, a 10-minute walk from

Kolymbítres, is the excellent **Hotel Kouros** (☎ 0284/51-565; fax 0284/51-000), with 55 spacious, full-amenity rooms and a freshwater pool in quiet, beautifully land-scaped grounds 100 meters from the beach; doubles go for Dr 18,750 ($79.75). **Camping Náoussa** (☎ 0284/51-595), about 60 yards from the beach, has hot show-ers, a kitchen, clothes- and dishwashing, and charges Dr 1,250 ($5.30) per person. Tent sites are free and tents can be rented for Dr 800 ($3.40).

North of the beach at Kolymbíthres, by the Áyios Ioánnis Church, is **Monastery Beach,** with some nudism, and the **Monasteri Club,** a bar-restaurant with music and beach service. Most of the other beaches west of Náoussa are overcrowded because of all the new hotels.

About 2 ¹/₂ kilometers north of Náoussa on an unimproved road is the popular **Langéri Beach.** A 10-minute walk further north will bring you to the nudist beach, with a gay and straight crowd.

Before you reach Langéri the road forks to the right and leads to **Santa Maria Beach,** one of the most beautiful on the island. It has particularly clear water and shallow dunes (rare in Greece) of fine sand along the irregular coastline. It offers some of the best windsurfing on the island. The excellent **Aristophanes Taverna** serves grilled fresh fish and meats and sometimes a feast of superb grilled astakós (local lobster) with wine, cheese, and salad for about Dr 12,500 ($53.20) for two. The Aristophanes also offers villas for rent. The nearby **Santa Maria Surf Club** provides windsurfing gear and lessons. **Santa Maria Camping** (☎ 0284/52-490; fax 0284/ 51-937) has the best campsite on the island, with two restaurants, a bar, a swimming pool, minimarket, cooking/eating area, laundry, bungalows, water sports, and 50 hot showers; Dr 1,250 ($5.30) per person, tent sites free.

Southeast of Náoussa, connected by public bus, is the fishing village of **Ambelás,** which has a good beach, some inexpensive tavernas, rooms to let, and several small hotels. The **Hotel Christiana** (☎ 0284/51-573) has 18 simple rooms (all with bath) with doubles for Dr 9,200 ($39.15) and a good restaurant.

About a half-hour's hike south of Ambelás along the east coast, past several undeveloped beaches, brings you to **Glyfádes** and just beyond it **Tsoukália,** which are said to be the place for "radical" windsurfers. Both beaches have a few studios to rent and a restaurant. The main north-south road is nearly a kilometer inland at this point.

The better east coast beaches can be reached by public bus from Parikía and Náoussa; buses leave hourly in the summer. Unfortunately, the road is well inland and you can't scope out the beaches from the bus window. Ask around about crowd conditions on the several beaches; once you've reached a beach, it's several miles to the next one.

Mólos, at the tip of a small peninsula is beautiful and convenient to the attrac-tive inland villages of **Mármara** and **Márpissa,** where there are rooms to let, so it can sometimes get crowded. The next beach south, **Píso Livádi,** was once the port for the marble quarries; it still has caïque service on the summer to Ayía Ánna on Náxos. Hotels and pizza parlors overcrowd its small, shallow sandy cove. **Logáras,** the next cove south, has a good sandy beach, though it's beginning to get the overflow from its busier neighbor. **Captain Kafkis Camping** (☎ 0284/51-595) at Píso Livádi is the nearest camping.

The next major beach, **Chrissí Aktí** ("Golden Beach"), a kilometer of fine golden sand, is generally considered the best beach on the island, and the windiest. It's become a major windsurfing center, the site of the 1993 World Windsurfing championship competition. There are two windsurfing clubs, the **Sunwind BIC Center** and **Force Seven,** with lessons for beginners and advanced surfers. Chrissí Aktí also has some tavernas, rooms to let, hotels, and even a disco and bar.

The community is about half a mile off the paved road, with a parking lot at the end for beach commuters. At the parking lot, the **Golden Beach Hotel** (☎ **0284/41-194**; fax 0284/41-195) has 35 rooms with beach views, doubles for Dr 13,800 ($58.70). Next door the newer 38-room **Amarilis Hotel** (☎ **0284/41-410**; fax 0284/41-600) has doubles with bath for Dr 17,250 ($73.40).

Many overnight visitors, however, head south to **Dríos**, a pretty village that is fast becoming a resort town, with hotels, luxury villas, waterside tavernas, and rooms to let. The **Julia Hotel** (☎ **0284/41-494**) has 12 rooms with doubles for Dr 7,350 ($31.25). The very nice **Hotel Annezina** (☎ **0284/41-037**) has 13 doubles with bath for Dr 7,950 ($33.75) and a good restaurant; it's located in the center of the town, next to a good supermarket and near the bus stop and the popular **Anchor Taverna.** Buses run from Dríos to Parikía five times daily, hourly in the summer.

Around the southern tip of the island is **Alikí,** now experiencing a construction boom; the sound of planes taking off from the nearby airport is deafening, and we don't recommend a visit. The next town west is **Poúnda** (which means "Point," and there are three Poúndas on the island, though this is the biggest and best known). It's also experiencing a construction boom and merits a visit only to catch the ferry to Antíparos.

Before we jump off to the neighboring island, there are several important sights on Páros we haven't covered yet, most importantly the valley of Petaloúdes ("Butterflies"), the marble quarries at Maráthi, and the medieval capital of Léfkes. There is also at least one good beach on the west coast, at **Ayía Iríni,** a secluded sandy cove just a couple of miles south of Parikía, visible from the main road just before the turnoff to Petaloúdes. There you'll find a taverna, the **Ayía Iríni Campgrounds** (☎ **0284/22-340**), and a handful of palm trees.

The valley of **Petaloúdes** is a lush oasis of plum, pear, fig, and pomegranate trees, about 4 miles (6km) south of Parikía. Take the beach road south of town for about 2 1/2 miles to the left-hand turnoff for the nunnery of Christoú sto Dássos ("Christ of the Forest"). The 18th-century nunnery itself will be of interest to some, though men are not permitted past the courtyard. Another name for the **valley of the butterflies** is *Psychopianí* ("soul softs") because it quiets the mind and lifts the heart. Kóstas Graváris opens his home daily from 8am to 8pm, closing for siesta from 1 to 4pm. He recommends you come in the early morning or evening when the butterflies are most active. The butterflies, actually tiger moths (*Panaxia quadripunctaria poda*), look like black-and-white striped arrowheads until they fly up to reveal their bright red underwings. They have been coming here for at least 300 years, because of the freshwater spring, flowering trees, dense foliage and cool shade, and are most numerous in July and August. The keeper's fee is Dr 800 ($3.40), and there is a small snack bar. Donkey or mule rides from Parikía to the site along a back road cost about Dr 2,000 ($8.50).

The inland road that branches off to the right just outside of town on the road from Parikía to Náoussa will take you up the side of the mountain to the **marble quarries at Maráthi,** source of the famous Parian marble, prized for its translucency and fine, soft texture, and used by ancient sculptors for their best work, including the *Hermes* of Praxiteles and the *Venus de Milo*. From the small farming village of Maráthi walk up to the deserted buildings that once belonged to a French mining company, that in 1844 quarried the marble to construct Napoleon's tomb. (The marble is simply too expensive for anyone to use today.) Take a flashlight, if you have one, to explore the tunnels.

Continue 1.3 miles to the village of Kóstos, and perched above it you'll find **Studio Yria** (☎ **0284/29-007**), where local craftspersons Stelio and Monika Ghikis produce functional earthenware that incorporates indigenous designs, including an abstract octopus motif. They also sell weavings and objects of cast bronze, forged iron, and Parian marble.

About 2 winding miles further south along the inland road you'll reach **Léfkes,** the medieval capital of the island. Its whitewashed houses with red-tile roofs form a maze around the central square. Léfkes was built in such an inaccessible location and with an intentionally confusing pattern of streets to thwart pirates. Test your own powers of navigation by finding the famous Ayía Triáda (Holy Trinity) Church, whose carved marble towers are visible above the town. You can continue on east to the villages of **Pródromos,** an old farming community; **Mármara** ("Marble"), where many of the marble houses have been whitewashed but some of the streets are paved with it; and the prettiest, **Márpissa,** with the ruins of a 15th-century Venetian fortress and the handsome monastery of Áyios Antónios. Continue on to Náoussa. (You can of course make the same trip in reverse order.)

If your time on Páros is limited, rent a moped or car for an around-the-island tour that might include a morning visit to Petaloúdes, and/or the marble quarries, Léfkes, and the villages, a stop for a good lunch in Náoussa, a stroll around the old town and harbor, then a swim at your beach of choice. There are a number of day tours offered by local travel agents for about Dr 3,000 ($12.75). **Páros Tours** (☎ **0284/21-582;** fax 0284/22-582) offers a variety of tours that cost from Dr 2,000 to Dr 4,000 ($8.50 to $17).

WHERE TO STAY
PARIKÍA

The port town has three basic hotel zones: the agorá, the harbor, and the beach. Most hotels now require reservations for July and August, and these should be made at least a month in advance. All written requests must be accompanied by a deposit equal to one night's rent. A follow-up phone call is recommended once you arrive in Greece, especially for those who haven't received written confirmation.

The gauntlet of room hawkers that meet you at the port gets increasingly daunting. If it's high season, you don't have a reservation, and you're exhausted, you might consider taking one—but take your time, as some of them will be well off the beaten path and not especially attractive.

The **Hotelliers Association of Páros** (☎ **0284/24-555** or 0284/24-556) has an information and reservation office at the entrance of Mavroyénous Square, behind the windmill and to the right.

AGORÁ

The agorá is the heart of Parikía, and it beats 24 hours a day, so it can get noisy. Accommodations in the quiet back streets are more enticing.

Hotel Argonauta. Agorá, Parikía, 844 00 Páros. ☎ **0284/21-440.** Fax 0284/23-422. 15 rms (all with shower). TEL. Including breakfast: Dr 11,000 ($46.80) single; Dr 14,000 ($59.55) double. EU, MC, V.

This charming and comfortable hotel is at the far end of Mavroyénous Square, behind the Emborikí (Commercial) Bank, so it's refreshingly quiet. The rooms are modern and well equipped with a few traditional touches; they're built around an inner second-floor courtyard. The owners, Soula and Dimitri Ghikas, make their spacious and attractive lobby feel like home.

⑤ Hotel Dina. Market St., Parikía, 844 00 Páros. ☎ **0284/21-325.** 8 rms (all with bath). Dr 10,500 ($44.70) double. No credit cards.

This small lodging is distinguishable from the neighborhood homes only by the discreet sign outside. The friendly proprietor, Dina Patelis, has simple, spotless rooms with blue-tiled bathrooms.

Hotel Platanos. Parikía, 844 00 Páros. ☎ **0284/24-262.** 11 rms (all with bath). TEL. Dr 17,200 ($73.20) double. No credit cards.

This small hotel, 350 meters south of the windmill and one block in from the *paralía* (waterfront), was highly recommended by reader Garry Wabba. The neighborhood is quiet, the rooms are comfortable, and Ursula Antonionou is a gracious hostess.

Pension Vangelistra. Parikía, 844 00 Páros. ☎ **0284/21-482.** 6 rms (all with bath), 2 apartments. Dr 10,500 ($46.70) double; Dr 11,900 ($50.65) apartment. No credit cards.

Call Yorgos and Voula Maounis, and one of their friendly English-speaking kids will help you find this cozy and attractive lodging in a quiet neighborhood. The rooms, all with balconies, are spotless. The flower-covered terrace brightens the whole street.

AT THE HARBOR

The harborside near the windmill is a convenient and lively place, but it's often too noisy for a good night's rest.

Hotel Georgy. Platía Mavroyénous, Parikía, 844 00 Páros. ☎ **0284/22-544.** 38 rms (all with shower). Dr 10,600 ($45.10) single; Dr 16,300 ($69.35) double. No credit cards.

Rooms facing the inner courtyard garden are the best choice. The Kontostavros family provides good service to their guests, and continental breakfast in their cafe costs Dr 400 ($1.70).

Hotel Kypreos. Parikía, 844 00 Páros. ☎ **0284/22-544** or 0284/22-448. 5 rms (all with shower). Dr 6,900 ($29.35) single; Dr 9,200 ($39.15) double. No credit cards.

This hotel is just north of the windmill. Anne, a warm and helpful hostess, offers neat, simple rooms that have double beds and balconies. Her husband has a car-rental shop here, and a night's stay at the Kýpreos might get you a discount on a car rental.

AT THE BEACH

The strip of hotels along Livádi beach—about a 10-minute walk north of the windmill, left coming from the ferry—all have three common features: bland decor, proximity to the crowded town beach, and sea views. Those we recommend, in order from the windmill are:

Hotel Argo. Parikía, 84400 Páros. ☎ **0284/21-367** or 0284/21-207. 45 rms (all with bath). TEL. Dr 13,400 ($57) single; Dr 15,500 ($65.95) double. V.

The Argo's cozy, overfurnished lobby may remind you of your grandmother's. There's an elevator, and the spacious rooms have balconies. Breakfast costs Dr 900 ($3.85).

Hotel Asterias. Parikía, 844 00 Páros. ☎ **0284/21-797** or 0284/22-171. Fax 0284/22-172. 36 rms (all with shower). TEL. Dr 12,650 ($53.85) single; Dr 16,100 ($68.50) double. AC, EU, MC, V.

This Cycladic-style hotel is the closest to the beach; it's one of the best hotels in the area, with a flowering garden out front. The spacious rooms have wooden shuttered doors that open onto balconies, all with sea views.

Hotel Páros. Parikía, 844 00 Páros. ☎ **0284/21-319**. 15 rms (all with bath). Including breakfast: Dr 11,500 ($48.95) single; Dr 13,800 ($58.70) double. MC, V.

This older but well maintained hotel has good value rooms, and Peter, the friendly owner, and his family will help make your stay pleasant.

Villa Ragousi. Parikía, 84400 Páros. ☎ **0284/21-671.** 10 rms (all with shower). Dr 13,200 ($56.17) single/double. No credit cards.

Several readers wrote to recommend this modern three-story house with good clean rooms, up the hill from the Taverna Skouna. Some of the rooms have balconies overlooking the bay. Gavrilla Ragousi speaks English and drives a cab during the day; ask for him at the taxi stand.

CAMPING

Camping Koula (☎ 0284/22-082) is north of the harbor, about 900 yards left from the ferry. It's the area's first choice campground, but in the summer it gets so busy that most people find it unpleasant. It costs Dr 800 ($3.40) per person; tents are free.

Parasporos Camping (☎ 0284/21-944) is a newer facility, south of Parikía on the road to Eloúnda. It has all the amenities on large, well-landscaped grounds. There's breathing room and quiet, even in busy July and August. It cost Dr 1,200 ($5.15) per person, tents are free.

SOUTH OF PARIKÍA

Hotel Yria. Paraspóros, 84400 Páros. ☎ **0284/24-154.** Fax 0284/21-167. 68 rms (all with bath), 12 suites. A/C MINIBAR TV TEL. Dr 25,750 ($109.55) single; Dr 30,800 ($131.15) double. AE, DC, EU, MC, V.

This new bungalow complex, 2½ kilometers south of the port, is just too good to be ignored. The architecture is traditional with a villagelike plan, so that not all rooms have a sea view, but the grounds are so beautifully landscaped and well maintained that you won't feel deprived if yours doesn't. There's a big handsome freshwater pool, a fair beach nearby, tennis and basketball courts, a children's playground, a spacious lounge, and a good dining room. The hotel offers an information desk, currency exchange, car rental, travel arrangements, laundry; fax, and mail service. The staff is well trained, friendly, courteous, and exceptionally helpful.

NÁOUSSA

If you haven't made reservations in the high season and are unable to find a room, try **Nissiótissa Tours** (☎ 0284/51-480), just off the east (left) side of the main square. In the quiet back streets surrounding the Hotel Minoa and in the area behind the Sagriótis Monument, you'll see a number of whitewashed abodes sporting signs such as Rooms, Chambres, and Zimmer.

Astir of Páros. Kolymbíthres Beach, 84401 Páros. ☎ **0284/51-797.** Fax 0284/51-985. 15 rms, 42 junior suites, 4 executive suites. A/C MINIBAR TV TEL. Dr 30,400 ($129.35) single; Dr 52,900 ($225.10) double; suites from Dr 64,800 ($275.75). AE, DC, EU, MC, V.

The best hotel on the island is west of Náoussa, off the south end of Kolymbíthres Beach. It's built like a Cycladic village and has a sumptuous garden. There's a private beach, a three-hole golf course, a good pool, Jacuzzi, tennis court, gym, and art gallery. The elegant reception area displays contemporary Greek art. The staff is especially attentive. The rooms are spacious; four rooms have handicapped access.

Hotel Fotilia. Náoussa, 84401 Páros. ☎ **0284/51-480.** Fax 0284/51-189. 14 rms (all with bath). TEL. Including breakfast: Dr 18,500 ($78.70) single; Dr 22,500 ($95.75) double.

Climb to the top of the steps at the end of town and to the left of the church you'll see a restored windmill behind a stone archway. The companionable Michael Leondaris will probably meet you with a cup of coffee or glass of wine. The rooms are spacious and furnished in an elegant country style, with crisp blue-and-white curtains that open to balconies that overlook the old harbor and bay.

Hotel Kontaratos. Ayíi Anáryiri Beach, 844 01 Páros. ☎ **0284/51-693** or 01/49-13-530 in Athens. Fax 0284/51-740. 33 rms (all with bath). TEL. Including breakfast: Dr 20,500 ($87.25) single; Dr 30,600 ($130.20) double. EU, MC, V.

One of the best hotels on Páros is on the beach east of Náoussa. The large rooms with views of the beach have large bathrooms with bathtubs. Most rooms have balconies. There's a large swimming pool and sun deck, a tennis court, and a private beach with water sports.

Hotel Petres. Náoussa, 84401 Páros. ☎ **0284/51-480.** Fax 0284/52-467. 16 rms (all with bath). A/C MINIBAR TEL. Dr 13,250 ($56.40) single; Dr 18,500 ($78.70) double.

Claire Hatzinkolakis has decorated her charming reception area with antiques and her rooms with loving care. The beds have handsome woven covers, hand-crocheted lace is draped over the lamps, and the walls have prints from the Benaki Museum. A kitchen and barbecue are available to her guests. Her "honeymoon suite" has her grandmother's marriage bed.

⑤ Kalypso Hotel. Ayíi Anáryiri Beach, 84401 Páros. ☎ **0284/51-488.** Fax 0284/51-607. 40 rms (all with bath). Including breakfast: Dr 13,500 ($57.45) single; Dr 20,600 ($87.65) double. AC, MC, V.

This very nice, traditional-style seaside hotel right on the beach east of town is built around a cobblestone courtyard. Many of the outer rooms have balconies overlooking the sea. The spacious upper-floor rooms are reached by an ornately carved wooden mezzanine, which overlooks the Kalypso's bar.

Papadakis Hotel. Náoussa, 84401 Páros. ☎ **0284/51-643.** Fax 0284/51-643. 16 rms (all with bath). Including breakfast: Dr 18,000 ($76.60) single or double. No credit cards.

If you like hillside locations, try the new Papadakis, which offers the best views over the village and bay. It's a brisk five-minute walk from the main square. Large rooms with balconies open onto a common patio. The highest rooms have the best views.

APARTMENTS

There are a number of newly built apartments and studios east town near Ayíi Anáryiri Beach. Most function like small hotels, with a manned reception desk, common switchboard, lounge, and sometimes breakfast service.

Batistas Apartments. Náoussa, 84401 Páros. ☎ **0284/51-058** or 01/97-57-286 in Athens. 8 apts. Dr 16,500 ($70.20) for two; Dr 26,500 ($112.75) for four.

Mrs. Batistas's homespun lace, crochet, and needlework give these handsome apartments an extra feeling of home.

Kapten Nikolas Apartments. Ayíi Anáryiri Beach, 844 01 Páros. ☎ **0284/51-340.** Fax 0284/51-519. 17 apts. TEL. Dr 16,500 ($70.20) for two; Dr 26,500 ($112.75) for four.

These handsomely furnished apartments, with marble-top tables and colorful furniture, are near the Kalypso Hotel. The neighborhood is quiet, and the sea views are lovely. Contact **Nissiótissa Tours** (☎ **0284/51-480;** fax 0284/51-189) for reservations.

Lily Apartments. Náoussa, 84401 Páros. ☎ **0284/51-377.** Fax 0284/51-716 or 01/ 95-89-314 in Athens. 17 apts. TEL. Dr 16,500 ($70.20) for two. EU, MC, V.

Lily Ananiadou has our favorite apartments in Náoussa. They're simple, pleasantly modern, and fully equipped with kitchens. The balconies overlook dry, scrub-brush hills.

WHERE TO DINE
PARIKÍA

The food on Páros has generally improved and become more international and sophisticated with the recent influx of foreign chefs and palates. We won't have to bring your attention to the neon-lighted gyros/pizza/burger joints near the port, and they certainly seem sufficient for the college crowd. Those interested in more elegant fare should head for Náoussa.

⑤ Aligaria Restaurant. Platía Aligarí, Parikía. ☎ **0284/22-026.** Appetizers Dr 600–Dr 1,350 ($2.55–$5.75); main courses Dr 1,250–Dr 2,300 ($5.30–$9.80). EU, MC, V. Daily noon–3:30pm and 6:30pm–midnight. GREEK.

You'll find this charming little place with green trim and white lace curtains to the left off Mavroyénous Square behind the Hotel Kontes. Owner Elizabeth Nikolousou is an excellent cook who prepares specialties like a light zucchini pie that disappear early. But even her standards, like stuffed tomatoes are special, and her servings are generous. She also has a good selection of Greek wines.

Argonaut Restaurant. Mavroyénous Square, Parikía. ☎ **0284/21-440.** Appetizers Dr 600–Dr 1,500 ($2.55–$6.40); main courses Dr 1,200–Dr 2,600 ($5.10–$11.05). EU, MC, V. Daily 8am–midnight. GREEK/INTERNATIONAL.

This unpretentious place on the upper end of Mavroyénous Square is dependable during all its long hours. Breakfasts are good and reasonably priced. Salads are fresh and generous. Grilled meats are well prepared, and the usual Greek standards are especially good.

Dionysos Taverna. Agorá, Parikía. ☎ **0284/22-318.** Reservations recommended in July and August. Appetizers Dr 500–Dr 1,200 ($2.15–$5.10); main courses Dr 1,200–Dr 2,750 ($5.10–$11.70). AE, EU, MC, V. Daily 6pm–midnight. GREEK/INTERNATIONAL.

This popular taverna has most of its seating outdoors, in a pretty garden filled with bright red geraniums. Inside, a flaking fresco depicts mortals frolicking around Dionysus, who is overseeing the sale of the Parian favorites: Lagari, a strong red wine, and Kavarnis, a dry white.

Hibiscus Cafe. Platía Valéntza, Parikía. ☎ **0284/21-849.** Appetizers Dr 500–Dr 800 ($2.10–$3.40); main courses Dr 1,000–Dr 2,000 ($4.25–$8.50). No credit cards. Daily noon–midnight. GREEK/PIZZA.

One of the few casual yet stylish places is on the paralía, about 100 yards south of the port. It's inexpensive and has a wide selection of snacks and brick-oven pizzas. Tables have sea views.

Levantis Restaurant. Market St., Parikía. ☎ **0284/23-613.** Reservations recommended Jul–Aug. Appetizers Dr 700–Dr 900 ($3–$2.85); main courses Dr 1,850–Dr 3,000 ($7.85–$12.75). AE, DC, EU, MC, V. Wed–Mon 7pm–2am. GREEK/EASTERN MEDITERRANEAN.

Dinner is served under grapevines that some of the older citizens remember being there when they were young. Vivacious Mariana is happy to recommend her favorite of the day, and her husband, Nikolas, offers a friendly glass of wine. The fish here can be disappointing, but the eastern specialties are excellent.

⑤ Poseidon Grill. Livádi Beach, Parikía. ☎ **0284/22-667.** Appetizers Dr 400–Dr 700 ($1.70–$3); main courses Dr 1,000–Dr 2,000 ($4.25–$8.50). No credit cards. Daily 8am–midnight. GREEK.

This somewhat fancier taverna near the town beach, across from the Stella Hotel, has a wide range of vegetable entrées and excellent fish. Share swordfish, grilled calamari, some mezédes, salad, and a bottle of Nissiótissa wine.

NÁOUSSA

Náoussa's main square has plenty of casual eating establishments. The **Náoussa Pâtisserie,** on the east side of the square, has delicious cheese pies, pastries, biscuits, and espresso. The village's **bread bakery** is past the church near Christo's Taverna.

Barbarossa Ouzerí. The waterfront, Náoussa. ☎ **0284/51-391.** Appetizers Dr 500–Dr 1,200 ($2.10–$5.10). No credit cards. Daily 7:30–11:30pm. GREEK.

This authentic ouzerí is right on the port. Old, wind-burned fishermen sit for hours nursing their milky ouzo in water and their miniportions of grilled octopus and olives. If you haven't partaken of this experience yet, this is the place to try it.

Christo's Taverna. Archilochus Street, Náoussa. ☎ **0284/51-442.** Reservations recommended Jul–Aug. Appetizers Dr 400–Dr 1,200 ($1.70–$5.10); main courses Dr 1,100–Dr 3,300 ($4.70–$14). No credit cards. Daily 7:30–11:30pm. EURO-GREEK.

Christo's is known for its eclectic menu and Euro-Greek style. Dinner only is served in a beautiful garden filled with red and pink geraniums. The color of the dark purple grape clusters dripping through the trellised roof in late summer is unforgettable. Classical music soothes as you dine on elegantly prepared, freshly made veal, lamb, or steak dishes.

Kavarnis Bar. Archilochus St., Náoussa. ☎ **0284/51-038.** Crepes Dr 900–Dr 2,000 ($3.85–$8.50); pasta Dr 1,200–Dr 2,600 ($5.10–$11.05). No credit cards. Daily 7:30pm–2am. CONTINENTAL.

This beautiful bar, just around the corner from the post office, takes you back to another time: Paris in the 1920s. Along with modern jazz, they serve elaborate cocktails and specialize in delectable crepes filled with everything from fruit to ice cream to meat. Try the famous cognac crepe.

۞ Lalula. Náoussa. ☎ **0284/51-547.** Reservations recommended Jul–Aug. Appetizers Dr 1,000–Dr 1,900 ($4.25–$8.10); main courses Dr 1,800–Dr 3,300 ($7.65–$14). No credit cards. Daily 7–11:45pm. GREEK/MEDITERRANEAN/VEGETARIAN.

Take a left at the post office and find this special place across from the Minoa Hotel. A gifted German restaurateur is responsible for the delicious and distinctive food, subdued decor, and interesting but unobtrusive music. There's a lovely little garden in the back. The cooking is lighter and more refined than usually found in Greece, and the menu is imaginative and eclectic, depending upon what's fresh at the market. Regular items include vegetable quiche, sweet-and-sour chicken with rice and ginger chutney, and fish steamed in herbs.

Minoa Restaurant. Minoa Hotel, Náoussa. ☎ **0284/51-309.** Appetizers Dr 350–Dr 900 ($1.25–$3.85), main courses Dr 1,000–Dr 3,300 ($4.25–$14.05). No credit cards. Daily 7:30am–midnight. GREEK.

Across from Lalula is one of the town's best tavernas. A feast of rich, old-fashioned Greek fare steeped in olive oil and oregano, with fresh bread and wine, will cost about $25 for two.

Pervolaria. Naoussa. ☎ **0284/51-721.** Appetizers Dr 400–Dr 1,250 ($1.70–$5.30), main courses Dr 1,250–Dr 3,500 ($5.30–$14.90). AE, V. Daily 7pm–midnight. GREEK.

This good restaurant is set in a lush garden with geraniums and grapevines behind a white stucco house decorated with local ceramics, about a hundred yards back from the port. Favorite courses here include schnitzel à la chef (veal in cream sauce with tomatoes and basil) and tortellini Pervolaria (with pepperoni and bacon), but his Greek plate with souvlaki and varied appetizers is also recommended.

PÁROS AFTER DARK

Warning: Several places on the strip in Parikía offer very cheap drinks or "buy one, get one free"—this is usually locally brewed alcohol that the locals call *bómba.* It's illegal, and it makes one intoxicated quickly and very sick afterward.

Just behind the windmill in Parikía is a local landmark, the **Port Cafe,** a basic kafenío lit by bare incandescent bulbs and filled day and night with tourists waiting for a ferry, bus, taxi, or a fellow traveler. The cafe serves coffee, pastry, drinks, and as a place for casual conversation.

The **Pebbles Bar** in Parikía plays classical music at sunset for those who want to start their evening in a mellow mood. The **Saloon d'Or** (☎ 0284/22-176), south of the Parikía's port, is the most popular place for starting the evening with fairly inexpensive drinks, and on good nights it gets the liveliest young crowd around. Continue south from Parikía along the coast road, turn left at the bridge, and about 100 yards on you should have no difficulty finding a complex with the **Dubliner** (☎ 0284/22-759), which has live music several nights a week; **Down Under,** an Australian place, we presume; and yet another **Hard Rock Cafe** (☎ 0284/21-113).

If you're not in the mood to party, Parikía offers several more elegant alternatives. The **Pirate Bar,** a few doors away from the Hotel Dina in the agorá, is a tastefully decorated bar with a stone interior and dark wooden beams; it plays mellow jazz, blues, and classical music but its drinks are slightly more expensive. Back on the paralía, there's a more sophisticated choice with a great view of the harbor, **Evinos Bar.** It's above the retaining wall south of the OTE, high enough from the madding crowd that you can hear the music and enjoy the scenery.

For partiers in Parikía, there's the **Rendezvous,** with pretty good rock music. **Black Bart's** (☎ 0284/21-802), midway on the paralía in Parikía, is a good place for loud music and more boisterous big drinkers.

The outdoor **Ciné Rex** (☎ 0284/21-676) in Parikía shows two features, often in English. Parikía has a number of discos in the back lanes of the agorá and at the far end of the paralía, though we won't hazard a guess about which will be hot during your visit.

There seems to be little of Greek entertainment on Páros, but if you're interested ask about the possibility of seeing a performance by **N.E.L.E.** This group performs traditional dances in costume, usually in Náoussa. The bars in Náoussa tend to be more sophisticated and considerably less raucous than in Parikía. A local friend recommends the **Sofrano Bar,** on the harbor in Náoussa, for relaxing. There's also an outdoor movie theater in Náoussa, **Makis Cinema** (☎ 0284/21-676), with nightly features usually at 10pm and midnight; these are often action films in English. The hot spot in Náoussa is still **Banana Moon,** about a 10-minute walk up the main street.

A SIDE TRIP TO ANTÍPAROS

Antíparos (meaning "Opposite Páros") is a popular refuge for those who find Páros too crowded. The two islands were once connected by a natural causeway. A deep cave full of fantastic stalactites was discovered on Antíparos during the time of Alexander the Great, and it's been a reason to stop off there ever since.

Excursion caïques leave the port of Parikía regularly (hourly in the summer) beginning at 8am for the 45-minute ride to the busy little port of Antíparos. There is also a shuttle barge for vehicles as well as passengers that crosses the channel between the southern port of Poúnda and Antípáros continuously from 9am; the fare is Dr 300 ($1.30), and you can take along your bike for free. There are also round-trip caïque excursions that include a visit to the cave from Parikía for about Dr 3,000 ($12.75) and from Náoussa for Dr 1,600 ($6.80).

The **cave** is a half-hour walk up from the boat landing or a two-hour hike from the port of Antíparos. From the church of Áyios Ioánnis, you'll have an excellent view of Folégandros (furthest west), Síkinos, Íos, and part of Páros. Visitors once entered the cave by rope, but a concrete staircase now offers more convenient if less adventurous access. The farthest reaches of the cave are now closed to visitors. Through the centuries visitors have broken off parts of stalactites as souvenirs and left graffiti to commemorate their visit, but the cool mysterious cavern is still an interesting contrast to a sun-flooded beach. Among those who have left evidence of their visit are Lord Byron and King Otto of Greece. The Marquis de Nointel celebrated Christmas mass here in 1673 with 500 paid attendants and explosions to add drama.

The town of Antíparos, which has a permanent population of about 500, has several travel agents, a bank with limited open hours, a post office, and a small OTE office.

The island has a number of pensions and rooms to let and several hotels. The **Hotel Artemis** (☎ 0284/61-460; fax 0284/61-472) at the end of the paralía has 30 comfortable rooms; a double with breakfast is Dr 12,500 ($53.20). The recently renovated **Hotel Mantalena** (☎ 0284/61-206) has 35 rooms with views of the sea and small fishing port; a double with breakfast is Dr 11,500 ($48.95). There's also **Camping Antiparos** (☎ 0284/61-221) with full facilities about a 10-minute walk north from the port.

Of the several eateries the most often suggested are: **Anárgyros,** on the port below the hotel of the same name; **Klimatariá,** inland about 100 meters; and the more expensive **Marios Taverna,** which features seafood dinners and local wine, near the square.

5 Náxos

103 nautical miles (191km) SE of Piraeus

Self-sufficient Náxos is the largest and most fertile of the Cyclades. Though it's seeing an increasing number of tourists, including groups, its abundant earthy charm has so far shown little sign of succumbing to the invasion. Its Hóra boasts the famous Portára, a portal to an ancient temple of Apollo, and its Kástro, an impressive 13th-century Venetian castle surrounded by a pleasant maze of pedestrian lanes. There's also plenty of interesting and inexpensive shopping. A well-developed resort area is just south of town. The interior of the island is unspoiled, with thriving agriculture, a number of interesting villages, and spectacular scenery, including Mount Zas, the highest point in the Cyclades.

ESSENTIALS

GETTING THERE   By Plane   Olympic Airways has two flights daily (three daily in the summer) between Náxos and Athens. For information and reservations call their office in Athens (☎ 01/96-16-161) or Náxos (☎ 0285/22-095).

By Ferry   There is one ferry daily (more frequently in the summer) from Piraeus. Service is presently irregular and offered by several carriers, so check schedules in Athens by calling the **Tourist Police** at **01/171** or the **Port Authority** 01/45-11-311, or call the **Náxos Port Authority** (☎ 0285/22-340). **Ilio Lines** (☎ 0285/ 42-24-772 in Athens or 0294/22-888 in Rafína) has hydrofoil service Sunday through Friday from Rafína. There is daily (several times daily in the summer) ferry connection with Íos, Mýkonos, Páros, and Santoríni. There is ferry connection several times weekly with Sýros and Tínos, less frequently with Folégandros, Rhodes, and Sámos, and once a week with Sífnos.

VISITOR INFORMATION   There's no official tourist information office; the commercial **Náxos Tourist Information Center** (☎ 0285/22-923 or 0285/24-525; fax 0285/25-200), across the plaza from the ferry pier (not to be confused with the small office on the pier itself, which is usually closed), is run by Despina and Kostas Kitini. Their office is the most reliable and helpful one on the island, and current bus and boat schedules are posted out front. They sell Olympic Airways and ferry tickets, book island excursions, make hotel and villa reservations, exchange money, hold luggage, help make card and collect phone calls, and have two-hour laundry service.

GETTING AROUND   Walking is the best way to experience Náxos because it gives you the opportunity to join the local pace and to meet the friendly inhabitants face to face. If you plan to explore the island's interior, catch a **bus** to a village that interests you, then explore it leisurely on foot.

You can't miss the **bus station** right in the middle of the port plaza on the north end of the harbor. Ask at the nearby KTEL office, across the plaza to the left, for specific schedules. There's regular service throughout most of the island two or three times a day, more frequently to the more important destinations. In the summer there's hourly service to the nearby south coast beaches at Áyios Prokópios and Ayía Ánna.

One of the most popular day trips is to Apóllonos, near the northern tip of the island. The bus only makes this two-hour trip twice a day, and the competition for seats is often fierce, so get to the station well ahead of time. In addition to the public buses, there are various **excursion buses** that can be booked through travel agents.

Bikes will suffice for getting to the beach and back, but the interior is too mountainous to bike. A **moped** or **motorcycle** might be your choice; the island's roads are fairly good and the traffic is sane. **Moto Náxos** (☎ 0285/23-410), on the Post Office Square, and **Stelios Rent-A-Bike** (☎ 0285/24-703), near the police station, have good selections. Expect to pay about Dr 4,000 to Dr 8,000 ($17 to $34) a day, including insurance, depending on size and season. Náxos has some major inclines that require a strong motor and good brakes.

A **Jeep** or **small car** might better suit your requirements, and most travel agents rent them. **ZAS Travel** (☎ 0285/23-444), near the bus station, rents buggies, cars, and Suzukis for about Dr 10,500 to Dr 18,000 ($44.70 to $76.60) per day, including full insurance, free mileage and road service, a map, and good advice.

You might also consider hiring a **taxi;** a half-day round-the-island tour should cost you about Dr 14,000 ($59.55). The taxi station (☎ 0285/22-444) is on the port. Find a compatible driver who speaks English well enough to act as a guide, bargain, and agree on a price before you depart.

FAST FACTS   The telephone office (**OTE**) is at the south end of the port; summer hours are daily 7:30am to midnight. Turn inland at the OTE, take the first right and find the **post office** on the left; it's open 8am to 2:30pm. The town **police** (☎ 0285/23-280) are off the north end of the port, up from the bus station, across from the elementary school.

The **Tourist Police Station** (☎ 0285/22-100) is two blocks behind the Panayía Pantanássa Church, just before the Agrarian Bank, about 200 meters south from the ferry pier; there's a list of hotels and private rooms there, and they'll make reservations for you.

Náxos has a good **Health Center** (☎ 0285/23-333), open 24 hours, just outside town on the left off Odós Papavasíliou, the main street off the port just after the OTE.

Banks all keep the same hours—8am to 2pm Monday through Thursday, 8am to 1:30pm Friday—but travel agencies change money during extended hours.

English language newspapers and periodicals can be found in an old shop behind and to the right of the Captain's Cafe, at the entrance to the Old Market, or at Zoom, on the harbor front.

You may want to find a good **map** as soon as possible, as **Hóra** (Náxos town) is old, large (with a permanent population of over 3,000), and complex. The free *Summer Náxos* magazine has the best map of the city. The new Harms-Verlag *Náxos* is the best map of the island. John Freely's guide *Náxos* (Lycabettus Press) is a short colorful account with excellent descriptions of walking tours.

WHAT TO SEE & DO

Pulling into the harbor, you can already see Náxos's most famous attraction, the Portára, off to the left; the pretty little church of Panayía Myrtidiótissa on an islet in the harbor on the right; and the most important attraction, the Kástro, above.

The **Portára** ("Great Door") and a foundation is all that remains of an ancient **Temple of Apollo,** which stands on the islet of Palátia. Before the Mediterranean rose, the islet was a hill attached to Náxos. It's now accessible by a causeway off the northern tip of the harbor. The temple was once thought to honor Dionysus, the island's patron, who rescued Ariadne, daughter of King Minos of Crete, who was abandoned on Náxos by the ungrateful Theseus after she helped him kill the Minotaur and escape the Labyrinth. The temple is now believed to be dedicated to Apollo, because of a brief reference in the Delian Hymns and because it directly faces Délos, his birthplace. On a clear day you can see that island through it. It was begun in 530 B.C. by the tyrant Lygdamis, but he was deposed before it was finished. Most of the marble was carted away to build the Kástro, but fortunately the massive posts and lintel were too big for the Venetians to handle.

The exquisite Venetian **Kástro,** the medieval citadel that dominates the town, is Hóra's greatest treasure, and you should allow yourself several hours to explore it. Begin by turning left off the first square and entering the **old town** through the lancet (pointed) archway on the right. The lower part of the old town, **Boúrgos,** where the Greeks lived when the Venetians ruled the island, is a pleasantly confusing maze of narrow cobblestone lanes. The Kástro ("Castle") itself, the domain of the Catholic aristocracy, was built by Marco Sanudo, nephew of the doge of Venice. It was probably constructed on the site of the ancient Mycenaean acropolis, in the 13th century when Sanudo declared himself the Duke of Náxos. It remained the seat of Venetian power in the Cyclades for more than 300 years.

By continuing up in any direction, you will reach the outer wall of the castle, which has three entryways. Inside you'll find various buildings, some being restored. Beginning at the northern gate you'll find the **Glezos Tower,** residence of the last dukes; then by turning left, **Sanudo's Palace** on the right; and across the plaza, the **Catholic Cathedral.** To the right behind the cathedral is the **French School of Commerce** and the **Ursuline Convent and School.**

The French School has housed schools run by several religious orders, and among its more famous students was the Cretan writer Níkos Kazantzákis, who studied here in 1896. It now houses the **Archaeology Museum,** which is open 8:45am to 3pm daily, 9:30am to 2:30pm, closed Tuesday; admission is Dr 500 ($2.15). Those interested in Cycladic culture will want to take some time here. One might hope for fewer items better displayed and labeled, but nevertheless the treasures are there to be seen, including Early Cycladic vessels that demonstrate growing refinement; some excellent examples of white marble figurines; and many objects from the prosperous Late Mycenaean period (1400–1100 B.C.) found near Grotta, including vessels with the octopus motif that still appears in local art.

North of the Kástro and Boúrgos is the **Greek Orthodox Cathedral,** built in 1789; it's well worth a visit. Material from several ancient temples were used in its construction. The granite pillars are thought to be from Délos. The interior is quite ornate, and the iconostasis is particularly noteworthy.

Next to the cathedral is the **ancient agorá,** which has been partly excavated. Further north is the area called **Grotta,** below which can be seen the underwater remains of a Cycladic village.

Hóra is a fine place for shopping, both for value and variety. Toward the north end of the paralía, near the bus station, you'll find **O Kouros** (☎ 0285/25-565), which has excellent copies of Cycladic figurines in Naxian marble, other reproductions, and interesting modern ceramics; credit cards are accepted. To the right and up from the entrance to the Old Market, you'll find **Techni** (☎ 0285/24-767), which has two shops. The first shop contains a good array of silver jewelry at fair prices; above it the second, the more interesting of the two, has textiles, many handwoven, and some by local women.

Continue south along the paralía to the OTE, turn left on the main inland street, Odós Papavasilíou, and continue up on the left side of the street until your nose leads you into the **Tirokomiká Proïónia Náxou** (☎ 0285/22-230). This delightful old store is filled with excellent local cheeses (kephalotíri, a superb sharp one, and milder graviéra), barrels of olives, spices, and other dried comestibles. It's also a good place to pick up a bottle of kítron, the island's famous sweet citron liqueur.

Follow any of the nearer streets south to reach **Court Square,** which is also called Cemetery or Post Office Square. The post office is to the north, and the **cemetery,** well worth a visit, is on the southwest corner. It's only a few blocks further to the town's beach and resort suburb of Áyios Yióryios.

Áyios Yióryios is lined three or four blocks deep with resort hotels, restaurants, and bars. It's swarming with tourists, and yet it remains remarkably civilized. You have to think almost everyone has come to enjoy a quiet and relaxing vacation.

Many people head further south by bike, bus, or caïque to the less crowded beaches at Áyios Prokópios and Ayía Ánna.

Áyios Prokópios is a longer, broader, cleaner fine-sand beach with a number of hotels, pensions, and tavernas built along the road back from the beach. The **Hotel Kavoúras** (☎ 0285/23-963) is a good rooming option; a double with private bath is Dr 8,000 ($34.05), and studios for four are Dr 10,500 ($44.70). Nearby at Stylída, the handsome new **Kouros Studios** (☎ 0285/24-964; fax 22-413) are among the most stylish and luxurious on the island, with air conditioning, a pool with hydromassage, and an excellent buffet breakfast.

Ayía Ánna, the next cove south, is much smaller, with a small port for the colorful caïques that transport beachgoers from the main port. The **Hotel Kapri** (☎ 0285/23-799; fax 0285/24-736) has 36 rooms and 12 studios; doubles with private bath are Dr 8,000 ($34.05) and studios are Dr 10,500 ($44.70); minibus service to Hóra is available several times a day. The **Iria Beach Hotel** (☎ 0285/24-022; fax 0285/24-656) has 21 apartments at Dr 9,250 ($39.35) for two, Dr 10,600 ($45.10) for three, with a restaurant, minimarket, and change bureau. **Taverna Gorgóna** (☎ 0285/23-799), at the pier where the caïques dock, has an excellent buffet dinner daily, with fresh grilled fish and meat, salads, vegetables, and complimentary wine.

Both beaches have windsurfing and are ideal day trips, but not for those seeking nighttime activities. **Camping Maragas** (☎ 0285/24-552) is a good facility at Ayía Ánna. **Camping Apollon** (☎ 0285/24-117) is closer to Hóra and the inland, with modern facilities and space for RVs.

Both Áyios Prokópios and Ayía Ánna are accessible over dirt roads by public bus in the summer, when school buses run vacation routes. They run almost hourly from Hóra and cost Dr 340 ($1.45). Ayía Ánna has caïque service from the small caïque jetty south of the Myrtidiótissa church islet in Hóra, hourly from 9:30am to 5:30pm for about Dr 700 ($3) each way. From Ayía Ánna it's a 10-minute walk north to Áyios Prokópios.

South of Ayía Ánna you'll find **Pláka beach,** considered the best on the island, a 5-kilometer stretch of almost uninhabited shoreline where nude sunbathing is common. You can reach it by caïque from Hóra in the summer or by walking south from Ayía Ánna.

Further south (16 kilometers from Hóra) is **Kastráki Beach,** with waters recently rated the cleanest in the Aegean and a 7-kilometer stretch of beach. The **Summerland Complex** (☎ **0285/75-461;** fax 0285/75-399) has 12 studios for Dr 19,700 ($83.85) and three apartments for Dr 26,500 ($112.75), a pool, gym, tennis court, children's playground, snack bar, and minimarket.

Further still (21 kilometers from Hóra), **Pyrgáki,** the last stop on the coastal bus route, offers excellent swimming in the large protected bay, and 4 kilometers further, **Ayiássos** has the small **Hotel Neräïda** (☎ **0285/75-301**), which has a restaurant.

Apóllonas, 54 kilometers northeast of Hóra near the northern tip of the island, is a popular excursion because it gives an ample introduction to the scenic wonders of the island on the way to one of the island's most touted attractions, the giant *koúros.*

By car, cycle, or moped, you can make a good round-trip tour of the interior of the island, which we will describe briefly in a somewhat counterclockwise order. You can make a similar tour, though not so easily, by public bus, and you can also book bus excursions to those places that pique your interest.

East from Hóra, left from the OTE along Odós Papavasilíou past the Medical Center, about a kilometer out of town you'll reach a fork in the road; take the one to the right toward **Galanádo,** where you'll find the handsome Venetian tower, **Pýrgos Belónia,** which was the fortified house of the local Italian rulers. (Towers were strategically located around the island as refuges from invading pirates. Fires were lighted on the tower roofs to warn the neighboring villagers and adjacent towers of an attack.) In front of the tower is the 13th-century church of **Áyios Ioánnis** (St. John), an interesting monument to Venetian religious tolerance: the left side is a Catholic chapel, and the right is Orthodox.

About 3 kilometers further along on the road to Sangrí, just off the right of the road, is the recently restored 8th-century Byzantine cathedral of **Áyios Mámas,** which was neglected during the Venetian occupation, but has recently been partly restored. **Sangrí** is a corruption of Saint Croix, the French name for the three villages near the monastery of **Tímiou Stavroú** ("True Cross"). The monastery has so many remains from the past that it's sometimes referred to as "Little Mistrá." At **Káto** ("Lower") **Sangrí,** the first village, is another ruined Venetian tower. South of the pretty little village of **Áno** ("Upper") **Sangrí** is the small Byzantine chapel of **Áyios Ioánnis Yiroúlas.** It was built over an ancient temple of Demeter and is accessible by foot or by an unimproved road off the main road south from Sangrí. Further south is the Byzantine castle of **T'Apaliroú,** the last stronghold on the island to fall to Marco Sanudo. West of Sangrí is **Kalorítsa,** with the ruins of a 13th-century monastery above a cavern containing three small churches.

From Sangrí, the road descends into the lush **Tragéa Valley** toward **Halkí,** where both the Byzantines and the Venetians built fortified towers. The lovely 11th-century white church with the red-tiled roof, **Panayía Protóthronos** ("Our Lady

Before the Throne"), is sometimes open in the morning. Turn right to reach the **Frankópoulos** (or **Grazia**) **tower;** the name says it's Frankish, but it was originally Byzantine; a marble crest gives the year of 1742, when it was renovated by the Venetians. Climb the steps for an excellent view of Filóti, one of the island's largest inland villages. Halkí's other tower (*pírgos*) is to the southeast. Northwest the **Apáno Kástro** commands the valley. This Mycenaean fortress, last renovated by the Venetians, was possibly a summer residence for Marco Sanudo.

You can go north to Moní, but we recommend you continue east to **Filóti,** at the base of Mt. Zas. This is a pleasant place to stroll and look at local life. In the center of town there's the church of **Kímisis tis Theotókou** ("Assumption of the Mother of God"), with a lovely marble iconstasis, and a Venetian tower. The town has several tavernas and a few rooms to let, as well as a number of abandoned houses, which may be available for long-term rent.

The main reason to stop in Filóti, however, is to begin a hike up **Mount Zas,** the high point of the Cyclades. It takes about three hours beginning west of town. There's an interesting **cave** near the top, which was in ancient times sacred to Zeus and later used during the Turkish occupation as a Christian chapel. On the western slope is the well-preserved Hellenistic tower, **Pírgos Himárou,** built by Ptolemy.

The road continues along the slope of Mt. Zas to **Apíranthos,** the most beautiful of the mountain villages. It has marble streets as well as marble embellishments on the interesting architecture, which incorporates elements of both the Cycladic and Venetian. There are also two Venetian towers and a small archaeological museum near the main square with interesting Cycladic finds. The museum is usually open 8:30am to 1:30pm, no admission charge. Inquire for curator. The people of Apíranthos were originally from Crete; they have their own peculiar and colorful customs. Some local weaving and needlework is sold by the village women, and **Stiastó** (☎ 0285/61-392) has a good selection of popular art, including good ceramics.

The road continues north toward Apóllonas, and you may want to turn left back toward Hóra at the crossroads about 4 kilometers north of Apíranthos. North the road becomes extremely winding passing through the pretty villages of **Kóronos** and **Skádo.**

There are a number of marble quarries in the area, but about 7 miles (11km) south of Apóllonas, you'll see steps leading off to the left to the famous **koúros,** a colossal statue 28 feet (nearly 10 meters) tall begun in the 7th century and abandoned probably because of the fissures that time and the elements have exacerbated. Some archaeologists believe it was meant for the nearby temple of Apollo, but the beard suggests that it's probably the island's patron deity, Dionysus.

Apóllonas itself is a small fishing village on the verge of becoming a rather depressing resort, with a sand cove and a pebbled public beach in full view. There plenty of places to eat, rooms to let, and a few hotels. We don't recommend a stay, but the **Hotel Kouros** (☎ 0285/81-340), on the beach at the far end of town is hospitable and well maintained, with doubles for Dr 8,500 ($36.15). Don't be tempted to take the coastal road back to Hóra, as the road itself is poor, the scenery is not attractive, and you would miss Moní.

Just south of **Moní,** near the middle of the island, is the important 6th-century monastery of **Panayía Drossianí** ("Our Lady of Refreshment"). These three unimpressive gray chapels huddled together contain excellent Byzantine frescoes. Visits by those properly dressed are allowed at all hours during the day, but you may have to ring the bell to get someone to let you in. There are a couple of tavernas and some rooms to let in Moní. If you continue back to Hóra along the more northerly route you'll pass several more marble quarries and between the villages of Kinídaros and Míli on the left, with some help from locals or a good map, you'll find two more koúri, not as large but more finely detailed, also abandoned because of flaws.

WHERE TO STAY

Hóra's broad paralía is too busy for quiet accommodations, so we recommend hotels in four nearby areas, all within a 10-minute walk of the port: Boúrgo, just above the harbor below the Kástro; Grotta, left (north) and up from the port; behind the town; and Áyios Yióryios, just south (right from the harbor) of town.

BOURGO

Hotel Anixis. Hóra, 84300 Náxos. ☎ **0285/22-122.** 16 rms (12 with bath). Dr 5,900 ($25.10) single/double without bath; Dr 9,900 ($42.10) single/double with bath. No credit cards. From the bus station, take the nearest major street (with traffic) off the port and turn right through the lancet archway into the Old Market area; follow the stenciled green arrows to the Anixis Hotel.

This small hotel near the Kástro's Venetian tower offers basic comfortable accommodations in this quiet, desirable area. Shared facilities are kept clean.

Hotel Panorama. Hóra, 84300 Náxos. ☎ **0285/24-404.** 16 rms (10 with bath). Including breakfast: Dr 6,000 ($25.55) single, Dr 9,200 ($39.15) double without bath; Dr 10,600 ($45.10) double with bath. No credit cards.

Just across from the Anixis, this family run hotel is a good choice for those who want to stay in this atmospheric neighborhood. The views live up to the name.

Chateau Zevgoli. Hóra, 84300 Náxos. ☎ **0285/22-993** (01/65-15-885 in Athens). 14 rms (all with bath). Including breakfast: Dr 17,000 ($72.35) double. V.

This recently restored Venetian mansion is easily the most attractive hotel in Boúrgos, and it's one of the most desirable on the island. The lobby/dining area has been charmingly decorated with antiques and family heirlooms by the gracious and discerning owner, Despina Kitini. Each cozy room is distinctively furnished in traditional style. The rooms have modern bathrooms and central heat. All rooms open onto the central atrium with a lush garden. (Inquire at the Náxos Tourist Information Center on the paralía.)

GROTTA

Apollon Youth Hostel. Hóra, 84300 Náxos. ☎ **0285/22-468.** 25 rms (70 beds). Dr 2,300 ($9.80) per person. No credit cards.

From the bus station, take the nearest major street (with traffic) off the port and continue up. Bear right after the school and police station, continue up past the Cathedral, and you'll find the well-managed youth hostel on the left.

🚭 **Hotel Grotta.** Hóra, 84300 Náxos. ☎ **0285/22-215.** Fax 0285/22-000. 20 rms (all with bath). TEL. Dr 9,800 ($41.70) single; Dr 13,800 ($58.70) double. No credit cards.

Follow the east coast road to the left after the school, and you'll find the friendly Lianos family's hotel off to the left. Spotless rooms have polished marble floors and large balconies. The attractive dining area has a gallery overlooking the sea and the Portára. If you call ahead, Mr. Lianos will meet you at the ferry.

BEHIND THE TOWN

Hotel Anatoli. Hóra, 84300 Náxos. ☎ **0285/23-999.** 26 rms (all with bath). TEL. Dr 10,500 ($44.70) single; Dr 12,700 ($54.05) double. V.

Turn left off the paralía at the OTE and continue up the main inland street, Odós Papavasilíou, about five minutes and find this newer hotel off to the left after the health center. It doesn't have sea views, but it does have a pool, and it's only a 10-minute walk to the town beach.

Mathiassos Village Bungalows. Hóra, 84300 Náxos. ☎ **0285/22-200** (01/29-18-749 in Athens). Fax 0285/24-700. 110 bungalows (all with bath). TV TEL. Dr 20,700 ($88.10) double; Dr 27,600 ($117.45) for four. AE, EU, MC, V.

This resort complex on the ring road behind the town is one of the most luxurious on the island. It has semi-attached bungalows spread through well-landscaped grounds. There's a swimming pool and sundeck, a tennis court, cafeteria, taverna, an ouzerí, and even a chapel. The bungalows are spacious, with patios or balconies. Refrigerators are available, making them especially suitable for families. It doesn't have sea views, but it offers bus service to the beach.

ÁYIOS YIÓRYIOS

From the edge of the port to the end of the town's sandy beach is a continuous strip of hotels, restaurants, and apartments three or four blocks deep. If you don't find a room in one of the hotels we suggest, you will be able to find one nearby.

Hotel Galini. Áyios Yióryios, Hóra, 84300 Náxos. ☎ **0285/23-999.** Fax 0285/24-916. 30 rms (all with bath). TEL. Including breakfast: Dr 10,300 ($43.80) single; Dr 12,400 ($52.75) double. No credit cards.

This hotel, 50 meters from the beach, and its sister, the **Sofia,** are both run by the charming Sofia, who has a green thumb, and her amiable son George. Clean, quiet rooms have marble floors and balconies with sea views and cooling breezes. Transportation is provided to and from the port if you have a reservation.

Hotel Glaros. Áyios Yióryios, Hóra, 843 00 Náxos. ☎ **0285/23-101.** Fax 0285/24-877. 13 rms (all with bath). Including breakfast: Dr 15,200 ($64.70) single/double. AE, V.

This well-kept hotel with comfortable, shuttered rooms with balconies is near the west end of the beach. Mr. Franjescos, the friendly owner, will pick you up at the port if you have reservations. He also has some very nice studios nearby.

Hotel Nissaki. Áyios Yióryios, Hóra, 84300 Náxos. ☎ **0285/25-710.** Fax 0285/23-876. 40 rms (all with bath). TEL. Including breakfast: Dr 14,700 ($62.65) single; Dr 18,400 ($78.30) double. AE, DC, EU, MC, V.

Just across the street from the Glaros, the Papadopoulos family owns and runs this comfortable hotel, which is built on a larger scale and has a pool. Many of its large, well-furnished rooms have balconies with beach and sea views. Its large restaurant serves three meals a day at the edge of the sand.

WHERE TO DINE

The food in Hóra is generally quite good, and there are a number of pleasant places to eat that we don't have room for. The **Bakery** (☎ 0285/22-613) on the paralía has okay baked goods at fair prices. Further north, across from the bus station, **Bikini** is a good place for breakfast and crepes. The **Braziliana Pâtisserie** (☎ 0285/23-777), near the post office, is a nice place for a sweet treat, and the nearby **Klimatariá** certainly looks worth a try.

Christos' Grill. Hóra. ☎ **0285/23-072.** Appetizers Dr 450–Dr 1,100 ($1.90–$4.70); main courses Dr 1,400–Dr 2,900 ($5.95–$12.35). No credit cards. Daily 6pm–1am. GREEK.

This small family run taverna is one street up from the paralía, just off the district road (next to the church that was once a synagogue). Christos and his wife serve fresh grilled fish and meat with a large assortment of side dishes. We recommend the delicious Náxos potatoes fried in olive oil.

❸ **Faros Restaurant.** Paralía, Hóra. ☎ **0285/23-325.** Appetizers Dr 700–Dr 1,850 ($3–$7.85); main courses Dr 900–Dr 3,350 ($3.85–$14.25). AE, DC, EU, MC, V. Daily 8am–4am. INTERNATIONAL.

The best, most varied and sophisticated food on the island can be found just across from the bus station. Inside the restaurant looks like a German country inn, the walls laden with antiques. The menu is rather astonishing, with such items as smoked trout on toast with cranberry-horseradish sauce; meatballs with gypsy sauce; pepper steak with broccoli and rice; and liver Berlin style with apple, onion, and roast potatoes. (Rumor has it that the smart Berliner who owns it will open a new restaurant soon, and we advise you to try to find it.)

Nikos. Paralía, Hóra. ☎ **0285/23-153.** Appetizers Dr 660–Dr 1,750 ($2.80–$7.45); main courses Dr 1,100–Dr 2,650 ($4.70–$11.30). MC, V. Daily 8am–2am. GREEK.

The most popular restaurant in town and one of the biggest and best is above the Commercial Bank. The owner, Nikos Katsayannis, is himself a fisherman, and the range of seafood available will amaze you. It's all excellent, but if you're not in the mood for fish, try the exohikó, fresh lamb and vegetables with fragrant spices wrapped in crisp phýllo (pastry leaves). The wine list is quite large, with lots of local and Cyclades wines. The ice-cream desserts are also delightful.

Papagalos Restaurant Bar. Court Square, Hóra. ☎ **0285/22-464.** Appetizers Dr 900–Dr 2,200 ($3.85–$9.35); main courses Dr 1,250–Dr 4,000 ($4.95–$17). No credit cards. Daily 10am–3pm and 6:30pm–midnight. INTERNATIONAL.

This casual Southern California–style eatery is just south of the cemetery off the Court Square. It has quite a variety of dishes, including New Orleans pork chops, Sorrentino chicken, filet mignon oriental in sweet hot sauce, and vegetarian dishes such as a veggie burger.

Pizzaria Grill. Hóra. ☎ **0285/22-083**. Main courses Dr 700–Dr 1,850 ($3–$7.85); pizza for two Dr 1,850 ($7.85). No credit cards. Daily 11am–1am. INTERNATIONAL.

One street back from the port, near the entrance to the Old Market, you'll find this a good place for pizza, baked pasta, and roast chicken.

NÁXOS AFTER DARK

Náxos doesn't compare to Mýkonos or Santoríni for wild nightlife, but it has a lively and varied scene.

Apostolis (☎ 0285/24-781), an ouzerí on the port near the ferry pier, or **Portára,** further north, are good places to enjoy the sunset. The **Bikini** serves good drinks at reasonable prices. **Fragile** (☎ 0285/25-336), through the arch in the entrance to the Old Town, is worth a stop. **Remezzo** and **Relax** are also recommended. You can always join the evening *vólta* (stroll) along the paralía. **The Loft** is an attractive place with a savvy barman. Behind the Rendezvous (*Panteboý*) Fast Food, you'll find **Dolphini,** which begins the evening with classical music and then segues into jazz or rock easy enough for conversation. Up in Kástro, **Notos** offers an even more sedate evening with mellow jazz.

Upstairs on the paralía, the **Greek Bar** is considerably livelier. The **Flamingo,** on top of the Agricultural Bank, will appeal to those with more sophisticated tastes. **Day and Night,** opposite the OTE, has a good blend of music which becomes more purely Greek in the early morning. At the end of the waterfront past the National Bank, you'll find the more sophisticated **Véngera** (☎ 0285/23-567), a designer copy of the bar of the same name on Mýkonos, which doesn't open until 9pm and doesn't get warmed up until much later; there's a garden if the rock gets a little much for you.

Next door, **Ecstasis** has a more eclectic blend of music. Around the block, the **Island Bar** (☎ 0285/22-654) offers good rock and soul after 10pm.

Dancers may want to try the **Ocean Club** (☎ 0285/24-323) down the block, or stroll on along to the west end of the Áyios Yióryios beach and check out the **Club Limani** on the promontory. At the other end of the beach is **Flisvos** (☎ 0285/22-919). **Náxos By Night,** back closer to town, has bouzouki music and dancing. More authentic Greek music is at **O Plátanos,** 4 kilometers east of town on the road to Mélanes.

The best place to take in the sunrise is probably through the big window of the Ocean Club.

6 Santoríni

126 nautical miles (233km) SE of Piraeus

Is Santoríni (*Thíra*) the lost island of Atlantis? One of the most southerly of the Cyclades, Santoríni is one of the most spectacular islands in the world. Hundreds of ships sail into its huge caldera left by the eruption of a titanic volcano more than 3,600 years ago. Cruise ship passengers hurry to the top of the precipitous cliff to the capital, Firá, for a couple of hours of shopping and the view. Thousands of people traveling on tours or independently arrive at its homely port of Atheniós to spend a night or two, maybe in one of the many rooms to let in one of several villages. Most take in Firá, and many visit the premier archaeological site at Akrotíri, see the sunset at scenic Ía, and maybe swim at one of the dark beaches.

ESSENTIALS

GETTING THERE   By Plane   Olympic Airways has several (six in the high season) daily flights between Athens at the airport at Monólithos, which also receives European charters. There is also daily connection with Mýkonos, service three or four times a week to and from Rhodes, two or three times a week with Iráklio, Crete, and even three times a week during the high season with Thessaloníki. For schedule information and reservations, check with their office in Firá on Odós Ayíou Athanassíou (☎ 0286/22-493), just southeast of town on the road to Kamári, or in Athens at ☎ 01/96-16-161.

By Ferry   There is **ferry** service to and from Athens at least twice daily by several companies; the trip takes 10 to 12 hours, but it's relaxing and a good opportunity to see most of the rest of the Cyclades. There is ferry connection several times a day with Íos, Mýkonos, Náxos, and Páros; daily ferry service with Anáfi, Folégandros, Síkinos, and Sýros. Check schedules with **Tourist Information** in Athens (☎ 01/171) or the **Port Authority** in Piraeus (☎ 01/45-11-311) or the **Port Authority** in Santoríni (0286/22-239). There is ferry connection two or three times a week to Skiáthos and Thessaloníki and once a week with Skýros and the Dodecanese islands of Kássos, Kárpathos, and Rhodes.

There is almost daily connection by **excursion boat** with Iráklio, Crete, for about Dr 5,000 ($21.25), but because this is an open sea route the trip can be an ordeal in bad weather.

The high-speed hydrofoil *Neárchos* connects Santoríni with Íos (Dr 3,300/$14.05), Páros (Dr 6,600/$28.10), Mýkonos (Dr 7,400/$31.50), Iráklio, Crete (Dr 9,000/$38.30) three times weekly in the low season, almost daily in the high season—if the winds are not too strong. Contact a travel agent for schedule information.

Most ferry tickets can be purchased at **Nomikos Travel** (☎ 0286/23-660) with offices in Firá, Karterádos, and Périssa. Almost all ferries now dock at Atheniós, where there are buses to Firá, Kamári, and Périssa. Ía-bound travelers should go to Firá and change buses there. Taxis are also available from Athiniós, but they cost nearly ten times the bus fare.

The exposed port at Skála, directly below Firá, is usually too unsafe for ferries. Cruise ships, yachts, and excursion vessels often drop anchor well out in the harbor from Skála, and passengers are shuttled to and from shore on small caïques (skiffs). If you dock at Skála, you can take the cable car (Dr 800/$3.40), ride a mule or donkey (Dr 1,000/$4.25), or walk up to Firá. It's a tough 45-minute hike but fairly pleasant down. We recommend a mule up and the cable car down.

Sometimes ships will stop below Ía, on the northern tip of the island, and caïques will transport passengers to shore, where donkeys are available for the ascent to the town.

VISITOR INFORMATION   There is no official government tourist office, but there are a number of helpful travel agencies, as well as some we're not so sure about. We recommend **Kamari Tours** (☎ **0286/22-666;** fax 0286/22-971), two blocks south of the main square on the right, which offers day trips to most of the island's sites and can help you find a room and rent a moped. **Damigos Tours** (☎ **0286/22-504;** fax 0286/22-266), on the main square, offers excellent guided tours, at slightly lower prices. **Nomikos Tours** (☎ **0286/23-660;** fax 0286/23-666), has three helpful offices in Firá.

GETTING AROUND   By Bus   Santoríni has very good bus service. The island's central **bus station** is just south of the main square. Schedules are posted on the wall of the office above it; most routes are serviced every half hour from 7am to 11pm in the summer, less frequently in the off season. (Jot down or remember the return times from your destination, as they will probably not be displayed there, and if you miss the last bus you'll probably have to call a taxi.) Destinations are displayed on the front of the bus, and fares are collected by a conductor after the bus is underway.

By Car   Most travel agents will be able to help you rent a car. You might find that a local company such as **Zeus** (☎ 0286/24-013) will offer better prices, though the quality of your vehicle might be a bit lower. Of the better-known agencies we recommend **Budget Rent-A-Car** (☎ **0286/22-900;** fax 0286/22-887), a block below the bus stop square in Firá, where a four-seat Fiat Panda should cost about Dr 19,500 ($82.95) a day, with unlimited mileage.

By Moped   Roads on the island are notoriously treacherous, narrow, and winding, with shoulders that give way easily on steep slopes. There are a number of serious accidents and several fatalities every year. You won't have any trouble finding a moped to rent, and you should expect to pay about Dr 3,000 to Dr 6,000 ($12.75 to $25.55) per day, depending on the size and season.

By Taxi   The **taxi station** (☎ 0286/22-555) is just south of the main square, though in the high season you should book ahead by phone. The drivers are better organized here than elsewhere in the Cyclades, though not any better mannered, but prices are standard from point to point. If you call for a taxi outside Firá, you will be required to pay the pickup fare.

FAST FACTS: FIRÁ

American Express   The **X-Ray Kilo Travel Service** (☎0286/22-624; fax 0286/23-600), on the main square, is the American Express representative in Santoríni.
Area Code   The telephone area code is **0286.**
Banks   The National Bank (open weekdays 8am to 2pm) is a block south from the main square on the right near the taxi station. Many travel agents also change money; most are open daily from 8am to 9:30pm.

Hospital   The small **Health Clinic** (☎ 0286/22-237) is on the southeast edge of town on Odós Ayíou Athanassíou, to the left after the children's playground.

Police   The **police station** (☎ 0286/22-649) is on Odós I. Dekigála, several blocks south of the main square, on the left. The port police can be reached at ☎ 0286/22-239.

Post Office   The **post office** (☎ 0286/22-238; fax 0286/22-698), open 8am to 1pm Monday through Friday, is up to the right from the bus station.

Telephones   The telephone center (**OTE**) is just off Odós Ypapantís ("Gold Street"), up from the post office.

WHAT TO SEE & DO

The topography of the island is dramatic. The sheer cliff around the huge Caldera rises in layers of brick-red, charcoal, lighter gray, pink, pale green—the result of a volcanic eruption that took place between 1647 and 1628 B.C., according to the latest interpretation of the evidence. The eruption was probably at least four times as powerful as the one in Krakatoa in 1883.

The Caldera, the crater of the volcano, measures 6 miles (10km) at its widest by 4 miles (7km) at it narrowest. The entire middle of the original island is all but completely gone, and even that little reappeared only relatively recently. The eruption itself buried the cosmopolitan city of Akrotíri, and the subsequent tidal wave inundated most of the Minoan cities on Crete and very nearly destroyed its civilization.

Was this Atlantis? Plato seems to have had no doubts that such a place existed. Solon heard about it from priests he visited in Egypt, who assured him that a great advanced civilization had disappeared in a deluge 9,000 years before. But suppose he added a zero to the number in his imperfect understanding of foreign speakers, and the priests had actually said 900. That would place the cataclysm at very nearly the same date modern geological science does. Have a look at Akrotíri before you dismiss this possibility.

The ancients called the island *Strongilí* ("Round") because of the shape of the Caldera, and *Kálliste* ("Most Beautiful"). The inhabited island west across the Caldera is **Thirassí,** part of the rim of the original island, and south of it is another small remnant, the uninhabited **Asprónissi** ("White Island"). The two smoldering dark islands in the middle are **Paléa Kaméni** ("Old Burnt"), the smaller and more distant one, which appeared in A.D. 157, and **Néa Kaméni** ("New Burnt"), which began its appearance sometime in the early 18th century. (Let us say right away that there are more interesting places to visit than the litter-strewn source of the smoke, though admirers of hot mud baths may find an excursion worthwhile. Do not jump into the volcano, as there are sharp rocks beneath the surface.)

The island was renamed *Thíra* in the 10th century B.C. in honor of a Dorian invader from Sparta, and that name has stuck with most Greeks. There is ample evidence of subsequent occupation by Hellenic, Roman, and Byzantine people. The Venetian crusaders gave it the name most of us know it by, Santoríni, after Saint Irene, the island's patron saint, who died in exile here in A.D. 304. About all that remains of the Venetian occupation besides the name are the remnants of the *kástro* in the village of Pírgos and a fortress wall in Embório.

In 1956 an earthquake registering 7.8 on the Richter scale destroyed about two-thirds of the housing on the island. Because it struck early in the morning, when most of the people were out working in the fields or on their boats, only 48 people were killed. After the quake, many islanders fled to other Greek ports, America, and Australia to begin new lives, and some of them have returned to rejoin the island's 11,000 inhabitants in the island's new industry, tourism. Wine production is also important to the economy and all over the island you'll see the vines coiled into baskets that protect the grapes from the extreme heat and aridity and keep them from being blown away by the strong meltémi winds. The volcanic soil prevented the phyloxera plague that ravaged most of Europe's vineyards during the last century, and the roots, many well over a century old, run deep into the porous soil, producing some of the finest white wines in the world.

Most people first step foot on the island in the homely port of **Athiniós** and are a bit appalled by the mob they have to fight their way through. Find your hotel driver or the bus with your destination on the front and climb on for the ride. Even if you don't already have a room, unless it's the very height of the season and you're dead tired, get on the bus to Fíra and start your search there. You may want to keep your eyes half-closed as the poor vehicle makes its arduous zigzag up between hairpin turns to the top.

At the crest you'll see the village of **Megalohóri** off to the right (south, in case you need reorientation), where those interested in wine can later find the Boutari south of town on the road to Akrotíri. The bus will turn left (north), and the pretty village of **Pírgos** ("Tower"), the oldest and highest settlement on the island, will be off to the right, and worth a visit later to its charming churches and old houses clinging to the ruins of the Venetian castle. The first village you'll pass through is **Messariá,** where the road to the right branches after about a kilometer, to the south to the island's major resort at Kamári and west to the airport and the small beach at Monólithos. (Those coming from the airport will be joining our tour now.)

Start getting ready for Fíra—that's the official spelling, though you will hear plenty of people, including islanders, saying *Fíra,* which is perhaps a confusion with *Thíra* (also spelled *Théra*), and of course also called Hóra. Just off to the right beyond the growing cluster of hotels as you pull into town is the village of **Karterádos,** an intriguing maze around a handsome old cathedral, which can be a convenient place to stay. The bus will stop just south of **Platía Theotokopoúlou** (El Greco, to you), the **main square,** which really isn't much, though it has a number of travel agencies and serves as a good point of reference.

If you want to head straight for the famous view, just climb the hill to **Odós Ypapantís ("Gold Street").** The shopping is to the right, and the **Cathedral of Panayía Ypapantís** is to the left. If you continue to the left past the modern Greek Orthodox Cathedral, which definitely deserves a look, you'll find the quiet **Platía Sarpáki,** but the chances are you'll want to turn right and join the crowd in the town's most acclaimed activity, **shopping.** If you're interested in fine jewelry, the prices are just a little higher than they are in Athens, but the selection is fantastic. **Porphyra** (☎ 0286/22-981), in the Fabrica Shopping Center near the Cathedral, has some impressive work. Santoríni's best known jeweler is probably **Kostas Antoniou** (☎ 0286/22-633), on Odós Ayíou Ioánnou, north of the cable car station. And there are plenty of shops between the two. Generally the further north you go the higher prices get, the less certain the quality, and the greater the pressure.

The **donkey station** is down to the left on little Odós Marinátou, and the lower, and much quieter street is called Ayíou Miná. (By following it north you could reach **Odós M. Nomikoú** (Nomikós Street), which follows the edge of the caldera all the way to the northern tip of the island.) At the north end of Gold Street you'll find the **cable car station.** The Austrian-built system, the gift of wealthy shipowner Evángelos Nomikós, can take you down to the port of **Skála** in two minutes. The cable car makes the trip every 15 minutes from 6:45am to 8:15pm for Dr 800 ($3.40), and it's worth every cent, especially on the way up—unless you'd prefer to take one of the well-cared-for donkeys or mules.

The **Catholic church** is about a block further to the north, to the right or left and around. (The island has a large and fairly influential Catholic population.) Up and to the right from the cable car station is the very attractive **Archaeology Museum** (☎ 0286/22-217), which has some Early Cycladic figurines, vases from Ancient Thíra, some interesting Dionysiac figures, as well as finds from Akrotíri. It's open Tuesday to Sunday 8am to 3pm; admission is Dr 500 ($2.15). (The famous frescoes are in the National Archaeological Museum in Athens, though rumors persist that a museum will be built to house them locally.)

Beyond the museum and to the left you'll find the **Mégaron Gízi,** a cultural center and museum in a handsome 17th-century mansion with paintings, old photographs, manuscripts, and maps. It's open daily from 10:30am to 1:30pm and 5 to 8pm; admission is Dr 400 ($1.70), children are free. Those interested in icons will want to continue through the gallery to the workshop of **Catherina Ioannidou** (☎ 0286/23-077).

North of Firá, both along pedestrian Odós Nomikoú and Odós 25 Martíou (25th of March), off the northwest corner of the main square, you'll reach the suburb of **Firostepháni** and beyond it **Imerovígli** ("Dayvigil"), the highest point along the lip of the caldera, from which a watch was kept for pirates. If you have the time and stamina, you really should take the spectacular footpath along the caldera; it's only 3 kilometers. You might even consider hiking all the way to the northern tip of the island, another 9 kilometers, to dramatic Ía (spelled *Oía* in Greek pronounced as we spell it).

Ía is the most beautiful and pleasantly unconventional village on the island, if not in the whole Cyclades. It's world famous for its spectacular sunsets. Wait for the crowds to depart and you'll find yourself in one of the most peaceful and sophisticated spots in the Aegean. It survived the 1956 earthquake better than any place on the island—which is not to say it escaped it entirely, and the damage still shows in places. The ruined **Lontza Castle** at the western end of town is the best place to catch the sunset. There is some new construction and much tasteful reconstruction. It gets more elegant every time we visit, and yet it retains much down-to-earth charm and remains a very special place and a very attractive alternative to pricey, hectic Fíra.

There are basically only two streets, the one with traffic and the much more pleasant inland pedestrian lane, Odós Nikólaos Nomikoú (the other end of the Nomikós Street that began in Firá), paved with marble, with a growing number of interesting shops, pleasant tavernas, and bars. There's a small **Naval Museum** (☎ 0286/71-156) in an old mansion, open Wednesday to Monday from 10am to 1pm and 5 to 8pm. The fishing port southeast below, **Arméni,** where ferries sometimes dock and you can catch an excursion boat around the caldera, has a small taverna.

One thing English-speaking foreigners can do in Ía more easily than just about anywhere in Greece is get married. Márkos Karvoúnis, of **Karvounis Tours** (☎ 0286/71-290 or 0286/71-209; fax 0286/71-291) has proven himself as good at arranging weddings (not marriages) as he is at making travel and accommodation arrangements. Visit his office on the marble pedestrian street to change money, make a metered long-distance call, rent a villa or room, book island day trips, or purchase ferry and plane tickets; AE, MC, V accepted. You can also call if you have questions between the hours of 10am and 2pm and 6:30 to 10pm, his time, from April through October. (The newer travel agencies on the bus stop square are staffed by unknowledgeable Athenians and charge higher rates for changing money.)

Many people find it unthinkable to visit a Greek island without a visit to a beach. Let's be honest and admit that Santoríni doesn't have the finest. (With all its other assets, it doesn't need them.) There's okay swimming west below Ía, off a cement platform at **Ammoúdi,** and down the gentler northern slope at **Baxédes** or **Mavrópetra.**

There are small beaches all along the east coast of the island, though none of them is anything to rave about, including **Paradise** and **Kolumbus** near the north end. **Monólithos,** near the end of the road to the airport has a small beach and a couple of tavernas, and a little further south **Ayía Paraskeví,** has a bit of beach and the small **Tomato Taverna,** which residents claim is one of the best on the island.

Kamári, a little over halfway down the coast, has the best beach on the island. It's also the most developed, lined by hotels, tavernas, restaurants, shops, and clubs. On the way to Kamári from Firá you can stop at **Canava Roussos** (☎ **0286/31-278**) to sample their wines at a reasonable price and purchase any you particularly like. Though the black pebbled beach at Kamári is often overcrowded, the resort itself remains quite pleasant, especially at night. It's altogether more attractive than the resort that's growing along the less crowded and scruffier beach at **Périssa,** to the south.

These two major beaches are separated by a headland called Mésa Vouná on which stands the ruins of **Ancient Thíra.** It was first inhabited by the Dorians in the 9th century B.C., though most of the buildings date from the Hellenistic era when the site was occupied by Ptolemaic forces. It has a few Byzantine remains. It's open Tuesday through Saturday 9am to 2:30pm and on Sunday and holidays until 1pm. You can reach the site by taxi or take one of the various excursions offered from Firá, including an ascent by mule for about Dr 4,500 ($19.15). Or you can hike; the shorter way is a half hour up from Périssa, but the more interesting way is from Kamári, which we recommend for your descent, as it passes a large cave with a small shrine and the only freshwater spring on the island. (Wear sturdy shoes and bring food and water.)

After you enter the site follow the path to the left, where you'll find a small shrine with symbols carved into the rocks: the eagle of Zeus, the lion of Apollo, and the dolphin of Poseidon. There's also a portrait of a Dorian admiral. Just south is the ancient Agorá and behind it the ruins of the Governor's Palace. On the southern end is a terrace thought to be the center for religious practices. It's considered the sanctuary of Apollo, with graffiti from about 800 B.C. giving the names of boys who danced naked in his honor. Nearby are the remains of houses with mosaics. From the theater the view is fantastic, with the sea 1,200 feet directly below, to the left the ancient port and beach of Kamári, and to the right the beach of Périssa.

Further up the same mountain is the **Monastery of Profítis Ilías,** built in 1712 on the island's highest point, now spoiled by communication towers and a NATO radar antenna. Part of the monastery has been converted into a museum of local culture. Because the population of monks has dwindled and objects have been stolen, the monastery is presently all but closed to visitors. (Those wishing to visit should try to make arrangements through a travel agency.)

South of the monastery, on the road to Périssa, is the handsome old village of **Embório.** Homes have been built into the ruins of its Venetian fortress, and life has a much more traditional pace and feel than elsewhere on the island. Further south, at the southernmost tip of the island is **Exomitís,** the best preserved Byzantine fortress in the Cyclades, with a small beach nearby.

Last and most impressive is the archaeological site of **Akrotíri,** near the southwest end of the crescent. It has given the world a fascinating look at daily Minoan life, provided the most astonishingly beautiful frescoes from the prehistoric world and along with other exquisite artifacts, and promises much more.

Akrotíri can be reached by public bus or private bus tour; **Damigos Tours** (☎ **0286/22-504**), on the main square, has expert and entertaining guides. Admission costs Dr 1,500 ($6.40), and the site is open from 8:30am to 3pm daily. Because the excavation is protected by a greenhouse-like roof it, gets quite hot by midday. The growing afternoon crowds and fine dust make it increasingly unpleasant, so go as early as possible. You can stop at the **Boutari winery** (☎ **0286/81-011**) afterward to sample some of this excellent company's fare, or hike over to the pebbly Red Beach for a swim and a seafood lunch.

You enter the Akrotíri site along the main street, and on either side are the stores or warehouses of the ancient commercial city. One room held 400 clay vessels stacked according to size. Another held large earthen jars, called *píthi*, some with traces of olive oil, fish, and onion inside. On down the street you'll come to a triangular plaza, and in front of you is the West House. This three-story home is also called the Captain's House because of the richly detailed fresco found on the second floor. It depicts a naval engagement, perhaps a battle, between Minoans and Libyans.

Continuing along the main street, you'll see other houses where other remarkable frescoes were discovered—all in fragments that have been meticulously reassembled. (The originals are in the National Archaeological Museum in Athens, which you should also definitely visit. Reproductions and photo postcards are available locally, and there is hope the originals will be returned to a new museum in Firá.) You can also see the "ghosts" of wooden parts of the structures and furniture, including that of a bed remarkably like ones still slept on by today's peasants.

WHERE TO STAY

Santoríni is packed in July and August, and if you plan to visit during that time you should make a reservation with a deposit at least two months in advance or be prepared to accept pot luck. Book your room yourself when possible, as travel agencies can add as much as 35% to your cost. Do not accept rooms offered at the port unless you are exhausted and don't care how meager the room and how remote the village you wake up in in the morning, and then commit yourself to one night only. Otherwise, it's probably better to pay a travel agent his fee to find a room that better suits your preference.

You will have to pay a premium for a hotel room with a Caldera view, especially in Firá, but the number of possible alternatives is remarkable. If you come between April and mid-June or in September or October— when the island is less crowded and far more pleasant—the rates can be nearly half the high-season rates we quote.

The barrel-roofed cave houses, built for earthquake resistance and economy, may at first strike you as rather cramped, dark and stuffy, but like most visitors you'll probably soon find them another part of the island's special charm.

Many of the island's best hotels don't have ocean views, and there are plenty of modest but perfectly acceptable little hotels all over the island. Many local people have built modern additions to their houses or separate apartments that can be quiet, comfortable, and more affordable.

Part of the expense on arid Santoríni is the cost of trucking water from Kamári, the only source of water on the island.

FIRÁ

Due to the noise in Firá, light sleepers may want to consider one of the more remote possibilities.

Hotel Aressana. Firá, 84700 Santoríni. ☎ **0286/23-900.** Fax 0286/23-902. 39 rms, 9 suites (all with bath) A/C TEL. Including breakfast: Dr 39,000 ($165.95) single; Dr 48,750 ($207.45) double; suites from Dr 61,000 ($259.55). AE, DC, EU, MC, V.

This newer hotel has just about everything you could ask for except a Caldera view—though it's only a block away, just beyond the Cathedral, across a small plaza from the Atlantis Hotel. The rooms are large, attractively furnished and very comfortable, but the big pluses are the large swimming pool and the location just beyond the action and near the view.

Hotel Kavalari. P.O. Box 17, Firá, 84700 Santoríni. ☎ **0286/222-347** or 0286/22-603. Fax 0286/22-603. 18 rms (all with bath) TEL. Including breakfast: Dr 18,650 ($79.40) single; doubles from Dr 30,200 ($128.60) double; triples from Dr 45,950 ($195.60). AE, MC, V.

This excellent hotel just below Gold Street has traditional-style accommodations. Each room is unique, comfortably furnished, colorfully decorated, and faces the Caldera. There are shared patios for enjoying the view. Some rooms have kitchenettes and cost a bit more.

Ⓢ Loucas Hotel. Firá, 84700 Santoríni. ☎ **0286/22-480** or 0286/22-680. Fax 0286/24-882. 20 rms (all with bath). A/C TV TEL. Including breakfast: Dr 20,600 ($87.65) single; Dr 25,600 ($108.95) double. MC, V.

This is one of the oldest and best hotels on the Caldera, with barrel-ceilinged "caves" built to prevent collapse during an earthquake. All units are newly renovated, and some have been enlarged. They're furnished with handsome blue furniture and have shared patios overlooking the Caldera. An excellent value for the location, amenities, and view.

Pelican Hotel. P.O. Box 5, Firá, 84700 Santoríni. ☎ **0286/23-113** or 0286/23-114. Fax 0286/23-514. 18 rms (all with bath) A/C TV TEL. Including breakfast: Dr 25,600 ($108.95) single; Dr 32,000 ($136.15) double. AE, DC, MC, V.

This attractive newer hotel is just north of the central square, so it doesn't have a Caldera view, but it's nevertheless a good choice. The spotless rooms are large and comfortable, the staff is friendly and helpful, and the breakfast includes fresh orange juice.

Pension Blue Sky. Firá, 84700 Santoríni. ☎ **0286/23-400.** 25 rms (all with bath). Dr 10,200 ($43.40) single; Dr 20,750 ($88.30) double.

This good new hotel just below town has a swimming pool. Continue down past the Pelican Hotel northeast off the main square, turn left at the supermarket, take the next right and find it about 100 meters down on the right. If they're full, ask about the Pension Soula across the street.

CAMPING

There's an excellent camp site at **Camping Santoríni** (☎ 0286/22-944) south of town and two youth hostels:

International Youth Hostel Kamares. Firá, 84700 Santoríni. ☎ **0286/23-142.** 66 beds, 80 more on roof, 14 showers. Dr 2,000 ($8.50). No credit cards.

The IYHF hostel, 200 meters north of the bus station, past the main square on the left, is newer, cleaner, and better managed than the Kontohori International. There are separate dorms for males and females, with bunk beds. No curfew.

Kontohori International Youth Hostel. Firá, 84700 Santoríni. ☎ **0286/22-722.** 48 beds. Dr 1,500 ($6.40). No credit cards.

This hostel, about 400 meters north of the bus stop, right off 25 March Street, offers clean dorm beds, hot showers, advice, and ferry tickets at a discount to their guests.

FIROSTEPHÁNI

This quieter and less-expensive neighborhood is just a 10-minute walk from Firá. The views of the Caldera are just as good, if not better. There are many rooms to let, and except in the high season, you can have your choice. Make reservations for the high season.

The **Hotel Galini** (☎ **0286/22-336**) is near the center of town, below the cliffside pedestrian lane. It has 15 units tiered down the cliff for excellent Caldera views, and there are separate entrances off a common veranda for privacy. Doubles go for Dr 16,400 ($69.80); AE, MC, and V are accepted. A little further north on the lane is the more luxurious **Hotel Heliovassílema** or **Sunset Hotel** (☎ **0286/23-046**). It's built in the traditional style; comfortable doubles with telephones cost Dr 19,500 ($83), and breakfast, served on the terrace with a Caldera view, is Dr 1,250 ($5.30) per person. The **Grotto Villas** (☎ **0286/22-141;** fax 0286/22-187) has 12 self-catering apartments, each with its own private terrace; studios for two cost from Dr 32,500 ($138.30).

The newer **Sun Rocks Apartments** (☎ and fax **0286/23-241**) has 22 units, with a swimming pool, breakfast, and laundry and grocery delivery service. Studios start at Dr 41,500 ($176.60). Just beyond them, **Nomikos Villas** (☎ **0286/23-887;** fax 0286/23-666) is our first choice among the luxury apartments and studios in Firostepháni. These thoroughly modernized traditional cave houses have bathtubs, telephones, television, and a swimming pool. Some units come with a kitchen and private terrace. Doubles start at Dr 32,500 ($138.30), apartments for four cost Dr 57,500 ($244.70), and six can share a villa for Dr 73,000 ($310.65). AE, MC, V are accepted.

IMEROVÍGLI

The next village north, where the "day vigil" was kept from the highest point on the Caldera, has a number of excellent accommodations. Outstanding among these is **Heliotopos** (☎ **0286/23-670** or 01/93-83-059 in winter; fax 0286/23-672). A perfect place for a honeymoon, it's a beautiful secluded traditional complex with eight studios (Dr 65,000 $276.60) and two suites (Dr 50,000/$212.75). Each unit is distinctively configured and decorated. There's an especially charming dining grotto and a sumptuous breakfast. All major credit cards are accepted. Nearby **Remezzo Villas** (☎ and fax **0286/23-030**) has eight units with kitchen and bath from Dr 34,000 ($144.70), three bedrooms from Dr 43,000 ($183). AE, MC, V are accepted.

ÍA

Ía has a wide variety of housing to suit just about any budget range; this includes a number of restored houses and villas that can accommodate up to seven people. Information and bookings are available from **Cycladic Environments,** P.O. Box 382622, Cambridge, MA 02238, ☎ **800/719-5260,** fax 617/492-5881. Rates begin at Dr 19,500 ($83) a night for two up to Dr 41,000 ($174.45) for six.

Karvounis Tours (☎ **0286/71-209;** fax 0286/71-291) books the **Armenaki Villas,** a more contemporary complex overlooking the village and Caldera. It has units for two at Dr 41,000 ($174.45), as well as other villas, private apartments, and hotel rooms.

Ía also has a few rooms to let, though they are harder to find and more expensive than in and near Firá. Some more conventional accommodations are:

Hotel Anemones. Ía, 84702 Santoríni. ☎ **0286/71-220.** 10 rms (all with bath). Dr 12,500 ($53.20) single/double. No credit cards.

Comfortable modern rooms at a good price. A superb view from the breakfast room.

Canaves Ía Traditional Houses. Ía, 84702 Santoríni. ☎ **0286/71-453;** fax 0286/71-195 or in Athens 01/89-42-441; fax 01/89-44-543). 15 houses (all with bath). MINIBAR TEL. Beginning at Dr 45,000 ($191.50) for two and Dr 80,500 ($342.55) for six. MC, V.

These exclusive houses are furnished in traditional island style, and they have views of the Caldera, fully equipped kitchens, and private terraces. The complex has a swimming pool with a bar.

Hotel Finikiá. Finikiá, 84702 Santoríni. ☎ **0286/71-373** (or in Athens 01/65-47-944). Fax 0286/71-338. 15 rms (all with bath). Dr 13,500 ($57.45) single; Dr 17,500 ($74.45) double. MC, V.

This new complex, just east of Ía, is in the traditional cubic style and has a good pool. Each room has its own personality and its own small front patio garden.

Hotel Fregata. Ía, 84702 Santoríni. ☎ **0286/71-221.** Fax 0286/71-333. 19 rms (all with bath). TEL. Including breakfast: Dr 18,600 ($79.15) double.

This is one of the better contemporary-style hotels, with a plant-filled breakfast room, a superb view, and a giant chess game on the roof.

Ía Youth Hostel. Ía, 84702 Santoríni. ☎ **0286/71-292.** Fax 0286/71-291. Including breakfast: Dr 4,250 ($18.10) per person.

This recently built international youth hostel is about 50 meters north of the bus stop square. The traditional dormitory-style rooms are comfortable, and the complex includes a minimarket, bar, restaurant, as well as telephone, postal, and travel service.

Laokasti Villas. Ía, 84702 Santoríni. ☎ **0286/71-343.** Fax 0286/71-116. 8 units (all with bath). TEL. Including breakfast: Dr 31,000 ($131.90) double; Dr 5,000 ($21.30) per extra person. AE, MC, V.

These eight small villas are furnished in the traditional style have kitchenettes and room for an additional person or two. The complex has a swimming pool, a reception room with fireplace, a cozy bar, and a breakfast room with a panoramic view toward the beach and coast. On the west side of the vehicle road.

Lauda Rooms and Houses. Ía, 84702 Santoríni. ☎ **0286/71-204** or 0286/71-157. 16 rms (2 with bath). Dr 15,800 ($67.25) single/double without bath; Dr 18,750 ($79.80) single/double with bath; Dr 25,000 ($106.40) house with kitchen.

These charming traditional rooms are pleasant even without a private bathroom. The priceless Caldera views make them a good value. Located below the pedestrian lane.

Museum Hotel. Ía, 84702 Santoríni. ☎ **0286/71-515** or 01/77-58-780 in Athens. Fax 0286/71-516. 9 apts (all with bath). MINIBAR TV TEL. Dr 37,500 ($159.55) for two; Dr 47,500 ($202.15) for three. MC, V.

In a restored museum on the pedestrian lane, these beautiful new apartments are stylishly and distinctively furnished. They have fully equipped kitchens, and there's a good pool in a quiet courtyard. The only thing they lack is an ocean view.

Perivolas Traditional Settlement. Ía, 84702 Santoríni. ☎ and fax **0286/71-309** or in Athens ☎ and fax 01/62-08-249. 14 units (all with bath). TEL. Dr 57,000 ($242.55) for two; Dr 68,800 ($292.75) for five. EU, MC, V.

What distinguishes these beautiful villas is that they are restored traditional houses and wineries; they have a rustic elegance that copies just don't have. They have domed bathrooms, kitchenettes, and patios. The complex has a good pool, a snack bar, breakfast veranda, laundry facilities, and parking.

KARTERÁDOS

Just 1¼ miles southeast of Firá, this attractive whitewashed traditional village offers a more sedate setting, if not the views. Several women in the village offer rooms attached to their homes at Dr 8,000 to Dr 12,000 ($34.05 to $51.05). The helpful local office of **Nomikos Tours** (☎ **0286/23-660**), on the main square, can help you find a room, exchange travelers checks, and arrange ferry tickets.

A few minutes from Karterádos's main square, near the bus station, the **Hotel Palladion** (☎ 0286/22-583), has simple doubles with baths and telephone for Dr 14,500 ($61.70). Breakfast (included) is served in the charming ground floor dining room, which is decorated with lace, flowers, and traditional embroidery. Further up the road, the **Hotel Cyclades** (☎ 0286/22-948), which looks like a whitewashed private villa, has 26 doubles for Dr 12,500 to Dr 18,500 ($53.20 to $78.70), breakfast included.

Readers have suggested several hotels. The **Pension George** (☎ 0286/22-351) is particularly recommended because of its gregarious host, George Halaris, and his English wife, Helen. The clean rooms have private baths; singles go for Dr 10,200 ($43.40) and doubles for Dr 14,000 ($59.55). The **Hotel Olympia** (☎ 0286/22-213) has a pool and 25 rooms (all with bath); singles cost Dr 14,000 ($59.55) and doubles go for Dr 19,500 ($83).

The **Villa Odyssey** (☎ 0286/23-681) has 17 rooms (all with bath) with singles for Dr 12,500 ($53.20) and doubles for Dr 17,200 ($73.20).

The best lodgings in Karterádos are at the **Santoríni Tennis Club Apartments** (☎ 0286/22-122 or 01/86-57-157 in Athens; fax 0286/23-698), created from abandoned 19th-century village homes. Some of these nine handsome villas have room for five people, and they're all equipped with kitchenettes and telephones. There's a swimming pool and two tennis courts. Doubles cost from Dr 35,000 ($148.95); AE, MC, V are accepted.

MESSARIÁ

This busy crossroads village has a number of acceptable hotels and one of the island's finest guest houses, the **Archontikó Argyroú** (☎ 0286/31-669 or in Athens 01/32-23-100; fax 01/32-16-855 in Athens). This beautifully renovated neoclassical mansion is furnished and decorated with authentic 19th-century antiques so exactingly that the salon is also a museum. It's open to the public daily except Wednesday mornings from 10am to 1pm and 4 to 7pm; the entrance and guided visit is Dr 1,000 ($4.25). There are six distinctive apartments available; the largest with room for four has a fully equipped kitchen, direct-dial telephone system, and daily maid service for Dr 55,000 ($234.05). The smallest, which has a modern bathroom, fridge, and telephone, costs Dr 25,000 ($106.40).

You'll also find one of the island's biggest and best hotels:

Santoríni Image Hotel. Messariá, 84700 Santoríni. ☎ 0286/31-874 or 0286/31-875. Fax 0286/31-174. In Athens 01/60-13-014; fax 01/63-91-193. 130 rms (all with bath). TEL. Including half board: Dr 42,500 ($180.85) double. AE, MC, V.

The architecture suggests a traditional decor, though it's thoroughly modern and rather elegant inside. The rooms are spacious by local standards, with high ceilings, marble bathrooms, central heat, and private patios or balconies. The complex includes a huge pool and a pool bar, a children's pool and playground, a lighted tennis court, snack bar, the chic Apollo bar, a large restaurant, a more formal supper room with piano bar, a nightclub, and conference facilities, all in beautifully landscaped grounds.

KAMÁRI

Most of the hotels at Santoríni's best and best-known resort are booked by tour groups in the summer. Those who visit in the spring or fall will probably be able to find a room on their own or through travel agencies. Visit the Firá or local office of **Kamári Tours** (☎ 0286/31-390 or 0286/31-455), which books most of Kamári's rooms as well as tours and cruises to other islands.

Kamári Camping (☎ 0286/32-452 or 0286/31-453) is an attractive facility 800 meters from the beach. It has 590 sites and costs Dr 2,000 ($8.50) per person.

There's a tourist information center, restaurant, cafeteria, minimarket, laundry, hot showers, public telephone, and bus service.

Akis Hotel. Kamári, 84700 Santoríni. ☎ **0286/31-670.** Fax 0286/31-423. 18 rms (all with bath). Dr 19,500 ($82.90) single; Dr 25,250 ($107.45) double. AE, MC, V.

This hotel is on the main street, just 30 meters from the beach. It has a cafe/cafeteria downstairs with good food, attested to by the local clientele.

Kamari Beach Hotel. Kamári Beach, 84700 Santoríni. ☎ **0286/31-216** or 0286/31-243 or 01/48-28-826 in Athens. Fax 0286/31-243. 92 rms (all with bath). Including breakfast: Dr 35,500 ($151.05) double. AE, DC, MC, V.

This superior hotel has the best beachfront location. All its rooms overlook the lovely pool below and the Aegean beyond it.

Korali Hotel. Kamári Beach, 84700 Santoríni. ☎ **0286/31-904.** 9 rms (all with bath), 2 apts. Dr 23,000 ($97.85) single/double. MC, V.

The handsome new hotel is behind the Korali Taverna. The rooms are attractive, quiet, and comfortable; each has its own entrance.

Matina Hotel. Kamári Beach, 84700 Santoríni. ☎ **0286/31-491.** Fax 0286/31-860. 27 rms (all with bath). Including breakfast: Dr 24,500 ($104.25) single or double; Dr 19,450 ($82.75) single or double without breakfast in pension annex. AE, EU, MC, V.

A thoroughly modern hotel, just a two-minute walk from the beach. If they're booked, ask about their nearby annex, Pension Matina.

Rooms Hesperides. Kamári, 84700 Santoríni. ☎ **0286/31-185.** 17 rms (all with bath). Dr 12,500 ($53.20) single/double. No credit cards.

Little English is spoken at this neat, modern pension in the middle of the pistachio orchard across from the Akis Hotel in town, but the owners are very friendly and hospitable. Excavations around the pension have revealed buried Byzantine ruins.

Venus Hotel. Kamári Beach, 84700 Santoríni. ☎ **0286/31-183.** 60 rms (all with bath). Including breakfast: Dr 25,350 ($107.85) single/double. MC, V.

This plush hotel next to the Kamari Beach has comfortable rooms done with touches of pastels and having white-on-white marble floors. There's central heating and radios.

MEGALOHÓRI

One of the island's most charming villages has Santoríni's finest hotel:

Vedema Hotel. Megalohóri, 84700 Santoríni. ☎ **0286/81-796** or 0286/81-797. Fax 0286/81-798. In Athens, ☎ 01/42-24-980; fax 01/42-23-851. In the U.S., 800/525-4800. 42 residences (all with bath). A/C MINIBAR TV TEL. Including breakfast: 1-bedroom apartment Dr 60,000 ($255.30); 2-bedroom apartment Dr 85,000–Dr 125,000 ($361.70–$531.90); 3-bedroom apartment Dr 140,000 ($595.75). AE, DC, EU, MC, V.

This member of "Small Luxury Hotels of the World" is justly proud of its attentive but unobtrusive service. The residences are set around several irregular courtyards much like those found in the village itself. Each apartment is unique, comfortable, and tastefully furnished; they have separate living rooms, marble bathrooms, central heat, refrigerators and bars, and twice-daily maid service. The complex has a nice swimming pool with a bar, the medieval chic Vedema restaurant with fine Mediterranean cuisine, the charming Canava Bar in a 300-year-old wine cellar, a souvenir and sundry shop, in-house laundry service, and an interesting art gallery with a new exhibition each month. The only false note is the poor acoustics in the conference hall.

PÉRISSA

This is generally a backpackers' beach, but Santoríni is so popular that some better hotels are springing up, but they're usually booked up by groups in the summer.

Périssa Camping (☎ **0286/81-343**), right behind the beach, has sites for Dr 900 ($3.85) per person; a tent is Dr 400 ($1.70) extra. It's the nude sunbathing center of Périssa. There are free hot showers for guests, a minimarket, a bar, snack bar, and a very active canteen with excellent music.

Périssa has two youth hostels; they're about 100 meters from the beach and are located across the main road from each other. The **International Youth Hostel Périssa** (☎ and fax **0286/81-639**) is better managed; it offers hot showers, a friendly atmosphere, and 42 beds for females, 40 for males, at Dr 2,750 ($11.70) per person. The **Youth Hostel Anna,** across the road, is doing as well as it can on its limited means. It has a friendly management and a good local reputation, and it costs slightly less.

Marco's Rooms, a spotless new family run pension, is a five-minute walk from the beach. It has 12 rooms (all with bath), marble floors, and balconies. Doubles cost Dr 10,500 ($44.70); MC and V are accepted; inquire at Marco's Taverna. **Darzeda Pension** (☎ **0286/81-236**), 60 meters from the beach above the bus stop at the north end of town, has 13 simple rooms, all with bath and refrigerator, some with balconies; doubles cost Dr 9,250 ($39.35).

The modern **Meltemi Hotel** (☎ **0286/81-119** or 0286/81-325; fax 0286/81-139), has 47 clean fresh rooms, all with baths and phones, and it's own pool. Singles cost Dr 10,000 ($42.55); doubles go for Dr 13,250 ($56.40); AE, MC, V are accepted. Newer air-conditioned apartments rent for Dr 20,500 ($87.25) for two, Dr 5,000 ($21.30) for each additional person.

AKROTÍRI

Just outside the village of Akrotíri you'll find the hotel most often recommended by Frommer's readers, **Villa Mathios** (☎ **0286/81-152**). It has a swimming pool, restaurant, and 25 rooms (all with bath). Dr 18,000 ($76.60) for singles, Dr 20,000 ($85.10) for doubles, including breakfast and transport.

WHERE TO DINE
FIRÁ

Generally the closer you are to the cable car, the steeper the tabs at restaurants (someone has to pay the outrageous rents) and the smaller the incentive for quality (those tourists will never be back). The **Kastro,** though, has a very good reputation. The better restaurants on Gold Street are nearer the Cathedral and include **Alexandria, Aris, Meridiana, Selene,** and **Sphinx.** The Chez Cat'rine on Mýkonos is famous and merits the prices it charges; the restaurant by the same name in Firá hopes you won't know the difference. *Note:* We've received numerous complaints about exorbitant charges for seafood and wine at several of the newer restaurants.

Aris Restaurant. Odós Ayíou Miná, Firá. ☎ **0286/22-840.** Appetizers Dr 300–Dr 1,500 ($1.30–$6.40); main courses Dr 1,250–Dr 3,000 ($5.30–$12.75). MC, V. Daily noon–1am. GREEK/INTERNATIONAL.

This excellent restaurant is on the lower pedestrian street, south of the donkey path down to Skála, and below the Loucas Hotel. The chef was formerly at the Athens Hilton. The dishes, mainly Greek, are updated and refined. The mezédes are delicious, especially the saganáki made with Náxos graviéra cheese and the dish-baked moussáka is superb. Try Aris Ziras's own white house wine.

How Akrotíri Was Discovered

During the construction of the Suez Canal in the 1860s a French firm, mining for pumice for making water-resistant cement, ran into some hard areas that turned out to be the walls of ancient buildings. A French geologist named Fouqué, interested in the eruption of the volcano came to investigate. Along with some locals, he discovered some vessels containing carbonized food, bits of frescoes, and metal tools—evidence that the inhabitants had been rather advanced. In the early 1930s, the Minoan expert Spyrídon Marinátos, noting the sudden and simultaneous abandonment of many Minoan settlements on Crete without evidence of warfare, began to formulate a theory of their inundation by a tidal wave following the eruption of the Thíra volcano. (The destructive tsunami following the eruption of Krakatoa was an important clue.) In 1967, Dr. Marinátos, following his hunch, brought a team to Akrotíri from the University of Athens. Under 15 feet of volcanic ash they struck archaeological gold, one of the most important discoveries of this century.

So far about 40 buildings have been excavated, just a small fraction of the city that remains buried. We are now sure that this was a Minoan outpost, probably an important and prosperous trading center, and that it had contact with Africa. We can also surmise that the inhabitants had ample warning of the impending disaster because no human remains, jewelry, or other valuable personal articles have been found.

Barbara's Café-Brasserie. Fabrica Shopping Center, Firá. No phone. Breakfast Dr 600–Dr 1,500 ($2.55–$6.40); sandwiches Dr 750–Dr 1,500 ($3.20–$6.40). No credit cards. Daily 9am–1am. INTERNATIONAL.

One of the best places for breakfast or a light lunch is up from the bus station toward the Cathedral. After 7pm, it becomes one of the least expensive bars in town, with beer for Dr 500 ($2.15), wine by the glass for Dr 600 ($2.55).

Crêperis House. Theotokopoúlou Square, Firá. No phone. Croissants Dr 300–Dr 600 ($1.25–$2.55); crepes Dr 600–Dr 1,250 ($2.55–$5.30). No credit cards. Daily 9am–3pm, 8pm–3am. INTERNATIONAL.

This good place for breakfast and light meals is on the north side of the central square.

✪ **Meridiana Restaurant Bar.** Odós Ypapantís, Firá. ☎ **0286/23-427.** Reservations recommended for dinner. Appetizers Dr 1,000–Dr 3,000 ($4.25–$12.75); main courses Dr 2,800–Dr 8,000 ($11.90–$34.05). AE, MC, V. Daily 11am–3pm, 7pm–1am. INTERNATIONAL.

On the second story of the Fabrica Shopping Center on Gold Street near the Cathedral, this excellent restaurant has views of both the Caldera and the town and island. The decor is informal and the service is relaxed. The food is meticulously prepared with little oil and salt, so that the subtle flavors of the distinctive spices can come through. The menu is large and varied, including piquant paella, chicken curry, pasta, teriyaki beef, and traditional Santoríni dishes. Desserts are also excellent.

❸ **Naoussa Restaurant.** Lagouder Shopping Center, Firá. ☎ **0286/24-869.** Main courses Dr 450–Dr 1,250 ($1.90–$5.30). V. Daily noon–midnight. GREEK/INTERNATIONAL.

Readers Anne and Roy Hart of Corvallis, Oregon, and our knowledgeable Greek friend Dimitris recommended this friendly family run place. The restaurant is on the second floor, above the shopping lane, uphill from the main street, north of the central square toward the cable car station. The menu isn't large, but it includes quite a variety, including a Mexican salad, five kinds of spaghetti, shrimps flambé, souvlaki oriental, chicken Americaine, and mixed grill—all in generous portions.

✪Sphinx Restaurant. Odós Mitropóleos, Firá. ☎ **0286/23-823.** Reservations recommended. Appetizers Dr 1,100–Dr 2,300 ($4.70–$9.80); main courses Dr 1,800–Dr 5,800 ($7.65–$24.70). AE, DC, MC, V. Daily noon–3pm, 7pm–2am. INTERNATIONAL.

This more formal restaurant near the Atlantis Hotel is especially recommended for those who like to get dressed up for dinner. A restored old mansion has been decorated with antiques, sculpture, and ceramics by local artists. The seafood specials and imaginative Greek dishes are fresh and superbly prepared.

ÍA

Snackers can try the **Minute,** on the pedestrian lane for ice cream and juice. There's a bakery next to the bus stop. In addition to the restaurants we list, **Koukoumavlos** (☎ **0286/71-413**) and **Kyklos** (☎ **0286/71-145**) are frequently recommended by locals and Frommer readers.

Katina Fish-Taverna. Port of Ía. ☎ **0286/71-280.** Appetizers Dr 250–Dr 1,250 ($1.05–$5.30); main courses Dr 1,250–Dr 3,500 ($5.30–$14.90). No credit cards. Daily 11am–1am. SEAFOOD.

One of the best places to eat in Ía isn't in town but rather down in the port of Ammoúdi, which is best reached by donkey. (Reader Paul Kemprecos of Orleans, Massachusetts, suggests that you may want to call a cab for the return trip to avoid their droppings.) Katina Pagoni is considered one of the very best local cooks, and the restaurant's setting beside the glittering Aegean is very romantic.

Neptune Restaurant. Odós Nikólaos Nomikós, Ía. ☎ **0286/71-280.** Appetizers Dr 500–Dr 1,500 ($2.15–$6.40); main courses Dr 1,200–Dr 3,200 ($5.10–$13.60). MC, V. Daily 7pm–1am. GREEK.

This very good place is on the pedestrian lane near the church square. It has a rooftop garden with a partial sunset view. All their typical Greek dishes are well prepared, and their vegetable specials are made with the season's best.

Restaurant-Bar 1800. Odós Nikólaos Nomikós, Ía. ☎ **0286/71-485.** Appetizers Dr 1,500–Dr 3,500 ($6.40–$14.90); main courses Dr 2,000–Dr 5,800 ($8.50–$24.70). AE, DC, EU, MC, V. Daily 6pm–midnight. INTERNATIONAL.

This establishment in a restored captain's mansion is certainly the most attractive restaurant in town. It has a large and varied menu that includes fresh muscles, spaghetti with fresh crab meat, and cold chicken with walnut sauce.

KAMÁRI

Agiris Taverna. Kamári village. ☎ **0286/31-795.** Appetizers Dr 250–Dr 1,000 ($1.05–$4.25); main courses Dr 1,100–Dr 4,000 ($5.10–$13.60). V. Daily 6pm–midnight. GREEK.

This old family run taverna, opposite the main church, has the best Greek food in the village. It depends on a loyal local clientele, so the quality of the authentic food must be kept high. Stuffed chicken is one of the delicious specialties.

✪ Camille Stephani. Kamári Beach. ☎ **0286/31-716.** Reservations recommended July–Sept. Appetizers Dr 950–Dr 2,500 ($4.05–$10.65); main courses Dr 2,250–Dr 5,000 ($9.55–$21.25). AE, DC, MC, V. Daily 1pm–4pm, 6:30pm–midnight. GREEK/INTERNATIONAL.

Even if you're not staying at Kamári, it's worthwhile to make a trip there to this excellent, more formal restaurant on the north end of the beach, 500 meters from the bus stop. You can take a moonlight stroll along the beach afterward. The special is a tender beef filet with green pepper in Madeira sauce.

Korali Taverna. Kamári Beach. ☎ **0286/31-904.** Appetizers Dr 600–Dr 1,800 ($2.55–$7.65); main courses Dr 1,100–Dr 4,500 ($4.70–$19.15). MC, V. Daily 8am–1am. GREEK.

This good casual place is in the pine grove on the north end of the beach. It has the usual Greek dishes, reasonably priced. The excellent fresh-grilled daily catch is priced according to supply and demand.

ELSEWHERE ON THE ISLAND

In Imerovígli, the places most often recommended by locals and other travelers are **Eleni's,** on the main square, and **Skaros Fish-Taverna** (☎ 0286/23-616). In Finikiá, just southeast of Ía, there's the excellent **Finikiá Restaurant** (☎ 0286/71-373) and the less-expensive **Yioryios Taverna** (☎ 0286/71-280). On the road from Firá to Karterádos there's the reader recommended **Restaurant Nefeli** (☎ 0286/22-557). In the village itself is the **Coral No. 2 Taverna** (no phone).

In Pírgos, the **Pírgos Taverna** (☎ 0286/31-346) is recommended by readers and islanders as a good place for traditional Greek food and music. In Megalohóri the **Vedema Restaurant** (☎ 0286/81-746), at the luxurious Vedema Hotel, is an excellent restaurant with a light Mediterranean cuisine. In Périssa **Marco's Taverna** (☎ 0286/81-205) is the best beachside eatery. **Makedonia,** on the main road, is popular for inexpensive pizza.

SANTORÍNI AFTER DARK

Firá has nightlife aplenty and in some variety. Most people will want to start the evening with a drink on the Caldera taking in the spectacular sunset. **Franco's** (☎ 0286/22-881) is still the most famous place for this magic hour, but be prepared to pay about Dr 2,500 ($10.65) per drink. **Archipelago** (☎ 0286/23-673) and **Canava Café** (☎ 0286/22-565) also have good views. For more reasonable prices, a bit more seclusion, and the same fantastic view, continue through the Canava Café and below the Loucas Hotel to the **Renaissance Bar** (☎ 0286/22-880).

Those visiting in August and September may be able to catch a performance of classical music at the **Santoríni Festival** (☎ 0286/22-220 for details), where international singers and musicians perform at the open-air amphitheater.

On the north end of the square, **Bonjour** is a good place to start looking for jovial company. Underneath the square, the **Kirathira Bar** plays jazz at a level that permits conversation.

Cross the main street and wander around the shopping area to find a number of smaller bars that come alive after 9pm. The **Town Club** appeals to clean-cut rockers, while the **Two Brothers** pulls in the biggest, chummiest, and most casual crowd on the island. A bit further north, the outdoor **Tropical Bar** attracts a louder, rowdier gang. For bouzouki, find the **Apocalypse Club** or **Bar 33.**

Discos come and go, and you only need to follow yours ears to find them. The **Koo Club** is the biggest, and the **Enigma** is still popular with those interested in good music. The **Tithora Club** is on the steps down to Skála. There's usually no admission charge, but drinks may run from Dr 1,000 to Dr 2,000 ($4.25 to $8.50).

In Ía, **Melissa's Piano Bar** is an excellent place to station yourself for the sunset—there's a Dr 1,200 ($5.10) minimum on its premium seats—and a good place for a light meal and live piano after 9pm. **Zorba's** is another good cliffside pub. **1800** is a more sophisticated bar, without a view.

Kamári has its share of bars. The **Yellow Donkey Disco** (☎ 0286/31-462) is popular with younger partiers, and the more sophisticated usually seek the chic **Valentino's,** near the bus stop.

In Périssa, there's usually a party crowd at **Taboo,** which often has live music after 7pm, and at the two branches of **Florida Disco,** with music from 10pm to 3am—all three venues are on the main vehicle street.

7 Folégandros

98 nautical miles (181km) SE of Piraeus

Most travelers who know of Folégandros, have seen it only when passing its rather forbidding northern coast, where precipitous cliffs rise up to almost a thousand feet. So far, relatively few have ventured up to experience the austere beauty of Hóra. Since Roman times, Folégandros has been used as a place of exile, and for the last decade, it's become a place of self-imposed exile. Those wanting to get away from the tourist hordes have discovered it, but for the present it remains unspoiled. The fewer than 1,000 inhabitants still go about their daily lives of growing barley in terraced fields, raising livestock, and fishing. In summer, they welcome visitors from Athens and a growing number of people from Italy, Scandinavia, and England. The island's limited facilities are fully booked in July and August, and reservations are necessary.

ESSENTIALS

GETTING THERE   Three ferries a week (six in the high season) stop at Folégandros on the Piraeus, Íos, Santoríni route. Two or three ferries (five in the high season) a week stop on the Náxos, Páros run. Two ferries (four in the high season) stop on the Sérifos, Sífnos, Mílos run. There's ferry connection once a week (three times in the high season) with Kímolos, Kýthnos, Síkinos, and Sýros.

VISITOR INFORMATION   The **Maraki Travel Agency** (☎ **0286/41-273**), is just around the southwest corner of the bus stop square in Hóra. They can exchange money, help with travel arrangements, and sell you a map of the island for Dr 600 ($2.55).

GETTING AROUND   There are no taxis on the island, no cars for rent, and no reason to rent one. As yet, there's not even any motorcycles for hire. The bus meets all ferries, and it makes eight or nine trips a day along the main road, which runs along the spine of the island. The bus fare is Dr 100 (45¢).

FAST FACTS   The **post office** and **OTE,** open weekdays 8am to 3pm, are right off the central square in Hóra. The **police** (☎ **0286/41-273**) are behind the post office and OTE.

WHAT TO SEE & DO

Visitors arrive in the unimpressive port of **Karavostássi,** where there's a decent beach and a few hotels and rooms to let. Campers may head south one kilometer to **Livádi Beach.** Most people, however, will jump aboard the bus that's waiting to chug the 4 kilometers up to **Hóra.**

Hóra is one of the most beautiful capitals in the Cyclades. Above it, the handsome all-white **Panayía Church** beckons you to climb the hillside for a closer look and incredible views. Even from the bus stop square, the sheer drop off the cliff offers a pretty awesome sight. On the right in the next square, you'll find the picture-perfect **Kástro,** built when Marco Sanudo ruled the island from Náxos in the 13th century. The town is centered around five closely connected squares, along and around which you'll find churches, restaurants, and shops.

About a kilometer south of Hóra is **Áyios Elefthérios,** the highest point on the island. Continue west by foot or bus to reach the village of **Áno Meriá.** The small farms there are so widely dispersed that they're barely recognizable as a community, though it's the island's second largest town. There's an interesting **Folk Museum,** open in the afternoons, with exhibits on local life.

Swimmers will want to get off at the first crossroad and walk down to **Angáli,** the best fine-sand beach on the island. There are a few tavernas and rooms to let. **Áyios**

Nikólaos, another good beach, is a couple of kilometers farther west. Yet another four kilometers will bring you to **Livadáki.** (In the summer there's caïque service to these beaches from Karavostássi.)

At the far northwest end of the island is the beach at **Áyios Yióryios;** it's an hour's walk beyond the last bus stop.

In the port of Karavostássi, you can hire a boat and guide to visit **Chrissospiliá,** a cave with stalactites and other curiosities, which is in the base of the cliff below the Panayía Church. This trip isn't for everyone as the current and winds drive the boat into the rock.

WHERE TO STAY

Beach types may want to stay at Karavostássi, a pebbled beach. The pleasant **Aeolos Beach Hotel** (☎ 0286/41-205) has 18 rooms, with doubles for Dr 11,500 ($48.95). Campers will want to head south to **Liváadi Camping** (☎ 0286/41-204). We recommend that you stay in Hóra, where there are also a number of good rooms to let.

Anemomilos Apartments. Hóra, 84011 Folégandros. ☎ **0286/41-309.** 17 apts. Dr 20,000 ($85.10) for two up to Dr 27,500 ($117) for five. AE, V.

Hóra's best and most traditional-looking luxury apartments are on the right up from the Hóra bus stop. They are all simply elegant, each with its own personality—one especially configured for the handicapped—most with sensational views.

✪ Cástro Hotel. Hóra, 84011 Folégandros. ☎ **0286/41-230** or 01/77-81-658 in Athens. Fax 0286/41-230. 10 rms. Dr 10,600 ($45.10) single; Dr 13,250 ($56.40) double. No credit cards.

Our favorite hotel is the Cástro, built in 1212 and fully renovated in 1992. The rooms are small—your private bathroom may be down the hall—but they're faithfully restored and comfortable. There's nothing like having a window with the ocean right under it 200 meters below. The charming owner, Despo Danassi, makes you feel at home and serves a homemade breakfast in antique dishes. Her family has owned the hotel for five generations.

Hotel Odysseus. Hóra, 840 11 Folégandros. ☎ **0286/41-239.** Fax 0286/41-366. 9 rms (all with bath). Dr 8,000 ($34.05) single or double. No credit cards.

This is Hóra's best budget choice. The rooms are simple, quiet, comfortable, and very clean. Sunsets from the Odysseus are splendid. It's on the west side of town, a few blocks beyond the OTE/post office, then left.

Polikandia Hotel. Hóra, 84011 Folégandros. ☎ **0286/41-322.** Fax 0286/41-323. 31 rms (all with bath). Dr 12,000 ($51.05) single; Dr 15,000 ($63.85) double. No credit cards.

This handsome new traditional-style hotel is on the left as you enter town. The rooms are large and comfortable with colorful furnishings. It's fully booked in July and August with group tours.

WHERE TO DINE

Hóra has a number of tavernas along the central squares. Locals recommend the **Poúnda** (☎ 0286/41-063), on the bus-stop square, and **Nikólaos** (☎ 0286/41-216) on the second square—its owner is especially friendly and informative. **Piátsa** (☎ 0286/41-274), on the third square, is a simple, family run taverna, with main courses costing from Dr 800 to Dr 2,000 ($3.40 to $8.50). **O Krítikos** (☎ 0286/41-218) is another local favorite known for its grilled chicken. In Áno Meriá, the **Iliovasílema Taverna** (☎ 0286/41-357) is known for its local specialties and sunsets.

FOLÉGANDROS AFTER DARK

Folégandros isn't exactly buzzing with nightlife, of course, but there is the large and fairly stylish **Bzut Disco,** on the south side of town beyond the last square. Just before the Bzut, on the left, is the small and mellow **Kaliteremi Music Bar.**

8 Sífnos

93 nautical miles (172km) SE of Piraeus

It's no longer a secret that Sífnos is the most beautiful of the western Cyclades. It's still a favorite destination for Greeks who want to escape the hordes of foreign tourists on the other islands and is becoming very crowded in July and August. The island was famed in antiquity for its gold mines. Each year the islanders were required to send a solid-gold egg to Délphi as a tribute to Apollo. One year they succumbed to their greedier instincts and substituted a gilded rock. Apollo (or his priests, at least) was incensed and cursed the island. This gave Polykrátes of Sámos all the excuse he needed to plunder the island, and the mines have since sunk into the Aegean. Since that time no gold has been found on the island, and its name means "Empty." Today it's full of charm, tranquility, well-tended fields, good restaurants, and easygoing people, both locals and visitors.

ESSENTIALS

GETTING THERE   By Boat   There's at least one boat daily from Piraeus. There's daily (twice daily in the summer) ferry connections to Sérifos and Mílos, and less frequent service to Kímolos and Kýthnos. There's a ferry connection four times a week with Santoríni; three times a week with Folégandros, Íos, and Síkinos; and once a week with Ándros, Crete, Mýkonos, Páros, Rafína, Sýros, and Tínos. There's also once weekly connection with the Dodecannese islands of Kárpathos, Kássos, Rhodes, and Sými. Contact the **Port Authority** in Piraeus (☎ **01/143** or 01/45-11-131) or in Sífnos (☎ **0284/31-617**) for information.

VISITOR INFORMATION   Your first stop should be the excellent **Aegean Thesaurus Travel and Tourism** office on the port (☎ **0284/31-804**). Located 20 meters north of the square up the pedestrian lane, this is a one-stop help center, where you can cash traveler's checks, pick up a bus schedule, and a good map of the island for Dr 700 ($3), book a flight, and avail yourself of their other services every day from 9am to midnight. All major credit cards are accepted. The main office of **Aegean Thesaurus** is in Apollonía (☎ and fax **0284/31-145**).

At **Siphanto Travel** (☎ **0284/32-034;** fax 0284/31-024), also highly recommended, you can book a room, buy ferry tickets, rent a car or motorbike, arrange excursions, and leave your luggage.

GETTING AROUND   Getting around Sífnos is one of its pleasures; many visitors come for the wonderful hiking and mountain trails. We don't think a car or moped is necessary.

By Car   Cars can be rented in Apollonía at **FS** (☎ **0284/31-795**) and **Aegean Thesaurus** (☎ **0284/31-145**). In Kamáres, **Siphanto Travel** (☎ **0284/32-034**) and **Sífnos Car** (☎ **0284/31-793**) rents cars.

By Bus   The island's bus system is fairly efficient. Apollonía's Platía Iróon is the central **bus stop** for the island. Buses run regularly to and from the port at Kamáres, north to Artemónas, east to Kástro, and south to Fáros and Platís Yialós. (Visit Aegean Thesaurus Travel for a schedule, see "Visitor Information," above.)

By Moped Apollonia has a few moped dealers, try **Yoni's** (☎ 0284/31-155) on the main square or **East Rider** (☎ 0284/31-001) on the road circling the village.

By Taxi Apollonía's Platía Iróon is also the main taxi stand, though there aren't a lot of them on the island.

FAST FACTS Visitor services are centered around Platía Iróon, which is the main square in Apollonía. The **post office** (☎ 0284/31-329) is open weekdays from 8am to 3pm, Saturday and Sunday 9am to 1:30pm in the summer. The **National Bank** (☎ 0284/31-237) is open Monday through Thursday from 8am to 2pm, Friday 8am to 1:30pm. The telephone center (**OTE**), just down the vehicle road, is open daily from 8am to 3pm, and in summer 5 to 10pm. (The news kiosk on the square has a metered phone for after-hours calls.) The **police station** (☎ 0284/31-210) is just east of the square, and a first aid station is nearby; for **medical emergencies** call **0284/31-315.**

WHAT TO SEE & DO

To ferry passengers, almond-shaped Sífnos appears to be a barren rock stretched lazily across the western Aegean. The island's west coast, dominated by the port of Kamáres where most visitors arrive, is much drier than the east. Most visitors arriving during the cooler weather (facilities are open from mid-April to late September) will want to base themselves at Apollonía, the island's inland capital.

In the high season, things get very busy. A room at the east coast beach resort at Platís Yialós is most highly prized, but the yachting crowd and lively cafes of Kamáres give it appeal also. If you're not a dedicated sun worshipper, head to Apollonía or the picturesque village of Artemóna.

Kamáres, on the west coast and the island's port, will be most visitor's introduction to Sífnos. Kamáres is fairly attractive and an okay place to stay. Its one street leads from the ferry pier through the town. The central part of Kamáres cove is a sandy beach, lined with tamarisk trees and dune grass. There are some fine isolated beaches north and south of Kamáres that can be reached by boat.

The town beach is the focal point of most people's day, but don't miss the shops, many of which are filled with the island's best-known contemporary commodity, ceramics. Sifnian ceramics and everyday pottery are exported throughout Greece; they're in wide use because of their durability and charming folk designs. One of the most interesting shops is the ceramics workshop of **Antonis Kalogirou** (☎ 0284/31-651) on the main harborside lane. Antonis sells folk paintings of island life and the typical pottery of Sífnos, which is manufactured in his showroom from the deep gray or red clay mined in the inland hill region.

From the Kamáres pier, you can hire a caïque to **Vathí,** a small coastal village due south, with a good sandy beach and a twin-domed **monastery of the Taxiarchs** that watches over the skimpily clad bathers. The town is also the site of some old potteries, which can be explored, and it has several tavernas. **Hersónissos** ("Peninsula") is an even better beach on the north coast that's accessible by a new unpaved road or by caïque from Kamáres. In the summer, travelers in Kamáres gather at the caïque port and bargain with fishermen, who usually charge about Dr 7,000 ($29.80) each way to Vathí and Hersónissos for a boat seating 10.

You can hop on a bus to **Apollonía,** the capital, which is sometimes called Hóra. It's the most interesting village on Síphnos and just 5 kilometers southeast of the port. The drive between Kamáres and Apollonía reveals the island's agricultural heart and the meticulous care given the fields. Every hillside is impeccably terraced with walls of schist and flagstone slabs. Rocky surfaces between higher walls serve as footpaths over the hills, and carved stone and marble steps between the olive and almond trees are common. Small Cycladic farmhouses with the occasional ornamental dovecote are scattered throughout, most sporting geraniums, hibiscus, or apricot trees. Apollonía is spread over three mounds in the foothills of Mt. Profítis Ilías, site of an 8th-century Byzantine monastery.

Apollonía's **Platía Iróon** (Heroes' Square) is the transportation hub of the island. All the island's vehicle roads converge here, and this is where you find the bus stop and taxi stand. The square has a monument to Sífnos's World War II veterans. Winding pedestrian paths of flagstone and marble slope down from the square and lead through this beautiful Cycladic village. Along the village's only car route are a few shops, a few small markets with island maps, a restaurant or two, and **Lakis Kafeneion,** an open air cafe near the square that is the island's hangout.

There's a small **Popular and Folk Art Museum** on Platía Iróon. It's open from July to September 15, 10am to 1pm, 6 to 10pm; admission is Dr 400 ($1.70). Left of it the main pedestrian street, Odós Styliánou Prókou, invites a stroll through town and up to the 18th-century church of **Panayía Ouranoforía,** on the highest hill. On the left of this lane near the museum, **Hersónissos** (☎ 0284/32-209) has a choice selection of contemporary jewelry and ceramics. There are several other contemporary ceramics galleries featuring the excellent work of Greek artisans in the winding back streets. **Mouses** ceramic gallery (☎ 0284/32-165) is 50 meters north of the main bus stop on the road to Artemóna.

Pretty **Artemóna** fans over a hillside crowned by two blue-dotted windmills and the remnants of others, just a 2-kilometer walk north from Apollonia. (You may want to take the bus up and walk down.) Some impressive neoclassic mansions, belonging to the island's oldest families, border the encircling outer vehicle road, and it's a pleasure to stroll around the village's quiet lanes. Though the community is obviously affluent, there is little ostentation and a pervading sense of peace and ease.

Kástro is a beautiful east coast village overlooking the sea, just 3 kilometers east of Apollonía, an easy walk except under the midday sun. Whitewashed houses, some well preserved and others eroding, adjoin each other in irregular chains circling the sheer cliff. The Venetians took Sífnos in 1307 and built the fortress on the foundation of the ancient acropolis. Venetian coats of arms are still visible above the doorways of the older houses that abut the fort. Within its maze are a few shops, rooms-to-let, and a small **Archaeological Museum,** open daily from 10am to 2pm. Below the town is a small pebble beach, where you can swim.

South of Apollonía the road passes through the pleasant village of **Exámbela.** Then off to the left is the active **monastery of Vrísis,** built in the early 17th century. It houses a collection of old manuscripts and religious artifacts. A little further south the road branches left to Fáros and right to Platís Yialós.

Fáros is a small resort with some good budget accommodations and tavernas. It can be an okay base if you don't find a room elsewhere. **Apokoftó** has a good long sand beach, and nude bathing is permitted at nearby **Fasoloú.**

The remarkably situated **monastery of Panayía Chryssopiyí** is built on a rocky promontory. It's said to have broken away from the island when two young women stalked by pirates prayed to the Virgin Mary for intervention. The double-vaulted whitewashed church houses a miraculous icon found glowing underwater by fishermen. There's good swimming immediately below the monastery and along the coast, where secluded bays protect swimmers from rough water.

Platís Yialós is the biggest and most southern of the west coast beaches. This long stretch of fine tan sand lines a shallow cove. It's a great place for beach bums, particularly in late May, June, and September, when the sea is warm but calm. From here, it's a half-hour walk east through the olive groves and intoxicating oregano and thyme patches over the hill to Chryssopiyí.

WHERE TO STAY
APOLLONÍA

Many young Athenians vacation on Sífnos, particularly on summer weekends, and it can be very difficult to find a room. **Aegean Thesaurus** (☎ and fax **0284/32-190**) can place two in a room in a private house with your own bathroom for Dr 7,000 to Dr 8,000 ($29.80 to $34.05); in a studio with a kitchenette for Dr 11,500 ($48.95); or in other accommodations ranging up to a stylish villa and sleeping six for Dr 60,000 ($255.30) per night.

Hotel Anthoussa. Apollonía, 84003 Sífnos. ☎ **0284/31-431.** 7 rms (all with bath). Dr 10,500 ($44.70) single; Dr 12,000 ($51.05) double. MC, V.

This hotel is above the excellent and popular Yerontopoulos cafe-patisserie. Although the street-side rooms offer wonderful views over the hills, they're recommended only to night owls in the high season, as they overlook the late-night sweet-tooth crowd. The back rooms are quieter and overlook a beautiful bower of bougainvillea.

Hotel Sífnos. Apollonía, 84003 Sífnos. ☎ **0284/31-624.** 9 rms (all with bath). Dr 8,200 ($34.90) single, Dr 12,000 ($51.05) double. AE, EU, MC, V.

This is the best hotel in the village, and it's the most traditional choice in terms of island architecture. It's located southeast of the main square, on the pedestrians-only street that leads to the cathedral. The hotel's manager, Helen Diareme, and her son Apostolos will do their best to make your stay comfortable. The Sífnos is open year-round.

Hotel Sofia. Apollonía, 84003 Sífnos. ☎ **0284/31-238.** 11 rms (all with shower.) Dr 6,200 ($26.40) single; Dr 8,600 ($36.60) double. No credit cards.

This recently built hotel is on the road circling the town, a two-minute walk north from the square. Most of the rooms are large and have private showers. Many have balconies overlooking the rooftops of the town. There's a supermarket on the ground floor.

ARTEMÓNA

Hotel Artemon. Artemóna, 84003 Sífnos. ☎ **0284/31-303** or 0284/31-888 in winter. Fax 0284/32-385. 24 rms (all with bath). TEL. Including breakfast: Dr 13,750 ($58.50) single; Dr 18,250 ($77.65) double. AE, EU, MC, V.

This quiet, comfortable hotel is on the road just before the platía. From the patios or balconies, you'll have a view of wheat fields and olive groves sloping down to the sea. The Artemon has a large terrace restaurant shaded by grape vines.

KAMÁRES

Kamáres has the biggest concentration of hotels and pensions on the island; you should make reservations by May if you plan to be in Kamáres during the high season.

Hotel Boulis. Kamáres, 84003 Sífnos. ☎ **0284/32-122** or 0284/31-640 in winter. Fax 0284/32-381. 45 rms (all with bath). TEL. Including breakfast: Dr 8,000 ($34.05) single; Dr 12,250 ($52.15) double. AE.

This recently built hotel is right on the port's beach. The large, carpeted rooms have balconies with beach views. There's a spacious reception area with a marble floor.

Hotel Kamari. Kamáres, 84003 Sífnos. ☎ **0284/31-709.** Fax 0284/31-709. 18 rms (all with bath). TEL. Dr 7,650 ($32.55) single; Dr 11,250 ($47.90) double. AE, MC, V.

This is a clean, attractive lodging with balconied rooms, at the quiet end of town, where the road and beach meet. The friendly and attentive management offers transportation to other villages by minibus and car rentals.

Hotel Stavros. Kamáres, 84003 Sífnos. ☎ **0284/31-641.** Fax 0284/31-709. 14 rms (10 with bath). TEL. Dr 6,400 ($27.25) single or double without bath; Dr 9,200 ($39.15) double with bath. AE, MC, V.

The same friendly management that runs the Hotel Kamari also tends this simple place on the paralía next to the church. The rooms are spartan but reasonably quiet, and the common showers are kept very clean.

PLATÍS YIALÓS

July and August bring the stormy meltémi winds and the many Greek and European tourists who return annually to this resort's few pensions and hotels. **Community Camping** (☎ 0284/31-786) is just 600 meters from the beach and charges Dr 750 ($3.20) per person with free showers for guests.

Hotel Benakis. Platís Yialós, 84003 Sífnos. ☎ **0284/32-221.** 24 rms (all with bath). Including breakfast: Dr 10,600 ($45.10) single; Dr 18,400 ($78.30) double. No credit cards.

This small hotel with a lovely sea view from its perch on the main road is run by the friendly, helpful Benakis family. The rooms are spotless, quiet, and comfortable.

Hotel Philoxenia. Platís Yialós, 84003 Sífnos. ☎ **0284/32-221.** 9 rms (all with bath). Including breakfast: Dr 12,800 ($54.45) single/double. No credit cards.

This small, simple hotel on the main street has large, clean rooms, some with balconies offering sea views.

Hotel Platís Yialós. Platís Yialós, 84003 Sífnos. ☎ **0284/31-324** or 0831/22-626 in winter. Fax 0284/31-325 or 0831/55-049 in winter. 26 rms (all with bath). A/C TEL. Including breakfast: Dr 26,250 ($111.70) single; Dr 31,750 ($135.10) double. No credit cards.

The island's best hotel is ideally situated overlooking the beach on the west side of the cove. A recent renovation has added modern tiled bathrooms with tubs; the ground-floor rooms have large private patios. Ceramics, painted tiles, and small paintings provide decorative touches. The Plateís Yialós's flagstone sun deck extends from the beach to a dive platform at the end of the cove. A bar and restaurant share the same Aegean views.

WHERE TO DINE
APOLLONÍA

Apostoli's Koutouki Taverna. Apollonía. ☎ **0284/31-186.** Appetizers Dr 400–Dr 1,000 ($1.70–$4.25), main courses Dr 1,250–Dr 3,200 ($5.30–$13.60). No credit cards. Daily noon–midnight. GREEK.

There are several tavernas in Apollonia, but this one on the main pedestrian street is the best for Greek food. The service, though, is usually leisurely. The vegetable dishes, most made from locally grown produce, are delicious.

Sífnos Cafe-Restaurant. Apollonía. ☎ **0284/31-624.** Appetizers Dr 350–Dr 900 ($1.50–$3.85); main courses Dr 1,000–Dr 2,800 ($4.25–$11.90). AE, EU, MC, V. Daily 8am–midnight. GREEK.

You'll find the best all-around place to eat in town along the main pedestrian street toward the cathedral. It's under a grape arbor, between the Sífnos Hotel and a quiet plaza. The breakfast menu offers fresh fruit juice and a dozen coffees. Choose from a variety of snacks, light meals, and desserts during the day. At sunset, have ouzo and mezédes. Go in and check out the refrigerator case displaying the catch of the day and other main courses when you're ready for a big evening meal.

ARTEMÓNA

To Liotrivi (Manganas). Artemóna. ☎ **0284/32-051.** Appetizers Dr 250–Dr 900 ($1.05–$3.85); main courses Dr 900–Dr 3,200 ($3.85–$13.60). No credit cards. Daily noon–midnight. GREEK.

The island's favorite taverna has a handsome new building. You can dine here down in the cellar, on the roof, or by the street. Find out why the Sifnians, who pride themselves on their fine, distinctive cooking, consider Yannis Yiorgoulis one of their finest chefs. Try his delectable kaparosaláta (minced caper leaves and onion salad); povithokeftédes (croquettes of ground chick-peas); or ambelofásoula (crisp local black-eyed peas in the pod). Or go for something ordinary like the beef fillet with potatoes baked in foil.

KAMÁRES

Captain Andreas. Kamáres. ☎ **0284/32-356.** Appetizers Dr 350–Dr 1,400 ($1.50–$5.95), main courses Dr 1,000–Dr 1,600 ($4.25–$6.80); fish Dr 2,500–Dr 16,000 ($10.65–$68.10) per kilo. No credit cards. Daily 1–5pm, 7:30pm–12:30am. SEAFOOD.

Captain Andreas, a favorite place for seafood, has tables right on the town beach. Andreas, the proprietor and fisherman, serves the catch of the day. It's usually simply prepared and accompanied with terrific chips or a seasonal vegetable dish.

Pothotas Taverna O Simos. Kamáres. No telephone. Appetizers Dr 350–Dr 1,250 ($1.50–$5.30), main courses Dr 800–Dr 2,000 ($3.40–$8.50). No credit cards. Daily 11am–midnight. GREEK.

This unobtrusive port-side place has a basic Greek menu, and everything is done well. The bread brought to your table is sprinkled with sesame seeds. Their horiátiki salad is made with locally aged mizíthra cheese. Fish is fresh and not expensive. The individually baked pots of moussaka are delicious.

PLATÍS YIALÓS

Ampari Cafe. Platís Yialós, No telephone. Snacks Dr 400–Dr 1,400 ($1.70–$5.95). No credit cards. BREAKFAST/SNACKS.

The "Ship's Hold," on the central beach, has two decks, cozy indoor and outdoor spaces, and a beach bar, where you can enjoy breakfast, light snacks, salads, and fresh fruit. It's a popular cafe/bar on weekends, when two local musicians bring out a lýa (fiddle) and a 200-year-old laoúto (lute) to play folk music.

Sofia Restaurant. Platís Yialás. ☎ **0284/31-890.** Appetizers Dr 200–Dr 900 (85¢–$3.85), main courses Dr 800–Dr 2,800 ($3.40–$11.90). No credit cards. Daily 9pm–1am. GREEK.

At the east end of the beach is the best restaurant for Greek peasant fare. It's popular for its outdoor terrace and large wine list. For many in Apollonía, the casual seaside ambience warrants an evening outing.

SÍFNOS AFTER DARK

In Apollonía, the **Argo Bar, Botzi,** and **Volto** on the main pedestrian street are good for the latest European and American pop at very loud volumes. In summertime, the large **Dolphin Pub** becomes a lively and elegant nightspot; it closes for the season in mid-September.

In Kamáres at sunset, you can seek relative tranquility near the beach at the picturesque **Old Captain's Bar.** Or join the yacht set drinking Sífnos Sunrises at the rival **Collage Club.** Later, the **Mobilize Dance Club** and the more elegant **Follie-Follie,** right on the beach, start cranking up the volume for dancing.

In summer, the **Cultural Society of Sífnos** sometimes hosts concerts in Artemóna, and local festivals offer folk music and dance.

9 Sýros

78 nautical miles (144km) SE of Piraeus

Unlike most of the Cyclades, Sýros does not rely on tourism as the mainstay of its economy. Its huge shipping industry, textiles, and inland greenhouses are the main sources of revenue. The islander's off-handed style with foreigners and the lack of tourist savvy can be rather refreshing. Sýros offers a rare opportunity to vacation as the Greeks do—on an island whose lack of beautiful sand beaches, archaeological wonders, and discos has spared it rampant overdevelopment.

Since antiquity Sýros's central position has made it a prosperous trading and shipping port. Excavations at Halandrianí have revealed the existence of an early Cycladic civilization from the third millennium B.C. After the Greek Liberation of 1821, the northern Aegean islanders who had been driven out by the Turks sought refuge on Sýros. Throughout the 19th century, Sýros flourished as a maritime center, and Ermoúpolis became the most important port in Greece.

ESSENTIALS

GETTING THERE   By Plane   There is one flight (two in the summer) daily from Athens. Call **Olympic Airways** at their Ermoúpolis office (☎ **0281/81-244** or in Athens ☎ 01/96-16-161) for reservations.

By Boat   Syros is connected daily (more frequently in the summer) by ferryboat to Piraeus, Ios, Náxos, Mýkonos, Páros, Santoríni, and Tínos; four or five times weekly to Andros, twice weekly with Folégandros and Sikinos; and once a week to Milos, Sífnos, and Serifos. All schedules should be checked with a local travel agent. **Syros Travel** (☎ **0281/23-338**) is on the harbor. These are also daily ferries from Rafina, but you should avoid the slow cargo boats.

VISITOR INFORMATION   The city of Ermoúpolis **Tourist Information Office** (☎ **0281/27-027**) and an office of the **National Tourist Organization** (☎ **0281/ 22-375**) are on the harbor. The main **National Tourist Organization** for the Cyclades (☎ **0281/26-725**) is on the second floor of the Town Hall, on the main square, and is open 8am to 2:30pm Monday to Friday.

Teamwork Holidays, on the paralía (harbor front) at Aktí Rálli 10 (☎ **0281/ 23-400;** fax 0281/23-508), is open daily to book rooms, handle travel plans, change money, sell Olympic Airways tickets, and arrange rental cars. They also offer a round-the-island half-day bus tour or a full-day beach tour by motor boat. **AA Sýros** (☎ **0281/27-711**; fax 0281/23-508) at the New Port sells boat tickets and changes money.

GETTING AROUND   By Bus   Getting around by bus is so easy and convenient that you will not need to rent a car or moped, though there are several rental places near the harbor. The **bus station** is on the harbor, midway along the paralía, Aktí Rálli, a left from the ferry quay. Buses circle the southern half of Sýros about eight times a day between 10am and 8pm, and more frequently in summer. The main route goes to Possidónia/Dellagrazia, Fínikas, and Galíssas. Buses to Vári and Megálos Yialós, the south coast beaches, run six times a day from Ermoúpolis, between 6:45am and 2:30pm—this makes late afternoon sunbathing an option only for those with mopeds or cab fare. Buses west from Ermoúpolis to Kíni run five times a day (hourly in summer) and return later in the evening.

By Taxi   The **taxi station** is on the main square, Platía Miaoúlis (☎ **0281/26-222**).

FAST FACTS   The **police** (☎ **0281/22-610**) and the **post office,** open 7:30 to 3pm weekdays, are south side of the main square, opposite the Town Hall; the **port police** (☎ **0281/22-690**) are nearby. The telephone center (**OTE**) is off the northeast corner of the main square, open 6am to 11pm daily. There's a **laundry** on Odós Protopapadáki, the second street back from the port, a couple of blocks right (east) from Odós Venizélou. For **medical emergencies** call **0281/22-555.**

WHAT TO SEE & DO
IN ERMOÚPOLIS

Ferries dock at Ermoúpolis ("the city of Hermes," god of commerce), which we recommend as a base for visitors. It's been the island's major port since ancient times. Today, Ermoúpolis is a busy harbor, enlarged by a huge modern breakwater that provides anchorage for many tankers and container cargo ships. Opposite the ferry quay across the harbor is the Neórion shipyards, which are no longer in use.

Above the city, the taller hill on the left (west) is **Áno Sýros,** the Catholic quarter. The hill to its right (east), topped with the blue-domed church, is called **Vrondádo.** The large neoclassic mansions overlooking the water are vestiges of Syros's prosperous past. Although they are now somewhat faded, they are nevertheless an important part of why Ermoúpolis has been named a national historic landmark.

From midport, right after the bus station, Odós Venizélou leads inland to the marble-paved **Platía Miaoúlis** (Miaoúlis Square), the heart of the city. The square is dominated by the grand neoclassic **Town Hall,** which is presently still being restored. (Even if Town Hall is closed at the time of your visit, check out the interior of the **Roma Cafe** below it.)

The **Archaeological Museum** is on the west side of Town Hall, beneath a clock tower. Its small collection includes some fine Cycladic sculptures from the third millennium B.C., two beautiful miniature Hellenistic marble heads, and Roman-era sculpture from Amorgós. It's open daily except Monday from 8:30am to 3pm, and entrance is free.

A couple of blocks northeast of the Town Hall, you'll find the 19th-century **Apollon Theater,** a smaller version of Milan's La Scala. It's has been totally rebuilt thanks to funding from the European Union. (Contact **Teamwork Holidays** at ☎ **0281/23-400** for information and tickets.) Northeast behind it is the lovely church of **Áyios Nikólaos,** with a green marble iconostasis carved by Vitalis. He also sculpted the monument to an unknown soldier in the garden near the entrance. A short stroll beyond the church will bring you to the neighborhood called **Vapória,** named after the steamships that brought it great prosperity.

The best street for shopping is two streets from the port, Odós Protopapadáki or Proíou Street, which is open to car traffic and chock-full of shops. Inexpensive sandals, espadrilles, costume jewelry, cotton sportswear, well-priced fashionable bathing suits, children's clothes, you name it, are all here. **Kira** (no phone) sells local pottery and other interesting artifacts. The town produce market is on Odós Híos, west of the main square; it's particularly lively on Saturdays. You shouldn't leave the market without trying the local specialty loukoúmia, better known as Turkish delight, and halvodópita, a sort of nougat.

Áno Sýros, the taller hill on the left, can be visited by local bus. By foot, it's a half-hour hike up Odós Omírou, then up the old stairs of Odós Andréa Kárga. This medieval quarter, with an intricate maze of streets, was built by the Venetians in the 13th century. Áno Sýros originally spread across the summit of both hills, where its inhabitants were protected from pirate raids. Several Roman Catholic churches stand here;

the most important of which is the **Church of San Giorgio.** The large buff-colored square building on the hilltop is the medieval **Monastery of the Capuchins.** Remnants of castle walls, stone archways, and narrow lanes will delight visitors.

The other hill, **Vrondádo,** with its blue-domed Greek Orthodox Church of the Resurrection, was built up after the Greek immigration of 1821. Its narrow streets, large marble-paved squares, and dignified mansions lend a certain old-world charm to the bustling inner city.

AROUND THE ISLAND

The island's east coast south of Ermoúpolis is lined with large and small piers. The huge **Neórion boatyards** once handled the construction and repair of vessels as large as 80,000 tons. In between their piers are the tiny caïques and larger fishing boats that supply tavernas around the island. The southern half of the island, particularly between **Áno Mána** and **Possidonía,** is neatly terraced with vineyards, wheat fields, tomato greenhouses, and fruit trees. (**Dellagrazia** is the Venetian name for **Possidonía,** the village dominated by the Madonna of Grace Church.) The vegetables produced here are exported to Athens.

There are a number of quiet beaches around the island, though none of them is anything special. Most bathing is off the rocky bluffs that jut from the tree-lined shore into the many bays and inlets on the south and west coasts. **Azólimnos,** southeast of the airport, is popular with locals for its cafes and ouzeries, but there are no accommodations there. **Vári,** on the southeast coast, is a fishing village that is becoming an important resort. **Achládi,** west across the headland, is considerably more pleasant; it's the best-sheltered beach on the island when the meltémi is blowing.

Mégas Yialós, as its name states, is the largest beach on the island and the prettiest on the south coast. Its sandy beach is shaded by tamarisk trees and is especially good for families because it's gently shelved. Across the southwest tip of the island, **Possidonía** is an attractive village with Italianate neoclassical mansions, often having Turkish-inspired wooden balconies and gingerbread trim. The beach at Possidonía is small and rocky. **Agathopés,** a 10-minute walk south of Possidonía, has a nice sandy beach and a little offshore islet. **Fínikas** ("Phoenix"), said to have been an early Phoenician settlement, on the northwest side of the bay, is another popular resort.

North across the headland, **Galissás** has the best sheltered beach on the island, a crescent of sand bordered by tamarisks, but it's a bit too popular in the high season, when it's overrun by backpackers. **Arméos beach,** south of town, is the local nudist hangout.

Kíni is a small fishing village with two beaches on sheltered Delfíni Bay, valued for its sunsets and a local family of bouzouki musicians. Kíni is on the west coast opposite Ermoúpolis, not on the southern bus route; the bus from Ermoúpolis makes the trip hourly in the summer. There are fairly late return bus trips to Ermoúpolis, so that you can enjoy a late afternoon at the beach and a leisurely dinner. Nudists will want to go north over the headland from Kíni to **Delfíni beach.**

The northern part of Sýros is mountainous and barren, with poor roads and few villages. The region has dairies that produce the popular San Michaeli cheese, milk, and butter that visiting Greeks love to take home. The northern tip of the island is thought to have been the home of the philosopher Pherecydas, whose best pupil was Pythagoras. A couple of caves there are said to be his summer and winter residences. **Kástri,** north of Halandrianí, is thought to be the one of the oldest settlements in the Cyclades, with the foundations of houses and remains of a cemetery that have provided important clues about early Bronze Age culture.

WHERE TO STAY
ERMOUPOLIS

There are a number of rooms to let in Ermoupolis, and you can check with travel agencies for listings by the local association. The small office of the **Sýros Hotelier Association,** right as you come off the ferry in Ermoupolis, can help you find a room in one of the better hotels.

There are also accommodations available in luxury apartments and renovated mansions, such as the **Mansion Vourlis** (☎ **0281/28-440** or 0281/81-561). Built in 1888 and recently fully restored, the Vourlis has doubles for Dr 22,500 ($95.75). The **Villa Maria** (☎ **0281/26-536;** fax 0281/81-556), Odós Hýdras 42, was built in 1902 and recently fully renovated; it has doubles for Dr 16,000 ($68.10) and furnished apartments for Dr 32,000 ($136.15).

Europe Hotel. Odós Stam. Proíou 24, Ermoúpolis, 84100 Sýros. ☎ **0281/28-771.** Fax 0281/23-508. 28 rms (all with bath). Dr 10,000 ($42.55) single, Dr 13,250 ($56.40) double. AE, DC, MC, V.

Rooms are small and simply furnished. All open onto an interior veranda overlooking a small garden. The church of the Assumption (Kímisis), where you can see an El Greco icon, is nearby. This pleasant hotel is a five-minute walk west of Platía Miaoúlis.

Ipatia Guesthouse. Odós Babayiótou 3, Ermoúpolis, 84100 Sýros. ☎ **0281/23-575.** 8 rms (5 with bath). Dr 7,250 ($30.85) double without bath; Dr 9,250 ($39.40) double with bath. No credit cards.

This lovely restored mansion dating from 1870 is uphill from the Áyios Nikólaos Church. What's truly special about the Ipatia is the Lefebvre family from Philadelphia, who run it. Several years ago, they were steered to rooms at the aging Ipatia; they fell in love with the hotel and then bought it. They now open it to guests and friends every June to September.

The high-ceilinged rooms have brass beds, stone floors, and simple Syriot furnishings. Frescoed ceilings, carved wooden doors, spotless rooms, and sloping stairs add enough charm to compensate for a little wear, though all is being continually updated.

Rooms at the Ipatia have a wonderful prospect over Vapória, the quarter with homes that abut the rocky Asteria beach. Some steps across from the hotel lead to concrete bathing platforms and a water-side taverna. In the winter you can contact the Lefebvres at 45 Tookany Creek Parkway, Cheltenham, PA 19012.

Kymata Hotel. Platía Kanári, Ermoúpolis, 84100 Sýros. ☎ **0281/22-758.** 8 rms. Dr 9,150 ($38.95) single or double. No credit cards.

Another restored neoclassical home can be found on Platía Kanári, near the ferry quay, across from the handsome Hotel Hermes. The Kymata has a simple style and scalloped stucco ceilings (an old anti-earthquake reinforcement technique). Great port views are had from its front rooms. Spacious, bright rooms are spotless, with modern showers tucked away inside. Open year round.

AROUND THE ISLAND

At Achládi, the seafront **Achládi Hotel** (☎ **0281/61-400**) has 13 simple but pleasant rooms, with doubles for Dr 6,250 ($26.60), and a good taverna.

At Possidonía (sometimes also called Dellagrazia), the attractive, 60-room Class B **Poseidonion Hotel** (☎ **0281/42-100**) has the best facilities; doubles cost Dr 15,300 ($63.75).

In Gallisás, the roadside **Hotel Francoise** (☎ 0281/42-000) has 34 rooms with private facilities; it's about five minutes from the beach. Rates are Dr 7,800 ($33.20) for a single, Dr 9,750 ($41.40) for a double. The **Maistrali Pension** (☎ 0821/42-059) is another choice, with balconied rooms only 76 yards from the beach. Singles go for Dr 9,750 ($41.40); doubles are Dr 14,500 ($61.70). **Dendrino's Rooms-to-Let,** near the bus stop, has been highly recommended by reader, Rev. Martin Peter. None of these places accept credit cards.

Galissás also has the island's two campgrounds: **Two Hearts** (☎ 0281/42-052), the more pleasant, better of the two, has a minibus which meets the ferries. **Camping Yianna** (☎ 0281/42-447), is about 100 yards from the beach and has its own open air disco, which goes until 1am or later—something to weigh carefully before unfurling your sleeping bag. The Yianna grounds also have a minimarket, snack bar, and restaurant. There's currency exchange, transportation to and from the airport, and an information service. Rates are Dr 1,250 ($5.30) per person; Dr 800 ($3.40) per tent.

Above Kíni, **Captain's Rooms** (☎ 0281/71-376) has nine modern furnished apartments, where two people are charged about Dr 15,000 ($63.85).

WHERE TO DINE

There are numerous zacharoplastía (confectioners) and patisseries in Ermoúpolis, and many feature homemade loukoúmi and serve coffee and café frappé. There are several eateries on Platía Miaoúlis, and **Pyramid Pizzeria** (☎ 0281/24-295) is a fashionable, more casual, and inexpensive choice.

Sunsets are particularly fine when viewed from **Tramps,** a snack bar and cafe on the east side of the paralia. There's also a very popular late afternoon and evening cafe next to the tourist office in the Customs House, by the ferry quay; it's the place to celebrate the comings and goings of friends. Also on the port, the **Bourba Ouzeri** and the **Yacht Club of Sýros,** the oldest in the Balkans, are both excellent places for ouzo and mezédes.

Some of the best restaurants in the city are found in the quiet streets of Vrondádo. You will have to search for **Lymberis' Koutouki** (which only has seven tables), the **Medousa,** and **O Tembelis,** all of which don't have phones. The **Taverna Folia,** Odós Athanasíou Diakoú 6, is well known for its pigeon and rabbit dishes.

There are also some excellent places up in Áno Sýros; the most famous of which is **Lilis** (☎ 0281/28-087), and you will probably want to call ahead for reservations and take a cab up. The **Katoga Taverna** is another very good choice for more traditional fare.

Cavo d'Oro. Paralía, Ermoúpolis. ☎ **0281/81-440.** Appetizers Dr 400–Dr 900 ($1.70–$3.85), main courses, Dr 1,300–Dr 2,400 ($5.50–$10.20). No credit cards. Daily 11am–midnight. SEAFOOD.

This clean, comfortable restaurant has indoor and outdoor seating near the center of the harbor front. A large selection of fish, squid, and octopus dishes are served very fresh, grilled or fried. The chef makes a piquant skordaliá (garlic dip that goes very well with fish), taramosaláta, hórta (greens), and other typical dishes to please the Greek clientele.

Eleana Restaurant. Platía Miaoúlis, Ermoúpolis. No telephone. Appetizers Dr 450–Dr 900 ($1.90–$3.85), main courses Dr 1,000–Dr 1,600 ($4.25–$6.80). No credit cards. Daily 11am–3pm, 7–11pm. GREEK/INTERNATIONAL.

Eleana has a varied taverna menu of vegetable dishes and meat casseroles. The interior is air-conditioned and the exterior opens onto the picturesque square.

AROUND THE ISLAND

Most of the tavernas at the various beaches and towns along the coast are at least acceptable, but few of them stand out. According to reader Rev. Martin Peter, **Nikos Restaurant** in Galissás "has delicious food and very good prices." In Kíni the **Iliovasílema** ("Sunset") is famous for its food as well as the spectacular sunset.

SÝROS AFTER DARK

In Ermoúpolis, the waterfront is the best place to be at sunset, and the **Allo Bar** is thought of as the most au courant. **Tramps** is more down to earth, with a good selection of music. The **Dizzy Bar** plays more relaxing music than its name might lead to expect. The music gets louder at **Highway,** and louder still at **No Name.**

You can also join in the evening vólta (stroll) around Platía Miaoúlis, or take a seat to watch it. There are of course several bars nearby, including **Café No. 9** (☎ 0281/22-018), which plays a variety of mellow music. Wander east a little later and follow your ears to several discos and dance bars.

For information and tickets to a performance at the **Apollon Theater,** contact Teamwork Holidays at **0281/23-400.** There's also the outdoor **Pallas Cinema,** east of the main square, which has two nightly showings, often in English.

Sýros was among the most fertile grounds for rebétika, and you will find this special music played more authentically in several bars outside town, such as **Dakrotsides Taverna** (☎ 0281/71-210), near Kíni, and the **Neráïda Bouzouki Club,** near Mána.

Up in Áno Sýros, where a square has been named after the great bouzoúki player Márkos Vamvakáris, **Rahanos** and chic **Lilis** (☎ 0281/28-087) have late-night performances on the weekends; reservations are a must.

9

The Dodecanese

by Michael C. Goldstein

The *dódeka*, or 12, islands that constitute the Dodecanese (Dodekánissos) form Greece's far eastern strategic border, within kissing distance of neighboring Turkey. From tiny Kastellórizo in the far south—just look at a map—to Pátmos at the northern end, they span a diverse touristic and geographic landscape that makes for pleasant travel. Like most of the islands, the Dodecanese have been or are actively in the process of being subjugated to the onslaught of European group tourism, continuing a long tradition in Dodecanese history.

From the Asian tribes of Anatolia in antiquity to the Crusaders in the Middle Ages the unfortunate 12 seem to be perennially in the way of this or that conquering horde. It's hardly surprising that these particular islanders, credited with organizing the rebellion against the Turks, are among the most politically minded people in all Greece and have often been leaders in new social movements.

Of all those who overran the islands, the Italians (who occupied the Dodecanese between 1913 and 1943) have left the greatest mark. Many older citizens speak the language fluently and hints of Italian taste crop up in the cuisine and culture of the region. Romans, Venetians, Genoese, and Crusaders constructed most of the islands' magnificent temples and fortresses. It was under Mussolini's direction that ancient and medieval sites on Rhodes and Kos were restored in a particularly Fascist style. Though repeatedly occupied by different nations, the Dodecanese have miraculously remained essentially Greek.

Of the major islands, **Rhodes** is the largest and the most cosmopolitan, with a wall of beach resorts on both sides of the main town that scream "Miami! Miami!" Don't let that put you off; we still love exploring the back cobbled lanes of the medieval Old Town and the picture-postcard village and acropolis of Lindos. One-and-a-half hours away by ferry is tiny **Sými,** once a secret and now a ballyhooed neoclassical gem that still draws "oohs" and "aahs" from its many day-tripping and longer-term guests. Nearby and north, where Hippocrates penned his famous oath, is **Kos,** which used to be a favorite for its antiquities and magnificent beaches, but has now become a playground for British and Scandinavian charter groups. **Kálymnos** has made a relatively successful transition from sponge island to tourist enclave. Donkeys still outnumber cars on little **Lipsí,** whose secluded beaches and tavernas are all within walking

The Dodecanese

Monastery of St. John and the
Holy Cave of the Apocalyse ❶
Panormítes Monastery ❷
Petaloúdes
(Valley of the Butterflies) ❸

GREECE
Athens ★
The
Dodecanese

PÁTMOS
Arkí
Agathoníssi
Kámpos (Valley)
Márathos
Megálo Chorió
Skála
Gríkos ❶
Lipsí
Frángos
Farmakoníssi
LÉROS
Pantéli
Lakkí
Xerókampos
Lévitha
Embórios
Arginóntas
Télendos
Massoúri
Myrties
KÁLYMNOS
Psárimos
Kálymnos
Lámbi
Mastichári
Tigáki
Kos
Asfendioú
Aghios Fokás
Kéfalos
Kardámena
KOS
Nimos
Vathýs
Yialí
Koutrá
Sými
Pédi
Mandráki
Emborios
SÝMI ❷
Anállipsi
Avláki
Astypálaea
Pachiá
Níssiros
Astypálea
Kandelioússa
Megálo Chorió
Pandeleímonos
Tílos
Livadiá
Rhodes
Sírna
Alímia
Ialysos
Fanés
Maritsa
Kalithéa
Tría Nissiá
Mandrikó
Soróni
Halkí
❸
Afándou
Émbonas
RHODES
Archánghelos
Monólithos
Laermá
Líndos
Apolákia
Messanágros
Ghennádi
Kataviá
Plimíri

Sariá
Diafáni
Ólympos
Spoá
KÁRPATHOS
Píles
Arkássa
Kárpathos
Armathiá
Frí
Kássos

Airport ✈
Car Ferry Routes ▬ – – – –

0 ▬▬▬▬ 37.6 km
25 mi
N

9622

335

distance from the friendly harbor village. In A.D. 95, **Pátmos** provided refuge for St. John the Divine, and still today embraces all who visit this friendly island.

1 Rhodes

250 nautical miles E of Piraeus

Ever since Julius Caesar vacationed on Rhodes, the Italians have coveted the island as a resort. They went a long way when, in the first third of this century, they occupied the island, built new buildings, renovated dilapidated ones, and improved the infrastructure.

The best beaches lie on the east coast of the island below Líndos, from Lardos Bay 26 kilometers south to Plimiri; our favorite stretch is between Lahania and Plimiri. Compared to the rest of this woefully overbuilt island there is little development; however, a strip of burgeoning resorts catering to Scandinavian, German, and English groups makes life along this coastline extremely difficult for individual travelers. The greatest concentration of Miami Beach–style monoliths is in the north, around the perimeter of Rhodes town, spreading over an area approximately 15 kilometers long along both east and west coasts. The interior section of Rhodes is mountainous and green, with small villages dotting its rugged terrain.

Rhodes town is the northernmost and by far the largest and most diverse city on the island, and makes the best base for sightseeing and beach going. Lindos, on the southeast coast, is a scenic gem, with an ancient acropolis, traditional architecture, and a lovely beach cove. Unfortunately, it's overrun with tourists and finding a room in July and August is almost impossible. Unless you have a reservation, stay in Rhodes. (Advance reservations here are also highly recommended.)

ESSENTIALS

GETTING THERE **By Plane** **Olympic Airways** offers one flight daily from Iráklion, Crete; three flights daily from Athens; three flights daily from Karpathos; one flight daily from Kos; four flights weekly from Páros; one flight daily from Mýkonos; three flights weekly from Santoríni, Kastellorizo and Kassos. Reservations and ticket information can be obtained from the **Olympic Airways Office,** Odos Ierou Lochou 9 (☎ **0241/24-571** or 0241/24-555). Flights fill quickly so make reservations early. **Air Greece** is a new, private airline, with up-to-date aircraft and better service than the established Olympic Airlines. It has daily service to Athens, costing Dr 9,500 ($40.45) less than the Olympic price for the round-trip fare. It also operates two flights weekly to Crete and to Thessaloníki. Tickets for Air Greece flights can be purchased at **Triton Holidays,** near Mandraki Harbor, Odos Plastira 9, Rhodes town(☎ **0241/22-508;** 0241/fax 31-625).

Taxis cost about Dr 1,500 ($6.40) between the airport and Rhodes town. There's a duty-free shop at Rhodes International Airport as well as an information desk with erratic hours.

By Boat Daily car ferries from Piraeus make a grueling 18-hour trip to Rhodes, and infrequent service from Rafina is even longer. There are four ferries weekly to Ághios Nikólaos, Crete, and Santoríni. Two to three (depending on the season) ferries weekly ply the Dodecanese waters to Tilos, Nissiros, Halkis, and Karpathos, while daily ferries service the more popular Sými, Kos, Leros, Kálymnos, and Pátmos. There's a once-weekly ferry to Astipalea via Kálymnos. Twice weekly you can take a ferry to Limassol, Cyprus, and then on to Haifa, Israel. There's a daily ferry to Sámos (in the Northern Aegean group) that continues on to Thessaloníki (northern mainland Greece). Your best bet is to check the **EOT office** or the **Tourist Information**

Archeological
  Museum of Rhodes **3**
Church of Our Lady
  of the Castle **4**
Clock Tower **5**
Municipal Baths **7**
Palace of the Villiers
  of the Isle of Adam **2**
Site where Colossus
  is believed to
  have stood **1**
Stadium **9**
Suleyman Mosque **6**
Theater **8**

Lighthouse
Information

Office for their printed schedule of weekly departures; they can tell you the travel
agents selling tickets to each boat.

There is daily hydrofoil service from Mandraki Harbor to Kos and Sými, and less
reliable service to Kálymnos, Leros, Pátmos, Kastellorizo, and Sámos. The advantage
of hydrofoils is that they make the voyage in half the time as the ferries. The down
side is that if the wind blows up the waves, then the sailings are canceled. There are
also daily excursion boats to Sými for Dr 3,000 to Dr 4,000 ($12.80 to $17), which
leave at 9am and return by about 5:30pm. Daily excursion can also be taken from
Kamiros Skála (an east coast port 19 miles south of Rhodes) to Halki.

Ferry boat and hydrofoil tickets as well as tickets to Turkey (see "Excursions to
Turkey," below) can be purchased from several agencies in Rhodes town on Amerikis
Street or from the very helpful **Triton Holidays** office near the entrance to the
Rhodes Old Town (see "Getting Around," below). In the Old Town, superfriendly
Christos of **Castellania Travel Service,** on Hippocrates Square, is your best source
of travel information and boat tickets.

VISITOR INFORMATION   At the **Greek National Tourist Office (EOT)**
(☎ **0241/23-655;** fax 0241/26-955), open Monday through Friday 7:30am to 3pm,
at the intersection of Makariou and Papagou streets, you can get advice about the
whole island, as well as check on the availability of accommodations. There's also a
helpful **Rhodes Municipal Tourist Office** (☎ **0241/35-945),** open Monday
through Friday from 8am to 7pm and Saturday from 8am to 6pm, down the hill at

Rimini Square near the port taxi stand. They have information and advice on local excursions, buses ferries, and accommodations.

GETTING AROUND   Rhodes is so big that you'll need public buses, group-shared taxis, a rental car, or an organized bus tour for around-the-island excursions. Within the town, walking is the best and most pleasurable mode of transport; you'll need a taxi only if you're going to splurge at one of the farther-out restaurants or if you're decked out for the Casino and don't want to be seen walking

By Bus   There's a good **public bus system** throughout the island; **EOT** and the **Tourist Information Office** publish a schedule of routes and times. From the **East Side Bus Station** on Rimini Square there are hourly buses to Faliraki, nine a day to Lindos, and several a day to the other east coast beaches. From the nearby **West Side Bus Station** on Averof Street, there are half-hourly buses to Kalithea and Ialyssos, four a day to Kamiros, one a day to Monolithos and Embosa, and several to the airport.

By Taxi   In Rhodes city, there's a large, well-organized **taxi stand** (☎ 0241/27-666 or 0241/64-712; for **radio taxis** call **0241/62-029**) in front of Old Town, on the harbor front in Rimini Square. There, posted for all to see and agree upon, are the set fares for sightseeing throughout the island. Since many of the cab drivers speak sightseer English, a few friends can be chauffeured and lectured at a very reasonable cost. Taxis are metered, but fares should not exceed the minimum on short round-the-city jaunts. For longer trips, negotiate cab rentals directly with the drivers.

By Car   There are several car-rental companies in each community, and a local travel agent may be able to give you the best price. We were extremely pleased with the car and the service from **Europcar** (☎ 0241/21-958; fax 0241/30-923) on Odos Oktovriou 28, which delivered the car to our hotel. Prices start at about Dr 14,000 ($59.60) per day.

By Tour/Cruises   There are several tour operators featuring nature, archaeology, shopping, and beach tours of the island. In Rhodes town, **Triton Holidays,** near Mandraki Harbor, behind the Bank of Greece, at Odos Plastira 9 (☎ 0241/21-690; fax 0241/31-625), is one of the largest and most reliable agencies. They offer a wide variety of **day and evening cruises, hiking tours,** and **excursions** in Rhodes, as well as to the other Dodecanese islands and to Turkey. We recommend their full-day guided tours, either to Lindos (Dr 5,500/$23.40) or their "Island Tour" (Dr 8,800/$37.45), which takes you to small villages, churches, and monasteries, including lunch in the village of Embona, known for its local wines and fresh, grilled meat. There is also a fascinating half-day guided tour to the Filermos Monastery, the Valley of the Butterflies, and to the ancient city of Kamiros (Dr 5,500/$23.40). Along Mandraki Harbor one can find excursion boats which leave for Lindos at 9am and return about 6pm (Dr 4,000/$17). For an in-depth island experience, Triton holidays also offers a combination package of car rental and hotel accommodation in four small villages around the island (Kalavarda, Monolithos, Prassonisi, and Asklepion), ranging from four to 10 nights.

CITY LAYOUT   Today, Rhodes City is divided into two sections, the Old Town, dating from medieval days, and the New Town. The **Old Town** is surrounded by the massive walls (nearly eight feet thick) built by the Knights of St. John and overlooks the harbor. The **New Town** surrounds the old one on all sides and extends south to meet the resort strip. At its north tip is the **town beach** in the area called **100 Palms,** and nearby **Mandráki Harbor,** once straddled by the Colossus, is now used as a mooring for private yachts and tour boats.

Walking away from Mandráki Harbor on **Plastíra Street,** you'll come to **Cyprus Square,** where most of the New Town hotels are clustered. Veer left and continue to the park where the mighty fortress begins. Opposite it is the **EOT office;** there is also a **Rhodes Municipal Tourist Office** down the hill at Rimini Square (see "Fast Facts," below, for information on both).

FAST FACTS: Rhodes City

American Express   The local American Express agent is **Rhodos Tours** (☎ 0241/ **21-010**), at Odos Ammochostou 23, in the New Town. They're open Monday through Saturday 8:30am to 1:30pm and 5 to 8:30pm.

Area Code   The area code for Rhodes City is **0241.**

Banks   The **National Bank of Greece,** on Cyprus Square, keeps extended hours for exchanging currency Monday through Thursday 8am to 2pm and 6 to 8pm; Friday 8am to 1:30pm and 3 to 8:30pm; 8am to 2pm on Saturday, and 9am to noon on Sunday. There are also numerous **currency exchange offices** throughout the Old and New Town, very often with rates better than those of the banks.

Emergencies   For medical emergencies call **Rhodes General Hospital** (☎ 0241/ **22-222**) on Erythrou Stavrou Street. For other emergencies call the **Tourist Police** (☎ **0241/27-423**) or dial **100.**

OTE/Telephone   The main OTE branch, open daily 6am to midnight, is located at Odos Amerikis 91 in the New Town. There is also a branch just off Simi Square, open daily from 7:30am to 11pm. You can also make overseas and long-distance calls at **Castellania Travel Service,** on Hippocrates Square, for the same price as phone cards rates. Other travel agencies also offer this service.

Pharmacies   The **International Pharmacy** (☎ **0241/75-331**), 22 A. Kiakou St. near the Thermai Hotel, provides worldwide medicine identification and compatibility. There is always a pharmacy open 24 hours on a rotation basis. Some drugs and antibiotics are available without prescription.

Police   The **police** (☎ **0241/23-849** or 100) in the Old Town are open from 10am to midnight to handle any complaints of overcharging, theft, swindles, or other price- or goods-related problems. There's a **Tourist Police** office (☎ **0241/ 27-423**) on the edge of the Old Town, near the port.

Post Office   The office on Mandraki Harbor is open Monday through Friday from 7am to 8pm. There is a small post office on Orpheon Street in the Old Town, open seven days a week for shorter hours.

THE MYTHOLOGY OF RHODES

The stories surrounding the origin and name of Rhodes are among the loveliest in Greek mythology. In the lofty heights of Mt. Olympus, Zeus, after his battle against the giants, was dividing the spoils of his victory among the other gods. Helios, the god of the sun, was gone when lots were cast for the division of earth. Upon his return, Helios appealed to Zeus to make some compensation, proposing that a piece of land, rising from the "foaming main," be granted as his sole possession. Zeus complied, and as Pindar wrote in the 5th century B.C., "From the waters of the sea arose an island, which is held by the Father of the piercing beams of light, the ruler of the steed whose breath is fire." The legend continues that Helios wed the nymph of the island, Rhodes, daughter of Poseidon, and was so taken with her beauty that he declared he would make the whole island an equal delight.

A further embellishment holds that a child was born of Helios and Rhodes, who in turn begat three sons: Kamiros, Ialysos, and Lindos. Each son established a great city and thus the wealth and fame of Rhodes spread throughout the world.

Identified with the Colossus, one of the seven wonders of the ancient world, and the impressive walled monastery of the Knights of St. John, Rhodes is today known by many as the most cosmopolitan resort in the Aegean.

WHAT TO SEE & DO IN RHODES CITY
EXPLORING THE OLD TOWN

The best introduction to the old walled city is through **Eleftería (Liberty) Gate,** where you'll come to **Simi Square,** containing ruins of the **temple of Venus,** identified as such by the votive offerings found at the site, and thought to date from the 3d century B.C. The remains of the temple are next to a parking lot (driving hours are restricted in Old Town), which rather diminishes the impact of the few stones and columns still standing. Nevertheless the ruins are a vivid reminder that a great Hellenistic city once stood within these medieval walls.

Simi Square also is home to the **Municipal Art Gallery of Rhodes** (open Monday through Saturday from 8am to 2pm), with additional hours Wednesday from 5 to 8pm) above the Ionian and Popular Bank. One block farther on is the **Museum of Decorative Arts** (open Monday through Friday from 8:30am to 3pm, Saturday, Sunday and holidays 8am to 1pm; admission Dr 600/$2.50) containing finely made Rhodian objects and crafts. Continue through the gate until you reach the **Museum Reproduction Shop** (with a precious painted tile of the Madonna above its door), then turn right on Ippiton Street toward the **Palace of the Knights.**

STREET OF THE KNIGHTS   This street (Ippotón, on the maps) is known as the Street of the Knights, and is one of the best preserved and most delightful medieval relics in the world. The 600-meter-long, cobble-paved street was constructed over an ancient pathway that led in a straight line from the Acropolis of Rhodes to the port. In the early 16th century, it became the address for most of the inns of each nation, which housed Knights who belonged to the Order of St. John. The inns were used as eating clubs and temporary residences for visiting dignitaries, and their facades reflect the different architectural details of their respective countries.

Begin at the lowest point of the hill (next to the Museum Reproduction Shop), at the Spanish house now used by a bank. Next door is the **Inn of the Order of the Tongue** (language) of Italy, built in 1519 (as can be seen in the shield of the order above the door). Then comes the **Palace of the Villiers of the Isle of Adam,** built in 1521, housing the Archaeological Service of the Dodecanese. The **Inn of France** now hosts the French Language Institute. Constructed in 1492, it's one of the most ornate of the inns, with the shield of three lilies (fleur-de-lis), royal crown, and that of the Magister d'Aubusson (the cardinal's hat above four crosses) off-center, over the middle door. Typical of the late Gothic period, the architectural and decorative elements are all somewhat asymmetrical, lending grace to the squat building. Opposite these inns is the side of the **Hospital of the Knights,** now the archaeological museum (see below).

The church farther on the right is **Aghía Triáda** (open 9am to noon daily), next to the Italian consulate. Above its door are three coats of arms: those of France, England, and the pope. Past the arch that spans the street, still on the right, is the **Inn of the Tongue of Provence,** shorter than it once was due to an 1856 explosion. Opposite it on the left is the traditionally Gothic **Inn of the Tongue of Spain,** with vertical columns elongating its facade and a lovely garden behind.

The Inn of France is open daily. The ground floor houses the Institut Français, but you can get a view of its garden and an occasional art show in the 2d floor gallery. The other inns are now used as office space or private residences and are closed to the public.

PALACE OF THE KNIGHTS   At the crest of the hill on the right, through the grand gates, is the amazing **Palace of the Knights** (also known as the Palace of the Grand Masters or Magisters), thought to be the original site of the ancient **Temple of Helios.** The palace, on Ippiton Street (☎ 0241/23-359), was neglected by the Turks (they turned it into a prison), and in 1856 was accidentally blown up, along with the Church of St. John. During the Italian occupation the Fascist government undertook the enormous project of reconstructing the castle. Only the stones on the lower part of the building and walls are original; the rest is the work of 20th-century hands. The palace reflects a happy Gothic style of architecture, with large bright windows flooding the interior with light. Inside, offsetting the dark weighty Renaissance furniture is a collection of pastel-colored Hellenistic, Roman, and early Christian mosaics "borrowed" from Italian excavations on neighboring Kos. The intricately painted urns are Japanese and were presented as gifts from Italy's allies across the Pacific. The palace is open Tuesday through Sunday from 8:30am to 3pm; admission is Dr 1,000 ($4.15), half price for children, Sundays are free.

From the Palace of the Knights, go back down Ippiton Street to Simi Square. The Church of the Virgin of the Castle will be on your left and the Archaeology Museum of Rhodes will be ahead on your right.

Church of Our Lady of the Castle   Formerly the Byzantine Museum of Rhodes, the Church of the Virgin of the Castle (☎ 0241/27-674) was reopened in 1988, occupying the renovated interior of this 11th-century church (also known as Our Lady of the Castle). Inside is a permanent exhibition of paintings of Rhodes from the early Christian period to the 18th century, including **icons, wall paintings,** and **miniatures.** The museum is open daily from 8:30am to 3pm; admission is Dr 500 ($2.10), children and students free.

ARCHAEOLOGICAL MUSEUM OF RHODES   Opposite you is the medieval hospital, now housing the Archaeological Museum of Rhodes, on Apelou Street (☎ 0241/27-657), with several exquisite **Greek sculptures.** The first floor is lined with **tombstones of knights** from the 15th and 16th centuries, many of which are festooned with extravagant coats-of-arms and wonderfully overblown inscriptions. One of the masterpieces of the collection of ancient works is a **funeral stele** dating from the 5th century B.C. showing Crito, the grieving daughter of Timarista, embracing her mother for the last time. It's an elegant and expressive example of classic Greek art. Equally stunning, on the second floor, is the petite **statue of Aphrodite,** sculpted 400 years later (Lawrence Durrell's "Marine Venus"), but also an extraordinarily beautiful work of the Hellenistic period. The head of Helios, patron deity of the island, was found near the site of the palace in this old city. Metallic rays, representing flashes of brilliant flames from the sun, were attached around the crown. There is also a fine collection of **ancient vases** and **jewelry** from Ialysos and Kamiros in the Knights' Hall. The museum is open Tuesday through Sunday from 8:30am to 3pm; admission is Dr 1,000 ($4.15).

OTHER SIGHTS   The **Mosque of Süleyman** and the **public baths** are two reminders of the Turkish presence in Old Rhodes. Follow Sokratous Street, away from the harbor; the mosque will be straight ahead near Panetiou Street. You can't miss it, with its slender, though incomplete, minaret and pink-striped Venetian exterior.

The **Municipal Baths** (what the Greeks call the **"Turkish baths"**) are housed in a 7th-century Byzantine structure. They warrant a visit by anyone interested in the vestiges of Turkish culture still found in the Old Town, and are a better deal than the charge for showers in most pensions. The **hamam** (most locals use the Turkish word for "bath") is located in Arionos Square, between a large old mosque and the Folk Dance Theater. Throughout the day men and women enter their separate entrances and disrobe in the private shuttered cubicles. A walk across the cool marble floors will lead you to the bath area, many domed, round chambers sunlit by tiny glass panes in the roof. Through the steam you'll see people seated around large marble basins, chatting while ladling bowls of water over their heads. The baths are open Tuesday through Saturday from 7am to 7pm; the baths cost Dr 850 ($3.55) on Tuesday, Wednesday, and Friday and only Dr 250 ($1.05) on Thursday and Saturday. The ticket sellers warn that Saturday is very crowded with locals.

The Old Town was also home to the Jewish community, whose origins date from the days of the ancient Greeks. Much respected as merchants, they lived in the northeast or **Jewish Quarter** of the Old Town. Little survives other than a few **homes with Hebrew inscriptions,** the **Jewish cemetery,** and the **Square of the Jewish Martyrs** (also known as Seahorse Square because of the seahorse fountain). There is a lovely **synagogue,** where services are held every Friday night; a small black sign in the square shows the way. The synagogue is usually open daily from 10am to 1pm and is located on Dosiadou Street, off the square. This square is dedicated to the thousands of Jews who were rounded up here and sent to their deaths at Auschwitz. If you walk around the residential streets, you'll still see abandoned homes and burned buildings.

After touring the sites of the old city, a walk around the walls is recommended (the museum operates a daily tour, Monday through Saturday at 2:45pm, beginning at the Palace of the Knights). The fortification has a series of magnificent gates and towers, and is remarkable as an example of a fully intact medieval structure. Admission is Dr 1,000 ($4.15).

EXPLORING THE NEW TOWN

The two major attractions within the confines of the new city are **Mandraki Harbor** and **Mount Smith.** The harbor is perhaps more famous for the **legend of the Colossus** than its present use. The Colossus, a 90-foot-tall image of Helios, was cast from 304 to 292 B.C., but tumbled down in an earthquake only 66 years after its completion. The shattered giant, one of the seven ancient wonders, lay on the ground for more than 800 years before it was hauled away and eventually carried through the Syrian desert by a caravan of 900 camels. It was probably melted down to make weapons. The exact site of the Colossus has never been firmly established. Myth makers and romantics have placed it on either side of Mandraki Harbor, where mighty ships from Rhodes and foreign ports could pass under its gigantic legs. Recently a psychic led some divers to the harbor, swearing they'd find big chunks of the Colossus. Large pilings were found, but Greece's culture minister denied they were part of the Colossus. Two columns capped by a stag and doe, symbols of Rhodes, mark the supposed location of the Colossus. More serious historians and archeologists place the site farther inland, near the once-standing Church of St. John and temple of Helios (now the Palace of the Grand Masters).

Mandraki also has a **Venetian-era watchtower,** three picture-postcard **windmills,** and **boats** of all varieties, from funky excursion boats leaving for Sými, to space-age hydrofoils, regal sailing vessels, and supersleek jet-powered yachts.

Mt. Smith is a modest hill named after an English admiral. It's north of the present city and the site of the ancient **Acropolis,** which dates from 408 B.C., which, with

Mt. Smith, the north shoreline, and the Old Town, once bordered the city. Traces of its north-south main street have been found under the modern New Zealand Street. On top of Mt. Smith are **remnants of temples** dedicated to Athena and Zeus Polieus. Archaeologists believe that this very large temple complex was easily visible to ships in the Straits of Marmaris, and therefore all treaties and allegiance documents between Rhodes and her warring neighbors were kept here. Below this are the three tall columns and a pediment that remain from the vast **Temple of Apollo.**

Below the Acropolis is a long **stadium** built into the side of Sandourli Hill. It was reconstructed by the Italians in the early 1940s, though some of the original tiers from the 2nd century B.C. can be seen. To its left is the totally reconstructed 800-seat **theater** once used to teach rhetoric (an art for which Rhodes was well known). In the vicinity are the remains of a **gymnasium,** and above it near the acropolis, a **nymphaeon** where **caves** and **water channels** indicate that here river goddesses may have been worshipped.

OTHER SIGHTS

Modern Rhodes has a number of other diverting attractions. Among them is the **Aquarium,** built by the Italians in 1938 on the northern point of the city. It displays an amazing variety of Mediterranean marine life, with the lower floor designed like an underwater grotto, its aquariums filled with fantastic denizens of the sea. There is also a small museum with stuffed and preserved sea creatures, mammals, birds and even genetic freaks, supplied by the local farmers. It's open daily 9am to 9pm; admission is Dr 600 ($2.55), students and children Dr 400 ($1.70).

As you walk along the waterside from the Old Town to the aquarium, you'll see a complex of massive Italianate buildings, erected by the Italian occupation authorities during the fascist era.

SHOPPING

Special tax privileges conferred on the Dodecanese islands means that many items such as **fabrics, woolens, designer-name clothing, shoes, leather goods, jewelry, booze,** and **tobacco** are cheaper here than in the rest of Greece, sometimes even less expensive than in the country of origin. **Greek handicrafts** and **folk art** are abundant, although you must seek out the genuine quality items among all the commercial souvenir-style goods. Don't forget to get a receipt; faulty merchandise (particularly jewelry) can sometimes be exchanged with tourist police help.

In the Old Town, you'll find classic and contemporary **gold** and **silver jewelry** almost everywhere. The top-of-the-line Greek designer **Ilias LaLaounis** has a boutique on Simi or Museum Square. The high-priced, high-quality **Alexander Shop,** one block from Socratous Street behind the Alexis Restaurant, offers stylish European work, elegant gold and platinum link bracelets and beautifully set precious gems. There are dozens of competitors in the crowded lanes in between. While you're on Socratous, stop in at the traditional **Kafeneion Turkiko** at no. 76 to rest your feet and have a coffee.

For imported **leather goods** and **furs** (the former often from nearby Turkey and the latter from Kastoria in northern Greece), stroll down the length of Socratous Street. Antique-ophiles should drop into the **Ministry of Culture Museum Reproduction Shop** on Ippitou Street, open from 8am daily, which sells excellent plaster and resin reproductions of favorite sculptures, friezes, tiles, and other works from throughout ancient Greece. True antiques can be found in a wonderful old building with a pebble-mosaic floor and an exotic banana-tree garden near the Knights Palace on Odos Panetiou 30, called **Kalogirou Art,** with furniture, carpets, porcelain and paintings. We found the prices of Turkish carpets, kilims, and Bucharan suzanni to be quite reasonable.

The New Town, especially Makariou Street and the crowded roads around the EOT office, features many **European boutiques** and well-known franchises, such as **Armani, Pull & Bear Clothing Company** (great Spanish clothes at cheap prices!), and **Lacoste.** The natural cosmetics company, the **Body Shop,** is at Odos Makariou 25, with a branch also in the Old Town off of Socratous Street. Nearby at no. 43 is **Benetton,** for anyone who forgot his resort wear and is contemplating a night on the town. There are also some great sales along Kyprou Street, with good prices for sportswear.

SPORTS & OUTDOOR ACTIVITIES

If it's activities you want, Rhodes City has them, too. Information on taking **folk dance lessons** can be obtained from the **Old Town Theater** (☎ 0241/29-085), where Nelly Dimoglu and her entertaining troupe perform, or by writing the **Traditional Dance Center,** Odos Dekelias 87, Athens 143, Greece (☎ 01/25-1080, in Athens). Classes run from June through the beginning of August, 30 hours per week; each week dances from a different region are studied. There are also shorter courses.

For more conservative jocks, try the **Rhodes Tennis Club** (☎ 0241/25-705) in the resort of Elli, or the **Rhodes-Afandau Golf Club** (☎ 0241/51-225), 19 kilometers south of the port. Fully equipped fitness centers can be found at **Body Center Rhodes** (☎ 0241/20-233), at 86 Lindou St., and at **Busy Bodies Health Club** (☎ 0241/20-345), at 45 Filerimou St.

No license in required for **fishing,** with the best grounds reputed to be off Kamairos Skála, Kalithea, and Lindos. Try hitching a ride with the **fishing boats** which moor opposite St. Katerina's Gate. For sailing and yachting information call the **Rodos Yacht Club** (☎ 0241/23-287) or the **Yacht Agency Rhodes** (☎ 0241/22-927;** fax 0241/23-393), which is the center for all yachting needs.

If you always wanted to try **scuba diving,** here's your chance. Both **Waterhoppers Diving Schools** (☎/fax 0241/38-146) and **Dive Med** (☎ 0241/28-040;** fax 0241/23-780) offer one-day introductory dives for beginners, diving expeditions for experienced divers, and courses leading to certification.

WHERE TO STAY
IN RHODES CITY

Hotels and pensions in the Old Town are cheaper and less sterile than those in modern Rhodes, and there's a special feeling along the dimly lit medieval streets. With all the following recommendations, reservations are suggested, at least six weeks in advance for the high season. Note that hotels open from late April to mid-October unless otherwise noted, and that rates drop up to 40% in the low season.

The true low-budget traveler will have a hard time in expensive Rhodes. If you can't get into one of the recommendations below, contact the Greek National Tourist Office for their list of rooms to let or look for one of the small pensions off Platia Martiron Evreon (Square of the Jewish Martyrs), near the harbor between the Aghia Ekaterini and Milon Gates. Off the square along Demosthenous Street are several inexpensive places, such as the **Artemis Pissa** (no phone), run by an old couple on 12 Dimosthenous, which charges Dr 1,500 ($6.40) for a dormitory bed. Most of these places actually have a certain charm with their inner courtyard gardens, are relatively clean, and are conveniently located. The **Rodos Youth Hostel** (☎ 0241/30-491),** in an impressive, partially restored 400-year-old building at Odos Erghiou, has 50 beds at Dr 1,800 ($7.65), breakfast for Dr 750 ($3.20), a common-use kitchen, hot showers, self-service laundry facility, a bar, and no curfew.

Note: Taxis are required to take passengers with luggage into the Old Town if so requested; there is a prohibition against entering this vehicle-free zone only for those without luggage. Insist on getting the service you've paid for and resist unscrupulous drivers who try to take you to commission-paying New Town hotels, such as the Bella Vista.

IN THE OLD TOWN

Expensive

✪ **S. Nikolis Hotel.** Odos Ippodamou 61, Rhodes 85100. ☎ **0241/34-561.** Fax 0241/32-034. 10 rms, 4 apartments, 4 suites (all with bath). TEL. Dr 16,000 ($68) single; Dr 18,000–Dr 22,000 ($76.60–$93.60) double; Dr 30,000 ($127.65) suite (including breakfast). AE, EC, MC, V. Open year-round.

If you are seeking the incomparable charm of staying in the Old Town, together with pleasure and comfort of a tastefully restored rustic lodging, this is the nicest place in Rhodes. The two lower rooms, with their 800-year-old stone arches, have air-conditioning and balconies overlooking a delightful inner courtyard. All of the rooms have modern tiled showers and heaters in case the chilling meltemi begins to blow. Owner, Sotiris Nikolis, and his Danish wife, Marianne, are the ultimate caring hosts, pampering their guests by providing every possible service from laundry to car rental and excursion boat tickets. The delicious and substantial breakfast is served on the roof-top terrace, with an outstanding view of the Old Town and the harbor. They also have attractive, nearby apartments for rent that come with a fully-equipped kitchen (rates equal the hotel's but without breakfast), as well as some simpler rooms to let. Their newest additions are four deluxe "honeymoon" suites, each with over-sized double beds, air-conditioning, fully equipped kitchens, TV; fax and video facilities, and even one bath with a built-in Jacuzzi. Check out their adjacent **Ancient Agora Bar and Restaurant** where, in 1990, a 10-ton marble pediment dating from the 2nd century was found beneath the medieval foundations.

Moderate

Hotel La Luna. Odos Ierokleous 21, Rhodes 85100. ☎ **0241/25-856.** 7 rooms (none with bath). Dr 11,000 ($46.80) double (including breakfast). No credit cards.

This small, delightful hotel is one block from the taverna-lined touristic Orfeous Street in a quiet residential neighborhood. It has a large, shaded garden with a cozy bar and breakfast tables. The real highlight is the setting of the common bathrooms—built into this old home is a genuine 300-year-old Turkish bath! Each eclectically decorated, high-ceilinged room has flower-print wallpaper, and though bathless, are spacious and bright. For 23 years, manager Tony Kaymaktsis has maintained a fresh, clean and very friendly place, and will regale you with stories of Ben Kingsley's stay during the filming of the British epic Paschali's Island.

Inexpensive

Andreas Pension. Odos Omirou 28D, Rhodes 85100. ☎ **0241/34-156.** Fax 74-285. 12 rms (none with bath). Dr 7,000 ($29.80) double. V.

A relief from the cardboard walls and linoleum floors which seem to constitute many of the town's budget accommodations, this well-run pension in a restored 400-year-old Turkish house offers attractive rooms, some of which have panoramic views of the town, others with wooden lofts which can comfortably sleep a family of four. Dmitri, a former barge captain, and his French wife, Josette, serve breakfast on a shaded terrace which has gorgeous vistas of the town and the harbor.

🟢 **Hotel Kastro.** Odos Arionos 14, Rhodes 85100. ☎ **0241/20-446.** 12 rms (5 with bath). Dr 6,000 ($25.55) double with bath; Dr 5,000 ($21.30) double without bath. No credit cards.

We delighted visiting this picturesque place, with simple, clean twin-bedded rooms, overlooking the Plateia Arionos and its 18th-century Turkish Baths. Owner Vasilis Caragiannos, a 75-year-old former marine commando and devout royalist, has created a beautiful inner garden, including hand-sculpted benches and friezes on the walls which depict events from his life and his fertile imagination. We loved the surrealistic painting on the garden wall with imaginative interpretations of Greek mythological characters. The courtyard is a great place for sitting in the evening with his dog, Rambo, and his land turtle, Papandreou, to watch the sunset over the harbor.

Maria's Rooms. Odos Menekleous 147-Z, Rhodes 85100. ☎ **0241/22-169.** 8 rms (3 with bath). Dr 6,000 ($25.55) double without bath; Dr 7,000 ($29.80) double with bath. No credit cards.

We like this pristine little pension near the Cafe Bazaar, which for price and quality merits high marks. The rooms are sparkling white, squeaky clean, and Maria is a warm and welcoming hostess.

Pension Minos. Odos Omirou 5, Rhodes 85100. ☎ **0241/31-813.** 17 rms (none with bath). Dr 8,000 ($34) single/double. No credit cards.

This clean and contemporary pension, though in a soul-less concrete edifice, is one of the best budget choices. Hostess Maria Lenti is an indefatigable cleaner and the airy large rooms with private sinks, the common toilets, and the showers all gleam. We preferred the balconied room no. 15 with its glorious view across the Old Town's minarets and domes to the harbor. Go to the minimarket or bakery across the street for a take-out breakfast or snacks, then dine like royalty on the scenic rooftop terrace.

Sophia's Rooms. Odos Aristophanous 27, Rhodes 85100. ☎ **0241/36-181.** 10 rms (all with bath). Dr 6,000 ($25.55) double. No credit cards.

For those who insist on private baths in the Old Town on a minimalist budget, you might try this otherwise nondescript place, with small, clean rooms. It is presided over by Sophia's 78-year-old mother, who speaks not a word of English. If sign language is insufficient, Sophia is usually present in the Cavo d'Oro Restaurant across the square, which she operates.

Spot Hotel. Odos Perikleous 21, Rhodes 85100. ☎ **0241/34-737.** 9 rms (all with bath). Dr 10,000 ($42.55) single/double. No credit cards.

Michalis Mavrostomos, a former New York construction foreman, impeccably maintains these spotless rooms and offers helpful travel information. Located near the harbor right off of Platia Martiron Evreon, it has a communal fridge and a small inner courtyard.

Sunlight Pension. Odos Ippodamou 32, Rhodes 85100. ☎ **0241/21-435.** 6 rms (2 with bath). Dr 6,000 ($25.55) single/double. No credit cards.

The small, modern rooms are satisfactory, although the two ground-floor rooms with bath are too close for comfort to the downstairs Stavros Bar, a popular late-night meeting ground, especially for British tourists.

IN THE NEW TOWN & ENVIRONS

The modern hotels, even in the New Town, are more expensive in Rhodes than on other islands. Mediocre breakfasts are usually exorbitant, and most bland establishments cater to group tours and are rarely available to individual travelers. We've listed below a few of the exceptions.

Very Expensive

Rhodos Imperial. Ialysou Avenue, Ixia, Rhodes 85100. ☎ **0241/75-000.** Fax 76-690. 353 double rooms and 51 deluxe suites. A/C MINIBAR TV TEL. Dr 43,500 ($185) double with sea view (including breakfast). AE, MC, V.

Located 4 kilometers out of the New Town, this luxurious megahotel, across the road from the beach, has every possible facility which you might desire: three swimming pools (one indoor); a fully equipped fitness club and spa; tennis club; and a beach with windsurfing, sailing, jet-skiing, paragliding, and even swimming. You can stash your kids in the supervised miniclub while you're working out in the gym or taking your syrtaki (dancing) or aerobic lessons, and use an in-house baby-sitter while attending one of the hotel's evening shows. We're sure that you'll find something to eat in one of the three restaurants, serving either Greek, Polynesian, or International cuisine.

✪ **Rodos Park-Suites Hotel.** Odos Riga Ferou 12, Rhodes 85100. ☎ **0241/24-612.** Fax 24-613. 30 deluxe suites and 30 double rooms. A/C MINIBAR TV TEL. Dr 50,760 ($216) double (including breakfast). AE, MC, V.

Finally the New Town has a bona fide luxurious hotel, with gleaming marble and polished wood interiors, designed to offer exclusive services to the most demanding traveler. If you want a Jacuzzi in your room, choose one of the suites, preferably one with a superb view of the Old Town walls. If you need to work off some the surplus calories from the 24-hour room service or the in-house gourmet restaurant, head down to the fitness center, hit the machines, and then get pampered with a Swedish or hydro-massage, a sauna, or a steam bath. The added attraction is the convenient proximity of being a few minutes walk from the Old Town, Mandraki Harbor, or the New Town shopping and dining areas.

Expensive

Kamiros Hotel. Odos Martiou 1, Rhodes 85100. ☎ **0241/22-591.** Fax 0241/22-349. 48 rms (all with bath). A/C MINIBAR TV TEL. Dr 23,300 ($99.15) double (including breakfast). AE, MC, V.

This renovated hotel is well located in the heart of town overlooking Mandraki Harbor, just a few blocks from the Old Town. The rooms are large, the bathrooms especially spacious, and double-paned windows make them especially quiet for the central location. The buffet breakfast is unusually substantial.

Moderate

❸ **Hotel Anastasia.** Odos 28 Octovriou, 46, Rhodes 85100. ☎ **0241/28-007.** Fax 0241/21-815. 20 rms (all with bath). Dr 11,000 ($46.80) double (including breakfast). No credit cards. Open year-round.

Set quietly back off the street down a green lane, this 65-year-old Italian mansion is a charming place to stay. Operated for the past 20 years by George Anghelou, it has pleasant rooms with five-meter-high ceilings, giving a feeling of light and space. It's only a 100-meter walk to the municipal beach and close to the restaurant district of the New Town. For the hotel residents and their guests, there is a rustic bar in the hibiscus-trellised garden.

Hotel Despo. Odos Lambraki 40, Rhodes 85100. ☎ **0241/22-571.** 64 rms (none with bath). TEL. Dr 14,000 ($59.60) double. No credit cards.

From the usual Class C fare, this decent hotel, in the heart of the New Town, is one of the best. It's so well managed that the 1950s-era black and white leather furnishings in the lobby don't show many signs of wear. Sunny, clean rooms have balconies.

Hotel Spartalis. Odos Plastira 2, Rhodes 85100. ☎ **0241/24-372.** Fax 0241/20-406. 79 rms (57 with bath). TEL. Open year-round. Dr 9,000 ($38.30) single; Dr 13,000 ($55.30) double. MC, V.

Facing the marina of Mandraki harbor, and only a short walk to either the beach, the Old Town, or the bus station, this well-aged hotel has a great location. Try to get one of the top floor rooms, which have the best views and full-sized bathtubs.

Marieta Pension. Odos 28 Oktovriou, 52, Rhodes 85100. ☎ **0241/36-396.** 8 rms (all with bath). Dr 10,000 ($42.55) double. No credit cards.

This clean, spacious pension is a welcome alternative to the overpriced New Town hotels. After running a supermarket in St. Louis for many years, Marietta Potsos returned home to Rhodes and opened this pleasant, home-style place in a 52-year-old traditional villa. The rooms are large and high ceilinged.

WHERE TO DINE
IN RHODES CITY

The Old Town is crammed with tavernas and restaurants, all hungry for tourist dollars. Hawkers stand in front of eateries and accost passersby—handing out business cards, ushering people in for a look at the kitchen, and finally strong-arming them into sitting down. It's all part of the game. The best way to handle a restaurant bully is to continue walking to one of the restaurants listed below. Lest you think that Old Town restaurants are strictly for tourists, many Rhodians consider this section of town to have some of the best food in the city, particularly for fish, although low-cost seafood feasts are an impossible contradiction.

Expensive

Manolis Dinoris Fish Taverna. 14A Museum Square. ☎ **0241/25-824.** Appetizers Dr 400–Dr 2,300 ($1.70–$9.80), fish from Dr 8,800–Dr 12,500 ($37.45–$53.20). AE, EU, MC, V. Year-round, daily noon–3pm, 7pm–midnight. SEAFOOD.

Housed in the stables of the 13th-century Knights of St. John's Inn, this restored building is a unique setting to enjoy delicious and fresh seafood delights. Either choose à la carte or the set menu, which includes coquille St. Jacques, Greek salad, grilled prawns, swordfish, baklavas, coffee, and brandy. We liked the quiet garden on the side, but in winter it's cozy indoors with a fire roaring in the old stone hearth.

Inexpensive to Moderate

✪ **Alexis Taverna.** Odos Socratous 18. ☎ **0241/29-347.** Reservations recommended. Appetizers Dr 600–Dr 2,300 ($2.55–$9.80), fish from Dr 6,800–Dr 12,000 ($28.90–$51) per kilo. AE, V. Mon–Sat noon–3pm, 7pm–midnight; Sun 7pm–midnight. SEAFOOD.

This fine restaurant sets the standard by which all other seafood restaurants are compared. Preserving the tradition of their grandfather, Alexis, who founded this well-aged taverna in 1957 at the time of Rhodes independence, brothers Yiannis and Constantine succeed in maintaining world-class standards on the otherwise over-commercialized Socratous Street. Lining the interior walls are photographs of notables who frequented the restaurant, such as Churchill, Onassis, Telly Savalas, and the commander of the U.S. Sixth Fleet. They so insist on quality and freshness, that they have built their own greenhouse on the outskirts of town to cultivate organic vegetables. We started with a bounteous seafood platter, with delicately flavored sea urchins, fresh clams, and a tender octopus carpaccio. The sargos, a sea bream–type fish, was charcoal-grilled to perfection. The creamy Greek yogurt with homemade green-walnut jam was a perfect ending for a superb culinary experience.

Cleo's Restaurant. Odos St. Fanouriou 17. ☎ **0241/28-415.** Appetizers Dr 1,000–Dr 1,700 ($4.25–$7.25), main courses Dr 1,700–Dr 3,950 ($7.25–$16.80). AE, EU, MC, V. Mon–Sat 7pm–midnight. ITALIAN.

This tranquil place, with its whitewashed courtyard and elegantly furnished two-story interior, is found down a narrow lane off the noisy Socratous Street. Owner, Romildo Fistolera, from Como, Italy, prepares the best Italian and nouvelle European cuisine in Rhodes, as well as having a superb wine selection from the lesser-known "boutique" wineries. We savored the homemade tagatelle with salmon sauce, and found the beef fillet with white mushroom sauce to be superb. Every day there is a choice of four different fixed-price three-course dinners that are especially good buys. For dessert, the creamy tiramisu is sinfully exquisite. The colorful, large wall-mural in the courtyard was painted by a Native American Indian.

⑤ Diafani Garden Restaurant. Opposite the Turkish bath, Arionos Sq. 3. ☎ **0241/26-053.** Appetizers Dr 350–Dr 800 ($1.50–$3.40), main courses Dr 700–Dr 2,400 ($3–$10.20). No credit cards. Daily noon–midnight. GREEK.

Several locals recommended this family operated taverna to us. The Karpathian Protopapa family cooks up fine traditional Greek fare at bargain prices. Sitting under the spreading walnut tree in the vine-shaded courtyard, we enjoyed the potpourri of the Greek plate and the splendid papoutsaki, braised eggplant slices layered with chopped meat and a thick, cheesy béchamel sauce, delicately flavored with nutmeg and coriander.

Dodekanisos. 45 Platia Evreon Martyron. ☎ **0241/28-412.** Appetizers Dr 600–Dr 3,000 ($2.55–$12.75), fish Dr 5,000–Dr 12,000 ($21.30–$51) per kilo. AE, MC, V. Year-round daily 11am–midnight. SEAFOOD.

This simple place on the square is very popular with the locals—the fresh fish is grilled on the coals, and we found the vegetables fresh, firm, and not oily.

⑤ Kafeneio Araliki. Odos Aristofanous 45. ☎ **0241/28-991.** Appetizers/snacks Dr 450–Dr 1,000 ($1.90–$4.25). No credit cards. Mon–Sat 11am–3pm, 7pm–1am. GREEK.

A kafeneio is a place to eat small plates of savory dishes while sipping retsina or ouzo. Off the tourist circuit, this picturesque hideaway, run by two superfriendly Italian women, Valeria and Miriam, became our favorite place to sit in the evening among locals and expatriates, and munch on the delightful vegetarian, fish, or meat mezedes. The upstairs gallery is especially charming, with seating either at tables or on an oriental-style platform with comfortable cushions for reclining.

Kafeneio Turkiko. Odos Sokratous. No phone. Drinks/snacks Dr 200–Dr 500 (85¢–$2.15). No credit cards. Daily 11am–midnight. No credit cards. SNACKS.

Located in a Crusader structure, this is the only authentic place left on the touristy Sokratous Street, otherwise replete with Swatch, Body Shop, Van Cleef, and a multitude of souvenir shops. Each rickety wooden table comes with a backgammon board for idling away the time while you sip on Greek coffee, juice, or have a yogurt and honey. The turn-of-the-century pictures, mirrors, and bric-a-brac on the walls enhanced our feeling of bygone times.

Kavo d'Oro. In alley off 41 Sokratous. ☎ **0241/36-181.** Appetizers Dr 500–Dr 1,250 ($2.15–$5.30), main courses Dr 800–Dr 2,800 ($3.40–$11.90). No credit cards. Daily 10am–midnight. GREEK.

This reliable and friendly eatery in an unpretentious covered courtyard offers Greek food just the way we like it: hot and fresh. We started with the Greek plate, with its variety of tsatsiki, taramasalata, dolmades, and other goodies. We relished the fried eggplant with melted cheese and fresh tomato sauce; the beef stifado, scented with rosemary, was a treat. Owner, Sophia, and her daughters, receive our compliments for good food at bargain prices.

Restaurant Latino. Odos Ippodamou 11. ☎ **0241/24-876.** Appetizers Dr 350–Dr 1,000 ($1.50–$4.25), pastas Dr 1,200–Dr 1,800 ($5.10–$7.65), pizzas Dr 1,450–Dr 1,900 ($6.20–$8.10). MC, V. Daily 6pm–1am. ITALIAN.

Our thanks to Heather Howard, of Beverly Hills, California, who sent us a letter raving about this place. We fancied the fettucini primavera, made with fresh vegetables, tiny shrimp, and a creamy garlic sauce. The sogliola (sole) meunière, served with baked potato, rice, and vegetables, was also very satisfying. We enjoyed dining on the roof garden with its fine views over the harbor, but on a windy day we would probably prefer to sit downstairs in the decorated inner courtyard. Massimo, from Rome, uses a wood-burning oven to produce great pizzas.

Ⓢ Yiannis Taverna. Odos Appelou 41. ☎ **0241/36-535.** Appetizers Dr 350–Dr 700 ($1.50–$3), main courses Dr 850–Dr 2,200 ($3.60–$9.35). No credit cards. Daily 9am–midnight. GREEK.

For a budget Greek meal, visit chef Yiannis's small place on a quiet lane behind the Kavo d'Oro. The moussaka, stuffed vegetables, and meat dishes are flavorful and well prepared by a man who spent 14 years as a chef in New York Greek diners. His Greek plate is the best we found in Rhodes, with an unbelievably large variety of tasty foods. Portions are hearty, it's cheap, and the friendly service is a welcome relief from nearby establishments. The breakfast omelets are a great deal, too.

IN THE NEW TOWN

Expensive

✪ Kioupia. Tris village. ☎ **0241/91-824.** Reservations required. Fixed-price meal of Dr 8,000 ($34.00) per person, wines and service extra. MC, V. Mon–Sat 8pm–midnight. GREEK.

Rated by the *London Guardian* as one of the world's 10 best restaurants, this unique place provided us with an exquisite gourmet experience that we shall treasure forever. Kioupia was founded in 1972 by the creative and artistic Michael Koumbiadis, called by Athenian society "the Colossus of Rhodes," who has discovered the true harmony in the taste of Greek traditional cuisine, using the best of local ingredients and village recipes. In the elegantly decorated, rustic old house, the meal began with a rinsing of hands in rosewater, and then a choice from three soups, including the unusual trahanas, a Greek wheat and cheese soup. And then, as in a fantasy from Arabian Nights, an amazing array of more than 15 delectable appetizers kept arriving at our table, each tantalizing our eyes and enchanting our palate. To mention just a few: sautéed wild mushrooms, homemade sausage with pistachios, pumpkin beignee (dumplings), savory braised red peppers in olive oil (the best we've ever tasted), pine nuts and eggplant purée, and more and more. These were accompanied by home-baked carrot bread and pastrami bread, served with a delicately seasoned butter. A waiter then came to our table and peeled a charcoal-braised eggplant, hand-mincing it with feta cheese, olive oil, vinegar, and an herbal creme—a true delicacy. The main dishes were equally superb—broiled veal stuffed with cheese and sprinkled with pistachio nuts with yogurt sauce on the side, and delectable pork souvlaki with yogurt and paprika sauce on the side. The toothsome desserts were a delight: "bitter love"—a panna cotta (custardlike dessert) with pine nuts, chocolate, and fresh confiture, light crepes filled with sour cherries and covered with chocolate sauce and vanilla creme, baklava prepared in the wood oven, and baked, fresh pineapple slices and nectarines! Many of the foods are prepared in a traditional wood-burning oven in clay pots, the faint smell of wood permeating the restaurant. In addition to reveling in the food, we also had utmost praise for the polite and attentive waiters, who knew how to pamper without being intrusive.

Moderate

Palla Historia (The Old Story). Odos Mitropoleos 108. ☎ **0241/32-421.** Reservations recommended. Appetizers Dr 900–Dr 1,500 ($3.85–$6.40), main courses Dr 2,500–Dr 4,200 ($10.65–$17.90). EU, V. Daily 7pm–midnight. GREEK.

This is one of the best restaurants in the New Town, well worth the 10-minute cab ride or 25-minute walk. Most of the clientele is Greek, drawn by the subtle cuisine and lack of tourists. We recommend the unusual mezedes: finely chopped beet salad; lightly fried zucchini; the country salad with potatoes, olives, and tomatoes; the fried cheese or mussels saganaki; then a fluffy greens and cheese soufflé, and delicious meatless dolmades. For our main course, we enjoyed the moist and tender pork cassoulet in a gingery-hoisin sauce, served with potatoes. A feast indeed.

Inexpensive

Break Delicatessen. Odos Sof. Venizelou 8. ☎ **0241/34-809.** Snacks Dr 350–Dr 1,400 ($1.50–$5.95). No credit cards. Year-round, daily 7am–3am. CREPES/SALADS/SANDWICHES.

Two blocks west of EOT, this is a New Age fast-food joint, actually much nicer than you'd imagine. The counter chef huddles over a crepe grill, turning out a dozen varieties priced as low as $1.50. If you want an inexpensive salad, burger, fried chicken, baguette sandwich, stuffed baked potatoes, spinach pie, or ice cream, it's here, and at all hours.

Harley Davidson Cafe. Odos 25 Martiou. ☎ **0241/26-406.** Snacks Dr 650–Dr 1,400 ($2.75–$5.95). No credit cards. Daily noon–midnight. SNACKS/DESSERTS.

Homesick? Set yourself down at the counter on leather chopper seats, listen to the American country music and soft rock, and have yourself a Wide Glide Burger, a Low Rider Chicken, or a Daytona Special Ice Cream. This is the first cafe of its kind in Europe, and it's a hit among the locals.

Kon Tiki Floating Restaurant. Mandraki Harbor. ☎ **0241/22-477.** Appetizers Dr 800–Dr 2,100 ($3.40–$8.95), main courses Dr 1,600–Dr 3,900 ($6.80–$16.60), fish Dr 7,000 ($29.80) per kilo. AE, MC, V. Daily 6pm–midnight. GREEK/INTERNATIONAL.

Still floating after 31 years of serving good food, this was one of Rhode's first decent restaurants, and it's still a great place to watch the yachts bobbing alongside while enjoying well-prepared, creative dishes, such as the sole valevska, with fillet of sole with shrimps, crabs, and mushrooms gratinéed in a béchamel sauce. The saganaki shrimp were exceptionally tasty, served with feta cheese, local herbs, and tomato sauce.

Salt and Pepper. Odos Petridi 76. ☎ **0241/65-494.** Reservations recommended. Appetizers Dr 400–Dr 1,050 ($1.70–$4.50), main courses Dr 1,400–Dr 2,400 ($5.95–$10.20). V. Daily (in winter closed Mon) 6:30pm–midnight. GREEK.

In this fine place frequented by discerning Greeks and the occasional fortunate tourists, genial host Spiros Diasinos succeeds in transforming Greek cooking into splendid, gourmet cuisine. He brings a selection of more than 10 mezedes to your table, each tastier than the next—let Spiros guide you in choosing your ideal selection. We delighted in the scrumptious calamari, stuffed with rice, tomatoes, and onion. The zucchini keftedes were subtlety flavored with mint, and the beet and wild spinach salad was the best we had ever tasted. After having the excellent snails in tomato sauce, the succulent butter beans, and the tasty black-eyed peas, we were so sated that we did not venture to try the appealing main courses, such as beef prepared in yogurt sauce. The homemade pitas, grilled on the coals and served with feta cheese spread and olive pate, were a nice addition to the meal.

RHODES CITY AFTER DARK

Outside of Athens, Rhodes has the most active nighttime scene in Greece. From Greek studs cruising the harbor for bombshell Swedish girls on vacation to the suave and sophisticated rich and near-rich who play high-stakes blackjack in the **Casino Grand Hotel,** Rhodes by night is brimming with energy.

For a different type of evening, try one of the many **outdoor cafes** lining the harborside of the New Town. There's a string of them under the lit arches outside the Agora (New Market). You'll have a good time watching the Greeks engage in **kamaki,** the ancient sport of girl-chasing (kamaki, actually, is Poseidon's trident, but you get the idea). Otherwise, at the north end and inland from the harbor, on G. Estatheadi Street, is the **Dimotikou Cinema,** which often shows American films in English (Greek subtitles). The **Palace Cinema** is south of Old Town on Dimokratias Street, near the stadium.

For entertainment of a strictly adult nature, try walking G. Fanduriou Street in the Old Town. On and around the street you'll find bars, music, and willing company. The party-scene street in the New Town is Iróon Politechniou Street; if you don't want to go home alone, this is the street to stroll through, as is the surrounding neighborhood.

CULTURAL ENTERTAINMENT

Sound and Light. Odós Papágou, south of Rimini Square, Old Town. ☎ **0241/21-922.** Admission: Dr 1,000 ($4.25), students Dr 500 ($2.15), children under 12 free.

The Sound and Light presentation dramatizes the life of a youth admitted into the monastery in 1522, the year before Rhodes's downfall to invading Turks. In contrast to Athens's Acropolis show, the dialogue here is more illuminating, though the lighting is unimaginative. Nevertheless, sitting in the formal gardens below the palace on a warm evening can be a pleasant and informative experience, and is heartily recommended to those smitten by the medieval Old Town. Twice-nightly performances are scheduled according to season (check the posted schedule) and include one performance in English.

Traditional Folk Dance Theater. Odós Adronikou, off Arionos Square, Old Town. ☎ **0241/ 20-157.** Admission: Dr 2,800 ($11.90), students Dr 1,500 ($6.40), children under 10 free.

The Greek folk dance show, presented by the Nelly Dimoglou Dance Company, is always lively. Twenty spirited men and women perform dances from many areas of Greece in colorful, often embroidered, flouncy costumes. The five-man band plays an inspired, varied repertoire, certainly more interesting than the amplified bouzouki emanating from the Old Town's new tavernas. The choreography is excellent, the dancers skillful, and even the set (an open square surrounded by two-dimensional Rhodian houses) is effective. There are presently performances Mondays, Wednesdays, and Fridays at 9:20pm from late May through early October. Check with tourist information for an updated schedule.

DISCOS & NIGHTCLUBS

There are hundreds of bars, nightclubs, and discos in and around Rhodes, ranging from the fanciest to the raunchiest. **Alex Diakou Street** is a parade of bars playing loud music, the best among them being **Memphis,** with its crazy cocktails and funky music, and **The 60's Bar,** with its reasonably priced drinks and mostly 1960s music with a touch of the 1970s. Nearby is **Garnier Bar,** with a lively dance floor and a beat for the over-25 crowd. If you're an Elvis freak, then try **Presley's Bar,** decorated with photos and memorabilia of the King and with a mellower sound from the 1950s and 1960s. Other popular places nowadays are the **Underground, Amazan, Incas, Zigzag, Colorado** (live, rock music), the popular **Le Palais Disco,** and the omnipresent **Hard Rock Cafe.**

The Old Town tends to be a bit less wild and loud, so if you're not up for a serious spree, you might head for the stylish **Symposium,** on Ippodamou off of lively Sokratous. Nearby, at Odos Omirou 70, the **Ancient Agora Bar** offers an even more sedate venue for actual conversation in unusual surroundings; there's even a no-smoking section.

Rhodes sports a variety of Greek nightclubs, where **bouzouki bands** strum and singers croon. **Minuit Palace** in Ixia and Melody Palace were considered the best clubs at our visit. The custom, as in many of the top clubs, is to send bunches of flowers and bottles of champagne to the stage in response to a heart-wrenching performance. Finally, when the act accelerates into an absolute orgasmic state, the crowd smashes plates with enthusiasm and spontaneity. At both, the international pop entertainers come on at 10pm, the Greek bouzouki kings at midnight. Admission is buried in the exorbitant drink and food charges; be sure to check the prices of what you're ordering so as not to pass out when you get your bill.

GAMBLING

Gambling is a popular nighttime activity in Greece. Rumor has it that there's a network of private high-stakes (and illegal) gambling dens scattered throughout the city. But for those who want to wager in a less subterranean atmosphere, saunter over to one of Greece's three legal casinos, the **Casino Grand Hotel,** in the Grand Hotel Astir Palace, Rhodes, off Othonos Amalias Street on the northwest side of the New Town. At the time of writing, Playboy International had just been chosen as the new concessionaire that will renovate the present casino, so we anticipate there will soon be a much improved, posher place to play your stakes.

EXPLORING THE ISLAND
LÍNDOS

Líndos is without question the most picturesque town on the island of Rhodes. Be warned, however, that it is often deluged with tourists; your first view of Líndos will be unforgettable for the wrong reasons. The Archaeological Society has control over all development in the village (God bless 'em!), and the traditional white stucco homes, shops, and restaurants form the most unified, classically Greek expression in the Dodecanese. Far too many vehicles are left by a towering, centuries-old plane tree whose roots are enclosed in a pebble-paved bench. Here, next to an ancient fountain with Arabic script, the old village women in black chatter in the shade, watching hundreds of skimpily clad tourists cross back and forth to the beach below.

Bear right into the maze before you, aim to get lost, and you'll find the basis for Líndos's aesthetic reputation. Avoid the Disneyland atmosphere of the high season. With luck the peasant blouses, ceramic plates, and rock-star posters (David Gilmore of Pink Floyd has a house here) hung along the shopfronts won't distract you from the village's architectural purity.

There are two entrances to the town. The first and northernmost leads down a steep hill to the bus stop and taxi stand, then veers downhill to the beach. At this square you'll find the friendly, extremely informative **Tourist Information Kiosk** (☎ **0244/31-227**; fax 0241/31-288), where Michalis will help you daily between April 1 and November 1 from 9am to 7:30pm. Here, too, is the commercial heart of the village with the Acropolis above. The rural clinic (☎ **0241/31-224**), post office, and OTE are nearby. The second road leads beyond the town and into the upper village, blessedly removed from the hordes. This is the better area for architecture enthusiasts.

Past the bus stop square and donkey stand you'll see "Acropolis" signs. A visit to the superb remains of the Castle of the Knights on a hill above the town will help to orient you. From the east ramparts of the castle you can see the lovely beach at St. Paul's Bay below and more of Rhodes's less-developed eastern coastline.

The Acropolis contains the ruins of one of Rhodes's three Dorian towns (settled by Lindos, one of Helios and Rodon's three grandsons), and within its medieval walls are the impressive remains of the Sanctuary of Athena, with its large Doric portico from the 4th century B.C. St. John's Knights refortified the Acropolis with monumental turreted walls and built a small church to St. John inside (though their best deed was to preserve the ancient ruins still standing). Stones and columns are strewn everywhere, and at the base of the stairs leading to their Byzantine church is a wonderful large relief of a sailing ship, whose indented bridge once held a statue of a priest of Poseidon. From the north and east ramparts you'll have the most wonderful views of new Líndos below, where most of the homes date from the 15th century. Dug into Mt. Krana across the way are caves left by ancient tombs. The Acropolis (☎ 0241/ 27-674) is open from 8:30am to 3pm Tuesday through Sunday. Admission is Dr 1,000 ($4.15), half price for children, Sunday free. If you want to conserve your energy for picture taking, a Dr 900 ($3.75) donkey ride is available at the town's entrance.

In Líndos, try to stay away from the village's commercial heart. Instead, stroll through the maze of narrow streets, and look for ancient scripts carved in the wooden door lintels. There's the Byzantine Church of the Virgin, Aghía Panagia, from 1479. Inside there are intricate frescoes painted by Gregorios of Sými in 1779. The floor is paved chochlakia, the Rhodian technique done with pebbles, and here it's a perfect sawtooth pattern of upright black-and-white stones, worn smooth over the centuries. After feeling it, scout out a chaise lounge on one of the two beaches encircling the main port to admire the luxury yachts docked at the point.

An elaborate local wedding took place there during our stay. Such glorious lace and embroidery were brought out for the bride and honored guests that afterward it was impossible to consider any of the comparatively primitive lace things for sale in the shops. Embroidery from Rhodes was coveted even in antiquity; it's said that Alexander the Great wore a grand embroidered Rhodian robe into battle at Gaugamila. And in Renaissance Europe, the French ladies used to yearn for a bit of Lindos lace.

Where to Stay & Dine in Lindos & Environs

In the high season (ironically, when the weather is hottest!) 4,000 resident tourists are joined by up to 10,000 day-trippers from Rhodes. Since no hotel construction is permitted, almost all of the old homes have been converted into pensions (called "villas" in the brochures) by English charter companies. However, in the peak season, the local **Tourist Information Kiosk** (☎ **0244/31-227**; fax 0244/31-288) has a list of the homes that rent rooms to individuals and will help to place you, though plan to pay Dr 6,000 ($25.50) to Dr 8,000 ($34) a bed in tiny rooms with shared facilities.

Triton Holidays in Rhodes (☎ 0241/21-690) books six-person villas for Dr 35,000 ($145.85) a day in the low season, including kitchen facilities (reservations are usually made a year in advance). If Lindos is booked or not to your taste, consider the attractive beaches to the south at Pefkas, Lardos, or Kalathos. **Heliousa Travel** (☎ 0244/44-057; fax 0244/44/041) in Lardos can help you find a room as well as with other travel needs.

Despite the huge number of restaurants in tiny Lindos, we just can't assume the risk of steering you to any in particular. However, on the beach, the huge **Triton Restaurant** would get our nod because you can easily change into your swimsuit in their bathroom, essential for nonresidents who want to splash in the gorgeous water across the way. It's not as overpriced as all the others, and you can eat a decent meal of typical stuffed tomatoes or moussaka for Dr 2,000 ($8.35) and chalk it off to "cabana rental." (There's a wimpy public shower right on the sand.)

Argo Fish Taverna. Haraki Beach, Rhodes. ☎ **0244/51-410.** Reservations recommended. Appetizers Dr 650–Dr 1,550 ($2.75–$6.60), main courses Dr 1,100–Dr 2,500 ($4.70–$10.65), seafood Dr 4,000–Dr 11,000 ($17–$46.80) per kilo. AE, MC, V. Daily noon–11pm. GREEK/SEAFOOD.

Ten kilometers north of Lindos is Haraki Bay, a quiet fishing hamlet with a gorgeous, crescent-shaped pebbly beach and this excellent seafood taverna. Consider stopping here for a swim and lunch on a day trip from Rhodes to Lindos. We appreciated the freshness of the food, and the nice variation on a Greek salad with an addition of mint and dandelion leaves with fresh herbs, served with whole-wheat bread. The lightly battered fried calamari were tasty and a welcome relief from the standard over-battered fare, and the mussels, baked with fresh tomatoes and feta cheese, were also nice.

Atrium Palace. Kalathos Beach, Rhodes 85100. ☎ **0244/31-601;** fax 0244/31-600. 171 double rooms and 2 deluxe suites. A/C MINIBAR TV TEL. Dr 38,000 ($161.70) double (including breakfast). MC, V.

Located 6 kilometers out of Lindos on the long beach of crystal-clear Kalathos Bay, this luxurious resort-hotel features an eclectic architectural design—a neo-Greek, Roman, Crusader, and Italian pastel extravaganza. The inner atrium is an attractive, tropical water garden of pools and waterfalls. The beautifully landscaped outside pool complex is a nice option to the nearby beach, and there's an indoor pool, sauna, and fitness club to keep you busy.

Ladiko Bungalows Hotel. Faliraki P.O. Box 236, Rhodes 85100. ☎ **0244/85-536.** Fax 0244/80-241. 42 double rooms suites. A/C TEL. Including breakfast: Dr 19,800 ($84.25) double. MC, V.

Anthony Quinn obtained permission to build a retirement home for actors on this pretty little bay, on the road to Lindos 3 kilometers south of the swinging beach resort of Faliraki; he never realized his plans, but the bay retains his name. We especially enjoyed the quiet and the convenient location of this friendly, family operated lodge, with nature-lover activities such as swimming, fishing, and hikes to nearby ruins and less-frequented beaches, and its proximity (20-minute walk) to noisy and bustling Faliraki.

Lindos Mare. Lindos Bay, Rhodes 85100. ☎ **0244/31-130.** Fax 0244/31-131. 123 double rooms suites. TEL. Including half board: Dr 41,000 ($174.50) double with sea view. MC, V.

An American couple, Maria and Roger Griffith, wrote that the Lindos Mare is the best and most accommodating hotel they've visited in their years of travel. We also fancied the ambience of the place, constructed steplike down the sloping hill toward the beach. A tram descends from the upper lobby, restaurant, and pool area to the lower levels of attractive Aegean-style bungalows, and continues onward down to the beach area, where there are umbrellas and water sports. It's only a 2-kilometer walk or ride into Lindos, although you just might want to stay put in the evenings with the in-house social activities, such as barbecue, folklore evenings, or dancing.

✪ **Mavrikos.** Main Square, Lindos. ☎ **0244/31-232.** Reservations recommended. Appetizers Dr 450–Dr 1,400 ($1.90–$5.95), main courses Dr 1,300–Dr 3,000 ($5.55–$12.75), fish Dr 8,000 ($34) per kilo. V. Daily noon–midnight. GREEK/FRENCH.

In 1933 the Italian governor of Rhodes commissioned the building of this restaurant and brought grandfather Mavrikos back from his job as a chef in France to prepare fine food. Grandsons Michalis and Dimitri continue the family tradition of fine Greek and French cuisine, such as the oven-baked lamb and fine beef fillets, with a large selection of tasty mezedes. The old restaurant and expansive shaded terrace has retained its special rustic charm—David Gilmore of Pink Floyd fame was so furious when they brought new, modern chairs, that Michalis quickly restored and returned the originals. The Mavrikos have also opened a great ice-cream parlor, Geloblu, serving homemade frozen concoctions and cakes, located within the labyrinth of the old town near the church.

SIGHTS & BEACHES ELSEWHERE AROUND THE ISLAND

The island of Rhodes is known for scenery, and an around-the-island tour provides is a chance to view some of its wonderful variations. The sights described below, with the exception of Ialysos and Kamiros, are not of significant historical or cultural importance, but if you get bored with relaxing, try some.

Ialysos was the staging ground for the four major powers that were to control the island of Rhodes. The ancient ruins and monastery reflect the presence of two of these groups. The Dorians ousted the Phoenicians from Rhodes in the 10th century B.C. (An oracle had predicted that white ravens and fish swimming in wine would be the final signs before the Phoenicians were annihilated. The Dorians, quick to spot opportunity, painted enough birds and threw enough fish into wine jugs so that the Phoenicians left without raising their arms.) Most of the Dorians left Ialysos for other parts of the island; many settled in the new city of Rhodes. During the 3rd to 2nd centuries B.C., the Dorians constructed a temple to Athena and Zeus Polius (similar to those on Mt. Smith), whose ruins are still visible, below the monastery. Walking south of the site will lead you to a well-preserved 4th-century B.C. fountain.

When the Knights of St. John invaded the island, they too started from Ialysos, a minor town in the Byzantine era. They built a small, subterranean chapel decorated with frescoes of Jesus and heroic knights. Their little whitewashed church is built right into the hillside above the Doric temple. Over it, the Italians constructed the Monastery of Filerimos, which remains a lovely spot to tour. Finally, Süleyman the Magnificent moved into Ialysos (1522) with his army of 100,000 and used it as a base for his eventual takeover of the island.

The site of Ialysos is open from 8:30am to 3pm Tuesday through Sunday. Proper dress is required, and admission is Dr 500 ($2.10). Ancient Ialysos is 6 kilometers inland from Trianda on the island's northwest coast; public buses leave from Rhodes frequently for the 14-kilometer ride.

The ruins at **Kamiros** are much more extensive than those at nearby Ialysos, perhaps because this city remained an important outpost after 408 B.C., when the new Rhodes was completed. The site is divided into two segments: the upper porch and the lower valley. The porch served as a place of religious practice and provided the height needed for the city's water supply. Climb up to the top and you'll see two swimming pool–size aqueducts, their walls still lined with a nonporous coating. The Dorians collected water in these basins, assuring themselves a year-round supply. The small valley contains ruins of Greek homes and streets, as well as the foundations of a large temple. The site is in a good enough state of preservation for you to imagine what life in this ancient Doric city was like more than 2,000 years ago.

You should think about wearing swimsuits under your clothes: There is a good stretch of beach across the street from the site, where there are some rooms to let, a few tavernas, and the bus stop. The site is open Tuesday through Sunday 8:30am to 3pm. Admission is Dr 500 ($2.10). Kamiros is 34 kilometers southwest of Rhodes town, with regular bus service.

Petaloúdes is a popular tourist attraction because of the millions of black and white–striped butterflies that have overtaken this verdant valley. When resting quietly on flowering plants or leaves, the butterflies are well camouflaged. Only the screaming of parents, the wailing of infants, and the Greek disco/rock blaring out of portable radios disturbs them. Then the sky is filled with a flurry of red, their underbellies exposed as they try to hide from the summer crush. The setting, with its many ponds, bamboo bridges, and rock displays, was too precious for us. (Real butterfly hounds should make it a point to stop on Páros, in the Cyclades, to see the only other Petaloúdes in Greece. There you'll find, as the Greeks call it, *psychopiana,* an elevated state of the mind and heart.) Petaloúdes is 25 kilometers south of Rhodes and inland; it can be reached by public bus but is most easily seen with a guided tour.

The healing thermal waters of **Kalithea,** praised for their therapeutic qualities by Hippocrates, have long since dried up, but this small bay, 10 kilometers from Rhodes town, is still a great place to swim and snorkel off the small beach in the tiny coves. Mussolini built a fabulous art deco spa here; its derelict abandonment still retains a magical grandeur of the past. Heading south, **Faliraki Beach** is the island's most developed beach resort, a testosterone-charged place, with every possible vacation facility imaginable—from bungee jumping and laser clay shooting to gyroscopic body spinners. The southern end of the beach is less crowded and frequented by the au naturel crowd. South of Lindos from Gennadi to Plimiri, there is a long, undeveloped stretch of deserted beach, mostly dark sand, pebbles and sand dunes; tavernas and rooms to let are available in those villages. At the southern tip of the island, for those who seek off-the-beaten-track places, is **Prassonissi** (Green Island), connected to the main island by a narrow sandy isthmus, with waves and world-class windsurfing on one side and calm waters on the other. There is lodging and food available here, including Prassonisi Club Studios.

Heading up the windy, western coast, one reaches **Monolithos,** with its spectacularly sited crusader castle perched on the pinnacle of a mountain. Five kilometers down the windy, rough road is the long stretch of **Fourni Beach,** deserted except for a few snack bars. Driving north through the picturesque village of **Siana,** nestled on the mountain side, you skirt the side of the island's highest mountain, **Ataviros** (3,986 feet) via **Agios Issidoros,** and arrive in **Embonas,** the wine capitol of the island and home to several tavernas famed for their fresh meat barbecues. This village is on the tour group circuit, and numerous tavernas offer meat and wine feasts accompanied by live Greek music and folklore performances. We stopped at **The Baki Brothers** (0246/41-247; Dr 2,500/$10.65 fixed-price dinner, Dr 1,800/$7.65 for lunch, children half price), where you're first invited to enter a large, walk-in refrigerator to select your preferred carnivorous delight, then you're served various mezedes (tsatsiki, beans, and Greek salad), while your individually weighed portion is grilled on the coals. During the meal the wine flows freely. We liked the white Ilios, the red Chevalier, and the premium label Emery. If you're into hiking, there's a five-hour round-trip trek from Agios Issidoros to the top of Mt. Ataviros—ask in the village for directions.

If you don't have time to do the whole island circuit, from Lindos you can take a short detour to Asklipio, with its ruined castle and impressive Byzantine church. The church has a mosaic-pebbled floor and gorgeous "cartoon"-style frescoes, which depict the seven days of creation (check out the octopus) and the life of Jesus. Returning to Lardos, you take the road inland that cuts across the forested hilly interior to Agios Issidoros and Embonas. It's worth making a short side trip (5 kilometers) from Laerma to the Thami Monastery, the oldest functioning monastery on the island, with its beautiful, though weather-damaged, frescoes.

SIDE TRIPS TO TURKEY

Crossing to the Turkish port of Maramais has become a standard excursion. There's a daily ferry (except Sunday) to Marmaris (two hours), which usually leaves in the afternoon and costs Dr 6,000 ($25.55) for a one-way fare, plus $10 to be paid upon your arrival in Turkey. A round-trip to Marmaris by hydrofoil (45 minutes each way) costs Dr 14,000 ($59.60) for a same-day return, or Dr 16,000 ($68) for an open return, with the $10 fee to be paid upon arrival in Turkey. The hydrofoils leave Mandraki Harbor at 8am, and return from Marmaris at 3pm, which is a very tight schedule to make a trip up to Ephesus and back. You must submit your passport to your travel agent a day in advance of departure in order to obtain port clearance. The Turkish Consulate is at 10 Iroon Polytechniou for those who need visas. Check with your travel agent for more specific details.

2 Sými

Approximately 255 nautical miles E of Piraeus; 24 nautical miles N of Rhodes

Tiny, rugged Sými is often called "the jewel of the Dodecanese." Arriving by boat affords a view of pastel-colored neoclassical mansions climbing the steep hills above the broad horseshoe-shaped harbor. Yialos is Sými's the port, and Horia its old capital. The welcome absence of modern-designed buildings is due to an archaeological decree that severely regulates the style and methods of construction and restoration for all old and new buildings. Sými's long and prosperous tradition of shipbuilding, trading, and sponge diving is evident in its gracious mansions and richly ornamented churches, scattered over the entire island. Islanders proudly boast that there are so many churches and monasteries that one could worship in a different sanctuary every day of the year.

During the first half of this century, Sými's economy gradually deteriorated as the shipbuilding industry declined, the maritime business soured, and somebody went and invented a synthetic sponge. Sýmians fled their homes to find work on nearby Rhodes or in the United States, Canada, and Australia. Today, the island's picture-perfect traditional-style houses have become a magnet for monied Athenians in search of real estate investments, and Sými has a highly touted "off-the-beaten path" resort for European tour groups trying to avoid other tour groups. The onslaught of tourists for the great part arrive at 10:30am and depart by 3pm.

ESSENTIALS

GETTING THERE   By Boat   Several excursion boats arrive daily from Rhodes; two boats are owned cooperatively (the *Sými I* and *Sými II*) and are booked locally in Rhodes through **Triton Holidays** (☎ **0241/21-690**). Round-trip tickets are Dr 3,000 to Dr 5,000 ($12.75 to $22.25), depending on the season. The boats all leave every day at 9am from Mandraki Harbor, stop at the main port of Sými, Yialos, then continue onto Panormitis Monastery or the beach at Pedi for sightseeing, before returning to Rhodes. There are daily car ferries from Piraeus, two ferries a week to Crete via Karpathos, and two local ferries weekly via Tilos, Nisiros, Kos, and Kálymnos. The hydrofoil also skims daily at 9am from Rhodes to Sými, and in the afternoon (except Thursday) at 3:30pm.

VISITOR INFORMATION   Information and a free guide pamphlet may be obtained in the Sými Town Hall, located on the Town Square behind the bridge. We recommend the friendly and helpful services of Nikos Sikallos of **Sými Tours** (☎ **0241/71-307;** fax 0241/72-292), at the end of the harbor between the Ionian Bank and the National Bank of Greece. They are open daily from 8am to 2pm and 5 to 10pm, and can provide you with maps and information, boat and hydrofoil tickets, airline tickets and reconfirmations as well as currency exchange. They also can assist you in locating the local **doctor** (☎ **0241/71316),** **dentist** (☎ **0241/ 71272)** or even the Laundromat. The free *Sými News* is a local paper with useful information.

GETTING AROUND   Ferries and excursion boats dock first at hilly Yialos on the barren, rocky northern half of the island. There's a pretty clock tower, on the right as you enter the port, used as a local landmark when defining the maze of vehicle-free lanes and stairs. Yialos is the liveliest village on the island and the venue for most overnighters.

Sými's main road leads to Pedi, a developing beach resort one cove east of Yialos, and a new road rises up to Horio, the old capital. The island's 4,000 daily visitors most often take an excursion boat that stops at the Panormitis Monastery or at the beach at Pedi. Buses leave every hour from 8am until 11pm to Pedi via Horio (Dr 200/85¢). The are a grand total of four taxis on the island, which charge a set fee of Dr 400 ($1.70) to Horio and Dr 500 ($2.13) to Pedi. Mopeds are also available, but due to the limited road network, you might do better using the public transportation and your two feet. **Sými Tours** (☎ **0241/71-307)** organizes bus, boat, and walking tours to the islands few site (see below for further information). Caïques (skiffs) shuttle people to the various beaches, Emborios, Aghia Marina, Ághios Nikólaos, and Nanu; the prices range from Dr 300 to Dr 1,200 ($1.30 to $5.10) depending on the distance.

FAST FACTS   The **OTE** (☎ **0241/71212**) and the **Post Office** (☎ **0241/71315**) are located about 100 meters behind the *paralía* (waterfront); they are open weekdays 7:30am to 3pm. The **police** station (☎ **0241/7111**), located nearby, is open 24 hours a day.

WHAT TO SEE & DO

Sými's southwestern portion is hilly and green. Located here is the medieval **Panormitis Monastery,** dedicated to St. Michael, the patron saint of sea-faring Greeks. The monastery is popular with Greeks as a refuge from modern life; young Athenian businessmen speak lovingly of the monk cells and small apartments that can be rented for R & R. (Beds go for Dr 1,500/$6.40; a room for a family of four with kitchen and shower costs Dr 5,000/$21.30.) Keep in mind that one cannot make reservations, and space is scarce in August. The whitewashed compound is appreciated for its verdant, shaded setting and for the 16th-century gem of a church inside. The taxiarchis Mishail of Panormitis boast icons of St. Michael and St. Gabriel adorned in silver and jewels.

The town of **Panormitis Mihailis** is most lively and interesting during its annual festival on November 8, but can explored year-round via local boats or bus tours from

Yialos. The hardy can hike there (it's 10 kilometers, about three hours from the town) and enjoy a refreshing dip in its sheltered harbor and a meal in the taverna as reward for their labors.

In **Yialos,** by all means hike the gnarled, chipped stone steps of the Kali Strate (the good steps). This wide stairway ascends to Horio (village), a picturesque community is filled with images of a Greece in many ways long departed. Heavy-set, wizened old women sweep the whitewashed stone paths outside their homes. Occasionally a young girl or boy or a very old man can be seen retouching the neon blue trim over the door-ways and shutters. Nestled between the immaculately kept homes dating back to the 18th century are abandoned villas, their faded trim and flaking paint lending a wistful air to the village. Renovated villas now rent to an increasing number of tourists. And where tourists roam, tavernas, souvenir shops and bouzouki bars soon follow. Commercialization has hit once-pristine Sými, but now it's still at a bearable level.

There's a small **museum** in Horio housing archaeological and folklore artifacts which the islanders consider important enough for public exhibition. You can't miss the blue arrows that point the way; it's open from 9am to 2:30pm Monday through Saturday.

Crowning Horio is the **Church of the Panaghia.** The church is surrounded by a fortified wall and is therefore called the kastro (castle). It's adorned with the most glorious frescoes on the island, which can be viewed only when services are held (7 to 8am or weekdays, all morning Sunday).

Sými is, unfortunately, not blessed with wide sandy beaches. Close to Yialos, the harbor, are two beaches: **Nos,** a 50-foot-long rocky stretch, and **Emborios,** a pebble beach.

You can take a bus to Pedi, from there you can take short walks to either **St. Nikolaos beach,** with trees providing shade and a good taverna, or to **St. Marina,** a small beach with little shade but having stunning turquoise water and views across to the mini islet of St. Marina and its cute church.

You can also join guided tours organized by **Sými Tours** (☎ **0241/71-307**). One includes a trip via truck to the tranquil monastery of St. Constantine, followed by a guided tour of the Panormitis Monastery and museum, and ending with a short cruise to the tiny islet of Sesklia for a barbecue lunch, relaxation, and swimming. For the hardier, we recommend the tour which includes a three- to four-hour walk from the monastery of St. Michael Mirello, through a fragrant landscape of thyme, sage, and oregano, to the secluded bay of St. Emilianos for a barbecue lunch, swimming, relaxing, and a boat ride back to Yialos (Dr 5,500/$23.40).

One local craft still practiced on Sými is shipbuilding. If you walk along the water toward Nos beach, you'll probably see boats under construction or repair. It's a treat to watch the men fashion planed boards into a graceful boat. Sými was a boat building center in the days of the Peloponnesian War, when spirited sea battles were waged off its shores.

Sponge fishing is almost a dead industry in Greece, and Sými's industry is no exception. Only a generation ago, 2,000 sponge divers worked waters around the island; today only a handful undertake this dangerous work, and most do so in the waters around Italy and Africa. Working at depths of 50 to 60 meters (in the old days often without any apparatus), many divers were crippled or killed by the turbulent sea and too-rapid depressurization. The few sponges that are still harvested around Sými—and many more imported from Asia or Florida—are sold at shops along the port. Even if they're not from Sými's waters, they make inexpensive and light-weight gifts for friends. Sponges run from a few hundred to several thousand drachmas, depending on size and quality. For guaranteed quality merchandise and an informative explanation and demonstration of sponge treatment, we recommend the **Aegean Sponge Center,** operated by Kyprios and his British wife, Leslie.

WHERE TO STAY

Many tourists bypass hotels for private apartments or houses. Between April and October, rooms for two with shower and kitchen access go for Dr 8,000 to Dr 9,500 ($34 to $40.40). More luxurious two-bedroom, villa-style houses with daily maid services rent for Dr 11,500 to Dr 17,500 ($48.90 to $74.50). The best way of tapping into this alternative is to visit **Sými Tours** (☎ 0241/71-307), located on the left-hand side of the harbor. They represent more than 100 properties, including two newly renovated villa-pensions above the Clock Tower: the six-room **Forei Pension** and the five-room **Hotel Marika;** both have private showers in the rooms and go for Dr 7,000 ($29.80).

The following listings are open from mid-April to mid October unless otherwise noted. Before mid-June and after mid-September, you can obtain up to 40% discounts from high season rates.

Aliki Hotel. Yialos, Sými. ☎ **0241/71-665.** Fax 0241/71-655. 15 rms (all with bath). A/C TEL. Dr 17,000 ($72.35) double with sea view; Dr 12,000 ($51) double without sea view (including breakfast). No credit cards.

This well-restored sea captain's mansion, dating from 1895, is the standard by which all Sými lodging is judged. It has elegantly styled rooms, some with dramatic waterfront views. As the Aliki has become a chic overnight getaway from bustling Rhodes, reservations are absolutely required. Five rooms have balconies.

Dorian Studios. Yialos, Sými. ☎ **0241/71-181.** 9 rms (all with bath). A/C TEL. Dr 12,000 ($51) double. No credit cards.

Located in a beautiful part of town only 10 meters from the sea, this is a rustically furnished, comfortable lodging, with a kitchenette in every room. Many of the studios have balconies or terraces overlooking the harbor, where you can enjoy your morning coffee or evening ouzo.

Hotel Nireus. Yialos, Sými. ☎ **0241/72-400.** Fax 0241/72-404. 30 rms (all with bath). TEL. Dr 16,000 ($68) double. MC, V.

This new hotel right on the waterfront has become a popular venue for vacationing Greeks. The traditional Sýmian style facade has been preserved. Inside, the new modern rooms are comfortable. Try your best to obtain one of the 18 rooms that face the sea; if you're fortunate, you might get one with a balcony.

Hotel Niriidis. Emborios Bay, Sými. ☎/fax **0241/71-784.** 9 Apartments (all with bath). TEL. Dr 11,000 ($46.80) double (including breakfast).

This is where you satisfy your dream of having your own little place on a quiet bay with crystal-clear water. Each attractive bungalow has a bedroom, bath, salon, kitchenette, and balcony facing the sea. At present, one either boats or walks (15 minutes from Yialos) to this place, but owner Michalis Tsabaris assured me that sometime in the future a road will be built. Hotel guests are supplied with free umbrellas and lounge chairs on the beach. With a bar on the premises and a taverna on the beach, what else could you possibly want?

Hotel Horio. Horio, Sými. ☎ **0241/771-800.** 17 rms (all with bath). A/C TEL. Dr 14,000 ($59.60) double (including breakfast). No credit cards.

Perched high on the shoulder of a hill, this cluster of gold and pastel blue small buildings blend naturally with the village around it. Rooms are plainly furnished and spotless; some have porches while others have balconies. It's in the center of the upper town above Yialos and about a 15-minute walk from Pedi.

WHERE TO DINE

Family Taverna Meraklis. Yialos. ☎ 0241/71-003. Appetizers Dr 400–Dr 1,000 ($1.70–$4.25), main courses Dr 850–Dr 2,400 ($3.60–$10.20). EU, MC, V. Daily 8am–midnight. GREEK.

This tiny storefront taverna—hidden on a back lane behind the Ionian and Popular Bank and away from the day-trippers—is welcome more as a respite from the crowds than as a great dining experience. From a limited daily menu, some small fish, stuffed vegetables, meat, and mezedes are served, all for moderate prices. Chefs Anna and Sotiris pride themselves on the home cooking, which is most evident in their fresh vegetable dishes.

Milo Petra ("The Mill Stone"). Yialos. ☎ **0241/72-333.** Fax 0241/72-194. Appetizers Dr 800–Dr 1,600 ($3.40–$6.80), main courses Dr 2,400–Dr 3,300 ($10.20–$14). V. Daily 7pm–midnight. MEDITERRANEAN.

Owners Eva and Hans converted this 200-year-old flour mill into an exquisite setting for a gourmet dining experience. Over the course of five years, they collected antique Greek furniture and fabrics to simply but elegantly decorate this most unusual space. (It even includes a 2,000-year-old grave visible through a glass window in the pebble mosaic and rose marble floor.) For whatever excuse, ascend to the toilet on the upper veranda to get the overall view of the wonderful interior. You may choose to dine either outdoors on the patio or inside to experience the open kitchen. Every day a different menu is printed. We were especially impressed by the lamb and fish dishes, using the wonderful Sýmian hill spices, and the homemade pastas, such as "ravioli Larissa," filled with potatoes and homemade cheese, and served in sage butter.

Muragio Restaurant. Yialos. ☎ **0241/72-133.** Appetizers Dr 400–Dr 1,400 ($1.70–$5.95), main courses Dr 1,000–Dr 3,000 ($4.25–$12.75). No credit cards. Daily 11am–11pm. Open all year. GREEK/SEAFOOD.

Opened in 1995, this has become big hit among the locals, who praise the generous main courses and quality of the food. Try the bourekakia, skinned eggplant stuffed with a special cheese sauce and then fried in a batter of eggs and bread crumbs. We were advised to try the extremely popular lemon lamb, but instead we chose the saganaki shrimps in tomato sauce and feta cheese, and were extremely delighted.

Nireus Restaurant. Yialos. ☎ **0241/72-400.** Appetizers Dr 400–Dr 1,200 ($1.70–$5.10), main courses Dr 1,300–Dr 2,500 ($5.55–$10.65). MC, V. Daily noon–11pm. GREEK.

We met people in Rhodes who extolled the fine cooking of Michalis, the chef of this superior restaurant located in the Nireus Hotel on the waterfront on Sými. Our kudos go to his "frito misto," a mixed seafood plate with tiny, naturally sweet Sými shrimps and other local delicacies, served with french fries and sliced tomatoes. We also recommend the savory filet of beef served with a Madeira sauce.

Taverna Neraida. Town Square, Yialos. ☎ **0241/71-841.** Appetizers Dr 300–Dr 800 ($1.30–$3.40), main courses Dr 800–Dr 2,800 ($3.40–$11.90). No credit cards. Daily 11am–midnight. SEAFOOD.

Following our time-proven rule that fish is cheaper far from the port, this homey taverna has among the best fresh fish prices (up to Dr 8,000/$34 per kilo) on the island, as well as a wonderful range of mezedes. Try the black-eyed pea salad and skordalia. The grilled daily fish is delicious and the very typical ambience is a treat.

3 Kos

200 nautical miles E of Piraeus

Group tourism has certainly taken its toll on lovely Kos. In the summer, foreign visitors—mostly brought in on cheap package tours—outnumber the island's 30,000 inhabitants nearly two to one, so we recommend you avoid it in the high season. In the spring and fall is a much better time to visit. Kos has more than its share of archaeological sites, unspoiled beaches, friendly people, and good food, but we only wish it were more Greek. (If you're interested in the authentic, you'll have to look hard or elsewhere.)

Since ancient times, Kos has been associated with the healing arts and the practice of medicine. Before the Dorian settlement of Kos in the 11th century B.C., Koans established a cult dedicated to the worship of Asclepios, the god of healing and medicine. Asclepios was either a son of Apollo (from whom he acquired his knowledge) or a mortal (perhaps the physician of the Argonauts) who was deified because of his great healing power. An Asclepion, a sanctuary dedicated to the god, was built so the sick could make offerings in order to receive a cure. Throughout the centuries Kos produced many notable doctors, but none more renowned than Hippocrates (born 460 B.C.), the so-called Father of Medicine. He established the first medical school and a canon of medical ethics that is, to this day, the code of doctors throughout the world.

Many first-time visitors prefer to settle in the northern port town of Kos, then explore the rich variety of archaeological and historical sights and sample the capital's lively nightlife. After examining the beaches on bicycle excursions, long-term visitors move out and find accommodations closer to the golden sand. Our recommendation for beach-goers is to head south to the Ághios Stefanos–Kefalos region on the southwestern side of the island.

ESSENTIALS

GETTING THERE   By Plane   Olympic Airways has two flights daily from Athens and three flights a week from Rhodes. The airport is in an out-of-the-way inland village 26 kilometers from Kos town, but Olympic provides bus service to and from their office (☎ **0242/28-330**) at Odos Vas. Pavlou 12. If you arrive on another flight, you must either take a taxi (Dr 3,500/$14.90) or catch a KTEL bus outside the airport to Kos town, Mastihari, Kardamena, and Kefalos.

By Boat   Three car ferries run daily from Piraeus via Pátmos, and there is infrequent ferry service from the port of Rafina. Kos is served by daily boats from Rhodes (both car ferries and excursion ships). It's connected to the other Dodecanese by local excursion ships, which include three to five times weekly sailings to Kálymnos, Pátmos, volcanic Nisiros, and Tilos, and occasional steamers to Astipalea and Halki. In summer, there are several caïques daily from the beach in Mastihari to nearby Kálymnos. There are currently a few hydrofoil companies operating daily between Kos, Leros, Kalymnon, Pátmos, and Sámos and two trips a week to Tilos. Tickets are sold at the various travel agencies near the port. We found Mourat Bourinakis at **Mouratti Tours** (☎ **0242/25-414;** fax 0241/21-281), near the port on Fereou and Ipsllandou Street, to be extremely friendly and helpful.

Ferry service to Sámos (continuing on to Lesvos and Thessaloníki) is an exhausting 11 hours going by the once-a-week slow boat. You can double-check schedules in Athens at **Tourist Information** (☎ **01/143**), the **Piraeus Port Authority** (☎ **01/45-11-311**), or the **Strintzia Lines** (☎ **0294/25-200**) in Rafina.

VISITOR INFORMATION   Your first stop should be the very helpful **Municipal Tourism Office** (☎ 0242/24-460), located at Odos Vas Gheorghio 1, near the east side hydrofoil pier (open 7:30am to 9pm Monday through Friday). They publish and freely distribute an extremely comprehensive tourist information magazine called *Kos Summer,* which includes maps. The **Tourist Police** (☎ 0242/22-444) are open 24 hours daily in the police station on Akti Miaouli. You can ask them about available rooms to let.

GETTING AROUND   Residents of Kos town can easily walk to most sights, and a stroll along the harbor or the busy back streets of the Agora is one of pleasures offered by the island.

By Bus   Public bus service is inexpensive (the highest fare is currently Dr 600 ($2.55) to far-off Kefalos) but infrequent. At the time of writing, there are five a day to Tingaki; four to Kardamena and Pyli; three to Mastihari; and two to Kefalos via Paradise and Kamari beaches; and two to Zia via Asfendion. Try not to get stranded at the beaches after sunset; a return taxi will be very costly. For current schedules and fares either contact the **Public Transport Office** (☎ 0242/26-276), or go directly to the bus station around the corner from Olympic Airways on Kleopatras Street. Local city buses leave frequently from the EOT office on the port, and pass by local sights such as the Asclepion.

By Bicycle/Moped   A bicycle is the preferable mode of transportation to nearby tanning—there are actually bike lanes heading east from town toward the Psalidi beaches. You can rent bikes all around town for prices ranging from Dr 600 ($2.55) for a simple one, to a serious mountain bike for Dr 3,000 ($12.75). Mopeds are fun for longer excursions and can be rented at many places around town for Dr 3,000 to Dr 6,000 ($12.75 to $25.50), including insurance.

By Taxi/Car   Taxis use meters on Kos, and most trips in Kos Town will not even exceed the minimum fare. However, the airport is a Dr 3,500 ($14.90) ride away, and beaches are even more. There is a taxi stand near the tourist office; call ☎ 0242/23-333 or 0242/27-777 to get a cab. Several companies rent cars and Jeeps—including **Avis** (☎ 0242/24-272) and **Eurodollar** (☎ 0242/27-550)—but this is an extravagance unless you do some heavy-duty exploring. Expect to pay Dr 20,000 ($85.10) per day including insurance and fuel.

FAST FACTS   For medical assistance contact the **Hippocrates Hospital** (☎ 0242/22-300) on Odos Ippocratou 32. The **OTE** (Monday to Friday 7:30am to 11pm, weekends 7:30am to 3pm) is on Vironos Street, and the **post office** (7:30am to 2:30pm) is on Venizelou Street; they are both about two blocks from the agora. You can find English-language newspapers at the **Foreign Press Agency** at Vasileos Pavlou 2. **Banks** are open from Monday to Friday from 8am to 1:30pm. How-ever, you can change money at many tourist offices throughout town until late in the evening.

WHAT TO SEE & DO

From the time of the Roman Empire to the Allied victory over the Germans in World War II, Kos was occupied and ruled by foreign forces. Nowhere is the legacy of foreign domination more apparent than in the area of the port and capital city, Kos (also called Hora). The town has a network of Greek and Roman excavations, as well as Byzantine remains, Venetian buildings, a medieval castle, and a Turkish Mosque, all within 1 or 2 square kilometers of each other. Only 5 kilometers northwest of Hora is the Asclepion, the most important archaeological site on the island. From July to September, you can catch the many art exhibitions, theater, and dance performances funded by the Kos Hippokratia Festival.

Kos's many archaeological sites can be seen in one day; consider touring the outdoor sites like the Odeoum, western excavations, agora, and plane tree after seeing the Asclepion, Roman villa, castle, and museum.

A DAY TOUR

The best way to get to all of these sites is by bicycle; if you're hardy (fit for about 12 kilometers of cycling) you can visit everything in a day. Starting from town, take the main road to the intersection of Koritsas, Alexandrou, and Grigoriou streets, and follow the signs for the Asclepion. You'll pass through the hamlet of **Platani,** also called "Turkish Town," where residents still speak Turkish. It's a great place to stop for an inexpensive snack; you might consider returning for dinner in the quieter evening hours. The **Clarisse Ceramic Factory,** on the left, is a good place to buy souvenirs. You'll know you're nearing the Asclepion when you enter an exquisite cypress-lined roadway.

The Asclepion   The Asclepion was excavated in the early part of this century, first by the German archaeologist Herzog in 1902, then by a team of Italians. The Italians unearthed the lowest of four levels of the terraced site. The second level is the Propylaea, thought to be where the treatment of the sick actually took place (sulfur springs and a Roman-era bath, on the left, were central to the ancients' idea of exorcising disease). This level of the Asclepion (the largest) was bordered by a Doric portico on three sides, and contained many rooms to house visitors and patients. A number of niches and pedestals were found here, as well as statues and other votive offerings. Don't miss the refreshingly cool drinking fountain next to the stairway; it is Pan who, from his shaded enclave, leaps out at the parched visitor. Continue climbing the magnificent stairway to the two upper terraces, both containing temples from the Greek and Roman eras.

In the center of the third level is the Altar of Asclepion and two temples, the left one dedicated to Apollo and the right to the original Temple of Asclepion. Pilgrims placed their votive offerings (sometimes of enormous value) in the cellar of these temples, before therapy. The Ionic temple on the left, with the restored columns, dates from the 1st century B.C., while the Asclepion Temple is from the beginning of the 3rd century B.C.

As you ascend the stairs to the highest level, look back toward Turkey and you'll see the 7th-century B.C. ally of Kos, Halikarnassos (present-day Bodrum), part of the Doric Hexapolis uniting Kos, Halikarnassos, and Knidos with the Rhodian cities Lindos, Ialyssos, and Kameros. The fourth story contains the once-monumental 2nd-century B.C. Temple of Asclepion. This huge sanctuary, built in the Doric style of contrasting black and white marble, must have been an awe-inspiring sight, visible for miles around.

The Asclepion (☎ **0242/28-763**) is open daily 8:30am to 3pm; admission is Dr 750 ($3.15), half price for students, Sunday free.

Western Excavation   Returning to Kos, veer right on Grigoriou Street and proceed until you reach the site of the Western Excavation, on your left; through the tall trees the Odeum is on your right. The Western Excavation, also known as the ancient Greek and Roman city, connects the site by two 3rd-century B.C. perpendicular roadways. Follow the road leading away from the Odeum until you come to the large reconstructed building on the right; it was originally thought to be a nymphaeum (a place where virgins were readied for the fulfillment of their destiny); later research led archaeologists to conclude that it was a public toilet! Nevertheless it's a great toilet, with a superb mosaic floor; you'll have to climb up on the right side of the building to peer inside. Across from the toilet is the Xystro, a restored colonnade from a gymnasium dating from the Hellenistic era. If you continue walking along the road, you'll come to a covered area that houses a lovely 2nd-century A.D. mosaic showing the Judgment of Paris and various Roman deities. The buildings in the center of the site are, like the Xystro, from the 3rd century B.C.; you should climb up to discover the fine marble parquet floor and remarkable mosaics (many of which are covered by a thin layer of sand for protection).

Walk back through the site along the road and make a left to arrive at the second part of the site. The remains here date from the Roman and early Christian eras. The highlight is the splendid mosaic in the House of Europa (the first on your left) depicting a lovely, terrified-looking Europa being carted away to Crete by Zeus (in the incarnation of a bull) for his pleasure.

Roman Sites   Cross the modern road and proceed to the Odeum, excavated during the Italian occupation of the island in 1929. Many of the sites on the island have exceptional carved marble, and the Roman-era Odeum is no exception. The famous sculpture of Hippocrates (among others) was found in the covered archways at the base of the Odeum.

Continue down the modern road to the restored Roman villa known as Casa Romana, adjacent to a Roman bath and a Greek Dionysian temple. It's a fascinating archaeological achievement and presents a unique opportunity to tour a complete Roman villa. Admission is Dr 500 ($2.10), half price for children and free Sunday. It is open Tuesday through Sunday from 8:30am to 3pm.

Hippocrates Tree   Follow the Odeum road for three blocks and turn left to see the recently re-landscaped ruins of the Dionysian temple. Continue down Pavlou Street, and to the right of the nursery on Kazousi Square you'll find the ancient Agora, a 2nd-century B.C. market. Walking along the edge of the Agora, toward the harbor, you'll come to Lozia Square. Here you'll find a Turkish mosque and the plane tree of Hippocrates, under which he was supposed to have taught his students. The stories about this poor tree have been concocted so as to compare it to the apple tree under which Newton achieved scientific enlightenment. It's extremely unlikely that this tree was alive in the doctor's time, but who knows? Anyway, you can't help feeling for the aged trunk that supports still virile, muscular branches, fortunately propped up with old columns and pedestals.

Castle of the Knights   Walk across the bridge and you'll be at the Castle of the Knights of Rhodes. When entering this impressive fortress, built in the late 14th century and restored by the Grand Masters d'Aubusson and d'Amboise in the 16th century, you'll see fragments of statues, columns, pedestals, and other architectural paraphernalia from ancient times. To some, it may look like a tag sale of worn-out classical items, but it underscores a ubiquitous phenomenon in Greece: Succeeding generations pulled down existing structures to build new edifices that were more appropriate to the time. You might spot whole doorways taken from houses located in the ancient city, or a giant slice of pure-white Doric column stuck in the middle of an extension wall.

The design of the castle was considered innovative because of its system of inner and outer walls and the numerous subterranean tunnels and rooms that facilitated covert movement within them. As if that weren't enough, the whole fortress was surrounded by a moat. The views of the harbor and beach from the top of the far wall are unsurpassed, but that's why they built it there in the first place. Admission is Dr 500 ($2.10), half price for students, and free on Sunday. It's open Tuesday through Sunday from 8:30am–3pm.

Archaeological Museum   For those tireless souls who need to see it all in a day, a visit to the Archaeological Museum (☎ 0242/28-326) is the grand finale. The central room contains finely executed 2nd-century A.D. mosaics and sculptures found at the House of Europa. The mosaic (completely intact and in color) depicts the two most famous figures in the Koan pantheon, Asclepios and Hippocrates. The "must see" in this museum's excellent collection of Hellenistic and Roman sculpture is the figure of a man assumed to be Hippocrates. Whatever his identity, the statue is a deeply expressive work, showing the pathos of a man who has taken on the suffering of the world. Admission is Dr 500 ($2.10), half price for children, and free Sunday. It's open from Tuesday through Sunday from 8:30am to 3pm.

Synagogue   As with the other Dodecanese islands, Kos once had a large and influential Jewish population. Today there is but one Jewish family that survived the Holocaust and still lives on the island; the few others have emigrated to Israel. What remains of their presence is a synagogue, built in 1935, that was recently bought by the municipality of Kos and restored as a cultural center and office building. Although there are no torahs or other holy objects within the building, it is quite a stately place with a fine courtyard and identifiable religious decor. Inside are stained-glass windows of rather plain though elegant design and a chandelier; there is also a sculpture by Alexandrous Alwyn (see Ziá under Asfendíon, below). (When asked about the building, some neighbors told us that they call it the "havra," or chatter place, because of the custom of congregations reading aloud at their own pace.) It's open Monday through Friday from 9am to 2:30pm; no religious services are held in the building.

WHERE TO STAY

If you come to Kos in July or August, try to arrive in the morning since it can be packed. If you've arrived without hotel reservation, then either accept the room offered to you by someone at the harbor and change the next day if it isn't suitable, or go to the **Tourist Police** (☎ 0242/22-444) for assistance. You can also turn to **Mouratti Tours** (☎ 0242/25-414; fax 0242/21-281), who may even be able to get you a discount on your hotel reservations. Within Kos, there are basically three areas for hotels: Lambi Beach to the west, the central area behind the harbor, and Psalidi beach to the east.

    Kos Camping (☎ 0242/23-275), operated by the friendly Gregoriandou family, is 2 kilometers out of town, opposite the eastern beach in Psalidi. Their minibus usually meets the ferries at the harbor, providing a free shuttle service. Located within a shady olive grove, it is clean and has a laundry, kitchen, taverna, hot showers, minimarket, and even bicycle and moped rentals. The sleeping bag charge is Dr 1,250 ($5.30) per night, with tents costing an additional Dr 700 ($3).

    The following listings are open from mid-April to mid October unless otherwise noted. Before mid-June and after mid-September, you can obtain up to 40% discounts from high season rates; polite bargaining may be of assistance.

Moderate

Hotel Kipriotis Village. P.O. Box 206, Psalidi Beach, Kos 85200. ☎ 0242/27-640. Fax 0242/23-590. 1,500 beds (all rooms with bath). A/C TV TEL. Dr 18,500 ($78.75) single; Dr 28,400 ($121) double; Dr 37,050 ($158) apartment for two (including breakfast). Dr 3,700 ($15.75) extra per person for half board. AE, MC, V.

If you wish to spend part of your vacation amidst loads of fun-seeking Europeans with all the possible holiday facilities, try this new luxurious resort complex, only 4 kilometers from Kos and right on the beach. We liked the way it was built as a village. All the two-story bungalows and apartments surround an attractively designed activity area, which includes five pools (one Olympic-size), tennis, volleyball and basketball courts, a state-of-the-art fitness room, sauna, hydromassage, Turkish bath, and solarium. There's a full day of supervised activities for children. With three restaurants and two bars, you never really have to leave the premises, although there is public transportation every 15 minutes into Kos town.

Hotel Theodorou. Odos G. Papandreou, Kos 85300. ☎ **0242/23-363.** 60 rms (all with bath). TEL. Dr 7,500 ($31.90) single; Dr 12,000 ($51) double (including breakfast). No credit cards.

This lively place is a three-story hotel filled with Northern Europeans who seem to be perpetually up for a party. The location is ideal for those in need of a beach only 20 meters from the lobby and close to the town's nightlife. The tariff is on the high side for clean but totally standard Class C accommodations; you're paying for the popular Psalidi Beach.

Inexpensive

✪ **Hotel Affendoulis.** Odos Evrepilou 1, Kos 85300. ☎ **0242/25-321** or 0242/25-797. 17 rms (all with bath). TEL. Dr 7,800 ($33.20) single; Dr 9,000 ($38.30) double. No credit cards.

Our number-one choice is this fine modern hotel on a quiet side street; it's a mere 200 meters from the eastern beach or only a short walk to the bustling commercial center of town. This spotless hotel, with its polished marble floors and white lobby decorated with local hand-painted ceramic and crafts, is the domain of the Zikas family, as helpful and gregarious a clan as you could wish. Alexis, who grew up frolicking on the island's beaches, is an infinite source of information and assistance on all matters of transportation, travel planning, and the vagaries of life. There is a shaded outdoor breakfast area (an additional Dr 800/$3.40 per person) and a much-used honor-system kitchen for drinks and snacks. The bright, balconied rooms have firm mattresses and are comfortably furnished with decorative touches.

⑤ **Pension Alexis.** Odos Irodotou 9, Kos 85300. ☎ **0242/28-798.** 12 rms. Dr 5,500 ($23.40) single; Dr 6,000 ($25.50) double. No credit cards.

For those on a tighter budget, we recommend this ultrafriendly place. The guest book is filled with praises: "friendliness, good nature, and informed hospitality" or "you have the best hotel in Greece, with breakfasts better than the most expensive hotels." What more needs to be said? The rooms share common spick-and-span facilities, including a homey kitchen and breakfast area. We particularly liked the spacious upstairs rooms with their clean parquet floors, balconies, and fine views of the harbor. The pension is in the Zikas family home, and the feeling of living in a Greek house remains.

Pension Anna. Odos Venizelou 69, Kos 85300. ☎ **0242/23-030.** 18 rms (all with bath). TEL. Dr 6,500 ($27.70) single; Dr 8,500 ($36.20) double (including breakfast). No credit cards.

If all else fails and you need a room, try this simple, family run place. Rooms are totally plain but comfortable, and the location is fairly quiet and convenient.

Pension Kalamaki Nitsa. Odos G. Averof 47, Lambi Beach Kos 85300. ☎ **0242/25-810.** 12 rms (all with bath). Dr 8,000 ($34) single/double. No credit cards.

Across the street from popular Lambi Beach is a simple pension above a liquor store. Rooms are basic but clean and have private showers. Although it's only a short walk to the beach, the sand and water are cleaner a bit farther away from town.

WHERE TO DINE

In town, the plethora of continental/pizza/burger/ice cream joints is disheartening, but with a little walking you can get a decent meal. Don't forget to try some of the local Kos wines: the dry Lafkos, the red Appelis, or the light subtle Theokritos retsina.

Arap (Palatano) Taverna. Platinos-Kermetes. ☎ **0242/28-442.** Appetizers Dr 400–Dr 900 ($1.70–$3.85), main courses Dr 900–Dr 2,100 ($3.85–$8.95). No credit cards. Daily 10am–midnight. GREEK/TURKISH.

Because of its proximity to Bodrum, Turkey, Kos has a number of tavernas serving both Turkish and Greek cuisine. This one is on the road to the Asklepion, about two kilometers south of town. Among the most popular Turkish dishes is imam biyaldi, stuffed eggplant.

Intermezzo Italian Restaurant. Bouboulinas St. Kos. ☎ **0242/22-334.** Appetizers Dr 1,050–Dr 2,300 ($1.70–$3.85), pastas Dr 900–Dr 2,100 ($3.85–$8.95). MC, V. Daily 6pm–midnight. ITALIAN.

When you walk into this wood-paneled interior with its plush furniture and Neapolitan music, you know you've left moussaka territory. The Italian chef only uses Italian pastas and bakes his pizza in a wood-burning oven. The rigatoni was superb, and we also liked the tagliatelli Gorgonzola. A nice change.

Platanos Restaurant. Platanos Square, Kos. ☎ **0242/28-991.** Appetizers Dr 450–Dr 1,900 ($1.90–$8.10), main courses Dr 1,200–Dr 3,200 ($5.10–$13.60). EC, MC, V. Daily noon–11:30pm. GREEK/INTERNATIONAL.

Situated in the best location in Kos overlooking the Hippocrates Tree, this place is in a gorgeous building that was a former Italian officer's club. Built in 1933, it's replete with arches and the original tile floor. We liked the interior decoration of warm colors and wood, and thought the patio was great. Try reserving a place on the upstairs balcony with its impressive vista. The Greek specialties are creatively prepared, such as the shrimps in tomato sauce with feta; the octopus stifado; and the unusual Hippocrates escalope, prepared with pork, cheese, mushrooms, and asparagus in a béarnaise sauce. Should you wish a change of palate, try the Indonesian fillet, with pineapple and curry sauce, or the oscar fillet, which is beef in béarnaise sauce with crab and asparagus. For a real splurge, have an Irish coffee flambé for desert. Cool, live saxophone and guitar music make for an all-around beautiful setting for a good dinner.

Taverna Ampavris. Ampavris St. ☎ **0242/25-696.** Appetizers Dr 400–Dr 600 ($1.70–$2.55), main courses Dr 700–Dr 2,500 ($3–$10.65). V. Daily 5pm–2am. GREEK.

We rate this the best taverna in Kos. It's outside the bustling town center on the way to Asclepion, and down a quiet village lane. In the courtyard of this 130-year-old house are served the best local dishes from Kos island. Their salamura from Kefalos is mouth-watering pork stewed with onions and coriander; the lahano dolmades, stuffed cabbage with rice, minced meat, and herbs, is delicate, light and not at all oily. The faskebab, veal stew on rice, is tender and lean, while the vegetable dishes, such as the broad string beans, cooked and served cold in garlic and olive oil dressing, are out of this world. Our kudos to Emanuel Scoumbourdis and his family who operate this fine place.

Taverna Mavromátis. Psalidi Beach. ☎ **0242/22-433.** Appetizers Dr 450–Dr 1,500 ($1.95–$6.40), main courses Dr 950–Dr 4,500 ($4.05–$19.15). No credit cards. Daily 11am–11pm. GREEK.

One of the best choices in town is this 30-year-old vine and geranium-covered taverna run by the Mavromáti brothers. It's a 20-minute walk southeast of the ferry port or accessible by the local Psalidi Beach bus. Their food is what you came to Greece for: melt-in-your-mouth saganaki, mint and garlic spiced souzoukakia, tender grilled lamb chops, and moist beef souvlaki. Prices are reasonable, and the gentle music, waves lapping at your feet, and shaded back patio are delightful.

Restaurant Olimpiada. Odos Kleopatras 2. ☎ **0242/23-031.** Appetizers Dr 450–Dr 900 ($1.95–$3.85), main courses Dr 700–Dr 2,100 ($3–$8.95). EU, MC, V. Daily 11am–11pm. GREEK.

Located around the corner from the Olympic Airways office, this is one of the best values for simple Greek fare. The food is fresh, flavorful, and inexpensive, and the staff is remarkably courteous and friendly. The okra in tomato sauce and the several vegetable dishes are a treat. Open year-round.

KÁLYMNOS AFTER DARK

To our minds, the port-side cafes opposite the daily excursion boats to Kálymnos are best in the early morning. A much more romantic alternative in the evening is the pricier, luxurious **Rendezvous Cafe,** on the east side. Here you can lounge in a striking modern environment or outdoors on the marble terrace, sipping cocktails to the many moods of live piano accompaniment. **Platanos,** across from the Hippocrates tree, has live jazz. If you're interested in boogieing, the lively **Playboy Disco,** at Odos Kanari 2, has the most impressive light and laser show. On Zouroudi there are two popular discos, **Heaven** and **Calua,** with its swimming pool. If you want to hit the bar scene, try the **Hamam** on Kountouriotou or **The Blues Brothers** on Dolphins Square.

EXPLORING THE ISLAND

Although there are many fascinating archaeological sites, the reason that most people come to Kos is for its wonderful beaches. The island lies on a 45° angle; at its tip, the port of Kos faces due northeast to Bodrum, Turkey.

THE BEACHES

The two best beaches are between Tigaki and Mastihari on the windward north coast and between Kefalos and Kardamena on the south. Both areas can be reached by bus; from Kos town the closer, crowded northwest coast beaches are a mere hour's bicycle ride away on a flat, scenic, reasonably quiet road which runs parallel to the main island route. In order to reach the more secluded southern beaches, you might consider moped travel.

Beaches Along the Northern Coast

Tigaki, 11 kilometers from Kos, is typical of the beach towns that deal almost exclusively with groups, but it's convenient for day tips by bicycle or bus, and has a pleasant sandy beach with water sports. If you wish to stay here, we found the **Tigaki Beach Hotel** (☎ 0242/29-258; fax 0242/29-309, 168 rms, Dr 21,000/$89.40 for double, including breakfast), with its pool, tennis court, and colorful gardens, to be the nicest. From here there's also regular caïque service to **Pserimos,** a small island off Tigaki that has decent beaches and a taverna.

Four kilometers further is **Marmari,** a little quieter place, but becoming increasingly popular with the windsurfing crowd. For horseback enthusiasts of all levels of experience (including children), try **Marmari Riding Center** (☎ 0242/41-783), which offers daily guided excursions on the beach and four-hour mountain rides on Wednesdays.

Down the coast is **Mastihari,** a quieter, charming fishing village with its own fine beach and many rooms to let. If you stroll down to the western end, you might find more secluded spots among the dunes. On your way check out the ruined basilica, with its mosaic floors. Simple rooms can be found in Mastihari, starting at Dr 6,500 ($27.65) for a double. For the best accommodations, we recommend the new **Mastihari Bay Hotel** (☎ **0242/5111;** fax 0242/51-659), which offers swimming pools, tennis courts, windsurfing, and a fully outfitted fitness room. Doubles with half board (one meal provided) go for Dr 17,000 ($72.35). From Mastihari, small excursion boats make the 30-minute crossing to Kálymnos several times daily.

Heading south, you'll pass through the village of **Antimachia,** known for its old windmill, which is still used to grind flour, and for its tavernas that specialize in souvlaki and game meat. Drive through the pine-forested picnic area of the **Plaka valley** with wild peacocks roaming around, until you get to a turn-off to the right towards **Limnionas.** If you're willing to brave the bumpy, unpaved road down to this secluded port with its crystal clear waters, you're guaranteed a scrumptious seafood feast at the **Limnionas Fish Taverna.** Owner, Yiannis, has a fishing boat in this miniharbor, and he supplies the catch from the boat straight to the grill and onto your plate. We had the tsatsiki, tuna salad, and Greek salad for starters, and then we relished maikaki, tiny sardinelike fish that you pop into your mouth, heads and all. The appetizers are Dr 500 ($2.15) apiece, and the juicy white snapper is Dr 2,500 ($10.65). Or just sit down with an ouzo and eat your octopus right off the grill. The calm waters behind the breakwater are a great place for a swim during your stay in this idyllic place.

Beaches Along the Southern Coast

We would probably avoid staying in **Kardamena,** a former fishing village that's now become a tourist resort. Heading south toward the almost connected villages of Aghios Stafanos and Kefalos, there is an enormous stretch of sand and stone visited by a mere fraction of the tourists who prefer to frequent the town beaches. These beaches, **Polemi, Magic** (our favorite), **Paradise, Camel, Bubble** (with water sports), and **Sunny** (with jet-skis), all have small snack-bars and are served by frequent bus service from Kos town.

The town of **Kefalos** (43 kilometers from Kos), overlooking the sea, used to be a wealthy place that relied more on income brought in by its many sailors and ship captains than by tourism. The seaside is now being rapidly developed, and the village has the largest number of consumer conveniences on the southern part of Kos, including a bank, post office, OTE, tavernas, and shops. Below the village, **Kamari Bay,** with its gray sand and gently arced cove, is gorgeous, although dominated by the **Club Mediterranee Resort.** On the middle stretch of beach, the superorganized **Surfpool Windsurfing School** caters weekly programs to German tour groups, but also rents K2 equipment for beginners or semipros by the day. Rates, including wetsuits, are Dr 5,000 ($21.30) per hour, or Dr 19,000 ($80) for five hours, which can be used up over several days. During the high season, brisk offshore breezes provide swift sailing but few waves, an ideal combination for racing back and forth parallel to the seashore. The colorful presence of so many Windsurfers and sailboats (rented at Club Med) make up much of Kefalos' scenic appeal.

Where to Stay & Dine in Kefalos

Newly developed Kefalos has many rooms to let with little personality, and a few good value hotels. Most of the beachside places have small restaurants, but there are two appealing casual places on the sand. **Restaurant Corner** (☎ **0242/71-223**) in the middle of the beach serves only those specials that take advantage of the day's fish catch (sold at Dr 8,000 to Dr 10,000/$34.05 to $42.55 per kilo). The octopus, lightly battered, fried, and served with oregano and lemon is great. **Captain John** (☎ **0242/71-152**) at the south end of the beach has an international menu, and draws the biggest morning crowd with its 8:30am opening and large variety of break-fast eats. Both places serve lunch and dinner daily, have reasonably priced food and local wines, and don't accept credit cards.

If you're into the **Club Mediterranee** (☎ 0242/71-311) scene with your days programmed with nonstop activities with the best of facilities on this beautiful stretch of beach, then we suggest you book through your local travel representative, or through **Mouratti Tours** (☎ 0242/25-414; fax 0242/21-281) in Kos—the package deals work out cheaper than the individual per night price.

Hotel Kokolakis. Kefalos, Kos. ☎ 0242/71-446. Fax 0242/71-496. 42 rms (all with bath). TEL. Dr 9,000 ($38.30) single/double (including breakfast). No credit cards.

This was one of the first hotels here and claims a prime location just off the quiet main street on the beach. Balconied rooms, most overlooking their small pool and the sea, are simple and whitewashed. There's a rattan bar next to the pool for snacks and drinks. The front desk will arrange car or Jeep rentals at good prices.

Sacallis Inn. Kefalos, Kos. ☎ 0242/71-010. 25 rms (all with bath). TEL. Dr 7,000 ($29.80) single; Dr 9,000 ($38.30). No credit cards.

Tony and Maria Sacallis operate this well-designed and very appealing inn. Large rooms are spick-and-span, with fresh carpeting, modern facilities, and tiled balconies, most overlooking the picturesque Kastri islet and the azure sea. There's a large beachside patio with a bar and a nice lawn, as well as a Greek/continental sea-view taverna.

ASFENDÍOU (RUSTIC VILLAGES)

The inland villages of **Ziá, Evangelístria,** and **Lagoúdi,** are all part of the Asfendíou region, a 30-minute drive from downtown Kos. These hamlets are situated halfway up the craggy peaks that form the island's geological backbone, placing them in forests of eucalyptus, pine, and fig and olive trees. During spring, the ground is littered with wildflowers of every hue, and the soft aroma of chamomile, oregano, mint, and sage perfumes the air. Locals hike these villages during the summer for the cooling breezes blowing across the mountain. There is a wonderful mix of stately churches, crumbling houses, active farms, and new construction, and the people everywhere seemed the friendliest on the island. We loved the quintessentially Greek ambience of this area.

The most efficient way to visit this area is by car, but we prefer taking the public bus, infrequent but cheap, and walking from town to town. In the village of Evangelístria, we happened upon an English artist's studio that's worth a visit. **Alexandrous Alwyn** is known for his bronze sculpture, though many of his highly eclectic sketches and paintings are also on display. His work is somewhat like Henry Moore's, only warmer and more expressive, and is set in a lovely courtyard outside of his studio; open daily. Ask any local for directions.

It's almost worth taking the trip solely for the superbly simple dining at the **Sunset Balcony** (☎ 0242/29-120), just west of the church in Ziá. We had Heineken beer and a large plate of more than a dozen mezédes, all of which were distinctive and delicious, and we finished with near-perfect souvlaki, all for less than $20 each. The sun setting over the Kos plains and the sea with several nearby islands is nearly as remarkable as it is on Santoríni.

From Zia, starting from the Kefalovrisi Church you can take an hour-long hike up the highest peak of Kos, with outstanding views in all directions. We enjoyed strolling around the unspoiled villages of **Agios Georgios** and **Agios Dimitrios,** and delighted filling our water bottles in the cool, fresh spring water flowing out of an ancient fountain shaded by a fig tree in Pyli, a good place also to stop and have a bite in the typical village taverna.

SIDE TRIPS TO TURKEY

Many visitors to Kos find themselves staring longingly at the Turkish coastline, imagining an excursion into exotic Asia Minor. Both Greek and Turkish excursion boats and hydrofoils presently leave several times daily from the main harbor. For schedules and prices, you can either question the boat skippers along the pier or ask the **Tourist Police** (☎ 0242/22-444), who can also inform you as to the required papers and fees, since politically motivated visa regulations and rules change frequently. You can also contact **Mouratti Tours** (☎ 0242/25-414; fax 0242/21-281), who speak Turkish and have a corresponding agency in Bodrum. At the time of writing, we encountered fees ranging from Dr 6,000 to Dr 7,000 ($25.55 to $29.80) one-way fare, Dr 10,000 to Dr 11,000 ($42.55 to $46.80) same-day round trip, and Dr 12,000 ($51.05) if you stay over and return at a later date.

YACHTING OUT OF KOS

Our dream way of traveling the Greek islands is in the time-honored Greek fashion: by boat. If you're an explorer at heart, love the sea, sun, and the spice of adventure, then consider chartering a yacht, which allows you the total freedom to go when and where you please. You can party in a lively port till the wee hours of the morning and then spend the next day anchored in a totally secluded pristine bay, scarcely touched by tourism. The charter boats afford opportunities for everybody—if you're inexperienced, you can learn the basics of sailing from qualified skippers, and if you're a sailor, you can participate as much as you wish in running the boat and improving your skills. It's also a great way to meet other "yachties" from around the world.

We were extremely impressed by SeaScape, which operates a sloop-rigged 53-foot luxurious fully equipped yacht with comfortable accommodations for 10 people (four double cabins and two singles). They consolidate couples and individuals for fabulous one- to two-week cruises for about $500 a person per week. Diane Edwards is a laid-back, experienced skipper, who's life's passion is sailing these waters and who knows and loves these islands and the island people. She can also help you find the right boat in an area to suit your experience level. **SeaScape's** contact in Seattle is ☎ 206/883-0961; they can also be reached via Donna Gross, SeaScape, P.O. Box 7022, Vero Beach, FL 32961.

You can also arrange charter yachts through **Mouratti Tours** (☎ 0242/25-414; fax 0242/21-281), who specialize in arranging cruises along the Turkish coast. The boats cost up to $1,000 per day including full board and accommodate up to 12 people—the agency will consolidate individuals and couples into larger groups. You can also just stroll along the pier, talk it up with a skipper of a local charter yacht, and try out your sea legs on a day's sail.

4 Kálymnos

183 nautical miles E of Piraeus

Most visitors to Kálymnos come on a day trip from Kos and only have time for a visit to one of the sponge treatment centers (plus a splash at the beach). Orient yourself while you're approaching the harbor at Pothiá, and it becomes obvious that the waterfront, packed with active boats, still dominates life here. To the left, silver-domed spires top the cream-colored Ághios Nikólaos Church, a treasure trove of icons and frescoes. Indeed, this is one of the most elaborate churches in the Dodecanese, as it was the object of tribute by the well-to-do sponge fishermen and their families. The barren hillside above the town is capped with a 30-foot-tall cross, standing alone as a beacon to the returning fishermen. To the right, built over the water, is the Christ Our Savior Church, whose rotund pink basilica is paired with a tall, slim clock tower.

In the middle of the pier is a modern bronze sculpture of a nude sponge diver, arms raised above his head, who, we suppose, should be viewed upside-down for maximum effect. He's the work of local sculptor Michael Kokkinos, whose many other sculptures pop up in the oddest, most pleasant places.

ESSENTIALS

GETTING THERE   By Ferry   One car ferry leaves daily via Leros and Pátmos from Piraeus; schedules should be confirmed in Athens at **Tourist Information** (☎ 0243/01/143) or at the **Port Authority** (☎ 01/45-11-311). There's also a daily boat from Myrties beach to Leros, and irregular service (about five times a week) to Kálymnos from the other Dodecanese islands. In the high season, there's twice-daily service to Kos and Pátmos. There are once-weekly connections to the Cyclades, Pythagorion on Sámos, and Iraklio, Crete. Schedules should be checked at the port of departure. Kálymnos is served daily, weather allowing, by the hydrofoil, which connects it with Sámos, Pátmos, Leros, and Kos. Boat tickets and departure information can be obtained from the helpful **Kálymnos Tours** (☎ 0243/28-329; fax 0243/29-656).

VISITOR INFORMATION   Midway on the harbor, near the Poseidon statue but set back from the paralía, is the **tourist information (EOT) hut** (☎ 0243/23-140), open daily 8:30am to 1pm and 2 to 7pm to provide maps and information on rooms to let, sightseeing, and boat and bus schedules.

GETTING AROUND   It's easy to walk around Kálymnos town (called Pothiá), but the island itself is large. During the summer there are roughly four buses an hour between Pothiá, Myrties, and Massouri. The bus departs from the front of City Hall; buses to Emborios run far less frequently (only three days at week when we were there).

Taxis pool individuals for a very modest Dr 350 ($1.50) for the beach run. A price list for other destinations is posted at the taxi stand on Plateia Kyprou. (See "Exploring the Island," below for information on taxi tours.)

Our favorite way to discover the island is by moped. We found **Costas Katrivesis,** located behind the port police, to be quite reasonable and helpful with small 50cc models including insurance for only Dr 2,000 ($8.50) per day.

FAST FACTS   Along Eleftherios Street (the harbor road) you'll find the **port police** (☎ 0243/29-304), the **National, Commercial and Ionian Banks,** and several travel agents, among them reliable **Kálymnos Tours** (☎ 0243/28-329; fax 0243/29-656). The **police** (☎ 0243/22-100) are north of Plateia Kyprou, and the **bus station** is on the waterfront, just south of the Aghios Christos Church. A few blocks inland from the harbor is the **taxi stand** (☎ 0243/29-555), and there you'll also find the **OTE** and the **post office**.

WHAT TO SEE & DO

You can't leave Kálymnos without learning something about the islanders' nearly extinct occupation: sponges. The industry dates from 1700, when divers, weighted by a stone belt, would dive 10 to 15 meters down (holding their breath), collecting up to 10 sponges per dive. The sponges, animals living in plantlike colonies on rocks at the bottom of the sea, were then cleaned and treated. In 1885, the Skafandre (a primitive diving suit) made it possible for the divers to remain underwater at depths of 30 to 40 meters for nearly an hour. In heavy, rubberized canvas suits, with an air tube attached to a fishbowl helmet, men would walk the sea bottom, cutting sponges with their knives and gathering them with racquet-style baskets. On board, other workers would trample the sponges to squeeze out the dark membrane and milky juices. Each May 10, the ships would depart Kálymnos for the annual harvest, after much celebration, prayer, and a blessing from the high priest of Ághios Nikólaos. On October 30, another festival was held to thank God for those who returned home safely.

The riskiness of this occupation, in which workers were crippled by the bends or died, has reduced the number of divers from several thousand to about 80. Today the fleets sail north to nearby Sámos and Ikariá, or south of Crete to the Libyan Sea, and the men wear modern scuba gear. The export of sponges has declined due to competition from plastic sponges and poorer-quality natural sponges processed in the Phílippines and Malaysia; pollution in the Mediterranean has also impacted the sponge industry. Nonetheless, on a reduced scale this industry still thrives. Incidentally, many Kalymniots immigrated to Florida after the World War II, settling in Tampa and Tarpon Springs to continue their trade off the coasts of the Bahamas.

POTHIÁ

To get to the **Astor Workshop of Sea Sponges** (☎ 0243/29-815) in Pothiá, take the stairs at the left of the pier, past the tavernas up into town. About halfway up, a cement path on your right leads to the workshop run by Nick Gourlas. Here you can see each stage of preparation: the sponges' blackish original color, their softening after being beaten with sticks to loosen pebbles and fibers, and the subsequent whitening after a bath in sulfuric acid. Think that's rough? You can watch one of the workers trimming them into a round shape with gardening shears. Sponges here are for sale according to their size and grade. The cheaper unbleached sponges are more durable for cleaning chores; the light ones with big pores are for bathing; the finest-quality smooth ones, with tiny pores, are for sensitive skin and cosmetic use. (The Astor Workshop has inexpensive rooms to rent right upstairs.) Next door is the **Dorellos Sponge Warehouse,** a more up-to-date (less charming) version of the sponge show and tell.

The sponge-fishing industry has left another cultural legacy as well—the **Museum of Kálymnos** (☎ 0243/23-113). A typical Kalymniot mansion, once owned by sponge magnate Mr. Vouvalis, has been donated by him to the city as a museum, and it's filled with local archaeological finds and personal and business memorabilia. The museum is in the Aghía Triada section, a few blocks (10 minutes' walk) up from the harbor near taxi square. Admission is free, and it's open Tuesday through Sunday from 10am to 2pm. You'll notice that almost every taverna or shop displays a barnacle-encrusted amphora or other ancient sea treasure brought back from the depths by the local fishermen.

WHERE TO STAY

When making a stopover in quiet Kálymnos during your grand tour of the Dodecanese, consider staying in Pothiá for a night until continuing on to your chosen retreat, or else use it as a base for a few days of exploration around the island. Upon your arrival, you will probably be met at the harbor by residents offering private accommodations. Pothiá's **Tourist Information Office** (☎ 0243/29-130) can also be a reliable source for rooms; expect to pay Dr 5,000 ($21.30) for a double with private shower in town and a little less in the villages.

The following listing are open from mid-April to mid-October unless otherwise noted. Before mid-June and after mid-September you can obtain up to 40% discounts from high season rates.

POTHIÁ

Arhontiko Hotel. Pothiá, 85200 Kálymnos. ☎ **0243/24-051.** Fax 0243/24-149.10 rms (all with bath). TEL. Dr 8,000 ($34.05) double (including breakfast). V.

Its name meaning "the mansion" or "noble house," this traditional island-style edifice was built in the last century by a wealthy sponge merchant, and it was first used as the governor's offices by the Turkish authorities. In 1912, it was purchased by the Karaphillis family, who tastefully renovated it as a small hotel in 1994. They mixed the original antique furnishings with other classic island furnishings. The rooms are comfortable and airy, with the 14-foot ceilings typical of these classic homes. Nikodimos Karaphillis is happy to provide you with a printed itinerary of a week's worth of excursions. It's open year-round.

🅢 **Hotel Panorama.** Ammoudara, Pothiá, 85200 Kálymnos. ☎ **0243/23-138.** 13 rms (all with bath). Dr 4,500 ($19.15) single; Dr 6,500 ($27.65) double. No credit cards.

We appreciated the hospitality of Themelis and Desiree Koutouzi, who opened this sparkling marble and stucco inn in 1989. It's located on the heights of central Pothiá, above sponge factory lane and removed from the hubbub of the town's center. Lower-level rooms have large patios, while all enjoy a wonderful breeze and fine views over the harbor. Try calling in advance to have some one meet you at the boat; it's a fairly strenuous uphill climb up many steps with your bags in tow.

Olympic Hotel. Pothiá, 85200 Kálymnos. ☎ **0243/28-801.** Fax 0243/29-314. 41 rms (all with bath). TEL. Dr 7,000 ($29.80) single; Dr 11,500 ($48.95) double (including breakfast). AE, MC, V.

In the Ághios Nikólaos part of town (named for the central church), sits this large, modern, all-white hotel, with four stories and a welcomed elevator. Large rooms have tiny bathrooms with showers, but good-sized balconies overlooking the harbor and the noisy paralía. Breakfast is served in the large, sunny lobby, and there's a rooftop terrace for snacking and sunning.

WHERE TO DINE

Afrismeno Kymna Ouzeri/Taverna Kosari. On the port. ☎ **0243/223-427.** Appetizers Dr 300–Dr 1,250 ($1.30–$5.30), main courses Dr 900–Dr 2,800 ($3.85–$11.90). No credit cards. Daily 11am–2am. GREEK.

This friendly taverna/ouzeri plays it both ways with grilled meat and fish, simple mezedes, and traditional stews. It's casual but delightful for a seaside lunch. Next to the Fast Food Pantelis, it has its own octopuses hanging out to dry. Make sure to order some cooked in the typical Kalymniot way.

Barba (Uncle) Petros Seafood Restaurant. Diamanti's Sq. ☎ **0243/29-678.** Appetizers Dr 300–Dr 350 ($1.30–$1.55), main courses Dr 600–Dr 1,700 ($2.60–$7.25), seafood Dr 5,000–Dr 7,000 ($21.30–$29.80) per kilo. No credit cards. Daily, year-round, 11am–midnight. GREEK, SEAFOOD.

"We don't give nothing not fresh," declares Theo Martha and his son, Petros, who for 14 years have operated this popular eatery. It's located at the northern end of the harbor, and an almost full-scaled caïque hangs above the entrance. The outside terrace is packed with long tables of locals who comprise 90% of its clientele. Don't be turned off by the menu with its glossy photographs of raw fish on beds of lettuce; rather walk into the bustling kitchen to choose your favorite fish from the day's catch, which will be grilled to perfection on olive wood charcoal. For a start, we enjoyed the deep-fried minced octopus balls, then absolutely reveled in the grilled calamari stuffed with fresh spinach and feta cheese. The grilled red snapper was served with lemon and olive oil sauce on the side.

⊗ Naftikos Omilos (Nok or Kálymnos Yacht Club). Behind the port police. ☎ **0243/ 29-239.** Appetizers Dr 300–Dr 350 ($1.30–$1.55), main courses Dr 600–Dr 1,700 ($2.55–$7.25). No credit cards. Daily 8am–3pm, 6–11pm. GREEK, SEAFOOD.

Do not expect the chic yacht club set in this delightful old seafarers' hangout, which is draped in fishnets and ancient barnacled amphori fished out of the island's waters. Old crusty island sailors and younger seamen sit either on the outside terrace overlooking the boats, or inside under the fabulous huge mural of a sponge fisherman floating above Pothiá town. Enjoy great Greek meals or simple, inexpensive fish and meat dishes such as grilled swordfish steak with garlic sauce and crisp french fries (Dr 1,190/$5.20), or afelia, pork pieces, and potatoes cooked in dry white wine and coriander (Dr 990/$4.30).

Ouzeri Meris. On the peralia in Christos. No phone. Appetizers Dr 400–Dr 1,000 ($1.75–$4.25). No credit cards. Daily 5pm–midnight. SEAFOOD, MEZEDES.

Octopus lovers, prepare yourselves for a treat! Try to find this treasure by sauntering down the paralía and looking for the sign with the painted octopus and with about 20 octopuses drying on a wire above the entrance. You can luxuriate over a plate of grilled octopus mezedes and an ouzo, or delight in the octopus balls, which are made from diced octopus and deep-fried in a light batter. By the way, the locals eat grilled octopus by dipping it into ouzo before chewing.

Poseidon Restaurant. On a lane off of main harbor road. ☎ **0243/23-149.** Appetizers Dr 550–Dr 1,200 ($2.40–$5.20), main courses Dr 1,500–Dr 3,500 ($6.40–$14.90). V. Daily, year-round, 8am–3pm, 6–11pm. GREEK.

Owner/chef Paul Douros has created a feeling of rustic island charm in this century-old stone building quietly set off the main road. With his steady clientele of yachtsmen, visiting Athenians and locals, he specializes in finely prepared, gourmet Greek cuisine, such as veal and vegetables baked in individual clay pots with wine and brandy.

Restaurant Zefteris. Christos St. ☎ **0243/28-642.** Appetizers Dr 400–Dr 800 ($1.75–$3.50), main courses Dr 700–Dr 1,400 ($3.05–$5.95). No credit cards. Daily 11:30am–11pm. GREEK.

When you get really hungry head straight for this restaurant in the Christos section of town, just off the harbor. Their quiet back garden and old-fashioned come-into-our-kitchen taverna is a treat. Try the plump souzoukakia or huge, freshly made dolmades. Open year round.

POTHIÁ AFTER DARK

One of Pothiá's better late-night drink and snack rendezvous is **Mike's Piano Bar** (☎ 0243/28-642), also called the Do-Re-Mi. This popular rusticated stone lodge attracts a cross-section of tourists, yachters, and Kalymniots until the wee hours of the morning and boasts live piano music in the winter. It's located next to the Tourist Information office, behind the portside Poseidon statue. If you are waiting for your ferry to arrive, try the open-air **Scirocco Cafe-Bar.** Its fine view of the Piraeus car ferry pier is the best place to nurse your drink and just hang out.

EXPLORING THE ISLAND

There's more to see on Kálymnos than Pothiá's sponges. A round-the-island tour may be taken in a taxi seating four, at about Dr 15,000 ($63.80) for eight hours or Dr 8,500 ($36.20) for four hours. If drivers Spyros or Manolis are available, you'll end up knowing more about Kálymnos than you ever imagined. Kim Moraitis at **Kálymnos Tours** also provides a bus tour around the island in English including a swim stop in Vathi four times a week (Dr 3,800/$16.20), and a full day round-the-island cruise that includes a swim and a Greek-style barbecue (Dr 5,500/$23.40). They also offer an adventurous full-day cruise that includes exploring the aquatic Kefalas cave, a barbecue on Nera, a deserted islet, and swimming and sunbathing in Vlihadia Bay. If that isn't enough to keep you busy, try the sunset cruise, the "Greek Night" with a folklore show and food served in a nearby village, or an adventurous day of scuba diving with a professional instructor.

If you are exploring the island on your own, head northwest by the oleander-lined road through **Chóra,** the old capitol with its Crusader castle of the Knights of Saint John overlooking the entire west coast of the island. You'll come to the consecutive beach resorts of **Kantouni, Panormos, Mirties,** and **Massouri,** all rather highly developed for mass group tourism with endless hotels, restaurants, and minimarkets along relatively nice gray sand and pebble beaches.

KANTOUNI-PANORMOS

5km from Pothiá

Where to Stay & Dine

✪ **Domus Roof Garden Restaurant.** Kantouni. ☎ **0243/47-959.** Reservations recommended. Appetizers Dr 450–Dr 850 ($1.95–$3.60), main courses Dr 1,200–Dr 2,400 ($5.20–$10.20). MC, V. Daily 12:30–3pm, 6:30pm–midnight. GREEK, INTERNATIONAL.

Perched on the second-floor terrace overlooking the beach and the glorious sunsets, this is our choice for the best cuisine and ambience on the island. We savored the food served by owner/host, Michalis Petridis, who tastefully designed this place. His fylla were the most delicious stuffed vine leaves we've tasted throughout the Dodecanese. The fresh and crispy salad was aesthetically prepared with a great homemade dressing, topped with grated Parmesan and bacon bits. We heartily recommend trying the local specialty, mououri, lamb stuffed with rice, baked overnight and fried with eggs. The Armenian lamb cooked with yogurt, and the spinach tagliatelle are also especially good. Make the effort to get here from wherever you are staying on the island.

Epicure Restaurant. Panormos. ☎ **0243/47-868.** Fax 0243/47-620. Appetizers 200-2,000 ($.85–$8.50), main courses Dr 1,000–Dr 2,500 ($4.25–$10.65). MC, V. Daily, 6pm–midnight. GREEK, INTERNATIONAL.

If you want to escape the bustling beach-side scene, try this fine eatery, off the main road. It offers oversized hamburgers, pork steak in wine with mushrooms, chef's lamb, and seafood dishes. Owner Nick Papamichail also offers a tasty vegetarian menu. Adjacent to the restaurant he has built the Elite Studio Apartments, designed in the traditional architectural style of the island and having many amenities, including fully equipped kitchen, phone, minibar, TV, room service, and even video films. Doubles go for Dr 10,000 ($42.55).

Hotel Elies. Panormos, 85200 Kálymnos. ☎ **0243/48-146.** Fax 0243/47-160. 64 rms (all with bath). TEL. Dr 14,000 ($59.60) double (including breakfast). No credit cards.

Two nice features distinguish this clean and comfortable hotel: an enormous domed multicolored skylight in the lobby and the lovely central courtyard filled with citrus trees. It's only a short, pleasant walk to the beach from the hotel. There's also a pool.

Kalydna Island Hotel. Kantouni, 85200 Kálymnos. ☎ **0243/47-880.** Fax 0243/47-190. 16 doubles, 32 studio apts. (all with bath). TEL. Dr 20,800 ($88.50) double. MC.

We liked the elegant look of this five-year-old fancier hotel, constructed in a traditional Aegean style, with individually designed bungalows around the large swimming pool. For the adventurous, the hotel offers scuba diving lessons, and for the rest of us, it's only a short walk down to the beach.

MYRTIES

To escape the crowded beaches, take one of the local boats that frequently ferry you across the shimmering crystal blue water to the small volcanic islet of Telendos. Explore the ruined monastery and castle and enjoy the small beaches with their tavernas and pensions around the minuscule village. A favorite Kálymnos folk story tells of a young princess who died so in love with her little island of Telendos, that its one hill acquired her reclined shape. Use your imagination to see the curve of her hip and the profile of her young face.

Where to Stay & Dine

Atlantis Hotel. Myrties 85200 Kálymnos. ☎ **0243/47-497.** 17 rms (all with bath). TEL. Dr 5,000 ($21.30) double. MC, V.

We met a Norwegian family that's come back nine consecutive years to this older hotel and restaurant, which offers the friendliest, homiest service in town. The large terrago-floored lobby is decorated with local ceramics and weavings. Bright, large rooms have big bathrooms and simple furnishings; most rooms come with a small kitchen and refrigerator. We preferred the second-floor rooms with balconies and fine sea views. Their popular taverna serves tasty seafood and grilled meats in the evenings at very reasonable prices.

Hotel Myrsina. Myrties 85200 Kálymnos. ☎ **0243/47-550.** Fax 0243/47-238. 40 rms (all with bath). TEL. Dr 9,000 ($38.30) double. MC.

This is one of the nicest, recently built hotels in this area with a large pool and grand sea views. Spacious balconies overlook the road to the bay, making the clean but ordinary rooms something special. The bad news is the group-tour hammerlock, so only a few rooms are available to individuals during the high season.

Themis Hotel. Myrties 85200 Kálymnos. ☎ **0243/47-230** or 0243/47-893. 9 rms (all with bath). TEL. Dr 8,000 ($34.05) double (including breakfast). No credit cards.

If you like the sound of waves lapping beneath your window, you should try this small hotel with balconied rooms right on the harbor. The hard-working Poullas family, which runs it and the busy restaurant downstairs, spent many years in Montreal where they perfected their veal Parmesan. If they're full, try across the street at either the newly renovated **Hotel Zepheros,** ☎ 0243/47-500, with its 30 doubles with baths at Dr 9,000 ($38.30), or **Katina Studios,** ☎ 0243/47-423, recently opened with 30 rooms, each with bath and kitchenette for Dr 10,000 ($42.50).

MASSOURI

Massouri, the best-developed resort on the island, is the next beach north of Myrties. Small hotels, private houses, restaurants, and tourist shops crowd the coastal road above a long, picturesque rock and sand beach. If you're the type who likes to be among loads of Scandinavian and British tourists, then you'll find it just up your alley, with friendly people, good accommodations and food, and a lively bar and disco scene. Since tour operators have a lock on many of the rooms during the high season, you can save time and perhaps even money by contacting either **Advance Travel** (☎ **0243/48-148)** or **Massouri Holidays** (☎ **0243/47-626)** for booking your hotel or private room.

Where to Stay & Dine

Aegean Tavern. Massouri. No phone. Appetizers Dr 300–Dr 600 ($1.30–$2.60), main courses Dr 700–Dr 1,800 ($3–$7.65). Daily, noon to midnight. GREEK.

George Pizanias returned home after many years of operating a Greek restaurant outside Atlanta and opened this charming new place above the street, located so you miss the passing vehicles and catch the evening breeze. The service is friendly and the food is fresh and suited to American tastes, with less oil than usual and attractively presented. We tried the standards like the country salad, moussaká, and saganaki—all superb.

The Continental Hotel. Massouri 85200 Kálymnos. ☎ **0243/47-836.** Fax 0243/47-331. 41 rms, (all with bath). TEL. Dr 9,000 ($38.30) double (including breakfast). MC.

We liked this recently built hotel with a small swimming pool and terrace overlooking the beach. Nickolas Lisgaris, the owner, helps you feel right at home in the spotless and comfortable rooms.

⑤ Fatolitis Apartments. Massouri 85200 Kálymnos. ☎ **0243/47-615.** 11 rms (all with bath). Dr 6,000 ($25.55) double. No credit cards.

This multitiered cluster of small apartments tumbles down from the main road below the cheerful wicker and flower-print decor of the Fatolitis Snack Bar. The family owners run a clean, stylish place with potted plants, large, sea-view verandas for lounging, and simple, natural wood furnishings. Two- and three-bed studios have a fridge and kitchenette. A great deal if you can book one.

Hotel Massouri Beach. Massouri 85200 Kálymnos. ☎ **0243/47-555.** Fax 0243/47-177. 30 rms (all with bath) TEL. 11 rms (all with bath). Dr 7,250 ($30.85) double (including breakfast). MC, V.

This beachside hotel has clean, modern rooms and with breakfast included is a good deal. The sea-view terrace with its small bar is wonderful. Make sure to request a room facing the sea to take advantage of their beachfront location.

Hotel Plaza. Massouri 85200 Kálymnos. ☎ **0243/47-134.** 63 rms (all with bath). TEL. Dr 12,000 ($51) double (including breakfast). No credit cards.

We liked the sea-facing doubles and the big pool with its own bar at this large group-oriented hotel. It's very spacious, with breakfast and dining areas geared to many clients, but it's a good value for the price.

Pink Elephant Bar. Massouri. ☎ **0243/48-106.** Daily, noon to midnight. DRINKS ONLY.

David and Elisabeth May, from England, met, fell in love with each other and with Massouri, and have stayed for the last four years operating this friendly pub which caters to a multinational crowd. The music is mellow, the service is friendly, and there are plenty of books to swap and magazines to read as you take a break from your heavy-duty vacationing.

Punibel Restaurant. Massouri. No phone. Appetizers Dr 500–Dr 1,000 ($2.20–$4.35), main courses Dr 1,200–Dr 2,300 ($5.20–$9.80). AE, V. Daily, noon to midnight. GREEK, ITALIAN.

Just recently opened, this place is the perfect place for your "Greeked-out" palate. First settle down on the terrace with a glass of house wine to enjoy a great view of the bay. Then try a 600-gram T-bone steak with french fries and salad for only Dr 1,400 ($5.95) or the scrumptious carbonara, spaghetti with white sauce, bacon, and egg for only Dr 1,200 ($5.10).

EMBORIOS

Leave the crowded beaches and endless tourist joints for a mere 13-kilometer drive from Massouri, past the beach of Arginonda and the 12-family village of Skalia, and you'll reach the end of the road, **Emborios.** You can do this by taking either the 9:30am bus from Pothiá, the daily excursion boat from Myrties, or a rented moped. With its 20 resident families, Emborios is the perfect place to enjoy peace and quiet on the village beach shaded by tamarisk trees. Hike half an hour to beautiful **Apitiki beach,** climb to the small Minoan castle on the hill, take a local fishing boat to Skalia cave, rent a canoe to explore the hidden inlets around the exquisite bay, or simply hang out in a quiet taverna on the beach. An ideal place for longer term Kálymnos visitors.

Where to Stay & Dine
Harry's Apartment and Paradise Restaurant. Emborios 85200 Kálymnos. ☎/fax **0243/ 47-434;** in winter 0243/29-050. 6 apts and 1 rm (all with bath) TEL. Dr 9,000 ($38.30) double. No credit cards. Appetizers Dr 500–Dr 700 ($2.20–$3), main courses Dr 1,000–Dr 2,000 ($4.25– $8.50), fish Dr 6,000 ($25.55) per kilo. GREEK, VEGETARIAN.

The Passas family has lived in Emborios for more than 380 years, and Harry carries on the family tradition with the finest lodging and restaurant in the village. These are the most spacious single-room apartments we found on the island, each with a fully equipped kitchenette. Harry, a very congenial host, will offer you helpful advice on all the wheres and hows and whys of the island. Harry's Restaurant was renamed Harry's Paradise Restaurant at the insistence of enthusiastic customers. Try the special Kálymnos salad with tomatoes, feta cheese, and homemade olive oil, served with special homemade bread. We especially flipped over the vegetarian moussaka, made with soya and mushrooms. Harry's is homemade Greek food at its best.

If Harry's is full, he will personally help find you alternate accommodations. You can also try **Pension Pizanias** (☎ 0243/47277) attached to the recommended Restaurant Themis. Eight very simple rooms go for Dr 5,500 ($23.40) a night.

VATHI

Eight kilometers northeast of Pothiá at the end of a long, winding mountain road is a long verdant valley filled with mandarin orchards. Vathi is the slender breathtaking fjord that penetrates the cliffs into the harbor village of Rena at the tip of this valley. Small caïques will boat you over to the picture-postcard beaches accessible only by sea—choose the beach of your preference from the photos on the pier. It is here that we vowed to return to spend more time during our next visit to Kálymnos.

Where to Stay & Dine
Hotel Gallini. Vathi 85200 Kálymnos. ☎ **0243/31-241.** 14 rms. TEL. Dr 6,000 ($26) double (including breakfast). GREEK.

This is our favorite place to stay on the island, situated right on this picture-perfect harbor. Rita and Yiannis Haralambis are great hosts—Yiannis wakes up early in the morning to milk his cows and then makes the tastiest yogurt you've ever had, topped by Rita's homemade syrup. Pure heaven.

There are other rooms and studios to rent in the village as well as four quaint tavernas: **Poppi, Palomitis, Harbour,** and **Faros.** A favorite of the yachting set, the Faros Taverna is located right on the water with its own little roped-off swimming area. Decorated in an attractive nautical style, it's a perfect place to munch on the home-baked bread, sip on wine straight from the barrel, and have a great meal in this spectacular setting, by candlelight and with Vivaldi playing in the background. Owner Michaelo Panayota lists the delectable specials of the day on a blackboard; he also provides live Greek music on weekend evenings.

5 Lipsí

7 miles N of Leros and E of Pátmos

Lipsí is the largest inhabited islet in this part of the Dodecanese, yet small enough so that it's only a 1¹/₂-hour walk to the most remote, secluded beaches on the opposite side of the island. It has a population of about 650 year-round inhabitants, who spend their peaceful lives farming, fishing, raising goats, and tending the small, but significant number of tourists who seek peace and quiet off the beaten track. It's a wonderful feeling to finally have escaped the drone of mopeds and the bustling, commercial tourist centers on the neighboring islands. Influenced by the religious beliefs radiated from nearby Pátmos, the locals have built more than 50 small white chapels with blue domes, which dot the barren hillsides. Avoid visiting in August, when boatloads of Italian tourists arrive on the island, straining its limited capacity and water resources.

ESSENTIALS

GETTING THERE   By Boat   Twice a week, the car ferry from Kálymnos stops here on its journey to Sámos via Leros; leaving Lipsí, it continues onward to Pátmos and Agathonisi. During the high season, when the weather permits, hydrofoils connect daily with Kálymnos, Pátmos, Leros, Kos, and Sámos. There are also daily trips by the two Lipsí-based excursion boats, *Anna Express* and *Rena II* to Leros and Pátmos.

VISITOR INFORMATION   Although there is a **Municipal Tourist Office** (☎ 0247/41-288) in the municipal building on the main square, we found the best source of information to be the friendly and knowledgeable **Anna Rizos,** the British owner of **Lipsos Travel** (☎ 0247/41-225), together with her husband, Manolis. As well as giving you the complete lowdown on Lipsí and on interisland travel, Anna also sells boat tickets, and can help you make international calls. She offers baggage storage, recent international newspapers, and even a paperback book swap.

You can get information about ship arrivals and departures also from the **Port Police** (☎ 0247/22-224) and the **local Police** (☎ 0247/41-222), which are located by the steps leading up to the main square.

FAST FACTS   On the main square are located the **OTE** and the **post office.** There's a supermarket attached to the Calypso Hotel that stocks just about everything you need, including fresh fruits and vegetables, for your day hikes to the beaches.

WHAT TO SEE & DO

Most of the island's population resides in or around the picturesque port town of Lipsí, which is the location all of the island's lodgings and commercial services. Housed in the same building as the Municipal information office is the rather amusing local **Ecclesiastical Museum,** with important "relics" such as "holy water" from the Jordan river.

To get to the several beaches scattered around the island, follow the excellent signposts in town and start walking with plenty of drinking water and snacks in your daypack. You can purchase a useful map showing walking paths and beaches at Lipsos Travel. If walking isn't your cup of tea, by the harbor there are small pickup trucks with wooden benches in the back that will taxi you on bone-jarring roads to the beaches. You can also get there by the several caïques and small excursion boats that line the harbor.

Lendou and **Kampos Beaches** are two pebbly beaches within 10 minutes' walk from town. Heading south for about a half an hour on the road, past small farmhouses and shepherds with their goats, you'll reach **Katsadia Beach,** with its two tavernas and plenty of shade. Mrs. Gabrielis cooks and operates the upper **Adonis Taverna,** while her good-looking, personable son, Christos, runs **Delilah Taverna,** which has an attractive shaded terrace and a superfriendly atmosphere. You can camp here for free under the shade of the pine trees. If you seek a more secluded spot, continue walking another 20 minutes to **Tourkomnima Beach,** on a pretty inlet of pristine water sheltered from the wind. **Platis Gialos Beach,** an hour walk northwest across the hillsides with panoramic views of nearby islets set in the azure sea, is considered by many to be the island's most beautiful beach. The long sandy beach has shade trees and a great taverna, operated by Kostas Makris—the former goalkeeper of the Rhodes soccer team—who grills chicken on a charcoal fire, and whose cold beer hits the spot.

We thank Wallace Herridge, a former Royal Air Force pilot, for telling us about a walk to **Kimissi Beach,** where you can visit 78-year-old Phillipas, a hermit-monk who lives in a small dwelling next to the chapel. He'll be pleased to relate stories of saints and miracles (in Greek, unfortunately), especially if you bring an offering of a small bag of rice or pasta.

For the Robinson Crusoes among you, ask Anna at Lypsos Travel about taking an excursion boat to nearby islets. **Makronissi** has one of the few remaining colonies of monk seals, an endangered species. Tiny **Marathi Island,** with its long, sandy beach and picturesque coves, reputedly has only one year-round inhabitant, a shepherd. But during the summer season Mr. Pandelis and Mr. Michalis operate two small tavernas and rent out rooms to those seeking quiet isolation (apart from the invasion of day trippers from Lipsí and Pátmos). Every Monday evening at 6:30pm the *Anna Express* excursion boat sails to Marathi for a fun evening of good food and live bouzouki and guitar music on the beach (Dr 3,000/$12.80).

WHERE TO STAY & DINE

In Lipsí town, there are several small pensions and studios that offer clean, comfortable doubles with bath for about Dr 5,000 ($21.30). Among those that have been recommended are: **Pension Flisvos, Studios Dreams** (with kitchenettes in the rooms), and **Rena's Rooms** (☎ 0247/41-242). Free, unofficial camping is available on Katsadia Beach, where Christos will help you set up under the pine trees.

Lipsí has five tavernas, three "fast-food" souvlaki joints, and two ouzerias, **Sophokles** and **Nikos,** where you can sit in the shade sipping your ouzo and munching fried calamari and other tasty mezedes. After eating dinner, stroll along the port to **The Rock,** a late night spot for meeting people, listening to modern Greek music, having a slow drink, and eating some more fried calamari.

Calypso Hotel and Restaurant. Lipsí town 85001. ☎/fax **0247/41-242.** 16 rms (all with bath). Dr 6,200 ($26.40) double (including breakfast). V.

This is the only hotel in town, located conveniently right by the harbor. The rooms are clean, and besides the squeaky door hinges, we were satisfied with the accommodations. We bought fresh, creamy yogurts downstairs in the Calypso Supermarket and savored them on our balcony overlooking the harbor. It's open year-round, together with the adjacent vine-shaded restaurant.

Delilah Taverna. Katsadia Beach, Lipsí 85001. No phone. Appetizers Dr 500 ($2.15), main dishes Dr 900–Dr 1,400 ($3.85–$5.95), fish Dr 6,000 ($25.55) per kilo, lobster Dr 7,000 ($29.80) per kilo. Daily noon–midnight. GREEK.

This is a wonderful, secluded place to have a light lunch, sitting under the shaded veranda, located right on the beach. At night, it's a moonlit stroll through the countryside along a decent road. In the evening Christos lights the oil lamps, cranks up the music, and provides the ambience for a delightful dinner. He mentioned to us that electricity is on the way, but promises that he'll maintain the same atmosphere.

Delphini Taverna. Lipsí 85001. ☎ **0247/41-257.** Appetizers Dr 500–Dr 900 ($2.15–$3.85), main dishes Dr 900–Dr 1,400 ($3.85–$5.95), fish Dr 5,000 ($21.30) per kilo. Daily noon–midnight. Open all year. GREEK.

We delighted in the home cooking of Anarhiros and his wife, Photeni, who possess that special touch to transform the familiar tsatsiki, octopus salad, and eggplant salad into a culinary delight. We especially relished the skordaya, eggplant fritters with garlic sauce. Lukas, the proverbial fisherman, brings in the daily catch, guaranteeing its freshness.

Yiannis Taverna. Lipsí 85001. No phone. Appetizers Dr 400–Dr 700 ($1.70–$3), main dishes Dr 900–Dr 1,400 ($3.85–$5.95), fish Dr 5,000 ($21.30) per kilo. Daily noon–midnight. GREEK.

For seven years, Maria and Yiannis Grillis have won praises from their many satisfied customers, who enjoy sitting on the shaded veranda above the harbor. Try their fresh meat specialties, either beef, veal, or goat, prepared in various tantalizing sauces.

6 Pátmos

163 nautical miles E of Piraeus

"Dear visitor, the place which you have just entered is sacred." Thus begins the brochure handed out to all who visit Pátmos's Holy Cave of the Apocalypse, the site where St. John the Evangelist wrote the Book of Revelations 1,900 years ago. From a distance, Pátmos is all gray stone: barren rocks and ascetic, just a rough-hewn pedestal for the huge walled fortress of the Monastery of St. John. Rounding Point Hesmeris reveals the hidden port of Skála, cluttered with bars, tavernas, and hotels. There's a Wild West quality about this small fishing port that's heightened by the gregarious locals who meet the boats. On isolated Pátmos, 12 hours by steamer from Piraeus, four hours by hydrofoil from Rhodes, the stagecoach has arrived. Blessed by the fact that organized tourism has not been allowed to take over the island, the development has been benevolently controlled.

Thousands of Christians make a pilgrimage to the religious shrines of Pátmos annually, but the majority arrive on Mediterranean cruise ships and depart the same day. Any traveler seeking peace and quiet, good-hearted, gentle Greek island people, and a disarmingly sophisticated social scene should stick around. Pátmos surprises all who stay long enough for a second look.

ESSENTIALS

GETTING THERE   By Boat   One car ferry leaves daily from Piraeus; schedules should be confirmed in Athens at **Tourist Information** (☎ **01/143**) or at the **Port Authority** (☎ **01/45-11-311**). There are daily car ferries to Leros, Kálymnos, Kos, and Rhodes. Ferries connect Pátmos to Ikaria four times a week and three times a week to Sámos (both in the Northeast Aegean group). Once a week the Sámos ferry continues on to Chios, Lesbos, Límnos, and Thessaloníki. During the high season, smaller and faster excursion boats cruise to Pythagorion, Sámos in less than three hours, making the round trip for Dr 3,500 ($14.90).

The fastest but most expensive method of transport is the hydrofoil that services Pátmos every day in the summer, operating on the route from Kos, Kálymnos, Leros, Pátmos, and Sámos, and reversing the direction in the afternoon. Your travel time is cut roughly in half, though summertime meltemi winds and high waves can occasionally prevent them from sailing. Contact **Astoria Shipping and Tourist Agency** (☎ **0247/31-205;** fax 0247/31-975) for schedules.

VISITOR INFORMATION　　There is a **Tourist Information Office** (☎ **0247/ 31-666**) right on the harbor on your left. They can help with accommodations on the island, including rooms, hotels, and houses. During the summer, they are open Monday through Friday from 9am to 11pm, Saturday and Sunday from 9am to 4pm. They also distribute the publication *Pátmos Summertime,* which is a good source of information and which contains maps of Skála, Chóra, and the entire island. The **Tourist Police** (☎ **0247/31-303**) are upstairs in the main square.

We found John and Nitsa Kamaratos, former Australian Greeks, of **Astoria Shipping and Tourist Agency** (☎ **0247/31-205;** fax 31-975), to be extremely helpful in providing general information, as well as for exchanging money, booking hotels, selling boat tickets, and arranging island tours.

Patmophiles will want to read resident Tom Stone's *Pátmos,* published by Lycabettus Press, and might be inspired to attend the English-language Catholic mass at St. Francis House held every Saturday night.

GETTING AROUND　　The port of Skála is compact enough to walk around with pleasure. Outside of Skála, goat paths lead up and over the many untouristed hillsides to wild, unexpected natural vistas. Hiking around the island will also bring you into contact with the lovely Patmian people, whose deep religious beliefs make them even more hospitable than the average welcoming Greek citizen.

By Bus　　From the ferryboat pier, the island's bus stop is directly ahead, a little to the left, behind the statue of Emmanuel Xanthos. Buses from Skála to Chóra run eight times daily, as per the schedule posted next to the stop; the fare is currently Dr 150 ($.65). (The hardier might actually enjoy the 30-minute uphill trek to the Monastery of St. John.) The entire island has only two other bus routes: to the beach at Kampos four times daily (Dr 160/70¢) and to the beach at Gríkos six times daily (Dr 200/85¢).

By Boat　　Local fishermen turn their caïques into beach shuttles during the summer season, and offer daily excursions to many of the island's private coves. Each night you can walk along the harbor and read the chalkboard destination signs hanging off the stern of every caïque. These small boats charge Dr 600 ($2.50) each way to Psiliámos or Lámpi and Dr 350 ($1.45) to Kampos each way.

By Taxi　　There are taxis (☎ **0247/31-225**) available in Skála, next to the post office. However, they're usually grabbed up by the repeat visitors or commuting residents who rush off the ferry before you. If you're interested in nighttime dining in Chóra, for example, walk over or call ahead to book one; fares to Chóra run Dr 700 ($2.90), depending on the time of day and season, plus a Dr 100 fee for radio calls.

By Car　　Contact **Rent A Car Pátmos** (☎ **0247/32-203**) on the port near the post office. Subcompacts start at Dr 14,500 ($60.40) per day.

By Moped　　Our favorite way to discover the island is by moped, which affords greater freedom of movement and is fun. Most Patmian roads are actually paved, so it's not as risky as elsewhere, but exercise caution on the gravel-filled, winding, hilly roads. There are moped rental shops aplenty in Skála. Theo, at **Mr. Moto Express**

(☎ 0247/32-088), was friendly and had a good selection of mopeds ranging in price from Dr 1,500 to Dr 3,000 ($6.40 to $12.75) per day.

ISLAND LAYOUT Pátmos has an unusually long tourist season, thanks to the moderating sea breezes that sweep across the island year-round. Most visitors stay at the east coast port of Skála at the island's narrow midriff, where the majority of the island's hotels and rooms are located. To the south, the hilltop Monastery of St. John dominates the port.

The jumble of whitewashed homes that cling to the fortresslike walls of this medieval monastery comprise Chóra (or "City"). Chóra has been the island's main town since the 11th century, and it's an architectural delight on the order of Lindos, Rhodes.

To the left (south) as you leave the ferryboat pier is the uphill road running east to Chóra, and the coastal road running southwest to the family beach resort at Gríkos. To the right (north) of the pier are the Skála town beach and the coastal route leading to the beach resort of Kámpos.

The island's two great Christian monuments, the Monastery of St. John and the Holy Cave of the Apocalypse, are of such historical and artistic significance that they should be seen by everyone visiting Pátmos.

FAST FACTS The **Hospital** (☎ 0247/31-211) is on the Skála-Chóra road. The **post office** is on the main square; it's open Monday through Saturday from 9am to 2pm, 5 to 8pm (10pm in summer). There is a **Laundromat** by the new port, and even a **newsstand** with day-old copies of the *Herald Tribune* for the news-starved island tripper.

A LOOK AT THE PAST

Since antiquity the isolated, arid island of Pátmos has been considered the "Siberia" of the Mediterranean world. Although many believe that Pátmos's inhabited history began with the founding of the Monastery of St. John in 1088, the island was originally colonized by the people of Caria in Asia Minor, who brought with them their cult worship of Artemis. Unexcavated ruins (from the 6th to 4th centuries B.C.) found on Kastelli Hill include the remains of an ancient acropolis, walls, temples to Apollo and Dionysos, and a hippodrome.

Pátmos's reputation as a Siberia fit only for banishment or exile began in the Hellenistic period. It is said that Orestes, son of Agamemnon and Clytemnestra, took refuge on Pátmos after he murdered his mother and her lover to avenge his father's death. Unfortunately, Orestes's lover, Erigone, was the product of his mother's illicit relationship, and the distressed woman brought Orestes to trial when she learned he had murdered her mother. The Erinyes (Furies) pursued Orestes throughout the Aegean until he landed on the isolated island of Pátmos. Orestes was acquitted by the gods, and after founding a temple dedicated to Artemis, left Pátmos to ascend the throne of Árgos.

The Romans immortalized the island by sending John the Theologian into exile there in A.D. 96 during the Emperor Domitian's wide-scale persecution of all Christians in the empire. Saint John (in the Book of Revelation) only makes this reference to his sojourn: "I dwelled in an island which is called Pátmos, as to preach the word of God and have faith in the martyrdom suffered by Jesus Christ."

For centuries after Saint John's historic visit, Patmians continued to trade with the mainland port of Miletus, their link to Asia Minor, and to adhere to the Artemis cult worship practiced in Ephesus. In 313 the Emperor Constantine officially recognized Christianity. Pátmos fell into relative obscurity, endured devastating raids through the Islamic period, and was eventually retaken by the Byzantine Empire.

In 1088, a devout monk, Christodoulos, went to Alexius I Comnenus to ask permission to found a monastery dedicated to Saint John on the island. Alexius realized the political favor such a bequest could earn him with the already powerful Christian church. The 1088 Chrysobull (Alexius's imperial decree that is still proudly displayed in the monastery) granted to the monks of Christodoulos "the right to be absolute rulers to all eternity." This Chrysobull (it also exempted Pátmos from government taxation or judicial interference and granted the monastery the right to own ships tax-free) shaped the future development of the island.

Pátmos's autonomous religious community flourished. The centuries of Turkish domination that withered Greek culture elsewhere left Pátmos almost untouched. The Monastery of St. John became the finest cultural and theological school in the country, even prospering under the Italian occupation. After World War II Pátmos was reunited with the Greek nation.

Today Pátmos is one of the few Greek islands that has benefited from tourism without having to sell its soul. The monastery's real estate monopoly ensured slow, careful development of the land. The monks never condoned nude or topless sunbathing; this has kept away the more risqué summer tourists. No military construction was permitted, so there is no commercial airport on the island (many foreign residents use Olympic's private helicopter landing pad in Skála). The revenue produced by Holy Land day-trip visitors is enough to keep Skála thriving; the less commercial sections of the island are supported by the elite foreign population. The fortuitous combination of historical and social factors has made Pátmos a unique, unspoiled island "sacred" to many.

WHAT TO SEE & DO

If you're lucky enough to be in Greece at Easter (late April or early May), try to book a room so that you can witness the Nipteras. It's a reenactment of the Last Supper that's only performed on Pátmos, in the square outside the Monastery of St. John, and in Jerusalem. The festivities and holy days extend from the Monday before Easter to the following Tuesday, when there's great feasting and dancing in Xanthos Square.

The Monastery of St. John. ☎ 0247/31-234.

The Monastery of St. John was founded in 1088 by the monk Christodoulos. Tall gray stone walls were constructed to protect the hilltop retreat from pirate raids, giving it the appearance of a solid medieval fortress.

Upon crossing the monastery's main threshold, the visitor is transported by the stillness and ethereal calm into a private world. Supported by heavy gray brick columns, the large covered cistern containing holy water in the center of the courtyard (an ideal bench for contemplation) held wine in the days when 200 monks inhabited Chóra. Except on major Greek Orthodox holidays, the monastery's religious activities are not as impressive as its museum-quality collection of manuscripts, religious icons, Byzantine art, and frescoes.

The Outer Narthex, to the left of the entrances, is richly painted with 17th-century frescoes depicting traditional tales from the life of St. John (a flashlight is needed for a thorough examination of the dark chapel). Tour guides meet the day-cruise visitors; their anecdotes of monastic life and vivid descriptions of the many parts of the monastery that are now off limits make joining a tour worthwhile.

For centuries the remarkable collection of more than 13,000 documents in the monastery library has drawn scholars to Pátmos. The earliest text is a 6th-century fragment from the Gospel of Saint Mark; on Pátmos there are 33 leaves of this priceless work, which has been divided among museums in Leningrad, Athens, Britain, the Vatican, and Vienna. The 1088 Chrysobull issued by Alexius I Comnenus granting the monastery sovereignty over Pátmos is displayed, as well as an 8th-century text of Job and Codex 33, the 10th-century illustrated manuscript of the discourses of Saint Gregory the Theologian. In the treasury are jewels and icons donated by Catherine II, Peter the Great of Russia, and other dignitaries, and the 4th-century B.C. marble tablet describing Orestes's visit to Pátmos.

After 200 years of tourist abuse (many valuable texts were taken back to Europe by visiting scholars) the library and original Treasury have been closed to view. One may visit the well-secured treasury-library-museum, where a sampling of the rich vestments, icons, and religious artifacts belonging to the monastery are displayed.

From the roof (now closed) one can see a spectacular panorama of the Aegean, including the islands of Ikaría and Sámos to the north, Léros, and beyond it, Kálymnos, to the southeast Amorgós, and in the far southwest Santoríni.

The monastery requests that you "Respect the Holy Places, our traditions, and our morals by your dignified attire, serious appearance, and your general behavior." Visiting hours change radically according to season, primarily geared to the comings and goings of cruise ships, but we suggest visiting between 9 and 10am (before the ships arrive). Contact tourist information (☎ 0247/31-666) for the current schedule; museum admission is Dr 500 ($2.10).

Holy Cave of the Apocalypse. ☎ 0247/31-234.

The Monastery of the Apocalypse was built at the site of the grotto where Saint John received his revelation from God. Located a five-minute walk below the hilltop monastery, it can be easily visited on the pleasant, vista-filled descent to Skála.

A rousing brochure written by Archimandrite Koutsanellos, Superior of the Cave, provides an excellent description of the religious significance of each niche in the rocks, and the many icons in the cave. The little whitewashed monastery that surrounds the cave was the 18th-century home of the Patmias School, an institute of higher learning unparalleled during the Turkish occupation. A large modern structure built after World War II to accommodate the school and a theological seminary dominates the barren hillside above Skála.

Appropriate attire is required (appropriate means no slacks for women, no shorts for anyone). This dress code applies when visiting any of the island's religious sites, including the several other monasteries and nunneries, which have fine frescoes and religious icons. Those with an interest in the significance of Pátmos in Christian history will be fascinated by Otto Meinardus's *St. John of Pátmos* and *The Seven Churches of the Apocalypse*, published by Lycabettus Press. Opening hours are roughly the same as the monastery.

The Simantiri House. ☎ 0247/31-360.

This house belonged to the Simantiri family for eight generations, beginning in 1625. Today this superbly restored Venetian-style Patmian mansion is open to the public, daily from 9am to 3pm and 5 to 8pm, for tours. The best way to find the Simantiri House is to ask for the Zoodochos Pigi Monastery; it's just down the street. Admission costs Dr 350 ($1.45). The **Zoodochos Pigi Monastery** (☎ 0247/31-256) is itself a treat to behold; it's open to the public daily from 9am to noon and 3 to 6pm; admission is free.

LOCAL LANDMARKS

If you stay on Pátmos long enough, you'll begin to hear about the hundreds of must-see sites cherished by the locals. We'll only explain two sites that you're likely to encounter.

A little way out in the harbor, opposite the Patmion Hotel, is a large red buoy that marks "Devil's Rock." This submerged plateau is marked not only as a warning to sailors—it keeps sinners on their toes! For here, nearly 2,000 years ago, according to local lore, the devil used to preach to citizens by communing with the spirits of their ancestors. The alternate telling of this folktale suggests that the devil was Kynops, a local magician sent by priests from the temple of Apollo to challenge Saint John's influence. In either case, one day the devil/Kynops offered to enlighten St. John himself, but when he dove underwater to display his powers, Saint John crossed himself and the devil was halted there, frozen in stone. Even though this is a convenient fishing perch, today the local fishermen avoid it because "the fish caught off this rock smell funny."

Another local landmark you might be curious about is the wrought-iron fencing that encloses a nondescript flat rock, toward the north end of the waterfront. Devoted Patmians have enclosed the stone slab where Saint John is said to have baptized more than 14,000 converts from among the local population.

SKÁLA

Skála is still small enough that most commercial activity is along the waterfront, with more recent development on the low hill behind the paralía, on unpaved back lanes two or three deep. If you walk from the ferry north to the well-marked Astoria Hotel, you'll pass the busy heart of town, Emmanuel Xanthos Square. In the maddeningly irregular, whitewashed lanes behind the square are some hotels and shops. From the square north along the waterfront are several small tavernas, hotels, and bars. Behind is the little "neighborhood" of Nethia, where some fine hotels are found. Ten minutes past Nethia on the path curving up to the right and over the hill is the local beach, **Órmos Melóï.**

WHERE TO STAY

There are not many hotels in Skála, so the best ones require reservations two to three months in advance, especially if you're planning to visit Pátmos during Greek or Christian Easter or in July or August. Last-minute planners should have no problem finding a private room in the surrounding hillside; upon your arrival you will probably be met at the harbor by residents offering private accommodations. If you're interested in renting a kitchenette apartment or villa, contact the **Apollon Agency** (☎ **0247/31356;** fax 0247/31-819) for more information.

At the nearby **Melóï Beach,** only 1¹/₂ kilometers from Skála, is the justifiably popular **Stefanos Camping** (☎ **0247/31-821**), also known as Pátmos Flower Camping. It's very convenient, with a mini market, cafe, communal kitchen, and tall bamboo groves providing shade at the tent sites. However, it does become very crowded in the high season; they charge Dr 1,200 ($5.10) for tents.

The following listings are open from mid-April to mid-October unless otherwise noted. Before mid-June and after mid-September you can obtain up to 40% discounts from high season rates; polite bargaining may be of assistance.

Adonis Hotel. Skála 85500 Pátmos. ☎ **0247/31-103** or 01/51-21-035 in Athens. Fax 0247/32-225. 23 rms (all with bath). TEL. Dr 11,000 ($46.80) single; Dr 13,500 ($57.45) double (including breakfast). No credit cards.

The Patmian style, white stucco and stone facade, and small rooftop neon sign distinguish this hotel from the many residences sprouting on the hillside. Fresh rooms, with harbor-view balconies (request the top floor), provide quiet and convenient lodging. New tiled bathrooms even have shower curtains. Breakfast is served on the shaded front porch, within scent of the jasmine-covered arbor.

Australis Hotel. Skála 85500 Pátmos. ☎ **0247/31-576.** 21 rms (all with bath). Dr 12,000 ($51) single/double (including breakfast). No credit cards.

The welcoming Fokas and Chris Michalis, who spent many years in Australia, run this small, friendly hotel in a blooming hillside oasis. The grounds are covered with bright bougainvillea, geraniums, carnations, fuchsias, dahlias, and roses; they were featured in *Garden Design* magazine. The pleasant communal porch, where breakfast is served, looks out on the harbor. Their son, Michael, rents mopeds and has three handsome new studios over his house on the old road to Chóra. Each has a well stocked kitchen and goes for Dr 12,000 ($51).

Blue Bay Hotel. Skála 85500 Pátmos. ☎ **0247/31-165.** Fax 0247/32-303. 22 rms (all with bath). TEL. Dr 10,800 ($45.95) single; 14,700 ($62.55) double (including breakfast). No credit cards.

Reader Robert H. Smith of El Cerrito, California, wrote to insist we consider this handsome new hotel about 200 meters left of the port. We found it every bit as quiet, immaculate, attractive, and comfortable, and the Karantani family as hospitable, gracious, and helpful as he said. It also has a bar and large balconies overlooking the harbor.

Castelli Hotel. Skála 85500 Pátmos. ☎ **0247/31-361.** Fax 0247/31-656. 45 rms (all with bath). TEL. Dr 9,100 ($19.50) single; Dr 12,600 ($28.25) double (including breakfast). No credit cards.

Guests are accommodated here in two white stucco blocks framed with brown shutters. The striking vista can be enjoyed from cushioned wrought-iron chairs on the balconies. Spotless rooms are large and have beige tile floors; the common lounge and lobby areas are filled with photographs, flower-print sofas, seashells, fresh-cut flowers from the surrounding gardens, and other knickknacks of seaside life. Such good care and charm make this a good value.

Hotel Effie. Skála 85500 Pátmos. ☎ **0247/31-298.** Fax 0247/32-700. 35 rms (all with bath). TEL. Dr 8,000 ($34) single; 11,400 ($48.50) double (including breakfast). No credit cards

Turn left before the Old Harbor Restaurant to find this recently built hotel on the quiet hillside. The rooms are large, light, spare, and spotless; they have balconies and somewhat limited views. Owners Effie and Nick make all their guests feel at home in the family atmosphere. It's open all winter, having central heating.

Hotel Hellinis. Skála, 85500 Pátmos. ☎ **0247/31-275.** Fax 0247/31-846. 40 rms (all with bath). TEL. Dr 9,000 ($38.30) single/double. V.

Located around the port, next to the Fina Station at the Melóï end of Skála, is this clean Class C lodging, with a fountain in front and a wonderful evening view across the harbor to the illuminated village and the sky-high monastery. It's run by Christodoulous Grillis and family, giving the otherwise plain accommodations some familial warmth. The family also keeps nine rooms to let nearby (Dr 6,000/$25.50 for two people).

Romeos Hotel. Skála 85500 Pátmos. ☎ **0247/31-962.** Fax 0247/31-070. 58 rms and 2 suites (all with bath). TEL. Dr 14,000 ($59.60) single, Dr 21,000 ($89.40) double, Dr 25,000 ($106.40) suite (including breakfast). EU, MC, V.

Of all Skála's newer lodgings, this one in the back streets behind the OTE is especially commodious. It has the biggest pool on the island and a quiet garden. Run by a Greek American family from Virginia, the Romeos has spotless rooms, with woven cotton upholstering, simple decor, and countryside-view balconies. Rooms are built like semiattached bungalows on a series of tiers across with views across to Mt.

Kastelli. The larger honeymoon suites, with matrimonial beds, full bathtubs, and a small lounge are another option. The only down side is the 10-minute walk to the port and the town center.

Skála Hotel. Skála 85500 Pátmos. ☎ **0247/31-343.** Fax 0247/31-747. 78 rms (all with bath). TEL. Dr 13,500 ($57.45) single; Dr 18,000 ($76.60) double (including breakfast). AE, EU, MC, V.

Tranquilly but conveniently situated well off the main harbor road behind a lush garden overflowing with arresting pink bougainvillea, this comfortable hotel has aged like a fine wine to become our favorite lodging in Skála. Annual improvements include the beautifully landscaped garden, a large pool with an inviting sundeck and bar, a large breakfast buffet, adjustable heat in all rooms, conference and meeting facilities, and even better and more personalized service. Host Captain Grillis, who skippers Caribbean cruises in the winter, and his staff offers guests the kind of hospitality one expects on such a sophisticated island. Some rooms have harbor views, but you'll have to reserve in advance.

WHERE TO DINE

Archontiko Restaurant. Chóra village. ☎ **0247/31-668.** Reservations necessary in high season. Appetizers Dr 750–Dr 1,450 ($3.20–$6.20), main courses Dr 1,400–Dr 3,000 ($5.95–$12.80). No credit cards. Daily 7:30pm–1am. GREEK/PROVINCIAL.

French owner Ghisleine Lesvigne spent 10 years lovingly restoring this nobleman's stone villa, built originally in 1645. Exposing the ancient walls and floors revealed a templar cross, an ancient well, and ceramic implements, which now decorate the premises. We enjoyed the ambience, with mellow lighting, woven tablecloths, and soft classical musical accompanying the attentive service and fine cuisine. Her French touch is evident in the homemade pâté with herbs of Provence and nuts in an onion marmalade. The grilled filet with herbs of Provence was tasty, tender, and prepared exactly as requested. We also enjoyed the spinach with creme and basil and the gratin dauphinois. The delectable, light chocolate mousse was a worthy coup de grâce to this gourmet cuisine.

Arion Cafebar. Paralía of Skála. ☎ **0247/31-595.** Snacks/desserts Dr 250–Dr 850 ($1.05–$3.60). No credit cards. Daily 8:30am–3am. CONTINENTAL.

Just as day cafe crowds favor the main square, sunset idlers seem to favor the harbor. The elegant old Arion, formerly a warehouse for salvaged metal from sunken ships, has high ceilings and exposed stone walls. Large old fans stir up a breeze above the long, broad, polished-wood bar. Ornate iron medieval-style wall sconces produce the intimate lighting. Late breakfasts, drinks, snacks, delicious ice cream concoctions, and coffee are served inside and out.

The Balcony (Jimmy's). Chóra village. ☎ **0247/32-115.** Appetizers Dr 450–Dr 900 ($1.90–$3.80), main courses Dr 650–Dr 2,500 ($2.75–$10.65). No credit cards. Daily 11am–11pm. GREEK/INTERNATIONAL.

After you have visited the monastery, have a treat by stopping in this unpretentious place with good food, reasonable prices, and a stupendous view toward Skála and the sea. Owner Jimmy the Greek is a real character and will regal you with stories from his earlier days living in Houston, Iowa, New Jersey, and driving a New York City cab for 15 years. We had a fresh village salad with a distinctive cheese, an excellent omelet, chicken with garlic and basil, a couple of beers, drank in the scenery, and came away completely satisfied.

Grigoris Grill. Opposite Skála car ferry pier. ☎ **0247/31-515.** Appetizers Dr 450–Dr 900 ($1.90–$3.80), main courses Dr 900–Dr 2,300 ($3.80–$9.80). No credit cards. Daily 6pm–midnight. GREEK.

One of Skála's better-known eateries, this place was formerly the center of Patmian chic. We recommend any of the grilled fish or meat dishes, particularly in the low season, when more care and attention are paid to preparation. Well-cooked veal cutlets, large, tender lamb chops, and the swordfish souvlaki are favorites. Gregoris also offers several vegetarian specials.

The Houston Cafe. Skála, near the harbor. No phone. Ouzo Dr 150 (65¢), beer Dr 250 ($1.06).

This old, traditional cafe is our favorite for experiencing Pátmos of yesteryear. A wood-beamed ceiling, pink and turquoise walls, and rickety Formica-top tables complement the decor of old boating posters, turn-of-the-century photographs, and antique decanters. In the 1920s, you could sit here and have a haircut, while sipping your coffee, which is still today made on the coals in the traditional Greek style.

The Old Harbor Restaurant. On the paralía of Skála. ☎ **0247/31-170.** Appetizers Dr 600–Dr 2,800 ($2.55–$11.90), main courses Dr 1,300–Dr 2,800 ($5.55–$11.90), seafood Dr 6,000 per kilo ($25.55). AE, MC, V. Daily 6pm–midnight. GREEK/INTERNATIONAL/SEAFOOD.

We especially enjoyed sitting on the upper terrace overlooking the crescent-shaped harbor with a blue neon cross gleaming on top of the opposite hill. We had received several recommendations of this place, and we found it to be quite adequate, with decent-sized portions and efficient service. The filet mignon was tender and cooked according to our request, and the swordfish steak was grilled just right.

ⓢ Olympia Taverna. Chóra village (follow signs to Vagelis). ☎ **0247/31-543.** Appetizers Dr 500–Dr 1,100 ($2.15–$4.70), main courses Dr 650–Dr 1,200 ($2.80–$5.10). No credit cards. Mon–Sat, noon–2pm, 6:30pm–midnight. Open all year. GREEK.

This taverna on picturesque Theofakosta Square, less frequented by tourists because of its low-key presence, is favored by the locals and by us as well for its traditional Greek home-style cooking. We tried the octopus yiuvetsi, the eggplants stuffed with meat, feta cheese and béchamel sauce, horta and beet salad, and a slab of their famous walnut cake, all delicious and inexpensive. During the summer they open the roof garden, with its great views, for open-air dining.

ⓢ Pantelis Restaurant. One lane back from Skála port. ☎ **0247/31-230.** Appetizers Dr 450–Dr 1,000 ($1.90–$4.25), main courses Dr 700–Dr 1,700 ($3–$7.25). No credit cards. Daily, 11am–11pm. GREEK.

One of Skála's older establishments serves delicious food at low prices in a comfortable, homey environment. A favorite with Patmians, it's located right behind the Astoria Complex. It has delicious lightly fried calamari and swordfish kebab, as well as a complement of vegetarian entrées.

The Patmian House. Chóra village. ☎ **0247/31-180.** Appetizers Dr 800–Dr 1,000 ($3.40–$4.25), main courses Dr 1,200–Dr 3,500 ($5.10–$14.90). No credit cards. Daily 7pm–midnight. Reservations advisable. GREEK/CONTINENTAL.

It shouldn't surprise you that sophisticated Chóra features one of the best and most interesting Greek restaurants in the entire country. It's set in a restored 17th-century dwelling on the back lanes behind Xanthos Square, and has been glowingly reviewed in *Vogue, The Athenian, European Travel and Life* and many other international publications. Victor Gouras, a Patmian gourmand who worked at the Tavern on the Green and other top New York restaurants, and his talented wife, Irene, have created the perfect place for that splurge evening. From several superb hors d'oeuvres we recommend Irene's special taramosalata, her gigantes (giant beans) in garlic sauce, spanakopita, or the tasty zucchini fritters. Their varied selection includes a superb rabbit stifado flavored with juniper berries, a tender, moist lemon chicken, a melt-in-your-mouth veal parmigiana, and a Patmian vegetarian specialty, melitzanes me revithia (an eggplant and chickpea casserole). Ask the Gouras family about any fish, steaks, or meat specialties of the day, and don't miss the diples, a honey-dipped dessert.

Plaza Kaffeterion. Main square of Skála. ☎ **0247/31-266.** Snacks/desserts Dr 300–Dr 800 ($1.30–$3.40). No credit cards. Daily 7am–midnight. CONTINENTAL.

Start your day in the lively square across from the post office. The favorites here are a continental breakfast or a hearty English or American breakfast. The Plaza is also popular for early evening drinks.

To Pirofani Fish Taverna. Central paralía of Skála. ☎ **0247/31-539.** Appetizers Dr 450–Dr 2,300 ($1.90–$9.80), main courses Dr 600–Dr 1,200 ($2.55–$5.10), fish Dr 7,500–Dr 8,500 ($31.90–$36.20) a kilo. No credit cards. Daily noon–3pm, 6–11pm. SEAFOOD.

This is our favorite for seafood, next door to the Skála Hotel. Begin with their special tsatziki, have grilled melanouri or barbounia, wine and salad, and it's a Patmian feast. Supplied daily by local fishermen, this is a casual, portside place for a Saturday night fish fry or grilled lobster.

PÁTMOS AFTER DARK

Skála has its bars, music clubs, and discos, such as the popular **Konsolato** and **Music Club 2000,** but we preferred the bar scene in Chóra. **Kafe 1673** is in marvelous building dating from that venerable year. Nearby is the **Stoa Kafe Bar,** another lively watering hole in a restored 300-year-old building. In Chóra head to Aloni Taverna for Greek dancing late Wednesday and Friday nights.

EXPLORING THE ISLAND

Other than the towns of Skála and Chóra, most of Pátmos's limited development has centered around the beach areas. Short-term visitors should allow a day to visit Chóra and the Monastery of St. John; after that, the island's exquisite beaches can be explored by foot (as we prefer) or by caïque excursions from Skála.

CHÓRA

The narrow, twisted lanes that encircle the monastery are lined with two-meter-tall white stucco walls surrounding the private residences of Chóra's elite international set. Even during siesta the ornately carved brown wood doors rarely open to reveal the elegant, stylish homes within. The town is a minimecca for the wealthy who scorn the splashier resort islands: actors, writers, publishers, diplomats, tycoons, and their friends. Chóra is like Bar Harbor, Newport, Malibu, and Positano; generations may pass, but the houses never change hands. Buyers interested in available villas are carefully (and silently) screened by the current residents. However, Chóra's exclusivity rarely affects the day visitor. The town's streets seem refreshingly deserted, even in the high season.

The wealthy who couldn't get into Chóra have built villas "down below," near the beaches. Their presence and their anonymity add the spice and mystique that make Pátmos such a special island.

Mr. Emanouil J. Fillieras, otherwise known as Manios, presides over the gift shop in the Monastery of St. John, but we also discovered that, as a real estate broker, he arranges rentals of private houses (particularly in Chóra) for intermediate- and long-term guests. If you're contemplating spending a few weeks or more on Pátmos (lucky you), and don't mind spending upward of Dr 240,000 ($1,000) a month for a two-bedroom, one-bath villa, give Manios a call at ☎ 0247/31-398 or 0247/31-407.

BEACHES

Pátmos has some very good beaches. The town beach, a sand and pebble patch just 500 meters from the ferryboat pier, offers no privacy; it's usually filled with Greek families who don't mind sunbathing in full view of the clothed tourists who stroll along the waterfront promenade.

The nearby **Melóï Beach,** just a 15-minute walk northeast of Skála, is a little more secluded though not the island's best. At Melóï, virile young Greek men who've come with their tourist girlfriends are likely to be playing cassette tapes of the latest European hits. "Nudity is Forbidden" signs are prominently posted, and the locals often complain when this rule is ignored. However, the beachside **Melóï Restaurant** (☎ 0247/31-888) is a good taverna and a very pleasant place to while away the evening.

It takes a moped, taxi (Dr 500/$2.10), excursion boat (same price as taxi), or sturdy legs (a 10-minute walk from the nearest bus stop) to reach **Agriolivádo Beach,** about 3 kilometers north of Skála. Along this unspoiled, tranquil sandy cove you'll find one taverna and some efficiency apartments.

KAMPOS

The next beach north of Agriolivado is **Ormos Kampos,** a sheltered cove populated with families. Its pale sand and rock beach is shaded by a few pine trees and the water is calm and shallow enough to make it ideal for children. Windsurfing, paragliding, sailing, and canoeing are available at the beach. **Acrogialo** (☎ 0247/32-590) is a popular restaurant on the beach that's not expensive. The Greek food and casual service are equally good, and proprietors Vasilis, Panormitis, and their dog and cat are great hosts.

Kampos village, on the hill above, has about 400 residents and is quite lively in the high season. There are very few rooms-to-let because most travelers rent homes long term, although a local travel agent may be able to find a room if any of the villas become vacant. Four buses a day ply the Skála-Kampos road every day, but most residents hop the frequent, inexpensive beach shuttles for the 20-minute ride.

There are also two small tavernas up the hill on Kampos Square. **Taverna Panagos,** with its rattan chairs and checkered-cotton tablecloths, is a delightful place to enjoy superb village cooking under the shade of the spreading ficus tree. The zucchini with thyme is succulent, and the eggplants in tomato sauce was so good we couldn't sponge the sauce up with our bread fast enough. We also tried the Patmian baby goat in lemon sauce—a treat. Appetizers range from Dr 350 to Dr 700 ($1.50 to $3) and main dishes go for Dr 550 to Dr 1,900 ($2.35 to $8.10). Next door is **Ta Kavourakia,** which is known for its seafood and has live bouzouki music every Saturday evening.

Between the beach and the village is a new, 37-room luxury hotel, the **Pátmos Paradise** (☎ 0247/32-590; fax 0247/32-740), with telephone and minibar in rooms, swimming pool, fitness center, sauna, and tennis and squash courts. We liked the gorgeous scenery from the balconies in every room. In the high season, a double room goes for Dr 31,000 ($132), including breakfast.

GRÍKOS

Four kilometers south of Skála is the resort village of **Gríkos,** where many foreigners have built villas for their summer holidays. As you descend from the coast road toward the shores of Grikou Bay, you'll see the islet of **Tragonísi,** its hills framing the large boulder that sits in the middle of the bay. This is called Kalikatsou, or "cormorant," by the Greeks, because of its appearance at the tip of a narrow, curved spit of land. The natural caves within this rock formation have been enhanced by human hands, leading Patmian author Tom Stone to speculate that monks might have inhabited these caves from the 4th to the 7th centuries, much as they did in Turkey's Cappadocia region.

Gríkos is a long-established resort with a very limited, pleasantly low-key hotel and restaurant scene. There's an okay, family oriented, pebble and sand beach right in town, with pedalos, Windsurfers, sunfish, and canoes for rent. The more private beach is in the cove just south at Petras.

Where to Stay & Dine

Hotel Artemis. Gríkos, 85500 Pátmos. ☎ **0247/31-555.** 24 rms (all with bath). A/C TEL. Dr 9,000 ($38.30) single; Dr 15,000 ($63.80) double (including breakfast). No credit cards.

Built in a traditional style, this place feels cozy. It's furnished simply and decorated with local handicrafts. All rooms have balconies facing the water. There's a TV room and a small bar downstairs adjoining a lush garden, where breakfast is served. If tennis is your sport, then you'll enjoy the well-maintained courts.

Patmian House Apartments. Gríkos 85500 Pátmos. ☎ **0247/31-180.** 8 apts (all with bath). Dr 12,000 ($51) two-bed apt. No credit cards.

The owners of Chóra's chic Patmian House Restaurant maintain eight attached villas in a flowering garden, just a few lanes inland from the beach. Each efficiency apartment has its own cooking facilities and is furnished in a spartan, easy-to-maintain beach house manner.

Petra Apartments. Gríkos 85500 Pátmos. ☎ **0247/31-035.** Fax 0247/32-335 or 01/80-62-697 in Athens. 25 apts (all with bath). TEL. Dr 20,000 ($85.10) apt for two. No credit cards.

The charming Stergiou family takes loving care of our favorite lodging in Gríkos. If the folks aren't home, Christos and his sheepdog Lumpi will happily show you around these stylish apartments, made into one- or two-bedroom units with small kitchenettes, compact bathrooms, and verandas with wonderful views over Gríkos Bay. Each is simply but carefully decorated, with the necessities of home plus some local color. It's a perfect family place, within a five-minute walk from the beach, but with an elegant outdoor bar for the adults. It's popular with Europeans in August, so early reservations are advised.

Stamatis Restaurant. Gríkos Beach. ☎ **0247/31-302.** Appetizers Dr 550–Dr 1,400 ($2.35–$5.95), main courses Dr 900–Dr 1,500 ($3.85–$6.40). No credit cards. Daily 10am–11pm. GREEK.

Eleni is the talented chef at the reliable restaurant located adjacent to the pier. The covered terrace is where diners consume prodigious amounts of fresh mullet, traditional Greek entrées, and drinks, while watching the yachts and Windsurfers.

Xenia Hotel. Gríkos, 85500 Pátmos. ☎ **0247/31-219.** 35 rms (all with bath). TEL. Dr 17,000 ($72.35) single/double (including breakfast). No credit cards.

The older but well-located Xenia is at the north end of the cove. Situated right on the beach, it's a perfect place for a quiet, idyllic seaside holiday. Most of the clean and spacious rooms overlook the bay, and it has a snack bar by the beach.

LAMPI AND PSILI AMMOS

To the north of Skála is **Ormos Lampis,** a beautiful beach famous for its wonderful striped and patterned smooth stones. The deep earth tones of cream, gray, lilac, and coral are particularly striking when wet, and a small bag of Lampi stones will make a wonderful addition to your aquarium back at home or just displayed on your windowsill. Daily excursion caïques that round Cape Geranos take about one hour from Skála, and the round-trip fare is Dr 1,500 ($6.40); one-way taxi fare is currently Dr 1,200 ($5.10). The last stop on the Kampos bus line leaves you about a 15-minute walk away. There are two tavernas on the beach. A saganaki flambe (Dr 700/$3) with a bottle of beer is the perfect beach snack at the **Lampi Beach Taverna** (☎ 0247/ 31-490). Further along the beach is the **Dolphin of Lambi Beach** (☎ 0247/ 31-951), whose mushroom balls with cheese and tomato (Dr 1,000/$4.25) are lip-smacking good. For those who seek quiet and romantic evenings on the beach, they also rent clean and comfortable rooms for Dr 8,000 ($34).

On the other side of the island's southern point is what's universally acclaimed as Pátmos's best beach: the kilometer stretch of **Psilí Ámmos** (Greek for "fine sand"). This protected cove, dotted with shade-giving salt pine trees and tucked in the craggy south coast, provides a special bathing experience. The water is shallow and calm until the afternoon, when breezes can bring waves, truly a rarity in the Aegean. It's only accessible by caïque—day trips from Skála are Dr 1,200 ($5)—or by a moped-worthy road then a hike. Because it's so isolated, nude bathing is as condoned as it ever will be on this orthodox island. There is even a small taverna that opens for great home cooking in the summer.

There are a few less-known beaches that are best reached by caïque. Among these are the twin pebble and sand coves beyond Kámpos, called **Vayiá** and **Livádi Déla Póthitou.** On the southern end of the island, on the opposite coast from Psilí Ámmos at a narrow crossover point between two bays, are two fine, rarely visited beaches near Gríkos, **Órmos Pétras** and **Órmos Diakoftoú.**

Central Greece 10

by Sherry Marker

Central Greece is less defined than much of Greece. Unlike the Peloponnese, clearly set off from the rest of Greece by the Corinth Canal, there's genuine disagreement as to just what is, and is not, part of Central Greece. Still, most Greeks would agree that Central Greece stretches from Boetia and Phocis in the south as far north as Thessaly. Some Greeks hold that Mount Olympus is the southernmost point in Northern Greece, while others consider Olympus to be the northernmost point in Central Greece, which the Greeks call Sterea Ellada. The name Central Greece dates from 1821, when the geographic area was the only section of continental Greece securely liberated from the Turks.

The thing to keep in mind when you set off for Central Greece is that you will be traveling through one of Greece's most varied landscapes. There's the shore along the Gulf of Corinth and the heights of Mount Parnassus. This is where Greece's most famous ancient oracle and most beautiful ancient site, Delphi, is located. There's the city of Thebes, famed for its magnificence in Mycenaean days, today an undistinguished modern town. There's the dusty plain of Thessaly and the extraordinary cliffs and promontories of the monasteries of the Metéora. And there's the lush, wooded mountain range of Mount Pelion, studded with small traditional villages. As if that weren't enough, there are famous ancient battle sites—Thermopylae and Chaironeia—and one of the famous beauty spots of Greece, the Vale of Témpe.

Some suggestions on how to tour Central Greece: If you are setting off from Athens, head via Thebes to Ossios Loukas and Delphi and try to spend two nights in Delphi. Then, head up to the Metéora for another night or two. From there, cross over to Volos and Mount Pelion, where you could easily spend a week relaxing in the mountain villages and taking in some of the best beaches. If you feel like some extra excursions en route, you'll find plenty of suggestions in what follows.

1 Delphi

110 miles (178km) NW of Athens

Delphi is the big enchilada of Greek sites. More than even Olympia, this place has everything: a long and glorious history, spectacular ancient remains, a superb museum, and a heartachingly beautiful location on the slopes of Mount Parnassus. Look up and you see the cliffs and crags of Parnassus; look down and you see Greece's most beautiful plain of olive trees stretching as far as the eye can see toward the town of Itea on the Gulf of Corinth.

Delphi is especially magical in the spring, when there's both snow and wildflowers on Parnassus—and relatively few tourists tramping around the site. But whenever you come here, you'll understand why the ancient Greeks believed that Delphi was the center of the world, the spot Apollo chose as the home of his most famous oracle.

ESSENTIALS

GETTING THERE   By Bus   There are five daily buses to Delphi from the Athens bus station at Odos Liossion 260 (☎ 01/83-17-096).

By Car   Take the Athens-Corinth National Highway 46 miles (74km) west of Athens to the Thebes turnoff. Continue west to Levadia. If you wish to stop at the monastery of Osios Loukas, take the Distomo turnoff and continue 5¹/₂ miles (9km) to Osios Loukas. Return to Distomo and continue via Arachova 16 miles (26km) or the seaside town of Itea 40 miles (65km) to Delphi. The approach from Itea is well worth the time, if you are not in a hurry.

VISITOR INFORMATION   The **area code** for Delphi is **0265.** Most services you may want are on Odos Frederikis. The **tourist office** is open 8am to 3pm and is often open 6 to 8pm in July and August (☎ 0265/89-920). The **post office** is open normal hours but is also sometimes open Sunday from 9am to 1pm. The **OTE** is open 7:30am to 3pm Monday through Saturday and Sunday 9am to 1pm. Both **banks** on Frederikis streets are planning to install ATM machines.

GETTING AROUND   If you can, you should walk everywhere in Delphi. Parking places are at a premium both in the village and at the site. If you have to drive to the site rather than making the five- to 10-minute walk from town, be sure to set off early to get one of the few parking places. Whether you walk or drive, keep an eye out for the enormous tour buses that barrel down the center of the road—and for the not terribly well marked one-way streets in the village.

A LOOK AT THE PAST

Pilgrims came to Delphi from all of the Greek world and much of the non-Greek world to ask Apollo's advice on affairs of state as well as small, personal matters. Unfortunately, the god's words were famously hard to interpret. "Invade and you will destroy a great empire," the oracle told Lydian King Croesus when he asked whether he should go to war with his Persian neighbors. Croesus invaded and destroyed a great empire: his own.

Delphi was also the site of the Pythian games, the most famous festival in Greece after the Olympics. The games commemorated Apollo's triumph over his oracular predecessor here, the snaky Python. Because Apollo was the god of music, the Pythian games had more artistic contests than the Olympic games. When you sit in the theater here, you can imagine the flute and lyre contests, the dances and plays, staged here every four years throughout antiquity to honor Apollo.

Like so many ancient sites, Apollo's sanctuary at Delphi was first neglected, then virtually forgotten, during the Christian era. Kings and generals looted Delphi of its treasures; later, locals hacked up the buildings to build their houses. The modern village of Delphi sat atop the ancient site until this century, when it was relocated just down the road so that archaeologists could help Delphi reclaim its past.

Central Greece

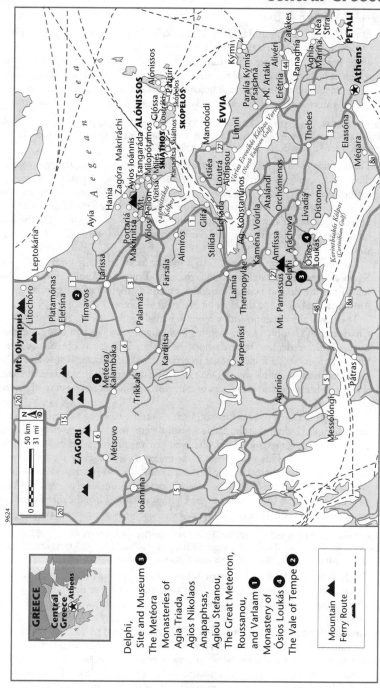

GREECE

Central Greece ★ Athens

Delphi,
Site and Museum ❸

The Metéora
Monasteries of
Agía Triáda,
Agios Nikolaos
Anapaphsas,
Agiou Stefanou,
The Great Meteoron,
Roussanou,
and Varlaam ❶

Monastery of
Ósios Loukás ❹

The Vale of Tempe ❷

▲ Mountain

┄ Ferry Route

WHAT TO SEE & DO

As at Olympia, the most important thing is to begin your visit as early as possible. Once you arrive, the first thing you have to decide is whether to visit the museum or the site first. Here's the main reason to head for the museum: Starting here gives you an overall understanding of the site and you'll certainly be able to visualize many of the important works of art that decorated the sanctuary on your visit. (Both the site and museum are sometimes relatively uncrowded for the hour before they close.)

The Delphi Museum. Delphi. ☎ **0265/82-313.** Admission Dr 1,200 ($5.10). Summer: Monday 11am–7pm, Tues–Fri 8am–7pm, Sat–Sun and holidays 8am–3pm. Winter: Mon 11am–5:30pm, Tues–Fri 8am–5:30pm, Sat–Sun and holidays 8am–3pm.

The first thing you'll see in the museum is a 4th-century B.C. **marble egg,** a copy of the yet older egg (or omphalos) that symbolized Delphi's unique position as the center (or naval) of the world. According to legend, when Zeus wanted to determine the earth's center, he released two eagles from Olympus. When the eagles met over Delphi, Zeus had his answer. You may still see eagles in the sky above Delphi, but more often than not, the large birds overhead are the less distinguished Egyptian vultures.

Each of the museum's 13 rooms has a specific focus: sculpture from the elegant **Siphnian treasury** in one room, finds from the **Temple of Apollo** in two rooms, finds from the Roman period (including a marble sculpture of the epicene youth **Antinous,** the beloved of the emperor Hadrian) in another.

The star of the museum, with a room to himself, is the famous 5th-century B.C. **Charioteer of Delphi,** a larger-than-life bronze figure that was part of a group that originally included a four-horse chariot. The wealthy Sicilian city of Gela dedicated this near monumental work to honor its tyrant Polyzalos's chariot victory here. The Charioteer is an irresistible statue: Don't miss the handsome youth's delicate eyelashes shading wide enamel and stone eyes, or the realistic veins that stand out in his hands and feet.

Although the Charioteer is the star of the collection, he's in good company here. Like Olympia, Delphi was chockablock with superb works of art given by wealthy patrons, such as King Croesus of Lydia, who gave the massive silver bull on display in the museum. And keep an eye out in the museum's last room for the tiny bronze ornament showing Ulysses clinging to the belly of a ram. When Ulysses and his men were trapped in the cave of the ferocious (but nearsighted) one-eyed monster Cyclops, they tied themselves to the bellies of the Cyclops's sheep. When the sheep went out to pasture, they carried the Greek heroes with them out of the cave to safety.

The Sanctuary of Apollo. Castalian Spring and Sanctuary of Athena Pronaia. ☎ **0265/82-313.** Admission Dr 1,200 ($5.10). Open Monday 11am–7pm (11am–5:30pm winter); Tues–Fri 8am–7pm (8am–5:30pm winter), weekends and holidays 8am–3pm.

The Sanctuary of Apollo is immediately beyond and just above the museum and the less well known Sanctuary of Athena is a 10-minute walk past the museum on the lower slopes of Parnassus. The Castalian Spring is between the two sanctuaries. If you can't visit everything here, spend your time at the Sanctuary of Apollo, stroll to the Castalian Spring, and then cross the Delphi-Arachova road to take a peek down at the Sanctuary of Athena. Be sure to buy a site map when you get your ticket to help you orient yourself at this sprawling site, many of whose monuments are unlabeled.

As you enter the Sanctuary of Apollo, you'll be on the marble Sacred Way, the road that visitors here have walked for thousands of years. The road runs uphill past the remains of Roman stoas and a number of Greek treasuries (including the Siphnian and Athenian treasuries, whose sculpture is in the museum). Cities built these small

Delphi Site Plan

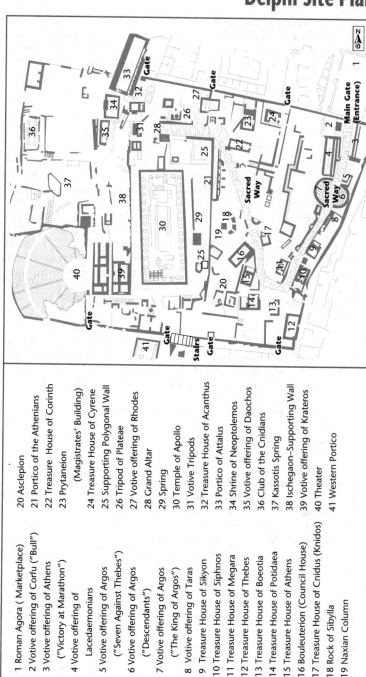

1 Roman Agora (Marketplace)
2 Votive offering of Corfu ("Bull")
3 Votive offering of Athens
   ("Victory at Marathon")
4 Votive offering of
   Lacedaemonians
5 Votive offering of Argos
   ("Seven Against Thebes")
6 Votive offering of Argos
   ("Descendants")
7 Votive offering of Argos
   ("The King of Argos")
8 Votive offering of Taras
9 Treasure House of Sikyon
10 Treasure House of Siphnos
11 Treasure House of Megara
12 Treasure House of Thebes
13 Treasure House of Boeotia
14 Treasure House of Potidaea
15 Treasure House of Athens
16 Bouleuterion (Council House)
17 Treasure House of Cnidus (Knidos)
18 Rock of Sibylla
19 Naxian Column

20 Asclepion
21 Portico of the Athenians
22 Treasure House of Corinth
23 Prytaneion
   (Magistrates' Building)
24 Treasure House of Cyrene
25 Supporting Polygonal Wall
26 Tripod of Plateae
27 Votive offering of Rhodes
28 Grand Altar
29 Spring
30 Temple of Apollo
31 Votive Tripods
32 Treasure House of Acanthus
33 Portico of Attalus
34 Shrine of Neoptolemos
35 Votive offering of Daochos
36 Club of the Cnidians
37 Kassotis Spring
38 Ischegaon–Supporting Wall
39 Votive offering of Krateros
40 Theater
41 Western Portico

temple-like buildings at Delphi for several reasons: to impress their neighbors and to store riches and works of art dedicated to Apollo. Take a close look at the treasury walls: You'll see not only beautiful dry-wall masonry but countless inscriptions. The Greeks were never shy about using the walls of their buildings as bulletin boards.

Alas, so many recent visitors were bent on adding their names to the ancient inscriptions that the Greek archaeological service no longer allows visitors inside the massive 4th-century B.C. Temple of Apollo, which was built after the 7th- and 6th-centuries B.C. temples were destroyed. In antiquity, one of the three Pythian priestess on duty gave voice to Apollo's oracles from a room deep within the temple. That much is known, although the details of what precisely happened here are obscure: Did the priestess sit on a tripod balanced over a chasm, breathing in hallucinatory fumes? Did she chew various herbs, including the laurel leaf sacred to Apollo, until she spoke in tongues, while priests interpreted her sayings? Perhaps wisely, the oracle has kept its secrets.

From the temple, it's a fairly steep uphill climb to the remarkably well-preserved 4th-century B.C. theater and the stadium, which was extensively remodeled by the Romans. Events in the Pythian festival took place in both the stadium and in the theater. In 1927, the Greek poet and eccentric Angelos Sikelianos and his equally eccentric wife, Eva, attempted to revive the ancient contests here (see the Sikelianos Museum, below). Today, the theater and stadium are used most summers for the Festival of Delphi, which, on occasion, has featured exceptionally unclassical pop music.

Keep your ticket as you leave the Sanctuary of Apollo and head along the Arakova-Delphi road toward the **Sanctuary of Athena** (also called the **Marmaria**, which simply refers to all the marble found here). En route, you'll pass the famous Castalian spring, where Apollo planted a laurel he brought here from the Vale of Témpe. Above are the rose-colored cliffs known as the **Phaedriades** (the Bright Ones), famous for the way that they reflect the sun's rays.

Drinking from the **Castalian Spring** inspired legions of poets in antiquity; at the time of our visit, poets had to find their inspiration elsewhere, as the spring was off limits to allow repairs to the Roman fountain facade. Poets be warned: Once an antiquity is closed in Greece, it often stays closed quite a while.

North of the Castalian spring, a path descends from the main road to the **Sanctuary of Athena,** the goddess of wisdom who shared the honors at Delphi with Apollo. As the remains here are quite fragmentary, except for the large 4th-century B.C. **gymnasium,** you may chose simply to wander about and enjoy the site without trying too hard to figure out what's what. The round 4th-century **tholos** with its three graceful standing Doric columns is easy to spot, although no one knows why this building was built, why it was so lavishly decorated—or what went on inside. Again, the oracle keeps its secrets.

The Angelos and Eva Sikelianos Museum. Admission Dr 200 (85¢). Open Wed–Mon 8:30am–3pm.

The road that leads steeply uphill through the village of Delphi ends at the handsome stone and brick Sikelianos home, now a museum commemorating the work of the Greek poet Sikelianos and his American wife, Eva. An artist, writer and, ultimately, costume designer, Eva helped her husband to stage Greek tragedies in Delphi's theater in the 1920s and 1930s. The couple's attempts to revive the Pythian games was not long-lived, but their desire to make use of Greece's ancient theaters had lasting effects, as all who have seen plays performed in the theater at Epidaurus know. This museum is a pleasant place to spend an hour and see Sikelianos's manuscripts and the beautiful costumes Eva designed. Few tourists visit this elegant home with spectacular views from most windows, cozy fireplaces, and the best bathroom in town.

SHOPPING IN DELPHI

Delphi used to be a good place to get nice gold jewelry, hand-loomed rugs, and antiques. At the time of our visit, most of the better shops were closed, one hopes temporarily. Still, along the main street, you'll be able to get all you need in the way of postcards, groceries, and souvenirs.

WHERE TO STAY

There's no shortage of hotels in Delphi and you can usually get a room here even in July or August. Still, if you want a room in a specific price category (or with a view), it's best to make a reservation. Finally, consider staying in nearby Arachova, where the hotels are usually less crowded and the restaurants are better (see below for Excursion to Arachova).

Amalia Hotel. Signposted on the Delphi-Itea Road. ☎ **0265/82-101.** Fax 0265/82-290. 184 Rooms. TEL. Double Dr 32,000 ($136.20). Rates include breakfast. AE, MC, V.

Like all the Amalia Hotels, the Delphi Amalia has all the creature comforts: swimming pool, several shops, restaurants, and a vast lobby. The Amalia is outside town, above the Delphi-Itea road, so you may not want to stay here unless you have a car. Most of the bedrooms face each other across a generous garden; nonetheless, when several tour groups are in residence, you are aware that you are not alone here.

Castalia Hotel. Vasileos Pavlou and Frederikis 13. ☎ **0265/82-205.** 26 rooms. TEL. Double Dr 17,250 ($73.40). Rates include breakfast. AE, DC, MC, V. Usually closed weekdays in January and February.

The Castalia, on Delphi's main street, has been here since 1938, but was completely remodeled in 1986. Actually, it looks more "traditional" now than it did originally, with attractive projecting balconies, a white stucco facade, and some nice touches (embroideries, hand-loomed rugs) in the bedrooms. The back bedrooms have fine views over the olive plain. If the Castalia is full, the Maniatis family may suggest that you try their other hotel, the Frederikis, at 38 Pavlou and Frederikis.

Ⓢ **Hotel Varonos.** Pavlou and Frederikis 27. ☎ **0265/82-345.** 9 rooms. Dr 9,200 ($39.15). AE, MC, V.

This small, family owned hotel has very clean, spare bedrooms with fine views out over the olive plain. If you can, take in the rooftop view. This is a very welcoming hotel: I once arrived here with an ailing gardenia plant, and the entire family pitched in to make sure that it was well taken care of during my stay.

✪ **Hotel Vouzas.** Pavlou and Frederikis 1. ☎ **0265/82-232.** Fax 0232-82-033. 59 rooms. TEL. TV. Dr 28,750 ($122.35). AE, DC, MC, V.

If you don't mind giving up the swimming pool at the Amalia, this is the place to stay—cozy fireplace in the lobby, spectacular views, and a short walk to everything you've come to see. That said, maybe you could persuade the owners that running a wide band at eye level through the dining room picture window is not very clever. The bedrooms and bathrooms here are very comfortable and the balconies not only have a table and chairs, but a welcoming pot of basil.

WHERE TO DINE

Frankly, we weren't enchanted with any of our meals here; the restaurants seemed desultory at best. Let's hope things improve in the future. Here are some places to eat in Delphi, though. (We're suggesting that you consider eating in Arachova, 5 miles north of Delphi.)

Taverna Vakchos. Odos Apollonos 31. ☎ **0265/82-448.** Main courses Dr 1,000–Dr 2,500 ($4.25–$10.65).

This small taverna gets many of its customers from the Youth Hostel next door. This means that the prices are very reasonable, the clientele casual, and the food basic.

Topiki Gefsi. Odos Pavlou and Frederikis 19. ☎ **0265/82-480.** Main courses Dr 2,000–Dr 3,200 ($8.50–$13.60). AE, DC, MC, V.

This large restaurant on the main street has a good view and reasonably good food. Unfortunately, as with most restaurants here, the staff is pretty sure that they'll never see you again and the service is consequently haphazard. That said, the stuffed vine leaves are quite good, and there are sometimes interesting stews on the menu. A guitar and piano duo sometimes appears in the evening.

SIDE TRIPS FROM DELPHI
ARACHOVA
6 miles (10km) N of Delphi

The mountain village of Arachova clings to Mount Parnassus some 950 meters above sea level. Arachova is famous for its hand-loomed rugs, including fluffy *flokakia, tagari* bags, and blankets. When several tour buses stop here during the daytime, this tiny village can be seriously crowded. Don't despair: Try to come back in the evening, when the shops are still open and the cafes and restaurants give you a chance to escape from the tourist world of Delphi to the village world of Greece. There's usually an energetic evening volta (stroll) on main street and if you climb the steep stairs to the upper town, you'll find yourself on quiet neighborhood streets, where children play and families sit out in front of their homes.

On the main street, have a look at the weavings in Georgia Charitou's shop **Anemi** (☎ 0267/31-701), which also has some nice reproductions of antiques. **Katina Panagakou** (☎ 0267-31-743) also has examples of local crafts.

For lunch or dinner here, try the **Taverna Karathanassi** by the coffee shops in the main street square with the lovely freshwater springs. You'll have simple family fare, served by the Karathanassi family; expect to pay about $10 for dinner. The nearby **Taverna Dasargyri,** which specializes in delicious koukouretsi (stuffed entrails), loukanika (sausages), and grills often has an almost entirely local crowd; dinner again about $10.

If you want to stay in Arachova, the **Xenia Hotel** (☎ **0267/31-230;** fax 0267/32-175) in town, with 43 rooms, each with a balcony, has doubles at Dr 15,000 ($63.80). The very pleasant **Best Western Anemolia** (☎ **0267/31-640**), with 52 rooms, on a hill just outside Arachova above the Delphi road, charges Dr 15,000 ($63.85) for a double Sunday to Thursday, Dr 23,000 ($97.90) a night for a Friday to Saturday stay, and Dr 26,000 ($110.65) for Saturday. Both these hotels are usually full winter weekends when Greeks flock here to ski Parnassus.

PARNASSUS
Parnassus is an odd mountain: It's difficult to see its peaks from either Delphi or Arachova, although if you approach from the north, you'll have fine views of the twin summits.

The good news is that you can drive the 27 kilometers from Arachova to the **ski resort at Fterolaki** 2,253 meters up Mount Parnassus in about an hour. The bad news is that the road and several incipient hamlets of ski lodges built by Greeks who vacation here are spoiling the mountain's isolation and much of its beauty. If you drive to Fterolaki in summer, don't expect to find any of the cafes and restaurants open. In winter, of course, things are livelier, with a dozen ski runs, several small shops, and a cafeteria (☎ 0234/22-689).

If you want to hike Parnassus, there are two possibilities: You can head uphill in Delphi past the Sikelianos house and keep going. Four hours will bring you to the upland meadows known as the Plateau of Livadi where shepherds traditionally pasture their flocks. As always in the mountains, it's not a good idea to make such an excursion alone. If you plan to continue on past the meadows to the Corcyrian Cave (known locally as Sarantavli, or "Forty Rooms"), where Pan and the Nymphs once were thought to live, or to the summits, you should check on conditions locally or with the **Hellenic Mountaineering Club** in Athens (☎ **01/32-34-555**). It's also possible to begin your ascent from Arachova, where you can get directions locally.

THE MONASTERY OF OSIOS LOUKAS

You'll probably want to see Osios Loukas en route to or from Delphi, although you could do the 60-mile round trip via Arachova as a day excursion. If you go to Osios Loukas via Levadia, pause at **Schiste** (Triodos), where three roads cross. This is the spot where the ancients believed that Oedipus unknowingly slew his father. Things got worse: Still unknowing, he married his mother and brought down tragedy on himself and his descendants.

Osios Loukas (the Monastery of Saint Luke) is a spectacular church and monastery founded in the 10th century, with much of what you see dating from at least the 11th century. This is not just a tourist destination: Devout Greek Orthodox visitors consider this a holy spot, something to keep in mind during your visit. This is not the place for sleeveless shirts, shorts, or a casual attitude toward the icons or toward the tomb of Saint Luke.

Osios Loukas is a lavishly decorated complex: Not just brick but a wide variety of different jewel-like polychrome marbles were used in the buildings. Along with the mosaics at Daphne, outside Athens, and the splendid churches of Thessaloniki, Osios Loukas's mosaics are among the finest in Greece. If you are lucky enough to be here when the **Katholikon (Main Church)** isn't too crowded, let yourself enjoy the changing light and shadow as it plays on the marbles and mosaics. Then head over to the smaller **church of the Theotokos (Mother of God),** with its lovely mosaic floor. If you have time left over, sit in the courtyard and imagine what Osios Loukas would have been like when hundreds, not today's handful, of monks lived and worshipped here.

2 Thebes

53 miles (87km) W of Athens off the Athens-Corinth National Highway

Thebes, which Homer called "seven-gated," was one of the most important Mycenaean settlements in Greece. The Athenian dramatist Agamemnon commemorated Thebes in his play *Seven Against Thebes,* and the poet Pindar was born here. When Alexander the Great captured Thebes in 336 B.C., he leveled the town, sparing only Pindar's birthplace.

Unfortunately, several 20th-century earthquakes have also leveled a good deal of Thebes, and the new city, though energetic, is not charming. If you're pressed for time, you might give Thebes a miss altogether, although the Archaeological Museum has a fine collection. There's no good hotel here, and several really down-at-the-heels ones, so we don't recommend staying here. As for food, you won't starve, but if you find a superior restaurant, please let us know. We haven't, despite many attempts.

ESSENTIALS

GETTING THERE   **By Car**   The turnoff for Thebes, just after Eleusis, is signposted on the National Highway. Allow two hours from Athens, due to heavy traffic and road works. It's also possible to reach Thebes by taking the Athens-Salonika highway north toward Lamia and taking the turnoff for Thebes.

By Bus   There are frequent buses from Athens, departing at Odos Liossion 260 (☎ 01/83-17-096), to Thebes, arriving at the bus station on Epaminondou Street in the center of Thebes (☎ 0262/275-13).

FAST FACTS   The **area code** for Thebes is **0262.** The **Post Office, OTE, Police (0262/28-551),** and several **banks** are on the main square.

WHAT TO SEE & DO

The Archaeological Museum. Odos Pindararou. ☎ **0262/27-913.** Admission Dr 500 ($2.15). Monday–Saturday 8:30am–3pm; Sunday 9am–2pm. Closed Tuesdays.

There's only one thing to detain you in Thebes: The Archaeological Museum, which is clearly signposted. If you've come by car, try to park on one of the side streets by the museum, which has a Frankish tower in its garden. Although the museum has a wide range of **pottery, inscriptions,** and **sculpture,** the **Mycenaean objects** are the highlight of the collection. There are several painted **Mycenaean sarcophagi,** some fine **gold jewelry,** and handsome **body armor.**

3 Two Famous Battlefields: Thermopylae & Chaironeia

THERMOPYLAE

120 miles (194km) N of Athens on the Athens-Thessaloniki highway

If you find yourself on the Athens-Thessaloniki highway, keep an eye out for the larger-than-life-size **statue of the Spartan king Leonidas** about half-way through the 4-mile-long Pass of Thermopylae that snakes between the mountains and the sea. One of the most famous battles in history was fought here in 480 B.C. during the Persian King Xerxes's attempt to conquer Greece. To this day, historians speculate on just how different the world might have been if Xerxes had succeeded, and Greece had become part of the Persian Empire.

When Xerxes invaded Greece in 480 B.C. with perhaps 100,000 men, soldiers from almost every city state in south and central Greece rushed to Thermopylae to try to stop the Persian king's advance. The Greeks might have succeeded in holding the narrow pass of Thermopylae had not a traitor told the Persians of a secret mountain path that allowed them to turn the pass. As Leonidas and his 300-man royal guard stood and fought at Thermopylae, the main Greek force retreated south to regroup and fight another day. When the fighting at Thermopylae was over, Leonidas and his men lay dead, but the Spartan king had earned immortal fame for his heroism.

The name *Thermopylae* (Hot Gates) refers to the warm springs that bubbled here in antiquity, when the pass was considerably narrower than it is now that centuries of silt have built up the seashore. Many of Thermopylae's springs have been partly diverted to spas, such as Kamena Vourla, but unfortunately, overdevelopment has seriously undercut the former charm of the seaside towns near Thermopylae.

CHAIRONEIA
81 miles (132km) NW of Athens on the Athens-Levadhia-Lamia highway

Just north of Levadhia, the Athens-Lamia highway passes **an enormous stone lion** that marks the site of the common grave of the Theban Sacred Band of warriors, who died here in the Battle of Chaironeia in 338 B.C. It was at Chaironeia that Philip of Macedon, with some 30,000 soldiers, defeated the combined forces of both Athens and Thebes and became the most powerful leader in Greece. It was also at Chaironeia that Philip's 18-year-old son Alexander first distinguished himself on the battlefield, when he led the attack against the superbly trained Theban Sacred Band, which fought to the last man. Philip's admiration for the Thebans's courage was such that he allowed them to be buried where they fell on the battlefield.

The lion itself, sitting on its haunches, with a surprisingly benign expression on its face, was erected by Thebes sometime after the battle. With the passing of time, the winds blew soil from the plain almost entirely over the lion. In 1818, two English antiquarians stumbled upon the lion's head and excavations in 1904 and 1905 led to the lion's restoration and re-erection here on the dusty plain of Chaironeia.

4 The Vale Of Tempe
202 miles (326km) N of Athens; 16 miles (27km) N of Larissa

This steep-sided 5-mile gorge between Mounts Olympus and Ossa has been famous since antiquity as a beauty spot. According to legend, this is where Apollo caught a glimpse of the lovely maiden Daphne, bathing in the Peneios River. When Apollo pursued Daphne, she cried out to the gods on nearby Olympus to save her—which they did, by turning her into a laurel tree (*daphne* in Greek). Apollo, who didn't give up easily, then plucked a branch from the daphne tree and planted it at his shrine at Delphi. Thereafter, messengers came to Témpe from Delphi, every nine years to collect laurel for Apollo's temple.

To this day, there are laurel, chestnut, and plane trees growing in the Vale of Témpe. Unfortunately, since virtually all north-south traffic in Greece now passes through the Vale, this is no longer the sylvan spot that was once the haunt of night-ingales. Still, if you're lucky enough to be here off-season, the sound of the gurgling river may be louder than that of touristic footsteps on the suspension bridge over the gorge. The car toll is Dr 500 ($2.15).

Keep an eye out for the remains of the "Kastro tis Oreas" ("Castle of the Beautiful Maiden") on the cliffs above Témpe and the little chapel deep in the gorge. Unfortunately, you won't have any trouble spotting the souvenir stands throughout the Vale.

If you possibly can, take an hour or two to visit the mountaintop village of **Ambelakia,** some 4 miles southeast of the Vale of Témpe. As yet, there are no hotels here, but ask Mr. Zachariadis, owner of the main taverna here, if there are any rooms available at Mr. Machmodies's home (a double around $40).

Ambelakia, whose name means "vineyards" in Greek, is perched amidst old oak trees on Mt. Kissavos. Astonishingly, this tiny village was an important center of cotton and silk production in the 17th century, with offices in far-off London. Today, little remains of Ambelakia's earlier wealth, but what does remain is well worth a visit: the handsome 19th-century **Schwartz House.** The Schwartz brothers were two of Ambelakia's wealthiest merchants and their handsome wooden house, with its overhanging balconies and elaborately frescoed interiors, is an absolute delight. Admission: Dr 800 ($3.40). Open somewhat unpredictably, but usually 9am–2pm.

The Wildflowers of Greece

Every spring, the arid Greek countryside is carpeted with a staggering variety of wildflowers. Small wonder that one of the oldest Greek poems, *The Homeric Hymn to Demeter,* celebrates meadows blooming with "roses, crocuses, lovely violets, irises and hyacinth and narcissus." High on the Pindus Mountains of Northern Greece shrub roses bloom, there are poppies as far as the eye can see on the dusty plain of Thessaly, and the wild iris flourishes on seashores deep in the Peloponnese. Even more astonishingly, poppies and oleanders continue to bloom on hillsides and even grow from tiny cracks in the marble blocks of fallen temples during the hottest summer months.

Greeks call almost all wildflowers just that—agria louloudia—and don't usually bother with specific names, although they do call the wild carnation *agriogarifalo.* The ancient Greeks thought that this little pink, red, or white flower was Zeus's particular favorite, just as the laurel was beloved of Apollo.

Like many Greek flowers, the more humble broom plant, whose vibrant yellow blossoms scent much of Greece each spring, is both beautiful and useful: After the broom blooms, its stalks are gathered and made into the brooms that you'll see being used throughout Greece. After the orchidlike caper flowers, the capers are gathered, pickled, and used in salads, along with the dried flowers of the richly scented herb oregano, whose distinctive taste makes Greek salads so unmistakably Greek.

5 Mount Olympus

241 miles (390km) N of Athens; 43 miles (70km) N of Larissa

Greece's most famous mountain range, home of the Olympian gods, towers above the plains of Thessaly and Macedonia reaching 9,751 feet (2,972m). From a distance, it's almost impossible to pick out Olympus's summit, Mykitas, nicknamed the "throne of Zeus," although the massive, gnarled, snow-capped range is often visible from Thessaloniki.

The first recorded successful ascent of the summit was in 1913, when two Swiss mountaineers with a local guide made it to the top. For such an imposing mountain, Olympus is surprisingly easy to climb, in large part because so many people since 1913 have climbed it. Consequently, there are a number of well-marked paths to the summit and shelters at Stavros (944 meters) and Spilios Agapitos (2,100 meters), where climbers can rest or even spend the night. In summer, these paths can be very heavily trafficked, with some elegant Greek women making the ascent in high heels.

Still, Olympus is a serious mountain and no one should attempt it alone. As always in the mountains, weather conditions can change for the worse without warning. Well into May, severe snow storms are not uncommon on the heights of Olympus—which helps to explain why the area has been developed in recent years as a ski resort.

ESSENTIALS

GETTING THERE   By Bus   Four buses that stop at Litochoro run daily from Athens to Katerini; seven daily buses run from Athens to Larissa, from which there is frequent service to Litochoro. All buses leave Athens from the station at Odos Liossion 260 (☎ **01/83-17-059**).

By Car Take the Litochoro exit on the Athens-Salonika highway.

By Train There are frequent daily trains from Athens to Larissa, however, the train trip takes longer than the bus.

VISITOR INFORMATION The **area code** for Litochoro is **0352.** The **Greek Mountaineering Club (GMC)** can be reached at **01/32-34-555** in Athens, 031/278-288 in Thessaloniki, or 0352-81-944 in Litochoro. The GMC can give you information on conditions on Olympus, which is usually climbable from June 1 through October 1, and they'll let you know whether you can just turn up, or need a reservation, at one of their overnight shelters. The **Spilios Agapitos** refuge can be reached at 0352/81-800; rates are rather flexible, but inexpensive.

CLIMBING MOUNT OLYMPUS

If you plan to climb Olympus, here are some suggestions. Purists will want to begin the ascent at the rapidly developing **ski resort of Litochoro,** while others may prefer to drive from Litochoro as far as Priona (11 miles/7km) and begin their climb there. On foot, it takes about four hours from Litochoro to Priona; by car, it's only an hour, but seems longer, due to the evil, twisting road. Fortunately, there's a small cafe at Priona, where you can reward yourself with a decent meal, or even a stiff drink.

From Priona, it's a two-hour climb, much of it over slippery schist slopes and knobby limestone outcroppings, to the **shelter at Spilios Agapitos.** If you don't mind communal quarters, this is the place to spend the night, especially since bedding and meals are both available. Most climbers begin the final two- to three-hour ascent at dawn and then do the entire descent, arriving back in Litochoro before dusk. The **Monastery of Agios Dionysios,** not far from Spilios Agapitos, is a good place to break your downward trek and enjoy the views. The monastery was destroyed by the Germans during World War II, but is now being rebuilt.

6 The Metéora

Kalambaka is 220 miles (356km) NW of Athens; the circuit of the Metéora monasteries is approximately 15 miles (25km)

As you drive across the plain of Thessaly, which can seem endless on a summer's day, you'll suddenly see a cluster of gnarled black rocks rising out of the plain. Some travelers have compared these crags to the mountains of the moon, but the fact is that the rock formations of the Metéora (the word means "in midair") are unique. Many geographers speculate that some 30 million years ago, all Thessaly was a vast inland sea; when the sea receded, sweeping the topsoil along, only rock formations were left behind. Over the millennia, the Peneios River and the wind carved the rock into the weird, twisted shapes that now rise some 984 feet (300m) above the plain. The Metéora is especially stunning in winter, when the Pindos range is capped with snow.

When you get closer to the Metéora and see that these sheer, slippery, seemingly unscalable rocks are topped with large monasteries, you'll probably find yourself asking two questions: *Why* did monks settle here and *how* did they build anything larger than a hut on the rocks? Small wonder that many monks believe that Saint Athanasios, founder of the first monastery here, the Great Meteron (Monastery of the Transfiguration), did not scale the rock, but was carried there by an eagle.

The first monks who came here were probably 10th-century ascetics who scaled the rocks, lived as hermits in caves, and spent their days in prayer and meditation. In fact, the word *monk* comes from the Greek for "alone." Over the centuries, more and more hermits and monks seeking to lead the solitary life made their way to the

Metéora, until by the 14th century, there were enough monks here for Saint Athanasios to found the Great Meteoron. While some monks continued to live alone and pursue the solitary religious life called "idiorrhythmic," others chose to live together and follow the cenobitic, or communal, life.

By 1500, there were 24 monasteries here, of which six—the Great Meteoron, Varlaam, Rousanou, Agia Triada, Agios Nikolaos Anapaphsas and Agiou Stefanou—are still inhabited and welcome visitors. Visitors, that is, who dress properly: long-sleeved shirts and skirts for women, slacks and shirts for men.

Visiting the Metéora is not recommended for those suffering from acrophobia, or any who might find it difficult to climb steep flights of stairs cut in the rock face. Still, even these vertiginous stepped paths are an improvement over what earlier travelers had to endure. When the English traveler Leake visited here in the 19th century, he was ferried up to the Great Meteoron in a net attached by a slender rope to a winch. Leake later wrote that, "Visitors' morale was not helped by persistent rumors that the monks only replaced the homemade ropes which held the nets when they broke—usually in mid air!"

ESSENTIALS

GETTING THERE   By Train   There are seven daily trains from Athens's Larissa station (☎ **01/82-13-882**) to the Kalambaka station (☎ **0432/22-451**). Allow at least eight hours for the Athens-Kalambaka trip.

By Bus   There are seven daily buses to Trikkala from the Athens terminal at Odos Liossion 260 (☎ **01/83-11-434**). Allow at least eight hours for the Athens-Kalambaka trip. There are frequent buses from Trikkala to Kalambaka. Several buses a day travel connect Kalambaka and the Metéora monasteries.

By Car   From Athens, take the Athens-Thessaloniki highway north to Lamia; from Lamia, take the highway northwest to Kalambaka. From Delphi, take the Lamia-Karditsa-Trikkala-Kalambaka highway north. Allow at least six hours for the Athens-Kalambaka trip.

VISITOR INFORMATION   The **area code** is **0432**. The **Police** (☎ **0432/22-109**) are near the bus station on Chatzipetrou Street. The **OTE** is signposted on the road out of Kalambaka to Metéora. The **post office** is signposted off the main square, where there are several banks.

GETTING AROUND   If you don't have a car, you may want to hire a taxi to visit the Metéora monasteries. Expect to pay about Dr 10,000 ($42.55) to visit the six monasteries usually open to the public. Your driver will wait while you visit each monastery and probably serve as a guide. Be sure you are in agreement as to how long you will have at each monastery; most drivers are content to wait 30 minutes at each monastery. If you want to make a longer visit, be sure to make this clear when you negotiate the fee.

WHAT TO SEE & DO

The road from Kalambaka through the Metéora takes you past Agios Nikolaos, Roussanou, the Grand Meteron, Varlaam, Agia Triada, and Agios Stephanos. If you only have time to visit one monastery, it should be the **Grand Meteoron.** Try to allow time for a leisurely visit here, so that you can chat with the monks and enjoy the stunning views through the forest of rocks from monastery to monastery. You'll find souvenir stands and be able to buy bottled water or soft drinks on sale outside each monastery.

We've listed the phone numbers for the monasteries, but don't be surprised if no one answers: Telephones and the monastic life are not really compatible. Also don't be surprised if you find one or more of the monasteries closed.

After visiting the monasteries of the Metéora, you may find it a relief to know that there's only one church to see back in Kalembaka: the 12th-century **Cathedral of the Dormition of the Virgin,** which is often locked. If it's open, take a look at the frescoes, which date from the 12th to the 16th centuries. You might also keep an eye out for the ancient marble blocks and column drums that the builders of this church pilfered from the earlier Temple of Apollo that once stood here.

THE METÉORA MONASTERIES

Agios Nikolaos Anapaphsas. ☎ 0432/22-375. Admission Dr 500 ($2.15). Open Daily 9am–6pm; often closed in winter.

This little 14th-century monastery, approached by a relatively gentle path, has splendid **frescoes** by the 16th-century Cretan painter Theophanes the Monk. Don't miss the delightful *Garden of Eden,* with elephants, fantastic beasts, and all manner of fruits and flowers. There's also a nice painting of *The death of Saint Ephraim the Syrian,* which shows scenes from the saint's life, including the pillar that he lived atop for many years in the Syrian desert.

At the time of our visit, there were no monks in residence at Agios Nikolaos and as tour buses often rush past to get to the Great Meteoron, you may find that you have this spot all to yourself.

Roussanou. No telephone. Admission Dr 500 ($2.15). Open daily 9am–1pm and 3–6pm.

Roussanou is relatively accessible, thanks to its new bridge. This 13th-century monastery is now a nunnery, whose inhabitants are usually much more jolly than monks. If the nuns offer you sweets while you sit in the courtyard between the refectory and the octagonal-domed church, be sure to leave a contribution in the church collection box.

The Great Metéoron. ☎ 0432/22-278. Admission Dr 500 ($2.15). Open Wed–Mon 9am–1pm and 3:20–6pm.

Although the Great Meteoron was founded in the 14th century, most of what you see here was built in the 16th century by monks from the Holy Mountain of Mount Athos. The **church** here is especially splendid, in the form of a Greek cross inscribed on a square, topped by a **twelve-sided dome.** Once your eyes get accustomed to the darkness, you'll be able to enjoy the elaborate **frescoes.** If you look up to the dome, you'll see Christ, with the four evangelists, apostles and prophets ranged below, the church fathers by the altar, and the liturgical feasts of the church year along the walls of the nave. There's also a rather bloodcurdling *Last Judgment* and *Punishment of the Damned* in the narthex.

After visiting the church, you may wish to sit a while in the shady courtyard, before visiting the **small museum,** which has a collection of **icons** and **illustrated religious texts.** Don't miss the wine cellar, whose enormous wooden barrels suggest that monastic life is not all prayer and meditation.

Varlaam. ☎ 0432/22-277. Admission Dr 500 ($2.15). Open Sat–Thursday 9am–1pm and 3:30–6pm.

A narrow bridge from the main road runs to this 16th-century monastery, which was named for a hermit who lived here in the 14th century and built a tiny chapel on this promontory. The **chapel,** considerably enlarged and decorated with **frescoes,** is now a side chapel of the main church. Varlaam's founders were two brothers from Ioánnina, who found the monastery and gentle lakeside scenery there too sybaritic for their tastes. Presumably the brothers found the Metéora's harsh landscape more to their liking: According to legend, they had to drive away the monster who lived in a cave on the summit before they could settle here.

The nicest thing about Varlaam is its **garden,** and the monk who sometimes sits here and is willing to chat with visitors.

Agia Triada. ☎ **0432/22-220.** Admission Dr 500 ($2.15). Open Daily 8am–1pm and 3–6pm.

It's not easy to say which of the monasteries has the most spectacular position, but Agia Triada would be near the top of most lists. Perched on a slender pinnacle, reached only by laboring up 140 steps, Agia Triada really does seem to belong to another world. The one monk who lives here is usually glad to see visitors and show them around the **church, refectory,** and **courtyard.** Don't miss **the winch,** for years used to bring supplies and visitors up here. If this monastery looks more familiar to you than the others, perhaps you remember it from the James Bond movie *For Your Eyes Only,* which was filmed here.

Agiou Stefanou.

Founded in the 14th century, Agiou Stefanou, now a nunnery, is almost on the outskirts of Kalambaka. A bridge from the main road makes it easy to get here and the nuns usually make you glad that you came. Sometimes, the nuns sell very reasonably priced embroideries.

Agiou Stefanou was badly damaged both in World War II and in the Civil War that followed. Many priceless frescoes were defaced and others were totally destroyed, but the monastery's most famous relic was saved: the **head of Saint Charalambos,** whose powers include warding off illness. There's also a **small museum** here, with ecclesiastical robes and paraphernalia.

WHERE TO STAY

Amalia. Outside Kalambaka on the Metéora road. ☎ **0432/81-216.** Fax 0432/81-457. 173 rooms, 2 suites. A/C, TV, TEL. Dr 32,200 ($136.20) double (including breakfast buffet); often less off-season. AE, DC, MC, V.

This large new hotel has two restaurants, a shop where you can get postcards and souvenirs, and a pool. Like other Amalia hotels, this one has large bedrooms that are tastefully decorated and bathrooms that have actual shower stalls. In short, this is a very comfortable place to stay, although you may find yourself feeling odd man out if all the other rooms are occupied by tour groups.

Divani Motel. Outside Kalambaka on the Metéora road. ☎ **0432/23-440.** Fax 0432/23-638. 165 Rooms. A/C TV TEL. Dr 20,000–Dr 32,000 ($85.10–$136); often less off-season. AE, DC, MC, V.

Like the Amalia, the slightly cheaper and less fancy Divani has a pool. One thing that may sway you toward the Divani: Rooms at the back have fine views out toward the Metéora.

Edelweiss. 3, El. Venizelou, Kalambaka. ☎ **0432/23-966.** Fax 0432/24-733. 48 rooms. TEL TV. Dr 12,000–Dr 15,000 double ($51–$63.80). MC, V.

If you want to be in Kalambaka itself, this is the place to stay. The Edelweiss is new, low-key but attractive and, a real plus, has a swimming pool. Some rooms have views of the Metéora.

Xenia. Outside Kalambaka on the Metéora road. ☎ **0432/22-327.** 22 Rooms. TEL. Dr 15,500–Dr 20,000 ($66–$85); often substantially cheaper off-season.

This hotel has been here a while and could use some redecoration. Still, it's considerably smaller than the Amalia and Divani hotels and, hence, usually quieter. In addition, the staff usually seems less harried here than at the larger hotels.

WHERE TO DINE

Gertzos. Economou 4, Kalambaka. ☎ **0432/22-316.** Main Courses Dr 1,000–Dr 2,200 ($4.25–$9.35). Usually closed November 1–Easter. GREEK.

This simple taverna has been in Kalambaka for more than 50 years, serving up the standard Greek fare, but also offering a number of dishes reflecting the owners' Greek heritage in Asia Minor. Unless it's so hot—as it can be in the summer here—that you feel you must order a cold drink, try one of the local wines.

Vachos. Plateia Riga Fereou. ☎ **0432/24-678.** Main Courses Dr 925–Dr 2,000 ($3.90–$9.35). Usually closed Nov–Feb. GREEK.

If you want to eat outdoors, head for Vachos, which has a small garden with views toward Metéora. As at Gertzos, the food here is so well prepared that even standard Greek dishes like zucchini and eggplant stuffed with rice and ground meat taste new and different. One plus here: There are usually several tasty sweets on the menu, so you don't have to finish your meal and then search out a Zacheroplasteion (Sweet Shop) for dessert.

7 Pelion

There comes a time on almost every trip when you need to take a brief vacation from your vacation. That's the time to head for Mount Pelion. Although it's possible to drive the circuit of Pelion's most handsome villages in a day, it seems a shame to rush through villages that preserve a sense of yesterday's leisurely pace at today's breakneck speed. If you can, spend a week here, staying in both a mountain and a seaside village. If you can't, try to spend at least one night here at one of the traditional settlement inns. For dinner, try one of the local specialties, such as bean soup (fasolada) or the spicy pepper and sausage stew (spetzofai).

In antiquity, Mount Pelion was thought to be the home of the centaurs, the legendary half-man half-horse creatures who roamed the hills and dales here. Although most centaurs had a reputation for brutish behavior, the wise old centaur Chiron helped to raise Achilles, the great hero of the Trojan war; Jason, who spent so many years searching for the Golden Fleece; and Asclepius, who became the god of medicine.

Presumably the centaurs found Pelion's lush green hills, with their plane, chestnut, and olive trees a pleasant change from the dusty plain of Thessaly. Certainly, generations of visitors have come to Pelion in search of cool breezes in summer and a glimpse, if not of centaurs, of traditional village life. Pelion's villages are among the most beautiful in Greece, shaded by enormous plane trees and watered by gushing springs. The architecture here is special, too: Most of Pelion's churches are low, three-aisled basilicas, often with large porches, rather than more familiar cross-in-square design. Pelion's stone houses, many with elaborately frescoed walls, slate roofs, and overhanging wooden balconies, are among the most handsome in all Greece.

In recent years, the Greek government has begun to worry that pell-mell development might threaten the beauty of Pelion's mountain and seaside villages. Consequently, the entire area now has a strict building code and some villages, such as Vizitsa, have been declared national landmark settlements. With luck these steps will help Pelion to preserve its unique architecture and character. In addition, the

GNTO's has established a number of "traditional settlement guest houses" by renovating abandoned village houses. These small inns give visitors a glimpse of traditional village life—and the visitors provide much-needed income for locals, who might otherwise have had to leave their beloved villages in search of work. Doubles at the traditional settlement inns are less than $100.

ESSENTIALS

GETTING THERE By Train There are seven daily trains from Athens's Stathmos Larissa (☎ **01/36-24-402**) to the Volos Station (☎ **0421/24-056**). The train takes at least six hours.

By Bus There are frequent daily buses to Volos from two Athens terminals: Odos Liossion (☎ **01/22-527**) and the corner of Grigoriou Lambraki and Lachana streets (01/83-17-186). Allow six hours for the trip. There are frequent daily buses from Volos to the Pelion villages. For schedules, check with the Volos bus station on Grigoriou Lambraki Boulevard (☎ **0421/33-254**) or the GNTO office at Plateia Riga Fereou (☎ **0421/23-500**)

By Car Volos is the jumping-off point for touring Pelion, and it's 200 miles (324km) northeast of Athens. To get to Volos from Athens, take the Athens-Thessaloniki highway; allow at least four hours. To reach Pelion from Volos, take Eleftheriou Venizelou Boulevard, which runs from the Volos harbor northeast out of town 3 miles (5km) to Ano Volos, the suburb of Volos that is the first town on Mount Pelion.

VISITOR INFORMATION The **area code** for **Volos** is **0421**. The Pelion villages have several area codes: For **Portaria** and **Makrinitsa**, it's **0421**; for **Milies** and **Vizitsa**, it's **0423**; and for **Zagora**, it's **0426**. The **Greek National Tourist Organization (EOT)** on Riga Fereou Square, Volos, is open Monday through Friday from 7am to 2:30pm (☎ **0421/23-500**). The **Tourist Police** at Odos Oktovriou 179 is open from 7am to 2:30pm (☎ **0421/27-094**). There are several banks on the main square in Volos.

WHAT TO SEE & DO

The thing to do on Pelion is to make haste slowly and enjoy the beauty of this unique region. From Volos, you can head around the peninsula in either a basically clockwise or counterclockwise fashion. Clockwise, this takes you from Volos through Ano Volos, Portaria, Makrinitsa, Hania, Zagora, Horefto, Tsangarada, Milopotamos, Miles, Vitizsa, Kato Lehonia, Agria, and back to Volos. Along the way, you'll probably make lots of stops to see the villages and to take in the spectacular views out over the Pagassitikos Gulf and Aegean. Here are some suggestions on what to watch for on your visit.

If you're very lucky, you may find someone in the cheek-by-jowl villages of **Anakassia** and **Ano Volos**, who will show you the **house with wall paintings** by the well-known early 20th-century primitive painter **Theophilos**, who was something of an eccentric. Long after anyone else, Theophilos dressed in a foustanella, the old Greek national costume of a short, white pleated skirt, long woolen hose, and heavy wooden shoes with turned-up toes—the same costume that the guards outside the Greek Parliament in Athens still wear. If you don't find the vital villager with the key to the house Theophilos decorated, don't despair: You can see examples of his frescoes showing figures from myth and history in the **Museum of Greek Folk Art,** Odos Kydathineon 17, Plaka, Athens.

The village of **Portaria,** although only 8 miles (14km) out of seaside Volos, is 600 meters up on the mountainside. The central square has the fountains and plane trees that make Pelion villages so charming, as well as several cafes where you can sample the local wine and cheese.

Portaria usually has fewer visitors than nearby **Makrinitsa,** whose handsome three-story houses flank the main square, which has fantastic sunset views back toward Volos. The **Diamantis cafe** in the main square and the **Church of Agia Triada** on the hill above the square both have examples of **Theophilos's work.**

If you want to stay in one of Makrinitsa's three small GNTO traditional settlement guest houses, the ✪ **Mousli** (☎ 0421/99-228), the **Xiradaki** (☎ 0421/99-250), and the **Sisilianou** (☎ 0421/99-556), it's a good idea to make a reservation well in advance through one of the hotels or the main office (☎ 0421/99-250). Doubles go for Dr 17,250 ($73.40). Reservations are particularly necessary at Easter and in early May, when traditional celebrations lure many Greeks here. All three of these inns are decorated with local weavings and some old furnishings; the Sisilianou overlooks the main square, while the Mousli and Xiradaki are off the square.

If you're here in summer, there's no reason to stop at **Hania,** which is currently being developed as a **ski center** for the **slopes at Agriolefkes.** In winter, information on ski conditions is available from the **Ski Center** (☎ 0421/96-417).

Zagora, Pelion's largest village, has a splendid 18th-century church with a bell tower that looks almost Alpine and several buildings with the exterior porches that were built to protect people not from the summer sun, but from the winter snow. If you are here in summer, you might want to head south from Zagora to the **fine beaches** at **Agios Ioannis** or **Milopotamos,** before continuing on to the villages of Milies and Vizitsa.

Milies has a splendid history. During the long years of the Turkish occupation, the school here (which you can still see today) helped to preserve Greek learning and culture. That tradition is continued today in Milies at the **small folk museum,** on the second floor of the Town Hall. Photographs, tools, household objects, and mementos from the Greek War of Independence give a glimpse of life in old Milies. Several books on Milies and Pelion in both English and Greek, as well as posters and postcards, are usually on sale here. The museum is usually open Tuesday through Sunday from 10am to 2pm and is sometimes open other days in the afternoon. Admission is free. An old mansion here is being converted into a GNTO traditional settlement inn.

Vizitsa, like Vathia in the distant Máni peninsula in the Peloponnese, was well on its way to becoming a ghost town when the GNTO began to restore eight houses here as ✪ small inns. Now, there are several simple tavernas in the village, as well as the inevitable souvenir stands. The GNTO office has a small display of local items and sometimes has weavings for sale. You'll probably have to take potluck with which inn you are assigned to, but if you arrive early and case the possibilities, you can lodge a specific request at the local **GNTO office** (☎ 0423/86-373). Doubles cost from Dr 16,100 to Dr 20,000 ($68.50 to $85).

It's hard not to have mixed feelings about what the GNTO has done in Vizitsa, which includes organizing **folk festivals** where traditional crafts are demonstrated. On the one hand, it's very pleasant to stay here and know that you are helping to revitalize a lovely area. On the other hand, it's hard not to worry that Vizitsa may end up being a kind of Greek Colonial Williamsburg: a living museum of outdoor history rather than a true village.

11 The Sporades

by John Bozman

The Sporades (Sporádes, "Strewn" Islands) have no important archaeological remains, so these verdant islands with fragrant pine trees growing down to the edge of golden sand beaches saw few foreign tourists until a couple of decades ago. Such natural charms, however, could not go unnoticed by the Greeks themselves in their desire to escape foreign hordes, and it was only a matter of time until the world became aware of these lovely islands and started beating a path there. Skiáthos, closest to the beautiful Mt. Pelion area and the major port of Volos, was the first to be discovered, developed, and touted. Soon, naturally, there were those looking for the next unspoiled island and the neighboring islands were put on the map.

The Sporades are no longer the excellent value they once were. Skiáthos and Skópelos are to the Sporades what Mýkonos and Páros are to the Cyclades and Rhodes and Kos are to the Dodecanese—the most popular islands, with excellent beaches, chic boutiques, a cosmopolitan following, and great scenic allure. **Skiáthos** is among the most expensive islands in Greece, rivaling Corfu in other ways as well; during the high season it's horrendously overcrowded, but in the spring and fall it remains a lovely and pleasant place. Skiáthos is well worth a visit, especially by those interested in a beach vacation, good food, and active nightlife.

Skópelos is nearly as expensive as Skiáthos in the high season—but not nearly so sophisticated nor as jaded. Its beaches are fewer and less impressive, but Skópelos town is among the most beautiful ports in Greece.

Alónissos is less developed for tourism and its port, Partitíri, is considered rather homely, but it has many of the attractions of its more famous neighbors, as well as people not yet spoiled by familiarity with too many foreigners.

Skýros, more remote, seems hardly a part of the group, especially as its landscape and architecture are more Cycladic. It too has a few excellent beaches, as well as a colorful local culture, and it remains a good destination for those who want to get away from the crowds.

1 Skiáthos

41 nautical miles (76km) from Volos

Skiáthos remained an isolated agrarian island until the early 1970s. Today it's known as one of the most cosmopolitan and exquisite islands in Greece, and this rapid change has created a few disturbing ripples. The island's inhabitants are eager for tourist bucks, but in general they haven't yet learned that quality and moderation will pay better in the long run. They can sometimes be shockingly ill mannered, and they depend too much on the importation of help, usually from Athens, which doesn't give a fig about the island or its visitors.

Yet Skiáthos retains much of its natural allure, and there is some sophistication, particularly among the foreigners who have been drawn by the island's beauty. For most visitors, the main attraction is the purity of the water and the lovely fine sand beaches. The island boasts of having more than 60, the most famous of which, **Koukounariés,** is considered one of the very best in Greece. If fun for you is crowds of foreigners relishing sun, sand, and sea, you're gonna love the place.

Laláría, on the less-developed north coast, much less accessible and so less crowded, has magnificent rock formations and is even more beautiful. The interior of the island is densely wooded. Within there are several pretty monasteries and the interesting old Kástro. Skiáthos town, sometimes called Hóra, is quite attractive, though it looks more Italian than Greek, with the handsome Boúrtzi fortress on its harbor, elegant shops, flashy nightlife, and excellent restaurants.

If there's any possibility of seeing Skiáthos before or after the period from July 20 to September 20, when the tourist crush is at its worst and the island's population of less than 5,000 is swollen to well over 50,000, you may find it fun and not too terribly expensive. If you don't like it or can't find a room, you can always take a hydrofoil to another, less-crowded destination. If you must visit during the high season, reserve a room well ahead of time and be prepared for the crush.

ESSENTIALS

GETTING THERE   By Plane   Olympic Airways has service daily (twice daily in April and May, five time daily June through September) from Athens; contact their office in Athens (☎ **01/96-16-161**) for information and reservations. Their office on Skiáthos (☎ **0427/22-200**) is on the main street in town. There is presently no bus service between the airport and town; expect to pay Dr 1,500 ($6.40) by taxi.

By Boat   Skiáthos can be reached by either ferryboat (three hours) or hydrofoil (75 minutes) from Volos or Áyios Konstandínos, and there is also ferryboat service from Kými on Évvia (five hours). In the high season, there are four hydrofoils daily from Volos, three from Aghios Konstantinos, and service from Thessaloniki (three hours).

In Athens, **Alkyon Travel,** Odós Akademías 97, near Omónia Square (☎ **01/ 38-43-220** or 01/38-43-221), can arrange bus transportation to Áyios Konstandínos and hydrofoil or ferry tickets.

For hydrofoil information, contact the **Ceres Hydrofoil Joint Service** at Piraeus (☎ 01/453-7107 or 01/453-6107), Skiáthos (☎ 0427/22-018), Áyios Konstandínos (☎ 0235/31-614), Thessaloníki (☎ 031/223-811), or Volos (☎ 0421/39-786) for schedules and details. For ferryboat information, contact the **Nomikos North Aegean Lines** in Volos (☎ 0421/25-688). Ferry tickets can be purchased through several local travel agents. (Skiáthos information is ☎ 0427/22-216 or 0427/22-209.)

Hydrofoils, excursion boats, and ferries dock at the port town of Skiáthos, also called Hóra, on the island's southern coast toward the east end of the island.

VISITOR INFORMATION   The **Mare Nostrum Holidays** Office (☎ **0427/ 21-463** or 0427/21-464; fax 0427/21-793), at Odós Papadiamándis 21, is open from 8am to 10pm daily and books villas, hotels, and rooms, sells tickets to many of the around-the-island, hydrofoil, and beach caïque (skiff) trips, books Olympic flights, exchanges currency, and changes all traveler's checks without commission. Katerina Michail-Craig, the charming managing director who speaks excellent English, is helpful, exceedingly well informed, and has lots of tasteful tips on everything from beaches to restaurants.

GETTING AROUND   By Bus   Skiáthos has public bus service along the south coast of the island from the bus station on the harbor to Koukounariés (Dr 300; $1.25) with stops at the various beaches between. A conductor will ask for your destination and assess the fare after the bus is in progress. Buses run six times daily in April and November; every hour from 9am to 9pm in May and October; every half hour from 8:30am to 10pm in June and September; and every 20 minutes from 8:30am to 2:30pm and 3:30pm to midnight in July and August.

By Car and Moped   Two reliable rental-car agencies are **Creator** at Papadiamándis 8 (☎ **0427/22-385**) and the local **Avis** licensee on the paralía (☎ **0427/21-458;** fax 0427/23-289), run by the friendly Yannis Theofanidis. Expect to pay Dr 16,500 to Dr 21,500 ($70.20 to $91.50) in the high season, somewhat less at other times. Mopeds are available from **K. Dioletta Rent a Car,** on Papadiamándis Street, starting at Dr 3,250 ($13.85) per day.

By Boat   The north coast beaches, adjacent islands, and the historic Kástro are most easily reached by caïque; these smaller vessels post their beach and island tour schedules on signs over the stem and sail frequently from the fishing harbor west of the Boúrtzi fortress. An around-the-island tour that includes stops at Laláría Beach and Kástro will cost about Dr 3,500 ($14.90).

The **Flying Dophin agent,** is right on the paralía, open 7am to 9:30pm; in the high season there are as many as eight high-speed hydrofoils daily to Skópelos and Alónissos and daily excursions to Skýros. Call **0427/22-018** or 0427/22-033 for up-to-date departure schedules. Tickets may be bought at their office or at most travel agencies. **Nomikos Lines** (☎ **0427/22-209** or 0427/22-276), at the base of Papadiamándis Street and the paralía, operates the ferryboats to the other islands.

FAST FACTS: SKIÁTHOS

American Express   Mare Nostrum Holidays at Odós Papadiamándis 21 (☎ 0427/21-463) is open 8am to 10pm daily.

Banks   There are many banks in the town, such as the **National Bank of Greece** on Papadiamándis Street, open Monday through Friday from 8am to 2pm and 7 to 9pm, Sun 9am to noon, closed Saturday.

Emergencies   For medical emergencies contact the **Skiáthos Hospital** (☎ 0427/ 22-040) or the **police** (☎ 0427/21-111).

Maps   Maps of all the Sporades and main towns are available at kiosks and travel agents. There is a good map of the island and town in the free magazine *Summer Skiáthos.*

Olympic Airways   Olympic Airways (☎ 0427/22-200), located on Papadiamándis Street about 200 meters from the port on the right side, is open Monday through Friday from 9am to 4:45pm; closed Saturday and Sunday.

Police   The **police station** (☎ 0427/21-111) is about 400 meters from the harbor on Papadiamándis Street on the left.

Post Office   The **post office** (☎ 0427/2-011) is on Papadiamándis Street, inland from the harbor about 300 meters on the right, and is open from 7:30am to 2pm Monday through Friday, closed Saturday and Sunday; they also exchange money.

Telephone/Telecommunications   The telephone center or **OTE** (☎ 0427/ 22-135) is next door to the post office on Papadiamándis Street, inland from the harbor about 300 meters on the right, and is open from 7:30am to 10pm Monday through Friday, 9am to 2pm and 5 to 10pm Saturday and Sunday.

WHAT TO SEE & DO

Skiáthos is a relatively modern town, built in 1930 on two low-lying hills, then reconstructed after heavy German bombardment during World War II. The handsome **Boúrtzi fortress** jutting out into the middle of the harbor is an islet connected by a broad causeway. Ferries and hydrofoils stop at the port on the right (east) of the fortress, and fishing boats and excursion caïques dock on the left (west). Two-story whitewashed villas with bright red tiled roofs line both sides of the harbor, with the handsome church of **Áyios Nikólaos** dominating the hill on the east side and the larger church of **Tríon Ierarchón** ("Three Archbishops") balances it lower on the west side.

The main street, with car traffic, that leads off the harbor and up through town is named Papadiamándis, after the island's best-known son, Alexándros Papadiamándis, an author who made his fame writing about island life and Greek customs in an idiosyncratic style and vernacular language that defies good translation into other languages. The **Papadiamándis House,** off the main street on the right a couple of blocks in from the port, has been turned into a museum filled with his works and memorabilia; it is open daily from 9:30am to 1pm and 4:30 to 7:30pm, closed Monday. On this busy street you'll also find several banks, the Olympic Airways office, the post office, the Mare Nostrum Holidays Office, the OTE, and the police station.

On the west flank of the harbor (the left side as you disembark the ferry) are several cheerful outdoor cafes, a few traditional small hotels, the excursion caïques for the north coast beaches, adjacent islands, and around-the-island tours, and in the corner, the broad steps leading up to the town's next level. Mounting the stairs above the Oasis Cafe will lead you to **Platía Tríon Ierarchón,** a stone-paved mall around the town's most important church, with many boutiques, bars, and ornate villas around it. The eastern flank is home to many tourist services as well as a few recommended hotels, and beyond it the harbor-front road branches right along the yacht harbor, an important nightlife area in the summer, and left toward the airport.

Skiáthos is most famous for its beaches, and we'll cover the most important ones briefly clockwise from the port. The most popular beaches are west of town along the 12 kilometers of coastal highway. You can rent an umbrella and two chairs at most beaches for about Dr 1,750 ($7.45) per day. The first **Megáli Ámmos**—the sandy strip below the popular group-tour community of Ftélia is so close to town and in such company—is hardly worth mentioning. **Vassílias** is usually also dismissed with a shrug. **Achládias** is said to have been very nice before it was overwhelmed by resorts. **Tzanérias** is thought to be a slight improvement, then further out on the Kalamáki peninsula, south of the highway, **Kanapítsa** begins to excite some interest, especially among those interested in water sports; **Kanapítsa Water-Sport Center** (☎ 0427/21-298) has water and jet skis, windsurfing, air chairs, sailing, and speed boat hire. Scuba divers may want to stop here at the **Dolphin Diving Center** (☎ 0427/22-520) at the big Nostos Hotel.

Across the peninsula, **Vromólimnos** ("Dirty Lake") is fairly attractive and usually relatively uncrowded, perhaps because of its unsavory name and the cloudy (but not polluted) water from which it comes; it offers waterskiing and windsurfing. **Ayía Paraskeví** is highly regarded. **Platánias,** the next major beach, is usually uncrowded, perhaps because the big resort hotels there have their own pools and sundecks. Past the next headland, **Troulos** is one of the prettiest because of its relative isolation, crescent shape, and the islets that guard the small bay. The major road north from the coastal highway here leads to the **Kounístria monastery,** a pretty 17th-century structure containing some beautiful icons, in a lovely spot with a nice taverna. Horseback enthusiasts should note that the **Pinewood Horse Riding Club** is located on this road.

The last bus stop is at the much ballyhooed **Koukounariés.** The bus—usually so packed with barefoot, bikini-clad tourists that it's a wonder it doesn't tip over—chugs uphill past the Pallas Hotel luxury resort. As the bus descends, it winds around the inland waterway, Lake Strofília, and then stops at the edge of a fragrant pine forest. Koukounariés means "pine cones" in Greek, and behind this grove of trees is a kilometer-long stretch of fine gold sand in a half-moon–shaped cove. Tucked into the evergreen fold are some changing rooms, a small snack bar, and the concessionaire for Windsurfers. The beach is extremely crowded with an easy mix of topless sunbathers, families, and singles, all out to polish their suntans. On the far west side of the cove is the island's Soviet-style, spartan Xenia Hotel, presently deserted. (There are many lodgings in the area, but because of the intense mosquito activity and tickytacky construction, we prefer to stay back in town or in a villa.)

Ayía Eléni, a short but scenic walk from the Koukounariés bus stop (the end of the line) west across the tip of the island, is a broad cove popular for windsurfing, because the wind is a bit rougher than the south coast beaches but not nearly as gusty as those on the north. Across the peninsula behind the deserted Xenia Hotel, 15 to 20 minutes of fairly steep grade from the Koukounariés bus stop, is **Banana** (still sometimes called Krássa), which is the island's most fashionable nude beach. It's slightly less crowded than Koukounariés, but with the same sand and pine trees. There's a snack bar or two, and chairs, umbrellas, and Windsurfers and jet skis can be rented. **Little Banana** is presently the gay beach.

Limonáki Xerxes, also called **Mandráki,** north across the tip of the island, a 20-minute walk up the path opposite the Lake Strofília bus stop, is a cove where Xerxes brought in 10 triremes (galleys) to conquer the Hellenic fleet moored at Skiáthos during the Persian Wars. It's pristine and a relatively secluded beach for those who crave a quiet spot. **Elía,** east across the little peninsula, is also quite nice. Both beaches have small refreshment kiosks.

Mégas Asélinos, east along the north coast, a windy beach where free camping has taken root, is linked to the coastal highway via the road that leads to the Kounístria monastery. Continue north when the road forks off to the right toward the monastery. There's also an official campsite and a fairly good taverna. **Mikrós Asélinos,** further east, is smaller and quieter, and you can reach it via a road that leads off to the left just before the monastery. Most of the other north coast beaches are only accessible by boat.

Kástro, the old fortress capital, was built in the 16th century when the island was overrun by the Turks, in its remote and spectacular site for security from pirate raids; it was abandoned shortly after the War of Independence when such measures were no longer necessary. Once joined to firm ground by a drawbridge, it can now be reach by cement stairs. The remains of more than 300 houses and 22 churches have mostly fallen to the sea, but three of the churches, with porcelain plates imbedded in their worn stucco facades, still stand, and the original frescoes of one are still visible. From this citadel prospect there are excellent views to the Kastronísia islet below and the sparkling Aegean. Kástro can be reached on foot, a two-hour hike from the port. Starting out on the uphill path just west of the harbor will take you by the monasteries of **Áyios Fanoúrias, Áyios Dionísios,** and **Áyios Athanássios** to Panayía Kardási, where the road officially ends. You can also reach Kástro by excursion caïque, by mule or donkey tour (available through most travel agencies), by moped via the latest road which runs to the north coast from just south of Ftélia.

Lalária, on the island's northern tip, near Kástro, is to our minds one of the love-liest beaches in Greece. One of its unique qualities is the Trípia Pétra, perforated rock cliffs, that jut out into the sea on both sides of the cove. These have been worn through in time by the wind and the waves to form perfect archways. From the shore these "portholes" frame a sparkling seascape. You can lie on the gleaming white pebbles and admire the neon-blue Aegean and cloudless sky through their rounded openings. The water at Lalária beach is an especially vivid shade of aquamarine because of the highly reflective white pebbles and marble and limestone slabs which coat the sea bottom. The swimming here is excellent, though the undertow can some-times be quite strong. If you swim through the arches against the brisk meltemi winds, you can play with the echo created inside them. Out in the water you can admire the glowing silver-white pebble beach and jagged white cliffs above it. There are many naturally carved caves in the cliff wall that lines the beach, providing pri-vacy or shade for those who've had too much exposure. Lalária can only be reached by caïque excursions from the port; the fare is Dr 4,000 ($17) for an around-the-island trip, which usually includes stops at one or more of the other sights along the north coast.

Skiáthos's north coast is much more rugged and scenically pure, with steep cliffs, pine forests, rocky hills, grottos, and caves.

Three of the island's most spectacular grottos—**Skotiní, Glázia,** and **Halkíni**—are just east of Lalária. Spiliá Skotiní is particularly impressive, a fantastic 20-foot-tall sea cave reached through a narrow crevice, just wide enough for caïques to squeeze through, in the cliff wall. Seagulls drift above you in the cave's cool darkness, while below, fish swim down in the 30-foot subsurface portion. Erosion has created spec-tacular scenery and many sandy coves along the north and east coasts, though none are as beautiful or well sheltered from the meltemi as Lalária beach.

Further along on the eastern peninsula of Poúnda, opposite the islet of Kamíni, Spiliá Kaminári is a huge roofless cave at the water's edge.

There are also two acceptable beaches on the east end of the island. Gray-sand **Mégas Yialós** and **Órmos Xánemos,** which can be reached by car, are both windy, unprotected coves that also suffer from proximity to the airport. Excursion caïques can also take you to the small island of **Tsougriá,** opposite Skiáthos town, where there's a small taverna and more isolated swimming.

If you take the first paved road to the left off the airport road and follow the signs, you can visit the island's most beautiful architectural site, the **Evangelístria monas-tery,** and beyond it on the mule path is the abandoned **Áyios Harálambos monas-tery.** Hikers may want to pick their way down to Lalária or continue west to Kástro. There are mule trips offered by the various travel agencies.

Skiáthos has excellent shopping. Merchandise is by no means cheap, but the quality is high and there is considerable variety. The highlight for Greek crafts and folk art is **Archipelago** (☎ 0427/22-163), adjacent to the Papadiamándis House. This bril-liantly put together space is the work of Marcos and Andrea Botsaris, an erudite couple who are among the premier collectors of folk art in the country. The exquis-ite objects of art and folklore, both old and new, largely come from outside of the Sporades, specifically from Epirus, Macedonia, Thrace, Lésvos, and the Peloponnese, and include costumes, jewelry, sculpture, painting, and all manner of objects.

A good place for clothing is **Aris** (☎ 0427/22-415), Odós Agliánou 4, where Maria Drakou sells bright, unusual dresses, T-shirts, and short, flirty, washable shirts hand painted with lively floral and abstract patterns. **Gallery Castello,** off Papadiamándis Street (☎ 0427/23-100), is run by Maria Vegena, a woman with an eye for the eclectic: Greek jewelry, ceramics, rugs, weavings and an assortment of objects varying from artistic to the everyday, old and new, make up the ever-changing inventory. We especially like Maria's taste in antique silver jewelry as well as weaving from Pelion, Epirus, and Crete. Open daily from 9:30am to 2pm and 6 to 11pm.

Galerie Varsakis (☎ 0427/22-255), on Tríon Ierarchón Square, above the fishing port, has another excellent collection of folk antiques, embroidered bags and linens, rugs from around the world, and other collectibles. We found very reasonably priced gifts, admired the superb antiques, and discovered that Harris, the proprietor, speaks English and is quite an original himself. **Island** (☎ 0427/23-377), on upper Papadiamádis (across from the OTE), is a pleasant surprise in the world of look-alike T-shirt shops; it stocks all-cotton shirts, designed and made in Greece, as well as other casual wear both attractively styled and priced. It's open daily 9:30am to 1:30pm and 5:30 to 10:30pm.

WHERE TO STAY

If you crave the restaurant/shopping/nightlife scene, or you've arrived without reservations at one of the resort communities, we'd recommend setting up a base for exploration in the port town. From here, you can take public buses to the beaches on the south coast or go on caïque excursions to the spectacular north coast. Many families prefer to rent two-to-four-bedroom villas outside of the town or overlook a beach, with only an occasional foray into town.

Between July 20 and September 20 it can be literally impossible to find a room in Skiáthos. If you're traveling at this time of year, try phoning ahead from Athens to book a room, or better still, book your accommodations well before you leave home. Many hotels will accept reservations when a deposit equal to one-third of the proposed rent is wired to them through an Athens bank, or if you book through an agency, is secured by check or credit card. (For those of you who make plans in advance, most of these hotels request that reservations by mail be made two or three months prior to the summer season.) If you're getting off the ferry cold and arrive between 8am and 10pm head to **Mare Nostrum Holidays** (☎ 0427/21-463), up Papadiamándis Street. They'll try to help you secure a place when all else fails.

Most of the "luxury" hotels were thrown up quickly some years ago and have since been managed and maintained poorly, so even if you prefer to stay in a beach resort, we recommend you check into one of the hotels in town and check out the possibilities before you commit to the rental of one of the smaller properties offered by the various agencies. If you do intend to book lodgings through an agency, expect to pay at least Dr 9,000 ($38.30) nightly for a first-class room, Dr 38,500 ($163.85) for a studio, or Dr 80,000 ($340) on up for a fully equipped three-bedroom villa on the beach. Most of these will be located on or near one of the island's popular beach resorts.

All over the hillside above the eastern harbor are several unlicensed "hotels," which are fairly recently constructed rooms to rent. Inquire from passerby when you're hotel hunting and you'll be surprised at which buildings turn out to be lodgings.

One of the most pleasant parts of town is the quiet neighborhood on the hill above the bay at the western end of the port. Numerous private rooms to let can be found on and above the winding stair/street. Take a walk and look for the signs or ask a passerby or neighborhood merchant.

Hotel Akti. Skiáthos, 370 02 Skiáthos. ☎ **0427/22-024.** 14 rms (all with bath). TEL. Dr 13,800 ($58.70) single; Dr 19,300 ($82.15) double. AE, EU, MC, V.

This thoroughly redone hotel has clean and tastefully furnished rooms. It's on the fairly noisy harbor-front street, however, and light sleepers should keep looking.

Hotel Athos. Ring Road, Skiáthos, 370 02 Skiáthos. ☎/fax **0427/22-4777.** 15 rms (all with bath). TEL. Dr 13,800 ($58.70) single; Dr 19,300 ($82.15) double. AE, EU, MC, V.

This hotel, which opened in 1991, is on the bypass road that skirts above the town. It should be especially attractive to those who wish to have ready access to the town without the bustle. The rooms, many facing the sea, are spotlessly clean and an especially good value in the low season.

Ⓢ **Hotel Australia.** Párodos Evangelístrias, Skiáthos, 370 02 Skiáthos. ☎ **0427/22-488.** 16 rms (all with bath). Dr 7,500 ($31.90) single; Dr 13,800 ($58.70) double; Dr 16,000 ($68.10) studio with kitchen. No credit cards.

Turn right off Papadiamándis Street before the post office, then take the first left to find this plain, clean, quiet hotel run by a couple who lived in Australia and speak English quite well. The rooms are sparsely furnished but comfortable, with small balconies, and guests can share the refrigerator.

Hotel Bourtzi. Odós Moraitou 8, Skiáthos, 370 02 Skiáthos. ☎ **0427/21-304.** Fax 0427/23-243. 23 rms (all with bath). MINIBAR TEL. Dr 12,400 ($52.75) single; Dr 12,900 ($54.90) double. No credit cards.

Mostly a group hotel but with a few rooms available to individuals, the Bourtzi Hotel is an attractive hotel in the middle of town. The back, garden-facing rooms are sure to be quieter. The owners also run the nearby 22-room Porthos Hotel. The facilities are quite similar to the Bourtzi, and like it, most rooms are contracted to agencies, but they're worth a try.

Hotel Meltemi. Skiáthos, 370 02 Skiáthos. ☎ **0427/22-493.** Fax 0427/21-294. 18 rms (all with bath). TEL. Dr 15,350 ($65.30) single; Dr 19,200 ($81.70) double (including breakfast). AE, EU, MC, V.

This comfortable modern hotel is on the east side of the harbor across from where the private yachts are moored. Spacious rooms all have private baths, though the front rooms, which face the harbor and have balconies, are noisy. Most rooms are booked by April, but give them a try; try to reserve at least three weeks in advance. Hosts Yorgo and Giuliana Rigas run a very friendly bar out on the waterside.

Hotel Morfo. Odós Anainiou 23, Skiáthos, 370 02 Skiáthos. ☎ **0427/21-737.** Fax 0427/23-222. 17 rms (all with bath). TEL. Dr 16,800 ($71.50) single; Dr 21,000 ($89.35) double (including breakfast). EU, MC, V.

Turn right off the main street at the National Bank, then left at the big plane tree, and find this attractive hotel on your left on a quiet backstreet in the center of town. You enter through a small, well-kept garden into a festively decorated lobby. Guest rooms are just comfortable and tastefully decorated.

Hotel Orsa. Skiáthos, 370 02 Skiáthos. ☎ **0427/22-430.** Fax 0427/21-736. 12 rms (all with bath). TEL. Dr 20,700 ($71.90) double (including breakfast). No credit cards.

One of the most charming small hotels in town is on the western promontory beyond the fishing harbor. To get there, walk down the port west past the fish stalls and Jimmy's Bar, go up two flights of steps and watch for a recessed courtyard on the left, with handsome wrought-iron details. Most of the rooms have windows or balconies overlooking the harbor and the islands beyond. A lovely garden terrace is a perfect place for a tranquil breakfast. Contact **Heliotropio Travel** on the east end of the harbor (fax 0427/21-952) for booking.

ON THE BEACH

Atrium Hotel. Platánias, 370 02 Skiáthos. ☎ **0427/49-345.** Fax 0427/49-444. 75 rms (all with bath). A/C TEL. Dr 52,000 ($221.30) double; Dr 67,700 ($288.10) double (with one meal). AE, EU, MC, V.

This is the handsomest of the "luxury" hotels, as most of them are slabs of concrete, and this one can claim some architectural quality and distinction. It has a beautiful Olympic-size pool on its own spacious plaza high above the Aegean. The public areas are luxuriously furnished with large white leather couches and tasteful touches of antique cabinets and old amphoras. The rooms are fully appointed and very comfortable, with large balconies and grand views. The hotel has a bar and restaurant, and water sports gear is available on the beach. (The hotel is across the road and up the hill from the beach.) The big flaw is a management and staff that knows little about service and manners and cares even less.

Troulos Bay Hotel. Troúlos, 370 02 Skiáthos. ☎ **0427/49-3909** or 0427/21-223. Fax 0427/ 21-791. 43 rms (all with bath). TEL. Dr 21,500 ($91.50) double; Dr 25,200 ($107.25) triple; Dr 28,800 ($122.55) studio. AE, EU, MC, V.

Though it's not exactly luxurious, this is our first choice of beach hotels. It's set in handsomely landscaped and well-kept grounds on the south coast's prettiest little beach. Like most of Skiáthos's hotels, it's mostly in the hands of groups, but it performs even for them, winning Thompson's "small and friendly award" three years in a row. The restaurant serves good food at reasonable prices, and the staff is refreshingly attentive and truly helpful. The rooms are large, attractive, and comfortably furnished; most have a balcony overlooking the gorgeous beach with the lovely wooded islets beyond.

WHERE TO DINE

The harbor and the lanes around Papadiamándis Street are lined with mediocre, overpriced tavernas and cafes. As is the case with most of the overdeveloped tourist resorts, there's a plethora of ice-cream parlors, fast food stands, and minimarkets, but there are also plenty of good and even excellent eateries. **Kypséli,** near the west end of the harbor serves a good English breakfast with eggs and bacon, fresh orange juice, toast, cake, and coffee for Dr 1,400 ($5.95), but an extra cup of coffee will cost you Dr 600 ($2.40). There is a number of attractive, well-regarded places above the west end of the harbor beyond Tríon Ierarchón church. Climb the steps to the left of the church under the awning at To Steki and you'll find **Stamátis Taverna,** recommended for traditional fare; then on the left, **Le Bistro** (which we review below); **Ánemos,** most often suggested by locals for seafood; **La Casa,** with Greek/Italian food; and up on the right, **Chez Julien,** with French cuisine.

✪ **Asprólithos.** Mavroyiáli and Koraí sts. ☎ **0427/23-110.** Reservations recommended. Appetizers Dr 400–Dr 2,750 ($1.70–$11.70); main courses Dr 1,500–Dr 5,500 Drs. ($6.40–$23.40), AE, EU, V. Daily 7pm–1am. GREEK/INTERNATIONAL.

Walk up Papadiamanti Street, a block past the high school, and turn right for a simply superb meal of light, updated taverna fare. You can get a classic moussaka here if you want to play it safe, or try specialties like artichokes and prawns smothered in cheese. Their excellent snapper baked in wine with wild greens is served with thick french fries that have obviously never seen a freezer. The main dining room is dominated by a handsome stone fireplace, and there are also tables outside where you can catch the breeze. An elegant ambience and friendly, attentive service.

Le Bistrot. Odós Martínou. ☎ **0427/21-627.** Reservations recommended. Appetizers Dr 900–Dr 2,750 ($3.85–$11.70); main courses Dr 1,800–Dr 4,800 ($7.65–$20.45). EU, MC, V. Daily 7pm–1am. CONTINENTAL.

This intimate, continental restaurant is easily spotted along with its twin, across the street, which functions as a bar, overlooking the water. Both the bar and the dining room are lovely spaces. The full-course meals are beautifully prepared from their own stocks and sauces. Swordfish, roast pork, and steamed vegetables should be savored slowly, so there will be room for their delicious desserts.

Carnáyio Taverna. Paralía. ☎ **0427/22-868.** Appetizers Dr 900–Dr 2,750 ($3.85–$11.70); main courses Dr 1,500–Dr 4,200 ($6.40–$17.85). No credit cards. Daily 8pm–1am. TAVERNA/ SEAFOOD.

One of the better waterfront tavernas is across from the Alkyon Hotel. It disappointed us during our most recent visit, but our favorites over the years have been exohiko, fish soup, lamb youvetsi, and grilled fish. The garden setting is still special, and if you're there late enough, you might be lucky to see a real round of dancing waiters and diners.

Kampouréli Ouzerí. Paralía. ☎ **0427/21-112.** Appetizers Dr 400–Dr 3,200 ($1.70–$13.60). Noon–1am. GREEK.

This ouzerí, toward the ferries on the waterfront, is one of the most authentic eateries in town, though it caters to a largely nonlocal crowd. You can have the authentic ouzo and octopus combo at Dr 550 ($2.35) or sample their rich supply of cheese pies, fried feta, olives, and other piquant mezedes (hors d'oeuvres).

Taverna Limanákia. Paralía. ☎ **0427/22-835.** Appetizers Dr 400–Dr 1,800 ($1.70–$7.65); main courses Dr 1,350–Dr 4,800 ($5.75–$20.45). MC. Daily 7pm–midnight. TAVERNA/ SEAFOOD.

Very much in the style of its next-door neighbor Carnáyio, the Limanákia serves some of the best taverna and seafood dishes on the waterfront. We vacillate about which of the two we prefer, but we've always come away feeling satisfied after a meal in this reliable eatery.

Taverna Mesóyia. Odós Grigóriou. ☎ **0427/21-440.** Appetizers Dr 600–Dr 1,600 ($2.55–$6.80); main courses Dr 1,000–Dr 2,250 ($4.25–$9.55). No credit cards. Daily 7pm–midnight. TAVERNA.

You'll have a hard time finding the best authentic traditional food in town, as this little taverna is in the midst of the town's most labyrinthine neighborhood, above the Tríon Ierarchón church, but when you find the very attractive Taverna Alexandros, you'll be just a turn or two away. Try the eggplant shoe (*melitzána papoutáki)*, the special chicken, or fresh fish in season. (They are refreshingly straightforward in admitting when something is frozen, as some fish must be at certain times of the year, when it's illegal to catch.)

☉ Stavros Gyros and Souvlaki. Tríon Ierarchón Square. No phone. Main courses Dr 650–Dr 1,325. ($2.75–$5.65). Dinner only 7pm–1am daily. GRILL.

This unassuming souvlaki stand with a green awning to the left of the Varsakis Gallery is one of our favorites in the Sporades. Outside you'll see pine picnic-style tables and a chalkboard menu offering souvlaki and lamb chops. Complement it with a peasant salad with feta, chase it all down with soda, beer, wine, or ouzo, and you'll be ready to tackle some more sights, and at a price that is unknown (to us, at least) in any other part of the island. Delicious and great value.

The Windmill Restaurant. Above Áyios Nikólaos church. ☎ **0427/21-105.** Reservations recommended. Appetizers Dr 1,200–Dr 2,300 ($5.10–$9.80); main courses Dr 1,800–Dr 3,400 ($5.55–$14.45). EU, V. Daily 7–11pm. INTERNATIONAL.

The town's most special dining experience is found at the top of the eastern hill beyond the white church with the clock. You couldn't ask for a better place to enjoy the sunset, and the menu has such distinctive dishes as smoked salmon and prawn filo parcels, spare ribs with barbecue sauce, and demi-spatchcock of chicken with bourbon glaze and chili sauce. Even the deserts are unusual, including lemon and orange terrine with butterscotch sauce and poached pears with red wine toffee glaze, and there are nearly two dozen wines to choose from, including the best from Greece.

SKIÁTHOS AFTER DARK

The **Aegean Festival** presents nightly performances of ancient Greek tragedies and comedies, traditional music and dance, modern dance and theater, and visiting international troupes in the outdoor theater at the **Bourtzi Cultural Center,** on the islet in the harbor, from mid-June until the beginning of October. (The center itself, open daily from 10am to 2pm and 5:30 to 10pm, hosts art exhibits in its interior.) Performances begin at 9:30pm and cost Dr 4,000 ($17), half price for students; call 0427/23-717 for information.

Skiáthos town has lively nightlife, more concentrated on each end of the port—and you might begin your evening with a volta (stroll) along the harbor—around and above Platía Tríon Ierarchón, and in the heart of town, especially along Odós Polytechníou, parallel to the main street and one block to the left (west).

The **Borzoi** (confusingly like Bourtzi), left off the main street, is the oldest club on the island and one of the most easily found, and you may want to check it out several times during the evening, which generally gets livelier toward midnight. Continue past it to find the **Banana Bar** (☎ 0427/21-232), for "surprising dance music," on the right; then the **Admiral Benbow Club,** for something more soulful. Across from the Benbow Club is the flashy **Spartacus,** and next door is the **Kazbar,** which claims to be the Aussie consul-general of Skiáthos and to rock to 3am. At the next intersection south you'll find **Kirki,** which plays jazz and blues, and the **Totem Musik Bar,** which the local young people recommend. **Vengera** (☎ 0427/21-935), also on Polytechníou, plays "real Greek music." **Down Town** (☎ 0427/23-102) plays jazz, rock, folk, and pop and has live music 10pm to midnight Wednesday and Friday.

Back across Papadiamándis Street, just before the post office, along Párados Evangelístrias you can find **Adagio** (☎ 0427/23-102), which is discretely gay and plays classical music and Greek ballads that allow conversation. Wander back down the main street to find **Kentavros Bar,** on the left beyond the Papadiamándis House, which plays heavier rock and roll.

On the east end of the harbor you'll find **Fresh, Cavos,** and **Kalua.** The **BBC Disco,** on the airport road just off the harbor, is said to be a good place for all-night dancing. The **Apothiki Music Hall,** wherever it may be, is said to have some of the best live Greek music.

On the west end of the harbor, **Jimmy's** (☎ 0427/22-816) promises the "getaway feeling." If you like to have videos with your drinks, try the **Oasis Cafe,** where the draft beer is only Dr 400 ($1.70) a stein, and if there's a game of any sort being played they'll have it on the tube. Further along the old harbor, just up the steps on the far side, you'll find the **Jailhouse Cafe,** which plays rock music and has a fun young menu with items like Cajun-style chicken and ribs with barbecue sauce; you can even have breakfast there. **Remezzo,** on the water near the old ship yard, gets rather wild downstairs but has a quieter upstairs if the scene gets too heavy for you.

Movie fans will want to find **Cinema Paradiso** (☎ 0427/23-886 or 0427/21-463), just beyond the ring road, which has two nightly showings of recent films in English, 8:30 and 11pm, Dr 1,500 ($6.40).

2 Skópelos

58 nautical miles (107km) from Volos

It was inevitable that handsomely rugged Skópelos would follow Skiáthos in its development, but it has done so more wisely and at a slower pace. Its beaches are not nearly so numerous or as pretty, but Skópelos town is one of the most beautiful ports in Greece, and the island is richer in vegetation, with wind-swept pines growing down to secluded coves, wide beaches, and terraced cliffs of angled rock slabs. The interior of the island is densely planted with fruit and nut orchards. The plums and almonds from Skópelos are famous and are liberally used in the island's unique cuisine. The coastline, like that of Skiáthos, is punctuated by impressive grottos and bays, and a camera will find frequent use.

ESSENTIALS

GETTING THERE   By Plane   To reach Skópelos by plane, you'll have to fly to nearby Skiáthos and take a hydrofoil or ferry to the northern port of Loutráki (below Glóssa) or the more popular Skópelos town.

By Boat   If you're in Athens, take a boat or hydrofoil from Áyios Konstandínos to Skópelos. **Alkyon Travel,** Odós Akademías 97, near Omónia Square (☎ **01/38-43-220** or 01/38-43-221), can arrange bus transportation to Áyios Konstandínos and hydrofoil or ferry tickets.

From north Greece, depart for Skópelos from Volos, which is closer and offers the option of a quick side trip to the Mt. Pelion region.

From Skiáthos, the ferry to Skópelos takes 90 minutes if you call at Skópelos town, or 45 minutes if stopping first at Glóssa/Loutraki; the fare to both is about Dr 990 ($4.10). Ferry tickets can be purchased at the Nomikos Lines office on the left side coming off the dock. The Ceres hydrofoil takes 15 minutes to Glóssa/Loutráki (four times daily; Dr 1,585/$6.75), and 35 minutes to Skópelos (eight times daily, Dr 1,850/$7.90). From Skiáthos, you can also hop on one of the many excursion boats to Skópelos.

It's possible to catch a regular ferry or hydrofoil from Alónissos to Skópelos (seven times daily; Dr 1,585/$6.75), or ride on one of the excursion boats. Expect to pay a little more on the excursion boats. If they're not full you can sometimes negotiate the price.

There are infrequent connections from Kými to Skópelos. Check with the Skópelos Port Authority (☎ 0424/22-180) for current schedules, as they change frequently. We feel that hydrofoils are worth the extra expense for hopping around the Sporades.

In the port of Skópelos town, hydrofoil tickets can be purchased at the Flying Dolphin agent, **Madro Travel** (☎ **0424/22-300** or 0424/22-145), immediately opposite from the dock; they're open all year and also operate as the local Olympic Airways representative.

VISITOR INFORMATION   The **Municipal Tourist Office** of Skópelos (☎ **0424/323-231**) is located on the waterfront, to the left of the pier as you disembark; it's open daily from 9:30am to 10pm in the high season. They dispense information as well as change money and reserve rooms.

The English-speaking staff at **Skopelorama** (☎ **0424/22-917** or 0424/23-250; fax 0424/23-243) run an excellent travel agency, located next door to the Hotel Eleni on the left (east) end of the port; they're open daily from 9am to 1pm and 5 to 10pm. They can help you find a room, exchange money, offer excursions and provide information; they know the island inside out and are really friendly folk.

Discover Skópelos, by Joanne Bramhall and Aneta Prosser, is a well-written guide of the island with photos and a fold-out map.

GETTING AROUND   By Boat   To visit the more isolated beaches, take one of the large excursion boats that visit more secluded beaches in a day and provide a barbecue lunch. These should cost about Dr 12,500 ($53.20) and should be booked a day in advance in the summer months. Excursion boats operate only in the peak season to Glistéri, Gliphóneri, and Sáres beaches, for about Dr 1,300 ($5.55). From the port of Agnóndas, there are fishing boats traveling to Limnonári, one of the island's better beaches.

By Bus   Skópelos is reasonably well served by public bus, and the bus stop in Skópelos town is on the east end of the port. There are four routes. Buses run the main route every half hour in the high season beginning in Skópelos and making stops at Stáfilos, Agnóndas, Pánormos, the Adrina Beach Hotel, Miliá, Élios, Klíma, Glóssa, and Loutráki. The fare from Skópelos to Glóssa is Dr 600 ($2.55).

By Moped and Car   The most convenient way to see the island is to rent a moped at one of the many shops on the port. The cost should be about Dr 2,800 ($11.90) per day. A Jeep at **Motor Tours** (☎ 0424/22-986), for example, will run around Dr 23,000 ($97.85), including third-party insurance; expect to pay a few thousand drachmas less for a Fiat Panda.

By Taxi   The taxi stand is in the middle of the waterfront, and taxis will provide service to almost any place on the island. Taxis are not metered, and you should negotiate your fare before accepting a ride; a typical fare, from Skópelos to Glossa, runs Dr 5,200 ($22.15).

FAST FACTS   The only **OTE,** or telephone center, on the island is in the middle of the waterfront Skópelos town, and there are also phone booths along the harbor, which require cards that can be purchased at the OTE or kiosks; press "i" for information in English. In Glóssa, Klíma, Moní Evangelístrias, Moní Prodromoú, Agnónda, and Pánormos you can try a kiosk, travel agent, or hotel for telephone service. The **post office,** which is located on the east side of the port, on the road behind the Bar Alegari, is open Monday through Friday from 8am to 2:30pm. The **National Bank of Greece** and the **Commercial Bank** are on the paralía; both are open 8am to 3pm Monday through Thursday, until 1:30pm Friday and 6:30 to 8:30pm Monday through Friday, 10:30am to 2pm Saturday. There's a **police station** in Skópelos town (☎ 0424/22-235). They can help you find a room as well as handle emergencies. There's a **self-service laundry** (☎ 0424/22-602), open daily except Sunday, just down the street from the Adonis Hotel.

WHAT TO SEE & DO

The ferries from Alónissos, Skýros, and Kými and most of the hydrofoils and other boats from Skiáthos dock at both Glóssa/Loutráki and Skópelos. Most boats stop first at Loutráki, a homely little port near the northern end of the west coast, with the more attractive town of Glóssa high above it. We suggest you stay on board for the trip around the northern tip of the island and along the east coast, getting a better sense of why the island's name means "cliff" in Greek, to the island's main harbor, especially if this is your first visit to the island. You'll know why as the boat pulls around the last headland into that huge and nearly perfect C-shaped harbor and you get your first glimpse of Skópelos town rising like a steep amphitheater around the port.

Skópelos town, also called Hóra of course, is one of Greece's greatest architectural treasures, on a par with Hýdra and Sými. The town scales the steep, low hills around the harbor and has the same winding, narrow paths that characterize the more famous Cycladic islands to the south. The town's many churches add much to the fantastic effect. Some of the older buildings are rather Italianate, the similarity enhanced by red tile roofs that replaced the old slate roofs tumbled by an earthquake in 1965. Other houses are of the more stolid Mt. Pelion design, and some are more Macedonian, with colorful wooden balconies. Even the newer buildings have been built in traditional style, so there is a pervasive sense of harmony.

To the right, as you leave the boat, are only a few of the town's 123 churches, which must be something of a record for such a small town. The waterfront is lined with banks, cafes, travel agencies, and the like. Interspersed between these prosaic offerings are some truly regal-looking shade trees. Many of the hotels are on the far left (as you leave the dock) end of the paralía. There are beaches on both sides of the harbor; Gliphóneri (or Áyios Konstandínos) beach, on the north end, is a 15-minute walk away, and there is a mediocre beach stretching south from town. The bus and taxi stand are near a giant plane tree about 200 meters to the left of the dock. Most of the shops and the OTE are up the main street leading off the paralía. The back streets are amazingly convoluted; the best plan is to wander up and get to know a few familiar landmarks.

A walk through the back streets and alleyways will delight almost anyone, and you can't stay lost for long. Flowering plants fill pots, small plots, the precariously overhanging wooden balconies, and even crevices all along the steep meandering streets. Here and there, you'll find an intensively cultivated garden with intricate trellises. A number of the whitewashed houses have had their green and gray slate roofs meticulously reconstructed. Old women sit outside in front of their houses in groups of three and four, knitting and embroidering, the speed of their needles nearly keeping up with their rapid conversation, though they're likely to smile and answer if you greet them. Old men still lead their donkeys up and down the narrow lanes, even as their grandsons wash the family car. Fishing and agriculture are still important sources of income.

Even the town's Venetian Kástro, which overlooks the town, has been whitewashed, so that it looks too new to have been built over an archaic temple of Athena and too serene to have been deemed too formidable for attack by the Turks during the War of Independence.

Once you have the town's architecture, you may be more interested in a visit to the **Folk Art Museum,** near the OTE. (It was being renovated during our most recent visit, but its usual hours are from 10:30am to 1pm and 6 to 11pm daily except Monday.) It is an old house furnished in the traditional style and contains displays of traditional dress, pottery, old photographs and exhibits of local crafts. There's also the new **International Center for Photographic Exhibition,** which will surely be of interest to shutterbugs.

Skópelos has a variety of galleries displaying local photography, ceramics, and jewelry. The Skópelos branch of **Archipelagos** (☎ 0424/23-127) is one of the best of these and can be found facing the waterfront near the bus stop. **To Sinnefo** (no phone) is located in the backstreets, off Velizaríou Street (one of the few named), and specializes in handmade puppets, mobiles, and marionettes. **Nick Rodies** (☎ 0424/22-779), whose gallery is located next door to **Skopelorama,** is from a Skópelos family that has made ceramics for three generations. His elegant black vessels, at once both classical and modern, are among the finest we've found in Greece. The studio is open daily from 9am to 1pm and 5 to 11pm, and credit cards are accepted.

There are five **monasteries** south of town, all strung along a pleasant path that continues south from the beach hotels. The first, **Evangelístra,** was founded by monks from Mt. Athos, but it now serves as a nunnery, and the weavings of its present occupants can be bought at a small shop there; it's open daily from 8am to 1pm and 4 to 7pm. The fortified monastery of **Ayía Bárbara,** now abandoned, contains 15th-century frescoes. **Metamóphosis,** very nearly abandoned, is very much alive on the 6th of August, when the feast of the Metamorphosis is celebrated there. **Prodromoú** is a 30-minute hike further, but it's the handsomest and contains a particularly beautiful iconostasis. **Taxiárchon,** abandoned and overgrown, is at the summit of Mt. Poloúki to the southeast, a hike recommended only to the hardiest and most dedicated.

There is basically only one highway on the island, with short spurs at each significant settlement. It runs south from Skópelos town, then skirts the west coast northwest to Glóssa, then down to Loutráki. The first spur leads off to the left to **Stáfilos,** a popular family beach recommended by locals for a good seafood dinner, which you must order in the morning. It was there that the tomb of the Minoan prince Stáfilos, which contained the sword now in the National Archaeological Museum, was found. About half a kilometer across the headland is **Velanió,** where nude bathing is common.

The next settlement west is **Agnóndas,** named for a local athlete who brought home the gold from the 569 B.C. Olympics, a small fishing village that became a tourist resort despite its lack of a beach. **Limnonári,** a 15-minute walk further west and accessible by caïque in the summer, has a good fine-sand beach in a rather homely and shadeless setting.

The road then turns inland again, through a pine forest, to **Pánormos,** with a sheltered pebble beach, which has become the island's best resort with a number of taverns, restaurants, hotels, and rooms to let, as well as water sports facilities. The road then climbs again toward **Miliá,** which is considered the island's best beach. You will have to walk down about half a kilometer from the bus stop, but you'll find a lovely light gray sand and pebble beach with the island of Dassía opposite and water sport facilities at the **Beach Boys Club** (☎ 0424/33-496). There are also isolated beaches between the two.

The next stop, **Élios,** is a town that was thrown up to shelter the people displaced by the 1965 earthquake. It's become the home of many of the people who operate the resort facilities on the west coast, as well as something of a resort itself. At **Káto Klíma** ("Lower Ladder") the road begins to climb to **Áno Klíma** ("Upper Ladder") on its way to Glóssa.

Glóssa means "Tongue," and that's what the hill on which the town built looks like from the sea. It was constructed during the Turkish occupation and was mostly spared during the earthquake; it remains one of the most Greek and charming towns in the Sporades. There are a number of rooms to let, a good hotel, and a very good taverna here, for those who are tempted to stay overnight. Most of the coastline is craggy, with just a few hard-to-get-to beaches. Among the best places to catch some rays and do a bit of swimming is on the small beach below the picturesque monastery of **Áyios Ioánnis,** east from town, which reminds many of Metéora. (Take food and water with you.) It's a winding 3 kilometers down to **Loutráki,** which has some rooms to let and places to eat, but we don't recommend a stay there.

If you're island-hopping, you might want to take advantage of Skópelos's two ports. The northern port at Loutráki/Glóssa is a short jaunt from Skiáthos, while Skópelos town is closer to Alónissos. Depending on where you've been and where you're going, consider starting at one end of the island, crossing to the other and moving on to the adjoining island.

Continuing in our clockwise course around the island we reach **Glistéri,** which is best reached by caïque from Skópelos town, a small pebbled beach with a nearby olive grove offering some respite from the sun. It's a good bet when the other beaches are overrun in the summer. You can also go by caïque to the grotto at **Tripití,** for the island's best fishing; the little island of **Áyios Yióryios,** which has an abandoned monastery; to **Gliphóneri** (or Áyios Konstandínos), the best beach just to the north of Skópelos town; and **Sáres,** the best beach just south.

The whole of Skópelos's 90 square kilometers is prime for biking, and the interior is still waiting to be explored. There's also horseback riding, sailing (ask at the Skópelos travel agencies), and a number of interesting excursions to be taken from and around the island. Skopelorama (see "Visitor Information," above) operates a fine series of excursions such as monasteries by coach, traditional Skópelos, a walking tour of the town, several cruises, and a day trip to Alónissos.

WHERE TO STAY

Skópelos is nearly as popular as Skiáthos. Because of its increasing flow of tourists, several new hotels have cropped up, especially in Skópelos town and at Pánormos. If you need advice about one of the in-town hotels or pensions or accommodations available in the outer limits, talk to Skopelorama or the officials at the town hall. Be sure to look at a room and agree on a price before accepting anything, or you may be unpleasantly surprised. To make matters confusing, there are few street names in the main, older section of town, so you'll have to ask for directions several times before finding your lodging.

New camping facilities have been constructed 7 kilometers from Skópelos town on the road above Agnóndas Beach. They offer dormitory accommodations with showers for budget prices (still no phone yet).

Hotel Amalia. 370 03 Skópelos. ☎ **0424/22-688** or 0424/22-033. 50 rms (all with bath). TEL. Dr 11,500 ($48.95) single; Dr 19,000 ($80.85) double (including breakfast). AE, EU, MC, V.

This handsome traditional style hotel is on the beach 500 meters from the port. The spacious lobby is attractively decorated in the colorful local style, and the hotel has a good large pool. Rooms are large with rustic-looking furniture. It's largely in the hands of groups but should have some spare rooms in the spring and fall.

Hotel Denise. 370 03 Skópelos. ☎ **0424/22-678.** Fax 0424/22-769. 25 rms (all with bath). A/C MINIBAR TEL. Dr 11,000 ($46.80) single; Dr 17,000 ($72.35) double (including breakfast). EU, MC, V.

One of the best hotels in Skópelos because of its premier location, clean facilities, and swimming pool, the Hotel Denise stands atop the village overlooking the town and commands spectacular views of the harbor and Aegean. The hotel was upgraded during 1991, but it still fits in well with the town's architectural style. Each of the Denise's four stories is ringed by a wide balcony. The rooms have hardwood floors and furniture. View rooms are among the best in town. As the Denise is very popular, before hiking up the steep road, call for a pickup and to check for room availability, or, better yet, reserve in advance.

☺ **Hotel Drosia.** 370 03 Skópelos. ☎ **0424/22-490.** 10 rms (all with bath). Dr 8,300 ($35.30) single; Dr 9,500 ($40.54) double.

This small hotel is next to the Denise, atop the hill overlooking the village. Having exceptional views, the Drosia is of the same vintage as the Denise but with slightly less expensive and well-equipped rooms. All in all, it represents very good value.

Hotel Eleni. 370 03 Skópelos. ☎ **0424/22-393.** 37 rms (all with bath). TEL. Dr 8,600 ($36.60) single; Dr 11,900 ($50.65) double. EU, MC.

The Hotel Eleni is a gracious modern hotel, 100 meters from the waterfront. All its rooms have balconies. Owner Charlie Hatyidrosis returned from the Bronx to build his establishment after many years of operating several pizzerias with his brother in New York.

✪ **Hotel Prince Stafilos.** 370 03 Skópelos. ☎ **0424/22-775** or 0424/23-011. Fax 0424/ 22-825. 70 rms (all with bath). TEL. Dr 19,500 ($83) single; Dr 36,800 ($156.60) double (including breakfast). AE, EU, MC, V.

The handsomest and most traditional hotel on the island is about a kilometer south of town. (They will give you a ride from the ferry dock.) The friendly owner, Pelopidas Tsitsirgos, is also the architect responsible for the hotel's special charm. The lobby is spacious and very attractively decorated with local artifacts. There's a pool, restaurant, and bars. A large buffet breakfast is served.

Hotel Rania. 370 03 Skópelos. ☎ **0424/22-486.** 11 rms (all with bath). TEL. Dr 9,200 ($38.30) single or double.

The Rania is down by the waterside, just beyond and to the left of the larger Amalia. Very simply furnished rooms have balconies and are reasonably well maintained. The Rania is one of the few hotels open year-round.

Pension Andromahi. Odós Velizaríou, 370 03 Skópelos. ☎ **0424/22-941.** 7 rms (all with bath). Dr 9,250 ($39.35) single; Dr 12,750 ($54.25) double. MC, V.

The Andromahi feels like an old-fashioned bed-and-breakfast with many homey touches and painted furniture. Our only hesitation, and it's fairly serious, is that it can be pretty noisy in the late evening. Other than that, this is a gem; open all year.

Pension Katarina. 370 03 Skópelos. ☎ **0424/23-307.** 7 rms (all with bath). Dr 12,500 ($53.20) single/double.

Built in 1991, this attractive pension commands a wonderful view of the town from its south side waterfront perch. We much admired the well-kept rose garden, as well as the attractive lobby and guest quarters. The only downside is that the Katarina is set just a couple of doors from two popular bars. Request a top floor, water-facing view room.

Skópelos Villas. 370 03 Skópelos. ☎ **0424/22-517.** Fax 0424/22-958. 36 units (all with bath). MINIBAR TEL. Dr 26,500 ($112.75) studio; Dr 31,000 ($131.90) apartment. No credit cards.

Each studio or duplex apartment is equipped with kitchen, private bath, and one or two bedrooms. The villas share a common swimming pool, barbecue, and snack bar where breakfast is served. The buildings are tastefully constructed as "traditional island houses." Each villa can comfortably sleep from two to six people.

PÁNORMOS

This pleasant little resort is on a horseshoe-shaped cove, halfway between Skópelos town and Glóssa. Here you'll find more than a thousand beds, several cafeteria-snack bars, and minimarkets. It's recommended as a base, especially as the best hotel on the island (the Adrina Beach Hotel, see below) is just above it. The **Pánormos Travel Office** (☎ 0424/23-380; fax 0424/23-748) is open from 9am to midnight. They have some nice rooms to let; offer telephone/fax services; can change money; rent cars, motorbikes, and speedboats; and arrange tours, including night squid fishing.

Adrina Beach Hotel. Pánormos, 370 03 Skópelos. ☎ **0424/23-373** to 375. (01/68-26-886 in Athens.) Fax 0424/23-372. 55 rms (all with bath). Dr 34,500 ($146.80) double; Dr 38,000 ($161.70) suite (including breakfast). AE, DC, MC, V.

This new traditional-style hotel, 500 meters above Pánormos, is presently the best on the island. Eight handsome units are ranked down the steep slope toward the hotel's private beach. The complex has a big saltwater pool with its own bar, a restaurant, bar, buffet room, spacious sitting areas indoor and out, a playground, and a mini-market. The rooms are spacious and tastefully furnished in pastels, each with its own balcony or veranda.

Affrodite Hotel. Pánormos, 370 03 Skópelos. ☎ **0424/23-150** or 0424/23-151. Fax 0424/23-152. 38 rms (all with bath). Dr 17,250 ($73.40) single; Dr 23,000 ($97.85) double (including breakfast). AE, MC, V.

This new hotel, built in a more modern and sprawling style, is inland across the road from the beach. It has a very nice pool and bar, and the rooms are large and comfortable, with varnished slate floors.

GLÓSSA

There are about 100 rooms to rent in the small town of Glóssa. Expect to pay about Dr 9,000 ($38.30) for single or double occupancy. The best way to find a room is to visit one of the tavernas or shops and inquire about a vacancy. If you can't find a room in Glóssa, you can always take a bus or taxi down to Loutráki and check into a pension by the water or head back to Pánormos.

Hotel Atlantes. Glóssa, 370 03 Skópelos. ☎ **0424/33-223**, 0424/33-756, or 0424/33-767. 10 rms (all with bath). TEL. Dr 7,150 ($30.45) single; Dr 9,250 ($39.35) double. No credit cards.

Owner and host Lee Chocalas, born in Mississippi but raised here, has returned to this island after a 30-year absence to build this comfortable hotel, across from the bus stop. All rooms have balconies looking down on the flower-filled garden or out to sea. If Lee has no room in the inn, ask him or George Antoniou at the Pýthari Shop (☎ 0424/33-077) in town for advice on a room to let.

WHERE TO DINE

There are a number of really good dining options in and around Skópelos town as well as a few well-recommended bars. Locals say that the best seafood can be found at Agnónda, but that you have to order it in the morning.

Anatoli Ouzerí. Skópelos. No telephone. Appetizers Dr 250–Dr 800 ($1.05–$3.40); main courses Dr 1,300–Dr 2,500 ($5.55–$10.65). No credit cards. Summer only 9pm–1am. GREEK.

You'll have quite a climb to reach this diminutive ouzerí high above the town, but we found the food superb, more than justifying the effort. Our meal featured several delicious mezedes (appetizers), including lightly fried green peppers, black-eyed peas with fresh spices, and an exceptional octopus salad. Lucky for you, the Anatoli is largely unknown except by residents or long-term guests, or you couldn't find a seat. If you're in luck, Yórgos Xindáris, the rail-thin proprietor/chef, will play his bouzouki and sing classic rebétika songs, sometimes with accompanists. If you come early or late in the season, bring a sweater.

Crêperie Greca. Skópelos. ☎ **0424/23-310.** Appetizers and main courses Dr 600–Dr 1,500 ($2.55–$6.40). No credit cards. Daily noon–3pm and 7pm–2am. CREPES.

If you like crepes don't miss Crêperie Greca. It's across from the Adonis Hotel, on the sloping street up from the waterfront bus stop. Zucchini and cheese or chicken and mushrooms are satisfying when you're really hungry. For drama, try the flaming fruit and cream crepes, all prepared by the French owner on a tiny burner.

Finikas Taverna and Quzeri. Skópelos. ☎ **0424/23-247.** Appetizers Dr 500–Dr 2,600 ($2.15–$11.05); main courses Dr 1,700–Dr 2,000 ($7.25–$8.50). No credit cards. Daily dinner only 7:30pm–2am. GREEK.

Tucked away in the upper backstreets of Skópelos is a picturesque garden taverna/ ouzeri dominated by a broad leaf palm. The Finikas may offer Skópelos's most romantic setting, perhaps by dint of its isolated location as well as its lovely garden dining area. Among the many fine courses are an excellent ratatouille and pork cooked with prunes and apples, a traditional island specialty.

Karávia Gelateria Cafeteria Snack Bar. Skópelos. ☎ **0424/22-970.** Breakfast Dr 600– Dr 1,000 ($2.55–$4.25); sandwiches Dr 500–Dr 900 ($2.15–$3.85); ice cream Dr 1,000– Dr 1,200 ($4.25–$5.10). No credit cards. Daily 8am–2am. BREAKFAST/SNACKS.

The Karávia with its attractive rattan furniture is the best place on the waterfront for breakfast. Its sandwiches are also good, and the ice cream concoctions are special treats. It's across from the bus stop and behind the World War II monument.

✪ L'Ouzerie Zaína. Platía Plátanos, Skópelos. ☎ **0424/23-310.** Fixed price Dr 5,500 ($23.40) for two. No credit cards. Daily 10:30am–3pm and 7:30pm–2am. FRENCH/GREEK.

The special cuisine prepared at this excellent new place fairly defies description but it's delicious and distinctive. We had a cool cucumber filled with a secret mix; muscles in wine sauce; keftédes (and not just your ordinary meatballs); cabbage rolls; Greco-French grilled chile rellenos; and chilled stuffed tomato. We had white wine, but you can order ouzo or tsipoúra, when it's available. We finished with a tart made with local prunes and walnuts and cognac.

Molos Taverna and Ouzeri. Skópelos. ☎ **0424/22-551.** Appetizers Dr 450–Dr 1,600 ($1.90–$6.80); main courses Dr 1,200–Dr 2,900 ($5.10–$12.35). Daily noon–2:30pm and 6pm– 1am. GREEK.

A local favorite right near the ferry on the paralía. Molos features many specialties, among them stuffed pork with cheese, garlic, and vegetables, abeloúrgos (stuffed chicken with ham, wrapped in grape leaves) and koukiar, a slice of thinly cut veal with eggplant, covered with a béchamel sauce. Molos is open year-round.

Platanos Jazz Bar. Skópelos. No telephone. Appetizers and main courses Dr 600–Dr 1,700 ($2.55–$7.25). No credit cards. Daily 5am–3am. BAR.

For everything from breakfast to a late-night drink, try the jazz pub Platanos. It's beneath the enormous plane tree just to the left of the ferry dock. Breakfast in the summer starts as early as 5 or 6am for ferry passengers, who can serve themselves German dip-style coffee, fruit salad with nuts and yogurt, and fresh-squeezed orange juice, all for Dr 2,000 ($8.50). Platanos is equally pleasant for evening and late-night drinks (expect to pay about Dr 1,200/$5.10). All is accompanied by music from their phenomenal collection of jazz records.

Spiro's Taverna. Skópelos. ☎ **0424/23-146.** Appetizers, main courses Dr 500–Dr 3,000 ($2.15–$12.75). Daily noon–midnight. GREEK.

Spiro's Taverna, to the left as you leave the ferry dock, is often packed with a crowd eager for their spit-roasted chicken. This simple outdoor cafe is popular with locals, expatriates, and travelers alike. It's open throughout the year.

☉ Taverna Koutoúki. Skópelos. ☎ **0424/22-380.** Appetizers Dr 350–Dr 1,100 ($1.50– $4.70); main courses Dr 900–Dr 2,400 ($3.85–$10.20). No credit cards. Daily 5:30pm–1am. GREEK.

You'll find this unpretentious excellent value taverna in a small grapevine-draped garden. The decor is basic, the music is traditional, the service is friendly, and the food is excellent, fresh, and hot. Some of its specialties are beef in a delicious sweet tomato sauce with garlic; meatballs; and pork stuffed with garlic. It's on the main back road, behind the Amalia Hotel near the Health Center.

GLÓSSA

Taverna Tagnanti. Glóssa. ☎ **0424/33-606** or 0424/3-076. Appetizers Dr 220–Dr 950 (95¢–$4.05); main courses Dr 1,000–Dr 3,300 ($4.25–$14.05). No credit cards. Daily 7am–midnight. GREEK.

This is the place to meet, greet, and eat in Glóssa. The food is inexpensive, the staff friendly, and the view spectacular. The menu is standard taverna style, but we enjoyed everything sampled. The Stamataki and Antoniou families run this and the nearby souvenir shop Pýthari; if asked, they'll even help you find a room in town. It's about 180 meters up from the bus stop.

SKÓPELOS AFTER DARK

The night scene on Skópelos isn't nearly as active as on neighboring Skiáthos, but there are still plenty of bars, late-night cafes, and discos. Most of the coolest bars are on the far (east) side of town; follow the plentiful signs above the Hotel Amalia to find the indoor **Kirki Disco** or continue on along the beachfront to find the outdoor **Karyatis;** on the way you'll pass **Akti Panorama** (☎ **0424/23-132**), a beachside taverna that often has live Greek music. The best place for bouzouki music is **Meidani,** in a handsomely converted olive oil factory approximately in the middle of town; it doesn't open until eleven or so, but there's a nice little bar just up from it, or you can wander around town checking out the night scene around Platanos Square, beyond and along the paralía. Don't forget the possibility of live music at the **Anatoli Ouzerí,** above the town.

3 Alónissos

62 nautical miles (115km) from Volos

Alónissos has been buffered from mass tourism by its more popular neighbors, Skiáthos and Skópelos. It remains largely undeveloped and unpretentious. The vast majority of the island is mountainous and green, covered mostly with olive trees and pines. The coast, especially along the inhabited southeastern part, is quite rugged and irregular, and there aren't a lot of beaches, but there are several very nice ones, all refreshingly lacking in motorboats, jet skis, and crowds, except in August when the island becomes an Italian possession. There are some good restaurants and a number of good hotels, and the islanders remain remarkably easygoing, open, and friendly.

ESSENTIALS

GETTING THERE   By Plane   The fastest way by plane is via Skiáthos with connection by hydrofoil. Although it's possible to fly to Skýros, there are many fewer boats and it's a much farther trip.

By Boat   Alónissos is on the ferry line with Skiáthos and Skópelos, so during the busy summer months there is regular daily service. The hydrofoils come and go seven times a day. Excursion boats from Alónissos's neighbors also operate on a daily basis throughout the summer. From Athens, depart from Áyios Konstandínos; **Alkyon Travel,** Odós Akademías 97, near Omónia Square (☎ **01/38-43-220** or 01/38-43-221), can arrange bus transportation to Áyios Konstandínos and hydrofoil or ferry tickets. From northern Greece, Volos is closer and offers the option of a quick side trip to the Mt. Pelion region. There's at least one boat a day arriving from either Volos, Áyios Konstandínos, or Kými (once weekly). In spring and fall, service to the island drops off considerably; check with the local **Port Authority** (☎ 0424/65-595) for the schedule.

VISITOR INFORMATION The **Ikos Travel Office** (☎ 0424/65-320; fax 0424/65-321) is right on the paralía. Pákis Athanassíou runs the agency and knows the island as well as anyone you're likely to meet, and he and his staff are the very best source of advice, help, and services, such as travel arrangements, including Olympic Airline tickets. They also have the best map of the island, prepared by Hans Jörg Rothenberger, a must if you plan to do any walking or hiking—and you should.

GETTING AROUND **By Bus** There is irregular bus service from the port in Patitíri to Old Alónissos four times a day, more frequently in the high season, less frequently in the off season. The fare is Dr 230 (95¢) one way. Tickets may be purchased on board or at Ikos Travel.

On Foot Alónissos, especially the southern part of the island, is easily visited on foot. Be sure to pick up one of the up-to-date maps from Ikos Travel.

By Moped and Car Mopeds and motorcycles are available in Patitíri for Dr 3,500 ($14.90) and up per day, depending on the size. A Jeep/truck can be rented for about Dr 28,000 ($119.15) per day, including insurance. Be very careful on the torturous mountain roads in the remote, northern parts of the island.

By Taxi The taxi stand (☎ 0424/65-573 or 0424/65-425) is on the right side of the port. The island only has three or four taxis. You have to be a firm negotiator to get a fair price. A taxi from Patitíri to Old Alónissos should cost about Dr 1,000 ($4.25) each way.

By Boat Most of the excursion boats to the nearby beaches leave the port sometime between 9 and 11am and cost about Dr 900 ($3.85) round trip. Ask at Ikos Travel about chartering a boat, or at least convincing a fisher to go to some of the nearby Lesser Sporades. Rental boats are available for approximately Dr 18,000 ($76.60) per day for a boat with a 9 horsepower motor.

FAST FACTS The **post office** is on the road to Hóra, the left-hand road off the harbor; it's open from 8am to 2pm Monday through Friday. The **telephone office (OTE)** is on the waterfront, but operates only in the summer; hours are from 7:30am to 9pm daily. There is a **doctor** who can handle most emergencies (☎ 0424/65-208). The local **pharmacy** is on the right-hand road, just off the harbor. The **police** have an office in Patitíri (☎ 0424/65-205). There is a newsstand up the left-hand road on the left with English language newspapers, magazine, and a few paperbacks.

WHAT TO SEE & DO

If recent history is a guide, then Alónissos, the least known and one of the most naturally attractive of the major Sporades, would have to be considered a star-crossed island. For many centuries Alónissos was a major producer of wine, and vineyards covered more than one-fourth of the island, then in 1950 phylloxera devastated the vines and contaminated the soil. The island is still unable to resume any significant production, though there are olive groves covering the hills.

Another trying year for Alónissos was 1965: A major earthquake hit the island, badly damaging the hilltop Byzantine capital, **Old Alónissos.** Roofs caved in and many walls cracked, but ironically the real damage was dealt by a military commission sent in to study the situation. Instead of recommending rebuilding the old town, they had the entire population of the capital moved to the minor port of **Paritíri** ("Winepress"). The homely, substandard housing of their "model community" created yet another blight on the island. (A Canadian film crew came to Alónissos a few years ago to make a documentary on how not to build a town.) However, purple bougainvillea now hides many of the architectural flaws, and islander's spirit has rebounded, so today the port can no longer be called ugly, and it has the familiar and pleasant blend of tavernas, hotels, and tourist services.

Patitíri has a small but well-sheltered harbor, with most services either along the waterfront or on one of the two main streets leading up off it: the left toward Old Alónissos, and the right toward Vótsi and points north. At the bottom of some steeply rising hills is a fairly small town. The hill on the right (north) as you leave the ferry has most of the town's hotels and private rooms to rent, many overlooking the harbor. There's another cluster of hotels on the southern side of the port beyond the small and rocky but acceptable town beach. The waterfront has the usual mix of cafes, hotels, fish tavernas, and shops.

The southeastern tip of the island, Marpoúnda, while not exactly off-limits, is dominated by the big **Marpoúnda Village Club,** which caters to fun-loving Italians, and you are unlikely to feel welcome there. Continue past the complex until you find a path leading off to the left through the pines and follow it down to **Vithísma,** a nicer beach that you will have to share with windsurfers in the summer. A little further along the upper trail you'll find **Megálo Mourtiá,** a pebble beach with a couple of tavernas and a path leading up to Old Alónissos.

Most people will want to make their first destination **Old Alónissos** (Paleá Alónissos, sometimes called Hóra, though most locals say Horió), the old Byzantine capital, with its spectacular views, especially at sunset. Many of the houses remain in ruins, while others were bought at bargain prices, mostly by English and German visitors, who have restored them. A few locals have also returned, and though the continuing restoration is for the most part faithful to the original architecture, the town has a rather sophisticated international feel.

Most of the foreigners come only for the summer, and until recently most people went without electricity and rejected modern comforts and conveniences for some greater psychic connection to the past. Some people use electricity only in the bars, tavernas, and shops, but still not at home. Tavernas, bars, minimarkets, a few rooms to let, and a growing number of art and craft shops have opened in the last few years, and it looks as if the capital may once again regain some of its lost dignity, as local resentment of the foreign invasion abates.

Even at its busiest, there is much tranquility, and even the derelict houses are interesting in what they reveal about the past, that includes the Venetians, who re-built the fortifications. It's a rather steep climb up a path, which begins near the post office, that will take you about an hour and requires sturdy shoes, so you might want to take the bus or a taxi up. We recommend you walk down, either along the more direct footpath during the day or along the vehicle road at night, unless you have a flashlight. Should you be fortunate enough to find a room, there's swimming a 20-minute walk north below the town at **Vrisítsa.** Coming down from Old Alónissos on the vehicle road you'll see Vrisítsa below on the left. The windmill there is being renovated, and it has some promise as a charming retreat.

The closest beach to the north of Patitíri is **Roussoúm Yialós,** which may suit less-ambitious beach seekers. Beyond it **Vótsi,** the island's second-largest settlement, with another well-protected harbor, is a fishing village that's becoming a resort. If you go to Vótsi by the vehicle road you'll pass the new **International Academy of Classical Homeopathy** on the left. (Ikos Travel can give you information about it.) There's a beach beyond Vótsi, **Spartínes,** but while you're moving you might as well continue on to **Miliá Yialós,** where pines grow down to the beach and the water is clearer, good for snorkeling. The next beach, **Chrissí Miliá,** has a more gradual slope into the Aegean, which makes it better for children, and it has a good taverna. **Kokkinókastro,** over the hill, is believed to be the site of ancient **Íkos,** and, as its name suggests, the pebbles on this beach are red. The remains of an even older settlement, one of the oldest in the Aegean, dating from the Middle Paleolithic, have recently been discovered there. It's a very pretty place, but you'll have to take a picnic and water if you want to spend the day. Beyond it, **Tzórtzi** is another pretty beach, with especially beautiful water, ideal for snorkeling. (You will probably not want to walk even this far, so you should catch a caïque in the port.)

Stení Vála, the last village of any size, with a fjordlike harbor, has a few tavernas, a market, a campsite, and enough rooms to mention it as a possibility for a stay. It's the gateway to the **National Marine Park,** which you cannot enter without special permission unless you are with a guided tour. **Kalamákia,** further north on the coast, also has a couple of tavernas and a few rooms. There's still plenty of territory to explore both along the coast and inland further north, but be aware that the roads are quite poor, the population quite sparse, and facilities meager if existent.

The coast also has a number of grottos of exceptional beauty, and there are several excursions run by Ikos Travel that take you along the coast. A short walk outside of Vótsi in Platsoúka, there is a cave that is particularly picturesque (it's most accessible on calm days). Alónissos offers opportunities for spear fishing, skin-diving, and underwater exploration of the ruins off Psathoúra, site of a huge modern lighthouse.

There are other minor islands off Alónissos, some of which can be visited by excursion boat in the high season. **Peristéra,** to the east, the largest and one of the closest, can be visited by excursion boat, and there are fine beaches within a 30-minute walk from where the boat docks at Vassilikó. On summer evenings boats carry parties out for special barbecues. **Kyrá Panayía (Pelagós),** which belongs to the Orthodox Church, has two abandoned monasteries and a cave that is often identified as the one belonging to the Cyclops Polyphemus, who Odysseus blinded. Beyond it **Yioúra** has another large cave that makes the same claim and a rare breed of wild goats. **Pipéri,** to their east, is a wildlife sanctuary, home to a small colony of monk seals and Elenora falcons.

WHERE TO STAY

There are quite a few private homes that rent rooms, and if you're looking to save money they're usually on a par with most of the Class D and some of the Class C hotels and pensions. Expect to pay Dr 5,750 to Dr 7,000 ($24 to $29.10) per person for a room. Most of the rooms are on the north side of the port, such as **Pension Lacy (☎ 0424/65-016),** run by one of the most gracious hostesses in town; a double runs Dr 6,900 ($28.75). By the time you arrive on Alónissos there may be accommodations available in the old capital. The folks at **Ikos Travel (☎ 0424/65-320;** fax 0424/65-321) can arrange to rent houses that sleep three to four people for Dr 15,000 to Dr 16,000 ($62.50 to $66.70).

Hotel Gorgóna. Rousoúm Yialós, 370 05 Alónissos. **☎ 0424/65-317.** Fax 0424/65-629. 17 rms (all with bath). TEL. Dr 13,250 ($56.40) single or double. No credit cards.

Take the right-hand road up from the harbor, continue east past the school, and look for a mural of a mermaid (gorgóna) flanking the front door of a hotel up on the right. The Hotel Gorgóna is one of the cleanest and quietest places in town, and all of the beds have firm, orthopedic mattresses. Request a sea-facing room; for the price, it's one of the best values in town.

Hotel Liadromia. Patitíri, 370 05 Alónissos. ☎ **0424/65-521.** Fax 0424/65-096. 24 rms (all with bath). TEL. Dr 13,800 ($58.70) single or double (including breakfast). EU, MC, V.

This is a very nice hotel on the right above the harbor. Many of its rooms have great views, and a roof garden provides an extra treat. The hostess, Maria Thansiou, an Alónissos original, has brought considerable style to this attractive inn. Lace curtains, wall hangings, murals, and wrought-iron fixtures distinguish this hotel from the average lodging.

✪ **Paradise Hotel.** Patitíri, 370 05 Alónissos. ☎ **0424/65-213** or 0424/65-160. Fax 0424/65-161. 31 rms (all with bath). TEL. Dr 13,800 ($58.70) single; Dr 18,400 ($78.30) double (including breakfast). EU, MC, V.

The Paradise Hotel, run by the gracious and gregarious Kostas, is also on the right above the harbor. You'll enjoy the new pool and relaxation area, late-afternoon drinks on the hotel's pine-shaded terrace overlooking the water-worn rocks, or a swim in the clean, clear sea below. The staff will arrange transportation from the dock.

VÓSTI

Pension Vótsi. Vótsi, 370 05 Alónissos. ☎ **0424/65-510** or 0424/65-066. Fax 0424/65-449. 15 rms (all with bath). TEL. Dr 9,200 ($39.15) double (including breakfast). No credit cards.

This handsome new pension is clean and quiet, with Pelion-style slate floors, ceiling fans in every room, and homey touches like hand-embroidered curtains. The friendly, relaxed family that operates it makes it feel even more like home.

STENÍ VÁLA

Theodorou Hotel. Stení Vála, 370 05 Alónissos. ☎ **0424/65-158** or 0424/65-558. Fax 0424/65-321. 10 rms (all with bath). MINIBAR TEL. Dr 7,900 ($33.60) single/double. No credit cards.

If you really want to get away from it all, this basic inn in Stení Vála, about halfway up the east coast of the island, may be what you're looking for. Transportation to the hotel is provided by Land Rover or boat. Rooms are very simply furnished but comfortable, and the village has two restaurants and a pub.

WHERE TO DINE

Argo. Patitíri. ☎ **0424/65-141.** Reservations not required. Appetizers Dr 600–Dr 1,800 ($2.55–$7,65); main courses Dr 1,250–Dr 11,500 ($5.30–$48.95). Fish priced per kilo. EU, V. Daily 10am–2am. TAVERNA.

This attractive outdoor taverna is on the cliffside around from the right (north) side of the harbor, with a view down the rocky eastern shore of the island. Late breakfasts are quite good. Fresh seafood is the specialty, and you can have the local lobster (astakós) for Dr 8,000 ($34.05) or crayfish (karavída) for Dr 11,000 ($46.80) per kilo.

Kamáki Ouzerí. Patitíri. ☎ **0424/65-245.** Appetizers Dr 500–Dr 2,400 ($2.10–$10.20); main courses Dr 850–Dr 4,000 ($3.60–$17). No credit cards. Daily 6pm–1am. GREEK.

The gregarious Spyros is in charge of the grill at this ultrapopular ouzeri, about 100 meters up the left-hand road off the harbor on the left. A wide selection of mezedes (appetizers) and fresh fish distinguishes this fine, but very basic eatery from the more touristed establishments. Probably the best food in town, especially for grilled seafood and fish.

Ouzerí Leftéris. Patitíri. No telephone. Appetizers Dr 500–Dr 950 ($2.10–$4.05); main courses Dr 800–Dr 2,800 ($3,40–$11.90). No credit cards. Daily 11am–4pm and 6pm–1am. GREEK.

Come here for the best bargain in town: an ouzo and hot plate combo, a bargain at Dr 400 ($1.70), including an assortment of mezedes. The Leftéris also has many

other salads, freshly grilled fish, and their delicious house specialty, saganáki shrimp
with onions, tomatoes, pepper, mustard, and feta.

OLD ALÓNISSOS

Taverna Astrofenyiá (Mina's Bar). Old Alónissos. ☎ **0424/65-182.** Reservations recommended. Appetizers Dr 700 ($3); main courses Dr 1,850 ($7.85). Daily 7pm–midnight from
June 1–Sept 30. INTERNATIONAL.

Good food, the island's best nightlife, and stunning views are all to be found at the
"Starlight," aka Mina's Bar. It's located on the top level of old Alónissos, in a dining area covered by a grape arbor. The food is surprisingly sophisticated, with such
dishes as artichoke hearts with a cream dill dressing and grilled swordfish with capers.
There's a good selection of wines. The vegetable moussaká is delicious and filling, and
the owner Iannis Toundas tries to use organic vegetables as much as possible in his
many tasty salads.

Taverna Paraport. Old Alónissos. No telephone. Appetizers Dr 400–Dr 1,000 ($1.70–$4.25);
main courses Dr 900–Dr 2,800 ($3.85–$11.90) Daily 9am–2pm and 6pm–1am. GREEK.

At the top of Old Alónissos village, head chef Ilias and family serve good standard
Greek taverna fare. There is live music about once a week.

STENÍ VÁLA

I Stení Vála. Stení Vála. **0424/65-545.** Appetizers Dr 400–Dr 1,200 ($1.70–$5.10); main
courses Dr 800–Dr 3,200 ($3.40–$13.60) Daily 7am–midnight. GREEK/SEAFOOD.

Locals consider this handsome taverna the best on the island, especially for seafood.
There's a large interior dining room and a spacious veranda with a good view of the
harbor and fjordlike cove. The cook's tirópita (cheese pie) is among the very best; it's
a large spiral filled with excellent feta and fried crisp in olive oil.

ALÓNISSOS AFTER DARK

The cafes, bars, and ouzerí near the port get fairly lively at night, and you don't have
much of a tour to make to see which one suits your fancy. **La Vie, Neféli,** and **Nine
Muses** are generally considered superior, and above the harbor on the right **On the
Rocks** is a good place for late-night dancing. **4 X 4 Disco,** up to the left off the road
to Old Alónissos, plays American and European rock, and a little further up the road,
Rebétika plays the best Greek music on the island. You might consider going on up
to **Mina's Bar** in Old Alónissos to get a little closer to the stars. **Elias Pub,** in Vótsi,
is also considered one of the island's best.

4 Skýros

25 nautical miles (46km) from Kými

Skýros is an island with good beaches, attractive whitewashed pillbox architecture,
and picturesque surroundings, and it has low prices and relatively few tourists. Why?
First, it's difficult to get to Skýros. The ferry to Skýros leaves either from the isolated
port of Paralía Kými, on the east coast of Evvia (with a two-hour boat ride to Skýros),
or from Volos (or the other Sporades), which is the starting point for a four-hour
hydrofoil ride to the island. Second, Greek tourists prefer the other, more thickly
forested Sporades. We find that Skýros's scruffy vegetation and stark contrast between
sea, sky, and rugged terrain make it all the more interesting.

Also, many Skyriots themselves have always been ambivalent, at best, about developing this very traditional island for tourism. Until recently there were only a handful
of hotels on the whole island. Since 1990, however, Skýros has seen a miniboom in

the accommodations-building business, and with the completion of a giant marina, it's setting itself up to become yet another tourist mecca. Direct charter flights from Europe, always a harbinger of accelerated change, now land at the island's airport. None of this should deter you, however; be assured that, at least for now, Skýros remains an ideal place for an extended stay.

ESSENTIALS

GETTING THERE   By Plane   Olympic Airway has two flights a week (daily in the summer) between Athens and Skýros. Call their office in Athens **01/961-6161** for information and reservations. The planes are small, so reserve well in advance. (You can also fly to Skiáthos and make a connection by hydrofoil, but this isn't such a good idea unless you'd like to have a look at the other Sporades first.) The local office Olympic Airlines representative is **Skýros Travel** (☎ **0222/91-123** or 0222/91-600). A taxi from the airport is about Dr 1,000 ($4.25) per person in a shared cab. A bus meets most flights and goes to Skýros town, Magaziá, and sometimes Mólos; the fare is Dr 400 ($1.70).

By Boat   There is only one ferry company serving Skýros, the **Lykomides Co.,** and it's owned by a company whose stockholders are all citizens of Skýros. A former ferry company provided great service in the busy summer months and lousy service in the off-season, so the citizens of Skýros bought their own boat, the *Lykomídes,* and only allow it to dock at Skýros. During the summers, it runs twice daily from Kými and Skýros (11am and 5pm) and twice daily from Skýros to Kymi (8am and 2pm); the trip takes about $2^{1}/_{2}$ hours. Off-season, there is one ferry each way, leaving Skýros at 8am and Kymi at 5pm. The fare is Dr 1,800 ($7.65).

For schedules to Kými, call **0222/22-020** in Kými. For Skýros ferry schedules, call **0222/91-790** or 0222/91-789. The Lykomídes office in Skýros and Kými sells connecting bus tickets to Athens; the fare for the $3^{1}/_{2}$-hour ride is Dr 2,850 ($12.15).

The **Flying Dolphin** now goes to Skýros five times a week, starting in mid-May, daily in July and August, from Skiáthos, Skópelos, and Alónissos. This is easily the most convenient way to go, though pricey compared to the ferry; one-way tickets cost Dr 10,500 ($44.70) for the four-hour-plus Volos-Skýros commute.

The tricky part of getting to Skýros by ferry is the connection with the ferry from the other Sporades islands. The off-season ferry from Skiáthos, Skópelos, Alónissos, and Volos is scheduled to arrive at Kými at 5pm but is frequently late. It's not uncommon to see the Skýros ferry disappearing on the horizon as your ferry pulls into Kými. You might have to make the best of the 24-hour layover and get a room in Paralía Kými. (We recommend the **Hotel Kými,** ☎ **0222/22-408,** or the older **Hotel Krineion,** ☎ **0222/22-287).**

From Athens, buses to Kými leave the Terminal B at Odós Lissíon 260 six times a day, though you should leave no later than 1:30pm; the fare for the $3^{1}/_{2}$-hour trip is Dr 2,850 ($12.15). From Kými you must take a local bus to Paralía Kými. Ask the bus driver if you're uncertain of the connection.

The ferries from Kými and Volos and hydrofoils from the other Sporades dock at Linariá, on the opposite side of the island from the town of Skýros. The island's only bus—sometimes they bring another over from the mainland—will meet the boat and take you over winding, curvy roads to Skýros town for Dr 220 (95¢). Depending on the mood of the driver, the bus will stop at Magaziá Beach, immediately north below the town next to the Xenia Hotel.

VISITOR INFORMATION   The largest tourist office is **Skýros Travel Center** (☎ **0222/91-123** or 0222/91-600; fax 0222/92-123), next to Skýros Pizza

Restaurant in the main market. It's open daily from 8am to 2:30pm and 6:30 to 11:30pm. English-speaking Lefteris Trakos is very helpful on many counts, including accommodations, changing money, Olympic Airways flights (he is the local ticket agent), long-distance calls, some interesting bus and boat tours, as well as Flying Dolphin tickets.

GETTING AROUND   By Bus   The only scheduled run is the Skýros-Linariá shuttle that runs four to five times daily; Dr 220 (95¢). Skýros Travel has a twice-daily beach excursion bus in the high season.

By Moped and Car   Mopeds and motorcycles are available in Skýros, near the police station or the taxi station, for about Dr 5,300 ($22.55) per day. A Fiat Panda can be rented for about Dr 15,000 ($63.85) per day, including insurance. The island has a relatively well developed network of roads.

By Taxi   Taxi service between Linariá and Skýros is available but relatively expensive, about Dr 2,000 ($8.50). Rates to other, farther destinations are similarly high.

On Foot   Skýros is a fine place to hike. The new island map, published by Skýros Travel and Tourism, will show you a number of good routes, and it seems to be pretty accurate.

FAST FACTS   The **post office** is near the bus square and is open Monday through Friday from 8am to 2pm. There's only one **bank** (with no extended hours), also near the bus square; it's best to bring plenty of drachmas to Skýros. The **telephone office (OTE),** open Monday through Friday only from 7:30am to 3pm, is 50 meters south of the bus stop.

WHAT TO SEE & DO

The boats dock at **Linariá,** a plain, mostly modern fishing village on the west coast, pleasant enough but not recommended for a stay. Catch the bus waiting on the quay to take you across the narrow middle of the island to the west coast capital **Skýros town,** which is built on a rocky bluff overlooking the sea. (The airport is near the northern tip of the island.) Skýros town, which is called Horió and of course sometimes Hóra, looks much like a typical Cycladic hill town, with whitewashed cube-shaped houses built on top of each other. The winding streets and paths that are called streets are too narrow for cars and mopeds, so most of the traffic is by foot and hoof. As you alight from the bus at the bus stop square, head north toward the center of town and the main tourist services.

Near the market, signs point up to the town's **Kastro.** It's a 15-minute climb, but worth it for the view, and on the way you'll pass the church of **Ayía Triáda,** which contains some interesting frescoes, and the monastery of **Áyios Yióryios.** The monastery was founded in 962 and contains a famous black-faced icon of St. George that was brought from Constantinople during the Iconoclasm.

A lion of St. Mark over the gate of the citadel identifies the structure as Venetian, but actually it's mostly Byzantine built atop a Classical foundation. According to myth, King Lykomídes pushed Theseus to his death from here. From one side, the view is over the rooftops of the town, and from the other the cliff drops precipitously to the sea.

The terrace at the far end of town is **Rupert Brooke Square,** where the English poet, who is buried on the southern tip of the island, is honored by a nude statue of *Immoral Poetry.* It's said to have greatly offended the local people when it was installed. You're more likely to be amused when you see how pranksters have chosen to deface the hapless bronze figure. The **Archaeology Museum** (☎ 0222/91-327) is just below on the steps leading down to Magaziá Beach. It has a small collection of Mycenaean and late Helladic funerary objects, proto-geometric vessels, and finds from the Roman period, and a reconstruction of a typical 19th-century house. It's open Tuesday through Sunday from 8:30 to 3pm; admission is Dr 500 ($2.15).

Nearby, the **Faltaits Museum** (☎ 0222/91-232), which is open daily in the summer from 10am to 1pm and 5:30 to 8:30pm; in the off-season just ring the bell and someone will open it for you; admission is free. The museum houses the private collection of Manos Faltaits, and it's one of the best island folk art museums in Greece. It contains a large and varied collection of plates, embroidery, weaving, woodworking, and clothing, as well as photographs, including some of the local men in traditional costumes from Carnival. There's a workshop attached to the museum where young artisans make lovely objects using traditional patterns and materials. The proceeds from the sale of workshop items go to the upkeep of the museum. The museum also has another shop in the town called **Argo,** on the main street (☎ 0222/ 92-158), which is open from 10am to 1pm and 6:30pm to midnight.

Local customs and dress are being better preserved on Skýros than on any island we know of. Older men can still be seen in baggy blue pants, black caps, and leather sandals constructed with numerous straps, and older women still wear their long head scarves. The embroidery you will often see women busily working at, as they gossip volubly, is famous for its vibrant colors and interesting motifs—such as people dancing hand-in-hand with flowers twining around their limbs and hoopoes with fanciful crests.

Peek into the doorway of any Skýrian home and you're likely to see what looks like a room from a dollhouse with a miniature table and chairs, and colorful plates—loads of plates hanging on the wall. During the Byzantine era, the head clerics from Epirus sent 10 families to Skýros to serve as governors. They were given control of all the land not owned by Mt. Athos and the Monastery of St. George. For hundreds of years these 10 families dominated the affairs of Skýros. With Kalamítsa as a safe harbor the island prospered, and consulates opened from countries near and far. The merchant ships were soon followed by pirates, and the ruling families went into business with them; the families knew what boats were expected and what they were carrying, and the pirates had the ships and bravado to steal the cargo. The pirates, of course, soon took to plundering the islanders as well, but the aristocrats managed to hold on to much of their wealth.

Greek independence reduced the influence of these ruling families, and during World War I hard times fell on them and they were reduced to trading their possessions with the peasant farmers for food. Chief among these bartered items were sets of dinnerware. Plates from China, Italy, Turkey, Egypt, and other exotic places became a sign of wealth, and Skyrian families made elaborate displays of their newly acquired trophies. Whole walls were covered, and by the 1920's local Skyrian craftsmen began making their own plates for the poorer families who couldn't afford the originals.

While we're on the subject of local eccentricities we might as well elaborate on the famous **Carnival of Skýros.** This 21-day celebration is highlighted by a four-day period leading up to Lent and the day known as Katharí Deftéra (Clean Monday). On this day Skýros residents don traditional costumes and perform dances on the platía. Unleavened bread, lagána, is served with taramasaláta and other meatless specialties. (Traditionally, vegetarian food is eaten for 40 days leading up to Pascha, Easter.)

Before this, and culminating on Sunday in the midafternoon, are a series of ritual dances and events performed by a group of weirdly costumed men. Some dress as old shepherds in dark animal skins with a belt of many sheep bells and wear a mask made of goatskin. Other men dress as young women and flirt outrageously. (Skýros has a long history of transvestism; it was here that Achilles was successfully beating the draft during the Trojan war by dressing as a woman until shrewd Odysseus tricked him into revealing his true gender.) Other celebrants caricature Europeans, and all behave outlandishly and rather aggressively, reciting ribald poetry, and poking fun at any and all bystanders. This ritual is generally thought to be pagan in origin and causes some people to reflect on the antics of ancient Greek comedy and even tragedy ("goat song"), with men playing all the roles, and catharsis as the aim.

According to local ethnologist Manos Faltaits, there are interesting connections with similar celebrations, such as the shepherd's feasts of Sicily, Bulgaria, Austria, and northern Greece. In those places, the festivities celebrate the victory of shepherds over farmers. In Naoússa, in northern Greece, the village divides into two factions and throws stones at each other; in other places they battle with wooden swords.

Skýros is also the home of a unique breed of wild **pygmy ponies,** often compared to the horses depicted on the frieze of the Parthenon and thought to be related to Shetland ponies. The Meraklídes, local Skyrians who care for these rare animals, have moved most of the diminishing breed to the nearby island of Skyropoúla, though tame ones can still be seen grazing near town. Ask around and you might be able to find a Meraklíde who'll let you ride one.

Skýros is also a good place for shopping, especially for the local ceramics. **Ergastiri,** on the main street, has interesting ceramics, Greek shadow puppets, and a great selection of postcards. For Skyrian plates try the small **shop at no. 307,** across from Fragoules hardware. Also popular for plates is the **studio of Yiannis Nicholau,** next to the Xenia Hotel; he makes all of the plates and also serves as the beer distributor for the island. Good hand-carved wooden chests and chairs made from beech (in the old days it was blackberry wood) can be purchased from **Lefteris Avgoklouris,** former student of the recently departed master, Baboussis, in Skýros town; his studio (☎ 0222/91-106) is on Konthili Road, around the corner from the post office. Another fine carver is **Manolios,** in the main market.

To get to **Magaziá,** continue down from Rupert Brooke Square. (If your load is heavy, take a taxi to Magaziá, as it's a hike.) From Magaziá, once the site of the town's storehouses (magazines), it's nearly a kilometer to **Mólos,** a fishing village, though the two villages are quickly becoming indistinguishable because of development. There's windsurfing along this more developed beach, and there are some fair isolated beaches beyond Mólos, with some nudist activity, but they're fairly exposed— the beaches and the people. There's a very good beach just below the Kástro, though getting to it is a bit of a problem. (We're sorry, but we just can't formulate any directions, and you'll have to ask—probably more than once.)

South of town the beaches are less enticing until you reach **Aspoús,** which has a couple of tavernas and some rooms to let. **Ahíli,** a bit further south, is where you'll find the big new marina, so it's no longer much of a place for swimming. Further south the coast gets increasingly rugged and there is no roadway.

We recommend you head back across the narrow waist of the island to **Kalamítsa,** the old safe harbor, three kilometers south of Linariá, which has a good clean beach and is served by buses in the summer.

The island is divided almost evenly by its narrow waist; the northern half is fertile and covered with pine forest, while the southern half is barren and quite rugged. Both halves have their attractions, though the most scenic area of the island is probably to the south toward **Tris Boukés,** where Rupert Brooke is buried. The better beaches, however, are in the north.

North of Linariá, **Achérounes** is a very pretty beach. Beyond it, **Péfkos,** where marble was once quarried, is better sheltered and has a taverna that's open in the summer. The next beach north, **Áyios Fokás,** is probably the best on the island, with a lovely white pebble beach and a taverna open in the summer. Locals call it paradise, and like all such places it's very difficult to reach. Most Skyrians will suggest walking, but it's a long hilly hike. To get there, take the bus back to Linariá, tell the driver where you're going, get off at the crossroads with Péfkos, and begin your hike west from there.

Atsítsa is another beach with pines trees along it, but it's a bit too rocky. It can be reached by road across the Óros Olýmbos mountains in the center of the island, and it has a few rooms to let and a holistic health and fitness holiday community. (Those interested in the **Skýros Centre** should contact it at 92 Prince of Wales Rd., London NW5 3NE, ☎ **071/267-4424;** fax 071/284-3063.) There's a sandy beach a 15-minute walk further north at **Kirá Panayía** that's a bit better.

The northwest of the island is covered in dense pine forests, spreading down to the Aegean. The rocky shore opens into gentle bays and coves. This area provides wonderful hiking for the fit. Take a taxi (Dr 4,000/$17) to **Atsítsa.** The cautious will arrange for the taxi to return in five or six hours. Explore the ruins of the ancient mining operation at Atsítsa, then head south for about $4^{1}/_{2}$ miles to **Áyios Fokás,** a small bay with a tiny taverna perched right on the water. Kali Orfanou, a gracious hostess, will provide you with the meal of your trip: fresh fish caught that morning in the waters before you, vegetables plucked from the garden for your salad, and her own feta cheese and wine. Relax, swim in the bay, and then hike back to your taxi. The ambitious may continue south for 7 or 8 miles to the main road and catch the bus or hail a taxi. This part of the road is mainly uphill, so walker beware. In case you tire or can't pry yourself away from this secluded paradise of Áyios Fokás, Kali offers two extremely primitive rooms with the view of your dreams, but without electricity or toilets (in the formal sense).

WHERE TO STAY

The whole island has only a few hotels, so most visitors to Skýros take private rooms. The best rooms are in the upper part of the town, away from the bus stop, where women in black dresses accost you with cries of "room, room." Walk beyond the platía, up the main street, investigate the rooms, and make your choice. A more efficient procedure is to stop in at **Skýros Travel Center.** The island of Skýros is somewhat more primitive in its facilities than the other Sporades, so before agreeing to anything check out the rooms to ensure they are what you want. Rates for in-town or beach rooms during the high season are about Dr 6,000 ($25.55); so-called Class A rooms run 6,750 ($28.70).

SKÝROS

Hotel Nefeli. Skýros, 340 07 Skýros. ☎ **0222/91-964.** Fax 0222/92-061. 12 rms (all with bath). TEL. Dr 11,250 ($47.85) single; Dr 15,800 ($67.25) double. AE, MC, V.

One of the best in-town options is built in the modern Skyrian style. Many rooms have fine views, and the large, downstairs lobby is a welcoming space, always filled at breakfast time. As the Nefeli is one of the better choices, you'd do well to reserve in advance.

Magaziá Beach/Molos

🄢 **Hotel Angela.** Mólos, 340 07 Skýros. ☎ **0222/91-764.** Fax 0222/91-555. 14 rms (all with bath). TEL. Dr 13,250 ($56,40) single or double. No credit cards.

This is among the most attractive and well-kept abodes in the Molos/Magaziá Beach area, located near the sprawling Paradise Hotel complex. All rooms are clean and tidy with balconies, but because the hotel is set back about 100 meters from the beach, there are only partial sea views. Nevertheless, the facilities and hospitality of the young couple who run the Angela make up for its just-off-the beach location, and it's the best bet for the money.

Paradise Hotel. Mólos, 340 07 Skýros. ☎ **0222/91-560.** 60 rms (all with bath). TEL. Dr 15,850 ($67.45) single; 18,500 ($77.15) double in the new building (including breakfast).

This pleasant hotel is at the north end of Magaziá Beach, in the town of Mólos. The older part of the hotel has 40 rooms; these more basic rooms run about 50% less. The newer part of the hotel has 20 rooms, and we suggest staying here because the rooms are better kept and have much better light. The hotel is somewhat removed from the main town, but there is a taverna on the premises and another down the street.

Pension Galeni. Magaziá Beach, 340 07 Skýros. ☎ **0222/91-379.** 13 rms (all with bath). Dr 11,900 ($50.65) single or double.

The small but delightful Pension Galeni has recently upgraded their rooms, so that they now all have private facilities. We like the front (sea facing) rooms on the top floor for their (currently) unobstructed views. The Galeni overlooks one of the cleanest parts of Magaziá beach.

Xenia. Magaziá Beach, 340 07 Skýros. ☎ **0222/91-209.** Fax 0222/92-062. 24 rms (all with bath). TEL. Dr 13,500 ($57.45) single; Dr 17,950 ($76.40) double (including breakfast). AE, DC, V.

The recently upgraded Xenia was built right on the beach and occupies the best location on Magaziá. In 1989, they added a controversial (and ugly) concrete break-water that's supposed to protect the beach from erosion. The rooms have handsome 1950s-style furniture and big bathrooms with tubs, as well as wonderful balconies and sea views.

Achérounes Beach

Pegasus Apartments. Ahérounes Beach, 340 07 Skýros. ☎ **0222/91-552.** 8 apts (all with bath). MINIBAR. Dr 11,600 ($49.35) studio; Dr 23,250 ($98.95) apartment. EU, MC, V.

The resourceful Lefteris Trakos built these apartments and studios that are fully equipped. Studios can accommodate two or three people, and apartments up to six. One of the pluses of staying here is the chance to see (and ride, if you're under 15) Katerina, a Skyriot pony.

Yirismata

Skýros Palace Hotel. Yírismata, 340 07 Skýros. ☎ **0222/91-310.** Fax 0222/92-070. 80 rms (all with bath). A/C TEL. Dr 18,000 ($76.60) single; Dr 26,000 ($110.65) double (including breakfast). AE, DC, EU, MC, V.

This out-of-the-way resort, about a mile north of Mólos, offers the most luxurious accommodations on the island. It has a lovely pool and adjacent bar, tennis courts, air-conditioned rooms, and a well-planted garden. The rooms are plainly furnished but comfortable, with large balconies. The beach across the road is an especially windy, rocky stretch of coastline, with somewhat treacherous water. The hotel has a sound-proofed disco, the most sophisticated on the island. Twice a day, there's a minibus into town. If you want to get away from it all and have some up-scale amenities to boot, it might be the place for you.

WHERE TO DINE

The food in Skýros town is generally pretty good and reasonably priced. **Anemos** (☎ 0222/92-155), on the main drag, is a good place for breakfast, with filtered coffee,omelets, and freshly squeezed juice. In the evening, the **Leventis** serve vegetarian pizza. Speaking of pizza, don't overlook the nearby **Skýros Pizza Restaurant** (☎ 0222/91-684), which serves tasty pies as well as other Greek specialties in generous portions.

The best bakery in town is hidden away up in the hills on the edge of Skýros town. Walk up along the stairs to the statue of *Immortal Poetry,* bear right up the whitewashed stone path, and ask a local. It's tucked away, but your nose will be your guide. (They also sell their bread in the market).

In Linariá, find **Kyría Maria,** over the headland near the power station, which is especially good for fish, especially if you ask her not to overcook it.

Christina's Restaurant. Skýros. ☎ **0222/91-311.** Reservations recommended in summer. Appetizers Dr 600–Dr 1,500 ($2.55–$6.40); main courses Dr 1,200–Dr 3,400 ($5.10–$14.45). No credit cards. Mon–Sat 7pm–1am. INTERNATIONAL.

This new restaurant down from the taxi stand is so sophisticated by local standards that some old hands call it pretentious—a definite change from the usual fare. The chef is Australian, and she brings a lighter touch to everything she cooks. Her fricasseed chicken is excellent, and her deserts are exceptional.

Maryétes Grill. Skýros. ☎ **0222/91-311.** Appetizers Dr 250–Dr 450 ($1.05–$1.90); main courses Dr 1,000–Dr 2,000 ($4.25–$8.50). Daily 1–3pm and 6am–midnight. GREEK.

One of the oldest and best places in town, the Maryétes is a second-generation–run grill that's equally popular with locals and travelers. The dining room is as simple as simple gets, so what you go for is the food. We recommend the grilled chicken and meat. There's a small sampling of salads.

⑤ O Glaros Restaurant. Skýros. No phone. Appetizers Dr 250–Dr 650 ($1.05–$2.75); main courses Dr 800–Dr 2,600 ($3.40–$11.05). No credit cards. Daily 7pm–1am. GREEK.

This venerable establishment serves from a very small list of traditional taverna fare. We've been regulars at this basic place on nearly every trip to the island over the past 10 years and can report that the moussaká is as good as ever. It's favored by locals in the busy summer season as a reward for staying open all year.

⑤ Restaurant Kabanero. Skýros. ☎ **0222/91-240.** Appetizers Dr 300–Dr 1,000 ($1.25–$4.25); main courses Dr 1,000–Dr 1,600 ($4.25–$6.80). Daily 1–3pm and 6am–midnight. GREEK.

This perpetually busy eatery serves the usual Greek menu: moussaká, stuffed peppers and tomatoes, fava, various stewed vegetables, and several kinds of meat. We found the preparation up to snuff and prices about 20% less than most of the others in town. A treat and one of the best dining values in town.

SKYROS AFTER DARK

If you've gotta dance, try the **Kastro Club** in Linariá, **Borio** on the road to Magaziá, or the **Skýros Club** in the Skýros Palace Hotel. Aside from these, there are few evening diversions other than bar-hopping on the main street. **Apocalypsis** draws a younger crowd. **Kalypso** attracts a more refined set of drinkers who appreciate their better-made but pricier cocktails. **On the Rocks** rocks. **Renaissance** is loud and lively. **Rodon** is best for actually listening to music. **Skyropoúla** can't quite make up its mind what it wants to do, but is worth finding.

12

Western Greece & Ioánnina

by John S. Bowman

Western Greece—traditionally understood as referring to the northwest of the country—is a relatively little known and little traveled region for most Americans and Europeans. It's quite different from the Greece that so many have become familiar with. Much of Greece is mountainous, so simply saying the northwest is dominated by the Pindos Mountains does not distinguish it, but the plentiful rainfall and generally more temperate climate seem to remove it from the travel poster Mediterranean. With its evergreen slopes, deep-set rivers and lush valleys, and villages with timbered houses with slated or tiled roofs, it seems more like an Alpine land. It's also one of the few places in Greece where you'll spend much of your time away from the sea. The region differs in yet another way that will affect visitors: It hasn't yet organized itself around tourism and foreigners. Which isn't to say that there aren't plenty of hotels and restaurants.

The pace of life in Ioánnina and other cities, not to mention in the villages, is governed by local customs. During the off-season, for instance, places such as the post office and information offices and laundries may be closed all weekend. Museum hours are cut back as are the hours of gift shops and many restaurants. And except for some staff in the hotels, better restaurants, and visitor information and car-rental offices, few people speak English, although they may speak Italian, French, or German. You may find yourself sharing a hotel with Greek commercial travelers, and it's hard to find your English-language newspaper or fresh-squeezed orange juice. Accepting this, then, here is a region of Greece that will reward the adventurous traveler with new perspectives—both those from spectacular mountain slopes and those from experiencing a different way of life. To make your acquaintance with this part of Greece, we recommend basing yourself in Ioánnina, the capital of Epirus and a city that offers a fine mixture of the historical attractions and modern amenities.

A LOOK AT THE PAST

Even in its history, western Greece (in particular Epirus, the northwestern corner) has often gone in different directions from the rest of Greece. It was settled by Greek-speaking peoples about the same time (ca. 2000 B.C.) as other parts of Greece, and over the centuries they worshipped many of the same gods and carried on much the same culture, as testified to by the exhibits in Ioánnina's

Archaeological Museum. But there were always many non-Greek peoples in this area, too, and this plus the remoteness meant that this region did not participate in the grand classical civilization. Their social organization remained more tribal, their leaders were small-time kings. The greatest of the Epirote kings, Pyrrhus (318–272 B.C.), was constantly making war, and his victories over the Romans outside Rome have given us the term *Pyrrhic victory* because won at great cost they came to nothing. Epirus itself was reduced to a Roman province after 168 B.C.

During the Middle Ages, the whole western region was constantly prey to invaders, and with the conquest of Constantinople by the Crusaders in 1204, some Greeks decided to set up a new state with Ioánnina as the capital, the so-called Despotate of Epirus. It never amounted to much and soon fell under the control of other peoples. Finally it was taken over by the Turks in 1431, and soon they controlled virtually all of Greece, although the Venetians and various other Western Europeans would gain possession of parts of western Greece.

It was near the end of this long phase that Epirus experienced its most dramatic moment in the spotlight of history, under the "Lion of Ioánnina," Ali Pasha (1741–1822). He was born in Albania and rose to prominence fighting on behalf of the Ottoman Sultan in Constantinople. But in 1788, Ali Pasha decided to set up a virtually independent domain with his capital in Ioánnina. An international celebrity in his day, visited by Byron among others, he was a cruel despot who boasted of killing 30,000 people, often in the most brutal fashion. The Ottomans tolerated Ali Pasha as long as they could, but in 1822 they sent a large force to capture him; he hid in a monastery on the islet off Ioánnina but was tracked down, killed, and beheaded.

When the Greeks rose up against the Turks in the 1820s, the southern part of western Greece, centered around Messolonghi, took an active role, but Epirus to the north did not join in. The southwestern district of Arta was freed from Turkish rule in 1881 but Epirus was not formally joined to Greece until after the Second Balkan War of 1913.

The region became a battleground two more times, against the invading Italians and Germans in World War II, and then in the Greek civil war. Since then it has enjoyed unparalleled peace and prosperity.

To make your acquaintance with this part of Greece, we recommend basing yourself in Ioánnina, the capital of Epirus and a city that offers a fine mixture of historical attractions and modern amenities.

1 Ioánnina

Ioánnina had long been a sleepy medieval town when Greeks fleeing Constantinople after its capture by the Crusaders in 1204 arrived to make it the capital of the Despotate of Epirus. The first Despot, Michael I, started building the walls that over the next centuries would be enlarged and strengthened by various conquerors—Greeks, Italians, Serbs, and Turks—to become the quite magnificent walled town that still exists.

ESSENTIALS

GETTING THERE   By Plane   Most foreigners entering western Greece by air will be taking one of the **Olympic flights** to Ioánnina from Athens—there are usually two a day. Several times a week, there are Olympic flights between Ioánnina and Thessaloniki. Olympic Airways also flies (about one a day) from Athens to Aktion, just outside Preveza, down on the southernmost coast of Epirus; from here you get a bus to Igoumenitsa and Ioánnina or even to the island of Lefkada, which is connected by a viaduct to the mainland.

By Ship   Igoumenitsa, on the coast opposite Corfu, is the point of entry to northwestern Greece for many people. During the summer, ferries connect to Corfu hourly and less frequently to Kefalonía, Ithaka, and Paxi. Numerous ferries and ships put into Igoumenitsa going to and from ports in Italy—Ancona, Bari, Brindisi; some of these connect to Pátras or Piraeus in Greece or even more distant ports such as Iráklion, Crete, or Cesme, Turkey.

During high season, there is also a ferry connecting Astakos—on the Ionian coast south of Preveza and north of Messolonghi—and the offshore islands of Ithaka and Kefalonía.

There are so many changes in scheduling of all these ships that it's useless to provide a lot of detail, but if you're concerned enough to want information in advance, contact **Milano Travel** in Igoumenitsa, located at Odos Aghion Apostolon 9, ☎ **0665/23565.**

By Bus   There are many possibilities for entering and leaving northwestern Greece by bus from distant points such as Athens or Thessaloniki; the former is a 7$^1/_2$-hour trip, the latter an eight-hour trip. This service is with the privately run **KTEL** line (☎ **01/512-5954** in Athens; **0651/27442** in Ioánnina).

By Car   There are several approaches to western Greece from distant points. From Athens, there are two main routes: One is the inland route north via Livadia, Lamia, Karditsa, Trikkala, Kalambaka, and Ioánnina. The second is via Corinth and then along the southern coast of the Gulf of Corinth to Rion, the ferry to Antirion, and then via Messolonghi, Agrinio, Arta, and Ioánnina. Alternatively, you can head to the Ionian coast after Messolonghi, and go up to Igoumenitsa via Astakos, Preveza, and Parga.

Coming from northeastern Greece, the preferred route from Thessaloniki is via Veria west to Kozani and Konitsa and then south to Ioánnina. Assuming that the former Yugoslavia has settled down enough to allow for transit, it should be possible to take the once well-traveled route from Skopje (now capital of the Former Yugoslavia Republic of Macedonia) down into northern Greece at Florina, and from there south to Kastoria and Ioánnina.

VISITOR INFORMATION   Ioánnina's **National Tourist Information** is located at Napoleon Zerva 2 (opposite the far corner of the central square) (☎ **0651/25086;** fax 0651/72148). Summer hours, Monday through Friday from 7:30am to 2:30pm and 5:30 to 8:30pm, Saturday 9am to 1pm; winter hours, Monday through Friday 7:30am to 2:30pm, closed Saturday and Sunday.

GETTING AROUND   By Bus   With enough time, you can see most of western Greece by bus, but as always, you would need lots of extra hours for the little side trips. Given the many mountainous roads and curves, however, many might prefer to let others do the driving. The **KTEL line** provides bus links between virtually all points in western Greece. Points to the north, northwest, and northeast (Igoumenitsa, Metsovo, Konitsa, Kastoria, and Thessaloniki) and Athens are serviced from Ioánnina's main bus terminal at Odos Zosimadon 4 (☎ **0651/25014**). Points to the south (Parga, Arta, Preveza, Astakos, Messolonghi, and Pátras) are serviced from a smaller bus terminal in Ioánnina at Odos Vizaniou 19 (☎ **0651/26286**).

By Car   Having your own or a rental car is probably the best way to experience the full variety of western Greece. Distances are not all that great, but then again trips take much longer than a map might suggest because of the many mountainous and curving roads.

By Taxi   There are so many switchbacks and hairpin roads that some people might prefer to take a taxi. Agree on a fee before you set out. Each hour's drive should cost about Dr 3,500 ($15); each hour's waiting, about Dr 1,000 ($4.25). Insist on a driver who speaks at least basic English, or a foreign language you understand—and you'll get a guide in the bargain. He in turn should get a generous tip.

FAST FACTS: Ioánnina

Airport   The Ioánnina airport is about 3 miles ($5^1/2$km) from the center of town; it's well serviced by public buses (nos. 1, 2, and 7) from the main square, but you will probably find it more convenient to take a taxi. The **Olympic Airline Office** (☎ 0651/23120) in Ioánnina is on the Central Square (at the far end). It's open Monday through Friday from 8am to 3pm. On Saturday, Sunday, and holidays, contact the office at the airport (☎ 0651/26218); it's open from 11:30am to 7pm.

Area Code   The area code for Ioánnina is **0651.**

Banks/ATMs   The branches of the big national banks in the main cities can handle all money exchanges; they also have ATMs that can process transactions on major credit and debit cards.

Bookstores   Dodonis Bookstore in Ioánnina has some English-language tourist material; it's located at Odos Mikhali Angelou 27 (☎ 0651/45332).

Car/Moped Rentals   Western Greece doesn't offer the choice in car or moped rentals as in more tourist-oriented parts of Greece. We have found that **Budget Rent-A-Car** in Ioánnina (Odos Dodonis 109, ☎ 0651/43901 or 0651/45382; fax 0651/45382) is the best to deal with. Paul Angelis is the genial manager. But don't expect to be rewarded by haggling during high season, because there are a limited number of vehicles for the influx of tourists. See "Getting Around," earlier in this chapter.

Climate   Keep in mind that western Greece is mountainous country well up in its latitude and with plenty of rainfall. Don't come much before late May or after early October and expect to find summer weather.

Embassies/Consulates   There are no U.S. or British consulates in this part of Greece. You would have to contact the embassies in Athens.

Emergencies   Dial the basic emergency number for all of Greece, 100.

Etiquette   Except for a few beach resorts on the Ionian coast, such as at Parga, you will be traveling through Greek cities and villages where beachwear is frowned upon. Casual wear, of course, is acceptable.

Holidays   Easter and the Christmas–New Year week draw many Greeks back to this region, and you should have reservations at this time for hotels, car rentals, boat ferries, and such.

Hospitals   The only major hospitals in western Greece are the two on the out-skirts of Ioánnina—one at Dourouti (some 4 miles/7km from Ioánnina) and the other at Hatzikosta (1 mile/2km). Other smaller cities and towns have clinics and plenty of trained doctors.

Luggage Storage/Lockers   Ioánnina's National Tourist Organization will store limited amounts of luggage in a pinch.

Mail and Post Office   Ioánnina's main post office is on Odos 28 Octobrio 3 (☎ 0651/26437). Its hours are 7:30am to 8pm except Sunday; in the off-season it's also closed on Saturday.

Maps   The National Tourist Organization in Ioánnina can sometimes provide a free map of Ioánnina.

Newspapers and Magazines   There's an excellent selection of foreign-language periodicals at **Athanasius Daktylithos,** Odos Pirsinela 14 (☎ 0651/28005). Hours are Monday through Saturday from 7:30am to 3pm and 5:30 to 9:30pm, and Sunday from 8am to 2:30pm and 6:30 to 8:30pm.

Police   The **Tourist Police** are located at Police Headquarters, Odos 28 Octobrio 11 (☎ 0651/25673). Their regular hours are from 7am to 2am.

Telephone, Telex, and Fax   The **OTE,** the National Communications Office, is on Odos 28 Octobriou 4. Open daily from 7am to 11:30pm.

Travel Agenies   In Ioánnina, one of the most helpful is the **Robinson Travel Agency** at Odos 8 Merarchias 19 (☎ 0651/29402; fax 0651/25071). See also "Visitor Information," above.

Transit Info   To contact the **KTEL bus line** in Ioánnina, call 0651/27442.

WHAT TO SEE & DO
A STROLL AROUND THE *FROURIO*: THE WALLED OLD TOWN & CITADEL

For many of those centuries that Ioánnina fell under the occupation of foreign conquerors, the city walls enclosed all the most important structures. There's virtually nothing of historic or architectural importance outside the citadel except on the islet of Nissi. Originally the fortress was separated from the mainland by a moat, which was crossed by three bridges. The moat has since been filled in. An esplanade now circles the lakeside below the walls, and there are several openings in the wall, but most people will enter the walls from the Platia Giorgio, which is lined by tavernas and gift shops.

A left turn from the Platia Giorgio onto Odos Ioustinianou leads (about two blocks) to the **Synagogue.** Dating from 1790, this white-walled synagogue, with a Hebrew inscription and a locked door, is distinctive enough to be interesting to those willing to track down someone who will let you in. (Inquire at the shop of Mrs. Allegra Matsa, Odos Anexartisias 18.) The Jewish community of Ioánnina traced its origins to Jews who came here at least by the 13th century. The Germans removed all 2,000 or so in 1941 and took them to labor and extermination camps. After the war, about 100 survivors came back, but today only some 50 Jews still live in Ioánnina. A small **Holocaust Memorial** is just outside the citadel, on the corner of Karamanlis and Soutsou streets.

If you continue on around the inside perimeter of the walls, you will come to a large clearing. From there, ascend a cobblestoned slope to the **Aslan Pasha Cami,** a 17th-century school with cells for Islamic scholars. Its **mosque** now houses the **Municipal Popular Art Museum.** During the summer season, it's open Monday through Saturday from 8am to 8pm, Sunday from 9am to 8pm; in winter, Monday through Friday from 8am to 3pm, Saturday and Sunday 9am to 3pm. Admission is Dr 600 ($2.60). The mosque was erected in 1618 on the site of an Orthodox church, razed by the Pasha to punish the Christian Greeks for a failed revolt (see "A Look at the Past," above). Entering the mosque, observe in the vestibule the recesses for shoes. The exhibits, which include traditional costumes, jewelry, weapons, documents, household wares, and such, are grouped around the three major religious-ethnic communities of Ioánnina: the Orthodox Greeks, the Muslims, and the Jews. There's an adjacent minaret, and when it and the mosque are illuminated each night, the scene from the lake is most entrancing.

In the opposite and far corner of the walled town is the **innermost citadel,** known by its Turkish name, *Kali.* Within it are the Victory Mosque (Fethiye Cami); the base of a circular tower; the remains of the palace of Ali Pasha, the cruel Albanian who dominated Epirus from 1788 until 1822; and what are alleged to be the tombs of Ali Pasha and his wife. The Greek army has long occupied this part of the citadel; its structures have been totally altered and entry is restricted, but plans are underway to establish a Byzantine museum here.

A BOAT TRIP TO THE ISLET OF NISSI (OR NISSAKI)

If you have only a day in Ioánnina, at least two to three hours (including an hour for a meal) should be given over to a visit to Nissi, the islet in Lake Pamvotis. Small boats leave from the quay below the fortress every half hour in the summer, from 6:30am to 11pm. In the off season, service is every hour—but note that the last boat leaves the island about 10pm. The fare is Dr 200 (85¢). The lake has unfortunately become overgrown with algae and is so polluted that local restaurants do not serve the fish taken from it (or so we've been assured).

The boat ride is barely 10 minutes and, day or night, provides a fine view of Ioánnina. You get off in what is virtually the lobby of three restaurants—each displaying its tank with seafood they want to cook up for you. Resist all until you are truly ready to eat. The specialties of these restaurants include eel, frog's legs, carp, crayfish, trout, and other imported fish.

The small village here is said to have been founded only in the 16th century by refugees from the Máni region of the Peloponnese, but its five monasteries predate this, and they are your destination. Take the narrow passage between the two restaurants, and signs are posted to your left and right. Following the signs to the left (east), you will come to the **Monastery of Panteleimon.** Although founded in the 16th century, it has been so heavily restored that little of the original remains.

Its interest today is that it houses a **small museum** devoted to the infamous **Ali Pasha**—numerous pictures, clothing, his water pipe, etc. It's open daily, and an attendant will come if it's closed. Admission is Dr 200 (85¢). The reason for such a display in a monastery is that Pasha had taken refuge here in 1820 and was eventually killed here in 1822 by Turks. You may even be shown holes in the floor where he is alleged to have been shot from below.

Directly beside this monastery is a second, the **Monastery of the Prodromos (St. John the Baptist),** but most people will want to move on to the western edge of the islet to the **Monastery of Aghios Nikólaos Spanos** (or **Moni Philanthropinon**). It's signed "Secret School" because it's claimed that Orthodox priests maintained a secret school here during the Turkish occupation. Founded in the 13th century, it was rebuilt in the 16th century, and magnificent frescoes were then painted on its walls. (There's no admission but it's customary to leave a gratuity with the caretaker.) Seldom does the public get to view such an ensemble of Byzantine frescoes so close up. Although the dim light can be a problem (bring a flashlight), you should be able to recognize such subjects as the life of Christ on the walls of the apse, God and the Apostles in the central dome, and the many saints. Most unexpected, however, are the portrayals of ancient Greek sages on the wall of the narthex as you enter—Apollonius, Aristotle, Cheilon, Plato, Plutarch, Solon, and Thucydides.

Practically adjacent to this monastery is another, **Aghios Nikólaos Dilios** (or **Moni Stratgopoulou**), the oldest (dating from the 11th century) on Nissi. Its 16th-century frescoes are also of some interest but are in poor condition. The fifth monastery, **Aghios Eleouses,** is closed to the public.

By now you have earned your meal on Nissi. Choose one of the restaurants (see "Where to Dine," below). And as you sip your wine, you can contemplate what such a locale means while enjoying the view.

AN ARCHAEOLOGICAL MUSEUM

Ioánnina Museum. Platia 25th March (behind clock tower on central Square). ☎ **0651/ 25490.** Admission Dr 500 ($2.15). Summer hours, noon–7pm, Tues–Fri 8am–6pm, Sat–Sun 8:30am–3pm; Oct 15–Apr 15, Mon–Fri 8:30am–3pm.

Housed in a modern building, this fine little provincial museum has just enough to engage anyone who has come this far. Most of the displays are from graves and burial sites in Epirus, but the range of items extends from Paleolithic implements through the Bronze Age to Roman times. Various bronze works are especially interesting, and there's the superb Attic-style sarcophagus (coffin) dating from the 2nd to 3rd centuries A.D., with carved scenes from the *Iliad*.

But undoubtedly, the display case that will surprise and interest most people holds some of the little lead tablets found at the Oracle of Dodona (see "Easy Excursion from Ioánnina," below). People from all stations of life came to Dodona and had some desire or query inscribed on a strip of lead that was then submitted to the oracle. Today we can read these actual pleas. Some are quite practical: Should I buy a certain property? Should I engage in shipping? Others have a religious tinge: To which god should we pray or sacrifice to get certain results? But the most intriguing are the personals: Is it better to marry? Shall I take another wife? Am I the father of her children? These tablets speak to us as do few remains from the ancient world.

ANOTHER STROLL AROUND IOÁNNINA

Ioánnina has become a busy commercial center for all of northwestern Greece and its streets can be filled with vehicles of all kinds generating noise and fumes, but there are some interesting retreats from this. One is the old **Turkish Bazaar,** down near the walled town and just off the main street, Odos Averoff. In its tiny shops you will still see men practicing the old crafts—metalsmiths, jewelry-makers, cobblers, tailors, and such. Proceeding up Odos Averoff you come to Platia Dhimokratias and then the **clock tower** (on the left). In the **gardens** behind this is the city's archaeological museum (see above). When you leave the museum, stroll across the broad terraced gardens built over the site of what was once the **walled Kastro,** where the Christians lived during the Turkish era. At the far corner is the **Cafe/Restaurant Litharitsia** (☎ 0651/20043, 0651/23085, or 0651/24954), with a fine view of the lake and distant mountains if you eat outdoors. Returning to the main street you are now on the **Central Square** (officially **Platia Pyrros),** also with its share of cafes and restaurants.

WHERE TO STAY

Ioánnina and its immediate environs don't offer luxury hotels or resorts, but that's not why you go there. There are, however, several quite special hotels and plenty of more-than-adequate accommodations.

EXPENSIVE

Xenia Hotel. Odos Dodonis 33 (up past the Central Square), Ioánnina 45221. ☎ **0651/ 25078.** Fax 0651/25089. 60 rms, all with baths. TV TEL. High season, Dr 26,000 ($111) double; low season, Dr 22,000 ($94). Rates include buffet breakfast. AE, DC, EU, JCB, MC, V. Open all year. Parking on grounds. Easy walking from center but public bus goes by.

This is Ioánnina's class act, and although the rooms are not exceptional (but certainly tasteful and comfortable) what you get for your money is a sense of seclusion in a park setting at the very heart of Ioánnina. The hotel is set well back from the street, and the rooms at the rear enjoy fine views. There's an outdoor cafe that allows you to relax in a park atmosphere; the indoor restaurant is highly regarded and certainly convenient if you don't care to explore Ioánnina's many others. The desk will see to basic needs (laundry, car rental, excursions), there is room service, and two conference rooms can handle up to 100. The hotel was renovated in 1988; its lobby and rooms have a discreet decor that will appeal to people who like an international feel to their hotels.

MODERATE

Hotel Olympic. Odos Melanidi 2 (one block off Central Square), Ioánnina 45220. ☎ **0651/25147.** Fax 0651/73008. 52 rms, all with bath. A/C TV TEL. High season, Dr 17,000 ($72) double; low season, Dr 13,000 ($55). EU. Open all year. Parking in lot across from hotel. Open all year. Walking distance of every place in town.

In several ways, the "coolest" hotel in town, the Olympic is the only one with air-conditioning, and it seems to attract the most sophisticated visitors—members of the diplomatic corps, government dignitaries, and such.

All that means nothing, of course, if *you* aren't made to feel welcome and comfortable, and you can be assured of both. The lobby is modest but the desk service (and 24-hour room service) are what count. Rooms have small refrigerators. The upper-story front rooms enjoy a view of the distant lake. You're in the center of town but the noise dies down by bedtime (and with air-conditioning your windows are presumably closed). Go with this if you like to be at the center of the action.

Hotel Palladion. Odos Botsari 1 (off 28th Octobriou), Ioánnina 45444. ☎ **0651/25856** to 9. Fax 0651/74034. 130 rms, all with tub or shower. TV TEL. High season, Dr 16,000 ($68) double; low season, Dr 13,000 ($55). Rates include continental breakfast. AE, DC, EU, MC, V. Open all year. Private parking lot in rear. Walking distance of every place in town.

We like this place for its combination of features: convenient yet quiet, a pleasant lobby backed up by a professional desk, no frills but good value. Rooms are not very exciting but everything works. (And when we asked to move from one because of lingering cigarette odor, this happened instantly and with no further questions.) There are conference facilities for up to 80 and the Palladion often hosts groups, but this doesn't interfere with your stay. The breakfast is nothing to write home about, but the free parking in the rear more than compensates for it.

INEXPENSIVE

Hotel Galaxy. Platia Pyrros (Central Square), Ioánnina 45221. ☎ **0651/25056.** 38 rms, some with shower, some with tub. TEL. High season, Dr 11,000 ($47); low season, Dr 8,000 ($34). Rates include continental breakfast. No credit cards. Parking in front. Walking distance of everyplace in town.

This is located just below the Central Square, but it's fairly well insulated from the noise of traffic. It's nothing fancy, just your basic Greek Class C—which means actually three C's: convenient, clean, and cheap. For the budget traveler.

WHERE TO DINE
MODERATE

La Fontantina. Odos Melanidi 2 (on ground floor of Olympic Hotel, one block off Central Square), Ioánnina 45220. ☎ **0651/25147.** Fax 0651/73008. Reservations recommended in high season for holidays and weekends. Main courses, Dr 1,100–Dr 3,500 ($4.70–$14.90). No credit cards. Daily 10am–midnight. GREEK/ITALIAN.

This is the house restaurant of the Olympic Hotel and has become a favorite gathering place for foreigners and Greeks who enjoy a sense of being at Ioánnina's crossroads. It's not that large, the decor is hotel classy, service is a bit standoffish, and the menu ranges from Greek standards to Italian standards. It's all tasty enough, but it's hardly gran' cucina. So you go here to take in the lively scene while you enjoy your spaghetti carbonara or your steak filet with one of the fine red wines from northern Greece—a Naoussa, an Amyntaion, or a Carras. Florence it's not, but La Fontantina offers a taste of upscale Ioánnina.

The Gastra Restaurant. Eleousa, along the Airport-Igoumenitsa Highway (4.3 miles/7km outside Ioánnina; 1 mile/1¹/₂km past airport, just before turnoff to Igoumenitsa). ☎ **0651/61530.** Reservations recommended in high season on weekend evenings; on Sundays, you are advised to leave it to the citizens of Ioánnina. Main courses, Dr 1,100–Dr 3,500 ($4.70–$14.90). No credit cards. Tues–Sun 1–5pm and 8pm–1am. Open all year. Public bus: 2. Restaurant is on right, with large sign displaying eating implements. GREEK REGIONAL.

This is a must for all those willing to try a special type of regional cooking that involves heaping red-hot embers over a *gastra*—the conical cast-iron lid that's lowered onto the baking dish holding the food (lamb, goat, pork, or chicken), which then roasts slowly to appear on your table as especially succulent meal. It's delicious. The restaurant also has other specialties: for an appetizer, try the *skordalia karithia* (walnut-garlic dip); for dessert, their special crème caramel.

In pleasant weather, you can eat out front in the shaded garden and watch your meal cooking in the open fireplace. In cooler times, you can sit inside the handsome restaurant. When the spirit moves, diners are encouraged to dance to the music. You go here for a leisurely experience, not just for the food. (And if it's too crowded and you need your gastra, proceed less than a mile after taking the left turn signed to Igoumenitsa to another such restaurant, the **Diogenes.**)

Pamvotis. Nissi Ioánnina (the offshore islet). ☎ **0651/81081.** Fax 0651/81631. Main courses, Dr 900–Dr 2,000 ($3.85–$8.50). EU, MC, V. High season, daily 11am–midnight; low season, daily 11am–10pm. Ferry boat from Ioánnina's lakefront. GREEK.

If you have only one meal to eat in Ioánnina, it has to be at one of the restaurants on the islet out in the lake. And if you ask around as to which is the best, you'll get a different answer from everyone. In fact, they're all about the same quality, so you choose one with a location that appeals. We like this one—located near the dock where the little ferries put in, so you get a lively scene along with the local specialties. (If you prefer a more natural setting, go on to the **Propodes Restaurant** at the side of the Aghios Panteleimon Monastery, which you'll want to visit. See "A Boat Trip to the Islet of Nissi (or Nissaki)," above.)

You can pick your lobster, *karavides* (a cross between crayfish and shrimp), trout, or other fish of the day right out of holding tanks. If you're game, try one of the two local specialties: frogs' legs or eels. The white Zitsa Primus, a slightly sparkling white wine from the region, is a perfect accompaniment to your meal and your time on Nissi.

INEXPENSIVE

The Pharos. Platia Mavili 13 (down along lakefront), Ioánnina 45444. ☎ **0651/26506.** Main courses Dr 900–Dr 2,500 ($3.85–$10.65). No credit cards. Daily 9am–10pm. Closed mid-Oct to Mar. Bus from center but only 10-minute walk. GREEK.

One of several restaurants set back from the lakefront, the Pharos should appeal to those who just want a good meal in a pleasant setting. In warm weather, you can sit in the square opposite or at the tables outside the restaurant; on cooler days, you can sit inside. The menu is traditional but with some variants. For an appetizer, try the fried peppers in a garlic sauce. For your main course, order whatever's being grilled that day, and get the pilaf instead of potatoes. Most main dishes fall in the Dr 1,000–

Dr 1,800 range ($4.25–$7.65), but if you're feeling ambitious, try the frogs' legs or crabs at Dr 2,500 ($10.65).

To Mantelo. Platia Georgio 15 (opposite the main entrance to citadel), Ioánnina 45444. ☎ **0651/25452.** Main courses, Dr 880–Dr 1,700 ($3.40–$7.25). No credit cards. Daily 10am–2am. Open all year. GREEK.

Here's one for those who prefer their Greek tavernas to look traditional and to attract Greeks. It's a no-frills place that gives you a front-row seat on the square outside the old walled town, where all kinds of characters congregate. For an appetizer, try one of the fried-marinated dishes—peppers, squash, or eggplant. Try any of the grilled dishes—veal, chicken, lamb—or the calves liver. If you're adventurous, try the lamb's head or boiled goat. In all cases, ask for the pilaf. The taverna can feel cramped when it's crowded, but that's what makes it Greek.

SHOPPING

If you get the impression that every third store in old Ioánnina is selling jewelry, silverware, hammered copper, and embossed brass work, you're right—these are the traditional crafts here. Many of the jewelry stores are really selling nothing but modern work in gold and silver and/or precious and semiprecious jewels. Be wary of "antiques" that may be offered in some shops—they may be little more than 60 years old.

There's an extended cluster of jewelry and gift shops opposite the walled citadel. One of the more interesting selections of metal work (and he also has water pipes) is at **Politis Douvflis,** at Platia Georgio 12.

Here and there you may see embroidered clothing or woven socks, but this is not a region known for delicate needlework.

2 Side Trips from Ioánnina

DODONA (OR DODONI)

Even if you aren't the kind who chases after every classical ruin, this is a rewarding site: a spectacular theater at one of the major oracles of the ancient world.

It's located only 20 miles (32km) from Ioánnina, so it could be visited in about two hours if you have a vehicle. The bus service is inconvenient; it's better to spring for a taxi—about Dr 5,000–Dr 6,000 ($21–$26) for the round trip, including an hour's wait. The first 4.3 miles (7km) are on a main highway due south (signed to Arta); the turn to the left becomes (after 3 more kilometers) an ascending and curving (but asphalt) road. This trip becomes part of the experience—you get the sense that you're on a pilgrimage to a remote shrine.

On arrival, you are on a plateau ringed by mountains. Admission to the sacred precincts is Dr 500 ($2.15). Hours in the high season are Monday through Friday from 8am to 7pm, Saturday and Sunday 8:30am to 3pm. In the off-season, it's open Monday through Saturday from 10am to 3pm.

The Oracle of Zeus here at Dodona traces its roots back to the early Hellenistic peoples who had arrived in northwestern Greece by about 2000 B.C. They themselves probably worshipped Zeus, but it now appears that at Dodona there was already some cult that worshipped a form of the earth goddess—possibly there was an oracle of sorts that based its interpretations on the flights of pigeons. In any case, by about 1400 B.C., it appears that the Zeus-worshipping Greeks had imposed their god on the site and turned the goddess into his consort, Dione.

By this time, too, the priests were linking Zeus's presence to the rustling leaves of an oak tree at Dodona and were interpreting these sounds as oracular messages. The Greeks set up a shrine around this tree, at first nothing more than a protective fence. Over the centuries they built more and more elaborate structures on the site, but the first temple to Zeus was not erected here until the 4th century B.C.

Eventually the oracle spoke through the bronze statue of a youth with a whip that was stirred by the wind to strike adjacent metal cauldrons, and the reverberating sound was interpreted. Many ambitious structures, both religious and secular, were erected at Dodona, but the oracle effectively ceased functioning in the 4th century A.D.—about the time when, it is claimed by some, the original oak died. The oak now on the site of the shrine is, of course, a recent planting.

Only traces of walls are left of other structures, but the **magnificent theater** survives, albeit, thanks to what was virtually a reassembling in the 19th century. The first theater was built in the 3rd century B.C. and was said to have seated 17,000. It was destroyed, but another equally large was built on the site in the 2nd century B.C. Later, the Romans converted it into an arena for gladiatorial contests. The theater was one of the largest on the Greek mainland and has almost the same marvelous acoustics as the famous (but smaller) one at Epidaurus. Even if you do not explore the other remains, just to sit in this theater for awhile is an evocative experience.

PERAMA CAVE

Only some 3 miles (5km) north of Ioánnina (the turnoff is past the airport), this cave—actually more a series of caverns—was only discovered in 1941, during World War II when people were seeking hiding places. It has since been thoroughly developed, with electric lights, steps, and handrails that allow for a perfectly safe walk through. It's open in the high season Monday through Sunday from 8am to 8pm; in winter, 9am to sunset. Guided tours set out about every 15 minutes from the well-signed entrance in Perama village; the fee is Dr 1,000 ($4.25). The guides often don't speak much more English than to repeat the names assigned to unusually shaped stalagmites or stalactites and they have an annoying habit of making everyone rush through (but in fact you can linger behind and join the next group).

Whether or not Perama lives up to its boast to be one of the most spectacular caves in the world, it's worth a visit if you haven't been in many such caves. *Warning:* At the very end, you must climb what seems like an endless number of steps to come out at the far end—but at least you're at a cafe!

METSOVO

This is a traditional mountain village that has become so popular that at times the original appeal can be overwhelmed by tourism at its worst. Still, many people find it satisfying—some even find it magical. It's about a 1¹/₂-hour bus ride east of Ioánnina. Although there are a couple of buses to Metsovo in the morning, there's really only one back from Metsovo in the late afternoon that allows for a day in the village—so either pay close attention to the always changing bus schedule or rent a car. (It can also be approached by bus from the east, coming from Athens or Thessaloniki.)

The village sits at about 3,320 feet (1,000m) above sea level, nestled among **peaks of the Pindos mountains,** so in addition to attracting day trippers, it draws serious **nature lovers** and **hikers** from all over Greece and Europe. Overnight accommodations are often strained, especially during Greek holidays. And because there are **ski slopes** nearby, Metsovo is also a popular destination even during the winter.

Assuming that you go there on a day's excursion, what you will experience is a village that has managed to maintain a certain style of architecture; traditional customs such as clothing and dances; several crafts such as weaving, embroidery, and wood work; and several food specialties. The buildings, of course, can be seen at all times just by strolling around. They're what most of us think of as an alpine-style—stone, with wooden balconies, and slate roofs. Some of the older people wear traditional clothing all the time, but the fancier costumes are only worn on Sundays and holidays.

If you want to see the **dances,** July 26 is the village's **feast day,** but also one of its most overcrowded days. The crafts are on display and sale in dozens of shops up and down the main street. Some of the wares are touristic and imported kitsch, but some are authentically local and handsome. The best of the latter are at the **Metsovo Folk Art Cooperative,** located about 50 meters from the Egnatia Hotel. The traditional Epirote foods can be sampled in several restaurants (see "Where to Dine," below).

Disneyland it ain't, but don't go to Metsovo thinking you're discovering a quaint native village. There's even a fairly ambitious conference center in town.

There remains yet another reason to go to Metsovo. It's the center (in Greece, at least) of **the Vlach people,** who claim descent from Latin-speaking Wallachians of what is now Romania. The Vlachs were originally shepherds who followed their flocks, and many still do just that; but over the centuries, many other Vlachs have settled down in northern Greece and prospered in crafts, commerce, and trade. Some of the wealthier Vlachs, however, have made their money from dealing in wool and other products from the flocks, and now many in Metsovo prosper from the tourist trade. Because the Vlachs wrote down little in their distinctive Latin-based language and because it's not taught in the schools, it's in danger of being lost as the new generation marry and move out of their relatively small circles. You'll find the Vlachs of Metsovo extremely congenial—and patient as foreigners constantly ask them to "say something in Vlach." (Don't expect your Latin to help much!)

In addition to walking about the village, there are several special attractions that should appeal to at least some. There's the **Museum of Folk Art** in the **Arhondiko Tositsa,** a 17th-century mansion that's been completely restored by Baron Michalis Tositsa, a wealthy Vlach living in Switzerland. With its paneled rooms, furniture, rugs, clothing, crafts, and domestic furnishings of all kinds, it's a superb example of how a prosperous family might once have lived in Epirus. The museum, located on a road above the main street, is open Monday through Wednesday and Friday and Saturday, 8:30am to 1pm and 4 to 6pm in summer; in winter, it's open the same days but from 3 to 5pm only. Admission is Dr 300 ($1.30).

Founded by another prominent Vlach from Metsovo, Evangelos Averoff-Tositsa, the **Averoff Gallery** is a museum of Greek paintings and sculpture from the last two centuries. Although it's a worthy institution that does admirable work, it's probably not what most visitors to Metsovo have come to see. Located above the main square, the museum is open in summer Wednesday to Monday from 9am to 1:30pm and 5 to 7:30pm; in winter, it's open Wednesday to Monday from 4 to 6pm. Admission is Dr 300 ($1.30).

Much more typical of Metsovo is the little church of **Aghia Paraskevi** on the main square, with its carved wood altar screen, silver chandeliers, and copies of Ravenna mosaics.

And if you can handle the half-hour walk down and an hour walk back up, you can visit the restored 14th-century **Moni Ághios Nikólaos.** A signed trail for this monastery leads off from the main square, and the resident warden will allow entry until 7:30pm during the high season. Its church has fine 16th-century frescoes (long lost until 1960).

WHERE TO STAY

If you want to overnight in Metsovo, there are 12 hotels to choose from. All of them are quite acceptable and all to some degree are decorated in the traditional style of the region. We can single out several.

Galaxias. On a terrace above the main square. ☎ **0656/41123.** Fax 0656/41124. 10 rms, some with shower, some with tub. TV TEL. High season, Dr 18,000 ($77) double; low season, Dr 12,000 ($51). Rates include continental breakfast. EU, MC, V.

If you want to be at the center of things, then this should be your choice. It has the restaurant singled out above.

The Hotel Victoria. About ¹/₂ mile (1km) from the main square. ☎ **0656/41761.** Fax 0656/ 41454. 37 rms, some with shower, some with tub. TV TEL. Regular rate season, Dr 19,000 ($81); Christmas holiday week, Dr 23,000 ($98). Rates include continental breakfast. EU, MC, V.

If you want a more natural setting and a bit more luxury, then try the Victoria. It too has its own fine restaurant.

Kassaros Hotel. ☎ **0656/41800.** Fax 0656/41262. 31 rms, some with shower, some with tub. TV TEL. High season, Dr 16,000 ($68) double; low season, Dr 11,000 ($47). Rates include continental breakfast. AE, DC, EU, MC, V.

For a location away from the square, but not as far as the Victoria, and as a favor to your budget, try the Kassaros Hotel. This is the perfect hotel for those who intend an extended or active stay in Metsovo, because the proprietor runs a travel agency, **Kassaros Travel,** Odos Tsoumaka 3, Metsovo 44200 (☎ **0656/41346;** fax 0656/ 41262). This agency can arrange for ski equipment, has a snowmobile for rent, and also has its own buses for excursions throughout Epirus.

WHERE TO DINE

Even if you spend only a few hours in Metsovo, you should try a meal at a restaurant that offers traditional Epirote fare. There are a couple decent ones along the main street (Odos Tositsa)—**Taverna Saloni** or **Taverna To Spitiko**—but we recommend the **Galaxias** (in the hotel of the same name, just above the main square) (☎ **0656/ 41202**). Main courses are from Dr 900 to Dr 1,700 ($3.85 to $7.25). It's open daily all year, from noon to 11pm. In warm weather, you can sit outdoors; in cooler weather, eat in the handsome dining room warmed by a cheerful fire. Try a meal of the local specialties. Start with the bean soup (*trachana*) and/or a cheese pie with leek. Move on to the spicy sausage or beef patties with leeks and celery baked in a pot. For dessert, try the baklava or yogurt but be sure to save room for one of the local cheeses, of the smoked variety (*metsovonay*), or the mild *vlachotiri*. To accompany your meal, ask for the local red wine, Katoyi, or since that's in short supply, just the house wine.

ZAGORI (ZAGORIA, ZAGOROHORIA) & THE VIKOS GORGE

For some, this might be a more appealing way to spend an extra day in northwest Greece than to visit Metsovo or Dodona or Perama Cave. The Zagori is the mountainous area just north of Ioánnina, a region of perhaps 400 square miles. The whole region is now part of the **Greek National Park System** and has about 46 villages. These have remained virtually unchanged through the centuries. The mountainous roads can make for slow going even to visit a few sites.

Becoming a part of the national parks system has put a stop to the unrestricted development that has spoiled so many locales in Greece; it's also required any new

---

Trekking into the Vikos Gorge

For those who want to go into the Vikos Gorge, the lower square of Monodendri offers one of the most accessible approaches. The path down into the gorge is signed there. But even to get to where the gorge begins to open out ahead of you is a rugged $4^1/_2$- to 5-hour walk—and then it would be still longer to come back up. So no one should attempt this without proper gear, supplies, and experience. The walk through the entire gorge—some 10 miles (16km)—is even more demanding. If you would like to go on even an abbreviated expedition, the best advice is to go with one of the groups organized by **Robinson Travel Agency** in Ioánnina, at Odos 8 Merarchias 19, ☎ **0651/29402;** fax 0651/25071. More experienced trekkers might prefer to contact the **Mountain Climbing Association of Ioánnina** (☎ 0656/22138) or the **Mountain Climbing Association of Papingo** (☎ **0653/41138** or 0653/41320), based in one of the Zagori villages (see below).

---

structures to be built in the traditional manner—stone buildings, slate roofs. But it has also so cramped life that young people leave and many of the villages are now all but abandoned. The villages you'll visit tend to be interesting rather than quaint, and much of the appeal of the excursion is in the scenery and such elements as the old bridges. Some disagreement exists as to which are villages, which are hamlets, and which are mere settlements.

The region's most spectacular sight is the **Vikos Gorge,** and for those who are up to it, this can be an excursion of its own.

Getting around the Zagori without your own vehicle is all but impossible. The few buses simply don't allow you to get to more than one destination and back to Ioánnina in a day, whereas with a car you can see pretty much all in a day. Even if you have only half a day, with a car you could visit one or two villages, view the Vikos Gorge from above, experience the scenery, and be back in Ioánnina all within four hours. Or you could join an organized tour.

Take the main road north out of Ioánnina toward Konitsa; the turnoffs are clearly marked. Your first destination should be **Monodendri;** you take the highway north and at 8 miles (13km) bear right; it's signed **Zagouria.** Make the detour to **Kipi** to see the famous 16th-century Turkish-style bridges, especially the triple-arched one (known as Plakidas). At about 22 miles (36km) (signed to Vikos Gorge) turn right and proceed on to about 24 miles (39km) where a sign (in Greek only) indicates a turn right into the lower square of Monodendri.

If you continue on the main road for about another half mile, you come to the upper square of Monodendri: Here is where you will find several modest hotels and decent restaurants, but unless you are needing such amenities, you need not go up there. If you want to have a meal while here, we recommend **To Petrino Dasos,** the little taverna on the right as you come up to the square. The **I Oxio,** a hotel and restaurant on the left, just opposite To Petrino Dasos, and the **Monodendri Pension and Restaurant,** at the top of the square, are also recommended. There's a cobblestone path that connects the upper square and lower squares.

If you have driven directly into the lower square, you will park there and then proceed on foot (following the sign) about 10 minutes to the lovely little 15th-century **Monastery of Aghia Paraskevi,** perched on the edge of the **Vikos Gorge.** The viewing areas here are well protected and this may be spectacular enough for most, but if you have no fear of heights and are sure-footed, you get back on the trail above the monastery and proceed on for several hundred yards to enjoy even more spectacular views of the gorge—but also more dramatic drops from the totally un-protected and narrow path. Definitely this is not for everyone.

If you do want another view of the gorge, you can drive up through the upper square and on for another 4^1/$_2$ miles (7km) (signed to Osia); you again leave your car and walk down a stone path to what is known as the **Vikos Balcony,** offering a truly spectacular view.

You are now ready to leave Monodendri and proceed on to **Papingo.** Drivers are usually advised to return all the way back to the main highway and then proceed north on it to the turnoff to Papingo. This is a 1^1/$_2$-hour drive (because you are first heading south again). If you are a bit adventurous—and more important, able to ask basic directions in Greek—you can take a perfectly fine asphalt road that cuts off an hour of that drive by going more directly to that highway. You turn right below Monodendri and head for Elafatopos; you will then come out onto the main high-way, turn right and proceed until a sign to the left indicates Papingo. The drive here offers the kind of scenery best described by a young English traveler we fell in with, Simon, when he said, "It makes you want to stop the car and get out and applaud."

There are two villages, **Megalo Papingo** and **Micro Papingo**—the first translated as "Big" and the latter as "Small"—and you will want to visit at least the first. Many regard this as the archetypal Zagori village, with its terrain, streets, homes, roofs, pub-lic buildings, and everything else seemingly all made of the same stone. Megalo Papingo has several cafes and restaurants as well as several modest hotels; you can al-ways be sure of a meal in Papingo but rooms can be booked up at various times of the year—such is the reputation of the Zagori in Greece and elsewhere in Europe.

We can recommend the **Hotel Koulis** (☎ **0653/41138**). A double is Dr 10,000 ($42); rates include private bath and breakfast. No credit cards.

Or if you want something more elegant, try the **Saxonis Houses** (☎ **0653/41615**), Dr 24,000 ($101) for a double. Rates include private baths and breakfast. No credit cards.

If you drive on another mile from Megalo Papingo, you'll come to Micro Papingo, which offers another vista. If you really want to get away from it all, stay at the little **Hotel Dias** here, with its "restaurant" (☎ **0653/41257** or 0653/41892); a double runs Dr 10,000 ($42), but that's probably negotiable.

After all this you are now only 39 miles (62km) from Ioánnina. You can return feeling you have seen the true Epirus.

The Ionian Islands

by John S. Bowman

The Ionian Islands, located off the northwestern coast of Greece, have long been a lure to select groups of Europeans, especially the British and Italians. In recent years these islands have attracted increasing numbers of visitors from many lands. No wonder, since these islands offer some of the loveliest natural settings in all of Greece, a distinctive history and lore, and some special archaeological and architectural sites.

The Ionian Islands are part of the great mountain chain that extends down from eastern Europe. Essentially they are nothing but the peaks of that chain that happen to protrude above sea level. They thus are both literally and figuratively linked to Europe in the way that many parts of Greece do not seem to be—specifically to Italy. Also their latitude (that of northern California) and relationship to major land masses accounts for a climate that has made for a natural environment quite different from that of the stereotypical Greek islands. More rainfall, for instance, supports a greener landscape, but a more temperate climate slightly cuts down the tourist season. The "high season" on these islands tends to run from June to September. That still leaves many months for visitors to enjoy the beautiful beaches, the spectacular vistas, the refreshing cafes, and fine restaurants to be found around these islands. The roads are generally in first-class condition, even if unavoidably steep and twisting. Accommodations range from luxury resorts to quiet little rooms on remote beaches. The local cuisine and wines offer numerous special treats—*sofrito* (a spicy veal dish), *bourdetto* (a spicy fish dish), and the Theotaki or Liapaditiko wines.

A word about just what the Ionian Islands comprise. Traditionally, they have numbered seven—indeed, the Greeks' name for this group is *Heptanisos* (or *Eftanisos*), "Seven Islands." Listing first the names with which they will be treated in this book and then the common variants, they include: Corfu (Kerkira); Paxos (Paxoi); Levkás (Lefkas, Lefkada); Ithaca (Ithaki); Kefalonía (Kefallinia, Cephalonia); Zákinthos (Zakynthos, Zante); and Kíthira (Cythera, Cerigo). The last named lies off the southeastern tip of the Peloponnese, quite removed from the others, and is no longer treated by the Greek government as an administrative part of the Ionian Islands. Meanwhile there are many more than seven islands in the archipelago along Greece's northwestern coast, including several that

Western Greece and the Ionian Islands

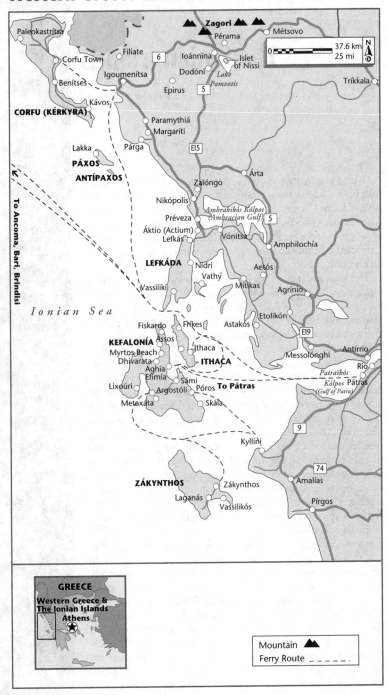

Zagori
Pérama
Métsovo
Paleokastrítsa
Filiate
Ioánnina
Islet of Nissi
Corfu Town
6
Dodóni
Benítses
Igoumenítsa
Epirus
5
Lake Pamvotis
Tríkkala
Kávos
CORFU (KÉRKYRA)
Paramythiá
Margaríti
Lakka
Párga
E15
Árta
PÁXOS
ANTÍPAXOS
Zalóngo
Nikópolis
Ambrakikós Kólpos
(Ambracian Gulf)
5
Préveza
Áktio (Actium)
Lefkás
Vónitsa
Amphilochía
LEFKÁDA
Nídri
Aetós
Vathý
Mítikas
Agrínio
Vassilikí
Ionian Sea
Etolikón
Fiskardo
Fríkes
Astakós
E19
KEFALONÍA
Assos
Ithaca
Antírrio
Myrtos Beach
Dhivarata
ITHACA
Messolónghi
Río
Aghía
Sámi
Patraïkós
Pátras
Efimía
Kólpos
(Gulf of Patra)
Lixoúri
Argostóli
Póros
To Pátras
Metaxáta
Skála
9
Kyllíni
74
ZÁKYNTHOS
Zákynthos
Amalías
Laganás
Vassilikós
Pírgos

To Ancona, Bari, Brindisi

0   37.6 km
     25 mi
N

GREECE
Western Greece & The Ionian Islands
Athens

Mountain
Ferry Route

are inhabited. For travelers, though, it's two of the six major islands that we single out here: Corfu and Kefalonía.

A LOOK AT THE PAST

It's in the fabric of their history that the Ionian Islands can trace certain threads that both tie them and distinguish them from the rest of Greece. During the late Bronze Age (1500–1200 B.C.), there was a Mycenaean-type culture on at least several of these islands. Although certain names of islands and cities were the same as those used to-day—Ithaka, Zakinthos, and Cephalonia, for instance—scholars have never been able to agree on exactly which were the sites described in *The Odyssey*. (This has never stopped tour guides and tourists from visiting these sites.)

When the Bronze Age faded into the "dark age," the islands slipped into obscurity until they were re-colonized by people from the city-states on the Greek mainland, starting in the 8th century B.C. The Peloponnesian War, in fact, can be traced back to a quarrel between Corinth and her colony at Corcyra (Corfu) that led to Athens's interference and eventually the full-scale war. By the end of the 3rd century B.C., the islands had fallen under the rule of the Romans. When Rome's power faded, the Byzantine empire absorbed the islands as a province near the end of the 9th century A.D. For the next several centuries, the Ionian Islands were prey to the various warring powers (and pirates) in this part of the Mediterranean—Byzantine Greeks, Franks from Western Europe, Normans from Sicily, Italians, and Turks. By the end of the 14th century, Corfu fell under the control of Venice, and during the next few centuries, Venice not only came to rule all the Ionian Islands but the Italian language and culture—including the Roman Catholic Church—came to predominate.

With the fall of Venice to Napoleon's France in 1797, the French took over and—with the exception of a period (1800–07) when the Ionian Islands experimented with a so-called Septinsular Republic—the French held sway until 1815, the end of Napoleon. The Ionian Islands then became a protectorate of the British; although the islands did experience peace and prosperity, they were in fact a colony. When parts of Greece gained true independence from the Turks by 1830—due in part to leadership from Ionians such as Ioannis Capodistrias—many Ionians became restless when they remained under the British. Attempts at gaining union with Greece culminated with Prime Minister Gladstone's granting this in 1864.

During World War II, the islands were at first occupied by the Italians, but when the Germans took over from them, the islands, especially Corfu, suffered greatly. In the decades since 1945, the Ionian islands have enjoyed unparalleled prosperity.

1 Corfu

There's Corfu the island and Corfu the town, and they aren't always the same place—or at least they don't necessarily appeal to the same vacationers. Corfu the island lures people who are essentially looking to escape civilization and head for the beach, with the search for a great fish dinner as the maximum exertion. The destinations on Corfu attracting sun-seekers range from the undeveloped little beaches, with a simple taverna and some rooms to rent, to spectacularly developed beach resorts, with restaurants that could hold their own anywhere. Then there's Corfu Town—European, you might at first conclude, but then again not quite like any other European city. And, there's the inland of this island, with lush vegetation and gentle slopes, modest villages and farms, and countless olive and fruit trees.

Whichever Corfu you choose, it will prove to be a congenial place. It was, after all, this island's ancient inhabitants, the Phaeacians, who made Odysseus so comfortable. Visitors today will find Corfu similarly hospitable.

ESSENTIALS

GETTING THERE   By Plane   Olympic Airways provides at least three flights daily from and to Athens and two flights weekly to and from Thessaloniki. One way for both routes is about Dr 20,000 ($85). The **Olympic Airways office** (☎ **0661/ 30180**) in Corfu Town is (for now at least) on Odos Polila 11, but many agents around town sell tickets. There are also numerous charter flights linking Corfu directly to many European cities, but most of these are package deals involving accommodations, etc. However, occasionally you'll see notices in travel agency offices in Corfu Town offering individual tickets on charter planes to European cities.

The Corfu Airport is located about 2 miles (4km) south of the center of Corfu Town. Fortunately, the flight patterns of most planes do not bring them over the city. There is no public bus into town, so everyone takes a taxi; a standard fare should be about Dr 1,500 ($6.40) but may fluctuate with the number of passengers, amount of luggage, and time of day.

By Ship   There are many lines and ships linking Corfu to both Greek and foreign ports. There are ferries almost hourly between Igoumenitsa, directly across on the mainland, and at least one daily to and from Pátras. There are daily ships linking Corfu to Brindisi; contact the **Minoan/Strintzi Lines** (☎ **0661/25232**) in Corfu. There is the **Hellenic Mediterranean Line** (☎ **0661/31569**) linking Corfu to Venice daily during high season. The **ANEK line** (☎ **01/3233481**) in Athens provides service several times weekly to and from Trieste and Ancona, Italy, while the **Ventouris Line** (☎ **01/0889280**) in Athens offers the same to and from Bari, Italy. (The ships to and from those Italian ports also connect with Pátras.)

By the way, Corfu Town is also one of Greece's official entry/exit harbors, with customs and health authorities as well as passport control. This is of special interest to those arriving from foreign lands on yachts. There are, of course, numerous marinas located around all of the islands.

By Bus   The private bus line **KTEL** offers service all the way from Athens or Thessaloniki, with a ferry carrying you between Corfu and Igoumenitsa on the mainland opposite. This mode of transportation also allows you to get on or off at main points along the way, such as Ioánnina. The buses are comfortable enough, but be prepared for many hours of winding roads.

VISITOR INFORMATION   The **National Tourist Organization** (☎ **0661/ 37638,** 0661/37640, 0661/39422, or 0661/37520) has recently moved to the first floor of a modern building (unnumbered) on the corner of Rizospaston and Polila in the new town, a block from the Post Office. Its hours are Monday through Friday from 7am to 2:30pm, closed Saturday and Sunday. Just as helpful are the two **Municipal Information Offices.** One is on Esplanade Square, open April through October only, Monday through Saturday from about 9am to 8:30pm, Sunday about 9am to 3pm. The other is down in the reception building at the New Port; its hours are Monday through Saturday from 6:30am to 1pm. They'll give you the standard brochure on Corfu with a fine map that can guide you around town; if you want a map of the island, they will sell you one for Dr 300 ($1.30).

GETTING AROUND   By Bus   Public buses, distinguished by their dark blue color, service Corfu Town, its suburbs, and nearby destinations. The semiprivate **KTEL buses,** painted green and cream, offer frequent service to points all over the island—Paleokastritsa, Glifada, Sidari, and more. The **KTEL office** (☎ **0661/39627** or 0661/39985) is located just off Leoforos Avramiou, up from the New Port.

By Taxi   In and around Corfu Town, a taxi is probably your best bet—sometimes the only way around, such as to and from the harbor and the airport. Although taxi drivers are supposed to use their meters, most don't, so you should agree on the fare before setting out. You may also decide to use a taxi to visit at least some of the sites outside Corfu Town; again, be sure to agree on the fare before setting out.

By Car   There are myriad car-rental agencies all over Corfu; even so, during high season it can be very difficult to get a vehicle on the spur of the moment. If you're sure of your time on Corfu, it's advisable to make arrangements, before departing home, with one of the established international agencies. If you haven't made prior arrangements, try **Greek Skies Travel Agency** (☎ **0661/39160;** fax 0661/36161) in Corfu Town at Odos Kapodistriou 20A.

By Moped   It's easy to rent all kinds of mopeds and scooters and motorcycles, but the roads are so curvy, narrow, and steep that you should be very sure that you are in absolute control of such a vehicle.

CITY LAYOUT   The **new town** of Corfu Town is relatively modern and even a bit cosmopolitan; its **Leoforos Alexandros** almost evokes Paris but not so its shops. You probably won't want to spend much time in this new town, except for visiting the Post Office (and its news stand outside), the National Tourist Information Office, and the telephone office.

You'll want to be spending most of your time in the **old town,** with its *cantouni,* Greece's largest complex of centuries-old streets and buildings, effectively unchanged and thoroughly inhabited. This is the kind of place where if you go out early Sunday morning, the streets resonate with the chanting of the priests and choirs from the many Orthodox churches. Meanwhile, the crown jewel of the old town is the **Liston,** the arcaded row of cafes were you can spend a lazy afternoon watching a cricket match on the great green of the adjacent **Esplanade** (or *Spianada*). For those whose idea of travel is a city with restaurants and shops, historical structures and interesting architecture, museums and street life, old Corfu Town can occupy visitors for many days.

FAST FACTS: Corfu Town

American Express   The official agent for Corfu is **Greek Skies,** Odos Kapodistriou 20A (☎ **0661/39160;** fax 0661/36161). American Express checks and charge cards, of course, are honored at many places throughout the island.

Area Code   The area code for Corfu Town is **0661.** For Paleokastritsa, it's **0663.**

Banks/ATMS   There are numerous banks in both the Old Town and New Town, many with ATMs that you can use either to borrow money or debit your home account through Visa and other cards.

Car Rentals   See "Getting Around," earlier in this chapter.

Embassies/Consulates   There is no U.S. Consulate on Corfu. The **British Consul** is at Odos Menekratos 1 (☎ 0661/30055); it is located down at the south end of the town, near the monument of the same name.

Emergencies   For general emergencies, dial **100.** For an ambulance, dial **166.**

Holidays   In addition to the usual Greek holidays and holidays, Corfu Town makes much of **Carnival** (the days before Lent). Four times a year it also parades the remains of the island's patron saint, St. Spiridon, through the streets of old Corfu: Palm Sunday, Holy Saturday, August 1, and the first Sunday in November.

Hospitals   Corfu Town's **General Hospital** is on Odos Julius Andreatti.

Luggage Storage/Lockers   There are two places to leave your luggage (for a fee), both across from the New Port Reception Building. One is directly across the avenue and above the Commercial Bank at Odos Avramiou 130—the sign is prominent; its present status seems unpredictable. The other is reached by walking up Avramiou to the building at no. 120, where you turn right into the side street, and then make a left; you will soon see a sign to an upstairs area where "Mrs. Maria" will guard your luggage for Dr 500 ($2.15) per item per 24 hours. She insists she is at home all the time, but it would be advisable not to arrive at too awkward an hour or with too little time to catch a boat.

Newspapers and Magazines   The best selection of foreign-language newspapers and periodicals is at either the kiosk newsstand right outside the main Post Office (See "Post Office," below) or at the little shop called **Kiosk** at Odos Kapodistriou 11 (behind the Liston).

Police   The **main police station** (☎ 0661/39575) is at Leoforos Alexandros 19 (catercorner from the post office). The **Tourist Police** (☎ 0661/30265) are at Odos Xenofontos Stratigou 1 (one flight up); it's just off the waterfront as you walk toward Solomou Square and to New Fortress.

Post Office   The main post office (☎ 0661/25544) is at Leoforos Alexandros 26. Open Monday through Friday from 7:30am to 8pm, Saturday 7:30am to 2pm, Sunday 9am to 1:30pm.

Restrooms   There are public toilets at the New Port Reception Building, in San Rocco Square, at the KTEL Bus Station, and at the Esplanade (opposite Kapodistriou 20, in a below-ground locale, having a prominent yellow structure that's actually an elevator for handicapped people).

Telephone, Telex, and Fax   The **main OTE office** is at Odos Mantzarou 9 (a small street between Rizospaston and the Municipal Theater). It's open every day 6am to midnight. There's a **branch office of OTE** at Odos Kapodistriou 34 (up a slope past Liston), but its hours are highly irregular. Best of all in terms of facilities and service is the **OTE branch** down at the New Port. It's open Monday through Sunday from 8am to 10pm; the staff there is really dedicated to helping foreigners.

Travel Agenices   There are many travel agencies, all over town, but Frommer loyalists have always fared well with **Greek Skies** (see "American Express," above). Proprietor Spyros Lemis and his staff will take care of your every need, from hotels and rooms to car rentals and airline tickets.

WHAT TO SEE & DO
ATTRACTIONS

Archaeological Museum. Odos P. Vraila-Armeni 1 (on the corner of Dimokritas, the boulevard along the waterfront). ☎ **0661/30680.** Admission Dr 800 ($3.40), free Sunday. Tues-Sun 8:30am–3pm.

Even if you're not a devotee of ancient history or museums, you should take an hour to visit this small museum. On your way to see its masterwork, as you turn left off the upstairs vestibule, you'll pass the **stone lion** dating from the Archaic Period (ca. 575 B.C.). Found in the nearby Menekrates tomb, which is along the waterfront, just down from the museum, the lion is thought to have originally rested on the tomb. You go around and behind this work to the large room with arguably the finest example of Archaic temple sculpture extant, the **pediment from Temple of Artemis.** The temple itself is located just south of Corfu Town and dates from about 590 B.C.

The pediment features the Gorgon Medusa, attended by two pantherlike animals. You don't need to be an art historian to note how this predates the great classical works such as the Elgin marbles—not only in the naïveté of its sculpture but also in the emphasis on the monstrous, with the humans so much smaller.

Not as important but interesting for comparison is the fragment from another **Archaic pediment found at Figare, Corfu.** Displayed in an adjoining room, it shows Dionysos and a youth reclining on a couch. It's only a century later than the Gorgon pediment, but already the humans have reduced the animal in size and placed it under the couch.

Museum of Asiatic Art. The Palace of St. Michael and St. George, north end of Esplanade. ☎ **0661/30443.** Admission Dr 1,000 ($4.25). Tues–Sun 9am–3pm. (*Note:* This museum was closed for renovations to host a European Economic Community Summit meeting, and its opening was scheduled for 1996.)

The building itself is of more than passing interest as an example of neoclassical architecture. It was constructed between 1819 and 1824 to serve as the residence of the lord high commissioner, the British ruler of the Ionian islands, to house the headquarters of the Order of St. Michael and St. George, and to provide the assembly room for the Ionian senate. When the British turned the Ionians over to Greece, this building was given to the king of Greece. As he seldom spent much time there, it fell into disrepair, until after World War II when it was restored and turned into a museum.

The works on display are mainly from the collections of two Greek diplomats. The centerpiece of the museum is the **Chinese porcelains, bronzes,** and other works from the Shang Dynasty (1500 B.C.) to the Ching Dynasty (19th century). There are also strong holdings of **Japanese works**—wood-block prints, ceramics, sculpture, watercolors, and netsuke (carved sash fasteners). You may not have come to Greece to appreciate Asian art, but this is one of several unexpected delights of Corfu.

Old Fort (Paleo Frourio). The Esplanade (opposite the Liston). Admission Dr 800 ($3.40), students Dr 400 ($1.70), seniors (over 60) Dr 500 ($2.15). Tues–Fri 8am–7pm; Sat, Sun, holidays 8:30am–3pm. During the summer there is a sound-and-light show several nights a week (in different foreign languages, so be sure to check the schedule) Dr 2,000 ($8.50).

Originally a promontory attached to the mainland, its two peaks—*koryphi* in Greek—gave the modern name to the town and island; the promontory itself was for long the main town (and appears as such in many old engravings).

The Venetians dug the moat in the 16th century at the time they were building the ambitious fortifications (most of which the British blew up when they left in 1864). These enabled the Venetians to hold off several attempts by the Turks to conquer this outpost of Christianity, most notably in a great siege of 1716 that was turned away with the aid of Marshal Schulenburg from Saxony. (The Venetians honored him with the statue now on the Esplanade opposite the entrance to the fort.)

Each peak is crowned by a castle; you can get fine views of Albania to the east and Corfu, town and island, to the west. The Doric-style Church of St. George was built by the British in 1830.

New Fortress. Best approached from Platia Solomou on the waterfront by climbing the flight of stairs that is Odos Velissariou. Admission Dr 500 ($2.15). Daily 9am–9pm. Inside the fort are a cafe, a souvenir shop, public telephones, and toilets.

Yet another of the mammoth fortresses built by the Venetians (1577–88), this will be appreciated by many people when viewed from a distance: It seems incredibly large and overpowering. Considerable parts of what we see were added by the French and then the English. The fortress served as a Greek naval installation until 1992.

Aficionados of old forts can wander through the labyrinth here, but many visitors will be content to enjoy the spectacular views around all points of the compass.

The Kalypso Star. Old Port, Corfu Town. ☎ **0671/46525.** Fax 0661/23506. Adults Dr 3,000 ($12.75), children Dr 1,500 ($6.40). Every hour 10am–6pm, night trip 10pm.

The *Kalypso Star* is a glass-bottomed boat that takes small groups on trips offshore and provides a fascinating view of the marine life and undersea formations.

Danilia Village. Located at Gouvia, 5 miles (8km) northeast of Corfu Town, on the road to Paleokastritsa. A visit here, including a meal, will cost an adult about Dr 9,000 ($38). Travel agents in Corfu can put you on a group tour for about Dr 12,000 ($51), which includes private bus transportation, a tour of the village, an evening meal (with all the wine you want), and the entertainment. For further information, contact the Corfu Town office at Odos Kapodistriou 38 ☎ 0661/36833. Mon–Sat 10am–1pm, 6pm–midnight. Bus: 7 from Corfu Town goes close by, then it's a 1-mile (2km) walk.

Not necessarily everyone's idea of why we go abroad, but clearly popular with many, is this working replica of a traditional Greek village. It includes fields being tilled, herds of goats and sheep, wine and olive presses, weavers, potters, a museum of farm objects, and an Orthodox Church. To the extent that it's almost impossible for most visitors ever to witness all this in real-life situations, it can be worthwhile and interesting.

If you do go, you should hold off until the evening session, when you can take a meal (at 8:30pm) at the taverna on the grounds, accompanied by Greek music and folk dancers.

A STROLL AROUND CORFU TOWN

Corfu Town is not the kind of city to make a concentrated tour through, with your face buried in a guidebook. Rather it's a browsers' town—the kind of place you want to stroll though in search of a snack or souvenir and serendipitously discover an old church or monument. But to gain some orientation, start with the Esplanade area that is bounded by the **Old Fort** (see above) and the sea on one side; the small haven below and to the north of the Old Fort is known as Mandraki Harbor, while the shore to the south is home port to the Corfu Yacht Club.

The Esplanade is bisected by Odos Dousmani. The north part has the field known as the *Platia,* where cricket games are played on lazy afternoons. At the north side of the Esplanade is the Palace of St. Michael and St. George, now housing the **Museum of Asiatic Art** (see above). If you proceed along the left (northwest) corner of the palace, you come out above the coast and can make your way around Odos Arseniou above the medieval sea walls (known as the *mourayia*).

On your way you will pass (up a flight of stairs on the left) the **Byzantine Museum** in the Church of Antivouniotissa, with its fine collection of religious art and artifacts. It's open Tuesday through Saturday from 9am to 3pm, Sunday 10am to 2:30pm. Admission is Dr 800 ($4.40).

You proceed along the coast road and come down to the square at the Old Port; above its far side rises the **New Fortress** (see above) and beyond this is the New Port. Off to the left of the square, with what remains of the 16th-century **Porta Spilia** (and past the building with the Tourist Police), is Platia Solomou. On the far side of this square, on Odos Solomou 7-9, is the **Shell Museum**, the collection of a world-ranging Corfiote, Sagias Napoleon. It's open daily from 10am to 7pm. Admission is Dr 500 ($2.15).

If you proceed up from Platia Solomou along Odos Velissariou, you come on your left to the 300-year-old **Synagogue,** with its fine collection of torah crowns. It's open on Saturdays from 9am.

If you're adventurous, you can now turn to your left and plunge into the section of Old Corfu known as *Campiello,* with its stepped streets and narrow alleys.

Back on the Esplanade, its south part has a bandstand and at its far end is the **Maitland Rotunda**, commemorating Sir Thomas Maitland, the first British lord high commissioner of the Ionian Islands. Past this is the **statue of Count Ioannis Kapodistrias** (1776–1836), the first president of independent Greece. Just outside the south end of the Esplanade is a school building that once housed the Ionian Academy.

If you proceed south along the shore road from this end of the Esplanade, you pass the **Corfu Palace Hotel** on your right; then the **Archaeological Museum** (see above), up Odos Vraila on the right. After two more blocks, off to the right on the corner of Odos Marasli, is the **Tomb of Menekrates,** a circular tomb of a notable who drowned about 650 B.C. Proceeding to the right here onto Odos Alexandras will bring you into the heart of the **new Corfu Town.**

The western side of the north half of the Esplanade is lined by a wide tree-shaded strip filled with cafe tables and chairs, then a street reserved for pedestrians, and then arcaded buildings patterned after the Rue de Rivoli in Paris. These two arcaded buildings were begun by the French, but were finished by the British. They are known as the **Liston,** a word derived from the English word *list* and given a Greek suffix; it refers to something like a "social register," the list of those whose social status allowed them to hang out under the arcades. Now anyone with the price of a cup of coffee (admittedly an expensive one) can sit here and enjoy the passing scene. In addition to cafes, there are a couple of restaurants and several shops also in the Liston. The upper stories are apartments.

At the back of the Liston is Odos Kapadistriou, and perpendicular from this are several streets that lead into the heart of **Old Corfu**—a mélange of fine shops, old churches, souvenir stands, eating places, and other stores in a maze of streets, alleys, and squares that make you feel you are in Venice without its water. The broadest and most stylish is Odos Nikiforio Theotoki. Proceeding up Odos Aghios Spyridon (at the north end), you come to the corner of Odos Filellinon and to **Aghios Spyridon Cathedral,** dedicated to Spyridon, patron saint of Corfu. A 4th-century bishop of Cyprus, Spyridon is credited with saving Corfu from famine, plagues, and a Turkish siege. The church hosts the saint's embalmed body in a silver casket, as well as precious gold and silver votive offerings and many fine old icons.

Proceeding up Odos Voulgareos behind the south end of the Liston, you come up along the back of the **Town Hall,** built in 1663 as a Venetian Loggia; it later served as a theater. In 1903, it was renovated (and its second story added) and turned into the Town Hall. Turn into the square it faces and you will feel you are in a Roman piazza, with its steps and terraces, the Roman Catholic Cathedral Church on the left, and reigning over the top, the restored Catholic archbishop's residence now housing the Bank of Greece. The street proceeding up the incline along the left side of Town Hall Square is **Odos Guilford,** named after the Lord Guilford, the eccentric Englishman who in the 1820s tried to introduce higher learning and culture to Corfu.

Again, you are invited to wander up and down and in and out the various streets and continue exploring Old Corfu.

SHOPPING

Bizarre. Odos Arseniou 27 (on outer waterfront road to Old Harbor), Corfu 49100. ☎ **0661/ 26384.**

This store has an eye-catching array of women's clothing, yet is a bit out of the way, so we thought we'd call it to your attention. To be frank, most of these clothes will appeal to the younger crowd, or at least women who like to dress dramatically. Most of the dresses, pant suits, jumpers, and whatnots are made in Greece, although some are from Asia—more earthy tones from the former, dazzling colors from the latter. The prices seem reasonable—a handsome knit sweater-jumper combination for Dr 8,000 ($34), for example. Open daily from 10am to 10pm in the summer, 10am to 3pm in the winter.

Elli—The House of Embroidery. Odos N. Theotoki 88, Corfu 49100. ☎ **0661/26283.**

Again, there are many shops selling handmade needlework and weavings, and we can't claim this one has anything all that much different in quality or pricing. But the owner, George Kantaros, seems willing to talk about his wares and discuss prices. In addition to the many handmade tablecloths, embroidered coverlets, lace doilies, and such, he has some small Greek rugs. Don't be surprised, however, to see the American-style quilts, which are imported from somewhere. Pick something you like and the price will seem fair. Open July through October 9am to 10pm; November through June, 9am to 2pm and 5 to 9pm.

Olive Wood. Odos N. Theotoki 131 (at far end, close to waterfront), Corfu 49100. ☎ **0661/ 47375.**

There are several shops in Corfu Town that sell products made from olive wood, and in general they are all about the same. We especially like this one, though, because the maker of most of the items can be observed working away inside. Salad bowls, boxes and vases, flutes, casks, and serving utensils are among the main objects. Prices are reasonable—a fair-sized salad bowl for Dr 6,000 ($26), serving fork and spoon for Dr 1,010 ($4.25). If you're looking for a typical Greek item as a gift, try olive wood. Open March through October 9am to 10pm.

Terracotta. Odos Filarmonikis 2 (just off N. Theotoki, the main shopping street). ☎ and fax **0661/45260.**

Although owned by a Swiss woman, Ruth Bossard, this elegant little gallery-shop sells only contemporary Greek work—jewelry, true one-of-a-kind pieces; ceramics; small sculptures; and wall plaques. Some of the work is by well-known Greek artists and artisans such as Theodoros Papayiannis; his small bronzes are both original and engaging. Nothing is cheap but everything is classy. Open daily from 9am to 9pm.

WHERE TO STAY

Corfu Town and the island of Corfu have an apparently inexhaustible choice of accommodations, but during the high season (July through September) many of these will be taken by package groups from Europe. Reservations are recommended if you have specific preferences for that period.

IN TOWN

Very Expensive

Corfu Palace Hotel. Leoforos Democratias 2 (along Garitsa Bay, just south of center), Corfu 491000. ☎ **0661/39485.** Fax 0661/31-749. 112 rms, 8 suites, all with tub and shower. A/C MINIBAR TV TEL. High season, Dr 66,170–Dr 85,800 ($282–$365) double; low season, Dr 39,000–Dr 53,690 ($166–$228), double. Rates include buffet breakfast. Children up to age 12 sharing room with cot, free without meals. AE, DC, EU, MC, V. Parking at hotel. Closed Nov–Mar. Five minutes' walk from Esplanade.

This is not only a grand hotel but an elegant one, with an atmosphere really more in the Swiss tradition of its owners than indigenous Corfiote. The landscaping creates a tropical ambience; the lobby and public areas bespeak luxury. All rooms enjoy balconies and views of the sea; their decor varies from Louis XIV to Greek rustic but all are roomy and restful. The guests can make use of the facilities of the nearby Corfu Tennis Club and Yacht Club; the Corfu Golf Club is 9 miles (14km) away. Aside from the splendid surroundings, superb service, and grand meals, the main appeal of this hotel is probably its combination of restful isolation above the bay with its proximity to the city center.

Dining/Entertainment: The hotel's two restaurants, the Albatross (a grill room on the poolside terrace) and the Panorama (with a view of the bay), serve both Greek and international menus; both vie for some people's idea of the finest eating on Corfu. Two bars; poolside buffet. Barbecue every Saturday.

Services: Concierge, room service, dry cleaning, laundry, newspaper delivery, baby-sitting.

Facilities: Three swimming pools (one outdoors, one indoors, one for children), sundeck, tennis nearby (outdoors, lit in evening), bicycle rental, game room, conference and banquet rooms (up to 200), car rentals, tours arranged, hairdresser, jewelry store, foreign-language books.

Expensive

Cavalieri. Odos Kapodistriou 4, (at far south end of Esplanade), Corfu 49100. ☎ **0661/ 39041.** Fax 0661/39283. 50 rms, all with baths. A/C TV TEL. High season, Dr 45,500 ($194); low season, Dr 26,000–Dr 28,250 ($110–$120). Rates include buffet breakfast. AE, DC, MC, V. Open all year. Parking on adjacent streets. Walking distance of old and new town.

If you like your hotels in the discreet old European style, this is for you; those who prefer a bit of glitz should go elsewhere. It's in an old (original parts 17th century) building with a small elevator; the main lounge is Italian-velvet; its restaurant is nothing special; service is low-key; rooms are spare. But it must be doing something right, advance reservations are usually required. Location is much of its appeal: Front rooms on the upper floors have great views of the Old Fort, so ask for them. Above all, literally, is the rooftop garden, which after 6:30pm offers drinks, snacks, and light meals along with a spectacular view. Even if you don't stay here, it's a grand place to pass an hour in the evening.

Moderate

Astron Hotel. Odos Donzelot 15 (waterfront road down to old harbor), Corfu 49100. ☎ **0661/39505.** Fax 0661/33708. 30 doubles, 3 singles, all with baths. TEL. High season, Dr 21,580 ($92) double; low season, Dr 14,690 ($63) double. Rates include continental breakfast. EU. Open all year. Parking at nearby lot. Walking distance of everyplace in town.

Recognizable with its yellow awnings as you enter or leave the port of Corfu, the Astron may strike those seeking a shiny new hotel as one that has seen better days. And indeed, this is a place for those who like to stay in a hotel that boasts of one of the oldest elevators in town. The lobby is a bit spartan, but the common rooms, including a TV room and a bar, are pleasant enough. And the bedrooms and bathrooms are large, the way they used to be in hotels. There's plenty of hot water (and heat in the winter). Most of all, this is a hotel for those who feel that if you're staying on an island you should be on the water. Definitely insist on a front room with a balcony for a glorious view of the harbor, the New Fort, and Vidos islet just offshore. Then you'll see why we recommend it.

Arcadion Hotel. Odos Kapodistriou 44 (catercorner from south end of Liston, facing the Esplanade), Corfu 49100. ☎ **0661/37671.** Fax 0661/45087. 55 rms, some with tubs, some with showers. TEL. High season, Dr 23,000 ($98); low season, Dr 16,600 ($71) double. Rates include buffet breakfast. No credit cards. Open all year. Public parking lot (fee) nearby.

If you like to be at the center of a city, you can't get much closer than this: When you step out the door, the Esplanade and the Liston are 50 feet away. Admittedly, this also means that on pleasant evenings (most of the time you'd be there) there's apt to be a crowd of young people hanging out in front of it; so it's probably not for early to-bedders, as you'd probably want a front room with its view over the Esplanade and Old Fort. In the mornings, however, you reclaim that area when you breakfast on the terrace. The lobby and common areas are beginning to look a bit tired, but rooms are clean and adequate. Definitely a hotel for those who like to feel they've left home.

Bella Venezia. Odos N. Zambeli 4 (approached from far south end of Esplanade), Corfu 49100. ☎ **0661/46500** or 0661/44290. Fax 0661/20708. 32 rms, all with baths. A/C TV TEL. High season, Dr 24,700 ($105) double; low season, Dr 20,000 ($85). Rates include buffet breakfast. AE, DC, EU, MC, V. Open all year. Parking on adjacent streets. Walking distance of old and new town.

Like the gold medal winner of the decathlon, this hotel may not win in any single category, but its combined virtues will make it many people's first choice. The building is a restored (in late 1980s) neoclassical mansion, with character if no major distinction. Its location is just a bit off center and lacks fine views, but it's quiet while still close enough to anyplace you'd want to walk to. The common areas are not especially stylish but have their personality. Although not luxurious, the rooms have an old-world charm. There is no restaurant, but there's a colorful patio-garden for breakfast and enclosed kiosk for light meals. Finally, its rates are below what other hotels of this caliber charge.

OUTSIDE TOWN
Very Expensive

Corfu Hilton. Odos Nausicaa, Kanoni, (some 3 miles/5km south of Corfu Town), Corfu 49100. ☎ **0661/36540.** Fax 0661/36551. 255 rooms, 11 suites, all with bath. A/C MINIBAR TEL. High season, Dr 38,000–Dr 52,000 ($162–$221) double; low season, Dr 32,000–Dr 40,000 ($136–$170) double. Buffet breakfast extra Dr 3,500 ($14.90) per person). Inquire at travel agents for special packages for extended stays. AE, DC, EU, MC, V. Open all year-round. Parking on grounds. Public bus (no. 2) stops 200 yards away, but a taxi is probably more in style.

This is a grand hotel in the contemporary manner—more like a resort in the range of its facilities and amenities. Its lobby sets the tone: spacious yet relaxed. The staff likewise is professional yet friendly. The grounds create a semitropical ambience. In addition to the two pools (one indoors, one outdoors), there's a lovely private beach down below. The famous locale known as Kanoni is a couple of hundred yards from the hotel. The island's airport is off in the middle distance—not a major problem, but you're advised to ask for a room facing the sea and away from the airport.

Dining/Entertainment: The main restaurant, the Eftanissa, serves a fixed menu for those paying on half board. The Eftanissa Grill overlooks the gardens; it serves a Greek and Continental menu. There's also a restaurant at the pool and a snack bar on the beach. The Kefi Bar has a pianist in the evenings.

Services: Concierge, room service, dry cleaning, laundry, baby-sitting, minivan to Corfu Town.

Facilities: Two swimming pools, health club, sundeck, 2 tennis courts (lit at night), water sports equipment, jogging track, bowling, billiards, table tennis, 20% discount at Corfu Golf Club 10 miles (16km) away, conference rooms (up to 500), car-rental desk, tours arranged, beauty salon, boutiques.

Casino: Occupying the rooms at one corner of the hotel's lobby, the casino actually belongs to the Greek National Tourist Organization. It's open from 8pm to 2am nightly.

Moderate

Archontiko Hotel. Odos Athanasiou 61, Garitsa (about 1 mile from center) Corfu 49100. ☎ **0661/36850.** Fax 0661/3829410. 10 rooms, 10 suites, all with tubs and showers. MINIBAR TV TEL. High season, Dr 20,670 ($88) double, Dr 36,400 ($155) suite; low season, Dr 14,040 ($60) double, Dr 19,500 ($83) suite. Rates do not include any meals (but breakfast is served). No credit cards. Parking on street.

Set one street back from the Garitsa Bay but facing a strip of park along the bay, this should appeal to those who value old buildings with unusual decor more than a fashionable location. The hotel is in a turn-of-the century mansion and some of the rooms have the original frescoed cathedral ceilings (although the furniture is a somewhat incongruous knotty pine). All rooms have large modern bathrooms. The suites can accommodate from three to six beds. You breakfast outdoors. The neighborhood is safe and quiet and the walk into town can be pleasant. A hotel for independent people.

Inexpensive

Hotel Royal. Odos Figareto 110, Kanoni (a few hundred yards before Hilton), Corfu 49100. ☎ **0661/37512.** Fax 0661/38786. 121 rooms, all with bath. TEL. Year-round Dr 13,000 ($55) double. Rates include continental breakfast. No credit cards. Closed Nov–Mar. Parking on grounds. Public bus: 2 stops 100 yards away but taxi is probably more in style.

This might be considered an alternative to the nearby Hilton if your desire is to stay outside Corfu Town but you can't afford the Hilton's rates. It's a kind of funky place—the architecture and decorations are neobaroque, but the lobby is filled with traditional works of art, the proprietor's personal collection. The most spectacular feature are the three swimming pools arranged in tiers—it's a great place to come back to with the kids after a day spent sightseeing. As with the Hilton, the airport is off in the middle distance, but the noise problem adds up to a relatively small portion of a day. It's a big hotel with a family atmosphere, and you can't beat the rates.

WHERE TO DINE
IN TOWN
Very Expensive

Chambor. Odos Guilford 71, Corfu 49100. ☎ **0661/39031.** Fax 0661/20112. Reservations recommended in high season; definitely a dress-up place in the evening. Main courses Dr 1,500–Dr 4,500 ($6.40–$19.15). EU, MC, V. Daily 9am–2am. GREEK/ITALIAN.

This is reputed to be the finest and most expensive restaurant in the center of Corfu Town, and it certainly lives up to the latter. Much of its appeal is its setting: On one of the terraces of Town Hall Square, you sit under umbrellas and, gazing at the illuminated Town Hall and Catholic Cathedral, you can feel you're in an Italian opera. The current chef is a Swiss-trained Greek and we wished his dishes had a bit more definition—the appetizers (expensive) were subtle to the point of blandness. But the *bourdetto*—a Corfu specialty of fish filet in a garlic-tomato sauce—was delicious. You could eat the cheapest items on the menu—spaghetti or moussaka for Dr 1,500 ($6.40)—have a glass of wine, and get out for Dr 5,000 ($21) per person, but then why go to such a place? More likely you'll end up spending at least twice that. It is overpriced, but we say, go for it if you're in a celebratory mood. When's the next time you'll get to be in an opera?

Expensive

Aegli Garden Restaurant. Odos Kapodistriou 23 (behind Liston), Corfu 49100. ☎ **0661/31944.** Fax 0661/26268. Main courses Dr 900–Dr 2,800 ($3.95–$11.90). AE, DC, EU, MC, V. Year-round 10:30am–midnight. GREEK/CONTINENTAL.

Located in the Liston, this old favorite offers seating indoors, under the arcades, or in the pedestrian-mall of Kapodistriou. The tasty menu attracts a lively crowd to all three locales in the evening. They take special pride in their Corfiote specialties, several of which are traditional Greek foods with rather spicy sauces—filet of fish, octopus, *pastitsada* (baked veal), *baccala* (salted cod fish), and *sofrito* (veal). If spiciness isn't your thing, try the swordfish or the prawns (shrimp). In fact, everything here is done with great care.

Venetian Well. Platia Kremasti (small square up from Old Harbor, behind Greek Orthodox Cathedral), Corfu 49100. ☎ **0661/44761.** Reservations recommended in high season. Main courses Dr 2,000–Dr 3,000 ($8.50–$12.75). No credit cards. Mon–Sat noon–midnight. Open all year. MIDDLE EASTERN/INTERNATIONAL/GREEK.

This is our candidate for the finest cuisine in Corfu Town. Its location should appeal to those whose idea of elegant dining is to sit at a candlelit table in a rather austere little square with a Venetian wellhead (1699) and facing a church at the opposite side. (When the weather changes, you sit in a stately room with a mural.) The atmosphere is as discreet as the food is inventive. There is no printed menu—you learn what's available either from a chalk board or from your waiter, and there's no predicting what the kitchen will offer on any evening. Start with the dark breads and the butter-cheese spread. For an appetizer (often not cheap), try something like the mushrooms baked in a light cheese sauce. Salads use seasonal vegetables so they vary from month to month. Main courses range from standard Greek dishes such as beef *giouvetsi* (cooked in a pot) to chicken Kasmir (with yogurt, paprika, and spices). Even the wines are a bit different, such as the Corfiote white Liapaditiko. In a word, everything about the Venetian Well has definition.

Moderate

NAOK (Nautical Club of Corfu). Odos Aghios Politekniou 2 (just south of and below the Esplanade), Corfu 49100. ☎ **0661/39230.** Main courses Dr 1,100–Dr 3,500 ($4.70–$14.90). V. Year-round 10am–5pm and 8pm–1am. Parking on street. GREEK.

This cafe-restaurant is on the upper stories of the private yacht club but is open to the public. (You descend to it by stairs from the upper waterfront sidewalk.) With its crisp blue-and-white decor, it offers a cool haven while you look out over the bay and watch the swimmers and boats below. Almost anything here will be well prepared—this is a favorite of Corfiotes—but the seafood is especially appreciated. Or try the chicken *pastitsada*, chicken and pasta with a tomato sauce.

Inexpensive

Bellissimo. Platia Lemonia (just off N. Theotoki), Corfu 49100. ☎ **0661/41112.** Main courses Dr 700–Dr 2,000 ($3–$8.50). Typical Greek selection Dr 1,500 ($6.38). No credit cards. 10:30am–11pm. GREEK/INTERNATIONAL.

This new (1995) restaurant gives promise of being a welcome addition to the Corfu scene—unpretentious but tasty. Located on a central and lovely town square (heavily bombed in World War II, but now restored), it's run by the Stergiou family, which had lived for many years in Canada. They offer a standard Greek menu with some "exotics," including hamburgers and chicken curry. Especially welcome is their Greek sampling plate—tzatziki, tomatoes-and-cucumber salad, *kephtedes* (meatballs), fried potatoes, grilled lamb, and souvlaki. At least at the outset they were charging less than most comparable places; catch them before they become fashionable.

Gloglas Taverna. Odos Guilford 16, Corfu 49100. ☎ **0661/37147.** Main courses, Dr 800–Dr 2,500 ($3.40–$10.65). No credit cards. Daily 11:30am–midnight. GREEK.

You want Greek taverna? You want authenticity? This is it, right on a corner in the heart of the old town, a block back from the Esplanade. You sit under a grape arbor among your fellow diners, a mixture of locals and tourists, who are all seeking no-nonsense taverna meals. You can go indoors if the weather demands, but it would be awfully crowded. The specialties of the house tend to be off the spit or grill—souvlaki (kebab), chicken, pork, and *kokoretsi* (lambs' intestines roasted on the spit). The cooked vegetables—green beans, eggplant, and whatever's in season—are also tasty. Take any of the above with a glass of the house red and you'll wonder why anyone wants to go to a fancier place.

CORFU TOWN AFTER DARK

Corfu Town definitely does have a night life, though, most people may be content to linger over dinner and then, after a promenade, repair to one of the cafes at the Liston, such as the **Capri, Serrano, Liston,** and **Europa**—all of which have much the same selection of light refreshments and drinks. Some may be drawn to a candlelit table at the **Cofineta Magnet,** at the north end of the Esplanade, just outside the Liston. For a real treat, ascend to the rooftop cafe/bar on the **Cavalieri Hotel** (see "Where to Stay," above). If you're seeking to get out of town for a change, visit the nightspots along the coast to the north between Corfu Town and the beach resort of Gouvia, such as **Ekati,** expensive, a typical Greek nightclub; **Esperides,** featuring Greek music; and **Corfu By Night,** definitely touristy. Be prepared to spend some money at these places.

During the summer months, there are frequent concerts by the town's orchestras and bands, mostly free, on the Esplanade. Corfu Town boasts the oldest band in Greece. The **sound-and-light** performances have been described in the listing for the Old Fort (see "What to See & Do: Attractions," above). In September there is the **Corfu Festival,** with concerts, ballet, opera, and theater performances by a mix of Greek and international companies. **Carnival** is celebrated on the last Sunday before Lent with a parade and a burning of an effigy representing the spirit of Carnival.

For those who like to gamble a bit, there's a well-known casino at the Corfu Hilton (see "Where to Stay," above), a few miles outside of town. Bets are a Dr 1,000 ($4.25) minimum and a Dr 250,000 ($1,064) maximum. It may not have the glamour of Monte Carlo, but it attracts quite an international set during the high season.

As for the younger crowd, there are any number of places that go in and out of favor (and business) from year to year. Among the more enduring up around the Esplanade are the relatively sedate **Aktaion,** just to the right of the Old Fort, and the **Tequila,** in an old mansion at Odos Kapodistriou 10, featuring the latest (and loudest) music. Young people seeking more excitement go down past the New Port to a strip of flashy disco bar/clubs—**Sax, Apokalypsis, Hippodrome,** and **Coca Flash.** Presumably, young women attracted to such places are aware of the type of young and not so young Greek males (pests at best) apt to hang out there. Also be aware that these clubs have a cover charge (usually Dr 3,000/$13, including a drink).

SIDE TRIPS FROM CORFU TOWN
ALBANIA

Here's one you didn't count on: A visit to the country of Albania, one of the last exotics left for even the seasoned traveler. Not too many years ago, this was one of those places that Americans were prohibited from visiting and most of the rest of the world had little interest in visiting. Since the early 1990s and the collapse of the Communist regime, Albania has extended its hospitality to everyone. If a day trip there appeals, try **Varthis Travel,** at Odos Donzelot-Arsenou 5 (the coast road above Old Port), ☎ **0661/31140;** fax 0661/31334. The boats set off at 9am; the trip is about 50 minutes; you're back about 7:30pm; the boat fare is Dr 6,000 ($25), but there is another Dr 7,000 ($30) fee for the visit to Albania; this includes a visa, lunch, folk dancing, and a conducted tour of the region where you put ashore.

KANONI/PONDIKONISI/ACHILLEION

Although these sites or destinations are not literally next door to one another, and have little in common, they are grouped here because they do, in fact, all lie south of Corfu Town and can easily be visited in half a day's outing. And they are all places that everyone who comes to Corfu Town will want to visit, even if they go nowhere else on the island. History buffs will revel in their many associations, and even beach bums cannot help but be moved by their scenic charms.

Kanoni is approached south of Corfu Town via the village Analepsis; it's well signed. Ascending most of the way, you come at about 2¹/₂ miles (4km) to the circular terrace (on the right) to the locale known as Kanoni, reflecting the fact that it was built as a gun battery position by the French. Unfortunately it has been commandeered by cafes and restaurants, but you can make your way to the edge and enjoy a wonderful view. Directly below in the inlet are two islets. If you want to visit one or both, you must retrace the road back from Kanoni a few hundred yards to a signed turnoff (on left coming back).

One islet is linked to the land by a causeway; here you'll find the **Monastery of Vlakherna.** To get to the other islet, **Pondikonisi ("Mouse Island"),** you must be ferried by a small boat (always available). Legend has it that this rocky islet is a Phaeacian ship that was turned to stone after taking Odysseus back to Ithaca. The chapel there dates from the 13th century, and its setting among the cypress trees makes it most picturesque. Many Corfiotes make a pilgrimage there in small boats on August 6. It's also the inspiration for the Swiss painter Arnold Boecklin's well-known work *Isle of the Dead,* which in turn inspired Rachmaninoff's music of the same name.

There is a causeway across the little inlet to Perama over on the main body of the island (the Kanoni road is on a peninsula) but it is only for pedestrians. So to continue on to your next destination, the villa of **Achilleion,** you must drive back to the edge of Corfu Town and then take another road about 5 miles (8km) to the south, signed to Gastouri and the villa of Achilleion. It's open daily from 9am to 4pm. Admission is Dr 700 ($3). Bus no. 10, from Platia San Rocco, runs direct to the Achilleion several times daily.

This villa was built between 1890 and 1891 by Empress Elizabeth of Austria, whose beloved son Rudolf had died in 1889 (the famous Mayerling affair). The empress identified him with Achilles, and so the villa is really a memorial to Rudolf (and her grief). Thus the many statues and motifs associated with Achilles (including the dolphins, for Achilles's mother was the water-nymph Thetis). As you approach the villa from the entrance gate, you will see a slightly Teutonic version of a neoclassical summer palace. The interior is a similarly eclectic assemblage of decorative elements. You will want to walk through at least some of the rooms, even if you do not care to examine closely all the memorabilia, family pictures, and such. Among the curiosities, however, is the small saddle-seat that Kaiser Wilhelm II of Germany sat on while performing his imperial chores. (He bought the villa in 1907, after Elizabeth was assassinated in 1898.)

The terraced gardens that surround the villa are now lush and tropical. Be sure to go all the way around and out to the back terraces. Only there will you see the most famous (and the most god-awful) of the statues Elizabeth commissioned (from Herter), *The Dying Achilles,* the 15-foot-tall Achilles that the Kaiser had inscribed: "To the greatest Greek from the greatest German." But even more impressive, step to the edge of the terrace and enjoy a spectacular view of Corfu Town and much of the eastern coast to the south.

If you have your own vehicle, you can continue on past the Achilleion and descend to the **coast between Benitses and Perama;** the first, to the south, has become a popular beach resort. Proceeding north along the coast from Benitses, you come to Perama (another popular beach resort), where a turnoff onto a promontory brings you to the pedestrian causeway opposite Pondikonisi (see above). The main road brings you back to the edge of Corfu Town.

PALEOKASTRITSA

It would probably be rushing things too much to suggest that you make this excursion in the other half of a day shared with the visit to Kanoni and the Achilleion (described above)—although it could be done in terms of sheer mileage and hours. Better to give each its own day, shared with walking around Corfu Town. But if you can make only one excursion on the island, this is certainly a top competitor with Kanoni and the Achilleion. Put it this way: If the latter is more for its historical associations, this is more for its natural attractions.

The drive there is northwest out of Corfu Town by well-marked roads. You follow the coast for about $5^1/2$ miles (8km) to Gouvia, then turn inland. The road eventually narrows but is asphalt all the way as you gradually descend to the west coast and **Paleokastritsa** (about 15 miles/24km). There's no missing it: It's been taken over by hotels and restaurants and all the other companions of modern tourism. There are several bays and coves that make up Paleokastritsa, and some are less developed than others, although all boast sparkling-clear turquoise water. Tradition claims it as the site of Scheria, the capital of the Phaeacians—and thus one of these beaches is where Nausicaa found Odysseus; in fact, no remains have been found to substantiate this.

You can continue on past the beaches and climb a narrow winding road to the **Monastery of the Panaghia** at the edge of a promontory (it's about a mile from the beach, and many prefer to go there by foot). Although founded in the 13th century, nothing that old has survived, but having come this far, it's worth a brief visit, at sunset if you could time it. It's open April through October, 7am to 1pm and 3 to 8pm.

More interesting in some ways, and certainly more challenging, is a visit to the **Angelokastro,** the medieval castle that sits high on a pinnacle overlooking all of Palaeokastritsa. Only the most hardy will choose to walk all the way up from the shore, a taxing hour at least. The rest of us will drive back out of Palaeokastritsa (about $1^1/2$ miles) to a turnoff to the left, signed **Lakones.** There commences an endless winding and ascending road that eventually levels out and provides spectacular views of the coast as it passes through the villages of Lakones and Krini. Keep going until the road takes a sharp turn to the right and down and you will come to the end of the line and a little parking area. From here you walk up to the castle—only 200 yards but seemingly longer because of the condition of the trail. What you are rewarded with, though, is one of the most spectacularly sited **medieval castles** you'll ever visit—you are now some 1,000 feet above sea level.

The original fort was erected by Byzantine warlords at least by the 13 century, then was greatly enlarged under the Venetians; not surprisingly, it was never taken by any of its several attackers. Little survives other than walls and chambers, but there is a chapel (dating from 1784).

It is traditional to eat at one of the restaurant/cafes on the road outside Lakones—the (appropriately named) **Bella Vista, Colombo,** or **Casteltron**—so as to enjoy your meal with the spectacular view. Be forewarned: During the high season and at the peak of mealtimes, these places are taken over by busloads of tour groups. If you have your own transport, try to eat a bit earlier or later. Speaking of your own transport, don't attempt to drive this road from the coast to the foot of the castle unless you are comfortable pulling over to the very edge of narrow roads (with sheer drops) to let trucks and buses by—something you will almost certainly have to do on your way down.

Back in Paleokastritsa, you have many choices for meals. The restaurants on the main beach strike us as over-touristy. (Did you come to the site of Homer's Scheria to eat at a place called Smurf's?) We prefer someplace a bit removed, such as the **Belvedere Restaurant** (☎ 0663/41583), high above the largely undeveloped cove before the main beach and serving fine Greek dishes at reasonable prices. Main courses range from Dr 900 to Dr 2,400 ($3.83 to $10.20); a complete dinner plate would cost Dr 3,000 ($12.80). It's open mid-April to late October from 9am to midnight.

If you like to eat where the action is, at the main beach the best value and most fun is to be had at the **Apollon Restaurant** in the Hotel Apollon-Ermis (☎ 0663-41211). Main courses are Dr 1,300 to Dr 3,000 ($5.75 to $12.77); special four-course meals are Dr 2,200 to Dr 3,500 ($9.35 to $14.90). It's open from mid-April to late October from 11am to 3pm and 7 to 11pm.

If you want to spend some time at Paleokastritsa, we still feel you'll enjoy getting away from the main beach. We like the **Hotel Odysseus** (just above the Belvedere Restaurant), where a double in high season goes for Dr 22,000 ($94), but this includes the obligatory half board (breakfast and dinner); ☎ 0663-41209; fax 0663-41342. There are 70 rooms, some with tubs, some with showers, and there's a swimming pool. It's closed from November to late April.

Slightly more removed on its own peninsula and fancier and pricier is the **Akrotiri Beach Hotel,** where a double in high season goes for Dr 29,900 ($123), including buffet breakfast; ☎ 0663-41237. All of the 250 rooms have baths, balconies, and views of sea. There's also a swimming pool. It's closed from November to mid-April.

On your way back from Paleokastritsa, you can vary your route back by heading south through the **Ropa Valley,** the agricultural heartland of Corfu. Follow the signs toward Lakones and Pelekas (although don't go into either of these towns). And if you have time for a beach stop, consider going over to **Ermones Beach** (the island's only golf club is located above it) or **Glifada Beach.**

2 Kefaloniá

This is a Greek island the way they used to be—a place that pretty much goes its own way while you make your way around and through it. Not to say that Kefaloniá doesn't have a full-service tourist industry—hotels (some fine ones), pensions, restaurants, cafes, bars, travel agencies, car rentals, the whole show. Indeed, there's hardly a place you'd care to stay (and some where you wouldn't) that a Kefalonían has not erected a building that offers rooms or "studios." By the way, Kefaloniá (along with Zakinthos) was virtually demolished by the earthquake of 1953, so most of the structures on this island have been built since then. Many of the more ambitious new homes belong to repatriated Kefaloníans who dispersed to North America or Australia or other quarters in the aftermath of that disaster.

Kefaloniá has several natural wonders that you'll want to see. A few historical buildings and archaeological sites will repay a visit. There are certainly many fine beaches.
But this is a place for the old-fashioned traveler. You are the outsider, the guest, the
transient; Kefaloniá is what's permanent and real. That's not a euphemism for an
island of picturesque poverty-stricken villages: It's long been one of the more prosperous and cosmopolitan parts of Greece, thanks to Kefaloníans' tradition of sailing
and trading in the world at large.

It also boasts of being the largest of the Ionian Islands, although you can pretty
much cover the whole island with two or three days of touring. But don't go looking for glamour or excitement or even significance. Come to Kefaloniá because you
want to see how some other people live, you want to spend some time in a pleasant
environment, you want to drive around and enjoy the spectacular vistas and lovely
countryside.

ESSENTIALS

GETTING THERE   As with most Greek islands, there are more possibilities of
getting to and from Kefaloniá during the summer months than off season. This has
to do with the same thing that cuts down on tourism during that season: the bad
weather, which eliminates smaller boats.

By Plane   There are at least three flights daily on **Olympic Airways** from Athens
(with some flights via the island of Zakinthos). The Árgostoli office (☎ **0671/28808**)
is at Odos Rokkou Vergoti 1 (the street between the harbor and the square of the
Archaeological Museum).

The airport for Kefaloniá is 5 miles south of Árgostoli. As there is no pubic bus,
everyone takes a taxi, which costs about Dr 2,000 ($8.50) into Árgostoli and about
Dr 1,200 ($5.10) out from Árgostoli.

By Ship   It can be guaranteed throughout the year that there is one car-passenger
ferry that leaves daily from Pátras to Sami; for details, call **Pátras Port Authority**
(☎ **061/277622**) or **Sami Port Authority** (☎ **0674/22031**). It can also be guaranteed that there is at least one car-passenger ferry daily from Killini (out on the
northwest tip of the Peloponnese) to Árgostoli via the **Strintzis Line,** and their main
office is in Athens (☎ **01/8236011**); at Killini and Árgostoli, they sell tickets right
at dockside. There's also a car-passenger ferry daily from Killini to Póros (on
Kefaloniá's southeastern coast).

Beyond these more or less dependable services, there are usually other possibilities
during the summer—ships to and from Corfu, Ithaka, Levkas, or other islands and
ports—but they do not necessarily operate every year. See "Getting There" at the
beginning of this chapter.

VISITOR INFORMATION   The **National Tourist Organization (EOT)** information office in Árgostoli is Odos Ioannnis Metaxa (on the harbor by the Port
Authority office); ☎ **0671/22248.** High season hours are Monday through Sunday
from 8am to 3pm and 5 to 9pm; low season, Monday through Friday from 8am to
3pm.

GETTING AROUND   By Bus   You can get to almost any point on Kelfalonia—
remote beaches and villages and monasteries—by **KTEL bus** (in Árgostoli, ☎ **0671/
22276** or 0671/22281). Bus schedules, however, are restrictive and may cut deeply
into your preferred arrival at any given destination. KTEL also operates its own special
bus tours to several of the major destinations around the island.

By Taxi   This is an expensive alternative to the buses, but in the case of those who
don't enjoy driving twisting mountain roads, it may be the best one. If you're based

in Árgostoli, go up to the Central (Vallianou) Square and work out an acceptable fare. A trip to Fiskardo, with the driver waiting a couple of hours, might run to Dr 20,000 ($85)—with several sharers, this isn't unreasonable. Aside from such ambitious excursions, taxis are used by everyone on Kefalonía. Legally the drivers are supposed to use their meters but many don't, so agree on the fare before you set off.

By Car There are literally dozens of car-rental firms, from the well-known international companies to hole-in-the-wall outfits. In Árgostoli, we found **Euro Dollar** at R. Vergoti 3a (☎ **0671/23613;** fax 0671/24452) to be reliable. But during high season, you'll find that rental cars are scarce, so don't expect to be able to bargain them down. A compact (as opposed to the many minimodels driven by many tourists) will come to at least Dr 16,000 ($68) a day (gas extra); better rates are offered for three-day and longer rentals.

By Moped/Motorcycle The roads on Kefalonía are asphalt and in decent condition, but they are often very narrow, lack shoulders, and when they are not twisting around mountain ravines they wind along the edges of sheer drops to the sea. That said, many people do choose to get around Kefalonía this way. Every city and town has places that will rent mopeds and motorcycles, with rates at about Dr 6,000 to Dr 8,000 ($25 to $34) per day for a two-seater.

FAST FACTS: Kefalonía

Airport The airport for Kefalonía is 5 miles south of Árgostoli. As there is no pubic bus, everyone takes a taxi, which costs about Dr 2,000 ($8.50) into Árgostoli and about Dr 1,200 ($5.10) out from Árgostoli.

Area Code The area code for Árgostoli, Lixouri, and Skala is **0671;** for Sami and Fiskardo, it's **0674.**

Banks/ATMS There are several banks in the center of Árgostoli with ATMs that can handle direct transactions with Visa or other debit and charge cards.

Holidays In addition to the usual Greek holidays, Kefalonía observes elaborate celebrations of its patron saint, Aghios Gerassimos, on August 16 and October 20. But be warned: The island's facilities are often overloaded during these occasions.

Hospitals The **Árgostoli Hospital** ☎ (0671/22434) is in Souidias Street, Árgostoli.

Mail and Post Office The post office in Árgostoli is on Odos Lithostrato (opposite no. 18), ☎ 0671/22124; open Monday through Saturday from 7:30am to 2pm. Closed Sunday.

Newspapers and Magazines The best selection of foreign-language periodicals in Árgostoli is at Leoforos Rizospaston 10 (just north of the Central Square).

Police Árgostoli's **Tourist Police** (☎ 0671/22200) are on Odos Ioannis Metaxa, across from the Port Authority.

Restrooms Public toilets (crude) in Árgostoli are at the bus terminal and at the far northwest corner of the central square known as Vallianou.

Telephone, Telex, and Fax Árgostoli's main telephone office (OTE) is at Odos G. Vergoti 8. Open April through September, Monday through Sunday from 7am to midnight; October through March, Monday through Sunday from 7am to 10pm.

Travel Agencies Many are found around Árgostoli, some specializing in transportation tickets, some in tours, some in accommodations, some in all and more.

One especially helpful agency for ship lines of all kinds is **Bartholomos** (☎ 0671/
28583; fax 0671/22809), at Odos 21st of Maiou 2 (a small street across from Port
Authority), Árgostoli. Maria speaks English, is most helpful, and will direct you
elsewhere for services (ships lines whose tickets they don't handle, car rentals, and
hotels elsewhere in Greece) her office cannot provide. Another helpful agency is
Filoxenos Travel (☎ **0671/23055;** fax 0671/28114), at Odos G. Vergati 2.

Transit Info   The **KTEL bus station** (☎ **0671/22276** or 0671/22281; fax 0671/
23364) is at Leoforos A. Tritsi (the harbor road by the market).

WHAT TO SEE & DO

Árgostoli is not only the capital and largest city of Kefalonía, it has far and away the
most diverse offering of hotels and restaurants. It's central to everyplace on the island
and allows you to go off on daily excursions to the beaches and mountains, yet return to a relatively cosmopolitan city. For these reasons, it makes a good base while
touring the island.

Kefalonía has some true "getaway" possibilities, and we note them along the way.
Árgostoli, to be honest, does not offer much in the way of old-world charm. But
whether walking along its waterfront boulevard, known locally as the *paralia*, and
observing the locals at work or sitting in its central square and watching your fellow
visitors relax, Árgostoli is the place to be on Kefalonía.

MUSEUMS

Historical and Folklore Museum of the Corgialenos Library. Odos Ilia Zervou (2 blocks
up the hill behind the public theater and the square with Archaeological Museum). ☎ **0671/
28835.** Admission Dr 500 ($2.15). Mon–Sat 9am–2pm.

Many so-called folklore museums, little more than typical rooms, have sprung up in
Greece in recent years, but this is one of the most authentic and satisfying. Its
displays include traditional clothing, tools, handicrafts, and objects used in daily life
across the centuries. Most engaging, too, is its large collection of photographs of pre-
and post-1953 earthquake Kefalonía. The gift shop has an especially fine selection
of items including handmade lace.

Archaeological Museum. Odos Rokkou Vergoti (Platia Museio—the square one block back
from the waterfront). ☎ **0671/28300.** Admission Dr 500 ($2.15). Tues–Sun 8:30am–3pm,
closed Mon.

To be honest, this is a museum that all except the most devoted archaeological buffs
can afford to pass up. It is mostly a collection of pottery from Mycenaean tombs on
the island, with few objects of general appeal.

A STROLL AROUND ÁRGOSTOLI

Árgostoli's appeal does not depend on any archaeological, historical, architectural, or
artistic particulars. Rather, it's a city for those who enjoy strolling or sitting around
a foreign land and observing the passing scene—ships coming and going along the
waterfront, Kefaloníans shopping in their own market and stores, children playing
in the **Central (Vallianou) Square.** There are plenty of cafes on the central square
and along the waterfront where you can sit and nurse a coffee or pastry or ice cream—
the **Paloma Patisserie** on the former and the **Hotel Olga** on the latter are as nice
as any.

If you do nothing else, though, walk down along the waterfront and check out the
Trapano Bridge, a shortcut from Árgostoli (which is actually on its own little peninsula) to the main part of the island. The bridge, more like a causeway, was built
by the British in 1813 and reconstructed since. About midway across is a small obelisk

placed there by the citizens of Kefalonía (originally with a plaque inscribed: "Glory of the British Nation"—since removed).

There are a couple of fine beaches just south of the city in the locale known as **Lassi,** which now has numerous hotels, pensions, cafes, restaurants, and all the rest of a tourist support system for the package groups that fly in from Northern Europe.

For those seeking more formal entertainment, **free outdoor concerts** are occasionally given in the central square. At the **Rex Cinema** (just off the Archaeological Museum Square), foreign films are shown in their own language. There's a quite new and grand **public theater** where plays are performed (in Greek). Young people looking for more action (and noise) can find a string of **cafes-bars-discos** on **Leoforos Rizospaston** (leading away from the north side of the Central Square).

If your style runs more to British-style pub crawling, try **the Old Pub House** (on a corner of tiny streets between the Central Square and the waterfront).

SHOPPING

It's a tribute to Árgostoli's still indigenous character that it has virtually nothing to offer visitors looking for stylish shops. The best souvenir might be a jar of Kefalonía's prized **Golden Honey** or **tart quince preserve** or a box of **almond pralines.** Another possibility, but difficult to transport, is a bottle of one of Kefalonía's **wines.** Even if you don't want to carry bottles around, you can visit one of the two major vineyards: the **Calliga Vineyard** (with its **white Robola** or its **red Calliga Cava**) or the **Gentilini Vineyard** (with its more expensive wines), both near Árgostoli. The National Tourist Organization Information Office on the waterfront will tell you how to arrange for a tour.

WHERE TO STAY

There is a fairly wide choice of accommodations on Kefalonía, from luxury hotels to basic rooms. But as indicated elsewhere, if you have specific requirements during peak times, you are advised to make reservations. **Filoxenos Travel** (☎ 0671/2355; fax 0671/28114) is experienced at satisfying such needs. We offer here a selection that we can recommend for Árgostoli.

EXPENSIVE

White Rocks Hotel and Bungalows. Platys Yialos (the beach at Lassi, outside Árgostoli), Árgostoli 28100. ☎ **0671/28332** or 0671/28335. Fax 0671/28755. 102 rms, 60 bungalows, all with bath. A/C TEL. High season, Dr 45,000 ($192) double, Dr 50,000 ($213) bungalow; low season, Dr 32,000 ($138) double, Dr 36,800 ($157) bungalow. Rates include half board (breakfast and dinner). AE, DC, EU, V. Closed end of Oct to end of April. Parking on private lot. Occasional public buses but most take taxis.

This is one of the better hotels on Kefalonía, located only a couple of miles south of Árgostoli just above two beaches—one small and private for the hotel, the other a larger public beach. You descend a few steps from the main road to enter an almost tropical setting. Its lobby decor is stylish but subdued, and that seems to characterize this hotel's rooms, amenities, and service. It has a fine restaurant with views, a bar, and a TV lounge. Its desk will take care of all your needs. But it makes no pretense of being a glamorous high-speed resort. It's the kind of low-key hotel where people catch up on reading they've meant to do all year.

MODERATE

Cephalonia Star. Odos I. Metaxa 50 (along waterfront, across from the Port Authority), Árgostoli 28100. ☎ **0671/23181.** Fax 0671/23180. 40 rms, some with shower, some with tub. A/C TV TEL. High season, Dr 16,100 ($69), double; low season, Dr 11,500 ($49) double. No meals included. V. Open all year. Parking on street.

A Class C hotel, but more appealing than many due primarily to its location along the bay, thus providing its balconied front rooms with fine views. (A mobile amusement park has been known to set up in August on the quay just opposite—but August all over Greece is a carnival.) Rooms are standard issue but clean and well serviced. There's a cafeteria-restaurant on the premises, but except for breakfast, you'll probably want to patronize Árgostoli's many fine eateries, all within a few minutes' walk.

Hotel Ionian Palace. Vallianou Square (the central square), Árgostoli 28100. ☎ **0671/ 25581.** Fax 9671-25585. 43 rms, all with bath. A/C TV TEL. High season, Dr 18,860 ($80) double; low season, Dr 12,500 ($53) double. Rates include buffet breakfast. AE, MC, V. Open all year. Parking nearby.

If you love hotels in the old European grand hotel style, this is the class act of Kefalonía. (Why it isn't classed higher is a mystery.) Vassilis Vassilatos, a native of the island, spent 15 years in New York with his family before returning to build this hotel in the neoclassical style and operate it in the best contemporary manner. The lobby, public areas, and rooms all share a tasteful, comfortable, and natural tone. The front rooms look out over the central square, but as no vehicles are allowed there, it's not noisy. Breakfast is served under the arcades. The evening meal may be taken at the hotel's own **Il Palazzino** restaurant, either indoors or outdoors; the menu has a strong Italian flavor and prices are surprisingly modest. This is the place to stay if you like to be in the heart of a city.

Hotel Miramare. Odos Metaxa 2 (far end of Paralia), Árgostoli 28100. ☎ **0671/25511.** Fax 0671/25512. 60 rooms, some with shower, some with tub. A/C TEL. High season, Dr 16,100 ($69) double; low season, Dr 10,350 ($44) double. Rates include continental breakfast. Closed Nov–Apr. Parking on street.

A relatively new hotel in an old-fashioned building: Facing the bay, it will make you feel you are on some Alpine lake or the Maine coast. The lobby is nothing special but there's a TV lounge and a small bar. Rooms, too, are standard, which is to say neat and clean. What recommends it is its location—slightly removed from the town's hustle yet within walking distance of anyplace you'd want to go. For those who like to feel they're abroad when traveling.

INEXPENSIVE

Lakis Apartments. Odos Metaxa 3 (one street back from waterfront, down near Port Authority), Árgostoli 28100. ☎ **0671/28919.** 8 rms, all with showers. High season, Dr 10,350 ($44) double; low season, Dr 5,750 ($24) double. Parking on street.

Located on a quiet little street midway between the central square and the waterfront, this modest hostelry offers something that most hotels can't: the proprietors, Jerry and Angelina Zervos, who spent many years raising their family in Chicago before returning to Kefalonía. Aside from their fluent English, they offer help and hospitality that no amount of drachmas can buy. Their rooms are good sized and clean; some have balconies. Staying here is more like being in a familiar apartment than in a remote hotel.

WHERE TO DINE

There's a fairly good selection of restaurants in Árgostoli, although several offer more of an Italian menu than Greek food. But in one of the restaurants listed below, you should try at least one of the two local specialties: *kreatopita* (meat pie with rice and a tomato sauce under a crust) and *crasato* (pork cooked in wine). Also, try one of the island's prized white wines, the modest Robola or the somewhat overpriced Gentilini.

MODERATE

Kefalos. Vallianou Square (southeast corner of central square), Árgostoli 28100. ☎ **0671/ 22655.** Reservations recommended for large parties. Main courses Dr 900–Dr 2,500 ($3.85– $10.65). AE, EU, MC, V. Daily 8:30am–midnight. Closed Nov–Apr. GREEK/INTERNATIONAL.

Recognizable by its red tablecloths and white umbrellas, this is one of several fine restaurants on the central square; we single it out because it offers a relaxed atmosphere, good service, and, above all, solid Greek dishes. For an appetizer, try their eggplant salad or the asparagus soup. For a main course, they have everything from octopus to steak filet but here's a place to try the kreatopita (the meat pie); if you like red wine with your meals, ask for the Ktima Calliga, a local vintage. All in all, a satisfying restaurant.

Old Plaka Taverna. Odos I. Metaxa 1 (at far end of waterfront), Árgostoli 28100. ☎ **0671/ 24849.** Reservations recommended for large parties in high season. Main course Dr 850– Dr 2,280 ($3.60–$9.70). EU, MC, V. Daily 9am–2am. Just far enough off by itself that you might want to take a taxi. GREEK.

An instance of how inconsistent Greeks can be in distinguishing tavernas from restaurants: Until 1994 this was a modest taverna located closer to the center; now, in its new location, it's become quite a stylish restaurant, with indoor and outdoor areas, but it retains the *taverna* in its name. It also retains quite modest prices and tasty Greek dishes. Any of the standard appetizers are especially fresh and lively. For the main course, the pork with (lightly flavored) garlic stuffing is a specialty as is the rabbit with (light) garlic sauce. This is a favorite with Árgostolians, which tells us it must be doing things right.

Patsoura's (Perivolaki). Odos Israel 1 (7 blocks along street leading north from central square), Árgostoli 28100. ☎ **0671/22779.** Main courses Dr 850–Dr 2,200 ($3.60–$9.35). V. June–Sept, noon–midnight; Oct–Apr 7–11pm. A 5-minute walk from central square along Leoforos Rizospaston. GREEK.

This has long been the favorite for those in the know, but it's been cited by so many guidebooks that now everyone stops by for its authentic Greek taverna ambience and food. Owner-chef Christianthou Pastoura presides over the tiny kitchen in the heat and hustle, while you relax in a fairly cramped garden-terrace and eat to the accompaniment of birdsong and insect-chirping. The perfect place to try either of the local specialties, kreatopita (meat pie) or *crasto* (pork in wine). Greeks love these unpretentious country-style tavernas, and you'll see why if you eat at Patsoura's.

SIDE TRIPS FROM ÁRGOSTOLI
LIXOURI

If you are in Árgostoli and have only a few hours to pass, take the **ferry** (with or without a vehicle) to Lixouri, across the bay. The boats leave every hour from the quay down by the Port Authority (and National Tourist Information Office). The city of Lixouri is not especially attractive, but the 30-minute ride (Dr 300/$1.30) provides you with fine views and refreshing air. You could also take a car or bus around the bay from Árgostoli to Lixouri, but it's a 20-mile (32km) trip. South of Lixouri are several **beaches,** including **Megas Lakos** and **Xi,** noted for its unusual red sand.

If you do have your own vehicle and are game for some exploring, the **peninsula** has **unspoiled villages, monasteries, churches** with fine altar screens, and enchanting scenery. There are hotels on this peninsula—including a fairly new luxury hotel at Xi Beach, the **Cephalonian Palace** (☎ 0671/93190). Doubles cost Dr 25,000 ($106). Rather than overnighting on the peninsula, most visitors will probably settle for a visit to the **Iakovatos Mansion** in Lixouri, a traditional Kefalonían house (that survived the 1953 earthquake) with some fine possessions.

FISKARDO/ASSOS/MYRTOS BEACH

This is probably the preferred excursion for travelers who have only one day for one trip outside Árgostoli. The end destination is **Fiskardo,** a picturesque port-village, which owes its appeal to the fact that it's the only such locale on Kefalonía to have survived the 1953 earthquake. Going or coming, you can also fit in a detour to the even more picturesque port-village of **Assos** and then reward yourself with a stop at **Myrtos Beach,** many knowledgeable peoples' candidate for one of the great beaches of all Greece.

You can make a round-trip Árgostoli-Fiskardo outing in one day with the **KTEL Bus Line** (daily except Sundays; Dr 2,000/$8.50) but then you can't fit in Myrtos or Assos. This is the occasion to rent a car. You leave Árgostoli via the Trapano Bridge and then follow the signs north to Fiskardo, barely 30 miles (48km) away but almost an hour's drive because of the winding mountainous road. At about 20 miles (32km) in the village of Dhivarata, there is a signed left turn down to the **Myrtos Beach.** With its white sand and smooth pebbles and its enclosed curve it often appears in photographs promoting Greece's wonderful beaches; all very well, but this also means that it's overcrowded in the high season. (Also, it has no shade, no toilets, and no restaurants.) We advise saving it for a brief swim after you've done Fiskardo and Assos.

Assos is another 7 miles (10km) up the upper coast road, again involving a (signed) left turn and a steep descent to the village. In some ways, Assos is more authentic than Fiskardo: It's almost a miniature village that sits astride a little isthmus that culminates in a promontory topped by a **16th-century Venetian castle** (and if you've come this far, go up to the castle to enjoy the spectacular view). Its harbor is tiny, modest rooms offer its only accommodations; a couple of cafes and simple tavernas provide its food. Most of its homes and accommodations are taken by well-heeled Greeks or Italians; during high season, hordes of day trippers descend on Fiskardo, photograph it from all points and angles, and then move on. In fact, it's one of those places whose appeal lies in viewing it from with a bit of distance. We can only hope it's left that way.

Fiskardo is an example of a picturesque village that's been so exploited that its original charms are all but overwhelmed. Its name comes from Robert Guiscard, a Norman adventurer who died in this port in 1085. Its charm depends on its many surviving **18th-century structures** and its intimate **harbor**—actually a series of little bays. In recent years this harbor has attracted an international flotilla of yachts from May through October, so do not go expecting to see a quaint Greek fishing port. Indeed, do not go expecting to see many Greeks: It's become a magnet for foreign visitors who come to dine and drink and gawk. The British in particular have established a major foothold here, renting large blocks of rooms through England-based agencies. In high season, Fiskardo is now on overload. Another unfortunate trend is the appearance of oversized facilities around the harbor, the most blatant being a minimall, The Fiskardo Center, with its restaurant, cafe, and "Hairstyling Unisex." That said, enough of the original Fiskardo survives to make it an appealing place to pass at least several hours.

There are plenty of restaurants around the main harbor to choose from. The "in" set seems to have settled at **Tassia's** (formerly Dendrino's), right at the center of the yacht harbor's *paralia*, but it can be expensive and crowded in high season.

Since a meal on the harbor seems de rigueur, we recommend the **Faros** (☎ **0671/41276**), over on the right curve. Main courses cost from Dr 1,100 to Dr 2,500 ($4.70 to $10.64). Prices are increased 10% on Sundays and holidays. It's open daily from 11am to midnight, closed November through April. Although more expensive than many comparable Greek restaurants elsewhere, its menu is inventive and the food tasty—dishes such as chicken *Katsantora* (roast chicken with a tomato sauce) or veal Kefalonían style (again, a tomato sauce).

An alternative is the **Panormos,** both a taverna and an inn located on the bluff that's up and around the right-hand curve of the yacht harbor. Here you can eat a lobster right out of the tank on a terrace with a fine view of a more natural bay. In fact, unless you like to stay right in the center of a tourist attraction, this or the adjacent bay offers an alternative to downtown Fiskardo. There are several hotels or apartment complexes situated on these largely undeveloped bays. The **Panormos Inn** asks Dr 11,500 ($49) for a double in high season, Dr 5,750 ($24) in low season; closed from mid-October to April.

Those interested in spending even a few nights in Fiskardo should probably deal directly with one of the **travel agencies** located there, especially since the very time you'd probably want to stay, so would hundreds of other people. Agents can arrange for anything from living quarters to boat rentals. We can recommend either **Fiskardo Travel** (☎ and fax **0674/41315** in season, 01/4297058 off-season, ask for Georgio) or **Aquarius Travel** (☎ and fax 0674/41306, ask for Tassos or Dimitri). Britons may prefer to deal with the **Greek Islands Club,** which specializes in waterfront apartments and houses; its main office is at 66 High St., Walton-on-Thames, Surrey KT12 1BBU, ☎ **0932/220477** or fax 0932/229346.

One of the fringe benefits of Fiskardo in high season is that you can get (small) ferry boats to Pisso Aetos, Ithaka, and Vassiliki or Nidri, Levkas, for day trips—or for permanently moving on. So although Fiskardo can no longer be described as a quaint village, it has several things to recommend it.

SAMI, MELISSANI GROTTO & DROGARATI CAVE

Many who come to Kefalonía arrive at **Sami,** the town on the east coast. The island's principal point of entry before tourism put Árgostoli in the lead, Sami is still a busy port. (In fact, in the Homeric age, ancient Sami was the island's capital.) Sami itself is nothing special although its harbor is framed by unusual **white cliffs.** Of more interest to travelers are the **two caves** to the north of Sami, both of which can easily be visited during a half-day excursion from Árgostoli.

The first is **Spili Melissani,** located only about 3 miles (5km) north of Sami, near the beach named Karavomilos. At a well-signed and organized entrance, you get into a small boat and are taken around a partially exposed, partially underground lake; its most spectacular feature is due to the sun's rays striking the water and creating a kaleidoscope of colors (open daily from 9am to 6pm; admission Dr 1,000/$4.25). It was once believed that this water flowed underground westward to a locale outside Árgostoli, **Katavothres;** it's now known that the flow is from Katovothres into Melissani.

On the road that leads away from the east coast and west to Árgostoli (about 2 miles/4km from Sami), there's a well-signed turnoff to the **Drogarati Cave,** (open daily, 9am to 6pm, admission Dr 800/$3.40). Known for its unusual stalagmites, its large chamber has been used for concerts (once by Maria Callas).

SKALA

Those who consider a Greek island primarily a place to go swimming may want to head to the southeastern tip of Kefalonía and **Skala.** But don't go expecting to find an unknown beach: It has long been discovered by British tourist "packagers." Compared to some of the more developed beach resorts in Greece, Skala is relatively natural—especially the beach itself, a mix of coarse sand and small gravel. Most all of the accommodations and eating places are located well back from and above it.

Even if you treat the beach at Skala as only a day trip—it's barely 25 miles (40km) from Árgostoli—the drive there offers several diversions. At about 6 miles (10km) from Árgostoli, you will see an impressive fort sitting on a pinnacle to your left; a signed turn to the left leads by a steep twisting (but hard-surface) road to the **Castle of St. George** (you must walk the last 200 yards). Originally a Byzantine fort but completely rebuilt by the Venetians in the 16th century, it's surprisingly well pre-served. At this same point is another turnoff (left) to **Metaxata,** a small village where Byron stayed for four months in 1823.

Back on the main road to the south, you proceed along the flank of **Mount Ainos,** the highest peak (5,341 feet/1,628m) on all the Ionian Islands. Ainos is famed for its endemic **fir trees,** the *Abies cephalonica,* which look much like a cedar. (If you want to ascend the peak by car, the approach is off the road between Árgostli and Sami.) Continuing southward on the main road, you'll pass turnoffs (to the right) to beaches such as **Lourdata.** At about 20 miles (30km) you pass through **Markopoulos,** a vil-lage distinguished for a peculiar phenomenon: Small snakes with a crosslike mark-ing on their heads begin to gather around a church in the days before August 15, the day of the Assumption of the Virgin; on the day itself these snakes supposedly dash for an icon of the Virgin in the church and then vanish until the next year. Celebrants come from all over Greece and some hold the (harmless) snakes to their chests. (It's been said that the local priests are not exactly passive observers of this phenomenon.)

After Markopoulos it is a long descent to the sea. Before Skala you will pass the turnoff to the beach of **Kato Katelios** (many tavernas and rooms to rent here). Skala is another couple of miles off to the southeast. The road's condition deteriorates (but remains asphalt) and when you feel you have reached the end of the world, you're at Skala. Except that suddenly the world reappears in the form of a small tourist resort—some small hotels, numerous pensions/apartments/rooms, cafes and restau-rants, and many souvenir shops. It's hard to get a solid meal at midday—this is a resort geared to people who breakfast about noon and eat their main meal in the evening. Although most of the facilities are removed from the beach by a strip of trees, the **Ippocampos Taverna** sits down near the beach; also down there is the finest hotel in Skala, **Tara Beach Hotel and Bungalows** (☎ 0671/83250; fax 0671/83344). Off-season from abroad, contact the Athens office at 01/9739179. In the high sea-son, doubles cost Dr 18,400 ($78); in the low season, doubles are Dr 11,500 ($49). It's closed November to April. At the south end of the beach, opposite the little Hotel Skala, are remains of a **Roman Villa** with interesting mosaics (2nd century A.D.). The site is well signed and is protected by a prominent shelter.

If Skala sounds like a place you'd like to spend some fixed time, your best bet would be to deal with the **Etam Travel Service,** which can make arrangements for rooms, transportation, and excursions. They can be reached in Skala at ☎ 0671/83101; fax 0671/83142. Or in Árgostoli, contact them at ☎ 0671/25651; fax 0671/25021.

14 Thessaloníki

by Tom Stone

Long overshadowed by the marbled brilliance of Athens's Classical past, Thessaloníki has only recently come to light as what one commentator has called "Greece's best-kept secret." Not only is it the country's second-largest city and *symprotévousa* or "co-capital," but with its location right on the edge of the spacious waters of the Thermaic Gulf, it's arguably the most beautiful of Greece's major metropolitan areas.

Certainly, it's the most cosmopolitan. While Athens (310 miles to the south) languished in the long twilight of its occupation by the Romans and Ottomans, becoming little more than a dusty, forgotten village as the center of Greek culture shifted to the Byzantine capital of Constantinople—Thessaloníki continued to prosper as a major center of trade between east and west and became not only the second city of the Byzantine empire but that of the Ottoman one as well. Thus, this long, uninterrupted intercourse with European as well as Oriental cultures has created within Thessaloníki's populace an openness to and curiosity about foreigners that makes visiting there a tourist's delight. It's also resulted in Thessaloníki's being named the 1997 Cultural Capital of Europe, a year-long designation that Thessalonians are certain to live up to with their customary charm and sophistication, as well as with a multiplicity of festivals and other artistic events of the first order.

A modern city rebuilt after a 1917 fire destroyed virtually its entire downtown area, Thessaloníki (often called Salonika) has a touch of Paris about it, with spacious boulevards, parks, and tree-lined streets that clearly reflect the national origins of the French architect Ernest Hébrard, designated to redesign it. Adding to this impression are a plethora of elegant boutiques and a quality of nightlife rivaled only by Athens.

Thessaloníki's location in the virtual center of Macedonia, of which it has been the capital since its founding in 316 B.C., also makes it a perfect place from which to explore not only the historical sites associated with Philip of Macedon and his son, Alexander the Great, but the splendid heights of Mt. Olympus and the marvelous beaches of the resort peninsulas of Halkidiki, all of which are no more than a hour's drive away. And within a day trip's reach are the fabled and fabulously beautiful monasteries of Mt. Athos and of the Metéora.

1 Orientation

ARRIVING

BY PLANE   From Athens   There are six daily Olympic Airlines flights to Thessaloníki, from very early in the morning until late in the evening. The flight lasts approximately 45 minutes and costs Dr 22,000 ($94).

From the U.S.   There are no direct flights to Thessaloníki. Connections can be made at a number of European cities, including London, Amsterdam, Brussels, Frankfort, Stuttgart, Munich, Zurich, and Vienna.

Thessaloníki's airport is 8 miles (13km) southeast of the city at Mikras. It's a 20-minute drive from the city center. A bus ride to the city costs Dr 115 (50¢), and a taxi would be about Dr 1,200 ($5). **Budget Rent-a-Car** (☎ 031/471-491) has an office at the airport.

A municipal bus plies between the airport and the train station every half hour and makes a stop on the northern end of Aristotelous Square, just opposite the Electra Palace Hotel. The trip takes about 30 minutes and costs Dr 115 (50¢).

BY CAR   From Athens   Take the National Road, a four-lane highway that's the best in Greece. The trip from Athens takes from six to eight hours. Much of the drive is extremely scenic.

From Europe   One must take the ferry from the Italian ports of Bari, Ancona, or Brindisi to Igoumenitsa on the northwest coast of Greece, and then drive across the Pindus Mountains to Thessaloníki. The trip takes from seven to eight hours and is scenically spectacular. The route via Ioánnina and Kalambaka to Larissa and the National Road is much less treacherous than the northern alternative through Kozani—particularly during the winter months—and is thus recommended. Also, the southern route will give you the opportunity to stop at Kalambaka and visit the monasteries perched on the awesome pinnacles of the Metéora.

Parking   This can be a problem in Thessaloníki as the downtown area is fraught with traffic and with drivers double-parking everywhere. But you may be lucky. Otherwise, try the outdoor **Municipal Parking Lot** just south of the Museum of Byzantine Culture at the eastern end of Vassilissis Olgas Street. Parking is free. It's about a 20-minute walk from the city center, but very near the White Tower and Archeological Museum. At night, however, it has recently become a gathering place for the city's transvestites.

BY TRAIN   Five daily express trains make the trip from Athens to Thessaloníki in about six hours, but most are extremely crowded, without air-conditioning, and subject to various unexplained delays. If you must take a train, then let it be on the overnight sleeper, which has well-appointed, isolated compartments for two and four passengers. Nothing, however, can be done about the noisy and sometimes bumpy ride on antiquated tracks. Reservations for sleeping compartments should be made many days in advance at the Larissa train station in Athens (☎ 01/323-6747). First-class tickets are Dr 8,800 to Dr 10,000 ($38 to $43); second class Dr 8,000 ($34); sleeper for two persons Dr 16,000 ($68).

In Thessaloníki, the train station is on Monastiriou Street, which is the extension of Egnatia Street west of Vadari Square, site of numerous shady bars. A taxi ride to Aristotelous Square and its nearby hotels takes about 10 minutes.

BY BUS   Ten daily buses from Athens make the trip to Thessaloníki in about seven hours, including a 20-minute stop at a roadside restaurant. Buses are air-conditioned, much less expensive than the trains, and usually arrive on time. Reservations should be made in advance at the Athens bus terminal, 100 Kifissou St. (☎ **01/514-8856**). A one-way fare costs Dr 6,800 ($29). The buses arrive in Thessaloníki at a stop opposite the train station, where there are always taxis (see also "By Train," above).

VISITOR INFORMATION

The main **Greek National Tourist Organization (EOT)** is at 8 Aristotelous Square (☎ **031/271-888** or 031/222-935). It's open Monday to Friday from 8am to 8pm and on Saturdays from 8:30am to 2pm. There's also a branch at the airport (☎ **031/ 471-170** or 031/473-212, ext. 215). A useful magazine to buy at virtually any newspaper kiosk is the quarterly *Pilótos,* which lists in Greek all of the cultural and entertainment goings-on in the city and has an English-language **"Blue Pages"** section at its end with all the important addresses and telephone numbers you could want, from the police to radio taxis to consulates, banks, bars, and cinemas.

CITY LAYOUT

The city of Thessaloníki rests on the northern coast of the Thermaic Gulf in the manner of a somewhat lopsided turban tilted slightly to the northwest. In its center, like a jewel on the forehead of the bay (if you will) sits the city's famous landmark, the **White Tower.** To the east sprawl the ever-expanding residential and suburban districts while to the west, situated in the area once defined by its fortresslike Byzantine walls, is the **commercial heart** of the city.

In this latter area, bounded on the south by the harbor and on the north by the rising heights of what is called the *Ano Polis* (the Upper City), are Thessaloníki's most important shops, markets, banks, agencies, hotels, restaurants, archaeological remains, and churches.

On its western edge are the shipping docks, customs building, warehouses, train station, and most bus terminals.

On the city center's eastern side, just north of the White Tower and outside of what was once the eastern gate, are the grounds of Aristotle University, the International Trade Fair, and the Archaeological and Byzantine museums. Between the latter and the White Tower are the Municipal Park and the State Theater.

The commercial area of the city is traversed by four main streets running on an oblique angle from the southwest to the northeast.

The largest, **Egnatia Street,** is laid down almost on top of the original Roman Via Egnatia and serves a similar purpose in that it connects Thessaloníki with both the western and the eastern areas of Northern Greece. Its two-way traffic runs straight across the northern side of the commercial district. On its western end at **Vardari Square** (the site of the ancient western gate) it connects with roads to the west, north, and east; on its eastern end (under the name of New Egnatia), it passes the university on the northern side of the International Fairgrounds and continues on to highways leading to the airport and to the peninsulas of Halkidiki in the southeast. Along its route in the heart of the city are a host of Thessaloníki's less-expensive discount shops dealing primarily in clothing, shoes, and electrical appliances. There are also a number of cheap hotels and modestly priced restaurants. Near its eastern end, straddling what used to be the route of the original Via Egnatia, is the triumphal arch of the Roman emperor Galerius.

The city's second most important commercial route is **Tsimiski Street,** which parallels Egnatia two blocks to the south and runs one way from east to west. Along and just off its tree-shaded length are the city's most prestigious shops and department stores, as well as its post office and banks.

One block south of Tsimiski and running one way from west to east, is **Mitropoleos Street,** so named because the Metropolitan Cathedral is situated near its center. Like Tsimiski, it hosts a number of the city's finest shops and boutiques.

Finally, another block to the south and running along the seaside promenade is **Nikis Avenue.** Also one way from west to east, it begins at the shipping docks and ends at the White Tower. Along its length is a virtually uninterrupted line of outdoor cafes and bars, as well as a few souvenir shops, a discotheque, and the U.S. Consulate.

The heart of downtown Thessaloníki is the spacious expanse of **Aristotelous Square,** which sits in its center bordering the sea. Ringed with outdoor cafes and restaurants, it's also the site of the city's major political rallies. Also here, on its north-eastern side, is the **Greek National Tourist Office.**

Running north and south and connecting Aristotelous with the city's other major square, Dikasterion, is **Aristotelous Street.** Here, along its arcaded sidewalks, are to be found a number of bookstores and stationery and record stores, as well as the downtown ticket office of the Greek national railway.

Dikasterion Square, the biggest in the city, rests on some of the site of the Roman marketplace and its partly wooded space now hosts a fine Byzantine church, a restored Turkish bathhouse, several basketball courts, and, on certain days of the week, an outdoor market in which Greek refugees from eastern Europe sell their wares from blankets on the sidewalk. The square is also the place where most local buses begin and end their runs to and from the heart of the city.

To the south of Dikasterion Square, across Egnatia and on either side of Aristotelous Street, are the city's **main market areas.** Here, one can find all kinds of produce and other items, including flowers and wonderful, freshly baked bread.

To the east of Aristotelous Street is the city's second main north-south route, **Aghias Sophias Street.** In its center, between Egnatia and Tsimiski, is the major Byzantine church of St. Sophia on a square of the same name. Along Aghias Sophias Street are a number of excellent clothing stores and eyeglass shops as well as, between the church and Egnatia, Thessaloníki's premier fast-food shops: Corner, Goody's, and, recently, McDonald's.

Opposite the northern side of the church, there begins a line of excellent shoe stores, which continues eastward to the rear of the church along Svolou Street.

Running diagonally southeast from the rear of the church directly to the White Tower is **Pavlou Mela Street,** which hosts a number of fine bars, cafes, and patisseries, while leading directly south to Tsimiski from virtually the same point are the tree-lined pedestrian walkways of Iktinou and Zevksidos streets, site of several outdoor cafes and restaurants.

Two blocks east of the rear of Aghias Sophias Square is Thessaloníki's major pedestrian walkway, **Dimitriou Gounari Street.** Beginning just below the Arch of Galerius and running south to Tsimiski Street, its shop-lined length covers, for the most part, a major Roman thoroughfare leading down from the arch to the imperial palace. The area containing the palace is now partially excavated and opens westward off the pedestrian walkway into the tree-shaded park of **Navarino Square,** crowded with outdoor cafes, bars, ice cream parlors, and tavernas and second only to Aristotelous as the city's major gathering place—although many of the artists and intellectuals who gather there would place it first.

Another two blocks east is **Ethnikis Aminis Street.** While it runs one-way south from Egnatia down to the State Theater and the White Tower, it becomes a two-way street above Egnatia at Sintrivaniou (Fountain) Square (the former eastern gate of the city) and leads into winding roadways which run outside the ancient walls to the **Upper City.**

On the hillside leading down to Thessaloníki proper from the Upper City is the old **Turkish Quarter,** where some of the finest Byzantine churches are located.

Just to the north of the Upper City is the **Ring Road,** which goes around Thessaloníki from the southwest to the southeast and connects the National Road from Athens with highways to Thrace and Halkidiki and the airport at Mikras along the sea to the east.

FINDING AN ADDRESS   Because of the orderly east-west, north-south arrangement of streets laid down by the French architect who rebuilt the city after the 1917 fire, finding an address in the city center is not difficult. Numbers begin at the eastern and southern ends of streets and go upwards, with even numbers on the right and odd numbers on the left. However, most Thessalonians think of addresses in terms of the cross streets or various well-known structures near them, and rarely use numbers.

Outside of the city center, particularly north of Egnatia Street, the problem is more difficult, as the streets begin to meander. Therefore, it's best to get a good map.

MAPS   The National Tourist Organization on Aristotelous Square gives out a free booklet called **"Thessaloníki and Halkidiki,"** with a good map of the main city streets and tourist attractions.

The best guidebook to the city and one that contains the best map is called *Thessaloníki* and is by Apostolos Papagiannopoulos. It's available in most bookstores. Try **Molxos's Bookstore** at 10 Tsimiski St.

The most detailed map but cumbersome to unfold is that published by **Welcome Tourist Guides.** It, too, is available at most bookstores.

2 Getting Around

You will find that in the city center most of the attractions, restaurants, and shopping areas are easily reachable by foot in no more than 20 minutes. Otherwise, taxis are your best bet, unless you are going to the Upper City. Taxis are reluctant to take this trip because there is little guarantee of a return fare down, and they may—unlawfully—refuse. If you're in the cab before you state your destination, there's little the driver can do but take you there.

BY BUS   The city is serviced by two types of buses. Those with double cars are boarded in the rear, where there is a conductor to make change and give you a ticket. Single-car buses are boarded in the front. With these, exact fare is required in the form of Dr 50, Dr 20, Dr 10, and Dr 5 pieces, which are deposited in a ticket-issuing machine situated behind the driver's seat. You should keep your ticket just in case a conductor boards the bus to check them. Fares vary according to the distance traveled and whether or not you're a student. It's up to the passenger to select the amount by pushing a button on the ticket machine. Yours will almost invariably be number 1, costing Dr 75 (30¢).

BY CAR   As noted above there is little reason to use your a car within Thessaloníki. Traffic is terrible and legal parking places are almost impossible to find.

Having a car to travel outside the city is, however, a boon and will allow you to see and enjoy a lot more than you would either with a bus or on a guided tour. The driving rules are those standard in Europe and most of the world except England.

Budget Rent-A-Car has offices at the airport (☎ **031/471-491**) and in the city at 15 Angelaki St. (☎ **031/274-272** or 031/229-519) opposite the International Fairgrounds.

Other rental offices are **Avis** (☎ **031/227-126** or 031/683-300), at 3 Nikis Ave., at the western end of the harbor, opposite the docks; and **Hertz** (☎ **031/224-906**), at 4 El. Venizelou St. on Eleftherias Square.

Rates vary with the model you rent, the season, and whether you want limited or unlimited mileage. In the summer, the charges for limited-mileage cars range from Dr 4,500 to Dr 11,000 ($20 to $47) a day, with the rate ranging from Dr 65 to Dr 110 (30¢ to 50¢) per kilometer. The rental price for cars with unlimited mileage ranges from Dr 45,000 to Dr 98,000 ($191 to $417) for three days. Prices in the low season are about 20% cheaper.

BY TAXI   Within the city, this is your best bet except, as noted, when you want to go to the Upper City. Your problem will be the language, so take along a map and show the driver where you want to go. Rates are extremely moderate when compared to those in the United States. A 20-minute ride should cost you no more than Dr 1,000 ($4.25). Tips are not expected. Make sure, however, that the driver turns on his meter and that, within the city limits, the rate that it uses is number 1. Number 2 is for outside the city limits, as when you approach the airport, and doubles the cost. There is an extra Dr 300 ($1.30) charge, however, for trips from the airport. After midnight, all fares on the meter are doubled.

BY FERRY/BOAT   It's possible to take ferries and boats from Thessaloníki to a number of Aegean islands, including Crete, Santoríni, Mýkonos, and the Sporades islands of Skiáthos, Skópelos, and Alónissos. Tickets can be purchased at the following agencies: **Karaharissis** (☎ **031/513-005** or 031/524-444), at the corner of Nikis and Kountouriotou streets, near Eleftherios Square; **Polaris Travel** (☎ **031/278-613** or 031/232-078), at 22 Pavlou Mela St., between Tsimiski Street and Aghia Sophia church; and **Zorpidis Travel,** 76 Egnatia St., corner of Aristotelous Street, 2nd floor (☎ **031/286-812** or 031/286-825).

FAST FACTS: Thessaloníki

American Express   The office is at 19 Tsimiski St. (☎ 031/239-797). It's open Monday to Thursday from 8am to 2pm and Friday from 8am to 1:30pm.

Area Code   Within Greece, **031.** From without, dial the country number, **30,** followed by Thessaloníki's code, **31.**

Airport   See "Arriving," earlier in this chapter.

Business Hours   All banks, offices, and stores are open Monday through Friday from about 9am to about 2pm year-round. Most then close for the siesta period. Some then open from about 5:30 to about 8:30pm, but only on Tuesdays, Thursdays, and Fridays. During the entire month of July, there are no evening hours at all. Bars and restaurants, etc., have continuous hours throughout the day and evening, with some staying open the full 24 hours.

Camera Repair   By far the best is that of **Sotos Damianides,** at 43 El. Venizelou St., corner of Egnatia Street, 3rd Floor (☎ 031/236-244 or 031/222-087). They do excellent work and speak very good English.

Car Rentals   See "Getting Around," earlier in this chapter.

Currency Exchange   All banks do this, as do most hotels and the central post office.

Dentist   The two Thessaloníki dentists most preferred by foreigners are **Dr. Dimitris Sirris** (☎ 031/275-868), 10 Aghios Theodoras St., off of Aghias Sophias

Street between Tsimiski and Ermou streets, and **Dr. Dimitra Konstantinidou** (☎ 031/815-526)**,** at 39 Vassilissis Olgas St., east of the Municipal Park. Both are excellent and speak English fluently.

Doctor   In Greece, almost all doctors specialize and there are few who fit in with the U.S. concept of a general practitioner. An excellent English-speaking doctor who happens to be a pediatrician but can also give you help in diagnosing your problem and finding the specialist you need is **Dr. Christos Chrysanthopoulos** (☎ 031/267-292), at 43-A Aghias Sophias St. In addition, the American Consulate (☎ 031/266-121 or 031/260-716) has a continually updated list of recommended doctors.

Drugstores   See "Pharmacies (Late-Night)," below.

Embassies/Consulates   The U.S. Consulate (☎ 031/266-121 or 031/260-716) is at 59 Nikis Ave., two blocks west of the White Tower. It offers a bare minimum of services.

Emergencies   There is an English-speaking **24-hour help line** (☎ 100) run by the **Greek Police.** This is the best number to dial for any emergency. Also try the **Greek Tourist Police** (☎ 031/254-870 or 031/254-871) at 4 Dodekanisou, near the eastern end of Tsimiski Street. The **Red Cross station** (☎ 031/530-530) is at 10 Kountouriotou St. For car breakdowns, call the Greek Automobile Touring Club, or ELPA (☎ 104). The **Greek National Tourist Organization** (☎ 031/271-888 or 031/222-935) can also be of great assistance, as can the U.S. Consulate, of course.

Eyeglass Repair   There are a number of shops on Aghias Sophias Street between Tsimiski and Egnatia streets. One of the best is **Lazarides,** 24 Aghias Sophias St. (☎ 031/263-192).

Hospitals   All Greek hospitals provide virtually free care for everyone including foreigners. However, they are terribly crowded and you may not find anyone who speaks good enough English for your purposes. There is an excellent private clinic, however, which takes Blue Cross/Blue Shield insurance. It's called **Aghios Loukás** (St. Luke's) and is located on the road to Panorama village northeast of the city (☎ 031/342-102 to 031/342-134). English is spoken there.

Hotlines   The police hotline is **100;** first aid is **166;** for car breakdowns, call **104.**

Information   See "Visitor Information," earlier in this chapter.

Lost Property   Call the Tourist Police at 031/522-656.

Newspapers/Magazines   Some sidewalk newsstands sell a limited number of English-language newspapers and magazines. Try the two on the northwest and southwest corners of Tsimiski and Aristotelous streets. For a much larger selection of everything from motor magazines to the *New Yorker,* go to **Molxos** at 10 Tsimiski St., corner of El. Venizelou Street.

Pharmacies (Late-Night)   Pharmacies alternate late-night hours. Lists and addresses of the ones open on a particular night can be found in the local newspapers and the windows of all pharmacies.

Police   The 24-hour emergency number is **100.** The Tourist Police number is 031/522-656.

Post Office   The main post office is at 45 Tsimiski St., just east of Aristotelous Street (☎ 031/278-924). Hours are Monday to Friday 7:30am to 8pm, Saturday 7:30am to 2pm, Sunday 9am to 1:30pm.

Radio The only classical music station is the Third Program at 92 FM. One of the best pop music stations is Star at 97.1 FM.

Restrooms All but the smallest eating places and bars have restrooms that you can request to use without embarrassment. There are three well-kept public toilets in the central area. One, the best, is under the dividing sidewalk on the south side of Tsimiski Street at Aristotelous Street. The second best is underground in the southeast corner of the Municipal Park near the White Tower. The third, clean but slightly seedy, is in Dikasterion Square, underground on the eastern side just behind the Turkish *hammam* (bathhouse). All have attendants who guard and clean the place and expect nominal tips of Dr 10.

Safety Thessaloníki is still an extremely safe city where women have no fear walking alone on the streets even in the wee hours. The only area to avoid is that around Vardaris Square, where bars in the area attract some very shady characters.

Taxis Radio-taxis in the city center can be called at 031/517-417. See also "Getting Around," earlier in this chapter.

Television There are numerous local channels offering a steady diet of English-language films with Greek subtitles. There's also CNN (off and on), Euronews, Eurosport, and MTV brought in by government transmitters and broadcast free to the public.

3 Accommodations

Because of Thessaloníki's long history as a center for national and international trade, its hotels have traditionally focused on serving the needs of commercial travelers rather than tourists. Thus, most are blandly functional, being little more than places to sleep for the night, while the few that aspire to a certain elegance are almost entirely lacking in charm. Those listed below have been chosen because they are both the best in their category and the most conveniently located.

Accommodations should be reserved in advance during both the summer and the winter seasons, as there are numerous trade fairs and associated cultural events throughout the year, particularly during September and October, when the grand International Trade Fair is quickly followed by the month-long cultural festival called the **Dimitria.** During this latter period, there is often a surcharge on the regular rates.

Should you not have a reservation and have trouble finding accommodations, check with the **Greek National Tourist Organization (EOT).** There's an office at the airport (☎ **031/471-170** or 031/473-212, ext. 215) and in the city center (8 Aristotelous Sq., ☎ **031/271-888** or 031/222-935).

VERY EXPENSIVE

Astoria Hotel. 7 Salaminos St. (corner of western end of Tsimiski Street), 54626 Thessaloníki. ☎ **031/254-902.** Fax 031/531-564. 12 singles, 72 doubles, 6 suites. A/C MINIBAR TV TEL. Summer, Dr 32,000 ($136) double. Off-season, Dr 26,500 ($113) double. Rates include continental breakfast. AE, MC, V.

Built in 1973, recent modernization in 1991 now makes this nine-story hotel second only to the Electra Palace (see below) among hotels in the city center, albeit a distant second. Redecorated throughout in the anonymous international style so popular in Greece, it's decidedly uncozy but well appointed and well serviced. Its location, on a busy intersection in the warehouse district of Thessaloníki, leaves much to be desired for all but the business people who make up most of its clientele. You should try to get a room on the upper floors in the rear, away from the traffic noise.

However, the hotel is within a short, five-block walk eastward to some of the more interesting areas of Thessaloníki, including its bustling shopping streets, indoor market, and spacious seaside promenade, not to mention the many fine eateries and bars to be found in the colorful adjoining quarter of Ladadika.

Electra Palace Hotel. 9 Aristotelous Sq., 54624 Thessaloníki. ☎ **031/232-221** to 031/232-229. Fax 031/235-947. 10 single rooms, 55 doubles, 5 suites. A/C MINIBAR TV TEL. Summer, Dr 46,200 ($197) double. Off-season, Dr 38,500 ($164) double. Rates include continental breakfast. AE, MC, V.

Built in 1972 and last renovated in 1986, this seven-story structure is the most elegant of Thessaloníki's older hotels. Along with the recently reopened Macedonia Palace (see below), it's where everyone who is anyone stays when visiting the city. Fronting the seaside expanse of Aristotelous Square with its excellent outdoor cafes, it's central to the finest shopping and dining areas of the city and a short walk from the main post office and virtually all bank branches. Its rooms are decorated in that anonymous international hotel style encountered everywhere, but they do have a certain upscale warmth. However, in choosing a room, keep in mind the fact that Aristotelous Square is often the site of loud and interminable political rallies and other events that not only make access to the hotel difficult but an early sleep impossible. So, while a view of the square and the sea would be preferable, this is not always the case.

Dining/Entertainment: The Four Seasons restaurant offers rather undistinguished international and Greek cuisine from 6:30am to 1am. The same kitchen serves the evening-only Executive restaurant, much cozier and more elegant, which also has live music and a changing program of vocalists. There's also a rather nice bar, the After Six.

Macedonia Palace. 2 Megalou Alexandrou Ave. 54640 Thessaloníki (on the seafront promenade ¹/₂ mile east of the White Tower). ☎ **031/861-400.** Fax 031/868-942. A/C MINIBAR TV TEL. Year-round Dr 60,000–Dr 65,000 ($255–$277) double. AE, DC, MC, V. Free parking outdoors, indoors at a price yet to be determined.

This recently reopened nine-story hotel was once by far the best in the city, in terms of both its superb seaside location and the quality of its service. Built in 1972 and renovated in 1995, it was closed for a two-year period from 1993 to 1995 and is now under new management. While the location is just as marvelous—far enough from the city center to be free of much of its heat and pollution, yet only a 30-minute walk along the sea from Aristotelous Square—the ability of its recently installed management to measure up to its former standards remains questionable. At the time of this writing, they have yet to do so. Of the hotel's 288 rooms, the best are those facing the sea, each with its private balcony. The decor is elegant but without much warmth or individuality.

Dining: The Symposium restaurant offers a variety of international dishes, while the Porfira specializes in French cuisine.

Facilities: A wall safe and an individual voice-mail system for every room. An outdoor swimming pool and indoor fitness club. There are two bars, the best being on the ninth-floor roof garden. 24-hour room service. Hairdresser.

EXPENSIVE

Hotel Olympia. 65 Olimpou St. (at the northern end of the Roman market), 54631 Thessaloníki. ☎ **031/235-421.** Fax 031/276-133. 15 single rooms, 100 doubles. A/C. Summer, Dr 28,800 ($124) double. Off-season, Dr 24,000 ($103) double. AE, DC, MC, V. Free parking on reserved street outside. Take Eleftherios Venizelou Street north and turn right at Kiprion Agoniston Square onto Olimpou Street.

Last renovated in 1980, the seven-story Olympia has a rather glitzy marbled lobby but is otherwise extremely unprepossessing in its rather functional decor. Nevertheless, its staff, mainly family, give this well-kept establishment a warm and welcoming ambience. The clientele—who can be seen making themselves at home in the lounge, where there is a bar and TV, and dining room—are predominantly business people, although the hotel is also a favorite of tour groups, mostly Greek and often students on an excursion. While not as centrally located as the Astoria and Electra Palace hotels, the Olympia is right by the city's flea and copper markets and the Roman agora. It's also two blocks away from St. Demetrios's church and the government ministry, which gives visas for visits to Mt. Athos. Rooms are best taken on the upper floors to avoid the early morning racket from the flea market.

Philippion. P.O. Box 19002, 56610 Thessaloníki (in the forest of Sheih-Sou to the north of the Upper City). ☎ **031/217-406.** Fax 031/218-528. 15 single rooms, 69 doubles, 4 suites. A/C MINIBAR TV. Summer, Dr 20,000 ($86) double; off-season, Dr 23,850 ($102) double. All rates include continental breakfast. AE, MC, V. Free parking. Take the Ring Road around Thessaloníki and exit at the sign labeled "Philipion." Shortly afterwards, another sign to the left will lead you to the hotel.

Dining/Entertainment: The Philipos restaurant is probably the best hotel restaurant in Thessaloníki and offers an ever-changing variety of Greek specialties such as mussels in hot pepper sauce, roast lamb, and shish kebab (*souvlaki*). There's an outdoor nightclub for the summer and an indoor one for the winter. These feature Greek singers and orchestras.

For those who cannot abide staying any city in the summer, but still want to spend time in one, this sprawling, modern four-story hotel complex, renovated in 1992, couldn't be more perfect. Or more convenient. It overlooks Thessaloníki from a forested hilltop just 15 minutes' drive from the city center (there are hotel shuttle buses leaving every half-hour), and yet is a vacation spot in its own right. There is a swimming pool, outdoor cafeteria, barbecue, and children's playground. The rooms are spacious, well appointed, and sunny, the best being on the third floor to the rear, with a view of the city. The clientele are mostly vacationing Greek families, who can be a bit noisy at times.

Finally, the hotel's proximity to the Ring Road makes it extremely easy to reach the airport (15 minutes away) and the main highways to Athens, Halkidiki, and Thrace.

MODERATE

Tourist. Mitropoleos 21 (one block west of Aristotelous Square), 54624 Thessaloníki. ☎ **031/276-335.** 37 rooms. Summer, Dr 12,000 ($52) double; off-season, Dr 10,800 ($46) double.

It shouldn't be so expensive, but it is, by virtue of its excellent location, which is just as central as that of the posh Electra Palace a block away. This three-story hotel, built about 1917 and last renovated in 1995, has no air-conditioning, no TV in the rooms, no bar or restaurant, doesn't accept credit cards, and has only recently added bathrooms to its double rooms. What it does have is the quiet grace of a turn-of-the-century townhouse, with high ceilings and tall, elegant doors and windows painted in soft gray and whites and bespeaking of a time when space was the amenity that mattered. It also has the family that runs it in a suitably gracious manner and keeps it quietly immaculate. Its clientele are mostly Greeks who have come there for years. If money is a consideration, but air-conditioning isn't, this is an excellent choice.

4 Dining

The cuisine of Thessaloníki has long been renowned throughout Greece for its delicate, aromatic character (a heritage of its historically close contact with the Levant) and the splendid variety of its game and hors d'oeuvres (*mezedes* or *mezedakia*). Recently, because the efforts of a number of enterprising young Thessalonians, it has now become better than ever before, perhaps the finest in all of Greece.

Even in the most expensive establishments the dress code is very casual, with ties and jackets rarely being worn. Reservations can be made, but the only guarantee that a table will be available when you arrive is if you get there before most Greeks come out to dine. Which is to say, you should try to eat lunch before 1pm and dinner before about 8:30pm.

The best of Thessaloníki's dining places fall into three basic categories: restaurants and tavernas that offer cuisine of a distinctly Thessalonian character, including game; fish tavernas; and *ouzeries*, which specialize almost exclusively in hors d'oeuvres. Those in the first category usually have an excellent selection of hors d'oeuvres, while the *ouzeries* may also offer more substantial main courses.

RESTAURANTS/TAVERNAS
EXPENSIVE

Aigli. Kassandrou and Aghiou Nikolaou streets (above the church of St. Dimitrios). ☎ **031/270-016.** Reservations recommended. Main Courses Dr 2,000–Dr 3,000 ($9–$13). Plus a Dr 2,000 cover charge when there is entertainment. No credit cards. Thurs–Sun 10pm–2:30am. Mon–Wed only open to private parties. Also available for luncheon bookings by large groups. GREEK/CONTINENTAL.

Established in 1992 in an exquisitely restored Turkish hammam, this is certainly the most beautiful restaurant in Thessaloníki. Indoors, one dines beneath the high double domes of the former bathhouse; outdoors, in the gardened grounds of an old, open-air cinema that now shows films in the summertime at 9pm and 11pm. The Aigli also used to boast the best haute cuisine in Thessaloníki, but the management has recently decided to shift its emphasis from cooking to entertainment and to booking the entire establishment for private parties. This is not to say that the food that is offered is not good; it just doesn't have the marvelous variety of regional dishes that its original chef, still part owner of the Bektsinar (see below), had concocted.

Specialties include chicken kebab, Turkish dolmades, and grilled filet of chicken breast. There is a wonderfully varied entertainment program. One night you might see a French chanteuse; on another, a group of Egyptian instrumentalists. Whatever it is, it is guaranteed to be exotic.

Bextsinar. 11-13 Katouni St. (one block west of the northern end of Eleftherias Square). ☎ **031/531102.** Reservations recommended after 9pm. Main Courses Dr 2,000–Dr 3,000 ($9–$13). DC. Daily 1pm–1:30am. GREEK/CONTINENTAL.

Established in 1989 by the same entrepreneurs and chef who later opened the above Aigli, this exquisitely renovated former warehouse was the first in what's now an explosion of bars and restaurants in the waterfront area of Thessaloníki known as Ladadika. One dines either on the small sidewalk outside or in the upstairs and downstairs wood-beamed dining rooms amidst a wonderfully eclectic collection of art deco furniture and other Greek artifacts in an atmosphere that's as tasteful and decorous as the surroundings. It's a favorite of the older and wealthier denizens of the city.

The food is wonderfully exotic—delicately flavored dishes that celebrate the influence of the Levant on Thessaloníki's cuisine. For hors d'oeuvres, sample the *bourekia* (spinach and cheese in filo pastry) and *manti* (ground mutton in filo). For the main course, try the *yourtlou kebab* (meatballs on pita with a curry-yogurt sauce) and *hounkair begienti* (stewed veal with puréed eggplant). Dessert specialties include *karidopita* (walnut cake) and seasonal fruits with yogurt, honey, and walnuts.

Krikelas. 32 Ethnikis Antistasis St. (an extension, going into the city from the airport, of the far eastern end of Vassilissis Olgas Street). ☎ **031/411-289.** Reservations necessary. Main Courses Dr 2,000–Dr 3,000 ($9–$13). No credit cards. Daily 11:30am–2am. GREEK.

Renowned throughout the country virtually since its opening in 1940, Krikelas is regularly patronized by visiting politicians, entertainment celebrities, and sports heroes, as well as by other Greeks from all walks of life. The brightly lit (and rather smoky) atmosphere is highly convivial and the food consistently excellent.

The specialties are its mouth-watering variety of hors d'oeuvres and whatever game is in season at the time. For hors d'oeuvres, try the special feta cheese, creamed with butter and hot green peppers, or the smoked gruyere from Metsovo. An interesting regional specialty is *spetzofai*, a mixture of seasonal vegetables and pungent country sausage. The spit-roasted lamb melts in your mouth. The game available depends on the season and could include quail, pheasant, rabbit, boar, and partridge. For dessert, try their homemade halvah with almonds. The wine list has a sumptuous variety of the very best in Greece at prices ranging from Dr 2,000 Dr 5,000 ($9 to $21) a bottle.

If you want a quiet dinner for two, get there before 8pm. After about 10pm, things become exceedingly but wonderfully boisterous.

MODERATE

Tiffany's. 3 Iktinou St. (on the pedestrian walkway between Tsimiski Street and the church of Aghia Sophia). ☎ **031/274-022.** Reservations recommended after 10pm. Main courses Dr 1,000–Dr 2,000 ($4–$9). Daily 11:30am–2am. No credit cards. GREEK/CONTINENTAL.

Established in 1970, Tiffany's is surprisingly inexpensive for a restaurant so upscale in decor, cuisine, and clientele, a large part of whom are knowledgeable, well-to-do Thessalonians. There's a lovely, tree-shaded eating area on the walkway and tasteful, subdued decor inside.

The cuisine is similarly tasteful and subdued. The specialty of the house is its *bifsteki*, ground beef patties with various sauces and stuffings. Try the *bifsteki Tiffany's*, which is stuffed with cheese and tomatoes. A more exotic offering is *hanoym borek*, a casserole of roasted pieces of chicken, ham, veal, and cheese.

Wolves. 6 Vassilissis Olgas St. (one block in and two blocks east of the Macedonia Palace Hotel). ☎ **031/812-855.** No reservations necessary. Main courses Dr 1,000–Dr 2,000 ($4–$9). No credit cards. Mon–Sat 12:30pm–1am; Sun 12:30–5pm. No. 3 bus from Aristotelous Square. GREEK.

This warm, dark-wooded, old-fashioned restaurant, established in 1977, has a cook reputed among locals to be the best in Thessaloníki when it comes to making a delicacy out of such basic Greek fare as pastitsio and moussaka. The name of the establishment is not indicative of anything on the menu; it's simply the sobriquet of the owner's favorite English soccer club.

This a place with no frills, where ready-made meals are served at all hours, making it perfect for families with kids. Try the roasted red peppers from Florina as one of your hors d'oeuvres. For the main course, sample the moussaka Wolves, the oregano-flavored stewed pork, and the batter-fried codfish in garlic sauce. Or take a look in the display counter in the kitchen at whatever mouth-watering specialty might be available that particular day.

INEXPENSIVE

To Makedoniko. 32 Giorgiou Papadopoulou St. (in the Upper City, inside the arch at the western end of the walls). ☎ **031/627-438.** No reservations. Main courses Dr 800–Dr 1,000 ($3–$4). No credit cards. Mon–Sat 9am–2am. Bus no. 23. GREEK.

You couldn't get more basically Greek than this. Rugged, rudimentary, and full of local color, To Makedoniko is a watering hole and eatery equally popular among the neighborhood working class and the downtown intellectuals, artists, and university students.

If you have the constitution to handle it, you must drink the local schnapps—*tsipouro,* a delicately perfumed but powerful variety of ouzo—with your hors d'oeuvres. While the limited menu can vary from day (or even from hour to hour), this writer's favorites have included pork riganato and mussels in a hot-pepper broth (*mydia saganaki*).

FISH TAVERNAS

The best fish tavernas are to be found in the suburbs of Aretsou, on the eastern side of the bay past the old summer palace of the Greek royal family at Kivernio, and in the neighboring district of Nea Krini. To get to both areas from the city center, go east along the seafront drive of Megalou Alexandrou and take a right at the stoplight at Themistokli Sofouli Street and continue along the coast.

Kavos. 59 Nikiforos Plastiras St. (near the seafront road in Aretsou). ☎ **031/430-475.** Reservations recommended after 9pm. Main courses Dr 1,500–Dr 7,000 ($6–$30). No credit cards. Daily 10am–2am. GREEK.

Somewhat more expensive than the rest of the many excellent seafood restaurants in the area, this brightly lit, no-frills taverna is known among Thessalonians as the best of its kind in the city. But beware the price of the fish: It's calculated by the kilo and is the most expensive thing you can eat in Greece. A good, medium-priced fish is one of the many varieties of sea bream or porgy called, in Greek, *sargós* or *lithríni.* The more expensive fishes are *barboúni* (red mullet) and *ksiflas* (swordfish).

Vrakos. 2 Mikras Asias St. (in Nea Krini, in a cul-de-sac off the seafront road towards Aretsou). ☎ **031/447-991.** Reservations recommended after 9pm. Main courses Dr 1,500–Dr 7,000 ($6–$30). No credit cards. Daily 12pm–2am. GREEK.

Almost as good as the Kavos and equally as low key. Its name means "rock," and it's so called because of its lovely situation on a rocky headland on the bay, where one dines on the terrace virtually on top of the water. Its specialty is shrimp in a hot pepper broth called "*saganáki.*"

OUZERIES

As can be gathered from the name, ouzeries are places specializing in ouzo and the hors d'oeuvres that go with them. One need not, however, drink ouzo—or for that matter, any kind of alcoholic beverage—to enjoy the marvelous variety of foods that they offer: octopus; meatballs; shrimp; squid; *taramasaláta* (fish roe puréed with oil and bread); *tzatziki* (cucumber, yogurt, and garlic); *melitzánasalata* (eggplant purée); cheeses; potato, beet, and bean salads, etc. The list goes on and varies from establishment to establishment, some with their own specialties found nowhere else. Since in most places you won't be able to understand the menu, it's always best to go with your waiter to look at the offerings and point out what you want.

EXPENSIVE

Aristotelous. 8 Aristotleous St. (in a cul-de-sac between office buildings on the east side of Aristotelous Street, just north of Tsimiski Street). ☎ **031/230-762.** No reservations possible.

For a variety of hors d'oeuvres, Dr 2,000–Dr 3,000 ($9–$13). No credit cards. Mon–Sat 10am–2am; Sun 11am–6pm. GREEK.

First on the list and the best. Highly popular with writers, artists, and everyone else in the know, it's constantly packed during the peak lunch and dinner hours, so you should come either early or late, or you'll end up waiting at least 20 minutes. Indoor and outdoor seating areas in between high-rise office buildings contribute to the crush and somehow the charm. You can and should linger for hours, which is why it's often so hard to get a table. The variety of hors d'oeuvres is sumptuous. Try the fried zucchini and eggplant; the feta cheese mashed with hot peppers and olive oil (*ktipiti*); and, for something more substantial, the stuffed cuttlefish (*soupiá*). Also delicious is the homemade halvah.

Totti's. 3 Aristotelous Sq. (southwest corner fronting the sea). ☎ **031/237-715.** No reservations necessary. Main courses Dr 2,000–Dr 3,000 ($9–$13). No credit cards. Daily 7am–2pm. GREEK.

Its outdoor dining area festooned with yellow and orange umbrellas and facing the broad east to west expanse of Thessaloníki harbor, this is perhaps the most soul-refreshing ouzerie in the city, particularly in the evenings when the sun sets into the sea in front of you. It's also a great place for breakfast. The food is typical ouzerie fare, but the tableware and other accouterments have considerably more elegance, which is reflected in the price. The service, however, as the waiters take their long walks to and from the interior kitchen, can be interminable.

MODERATE

Apróopto Light. 6 Zevksidos St. (a pedestrian walkway off the eastern end of the church of Aghia Sophia). ☎ **031/241-141.** No reservations. Main courses Dr 1,000–Dr 2,000 ($4–$9). No credit cards. Daily 12pm–1:30am. GREEK.

Highly popular with professionals of the nearby State Theatre and other artistic types, this place serves excellent hors d'oeuvres as well as some main course dishes. Its relatively small, well-decorated sidewalk and interior dining area are usually packed and rife with conviviality. Try the mussels with spinach and the leeks à la Parisienne as well as the *taganaki*, a cheese and potato dish.

INEXPENSIVE

Thanasis. Just inside the main entrance of the western end of the Modiano Market. ☎ **031/274-170.** Reservations necessary after 10pm. Main courses Dr 1,000 ($4). Daily 7am–5am. No credit cards. GREEK.

The sign over the door reads "H Mypobolos Smyrnh" (pronounced "*ee-me-RO-volos SMEAR-ni*") and translates as "Miraculous Smyrna," but everyone knows it equally well by the name of its marvelously genial owner, Thanasis. He and his wife and relatives labor incessantly during market hours to satisfy the cravings of a seemingly endless number of market workers, business people, artists, prostitutes, actors, and various other characters from the high and low walks of Thessaloníki life—including, quite often, gypsies and their dancing bears—who crowd into and around this boisterous eatery to sample its superb food and exhilarating atmosphere. Recently, Thanasis has acquired a partner who financed the expansion of the restaurant in both size and hours; and, consequently, it has now become one of the hottest late-night establishments in town, with dancing and drinking going on well into the wee hours. The food, however, is the same from morning to morning. Aside from the hors d'oeuvres, Thanasis and his family offer a delicious potato salad, cheese croquettes, squid stuffed with cheese and rice, grilled fish and meats, and an excellent batter-fried cod (*bakaliáro*). A real taste, in every sense of the word, of Greek life as it is truly lived.

5 Attractions

One of the great rewards of visiting Thessaloníki is uncovering its past. Beneath the robust charm and cosmopolitan sheen of this sparkling modern city lies a continuum of historical richness that's barely hinted at on its surface. As Athens is considered the repository of the glory that was classical Greece, so Thessaloníki is the same for most of the rest of its history, from the Macedonian and Hellenistic civilizations of Philip and Alexander in the 4th century B.C. through to the end of the Ottoman occupation in 1912. Throughout this period, it was mainland Greece's preeminent city. During the Roman occupation, it was the seat of the co-emperor, Galerius, and was visited twice by St. Paul in A.D. 49 and 56. When the Roman empire became Christianized, Thessaloníki was second only to Constantinople as the major city in the Byzantine Empire. It maintained its stature during the Ottoman rule, when it rivaled Istanbul as the major trading and administrative center of the empire.

But it's a historical mosaic that survives today only in bits and pieces, much of it destroyed or scattered by the succession of civilizations that took over the city or by such disasters as the great fire of 1917, which eradicated most of the city's colorful bazaars and distinctive Turkish, Jewish, Frank, and Greek quarters.

Thus, a bit of exploration is required to put the picture back together again: Visits to Thessaloníki's marvelous archaeological and Byzantine museums will provide the most brilliant details, while walking tours around the city with visits to its walls, towers, monuments, hammams, and churches will both outline the shape and fill in the gaps. In the process, it's hoped that you will get to know the Thessalonians and find that there's still very much of the city's past alive in its present.

THE TOP ATTRACTIONS

As noted above, one of the great joys of being in Thessaloníki is learning about its past. Thus the city's top attractions are its museums, ancient Roman monuments, Byzantine churches, and Ottoman edifices. All of these are grouped reasonably close together and can be visited, on foot, in a single day.

The Archaeological Museum. Corner of Angelaki Street and Stratou Avenue (opposite the south side of the International Fairgrounds). ☎ **031/830-538.** Admission Dr 1,500 ($6.50). Tues–Sun 8am–7pm, Mon 12:30–7pm. Bus no. 58 from Dikasterion Square or bus no. 11 heading east from anywhere on Egnatia Street.

The collection of this spacious, elegant museum encapsulates Macedonian and Thessalonian history from its Neolithic beginnings through the Roman occupation. Most impressive are objects taken from various Macedonian tombs, particularly those found in Vergína in the undisturbed tomb of Alexander's father, Philip of Macedon, and his family. Also on view is bust of the Emperor Galerius, who built the Rotunda and the Triumphal Arch (see below in this section and "More Attractions," below).

Museum of Byzantine Culture. Stratou Avenue (just west of the Archaeological Museum). ☎ **031/868-570.** Free admission temporarily. Mon–Sat 4–9pm, Sun 8am–2:30pm. Bus no. 58 from Dikasterion Square or Bus no. 11 heading east from anywhere on Egnatia Street.

Partially opened in early 1995, this modern, red-brick Byzantine-inspired structure is not expected to have the full extent of its permanent exhibits on view until sometime in 1996. When it does, it will have an extraordinary and stunning representation of the 1,100-year development of Byzantine culture from its early beginnings in the Roman world through the age of the iconoclasts to its full Thessalonian flowering during the era of the Paleologos dynasty. On view will be not only icons and other religious objects, but a full range of secular artifacts as well. A must-see, as impressive and important as the treasures from Philip's tomb in the Archaeological Museum (see above, in this section).

The White Tower. Nikis and Pavlou Mela streets on the seaside promenade just south of the Archaeological Museum. ☎ **031/830-538.** Admission Dr 800 ($3.40). Mon 12:30–7pm, Tues–Fri 8am–7pm, weekends and holidays 8:30am–3pm. Bus no. 58 from Dikasterion Square or bus no. 11 heading east from anywhere on Egnatia Street.

Once a prison and place of execution during the Ottoman reign, this is now the city's most famous landmark. Within its beautifully restored interior are a number of "satellite" exhibitions organized by the Museum of Byzantine Culture (see above in this section). These include a beautiful selection of icons, frescoes, coins, reliefs, and glasswork from the museum's collection.

The Rotunda. Aghios Giorgos Square at Fillipou Street (one block north of the juncture of Egnatia and Dimitrios Gounari streets, just above the Arch of Galerius). ☎ **031/213-627.** Free admission except for special events. Temporarily closed. Bus no. 10 or 11 heading east from anywhere on Egnatia Street.

This was apparently intended to be the mausoleum of the Roman co-emperor Galerius (A.D. 293–311) but his successor refused to have him buried there. Converted into the church of St. George during the Byzantine era, it contains beautifully done 4th-century mosaics of early Christian saints. The minaret outside was placed there by the Ottomans. The entire structure is still in the process of being restored after having been damaged by an earthquake in 1977 and, except for a rare art exhibit or concert, is usually closed to the public, but could open at any time.

Church of Aghia Sophia. Aghia Sophia Square, corner of Aghia Sophia and Ermou streets, between Tsimiski and Egnatia streets. ☎ **031/270-253.** Free admission. Open 8am–9pm. There is no convenient bus along this route. Get off any bus at the corner of Egnatia and Aghia Sophia streets and walk one block south.

Huge and somber, this church is worth visiting primarily because of its beautiful mosaics of the Ascension and the Virgin Mary with the infant Jesus. Originally, the Virgin Mary held a cross (still partly visible), but after the doctrinal defeat of the Iconoclasts, who did not believe it was proper to either create or venerate images of divinity, the figure of Jesus replaced the cross.

Church of Aghios Dimimtrios. Corner of Aghiou Dimitriou and Aghiou Nikolaou streets, one block north of the Roman market. ☎ **031/270-008.** Free admission. Tues–Sun 8:30am–3pm. To get to the Upper City and the Church of Aghios Dimitrios, take the no. 22 or 23 bus, which leaves about every 10 minutes from the southeast side of Eleftherias Square, just off the harbor promenade two blocks west of Aristotelous Square. Its route, with various stops along the way, goes up El. Venizelou Street, turns eastward on Aghiou Dimitriou Street, passes the church where there is a stop, and then wends its way to the Upper City. On a good day, the trip to the top takes about 20 minutes.

This was built in the 5th century to honor the city's patron saint, who was executed in 303 by the emperor Galerius in the Roman baths that lie beneath the church's apse. It was burned down in the great 1917 fire and rebuilt during the years 1926 through 1949. Its interior still bears signs of the fire. One can visit the crypt below the apse, which was uncovered during the rebuilding of the church and has now been impressively restored.

The Alatza Imaret. Dimitrion Square, just off Aghiou Nikolaou Street, half a block north of Kassandrou Street, 1½ blocks north of the church of Aghios Dimitrios. ☎ **031/278-587.** Free admission. Open intermittently for exhibitions. Bus no. 22 or 23 from Eleftherias Square or stops along El. Venizelou Street north to Aghiou Dimitriou Street. Get off at the church of Aghios Dimitrios and walk north on Aghiou Nikolaou Street.

Its name means "many-colored" from the tiles that covered it during the Ottoman reign. Formerly an almshouse, it now hosts various cultural exhibitions under the aegis of the city government. With the exception of the Aigli restaurant (see "Dining," above), it's the best-preserved Turkish structure in the city and well worth seeing because of that.

Atatürk's Birthplace. 151 Aghiou Dimitriou St. (eight short blocks east of the church of Aghios Dimitrios). ☎ **031/269-964.** Free admission. Daily 9am–1pm, 2–6pm. Bus no. 22 or 23 from Eleftherias Square or stops along El. Venizelou Street north to Aghiou Dimitriou Street. Entrance through the front gate of the Turkish consulate, passport necessary.

Just behind the consulate, this rather unimpressive wood-framed house was the birthplace of the man who created the modern Turkish state and became its president. His real name was Mustafa Kemal, and he was born in Thessaloníki in 1881. Given to Turkey as a present by the Greek government in 1933, the house has been restored and furnished to reflect the way it must have been at Atatürk's birth. It contains numerous photos of the man, young and old, various letters and papers as well as cases containing the clothes and uniforms he wore. There is an excellent booklet in English available with all the relevant information as well as photos.

MORE ATTRACTIONS

The following provides information about sights that lie along your walking tour routes (see "Walking Tours," below).

The International Fairgrounds. Entrances at the corners of Angelaki and Tsimiski streets, and Angelaki and Egnatia streets. Free admission except during scheduled exhibitions, when the entrance price varies. Open daily 8am–10pm, although this varies according what exhibitions are being held.

Built in 1926 on the site of the Turkish cemetery, this is the modern manifestation of a tradition of trade fairs that goes deep into Thessaloníki's Byzantine past, and it's intimately connected to religious festivals that were and are still held for the city's patron saint, Aghios Dimitrios. These latter festivals were originally held within the city walls from October 20 to 26 while concurrently, outside the walls, merchants would gather to trade their wares. Nowadays, the major International Trade Fair is held for two weeks in mid-September and is followed in October by a month of cultural festivities called the **Dimitria,** with St. Dimitrios's Day being celebrated only on October 26.

The fairgrounds are host to numerous other commercial exhibitions throughout the year and its domed Palais de Sport is the home court of the Aris and PAOK professional basketball teams as well as being the site of numerous musical events.

The Arch of Galerius. Just below the Rotunda on Egnatia and Dimitriou Gounari streets. Any bus going eastward along Egnatia Street will take you there.

Known to Thessalonians as *ee kamára* ("the arch"), this was erected by the vainglorious Galerius in about 305 to celebrate a dubiously pyrrhic victory against the Persians. It straddles what was once the course of the original Via Egnatia.

The Roman Agora. Just north of Dikasterion Square in the center of Egnatia Street. Any bus going east or west along Egnatia Street will take you to Dikasterion Square.

This was uncovered in 1962 when ground was being dug for a new courthouse (*Dikasterion*). Construction of the courthouse was abandoned and the excavation of the agora has been slowly proceeding ever since. The small amphitheater within has recently been the site of summer music concerts.

The Byzantine Walls

Although now visible only in sections in the upper parts of Thessaloníki, these massive walls once encircled the entire city, including its seafront, and were studded with towers. During the Byzantine era, the original Macedonian walls were considerably fortified and remained that way through most of Ottoman reign. In 1866, the Ottomans, having subdued piracy in the area, began razing the lower walls with an eye to attracting European maritime trade. The only structure left standing because it was in full use as a prison and place of execution was the White Tower (see "The Top Attractions," above).

The Tower of Trigoniou

On the eastern corner of the walls of the Upper City, this commands a marvelous view of Thessaloníki and its harbor and is adjacent to a number of very refreshing sidewalk cafes.

SPECIAL-INTEREST SIGHTSEEING
BYZANTINE CHURCHES

In addition to the major churches listed in "Top Attractions," above, there are a number of smaller churches scattered throughout the city that exhibit virtually the full range of Byzantine styles from the 6th to the 14th century.

Located in downtown Thessaloníki (see "Walking Tour 1," below) are the following:

- The mid–5th-century church of **Panaghia Archiropiitas,** on the eastern side Aghia Sophia Street just north of Egnatia, is the oldest surviving church in Thessaloníki and has some excellent 11th-century frescoes and mosaics.
- The tiny, charming church of **Panaghia Chalkeon** (Virgin of the Copper Workers) lies just outside the copper district, embedded in the southwestern corner of Dikasterion Square. An excellent example of the domed, cruciform style, it was completed in 1028.
- The 14th-century churches of **St. Panteleimon** and **Metamorphosis.** These are just west of the Arch of Galerius on either side of Egnatia Street at the intersection of Palio Patron Germanou Street and Iasonnidou streets. They are notable for their decorative Macedonian brickwork and thrusting, cylindrical domes.

Located in the Turkish Quarter (see "Walking Tour 2," below) are the following:

- Near the top and center of the quarter is the tiny and utterly captivating church of **Osios David,** the second oldest in the city and chapel of the Monastery of Latomos. Built at the end of the 5th century, it was later made into a mosque and lost its western side. There is now virtually nothing left but a line of pews and its apse. But in the half-dome of the apse is a superb mosaic of Christ as a beardless, almost Orphic figure as seen in the vision of Ezekiel. This was hidden from the Turks for centuries by a thin layer of plastered calfskin and, it is said, miraculously discovered on Greek Independence Day 1921 by an Orthodox monk from Egypt, who had been told in a vision to go and pray there. When he did, an earthquake uncovered the mosaic. And the monk expired on the spot.
- On the eastern side of the quarter is the 14th-century church of **Ághios Nikólaos Orphanos.** Rich with frescoes, it has a wooden outer narthex that was added with intriguing effect in later years.

- On the western side of the quarter is the church of **Profitis Ilias.** Built on the site of a Byzantine Palace in about 1860, its construction is in a cruciform-dome style similar to many churches on Mt. Athos, and it has some good but unfortunately damaged frescoes.

WALKING TOUR 1
Lower Thessaloníki

Start: The Greek National Tourist Office, Aristotelous Square.
Finish: Aristotelous Square.
Time: 2 to 3 hours.
Best Times: Tuesday through Saturday mornings.
Worst Times: 1 to 4pm in the summer.

Begin your tour along the harborfront at:

1. **The Greek National Tourist Office, Aristotelous Square.** Here you might want to pick up a free brochure about Thessaloníki that has basic information and a very serviceable map, as well as excellent photographs.

From the office, you emerge onto Aristotelous Square and turn right, crossing Mitropoleos Street and walking under the curving arcade one block north to:

2. **Tsimiski Street.** This is the main shopping artery in the city. The two kiosks across Aristotelous Street to your left sell English-language newspapers and magazines. Two to three blocks further to the left are the principal banks, including American Express, Molxos's bookstore, and Lambropoulos, the main department store. On the other side of Tsimiski Street a half block to your right is the central post office.

Walk one block to your right (eastward) to the other side of Aghia Sophia Street. If you want to have a coffee before continuing, there is no better place than **Family,** on the corner one block to the south. It has the best coffee, cake, and ice cream in the city.

Otherwise, go one block north up Aghia Sophia Street to the circular square on which is:

3. **The Church of Aghia Sophia.** (See "The Top Attractions," above.) The name means "Holy Wisdom," and it's modeled after the church of the same name in Constantinople (Istanbul). Inside its rather gloomy interior are some excellent mosaics.

On leaving, turn to the left and circle around to the rear of the church onto Svolou Street. Follow this east to Palio Patron Germanou Street. To the south across this street, you will see a diagonal street (Loui) heading southeast. Follow this into:

4. **Navarino Square and the Palace of Galerius.** This spacious, tree-shaded square is full of very nice cafes, bars, and restaurants and is the gathering place of Thessaloníki's artists and intellectuals. On its eastern side, exposed in excavations below street level, are the remains of the Roman palace of the Emperor Galerius. Most intriguing is the octagonal structure in the southeastern corner of the square, which is assumed to have been Galerius's throne room. In it was found an arch with the bust of Galerius on one side and a female figure representing Thessaloníki on the other. This is now on display in the Archaeological Museum.

Running north and south on the eastern side of the square is the pedestrian walkway of Dimitriou Gounari Street, where there are several more exposed

Walking Tour 1—Lower Thessaloníki

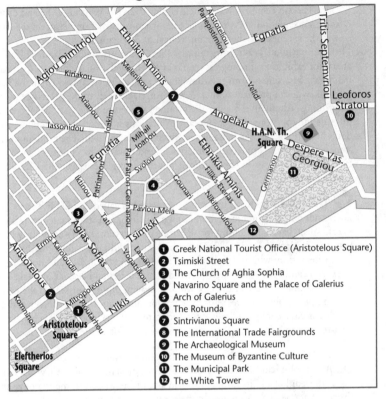

1. Greek National Tourist Office (Aristotelous Square)
2. Tsimiski Street
3. The Church of Aghia Sophia
4. Navarino Square and the Palace of Galerius
5. Arch of Galerius
6. The Rotunda
7. Sintrivianou Square
8. The International Trade Fairgrounds
9. The Archaeological Museum
10. The Museum of Byzantine Culture
11. The Municipal Park
12. The White Tower

ruins. This was part of a Roman complex that led from the palace south to the sea and north (your direction) to:

5. **The Arch of Galerius.** (See "Top Attractions," above.) Originally this was a four-sided domed structure of which there remains only the large eastern arch and the smaller northern one. The arches thus spanned the Via Egnatia as well as the passageway leading from the palace to your next destination:

6. **The Rotunda.** (See "The Top Attractions," above.) Once the repairs to damage from a 1977 earthquake have been completed, it's intended to be a museum for Christian art.

On leaving the Rotunda (if you can get in), return to the arch on Egnatia St. and head east (left) toward the fountain on:

7. **Sintrivianou Square.** This square and its fountain mark a spot that was once just inside the ancient eastern gate of the city.

Outside of this gate were the city's traditional burial grounds, not only of the Christians but of the Jews and Muslims as well. Of these cemeteries, only those of the non-Orthodox and Orthodox Christians remain and are to be found one block north of the fountain, at the end of Ethnikis Aminis St.

The Jewish cemetery was dug up in 1949 when ground was broken for the University of Thessaloníki as only 1% of the city's once thriving Jewish community had survived the Nazi occupation. On the campus, which begins on the northern corner of Ethnikis Aminis and Egnatia streets, headstones from the cemetery can still be found.

The Turkish cemetery was demolished in 1926 (14 years after the end of the Ottoman occupation of Northern Greece) when construction began on the large area to the southeast of the fountain, your next destination:

8. **The International Trade Fairgrounds.** (See "More Attractions," above.) If there are major exhibitions in progress, you may be charged a small entrance fee at the main gate just across from the fountain. If you do not want to enter the fairgrounds, you can proceed southeast along Angelaki Street to the other side of the fairgrounds. Alternatively, enter the grounds and make your way through them towards the southeast. If there are any exhibitions in progress that interest you, don't hesitate to enter the buildings in which they are housed. The exhibitions can sometimes be quite impressive. Otherwise, head towards the large, spindly structure that you will see in the southeast towering over the rest of the fairground buildings and:

☕ **TAKE A BREAK**   This spindly structure is called the **OTE Tower** and houses not only telecommunication facilities but also, at its top, a circular, glassed-in cafe-snack bar that is a must for sightseers in Thessaloníki. It's open daily from 9am to 12:30am (☎ 031/222-740). An elevator will take you to the top (4th) floor where, from within the comfort of its elegantly styled, air-conditioned confines, you can have a moderately priced drink or coffee and a snack and take in a superb panoramic view of the city without moving from your seat as the entire room imperceptibly revolves 360° over a 30-minute span. If you are lucky and the weather is clear enough (usually only during the winter), you will also be able to see Mt. Olympus looming across the southwestern side of the gulf.

Across Stratou Avenue just to the south of the tower is:

9. **The Archaeological Museum.** (See "The Top Attractions," above.) When looking at the skull of Philip II, note the evidence of the wound in the right eye and the fact that one of the shin guards (greaves) is shorter than the other. Since it was known that Philip had a limp and also was wounded in the eye by an arrow, these finds served as additional confirmation that the tomb was indeed his.

On leaving the museum, turn right and then right again and walk along Stratou Street opposite the fairgrounds. One block to the east is a large two-story modern brick structure:

10. **The Museum of Byzantine Culture.** (See "The Top Attractions," above.) It is interesting to note that although a Byzantine museum had been planned for Thessaloníki as long ago as 1913 (one year after Northern Greece had been freed from Ottoman rule), the same 1914 law that allowed the foundation of the Christian and Byzantine Museum in Athens held up the establishment of a similar one in Thessaloníki for more than 60 years. It was only in the climate of national unity that followed the fall of the junta in 1973 that an architectural competition was announced in 1977. But it was not until 1984 that the land, then owned by the national Ministry of Defense, was finally given over for its use. This should give you an idea of the intensity of the competition between Athens and Thessaloníki. Or rather, of how jealously Athens sometimes guards its supposed superiority over Thessaloníki, and how insecure it feels about it.

On leaving the Byzantine museum, return back along Stratou Street to the Archaeological Museum and turn left at its front, crossing the diagonal of Angelaki Street to the broad, cafe-lined walkway in front of you that is the center of:

11. **The Municipal Park.** In addition to the cafes and restaurants on the walkway, the main attraction of this park is the marvelous children's playground), which

is in the middle of the park just to the right (west) of the walkway as you face the harbor.

☕ **TAKE A BREAK**   At any one of the several cafes you will see along the walkway. They offer coffee, sweets, snacks, and soft and alcoholic drinks.

Afterwards, follow the walkway across the wide boulevard of Megalou Alexandrou Avenue. On the opposite side of the street half a block to the right (west) is an excellent kiosk offering the widest selection of foreign-language newspapers and magazines outside of Molxos's bookstore.

"Megalou Alexandrou" means "Alexander the Great" and, at the end of the walkway on the waterfront promenade, there's an enormous bronze statue honoring him.

About 100 yards to the west of Alexander's monument along the seaside promenade is:

12. **The White Tower.** (See "The Top Attractions," above.) When it was unpainted and in use by the Turks as a place of execution, it was known to the people of Thessaloníki as "the Bloody Tower." Then, when the Turks tore down the lower walls of the city in order to facilitate trade with Europe, they painted the tower white, perhaps to placate European sensibilities. Since then it has become the city's most famous landmark.

Across the street from the tower is an imposing building that houses the stage and administrative offices and rehearsal rooms of the **State Theater of Northern Greece** (see "Thessaloníki After Dark: The Arts," below).

After you leave the tower, take a stroll eastward along the seaside promenade and take a break, if you like, at one of the many cafes lining the sidewalk opposite. Or, continue on to your morning starting point, **Aristotelous Square.**

☕ **WINDING DOWN**   It should now be lunch time and the perfect opportunity to eat at one or another of Thessaloníki's best *ouzeries*: **Totti's,** on Aristotelous Square, or the **Aristotelous,** 1¹/₂ blocks north of the square off the right (eastern) side of Aristotelous Street. See the "Dining" section, above, for details.

WALKING TOUR 2
Upper Thessaloníki

Start: Eleftherios Square, two blocks east of Aristotelous Square.
Finish: Modiano Market.
Time: 2 to 3 hours.
Best Times: Tuesday through Saturday mornings.
Worst Times: 1 to 4pm in the summer.

Begin your tour along the harborfront at:

1. **Eleftherios Square.** On the eastern side of the square there is a bus stop for the no. 22 and 23 buses that will take you on an often picturesque 20-minute ride through the commercial district, past the great church of Saint Dimitrios, and up through the winding streets of the old Turkish Quarter to the main gate of the Upper City. This main gate is called "*ee portára*" and the Upper City variously known as the "*áno pólis*," which means just that, or "*Ta Kástra*," a reference to the many castlelike towers that once bristled on the walls.

If you don't want to take the bus, you can try to get a taxi, but drivers have been known more often than not to refuse to take you there once they know the destination. This is because the area is poor and fares going down are not easy to find.

If you take a taxi, tell the driver to let you off at the main square (*ee platía*) of the Upper City.

If you take the bus, don't get off at the stop just to the left of the main gate; stay on it as it travels west along the walls. This will allow you to have a look at the humble but colorful homes on that side of the city. The bus will then turn around and come back along the walls to the arch which enters the massively tree-shaded main square. Get off there.

☕ **TAKE A BREAK**   Either at one of the cafes in the square or outside the arch that enters it, where there is a fine view of the city below.

To the east of this arch on the outside of the walls is the entrance to:

2. The Tower of Trigoniou. This is the second most famous Byzantine tower in the city. It's open throughout the day and evening. There are no exhibits inside, but its top offers a superb, eagle's-eye view of Thessaloníki and its harbor.

After you leave the tower, go back through the arch to the main square and take a walk through:

3. The Upper City. Just inside the arch are two roads. The one to the left follows the main street as it curves around and goes out through the main gate, about a 10-minute walk through a rather drab commercial district, which ends, however, at a lovely, spacious grassy area just inside the gate.

The road to the right curves around to the rear of the city, where there are other Byzantine walls and the infamous **castle of Eptapyrgiou.** Once a Byzantine castle, this became infamous as one of the most abominable prisons in Greece (it was finally closed in 1988) and is responsible for the original population of the area by destitute families of the inmates. You cannot get inside today, although there are plans to reopen it as a tourist attraction. For this reason, you may not want to walk there, as it takes about 20 minutes, some of it uphill. If you do, return back to the square and then follow the curve of the main street around to the main gate.

Go out the main gate and cross the street to the right. There you will find the entrance to:

4. Vlatades Monastery. Called "*Moní Vlatádon*" in Greek, the grounds of this wonderfully peaceful monastery contain a number of Byzantine and modern structures, the most significant of which is the side chapel of the central church, which is dedicated to streets Peter and Paul. Tradition says that it's built on the spot where Paul preached on his first visit to Thessaloníki in A.D.49.

On leaving the monastery, turn left and walk west on Eptapygiou Street outside the walls. About 100 yards on, you will come to a set of broad stairs on your left, at the bottom of which is a small square. This is the beginning of:

5. The Turkish Quarter. Once considered the choice residential district in Thessaloníki because it would catch the breezes coming off the gulf in summer (downtown Thessaloníki then being bordered by walls on the seafront), this area fell into disrepair after the Turks departed in 1912, and has only recently begun to come back into favor. Funds from European Community have been used to recobble its marvelous maze of winding streets and young Thessalonians are buying and renovating its picturesque Ottoman houses. If you don't stop along the way, a walk through this district from the Upper City down to the harbor takes

Walking Tour 2—Upper Thessaloníki

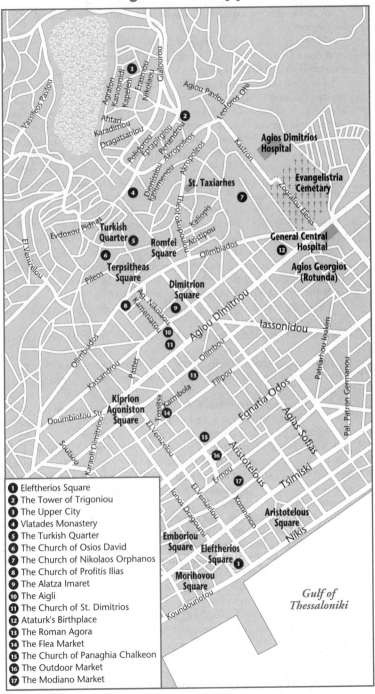

1 Eleftherios Square
2 The Tower of Trigoniou
3 The Upper City
4 Vlatades Monastery
5 The Turkish Quarter
6 The Church of Osios David
7 The Church of Nikolaos Orphanos
8 The Church of Profitis Ilias
9 The Alatza Imaret
10 The Aigli
11 The Church of St. Dimitrios
12 Ataturk's Birthplace
13 The Roman Agora
14 The Flea Market
15 The Church of Panaghia Chalkeon
16 The Outdoor Market
17 The Modiano Market

about 20 minutes, even though it looks like much more from the top of the stairs leading into it.

When you reach the tiny square at the bottom of the stairs, cross it and turn right down Dimitri Poliorkitou Street. Three houses down on your left, you will see a small set of stairs (and a sign to "Osios David") to a street leading down the hill. Go down this street and take your first left, following the winding descent of the street as it curves right to the entrance of:

6. The Church of Osios David. For details on this most enchanting of churches, see the section under "Special-Interest Sightseeing: Byzantine Churches," above.

When you leave the church, turn right and continue your cobblestoned descent a short distance to the first intersection. Here you will come to the rather bizarre sight of a house covered with sheets of tin with writing on them. This is the "palace" of the self-proclaimed "King of the Greeks." Written on the tin are his proclamations about the state of the world and dire prophecies about its imminent end if such things as pollution are not taken care of. Crazy? You decide.

From the "palace" continue downhill along Akropoleos Street to Romfei Square, a narrow open space to your left (east). If you are interested in seeing additional Byzantine churches, follow the directions to nos. 6 and 7 below in this walking tour. Otherwise, continue down Akropoleos Street to the next corner, Kassandrou Street, and turn right. A two-and-a-half block walk will take you to no. 8, the Turkish almshouse called the Alatza Imaret.

To see the first church, follow the street on the northern side of the square, Eolou Street, eastward to:

7. The Church of Nikolaos Orphanos. For details, see "Special-Interest Sightseeing: Byzantine Churches," above.

Afterward, return to Romfei Square and walk west along Eolou Street to:

8. The Church of Profitis Ilias. Again, for details, see "Special-Interest Sightseeing: Byzantine Churches," above.

After you have left the church, go back one block east and turn right down Aghiou Nikolaou Street. One and a half blocks down the street, you will see a small street leading off to the left (east). This will take you directly to:

9. The Alatza Imaret. For details, see under "More Attractions," above. With all the talk of Ottoman prisons and brutality, it is often forgotten that Muslims were, and are, particularly beneficent in their treatment of the poor and in their tolerance of others' faiths. As an almshouse, the Alatza Imaret dispensed food and alms to the destitute. And, had it not been for the Ottoman's respect for other religions, the Christian churches you have seen and are about to see would no longer exist. Notice that in Thessaloníki there are no extant mosques, only baths and almshouses.

On leaving the Imaret, turn down Aghiou Nikolaou at Kassandrou Street. On the southwestern corner is a former Turkish hammam (bathhouse), now beautifully restored and converted into one of the best restaurants (and nightclub and movie house as well) in the city. It's called:

10. The Aigli. From 9am on, this is open daily throughout the day for sightseeing only (except for special group lunches) and is well worth a brief visit. Also see "Where to Dine," above, for more information. One block further down Nikolaou Street, at the corner of Aghiou Dimitriou Street, stands:

11. The Church of St. Dimitrios. For centuries it was believed that this 5th-century church was built on the site of Roman baths where, in 303, St. Dimitrios was martyred for preaching the Christian faith in Galerius's capital. However, this was taken on faith rather than proof. It was not until 1926 that workmen repairing the damage of the 1917 fire uncovered the baths below the transept and found there a cross-shaped reliquary containing a vial of blood-soaked earth—virtual proof positive that this was indeed the very place where Dimitrios had been executed. For more details, see the listing for the this church in "The Top Attractions," above.

Across Aghiou Dimitriou Street from the entrance to the church is a small park dividing the upper end of Aristotelous Street. One block to the south is the Roman agora. If, however, you are interested in things Ottoman, you might want to take a detour to:

12. Atatürk's Birthplace. This is an eight-block walk east of the church along the same side of Aghiou Dimitriou Street. It will take about 10 minutes.

It surprises many people to know that the George Washington of modern Turkey was born in Thessaloníki (in 1881) and participated there in the Young Turks' movement that precipitated the fall of the sultanate and established Turkey as a republic. See "The Top Attractions," above, for more details.

If you visit Atatürk's birthplace, return to the front of the church, cross Aghiou Dimitriou Street and walk down the park-divided Aristotelous Street to:

13. The Roman Agora. For details, see the section under "More Attractions," above.

☕ TAKE A BREAK   At any one of the sidewalk cafes and tavernas along the park and facing the agora on Olimpou Street. The ones along the park are rather expensive. On Olimpou Street, just to the left of Aristotelous Street, there is, however, a much cheaper and wonderfully old-fashioned Greek cafe, "O Pavlos."

Stay on the northern side of the agora and walk west along Olimpou Street to the corner of Tositsa Street and turn left. This is the beginning of:

14. The Flea Market. Lining Tositsa Street are a number of antique and second-hand stores selling a variety of goods from new furniture to old magazines and clothes and coins, pistols, and, occasionally, some excellent antiques. Often, however, the best and most interesting buys are spread out on the street and sidewalks or in the backs of trucks. These are brought in in the early morning by enterprising merchants who have been scouring the outlying villages for goods.

To the east and south of the flea market is the **coppersmiths' district,** which has been there since Byzantine times. It was in this area that St. Dimitrios was arrested for preaching the gospel. To get there, turn left at the end of Tositsa Street and walk two blocks to the edge of Dikasterion Square. Turn right along the square. Two blocks down is Klissouras Street. Along this street are the best copperware stores, most of which make their own goods and sell them at prices much cheaper than the tourist shops.

At the southern corner of Dikasterion Squre and Egnatia Street is a beautiful Byzantine church dedicated to the Virgin of the Coppersmiths:

15. The Church of Panaghia Chalkeon. See under "Special-Interest Sightseeing: Byzantine Churches," above, for further information.

Directly across Egnatia Street from this church is a narrow sidestreet leading into:

16. The Outdoor Market. This is perhaps the nearest you will come to experiencing Thessaloníki as it must have been in the commercial heyday of the Ottoman Empire—a lively, bustling hodgepodge of spice sellers, clothing stores, basket weavers, flower shops, tinsmiths, leather workers, souvlaki stands, tavernas, bakers, candlestick makers, fish mongers, butchers, and produce sellers. Take a stroll through the wandering byways of the market, but don't stop here to eat. There are much more interesting places just to the south, across Ermou Street, where you will enter the covered, square-block expanse of:

17. The Modiano Market. Built in 1922 and 1923 by a Jewish architect named Modiano, this market has three entrances along Ermou Street and three corresponding ones along its southern side, Vassilis Irakliou Street. There is an additional entrance on its western side off of Komninon Street. On Ermou Street the entrance on the left (towards Aristotelous Street) leads exclusively into the seafood market. The other two lead into the main market, where there is a sumptuous variety of meats, fruits, vegetables, and breads, as well as a number of cafes, ouzeries, and tavernas.

☕ **WINDING DOWN**   If you can, try to get into the marvelous ouzerie called **Thanasis** (see "Dining," above). Even if it's full, it's still worth passing by just to imbibe the atmosphere. Otherwise, or in addition, try the **Kentriki Stoa,** a newly opened cafe-snack bar perched above the roofs of the vegetable stalls at the southern end of the market. From here, behind a glass partition, one gets a marvelous, pigeon's eye view of the swirling activities of the market below.

ORGANIZED TOURS

Inasmuch as most of the important sights of Thessaloníki can and should be visited on foot, taking an organized tour of the city is rather against the point. Tours to the outlying attractions, on the other hand, are highly recommended, as the buses are comfortably air conditioned and the guides invariably well trained, with good to excellent English, and full of all the information you could possibly want, and more.

Highly recommended is the tour to the "Philip and Alexander Sites" of Pélla, Vergína, and Dión. Particularly the latter two, Vergína offering a most stunning view of the Royal Tombs where the treasures shown in the Archaeological Museum were found, and Dión being the site of the most important and impressive archaeological excavations presently going on in all of Greece. This entire tour takes a very comfortable six hours or so with a stop for lunch.

Also recommended is a day cruise around the holy peninsula of Mt. Athos at the eastern-most end of Halkidiki. There is some spectacular scenery to be seen as well as some extraordinarily beautiful monasteries. This tour is particularly recommended to woman, as it is the closest they will be able to get to the female-forbidden grounds of this bastion of masculine virtue.

Tours within the city and to the Philip and Alexander Sites as well as day cruises to Mt. Athos can be booked at **Zorpidis Travel,** 76 Egnatia St., 2nd Floor (☎ 031/286-812 or 031/286-825). They are the best in Thessaloníki and can handle all of your traveling and touring needs.

OUTDOOR ACTIVITIES

Because of pollution in the bay and the frenetic nature of traffic in the city, outdoor activities such as swimming, boating, fishing, and biking are not recommended.

Beaches   As noted above, any beaches within the bay of Thessaloníki are too polluted to be entirely safe, although people do swim there. Those in the communities of **Perea** and **Aghia Triada** (10 to 15 miles along the bay east of the city) are considered reasonably safe. Just past Aghia Triada, on the headland of the bay, is the Greek National Tourist Organization facility of **Akti Thermaikou,** which also has a children's playground as well changing cabins, snack bars, and tennis courts (☎ 0392/513-52).

Horseback Riding   The **Thessaloníki Riding Club** (☎ 031/270-676) is located in the countryside northeast of the city, off the road to the hilltop community of Panorama. Directions for getting there are too complicated for this space, but the owners speak English and can ably assist you.

Jogging   Traffic pollution can be partly avoided by jogging along the spacious waterfront promenade east of the White Tower. It is, however, solid cement; there are no dirt footpaths anywhere in the city set aside for this purpose.

Tennis   Within the city, there are outdoor courts to be rented at the **Poseidonion Athletic Center,** next to the seaside amusement park at the foot of the 25th of March Street (☎ 031/428-453). Outside the city, there are courts on the beautiful, tree-shaded campus of the American-owned **Anatolia College** on the road to Panorama (☎ 031/301-071), about a 20-minute drive. There are also facilities at **Akti Thermaikou** (see "Beaches," above).

6 Shopping

There are two categories of shopping in Thessaloníki. First there are the products of local craftspeople, such as coppersmiths and jewelers, where real bargains are to be found. And there are imported goods, such as clothing from Italy and France, where customs duties make the cost prohibitive. In both instances, there is relatively little from which to choose. However cosmopolitan it may be, Thessaloníki is still a small city, and still geared to serving the needs of its populace, not the tourist trade.

The Shopping Scene   The best shopping area in town is in the city center along the east-west lengths of Tsimiski, Mitropoleos, and Proxenou Koromila between Pavlou Mela Street (the diagonal connecting the church of St. Sophia with the White Tower) and the north-south vertical of Eleftherios Venizelou Street. In this area are the city's few department stores, many boutiques selling the very latest in very expensive men's and women's haute couture, shops selling jeans and casual clothing, shoe stores, jewelry and antique stores, several record shops selling both Greek and foreign items, the best English- and French-language book and magazine store in town, and a number of confectionery stores.

Store Hours   In Thessaloníki, old-style, pre-European Community shopping hours, unfathomable to foreigners, are still in force. Shops open at about 9am and close around 1:30 or 2pm for the afternoon siesta. On Tuesday, Thursday, and Friday evenings, some (but not all) reopen from about 5:30 to 8:30pm. During July, however, all shops are closed in the evenings. Therefore, to be safe, plan to do your shopping in the mornings.

SHOPPING A TO Z
ANTIQUES
Relics. 3 Giorgio Lassani St. (1 block east of the Mitropoleos Cathedral off of Mitropoleos Street). ☎ **031/226-506.**

Relics offers the best variety of high-quality antiques in the city, from silver- and glassware to jewelry, ceramics, prints, art nouveau lamps, and Victorian-era dolls. You pay, however, for what you get. Open Monday through Saturday during the regular shopping hours.

ART
Art Forum. 29 Nikiforo Foka St. (off of Tsimiski Street 1 block east of Navarino Square). ☎ **031/224-060.**

A rapidly emerging new gallery that shows great taste in selecting the very best of contemporary Greek art. Open Monday, Tuesday, Thursday, and Friday from 10am to 2:30pm and 6 to 9pm. Closed during July and August.

Terra Cotta. 13 Smirnis St. (1¹/₂ blocks north of the U.S. Consulate between Nikis Avenue and Mitropoleos Street). ☎ **031/220-191.**

The very best gallery in Thessaloníki. Features works from all of the most famous contemporary Greek artists, such as Fasianos, as well as those of the emerging generation. Open Monday, Tuesday, Thursday, and Friday from 10am to 2:30pm and 6 to 9pm. Closed August 1 to 20.

BOOKS

Molhos. 10 Tsimiski St. (between El. Venizelou and Dragoumi streets). ☎ **031/275-271.**

A family run bookstore where English and French are spoken with helpful, fluent charm, Molhos offers the best selection of foreign-language books, magazines, and newspapers in the city. Check the upstairs room, where the more literary works are to be found, including books about Greece (and Thessaloníki) in English that are more than a cut above the normal tourist fare. Open Monday through Saturday during the regular shopping hours.

CONFECTIONARIES

Agapitos. 53 Tsimiski St. (between Aghias Sophias Street and Karolou Dil streets). ☎ **031/279-107.**

In a city where sweetness is next to godliness, this venerable establishment is the best. There are a wide variety of items to choose from, all made with great, mouthwatering, high-caloric care. Open Monday through Saturday during regular shopping hours.

COPPER WARE

Adelphi Kazanzidi. 12 Klissouras St. (running off the western side of Dikasterion Square, 1 block north of Egnatia Street). ☎ **031/262-741.**

A family run store that has passed down its copper-working skills from generation to generation. Numerous finely crafted copper-ware items from wine carafes to skillets, water heaters, trays, etc., all done on the premises and by hand. Open Monday through Saturday during regular shopping hours.

CRAFTS

Skitso. 11 Grigori Palama St. (1 block west of the intersection of Pavlo Mela and Tsimiski streets). ☎ **031/269-822.**

This store sells a delightful variety of handmade objects, mostly in wood, including puppets, ships, crosses, and children's toys. Open Monday through Saturday during regular shopping hours.

DEPARTMENT STORES

Lambropoulos. 18 Tsimiski St. (1 block west of Aristotelous Street, corner of Komninon Street). ☎ **031/269-971.**

The best in the city with five floors full of everything and anything you might want, from cosmetics to basketballs. Open Monday through Saturday during regular shopping hours.

GIFTS/SOUVENIRS

ZM. 1 Proxenou Koromila (1 block east of Aristotelous Square). ☎ **031/240-591.**

Pronounced *"zeeta mee"* (as in the alphabet), this gift shop offers three floors of expensive but well-crafted Greek souvenir items such as worry beads, pottery, folk art, rugs, toys, handcrafted caïques, prints, and a few antique silver place settings and jewelry. An extremely tempting place to browse. Open Monday through Saturday during regular shopping hours.

Tanagrea. Vogatsikou Street (1 block east of the Metropolitan Cathedral between Mitropoleos and Proxenou Koromila streets).

An impressive selection of handcrafted items by a stable of extremely skilled artisans employed by this well-known chain of stores, which also has outlets in Athens, Crete, and Spetsai. Ceramics, pewter, silver, leather goods, paintings, glassware, and jewelry. Open Monday through Saturday during regular shopping hours.

FOOTWARE

Pak. 3 Aghias Sophias Square (opposite the north side of Aghia Sophia church). ☎ **031/ 274-863.**

This shop offers a wide selection of high-quality Greek shoes from hiking boots to high heels at very acceptable prices. There are also foreign brands, but these are much more expensive. Open Monday through Saturday during regular shopping hours.

JEWELRY

Marina. 62 Mitropoleos St. (1 block east of the Metropolitan Cathedral). ☎ **031/238-361.**

Specializing in gold, but not exclusively, the eponymous owner offers her own designs as well as copies of the works of the famous Greek jewelers such as Lalaounis, with whom she has apprenticed. Open Monday through Saturday during regular shopping hours.

LEATHER WARE

Falli. 11 Askitou St. (southwest corner of the outdoor market, near Ermou and El. Venizelou streets). ☎ **031/229-197.**

The best of several leather-good shops in the area that make and sell shoulder bags, backpacks, attaché cases, sandals, etc. Some of these items are of very high quality at very reasonable prices. You should bargain. Open Monday through Saturday during regular shopping hours.

MARKETS

Modiano. Two square blocks east of Aristotelous Street between V. Irakliou Street to the south and Egnatia Street to the north.

This is the great municipal market of Thessaloníki: a bustling cornucopia of vegetables, fruit, meats, fish, breads, spices, delicatessens, ouzeries, and whatever else you can (or cannot) think of. There are two sections: the least expensive, outdoor area just south of Egnatia Street, and its covered counterpart to the south across below Ermou Street. You can buy almost anything you want in this area, and even if you don't, it's still one of the great attractions of the city.

Flea Market. Tositsa Street (running diagonally east from El Venizelou Street 3 blocks north of Egnatia Street).

While this street has numerous permanent stores (selling old medals, coins, swords, pistols, lamps, etc.—most overpriced)—the real attraction here are the goods spilled out on the sidewalks from trucks bringing in their wares from the villages in the early mornings. Most of it is junk, but interesting junk, and sometimes there's a real pearl shining among the shells.

MUSIC

Blow Up. 6 Aristotelous St. (on the eastern side of the street, a block north of Tsimiski Street). ☎ **031/233-255.**

Both this store and Patsis (see below) have excellent selections of Greek music well displayed in their windows and on the shelves. The difference is in the service: The owner of Blow Up not only speaks English but is a nice guy as well. Open Monday through Saturday during regular shopping hours.

Patsis. 39 Tsimiski St. (corner of Aristotelous Street). ☎ **031/231-805.**

Excellent selection of Greek music. Open Monday through Saturday during regular shopping hours.

PERFUME

Aroma. 62 Mitropoleos St. (1 block east of the Mitropoleos Cathedral). ☎ **031/286-010.**

This little shop with its enticing rows of colored perfume jars offers a multitude of scents, copying famous perfumes or mixing ones of your own choosing at extremely reasonable prices. Open Monday through Saturday during regular shopping hours (see "Store Hours," above).

TOYS

Fokas. 50 Tsimiski St. (east of Aghias Sophias Street). ☎ **031/276-774.**

A department store in whose basement you can find some adorable, Greek-made wooden children's toys. See also Skitso listed in "Crafts," above.

7 Thessaloníki After Dark

Thessaloníki does not really awaken until after dark, and when it does, it seems at times as if the entire populace has come out to amuse itself. In addition to the cultural festivals held in the fall, numerous theatrical events and pop and classical concerts take place year-round. Meanwhile, the city seems festooned with enough bars and music and dance clubs to serve a population twice its size, yet all of them are crowded to the bursting point and more open every year.

While there a number of publications listing the various events, and posters splattered everywhere announcing them, they will be all Greek to you, so the best thing to do is to ask for information on special events at your hotel or at the National Tourist Organization office on Aristotelous Square.

THE DIMITRIA FESTIVAL

In honor of the patron saint of Thessaloníki, St. Dimitrios, whose name day is October 26, this prestigious month-long cultural festival runs annually from the beginning to the end of October and includes the Greek Film Festival as well as many theatrical and musical events, all of them performed by major and minor artists from all over the country.

THE PERFORMING ARTS

The **State Theatre of Northern Greece** (Kratikó Théatro) has two venues. In the winter it puts on plays in its home, the State Theatre, which is opposite the White Tower (☎ 031/223-785), and, in the summer, at the **Forest Theatre** (Théatro Dásous), an open-air amphitheater located in the forested hilltop area east of the Upper City (☎ 031/218-092). It presents both ancient and modern Greek plays, as well as Greek translations of foreign plays, including those by such well-known authors as Beckett, Miller, and Tennessee Williams. Major Greek directors are brought in and some, but not all, of the productions are quite stunning. Temporarily closed for renovations, it's expected to reopen for the cultural festivals in 1997.

In summer, the Forest Theatre, which has a marvelous view of the city, also hosts lively, well-attended concerts by popular Greek singers and composers, as well as by visiting ballet companies.

In the winter, the State Theatre occasionally gives its stage over to visiting foreign companies presenting both plays and ballets. Visitors have included the National Theatre of England and the Bolshoi Ballet.

Mention should also be made here of the outdoor **Garden Theatre** (Theatro Kypou) in the Municipal Park to the east of the State Theatre. While part of the State Theatre complex, it's rented out by various local groups who present a variety of cultural events from music to ballets, plays, and musical comedies. All are in Greek, but some can be quite accomplished and entertaining.

The **Municipal Orchestra of Thessaloníki** performs at the Aristotle University concert hall on Nea Egnatia Street, opposite the northern entrance of the International Trade Fairgrounds, from September until May (☎ 031/283-343). Its repertoire includes the works of modern Greek composers as well as the standard classics, which it plays with great distinction before a highly appreciative audience.

THE BAR, CLUB & MUSIC SCENE

In the summer, virtually all of the best bars and music and dance clubs within the city shut down. Some then immediately reopen branches either in the resort areas of Halkidiki or along a section of the road leading east along the coast, about a mile before the airport. This, plus the fact that new or newly decorated and renamed venues are constantly opening while others go out of fashion and close, makes it virtually impossible to recommend any with any certainty.

There is one place, however, that can be recommended without hesitation. Not only is it both a permanent fixture of Thessaloníki nightlife winter and summer, but it incorporates by far the best of the bar, music, and club scenes in the city:

The Mylos. 25 Andreadou Giorgiou St. ☎ **031/516-945.** Go west on Tsimiski Street to its end and turn left onto October 28th Street. At the first traffic light, turn right onto Andreadou Giorgiou. It's near the end of the street on the right and can't be missed.

Within the grounds of an old, wonderfully restored multibuilding flour mill, the Mylos (pronounced *"MEE-los"*) complex contains a music club for blues, folk, jazz, and pop groups, a nightclub featuring Greek singers and comedians, a bar-discotheque, an outdoor concert stage and movie theater, a cafe, an ouzerie, and several exhibition rooms and art galleries. Opened in 1990, it has quickly established itself as one of the top musical venues in the country and features a constant stream of talent from within Greece and abroad.

There's so much to do and see here that it's best to go early and spend the evening, eating perhaps at the ouzerie, having coffee at the cafe, strolling among the exhibits, and attending one or both of the clubs. This is what the locals do, en masse, so it's best to arrive before 9pm, particularly if you want to get a place at the clubs, which open at 10pm and are mobbed. Reservations for the clubs can be made at the above number. There's a cover charge that varies with the entertainment—usually between Dr 2,000 and Dr 3,000 ($9 to $13), and drinks cost between Dr 500 and Dr 1,000 ($2 to $4).

The ouzerie, cafe, and galleries are also open during the daytime from about 11am on.

ONLY IN THESSALONÍKI

Taking what the Greeks call a *volta* (a stroll) along the seaside promenade, particularly at sunset or under a full moon, is one of the great pleasures of being in

Thessaloníki. Start at Aristotelous Square, perhaps with a coffee or a drink or sweets at one of its many cafes and walk east past the White Tower and toward the bright lights of the city's amusement park at the other end of the promenade, about 2 miles distant. Along Nikis Avenue, which borders the promenade in the city center, are a number of cafes and bars. At the White Tower, there are usually peanut vendors and, occasionally, the city's only **horse-drawn carriage** for rent.

You might also decide to take an hour's **cruise around the harbor** on the various small boats that dock just east of the tower. Several companies make the trip, but the best of these is **Ampari Lines** (☎ 094/359-330), which has cruises scheduled every two or three hours from 12:30pm to 3am. The cost is Dr 1,000 ($4). Coffee, fruit juices, and beer are served on board.

LATE-NIGHT BITES

Corner. 28 Aghias Sophias St. (on the east side of the street, between the church of Aghia Sophia and Egnatia Street). ☎ **031/273-310.** Also at 6 Ethnikis Aminis St. (1 block north of the White Tower, behind the State Theater). ☎ **031/273-039.**

Open daily 24 hours a day, this is where you can get, among other delicacies, the best pizzas in town. Alcoholic drinks are also served. See "Dining," above.

Xatzi. 50 Eleftheriou Venizelou St. (just north of Egnatia Street). ☎ **031/279-058.**

Established in 1908 and passed down from generation to generation, this tiny shop with seven tables is the perfect place to go for a midnight sweet. They have a superb selection of Levantine pastries and desserts (ask for the illustrated catalogue) whose recipes have not changed an iota since its opening.

The Philip & Alexander Sites of Northern Greece

by Sherry Marker

Every year, more people head north to Macedonia to see the cluster of ancient sites associated with Philip of Macedon (382–336 B.C.) and his famous son Alexander the Great (356–323 B.C.). In part, this is because word is getting out about just how congenial Thessaloníki, Macedonia's capital and Greece's "Second City," is. Until recently, Thessaloníki was virtually as undiscovered as some of the more remote Aegean islands. Now travelers are enjoying the pleasures of this seaside port city with its views of Mount Olympus. And, en route to and from Salonika, and on day trips, travelers are beginning to explore Macedonia.

Many of those visiting Northern Greece these days are Greeks, whose interest in things Macedonian was enormously intensified a few years ago when, just across the border, the former Yugoslavian district of Macedonia proclaimed itself a republic. How dare these non-Greeks take the name of Macedonia, Greeks asked—forgetting that their own ancestors had not considered Philip of Macedon a Greek! Most of all, Greeks were furious that Philip's best-known royal symbol, a star with 16 rays, appeared on the new Macedonia's flag. Throughout Greece, all the way south to the tip of the Máni peninsula, Greeks debated whether the new self-styled Macedonia had imperialistic aims. For once, Greece's long-standing enmity with Turkey was virtually ignored, as Greeks painted "Macedonia is Greece" on virtually every road and wall in the country.

Things have calmed down a bit now that the new Republic of Macedonia has changed its flag, but Greeks are still rediscovering their ancestral links with Philip of Macedon, the northern king who conquered Greece in 338 B.C.

The renewed interest in Philip, Alexander, and Macedonia itself has led the Greek Archaeological Service to redouble its efforts to excavate the Macedonian royal sites and build site museums. And that, of course, means that there's much more to see above ground than there was even a few years ago. In short, this is an excellent time to visit Macedonia and spend time retracing the footsteps of Philip and Alexander.

The only enjoyable and efficient way to see the places where Philip of Macedon and his son Alexander the Great lived and reigned is by car or with a tour. Several Athens-based companies, such as **Chat** and **American Express,** offer tours of Central and Northern Greece that take in the most important Macedonian sites. In addition,

Doucas Tours, Odos Venizelou 8, Thessaloníki (☎ 031/261-249) offers day trips to Pélla, Edessa, Veria, and Vergína ($70), and others to Philippa, Kavala, and Amphípolis ($50). The day of the week that these tours are given tends to vary, and it's vital to make an advance reservation.

In Thessaloníki, information on Doucas and other tours, such as the archaeologically oriented tours given by **Zorpidis Travel,** 76 Egnatia St. (☎ 031/286-82-56), is available from the **Greek National Tourist Organization (EOT),** Plateia Aristotelous (☎ 031/271-888), which is usually open Monday to Friday 8am-8pm and Saturday and some Sundays 8am-8pm.

1 Pélla

24 miles (40km) W of Thessaloníki

Pélla is easy to spot. It's right beside the highway you take to get there. The **Pélla Archaeological Site and Museum** (☎ 0383/311-60) is usually open weekdays 8am to 7pm, and weekends and holidays 8:30am to 3pm. Separate admission to the site and museum is Dr 500 ($2.15). Unfortunately, the things you'd most like to see—the palace where Philip and his son Alexander the Great were born and the theater where the great Athenian playwright Euripides's *Bacchae* had its first performance—have not yet been found by the excavators. Still, parts of the ancient agora and several streets lined with house foundations have been excavated.

The ancient town of Pélla seems to have covered at least 5 square miles on what today is a dusty plain. In antiquity, Pélla's situation was more appealing: A navigable inlet connected the city to the Thermaic Gulf. Over the centuries, the inlet silted up, leaving Pélla landlocked, but in Philip and Alexander's day, ships would have sailed here from the Thermaic Gulf.

The best thing about Pélla is not the site itself, but its **small museum,** with the glorious **pebble mosaics** found in some of the 4th-century B.C. homes excavated here. The two best-known mosaics show the god of wine Dionysios riding a leopard, and a lion hunt. The lion hunt is worth looking at not just for its powerful depiction of two youths and a slathering lion, but because this mosaic may show Alexander himself. Some scholars have suggested that the mosaic records the incident when the young Alexander was saved by a friend from a lunging lion. Others suspect that it's too good to be true that the mosaic actually shows that famous incident and suggest that this is simply a genre scene of a hunt. You can compare the marble bust of Alexander in the museum with the youth under attack in the lion hunt and decide whether you think they both show the young prince.

When you finish your visit here, you may want to take in the scenic town of **Edessa,** 27 miles (45km) west of Pélla, a cliff-top town with bubbling waterfalls and several pleasant small cafes and restaurants. This is not a good place to go on summer weekends, when many Thessalonians come here to escape the summer heat.

2 Vergína

38 miles (62km) W of Thessaloníki; 12 miles (20km) S of Pélla

Vergína (whose ancient name was Aigai), where Philip lived when not at Pélla and where he died in 336 B.C., is the most important of the royal Macedonian sites. The **Vergína Site and Museum (Royal Tumulus and Tombs)** (☎ 031/830-538) is open Tuesday to Sunday from 8:30am to 3pm. Admission to the site is Dr 500 ($2.15) and entrance to the museum is Dr 1,200 ($5.10). Vergína is just outside the hamlet of Palatitsa and is very well signposted. You may want to begin by visiting the spot where Philip died: the theater, which was unearthed in the 1980s. Work is continuing on the rest of the site but as yet, little of what must have been a splendid palace has been unearthed. Preliminary excavations suggest that the palace was enormous, with an inner courtyard 147 feet square. You can see the bases of some of the 60 columns of the courtyard's Doric colonnade still in place. The palace also had a long airy veranda running the length of its north side, overlooking the theater. It's quite possible that the royal family watched some spectacles in the theater from the comfort of the palace veranda. Unfortunately for Philip, that's not what he did on the fatal day in 356 B.C., when he was assassinated en route from the palace to take in a performance at the theater.

As you drive from the site of Vergína to the Royal Tombs Museum, you'll notice hundreds of low mounds on the gentle hills of the Macedonian plain. These are some of the more than 300 **burial mounds** found here, some dating from as long ago as the Iron Age, but many from the time of Philip himself. Virtually all of these graves were robbed in antiquity but fortunately, and almost miraculously, the tomb identified as that of Philip himself was undisturbed for almost 2,000 years. How it was found is one of the great stories of archaeology, well deserving a place beside accounts of how Schliemann found Troy and excavated the Tomb of Agamemnon at Mycenae.

Vergína's first excavator, the French archaeologist Leon Heuzey, prophesied in 1876 that when Vergína was fully excavated, "the importance of its ruins for Macedonia will be comparable to Pompeii." In the 1930s, the Greek Archaeological Service began to work here and uncovered several tombs that looked like small temples. For years, the excavators nibbled away at the largest burial mound of all, the **Great Tumulus,** measuring 110 meters across and 12 meters high, containing a number of burials. One tomb they found was almost totally destroyed, another well preserved, but robbed. Still, head excavator Manolis Andronikos remained convinced that he was excavating ancient Aigai, Philip's capital city, and might yet find Philip's own tomb.

Finally, in 1977—on the last day of the excavation season—Andronikos and his workers opened the massive marble gates of the last remaining tomb. As Andronikos later wrote in *Vergína: The Royal Tombs:*

> *We saw a sight which it was not possible for me to have imagined, because until then such an ossuary (container for bones) had never been found . . . all-gold . . . with an impressive relief star on its lid. We lifted it from the sarcophagus, placed it on the floor, and opened it. Our eyes nearly popped out of our sockets and our breathing stopped; there unmistakably were charred bones placed in a carefully formed pile and still retaining the colour of the purple cloth in which they had once been wrapped. . . . if those were royal remains . . . then . . . had I held the bones of Philip in my hands?*

Andronikos, and virtually all of Greece, answered his question with a resounding "Yes," in large part because of the other objects found in the tomb. The gold wreaths, Andronikos felt, were too fine to belong to anyone but a king. And surely the little ivory portrait heads were the spitting images of Philip and Alexander themselves. And, most persuasive of all, what about the bronze greaves (shin guards) found in the tomb? Were they not of unequal size? And was not Philip known to have legs of different length, due to an early injury?

It's difficult to overestimate the Philip fever that swept through Greece when Andronikos announced that he had found Philip's tomb and identified Vergína as Ancient Aigai, Philip's capital city. Although some scholars have questioned whether

Philip & Alexander

When Philip was born in 382 B.C., most Greeks thought of Macedonians—if they thought of them at all—as one of the rude northern tribes of barbarians who lived in the back of beyond. Macedonians, after all, were not even allowed to participate in the panhellenic games at Delphi. Clearly, this irritated Philip. By 346 B.C., after conquering a number of Athenian colonies and allied cities, Philip had won a place on Delphi's governing board. A few years later, in 338 B.C., despite Demosthenes's best oratorical efforts to alert the Athenians to Philip's intentions, the Macedonian king had conquered all Greece. Two years later, Philip was dead, cut down as he strolled to see a performance in the theater at his capital city of Vergína. Some said that his young son Alexander was behind the assassination, while others wondered how the unproven youth could rule Macedonia, let alone Greece.

No one, except perhaps Alexander himself, could have imagined that by the time he died at 33, he would have conquered much of the known world as far east as India. Alexander's early death makes it impossible to know what he would have done with the rest of his life once he had no new worlds to conquer. Some scholars think that Alexander was a visionary bent not just on conquering, but on uniting the world into a "brotherhood of man." This, they suggest, is why Alexander contracted so many foreign marriages and accepted conquered princes into his retinue. Other scholars, more cynical, think that both Alexander's marriages and his use of former enemies were simply shrewd political moves. The truth probably lies somewhere in between the two theories.

In any event, after Alexander's death, his former comrades turned on one another and destroyed his empire. Within a few generations, Macedon was once more a northern kingdom in the back of beyond, living on memories of its brief period of international importance.

this is, in fact, Philip's tomb, those scholars are not Greek. Greeks regard with horror any suggestion that this splendid tomb may have belonged to Arrhidaeos, the son of Philip known only for his lack of distinction.

The arched roof of the **Royal Tombs Museum** re-creates a sense of the Great Tumulus itself, as does the passageway leading into the tomb area. Each of the five tombs is protected by a glass wall, but seeing the tombs this way is the next best thing to being able to stand inside them. Give your eyes time to get accustomed to the darkness and then enjoy the lovely decorative paintings on the facades of the templelike tombs. And, of course, be sure to see the treasures from these tombs now on display in the Archaeological Museum in Thessaloníki.

If Vergína has whetted your appetite for royal tombs, you might consider heading north to **Leukadia,** 12 miles (20km) south of Edessa in the beautiful **foothills of Mount Vermion.** Be warned: This is one of those excursions filled with suggestions like "ask for directions in the village" and "ask if the custodian will accompany you and open the tombs." If you're lucky and find the custodian and the tombs, you'll get to see three spectacular tombs. The 3rd-century B.C. **Great Tomb** is decorated with paintings of battles of Lapiths and Centaurs and Greeks and Persians. The **Kinch Tomb** (named after its discoverer) and the **Tomb of Lyson and Kallikles** are decorated with paintings of funeral swags of pomegranates and snakes, a symbol of both the underworld (since snakes often live underground) and rebirth (because snakes shed old skins for new ones). The claustrophobic may find the descent down a dank shaft into the Tomb of Lyson and Kallikles unappealing. If the custodian does take you to see these tombs, you should slip him at least Dr 1,000 ($4.25) along with your thanks.

If an excursion to Leukadia seems too much like work, try the town of **Veria** (Veroia), 9 miles (15km) northwest of Vergína. Veria is in the throes of development, but still has a number of old streets with wood houses, small Byzantine churches, and a fine small museum with finds from local sites. Admission is Dr 500 ($2.15). It's open Tuesday through Sunday from 8:30am to 3pm. Veria's small restaurants serve food that is almost invariably better than that dished out at the tourist places at Vergína.

About halfway between Veria and Edessa, on the slopes of Mt. Vermion, several **vineyards** are open to visitors. At Naoussa, a region famous for its wine, the **Stenimachos Winery,** run by the **Boutari vintners,** is open to the public. Tours of the winery are given most work days and are sometimes offered in English. For information call **0332/42-687,** or check with the **GNTO** in Thessaloníki (☎ **031/271-888**).

3 Dión

48 miles (78km) S of Thessaloníki on the E/75; Dión is outside the village of Dio, about 5 miles (8km) W of the Dión sign on the E/75, the main Athens-Thessaloníki highway

Dión has a lovely site, just outside the Vale of Témpe, in the foothills of Mount Olympus. This is an unusually green spot, with pine groves and farm fields watered by springs fed by the melting snow that clings to Olympus's peaks year-round. The **Dión Archaeological Site and Museum** (☎ **0351/53-206**) is open Tuesday to Sunday from 8:30am to 3pm. Admission to the site is Dr 800 ($3.40) and entrance to the museum is Dr 800 ($3.40). If you can, bring a picnic and linger here a while after you visit the site and museum.

Dión's constant water supply led both Philip and Alexander to establish military training camps here. Philip bivouacked here before he marched south to conquer Greece, and Alexander drilled his men here before heading east to conquer Asia.

According to a story preserved by the 2nd-century A.D. biographer Plutarch, it was at Dión that Alexander, then only eight, first saw Bucephalos, the handsome black stallion soon to be his favorite mount. Philip himself had bought the horse, but found that neither he nor any of his men could ride it. Alexander asked his father if he could have a go at taming the creature. Muttering that if he could not tame the horse, an eight-year-old hardly could, Philip nonetheless agreed to give Alexander a chance. Immediately, Alexander turned Bucephalos so that he could not see his shadow; then the boy leapt onto his back and they galloped away. When the young prince returned from his ride, Philip said, "My son, look for a kingdom equal to you. Macedonia is too small."

Although Dión was an important military camp, it was not merely the Fort Bragg of antiquity. There was a theater here, and sanctuaries to the healing god Asclepius, the nurturing goddess Demeter, and the popular Egyptian goddess Isis. Copies of some of the statues found in the sanctuaries have been erected at the site, while the originals are safely tucked away in the museum.

The Dión museum is a heartening example of what a provincial museum can be when it's well funded and well cared for. An English video and museum labels in English help foreign visitors to understand the importance of what they are seeing, while models of the ancient site make the Dión of Philip and Alexander easy to visualize. Exhibits include statues of the children of Asclepius, lined up as though posing for a family photo; grave monuments; votive offerings; and, best of all, a wonderful copper water organ, probably made in the 2nd century A.D. that would be the hit of any music hall today.

There's a string of cafes and restaurants directly across from the museum; friends report having a good meal at the **Dionysios,** which serves good roast goat, loukanikia (sausages), and the usual chops and salads. Expect to pay about Dr 1,500 ($6.40) for lunch or dinner unless you go overboard on the roast goat, which is priced by the kilo and may bring your tab to $10.

If you want to spend the night here, check to see if the small hotel under construction in the village of Dio at the time of our visit is open.

4 Pýdna

34 miles (55km) S of Thessaloníki on the E/75, the main Athens-Thessaloníki road. The site of Pýdna is E of the E/75 near the hamlet of Kitros.

Only the most devoted fan of Philip and Alexander would make the pilgrimage to the unexcavated site of the harbor town of Pýdna, one of the first colonies that Philip seized from the Athenians. Still, as you whiz past the turnoff on the E/75 you may want to remember that it was at Pýdna, in 168 B.C., that the Romans conquered Macedonia and put an end to the remnants of the empire won by Philip and Alexander.

5 Amphípolis

63 miles (102km) E of Thessaloníki

If you find yourself heading east from Salonika, perhaps en route to Turkey, keep an eye out for the enormous **Lion of Amphípolis** that sits beside the main Athens-Istanbul highway looking out to sea. No one is really sure when or why the lion was erected, although there are lots of theories, of which the most popular is that it honors a 2nd-century B.C. former sailor who made good by becoming governor of Syria.

Philip conquered Amphípolis in 358 B.C., eager to get his hands on the rich mines it controlled in Mt. Panagaeum, which looms above the coast road. Amphípolis was an important town in Roman times, and there are **extensive ruins** of churches, temples, stoas, and baths on the acropolis in the hills above the lion. If you want to explore the ancient site, take the Drama road and then head up the unpaved road toward the **acropolis,** which you'll probably recognize by its **ancient walls.** Be sure to take water and a sun hat, as this site has virtually no shade and no refreshment stand (and no admission charge).

6 Phílippi

112 miles (181km) E of Thessaloníki; 9 miles (14km) E of Kavalla

Not content with conquering Amphípolis, Philip founded this city, which he modestly named after himself, in attempt to control the mines of Mt. Panagaeum. But that's not why Phílippi is famous: in 42 B.C., Brutus and Cassius were defeated here by Octavian and Antony. After the battle, both Cassius and Brutus, whom Shakespeare called "the noblest Roman of them all," committed suicide on the battlefield.

The **Phílippi Site** (☎ **051/516-470**) is open Tuesday through Sunday from 8:30am to 3pm. Admission is Dr 800 ($3.40). As it happens, little remains here from the time of either Philip or Brutus. Nonetheless, Phillipi is well worth visiting for its splendid and quite enormous **2nd-century A.D. basilica** (a large church) and its even larger **6th-century A.D. basilica.** This later Phílippi basilica was so huge, in fact, that its dome collapsed almost before the church could be consecrated. Some scholars think that when architects in Constantinople got word of the basilica dome disaster at Phílippi, they modified their plans for the dome of Highia Sophia (Saint Sophia), which remains in place to this day.

16 The Northeastern Aegean Islands

by John Bozman

The islands in the northeast Aegean are among the least visited of the major Greek islands, sometimes because they are fairly inaccessible, but usually because they are simply not as well known. This far-flung group of islands also in general lacks close historical and even in some cases geographic association. For the sake of convenience, they can be further divided into the eastern islands of Sámos, Híos, and Lésvos (Mytilíni) and the northern islands, including Límnos, Samothrace, and Thásos. The division reflects both physical and cultural differences.

The better-known eastern islands are more autonomous; they all share a cultural (and transportation) connection with Turkey, as well as that country's exotic, Asian heritage. The smaller northern islands, though less visited by foreigners, in July and August become extensions or weekend resorts of Thessaloníki and the larger mainland cities.

The Northeastern Aegean islands are spread out and rather difficult to hop between; therefore, we recommend you limit your ambition, especially if your time is limited. If you only have a week to travel, limit your itinerary to two islands. We suggest you fly from Athens to Sámos and make your base Sámos town for three or four nights. See Pythagório, the Efpalínios Tunnel, the Archaeological Museum, and at least one of the island beaches. Take a day trip to the incredible archaeological site at Ephesus, Turkey, one of the Seven Wonders of the Ancient World.

Take a ferry or hydrofoil to Híos and arrange accommodations in the village of Mestá or on the northeast coast at Kardámila for two or three days. Visit the medieval villages in the south of the island, especially Piryí, and at least one of the island's exquisite beaches. Fly back to Athens.

If you have a few more days and your visit is in the spring or fall, take a ferry or hydrofoil on to Lésvos and spend them at Mólyvos, then fly back to Athens.

1 Sámos

174 nautical miles (322km) NE of Piraeus

Sámos is an attractive and pleasant island, mountainous and green. Its peaks are the highest in the Aegean islands, and sections of the scenic interior are as thickly forested as any in the region. It has a

The Northeastern Aegean Islands

BULGARIA

0 45 km
   28 mi

N

TURKEY

Kavála

Alexandroúpolis

Thássos (Liménas)
Makryámmos
Limenária Panaghía

SAMOTHRÁKI
Hóra
Mt. Fengári

Gallípoli

Sea of Marmara

THÁSSOS

Kamariótissa

Canakkale

A e g e a n

S e a

Gökçeada

TURKEY

Kórnos
Mýrina
Skandáli

LÍMNOS

Ayvalik

Pergamon

Mólyvos
(Míthymna) Mandamádos

LÉSVOS (Mytilíni)
Éressós   Pétra

Skála Eressós Ayiássos   Mytilíni

Plomári

Skýros

Psará   HÍOS
Kardámíla   Inoússes

Izmir

Híos Town

Pasalimáni   Çesme

Mestá   Piryí

Ephesus
Kuşadasi
Kokkári   Sámos
Karlóvassi
SÁMOS   Mytilíni
Pythagório
Psilí Ámmos

IKARÍA

GREECE

Athens

The Northeastern
Aegean Islands

531

long and honorable history and abundant evidence to prove it. During the 6th-century B.C., in the glory days of the Ionian civilization, Sámos lead the field in its contributions to art, architecture, and science. The island's favorite son, Pythagoras, is the most notable in a long list of luminaries that includes the philosopher Epicurus, Aesop of fables fame, and the mathematician Aristárchos. Herodotus devoted a large portion of his *History* to the island.

Because Sámos is one of the closest Greek islands to Turkey, it's a particularly convenient crossover point for those who want to visit Ephesus, one of the most important archaeological sites in Asia Minor. We recommend a brief stay to see Sámos's historic sites, combined with an excursion to the unforgettable splendor of Ephesus.

ESSENTIALS

GETTING THERE   Although there is ferry connection from Piraeus to Sámos, it's a long trip. The best way to get there is to fly.

By Plane   Olympic Airways has three flights daily (five daily in the summer) between Athens and Sámos. The Olympic office (☎ **0473/27-237**) in Sámos town is at the corner of Kanári and Smýrnis streets. In Pythagório, there's an Olympic office at Odós Lykoúrgos 90 (☎ **0473/61-213**). From the airport, you can take a taxi to Sámos town (Dr 3,000/$12.75) or Pythagório (Dr 1,200/$5.10), then catch a public bus to other parts of the islands.

By Ferry   There are daily boats (sometimes two) from Piraeus via Náxos, Páros, and Ikaría to Karlóvassi and Sámos town in the high season.

Pythagório has ferry connection to Híos four times weekly, to Ikaría three times, and to Lésvos, Límnos, or Rhodes twice weekly. Five times a week, there are car ferries to Páros, four times to Léros, Kálymnos, or Kos, twice-weekly to Náxos, and once to Mýkonos. In summer there's hydrofoil service to Híos and Lésvos from Sámos town. In the summer there is hydrofoil connection from Pythagório to Pátmos and Kos. Smaller excursion boats leave Pythagório for Pátmos four times weekly—this can be a rough trip—and the larger, smoother-sailing steamers make the trip three times a week. There is one trip weekly to Kavála and Thessaloníki on the mainland. Call the port authority in Piraeus (☎ **01/45-11-311**) or Sámos (☎ **0273/27-318**) or Pythagório (☎ **0473/61-225**) for schedule information.

VISITOR INFORMATION   The **Sámos EOT (telephone office)** (☎ **0273/28-530** or 0273/28-582) is a half block in from the port, one lane from the main square. It's open daily from 8am to 2:30pm, with extended hours (daily 7:30am to 10pm) in the high season. The EOT is staffed by local people who are very helpful and informative; they won't make room reservations by phone but will help you find accommodations once you're at their office.

International Travel (☎ **0273/23-605**; fax 0273/27-955), the agency nearest the port in Sámos town, is one of the best and friendliest; they can help you with travel arrangements, including excursions to Turkey, find accommodations, change money at good rates, and store your luggage for free. **Samina Travel,** up the harbor front at Odós Them. **Sofoúli 67** (☎ **0273/28-841;** fax 0273/23-616), is also helpful and can change money and assist you in arranging day trips and plane tickets. **Pythagoras Tours** (☎ **0273/27-240**), also on the harbor front, is one of the many that sell ferry tickets.

GETTING AROUND   By Bus   There's good public bus service on Sámos; the Sámos town **bus terminal** (☎ **0273/27-262**) is inland from the south end of the port on Odós Kanári. The bus makes the 20-minute trip between Sámos town and Pythagório frequently. Buses go to Kokkári and the inland village of Mytilíní seven times a day. There are four buses daily from Pythagório to Iréo (near the Heraion), and there is also service to Pírgos, Marathókambos, and Votsalákia beach. Call for schedules.

By Boat   Excursion boats from the Pythagório harbor go to Psilí Ámmos beach (on the east end of the island) daily, and to the island of Ikaría three times weekly. There is a popular day cruise to the sandy beach on Samiopoúla, a small island where there is a taverna and rooms to let.

By Car   We recommend **Aramis Rent a Motorbike-Car** (☎ **0273/23-253**; fax 0273/23-620), 200 meters left from the harbor in Sámos town and near the bus station in Pythagório (☎ **0273/62-267**) for the best prices and selection. Expect to pay about $75 per day. There are plenty of other agencies, so shop around. You'll probably find rates cheaper in Sámos town than elsewhere.

By Taxi   The most common taxi fare, from Sámos to Pythagório, is Dr 2,500 ($10.65). You can book an all-day taxi for an around-the-island tour. Count on paying about Dr 3,600 ($15.30) per hour or Dr 22,500 ($95.75) for a full day by negotiating with a driver at one of the port-side taxi stands, or booking by phone (☎ **0273/28-404** in Sámos or **0273/61-450** in Pythagório).

By Bicycle or Moped   You can rent a bicycle or moped in Sámos from several shops near the central square. In Pythagório, **Nikos Rent a Motor Bike** (☎ **0273/61-094**) on Odós Lykoúrgos has rates that include helmets: bikes go for Dr 1,400 ($5.95), Vespas for Dr 3,000 ($12.75), and two-person mopeds from about Dr 5,000 ($21.75) a day.

FAST FACTS: SÁMOS TOWN

Currency Exchange   Sámos has a branch of National Bank of Greece on the port (open from 8am to 2pm Monday through Thursday, till 1:30pm Friday). Several travel agents change money at a less favorable rate but stay open daily from 8am to 10pm.

Consulates   There is a British Consulate on Sofouli Street in Sámos town (☎ **0273/27-314**).

Emergencies   In Sámos, call the local police at **0273/22-100,** all hours of the day.

Hospitals   The hospital (☎ **0273/27-407** or **0273/27-426**) is in Sámos town.

Police   The police station (☎ **0273/27-333**) is near the Credit Bank at the south end of the central square, Platía Iroon (Heroes Square).

Post Office   The main post office is on the central square, across from the municipal garden.

Telephone/Telecommunications   The OTE (telephone center) is on the central square across from the post office, and it's open daily 24 hours.

WHAT TO SEE & DO

Large, almond-shaped Sámos has three ports. The ferries from Piraeus and the Cyclades normally stop first at Karlóvassi, on the northwest coast, then continue on to Sámos town, on the northeast coast.

Sámos town (also called Vathí) is an old port that has undergone extensive development, but it remains an essentially Greek town with lots of commerce and color. The most important sights in Sámos town are the fine Archaeology Museum and the picturesque old quarter known as Ano Vathi.

The **Archaeology Museum** (☎ **0273/27-469**) has displays in two buildings, and you can spend an hour just reading the excellent text accompanying the exhibits.

Particularly impressive is the large and various collection of votives, mostly bronze, found at the Heraion, illustrating its prestige in the ancient world by their value and extent—all of Greece, the Near East, Egypt, Cyprus, even Spain. The newest building houses sculpture, including the largest (5.5 meters) standing *koúros* (Greek statue of a nude male youth) extant and a group of six archaic statues found at the Heraion. Sámos was the sculpture center of Greece; being much in demand, many of the island's best sculptors (especially adept in casting) traveled all over the Hellenistic world to create their art. The museum is open from 8:30am to 3pm, Tuesday through Sunday; admission is Dr 800 ($3.40).

Áno Vathí, the upper town, is a charming quarter with narrow winding streets and neoclassical houses. It's a quiet residential area that retains a lot of it original villagelike character. To reach it continue on beyond the museum.

There are also beaches near Sámos town, the closest and best being **Plaz Gagoú,** west across the harbor, and **Kalámi,** the town beach, a short walk left (north) from the port.

A few kilometers east of town, you can climb a path to the **monastery of Zoödóhou Piyís** for a good look at Turkey. On the southeastern tip of the island, at **Possidonió,** you will be even closer and can find a very good taverna for seafood. West along the coast is the better of the island's two beaches called **Psilí Ámmos.**

Pythagório, south across the island from Sámos town, is a charming but overcrowded modern resort, built on the site of an ancient village and harbor. It's named after the most notable of all Samians, Pythagoras, the great mathematician and philosopher. Under the autocrat Polykrates, what Herodotus called "three of the greatest building achievements of the world" were accomplished: the mole for the harbor was laid, where the jetty is today; the Efpalinion Tunnel was completed; and the Heraion was enlarged, making it the largest of all ancient Greek temples. Columns from the city fortifications and an unexcavated theater are visible on the left side north of the port. There are also remains of Roman baths about a kilometer west of town, open Tuesday through Saturday from 11am to 2pm.

You may like Pythagório enough to stay there despite its crowds. Although groups are said to have a lock on 80% of the rooms, there may be a few available during your visit. The **Pythagorio Municipal Tourist Office** (☎ 0273/61-022) is on the main street, Odós Lykoúrgo Logothétou, one block up from the harbor. It's open daily from 8am to 10pm. They will help you find a room and exchange money. The local **police** (☎ 0273/61-333) are also on the main street. **Samina Travel** has an office on the port of Pythagorio (☎ 0273/61-583); see the friendly Pavlo for advice. The **post office** is four blocks up from the harbor on the main street; the **OTE** is on the *paralía* (waterfront) near the pier. Alex Stavrides runs a **Laundromat** off the main street on the church street; it's open 9am to 9pm daily, till 11pm in summer. The **bus station** (actually just a couple of benches under a tree) is like nearly everything else, on the busy main street, on the left, five or six blocks up from the harbor.

The **Efpalinion Tunnel** (☎ 0273/61-400), one of the most impressive engineering accomplishments of the ancient world, a 1,050-meter-long waterway through the mountain above Pythagório, is about 2 kilometers northwest of town. It was excavated to transport water from mountain streams to ancient Sámos. Efpalinos directed two teams of workers digging from each side, and after nearly 15 years they met remarkably close to each other. The tunnel caved in during the 17th century when Sámos was devastated by a series of earthquakes. A few years ago, a German engineering team completed eight years of work to clear the tunnel of debris and rock, and they revealed this astonishing achievement.

You can walk up to the tunnel, a 45-minute moderate climb, by following the signs up from the west end of town, or you can take a taxi from Pythagório for about Dr 600 ($2.55). Some of the spaces are tight and slippery, but presently you can walk about a third of the way into the tunnel. Though it's lighted, you should bring a flashlight. It's open daily except Monday from 9am to 2pm, according to official sources. The hours are in fact erratic, so you should call ahead to determine if it's open, as they often close the tunnel for repairs. Officially the entrance fee is quoted at Dr 500 ($2.10), but it's often free.

The **Heraion** (☎ **0273/27-469**), the sanctuary of Hera, is southwest of Pythagório at Iréon, a rather lackluster resort. All that survives of the greatest of all Greek temples is its massive foundation, a lone reconstructed column, and copies of the original statuary, which can be seen in the archaeological museum. The temple was originally surrounded by a forest of columns, one of its most distinctive and original features. In fact, rival Ionian cities were so impressed that they rebuilt many of their ancient temples in similar style. The Temple of Artemis in nearby Ephesus is a direct imitation of the great Samian Structure. The Heraion was rebuilt and greatly expanded under Polycrates; it was damaged during numerous invasions and finally destroyed by a series of earthquakes. A good way to visit is by bicycle, as the road from Pythagoria is flat, or you can walk for about an hour or so. The few buses a day usually leave Sámos or Pythagorio in the afternoon. The site is open from 8:30am to 3pm Tuesday through Sunday. Admission is Dr 600 ($2.50), free Sunday.

In **Mytilíni** is an attractive little town northwest of Pythagória and southwest from Sámos town. Many of the best-known paleontological remains in Greece, mostly finds excavated from the nearby Stephanidis Valley, are on display in the **paleontological museum** (☎ **0273/51-205**). It's open Monday through Saturday from 8:30am to 2pm and 6 to 7:30pm; admission is Dr 500 ($2.15). There is bus service to Mytilíní three times a day from Sámos or Pythagório.

From the south of Mytilíní, the road continues west through the fertile interior of the island through **Pírgos**, the honey capital of the island. Due west but accessible by a more circuitous route, is the most rapidly developing part of the coastline on Marathókambos Bay, along the southwestern shore. The once-tiny village of **Órmos Marathókambos** has several tavernas and a mushrooming number of hotels and pensions; its rock and pebble beach is long and narrow, with windsurfing an option. A couple of kilometers further west of Órmos Marathókambos is **Votsalákia,** a somewhat nicer beach.

The road continues north from Órmos Marathókambos to **Karlóvassi,** the least touristed of the three major ports. There's a harbor, nearby beaches, and a scattering of hotels. **Potámi,** west of Karlóvassi, has an excellent beach.

Midway on the north coast road between Karlóvassi and Kokkári is the **Platanákia region** of villages, set on steeply terraced hills. This is where Sámos' famous muscadine grapes grow. Samians call Platanákia "paradise." A narrow road leads south from the coastal highway though cool densely wooded valleys with rushing streams and up through terraced hills to mountain hamlets. To visit this area from Sámos town, drive west past Kokkári; after about 18 kilometers, there's a left turn to Aïdónia and Manolátes.

You might stop at the **Paradisos Restaurant** (☎ **0273/94-208**), a large garden cafe located just at the Manolátes turnoff from the coast highway. Mr. Folas, the owner, worked in vineyards many years and makes his own wine from the excellent Samian grapes. Mrs. Folas's tirópita (fresh baked after 7pm) is made from local goat cheese and butter; it's wrapped in a flaky pastry. Paradisos is open daily for lunch and dinner and also has a few rooms to let.

About 15 minutes up the winding country road to Manolátes, two more "country" tavernas have found a spot under the evergreens beside a stream. Near **Aïdónia** ("Nightingale"), there's a clear mountain spring that attracts scores of songbirds and is a delightful watering and washing spot.

Manolátes is further up the road and is now accessible by car—it's a peaceful, half-hour hike uphill if you have the stamina. You'll be rewarded by a marvelous view of the steeply tiered vineyards strung along the foothills of Mt. Ambelos (1,140 meters high) and down to the deep-blue sea. This small hamlet is a typical Samian village, with stucco homes and red-tiled roofs. The narrow cobblestone streets are so steep that you may find yourself bending forward to avoid falling backward. Manolátes has a simple taverna and a small snack bar, deeper in the pedestrian lanes, with panoramic views.

The line of beaches that extend westward from Avlákia to Kokkári are composed of large gray sand and pebbles. They're fairly wide and attractive, but be forewarned that the winds on this side of the island are notoriously strong, and you may have to move on to sunbathe comfortably.

Kokkári is about 10 kilometers west of Sámos town on the north coast highway. Up until a decade ago, it was a traditional Greek fishing village with small cobbled back streets and a few tavernas. Off in the distance are green brush-covered hills. Today it's filled with small hotels, pensions, and rooms to let in many of the town's older homes. There are many waterside cafes and chic boutiques. Its small-scale commercialism, though dense, is very appealing and draws hordes competing for its few rooms and hotels in the summer months. Kokkári has pedestrian bridges and walkways and is still very charming in the spring and fall.

A SIDE TRIP TO TURKEY

During the high season there are usually two boats a day between Sámos and Kusadasi, Turkey, a popular, well-developed resort 20 minutes from the magnificent archaeological site at Ephesus. A one-way trip to Kusadasi runs Dr 14,000 ($59.60), while a round-trip ticket (including a guided tour of Ephesus and a same-day return) costs Dr 22,500 ($95.75). If you decide to buy a round-trip ticket but wish to stay in Turkey for longer than a day, you'll have to pay an extra port tax. Many travel agencies sell tickets to Turkey. Boats depart from both Sámos town and Pythagório.

WHERE TO STAY
SÁMOS TOWN

The accommodations in Sámos town are usually booked by European tour groups during July and August. Ask the EOT (Greek National Tourist Organization) for help in finding a private room. A double room with private bath usually rents for approximately Dr 9,000 ($38.30). You can also inquire at **Samina Travel** (☎ 0273/ 28841), which is usually open April 15 to October 31.

Aeolis Hotel. Odós Sofoúli 33, Sámos, 831 00 Sámos. ☎ **0273/24-316.** Fax 0273/28-063. 57 rms (all with bath). A/C. Dr 11,900 ($50.65) single; Dr 17,850 ($75.95) double (including breakfast). MC, V.

This attractive hotel is easily the best on the port. Even the front rooms are quiet, as the windows are double-paned. The friendly owners take excellent care of it and are planning to add a swimming pool and Jacuzzi on the top floor.

Emily Hotel. Odós Grámmou and Odós 11 Noemvríou, Sámos, 83100 Sámos. ☎ **0273/ 28-24-691.** 19 rms (all with bath). A/C TEL. Dr 11,900 ($50.65) single; Dr 15,800 ($67.25) double (including breakfast). AE, V.

You'll find this charming new hotel several blocks up from the port on the small street between the Sámos Hotel and the Catholic Church. The rooms are spacious, attractively furnished, and especially quiet. Most have their own balcony.

Hotel Paradise. Odós Kanári 21, Sámos, 83100 Sámos. ☎ **0273/23-911.** Fax 0273/28-754. 48 rms, 2 suites (all with bath). A/C TEL. Dr 14,550 ($61.90) single; 15,870 ($67.55) double (including breakfast). EU, V.

This stylish hotel has well-landscaped grounds and a large swimming pool set in the back garden. It's a convenient midtown location—near the bus station, back from the harbor, and a bit removed from the tourist crush. It's booked fairly solid by groups. There's a large snack bar, evening cocktail bar, and pretty breakfast room. The rooms are painted a cool blue and tastefully decorated. They have balconies and a full bath tub.

Hotel Sámos. Odós Sofoúli 33, Sámos, 831 00 Sámos. ☎ **0273-28-378.** Fax 0273/23-771. 105 rms (all with bath). TEL. Dr 9,200 ($39.15) single; Dr 11,850 ($50.40) double (including breakfast). EU, MC, V.

This comfortable lodge, with a popular cafe bar out front, is the closest to the ferry. The facade has been restored to resemble a classic Samian-style mansion. Inside, there's an elevator and wall-to-wall carpeting. Spacious, simple rooms are superclean with first-rate service. We recommend the rooms in the back of the hotel, which are quieter and have larger balconies. All in all, a good value.

Pension Avli. Odós Lykoúrgou, Sámos, 831 00 Sámos. ☎ **0273/22-939.** 20 rms (10 with bath). Dr 4,500 ($19.15) single/double without bath; Dr 6,500 ($27.65) single/double with bath. No credit cards.

Probably the most charming pension on the island, this is a restored convent. Complete with a crypt, it has a grand marble courtyard filled with plants and breakfast tables. Spyros tends his home well. The 10 rooms without bath are simple but spotless; they have their own water closet and the common showers are down the hall. His modernized rooms with private bath are often reserved by groups, but inquire about their availability.

⑤ Pythagoras Hotel. Odós Kalámi, Sámos, 83100 Sámos. ☎ **0273/28-422.** Fax 0273/27-955. 17 rms (all with bath). Dr 4,800 ($20.40) single; Dr 7,250 ($30.85) double. MC, V.

Plain but comfortable, this older family hotel is about 500 meters left from the port on the way to the town beach. The seaside rooms are quiet, except for the surf and birds singing in the trees. The neighborhood cafe downstairs serves a good, inexpensive breakfast.

Sibylla Hotel. Platía Ayíou Nikoláou. Sámos, 831 00 Sámos. ☎ **0273/22-396.** 20 rms (all with bath). Dr 5,500 ($23.40) single; Dr 8,350 ($35.55) double. No credit cards.

This pretty, very clean hotel, a couple of blocks in from the middle of the port, off the northwest corner of St. Nicholas Square, is popular with tour groups but a good choice if you can get a room. The building was originally a tobacco factory, but it has been renovated in the old villa-style of the local mansions.

PYTHAGÓRIO

Pythagório is almost completely at the service of European tour groups. If you land there roomless, head for the town's tourist office, one block off the paralía on the main street. They'll help you find one of the many private rooms, which should cost approximately Dr 7,250 ($30.85) for a double room with private bath. Or inquire at Rhenia Tours (☎ **0273/61-589**) or Samina Travel (☎ **0273/61-583**), open April 15 to October 31.

Captain Fragoulis. Pythagório, 83103 Sámos. ☎ **0273/61-473.** 9 rms (all with bath). Dr 6,325 ($26.90) single; Dr 9,375 ($39.90) double (including breakfast). No credit cards.

This personal little pension has a mostly rustic stone facade. There's a wonderful view of Pythagório from its location on the road back to Sámos. The good captain's son-in-law is an artist, and he's lent his touch to the decor of this well-maintained hostelry.

George Sandalis Hotel. Pythagório, 83103 Sámos. ☎ **0273/61-691.** 14 rms (all with bath). Dr 8,625 ($36.70) single; Dr 12,000 ($51.05) double (including breakfast). No credit cards.

Above Pythagório, this homey establishment has tastefully decorated rooms and balconies with French doors. The rear rooms face quiet hills and a lovely flower garden. The Sandalises spent many years in Chicago and are gracious hosts.

⑤ Hotel Alexandra. Odós Metamórphoseus 11, Pythagório, 83103 Sámos. ☎ **0273/61-429.** 12 rms (8 with bath). Dr 5,600 ($23.85) double without bath; Dr 6,785 ($28.85) double with bath. No credit cards.

The Alexandra is a quiet pocket of good value, a small hotel on a tranquil lane, near the church. The downstairs rooms are old-fashioned, with high ceilings and a shared bath. The plain upstairs rooms are newer and have private baths. It's run by the kind and friendly Manolaros family. All will enjoy the shade garden and the company of Dimitri and his son, John.

Hotel Evripili. Pythagório, 83103 Sámos. ☎ **0273/61-407.** 10 rms (all with bath). Dr 7,500 ($31.90) single; Dr 9,300 ($39.55) double (including breakfast). No credit cards.

Across the lane from the new Hotel Labito, this 400-year-old some mansion has compact, comfortable guest rooms, most with balconies. Austrian tour groups often fill the place in July and August, but you can check in the cozy basement breakfast lounge about room availability.

Hotel Hera II. Pythagório, 831 03 Sámos. ☎ **0273/61-319.** Fax 0273/61-196. 7 rms (all with bath). A/C TEL. Dr 16,600 ($70.65) single; Dr 18,725 ($79.65) double (including breakfast). No credit cards.

Hotel Hera II is situated on the hillside off the road back to Sámos. This small, luxurious neo-Baroque villa has drop-dead views over the harbor below. Rooms, with piped-in music, are elegantly simple. The service is first-rate, except during July and August, when group-booked tourists take over.

⑤ Hotel Labito. Pythagório, 83103 Sámos. ☎ **0273/61-086.** Fax 0273/61-085. 69 rms (all with bath). A/C TEL. Dr 14,750 ($62.75) single; Dr 17,325 ($73.85) double. No credit cards.

This beautiful new hotel, designed to resemble rows of two-story Samian mansions painted classic lemon-yellow with green and white trim, is a welcome addition in the heart of the village. Set just two lanes behind the port, it's an ideally quiet and convenient location. The marble lobby, simply decorated breakfast and bar areas, and the pastel pink or blue room furnishings add a touch of luxury. The best value in town.

Hotel Olympiada. Pythagório, 83103 Sámos. ☎ **0273/61-490.** 10 rms (all with bath). TEL. Dr 5,500 ($23.50) single; Dr 10,700 ($45.55) double. No credit cards.

Next to the pricey Hotel Hera II (see above), this attractive, newly built hotel has pleasant plantings and a good view of the harbor. Not recommended for those with a lot of luggage, it's about a 15-minute walk from the paralía, a steep uphill climb. The well-kept rooms are good value.

KOKKÁRI

The **Tourist Office** (☎ 0273/92-333) will do its best to help you find a room; expect to pay Dr 6,600 ($28.10) for a room with bath, Dr 5,600 ($23.85) without. Some hotels will subrent group-tour booked rooms; they'll charge at least Dr 10,000 ($41.65) for two. We can recommend the simple twin-bedded rooms, with private toilet and showers (some with balconies), handled by the **Cafe Manos** (☎ 0273/92-217) on the west end of the waterfront. They manage a small, brown-shuttered building and around the corner from it, the **Pension Christos,** both inland just off the east end of the waterfront. **Sophia Rooms-to-Let** (☎ 0273/92-431) is above the west waterfront, so rear-facing water-view rooms will be the quietest. Both places charge Dr 5,500 ($23.40) for a single or double room.

Hotel Olympia Beach. Kokkári, 831 00 Sámos. ☎ 0273/92-353. Fax 0273/92-457. 11 rms (all with bath). TEL. Dr 13,250 ($56.40) single/double (including breakfast). No credit cards.

This is a bright, clean place overlooking the beach. It's often booked by European groups. If you do stay here, try to secure a sea-facing room, or you might find the road noise disturbing. The same management has recently built the **Hotel Olympia Village** (☎ 0273/92-420) on the road into Kokkári. Though the facilities are nice, the location is not especially appealing.

WHERE TO DINE
SÁMOS TOWN

The food on Sámos is mostly tourist-quality, mediocre, and fairly expensive. The local wines can be excellent. (Byron exclaimed, "Fill high the bowl with Samian wine!") A preferred wine is the dry white called Samaina. There's also a delicious relatively dry rosé called Fokianos. The Greeks like sweet wines, with names like Nectar, Dux, and Anthemis. Almost any restaurant on the island will serve one or all of these wines.

Christos Taverna. Platía Ayíou Nikoláou. ☎ 0273/24-792. Appetizers Dr 500–Dr 1,000 ($2.10–$4.75); main courses Dr 700–Dr 2,200 ($3–$9.35). No credit cards. Daily 11am–11pm. GREEK.

This simple little taverna, under a covered alleyway decorated with odd antiques, is left off the small square as you come up from the port. The food is simply prepared and presented; it comes in generous portions and is remarkably good.

☉ Gregoris Grill. Odós Smýrnis. ☎ 0273/22-718. Appetizers Dr 300–Dr 650 ($1.25–$2.70); main courses Dr 600–Dr 1,800 ($2.50–$7.50). No credit cards. Daily 7–11:30pm. GREEK.

About 100 meters up from the paralía and around the corner from the Olympic Airways office, the Gregoris isn't much to look at, but the lamb chops are delicious and everything is cooked just right. The service is ultrafriendly, though little English is spoken. Prices are cheap.

Pergola Restaurant. Sámos town. ☎ 0273/28-794. Appetizers Dr 800–Dr 2,800 ($3.40–$11.90), main courses Dr 900–Dr 3,400 ($3.85–$14.45). EU, MC, V. Daily 6pm–midnight. CONTINENTAL.

The very attractive Pergola is in an isolated garden of lemon and pomegranate trees in an undeveloped neighborhood, one long block from the bus station away from the port. Filet marsala, seafood dishes, spaghetti, and seasonal specials are prepared with European taste buds in mind. It's a very pleasant change from typical taverna fare.

Restaurant Medusa. Odós Sofoúli 25. ☎ 0273/23-501. Appetizers Dr 600–Dr 2,200 ($2.55–$9.35); main courses Dr 1,600–Dr 3,200 ($6.80–$13.60). No credit cards. Daily 9am–1am. INTERNATIONAL.

This very popular cafe/restaurant serves a huge variety of snack foods, including pizza, sweet and savory crepes, grilled meats and fish, pasta, salads, and even some Greek standards. Though a bit pricey, particularly for drinks, the Medusa has port-side views and well-prepared food. They play Greek pop music.

PYTHAGÓRIO

There are a few places to recommend in Pythagório, and prices at this resort are higher than what you'd pay in Sámos town.

Experides Restaurant. Pythagório. ☎ **0273/61-767.** Reservations recommended in summer. Appetizers Dr 450–Dr 1,400 ($1.90–$5.95), main courses Dr 1,200–Dr 4,000 ($5.10–$17). No credit cards. Daily 6pm–midnight in summer, noon–midnight rest of year. INTERNATIONAL.

This pleasant walled garden is a few blocks inland from the port, and west of the main street. There are uniformed waiters and a dressier crowd. The continental and Greek dishes are well presented and will appeal to a wide variety of palates. We resented the frozen french fries served with their tasty baked chicken, but the meats and vegetables are fresh.

The Family House. Pythagório. No phone. Appetizers Dr 500–Dr 2,800 ($2.10–$11.90), main courses Dr 750–Dr 4,000 ($3.90–$17). No credit cards. Daily 6pm–midnight. GREEK/CONTINENTAL.

This casual garden, enlivened by Christmas tree lights strung through some white-washed citrus trees, is found a block east of the main street, below the main church. The Greek food is tasty and not overcooked. There's a respectable selection of pasta and seafood dishes for those who shun moussaka.

☻ I Varka. Paralía, Pythagório. No phone. Appetizers Dr 250–Dr 1,000 ($1.05–$4.25), main courses Dr 1,200–Dr 3,400 ($5.10–$14.45). No credit cards. Daily May–Oct noon–midnight, Jul–Aug 6pm–midnight. SEAFOOD.

This ouzerí/taverna (pronounced *E varka*, "The Boat") is in a garden of salt pines at the south end of the port. Delicious fresh fish, grilled meats, and a surprising variety of mezedes (appetizers) are produced in the small kitchen, built within a dry-docked fishing boat. The grilled octopus, strung up on a line to dry, and the pink barboúnia or clear gray mullet, all cooked to perfection over a charcoal grill, are the true standout of a meal here.

Restaurant Pythagora. Paralía, Pythagório. ☎ **0273/61-371.** Appetizers Dr 500–Dr 1,200 ($2.10–$5.10), main courses Dr 1,400–Dr 3,200 ($5.95–$13.60). No credit cards. Daily 11am–1pm. GREEK.

Of the many port-side cafes, this is one stands out for its freshly made Greek specialties, its good selection of continental alternatives, and the gorgeous view of the harbor.

KOKKÁRI

Taverna Ávgo Tou Kókora. Kokkári. ☎ **0273/92-113.** Appetizers Dr 600–Dr 1,600 ($2.55–$6.80), main courses Dr 1,400–Dr 3,000 ($5.95–$12.75). No credit cards. Daily noon–1am. GREEK.

This chic seaside cafe has a refreshingly diverse menu and a postcard-perfect setting. (The fanciful name means "Cock's Egg.") You'll find the island's biggest assortment of mezedes as well as a variety of grilled meats and fresh fish. Several dishes play on the name of the establishment.

SÁMOS AFTER DARK

The hottest disco in Sámos town is **Metropolis,** behind the Paradise Hotel. **Totem Disco,** 3 kilometers from town on the main road to Pythagorio, looks as though it could get lively. For bouzouki, there's **Zorba's,** out of town on the road to Mytilíní. Sámos Town's "in" place is the **In Music Bar,** near the central square. There are several other bars of various kinds on the lanes just off the port. **Number Nine,** at Kephalopoúlou 9, beyond the jetty on the right, is one of the oldest and better known.

Nightlife in Pythagório is much more restrained. The **San Lorenzo,** above the port on the Sámos road, and **Labito,** on the village's back lanes, are considered two of the island's best discos.

2 Híos

153 nautical miles (283km) northeast of Piraeus

"Craggy Híos," as Homer dubbed it—and he should have known, as it was probably his home—remains very much unspoiled, and that's why we recommend it to you. The black pebble beaches on the southeast coast of the island are famous and not neglected, but there are white sand beaches on the west coast that look as though they only see a few hundred people in an entire year. Such beaches on the Cyclades would get that many visitors in an hour. There is a monastery in the middle of the island, Néa Moní, that challenges any in Greece for the grandeur of its location and surpasses them with the beauty of its Byzantine mosaics. There are unique medieval villages in the south—Piryí is truly fantastic—and the major crop, mastic (a tree resin used in chewing gum), is grown nowhere else in the world. The north of the island offers excellent hiking opportunities, and the clear waters are superb for swimming, diving, and fishing. The people are known for their good humor; they still enjoy sharing their island with visitors, and money is not their only motive. Enjoy it while you still can. For now Híos remains an ideal destination for those who want to escape the hordes and one of the most exotic places from which to cross over to Turkey.

ESSENTIALS

GETTING THERE   By Plane   Olympic Airways has flights four times a day between Athens and Híos. There is connection twice a week with Lésvos (Mytilíní) and Thessaloníki. The Olympic office in Híos town is in the middle of the harbor front (☎ 0271/24-515). To contact the airport, call ☎ 0271/24-546.

If you arrive by plane, count on taking a cab into town. Taxis to and from the airport are about Dr 1,250 ($5.30) for the 7-kilometer ride.

By Ferry   One car ferry leaves daily for Piraeus via Sámos, then continuing on to Lésvos. There is once-a-week service to Thessaloníki, Kavála, and the Dodecanese. Excursion boats service Híos from Pythagório, Sámos, four times a week. Check with the Híos Port Authority (☎ 0271/44-432) for current schedules and prices.

VISITOR INFORMATION   A helpful **Tourist Information Office** is located at Odós Kanári 18 (☎ 0271/44-389), the second street from the north end of the harbor. They will assist you in finding a room. The office is open daily in summer 7am to 2:30pm and 6:30 to 9pm Monday through Friday; 10am to 1:30pm on Saturday, 10am to 12pm on Sunday. The **tourist police** (☎ 0271/44-427) are headquartered at Odós Neoríon 35.

Another mine of information is **Híos Tours** (☎ **0271/29-444;** fax 0271/21-333); they're located at Leofóros Egéou 84, on the haborfront. It's open daily from 8:30am to 1:30pm and 5:30 to 8:30pm except Sunday (6 to 8pm only). They will assist with a room search and offer a possible discount. Híos Tours or the tourist office will change money after the port-side banks' normal hours.

The free *Híos Summertime* magazine has a lot of useful information, as well as maps of the city.

GETTING AROUND   By Bus   All buses servicing the island leave from Híos town. The blue buses, which leave from the **blue bus station,** on the north side of the Central Park, serve local destinations. The green long-distance buses leave from the **green bus station,** a block south of the Central Park. There are four buses a day to Mestá (Dr 380/$1.60); eight a day to Piryí (Dr 380/$1.60); five to Kardámila; and only two buses a week to Volissós, on the northwest coast.

By Car   Híos is a large island and fun to explore, so carpooling really pays off. If you wish to rent a car, try **Vassilakis Brothers Rent-A-Car,** at Odós Evgenías Hándri 3 (☎ **0271/23-205;** fax 0271/25-659).

By Taxi   Taxis are easily found at the port, though the **taxi station** is beyond the OTE, on the northeast corner of the central square. Fares run Dr 3,800 ($16.15) to Piryí and Dr 4,800 ($20.40) to Mestá.

By Moped   Híos is a great place for moped riding, with good roads and terrific scenery. There are several moped-rental shops on the port. A fully insured Honda 50, suitable for two, runs about Dr 4,400 ($18.70) per day. Expect to pay a few hundred less for a moped.

FAST FACTS   The **tourist police** (☎ **0271/44-427**) are headquartered at Odós Neoríon 35. The **telephone center (OTE)** is across the street from the Tourist Office. The **post office** is on Odós Omírou, the second street from the south end of the harbor.

WHAT TO SEE & DO

Boats dock at **Híos** (often spelled Chíos) town, the largest town on the island and a thriving Greek port. It doesn't look typically Greek and isn't particularly attractive. Most of the city was built after a destructive earthquake in 1881, and the square modern architecture is by no means pretty. The central square, **Platía Vounakíou** (or **Plastíra**), is a couple of blocks in from the north end of the west side of the harbor. It's the heart of the city and is definitely Greek as well as a bit Turkish. Behind the square is the city's **central park.** To the square's south is the **bazaar,** a maze of market lanes, where you can find an astonishing range of merchandise.

The former mosque, east from the central square, houses the island's **Byzantine Museum.** It's open 10am to 1pm daily except Monday, with free admission. The displays, a clutter, seems to be mostly marble gravestones.

The town's **Kástro** is north of the central square behind the **Town Hall.** It was built by the Genoese, and all but the inland walls were destroyed by the earthquake. You can enter through the **Porta Maggiora** and investigate what remains of the old Jewish and Turkish quarters. The small tower to the right as you enter is the **Justiniani Museum,** which houses a collection of icons and mosaics, but it was closed during our last visit.

If you're interested in museums, head south to Odós Koráï, the next to the last street off the west side of the harbor (after the post office). Find the **Argenti Museum** near the **cathedral,** on the top floor of the **Koráï Library.** It's open Monday through Friday from 8am to 2pm and Saturday from 8am to 12:30pm; admission is free. The museum houses portraits of the local aristocracy and copies of Eugene Delacroix's *Massacre of Híos,* a masterpiece depicting the Turkish massacre of the local population in 1822 that helped galvanize European opinion against the Turks. (Actually, the Samians were to blame for starting an insurrection. Híos suffered the slaughter of 30,000 Greeks, another 45,000 were enslaved, and the island's vineyards were uprooted.)

There's also a small **Archaeology Museum** (☎ 0271/44-239), at Odós Michálon 5, south off the southwest corner of the harbor. This too was closed during our last visit. It's said to be a typical island archaeology museum with miscellaneous local finds, plus a letter from Alexander the Great to the local people.

South of town, **Kámbos** (or Campo) is a fertile plain that was staked out by the Genoese aristocrats. Lining the coast road, which leads south toward the airport, are mansions (some from the late 19th century and other dating from as early as the 14th century). These are in various states of repair and are distinctly Italian in design— golden ochre in color with strong horizontal lines. This is an interesting quarter to wander the narrow lanes in search of glimpses into the gardens and courtyards inside the high walls. Unfortunately this area is being developed, and there are already Scandinavian, Dutch, and German tour groups being brought in.

The nearest beach to town is **Bella Vista,** but it's often crowded. The fine-sand beach of **Karfás,** further south, is much better; it can be reached by a local (blue) bus. The best beaches are further south near the southern end of the island, beginning at **Kómi,** which has a white sand beach.

A couple of kilometers further south, **Emborió** is considered the island's best beach. Emborio is a small fishing village built around a volcanically formed cove. The water appears black from the dark smooth stones on the ocean floor. Men wade knee-deep to catch squid and pry off crustaceans. Snorkelers explore the colorful seabed. The small man-made black-pebble beach is filled with families. Just over those rocks to your right is a beach that will knock your socks off, **Mávra Vólia.** Walking on the smooth black rocks feels and sounds like marching through a room filled with marbles, and the sound reverberating against the rough volcanic cliff behind. The panorama of the beach, slightly curving coastline, and distant sea is an incredible experience. There are regular buses from Híos town or from Piryí (8 kilometers away) to Emborió.

Híos offers the adventurous visitor many more remote sandy coves on the west coast. In the intact medieval villages, you can rent a room in a 700-year-old house. The most interesting of these villages are Piryí and Mestá. Both are in the mastic region, in the southern half of Híos, so named because of the gum trees that still grow in the countryside. (The word *mastic* in the Phoenician language was *chio,* which may account for the island's name.) Piryí is known throughout Greece for the distinctive gray-and-white geometric designs that decorate the facades of most of its buildings. Mestá, and many of the hamlets surrounding it, including Olýmbi and Véssa, are architectural gems. These villages of two-story stone-and-mortar houses are linked by narrow vaulted streets and quiet squares.

If your tour around the island takes you to the interior sections—and it should— you'll likely encounter huge swaths of the landscape that have been burned. This is from a series of calamitous fires that spread throughout the island in 1988. The most interesting excursion is to the mastic villages, beginning with Armólia, and including Piryí, Olýmbi, Mestá, and Vessá; then continuing back along the western coast to the ghost town of Anávatos; and finally to Néa Moní, the 11th-century monastery in the center of the island. Or you can make the tour in the opposite direction, west from Híos town.

Piryí is the only village in Greece decorated with distinctive white-and-gray graffiti. From the main *platía,* the view is like some strange Neo Geo or Op Art cityscape. On the main square in Piryí is the 12th-century Byzantine chapel of Áyii Apóstoli; it was built in the style of the earlier Néa Moní. It's a tiny jewel, with 17th-century frescoes that are still in good condition.

Mestá is quite different from Piryí. This remarkable 14th-centry fortress village was built inside a system of walls. Corner towers and iron gates helped to fend off invaders. The meter-thick walls create a labyrinth of streets that will charm, delight, and disorient you. Though many of the town's young people have moved away, life is thriving in Mestá, thanks to the many renovation projects. The arch-roofed houses that have withstood centuries of earthquakes. Life is slow and quiet here. It's a perfect place for a quite retreat.

Mestá has two beautiful churches. The newer one, only 120 years old, is the fourth largest in Greece and one of the wealthiest. Its ornate frescoes, massive chandeliers, and lovely icons make it worth a stop on your trip through the main square. The older church, Paleós Taxiárchis, is deep within the village. The gatekeeper lives across the street. Byzantine frescoes have been revealed beneath plaster that covered them during its use as a Turkish mosque. Both churches are dedicated to the patron saints of the village, Michael and Gabriel.

Five nuns live a quiet life at **Néa Moní,** a medieval church built in 1042 by craftsmen, who were sent from Constantinople by Emperor Constantine VIII to replace an earlier monastery, and it has been called "New Monastery" ever since. One of Greece's prettiest monasteries, it has an octagonal chapel. Its interior is highlighted by exquisite mosaics of marble white, azure blue, and ruby red on a field of gold tiles. The dreamy expressions of the figures have an other worldly quality. Not completely restored, these are the most beautiful Byzantine mosaics in Greece. If you've visited the Kariye Camii in Istanbul, the high quality and style of these mosaics should be familiar (though the work in Istanbul is more recent, this was restored after an 1881 earthquake). These at Néa Moní are the best of their kind, not technically a match with those at Óssios Loukás and Dafní but outshining them in the sweet subtlety of expression.

Be sure to wander to the back of the monastery for the view of the valley below and Híos town. Look into the cistern, a cavernous vaulted room with columns (bring a flashlight); it's to your right as you come through the main gate. The small chapel at the entrance to the monastery is dedicated to the martyrs of the 1822 massacre by the Turks, who also damaged the monastery itself. The skulls and bones are the victims themselves. There are only a few buses each week (the schedule is posted at the station) to Néa Moní. You may have to take a moped, car, or taxi. It's open daily except from 1 to 4pm (the nuns' nap time) and after 8pm.

On the west coast of Híos, directly across from the main town, are a series of coves and beaches between Órmos Elinátas and Órmos Trachiloú. About a kilometer northwest of the town of **Lithí** there's a shallow cove with mooring for colorful fishing boats, a few tavernas, and a few rooms to let. **Agistri** (☎ **0271/73-469**), above the far end of the beach, is the most enticing, with six rooms for Dr 5,500 ($23.40). A bit further north there's a long stretch of fine white pebbles and stones, where nude bathing is common. If you intend to go to the west coast, consider renting a car or moped for the long, winding road, because there is only infrequent bus service to Lithion.

The north of the island is craggier, and the fishing and diving off the rocks is superior. The road north from Híos is more picturesque, and there are various small resorts, such as **Vrondádos** and **Langáda,** in the rocky coves, many with good tavernas. Although no one knows for sure where Homer was born, most historians believe that he was from Híos. The "Stone of Homer," where the blind poet was supposed to have sat when he composed his legendary works, is outside Vrondádos in a grove of olive trees, at the ancient site of the Temple of Cybele and Rhea.

The most attractive town on the island is **Kardámila,** on the northeast corner, an enclave of shipowners and affluent ship officers and crew. The elite families that control Greece's private shipping empires tend to congregate behind high stone fences on secluded islands—a point of pride for locals. The names Onassis, Livanos, Karas, Pateros, and Chandris are only part of Híos's modern-day pantheon. Some local families came to the island from Smýrna (now Izmir) during the massive population exchange between Greece and Turkey. The declining merchant navy still employs the majority of the workforce, and Kardámila is still affluent enough to resist going after tourist bucks. There's only one hotel here and very little in the way of tourist services, and that's why it's so refreshing.

Nagós, northwest across the headland, is another pleasant seaside village that offers some great black-sand beaches. Most people go to the beach right near the town, but it can sometimes become crowded. The secret is to hike to the two small beaches a little to the east. To get there, take the small road behind the white house near the windmill. To get to Nagós you'll have to take the Kardámila bus and hope that it'll continue the 5 kilometers to the beach. If not, you can usually get a ride by waving down a private car. (There aren't enough hitchhikers on the island yet to make anyone wary.)

Híos is ringed by several private islets. The most famous of these is **Inoússes,** an 18-square-kilometer island, that's home to 30 multimillionaire families, who are said to control 25% of Greece's 2,700 registered-vessel merchant fleet. Constantine Lemos, who supposedly grosses $1 million a day, is only one among many who form the tightly knit society on Inoússes. The social life on this private isle is rumored to be as wild as anything in Greece. Daily excursion boats ply the short distance between Híios and Inoússes for beach, fish, and island tours. Híos Tours can arrange such a day trip for about Dr 7,000 ($29.80).

There are also excursions to the island of **Psará** from **Limniá,** near Vollisós on the west coast.

A SIDE TRIP TO TURKEY

During the summer, there are daily departures to Çesme, Turkey, from the port of Híos. The round-trip price is about Dr 16,000 ($68.10); this includes a bus tour of the city of Izmir, or a two-hour bus ride and tour of Ephesus, and all taxes. Off season, boats run less frequently; check with the port-side travel agents such as Híos Tours. *Note:* Çesme is a 45-minute bus ride from Izmir on the Aegean coast, where buses run frequently to Istanbul and all the coastal cities including Ephesus.

WHERE TO STAY

If you're just arriving on Híos, you might consider finding accommodations in the town before setting off for one of the island's many special villages (prettier and cheaper; though, from these, you'll need your own transportation to sightsee). Híos town has a large number of private rooms; you can expect to pay about Dr 6,500 ($27.65) for a double. Contact the tourist office for references.

Híos Town

Hotel Kyma. Odós Evyeniás Handrí 1, Híos, 821 00 Híos. ☎ **0271/44-500.** Fax 0271/44-600. 59 rms (all with bath). A/C TEL. Dr 12,650 ($53.85) single; Dr 16,500 ($70.20) double (including breakfast). No credit cards.

Our favorite in-town lodging was built in 1917 as a private villa for John Livanos. (You'll notice the portraits of the lovely Mrs. Livanos on the ceiling in the ground floor breakfast room.) Though the hotel is of historic interest (the treaty with Turkey was signed in the Kyma in 1922), most of the architectural details, other than in the lobby area and breakfast room, are gone. All the rooms have been renovated in a modern style. Many rooms have views of the sea, and a few have big whirlpool baths, and the management, under the smart direction of the venerable Mr. Spordílis, is friendly, capable, and helpful. They also serve an excellent breakfast, complete fresh tangerine juice, thick yogurt, tea and coffee of all varieties, and fresh fruit.

Pension Yiannis. Odós Mihaíl Livanoú 48-50, Híos, 821 00 Híos. ☎ **0271/27-433.** 13 rms (10 with bath). Dr 6,750 ($28.70) single/double without bath; Dr 9,700 ($41.25) single/double with bath. No credit cards.

A good value, this pleasant pension is one street off the south side of the harbor. The friendly hostess, Irene, grew up in New Jersey and New York. She allows you to share her refrigerator. The rooms are clean and fine, and the garden behind it is a treat.

Rooms Alex. Odós Mihaíl Livanoú 29, Híos, 82100 Híos. ☎ **0271/26-054.** 6 rms (2 with bath). Dr 5,500 ($23.40) without bath; Dr 6,600 ($28.10) with bath.

Another good value place south of the harbor, with clean rooms and a roof garden with a sea view. Alex, who speaks English very well, will meet you at the harbor or airport if you call.

Outside of Híos Town

There are a great many rooms and apartments for rent in the Vrondádos beach area north of Híos town. Contact Tourist Information or **Híos Tours** (☎ **0271/29-444**) for specific recommendations.

Kardámila

Kardámila, on the northeast coast, is our choice of the resort towns, because it's prosperous, self-sufficient, and very untouristy.

Hotel Kardámyla. Kardámila, 82300 Híos. ☎ **0272/23-353.** Fax 0271/23-354. 32 rms (all with bath). A/C TEL. Dr 13,500 ($57.45) single; Dr 17,125 ($72.85) double (including breakfast). No credit cards.

This modern resort hotel was built for the guests and business associates of the town's shipowners and officers, and it has its own small beach. The rooms are large and plain, with modern bathrooms and balconies overlooking the beach. The excellent Theo Spordílis has taken over its management, so you can be sure the service will be good.

Karfás

Karfás, 7 kilometers south of Híos town around Cape Ayía Eléni, is an exploding tourist resort. Its fine sandy beach is lined with expensive Greek all-inclusive holiday hotels.

Golden Sand Hotel. P.O. Box 32, Karfás, 82100 Híos. **0271/32-080.** Fax 0271/31-700. 108 rms (all with bath). A/C MINIBAR TEL. Dr 18,000 ($76.60) single; Dr 20,900 ($88.95) double, depending on season. AE, EU, MC, V.

The Golden Sand is one of the earliest Karfás beach resorts, an attractive, group-oriented, two-story lodge with a large roof deck and marble floors throughout. It also has a large pool, its own private beach, satellite TV, and radios in large guest rooms. The breakfast area is airy and spacious. There's even a beauty salon and kids playground. Between mid-June and mid-September a compulsory half-board plan is in effect, adding Dr 3,200 ($13.60) per person, per day, to the high season rates above.

TRADITIONAL VILLAGES

There are a few centuries-old villages in Greece that seem timeless, where life seems to have changed as little as the buildings themselves. Many of these villages are studied and appreciated for their unique style of organic construction. Unfortunately, the younger members of the community have left these villages for economic and social reasons. Mestá, 36 kilometers southwest of Híos town, is just such a village. Fortunately, the Greek government acquired 33 old abandoned homes there to protect them from further deterioration. Four of these homes, originally built more than 500 years ago, have been restored and opened by the Greek National Tourist Organization as part of its Traditional Settlements Program. The admirable Dimitri Pipidis (☎ 0271/76-319) manages the four houses, and each comes equipped with a kitchen, bathroom, and enough sleeping space for two to six people. The price is determined by the number of beds: for one bed Dr 8,800 ($37.45); two beds, Dr 10,000 ($42.55); and three beds, Dr 11,500 ($48.95).

You can visit Dimitri's office on the central platía in Mestá. If the houses are booked, Dimitri will assist you in finding one of many private rooms in Mestá. A typical room runs Dr 7,500 ($31.90) depending on the house and season. For the high season, make your reservations early—a must in the busy summer months.

There are also private rooms for rent in Piryí, though it's so busy with day trippers that we find Mestá much more relaxing. One such place is **Astra Rooms** (☎ 0271/71-149) where very simple rooms (without bath) go for Dr 2,800 ($11.90) a bed per night. Astra is located one block off the main platía, where several businesses offer nearby rooms to let.

WHERE TO DINE

The more sophisticated islanders prefer to take a short drive, south or north of Híos town, for fine cuisine. Starting with the beaches, the taverna **Giamos** on Karfás beach is known for its good meat courses. If you're in Emborio or Pasalimani, make sure you try the fish and squid. Both of these villages are known for their seafood, and you can watch the fishermen bring in their catch right in front of your table. The same is true just north of Vrondados at the **Ormos Lo Restaurant,** near the public beach.

Apolaisi. Ayía Ermióni Village. ☎ **0271/31-359.** Appetizers Dr 600–Dr 1,500 ($2.55–$6.40); fish from Dr 10,000 ($42.55) per kilo. No credit cards. Daily 5pm–midnight. SEAFOOD.

About 8 or 9 kilometers south of Híos town, this delightful fish taverna, with a candlelit terrace, is run by Yiorgo Karanikola. Dine on fried calamari, grilled fish, and an assortment of salads while fishers below take their boats out for their night's work. You'll need to take a taxi to get to Apolaisi. Plan on a 10- to 15-minute ride.

Híos Marine Club. Odós Nenitoúsi 1. ☎ **0271/23-184.** Appetizers Dr 300–Dr 1,500 ($1.25–$6.40), main courses Dr 650–Dr 3,200 ($2.75–$13.60) EU, MC, V. Daily noon–2am. GREEK.

This good, simple taverna serves the usual Greek dishes, pasta, grilled meats, and fish.

Iviskos. Central Square. No telephone. Snacks/desserts Dr 400–Dr 2,800 ($1.70–$11.90). Daily 7am–2am. CONTINENTAL.

Iviskos serves excellent bread with their breakfast, and they also serve a dynamite Black Forest cake until 2am. This is the place for light eats and people-watching.

Paradise (Yiorgo Passa's). Langáda Village. ☎ **0271/74-218.** Appetizers Dr 600–Dr 2,800 ($2.55–$11.90); fish from Dr 10,000 ($42.55) per kilo. No credit cards. Daily 11am–2am. SEAFOOD.

Langáda is a fishing village with a strip of five or six outdoor fish taverns lining the harbor. Known for its excellent restaurants, it's about 20 kilometers north of Híos. Our favorite place in Langáda was Yiorgo Passa's Paradise Snackbar. His place is the first on the left as you walk down to the waterfront. Prices are low, portions are generous, and the ambience is warm and friendly. *Note:* There are evening dinner cruises to Langáda from Híos; check with Híos Tours about the schedule and prices.

Theodosiou Ouzeri. Paralía, Híos. No phone. Appetizers Dr 400–Dr 3,500 ($1.70–$14.90). No credit cards. Daily 5pm–midnight. GREEK.

In the evening, many residents prefer to pull up a streetside chair at a cafe along the waterfront and sip an ouzo or slurp a chocolate sundae. Of the many cafes on the paralía, we like Theodosiou Ouzeri, located on the far right (north) side of the port, for both the scene and its menu.

Zerbas. Odós Neoríon 1, Híos. ☎ **0271/44-709.** Appetizers Dr 400–Dr 2,300 ($1.70–$9.80); main courses Dr 1,000–Dr 2,200 ($4.25–$9.35). EU, MC. Daily noon–2am. GREEK/ INTERNATIONAL.

This new restaurant on the north end of the harbor is easily the most attractive of the waterfront establishments. The food is as good as the handsome decor promises. Try their specialty, grilled chicken—a hit with local diners.

HÍOS AFTER DARK

Most people in Híos entertain themselves along the harbor front and around the central square, strolling up and down the streets, sitting at the cafes, and playing a game of pool at one of the pool halls. There are a few sophisticated bars, including **Kavos** and **Remezzo.** There's also a disco, **Neraïda** (☎ **0271/20-149**), at Leofóros Enósseos 3. **Karnayio** is another disco on the road to the airport.

The **Omírio** (Homeric) **Center** (☎ **0271/24-217**), off the southwest corner of the main square sometimes hosts visiting musicians.

3 Lésvos (Mytilíni)

188 nautical miles (348km) northeast of Piraeus

Lésvos, very often called Mytilíni, after its capital, is the third-largest island in Greece, with a population of nearly 120,000. On the southeast coast, Mytilíni is a small bustling city, and its port is one of the busiest in Greece.

The island is very irregular, with huge tear-shaped bays cutting into the west and south coasts of the island. There are important concentrations of tourism on the north coast at beautiful Mólyvos (which, to add to the confusion, is called by its ancient name of Míthymna nearly half the time) and south at Plomári. Sappho's hometown, Eressós, is near the northwest coast of the island. Within the island's irregular triangle there is amazing diversity: Parts of the island are industrialized; parts are fertile (with about 12 million olive trees); parts are mountainous with chestnut and pine trees; and parts are desertlike plain. There are even a few marshy areas to round out the picture.

ESSENTIALS

GETTING THERE   By Plane   Olympic Airways has three flights daily to Mytilíni from Athens. There are connections 10 times weekly with Thessaloníki, three times weekly with Límnos, twice weekly with Híos. The Olympic Office in Mytilíni (☎ **0251/28-660**) is at Odós Kavétsou 44, about 200 meters south of Ayía Irínis park. To get there, walk south from the harbor; turn left before the World War

II monument, a metal statute of a woman holding a sword; turn right and find it on the right. An airport bus meets flights; the fare to Mytilíni costs Dr 380 ($1.60).

By Boat   There's one boat daily to Lésvos from Piraeus, stopping at Híos. There's one boat weekly from Rafína. Two or three boats call weekly from Kavála, stopping at Límnos; one boat weekly from Thessaloníki, stopping at Límnos. There are daily boats to and from Híos.

In the summer **Ilios Lines** and **Gianmar** hydrofoils connect Lésvos with Alexandroúpoli, Híos, Kávala, Límnos, Pythagório (Sámos), Pátmos, and Sámos town.

Call the **Maritime Co.** (☎ **0251/23-720**), the **port authority** (☎ **0251/28-888**), or the **port police** (☎ **0251/28-647**) for current schedules.

Once you get to Lésvos, double-check the boat schedule for your departure, as the harbor is extremely busy in the summer and service is often inexplicably irregular. Many of the ferries to Mytilíni are scheduled to arrive at midnight, but are as late as 2:30am. The late boats are not necessarily met by people with rooms to let, so do be sure to call ahead for accommodations. If you're stuck, you can always wake up the night clerks at the following two places: the **Blue Sea Hotel** (☎ **0251/23-994**), across from the ferry quay at Koundouriótou 91; doubles cost Dr 17,900 ($76.15); or the **Hotel Sappho,** midway down the harbor front at Koudouriótou 31 (☎ **0251/ 22-888**), where doubles cost Dr 11,400 ($48.50).

VISITOR INFORMATION   The **Greek National Tourist Organization (EOT)** is in Mytilíni at Odós Aristárhou 6 (☎ **0251/42-511;** fax 0251/42-512). It's behind Customs, to the left (east) from the ferry quay. They're open daily from 8am to 2pm with extended hours in the high season. They have a complete listing of hotels, pensions, and rooms throughout the island. They'll make calls to arrange accommodations.

GETTING AROUND   By Bus   Lésvos has an expensive, infrequent, and metered bus system. There's daily service in summer to Kaloní and Mólyvos (four times), to Mandamádos (once), Plomári (four times), and to Eressós and Sigrí (once). The round-the-island KTEL buses can be caught in Mytilíni at the south end of the port behind the Argo Hotel. The local bus station is in Mytilíni near the north end of the harbor, near the Popular Arts Museum.

By Car   There are many car-rental offices on the port in Mytilíni. In the off season, you can bargain for better rates. **Europcar** (☎ **0251/43-311**) has offices in Mytilíni and a desk at the airport (☎ **0251/61-200**). Expect to pay Dr 16,500 ($70) a day without gas for a Fiat Panda.

By Boat   **Aeolic Cruises** (☎ **0251/23-960;** fax 0251/43-694) offers daily boat excursions around the island during the high season from its port-side office in Mytilíni.

By Taxi   Lésvos is a big island. The one-way taxi fare from Mytilíni to Mólyvos is Dr 10,000 ($42.55). Taxi fare from Mytilíni to Eressós or Sígri is Dr 12,500 ($53.20). The taxi stand in Mytilíni is near the local bus station near the north end of the port and the Popular Art Museum.

FAST FACTS   The telephone area code for Mytilíni is **0251,** for Mólyvos (Míthymnma) and Eressós it's **0253,** and for Plomári it's **0252.**

The **tourist police** (☎ **0251/22-776**) are located near EOT, left (east) from the ferry quay. The **Vostáni Hospital** (☎ **0251/43-777**) on Odós P. Vostani, just southeast of town, will take care of emergencies. The **post office** and the **telephone center (OTE)** are on Odós Vournázon, a long block inland behind the Town Hall.

THE MYTHS OF LÉSVOS

It's impossible to think about Lésvos without the island's two most obvious, related associations: the love of women for women and the great classical poet Sappho, who Plato dubbed the Tenth Muse. Legends abound about the origin of the former, some suggesting that it developed as the practise of a cult or of college devoted to Aphrodite (possibly founded by Sappho), others theorizing that the island became lesbian when the Athenians wreaked vengeance on its inhabitants after a failed rebellion by slaughtering all its men.

Sappho herself is an equal mystery because so little of her writing has survived—though that little confirms that she was indeed one of the greatest of lyric poets. What is known is that she lived in the 7th century B.C. and was born in the village of Eressós on the northwestern part of the island. She wrote openly about love and desire, of men and women: "Love's unbound my limbs and set me shaking, / A demon bittersweet and my unmaking." To confuse matters further, certain probable embroideries have been added to her biography. She is said to have fallen in love with an attractive younger man, Phaon, who she followed across the sea to the mainland, and that in despair at his rejection she flung herself to her death off the white cliffs of Lefkáda. We are fairly certain that she had a daughter, that she had a sort of finishing school for aristocratic young women, and that she composed some truly immortal poetry.

Lésvos was in ancient times an important artistic center, famous for its academies and symposia, and there is still a festival each May called "The Week of Prose and Arts." Theophrastus, director of the Athens Academy, was from Lésvos, and both Aristotle and Plato went to Lésvos to teach and study. The maxims "Know thyself" and "Nothing in excess," inscribed on the Temple at Delphi, were taken from the writings of Pitticus, one of the Seven Sages of Greece and a tyrant of Lésvos. The philosopher Epicurus came to Lésvos from Sámos to study and write, "Pleasure is our first and greatest aim."

WHAT TO SEE & DO

Most people arrive on Lésvos at the big and busy harbor of **Mytilíni** and immediately rush away. Yes, it's more like a mainland city than an island capital. It has a big-city ambience more like Thessaloníki than any other Aegean backwater. Mytilíni is not to everyone's taste, especially at first glance, but we recommend you take another look. Take a stroll around town and take in the amazing array of architecture.

The most important sites are the excellent Theophilos Museum in nearby Variá, the port, and the ornate, peaked dome Church of St. Therapón. The port street (or *Prokymaía*) is **Odós Koundouriótou;** it's the most important area of the city for tourists, with nearly all services and shops. Ermoú Street, parallel to the harbor, is the main commercial thoroughfare. There are many grand old garden villas scattered around town, especially near the archaeological museum, west of the port. To the north, toward the fortress, Mytilíni's crumbling ochre backstreets contain a mix of traditional coffeehouses, the studios of artisans, and food vendors, along with stylish shops selling jewelry, antiques, and clothing.

The new **Archaeological Museum of Mytilíni,** at Odós Eftalíou 7 (☎ **0251/ 28-032**), has a fine sculpture collection. The museum exhibits finds from the Bronze Age up to the Hellenistic era from Thérmi and Mólyvos, including the latest excavations, and a rich selection of mosaics, sculpture, and tablets. It's open Tuesday through Sunday from 8:30am to 3pm; admission is Dr 500 ($2.10).

The **Popular Museum** (☎ 0251/41-844) is in a small white house near the local bus station on Koundouriótou Street. Its current curator and guide, Ioánna, will give you an excellent tour of its fine embroideries, eccentric pottery (much of which came from Cannakale, Turkey), costumes, and historical documents. It's open Monday through Saturday 8:30am to 2pm; admission is Dr 250 ($1.05).

The **Theóphilos Museum** is the former house of folk artist Hatzimichális Theóphilos (1868–1934), who emigrated from the Mt. Pelio region to paint on Lésvos. It's about 3 kilometers south of town in Variá. His watercolors of ordinary people, daily life, and local landscapes are widely celebrated. They are also exhibited at the Museum of Folk Art in Plaka, in Athens. The museum is hung floor to ceiling with Theóphilos's extraordinary canvases. Be sure to take in the photographs showing the artist dressed as Alexander the Great. He would travel around Greece dressed as the fallen soldier, and little costumed boys posed as his soldiers. The museum is open Tuesday through Sunday from 9am to 1pm and 4:30 to 8:pm; admission is Dr 300 ($1.25).

The mildly compelling **Teriad Library and Museum of Modern Art** is next door to the Theóphilos Museum. It's in the home of the noted art critic Stratis Eleftheriadis-Teriad. Copies of his published works, including the *Minotaure* and *Verve* magazines, as well as his personal collection of works by Picasso, Matisse, and other modern artists are displayed. It's open Tuesday through Sunday from 9am to 1pm and 5 to 8pm; admission is Dr 500 ($2.10).

The **Kástro,** to the north of the city, was founded by Justinian in the 6th century. It was restored and enlarged in 1737 by the Genoese, who incorporated columns from a 7th-century B.C. temple of Apollo. In the summer, it's used as a performing arts center and is often with popular Greek singers. There's also an **ancient theater** to the east above the town and a well-preserved **Roman aqueduct,** thought to have been built in the 2nd century, near Moria, a short distance north from Mytilíni.

The east coast road, leading up to **Mandamádos,** is the most scenic on the island; olive and fruit trees grow down to the water's edge and thermal springs form warm pools that attract bathers. **Mólyvos** (Míthymna), at the northern tip of the island's triangle, is a castle-crowned village with stone and pink-pastel stucco mansions capped by red-tile roofs. The town overlooks the sea and a modest harbor. Its pebble beaches overflow with sunbathers and swimmers.

The legend told most often about Mólyvos concerns Arion, a 7th-century B.C. poet-musician and contemporary of Sappho. Apollo told Arion in a dream that the sailors who were returning with him to Lésvos were going to kill him for the prize he had won in a music contest. The events unfolded as Apollo had prophesied, and when Arion was granted one last wish, he asked the sailors if he could play his lyre. They consented and Arion played and at the very last moment jumped into the sea. He was picked up by a school of appreciative dolphins, who carried him on their backs to the shores at Molyvos. Historians believe that the story is based at least partly on fact.

Although there are now altogether too many souvenir shops selling neon-green plastic back scratchers and the like, the village of Mólyvos is still a wonderful place to soak up a lot of Greek atmosphere. Some of the village men seem to live in cafes, studying their ouzo; bright, colorful geraniums and roses decorate balconies and windowsills; the streets, alleyways, and passages are laid out in an unfathomable pattern; and the women are always working. In Mólyvos, you can wander up to the Genoese fortress, stroll along the port, or swim at the local pebble beaches.

Seven kilometers south of Mólyvos is the enterprising village of **Pétra.** This fishing village, with an enormous rock in its center, has a Women's Agricultural-Tourist Cooperative program that welcomes visitors to live in local homes.

The paved road to Mólyvos meets the westbound road at **Kalloní,** a sardine center, 4 kilometers north of Lésvos's largest inland body of water. The western half of the island is the least visited; sandy beaches run the length of the coast from Sígri to Skála Eressós. The villages on this part of Lésvos are as serene as one finds on the island.

Eressós, the winter village, and its summer neighbor, **Skála Eressós** (4 kilometers south), have become a full-scale resort. This has nothing to do with Eressos being the birthplace of Sappho, or the lesbian community that makes pilgrimages there; the beach there is the best on Lésvos. It's a wide, wonderful, dark-sand stretch. A long stretch of sandy beaches and coves extends north from there to Sígri. When you return from the beach to the village, you can visit the **archaeology museum,** behind the Church of St. Andrew, the Byzantine-era fortress (closed Monday), or the 5th-century basilica, Áyios Andréas.

Most people who come here stay at the beach at summer homes and private rooms, but a few prefer the village of Eressos. The **Cooperative Tourism and Travel Agency** (☎ 0251/21-329) in Mytilíni has a list of available rooms.

Plomári is 40 kilometers southwest of Mytilíni. Still having the character of a fishing village, it's very much like Mólyvos, though it's not as pretty. It's one of Greece's major ouzo centers and is a growing resort center. If you're there when the potent drink is being distilled, your nose will catch the fennel scent wafting in the breeze. It's been able to accept tourist development without completely selling its soul. The village has very different architectural appeal than Mólyvos but also offers winding streets, mysterious passageways, outdoor cafes, a scenic harbor, and a relaxed pace. Plomári is especially known for its potent ouzo (the Ouzo Festival is held each July), as well as fresh shrimp, red hot peppers, and locally produced mushrooms. Unfortunately, hotel rooms are very hard to find. Plomári's in-town beaches are fine for swimming, but travel a few kilometers east to **Áyios Isodóros** for better water, a long pebble beach, and a growing number of pensions and condos.

Due west on Lésvos's south coast is the popular sand beach at **Vaterá.** It's 8 kilometers long, 30 meters wide, and often jammed. Keep walking and you're bound to find an empty spot.

A really enjoyable day trip is to the rural hamlet of **Ayiássos,** 23 kilometers west of Mytilíni. There local craftsmen still turn out their ceramic wares by hand. The town, built up on the foothills of Mt. Ólýmbos, consists of traditional gray stone houses. Some of these are painted in pastels and have wooden "Turkish" (Ottoman) balconies that are covered in flowering vines. The town has narrow cobblestone lanes and modest churches. There are excursion buses from Mytilíni, or you can share a taxi for about Dr 6,500 ($27.65) for the one-hour, 25-kilometer ride.

A SIDE TRIP TO TURKEY

From Lésvos, there's direct connection to Turkey via the port of Ayvalik; only about 3,000 tourists make the crossing annually. During the high season, ships to Turkey sail daily except Sunday. Tickets for the Turkish boats are sold by **Aeolic Cruises Travel Agency** (☎ 0251/23-960) on the port in Mytilíni; the fare is about Dr 16,500 ($70) round trip. You need to submit your passport one day in advance of departure. Ayvalik is a densely wooded fishing village; it makes a refreshing base camp from which to tour Pergamum or ancient Troy. An all-inclusive tour to Pergamum with lunch, bus, and round-trip boat fare costs about $80.

WHERE TO STAY
MYTILÍNI

Mytilíni has a number of older hotels on the port, most of them hardly worth mentioning. The helpful EOT office can also advise you about the availability of private rooms. The **Cooperative Tourism and Travel Agency** (☎ **0251/21-329;** fax 0251/41-268) at Odós Konstantinoupóleos 5, next to the bus station, will help you find rooms in any of the island's rural areas.

Hotel Blue Sea. Odós Koundouriótou 91, Mytilíni, 810 00 Lésvos. ☎ **0251/23-995.** Fax 0251/29-656. 61 rms (all with bath). TEL. Dr 11,500 ($48.95) single; Dr 17,900 ($70.75) double. EU, MC, V.

This older hotel, on corner of the port near the ferry quay, was recently remodeled. It's been outfitted with double-paned windows, so now it's not only conveniently located but quiet enough for a good night's sleep.

Hotel Erato. Odós P. Vostáni, Mytilíni, 81000 Lésvos. **0251/41-160.** 22 rms (all with bath). TEL. Dr 6,900 ($29.50) single; Dr 11,250 ($47.85) double. EU, MC, V.

The bright rooms, with balconies, have well-scrubbed baths. The staff is friendly and helpful. Many of the rooms suffer from the noise of cycles ripping by, so check yours out before you commit. Open all year-round, this four-story lodging was converted from a medical clinic.

Salina's Garden. Odós Fokéas 7-9, Mytilíni, 810 00 Lésvos. ☎ **0251/42-973.** 8 rooms (2 with bath). Dr 5,700 ($24.25) single; Dr 7,600 ($32.30) double. No credit cards.

These clean, rustic rooms, are arranged around a lovely garden. It's not far from the old fortress in town. There's no Salina here, just a friendly, English-speaking Greek family who create a relaxed, mellow atmosphere. They also rent motorbikes for a reasonable price. Very popular with budget travelers, this place fills up fast, so call ahead.

MÓLYVOS

In Mólyvos, the **Tourist Information Office** (☎ **0253/71-347**) maintains a list of private rooms to rent, many of which are up on the hill near the ochre-colored castle. A Class A room in Mólyvos typically starts at Dr 7,000 ($29.80).

Hotel-Bungalows Delfinia. Mólyvos, 811 08 Lésvos. ☎ **0253/71-315.** Fax 0253/71-524. 65 rms, 57 bungalows (all with bath). MINIBAR TEL. Dr 16,000 ($68.10) single; Dr 22,150 ($94.25) double; Dr 31,625 ($134.60) for bungalow with half-board plan (all rates include breakfast). AE, DC, V.

Open year-round, this contemporary white stucco and gray stone resort is in a panoramic setting above the port and beach. It's a good value. Room service and one-day laundry can go a long way toward making a vacation special. The rooms are simple. On the large well-kept grounds, there's a saltwater swimming pool, table tennis, snack bar, basketball, volleyball, and tennis facilities.

Hotel Olive Press. Mólyvos, 811 08 Lésvos. **0253/71-205.** Fax 0253/71-246. 41 rms, 9 studios (all with bath). TEL. Dr 14,000 ($59.70) single; Dr 18,860 ($80.25) double (including breakfast), Dr 28,840 ($105.70) for studio without breakfast. AE, DC, V.

The most charming hotel in town is built down on the water in the traditional style. The rooms are on the small side, but they're quiet and very comfortable. They have terrazzo floors, handsome furnishings, and bathtubs with shower curtains. Some of the rooms have windows opening onto great sea views, with waves lapping just beneath the windows. There is a nice inner courtyard with several gardens. The staff is gracious and friendly.

Nicholas Prokopiou Rooms to Let. Odos Eftaliotou 22, Mólyvos, 81108 Lésvos. ☎ **0253/ 71-403.** 4 rms (none with bath). Dr 6,325 ($26.90) double; Dr 7,600 ($32.30) triple. No credit cards.

This lovely unnamed stone house in the old part of town has clean double-bedded rooms and kitchen facilities. You can dine in a secluded, verdant garden.

Sea Horse Pension (Thalássio Álogo). Mólyvos, 81108 Lésvos. **0253/71-320.** Fax 0253/ 71-374. 14 rms (all with bath). Dr 7,900 ($33.605) single; Dr 9,000 ($38.30) double (including breakfast). No credit cards.

A cluster of recently built Class C hotels are set below the old town, near the beach. Among them is this smaller, homier pension. The friendly manager, Stergios, keeps the rooms, with good views, tidy. There's also a restaurant and an in-house travel agency.

PLOMÁRI

In Plomári, we like **Pension Lida** (☎ **0251/44-320**). It's located in two handsome old villas right in town; doubles with sea views and private baths are Dr 8,250 ($35.10); breakfast (included in the rates) is served on a little garden balcony. The **Cooperative Tourism and Travel Agency** (☎ **0251/21-329**) in Mytilíni has a list of rooms for rent in the area.

WHERE TO DINE
MYTILÍNI

Mytilíni, with its youthful, somewhat avant-garde population, has even more portside cafes and tavernas than your average bustling harbor town. At the southern end of the port (opposite the new docks) are several small ouzeris, specializing in grilled octopus, squid, shrimp, and local fish. Small portions of tzatziki, potatoes, and olives accompany wine or one of the many types of ouzo from Plomári. The cluster of chairs around the small lighthouse at the point is the most scenic (as well as the windiest) of these places. For après ouzo there are several cafes, but on soccer night it's almost impossible to get a seat.

Averof 1841 Grill. Paralía, Mytilíni. No phone. Appetizers Dr 300–Dr 1,200 ($1.25–$5.10), main courses Dr 600–Dr 3,200 ($2.55–$13.60). No credit cards. Daily 11:30am–11:30pm. GREEK.

This taverna, located midport near the Sappho Hotel, is one of the better grills around. It has particularly good beef dishes. Try any of their tender souvlaki or the lamb with potatoes.

MÓLYVOS

Mólyvos has quite a few good possibilities, including the **Olive Press,** down by the sea, which serves an excellent breakfast.

Melinda's. Mólyvos. ☎ **0251/71-787.** Appetizers Dr 350–Dr 900 ($1.50–$3.85); main courses Dr 1,000–Dr 3,200 ($4.25–$13.60). No credit cards. Daily 7pm–1am. INTERNATIONAL.

This restaurant offers a scrumptious vegetarian menu. The carrot-and-currant salad, brown rice, vegetable-and-hazelnut salad, and nut roast with a spicy sauce are excellent. Main course meat dishes are also served. The service and ambience are also fine.

Tropicana. Mólyvos. **0251/71-869.** Snacks/desserts Dr 400–Dr 2,800 ($1.70–$11.90). No credit cards. Daily 8am–1am. CAFE FARE.

After lunch or dinner, stroll up into the old town to sip a cappuccino or have a dish of ice cream. This outdoor cafe under a plane tree has soothing classical music and a most relaxing ambience. The owner, Hari Procoplou, learned the secrets of ice creamery in Los Angeles.

ERESSÓS

In **Eressós,** we enjoyed dining along the water, and found one good place to the far left as you face the sea. The **Arion Restaurant** (otherwise know as The Boy on the Dolphin, ☎ **0251/53-384**) serves a delicious moussaka and Greek specialties that have a vaguely English touch. It's open for lunch and dinner.

For a great fish meal, take the first right turn past Áyios Isodóros and go about 2 miles to the town of Ayía Várvara. Fresh swordfish steaks are Dr 1,900 ($8.10) per person at **Blue Sea** (☎ **0251/32-834**). At night, you sit under the stars, right beside the unspoiled rocky coastline. There are also a few rooms available here.

MYTILÍNI AFTER DARK

In Mytilíni, there's plenty of the nightlife on either end of the harbor. The east side tends to be younger, cheaper, and more informal. The more sophisticated places are off the south end of the harbor. There's also the outdoor **Pallas Cinema** nearby. Don't forget that there might be entertainment at the Kástro.

Nighttime in Mólyvos revolves around bars, and bars are aplenty. Among the hottest spots, when we last visited, was **Perlita. Koukos** is supposed to attract a largely gay following. A local favorite, the **Castro Bar** has been known to host an active pickup scene.

As you approach to Mólyvos, you may notice a really strange structure to the right on the outskirts of town. A cantilevered deck with a mast and a sign says "boat-spirit-music." That's **Gatelouzi,** said to get very lively at night.

Vangelis Bouzouki (no telephone) is Mólyvos's top acoustic bouzouki club. It's located west from Mólyvos on the road to Efthaloú, past the Sappho Tours office. After about a ten-minute walk outside of town, you'll see a sign that points to an olive grove. Follow it for about another 500 meters through the orchard until you reach a clearing with gnarly olive trees and a few stray sheep. You see the circular cement dance floor, surrounded by clumps of cafe tables, you've found it. Forget about the food, but have some ouzo and late-night mezedes, and sit back to enjoy the show.

4 Límnos

186 nautical miles (344km) northeast of Piraeus

Límnos is pretty much all alone out in the middle of the northeastern Aegean, guarding one of history's most strategic locations, the Dardenelles (or the Hellespont, as it was called in antiquity). The strait between Europe and Asia connects the Aegean with the Sea of Marmara and the Mediterranean with the Black Sea.

It's a rugged volcanic island, nearly treeless due as much to overgrazing and recent fires than the volcano eruptions of antiquity that made it the home of Hephaestus (Vulcan to the Romans), god of fire and metalwork. In the spring it's green with low-growing scrub and abundant wildflowers worthy of close inspection, but by fall it has be scorched sere, the color of cinnamon. It's the home of some very important military installations and one of Greece's best and best-known resort, the Akti Mirina.

ESSENTIALS

GETTING THERE   By Plane   Olympic Airways has three flights daily between Límnos and Athens, and one connection daily with Thessaloníki, and three times a week with Lésvos. Their office (☎ **0254/22-478**) is on Odós Garoufalídou, in

Mýrina. The airport bus departs from Mýrina to the airport 90 minutes before flight time and costs Dr 250. ($1.05).

By Boat   Getting to Límnos isn't much of a problem from northern Greece. It's connected by boat to Kavála four times weekly and to Lésvos three times weekly. There is infrequent service to and from Híos, Samothrace, Alexandroúpoli, the Dodecanese, and Kými, on Évvia. There is also connection with Rafína four time a week, with Piraeus three times a week, and with Thessaloníki twice a week. In summer there is hydrofoil connection with Híos, Lésvos, Sámos, and Pátmos. The schedule changes often, so you'll have to contact the **Límnos Port Authority** (☎ 0254/ 22-225) or the port authority or travel agency from your point of origin.

VISITOR INFORMATION   Mýrina has two helpful travel agencies: **El Travel** (☎ 0254/24-988; fax 0254/22-697), on the far east side of the public square on the harbor, and **Petridou Travel** (☎ **0254/22-309**; fax 0254/22-129), just around the corner to the right of the public square.

GETTING AROUND   By Bus   In Mýrina, The central **bus station** (☎ 0254/ 22-464) is three blocks up from the taxi square; turn right and find it on the left. A schedule is posted, but you're not likely to find much on it. Except for Moúdros and Kondiás, most places on the island get service only once a day, usually in the afternoon.

By Bicycle   There are bicycles for rent in Mýrina, and they are an inexpensive and sufficient means of transportation.

By Boat   There are caïques on the north side of the harbor in Mýrina; they offer service to the various beaches and the grottos at Skála. The price is negotiable, and they will leave when they're ready.

By Car   You can rent a small Jeep from almost any of the travel agents in Mýrina for about $70 a day.

On Foot   You can visit all of Mýrina, the Kástro, and the beaches on either side of town easily by foot.

FAST FACTS   From the port of Mýrina, continue up to your right past the **city hall** and the Aktaeon Hotel; then turn left to find the main street, Odós P. Kída. Most services are found within a few blocks along this main street. The **taxi station** marks what might conveniently be called a **central square.** The **telephone center** (**OTE**) is to your right, as are two **banks.** The **post office** is to your right and then around to the left. Continue to your right along Odós Garoufalídou to find the **police station** (☎ 0254/22-200); the **tourist police** can be reached at (☎ 0254/ 22-201). There's a self-service **laundry** (☎ 0254/24-392) on Odós Garoufalídou across from the Olympic Airline office. It's open from 8:30am to 2pm and 5 to 11pm, and the friendly women who run it will probably do your laundry for you. Continue a block past the police station and turn left to find the **hospital** (☎ 0254/ 22-222).

WHAT TO SEE & DO

The first thing you notice as you pull into Mýrina, the capital and port, is the Kástro that dominates it, solid evidence of the island's military history. We suggest that you investigate the town first, which is a pleasant, easygoing place once you get past the crush at the ferry quay. You'll probably have to look closely to recognize much distinction in the architecture, but there's more than a trace of both the Turkish and the Thracian in it. There's pleasant shopping up along the main street, for antiques, preserves made from the local black plums, Limnian honey (a favorite of the gods), the famous Limnian wines (red and rosé, "Kalavaki," Aristotle's favorite, a dry white, and the sweet "Moschato"), and the local pottery.

It won't be long until you notice the presence of the military. They may have even escorted you ashore. Young soldiers casually mill through the town, smiling and joking, and their good humor is infectious.

You may want to wander back to the right through the maze of narrow streets to the paralía (Navaroú Koudouriótou) and have a walk along the beach, past some nice hotels and cafes. The first beach is called **Romeïkos Yialós** ("Roman Beach"—the Greeks have called themselves Romans since the early Byzantine period). The second beach is **Ríha Nerá;** that's the famous and expensive resort of Akti Mirina off at the other end (see "Where to Stay," below).

The island's **cathedral** and **Archaeology Museum** (☎ 0254/22-990) are along the paralía. Newly overhauled, the museum was named one of the best three small museums in Europe. It's usually open Tuesday through Sunday from 8:30am to 3pm; admission is Dr 500 ($2.15). It contains finds from three of the island's important ancient sites: Polióchni, the Ifestía (sanctuary of Hephaestus), and the sanctuary of the Kavíri. (These actual sites, by the way, are very ancient and obscure, and will be of interest only to the most avid.)

Next you may want to tackle the **Kástro.** In classical times this was the site of a temple of Artemis; later it was a Roman site, then Byzantine, then Venetian, then Genoese, then Turkish.

An important military site is muddy **Moúdros Bay,** across the island. This was the Allied naval base during World War I for the disastrous Gallipoli campaign. On the bay is the rather depressing second town of the island, **Moúdros,** and a British Commonwealth cemetery with 800 graves.

The volcanic past of the island is everywhere apparent, and it's little wonder that Hephaestus was worshipped here—or that his myth grew up in association with this island, which was home to some of the earliest metallurgy we know of. It's probably not mere coincidence that the ancients valued their metalworkers so much that they sometimes cut their Achilles tendon, so that they could not escape, and that the smithy god should be lame. Born ugly, Hephaestus was rejected by his father Zeus, and as Milton wrote "Dropt from the zenith like a falling star, on Límnos, the Aegean isle." Here he fashioned shields and spears for the Olympians and created a race of cast-gold robotic maidens who stoked the fiery furnace that caused the volcanic disturbances.

Another local myth says that Aphrodite once made the island's women smell repulsive to their husbands because the men had favored Hephaestus over her during the couple's tempestuous marriage. The women grew angry with their men's rejection, poisoned their wine, slit their throats, and threw them into the sea from the cliffs above Akti Mirina. For a while Límnos was inhabited only by women, until the Argo and its crew pulled into Límnos's snug harbor to repopulate the island.

WHERE TO STAY

Private rooms are available on the island. As the Limnians will often double the "expected" rate for the few tourists they meet, you should bargain.

Aktaeon Hotel. Odós Arvanitáki, Mýrina, 814 00 Límnos. ☎ **0254/22-258.** 14 rms (12 with bath). Dr 4,400 ($18.75) without bath, Dr 10,100 ($43) double without bath, Dr 12,650 ($53.80) double with bath. No credit cards.

This older hotel on the harbor front might be a little better maintained, but it still has some charm, is convenient, and open year-round.

Akti Mirina. Mýrina, 814 00 Límnos. ☎ **0254/22-681.** Fax 0254/22-382. 125 bungalows (all with bath). A/C MINIBAR TEL. Dr 66,000–Dr 138,000 ($280.85–$587.25) double bungalows; Dr 132,250–Dr 147,200 ($562.75–$626.40) suites. AE, EU, MC, V.

This famous resort, one kilometer west of town north of the Kástro, beyond the town beaches, is a very nice place indeed, with three restaurants, several bars, a private beach, a heated sea-water swimming pool, water sports, minigolf, and tennis facilities. Along the shore are wonderful climbing rocks. These plush amenities and a modern convention center are responsible for attracting more tourists to the island than any other local asset. We still think they must be kidding about the prices.

Hotel Lemnos. Odós Arvanitáki, Mýrina, 814 00 Límnos. ☎ **0254/22-153.** Fax 0254/23-494. 26 rms (all with bath). Dr 9,900 ($42.10) single; Dr 13,200 ($56.15) double; Dr 15,400 ($65.55) triple. MC, V.

This new hotel on the harbor is attractive, clean, comfortable and quiet. The owners, Harry Geanopoulos and Bill Stamboulis, spent many years in New Jersey, so they speak English. A good night's sleep is offered at a fair price.

Hotel Sevdalís. Odós Garoufalídou 6, Mýrina, 814 00 Límnos. ☎ **0254/22-303.** Fax 0254/22-382. 36 rms (all with bath). A/C TEL. Dr 12,075 ($51.40) single; Dr 15,525 ($66.05) double. No credit cards.

This well-maintained older hotel is above the taxi square, near the Olympic Airways office, about 300 meters off the port and 700 meters from the beach. There's a lounge with TV and a bar for guests.

WHERE TO DINE

The **Avra,** next to the Port Authority near the port, is a good basic place with fair prices. It doesn't have a menu, and you go inside and choose from the steam table. The best place for seafood is behind the sheltered fishing boat mooring.

MÝRINA AFTER DARK

There's plenty of nightlife in Mýrina along the paralía north of the Kastro and in the middle of town, though you'll share it with a number of very pleasant soldiers. The **Disco Avlonas Club** (☎ 0254/23-885) is 2 kilometers out of town on the road to Thános. The **Gitonia Ton Angelon** (☎ 0254/23-345) in Áyios Dimítrios; its advertising promises "a new proposition for your night's entertainment."

Appendix

Basic Greek Vocabulary

Greek is relatively easy to pronounce. Every syllable in a word is uttered as written, and words of more than one syllable almost always have a stress accent. The pronunciation guide on the next page is intended to aid you as you go over the basic words and phrases listed in this appendix. While your pronunciation may not be perfect, you'll find that people in Greece will quickly warm to you if you try to speak to them in their own language.

The transliteration of Greek into English presents a special problem, because there is no recognized standard system to go by. Thus, for example, the island of ΑΙΓΙΝΑ is variously spelled Aegina, Aiyina, and Egina, while the name ΓΕΩΡΓΙΟΣ shows up in English as Georgios, Gheorghios, and Yeoryios, to cite only some of the variants. So, don't be surprised if you see a street or town spelled differently on your map or on a signpost. (If you can read the Greek, you have the game won!)

GREEK ALPHABET

GREEK ALPHABET	NAME	TRANSLITERATION	PRONUNCIATION
Α, α	álfa	a	f*a*ther
Β, β	víta	v	e*v*ade
Γ, γ	gámma	gh *or* y	*y*es
Δ, δ	délta	d *or* dh	*th*en
Ε, ε	épsilon	e	*e*gg
Ζ, ζ	zíta	z	*z*one
Η, η	íta	i	mach*i*ne
Θ, θ	thíta	th	*th*in
		i	*i*s
Ι, ι	yóta	y (semi-consonantal)	na*ti*on
Κ, κ	káppa	k	*k*ey
Λ, λ	lámbda	l	*l*amb
Μ, μ	mí	m	*m*other
Ν, ν	ní	n	*n*et
Ξ, ξ	xí	x	a*x*e
Ο, o	ómikron	o	*o*ver
Π, π	pí	p	*p*et
Ρ, ρ	ró	r	bu*rr*o (with a slight trill)
Σ, σ, ς*	sígma	s	*s*ee
Τ, τ	táf	t	*t*op
Υ, υ	ípsilon	y *or* i	p*y*ramid
Φ, φ	fí	f *or* ph	*ph*ilosophy
Χ, χ	chí	ch *or* h	Scottish lo*ch* or German *ich*
Ψ, ψ	psí	ps	la*ps*e
Ω, ω	oméga	o	*o*ver (but slightly longer)

*The letter ς occurs only at the end of a word; σ occurs elsewhere in a word. For example: σεισμός "earthquake."

DIPHTHONGS	TRANSLITERATION	PRONUNCIATION
ΑΙ, αι	ai, ae, *or* e	like *e* above
ΕΙ, ει		
	i	like *i* above
ΟΙ, οι		
ΟΥ, ου	ou	Lou*v*re
ΑΥ, αυ	av before vowels and some consonants	a*v*ert
	af before other consonants	a*f*firm
ΕΥ, ευ	ev before vowels and some consonants	le*v*el
	ef before other consonants	le*f*t

DOUBLE CONSONANTS	TRANSLITERATION	PRONUNCIATION
ΓΓ, γγ		
	ng nasalised	a*ng*le
ΓΚ, γκ		
ΜΠ, μπ	b	*b*ar
ΝΤ, ντ	d (at the beginning of a word)	*d*andy
	nd (in the middle of a word)	da*nd*y
ΤΣ, τσ	ts	hi*ts*

WORDS & PHRASES

Airport	**Aerodrómio**
Automobile	**Aftokínito**
Avenue	**Leofóros**
Bad	**Kakós,-kí,-kó***
Bank	**Trápeza**
The bill, please.	**Tón logaryazmó(n), parakaló.**
Breakfast	**Proinó**
Bus	**Leoforío**
Can you tell me?	**Boríte ná moú píte?**
Car	**Amáxi**
Cheap	**Ft(h)inó**
Church	**Ekklissía**
Closed	**Klistós, stí, stó***
Coast	**Aktí**
Coffeehouse	**Kafenío**
Cold	**Kríos,-a,-o***
Dinner	**Vradinó**
Does anyone speak English?	**Milál kanís angliká?**
Excuse me.	**Signómi(n).**
Expensive	**Akrivós, -í,-ó***
Farewell!	**Stó ka-ló!** (*to person leaving*)
Glad to meet you.	**Chéro polí.****
Good	**Kalós, lí, ló***
Good-bye	**Adío or chérete****
Good evening	**Kalispéra**
Good health (cheers)!	**Stín (i)yá sas** or **Yá-mas!**
Good morning	**Kaliméra**
Good night	**Kaliníchta****
Hello!	**Yássas or chérete!****
Here	**Edó**
Hot	**Zestós, -stí, -stó***
Hotel	**Xenodochío****
How are you?	**Tí kánete or Pós íst(h)e?**
How far?	**Pósso makriá?**
How long?	**Póssi óra or Pósso(n) keró?**
How much is it?	**Pósso káni?**
I am from New York.	**Íme apó tí(n) Néa(n) Iórki.**
I am lost or I have lost the way.	**Écho chathí or Écho chási tón drómo(n).****
I'm sorry, but I don't speak Greek (well).	**Lipoúme, allá dén miláo elliniká (kalá).**
I don't understand, please repeat it.	**Dén katalavéno, péste to páli, sás parakaló.**

*Masculine ending -os, feminine ending -a or -i, neuter ending -o.
**Remember, *ch* should be pronounced as in Scottish *loch* or German *ich,* not as in the word *church.*

I want to go to the airport.	**Thélo ná páo stó aerodrómio.**
I want a glass of beer.	**Thélo éna potíri bíra.**
It's (not) all right.	**(Dén) íne en dáxi.**
Left (direction)	**Aristerá**
Ladies' room	**Ghinekón**
Lunch	**Messimerianó**
Map	**Chártis****
Market (place)	**Agorá**
Men's room	**Andrón**
Mr.	**Kýrios**
Mrs.	**Kyría**
Miss	**Despinís**
My name is . . .	**Onomázome . . .**
New	**Kenoúryos, -ya, -yo***
No	**Óchi****
Old	**Paleós, -leá, -leó***
	(pronounce palyós, -lyá, -lyó)
Open	**Anichtós, -chtí, -chtó***
Pâtisserie	**Zacharoplastío****
Pharmacy	**Farmakío**
Please	**Parakaló**
Please call a taxi (for me).	**Parakaló, fonáxte éna taxi**
	(yá ména).
Post office	**Tachidromío****
Restaurant	**Estiatório**
Restroom	**Tó méros** *or* **I toualétta**
Right (direction)	**Dexiá**
Saint	**Ághios, aghía,** *(plural)* **ághi-i**
	(abbreviated **ag.***)*
Shore	**Paralía**
Square	**Platía**
Street	**Odós**
Show me on the map.	**Díxte mou stó(n) chárti.****
Station (bus, train)	**Stathmós (leoforíou, trénou)**
Stop (bus)	**Stási(s) (leoforíou)**
Telephone	**Tiléfono**
Temple (of Athena, Zeus)	**Naós (Athinás, Diós)**
Thank you (very much).	**Efcharistó (polí)****
Today	**Símera**
Tomorrow	**Ávrio**
Very nice	**Polí oréos, -a, -o***
Very well	**Polí kalá** *or* **En dáxi**
What?	**Tí?**
What time is it?	**Tí ôra íne?**
What's your name?	**Pós onomázest(h)e?**
Where is . . . ?	**Poú íne...?**
Why?	**Yatí?**

*Masculine ending -os, feminine ending -a or -i, neuter ending -o.
**Remember, *ch* should be pronounced as in Scottish *loch* or German *ich,* not as in the
word *church.*

NUMBERS

0	**Midén**	17	**Dekaeftá**	151	**Ekatón penínda éna**	
1	**Éna**	18	**Dekaoktó**	152	**Ekatón penínda dío**	
2	**Dío**	19	**Dekaenyá**	200	**Diakóssya**	
3	**Tría**	20	**Íkossi**	300	**Triakóssya**	
4	**Téssera**	21	**Íkossi éna**	400	**Tetrakóssya**	
5	**Pénde**	22	**Íkossi dío**	500	**Pendakóssya**	
6	**Éxi**	30	**Triánda**	600	**Exakóssya**	
7	**Eftá**	40	**Saránda**	700	**Eftakóssya**	
8	**Októ**	50	**Penínda**	800	**Oktakóssya**	
9	**Enyá**	60	**Exínda**	900	**Enyakóssya**	
10	**Déka**	70	**Evdomínda**	1,000	**Chílya***	
11	**Éndeka**	80	**Ogdónda**	2,000	**Dío chilyádes***	
12	**Dódeka**	90	**Enenínda**	3,000	**Trís chilyádes***	
13	**Dekatría**	100	**Ekató(n)**	4,000	**Tésseris chilyádes***	
14	**Dekatéssera**	101	**Ekatón éna**	5,000	**Pénde chilyádes***	
15	**Dekapénde**	102	**Ekatón dío**			
16	**Dekaéxi**	150	**Ekatón penínda**			

CALENDAR

Monday	**Deftéra**	Friday	**Paraskeví**	
Tuesday	**Tríti**	Saturday	**Sávvato**	
Wednesday	**Tetárti**	Sunday	**Kiriakí**	
Thursday	**Pémpti**			

January	**Ianouários**	July	**Ioúlios**	
February	**Fevrouários**	August	**Ávgoustos**	
March	**Mártios**	September	**Septémvrios**	
April	**Aprílios**	October	**Októvrios**	
May	**Máios**	November	**Noémvrios**	
June	**Ioúnios**	December	**Dekémvrios**	

*Remember, *ch* should be pronounced as in Scottish *loch* or German *ich*, not as in the word *church*.

MENU TERMS

Hors d'Oeuvres—Orektiká

Choriátiki saláta "Village" salad ("Greek" salad to us)
Chórta Dandelion salad
Domátes yemistés mé rízi Tomatoes stuffed with rice
Melitzanosaláta Eggplant salad

Piperiés yemistés Stuffed green peppers
Saganáki Grilled cheese
Spanokópita Spinach pie
Taramosaláta Fish roe with mayonnaise
Tirópita Cheese pie
Tzatzíki Yogurt-cucumber-garlic dip

Fish—Psári

Astakós (ladolémono) Lobster (with oil-and-lemon sauce)
Bakaliáro (skordaliá) Cod (with garlic)
Barboúnia (skáras) Red mullet (grilled)
Garídes Shrimp
Glóssa (tiganití) Sole (fried)

Kalamarákia (tiganitá) Squid (fried)
Kalamarákia (yemistá) Squid (stuffed)
Karavídes Crayfish
Oktapódi Octopus
Soupiés yemistés (Stuffed cuttlefish)
Tsípoura Dorado

Meats—Kréas

Arní avgolémono Lamb with lemon sauce
Arní soúvlas Spit-roasted lamb
Arní yiouvétsi Baked lamb with orzo
Brizóla chiriní Pork steak or chop
Brizóla moscharísia Beef or veal steak
Dolmadákia Stuffed vine leaves
Keftedes Fried meatballs
Kotópoulo soúvlas Spit-roasted chicken

Kotópoulo yemistó Stuffed chicken
Loukánika Spiced sausages
Moussaká Meat and eggplant
Païdákia Lamb chops
Piláfi rízi Rice pilaf
Souvláki Lamb (sometimes veal) on the skewer
Youvarlákia Boiled meatballs with rice

Index

WHEREVER YOU TRAVEL, *H*ELP IS NEVER FAR AWAY.

From planning your trip to providing travel assistance along the way, American Express® Travel Service Offices are always there to help.

Greece

American Express Travel Service
2 Hermou Street, Syntagma Square
Athens
1/3244976

Acteon Travel Agency (R)
Port Square
Ios
286/91343

Greek Skies Travel (R)
20A Capodistria Street
Corfu
661/33410

Delia Travel Ltd. (R)
At The Quay
Mykonos
289/22322

Adamis Tours (R)
23, 25th August Street
Heraklion, Crete
81/246202

Albatros Travel (R)
48 Othonos Amalias Street
Patras
61/220127

X-Ray Kilo (R)
Main Square
Fira-Santorini
286/23401

Rhodos Tours Ltd. (R)
23 Ammochostou Street
Rhodes
241/21010

Travel

http://www.americanexpress.com/travel

American Express Travel Service Offices are found in central locations throughout Greece.

In case you want to see the world.

At American Express, we're here to make your journey a smooth one. So we have over 1,700 travel service locations in over 120 countries ready to help. What else would you expect from the world's largest travel agency?

do more

AMERICAN
EXPRESS

Travel

http://www.americanexpress.com/travel

In case you want to be welcomed there.

We're here to see that you're always welcomed at establishments everywhere. That's why millions of people carry the American Express® Card – for peace of mind, confidence, and security, around the world or just around the corner.

do more

Cards

In case you're running low.

We're here to help with more than 118,000 Express Cash

locations around the world. In order to enroll, just call

American Express before you start your vacation.

do more

Express Cash

And just in case.

We're here with American Express® Travelers Cheques and Cheques *for Two*® They're the safest way to carry money on your vacation and the surest way to get a refund, practically anywhere, anytime.

Another way we help you...

do more

Travelers Cheques